WHAT IS TO BE DONE WITH THE PROFITS FROM THE SALE OF THIS BOOK.

Resolved, That the Howard Association of Memphis thanks Mr. J. M. Keating for the very generous gift of his work, entitled: "A History of the Yellow Fever," the copyright, and all rights, title to, or profits in which he has transferred to the Howard Association of Memphis; and,

Resolved, That the proceeds of the sale of such work, after the first edition of five hundred copies, which are hereby reserved for free distribution by the Association, shall, as he requests, be applied to the building of a Monument to the Physicians, Nurses, Members of the Howard Association and Citizens' Relief Committee, who died in Memphis during the epidemic of 1878.

Adopted unanimously, January 6, 1879.

The History of the Yellow Fever Epidemic of 1878

IN
MEMPHIS, TENNESSEE

Embracing a Complete List of the Dead, the Names of
the Doctors and Nurses Employed, Names of All
Who Contributed Money or Means, and the
Names and History of the Howards,
Together with Other Data,
and Lists of the Dead
Elsewhere

J. M. Keating

HERITAGE BOOKS
2008

HERITAGE BOOKS
AN IMPRINT OF HERITAGE BOOKS, INC.

Books, CDs, and more—Worldwide

For our listing of thousands of titles see our website
at
www.HeritageBooks.com

A Facsimile Reprint
Published 2008 by
HERITAGE BOOKS, INC.
Publishing Division
100 Railroad Ave. #104
Westminster, Maryland 21157

Copyright © 1879 The Howard Association of Memphis

Copyright © 2008 Heritage Books, Inc.

— Publisher's Notice —
In reprints such as this, it is often not possible to remove blemishes from the original. We feel the contents of this book warrant its reissue despite these blemishes and hope you will agree and read it with pleasure.

International Standard Book Numbers
Paperbound: 978-0-7884-7693-8
Clothbound: 978-0-7884-7694-5

INTRODUCTION TO REPRINT

Memphis endured ten weeks of unimaginable horror in the late summer and early fall of 1878. Although it was not the city's first experience with yellow fever, the earlier outbreaks produced nowhere near the toll exacted on the city during the epidemic of 1878. Memphis was not alone. All along the Mississippi, Tennessee, and Ohio river valleys, more than 200 places were hit in the 1878 epidemic and 20,000 died. Memphis suffered the greatest losses. This book, compiled immediately after the epidemic, is a valuable record of fatalities and efforts to cope with the dead and dying. Later accounts enable a better understanding of the scope and circumstances of this tragedy.[1]

The yellow plague reached Memphis with the first confirmed death on August 13. Two days later, twenty two new cases were reported and the day after that, thirty three. The panic was on. Any road leading out of Memphis was crowded with vehicles of every kind. People fought for seats on boats and trains. Inside of ten days, some 25,000 people poured out of the city. Those who could went to relatives in inland places. Evacuation centers were set up, and many refugees were housed in tent cities in the country. The end finally came in late October when the first frost occurred on the 18th and there were no new cases by October 29. Cold weather stopped the mosquito larvae from hatching, thereby breaking the cycle of the disease.

Among the several relief organizations caring for those who were unable to leave Memphis were the "Howards" (the Howard Association of the City of Memphis), modeled after the group in New Orleans specifically organized to cope with yellow fever epidemics. Named for the distinguished English philanthropist, John Howard, the "Howards" were a group of approximately forty businessmen who raised money, secured doctors and nurses, and at the risk of their own lives, stayed in the city to supervise care of the sick and sanitary burials of the dead. Thirty of them got the disease, and eleven died. Of the Howard doctors, fifty-four came down with the fever and thirty-three died.

The epidemic had a profound impact on the economic, social, and political life of Memphis and surrounding areas. From being one of the Mississippi Valley's most pestilent and unsanitary cities, Memphis set out to become one of the cleanest. Yellow fever hit the city again in 1879 but was much less virulent; from 2,000 cases there were 583 deaths. Although other places were hit in 1888, 1897, and 1899, Memphis never again had any cases of the yellow plague. Once it was established that the mosquito was an essential element in its spread and could be controlled, yellow fever disappeared from American cities after 1906.

The above mentioned Howard Association was responsible for the original publication of this book in 1879. In what may have been its last contribution to the city, it saw that this account of the 1878 epidemic was written. It serves as a lasting memorial to the thousands of individuals whose names are recorded herein, those who recovered, those who died, and those who did what they could to help its victims, as well as the many individuals and organizations who sent food and supplies to aid the beleaguered city.

This history of the 1878 yellow fever epidemic in Memphis is of value to the medical historian for its detailed account of the valiant efforts of the medical profession to cope with an unknown enemy of frightening proportions, and of the volunteers, men and women, blacks and whites, who courted certain death by staying the city to do what they could to help while more than half of the population had fled.

The book is of value to local historians because it cites many towns and localities throughout the south that were also impacted by the 1878 epidemic, both directly by illness and death, and indirectly by changes in social and economic circumstances.

Genealogist and author, Dorothy Williams Potter points out that this book may be the only record of some of the deceased, such as minor children. In addition, the lists cover a much wider area than Memphis, and one finds deaths published for thirty other Tennessee towns, for forty-four Mississippi towns, and for areas in Arkansas, Alabama, Kentucky, and Louisiana, including New Orleans. "Thus," she said, "the book is of great value to genealogists and family historians who may discover the fate of lost Southern families."

This reprint edition is taken from a copy of the original edition that belonged to Matthew W. Wheeler (1855-1921) of Milan, Tennessee, and was provided to Heritage Press by his grandson, Glynn P. Wheeler of Birmingham, Alabama. The addition of an index prepared by Heritage Press provides easy access to the thousands of names of individuals and families caught up in this tragedy.

Annie Ford Wheeler

Samford University Librarian, retired.

Former lecturer and director of the Institute of Genealogy and Historical Research, Samford University, Birmingham, Alabama.

---

[1] Bernard A. Weisberger, "Epidemic," in *American Heritage*, 35:6, 1984, p. 57-64; Shields McIlwaine, *Memphis Down in Dixie*, E. P. Dutton, ca. 1984, p. 167-177.

DEDICATION.

TO THE MEN AND WOMEN WHO VOLUNTEERED THEIR LIVES FOR THE FEVER-STRICKEN CITIZENS OF MEMPHIS IN 1878; TO ALL WHO CONTRIBUTED FOOD, CLOTHING, OR MONEY TO SUCCOR THE SICK, RELIEVE THE DESTITUTE, AND BURY THE DEAD, THIS HISTORY OF A TERRIBLE SCOURGE AND RECORD OF A GREAT PUBLIC CALAMITY, IS GRATEFULLY AND RESPECTFULLY DEDICATED,

BY J. M. KEATING.

GRATEFUL AND HEARTFELT THANKS.

TOWARDS the close of the epidemic of 1878, the Howard Association and the Citizens' Relief Committee, in the name and in behalf of the dead, of the sick, the convalescent, and the suffering citizens of Memphis, thanked the people of the world in terms of heartfelt gratitude for the kind consideration, sympathy, and generous charity of which, in common with their fellow-citizens of other cities and towns of the South, they had been the objects and recipients during the awful visitation. On the 28th of November, 1878, being Thanksgiving Day, at an immense mass-meeting composed of representatives of all classes of the lately returned people of Memphis, the following preamble and resolutions were unanimously adopted:

WHEREAS, We, the citizens of Memphis, who were absent during the recent pestilence, mindful of the individual heroism displayed in behalf of our deeply-afflicted people, and of the generosity, consideration, and aid extended to them by a sympathetic world, desire to testify our appreciation in a manner which will not only prove acceptable, but in a way by which it will be sure to reach all those to whom we owe so much; therefore, on this the 28th day of November, 1878 — a day set apart by the President of the United States, and by the Governor of this State, as one of thanksgiving and prayer — we, deeming such day and such time most appropriate, and being in solemn mass-meeting assembled, do hereby publicly express our gratitude —

First,—To the President of the United States, the Secretary of War, and other members of his cabinet.

Second,—To the Governor and Treasurer of the State of Tennessee.

Third,—To the municipal authorities, merchants' exchanges, chambers of commerce, cotton exchanges, bankers and underwriters of the United States and Canada.

Fourth,—To the commercial bodies of Europe, and the représentatives abroad of the American Government.

Fifth,—To the churches, Sunday-schools, and benevolent associations in all sections of the Union.

Sixth,—To the press of the United States.

Seventh,—To the theatrical managers and members of the dramatic and musical professions.

Eighth,—To the officers, members, nurses, and employés of the Memphis Howard Association.

Ninth,—To the Howard Medical Corps, its officers and members.

Tenth,—To the volunteer physicians and nurses from other sections.

Eleventh,—To the officers, members, and employés of the Citizens' Relief Association.

Twelfth,—To the officers and employés of the commissary department of the Citizens' Relief Association.

Thirteenth,—To the clergy and religious orders of Memphis, and volunteers from abroad.

Fourteenth,—To the employés in the Memphis post-office.

Fifteenth,—To the Memphis daily press.

Sixteenth,—To the working committees of the Odd Fellows, Masons, Knights of Honor, Knights of Pythias, Ancient Order of Workingmen, Independent Order of Mutual Aiders, and other benevolent organizations.

Seventeenth,—To the mayor and other city officials, and to the police and fire departments of Memphis.

Eighteenth,—To the military companies, white and colored, who remained on duty during the pestilence.

Nineteenth,—To the Memphis and Louisville, the Memphis and Charleston, the Mississippi and Tennessee, and other railway lines; and to the Memphis and Ohio River and the Anchor Line Packet Companies.

Twentieth,—To the officers and employés of the Memphis banks, of the Southern Express Company, and of the Western Union Telegraph Company.

Twenty-first,—To the charitable of the known and unknown people not connected with any charitable or philanthropic association — persons from every walk and station in life, both lofty and humble; and to the many who, sacrificing interest, safety, the ties of kindred and the comforts of home, risked all in the humanitarian mission to which they had dedicated their lives.

Twenty-second,—To the women of America, whose hearts went out towards the sick and afflicted of the land.

Twenty-third,—To the martyred dead, we feel but can not express our gratitude; yet, in all the days to come, their memories shall be kept green, and their names go down in the annals of our city, honored, revered, and blessed. It would be a pleasing though melancholy task to call the roll of our illustrious dead, and let our grateful hearts respond in fitting tribute to their many virtues; but to a list so long, where every virtue is conspicuous, your Committee believes this to be not the time nor the place to mention individual merit. To do justice to the memory of any one of a hundred whose names might be suggested, would occupy more time than is now at your disposal; hence it is we restrain our inclination to mention names, and leave to each of you the sacred privilege of recalling the pleasant memories which cluster around our hallowed dead.

PREFACE.

This history of the yellow fever, and record of the epidemic of 1878, in Memphis, had its origin in the wish expressed by a large number of intelligent citizens, at home and abroad, who desired that the origin, progress, and results of the recent epidemic, especially, might be rescued from the evanescent columns of the daily press and put in an enduring form — a monument testifying to the sufferings of the people of Memphis, the unparalleled losses of life, to the humanity and overflowing charity of their fellow-countrymen of all the States, and the people of many of the nations of Europe; and, above all, to the heroism of the women and the men who illustrated, as physicians and nurses, with a sublime self-abnegation, the first and chiefest of Christian virtues.

All the known and well authenticated sources of information have been freely availed of, and it is believed that nothing has been omitted that could increase the value of the book as a history of the yellow fever and complete record of the epidemic of 1878, from the occurrence of the first to the date of the last known case.

The author has, it will be seen, confined himself to facts, and has not indulged, as he could wish, and they deserve, in extended panegyrics of those who so nobly perished at the post of duty, or of those who, doing their duty, survived the ordeal of death. Want of space forbade. The nature of their employment will sufficiently speak the added danger, if any, encountered by each, whether Howard or citizen; and the official station they filled will mark those for special remembrance by the world, who, by their courage, zeal, and efficiency, were the life and inspiration of the comparative few who performed what, to them, was a sacred duty.

All cause of jealousy, complaint, or offense has been studiously avoided, while nothing has been omitted that was deemed essential to the "truth of history." The time allowed for the work has been brief, but it is hoped it will be found worthy alike of the living and the dead; a record of duty done, a history of those who have passed away, leaving us a lesson of gentle ministrations, of heroic warfare, of strained endurance, of patient resignation, of cool, calm courage, and of Christian fortitude.

The epidemic of 1878, when the numbers exposed, the numbers who sickened, and those who died, are taken into account, must be set down as one of the greatest calamities of modern times, marking an epoch in our history and expressing a period memorable for all time.

Trusting that the lesson it teaches will not be lost upon those whom it most immediately concerns, the author commits his work to the considerate judgment of his readers, praying their indulgence for such demerits as to them may appear.

MEMPHIS, *May*, 1879.

CONTENTS.

	PAGE
HISTORY OF THE YELLOW FEVER	11–73
CHRONOLOGY OF YELLOW FEVER	75–98
EPIDEMIC IN MEMPHIS, 1878	99–144
INCIDENTS OF THE EPIDEMIC	145–194
METEOROLOGICAL	195–206
THE DEATHS OF 1878	207–266
QUARANTINE AND SANITATION	267–326
APPENDIX (Reports of Howards, etc.)	327–443
INDEX	445–454

HISTORY OF THE YELLOW FEVER.

A HISTORY OF THE YELLOW FEVER.

I.

THE Yellow Fever, or, as Dowell prefers to term it, *febris typhus icterodes*, or *febris cum nigro vomito*, the *fievre jaune* of the French, and *negro vomito* of the Spanish, was known to the Caribs, according to Breton, who wrote in 1655, by the French equivalent of *coup de barre*, expressive of the muscular pains of the fever, as if produced by blows from a stick. Like Asiatic cholera and the small-pox, it is assigned to that class of diseases known as *zymotic* (from *xyma*, the Greek word for yeast). These diseases are produced by invisible germs floating in the atmosphere, which, taken into the blood through the lungs, are afterward propagated by the excreta and invisible emanations of the patients. The yellow fever is claimed by some to have originated and to have prevailed epidemically* in Africa, though Cortez found it prevailing in Mexico, to whose people it was known by the name of *matzlazahuatl*; and the Indians of San Domingo and other West India Islands were decimated by it before and soon after the discovery of America. It is unknown in Asia, Australia, or the islands of the Pacific; and it was unknown to Europe until after the discovery of America by Columbus. Dowell says that "it was undoubtedly introduced from Africa to America [he does not say when, nor does he tell us why, if it is an African fever, the negroes in this country are so largely exempt from it]; that it existed in Africa, eastern Asia, and southern Europe, long before the establishment of the Greek and Roman empires, is generally well established by Hertado, even running back a thousand years before Christ; that it has now become endemic along the coasts of Africa—both east and west—as well as in the West Indies and northern coast of South America, no one doubts [and he ought to have added the

---

* Epidemic diseases are those which attack at the same time a great number of people, depending on some temporary accidental and generally inappreciable cause: differing, in this respect, from endemic diseases, or those developed under the influence of some constant or periodic cause. Many diseases, ordinarily sporadic, may become epidemic (as yellow fever) under certain ill-understood conditions; or some new disease, introduced by contagion or other favorable circumstances, may spread epidemically.

coast of Mexico and Gulf and south Atlantic coasts of North America]; and that in all these districts its has its epidemic years and its years of nearly entire exemption is also well known." Dowler, on whose authority Dowell in other respects lays great stress, states that, on the contrary, "The slightest notice of yellow fever is nowhere found among ancient writers, although they have not failed to record, incidentally or directly, the time, place, and progress of numerous epidemics with more or less particularity, so that these characteristics may now, after the lapse of so many centuries, be ascertained. It is now nearly 3,000 years since the first temple arose in honor of Æsculapius; four or five centuries later, he was worshiped at Rome, where epidemics became both frequent and fatal. Homer opens his great poem by alluding to an epidemic that destroyed dogs, mules, and men; another, 430 years before Christ, most destructive at Athens, was very minutely described by Thucydides, himself having suffered by it. An epidemic also fell under the observation of Hippocrates, whose treatment of it was reckoned so successful, that he was presented with a massive crown of gold and the highest public honors. Five years later, Athens was again visited. Many epidemics prevailed at Rome before our era. In 263 and 212 (at the siege of Syracuse), and in 131 before Christ, the Roman and many other nations suffered from pestilential visitations, as mentioned directly or indirectly by ancient authors. Near the commencement of the Christian era, Celsus, and in the next century, Galen, gave the world their learned works on medicine. In the sixth century the plague was general; and, in A. D. 565, small-pox was first described in France, as it was in the tenth century by the Arabian physicians, Rhazes and Avicenna. Before the middle of the 13th century, medical schools existed at Montpelier and Damascus. The Parisian College of Surgery soon followed. Descriptions of scurvy and plica were soon after recorded. Books on medicine, too, appeared in greater number; and some new diseases were described in the 14th and 15th centuries, such as whooping-cough, the sweating sickness, and St. Vitus' dance, which later was epidemic on the Rhine. During this long period, so briefly sketched, yellow fever does not appear to have been noticed until the discovery of America by Columbus. Had it prevailed in ancient times, its prominent features, so very remarkable, at least in its advanced stages, would, doubtless, have been recorded."* It is said to have made its first appearance on this side of the Atlantic in the West Indies, in 1647; but the late Noah Webster has shown that it prevailed among the Indians of New England in 1618, and again in 1746, and at other periods. It is also said to have scourged Mexico many years before the Spanish conquest. It certainly prevailed in Central America in 1596. Epidemics of it have occurred as far north as Quebec, as far south as Montevideo, as far east as Spain, and as far west as Mexico. It is endemic in Brazil, the West Indies, Venezuela, New Grenada, Mexico, the Gulf coast, and along the south Atlantic coast of

---

* The weight of evidence is with Dowler, and yellow fever would seem to be an American, and not an African fever.

the United States, as far north as Charleston. It is uncommon in elevated regions, but deaths have occurred from it at New Castle, Jamaica, at the height of 4,000 feet; and, if the statement be true that ancient Mexico was visited by it, then it has been epidemic at a height of between 7,000 and 8,000 feet above the level of the sea. Dowell says, "That along the sea coasts and in the islands of the tropics it has never occurred above 3,000 feet, while under the equator it has occurred at 4,000 feet." Since 1668 it has many times prevailed epidemically in the New England, the Middle, the Western, and the Southern States of the Union, at a fearful sacrifice of life and cost of money. Dowell, writing in the first part of 1878, before the dreadful visitation of that year, which cost the country more than 25,000 lives and $200,000,000, says, "That yellow fever had [up to 1877] visited 228 cities and towns and 28 States of the Union, appearing 741 times, and causing 65,311 deaths" [of which we have record, and as many more, perhaps, of which we have not]. Dr. Bell, of Louisville, declares it an indisputable truth that, beyond 45° north latitude and 23° south latitude, the disease is but rarely or never felt, and it is rigidly confined between 20° east longitude and 30' north. In the West India Islands, on the west coast of Africa, and the continent of America the ravages of yellow fever are most frequently felt. The conspicuous zones for it are Barbadoes on the east, Tampico on the west, Rio Janeiro on the south, and Charleston on the north. Within this area the disease is perpetually present at some point." Dowell says, "That it can not live in a temperature above 212° nor below 32° Fahrenheit, or 100° centegrade; consequently, no patient will take the disease where the temperature is below freezing [see contradiction a few lines below], and you may steam a ship to boiling, and kill out all contagion, and make it clean and healthy, by raising the heat to 212° [or, as some others insist, by freezing it by the new refrigerating process of Gamgee]; that he has known non-intercourse to prevent it; *but, after a slight frost or two, the men were permitted to come to town, and there occurred several cases and one death*, in 1865, January 5th [and yet he says no patient will take the disease at a temperature below freezing point]; and that the cause is increased by meteorological changes of months' duration; and this is the cause of the belief of some that it comes in the air. It develops in from two to nine days, but cases have been known where patients have had it in them 23 days. The true cause is an animalculæ, so small that we have been unable yet to develop it, though there are some efforts being made in that direction, which foreshadow success." But they have not yet made their appearance. Dr. Bennett Dowler, an authority who shares the esteem of all students of the subject with Stone, Flaget, Bell, and many others, declares positively that it has originated spontaneously in more than one instance in the United States: and, so originating, has raged epidemically. The Commission appointed by the Board of Health of New Orleans in 1853, to inquire into the causes of the epidemic of that year, declared positively that it originated there, and was aggravated to a fearful intensity by the filthy condition of the city. The medical experts recently appointed by Congress, deny the position of Dowler, of the New

Orleans Commission of 1853, and of Bell, although these, as will be shown later on, are fully sustained by a weight of authority at least equal to that of the Commission, and by the fact that yellow fever has become naturalized in the West Indies,* in Mexico, in Brazil, and in New Orleans. They declare that "yellow fever is not domiciled in the United States, and that every epidemic that has occurred has been in chronological sequence to the countries south of us, with which we are in communication." They deny that it has ever originated indigenously in this country, and assert that it is always the result of importation, and invariably prevails in some sea-port before attacking the interior. Yet they say cases have occurred here where the specific poison, when hidden from the cold in sheltered places, has given rise the succeeding summer to scattered cases. It is transmitted, they also contend, by steam and sailing vessels, barges, personal clothing, baggage, ordinary merchandise; also by yellow fever patients, who are responsible for more epidemics, they say, than all other causes, though instances are not wanting where they failed to occasion other cases.

The yellow fever is a fever of one paroxysm continuously from 24 to 72 and and sometimes 96 hours. According to Dr. Faget, of the faculty of Paris, who, during a residence of 25 years in New Orleans, has closely observed it, "it is strongly individual in its characteristics. For, whereas, in paludal fevers there are generally two or more paroxysms, sometimes a continued series of them, yellow fever has but one single paroxysm. And, whereas, in the former the period of defervescence, during which the temperature regains its normal degree, is only from 30 to 48 hours, in the latter it averaged 96 hours. In paludal fevers there is a perfect concord between the line of the pulse and that of the temperature, while in yellow fever the line of the pulse descends, but that of the temperature maintains itself or rises." According to the observations of Dr. Faget and others, made during the epidemic of 1870, in New Orleans, "it should be six or seven days ($6 \times 24 = 144$ hours)." In summing up the march of the temperature, Dr. Faget says, the fever "is characterized by a unique paroxysm, with an effervescence of one to three days, followed by a defervescence of four to seven days, without any stationary stage." The duration of the yellow fever is stated by Dr. La Roche to be three days—"a febrile stage of about seventy hours' duration, more or less, is succeeded by a period of complete cessation of fever."

Dowler declares it to be non-contagious and to result from an antecedent wholly unknown. And Dupuy de Chamberry, whom he quotes, states positively that "the yellow fever of this place (New Orleans) is a disease *sui generis*, the product of local causes, and is never contagious or exportable." Dr. Dowell, the latest medical writer on yellow fever, describes it "as an eruptive or exanthematous fever, infectious or contagious from persons or clothes under circumstances not yet known." The medical experts appointed by Congress in December, 1878, declare it to be a specific disease produced by the introduction into the human organism of a specific poison, and that, though this specific

---

* If it did not originate there or in Mexico.

poison has never been chemically or microscopically demonstrated, nor in any way made evident to the human sense, they deem it safe to assume that it is material and particular, is endowed with ordinary properties, and is subject to the ordinary laws of material substances. They also hold that it is organic — is endowed with the vital properties of growth and reproduction; that it is not malarial; but the concurrence of local conditions favorable to the evolution of it seems to be necessary to the evolution of yellow fever epidemics. Atmospheric air, they admit, is the usual medium through which the infection is received into the human system; it is not carried by atmospheric currents, they say, nor by any modes or vehicles of conveyance other than those connected with human traffic and travel. The white race is most susceptible to it, and all colors intermediary between that and the negro less and less in degree as they approach the African, who suffers least of all from it. The period of incubation, they hold, varies from two to five days — second attacks are of rare occurrence — and it can be destroyed by extreme heat and cold and by chemical disinfectants where they can be concentrated. Dr. L. S. Tracey, in the *Popular Science Monthly*, a publication of the highest scientific character, regards the germ and development theory with favor. He says: "Yellow fever occupies a singular position between the contagious and non-contagious diseases. The poison is not, like that of small-pox, directly communicable from a sick person to a well one; but, although the emanations of the sick are connected with the spread of the disease, they seem to require an appropriate nidus in which to germinate and develop. This nidus must be warm and moist, and there the germs, whatever they are, lie and grow or, in some way, develop until they are able to migrate. The germs are portable, and may be conveyed in baggage or merchandise (*fomites*) for hundreds or thousands of miles. If not so conveyed, its progress is very slow. In 1822, in New York, when it gained a foothold in Rector Street, it appeared to travel about 40 feet a day until killed by the frost. It often leaves a house or a block intact, going around it and attacking those beyond, with no assignable reason. A thin board partition seems to have stopped it on Governor's Island in 1856, and an instance is related where it attacked the sailors in all the berths of one side of a ship before crossing to the other. Such apparent vagaries are, in the present state of our knowledge, inexplicable."* Dr. William Schmoele, of Philadelphia, in an essay on the cause, the fusion, localization, prevention, and cure of cholera and yellow fever, holds to the same theory, but lays particular stress on propagation by the patient. He says: "The parasites causing the yellow fever, although also of exclusively tropical origin, appear somewhat capable to be reproduced, during the heat of summer, wherever the thermometer of Fahrenheit ranges above 86 degrees, in more northern latitudes, outside of the human alimentary tube, especially if imported by patients, and deposited with their excrements, in warm, damp, and filthy localities, presenting all the additional conditions of development of minute vermin. Their chief diffusion, however, in northern climes, is effected by

---

* They have always been characteristic of it. All the medical and newspaper records treat of them.

reproduction of the seeds in the bowels of patients, and by their direct dissemination through the vapors of the excrements, which deposit them on articles of food, or in the mouth of new victims, thence to be carried, with the food, into the digestive tube." Dr. Chopin, Health Officer of New Orleans, a medical authority of high repute and yellow fever expert, describes yellow fever most nearly in accordance with the general experience in Memphis in 1878. He says "it is an exotic, and that its germ is a living organism capable of rapid reproduction under given conditions; that it multiplies itself, first on surfaces and then in the atmosphere, until it becomes epidemic. It is a self-limited disease, like all specific diseases; that it must run its course, and nothing that we know of can stop its progress. Like scarlet fever, measles, small-pox, and cholera, it will go on unchecked as long as the poison is in the system. Then, through the influence on the nervous system, tissue changes occur, which produce disorganization and death, unless it is checked." Dr. J. M. Clements, of Louisville, attributes the yellow fever poison to some order of fungus plants indigenous to the tropics, but as yet undiscovered, and says "that the germs or spores are transported by strips, and finding in the place attacked the conditions of filth, heat and moisture breeds in such numbers as to poison the air and lay human life under contribution." He rests his theory upon the experiments of Prof. J. H. Salisbury, of Cleveland, Ohio, who claims to have ascertained that intermittent and remittent fevers are caused by the introduction into the system of cells or spores emanating from certain species of algoid plants, called Palmellæ, which belong to the lowest known vegetable organism. To these species of plants he applies the generic name, *Semiasma*, signifying earth miasm, and he also calls them ague plants. Prof. Salisbury claims that this discovery is based on the following facts: "A microscopical examination of the salivary secretions and mucous expectoration, in the morning, of persons living in a malarious region showed cells of an algoid type, resembling strongly those of the palmellæ, to be the only bodies constantly present; and these bodies were invariably absent from the same secretions examined from persons residing above the summit plane of ague. The palmelloid cells were obtained by suspending plates of glass, over night, near broken ground, in places whence malarious emanations were known to arise. The so-called ague plants were invariably found in numerous localities in which intermittent fever prevailed, and in no instance were they found where this disease did not occur. Cakes of surface soil from a malarious locality, which were covered with the palmellæ, were carried to a high, hilly district, situated five miles from any malarious locality, where a case of malarial fever had never been known to exist. These cakes were exposed on the sill of an open second-story window, opening into the sleeping apartment of two young men. A plate of glass suspended over them during the night was found to be covered with palmelloid cells and spores. Both the young men had intermittent fever, one on the 12th day, the other on the 14th. No other members of the family were affected." The theory of Prof. Salisbury, accounting for the origin of remittent and intermittent fevers, and which is thus advanced by Dr. Clements, of Louisville, to account for the origin of yellow fever, is sustained by the experiments of Dr. Emil Querner, of Philadelphia, whose investigations into the causes of diphtheria leads him to the following conclusions: "After a laborious and scrutinizing investigation into the cause of a large number of cases of diphtheria that have come under my care during several years past, I have almost arrived at the conclusion that the primary infection of an individual comes from the fungi which are found as spots of different colors on the exterior of fruits, particularly apples. As far as the power of my microscope has shown, these fungi seem identical with the fungi from a diphtheritic ulcer, and last autumn I traced a number of cases, at one time five together in one family, back to the eating of apples picked from the ground in orchards without previously cleaning the fruit by rubbing or washing. The prevalence of this dreadful disease in the last three decades may be well accounted for by the fact that the appearance and flourishing of lower vegetable and animal organisms is periodical, of which we have examples in the potato-disease, the disease of the grape-vine, and cholera, which latter has been ascribed to a fungus growing on the ears of rice in East India, and carried in the human body as a contagion all over the globe, and in many other cases. Of course, any person infected with the disease from the primary cause may be the center of infection for others. Why many persons eat fruit with fungi on them with impunity is explainable simply on the ground that the susceptibility for disease differs greatly in individuals, and that, for instance, for the propagation of fungi upon the mucous membrane upon the pharynx there may exist a previous catarrhalic affection, with a spongy condition of the same. It is my opinion that in times of epidemic diseases almost every one takes the contagion into his system, but that for the development of the disease a certain predisposition, or some additional cause, is necessary. Thus, cholera breaks out in an individual only after the cooling off of the abdomen; and small-pox attacks timid persons often after being frightened by the sight of a pitted face of a convalescent patient from a distance. Thus, also, the impunity of physicians who treat such diseases with a zealous and investigating mind, and with a fearless interest in every case, may be accounted for; their nervous energy resisting the tendency of their vital power to succumb to the contagion. By this, I wish only to give a hint for further investigation in this matter, for certainly it is time that the medical profession should discover more of the hidden causes of zymotic diseases, which bring so much havoc among the human race."

Dr. J. P. Davidson, of New Orleans, very emphatically agrees with the experts appointed by Congress. He says "that yellow fever is exotic, and never originates locally except under peculiar circumstances of limited domestication, as when an epidemic has prevailed, or in certain years when a few cases have occurred, and periodically, after importation, the ensuing winter has been so mild that the mercury has not fallen repeatedly below 32°—the special cause, germs, if you will, survive the winter, and when the summer heat attains its maximum, they multiply sufficiently to impart the disease." He also holds "that it is due to a living, organized microscopicentity, vegetable or animal, which generated out of pre-existing germs under favorable circumstances, propagates itself indefinitely when these peculiar and essential conditions exist." Dr. Gaillard, of Louisville, is of opinion that yellow fever will not originate out of its zone; that carried beyond it and introduced into filthy cities, its favorite, if not essential nidus, it will spread and decimate, and will bring ruin and desolation in its train. Dr. Happholdt, who was conspicuous as a volunteer physician in Memphis during the epidemic of 1873, and who had previously had an extended experience with yellow fever as Health Officer of Charleston, in a pamphlet history of that visitation, declares that "yellow fever is peculiarly a disease of cities, where large numbers of persons are crowded together, and effete animal matters are allowed to putrefy in the atmosphere; but it is not proved that filth, garbage or noxious gases from rotting animal or vegetable matter can any more produce yellow fever than they can small-pox; though it is almost certain that they do so vitiate the atmosphere as to render it a proper nidus for the reception and proliferation of the essential epidemic germ, be it what it may; whether of fungoid growths, or germinal masses derived from normal cells, or analogous to yeast or other ferment, which, by virtue of catalytic action, is capable of producing deleterious changes in the constituents of the body. Assuming that all the destructive changes which the blood undergoes in yellow fever are due to the contact of certain infinitesimal particles, it may be readily conceived that after entering the organism and affecting its vital constituents, they may reproduce themselves, and, from their extreme minuteness, permeate the tissues and escape from it by the skin, the breath, and the excretions. When without the body, they may continue to multiply themselves indefinitely if the surrounding atmosphere be in a favorable condition; and floating about the air, impregnate water and food, and attach themselves to clothing, bedding, or other material, and so admit of transportation, and gaining access to the bodies of persons suitable for their reception; or these particles may lose a portion of their contagious vitality and be no longer capable of originating other germs that can propagate the disease, or being introduced into localities not favorable to their development, occasion only a few sporadic cases. But we are not assured that all the germs perish, after the cessation of their action, by the intervention of cold weather. Many may but hibernate in sheltering situations to be revivified and aroused into action by warm weather and other favoring circumstances." Assistant Surgeon Harvey E. Brown, of the United States Army, holds that the yellow fever is an acute, infectious disease, which originated in Africa,* and has become naturalized in the West Indies, and that it never has had an existence in the United States except in consequence of the importation and subsequent development and production of its active or germinal principle. The nature of the germ is unknown, and he says that "the transmission of yellow fever is not effected by means of a contagion or exhalation given off from the bodies of the sick, as is the case with small-pox, erysipelas, and the eruptive fevers, but the unknown poisonous principle probably exists in extremely minute particles or germs which impregnate and render noxious the

---

*He does not say when or in what part of Africa, and in that regard is as vague and indefinite as the majority of his brethren.

discharges from the stomach, bowels, and skin of any person undergoing an attack of the disease. These germs may attach themselves to clothing, bedding, carpets, and furniture in a sick-room; they may penetrate the walls and wood-work of a house, or the hold of a ship; when, by the general prevalence of the disease they become numerous, they may poison the atmosphere of a street or even of a whole town; they may contaminate and render dangerous drinking water, cess-pools, privy-vaults, and all places where the offal of houses is thrown. They have the power of self-production outside of the human body; hence but an infinitesimally small quantity of the original virus need be imported to produce a wide-spread epidemic. They are killed or rendered innocuous by certain substances known as disinfectants, among which may be mentioned a high degree of heat, carbolic acid, sulphate of iron (commercial copperas), nitrous and sulphurous acid gases, etc. A temperature of 32° Fahrenheit destroys their vitality. Should any of these germs hibernate and survive through a winter, it is found that on the return of warm weather they are revivified, but have parted with a portion of their vitality, and are no longer capable of self-reproduction; hence in the second season they only give rise to isolated or sporadic cases, and do not produce an epidemic. It has been found by actual experience that those cities and towns exposed to the disease, which are neglectful of sanitary laws, those localities in towns which are the filthiest, and those individuals who are the most careless or indifferent in their moral and physical habits are the greatest sufferers." It follows from the foregoing that while neglected streets, alleys, and yards, and defective drains and sewers, vaults, sinks, and cess-pools, rotten vegetable matter, or filth of any kind, can no more originate yellow fever than they can small-pox, yet their presence in the vicinity of human habitations affords a richly-manured soil for the imported germ to arrive at its fullest malignancy. The danger to a community cognizant of and having a due regard for the well-known laws of modern sanitation is reduced to a minimum, that to one ignorant or indifferent to them is intensified to a maximum. Dr. Hughes, of St. Louis, also contends for the germ theory and that an atmosphere below 32° kills. Dr. Mitchell, of Memphis, and nearly the whole corps of medical experts under him during the epidemic of 1878 took the same view.

Dr. Ford, of St. Louis, believes, on the contrary, in the principle of fermentation—that yellow fever was existent in the form of dry particles of dust everywhere it had been once, but that the cold would repress their activity—in that cold would render the person less receptive, and his body would not be in a condition to induce the fermentation of the dry dust. He says that "a person might go into a cold climate with the dry dust or active principle of yellow fever upon him, and while he remained in that cold climate he would not be afflicted with the disease, but if he went to a warm, malarial climate, he would be very apt to be stricken down. In other words, cold did not kill the vitality of yellow fever, but simply repressed it." He, however, admitted the efficacy of proper sanitary regulations to prevent a man's system from getting into the condition necessary to fermentation of the particles.

Professor P. Stille, of Mobile, differs from all the preceding authorities, and advances a novel theory to account for the origin of yellow fever. He attributes it to the Gulf Stream. Calling attention to the equable atmospheric conditions of the tropical lands of both hemispheres, he says: "Coming up the south-east, across the torrid zone, is an ocean current which, where it sweeps around the north coast of South America, is called the Guiana Current. It makes its way directly into the Gulf of Mexico, where it takes the name of the Gulf Stream. After washing the smaller islands of the West Indies, it forces itself with great strength through the narrow channel between Cuba and Yucatan, and rushes all around the shores of the gulf, taking its turn toward the east, and quitting the land immediately after passing the southern point of Florida. Within the gulf its temperature stands at from 85° to 89°, but soon after having passed Florida its temperature goes suddenly down to 65°, and finally to 54° and 50°. Now, if we examine every part of the sea we shall find no other spot where a warm current washes the land at any thing like so high a temperature as is exhibited in the Gulf of Mexico. A goodly portion of the time the temperature of the water stands entirely above that of the air, consequently a heavy mist is taken up. In other words, the atmosphere is completely saturated with moisture to such an extent as to render it too heavy to rise in obedience to the usual laws governing evaporation, the high temperature of the land preventing condensation. As a result, there lies upon the surface of the low country a thin stratum of air so heavy and so damp as to tempt us strongly into coining *subaqueous* as a designation by which to represent its condition. For proof that such conditions do arise in all cases where the water stands at a temperature higher than that of the air, we refer you to Fitch's *Physical Geography*, page 142; and for proof that they exist in the West India Islands, see Humboldt's *Island of Cuba*, page 172. And here, in my humble judgment, we have arrived at a knowledge of the main conditions necessary to the propagation of the yellow fever: A stratum of atmosphere saturated with moisture to such an extent as can only occur under like circumstances as exist in the West Indies, and a tropical clime such as prevails there, and is every now and then, as I contend, carried into regions far above its natural lines. This thin stratum of heavy atmosphere is carried from the ocean equator and thrown upon our shores from the gulf breezes, so called, but in ordinary seasons the low temperature of the earth condenses the moisture permanently before it has passed far inland. In seasons like the present, however, when there have been two summers together, as it were, the earth with us is too warm to admit of permanent condensation. A portion of the moisture may fall as heavy as dew, but the rising temperature of the morning will take it up again, and hence it will be carried on, wave after wave, as it were, until it has reached its final stopping point, possibly many degrees above the shores of the Gulf of Mexico. The immediate agent working in yellow fever (be it living atom or fungus) is semi-aquatic in its nature, perhaps, and therefore always finds itself at home in this peculiar character of heavy and wet atmosphere; hence it flourishes wherever a footing can be secured in it, and fattens upon its human victims the more the further it gets from its nursery bed and finds them the less acclimated against its effects. This heavy atmosphere theory would explain why yellow fever is mainly confined to the low grounds—in all cases waves of heavy atmosphere, like currents of water, find their ways through the depressions upon the surface of the earth. If our Gulf breezes should drive them inland, they would very naturally roll up the valleys of our rivers." Dowler quotes a similar theory advanced by the Faculty of Paris, in 1665, to account for the ravages of the black plague* now threatening the world in southern Russia and northern Brazil. He says: "In France, the medical faculty of Paris assembled in order to find out the causes and devise sanitary measures to arrest the progress of the epidemic. The doctors, after due deliberation, in a solemn official manifesto, or medical bull, decided in the most positive manner that the epidemic was 'owing to the constellations which combatted the rays of the sun, and the warmth of the heavenly fire which struggled violently with the waters of the sea, originating a vapor in the great eastern sea of India, corrupted with fish, enveloping itself with fog. Should the same thing continue not a man would be left alive, except the grace of Christ preserve him. We are of opinion that the constellations, with the aid of nature, strive, by virtue of their divine right, to protect and heal the human race, and to this end, in union with the rays of the sun, acting through the power of fire, endeavor to break through the mist.' The faculty at the same time predicted, in the most oracular manner, the future movements of the aforesaid constellations: 'Accordingly, within the next ten days, until the 17th of the ensuing month of July, this mist will be converted into a stinking, deleterious rain, whereby the air will be much purified. Now as soon as this rain announces itself by thunder or hail, every one of you should protect yourself from the air; and as well as after the rain, kindle a large fire of vine wood, green laurel, wormwood, chamomile, etc., until the earth is again completely dry, and three days afterwards no one ought to go about; only small river fish should be used; rain-water must be avoided in cooking; bathing is most hurtful, and the least departure from chastity fatal.'"

Dr. Labadie, in his report of the epidemic of 1864, at Galveston, reviewing the existing theories as to the origin and means of propagation of yellow fever, rather favors the explosive theory. He says: "What causes the rise and progress of this disease is a question hard to answer. Some say it is caused by a marsh miasm, under an atmosphere of over 90° Fahrenheit. Others contend that it is a peculiar subtle poison that explodes in the air, like an inflammable substance, communicates itself to certain points; and those who may happen to inhale or swallow more or less of it come under its influence after a certain number of hours—to as long as twenty-four days—which, when exploded in the stomach, or is absorbed by the blood from the lungs, finds its seat of infection in the stomach, which it first inflames to such a degree as to cause those violent pains witnessed; leaving its impress there, it soon

---

* Which, Dowell says, appears to resemble yellow fever in many respects.

leaves to do its work. The system becomes so depressed, so exhausted, that all the muscular force is gone. The walls of the stomach, no longer protected by the muscular fibres, a degree of relaxation follows; the capillary vessels relaxed soon bleed; this blood, mixing with a rank acid of the stomach or bowels, they neutralize each other, hence chocolate-colored vomit; but if this blood meets a strong acid, it becomes black, and, perhaps, carbonizes at times in small particles, hence black vomit more or less profuse."

Dr. Warren Stone, an authority held in as high esteem as any other, and a physician whose name in New Orleans was, for more than thirty years, as a household word, in the course of a lecture, delivered in Bellevue Hospital in the winter of 1867, sustained the wave or cycle theory, but as to other points agreed with Dowler and Dowell. He says: "It is a disease peculiar to warm latitudes, but its limits could not be defined by any exact temperature or climatic conditions, for exceptions would frequently occur to falsify any such restrictions. Nothing more definite can be said than that it is a disease incident to warm climates, and induced by a peculiar poison, totally intangible, and disconnected from any known causes of disease. There is no combination of filth, no combination of circumstances calculated to deteriorate health and excite typhoid or typhus fevers that had any thing to do with the generation of yellow fever. This remarkable fact is not generally known. Some Federal officers have taken credit to themselves for keeping yellow fever out of New Orleans during their occupation of that city; but it is a notorious fact that the city was not cleaner then (1862) in the suburbs and lower districts than it had often been before. The weather happened to be cooler, and there was less rain; but there was no material difference in any other respect. The city of New Orleans had been exempt from the fever for some years previously, when there was no quarantine whatever. Yellow fever has existed upon high and healthy latitudes, and proved as virulent there as in low regions. The Magnolia ridge, back of New Orleans, is one of the healthiest regions in the world, yet the yellow fever has proved quite as destructive there as in less favored regions. Indeed, the disease has always been more violent in the country, when it once prevails there, than in cities. In regard to the ætiology or causes of yellow fever, there has always been much dispute. It has been a question whether it is imported or is of local origin. It certainly has not been imported in ships. The epidemic influence is wafted through the atmosphere in waves or cycles, and always made gradual and regular approaches; so that in New Orleans we know when it is coming by its prevalence in the islands of the gulf and places south of us. In the year 1851 it began in Brazil, and after passing over the northern part of South America and the West India Islands, it reached New Orleans in 1853. In 1855 it had traveled as far as Memphis, and was severe in many of the interior towns. Its history in New Orleans the present year is remarkable. It first appeared in a mild form, and in several places at once, in the month of June, and, although the weather was favorable to its spread, it did not increase in intensity, and only about nine cases occurred per week. These cases evidently originated in the city. But later in the season a fresh wave approached from the direction of Mexico, appearing in a violent form in Indianola, Galveston, and New Iberia, and, lastly, in New Orleans, where it appeared in a severe form and in increasing ratio, although the weather was of the kind considered unfavorable to its propagation. This was the general history of the disease. It fixed upon a place and ran its course, increasing in a definite ratio, declining in the same way, and finally disappearing, but, for the time being, affecting all who were subject to attack and exposed to its influence. Debility and other reasons render some persons more susceptible than others to the peculiar poison; but this is the case with all diseases." Dr. P. V. Schenck, of St. Louis, in an exhaustive treatise, published during the epidemic of 1878, also upholds the wave theory. He says: "Yellow fever is an infectious disease, but it is neither miasmatic nor contagious. The poison of yellow fever is not generated in the human system; it is generated externally; it attacks persons, and may be carried in vessels and trunks; for the presence of the disease an imported germ, or descendant of an imported germ, is necessary. The old discussions which have so long disturbed the profession are at an end, and the mind will be no longer swayed like a pendulum beyond the point of a stable equilibrium. Even when the Royal Academy of Medicine were undergoing a lively debate; and when Dr. Chevrin was on his six years' journey of investigation; and when Drs. Pym and Bryson, of England, were quarreling over the facts in the Bann and Eclair cases; while the stupid Health Board of England were trying to break down quarantine; while old Dr. Hosack, of this country, was venting his wrath on those who believed in non-contagion, ' as juniors in knowledge and in years, and as the unfledged opinion and speculations of men of the closet, who have had but few opportunities to test them at the bedside,'—even then, if you will carefully examine the facts, you will find it to be impossible, out of the many old epidemics, to affirm of any one of them that it had been introduced by contagion. Bancroft has brought a mass of testimony and fact upon this subject. Dr. Porter, with his vessels, meets in mid-ocean with an infected vessel: his officers and crew intermingle, and they leave unharmed. A vessel lying at Havana, surrounded by infected vessels, in front of an infected city, is unharmed. The fourteen men who went to New York from Governor's Island, visited in the most thickly and filthy portions of that city; nine of them died, yet none of the citizens took the disease—indeed, so far as known, no case is on record in which a person having the disease in a previously healthy quarter, has become the starting point of a local epidemic. In yellow fever we meet with a non-contagious disease; the living person, though sick, will not propagate it—it is not reproduced in his system; the disease is of exotic origin, and, in order to become epidemic, it must be carried by the wave. It has its periods of rest and of activity. It travels three times as fast in tropical regions as it does higher up. It may hibernate, and resume its march the summer following; it may take one-half of a city this, and finish its work the next summer. It travels at the rate of about forty feet a day. Dr. Stone used to compare its course and mode of travel to a tax-collector—from house to house along a street before it diverges. It is most active in its operations near the surface of the earth, attacking a larger proportion of persons on the ground floor; it is more active at night than in the day-time; it may attack a single block or district in a city, as, for instance, in 1870, New Orleans suffered from yellow fever. It was confined to a portion of the second district, twelve blocks by four. In 1872 it was in the fourth district. In 1873 it appeared in all the districts in the city, and was epidemic, but disinfectants so modified the disease that it did not become a general epidemic, whilst higher up the river, Shreveport and Memphis passed through the terrors of a fatal epidemic. In 1874, New Orleans again escaped, while Pascagoula and Pensacola suffered. Walls may stop the progress of yellow fever; as, for instance, the inmates of the calaboose in New Orleans generally escape; even a partition of boards may intervene, as reported by Dr. Nott, from Governor's Island, in 1867. Dr. Parkes says that in the West Indies it has repeatedly attacked a barrack, while no other place on the island was affected. At Lisbon, Cadiz, and many other places, it has attacked only one side of a street. In the West Indies it has repeatedly commenced in the same part of a barrack. It has been known to attack every house in a neighborhood save one; to attack all the sailors in the berths on one side of a man-of-war before reaching over on the opposite side."

Dr. W. A. McCully, of Independence, Mo., a very intelligent physician, who volunteered and was devoted to the work in Memphis in 1878, writes of his experience during that epidemic, and one that prevailed at Key West, Florida, in 1864, while he was a surgeon of volunteers in the Federal army. It will be seen, from what he says, that notwithstanding a strict quarantine, enforced by an adequate military force, there were some seemingly spontaneous cases of fever in 1865. He says: "In the winter of 1864 and 1865 stringent sanitary regulations were enforced on the island of Key West and Fort Taylor. In March, 1865, a strict quarantine was ordered by Brig.-Gen. John Newton, which I enforced with the assistance of the army and navy. A number of cases occurred during the summer of that year, but all of a mild type, the mortality being but two per cent. The local conditions were such that the germs could not propagate, and in my opinion to them we must generally ascribe the malignancy of the disease. I left Key West in 1866, and never saw yellow fever again until the recent epidemic at Memphis, Tenn. The disease there exhibited the same phenomena as at Key West and Havana, except that it was frequently complicated with malarial fever. Patients sometimes would have intermittent fever precede, and at others follow yellow fever. Relapses were more frequent. A failure to treat the miasmatic complications was the cause of considerable mortality, I thought, at Memphis. I made thirty autopsies at Key West, and a number at Memphis, with almost identical results. The same lesions were observed in all, modified by malaria, suppression of urine, or some other complication. The observations made at these places lead me to the following conclusions:

"1st. That yellow fever is produced by a specific germ.

"2d. That the impression on the individual organization is as specific as that produced by typhoid or the eruptive fever, and protects it from subsequent attacks.

"3d. That race or acclimation affords no protection against contracting the disease. That the African race suffered less with small mortality, while the white race, especially those of sanguine temperament, suffered severely with heavy mortality. Being accustomed to the climate certainly diminished the mortality.

"4th. That the germs propagate within and without the body; the spread of the disease depending on cess-pools, sewers, filth and personal contact, the temperature and other meteorological conditions being favorable.

"5. That a temperature below 70° is unfavorable to the propagation of the germs, and if continuous will destroy them.

"6. That where the temperature produces frost sufficient to exterminate the germs it is probably a preventable disease by quarantine alone; but should it be introduced, its benign or malignant type will depend entirely upon the sanitary condition of our villages, towns and cities.

"7. I believe the disease may be introduced into any part of our country where there is a continuous daily temperature above 72° for two months."

The Commission of Allopathic Physicians* appointed by the Congressional Committee to investigate and report upon the origin and causes of the yellow fever epidemic of 1878, state that "the concurrence of local conditions favorable to the evolution of the yellow fever poison seems to be necessary to the evolution of yellow fever epidemics; but, as to the nature of these favorable local conditions, we have no positive knowledge. In a negative way, we know that yellow fever often fails to swell into epidemic prevalence when high summer heat, atmospheric moisture, marsh malaria, and abundant filth are all present; so that there must be some *conditio sine qua non* other than any or all of these. The discovery of this unknown factor in the generation of yellow fever epidemics would be a great boon to humanity." Dr. P. V. Schenck, of St. Louis, who, in a well-prepared paper — from which one quotation has already been made — shows that yellow fever has a home lacking in sanitary conditions; it migrates; it is carried in baggage and in the hold of ships, and by a wave power; and that it requires humidity and a continuously high temperature. But these are not causes. He says: "It is not generated by bilge-water; unsanitary conditions won't produce it. Constantinople has filth and the plague, but no yellow fever; India, heat and cholera, but no yellow fever. Heat and humidity exist without the disease. Mauritius, in the Eastern, compared with Jamaica in the Western, Seas, has a mean annual temperature (80° Fahrenheit) almost the same; the fluctuations and undulations are not excessive, and the humidity nearly the same. The rain-fall (sixty-six to seventy-six inches) is similar; the geological formations not dissimilar. Yet, with all these points of similarity, the diseases are very different. At Jamaica the

---

* The following are the names of the gentlemen composing the Commission: John M. Woodworth, M. D., President; Stanford E. Chaillé, M. D., Secretary; S. M. Bemiss, M. D.; Jerome Cochran, M. D.; M. S. Craft, M. D.; Samuel A. Green, M. D.; Thomas S. Hardee, C. E.; R. W. Mitchell, M. D.; Jacob S. Mosher, M. D.; W. H. Randle, M. D.; Louis A. Falligant, M. D.; R. M. Swearingen, M. D.

yellow fever is often epidemic, at Mauritius it is unknown. The ground is not tenable, therefore, that has been taken by some of the most eminent English practitioners in the West Indies, as well as prominent men in this country, that the yellow fever may be occasioned through the agency of a tropical sun, independent of any other cause. Dr. Bryson, who has studied this question, thinks that yellow fever is not a distinct disease, but only an exaggerated bilious fever, and quotes the celebrated case of the ship *Bann*, where there was no fever when they left—the first case was nothing but malarial fever. The cases after this assumed the type of yellow fever, which became so bad that they were compelled to abandon the cruise and go to Ascension Island for relief. He also quotes the Leclair case; and he accounts for these cases, that the disease, owing to local cause, changed its type. Dr. Fenner says that, in regard to yellow fever in New Orleans, the fevers there are intermittent, remittent, and continued, alternating in type, and running into each other. In summer and autumn they have a decided tendency to crisis by hemorrhage; this makes yellow fever. Dr. Hanson has observed that often malignant intermittent fevers precede the outbreaks of yellow fever epidemics.* The cause of miasmatic diseases is a specific excitant of disease, known as miasm, which propagates outside of, and is disconnected from, a previously diseased organism. But this disease does not occur, like marsh fevers, at regular periods; it occurs where there is the least malaria; it avoids the country, with its marshes, and seeks the city. In Charleston the people flee to the marsh lands in order to avoid the disease. Others contend it is owing to decomposing animal or vegetable matter; in other words, to an unsanitary condition of our large cities. Under such circumstances the disease could be produced at will, but we find that sanitary measures, in the ordinary acceptation of the term, have no power to arrest an epidemic wave. Besides these migrations of yellow fever have not occurred when the most unsanitary conditions would tempt it. During the whole of the war of the Revolution, and of the late war, when the military and naval operations on our coast, and the communication with the West Indies, were greater than at any other time; when, during the Revolution, large bodies of troops were accumulated in the Antilles and landed in our country direct from there, and every circumstance seemed combined that could generate and propagate disease, still during that time yellow fever was a disease entirely unknown, and unknown at points where it previously and has since prevailed with terrific force. When we state that yellow fever will attack the healthy villages equally with the dirty alleys of cities, the palace with the hovel, do not understand that a person placed under superior hygienic conditions is as liable to receive disease and that he will not recover from it sooner than one otherwise placed. From the earliest cultivation of medical science, certain states or conditions of the atmosphere have been recognized as powerfully influencing the production of the cause of disease. Hippocrates and Galen attributed to change in the air, though the

---

* This was the cause in Memphis in 1873 and 1878. In the first named year cholera and small-pox also prevailed.

former speaks of unknown divine principle, to the operation of which he supposed pestilential diseases might be owing. Some attribute to an electric operation; others speak of the epidemic constitution of the air; others, to some hidden or occult qualities derived from exhalations of the bowels of the earth. But now these ideas are, since the discovery of germs, put down among the curiosities of our literature."

The Homeopathic Commission, whose expenses were borne by that philanthropic lady, Mrs. Thompson, of New York—who also paid the expenses of the Woodworth (or Allopathic) Commission—after some weeks of personal investigation at the principal points affected by the fever in 1878, made a report of fifty-six pages, which contains matter of great value, but which unfortunately is interwoven with much of aggressive criticism of allopathic treatment which, in the eyes of those at least who are attached to the old school, is reprehensible especially in view of the importance of the subject under investigation. Treating of the causes of yellow fever this Homeopathic Commission * reports that it is a specific disease, entirely independent of malaria, occurring rarely a second time in the same person, infectious and capable of transmission to any distance by means of fomites or infected material. The yellow fever germs—for we accept provisionally the germ theory of the disease—are indigenous to the West Indies and perhaps to the west coast of Africa, and have been thoroughly naturalized in many localities in the southern portion of the United States. They were imported into New Orleans during the last quarter of the eighteenth century, and have existed in the soil or atmosphere of that place ever since, either in a latent or an active condition. They may lie dormant for many years consecutively, and they require a concurrence of causes to develop them into a state of disease-producing activity. Some of the factors which seem to be favorable to the excitation of the yellow fever germ are the following:

Low, swampy ground, near the level of a tropical sea.

Long continuance of very high temperature, following heavy rains.

Long continuance of south and east winds.

Aggregations of human beings with the excreta of their bodies in small spaces. A crowded and dirty ship may be a nidus for yellow fever, as well as a crowded and dirty city.

Long continuance of calm weather, unbroken by thunder-storms.

Exposure of decaying vegetable and animal matter to a burning sun.

Inefficient drainage and the general accumulation of filth, especially the city garbage.

Deficiency of ozone in the atmosphere.

Pestilential exhalations from an upturned soil.

---

* This Commission was composed of the following named gentlemen: Wm. H. Holcombe, M. D., of New Orleans, Chairman; T. S. Verdi, M. D., of Washington City, Sec'y; Bushrod W. James, M. D., of Philadelphia, Penn.; W. L. Breyfogle, M. D., of Louisville, Ky.; J. P. Dake, M. D., of Nashville, Tenn.; E. H. Price, M. D., of Chattanooga, Tenn.; F. H. Orme, M. D., of Atlanta, Ga.; L. A. Falligant, M. D., of Savannah, Ga.; Lucius D. Morse, M. D., of Memphis, Tenn.; W. J. Murrell, M. D., of Mobile, Alabama; Thomas J. Harper, M. D., of Vicksburg, Miss.

When the yellow fever germ has been waked into activity by these causes, it may be transported to places where none of them exist. It seems that a certain concurrence of several of the above factors is necessary to the generation of yellow fever. There is probably one combination in one epidemic, and a somewhat different combination in the next epidemic. An epidemic may be mild or severe according to the number and force of the concurring causes. There may also be other unknown but discoverable factors, which may be necessary at one time to produce an epidemic and not necessary at another. No one of the above suggested causes could excite an epidemic by itself, and it is not probable that they all ever concurred equally to the formation of the disease. The most extensive collections and comparison of facts are necessary to illumine the very great darkness which lies upon these complex questions. The naturalized yellow fever germs may receive so slight a stimulus as to produce only a few sporadic cases. Or they may be vitalized in certain localities to such a degree as to occasion quite an outbreak in those localities, not easily communicated to other quarters. Or, thirdly, the disseminated germs may be vivified in all directions, and a general epidemic excited. Or, lastly, the naturalized germs may lie entirely quiescent until fresh and active germs are brought in from foreign ports, which then act as sparks to ignite the inflammable material already existing. We thus have four shades or degrees of yellow fever visitation: sporadic cases, local and limited outbursts, epidemics from naturalized germs, and epidemics from importation. In sporadic cases and limited outbreaks the specific nature of the fever is not clearly brought to light, and it is sometimes difficult to diagnose it from the dominant malarial or bilious diseases. The imported epidemic, whether from Havana to New Orleans or from New Orleans to Memphis, etc., etc., is always a more quick-spreading and malignant disease than that arising from our naturalized germs. The comparative mildness of the late epidemic in New Orleans is one out of several reasons for believing that the disease was of local origin. The yellow fever of domestic origin can only be prevented by local sanitary measures. So long as the public authorities ignore the crying evils at home, and watch only for the enemy at the sea-side, we shall continue to be scourged with repeated epidemics of yellow fever. Quarantine may or may not keep out the tropical foe, but our utmost energies should be concentrated against the enemy which has been domiciliated in our households for nearly a century. Is there any personal prophylactic against yellow fever? None which has the least scientific value. Quinine is probably serviceable when malarial fevers are simultaneously prevailing, not because it has any power against yellow fever, but because an attack of malarial fever, preventable by quinine, might, if allowed to occur, precipitate an attack of yellow fever. Quinine for intermittents, belladonna for scarlet fever, and vaccination for smallpox, are the only prophylactics which have commanded even the partial belief of the profession. They are all confessedly homeopathic in their actions; and we confidently believe, if prophylactics for yellow fever, or any other disease, exist, that they will be found only by study and experiment in that direction. The poison of the rattlesnake produces an artificial disease bearing a remarkable resemblance to yellow fever, and it has proved a remedy of considerable value in the malignant forms of that affection. Inoculation with this poison was used extensively at Havana many years ago, under the auspices of an erratic genius who, it is said, assumed the venerable name of Humboldt. The results are differently stated by the friends and enemies of the experiment, but, as the quantity inoculated was entirely too great, and large doses of antidotal remedies were simultaneously administered, it may be fairly presumed that such an experiment had no real scientific value. Whether the poison, cautiously used, either hypodermically or in small doses by the mouth, may not produce a substitutive disease, which, for that season at least, might prevent an attack of yellow fever, is a question certain to command further consideration." It will thus be seen that the homeopathists do not believe in prophylactics, as little do the allopathists, who have had a wider and more extended experience with the fever. Beyond the reach of successful contradiction, it may be asserted that there is no known preventive of yellow fever. This has been proven in every epidemic; but especially in the last, that of 1878 in Memphis, and so strongly as to set the question at rest forever. Those who resorted to lime-water, to sulphur in the boots, shoes or stockings, to sulphur and gin, to regulated quantities of gin, to liver-pads, to garlic, to onions, to quinine, to cathartic pills, calomel, chlorinated lime, or any thing else, invariably proved easy victims, and died rapidly. The system was, by means of these poisons—for such they proved—either diseased or depleted; every additional dose or every additional effort only increasing or intensifying the fear which induces a resort to prophylactics. One case of many such within the author's knowledge may be mentioned. It was that of a man who ordinarily enjoyed good health, who left the city at the outset of the fever, but returned for the purpose of transacting some business. By the time this was accomplished, shot-gun quarantines were established, and he was compelled to remain. Demoralized by this enforced imprisonment in the doomed city, he had recourse to garlic and onions, which he used three times each day; and to sulphur, which he used in his stockings; and to sulphur and gin, of which he drank as his fears prompted. He was taken with the fever and died on the fourth day. All the physicians of experience advised against prophylactics, though there were not wanting a few of the faculty who had a pet preventive. Dr. Luke P. Blackburn, writing of his experiences in Hickman, in 1878, says that "those who had been taking quinine as a preventive also fell an easy prey. Quinine was an irritant, and usually opened the system to the attack of the disease. In my opinion much of the mortality of Memphis, Grenada, and other cities was due to the extravagant use of quinine and the saturation of the air with carbolic acid. Instead of the latter assisting in the suppression of the disease, it but increased the effect of the poison and made the fever more deadly. Those who had escaped easiest were those who lived temperately, were not frightened, and did not take 'preventives' too often recommended." A clergyman, who writes as if he had had some experience, says what every sensible layman as well as physician must endorse, as follows: "For individuals who are obliged to remain in an infected locality, there is no preventive so effectual as keeping the system in a general state of good health. Let a man breathe fresh air as much as possible, eat nutritious food moderately and regularly, take plenty of sleep at seasonable hours, bathe freely, and above all avoid the use of stimulants; by so doing he will reduce the danger to a minimum and be likely to escape, while strong men of irregular habits are stricken down by his side. An equable mind, which comes of a firm trust in God and an implicit reliance on His providence, is not the least valuable preventive of this as of every other disease."

II.

SPORADIC or epidemic yellow fever is not always to be attributed to the same causes, notwithstanding Dr. Dowell, of Galveston, says that in nineteen cases out of twenty it will be found to have been introduced or imported. Dr. Bennett Dowler, in his excellent pamphlet, "The Epidemic in New Orleans," tells of an outbreak of it in Gallipolis, Ohio, in 1796, which killed one-half the army and the inhabitants in ten days. This place, which also suffered in 1878, was at that time a new settlement, quite in the wilderness, and isolated from all others, having communication with the Atlantic cities only at long intervals and under favoring conditions of weather and of roads. Mr. A. Elliott, in his journal of a voyage down the Ohio in that year, referred to in the report of the surgeon-general of the army, says the disease raged violently, the fatal cases being generally attended with black vomit. "The fever," he says, "could not have been taken there from the Atlantic States, as my boat was the first that descended the river in the spring. Neither could it have been taken from New Orleans, as there is no communication up the river at that season of the year." In the fall of 1823, yellow fever of a high grade suddenly appeared at Fort Smith, Arkansas, and prevailed epidemically, without so much as a suspicion of exposure to contagion, according to the official report on file in the office of the surgeon-general of the army. The theory here suggested, that this disease, if not localized or indigenous to this country, may originate under favoring conditions, is borne out to some extent by a tabulated statement furnished in an article that appeared in *De Bow's Review* for December, 1853, immediately after what was, until last year's experience in Memphis, considered the most dreadful of its visitations in this country. The table shows the number of cases and deaths, from the year 1822 to 1849, inclusive, which occurred in the Charity Hospital. The figures are perfectly authentic, having been taken from the official records. These figures bear very significantly upon the proposition with which the writer prefaces his remarks, to wit: "That the yellow fever originates here,

A HISTORY OF THE YELLOW FEVER.

no instance of its ever having been imported being as yet well proved." The table, be it understood, represents only the cases and deaths at the Charity Hospital for the years respectively mentioned:

YEARS.	TOTAL CASES.	DEATHS.	YEARS.	TOTAL CASES.	DEATHS.
1822*	337	239	1836	6	5
1823	1	1	1837*	993	442
1824	167	108	1838	22	17
1825	99	49	1839*	1,086	452
1826	24	5	1840	3	3
1827	372	109	1841*	1,114	594
1828	290	130	1842*	425	211
1829	436	215	1843*	1,086	487
1830	256	117	1844*	169	83
1831	3	2	1845	1	0
1832*	18	26	1846	146	96
1833*	422	210	1847*	2,479	895
1834*	150	95	1848*	1,226	420
1835*	505	284	1849	1,055	545
			Total,	12,913	6,332

It thus appears that during these twenty-eight years there were thirteen epidemics in New Orleans, and at least five other seasons of heavy mortality from yellow fever when it did not please the authorities to declare an epidemic. It will be seen that there was not a single year in which the yellow fever did not appear at the Charity Hospital, and that the average number of deaths annually from that cause was more than 200. The author of this article in *De Bow* argues from the statistics of the year 1853, and from those of all the preceding years as far back as 1822, that the yellow fever is indigenous to New Orleans, and that it depends upon purely local conditions from year to year whether or not it will become epidemic. All accounts agree—and he quotes copiously from the contemporaneous press—that the sanitary conditions in 1853 were unusually and unprecedentedly bad; that at no time within the memory of man had the streets been as filthy and the policing of the city as negligently and criminally mismanaged. To these causes is attributed the frightful mortality of 1853 as compared with other years. Strengthening these conclusions, Dr. Simonds, of New Orleans, declared (and gave the figures to prove) that the yellow fever was treated in the Charity Hospital every year for thirty years, up to 1849. "So," as Dowler says, "that the stream of yellow fever, with whatsoever of contagion it may possess, is uninterrupted, no year having been wholly exempt in this institution, not to name the city at large." The commission appointed by the Board of Health of New Orleans, in 1853, to inquire into the origin, propagation, or mode of transmission of the then late epidemic of yellow fever,—sewerage, quarantine, and the sanitary condition of that city,—after a long and laborious investigation, reached the same conclusion. They say "that yellow fever is not a disease personally contagious; that its infectious properties are only communicable in a foul or infectious atmosphere; that is, that a foul vessel or individual with the disease will only propagate it under atmospherical and local conditions similar to that which furnished its na-

---

* The years marked (*) are those in which the fever was declared epidemic.

tivity. That although vitiated or infectious air may be conveyed in goods and in various ways to distant places, ventilation speedily dissipates it; and that if disease results, where it is much concentrated, or with very susceptible individuals, it extends no farther, except under the conditions above specified.* But further than this, the commission—after most careful scrutiny into the actual occurrences of the first irruption of the fever, its spread, the character of its localization, the persons most liable and suffering, from whatever class and country—have converted presumptive proof into positive certainty, that the fever originated with us; that its fatal malignity and spread were justly attributable to a very remarkable concurrence and combination of atmospheric and terrine causes, always particularly fatal to human health and life." Dowler strengthens this indigenous theory by the citation of another instance of epidemic yellow fever which could not otherwise be accounted for. It occurred in 1797, at New Design, a small town fifteen miles from the Mississippi River and twenty from St. Louis. It carried off one-fourth of the inhabitants. Not even one person had visited the place from places where the fever prevailed. Still another instance is furnished by the same distinguished author. He says

---

* Dr. Drake, of Nashville, at a meeting of the Davidson County Medical Society, on the 15th of March, of this year, 1879, in a speech worthy of the subject and of the distinguished body before which it was made, sustains the position taken by the New Orleans Commission of 1853, and fortifies it by facts as follows: "The testimony of Dr. Wilkes and others suggest some very important deductions. Dr. Webb returned from Memphis [in 1878] to his home carrying the germs of yellow fever about his clothing. His wife and children took the disease and died, and yet he escaped. How was this? His duties kept him in the open air, more or less, while the female inmates of his family were more or less confined to the house, where the germs found a lodgment from his cast-off clothing. In this room the poison evidently existed in the greatest quantity; and the constant occupants were the first to suffer. At Jackson, a gentleman who had been to Memphis [1878] hung up his clothes in a wardrobe, the weather being warm. After several days his wife opened the door and took the garments out. We would suppose that in a close, hot room the poison would multiply itself in this time until the air would be heavy with it; and so it seemed in this case, for the lady took the yellow fever and died, followed in due time by the rest of the family. Why was not the importer of the disease the first to take it? He had the germs with him most certainly. Evidently, the poisoned atmosphere around him while *en route* was too much diluted by fresh air to affect him beyond his powers of ordinary resistance. The inmates of his house were differently situated; confined in-doors, they breathed the poisoned atmosphere generated in unwholesome quantities, and so were the first victims, while his habits led him out into the open air, and he only took the disease when he was confined at home ministering to the sick. Again: the inhabitants of the tents in the neighborhood of Memphis principally escaped for the same reason, namely, that they were not exposed to an atmosphere sufficiently charged with the poison to produce morbific effects. This seems to be the only solution; for, if the active malific cause was general in its operations—atmospheric, and not specific—then those people would surely have suffered and died as they did at the city a few miles away. So it seems, from all this, that the danger from yellow fever grows in proportion to the stagnation and confinement of the air in a given quarter. Infected rooms become dangerous in proportion to the want of ventilation; and cellars, for obvious reasons, would be charged to saturation. The holds of vessels and the apartments of freight cars would become particularly dangerous."

that early in the summer of 1800, "the then Intendant of Cuba, El Sr. Don Pablo Valiente, chartered the ship *Dolphin* to take himself, family, and suite to Spain, touched at Charleston, and, having anchored in the Bay of Cadiz, he went ashore with his party two days after, on the 8th of July. A month later the yellow fever appeared in Cadiz; whereupon Valiente was arrested upon a criminal charge, for having imported yellow fever contagion from Havana and Charleston. The former he left in May, the latter he touched at on June 2d, and left eight days after. At neither place was there any yellow fever. No yellow fever appeared on board of the *Dolphin* during the voyage, though three of the sailors had died. The Intendant, after eleven months' imprisonment, was acquitted at Seville, and was afterwards promoted by the government, probably as a compensation for his wrongs." Another case is that of the visitation in Philadelphia, in 1853, which was attributed to the bark *Mandarin*, which had arrived from Cienfuego. An investigation by Dr. W. Jewell, of the College of Physicians, resulted in the declaration that—" 1st, No disease of a malignant type prevailed in the city previous to the arrival of the *Mandarin;* 2d, That none of the seamen of the *Mandarin* sickened ; 3d, That none of the laborers employed in unloading the *Mandarin* had taken the disease ; . . . . 6th, That in no case has the disease been communicated to any person visiting or engaged in attendance upon the sick ; and, 7th, That not a single instance can be met with having its origin to the south of where the *Mandarin* lay last." Dr. Heustis—in his work on Epidemic Fevers, published at Cahawba, Alabama, in 1825—in his account of the epidemic in Pensacola, in 1822, offers additional testimony in the same direction. He says: "It was pretended by the advocates of imported contagion that the fever was brought in a vessel which arrived from New Orleans about the beginning of August. The captain of this vessel was among the first that sickened and died of the malignant fever, and this after his arrival in Pensacola. . . . . The opinion of one of the most respectable physicians in Pensacola was, that the disease originated entirely from local causes. Such, also, was the conviction of the Board of Health." Dowell, on page 19 of his *Yellow Fever*, although favoring quarantine, says: "Yellow fever occasionally leaves its habitual, assumes a migratory character, traveling over great extents of country, not infrequently breaking through the most rigid quarantine. But in these migrations it seems to have a prescribed course, along which it pays no respect to any impediments placed in its way; but places in its line of travel [as in 1878] are often protected by non-intercourse, and hence the importance of quarantine." Quoting from such high authorities as Doctors Warren Stone, J. C. Nott, Hunt, Jones, Fenner, and Bennett Dowler, Dr. Dowell continues: "These great migrating epidemics revolve in a wave, hurling their terrible influence in a great and sometimes very extended area, often continuing their march during successive years—as the one which commenced in Rio Janeiro, in 1850, and culminated its devastating course at Norfolk, in 1856, putting to flight all theories about local origin and the protections of sanitary cordons or quarantine restrictions." Illustrating the irresistible force with which these great yellow fever epidemics sweep over the country, the following is copied from Dr. Bennett Dowler, perhaps the first among medical authorities on yellow fever. He says: "The geographical area of yellow fever in 1853, as compared with former invasions, was greatly extended, including Florida, Alabama, Louisiana, Mississippi, Arkansas, and Texas. Six States of the Union*—a vast territorial expansion of alluvial, diluvial, and tertiary formations; valleys, dry prairies, elevated plateaus, irregular terraces, low undulating hills, bluffs, and pine woods, interspersed with bayous, lakes, shallow basins, shaking prairies, large bays, dense cypress swamps, canebrakes, colossal grasses, inundated plains—a vast region, undisturbed by volcanic action, where the geological or telluric causes of disease, if such be really regarded as causes, must be nearly uniform. Of these States, five are washed by the almost tideless Gulf of Mexico, presenting a vast, depressed, marshy, sandy, shelly, rockless litoral, which covers from the Rio del Norte to the peninsula of Florida, deeply indenting the Temperate, yet approaching the Torrid Zone; having low, outlying islands in front and numerous great rivers flowing through the background; bringing detrital matter from the high lands and primitive formations of several mountain chains, with tertiary limestone and coral reefs trending along its eastern portion upon the Floridian peninsula." The British report on yellow fever and quarantine of 1852 enumerates ninety-six towns and villages of Spain wherein yellow fever has prevailed in this century, many of them far inland, high, dry, rocky, and hilly, and among the mountains; as, for instance, Gibraltar, where it has prevailed fatally. Bennett Dowler also mentions the fact that the yellow fever prevailed in Tampico and Vera Cruz in 1846, '7, '8, and in New Orleans in 1847; and that, though a large proportion of the American army, going to and returning from the Mexican war, passed through those places, they did not contract or spread the disease, nor did it prevail among the American shipping. Dr. T. J. Heard, of Galveston, who has treated yellow fever, and is one of the most eminent physicians of that city, says that from the "year 1839 to 1853 he had no reason to believe in the communicableness of the disease, either by infection or contagion. In 1853, however, Mr. B. R. Rucker, Postmaster at Washington, on the Brazos River, was taken down with the fever. Washington at that time was a distributing point for the surrounding country, and the Galveston and Houston mails came to the town at night, when Mr. Rucker would open them. Yellow fever was at that time raging in both Galveston and Houston, and Mr. Rucker undoubtedly caught the disease from infected mail-bags.† He conveyed the disease to his family, but further than this it did not spread. About the middle of October, 1853, Mr. Richard Niblett, now of Brenham, owned a drinking saloon in Washington. He received his ice from Houston every night, and opened it personally. He had a most violent attack of fever.

---

* In 1878 it was confined to eight States (embracing five of the above six): Kentucky, Tennessee, Alabama, Missouri, Ohio, Mississippi, Arkansas, and Louisiana.

† The postmaster at Covington, Tenn., was the only person there who had the fever in 1878. He died. He received a heavy mail that had been detained at the Memphis office for some time, opened it, and from it inhaled the poison which in three days killed him.

About the last of the same month, Joseph Brooks and wife, of Navasota, had the fever in New Orleans and came to Washington, stopping at the house of a Mr. Hurse, in the suburbs of the city. Mr. Hurse, his wife, and two children, caught the fever and died. In 1863, about October 1, a man from Orange came to Houston with his wife and stopped at a house near Kennedy's mill. When Dr. Heard arrived the man was dead, and his wife lay dying of yellow fever. The disease extended in the immediate neighborhood, and took a direct course along Buffalo Bayou, following the direction of the prevailing wind. About December 1, 1864, Mrs. Vincent, sister of ex-Lieut.-Gov. Henderson, fled from Houston on account of the yellow fever. A negro left behind took the disease, and, as there was a great lack of blankets, an old carpet was used instead. On his recovery the carpet was stowed away in the garret. Six weeks afterward Mrs. Vincent returned, and, going into the garret, took the carpet out to air it. Four days after this she had a most violent attack." The *Natchez Democrat* published the statement, during the epidemic of 1878, that the year 1819 was distinguished by the prevalence of a remarkably malignant type of yellow fever: "The weather was generally hot and sultry, and there were few and light showers of rain. Unlike its usual course, the fever did not spread, but broke out in widely different localities at one and the same time, raging on the same day in Boston and New Orleans. The pestilence ascended the southern rivers, attacking not only the large cities, but extending also into the country. . . . Of the southern cities Natchez was the greatest sufferer. A destructive flood had that year swept over the lower town and surrounding country, and when the waters subsided they left the usual amount of sediment and debris, covering hundreds of acres. This was not removed, and the heated rays of the sun rendered it a putrid mass of infected matter. Besides, the streets were overflowed and the cellars filled with water. Early in July intermittent and remittent fevers began to prevail, which gradually assumed a malignant type. By September yellow fever was fully developed, and became so general and so deadly that as many of the population as possibly could fled, and only nine hundred and ten remained to take their chances. The poor were removed to a more healthy locality, and cared for at the city's expense. Those who remained suffered terribly, and, as was the case with the epidemic of 1878, no class escaped. Many domestic animals were infected with the disease and died, and even the wild deer in the adjacent forests are said to have died from it." Dr. Labadie, of Galveston, says: " . . . That it takes its origin amongst us, I believe that all old settlers will agree with me; hence quarantine laws and regulations must always become a dead letter. Our city Fathers did once pass a quarantine law, and built a hospital on Mosquito Island, now Fort Point. By day and by night they had men and drays clearing yards, alleys, etc. Every blade of grass was pulled up. Never was a town more clean and nice. Whilst we were comforting ourselves in our happiness and certainty in our supposed security, and no steamship to arrive, as they had left for the North to be repaired, and no arrivals from New Orleans or any other port, a servant, a German girl, in the

employ of W. J. Berlocher, living on the strand, was taken sick and died with the black vomit before any one was aware of her real disease. She was a stranger, had not been out of the house for weeks, and had only been about four months at this place from Germany. About that time many were taken sick, and it went on increasing. The poison had inflamed all strangers and the atmosphere: our quarantine had become a dead letter. It spread out rapidly, destroying about 400 lives before frost put an end to its effects. A few years ago it broke out in one house on Tremont Street, and, before three days had passed, two deaths were reported. On the following day seven new cases were reported, and it went on as usual, doing its work of death. There had been no communication within two weeks previous. The first victims had been living here only a few months. It carried many natives to their long home as well as 300 unacclimated persons. It is believed that yellow fever can not be personally communicated: it must be inhaled: it is an atmospheric poison. If so, the strong gulf winds that visit us at this season seem to be unable to blow it away. If it proceeds from the soil, we have seen the waters of the gulf rise and wash over a great portion of our town to the bay; much rain has fallen upon our streets and yards, filling every sink, washing the whole surface of the soil as clean as sand could be washed, yet the disease progressed in its direful work steadily, as if neither winds, thunder and lightning, overflows or rains, had visited us at all. It is attached to the sills and under-floors of our houses (perhaps so, in a shape most imperceptible to the eye). This matter or animalculæ may be carried from place to place in goods, clothing, packages, etc., and, finding a suitable atmospheric pressure, may easily multiply or propagate itself in the air. So it may go on increasing, advancing slowly from place to place, even contrary to strong currents of wind, and harbor in particular places to increase. In this belief quarantine regulations may be of service. This animalculæ matter, or subtle poison, once inhaled, may be some days in the stomach or linings before it takes effect on the system; hence a person may travel many days before he is taken sick. It matters little where he goes, it will do its work sooner or later. I have read of cases of black vomit in Chicago being traced to New Orleans. I have seen cases in St. Louis of twenty-four days from New Orleans—in 1828; some often twenty days from that infected port die of black vomit. To see new cases of yellow fever ten, and even twenty, days after the appearance of a white frost, sustains me in the opinion that it is not possible to know who has inhaled or who has not inhaled the poison on leaving an infected place: and who can tell when this poison was inhaled? I dare say it will be difficult to contract the disease twenty days after a white frost. Doubtless, a frost does destroy this matter, or this subtle poison, yet many times this mysterious and awful disease comes and goes we know not how. . . . *
For many years my thermometer has stood from 90 to 100°, yet no yellow

---

* In Alexandria, La., the heavy frosts of October and November, 1853, had no appreciable effect upon it. The epidemic, which almost decimated that town, went on to its limit of life regardless of conditions.

fever appeared among us. When writers say it requires a heat of 90° or upward to produce the poison, there must be other conditions in the atmosphere to bring it about, or to cause this matter to hatch and multiply. Does it not require a peculiar state and exposure to the atmosphere to cause weevil to breed in a grain of corn or in a barrel of flour? Some years these are more in number than usual. If it is in the air or atmosphere, has it a center to hold itself? can not the strong gulf winds that we have blow it away? We know they have no influence over it whatever. The present epidemic has passed away from us without a frost, yet we witness no peculiar change in the season from any other. .... It has appeared for several years in succession after hard frosts and winters; it has followed or continued its deadly march after very mild winters; hence, we have no possible means of telling what portion of the South will be exempt. It comes without giving warning, and we only know it is among us by several cases being taken down within a week, and by its unmistakable marks on the body after death, and by black vomit." Dr. J. M. Reuss, accounting for the epidemic of Indianola, Texas, in 1867, says the fever was introduced by a pair of second-hand blankets,* sold by some persons connected with a small craft which had arrived from Vera Cruz, where it was raging a few days before the 20th of June. Two young men, who had only examined these blankets, were attacked, and one of them died of black vomit. A negro woman, who nursed one of them, also died of well-marked yellow fever. A lady from New Orleans, where the fever also raged, was taken sick at the hotel, and is supposed to have been another medium for its spread. Besides, as was the case in Memphis in 1873 and 1878, fever of a continued and dangerous form prevailed, which confused the physicians. Dr. Reuss says he himself had several cases of fever of a more malignant type than the common climatic fevers of that region. The first death occurred on the 24th of June, and in less than a week the whole business part of the town was struck down as by lightning, there being by that time between 125 and 150 cases, out of a population of 1,000. It reached its acme in two weeks, and lingered in the suburbs for over a month. The poison was most fatal at night, and generally took hold of nurses and doctors when it reached their places of residence. Dr. S. W. Welsh, of Galveston, traces the origin of the epidemic in that city in 1867 to a young German, who arrived from Indianola on the 28th, and to a per-

---

* Dr. Jacob S. West, of Texas, cites two cases where the yellow fever was introduced by sacks of coffee. Both occurred in 1867. At Liberty, Texas, a sack of coffee landed two miles from the town, from the steamboat Ruthven, which, coming from Galveston, was refused permission to land at the town. This sack of coffee was taken to Liberty on a dray, through an atmosphere, up to that time, perfectly healthy; but all who shared the coffee were taken with yellow fever, which spread with disastrous effects. The second case was that of a sack of coffee hauled fifteen miles in an open wagon, from Corpus Christi, where the fever prevailed, to a point near Meansville, where it was divided among the purchasers. Not one of these escaped; all of them were seized with yellow fever, and many of them died. But those who did not so share were, singularly enough, exempt. The conditions necessary to its spread were not there.

son who arrived on the 22d from New Orleans. In a few days the fever had complete possession of about a square mile of the city, "while," he says, "its origin would not seem to be connected with any particular meteorological conditions adequate to account for the disease, it is unquestionably true that the climatic conditions were highly favorable to its spread, given a starting point. The month of May was temperate, showery, pleasant, and remarkably exempt from all febrile diseases; nor was there any thing to be observed in the type of diseases to foreshadow yellow fever. June, however, was a month of uninterrupted hot weather, the thermometer ranging daily from 85° to 90°, with a breezeless and stifling atmosphere. Toward the close of the month, from the 20th of June to the 5th of July, a period of two weeks, there was heavy falls of rain daily, literally flooding the streets, and accompanied by unusual electrical phenomenon. In the intervals the sun shone brightly and with intense heat. The city was in good sanitary condition, and every precaution taken, and every thing had been done by the authorities that could ward off the dreadful visitation. Notwithstanding this, by the end of July the fever prevailed epidemically. It spread to Houston and to all the towns on the Central Railroad, committing ravages far beyond decimation. The popular and oft-expressed belief that a frost was absolutely required to put an end to—to arrest and extinguish—an epidemic of yellow fever, was falsified by the events of this season. There was, up to the 8th of January, more than two months after the cessation of the epidemic, no frost, no freeze, and only a few days of cool north wind. Yellow fever obeys, I am persuaded, certain laws, as fixed and immutable as those which govern the growth, development, and decay of organized matter. In the execution of such laws, the rise and fall of the thermometer can exert only a limited and temporary influence, can only retard and hasten the march of epidemics. Look to Havana, Vera Cruz, and other localities where yellow fever is indigenous, and where the temperature never falls to the freezing point, and yet in those cities the disease, after having run its course, obeys the laws which must everywhere control it, subsides, and finally disappears in the latter part of summer or first of autumn, to return with renewed virulence the succeeding spring, and run its destined course and subside as before."

Dr. Welsh, concluding his report, extended so as to cover all the points in Texas attacked in 1867, says: "The remarkable uniformity in all the reports from all parts of the epidemic district, as respects the range of temperature, winds, and rains, must have arrested the attention of the reader. The winds were, with few exceptions, from the north, north-east, and southwest. The wind from these quarters during the summer months are not what are known as northers proper, which are, as a rule, associated with a low range of temperature, and blow with great force continuously for two or three days, and are very dry, having been wrung of their moisture in their course over the high range of mountains between Texas and the Pacific; but are mere puffs alternating with dead calms, the temperature being at the same time extraordinarily high, and the atmosphere saturated with moisture. Singular influences clearly obtained throughout all the region of the State denominated the epidemic district. . . . . There seems to be but one opinion, so far as I have been able to extend my inquiries, as respects the putrid state of the atmosphere in all the localities attacked by the fever. The odor, which was broadcast in the atmosphere of the cities and towns where the epidemic raged, was offensive in the extreme. This is an odor so peculiar as that, to be appreciated, it must be experienced. It is not confined to houses, but often pervades the atmosphere of certain districts of the infected locality, where it most seemingly concentrated; then a larger proportion of the susceptible are attacked and the disease is most malignant. Is this one of the sensible properties of yellow fever poison, or does the poison determine certain chemical laws with an atmosphere reeking with almost every imaginable impurity consequent on active decomposition and exhalation of animal and vegetable matter, that result in the production of this odor? Is this the subtle and mysterious influence which, while it casts a death-like torpor over the vaso-nervous system, determines the most intense hyperæsthesia of the nerves of common sensation? Time and future observation must resolve the problem. I infer a relatively small amount of ozone to exist in such an atmosphere." Dr. R. H. Harrison, in his account of the epidemic at Columbus, Texas, in 1873, says: "The health of the town was much worse than usual. During June, July, and August the wind was steady from the south, sweeping whatever of malarial or other poison might have been developed along the river away from the town. Intermittent, remittent, and bilious fevers prevailed, with nothing unusual to mark their course. In one or two instances there was a marked hemorrhagic tendency. One such case ended in black vomit. Cases after this continued to multiply, aggravating, perhaps, the cause of the visitation. The low lands near the river had been overflowed four or five times between the months of April and November. One of these, occurring about the 25th of August, was remarkable for the enormous quantity of dead fish which floated down stream. The column of floating putridity was scarcely broken for two days and nights, and, the current being strong, the quantity which passed is altogether beyond computation. Occasionally they were floated away from the main current and lodged in the drift-wood of the overflowed land, where, coated with a thin sediment from the midday flood, vast quantities of them were left to swelter and decay. The source from whence they came and the cause of their death are questions that, up to the present time, have defied scrutiny. On the 2d of October the last of these overflows occurred. The weather was hot and sultry, and although there was no dead fish to be seen in the turbid waters, the stench from it was intolerably nauseating—the odor of rotting fish and weeds combined. Occasionally the skeleton of a fish with fragments of flesh in an advanced state of decomposition might be seen floating just beneath the surface. Other carcasses were also floating down the muddy torrent in abundance, some in advanced states of decomposition, and others but recently dead. The condition of affairs was now calculated to excite the most alarming apprehensions in all reflecting minds. Surrounded by a flood of filthy, stinking waters; the streets and vacant lots of the town covered with a rank growth of matured weeds, which were falling down and rotting rapidly under the influence of repeated rains and a high temperature; numbers of carcasses of dead hogs and dogs were found decaying in various parts of the town; privies were unpoliced; and, to aggravate this multitude of evils, a city government that, whenever it was addressed upon the subject of a sanitary police, insisted upon establishing quarantine against some place that it imagined had yellow fever. And, as if intent to precipitate us into an epidemic, at this juncture this government passed an ordinance requiring the hogs, our only scavengers, to be removed from the streets, thus leaving the offal from our kitchens to add its noisome effluvia to the mass already on hand. The result is not difficult to imagine. While the city government continued from time to time to adopt quarantine ordinances, the health of the town grew gradually worse, the number of cases increased, and the attacks were more violent, frequently terminating on the seventh or ninth day. By the 7th of October every member of the faculty was busy, and, by the 18th, yellow fever was announced, and the usual demoralization of the whole population set in. Calvert was prepared for the yellow fever in 1873 by the prevalence, during July and August, of malarial fever of an obstinate and unyielding character. While in this condition a young man named Hughes arrived from Shreveport, who was taken down with the yellow fever a few nights after his arrival, and in a few days died. Dr. Coleman, who attended him, made an attempt to have his bedding burned and the room fumigated, but the bedding, instead of being burned, was thrown upon the roof of a little house almost at the foot of Main Street, and left there three weeks in the sun. The prevailing wind blowing up the street, the whole town soon became impregnated with the poison." Dr. McCraven insists that the yellow fever which prevailed epidemically in Houston in 1848 originated there; that the city was badly drained and filthy, and there was not much rain during the latter part of summer, making it remarkably dry. He believes that no one had a second attack, as did Dr. Stone, of New Orleans; and he believes that animal filth is the food of the yellow fever, and that it will not spread in a clean city. Dr. Bennett Dowler declares that, from 1796 to 1853, it is almost certain that several cases of yellow fever have occurred every year in New Orleans, often only four or five. Baron de Carondelet, in 1801, recommended that the stagnant waters of the city be drained into Canal Carondelet: he regarded them the cause of much mortality from fatal fevers, among which he included yellow fever. Dr. Cartright and Dr. Merrill (lately of Memphis) state that, in their opinion, the epidemic of 1823 originated in Natchez, and was not imported. In 1853, according to Dowler, the heavy frosts at the close of October and beginning of November did not appear to have any marked influence upon the epidemic. He also says that about the 25th of October — and until frost appeared for a few nights at many of the interior towns of Louisiana, but which did not in a marked degree arrest the march of the epidemic — warm weather, however, soon returned, but this did not revive the epidemic in places where it had declined,—as in New Orleans and many other places, where the return of absentees and the influx of strangers did not reproduce the epidemic. In Clinton, La., where the fever began a month before the frosts above alluded to, the fever did not disappear; on the contrary, after the 10th of December many persons died, among them several negroes. "All the lessons of philosophy teach," says Dowler, "that yellow fever has a cause or combination of causes, without which it can not appear; with which, it can not fail to appear, being not the less certain because unknown in the present state of science. Its antecedents and sequences must prove when known as invariably connected and simple as any part of physics. Fortunately the conditions if not the causes of yellow fever are to a considerable extent known: for example, it is known to be connected, no matter how, with the warm season of the year; with unacclimated constitutions; with aggregations of people in towns and villages, and it rarely attacks rural populations unless they crowd together so as to become virtually towns."

And he might have added, that it is subject to a law of periodicity, that it reaches its zenith in a given time and declines without regard to climatic conditions or other influences, such as the continued unsanitary state of the public highways. In New Orleans, in 1853, the climax was reached on the 53d day of the epidemic; in 1858, on the 56th day; in 1867, on the 56th day; and in 1878, on the 57th day. In Memphis, in 1867, the fever reached its climax on the 40th day; in 1873, on the 40th day; and in 1878, on the 44th day—in every instance declining in the same ratio as it advanced.

That yellow fever can be imported and may be engrafted by conditions which, if they do not originate, certainly promote it, is apparent in the case of Louisville, from which we have this tardy confession in the *Age*, a weekly paper remarkable for its candor, for its freedom from sectional or political bias, from personal considerations or control, and that is amongst the best of our current publications for fair dealing, truth-telling, and trenchant, fearless criticism. It says, in the number for February 22, that "Many credulous persons in Louisville, relying implicitly upon the opinions of the doctors and the solemn assurances of newspapers last summer, laughed at the idea that indigenous yellow fever existed in the city. It is we believe with a single exception admitted now, however, that the dreadful disease not only existed here, but proved quite fatal in a number of cases. Fortunately it was not developed until late in the season, and the cool weather of September, followed by the frosts of October, retarded its propagation. It is interesting to discover the methods that were adopted to mislead the public. One of our most prominent physicians, writing in a late number of the *Medical News*, frankly discloses how the result was accomplished *secundum artem*. 'W. M.,' says he, 'had all of the usual symptoms of yellow fever, well marked, and died on the fifth day,' but, 'knowing that a public announcement of a death from this cause in a citizen would be disastrous to the business interests and social quiet of Louisville, it was decided to call the disease '*gastro enteritis*.' The death certificate, however, was brought to the physician in charge, 'filled out as *malarial fever*,' and the physician signed it. The cloud was a camel, a weasel, or a whale, any thing to suit the exigencies of the case." And here it is proper to remind all the communities north of Memphis, even so far as St. Paul, that yellow fever has many times prevailed epidemically even in bleak and cold New England; that it only needs conditions to prevail again and play havoc among the people of the Northern cities as it has within the past forty years among the people of the Southern. It must be remembered that the conditions necessary for the propagation of the disease one day are not those of another, hence the best doctors, like Chopin, of New Orleans, are not ashamed to confess that they know nothing about it, save as it develops itself in patients.

From the preceding it will be seen that, on the best authorities, every theory advanced touching the birth in Africa and origin in America, or its islands, of yellow fever, has been contradicted, and that the theories of geographical or zone limit, of altitude, of germ or fermentation origin, of development, of contagion or infection, of its naturalization in the United States and the effect of sanitary conditions to increase and intensify it, all have partisans who contend for each with zeal, every one of them furnishing more or less data with which to fortify positions that are taken only to be destroyed by others. It only remains, then, to furnish a case or cases in contradiction of the power of frost to kill it, and the conclusion of Dr. Chopin, of New Orleans, is irresistible, *that we really know nothing about yellow fever; that it is a law unto itself in its tenacity of life as well as in its inception, growth, and progress in development, how long it takes to incubate in the human system and the strength it must reach to prevail epidemically, to leap, as it did in Memphis in 1878, in three days, from one to one hundred cases.* First, we have the case of Mr. Joyner, a well-known merchant of Memphis, who had not been in the city during the epidemic, and who went down to George Hunt's plantation, near Horn Lake, Miss., to look after the estate of a deceased relative, late in December. He slept, it is said, in a bed occupied by a person who had died of the fever during the epidemic. However that may be, he contracted the disease in that place, and died at his home in Memphis, whither he had been removed. There had been much cold weather for a month before, the thermometer ranging lower than 32°, and the house where the disease was contracted, like nearly all houses in the South, was built more with a view to comfort in the heats of summer than to repelling the extreme colds of winter, so that it must have been thoroughly exposed and brought under the influence of the very low temperature which prevailed before his arrival. New Orleans furnishes another case that shames the temperature theory (an exceptional case, to be sure, like that of Joyner's), still a case that can not be overlooked. The New Orleans *Times* made a full report of it, giving names, locality, date, and the temperature of the room of the patient before and after the attack, and during sickness. It said: "Probably the most remarkable case of yellow fever ever recorded, and one which stands seriously in the way of many accepted theories, is that which has recently occurred in this city, in the person of Nellie, daughter of Mr. S. E. Carey of this city, aged five years. After an absence from the city of seven months, the child left Chicago December 18, when the temperature was 0—2° Fahrenheit, in the sleeping-car

'Autocrat,' which, with bedding just washed, had been exposed to the intense cold for fifty-one hours. She arrived in this city at noon, December 21, and was immediately conveyed to Mr. Carey's residence, No. 199 Louisiana Avenue. The house had been thoroughly cleaned in the spring, freshly kalsomined and frescoed, and moreover had not had a case of fever in it during the summer. On the 26th, Dr. Joseph Scott was summoned. He found the child suffering from severe supra-orbital, temporal, and epigastric pains; surface of body cool and slightly perspiring; pulse, 120; temperature (between teeth and cheek), $104\frac{3}{5}°$. Temperature of the room, $41°$. He visited her five times during the next twenty-four hours, pursuing the usual expectant treatment. Shortly after the last of these visits he was hastily resummoned, and found that black vomit had supervened. Dr. Joseph Jones examined the discharge and pronounced it to be from true yellow fever. Dr. Scott speedily checked the vomit. The fever lasted eighty-one hours, with thermal and sphygmic lines horizontal; then the pulse and temperature gradually declined to normal. On the second and third days albumen was found, and the sclerotics were imbued with the usual tint. In fine, every pathognomonic symptom of yellow fever was strongly marked, so much so that this might be regarded as a typical case. The theory that yellow-fever poison is destroyed by a temperature of $32°$ Fahrenheit is strongly controverted in the fact that the house had been exposed to even greater cold. The view that a temperature of at least $60°$ is required for its development finds contradiction in that the temperature of the room where the child sickened was only $41°$. Surely it can not be urged that the period of incubation extended from May to December; and on the other hand, what might have been the fomites conveying the germ, when it is an assured fact that there had been no fever in the house during the summer, and that neither had the child been outside the house nor had any one visited it. In fact, all accepted etiological and semeiological principles in yellow fever science seem to have been utterly set at defiance in this truly remarkable case. It surely can not be claimed that this was a case of bilious remittent fever, or of malarial type, when every symptom was in perfect accordance with the most marked type of yellow fever in its monoparoxysmal form. Here we have strong confirmation of the germ theory, and the alleged power of the seeds to hibernate; evidence adverse to the theory that cold will kill the poison, or that a test of $60°$ is necessary to develop it; and facts strongly pointing to the spontaneous reproduction of the disease at all times, even in cleanly and healthy localities. So clear and easily attainable are the circumstances surrounding it, that it is eminently worthy of rigid investigation and of being placed upon the records of science."

III.

Having thus given many, if not all, of the various theories advanced touching the origin, causes, propagation or means of transmission of yellow fever, the diagnosis and treatment of it are next to be considered. Dr. Happoldt, before referred to as a physician of high standing, gives the following as the result of his experience in Memphis in 1873: "Most cases," he says, "of whatever nature, were ushered in by a chill, followed by a fever, with a pulse and temperature to which the succeeding phenomena would correspond. The attack was so violent in some cases that death occurred within thirty-six hours. Great prostration was frequent from the beginning, in serious cases. The eye did not often exhibit the bloodshot, glistening appearance, and inquisitive, anxious stare; but frequently presented a mere suffusion with an expression of apathy; sometimes there was pain in the eye-balls, with intolerance of light. The face was sometimes injected, pale or waxy. The tongue was rarely furred at first; it would become red, cracked, and dry in hemorrhagic cases, and sometimes became darkly discolored, even when black vomit did not occur. Headache and rachialgia were generally constant during the first and second days; and pains in the joints common in children; and sometimes in adults they would simulate those of gout, rheumatism or dengue. The skin was most generally moist from the beginning, and became more so as the disease progressed; in some cases the perspiration was profuse and clammy, emitting a peculiar, disgusting odor; but its abundance afforded no relief to the patient—not apparently affecting the temperature. Insomnia and restlessness were constant during the febrile paroxysm. Delirium—mild or furious—was not uncommon, especially in female and nervous persons. Thirst was frequently an urgent symptom from the first. Anorexia was constantly present throughout the disease; the loathing of food was sometimes so great that liquid nourishment would induce nausea in many instances, even in those which terminated favorably. Pain and tenderness over the region of the stomach were sometimes distressing, even in favorable cases, and occasionally it would extend to the abdomen. In some cases, chiefly among adults, nausea and vomiting of bilious matter occurred in the inception of the disease, generally followed by biliary dejections, and accompanied with an icteric hue of the skin; pain in the region of the spleen usually attended these symptoms. Hemorrhages occurred, generally, late in the disease, mostly passive, and from the mucous surfaces. Uterine hemorrhage was constant in menstruating females; many miscarriages occurred; some women were delivered of still-born children at their full term. The temperature frequently fell during convalescence much below the normal standard. The pulse, whatever may have been its force and frequency, after it had declined, generally became weak and slow, sometimes falling below forty beats to the minute. In these cases convalescence was protracted; the appetite was perverted; and dyspeptic symptoms, with a weak heart, remained for months afterwards. Cutaneous eruptions of various kinds appeared in many cases after the subsidence of the febrile paroxysm, and also during convalescence. In some instances the eruption was confined to particular parts of the body—generally to the thorax, back, arms, and thighs; and sometimes to the brow alone. The urticarous, roseolous, and eczemous were the most common. The eruptions which appeared during and after convalescence were the most annoying, continuing longer than a week, and giving rise to intolerable itching; and in some cases the desquamation of the cuticle was as great as that occurring in a pronounced case of scarlatina. During and after convalescence boils and abscesses frequently made their appearance; they were confined to no particular part, and were sometimes so numerous, and gave rise to so much discomfort, as to confine the patient in-doors for several weeks. Swellings of the salivary glands, gums, and tongue were of common occurrence during the latter part of the disease. Suppuration of one of the parotid glands occurred in several cases; but in one case only, in the practice of Dr. W. J. Armstrong, did 'both of the parotid glands become inflamed quickly after the attack of the fever; and rapidly went on to suppuration and total destruction of the glandular structure, with sloughing of the parenchymatous tissues, leaving a cavity behind each angle of the lower maxilla an inch deep, by three-fourths of an inch in diameter.' In some cases a typhoid condition substituted convalescence; in many, an icteric hue of the skin and eyes remained for weeks. Bright's disease and albuminuria were among the sequelæ; generally occurring some weeks after convalescence, and were of the most serious character. Relapses occasionally occurred, and were almost always fatal. Death appeared to be due to feebleness of the heart. The greatest number of fatal cases appeared to be due to the direct sedative action of the poison of the disease. Death by coma and convulsions was most common in women and children. Uræmic poisoning, with or without black vomit, was most generally the outlet of life among adults, whose stomachs and kidneys had been impaired in function or structure from habitual dietetic indiscretions, from pernicious drugs, or from having undergone super-sudation. Whatever views may have been entertained of the special pathology of individual cases, occurring during the epidemic, it was from the master poison that the greatest danger was to be apprehended, and to which all efforts were to be directed. Every kind and variety of diseased action would wear its livery; and it was folly to burden the mind with useless distinctions, and attempt to treat any other disease without being ever conscious that the exhibition of special means should not be those inimical to the medical constitution existing at the time. For reasons before stated, a diversified treatment was required, according to the character of the case presented; and remedies were as varied as the diverse opinions entertained of the nature of the epidemic. Mercury and quinine were relied upon chiefly by some. Dr. Mallory, in his account of the epidemic, states that he gave a cathartic dose of calomel in the commencement; and that 'after purgation, the remedy was continued in small doses until ptyalism was induced.' His patients 'recovered without manifesting any inconvenience, in many instances, from its employment. Suppression of the urine did not appear in a single instance among the eighty-one patients on whom this treatment was employed.' One of those who used quinine in all cases, gave it in one-grain doses, in combination with the same quantity of calomel, every hour, until ten doses had been taken; and then gave the quinine alone every two hours until the fourth day, when stimulants were given as required. Dr. Luke P. Blackburn, of Louisville, who had charge of the Walthall Infirmary, believing yellow fever to be similar to the exanthemata, treated it with warm drinks and foot-baths, with sufficient covering. Neither purgatives nor diuretics were given until convalescence was established; though the vinous and stronger alcoholic stimulants were freely allowed. He believed that the poison was eliminated by the skin solely; and he looked upon 'the fæcal matter, coated over with bile, as being the most soothing coat which the bowels can have in the first stage of the disease.' According to his judgment, quinine was fatal in yellow fever. Some physicians employed neither mercury nor quinine, using gentle purgatives or aperients at first, and enemata when needed later in the disease. During the febrile paroxysm, warm diluents, as orange-leaf tea, etc., were generally resorted to. By some lemonade was preferred, and champagne and other wines allowed. To promote the action of the kidneys, the salts of potash or ammonia, with or without the spts. nitric ether, were commonly used. The effort was made by some to abort or resolve the febrile paroxysm by means of such depressing agents as gelseminum, aconite, digitalis, or veratrum viride; and for irritable stomach, chloroform, creosote, nux vomica, and Fowler's Solution of arsenic were prescribed. The hydrate of chloral and bromide of potassium, or morphia, were used to promote sleep. Carbolic acid and the sulpho-carbolate of sodium were tried when black vomit occurred. The spirits of turpentine, acetate of lead, and the preparations of iron were given for the relief of hemorrhages. Vinous, distilled and fermented liquors were almost always used during convalescence. These are among the articles of materia medica asserted to have been prescribed. Hot mustard pediluvia were invariably used by all, and cold sponging of the upper extremities by many. Sinapisms or blisters to the epigastrium to relieve gastric distress were in general use. Dry and wet cups, blisters, and warm fomentations were applied to the region of the kidneys in cases of suppression. My views of the pathology and treatment of yellow fever have undergone no essential change since 1854, when I denied the efficacy of Blair's formula expressed by the symbol XX by XXIV; and those of my acquaintances who attempted to carry out his precepts have been forced to abandon it. Quinine in scruple doses, in some epidemics, may do good when it is combined with calomel, but I believe that the beneficial effect is due more to the mercurial than the alkaloid. While rejecting this heroic treatment of Blair's, I also rejected the expectant as well as the sedative, which has not yet gone out of fashion with some; neither can I attach much importance to the internal administration of diuretics or diaphoretics, which have been thought eliminative, in consequence of their nauseating effects on the stomach. If we can not remove the cause of diseased action, we should attempt to annul it or counteract its effects. The cause of yellow fever, now recognized to be a peculiar zymotic poison, acting as a destructive ferment, depresses and perverts the vital and functional forces, gives rise to great excitement of the circulation and torpor of the glandular and secretory organs. The intense eremacausis of the tissues, and high combustion acting through the blood, may produce, in a short time, destructive changes in the most important organs of the body. The indications for treatment are obvious, and are to remove all offending matter from the *primæ viæ* and rouse the emunctories to action, and are best fulfilled by the administration of mercurials and salines, and promoting their action by warm diluents; at the same time that we attempt to reduce the temperature by sponging the upper extremities with ice-cold water, and assist in equalizing the circulation by revulsives to the surface of the abdomen, and hot stimulating pediluvia. These are, I believe, the best means of disgorging the glandular apparatus and equalizing the circulation preparatory to the use of agents which tend directly to counteract the destructive fermentation which is going on in the blood. All spoliative and depressing medication should now cease, though the action of the skin and kidneys should be promoted without disturbing the stomach; for upon the proper performance of their functions will depend the progress of the case and the impending lesion of the heart. Here judgment comes into play; and upon a recognition of the true pathological conditions of each individual case, and a knowledge of the therapeutical properties of the remedial agents adapted for its relief, will depend the result; always provided that the patient can be placed in a position suitable to his condition, and have all the agreeable surroundings which are required. Bland and nutritious liquid food should be regularly given to sheathe the lining of the stomach, and neutralize or dilute the gastric juice; but warm drinks for other purposes are to be discontinued. Crushed ice, or ice-water, may be used for their refrigerant effect only; but the urgent thirst, which necessarily ensues from the elimination of the watery elements of the blood by the induced catharsis, must be allayed by cool, pure water, or refrigerant, agreeable beverages, mixed with good wine; otherwise, inspissated blood will engorge the kidneys, and the case will be materially injured. The practitioner will always have to regard the idiosyncrasy of his patient, and be governed by the peculiarities of each case. After sufficient catharsis has been induced, wine, and even the stronger alcoholic stimulants, are more efficient than any other class of medicines. They will be found, in manageable cases of yellow fever, almost a *sine qua non*, preventing, *ceten paribus*, the supervention of the destructive changes which might otherwise occur, thus making a simple, mild case, which, if allowed to run its course expectantly, or attempted to be jugulated heroically, would become a "full-fledged" one, either to drag its slow course along, or terminate fatally. After congestions or other complications have occurred, it is too late to expect a specific action from the preparations of alcohol; but still, either with or without quinine and citric acid, its supporting action is required to stimulate the heart and equalize the circulation; and in malarial complications, its combination with quinine is the best for the exhibition of this salt. For irritable stomach, when the tongue is red and dry, and the thirst urgent, ice will not succeed so well as ice-cream or sherbet, or cool vinous drinks delicately prepared to suit the taste of the patient. Stimulating embrocations, sinapisms, or blisters over the epigastrium, in connection with the above treatment, have given relief to the most distressing symptoms. The hydrate of chloral and bromide of potassium, or the salts of morphia and camphor-water, are of questionable utility in this disease. If no complications arise, no drugs are to be given; the patient should be made comfortable by a proper regulation of diet and hygiene; and if there be no contra-indications, vinous, fermented, or distilled liquors, in quantities and combinations to suit the condition of the patient, should be allowed. The use of alcohol in the treatment of pyæmia, and its property of lowering the temperature in pyrexia, has, of late, attracted much attention; and the medical reader is competent to form an opinion on the subject.* I will briefly sum up, from the results of my own researches and those of others, the theory of the modus operandi of this agent, and would most respectfully call the attention of the profession to its action in yellow fever. In a state of health, alcohol does increase the animal heat, especially when the system is depressed by cold; when there is diminished capillary circulation and reduced temperature, by virtue of its combustible nature; and it resolves congestion of the lungs in incipient pneumonia by arousing the nervous forces and equalizing the circulation. In a state of fever it diminishes the temperature at the same time that it sustains the action of the heart; and this is explicable from the fact, that while rapidly oxidized itself, it prevents the oxidization of the tissues; therefore, by arresting the frightful combustion which obtains in yellow fever, it diminishes the temperature; and by arousing the latent vital energies, it equalizes the circulation and relieves engorgements or congestions. Another explanation is, that it acts within the animal economy as it does without, by preventing or arresting the putrefactive or fermentative process, each of which is attended by heat. It may yet be proved to be the best antidote to all zymotic poisons, as well as to the bites of venomous animals. When the temperature of the blood is too much increased, as it is in yellow fever, its saccharine elements can not be converted into alcohol (as I contend does take place in a state of health); but the acetous fermentation is induced instead, similar to what always occurs when the mash—prepared for the induction of the alcoholic fermentation—is subjected to a too great degree of heat. Under the conditions present in a marked case of yellow fever, we can readily conceive how, in a short time, the whole mass of the blood may become acetified, and so changed that the emunctories cease to act at all, and

---

* Dr. Austin Flint, Jr., of New York, has recently declared himself in favor of alcohol as a specific in cases of fever.

the functions of the economy are in abeyance, in consequence of the circulation of a fluid other than that which nature has designed for the maintenance of their action. The kidneys becoming as impermeable and useless as a foreign body, the abnormal death fluid seeks the great work-shop of the system, and oozes through its parietes, to be known to the observer as *black vomit*. The moral treatment is by no means unimportant in yellow fever. Fear being the most potent agent for evil, the patient should not be alarmed by being made acquainted with the nature of his case; neither should those nearest him be better informed, unless absolute necessity arises. The medical attendant should never betray doubt or anxiety as to the result; a confident look, kind words, and a manifestation of a friendly interest in behalf of the patient, encouraging him to hope for a successful issue, will do more good than medication. None but congenial, cheerful, and discreet persons should be allowed access to the sick-room; the exclusion of all disagreeable or depressing influences should be enforced, and the patient should be relieved of all personal cares of whatever nature, and feel himself perfectly secure in the hands of those to whom his physician has intrusted the management of his case."

Dr. R. W. Mitchell, recently appointed a member of the National Board of Health, who, as Medical Director of the Howard Association of Memphis, in 1878, enjoyed unusual opportunities for obtaining a thorough knowledge of the effects of yellow fever upon the human system, and of the value of almost all the known remedies, and who enjoyed the confidence of every physician who served under him as well as that of the public at large, by request furnishes the following as his method of treatment, which, it may be remarked, was very successful: "The natural history of yellow fever suggests the plan of treatment which observation and experience have proven to be the best. Being a self-limited disease, and one of very short duration, what could possibly be the aim of rational treatment beyond warding off complications and sustaining nature? To fulfill this indication, I have sought always to enforce absolute rest of mind and body during the entire course of the disease, to the full establishment of convalescence; to protect my patients from all perturbing and deleterious influences, such as might arise from the conversation of injudicious friends, or from changes of temperature; to watch the bodily secretions, and insure as perfectly as possible the performance of the various functions. The first objects requiring attention in a case of yellow fever, are the bringing about of reaction after the chill, and free evacuation of the bowels. The first is quite easily attained by means of the hot mustard foot-bath, and moderate covering with blankets. The second is, in most instances, best accomplished by a dose of castor-oil. Sometimes, when the attack is ushered in with nausea and a coated tongue, a few grains of calomel, followed in six hours by oil, or one of the saline aperients, is better practice. Having attended to these matters, I now lay medicine aside, unless the pains in the head and back are violent or delirium is present. To relieve these symptoms I prefer to make use of a combination of bromide potassium and tincture gelsemium — 15 grains of the first, and as many drops of the second — every two hours during the first day of the fever. Gentle perspiration, not free sweating, should be maintained for 15 or 18 hours by the foot-bath, suitable covering, and warm sage or orange-leaf tea. As a rule, no food of any kind should be administered during the continuance of the fever, unless the patient is very feeble, or the fever is disposed to run over three days. Under such circumstances, milk and lime-water, or rice-water, in small quantities, should be given at short intervals. Pellets of ice may be given to all patients in the beginning, and to the close. Having discontinued those remedies calculated to keep up perspiration, the closest attention should be given to the bodily temperature. If the clinical thermometer shows that this temperature is not above 102°, I instruct the nurse to sponge the entire body, under cover, every few hours with common whisky. If, however, the temperature goes above this figure, and reaches 104° or 105°, the whisky must be freely applied every hour, and as cold as ice can make it. To be effectual, each sponging should be continued for 20 or 30 minutes. A faithful nurse, who does not mind hard work, will in a few hours bring the temperature down two or three degrees. Patients thus treated, long for a return of the time for sponging, and will often beg for it: it relieves pain, soothes the troubled nervous system, and induces sleep. It also insures proper action of the kidneys, and serves to ward off that state of things in the stomach which gives rise to black vomit. The essence of treatment, then, in yellow fever, is to be found in keeping the digestive organs at perfect rest, by giving them nothing to do; in keeping the temperature of the body as near the normal as possible; and in warding off congestion of the liver and kidneys by making appeals to the skin. Should suppression of urine arise in a patient with high temperature, the best means of relief is the application of poultices of ice and salt over the loins. This application is made for 15 or 20 minutes, then removed and reapplied in half an hour. For the relief of suppression of urine in one whose temperature is nearly normal, I know nothing of much value. Allusion has been made to the good effect of cold sponging in keeping off black vomit. In addition to this, mustard plasters or blisters over the pit of the stomach may be required; but to do good they must be applied early. The nausea and vomiting with which attacks of yellow fever are ushered in, are not usually serious, and no special medication is required for their relief. When the fever subsides, we begin to repair the shattered strength of the patient by the administration, at short intervals, of a teaspoonful of milk and lime-water. After awhile, chicken-water or beef-tea may be substituted for this. Thirst may now be allayed by water in small quantities, and by the German seltzer-water. Should the temperature fall below the normal, and the pulse drop down to 50 or less, a little brandy may be added to the nourishment; but as a rule it is very seldom that stimulants can be used advantageously or safely with temperate subjects. Much harm has been done, and many lives destroyed, by the administration of champagne and whisky during the stage of calm which follows the subsidence of the fever. We go on, then, adding little by little to the nourishment, but not allowing solid food until nearly a week of convalescence has been reached. During all this time confinement to the horizontal position is rigidly enforced. When the blood has been renewed by food, and the strength in a measure restored, the patient is allowed to leave his bed. The reactionary fever, which in many cases follows the stage of calm, is usually very moderate, and requires no treatment but sponging. In very many cases malarial fever appears about the fourth or fifth day of convalescence: it comes in the evening, very insidiously, and the patient complains of having had a restless night. This is repeated for two or three days, and the patient dies. I saw many such cases during the past summer, and also observed that these attacks yielded to quinine if given promptly. Late in the season, I found it an advantage, in cases in which there seemed to be a malarial element, to commence the treatment of the disease by the administration of one or two ten-grain doses of quinine. Some patients seem stricken with death at the very outset of their attack, and for these no treatment is of any avail. In a large majority of the cases recovery ensues if the plan of treatment here described be scrupulously followed."

Dr. G. B. Thornton, who, like Dr. Mitchell, had the fullest public experience during the yellow fever epidemics which scourged Memphis in 1867 and 1873, was, as in the latter year, in charge of the City Hospital in 1878. A victim of the fever twice, he writes as one should who adds to knowledge acquired by an extended practice, that of a personal nature. He gives the following, by request, as his method of treatment: "Believing that yellow fever is a specific disease, a blood poisoning caused by a peculiar miasm against which medical prophylaxis has proven inefficient, and that active heroic medication to arrest it, when once established, is not only useless but positively injurious, the successful treatment has to be by such medication and management as will alleviate suffering and assist nature to throw off or eliminate this poison from the system. There is a fixed course the disease must run, or, in other words, an evolution which must follow as a consequence of this blood toxemia. Therefore, assuming that the treatment must be essentially of this auxiliary character, it becomes an important question to do nothing that will interfere with the efforts of nature to eliminate this poison. While the disease can not be cut short or aborted, as an ordinary malarial fever, it can be modified and rendered more tolerant to the patient by judicious medication and nursing. Ordinarily I commence my treatment by a mercurial cathartic, followed, if necessary, in six or eight hours, by castor-oil. After the bowels are once thoroughly moved cathartics are no longer indicated during the course of the disease. Quinine, if admissible at all, should be administered early in the attack, in the cold stage which precedes the fever. In anticipation of the fever it is thought, and I will not assert to the contrary, that given at this time in a positive dose, say ten grains, the fever is modified, and the temperature kept down. After the febrile stage is once established, my experience and observation is, quinine is positively injurious. It does no good towards eliminating this poison, and only complicates the case by aggravating the gastric and cephalic disturbance. After a warm foot-bath, the patient should be placed between blankets, and blankets enough used as cover, as not to oppress but keep the skin gently acting without exhausting perspiration. Woolen blankets are the best covers for yellow fever patients; they absorb perspiration without causing the inconvenience that these fluids would on cotton goods; they also allow the exhalations of the body to escape through their meshes without injury. Bedding should not be changed until convalescence is well established. Such medication should be used as will promote and keep up the action of the kidneys and this mild perspiration. To alleviate thirst, drinks possessing some diuretic property should be given in such quantities and at such intervals as not to offend the stomach. When equally agreeable to the patient, and not contra-indicated by any symptom that may exist, I prefer warm drinks, or, at least, of the temperature of ordinary cistern water, to either ice or iced water. The latter produces a decided unpleasant feeling in the stomach, amounting in some instances to a pain (at least that was my experience), and has no advantage over the former in allaying thirst. Rinsing the mouth with cold water, contributes very much towards alleviating this symptom. To relieve muscular soreness and promote gentle perspiration, and sometimes induce sleep, sponging the body and limbs with warm or tepid water, or water medicated with vinegar, ammonia, alcohol, or whisky. This should be done without exposing the patient to the air, or subjecting him to physical exertion. Unless it is properly done it had best not be attempted. Mental and physical quietude is an essential feature in the treatment, and every thing should be done to preserve this that does not interfere with the course of the disease. Opiates, as a rule, should be prohibited. There are some instances in which a cautious use of them is not only admissible, but demanded; but, like quinine, they can not be used indiscriminately: the judgment and discretion of the practitioner can alone decide when to use either. When good does not follow their use, harm certainly does. Opiates are likely to be followed by irritability of stomach and arrested action of the kidneys: to preserve the integrity of these organs is an important and may be an essential feature. In the secondary fever, as a rule, where there is no complication, no medication is required. A judicious administration of diet then takes the place of medication. This should be of a fluid character, given in such quantities and at such intervals as the stomach will appropriate without causing unpleasant symptoms. Approaching convalescence should be watched as closely as the first stage of the disease. Stimulants of some character are necessary in the majority of cases, and no arbitrary preference can or should be for a particular stimulant. Brandy or whisky are, as a rule, my preference, though in some cases one of the wines act better; and with some, as convalescence progresses, the malt liquors are preferred and act best. Special symptoms, as they arise during the course of the disease, such as diarrhœa, irritable stomach, black vomit, hemorrhage from any outlet, suppression of urine, and delirium, of course demand specific medication to combat. To guard against or meet an indication which may arise from a preëxisting infirmity, the general principles of practice are applicable, guarding against any therapeutic remedy that may be contra-indicated by the main disease."

Dr. R. B. Nall, surgeon in charge of Camp Joe Williams,* who was so fort-

---

* Situated seven miles from Memphis, on the line of the Mississippi and Tennessee Railroad.

unate, notwithstanding the exposures his patients were necessarily subjected to, not to have even one case of relapse, furnished, by request, the following as his method of practice: "To deal in the various theories advanced by men who have spent years of devotional industry in the attempt to explain the nature of the insidious matris morbi of yellow fever, is beyond the intention of this paper; the object is to prove that whatsoever has been administered to the sick as a curative agent, based either on scientific principles or empyrical notions, have all alike been barren of fruit. The sanitarian and scientist, assisted by the charity and generosity of the educated masses, have failed to check its fearful ravages, even under favorable meteorological conditions. The inhabitants of Camp Joe Williams were composed in the main of citizens of what was then known as the "infected district" (Poplar, Washington, Adams, etc.), who were removed by a detailed police force, under the vigilant supervision of the Citizens' Relief Committee, to the camp. On their arrival, every article of clothing or bedding which favored the propagation of the disease, was, by order of the surgeon in charge, consumed by fire. Of course, among so many hundred people, cases were soon developed, and most of them run that fatal course which is so characteristic of the disease. The remarkable and favorable feature of Camp Williams was that the disease did not spread among the inhabitants, nor did those who visited the camp from the surrounding country contract the disease. Those who visited the city soon died, or were quite ill for a time, while he or she who feared the place of death steered clear. Parties from the infected district joined those from the non-infected, living in common, occupying at night a small A tent—the former die, the latter escape. Every case which happened substantiated these facts. The details of several cases may not be out of place. The first case that happened was Mr. E., a painter; the disease run the usual fatal course, and on the fourth day he died. He was cared for assiduously by two friends, a lady and gentleman. Neither of these took the disease. Mrs. D. arrived at camp from the infected portion of the city. She took the fever a few days after her arrival. She and her husband occupied a small, close tent, during her illness, even sleeping together in the same bed. She recovered; he escaped the fever entirely. Another striking illustration of the non-contagious character of the disease is the following: Mrs. S., aged 40, the mother of four children, developed a case of fever. She was ordered to the hospital, her children to be cared for some distance from the hospital, in tents. One day these children took advantage of a favorable opportunity, stole away to the hospital, in which their mother lay sick of the fever, and in which several had died. During my evening visit to the mother, I found them gathered around her bed. My first intention was to have them immediately removed to their isolated quarters. But the children wept and entreated that they might be permitted to remain with their mother, while she argued that she could not survive, and begged that I would let them remain with her. The mother recovered; none of the children were attacked. In the wards of the male hospital were employed eight male nurses, five of whom, after nursing for three or four weeks among fifteen or twenty patients in all stages of the fever, thinking themselves proof against the disease, determined to go to the city and there offer their services, because of the higher price paid nurses by the Howard Association. I advised them fully as to the dangers of the city, nevertheless they went and remained there several days. The sick were all bountifully supplied with nurses from a distance; they were therefore unable to obtain positions, and consequently returned to camp. Four of these men died of the fever in the hospital in which they had nursed, the other was found dead between the city and the camp, a short distance from the latter—the result, I believe, of debauchery and fever. The three nurses who did not visit the city, but remained in the hospital during the epidemic (seventy-two days), nursed and buried their confederates, but were not attacked themselves. Every physician, except Dr. T. O. Summers, of Nashville, who was officially connected with the camp, and who visited the city, either died or had the fever, while I, who left the city early and never visited the infected district before I left for camp, escaped the disease. During the fatal illness of the late Dr. Sample, of Austin, Miss., I remained in the tent with him the whole time—four or five days; I was convalescing from a severe attack of bilious fever, but entirely escaped the fatal disease. From observations of Camp Joe Williams, I am driven to the conclusion that yellow fever, under favorable meteorological conditions, intense heat and humidity—particularly the former—finds a nidus or pabulum in the exhalations which emanate from the excreta of human beings."

Dr. Laski, a German physician, who, according to his own statement, had some experience in Asia with the black plague, and in Africa with the cholera, before settling in Memphis, where he has practiced for years, and where he had three experiences of epidemic yellow fever—in 1867, 1873 and 1878—treated his patients very successfully. He gave them castor-oil in simple doses so long as the discharges from the bowels were hard and dark; camomile tea to keep up perspiration; washing the body under the clothes with a wash composed of water tempered by alcohol, ammonia, camphor and common salt. To tone up the patient, he gave good cognac or the best whisky.

Dr. Luke P. Blackburn, of Kentucky, a noted yellow fever expert—whose experience is equal to that of any living physician, extending, as it does, not only over this continent, but to the Bermudas and the West India Islands, his latest experience being at Hickman, Ky., in 1878—gives his treatment as follows: "The patient should be placed in bed in a horizontal position; should not under any circumstances be allowed to arise from that bed; should be well covered with blankets; a foot-tub of hot water without mustard should be introduced under the blankets; the patient lying upon his back, should flex his lower limbs and place his feet in the tub; the covering should be tucked well around him, close up to his neck; he should be given hot tea, composed of balm, sage, elder blossom, boneset, corn-shock, or orange- or lemon-leaf. At the same time he should be permitted to drink ice-water or to take crushed ice in sufficient quantities to allay his thirst. Free and continuous perspiration should be kept up. After the foot-tub has been removed, if the action of the skin should cease and the forehead become dry, the feet should be at once replaced in the tub and the ptisan, or hot tea, should be used as before. The fever will continue from twenty to ninety hours. When it has passed off the blankets should be gradually withdrawn from the patient; stimulants, such as ale, porter, pure rum, and French brandy should be freely given. I prefer Cook's Imperial St. Louis native wine to any stimulant I have ever used. Nourishment, such as rice-water, or corn-meal gruel, or chicken-water should be given cautiously and sparingly. Should there be a spontaneous movement of the bowels, as will occur in many cases from the irritation of the mucous coat of the stomach and bowels, that tissue which is first assaulted by this disease, give no opium, no preparation of opium, nor any thing to check that action. It is the crisis of the disease as it is in measles. The fever will pass off in five hours, and the patient will recover rapidly without fear of a relapse. Should the perspiration have a glutinous, gummy touch, you may expect your patient to recover with watchful and careful nursing. But should the perspiration have a sensation like that of pure water, showing that there is no vicarious action by the skin, which gives relief to the liver and kidneys, you may know that your patient is in great danger. You will find upon an examination the tongue red and tremulous, covered with a short white fur, with great gastric fetor of the breath. It is then all important to apply the cups or leeches to the pit of the stomach in order to prevent that degree of inflammation which destroys the coat of the stomach. If neither cups, leeches, nor blisters be applied, the patient will complain of the sensation of a ball in his stomach in thirty-six hours. And in twelve hours thereafter he will throw off blood that is exuded into the stomach, known as black vomit, which has the appearance of coffee-grounds floating in an amber-colored fluid. If there be any doubt as to the character of the matter ejected from the stomach, you can at once decide upon its character by dipping a white handkerchief or linen cloth into the matter ejected from the stomach, and exposing it to the sun for a few moments. If it be the *vomito*, or genuine black vomit of yellow fever, it will impart a sanguine or bloody tinge to the cloth or handkerchief. If it be bile, which never occurs in yellow fever, it will impart a yellow tinge."

Dr. Marvin Huse, Physician of the Yellow Fever Hospital, of Louisville, where nearly two hundred cases were treated, "found that there were two classes of cases: one in which the temperature ranged from 100° to 106°, with a hot dry skin; and a second, where the temperature ranged between 97° and 100°, with a cold, clammy, and much yellower skin. The latter variety was more fatal. The symptoms were, in the main, like those of former epidemics, but a number of interesting characteristics were noted. The pulse was always so irregular as to be of help in the diagnosis. It ranged from thirty-five to one hundred and forty beats a minute. It bore no relation to the temperature. The fever was a continued one. It had remissions, but not intermissions. The fauces were red and swollen; the tongue, eventually, dry and cracked, unlike the flabby and enlarged tongue of malarial fever. From the skin there exhaled the peculiar rotten-hay odor always noticed. Herpetic eruptions about the mouth and nose were frequent. The urine had at first a high specific gravity, falling as the disease progressed. It was small in amount at first, also, and suppression with uræmia was always to be looked out for. It generally contained bile, and *always* albumen, the amount, however, varying very much. There were also granular casts. The amount of albumen and casts was in proportion to the severity of the disease, and furnished a valuable aid in prognosis. Vibrios and bacteria were found in the breath and the blood. The proportion of white blood-corpuscles was increased. Black vomit occurred in half the cases, and did not prove so very unfavorable a symptom, as a third of those thus affected got well. There were melænic stools, as usual. A hemorrhagic tendency was constant, but was easily controlled by a spray of Monsel's solution. The blood oozed from the mouth, eyes, nose, ears, etc. Just before death, the temperature generally fell to 97°. After death it gradually rose, sometimes to $106\frac{1}{4}°$ in the axilla, the body remaining warm for twelve hours. The average duration of the disease was four days. Very careful post-mortem examinations were made, the kidneys and liver giving the most uniform lesions. The stomach showed no erosions, congestion, or catarrh. The hemorrhages from it were passive ones. The liver was enlarged, and generally of some shade of yellow. The microscope showed more or less fatty infiltration and fatty degeneration, with occasionally increase of connective tissue. The kidneys always showed, under the microscope, the tubules choked with finely granular *débris* and epithelium, or in other places empty and denuded of epithelium. There were no important changes in the other organs. The treatment consisted in at once exerting the emunctories to action, especially the skin and kidneys. The patient was then kept cinchonized, and the various symptoms combated as they arose. The cases brought to the hospital were uniformly bad ones, the disease generally being in the second stage when they were received. The patients had previously suffered from neglect and exposure, and the mortality therefore of thirty-one is not considered high. None of the physicians, attendants, or visitors at the hospital caught the disease, although no especial pains were taken in the way of protection and disinfection."

Dr. Chopin, President of the New Orleans Board of Health, in his instructions to the people of that city, at the outbreak of the late epidemic, says of the yellow fever, that its "onset is more apt to be sudden and violent than that of the other fevers which prevail here, and more apt to occur at night. Frequently, but not invariably, a chill precedes the fever. There is violent pain in the forehead at the beginning, soon followed by severe pain in the lower part of the back. The eyes are red and glistening. Any individual affected as above described, should immediately go home, go to bed, and send for a physician without delay. Without waiting for his arrival, a hot foot-bath should be taken, and perspiration encouraged by warm drinks and a moderate cover in bed. If there should be any delay in the arrival of the physician, a simple purgative should be taken; and, if the attack comes on soon after eating, an emetic of ipecac or mustard would be advisable. Prompt treatment is of the utmost importance in this disease; and it should be understood that persons ought not to walk about after falling sick, nor get up at all after once going to bed, until the attack is over."

Dr. William H. Fall, of Cincinnati, gives his method of treatment as follows: "In the case of the sponge and vapor baths, the results were of undoubted benefit. The patients always expressed themselves as feeling much better after their use, and frequently requested that they might have them more often. I did not resort to hot or tepid-water baths, as I found the sponge and vapor baths to answer all purposes. I highly approve of their use in this disease, provided the patient is strong enough to bear them; but where there is much prostration, they are objectionable. Absolute rest of mind and body is of the greatest importance, and whatever occurs to mar it is injurious to the patient. Vapor and sponge baths may be given to the patient while in bed, and therefore can not produce any injurious results, while on the other hand they may be of decided benefit. They may be used in any stage of the disease. Every thing necessary for their use is to be found in every household, while portable bath-tubs are frequently absent. In reference to the use of the cold bath in this disease, I can not speak from experience, as I did not resort to it. It can not, however, be made use of, except in the first stage of the disease, and even then I doubt the propriety of its use. Ice-pellets and crushed ice were given freely to each patient, and were taken with relish. Lime-water was successful in allaying the irritability and acidity of the stomach, even after black vomit had occurred, and I regard it as one of the best agents we can employ. Iced champagne was made use of in cases Nos. 3, 4, and 5, and was very refreshing to the patient, agreeable to the taste, and arrested irritability of the stomach. Lemonade was given in two cases, but in each disagreed with the stomach, and was vomited. I do not approve of its use because of its excessive acidity. The salicylate of soda was given in three cases, and good results were obtained from its use. In the case of Smith, who recovered, no urine was passed for twenty-four hours, but after commencing the acid, the flow was reëstablished. I think if it had not been resorted to, combined with the use of the bath, he would most certainly have died of uremic poisoning. Cases 4 and 5 did well under its use until Tuesday night, when the sudden change of temperature produced such a change for the worse in their condition, that they did not rally from it. It has been remarked that northern breezes are killing to yellow-fever patients, and such was the result in these cases. I was forcibly struck with the effect the change of temperature produced upon them, and although every effort was made to shield them, it was unavailing. The salicylate of soda is a diuretic, diaphoretic, and antiseptic, and the symptoms and course of the disease clearly indicate it as a proper remedy in the treatment of yellow fever, and I think we are justified in giving it a further trial."

Mr. J. Livingston, of 52 Camp Street, New Orleans, who joined the Howard Association as far back as 1841, and has passed through every epidemic in that city, in a pamphlet published after the epidemic of 1878, offers to the public the ammonia cure, which, if the results he gives are well established, would seem to be advanced beyond the domain of theory and into that of fact. He says: "During last summer I talked much about my treatment. Physicians would not listen, and non-professional persons had their doctors, who, in their opinion, could give yellow fever the fits. Occasionally some of the unlearned thought they would, if occasion required, use the remedy suggested. One old man, a stranger to me, was particular in writing my prescription. A few weeks after he sent me word that his child was saved by the application. He could get no physician, and so expended twenty-five cents for ammonia and camphor and applied it as directed. The second day the physician came and found the child out of danger, and that his services were not required. In riding in the cars one day I explained my theory to a lawyer. Not long since I met him and he thanked me for saving his two children; 'for,' said he, 'two days after my conversation with you two of my children were taken with the fever, and on applying the liquid it acted as described.' He employed a homeopathic physician and explained what he had done. There were other cases reported to me, but as I never saw any of them I can not assert positively that the remedy was effectual, relying upon statements to me as to the results. I will cite particularly one case under my own observation. The patient, about forty-five, was in the early part of October taken with the fever. It was an aggravated case, with great heat, excruciating pains in the back and head, and with hemorrhage of the nose and gums, injected or congested eyes, tongue on the sides very sore, palate and roof of the mouth the same. It was a genuine case of hemorrhagic yellow fever. The hemorrhage commenced with the attack, and I was fearful that there was internal hemorrhage, or that it would soon take place. Cases of this description are nearly always fatal, and terminate with black vomit. This was my experience. As soon as I could I applied aqua ammonia, with an equal portion of spirits of camphor, commencing at the head, rubbing it well, then the spinal column—in fact, all over the body. But two applications were made. In an hour or less time the temperature of the body was much reduced and the pains all gone. The patient seemed, after the second application, inclined to sleep. The heat and pains never returned. Hemorrhage from the gums and nose continued for several days. On the arrival, in the evening, of an homeopathic physician, he found his patient free from fever and pains. On the third day he advised rubbing spirits of turpentine over the region of the kidneys, and gave a few drops of the spirits of sweet nitre, to be followed by watermelon tea. The urine which flowed after was not bloody, but of such a deep red color as to appear as if it was bloody. No nourishment was taken until the fifth day, and then in the shape of beef-tea. After this I gave chocolate, and eggs boiled very soft, stimulants in the way of weak brandy and water, a little krug, and English ale. I told the patient that all the internal organs were similar to the nose, gums, tongue and eyes, and that as soon as all the soreness and inflammation disappeared the inflammation of all the other organs would also be gone. From the externals I judge of the appearance and condition of the internals. On the tenth day the patient sat up and could take more nourishing food. Any indiscretion in eating, in this case, before the healing of the nose, gums, etc., had taken place, would have brought on a relapse. This was an undoubted case of very malignant yellow fever. The application used terminated the fever, arrested combustion, prevented internal hemorrhage, and rendered black vomit impossible. It is my conviction that no medical skill could have saved this patient. A continuance of the fever for twenty-four or forty-eight hours could not but have produced black vomit. The alkali neutralized the poison, and the fever disappeared. This and other cases impressed upon me the conviction that the right remedy had been applied at the right time. My next and concluding article will suggest the course to be pursued in the treatment of this fever. I have never observed any benefit from the administration of drugs. My conclusions were these: the process of digestion begins in the mouth, where the food is cut, crushed and ground. As it is reduced to a pulp it is moistened by the saliva, a digestive fluid, which is secreted from the blood by three sets of glands called the parotid, submaxillary, and sublingual. As soon as the food is mixed with this saliva it enters the stomach, and it there is acted upon by the gastric juice which is secreted by the glands of the stomach, and is converted into what chemists call chyme. It then passes into the intestinal canal, is acted upon by the pancreatic juice, and by the bile from the liver. These change the chyme into chyle, and in that condition it is then, by innumerable absorbents, distributed to the various parts of the system, supplying such matter as these various parts need. After all the nutriment is extracted, the chaff and husks, if I may so say, pass out of the system. In a healthy organization but very little goes out as excrementitious matter. This whole digestive apparatus, so very complicated, becomes inactive by the action of the poison, and all know that food can not be digested by a yellow fever patient. A piece of good beefsteak would be as fatal in the early stages of this fever as poison. Now, since the process of digestion is arrested, how is it possible for drugs to be acted upon, and how, since every absorbent is inactive, could the drugs be distributed throughout the system? It is impossible, according to my view. Hence, no treatment is preferable to medicines. As soon as combustion ceases, which it does after the poison is neutralized, the whole internal organism is left in an inflamed condition, just as the gums, nose and tongue were, in the case described, or I might say the whole was in a *raw* condition. Medicine can not be applied to a raw surface. Mucilaginous drinks should first be given. They are emollients and soothe the irritated surface. They contain also some nourishment. I would give gum arabic water, flaxseed tea, mucilage of boiled okra or slippery-elm bark. At first the mildest emetic should be given, and then a purgative of some of the preparations of magnesia, or a cooling cathartic, and afterwards diuretics, if necessary. But in comparatively mild cases diuretics will not be needed, for if the mixture is applied soon after the fever appears, combustion ceases, the internal organism will in two or three days be restored to its normal condition. The profession have a mistaken idea that the yellow fever has a particular spite against the kidneys. They are in no worse condition than the other glands; but because there is no visible manifestation that the kidneys do secrete, *ergo* the conclusion has been that the kidneys are in the most disorganized state. Every gland is in the same condition as the kidneys. The system, after the poison is destroyed, must have time to heal, and food and medicines arrest the healing process. It is known to all that any indiscretion in eating when the patient feels well, but before strength has been gained, is apt to produce a relapse, often terminating fatally. Keep the patient in bed as long as possible; a day or two more, even after he feels well, may prevent a relapse. Mucilaginous beverages, chocolate, eggs boiled very soft, and stimulants, the first few days will suffice. In conclusion I have demonstrated, I think—my theory—that the fever is caused by an acid poison—that aqua ammonia, being an alkali, destroys the poison and ends the fever. I always add about equal parts of spirits of camphor, acting under the impression that camphor is a sedative, and slightly narcotic, and that it has the tendency to quiet the nervous system. My theory is a plain remedy, cheap and always at hand, and if it does not cure, it can not kill."

Dr. Dowell, in his diagnosis and cure of yellow fever, says that "this disease usually comes on with slight chilly sensation, even preceded by a few hours or a few days of languor and general malaise. These chills or rigors last for a few minutes or a few hours, and terminate in a fever of not a very high grade: pulse about 100, respiration about 20, and heat about 36 centigrade, (102 F.); acute pain in head, back, and loins, sometimes vomiting mucous and undigested substances, and when severe mixed with specks of blood, which is a grave symptom in the first twenty-four hours of the fever. Patient very nervous, tremulous, easily excited, startles at any noise. This is especially so in children; fever continues regularly for twenty-four to sixty-four hours, generally abating in thirty-six hours, when there is a calm; this calm lasts for a few hours or a day, when it terminates in convalescence, or the fever will return. In four or five days, say about the fifth day, patient's eyes will become tinged with yellow, and finally the whole skin will become yellow, like the yellowness of slight bruise or contusion. The skin does not turn yellow in more than one case in six, and many die before there is the least yellowness even in the eyes; not more than one in three turn yellow that die of black vomit. When there is vomiting and sick stomach from the rise of the fever, the patient is liable, between or after the third day until final recovery, to vomit up specks of blood and mucous, which will become blacker, and finally a blackish brown-red, of the consistency of chocolate or coffee, but free from lumps. This is the pure vomito pristo, or black vomit, which is the only positive sign of the disease, and I believe it is unlike any thing seen in any other pathological condition. I have not seen any thing like it in my professional life. I have seen, in congestion of the stomach, black matter, sloughs of the mucous coat, and specks of blood, generally with some small green specks. This is common with malarial fevers with congestion of the stomach, and these symptoms may occur in yellow fever, but the brownish-black semi-fluid effusion in yellow fever is very different. This effusion may be in small quantities, leaving specks on the handkerchief or on the bed, or it may come up involuntarily, or may be spit up, or there will be pint after pint for hours, or even for two or three days. Patient at this stage is very restless, sighs, halloos, screams, attempts to get up, falls about, half-conscious, and can't tell why he can not lie still, nor can he give a reason why he cries out. Skin begins in this stage to become yellow, if patient does not die in a few hours; first a bright jaundice yellow, then a livid yellow, almost a contused black. In spots over the body blood will ooze out, nose will bleed, blistered and cupped surfaces will bleed, and show no disposition to heal. Urine is generally natural in this stage; will not stain the shirt, as it always does in jaundice. This fact is very important, for this yellowness occurs in hæmaturia miasmatica, and the species of delirium also occurs in that disease, but we seldom have hemorrhage from the kidneys in yellow fever. Most often there is a suppression of urine, and though it may be scant, it is rarely more yellow than natural. Black vomit is the last symptom, for the patient generally dies either in a few hours or a few days after throwing it up. The quantity thrown up does not indicate the fatality or hasten dissolution, for only a few mouthfuls seem to be as fatal as bowls full. This black stuff is often found in the bowels when not vomited up, and not more than one in three that die throw it up. Hence the great difficulty in diagnosing this fever. I summarize the following symptoms, to be specially noticed in the order I have put them down:

"1st. Chill, rigors along the spine.

"2d. Pain in head, very severe in most cases.

"3d. Fever not very high, tending to perspiration if kept free from a draft.

"4th. Stage of calm about third day. Fever lasts but twenty-four hours, at least in children, and may run on without interruption for at least five days.

"5th. No second chill unless patient has been subject to intermittent fever, when he will often have regular paroxysms each day, or every day for three days, when it will assume a typhoid type, with red edges to tongue, dark brown coat in center, and on the fifth and later there will be more or less dryness, and a disposition to crack and bleed. This will be especially the case if the patient is kept from hot water or made to drink hot teas." Dr. Dowell gives his treatment as follows: "No nurse should be put in charge of a case who will not follow directions of doctor or doctors in attendance. This is a great curse in this city, many taking upon themselves to change their medicines as well as openly violate the doctor's instructions; such should always be discharged—the doctor or nurse should be discharged at once. There must be no divisions of these persons, or the patient will most assuredly die. There are so many opinions as to how a patient should be nursed; I will only give my own plan, and what I wish all nurses under my directions to follow; but one thing all should remember, to make no change from doctors' directions. Doors should not be opened that were ordered to be closed, nor windows. All drafts of a sudden character should be strictly avoided—what I think a nurse should do and might do without the instructions of a doctor—and this is what I recommend: When chill comes on patient should be put to bed and comfortably covered, not too hot nor too cold, patient's feelings to be duly consulted in this. If patient has eaten only a few minutes before, an emetic of mustard or ipecac may be given, to remove all the undigested substances in the stomach, as well as make the patient sweat, and to stop the chill. If, however, he has eaten one or two hours before, a dose of castor-oil with a little brandy should be given, and repeated if it does not act, to remove all indigestible substances from the intestinal canal, which if left might irritate and cause serious gastric congestion, and finally prepare the way for the black vomit. If by this time the chill is over, the patient is perspiring moderately, he should be left alone. But if there is a dry skin and thirst, he should have warm teas: orange-leaf is perhaps the best, but flax-seed is good, sage is good, and even China tea. This should be taken as freely as patient wants, but should not be forced upon him. Feet should also be put in hot mustard bath, and kept in a sufficient length of time to cause perspiration, and then returned to bed and free from draft, which I think is bad at any and all stages of the disease. If patient gets too warm or sweats too profusely, the cover should be partially moved, and if there is pain in the head, the temporal arteries beating, cold cloths should be freely applied, with either nitre or muriate of ammonia in the water, or ice, if deemed necessary; but these should be used with caution, and, when once begun, must be continued. I use them but seldom, preferring plain cistern water, which may be discontinued or renewed at the desire of the patient. If patient vomits, no emetics should be used; no hot teas, especially if there be specks of blood in the vomit. Mustard plasters should be put to stomach at once, and ice pounded like snow used if patient desires it, instead of teas. If the vomiting continues or the stomach becomes sore, then patient should be cupped at once and freely. This being done, then for the doctor's prescription. When the fever appears to run high, and the pain in the back and head is great, I give the following:

"℞: Hyd. ch. mitis;
Quinæ sulphatis;
Opii et ipecac pulvis:
(F. charts, No. 4:) āā grs. xij.
Sig.—One every three hours."

"This is repeated as long as the fever lasts, lessening the dose or increasing the length of the intervals, from three to six hours, according to circumstances. All tending to congestions is carefully guarded against, and remedies directed to the point; all local pains are at once subdued. These are generally done by mustard plasters, cups, and blisters. If skin is still hot I give tincture of aconite, in ten-drop doses, every two or three hours, sometimes using sweet spirits of nitre with aconite. This treatment is continued until the fever subsides and the stage of calm comes on, which would be in thirty-six or fifty-six hours after the fever rises. If patient is much exhausted and pulse feeble I give brandy toddy, as much as patient wants, but will not force it on him; if there is restlessness I give valerianate of zinc, in from five- to ten-grain doses, as often as necessary. This is better than morphine; but I have used morphine with good results, if patient can not sleep. If there is retching or vomiting at this stage, I have used, with the best results, the following:

"℞: Brandy, ℥iv;
Creosote, ℨj;
Morphine, grs. iv : M.
Sig.—Give tablespoonful every three hours, or according to circumstances, in a little water."

"I generally put a blister over the stomach, which is generally swollen, sore and tender to the touch at this stage of the disease. Blister is closely watched and cuticle kept on if possible, dressed with glycerine and covered with oil-silk, for they are apt to bleed, and will mortify if they are not well attended to. Should black vomit come in spite of all our efforts to keep it back, I continue the brandy and creosote mixture, and alternate with tincture chloride iron, in five to thirty drops every two hours, between the brandy or the solution of perchloride of iron or tannin. The latter does not corrode. By this treatment twenty-three cases of black vomit recovered under my charge, in 1867. I never give quinine in this stage of calm, or while the fever is off, to a patient with yellow fever: just the reverse of intermittent fever. It chills the patient, makes the skin very cold, and causes a cold and clammy sweat, very weakening to the patient. I allow my patients lemonade, as they want, throughout the disease; and this must be closely watched or it will produce serious ptyalism, which should be avoided. When only partial it is a good, favorable sign; but if severe, will often prove fatal by producing sloughs and hemorrhages. Where the kidneys do not act I use freely sweet spirits of nitre, tincture of buchu, or spirits of turpentine, in the usual doses. If a stimulant is necessary in this condition I use gin instead of brandy. Patient should be allowed food whenever called for, which should be light and nutritious, such as beef-tea, tea and coffee, to suit patient's taste. Black meats, as pigeons, ducks, Guinea chickens, venison, etc., in moderation. Patient must be gently fed when fever goes off, if there is no bad symptoms, or he will sink and the stomach prey on its own membrane, and nausea and vomiting will follow. There is no disease that requires as close watching as yellow fever, and none in which judiciously administered medicines will do more good. Patient should be watched from the stage of calm, or after the fever leaves, until complete reaction is restored, and should not be allowed to get out of bed, if possible, using bed-pan on all occasions. They will faint easily, and to faint is very dangerous at this stage, as the blood is so fibrinated that clots will form in the heart and arteries and patient die from embolism. Patient must take no unusual exercise for six weeks, or be exposed to damp or wet; must carefully avoid all sudden changes, all mental excitement as well as physical. Relapses do not often occur from very trifling causes, and a relapse is much worse than the original disease, and must be combated with the same remedies, but as a general thing will have to be used in much smaller doses, or the patient will sink. I have thus given the plan with which I have treated over two thousand cases, with about twenty-five per cent. loss, in hospital, taking all the cases as they come, and in private practice about ten. In children about five per cent. In 1867 I treated fifty-nine cases from the time they took their bed until their final recovery, in the hospital (all grown persons—sailors and employés), and only lost three—my assistant surgeon, laundress, and one sailor from a revenue cutter. In 1867 I treated forty-two children, and did not lose a single case (I mean children under twelve years). Three had black vomit."

Dr. Warren Stone, in his Bellevue Hospital lecture, diagnoses the disease and prescribes his treatment of the disease as follows: "In the well-marked cases there was rigor, pains in the head, back, and limbs, and sometimes a peculiar capillary engorgement, particularly in the eye. If the patient is placed in bed at once, with a little assistance he breaks into a sweat, as in common intermittent fever; this gives some relief, but not much. The pains continue; but if the case is favorable, it will go on until the sweating and heat subside together at the end of three days. The patient must be kept perfectly quiet; and if he is then nourished, he will have no return of the suffering. He must not even be allowed to raise his head. If he gets up, a faintness comes over him, and the whole process is often renewed, with the addition of nausea and loathing of food. In this case he almost certainly dies. This is the history of favorable cases. Purgatives are not essential, and many do much harm. A mild dose of oil may be given if there is any thing in the stomach likely to ferment and prove irritating. A simple injection may prove useful. If patients were seen in the beginning, I gave them, as soon as perspiration began, a full dose of quinine. There is no doubt of its good effect in quieting pains and promoting perspiration. Sometimes a second dose would be advisable the following morning. This was all that could be done, beyond regulating the drink and nourishment. There was nothing more to do. There was no organic disease. Nothing was revealed by dissection. The poison caused a peculiar condition of the blood, which afterwards showed itself in the skin. There were many little points in the treatment which, in the aggregate, were of vast importance. In regard to the application of ice to relieve the pains in the head, it was common, but not advisable, and afforded only temporary relief. The reaction from it was dangerous. Cups to the head, stomach, and back were much used at one time; but only in cases of plethora were they of service. Simple applications of mustard were generally sufficient to relieve the pain in the back. Absolute rest and nourishment were of the highest possible importance. Any form of stimulant may be given that the patient prefers; but malt liquors are the best. Brandy may often be given, even with the fever. Beef-tea is necessary, and if the stomach can not retain it, it must be given by injection. Where there is acidity of the stomach, small doses of bicarbonate of soda, combined with the one-thirty-second part of a grain of morphia, had often an excellent effect. Sponging the patient is grateful and appropriate, but on no occasion must he be disturbed by the treatment. There is much in anticipating certain symptoms. If there is a disposition to delirium and wandering, it may be guarded against by mild anodynes and stimulants. If this delirium is allowed to continue, the patient becomes comatose, and dies. It must be remembered that yellow fever patients are wholly irresponsible, and though they may talk reasonably, they do not appreciate their own condition. It was exceedingly difficult to keep patients quiet in bed; yet it was the most essential part of the treatment. I once saved an intelligent sea captain, during one of the epidemics, by threatening to cut his throat if he dared to stir from a given position in the intervals of my visits. The treatment of yellow fever is simple. In old times, people thought because it was a mighty disease it needed mighty remedies; and, when I first went to New Orleans, it was customary to give sixty-grain doses of calomel, and even more than that; and yet some patients even then got well. With rational treatment, a large proportion will recover. The chief difficulty lies in preventing the patient from committing fatal acts of indiscretion in the absence of his physician. It should be remembered that every thing depends on rest and nutrition, and that nothing can be gained by depletion. It is even better to allow the bowels to remain unmoved for five or six days than to run the risk of giving active purgatives."

Samuel B. Washburne, late a captain of the volunteer navy of the United States, furnishes the following method of treatment. He says: "My first knowledge of the pestilence was in New Orleans, at the time it prevailed so frightfully in 1847. I think that was the year. I was then the first mate of the ship *Herculean*, Captain Isaiah Chase. We went to New Orleans in the month of August, to take in a cargo of cotton for Liverpool, and were in port for weeks when the fever was at its height, and expecting every day to be stricken down. During this time I watched the progress and treatment of the disease; and Captain Chase and myself determined on the treatment we would pursue in case either of us or any of our crew should be attacked. Having, after great delay, got our cargo on board, with much difficulty we shipped a crew. The shipping-agent delivered the men on board one evening, and we were immediately taken in tow, and on the next morning we were in the Balize. Early in the day symptoms of the fever were developed among the crew. Without losing a moment, Captain Chase and myself applied the remedies we had agreed upon. The patient was covered all over with thick woolen blankets, and his feet put into a tub of very hot water, well charged with mustard. After half an hour, and when in a full perspiration, two men with coarse, dry towels gave him a thorough rubbing down, until the whole body was in a glow, and the circulation in a good state. He was then put to bed and covered with blankets. In another half-hour an immense dose of castor-oil was administered. The patient was not permitted to leave his bed, but was kept very quiet, and limited to a very light and careful diet. No other medicine was given except an occasional dose of oil. We had four cases, and all recovered. In July, 1850, I found myself at Para, under the equator, in command of the ship *Edward Henry*. The yellow fever was then raging there with a malignity and fatality almost without a parallel. All business was suspended for more than two months, and the death rate was fearful, particularly among the shipping. There were many vessels in port that *lost every man on board, officers and crew*. Every single man on my ship was attacked. I was fully prepared, and had determined to apply the same treatment as on the *Herculean*. The American consul advised me, in the event of the fever breaking out, to send my men to the hospital on shore; but I declined, preferring to treat them myself. It was well I did so, for scarcely a sailor who went to the hospital ever came out alive. As soon as a man showed the least symptoms of the fever, I put him through the same course of treatment as I have stated, and every man recovered. As for myself, I happily escaped the fever both in New Orleans and Para, but had an attack of it at Brashear City, Louisiana, in the summer of 1863, when in command of the United States iron-clad steamer *Nyanza*. My attack was a light one, and yielded readily to the remedies I had so successfully applied to others."

Two contrasting cases are those offered by Dr. George W. Moore, of the Hernando Road, near Memphis, and Dr. E. J. Pitts, of Shreveport, La. The latter gives his personal experience of the ice treatment. He says: "In

Navisota, Texas, in the fall of 1867, I was attacked about midnight, but did not call a physician (Dr. Jones) until next morning, and he pronounced it yellow fever of the most malignant type, as did all other physicians whom he consulted. I was given a most active purgative, of which I think the principal ingredient was calomel, and took quinine during the day in great quantities; but my fever did not abate in the least, but rather grew worse. The next day I was so reckless of life that I resolved to try an experiment to kill or cure; my main object was to relieve myself of pain. So I hired the waiter to bring a tub of cold water in my room and put sufficient ice in it to make it almost in the freezing state. I drank often of ice-water, though little at a time, and swallowed pounded ice in lumps almost as large as my thumb; this threw the heat on the outward surface. I then wet my head and neck, and gradually got in the tub of ice-water and bathed my whole body freely for five or ten minutes, until I felt unpleasantly cold, and then immediately got in bed and wrapped up warmly, and soon got in a profuse perspiration, and fell into a pleasant slumber which lasted four or five hours. When I awoke I was entirely free from fever and from all pain, and was entirely well in a few days."

Dr. Moore's treatment is of another extreme, and is thoroughly heroic. He says: "I may premise by stating that I have a long experience in a disease known to the profession as 'malarial hæmaturia' or 'swamp fever.' It has prevailed extensively in the Mississippi swamps. The treatment which I pursue has been successful in every case, no matter how malignant. Now, as I consider malarial hæmaturia nothing more than a bastard form, or rather the twin-sister of yellow fever, I have adopted the same course of treatment in the present epidemic; and I am happy to add, that in every case, no matter how malignant, my cases have got well when called before the death symptoms (of black vomit or suppression of urine) have supervened. Now for a slight synopsis of the treatment I pursue. If called early in the disease, I give calomel ten grains, with one-half grain of ipecac; in four to six hours I scour out the bowels with oil and terpentine; on the first decline of fever I give from three to five grains of quinine every two hours until twenty or thirty grains are taken: sometimes combine a small portion of Dover's powders to allay nervousness and restlessness. From the beginning I order hot foot-baths, with plenty of mustard, also large mush and mustard poultices over the bowels. I also use a saturated solution of the chloral of potassa all through the disease to act on the secretions. As a nourishment I use beef-tea or chicken-water."

Two other and equally remarkable contrasts in treatment are furnished, the one by Mrs. Jane G. Swisshelm—who recommends hot water compresses and packs, with homeopathic medicines for internal treatment—the other Dr. S. Alexander, of Clinton, Miss., which is almost as heroic as Dr. Moore's, though with different (root) remedies. He says: "The treatment should be varied according to present indications, but always cleansing, stimulating, and sustaining. If you find your patient in the first stage with the chill upon him, give him strong, stimulating teas, as good composition or bayberry, African and wild ginger, equal parts; or ginger and bayberry in sage tea; or sage, or catnip, bayberry and cayenne; or bayberry, boneset, and ginger. If a free use of any of the preceding teas should have a tendency to produce vomiting, give a teaspoonful or more of lobelia-powder in a cup of the tea, to make him to do it well and thoroughly, and prevent that congestion which makes him vomit too much. Nine cases out of ten should be vomited at once to cleanse the stomach. Much attention should be paid to the surface. It should be thoroughly cleansed either by the vapor bath, the warm bath, or warm water and soap (the first is the best), and if hot, dashed with cool alkaline water after it; if cool, rubbed with a liniment made of a tablespoonful of cayenne in half a pint of good cider vinegar. While chill or fever is on, the thirst can be allayed by acidulated drinks, as with vinegar, lemonade, sumachberries, simple grape-juice, apple-water, etc. Good tonic bitters should be freely given after the system is thoroughly cleansed and the fever is off—not before. If the bowels are inactive, give enemas of a tea of equal parts of cayenne, lobelia, and slippery elm. If they are too loose give one of these, and follow its action with one of bayberry (or some other good astringent) and ginger and cayenne. Remember to bring the action to the surface as soon as you can, and maintain it there in a gentle softness of the skin, not profuse perspiration, which would prostrate, but just a comfortable freedom from heat and dryness. As soon as the stomach is cleansed and the action of the surface is restored, give enough of the following to move the liver and the bowels gently: say, one grain of the extract of mandrake, two grains of the extract of black root, and five grains of rhubarb. Should this dose fail to act in from six to eight hours, use the best Alexandria senna, in small doses, until the object is accomplished. Before and after the action of the medicine give a wine-glass of Virginia snake-root tea, with sage or pepper tea as a sudorific. The stomach cleansed, the action of the surface being restored, the liver and bowels being relieved, all that is wanting to complete the cure is good nursing, close attention, a judicious repetition of the same means as the exigencies of the case may demand. Convalescence of this disease requires to be watched with peculiar care."

Dr. Masderville, physician to Charles IV, published in New Orleans, in a work dedicated to the Governor Baron de Carondelet, in 1796, the following as a safe treatment: "An antimonial mixture, in viper water; five ounces of emetic wine; one ounce of cream of tartar; a teaspoonful for a dose. After the fifth day give an electuary of salt of wormwood, tartar emetic, and Peruvian bark, in divided doses." The third and last remedy (lavement), called the blessed laxative, was composed of antimonial wine-water, honey, and oil. He rejected cordials, blisters, and blood-letting. He considered life as residing in the blood, as declared by Moses (Leviticus xvii, 14), and denounces venesection as dangerous for that reason, as life and health depend upon it. He maintains that his method is a true specific against all the fevers of Spain and America, as he knew from an experience of twenty years. His most Catholic Majesty commanded the Spanish physicians to follow his prescription and to prescribe nothing else. He blamed the physicians of Havana for not having adopted this "blessed" method of treatment.

Dr. Mitchell, of New York, who was born in 1763, and died in 1831, Dowler says, learned alike in physic, physics, and politics, influential at home and abroad, exercised at the beginning of the present century an influence over the public mind rivaling that of Dr. Rush. This great New York professor and Member of Congress claimed to have discovered the demon of all epidemics, particularly that of yellow fever, called by him Septon, that reigned by virtue of the principle of Acidity in the earth, air, and water, causing corruption everywhere; whereupon, he inaugurated Alcalinity into power with a scrub broom in one hand and a bucket of lime-water or soap-suds in the other, by which only "Grim Septon" could be conquered. Dr. Mitchell moved, in Congress, the appointment of a committee with the view of reporting on the purification of ships by alkalies in order to destroy this pestilential Septon. The Secretary of the Navy adopted the theory, or at least the practice, which latter he ordered to be carried into effect. Books, pamphlets, and letters soon appeared against Septon and for Alcalies. The next year an article appeared in the *Medical Repository*, having the title following: "Dr. Chalmers on the Acidity of the Atmosphere of South Carolina." The fading of goods, the rusting of metals, and other effects of atmospheric acidity were gravely announced as indubitable proofs of this theory. Dr. Hosack and many others adopted Dr. Mitchell's theory of Septic acid as being the cause, and alkalies as the preventive of yellow fever. Lime-water and the like were reckoned to be vastly important in neutralizing the Septic acid, which was considered very corrosive, particularly after black vomit appeared. Dr. Cathrall, of Philadelphia, read a paper before the American Philosophical Society on the analysis of black vomit, in which he asserted that there was an acid in this liquid which was inert to the taste and smell, and harmless when swallowed.

In their report to Congress, the Homeopathic Yellow Fever Commission of 1878 state that, in their treatment for yellow fever they did not have recourse to any of the allopathic remedies. Some acknowledged the occasional use of an anodyne to produce sleep in cases of extreme wakefulness or restlessness. Some gave a little carbonate of soda for sick stomach, or sulphurcarbolate of soda for black vomiting, or frictions or enemata of quinine in collapse. One supplied a blister or two, a kind of coarse, external homeopathy! another gave watermelon-seed tea for suppression of urine. Foot-baths, sponging, enemas, warm and cold applications, frictions, stimulants, regulations of diet and of covering, of the temperature of the sick room, and ventilation of the same, were resorted to. "The great therapeutic question of the first stage," they say, "is how to reduce the extreme high temperature, which, if long continued, will inevitably destroy the integrity of the blood and arrest the processes of nutrition in the molecules of every organ of the body. The homeopathic physician would take Aconite, the great homeopathic antiphlogistic, and giving it in very *small doses frequently repeated*, would equalize the circulation, quiet the nervous system, and reduce the temperature in a gradual and satisfactory manner, without the possibility of doing the least harm. Leaving nature all her strength and her resources unimpaired, he would do the greatest amount of good practicable under the circumstances of each case. The whole secret consisted in selecting the remedy according to the homeopathic law, and in using it in very small doses frequently repeated. The last fact we can best illustrate by saying that water dropped, drop by drop, upon a stone, will make more impression upon it than a thousand times the quantity dashed against it at once. The homeopathic physician has more genuinely homeopathic remedies for the second stage than for the first, among them the giants arsenic, crotalus, and carbo vegetabilis. Here, too, he gives smaller doses, and with still better effect. He has more recoveries after black vomit. He checks hemorrhages without the use of that relic of surgical barbarism, the actual cautery, which was actually used upon a little child in New Orleans last summer. He restores the secretion of urine without diuretics. He rouses his patient from a deeper collapse, and saves him from the most desperate condition. The action of homeopathic remedies in the second stage of yellow fever frequently reminds us of their similar efficiency in the collapsed stage of Asiatic cholera."

The homeopathic commission quote, as an endorsement which they seem to lay particular stress upon, the treatment followed by Dr. Charles Belot, of Havana, Cuba, who has passed through eighteen epidemics, and has treated about a thousand patients annually. That gentleman says: "One very good auxiliary, which should never be neglected in resisting local congestion, and to diminish the plasticity of the blood, is the tincture of aconite. This remedy, given in doses of six drops in twelve ounces of water, administered by spoonfuls every hour, has a truly magical power. The pulse becomes softer, and its frequency diminishes, whilst the heat of the skin subsides as perspiration is established. It should never be neglected in the first or congestive period." Dr. Belot has also discovered that *arsenic*, pronounced by the concurrent voice of all our physicians to be the best remedy in the second stage, is, in reality, a magnificent remedy in the malignant cases of yellow fever. Hear him again: "Towards the end of the second period, when the vomiting can not be arrested, when the patient has continual nausea, when the vomit contains bile or mucosities, filled with blackish or sanguinolent streaks, there is no better remedy than arsenic. Prescribed under fitting circumstances, arsenic often brings unhoped-for amelioration. As for arsenic, whilst it may be difficult to appreciate its action in theory, its happy influence in this case is as certain as that of sulphate of quinine in intermittent diseases."

The Rev. C. K. Marshall, of Vicksburg, a gentleman who enjoys the confidence of all who know him; who has always been held in the highest esteem by his fellow-citizens of Mississippi, and who has had a life-time experience with yellow fever, warmly endorses the homeopathic treatment, and predicts its triumph over all others in the future. He says, writing in 1878: "The result of my observation is, that no treatment yet compares with the homeopathic. I will give some facts: One lady here has treated from fifty to seventy cases without the loss of one. She is a brave, womanly woman, who had never had the fever, and went among her neighbors, colored and white, because physicians could not be had, until stricken down herself, and her husband also. But they were treated by the same method, and recovered. I know several other ladies of clear heads, cool and calm spirits, who have done the same thing, only not to the same extent, but with success. Our regular homeopathic physicians were both originally allopaths. They both are quite advanced in years, but somehow have not faltered on account of years, though one of them fell sick of the fever; but he is all right again. They have been most laborious; and probably no two physicians have seen as many patients or lost as few, for no remedies can save all. One of these physicians had three sons, young men, away in business in places where the fever had not planted its black banner. He sent for them, one at a time, to come home and be sick, have the fever, and prepare for more useful lives as physicians. They came, and he has got all through but one, and he is waiting, as confident his father will bring him through as he is of his name. Indeed, I could fill pages with interesting facts about this treatment. But it will be treated with respect hereafter; and why not? The allopathic physicians have each a method of cure. Of forty together, it is doubtful if five practice alike. The populace see this. Dr. Chopin, of great and just celebrity, says to the physicians of New Orleans: 'Experiment! experiment!' The people have seen, what they call by pretty hard names, the sacrifice of valuable lives by these dreadful 'experiments.' Is it to be wondered at that they are trying experiments with the 'little sugar pellets that amount to nothing?' The system makes converts here daily."

It was remarked by Dr. Dowell, and other well known medical experts, who practiced in Memphis in 1878, that the yellow fever of that year was peculiarly virulent and violent, and particularly fatal. Most of the methods of treatment given in this chapter were resorted to, and often with gratifying results. Others not here reported, which were of a thoroughly heroic character, were in some cases remarkably successful. But generally, the treatment set forth by Dr. Mitchell was that resorted to, and which proved most satisfactory in its results and most successful. In New Orleans, also, experience forced the conviction that the visitation which last year afflicted so large a scope of country was not only wholly unparalleled, but phenomenal. The veteran of half a dozen epidemics did not pretend to disguise his amazement. "The disease," the New Orleans *Times* reported, " admitted the bewildered disciple of Esculapius into entirely new realms. Tenets which in that region had been articles of faith for more than half a century, suddenly collapsed and vanished into thin air. No sooner did the astonished believer in the immunity of all who were 'to the manner born' find himself confounded by the death of half a score of native patients, than he is met with the new heresy—judicious nourishment is not a death warrant. From a time when the memory of man runneth not to the contrary, it had been an axiom in this city, that an era of convalescence is an era of starvation. Bronze John invariably came in the orthodox way: light fever, gradual delirium, a sharp tussel, slow convalescence, and almost total abstemiousness. The convalescents of 1853 went for three months without daring to eat a full meal. '*Maintenant nous avons change tout cela.*' There were patients of the epidemic of 1878, on the contrary, who ate the leg of a broiled spring chicken forty-eight hours after the fever made his conge. The popular belief in blankets seemed to be completely extinguished. Light covering, often a single sheet, and perfect ventilation, appeared to be the triumphal path towards rapid recovery and wholesome recuperation. The reasons set forth for this phenomena are thus set forth by a physician: 'I,' he says, 'can divide my cases into two general classes—wet and dry. All are different, but this subdivision separates them sufficiently to be clearly understood. A sick person with a moist skin yields readily to the ordinary treatment, and can be purged and quinined to one's heart's content; but the dry skin and hot fever is a dangerous subject, and a physician is justified in adopting any method that will take him out of that dilemma. Sheets dipped in hot water, fanning, constant sponging, if they will diminish temperature, should be resorted to; but, very naturally, each individual requires special treatment, and that is the only general rule.' Another successful practitioner gave light nourishment, even at the risk of slightly increasing the temperature, insisting that the patient should be sustained to withstand a fearful drain upon the vitality. There were many physicians who clung to the ancient methods, insisting upon low diet with as much tenacity as they did thirty years ago. Many of these were successful, but all conceded that the disease which afflicted the South in 1878 was extremely dangerous in type, peculiar in character, and, in short, wholly different from the yellow fever as heretofore experienced and known." There is not a word of this that those who have experienced the fever, or who have had experience in yellow fever epidemics, will not endorse, and with it the following very positive utterances of Dr. Chopin, as to remedies: " *We know of nothing in the way of remedies which will check the disease. I know of none.* Every kind of treatment meets with about equal success, or the results vary very little. Of course, common sense in the application of the treatment will do more than could be obtained without its exhibition. *Yet we are at a loss to know how to check the ravages of the fever when it attacks the human body.*"

CHRONOLOGY OF YELLOW FEVER.

CHRONOLOGY OF YELLOW FEVER.

The visitations of yellow fever to this and other countries, whether epidemic or not, so far as any record of them has been preserved, follow in regular sequence, its origin, causes, methods and means of propagation and of transmission, diagnosis, and cure. It has never made its appearance in Asia nor in Australia; nor in any of the Islands of the Pacific Ocean; and it has only been felt sporadically on the Pacific coast of North and South America. In Europe it has invaded Spain, Portugal, Italy, France, and England. In South America it has prevailed in British Guiana, Columbia, Peru, Bolivia, Buenos Ayres, and the Brazils. In North America it has invaded Honduras, Mexico, all the West India Islands, Canada, and the following States of the Union: Maine, Vermont, Massachusetts, Rhode Island, New Hampshire, Connecticut, New Jersey, Pennsylvania, New York, Delaware, Maryland, Illinois, Indiana, Missouri, Ohio, Kentucky, West Virginia, Virginia, North Carolina, South Carolina, Georgia, Alabama, Tennessee, Mississippi, Arkansas, Louisiana, Florida, Texas; also the Indian Territory. It is said to have originated in Africa; but of this we know nothing. Except the reference to Hertado, by Dowell, we have not a word with which to hinge that continent to the scourge. We have no data of its ravages on the "dark continent," no record of its visitations. So far as these have been preserved, they are confined to Europe, to North and South America, and to the West India Islands, as will be seen from the following chronological statement:

1596 to 1699.

The first authentic record we have of the appearance of the yellow fever is that which occurred in Central America in 1596. Subsequently we hear of it in New England among the Indians in 1618. After that in the Island of St. Lucia in 1664, where it killed over 1,411 out of a population of 1,500 soldiers, being in the ratio of 1 in 1.06 of the whole number. We next hear of it in the same place in 1665, when, out of 500 sailors, 200 died, being 1 in 2.5; and again in 1666, when every man, woman, and child of 5,000 died. New York, in 1668, was visited by it for the first time; Boston in 1691, and again in 1693. Philadelphia was visited, for the first time, in 1695. In 1699 it again visited that city, the mortality being given as 220, which no doubt was very heavy, as the inhabitants were but few in numbers, the place being then only seventeen years old.

having been laid out by William Penn in 1682. Charleston, S. C., was also visited for the first time this year, but what the mortality was we have no means of knowing.

1702 to 1799.

1702.—The yellow fever broke out in New York and raged with great fury until the thirtieth of September, the mortality reaching 570. It also appeared at Biloxi, Miss., in that year, which was its first visitation on the Gulf coast.

1705.—Mobile, and at the same time in Cadiz, Spain—its first appearance in Europe.

1728.—Charleston, S. C.

1731.—Cadiz again suffered.

1732.—Charleston, S. C. In this year it commenced in May and continued until October, a period of nearly four months, some weeks beyond the limit it usually takes—ninety days.

1733.—Cadiz.

1734.—Cadiz; also in St. Domingo, where the mortality was as high as 1 in 5 of the population, and 1 in 2 of the number of cases. Charleston also suffered in that year.

1739.—Charleston, S. C.

1741.—Philadelphia suffered a loss of 250. New York was also visited in that year; and the village of Holliston, Middlesex County, Mass., twenty-five miles from Boston, suffered a loss of 15 souls.

1742.—New York and Philadelphia were both visited.

1743.—New York and Philadelphia again visited, the former losing 217 persons. New Haven, Conn., had this year its first visitation, and Catskill on the Hudson River.

1744.—It appeared almost simultaneously in Philadelphia and Cadiz.

1745.—Charleston, S. C., New York, and Stamford, Conn., were invaded.

1746.—Albany, N. Y., commencing in August.

1747.—New York and Philadelphia; also Norfolk, Va., for the first time.

1748.—New York and Charleston again, the latter after an interregnum of two years.

1753.—Charleston, S. C.

1755.—Charleston, S. C.

1761.—Charleston, S. C.

1762.—New York, Charleston, and Philadelphia. In the latter city it began in August and continued until November.

1763.—Nantucket Island, Mass., lost 259 persons by it, which must have been a very severe mortality.

1764.—Pensacola, Fla., received its first visitation. Cadiz also received a call.

1765.—It broke out afresh in Pensacola, Fla., and carried off 125 persons. Mobile also suffered from it during that year.

1766.—Mobile again.

1768.—Charleston.

1769.—New Orleans.

1770.—Charleston.

A HISTORY OF THE YELLOW FEVER.

1790.—New York, commencing in August and ending October 15th.
1791.—New York, New Orleans, and Philadelphia.
1792.—Charleston and New York.
1793.—In New Grenada it appeared among the sailors, the proportion of deaths to cases amounting to 1 in 3 of sailors; soldiers and white inhabitants, to 1 in 5; and of a total of 1,130 of the soldiers alone, 630 died, being in proportion to population 1 in 1.8. It also visited New York, New Orleans, Southwark, and Kensington, both the latter in Philadelphia County, Pa.; also the city of Philadelphia, commencing there in the month of August and ending in December, the deaths footing up the fearful total of 4,041; the ratio of mortality being 1 in 10 of the population.

1794.—It occupied a wide extent of territory—Catskill, N. Y., New York City, New Haven, Conn., Providence, R. I. Philadelphia, Norfolk, Va., Charleston, S. C., New Orleans, and Baltimore. The same year it prevailed in Havana, Cuba, where the mortality in proportion to numbers was 1 in 1.1 on some ships, and 1 in 1.1 in proportion to the whole number of cases. It also this year (1794) attacked Sir Ch. Grey's Army, in the Windward and Leeward Islands, and of an estimated population of 12,000, there was a mortality of 6,012—being 1 in 2.

1795.—It appeared for the first time in West Neck, Suffolk County, N. Y., and in New Orleans, Baltimore, Boston, Charleston, Norfolk, Va., and New York. In the latter city there was a mortality of 730. In Huntington, Suffolk County, on Huntington Bay, N. Y., the disease also appeared, and at Bristol, R. I., on Narragansett Bay; also at Providence, R. I.

1796.—It appeared for the first time in Chatham, Middlesex Co., Conn., commencing in August, and resulting in a mortality of 9. New Orleans also suffered that year, *Dowler says*, for the first time. Newburyport, Mass., was also visited this year for the first time; and Boston, Mass., commencing in August; also New York, and Gallipolis, Ohio, on the Ohio River, where half the garrison and many of the French settlers died in ten days. It also appeared in Philadelphia, Bristol, R. I., Charleston, S. C., Norfolk, Va., Wilmington, N. C., and St. Nicholas in the Island of San Domingo, where the mortality is set down as 1 in 2; also the Island of Guadaloupe, where, out of a population estimated at 20,000, there was a mortality of 13,807, being a proportion to population of 1 in 1.47. In the same island (in 1796), out of 367 artillerymen there was a death-list of 129, being a proportion to population of 1 in 2.8. It also prevailed in New Grenada that year.

1797.—It prevailed in New Orleans and Baltimore, commencing in August and ending in November; also in New Design, St. Louis Co., twenty miles below St. Louis, Mo., where 57 deaths resulted, being more than one-fourth of the inhabitants. In New York, Charleston, S. C., and Philadelphia, commencing August 1st and ending October 15th, with a mortality of 1,300 — 1 in 50 of the entire population. In Norfolk, Va., Bristol, R. I., and Providence, R. I., commencing at this last mentioned point August 13th, and ending the same month, with a mortality of 45.

1798.—It prevailed in Hartford, Conn., New London, Conn., on Thames

River, three miles from the ocean, commencing August 26th and ending November, with a mortality of 81. Also in Norwalk, Conn., Stonington, Conn., on Long Island Sound; New Castle and Wilmington, Del. The last-mentioned place suffered a loss of 255 persons. Baltimore also lost 200 persons. Boston and Salem, Mass., were visited; also Portsmouth, N. H., three miles from the ocean, commencing in August and ending in October, mortality, 100. It swept Burlington, N. J., twenty miles from Delaware Bay; also Port Elizabeth, N. J., commencing August 9th and ending in September, with a mortality of 6. Woodbury, N. J., Albany, N. Y., Greenfield, Saratoga Co., N. Y., far inland, Huntington, N. Y., New York City, commencing in August and ending in November, the mortality being 2,080. Chester, Pa., on Delaware River, mortality 50. Marcus Hook, Pa., on Delaware River, Philadelphia, Pa., commencing August 1st and ending November 1st, with a mortality of 3,500, being 1 in 15.50 of the entire population. Westerly, R. I., on Pawcatuck River, Charleston, S. C., Norfolk, Va.; Petersburg, on Appomattox River, Va., also City Point, on James River, Va., both for the first time; also the Island of St. Domingo, where, out of a population of 25,000 soldiers, the mortality in proportion to population was 1 in 1.14.

1799.—New Orleans, Baltimore, New York, commencing in July and ending in November, mortality 76. New Berne, N. C., on the Meuse River, for the first time. Bald Eagle Valley, in the center of Pennsylvania, Nittany, Centre Co., Pa., far inland, Philadelphia, commencing in July and ending in November, with a mortality of 1,000; the Island of Guadaloupe. Charleston suffered a mortality of 239. Norfolk, Va., was also visited. This year, on the ship *Delaware*, where the number of cases reached 40, there was a mortality of 20, being a proportion of 1 in 2.

1800 to 1879.

1800.—This year the yellow fever appeared in Hartford, Conn., New Orleans, Baltimore, Boston, New Bedford (on Buzzard Bay), Mass., New York, commencing in September and ending October 14th. The mortality in the Marine Hospital in that city was 21. Washington, N. C., on Tar River, Philadelphia, Pa., Providence, R. I., where 134 died; Charleston, S. C., which suffered a mortality of 184; Norfolk, Va., commencing July 26th, ending October 30th, mortality 250; Wilmington, N. C., Vera Cruz. In Cadiz, out of a population of 71,491, 57,499 remained in the city. The number of cases was 48,520, the mortality 7,387, being in proportion to the entire population 1 in 9.56, and to population remaining 1 in 7.67. The deaths, in proportion to cases, were 1 in 6.42. In the Cadiz Hospital, the proportion of deaths to cases was 1 in 2. At Zeres, Spain, with a population of 33,000, the number of cases aggregated 30,000, mortality 12,000 to 13,000, being in proportion to population 1 in 2.54, and to cases 1 in 2.5, or 1 in 3. At Puerto Santa Maria, counting a population of 20,000, the mortality was 400, being 1 in 50. At San Lucas, with a population of 18,000, the mortality was 3,000—1 in 6. At Ecija, containing 40,000 inhabitants, the number of cases was 400, mortality 100—1 in 4. At Seville, with a population of 80,568, the number

A HISTORY OF THE YELLOW FEVER. 81

of cases is recorded at the extraordinary figure of 76,488, the mortality being 14,685; in proportion to population, 1 in 5.5, in proportion to cases, 1 in 5.21. At the General Hospital, in the same city, the number of cases was 2,365, mortality 1,556, being 1 in 1.45. At Santa Caridad (Seville) the number of cases was 81, mortality 44, proportion 1 in 2. In Havana, 9,977 perished from yellow fever.

1801.—New Orleans, Baltimore, and New Bedford, Mass., were visited; also New York, commencing September and ending October; mortality, 16. One hundred and forty died, in October, at Queensborough, Orange Co., N. Y. Philadelphia, Pa. (sporadic), Black Island, R. I., on Long Island Sound, some continuing for nearly six months, commencing in June and ending in December. Norfolk, Va. At Seville, number of cases 1,100, of which 660 resulted fatally, being a proportion of 1 in 1.75. Savannah, Norwich, Conn., Charleston; Havana, population within and without the walls 95,000, mortality 2,366. Vera Cruz, Jamaica, St. Domingo, Medina, Sedonia (Spain). At Leghorn, Italy, 150 died daily for several months.

1802.—Portsmouth, N. H., deaths, 10; Wilmington, Del., mortality 86; New Orleans, Baltimore, Boston, mortality 60; New York, mortality (at Marine Hospital) 2; Philadelphia, mortality 307; Charleston, S. C., mortality 96—more than half the attacked recovered; Norfolk, Va.; St. Domingo, population 40,000 (principally soldiers), estimated number of cases, 27,000, mortality 20,000; proportion, 1 in 2, proportion to cases, 1 in 1.33, 1 in 1.2; Martinique, population, 11,085 (principally soldiers), estimated number of cases, 8,673, mortality, 2,891; proportion to population, 1 in 3.8; proportion to cases, 1 in 3; Guadaloupe (1802), 7; population, 16,363, mortality 5,057; proportion to population, 1 in 3.2. Mortality (in 1802) in West Indies, among French troops, 57 per cent. Vera Cruz, 428 cases admitted into the Hospital of St. Sebastian, of which number 60 died; in the city 1,500 died of fever.

1803.—Alexandria, Va., commencing August 1st, mortality 200; New Haven, Conn., New York, commencing July 18th and ending in October, mortality 6,700; Lisburn, Pa., nine miles from Harrisburg, commencing in August; Philadelphia, mortality 195; Charleston, S. C., 200 to 300 deaths; Winchester, Va., Norfolk, Va., Catskill, N. Y., commencing August 10th and ending September 28th, mortality 8. Martinique, last six months of 1803 and first six months of 1804,* number of cases, 2,462, mortality 546; proportion to cases, 1 in 4.5; Guadaloupe, 3,500 troops, mortality 2,700; proportion to population, 1 in 1.3. Out of 3,700 population 2,900 died. Vera Cruz (hospital), population 16,000 to 17,000; number of cases 428, mortality 69; proportion to population, 1 in 2.40, proportion to cases, 1 in 6.2; total mortality, 1,310. Mortality in West Indies (in 1803) among French troops was 35.7 per cent. At Malaga, 48,015 inhabitants remaining out of 51,745, 16,517 cases resulted, of which 6,884 proved fatal, being 1 in 4.1 of remaining population, and 1 in 2.4 of cases. Some accounts say that 12,000 to 13,000 died. At Barcelona, of 73 cases 30 died, being 1 in 2.43. In Havana 4,766 died.

---

* This is the most extraordinary of all the extraordinary freaks of this terrible disease.

1804.—At Cadiz the number of cases is stated to have been 5,000, and the mortality from 2,000 to 2,800, being about 1 in 2. At Ecija the mortality was 3,802, being in proportion to population 1 in 10. At Carthagena, with a population of 33,222, the mortality amounted to 11,445; other accounts say 14,940. At Malaga, out of a population remaining in the city of 36,054, 11,464 died, being 1 in 1.67. Other accounts say, out of a population of 110,000 only 7,000 escaped—26,000 dying in four weeks. At Alicant, population 13,000, number of cases, 9,000; the mortality was 2,471, being 1 in 3.64 of number of cases. *The population of Spain diminished one million; the official report of deaths from yellow fever amounted to 124,000 for the year.** At Gibraltar, the population being estimated at 10,000, the mortality reached 5,946, being a proportion of 1 in 2. At the hospital in Gibraltar, out of 2,754 cases 894 proved fatal, being 1 in 3.1; other accounts say, out of a population of 15,000 nearly 2 out of 5 fell victims. At Leghorn 48,000 inhabitants out of 60,000 remaining in the city, there was a mortality of 655. In the hospital (same city) number of cases, 164; 56 died, being 1 and 3. In Spain (during 1804) not less than twenty-five cities and towns were visited by the fever, the population of which amounted to 427,228, of which 52,559, or 1 in 8.12 perished. In some places, the number of persons affected amounted to 1 in 2.78 of the population, the extreme being 1 in 1.18 and 1 in 5. In twenty-one, the average proportion of deaths to the number afflicted was 1 in 3,087, the extreme being 1 in 1.3 and 1 in 6.42, while two hospitals gave a mortality of 1 in 2.15 of the number admitted, with extremes of 1 in 11 and 1 in 2.82. New Haven, Conn., New Orleans, West Point, N. Y., Charleston, S. C., Norfolk, Va., Winchester, Va., twenty miles from the Blue Ridge Mountains, during the month of July. The mortality in the West Indies, among the French troops, was 29.3 per cent.

1805.—New Haven, Conn., Baltimore, Boston, Gloucester City, N. J., on Delaware River, New York, commencing in June and ending in October, mortality 340 (302). Quebec, near the 47th parallel of north latitude, more than 300 feet above tide-water, was for the first and last time invaded by the fever in the middle of August; but September setting in very cold, the disease was not of long duration, though it was nearly as severe as that of the West Indies in malignity, especially among the troops. Of one company of 55, belonging to an English regiment, all perished except six. In Barbadoes, of 278 soldiers recently arrived from England, 70 died in 23 days. Chester Co., Pa., on Delaware River, Philadelphia, mortality 3,400. Westerly, R. I., on Pawcatuck River, Charleston, S. C., Norfolk, Va. Mortality in the West Indies, among French troops, 40.4 per cent. Providence, R. I., commencing July 19th ending August, 30 cases, 10 deaths. In Havana, 85 out of 100 American seamen died.

1806.—New York, commencing in June, ending in November. No mortality reported in Marine Hospital. Newport, R. I., Richmond, Va.

1807.—St. Augustine, Fla., on Matanzas Sound, 2 miles from the sea; Sa-

---

* The heaviest mortality from yellow fever on record.

vannah, Ga. New York, mortality (at Marine Hospital) 3 (20 cases in all). Philadelphia, mortality 3. Charleston, S. C., mortality 162.

1808.—Savannah, Ga. New York, mortality (at Marine Hospital) 1. Saint Mary's, Ga., nine miles from the sea, commencing September 5th and ending in October, mortality 84—half the population of the town which remained.

1809.—New Orleans, Brooklyn, N. Y., commencing July, ending September, mortality 40. New York, mortality (at Marine Hospital) 2. Philadelphia, Pa. (sporadic), Charleston, S. C., (sporadic).

1810.—New York, mortality (at Marine Hospital) 1. Philadelphia, mortality 3. Havana, 4,305 deaths, Gibraltar (sporadic), Cadiz and Carthagena severe.

1811.—Pensacola, Fla., New Orleans, Saint Francisville, La., on the Mississippi River, Perth Amboy, N. J., Philadelphia, Pa., mortality 5.

1812.—Philadelphia, mortality 3. New Orleans, Charleston, S. C., St. Christopher, W. I., number of cases 422, mortality 118; proportion to cases 1 in 3.58. Cadiz, epidemic.

1813.—Philadelphia, Pa., mortality 6; also prevailed in Spain.

1813.—At Cadiz, population 130,000, the mortality is estimated at 4,000, being 1 in 32.5. At Gibraltar, 12,501 remaining out of a population of 20,501, the number of cases amounted to 2,847, and the mortality 904, being 1 in 3.4 of proportion to cases.

1814.—Philadelphia, Pa., mortality 7. At Gibraltar (in hospital) number of cases 726, mortality 114, being 1 in 6.36; among civilians there were 132 deaths. Cadiz, epidemic.

1815.—Philadelphia, mortality 2. New York, mortality (at Marine Hospital) 7. Island of Jamaica, proportion to cases 1 in 4.

1816.—New York—no mortality noted at Marine Hospital. Philadelphia, Pa., mortality 2. Martinique, from August, 1816, to close of 1817, number of cases 327, mortality 61; proportion to cases 1 in 5.36. Barbadoes, 390 men, mortality 90; proportion to cases 1 in 4.33; twenty-five officers, mortality 10; proportion to cases 1 in 2.5.

1817.—New Orleans, from June 18th to December, mortality 800; other accounts say mortality for five months 1,142. Natchez, Miss., commencing September and ending November 9th, mortality 9; other accounts say 134 died. Whitsell's Landing, twenty miles below Natchez. New York, mortality (at Marine Hospital) 4; Charleston, S. C., commencing in July and ending in November, mortality 272. Mt. Pleasant, S. C., on Wingaw Bay, West Feliciana Parish, La., Baton Rouge, La., on Mississippi River.

1818.—New Orleans, mortality 1,151. New York, mortality (at Marine Hospital) 4. Martinique, number of cases 1,982, mortality 697; proportion to cases 1 in 2.82. Trinidad, W. I., proportion to cases 1 in 2.54.

1819.—At Xeres, population 45,000, number of cases 1,262, mortality 408. At Cadiz, population 72,000, number of cases 48,000, mortality 5,000. At Seville, number of cases 346, the mortality being 217. Fort Claiborne, Ala., on Alabama River, commencing July 4th, ending December 1; Fort St. Stephen, Ala., on Tombigbee River, commencing July 4th, ending December 1; Mobile, Ala., commencing August 15th, ending in November, mortality

A HISTORY OF THE YELLOW FEVER.

274. New Haven, Conn., Savannah, Ga., Alexandria, La., on Red River, New Orleans, commencing July 1st, mortality 2,190. Mr. Nuttal, the naturalist, in his book of travels, estimates the victims at from 5,000 to 6,000, which very much exceeds probability. West Feliciana Parish, La., Baltimore, commencing July 21st, ending October 30th, Natchez, Miss., commencing September and ending December, mortality 180. New York, commencing in August, mortality 37. Philadelphia, mortality 13. Charleston, S. C., commencing in August and ending in October, mortality 177. Boston, Baton Rouge, La., on Mississippi River, Jamaica. In 1819, '21, '27, proportion to cases 1 in 2, 1 in 4, 1 in 1.08. In 1819, '22, '25, '27, proportion to cases 1 in 2. In 1819 two regiments, proportion to cases 1 in 2, 1 in 1.7. Bermuda, number of cases 208, mortality 32; proportion to cases 1 in 13. Havana, 5,162 victims.

1820.—Middletown, Conn., commencing in June, Savannah, Ga., Bay of St. Louis, La., at mouth of Mississippi River, commencing in August, New Orleans, commencing in July, deaths in hospital, 82. Baltimore, Shieldsboro, on St. Louis Bay, commencing August 20th. New York, mortality (at Marine Hospital) 2; 150 died from August 21st to October 20th. Philadelphia, Pa., commencing July 24th, mortality 84. Barbadoes, proportion to cases 1 in 2.56. At Xeres the proportion to cases was 1 in 2. At Siguenza, number of cases, mortality 212, being 1 in 1.8. At Carlotta, population 733, remaining 473, cases 195, mortality 122.

1821.—Mobile, Ala., St. Augustine, Fla., commencing in August, mortality 140. Forty deaths took place in the garrison in a body of 120 soldiers. Baltimore; New York, mortality (at Marine Hospital) 16. Wilmington, N. C., commencing August 9th. Norfolk, Va., commencing August 1st. Martinique: number of cases 686, mortality 235; proportion to cases 1 in 3. Malaga, number of cases 21, mortality 17, being 1 in 1.3. Tortosa, 5,000 remaining out of 15,000 inhabitants—2,356 died. Barcelona, 70,000 remaining out of 145,000, number of cases 14,000, mortality 9,730; proportion to cases 1 in 1.33. At Seminary Hospital (same city) 1,739 cases, mortality 1,265; General Hospital, 830 cases, mortality 749; Marine Hospital, number of cases 79, mortality 55. Lazaretto of V. Queen of Peru, number of cases 56, mortality 39. City and suburb, according to Adouard, number of cases 20,625, mortality 1,600 to 1,700. Palma, 12,000 inhabitants remaining, number of cases 7,400, mortality 5,341.

1822.—Mobile, Ala., Pensacola, Fla., commencing August 12th, ending October 10, mortality 257. Alexandria, La., on Red River, Baton Rouge, La., on Mississippi River, mortality 60. New Orleans, La., commencing September 1st, mortality 239. Baltimore, New York, commencing July 10th, ending November 5th, mortality 230; other accounts say 243 out of 414 the number attacked. Charleston, S. C., commencing in June, ending in August, mortality 2.

1823.—Fort Smith, Ark., on Arkansas River, yellow fever of high grade prevailed without a suspicion of exposure to contagion. Ascension, La., on Mississippi River, New Orleans, commencing August 23d, mortality 1 (only 2 cases). West Feliciana Parish, La., Natchez, Miss., commencing August 10th,

A HISTORY OF THE YELLOW FEVER.

ending October 18th, mortality 312. Brooklyn, N. Y., New York, mortality (at Marine Hospital) 5. At Martinique (hospital) the proportion of deaths to cases was 1 in 2.5, 1 in 3. Port du Passage, seven leagues east of Bayonne, population 3,000; 1,200 remaining—101 cases, mortality 40, being 1 in 2.5. This locality, one of the finest ports in Europe, is represented to be unsurpassed for general salubrity.

1824.—Mobile, New Orleans, commencing August 4th, mortality 108. New York, mortality (at Marine Hospital) 8. Charleston, S. C., commencing in August, ending in November, mortality 235. Key West, Fla.

1825.—Mobile, Ala., commencing in September. Pensacola, Fla., New Orleans, commencing June 23d, mortality 49. Natchez, Miss., commencing August 20th, ending November, mortality 150. Washington, Miss., near Natchez (inland), commencing August, ending November, mortality 52. New York, mortality (at Marine Hospital) 1. Charleston, S. C., commencing August, ending September, mortality 2. Martinique, number of cases 1,464, mortality 388; proportion to cases 1 in 3.8.

1826.—Apalachicola, Fla., on Apalachicola Bay, New Orleans, commencing May 18th, mortality 5. New York, mortality (at Marine Hospital) 2. Norfolk, Va., commencing September 1. Guadaloupe, number of cases 386; mortality 128; proportion to cases 1 in 3.

1827.—Mobile, Ala., commencing in August. Pensacola, Fla., Savannah, Ga., Alexandria, La., Baton Rouge, La., Donaldsonville, La., on Mississippi River, New Orleans, commencing July 19, mortality 109. West Feliciana Parish, La., Natchez, Miss. New York, mortality (at Marine Hospital) 4. Charleston, S. C., commencing in August, ending in November, mortality 64. Jamaica, W. I., population 300, mortality 184; proportion to population 1 in 1.6.

1828.—Mobile, New Orleans, commencing June 18th, mortality 130. New York, mortality (at Marine Hospital) 0. Charleston, S. C., commencing in August, ending in September, mortality 26. Gibraltar, population 20,652; cases 6,715, mortality 1796, being 1 in 3.73; troops 3,652, cases 2,014, mortality 515—1 in 3.91; civilians, 17,000; cases 4,701, mortality 1,281, being 1 in 3.6.

1829.—Mobile, commencing September 14th, mortality 130. Key West, Fla., Baton Rouge, La., on Mississippi River, New Orleans, commencing May 23d, mortality 215. Opelousas, La., seven miles from head of navigation, West Feliciana Parish, La., commencing September 22d. Natchez, Miss., commencing September 1st, ending November, mortality 90. Rodney, Miss., on Mississippi River, Shieldsboro, on St. Louis Bay, commencing August 5th. New York—no mortality at Marine Hospital.

1830.—Bay St. Louis, mouth of Mississippi River, New Orleans, commencing July 15th, mortality 117. New York, mortality (at Marine Hospital) 1.

1831.—Alexandria, La., on Red River, New Orleans, commencing June 9th, mortality 2.

1832.—New Orleans, commencing August 15th, mortality 18. New York, mortality (at Marine Hospital) 1.

1833.—New Orleans, commencing July 12th, mortality 210. New York, mortality (at Marine Hospital) 2. Columbia; Texas, on Brazos River, Guadaloupe; Basseterie, W. I. (soldiers), number of cases 137, mortality 47.

1834.—Pensacola, Fla., commencing August 23d. New Orleans, commencing August 28th, mortality 95. New York, mortality (at Marine Hospital) 1. Charleston, S. C., commencing August, ending October, mortality 49.

1835.—New Orleans, commencing August 23d, mortality 284. New York, mortality (at Marine Hospital) 2. Charleston, S. C., commencing August, ending September, mortality 25. Suwanee, Fla., on Suwanee River; New Orleans, commencing August 24th, mortality 5.

1837.—Mobile, commencing September 20th, ending November, mortality 350. Alexandria, La., on Red River, Baton Rouge, La., on Mississippi River, New Orleans, commencing July 24th, mortality 442. Opelousas, La., commencing October 20th, ending November. Plaquemine, La., on Mississippi River, Washington, La., Natchez, Miss., commencing September 8th, ending November 25th, mortality 280. Havana, 1 in 10; Havana (Belot's Hospital) 1 in 6.48.

1838.—St. Augustine, Fla., two miles from the sea, on Matanzas Sound, Mobile, New Orleans, commencing August 25th, mortality 17. New York, mortality (at Marine Hospital) 8. Charleston, S. C., commencing August, ending November, mortality 351. Martinique, W. I. (in 1838, '39), number of cases 1,344, mortality 223; proportion 1 in 6. October 1 ('38 to September 30, '39), number of cases 1,202, mortality 150—1 in 8. Barbadoes, proportion to cases 1 in 4.25. Dominica, population 131; soldiers, number of cases 100 men, 6 officers, mortality 35 men, 3 officers; proportion to cases 1 in 3 men, 1 in 2 officers. Georgetown (Demarara), Seamen's Hospital, number of cases 2,071, mortality 404; proportion to cases 1 in 5.12.

1839.—Pensacola, Fla., St. Augustine, Fla., commencing August 15th. Tampa, Fla. (head of Tampa Bay), Mobile, commencing August 11th, ending October 20th, mortality 650 (average mortality to cases 1 in 7). Augusta, Ga., Alexandria, La., Franklin, La., on Teche River, Natchitoches, La., on Red River, New Iberia, La. (southern part of La.), New Orleans, commencing July 23d, mortality 452. Opelousas, La., commencing August, ending November. Plaquemine, La., on Mississippi River, Port Hudson, La., on Mississippi River, West Feliciana Parish, La., commencing August 28th, St. Martinsville, La., on Teche River, Washington, La., Biloxi, Miss., after an interval of 136 years, Natchez, Miss., commencing September, ending November, mortality 235. Shieldsboro, Miss. (on St. Louis Bay), Vicksburg, Miss., New York, mortality (at Marine Hospital) 4. Charleston, S. C., commencing June, ending October, mortality 22. Galveston, commencing September 30th, ending October 11th, mortality 250. Houston, Texas, Martinique, W. I., first three months of 1839, 92 cases, 19 deaths; proportion 1 in 4.5.

1840.—New Orleans, commencing July 25, mortality, 3; Charleston, S. C., commencing August, ending October, mortality 22.

1841.—Pensacola, Fla., St. Augustine, Fla., mortality 26; St. Joseph, Fla., near Gulf of Mexico, Mobile, Key West, commencing June, mortality 26; New Orleans, commencing July 27, mortality 594; Port Hudson, La., commencing September, ending October; Charleston, S. C., Barbadoes, W. I., proportion to cases, 1 in 2. Dominica, 204 cases, mortality 55; proportion to cases, 1 in 3.7.

1842.—Pensacola, Fla., Mobile, commencing August 20, mortality 60; New Orleans, commencing July 30, mortality 211; Opelousas, La., Barbadoes, W. I., proportion to cases, 1 in 5.6.

1843.—Pensacola, Fla., Mobile, commencing August 18, ending November 5, mortality 240; Baton Rouge, La., commencing October; New Orleans, commencing July 5, mortality 487; Port Hudson, La., West Feliciana Parish, La., commencing August 28; Rodney, Miss., commencing September 6; New York, mortality (at Marine Hospital) 5; Charleston, S. C., Guadaloupe, W. I. (sailors and troops), population, 2,757; number of cases, 772, mortality 183; French war steamer *Gomez*; number of cases, 165, mortality 17; proportion, 1 in 9.7. Guadaloupe, Basseterie, 96 cases, 64 deaths.

1844.—Pensacola, Fla., Mobile, New Orleans, commencing July and ending September, mortality 148; Natchez, Miss., Woodville, Miss., New York, mortality (at Marine Hospital) 2; Galveston, Texas, commencing July 5th, mortality 400; Houston, Texas.

1845.—Pensacola, Fla., New Orleans, mortality 2; Boa Vista, W. I., Porto Sal Rey, proportion to cases, Portuguese, 1 in 1.8, English and American, 1 in 1.1, natives, 1 in 13.4; Boa Vista, in all localities, Europeans, 1 in 1.16, natives, 1 in 15.4.

1846.—Pensacola, Fla., New Orleans, commencing August and ending October, mortality 160; West Feliciana Parish, mortality 1; Thibodeaux, La., commencing September 20th and ending October; New York.

1847.—Pensacola, Fla., mortality 76, average mortality to cases 1 in 7; Alexandria, La., on Red River, Algiers, La., opposite New Orleans, Baton Rouge, La., on Mississippi River, Bayou Sara, La., on Mississippi River, Burat Settlement, on Mississippi River, Covington, La., 45 miles north of New Orleans, Mandeville, La., on Lake Pontchartrain, Lafayette, La., near New Orleans, commencing June 22d; New Orleans, commencing August and ending in December, mortality 2,259; Plaquemine, on Mississippi River, Biloxi, Miss., Pascagoula, Miss., Pass Christian, Miss., Rodney, Miss., Vicksburg, Miss., New York, Galveston, commencing October 1st and ending November 26th, mortality 200; Houston, Texas.

1848.—Pensacola, Fla., Mobile, mortality 75; New Orleans, commencing June and ending November, mortality 850; West Feliciana Parish, La., Natchez, Miss., commencing June and ending November; New York, commencing August 12th, with a mortality of 12 at Marine Hospital; Stapleton, Staten Island, New York, commencing August 23d; Tompkinsville, Staten Island, commencing August 23d; Mt. Pleasant, S. C., Houston, Texas.

1849.—Mobile, mortality 50; New Orleans, commencing August and ending December, mortality 737; Charleston, S. C., commencing August and ending November, mortality 125.

1850.—New Orleans, commencing July and ending Oct., mortality 102; Cayenne, W. I. (hospital), number of cases 685, mortality 148; proportion 1 in 4.63.

1851.—Mobile, New Orleans, mortality 16.

1852.—Savannah, Ga., mortality 19; New Orleans, commencing July and ending December, mortality 415; Washington, La., Woodville, Miss., New York, mortality of 1 at Marine Hospital; Charleston, S. C., commencing August and ending November, mortality 310; Ft. Moultrie, in Charleston Harbor, Mt. Pleasant, S. C., on Wingaw Bay, Indianola, Texas, commencing in September; Norfolk, Va., commencing August 7th; Portsmouth, Va., Port Royal, W. I. (population 12,611), mortality 727—1 in 17.34; St. Pierre (population 20,360), mortality 1,200, proportion to population, 1 in 17; Barbadoes, W. I., troops (population 1,380), number of cases 879, mortality 173; proportion to population, 1 in 7.9, proportion to cases 1 in 5.08; steamer from St. Thomas to Southampton, month of November, number of cases 124, deaths 50; proportion, 1 in 2.3.

1853.—Milton, Fla., near Pensacola Bay, Pensacola, Fla., commencing July 9th; Tampa, Fla., head of Tampa Bay, commencing in September; Mobile, commencing July 13th and ending Nov. 1st, mortality 115 (Dr. Dowler gives an estimate of 1,072); Cahawba, Ala., on Alabama River, Citronelle, Ala., on Mobile & Ohio R. R., Dog River Cotton Factory, Ala., five miles from Mobile, commencing Aug. 8th; Demopolis, Ala., on Tombigbee River, Hollywood, Ala., on Tombigbee River, Montgomery, Ala., on Alabama River, commencing September and ending November, mortality 35; Selma, Ala., commencing Sept. 17th and ending Nov. 13th, mortality 32; Spring Hill, Ala., Columbia, Ark., commencing in June; Grand Lake, Ark. (on Mississippi River), Napoleon, Ark. (on Mississippi River), Key West, Fla., during August, mortality 112; Savannah, Ga., Alexandria, La., the disease carried off from one-fifth to one-sixth of the population; Algiers, La. (opposite New Orleans), Bay St. Louis, La Bayou Sara (on Mississippi River). New Orleans, commencing May, ending December, mortality 7,970, or variously estimated at from 8,000 to 10,000. Dr. Dowler says the greatest number of deaths in New Orleans was in August, amounting to 5,189, or, by adding all the deaths, 6,235, an average exceeding 201 per day—about 9 every hour, 1 every six or seven minutes for a whole month. His total, from May 26th to October 22d, by yellow fever, is 7,782; total unnamed (mostly yellow fever), 669; in all, 8,228, without enumerating deaths from October 22d to December 22d. He estimates the whole mortality at 8,400. Dr. Edward H. Barton, in his report to the Commission, states that the total mortality during the year, not only those certified to be such, but a large proportion of the "unknown," supposed to be such from a want of proper records, is estimated, upon all grounds of probability, to have been 8,101. . . . . The total number of cases of yellow fever in 1853 was 29,020, which was the largest number of cases of yellow fever which ever afflicted this city (New Orleans). But 8,101 deaths out of that great number of cases is only 27.91 per cent., or 1 in 3.58, the least mortality which had ever occurred in a great and malignant epidemic of the dread disease. Centreville, La. (on Teche River), commencing September 18th, ending November 18th; Clinton, La., commencing September 1st, ending December, mortality 75; Cloutierville,

A HISTORY OF THE YELLOW FEVER. 89

La., commencing August 14th, ending December 14th; Franklin, La., commencing October 19th, ending November 24th, mortality 2; Lake Providence, La. (on Mississippi River), reported to have lost 120; Opelousas, La., Pattersonville, La. (on Teche River), commencing August 8th, ending December, mortality 45; Plaquemine, La. (on Mississippi River), commencing September, ending October; West Feliciana, La., St. John Baptiste, La. (on Mississippi River), Shreveport, La. (on Red River), commencing September, ending December, destroying about one-fourth of the population; Thibodeaux, La. (on Bayou La Fourche), mortality 160—more than one-third of the 500 persons remaining; Trenton, La. (on Washita River), Vidalia, La. (on Mississippi River), commencing August 15th; Washington, La., commencing August 15th; Biloxi, Miss. (after an interval of five years), Brandon, Miss., commencing September 15th; Clifton, Miss., commencing August 28th, ending October; Natchez, Miss., commencing July 17th. Fort Adams (about 200 miles above) was visited with the fever. Grand Gulf, Miss. (on Mississippi River), Greenwood, Miss. (on Yazoo River), mortality 9; Jackson, Miss. (on Pearl River), Pass Christian, Miss., Petit Gulf Hills, Miss. (on Mississippi River), Port Gibson, Miss., Rodney, Miss., Woodville, Miss., commencing August 9th; Pascagoula, Miss., Yazoo City, Miss., commencing September 1st; New York (14 mortality at Marine Hospital), Philadelphia, commencing July 19th, ending October, mortality 128; Brownsville, Texas (on Rio Grande), commencing September 23d, ending December 23d, mortality 50; Memphis, Tenn. (cases brought from New Orleans), Hackley, Texas (near Buffalo Bayou), Houston, Texas (on Buffalo Bayou), Indianola, Texas, Liverpool, Texas, commencing August, mortality 4; Cypress City, Texas, Galveston, Texas, commencing August 16th, ending November 28th, mortality 536; Richmond, Texas (on Brazos River,) Saluria, Texas (on Matagorda Island). Baton Rouge, La., was, early in November, reported officially to have lost 202 by the epidemic. Natchitoches (more than 400 miles from New Orleans, on Red River), suffered severely. Dr. Dowler says: "The maximum mortality of the yellow fever of 1853 arrived sooner in the season than usual, and is more truly represented by that of the plague in London, in 1665, namely, June, 590 deaths; July, 4,129; August, 20,046; September, 26,230; October, 14,373; November, 3,449; total, 68,817."

1854.—Pensacola, Fla., Mobile, Montgomery, commencing September, ending November, mortality 45; Key West, Fla., Augusta, Ga., Savannah, Ga., commencing August 5th, mortality 580; Alexandria, La. (Burat Settlement, below New Orleans), commencing September 22; Cloutierville, La., on branch of Red River, Franklin, La., Jeanneretts, La., commencing October 7th; Jesuits' Bend, La., commencing September 12th; New Orleans, commencing July, ending December, mortality 2,423; Pattersonville, La., commencing September; Point a la Hache, La., on Mississippi River, commencing in October; St. Mary's Parish, La., on Gulf of Mexico, commencing September, ending October; Thibodeaux, La., commencing September 12th, ending October; Washington, La., Brandon, Miss., on Pearl River, commencing September 23d, ending November 18th; Jacksonville, Miss., St. Louis, Mo., 2 deaths. New

York, mortality (at Marine Hospital) 20; Beaufort, N. C., Philadelphia, Charleston, S. C., commencing August, ending November, mortality 627; Columbia, S. C., Georgetown, S. C., commencing August 20th, ending October 28th; Mt. Pleasant, S. C., Galveston, Texas, commencing August 9th, ending November 5th, mortality 404; Houston, Texas, Portsmouth, Va., Norfolk, Va., commencing October, ending November 2d, mortality 3.

1855.—Milton, Fla., near Pensacola Bay, Montgomery, Ala., commencing September, ending November, mortality 30; Alexandria, La., commencing September 13th; Carrollton, La., commencing May 18th; Centreville, La. (on Teche River), commencing September, ending October, mortality 1; New Orleans, commencing June, ending December, mortality 2,670; Pattersonville, La. (on Teche River), commencing September; Canton, Miss., Cooper's Wells, Miss., commencing August 23d, mortality 13; Natches, Miss., Pass Christian, Miss., Woodville, Miss., commencing September; St. Louis, Mo., commencing August 14th; New York, mortality (at Marine Hospital) 5; Memphis, Tenn., mortality 65; Bellville, Texas, 110 miles east of Austin, Gosport, Va., on Elizabeth River, Norfolk, Va., commencing June 30th, and ending October, mortality 1,807; Scott's Creek, Va., commencing June 29th, and ending July 29th; Portsmouth, Va., commencing August 1st, ending October, mortality 1,000.

1856.—New Orleans, commencing August, ending November, mortality 74; Bay Ridge, Long Island, N. Y., Brooklyn, N. Y., commencing July 14th; Governor's Island, New York Harbor, commencing July 29th; Gowanus, near New York, Red Hook, on Hudson River, N. Y., Yellow Hook, N. Y., Charleston, S. C., commencing August, ending November, mortality 211; Mt. Pleasant, S. C.

1857.—Jacksonville, Fla., New Orleans, commencing June, ending December, mortality 199; Charleston, S. C., commencing September, ending November, mortality 13; Mt. Pleasant, S. C.

1858.—Pensacola, Fla., Mobile, Savannah, Ga., Baton Rouge, La., Algiers, La., opposite New Orleans, Franklin, La., McDonoughville, La., New Orleans, commencing June, ending October 10th, mortality 3,889; Plaquemine, La., Biloxi, Miss., after an interval of four years; Natchez, Miss., Pass Christian, Miss., Vicksburg, Miss., Woodville, Miss., Charleston, S. C., commencing July, ending December, mortality 717; Fort Moultrie, Charleston Harbor, commencing August 15th; Galveston, commencing August 27th, ending November 14th, mortality 344; Houston, Tex., Indianola, Tex., on Matagorda Bay, Brownsville, Tex., on Rio Grande River, commencing August, ending November, mortality 41.

1859.—Brazoria, Tex., near Gulf of Mexico, Cypress City, Tex., Edinburgh, Tex., on Rio Grande, commencing in July, mortality 13; Houston, Tex., Indianola, Tex., Richmond, Tex., on Brazos River, Sugarland, Tex., on Brazos River; New Orleans, only 91 deaths.

1860.—New Orleans, 15 deaths.

1861.—Not a single case reported from any quarter.

A HISTORY OF THE YELLOW FEVER. 91

1862.—Tortugas, Fla., Gulf of Mexico, mortality 4; Key West, Fla., commencing June 20th, and ending October, mortality 71; New Orleans was attacked after an escape of three years; Smithville, N. C., Wilmington, N. C., commencing August 6th, ending November 17th, mortality 446; Charleston, S. C., Hilton Head, S. C., commencing September 8th, ending October 25th; Corpus Christi, Tex., Indianola, Tex., Matagorda, Tex., mortality 120; Brownsville, Tex.

1863.—Pensacola, Fla., commencing August 25th; New Orleans, nearly 100 cases, with two officially recorded deaths; Beaumont, Tex., on Neches River, Matagorda, Tex., on Matagorda Bay, Sabine City, Tex., commencing July, ending October 1st, mortality 14.

1864.—Key West, Fla., New Orleans—more than 200 cases, with 57 deaths; Beaufort, N. C., commencing September 25th, ending November 17th, mortality 68; New Berne, N. C., commencing September, ending November, mortality 700; Charleston, S. C., commencing July 27th, Galveston, commencing September 1st, ending November 20th, mortality 259; Houston, Tex., Millican, Tex.

1865.—Key West, Fla.

1866.—Memphis, Tenn. (sporadic cases); Galveston, Tex.

1867.—Pensacola, Fla., commencing July 24th, mortality 34; Tortugas, Fla., commencing July 4th, mortality 38; Fort Morgan Island, Mobile Bay, commencing August 13th; Montgomery, Ala., on Alabama River, commencing August 13th; Key West, Fla., New Iberia, La., New Orleans (after an escape of two years), commencing June 10th, ending December 22d, mortality 3,093; Opelousas, La., Washington, La., Alleyton, Tex., commencing September 4th, ending December, mortality 45; Anderson, Tex. (140 miles east by north of Austin), Austin, Tex. (above navigation on Colorado River), Bastrop, Tex. (on Colorado River), Brenham, Tex. (twenty miles from Brazos River), Calvert, Tex. (between Brazos and Navasota River), Chapel Hill, Tex. (near Brazos River), commencing August 6th, ending December, mortality 123; Corpus Christi, Tex., commencing August; Danville, Tex.; Memphis, Tenn., mortality 231; Goliad, Tex. (on San Antonio River); Galveston, commencing June 26th, ending November, mortality 1,150; Harrisburg, Tex. (on Buffalo Bayou); Hampstead, Tex. (fifty miles from Houston), commencing August 9th, ending November 26th, mortality 151; Huntsville, Tex., commencing August 9th, ending October 19th, mortality 130; Independence, Tex. (80 miles south of Austin), Indianola, Tex., commencing June 20th, mortality 80; Lagrange, Tex., commencing August, ending November, mortality 200; Liberty, Tex. (on Trinity River), Millican, Tex., commencing October 15th, ending November 12th, mortality 4; Navasota, Tex., commencing August 12th, ending December, mortality 154; Oldtown, Tex. (near Indianola), commencing October 13th, Port Lavaca, Tex., commencing July 3d, ending October 29th; Rio Grande City, Tex., mortality 150; Victoria, Tex., commencing August 1st, ending December 25th, mortality 200.

1868.—Baltimore—a few imported cases.

1869.—Milton, Santa Rosa County, Fla. (near Pensacola Bay), Hampton Roads, Va., in Harbor.

1870.—Montgomery, Ala., commencing August 22d, ending November 19th, New Iberia, La., New Orleans (after an interlude of two years), commencing May 16th, ending in December, mortality 587; Port Barre, La., Ville Platte (on Bayou Teche, La.), Governor's Island (New York Harbor), commencing September, ending October 26th, mortality 49; Philadelphia, commencing June 29th, mortality 18; Houston, Tex., ending in October, mortality 1.

1871.—Tampa, Fla., head of Tampa Bay, Cedar Keys, Fla., Gainesville, Fla., New Orleans, commencing August 4th, ending October, mortality 55; Vicksburg, Miss., Beaufort, N. C., Cincinnati, Ohio, Charleston, S. C., commencing July 19th, ending November, mortality 213; Beaufort, S. C., commencing August 5th, ending November 21st, mortality 7.

1872.—New Orleans, La., commencing August 28th, ending November 30th, mortality 40; New York.

1873.—Pensacola, Fla., commencing August 14th, ending November 19th, mortality 62; Montgomery, Ala., commencing September 4th, ending November 10th, mortality 102; Pollard, Ala., Little Rock, Ark., Bainbridge, Ga., on Flint River; Cairo, Ill., at junction Ohio and Mississippi River, commencing September 21st, ending September 25th, mortality 17; Louisville, Ky., on Ohio River, commencing September 22d, ending October 15th, mortality 5; New Orleans, commencing July 4th, ending November 18th, mortality 225; Shreveport, La., on Red River, commencing August 12th, ending November 10th, mortality 759; New York, commencing May 23d, ending October 30th, mortality 18; Cincinnati, Ohio; Memphis, commencing September 14th, ending November 9th, mortality 2,000; Baltimore; Columbus, Texas, on Colorado River; Corsicana; Texas (180 miles north-east from Austin); Corpus Christi.

1874.—Cuba; Pensacola, vessel in harbor with a few cases on board.

1875.—Key West, Fla., epidemic; Vera Cruz, Mexico; Fort Barrancas, Fla., Fort Pickens, Fla.; Pascagoula, Miss.; Cuba; Mobile; New Orleans; New York, vessel in harbor with crew sick.

1876. Savannah, Ga., epidemic; New York, 2 refugees from Savannah died; Charleston, S. C. (sporadic).

1877.—Havana, and Fernandina, Fla., epidemic.

1878.—Abingdon, Washington County, Va., Judge L. V. Dixon, refugee from Memphis, died September 17th; Athens, Ala., 2 cases, 2 deaths; Augusta, Ark., on White River, 7 cases, 7 deaths; Bartlett, Shelby County, Tenn., (eleven miles from Memphis) population 350, 35 cases, 23 deaths—proportion of deaths to cases 1 in 1.2; Baton Rouge, La., population 6,500, number of cases 2,716, deaths 201—proportion of deaths to cases 1 in 13; Bayou Sara, La., on Mississippi River, population 700, number of cases 250, deaths 13—1 in 19; Bay St. Louis, Miss. (summer resort), population, including visitors, 6,000, number of cases 546, deaths 83—1 in 6.2; Bayou Goula, La., on Mississippi River, 1 death—a refugee; Beech Grove, Tenn., 1 death—a refugee; Bell's Depot, Tenn., 5 cases, 3 deaths; Berwick City, La., population 150,

A HISTORY OF THE YELLOW FEVER. 93

cases 50, deaths 1; Bethel Springs, Tenn., 1 case, deaths 1; Biloxi, Miss., population 960, number of cases 216, deaths 56—1 in 4; Bolton, Miss. (twenty-seven miles from Vicksburg), population 200, number of cases 168, deaths 47—1 in 3.2; Bovina, Miss., ten miles from Vicksburg, population 100, number of cases 65, deaths 17—1 in 4; Bowling Green, Ky., number of cases 48, deaths 26—1 in 2; Brooklyn, N. Y., Navy Yard, 2 deaths; Broussard, La., 1 death; Brownsville, Tenn., population 4,026, number of cases 844, deaths 212—1 in 8; Buntyn, Tenn., five miles from Memphis, included in Memphis report; Buras, La., 2 deaths; Byram, Miss., cases included in Jackson report; Cairo, Ill., on Mississippi and Ohio rivers, population 6,300, number of cases 43, deaths 32—1 in 1.34; Canaan Landing, La., on Mississippi River, number of cases 28, deaths 6—1 in 5; Canton, Miss., twenty-three miles from Jackson, population 2,143, number of cases 936, deaths 176—1 in 5.3. Cayuga, Miss., on Big Black River, number of cases 38, deaths 9—1 in 4; Caledonia (on the Ohio River), one case from the steamer *Golden Crown*; Chattanooga, Tenn., on Tennessee River, population 12,500, number of cases 693, deaths 197—1 in 4; Cincinnati, Ohio, number of cases (all refugees), 49, deaths 19—1 in 1.2; Clinton, Hickman County, Ky., 2 cases, no deaths; Clinton, La., population 1,000, number of cases 187, deaths 43—1 in 4; Collierville, Tenn., twenty-five miles from Memphis, population 500, number of cases 121, deaths 48—1 in 2.2; Cook's Landing, La., population 35, number of cases 15, deaths 4—1 in 4; Courtland, Lawrence County, Ala., 1 death—Memphis refugee; Covington, Tenn., population 1,200, the Board of Health advising, the population fled the town—1 death occurred; Cox's Landing, Miss., number of cases 12, deaths 4—1 in 3; Dalton, Ga., 3 cases, 2 deaths—refugees from Chattanooga; Danville, Ky., 1 death—a refugee from Holly Springs; Dayton, Ohio, on Miami River, 1 death and some few cases—all refugees from the South; Decatur, Ala., population 1,200, number of cases 187, deaths 51—1 in 3.3; Delhi, La., forty miles from Vicksburg, population 250, number of cases 168, deaths 34—1 in 5; Donaldsonville, La., and Ascension Parish, on Mississippi River, population of town 1,500; number of cases 484, deaths 83—1 in 5.3; cases in parish, 1,373, deaths 179—1 in 7.3; Dry Grove, Hinds County, Miss., and vicinity, number of cases 203, deaths 50—1 in 4; Duck Hill, Montgomery County, Miss., number of cases 36, deaths 14—1 in 2.3; Dunboyne, a plantation near West Plaquemine, La., 3 deaths; Durant, Holmes County, Miss., 1 death; Edward's Depot, Hinds County, Miss., 3 deaths; Erin, Houston County, Tenn., population 723, number of cases 38, deaths 10—1 in 4; Eureka, La., 1 death; Fernandina, Fla., on vessel in harbor, 3 seamen died; Fillmore, Ky., 1 death—a refugee from New Orleans; Florence, Ala., population 2,500, number of cases 138, deaths 50—1 in 2.3; Frayser Station, Tenn., included in Memphis; Friar's Point, Miss., on Mississippi River, population 1,200, number of cases 25, deaths 7—1 in 3.3; Fulton, Ky., population 1,700; number of cases 12, deaths 5—1 in 2; Gadsden, Tenn., population 350, number of cases 6, deaths 4—1 in 1.3; Galway, Fayette County, Tenn., population 60, number of cases 13, deaths 8; Gallipolis, Ohio, on Ohio River, population 3,700, number of cases 51, deaths

31; Galman Station, Miss., deaths among Vicksburg refugees; Garner Station, Miss., population 200, number of cases 31, deaths 13; Germantown, Shelby County, Tenn., population 253, number of cases 81, deaths 45; Gills Station, Tenn., three miles from Memphis, 1 death; Grand Junction, Tenn., on M. & C. R. R., 201 cases, 82 deaths—1 in 2.2; Greenville, Miss., on Mississippi River, population 1,350, number of cases 1,137, deaths 387—1 in 3.40; Grenada, Miss., 100 miles from Memphis, population estimated at 2,000, number of cases 1,468, deaths 367—1 in 4; Gretna, La., three miles from Algiers, population 900, number of cases 210, deaths 60—1 in 3.2; Halifax, Nova Scotia, H. M. S. *Bullfinch*, most of the crew down; mortality heavy; Handsboro, Harrison County, Miss., population 400, number of cases 110, deaths 15—1 in 7; Harrisonburg, La., on Ouachita River, population 275, number of cases 30, deaths 10—1 in 3; Haynes' Bluff, Miss., on Yazoo River, number of cases 160, deaths 19—1 in 8; Henderson's Landing, La., on Mississippi River, population 25, number of cases 16, deaths 5—1 in 3; Hernando, Miss., population 1,000; number of cases 179, deaths 75—1 in 2.2; Hickman, Ky., on Mississippi River, population 1,950, number of cases 454, deaths 180—1 in 2.2; Holly Springs, Miss., population 4,000, number of cases 1,240, deaths 346—1 in 3.2; Huntsville, Ala., number of cases 33 (all imported), deaths 13—1 in 2.2; Jackson, Miss., population 3,000, number of cases 326, deaths 77—1 in 4.4; Key West, Fla., population 5,000, number of cases 162, deaths 39—1 in 4; King's Point, Miss., on Mississippi River, 92 cases, 6 deaths—1 in 15; Knoxville, Tenn., the only cases were refugees—not recorded; La Fourche Crossing, La., population 1,800, number of cases 235, deaths—1 in 12; Labadieville, La., and vicinity, 760 cases, 150 deaths—1 in 5; Lagrange, Tenn., population 712, number of cases 152, deaths 37—1 in 4; Lake, Scott County, Miss., population 400, number of cases 268, deaths 64—1 in 4; Lawrence Station, Miss., number of cases 16, deaths 5; Lebanon Church, Miss., total cases 192, deaths 44—1 in 4.2; Leighton, Calvert County, Ala., 1 refugee died; Lewes, Delaware, on Delaware Bay, 4 out of a crew of 8 died on a vessel in the Bay; Lockport, N. Y., a Memphis refugee died; Logtown, Hancock County, Miss., 40 cases, 9 deaths—1 in 4.2; Louisville, Ky., number of cases 126, deaths 34—1 in 4; McCombs City, Pike County, Miss., cases 7, deaths 3; McKenzie, Carroll County, Tenn., 14 cases, 4 deaths; McNairy (a plantation six miles from Dry Grove, Miss.), 36 cases, 9 deaths—1 in 4; Mandeville, La., a few cases, with 3 deaths; Martin, Weakly County, Tenn. (population 515), number of cases 126, deaths 34—1 in 3.3; Mason, Tipton County, Tenn. (population 260), number of cases 61, deaths 24—1 in 2.2; Memphis, Tenn., number of cases 17,600, deaths 5,150—ratio of mortality to cases, 1 in 3.3, to population, reduced to about 19,500, a fraction less than 1 in 4; Meridian, Miss. (population 3,000), number of case 382, deaths 86—1 in 3.4; Michigan City, Benton County, Miss., 2 cases, 2 deaths; Milan, Gibson County, Tenn. (population 2,025), number of cases 26, deaths 11—1 in 2.2; Mississippi City, Miss. (population 300), number of cases 165, deaths 19—1 in 8.2; Mobile, Ala. (population 32,000), number of cases 288, deaths 80—1 in 3.2; Morgan City, La. (population 1,000), number of cases 540, deaths 108—1 in 5; Moscow, number of cases 75, deaths 33—1 in 2.4; Mulatto Bayou, Miss., 1 case, 1 death; Nashville, Tenn., 96 cases (all refuges from infected places), deaths 18—1 in 5.4. On the 6th of August fever broke out on the steamer *Mary Houston* at New Albany, Ind., which had recently arrived from New Orleans, creating alarm there and at Louisville. Fondy Carroll, from the same vessel, had previously died in Louisville of the fever, on the 1st of August. New York City, four Memphis refuges died—no other cases; Norfolk, Va., several cases on vessel in harbor, 1 proving fatal; Nubbin Ridge, Shelby County, Tenn., 2 cases, 2 deaths; Ocean Springs, Jackson County, Miss. (population 450), number of cases 86, deaths 28—1 in 3; Ozyka, Pike Co., Miss. (population 450), number of cases 350, deaths 53—1 in 6.2; Paincourtville, La. (population 400), number of cases 150, deaths 13—1 in 12; Paris, Tenn., 118 cases, 28 deaths—1 in 4; Pass Christian, Miss. (population 1,250), number of cases 200, deaths 27—1 in 7.3; Pascagoula, Jackson County, Miss. (population 650), number of cases 17, deaths 4—1 in 4; Pattersonville, La., and vicinity, number of cases 300, deaths 93—1 in 3.4; Pearlington, Hancock County, Miss. (population 500), cases 5, deaths 1; Philadelphia, Pa., 2 Vicksburg refugees, the only cases known; Pensacola, Fla., crew of a brig in harbor the only cases; Pittsburgh, Pa., 1 death, from Steamer *Porter;** Plaquemine, La., on Mississippi River

---

* The history of the steam-tug *John D. Porter* is one of the most interesting episodes of the epidemic of 1878. For two months she, with two barges, moved up the Mississippi and Ohio rivers, a floating charnel-house, carrying death and destruction to nearly all who had any thing to do with her. Twenty-three persons died on her from the time she left New Orleans until she anchored near Pittsburgh. From her the fever was taken to Gallipolis, Ohio, where, out of 51 persons attacked, 31 died. When the *Porter* landed three miles below Gallipolis, on the morning of the 19th of August, the engineers refused to remain any longer at their post of duty. A strong guard was placed over the tug and her barges to prevent any one from landing from her. There were ten cases of fever on board at the time, three of them very ill, among the number the Captain, John Bickerstaff. Engineer Charles De Grelman, of Pittsburgh, and William Koehler, from Pomeroy, had previously died. Notwithstanding the guards, some of the crew went ashore, and were eventually followed by all the rest but two, who were too sick to leave. With these Dr. Carr, of the Board of Health of Cincinnati, remained, heroically refusing to leave his post of duty until one of them died and the other recovered. After this result, he went ashore at Gallipolis and did what he could for the plague-stricken people. While there, among others, his attention was called to a case of yellow fever ten miles out from the place, and, in company with a resident physician, he rode out in a buggy to the house of a small farmer by the name of Buck, or Burke, whose son was the victim. Dr. Carr arrived at the place after night-fall, and found the farmer sitting at a watch-fire of pine-knots in front of his domicil, afraid to enter it, lest he should catch the yellow fever. The doctor made known the object of his visit. The man was glad to see him, for he said that all the rest of the family had gone, scared away by his boy's horrible sickness. He thought his boy was dead, for he had not heard him for several hours, and did not dare to enter the house. While they were talking a groan was heard in the house. Dr. Carr took a brand and entered, and, following the directions of the father, found the bedroom, but not the patient. The place was in a state of disorder, and was filthy. An abominable stench pervaded it, and the three ground-floor rooms were smeared all over with black vomit and other unutterable excreta of the wretched victim. It was a sickening sight. Dr. Carr came out and told the father that

(population 1,500), number of cases 950, deaths 117—1 in 8; Point a la Hache, La., on Mississippi River, 4 cases, all fatal; Point Pleasant, La., 60 cases, 13 deaths—1 in 4.2; Port Eads, La., 62 cases, 14 deaths—1 in 4.2; Port Gibson, Miss. (population 1,500), number of cases in town and vicinity 1,340, deaths 294—1 in 4.2; Port Hudson, La. (population 200), number of cases 74, deaths 12—1 in 6; Raleigh, Tenn., 9 miles from Memphis, cases 64, deaths 18—1 in 3.2; Richoc, a plantation near Franklin, La., 62 cases, 18 deaths—1 in 3.2; Rocky Springs, Miss., cases 127, deaths 39—1 in $3\frac{3}{4}$; St. Gabriel, La. (population 425), cases 132, deaths 38—1 in $3\frac{3}{4}$; St. James, La., 36 cases, 4 deaths—1 in 9; St. Louis, Mo., 116 cases, 46 deaths—1 in 2.2—principally among refugees; Senatobia, Tate County, Miss. (population 1,400) cases 26, deaths 7—1 in 4; Somerville, Fayette County, Tenn., number of cases 151, deaths 56—1 in 2.3; Southwest Pass, on Mississippi River, cases 26, deaths 8; Stephenson, Ala., 5 cases, 2 deaths; Stoneville, Miss., and vicinity, 110 cases, 80 deaths—1 in 1.2; Summit, Pike County, Miss., a few cases and 3 deaths; Sunflower, Miss., on Mississippi River, 48 cases, 15 deaths—1 in 3; Tallulah, La., and vicinity, number of cases 33, deaths 4—1 in 8; Tangipaha, La., and vicinity (population 300), number of cases 178, deaths 69—1 in 4; Terry, Hinds County, Miss. (population 225), number of cases 10, deaths 5—1 in 2; Terrene, Ark., on White River, cases 21, deaths 19; Thibodeaux Parish, La., total cases in parish 1,800, deaths 175—1 in 10;

---

the young man was not inside. "He must be in there somewhere," replied the man, "for I heard him groan just now." Dr. Carr replenished his light and reëntered, and after a careful search found what he thought at first was a negro, covered with black and filthy clothing, in a dirty corner behind the cooking-stove. It was the wretched, abandoned, and dying youth, covered with filth, who, in his delirium and search for water, had crawled all over the dirty floors of the cabin, and, finally exhausted, sank down in the corner to die. Dr. Carr learned that for twenty-four hours no one had been near the poor wretch. His own flesh and blood forsook him and fled, and there he suffered and died in a manner that freezes one's blood to think of. Such was the dread which the pestilence originated, and such the fearful condition of brutal indifference to all but self, which it in many instances developed. The *Porter* was afterward put in proper sanitary condition by her owners, and her two barges were destroyed. Many other steamers passed up from New Orleans in August, to which was refused clean bills of health. Among them the *John A. Scudder*, on which one case developed on the 7th of August—a lady—who was put off at Refuge Landing, Miss., and there died. The *Golden Crown*, which passed up some days before, and at Memphis put off several passengers, was not allowed to land at any of the points above. She tried to evade the quarantine, it was said, as she did at Memphis, notwithstanding Dr. Lawrence refused to give her a clean bill of health, and Dr. John Erskine compelled her to anchor in the stream. William Warne, one of the first cases (the first reported by the Board of Health), had been a deck-hand on the *Golden Crown*. At Cairo she was ordered off, but at Mound City she landed all that remained of her passengers on the 19th, all well. At Shawneetown, Ill., as she approached, a military company was sent down to the river to prevent her landing. Her answer to this demonstration was what the local papers termed a piece of bravado. She fired one gun, as a salute to the military, and all hands turned out on the decks, and went to fiddling, dancing, and frolicking. The steamer *Mary Houston* also passed up with fever on board, which developed at New Albany, on the 6th, to an alarming extent, several of those attacked dying.

A HISTORY OF THE YELLOW FEVER. 97

Tuscumbia, Ala. (population 1,300), nearly all left, and disease was confined to Memphis refugees and colored people of the town; cases 119, deaths 31—1 in 4; Tuscaloosa, Ala., 2 cases, 2 deaths; Valley Horn, Miss. (Horn Lake), cases 30, deaths 17—1 in 2; Vicksburg, Miss., Washington, D. C., 5 cases, 5 deaths—all refugees from infected places; Water Valley, Miss. (population 3,000), number of cases 146, deaths 47—1 in 3; White Haven, Shelby County, Tenn.; Whistler, Ala., a few cases of refugees, one of whom died; Williston, Tenn. (population 200), cases 16, deaths 11—1 in 1.2; Winchester, Tenn., one refugee died; Winona, Montgomery County, Miss., of a population of 1,700 all fled but 200, number of cases 27, deaths 9—1 in 3; Wythe Depot, five miles from Memphis, 16 cases, 7 deaths—1 in 2.2; Yazoo City, Miss., on Yazoo River, number of cases 17, deaths 7—1 in 2.2.

1879.—Rio Janeiro, Para, and the north-western provinces of Brazil. Also Santo Domingo, and Cuba, West Indies. New Orleans, La., one case (imported), March 31st. The United States steamer *Plymouth*, which sailed from Boston March 15th, for a cruise to the West Indies, returned to that city April 4th, yellow fever having broken out when three hundred miles southeast of Bermuda. The boatswain died of the disease. The ship returned from the West Indies last autumn with yellow fever on board, and it was thought that fumigation and the frosts of a very severe winter in Boston had destroyed all the germs.* The Mobile *News*, of the 16th of April, states that

---

* The first two cases were announced on the 23d, eight days from the date of departure of the *Plymouth* from Boston, the vessel being in good condition and the crew in perfect health. She was on her way to Guadaloupe, but when she reached latitude 22 north, a short distance from Bermuda, the fever made its appearance. The *Plymouth* had several cases of yellow fever on board her while at Santa Cruz, in November of 1878. Two of them resulted in death, the others recovered. She sailed at once for the north, where she could be frozen out during the winter, as that had usually been considered a perfect preventive of the spread of the disease. She lay all winter in Boston, where every thing known to sanitary science was used to disinfect her of the germs of yellow fever. She was entirely broken up, the stores landed and exposed to a freezing temperature, and the ship thoroughly fumigated several times. A part of the time the ship was in a dock, where large quantities of ice remained, and the temperature frequently reached a point below zero. The water in the tanks and buckets in the store-rooms were constantly frozen, and when she was removed from the dock and fires lighted under her boilers, she was so thoroughly chilled that for several days the water remained frozen in her bilges. When the *Plymouth* left Boston all men of weak constitution or susceptible of climatic influences were removed from her, and she went to sea with a crew entirely healthy. Yet, notwithstanding all these precautions, yellow fever made its appearance, as above stated. But the most curious and remarkable fact of all is that the first man attacked, Richard Sanders, machinist, had his hammock slung in the precise place of the man who first showed symptoms of yellow fever in Santa Cruz in November last. For the present the *Plymouth* is in quarantine off the Portsmouth navy-yard, where every precaution has been taken to prevent intercourse with the shore. All the sick on board were taken to the quarantine hospital, and all her crew have been removed from on board. There was, after her arrival in Boston, one death from yellow fever, Peter Egan, the boatswain's mate, who was the second and last case on board. Richard Sanders, who was the first to show symptoms of the disease, recovered. This experience of the *Plymouth* agrees with the two cases of death by yellow fever—

the bark *Viscount Canning*, Murphy, arrived in the lower bay on Monday, in ballast, from Rio Janeiro, having left that port on the first of February. There had been two deaths from fever, the last one on February 14th. Captain Murphy visited the city on Tuesday, to see if the bark would be allowed to come up. The Board of Health took the matter under consideration, and in the meantime Captain Murphy was asked to return on board until some definite action was taken, for, although there might be no danger of contagion, yet, in the feverish condition of public sentiment, it was best to run no risk.

---

one in New Orleans, the other in Memphis—given in the closing pages of the first division of this book, and enforces the conclusion there stated that frost does not kill the germs; yet it is only just that Mr. Gamgee's opposing views be given, especially since the National Government has appropriated $200,000 for the purpose of fully testing his freezing apparatus. He says that the "United States vessel *Plymouth* was not thoroughly disinfected by the operation of natural frost, as alleged, while last winter in Boston. The report is that fire was kept up uninterruptedly in the captain's cabin, and moreover that the presence of water around the hull would preserve a temperature on the decks below the water line sufficiently high to keep the germs alive. Mr. Gamgee insists that cold air must be forced into the lower holds of ships by artificial means to make the freezing process successful."

The Surgeon-General of the U. S. Navy has furnished the following facts in regard to the last outbreak of yellow fever on the United States steamer *Plymouth*: "On Nov. 7, 1878, four cases of yellow fever occurred on board the vessel while lying in the harbor of Santa Cruz; these were removed to the hospital on shore, and the ship sailed to Norfolk. Three mild cases occurred during the voyage, and the *Plymouth* was ordered to Portsmouth, N. H., thence to Boston. At the latter port every thing was removed from the ship and all parts of the interior freely exposed to a temperature which frequently fell below zero, the exposure continuing for more than a month. During this time the water in the tanks, bilges, and in vessels placed in the store-rooms was frozen. One hundred pounds of sulphur was burned below decks, this fumigation continuing for two days, and the berth-decks, holds, and store-rooms were thoroughly whitewashed. On March 15th [1879] the ship sailed from Boston southward; on the 19th, during a severe gale, the hatches had to be battened down, and the berth-deck became very close and damp. On the 23d two men showed decided symptoms of yellow fever, and on the recommendation of the surgeon the vessel was headed northward. The sick men were isolated, and measures adopted for improving the hygienic condition of the vessel and crew. The surgeon reported that he believed the infection to be confined to the hull of the ship, especially to the unsound wood about the berth-deck, all the cases but one having occurred within a limited area; and that, while the *Plymouth* is in good sanitary condition for service in temperate climates, should she be sent to a tropical station, probably no precautionary measures whatever would avail to prevent an outbreak of yellow fever."

THE EPIDEMIC IN MEMPHIS, 1878.

THE EPIDEMIC IN MEMPHIS, 1878.

I.

To reach some of the causes inducing the awful havoc of the yellow fever epidemic in Memphis, during the months of August, September, October, and November, 1878, and the impoverished and helpless condition of her people, it will be necessary to review a part at least of the history of that city. By a mismanagement, the result of the ignorance of the city legislators and the indifference of the better classes of her people, during a few years, Memphis was reduced, in January, 1878, to bankruptcy. Her debt, floating and bonded, then amounted to more than $5,500,000. Her taxable wealth, which before the civil war was estimated at $28,000,000, was reduced to $18,000,000, and of that $6,000,000 had been bought in by the State at tax sales, having been delinquent for years. The population had doubled, but the volume of trade was only a slight increase over that of 1860. Negroes, who, under the system of slavery, which prevailed up to the breaking out of the civil war, had been productive laborers in the cotton fields of the adjoining States, attracted by the excitement it affords, flocked to the city, where at least one-third of them were added to the ranks of the very poor, and either as petty thieves or worthless paupers, depredated upon the industrious few of their own color, but for the most part upon the thrifty whites. Thus the non-producers—those who consume without laboring and live without the least regard for the obligations of good citizenship—were increased to the proportions of a small army. Besides this, taxation was high. Economy in public as in private affairs was unknown. The period between 1865 and 1873, it will be remembered, was one of extravagance throughout the Union. Municipalities were freely bled for, in some cases, unnecessary public and semi-public improvements. Appropriations of public monies were made in the most reckless way. There was no provision for the morrow, no consideration for the future. Promises to pay were lavishly issued. Wall Street was in many instances supplicated to take the bonds of solvent corporations at two-thirds of their face value. Capital was aggressive, predatory, and supreme. Nearly every county and town was busy issuing scrip or bonds. It was a period of wanton waste that by the light of the intelligence usually characteristic of the American people is without excuse. Thousands of miles of railroad were built that have not and will not for years to come pay dividends. The life insurance mania was at its height. To incur obligations without the means to meet them when pay-day came round seemed to be the order of the day. Extravagance raged as an epidemic. Swindlers and rogues were everywhere reveling in ill-gotten gains. The people were blind to their folly, and infatuated by the fictitious evidences of progress. The destructive demon of bankruptcy was hovering over the land preparing for his work. Memphis was no better than New York. Theft was not committed as was the case in the great metropolis, but ignorance and incapacity were working as great a wrong. Taxes were levied, but were not collected. The current expenses could not be met. Scrip was resorted to. The city government went into the banking business, and scattered its promises to pay broadcast. There was at one time as much as $960,000 of it afloat. It was sold as low as twenty-three cents on the dollar. When the policemen, firemen, and other employés could not get par for it, they petitioned the General Council to have the difference made up to them. This was for some time done, but always by a fresh issue of scrip. The county, at the same time, under the government of commissioners, was engaged in the same method of slow but sure financial suicide. The press expostulated; it was not heeded. Those who controlled municipal affairs had no regard for public opinion. The property owners seemed to be, if they were not wholly, indifferent. The merchants were too busy with their private affairs to pay any attention to those of the public, and the people generally were so absorbed in the work of rehabilitating their homes despoiled by the war as to be careless of the recklessness of their representatives. They did not see, they would not see, that a crop of wholesale ruin was being sown in a soil all too productive. There were not wanting spasmodic attempts at "retrenchment and reform," but these occurred at rare intervals. The stream of ruin steadily increased in volume and violence until at last it reached a point where a halt was called to prevent utter and entire loss. When the debt had reached the enormous sum of $5,500,000, the State, as has been stated, had taken possession of one-third of the realty for delinquent taxes, leaving only $12,000,000 worth to bear the burdens imposed for the support of the State, county, and city governments. The city, while this monument of folly was in course of construction, had passed through six epidemics—one of war, one of reconstruction, two of yellow fever (1867 and 1873), one of cholera, and one of small-pox. Up to 1878, for twenty years, Memphis had been the center of an extraordinary political agitation, of the passion and prejudice of the two sections, of the heat and strife of civil commotion, the uncharitableness of sectional animosity and the bitterness of party politics. In all that time there was not a single year of repose, of quiet, steady conservative endeavor, such as was before the war characteristic of the cities and towns of the South. The public pulse beat feverishly, and the very uncertainties of life became a provocation to wastefulness and extravagance. That under such circumstances Memphis survives to-day is a special wonder to all familiar with her wayward and untoward history. In any other country, and by any other people, she would long since have been abandoned and given over to decay and ruin. Having thus suffered, and living in a constant ferment of excitement, it is not to be wondered at that in August of 1878 the mere rumor of a possible epidemic of yellow fever precipitated a panic among the people. This was initiated early in May, when the question of quarantine was agitated with a view to prevent a visitation of the disease then known to prevail in epidemic form in the West Indies. This agitation monopolized the public mind for several weeks, but was eventually disposed of by the General Council, which, although petitioned thereto by the whole body of merchants and business men, refused to permit its establishment. On this Dr. Mitchell, President of the Board of Health, resigned, and was succeeded by Dr. Saunders who, aided by a prompt subscription of funds by the merchants,* immediately set about improving the sanitary condition of the city, which was disgraceful in the extreme. Miles of Nicholson pavement were decaying and sending forth a poison that none in the city limits could avoid, and the soil was reeking with the offal and excreta of ten thousand families. There was no organized scavenger system, no means by which the ashes and garbage could, as it should be, daily carted away. The accumulations of forty years were decaying upon the surface; a bayou dividing the city, and which was the receptacle of the contents of privies and water-closets, was sluggish and without current, owing to the want of water and the fact that there had been scarcely any rain for several weeks. Dead animals were decaying in many parts of it, and the pools which had formed at the abutments of the several bridges were stagnant and covered with a scum of putridity, emitting a deadly effluvia. The cellars of the houses in the leading thoroughfares were also alembics, in which were manufactured noxious gases which stole out and made the night air an almost killing poison. The streets were filthy, and every affliction that could aggravate a disease so cruel seemed to have been purposely prepared for it by the criminal neglect of the city government, who turned a deaf ear to the persistent appeals of the press. But they were not wholly to blame; the charter, under which they acted, was so worded as to provide but little funds for sanitary relief, and no relief in case of the dreadful emergency of an epidemic, notwithstanding 1867 and 1873. Every interest was carefully guarded and provided for, save that of the health and lives of the people. They must either take care of themselves—that is, be prepared to abandon their homes when yellow fever or cholera made its appearance—or be ready to meet death. Ignorant of the laws of life, its framers denied to themselves and their fellow-citizens the advantages of a growing intelligence in regard to sanitary affairs. But even these were not much to be blamed; their ignorance of sanitation curses every city in the land; for what municipality in the Union is to-day in a condition to resist epidemic disease if once it secures a foothold under the conditions necessary to its rapid propagation? Perhaps Boston, no other could. Defective sewerage,† if nothing else, dominates all attempts at

---

* The city treasury was empty.
† Dr. T. P. Corbally, in an article on the "Brooklyn sewers," which appeared in the April (1879) number of the *Sanitarian*, takes the ground that "The system is radically wrong, and that the sewers, accepting them as they are, have been managed with a degree of negligence which becomes criminal in view of the danger which such negligence causes to the health and the lives of the people." To sustain this position, he adduces a great deal of proof, the best of which is contained in an extract, which he

perfect sanitation, and the clamors of the gutter politicians are more effective than the warnings and appeals of skilled sanitarians. Seaboard cities have permanent pools of filth at every dock, and those inland pour into the rivers on the banks of which they are built a continuous stream of nameless nastiness that increases with the population. The quarters of the very poor are, for want of suitable provision or accommodation, as bad as those of many of the older cities of Europe. Instead of being an example, as we are in so many other respects for the world, ours, in sanitary matters, are, many of them, little better than the poorest cities of the least advanced nations of Europe. We have gas and water in our houses, but we have also water-closets, which are so many means of escape for the most subtle of all the life-destroying gases.* After the experiences of 1873, it was hoped by the press that the citizens of Memphis, so far as they could, would compel a reform that would enhance the value of human life. Instead of that they permitted the passage of the new charter, which cheapened it by preferring remedies for

---

quotes from the Report of the Engineer to the Board of Health of Brooklyn, as follows: "During storms, when the sewers are in a measure gorged, and the increased flow within them is backed into the house-drains, the rush of water with so great a fall through the leader will render its use as a ventilator for the drain entirely out of the question, and the gases in the drains will be forced somewhere into the house. Its failure as a ventilator occurs during the very time when it is most needed, by reason of the increased pressure having been brought upon all the traps communicating with the drain." Again, "The inhabitants are clamorous to be free from foul sewerage in their cellars, and to be saved the expense of cleaning them whenever they are flooded. The property has been assessed for the construction of these sewers, and successive Health Boards have compelled the owners to connect their houses with these elongated cess-pools"—cess-pools that make life as cheap on the average in Brooklyn as in New Orleans, which, as Dr. Holt, of that city, claims, rests upon a dung-heap. And New York, Cincinnati, Pittsburgh, Baltimore, Philadelphia, Chicago, St. Louis, and, no doubt, San Francisco, are quite as bad. The sewerage systems of these, and nearly all our cities, are nothing better than so many "elongated cess-pools," from which the gases escape "somewhere in the houses," resulting in typhoid fever, small-pox, scarlet fever, diphtheria, croup, and meningitis, which carry off so many persons as to bring the average of deaths up to, in some cases above, that of New Orleans. From this death-dealing poison there is only one escape, and that is by the destruction by fire of excreta, ashes, and debris and offal of every description. Fire is the purifier. In every ward of every city in the country, and in every town, furnaces for this purpose should be erected. Water-closets should be done away with, and the sewers should alone be used for carrying off the surface water of the streets and the waste water of the houses; and from them large ventilating pipes should lead into the sanitary furnaces, so that any lurking or latent poisons might be drawn off by the draught created by the fire, into which it would pass to be consumed. Sewer-gas is to-day killing more persons every year than the yellow fever in its worst periods of epidemic, and so long as water-closets are allowed to exist it will continue to kill, just as, until a better sanitary system obtains in the southern cities, visitations of yellow fever may be expected.

* Among the many disorders which may arise from the effluvia of drains and sewers, two additional ones have been recently mentioned in the English journals for the first time, viz., abscess of the cervical glands, and a tendency on the part of ulcerated surfaces to become sluggish and to yield to no ordinary management. Sometimes these ulcers take on a diphtheritoid appearance.

every thing else but the public safety. A few thousand dollars were set apart for that purpose, scarcely enough for a month of effective sanitary work. An efficient Board of Health thus found its hands tied. It could do next to nothing, and confronted by an ignorance so obtuse and besotted as to reject all instruction, its members became disheartened. In this condition the rumors of yellow fever fell upon the public ear full of evil portent, and the hope of the people fell to zero. Apprehensions thus awakened were quickened almost beyond control by the publication, in the morning papers of the 26th of July, of the fact that the yellow fever had made its appearance in New Orleans and threatened to become epidemic. The tardiness with which this information reached the doomed city was not due to any want of diligence on the part of the State or city health authorities. Dr. Maury, of the State Board, wrote to Dr. Chopin, of the New Orleans Board, on the 21st of May, asking for information. He received a curt reply that he (Maury) would receive official information regularly, and that he (Chopin) would not conceal any thing from the public. He stated additionally that the *Borussa*, from Liverpool, via Havana, was then quarantined below the city with six cases of yellow fever on board. Dr. Chopin was evidently on the *qui vive*. But notwithstanding his vigilance, the steamer *Sudder* passed up to the city wharf on the 23d. The purser of that vessel, who had evaded quarantine, sickened and died of yellow fever. In him it is asserted that the epidemic had its origin, and from him it spread. Dr. Maury continued to receive the New Orleans weekly health reports, according to the health officer's promise, but no cases of yellow fever were found in them; nor was any warning of even the existence of the disease conveyed until the 26th of July, when the newspapers of the country published Dr. Chopin's letter to Dr. Woodworth, Supervising Surgeon of Marine Hospitals at Washington, although it is well known that cases occurred before, and were reported about the 13th of July, and that the malady had been making havoc in the neighborhood of the refuge of the purser and mate of the death-freighted *Sudder*. But slow as the sad news was in reaching Memphis, it came all too fast. So soon as it was verified, the health officer, Dr. John Erskine, notified the city authorities, who, at last, but only when the whole population was worked up to a point of dread, in some cases bordering on insanity, gave consent to the establishment of the quarantine which they had refused to provide for only a few days before. The doctor, a noble example of official zeal, professional enthusiasm, and manly independence, at once perfected arrangements, and quarantine stations were established on the Memphis and Charleston Railroad, at Germantown, some twelve miles from the city, on the Mississippi and Tennessee Railroad, at Whitehaven Station, eight miles from the city, and on the river at the lower or southern point of President's Island. It was believed that this would prove effectual, especially as the railroad and steamboat officials had promised to second it by a rigid surveillance over passengers and baggage; and the people on the lines mentioned, and all along the river, for their personal safety, talked of or had already taken measures to enforce, in each case, local quarantine, by a decided exhibit of power in the form of a hastily formed militia or police force. These measures and assurances had some effect with most of the people of the city, but there were a few who, in a purely idle spirit, some of them because they had nothing else to do, went about expressing their own fears, and with an assumption of wisdom which neither their experience, habits, or education would warrant, predicted the direst consequences to the city. The uneasy feeling thus kept alive by the shiftless and thriftless gossips of the street, was aggravated by the announcement, on the 2d of August, of a case of yellow fever at the City Hospital—a steamboatman, who died at quarantine on the 3d— and by the dispatches from New Orleans, which every day gave an increased number of cases, and a mortality that, in proportion, was much larger than had before been known in that city. On the 9th of August, rumors prevailed that the fever had made its appearance in Grenada, Miss., the southern terminus of the Mississippi and Tennessee Railroad. Inquiry by telegraph, made on the 10th by citizens of Memphis, brought the most positive contradictions. But on the very day these were published in the newspapers there came a most anxious call for nurses and physicians. This appeal was responded to by the Howard Association,* Butler P. Anderson and W. J. Smith volunteering their services. These gentlemen left the city on the afternoon train and reached Grenada that night. On Monday, Anderson telegraphed to the *Appeal* that yellow fever, of the same type as that which cost Memphis 2,000 lives in 1873, prevailed epidemically, that twenty new cases had developed during the twenty-four hours since his arrival, and there was then a total of one hundred cases, none of which had so far yielded to treatment. The publication of these facts, and others from other sources of information, on the 13th of August, had the effect of exciting the people of the city to the last degree of alarm. Business was neglected. Men met in groups and discussed the news, and the probability of Memphis being attacked, little dreaming that already the fever had made a lodgment in the city, and had taken its second victim,

---

*The parent Association was organized twenty-five years ago (1853) in New Orleans, when it and other cities of the South were so cruelly afflicted with the fever, and such horror and panic were excited that husbands deserted their wives, parents their children, and the ties of common humanity seemed shattered. Napoleon B. Kneass, now of Philadelphia, but formerly a merchant of New Orleans, says that the organization originated in his store, among his clerks, especially two of them, whose mother was from San Domingo, and had seen much of the epidemic. They went about the city, hunted up new cases, and furnished the sufferers with medicines prepared by her and found effective in Hayti. From these clerks, as a nucleus, the Association was formed. Young men of wealth joined it, and the name of Howard was adopted, in honor of the renowned English philanthropist. They obtained medicines, nurses, and physicians, and established agencies in all the towns and cities that had been, or were likely to be, infected, binding themselves to act together at every reappearance of the pestilence. This body increased rapidly in numbers and means, and before the civil war it was one of the richest benevolent societies in the country. That bitter contest left most of its members poor, and the Association has been crippled in its power to do good. Until recently they never asked for aid, but any contributions to the cause were received, and distributed according to existing need. They divide the town or city into districts, to each of which members are assigned, and, when the disease reveals itself, each case is immediately reported to headquarters. The visiting committee at once investigates the matter, physicians and nurses are employed, and every thing is done that can be done to relieve the patient.

perhaps more. The death of Mrs. Bionda, an Italian snack-house keeper, was announced on the 14th as the first case originating in the city.* This increased the general fear. The little company of panic-stricken citizens was increased to a regiment, and in that ratio every hour until the next morning (the 15th), when the announcement of twenty-two new cases gave a fresh impetus to their dread, and, passing all bounds and limits of sense, thinking only of their personal safety, many of them indifferent to their fate, so they could get away from the now-admittedly-infected city, sought safety in flight. The announcement of thirty-three new cases on the 16th confirmed most of those who were willing to take their chances that an epidemic threatened, and a hegira ensued, which increased the feeling that inspired it, until at last the whole population was precipitated into a panic, surpassing all powers of description, and which deadened all human sympathy, all the kindlier emotions of the human heart, all feeling of kinship, all regard for neighborly claims, and in some cases all natural affection. The croakers were jubilant. "I told you so!" was often repeated. Business was almost as suddenly stopped as the fever began. Stores and offices were hastily closed. *Sauve que pute* was the order of the day. The future, which only a few short weeks before seemed so bright, was forgotten in dread of the pestilence, which, in the brief space of forty-eight hours had claimed fifty-five victims. Men, women, and children poured out of the city by every possible avenue of escape. A few steamboats were filled, but these were

---

* This is not true. It was ascertained, after the epidemic was fairly established, that many cases had occurred before her's. Mrs. C. W. Ferguson, boarding at the residence of Attorney-General G. P. M. Turner, 279 Second Street, states that on the 21st of July a colored man came up the river, whose wife was cook for Mr. Turner. This woman had a residence in the yard back of the Turner house, and abutting on an alley which runs from Second to Main Street. Her husband had been taken with a severe chill on the boat on the morning of the day on which he landed, and when he reached his home had a very high fever for several days. For this his wife treated him with hot teas, and he recovered. Subsequently, and about ten days after his arrival, Mr. Turner's two children were taken with well-marked cases of yellow fever. One of them died, and the other recovered. In the meantime, a young man named Willie Darby, an employé of Farrell, the oyster-dealer, who lived at 277 Second Street, and who was in the habit of passing to his meals through the alley infected by the colored man, although he slept in the third story of his house, was taken with the fever, but recovered. He was nursed by his aunt, and was not visited by a doctor. His was the second case; it occurred on the 25th of July. The good woman who saved his life took the fever and died, as did nearly all who lived in the house or in the houses near by. Mrs. Zack (white), who resided on the opposite side of the street, died of the fever on the 5th of August, and her brother-in-law, taken on the 10th, died on the 13th, the day before Mrs. Bionda died. About the 1st of August, the steamer *Golden Crown* landed three ladies, who were taken to the residence of Esquire Winters, on Alabama Street, and among them the fever developed, it was reported, about the 10th of August. All in this house but the 'Squire were attacked, but recovered. Before this, Mr. John Campbell, whose house was opposite that of Mr. Winters, was taken sick, and died, it was reported at the time, of congestion, but afterward was proven to be yellow fever, as his wife and many others were subsequently attacked in the same way, and developed well-defined cases of yellow fever.

for the most part shunned, especially by those who had the means for railroad travel, and had mind sufficient left to think of the possibility of their becoming charnel-houses, subject to the quarantines and freaks of folly of populations equally scared and bent upon their own safety. Out by the country roads to the little hamlets and plantations, where many of them were welcome guests in happier days; out by every possible conveyance—by hacks, by carriages, buggies, wagons, furniture vans, and street drays; away by batteaux, by any thing that could float on the river; and by the railroads, the trains on which, especially on the Louisville Road, were so packed as to make the trip to that city, or to Cincinnati, a positive torture to many delicate women every mile of the way. The aisles of the cars were filled, and the platforms packed. In vain the railroad officials plead, in vain they increased the accommodations. The stream of passengers seemed to be endless, and they seemed to be as mad as they were many. The ordinary courtesies of life were ignored; politeness gave way to selfishness, and the desire for personal safety broke through all the social amenities. If there was no positive indecency exhibited, there was a pushing, noisy, self-asserting, and frenzied rudeness, that was not abashed even in the presence of refined, delicate, and sensitive women. There was only one thought uppermost, and that was increased to an inexpressible terror. Men, refused admittance to the cars, took forcible possession of them, making such an exhibit of will, backed by arms, as deterred even the few policemen present from any interference. But with these there was more sympathy with than opposition to this rude rebellion against routine, custom, order, and social law. If they made any efforts to prevent these assaults upon the rules and rights of the railroad companies, it was altogether by words, and not deeds. No arrests were made—not even when the windows of the cars were opened from the outside, and men and boys were thrust in, over and despite the expostulations of the respectable women who occupied the seats. The cars of the trains for several days went out literally packed to suffocation with people. Every station and town had shortly its quota of refugees from Memphis, who, still inspired by the apprehensions which urged them to abandon their neighbors, and leave business and property to a possible fate they at no time dreamed of, spread the panic, some of them carrying with them the seeds of the disease which, with time and conditions to propagate, afterward brought to their hospitable and generous hosts the misery and death which then plagued their relatives and friends. To the cities of the far north and the far west they fled, too many of them to die on the way, like dogs, neglected and shunned, as if cursed of God; or, to reach the wished-for goal, only to die, a plague to all about, carrying dismay to those who even then were busying themselves for the relief of the stricken cities of the South. In less than ten days, by the 24th of August, twenty-five thousand people had left the city, and, in two weeks after, five thousand others were in camp, leaving a little less than twenty thousand to face consequences they could not escape. Some had walked away, having no means to pay for transportation, and, in Arkansas, many were forced to leave the trains and camp in the forest, unprepared as they were for a mode of living which not even the hardiest can encounter without risk to health and life. Shot-gun quarantines were by this time (the 26th of August) established at nearly all points in the interior, as well as upon the river; and, without leave, license, or law, trade was embargoed and travel prohibited. For the sake of humanity, men became inhuman. For the sake of saving those out of the fever's reach from its touch or taint, they denied a refuge to those who were fleeing from it. Law was everywhere suspended, but order was maintained. Even rogues for a time forgot their occupation, and the rash who were addicted to folly were sobered by the fear of the unseen foe by this time making itself felt where assurances were held out to the last, based upon the stupid zone theory, that it could neither find lodgment nor live.

II.

By the last week in August the panic was over in the city. All had fled who could, and all were in camp who would go. There was then, it was estimated, about three thousand cases of fever. Most of the white men who were not in bed, and who were to be met upon the streets, were engaged in the work of relief, either as physicians, nurses, as Howard visitors, or as members of the other organizations which did such noble service. The weather continued intensely hot and dry. During this month (August), it averaged 82.2° as compared with 79° for the same month in 1873. In September, it averaged 72° as compared with 71° in the same month in 1873. In October, 60.8° as compared with 56° in the same month in 1873, and in November, 57.8° as compared with 49° in the same month in 1873.* The drain of the physical energies, induced by this long-continued heat, was as fearful as the strain on the mind and heart, induced by the destruction of the fever. From either there was neither re-

---

* Dr. Schenck, of St. Louis, insists that yellow fever is a disease of the tropics, and occurs during July, August, and September. Exceptions to this have occurred in the West Indies, where they had a severe epidemic in February. Dr. La Roche states that during July Philadelphia has had seven epidemics to commence. New Orleans (from 1817 to 1853), fourteen; New York, three; Boston, two. During the month of August Philadelphia had three; Charleston, six; New York, two; Providence, Rhode Island, two. Yellow fever being a disease of the tropics, it requires a high temperature; it never spreads where the thermometer stands at less than 72° Fahrenheit. It has been proven in Philadelphia, in a series of years embracing many epidemics, that it occurred in no year when the average thermometer at 3 o clock P. M. was under 79° during the summer, and that the extent and malignancy of the disease were proportionate to the extent in which it exceeded that height, and that the average temperature of June and July, at that hour, governs the season in relation to health, insomuch that if by the first of August in any year the average shall be below that degree, they feel confident that during that season yellow fever will not occur. Dr. Barton says that in every instance in yellow fever epidemics in New Orleans great heat was the predominant condition; and it was remarked that the return of the intense heat reproduced the fever two or three times. In the months of May and June preceding the epidemics at New Orleans,

lease nor relief. An appalling gloom hung over the doomed city. At night, it was silent as the grave, by day, it seemed desolate as the desert. There were hours, especially at night, when the solemn oppressions of universal death bore upon the human mind, as if the day of judgment was about to dawn. Not a sound was to be heard; the silence was painfully profound. Death prevailed everywhere. Trade and traffic were suspended. The energies of all who remained were enlisted in the struggle with death. The poor were reduced to beggary, and even the rich gladly accepted alms. At midday a noisy multitude of negroes broke in upon the awful monotony of death, the dying, and the dead, clamoring each for his dole of the bounty which saved the city from plunder and the torch. When these had gone to their homes, now fast being invaded by the fever, the cloud of gloom closed down again and settled, thick, black, and hideous, upon every living soul. Even the animals felt the oppression; they fled from the city. Rats, cats, or dogs were not to be seen. Death was triumphant. White women were seldom to be met; children, never. The voice of prayer was lifted up only at the bed of pain or death, or in some home circle where anguish was supreme and death threatened, as in a few cases he accomplished total annihilation. Tears for one loved one were choked back by the feeling of uncertainty provoked by the sad condition of another. In one case a family of four was found dead in the same room, the bodies partially decomposed. There were no public evidences of sorrow. The wife was borne to the tomb while the husband was unconscious of his loss; and whole families were swept away in such quick succession that not one had knowledge of the other's departure. Death dealt kindly by these. In a week father, mother, and sisters and brothers were at rest, at peace. There was no mourning; no widow, no orphans. The parents went first; in a few hours the children followed. In some cases one of the parents was left dazed, stunned, in a condition beyond tears and bordering on insanity. In one such case, a mother, thus left, turned from her griefs with a brave heart, sustained by a holy trust, to nurse the sick. Her losses and trials deepened her sympathies and enabled her to appreciate the disheartened, almost demented, condition of those yet in the valley of the shadow, through which she had passed. She entered the sickroom with all the confidence of a martyr and dispensed the holy and comforting assurances of a saint. There was almost healing in her touch. A man also, thus bereft, who, in one short week, buried all his pets, who rose from a sick-bed to lay his wife away forever, also became a nurse, and for weeks, un-

---

the average temperature at midday was 83.75°. In Brazil and Demarara it is noticed that whenever the disease varied or changed, it was usually preceded by variation of temperature. Though Dr. Parks states that the observations at Lisbon (in 1857), made by Dr. Lyons, shows that there is no relation to the dew point in an epidemic of yellow ever, yet the experiments in the South show that the dew point of yellow fever is 70° to 80°; the disease rarely exists when it is under 60°. It is a common phrase to call the clear days of the season of the disease "yellow fever weather;" they are characterized by being very hot in the sun and cool in the shade, such days as when you are burning on one side of the street and on the other side you feel an inclinatian to button up your coat. During the worst periods of the epidemic at Galveston in 1867, the most frequent wind was from the east; still more remarkable was the frequency and long duration of calms.

A HISTORY OF THE YELLOW FEVER.

til the epidemic closed, went about doing good. Another woman heroically nursed and buried her husband and three children, and then lay down—a walking case—and, as she said, gladly welcomed death. Others, as sadly bereft, vainly prayed for death to release them from sorrows that could not be assuaged. Sadder cases than these were the orphans, who lost both parents, children who were dropped from comfort into poverty and robbed in a few hours of the care, protection, and guidance of loving parents, to become a public charge and the inmates of public asylums. A time came when the care of these little ones was as great an anxiety to the few who were left to manage affairs as the burial of the dead. The asylums were already full, and their inmates were bearing their share of the awful burden of death. The people of Nashville kindly and generously volunteered their aid. They took the children, and the relieved citizens turned their attention to the unburied bodies that were emitting the most noisome stenches, death-breeding and death-dealing. Some of these were found in a state little better than a lot of bones in a puddle of green water. Two bodies were found on a leading street in so advanced a stage of decomposition that they were rolled in the carpets on which they had fallen in the agonies of dissolution and were lifted into boxes, in which they were hurried to the potter's field and buried. Half the putrid remains of a negro woman were found in an outbuilding near the *Appeal* office; the other half had been eaten by rats, that were found dead by hundreds near by. A young gentleman, well known as a merchant, died in his room alone, after, it is supposed, a forty-eight hours' illness, and was only traced by the gases from his body, which was found so far advanced in putrefaction that it was with difficulty any one could be found to bury it. More than sixty unburied bodies were found by the burial corps, hastily organized by the Citizens' Relief Committee. Many of these were put away in the trenches where the paupers and the unknown sleep peacefully together. The carnival of death was now at its height. Women were found dead, their little babes gasping in the throes of death beside the breasts at which they had tugged in vain. One case is recalled where the babe was literally glued to the bosom, where it had found food and shelter, and perhaps expired at the same moment as the mother, whose love was evidenced even in a death embrace. Others passed away after the labors of birth had supervened upon the fever—mother and child being buried in the same grave. The penalties of maternity, which always command the tenderest solicitude and sympathy, were paid in nameless agonies, leading in all but two cases to forfeiture of life. No words can convey an idea of the peculiar sufferings to which women were subjected; some who had passed safely into the vigor of old age, were again taxed with functions long since silenced, and in the moment of death, and even after it, this curse of the sex asserted itself to an amazing and an astonishing degree. Not a few were affected with swellings that took on the form of goitre, increasing the disgusting consequences of a disease that to the patient is one of the most offensive—as much so as small-pox, or the black plague of the East. Its effects upon men were equally forbidding. It was no respecter of persons; good and bad went down together, but those whose physical system had been impaired by diseases which are a special pen-

8

alty of lecherous excesses, died soonest. Peculiarly a disease of the nervous system, it was fatal to those whose energies had been exhausted by debauchery. But neither cleanliness nor right living were a shield to stay the hand of this destroyer. He invaded the homes of the most chaste, and the den of the vilest. He took innocence and infamy at the same moment, and spread terror everywhere. Where sorrow was so general there could be no parade of it. There were no funerals, and but few demands for funeral services. The luxuries of woe were dispensed with. In most cases the driver of the hearse and an assistant comprised the funeral party. Not unfrequently many bodies were left in the cemetery unburied for a night, so hard pressed were the managers for labor, and so numerous the demands upon what they had. The bell at the grave-yard gate was for a long time tolled by a lovely girl, who for weeks was her father's only help. She kept the registry of the dead, and knew what the havoc of the fever was; yet she remained at her self-selected post, her father's courageous clerk, until sickness conquered her physical energies; but she recovered, and after a few days resumed her place, keeping tally until the plague itself was numbered with the things that were. No bell save that of death was tolled. The churches were closed. The congregations were dispersed. The members were far apart. Some were safe, many were dead. Only a few survived, and these were manifesting their faith by works. The police* were cut down from forty-one to seven. Their ranks were recruited, and again were thinned. They were a second and a third time filled up, and yet death was relentless. He was jealous of all sway but his own. The fire department† was cut down to thirteen. One by one they fell, dying at their posts; yet those who remained were always ready, with their comrades of the police force, to protect and save the lives and property of their fellow-citizens. Their bells, too, were silenced out of tender regard for the sick—so changed do rugged and even rough men become in the presence of an overwhelming and incomprehensible calamity. Their hearts went out in sympathy to all alike. The city was to them as one house, and all the stricken inmates of one family, to which they themselves belonged. They were pervaded by the spirit of the Howards, of the Citizens' Relief Committee, and of all the organizations for the relief and succor of living or dead—the spirit of charity. Fortunately there were but few fires, and these made no great demand upon the exertions of the department. But petty thieving prevailed as an epidemic. This was, however, principally confined to food and clothing, and wood or coal,

---

* Of the Police Department, twenty-seven out of a total of forty-eight men were attacked, of whom ten died and seventeen convalesced. The dead are as follows: Captain William Homan, Sergeant James McConnell, and Patrolmen James McConnell, William Unversagt, I. J. Huber, W. H. Sweeney, M. Cannon, M. M. Allison, Fred. Restmeyer, and Tim Hope.

† The following named members of the fire department died: Capt. P. Haley, Jno. Considine, Patrick Cronin, J. R. Luccarnia, Thomas Brennan, Felix Plaggio, Dennis Sullivan, Michael Fenny, Martin Carney, Michael Farrell, Tony Griffin, Jno. Leech, Patrick Connell, B. Lunch, Frank Saltglamaohia, Frank Frank, Jno. Heath, C. E. Riorden, James Hannon, Austin Beatty, Sam'l Townsend, Edward Moran, Edward Lee, Thomas Heath.

or both. A few who came to nurse died, leaving full trunks of silverware, bijoutere, bric-a-brac, and clothes, to prove how industriously they could ply two trades, and make one cover up and make up for the deficiencies of the other. A few, also, of them made themselves notorious for lewdness and drunkenness. To these many deaths are due. They shocked decency and outraged humanity. They were no better than the beasts of the field. Male and female, they herded together in vileness. They made of the epidemic a carnival. It was the one opportunity they had been looking for above all others. But the worst of them were cut short in their career; only one or two escaped. Many were sent whence they came; many others, a majority of them, died. They were taken in the midst of their transgressions. One of these, a woman, who could not, or would not, control her appetite for strong drink, while stupefied from wine and brandy, allowed a poor woman to leave her bed, naked as when born, and wander out into the country on an inclement night, calling as she went, for the husband who had preceded her to the grave by a few days. Two others, men, were found helplessly drunk, lying half-naked upon the floor, beside the dead body of the patient, whom the attending physicians said ought to have recovered. In the house of an ex-judge, whence a whole family had been borne to the grave, the victims of neglect, four such nurses died, and in the two trunks of one—and the worst of them, a woman of seeming refinement—there was found the family plate and wearing apparel of the judge's wife, then absent in Ohio. This woman and her paramours fell victims to the fever which they invited by their debauchery, and hastened by their excesses. In the whole range of human depravity there are few parallels to these cases. They illustrate the extremes of degradation; they sounded the lowest depths of vice, and shamed even the low standards of savage life. At a time when the hearts of nearly all were filled with sorrow and weighed with care, a few like these indulged in orgies that were an extreme contrast to the prevalent solemnity and sadness; they gave way to the vilest and most brutal of human weaknesses, and surrendered themselves to a shamelessness that at any time would horrify decency. It was deliberate lechery. There was nothing in the surroundings, or in the life, which was hurried forward with such rapidity to death, to prompt or encourage lewdness; on the contrary, there was every thing to forbid and repel it. Those, therefore, who gave themselves to it, did so in obedience to a propensity deliberately nursed, any, the faintest, expression of which makes one shudder, even at this distance of time, to contemplate. Out of these cases of excess grew a statement of wholesale rape of white women by negro male nurses. No charge ever made was so baseless, so wanton, so cruel, so unjust. This class of the population, whatever they may have been to each other—and not a few of them were inexcusably neglectful, and even brutally indifferent to each other's wants and woes—were deferential and respectful to the white race, and as soldiers, policemen, and nurses were earnest, honest, and devoted.* Not even one of them attempted a crime that

---

* The following list of colored soldiers, who died during the epidemic, attests their devotion and their courage: *McClelland Guards*—Peck, sergeant; Cobb, sergeant; Harris, private; Lane, private; Crutcher, private; Carey, private. *Zouave Guards*—W. N. Hanson, lieutenant; A. W. Brown, private; Tom Lewis, private.

would have courted and been punished by instant and merited death. Idle many of them were, and shiftless and thriftless, as is to be expected of those who are in the A, B, C of civilization; but they were neither cruel nor criminal in this direction. The only case of the kind that was reported, was that of a young white man, who was arrested charged with outraging the person of a woman who, herself, had called him to nurse her. Investigation, extending over many months, proves this to have been baseless, and that the woman invited the exhibit of depravity on which the charge was based.* A contrast to this debauchery was furnished by a few of those whom society deliberately abandons to a shameless life. One unfortunate " woman of the town "—a phrase that only too well tells her trade—gave up her house to be used as a hospital; and herself, until she fell in the act, nursed the sick, and closed the eyes and covered the faces of the dead. Others, doomed like her to become a curse instead of a blessing to humanity, followed her example. One such came from a great city of the West, disguised as a widow, and faithfully and assiduously continued to do her duty, running the gauntlet of death every hour; even after all, like her, were denounced in her presence as irreclaimable, and abandoned of God, by an earnest Christian woman, whom she nursed to convalescence. The physicians were greatly aided by hundreds of faithful and competent nurses—men and women of experience. These are indispensable to recovery. Where they were not to be had, and patients recovered, it was regarded as little less than miraculous. But not all of the deaths were attributable to ignorant or badly-disposed nurses. The patients themselves, many of them, were solely responsible; some died of fright; not a few died after but a few hours in bed—what is known as walking cases—victims of their stubbornness in refusing to yield to treatment. More than three hundred died in the convalescent stage—one from the simple exertion of writing a note, another from changing his position in bed, another from reading newspapers, another from reading letters, another from drinking tea and eating toast; and others, not a few, from sexual excesses, which were sure to end in death. One man, whose convalescence seemed certain, dropped dead only a few steps from the saloon where, a moment before, he had indulged himself in a glass of beer. A treacherous disease, the yellow fever usually leaves its victims in that condition where the spirit is willing but the flesh is weak. In vain doctors advised and the press plead. Deceived by the clearness of their mental vision, convalescents, to the last, continued to take counsel of their fancied strength, and threw away their lives. The horrors of the fever were thus increased, and the despair of the living was made more desperate. But there were not wanting some cases of another character: a few who were afflicted with chronic complaints found themselves completely restored to all

---

* The young man referred to was found by a woman nurse helplessly drunk, lying across the body of the dying woman, who was naked and exposed. The nurse, who declared to thus finding him, was, on the trial, proven to be herself in love with him, and that her jealousy of the poor creature, whose weakness for him had induced her to call for him to nurse her, impelled her to make a charge that was groundless. A few hours after the arrest of the young man, his alleged victim died, a typical case of yellow fever.

their faculties by attacks of the fever. One such case was that of a little girl approaching her twelfth year, who had, three years before, lost both hearing and speech; she was paralyzed also on one side, and was afflicted with something akin to St. Vitus' dance on the other; thus, more dead than alive, a burden to all about her, she was attacked by the fever, a long siege of which she not only withstood, but emerged from completely restored. Her hearing and speech came back to her, the paralysis disappeared, and with it its opposite, the excessive nervous affliction; her nerves were completely restored to their normal condition, and she is to-day mistress of all her powers of mind and body, as fresh and vigorous as if they had never been impaired. Thus while some were crippled for life, all their functions partially or wholly suspended, others were restored to powers, the exercise of which they indulged in at first as if not sure of them, as if they could not trust their suddenly acquired sense of them. But these blessed results were so few as to be a special wonder, bordering on the miraculous.

III.

On the 14th of September, the day of the heaviest mortality, many buoyant natures succumbed. They looked about them for convalescents, but they were not to be found; a few were reported, but they seemed nearly all of them to have been permanently disabled. The cry for food, for clothing, for money, for doctors, for as many as a thousand coffins, went out by telegraph to the ends of the earth, and a prompt and generous response came back. By telegraph, by express, through the banks, by private hands, money was forwarded by hundreds, by thousands of dollars—New York City alone sending altogether $43,800. Long trains of railroad cars were loaded with provisions and clothing, and medical supplies were sent in plethoric abundance, accompanied always with a heartfelt sympathy, and often by advice and by theories of treatment, earnest, but generally ill-advised. One train came almost altogether loaded with coffins. The people of the North were especially urgent; it seemed as if they could not do enough. "We send," they said, "what we can; but you, who know what you need, must ask—'Ask, and ye shall receive.'" The Republic, to its remotest confines, was moved, as if by a divine impulse. The leading artists of the lyric, as well as the dramatic stage, were especially conspicuous in good gifts, in generous contributions. Personally, they gave freely, and, with the aid of their brothers and sisters less gifted, gave benefits that netted large amounts. No class surpassed them in the expression of a profound sympathy, or in the efforts they made to mitigate, as far as possible, the results of the dreadful visitation. The miner in the Nevada hills, the ranchero in far California, and the farmer in distant Oregon vied, in dispensing a charity equal to the growing exigencies of the time, with the people of the older States of the East, where organiza-

tions in every city and village were eagerly engaged in the good Samaritan work. This contagion of kindness passed beyond the limits of our own country, and France paused amidst the festivities of her International Exhibition to express her sympathies and send her share of succor. England, too, and Germany, were early in the field; and from India and Australia, as from South America, contributions poured in upon a people who have vainly tried to express their gratitude for it all. Hundreds of men and women volunteered as nurses, who were destined to a speedy death. They poured in from all the States. Those from the South Atlantic and Gulf coast cities were especially welcomed on account of their experience, and because they had had the fever, or were acclimated by long residence in cities or sections of the country that had been frequently visited by it. They were to a certain extent proof against it. Northern and Western men and women, on the contrary, had hardly begun work ere they fell victims to it. They went down so fast that the medical director of the Howard Association, Dr. Mitchell, felt called upon to admonish them as they arrived of their liability, and give them the option of returning to their homes. In but few instances they refused to go back. They came, and they would remain to nurse. So long as they could, they did so patiently and assiduously. A long line of graves in Elmwood Cemetery tells the story of their fidelity to a mission that was one purely of mercy and loving-kindness; to which they brought great powers of endurance, a much needed discretion, and the courage of the veteran of many wars; some of them a previous preparation in the best hospitals of the country. Moved to the work by a feeling the most profound that can stir the human heart, they began where their dead comrades left off, eventually, and in a few hours sometimes, to fall on the spot hallowed by their martyrdom. Like the advancing column of a forlorn hope, on which the fate of empires hang, they pressed forward in the face of a foe whose mysteries have never yet been fathomed. The sense of danger was dumb; the sense of duty was eloquent. If they had moments when the step faltered, the hand became unsteady and the heart wavered, it was never known but to themselves. Theirs was a work of love, to which they grew the more the demands of the unfortunate pressed upon them. They lived to save life, and died in an heroic effort to conquer death. They fought nobly against dreadful odds. Out of a population of not more than 20,000, they lost 5,150, 1 in 4 of the whole number, or 70 per cent. of the white people who remained in the city.*
By comparison with the statistics of other campaigns with this fever, these,

---

* The medical estimate puts the total population, during the epidemic, at 19,600, and the total sick at 17,600, the deaths, as stated, being 5,150, a little less than one-third. Members of the Howard Visiting Corps, who have resided in the city many years, and know it well, and whose business, during the epidemic, it was to visit every ward, every day, say that at no time was there more than 20,000 persons in the city, if so many; and that of these fully 14,000 were negroes, leaving only 6,000 white people. Of the 14,000 negroes, 946 died of the fever, and of the 6,000 whites 4,204 died, being 70 per cent. of the whole number. Not more than 200 white people escaped the fever, and most of these had been victims of it in previous epidemics.

though significant of the havoc it made, were not so discouraging as annihilation.* So long as all were not sick or dead there was some hope. Building on this hope, inspired by narrow escapes, they continued to the last, growing fewer in numbers every day, so that only a squad of a once division could answer to the roll-call on the day of discharge. The doctors fared no better than the nurses. Death revenged himself upon them. Less exposed to the poison than the nurses—who were confined for days to the same rooms as their patients—and with some advantage of exercise in the open air, riding or walking, it was hoped they would escape in numbers sufficient to justify the hazards they took. It did not prove so. Their proportion of sick and dead was quite equal to the general average.† The physician could not heal himself. Some of them, as some

---

* Nearly as bad as this, in proportion—worse when the greater number is considered—is the havoc of small-pox, fever, and dysentery (and some think the black plague) in Brazil. Of this a New York *Herald* correspondent writes that paper as follows: "The whole number of registered deaths in November for the two cemeteries of San Juan Baptista and Lagoa-funda was 11,075. Of these 9,270 were small-pox cases. But I think we must add to this at least one thousand buried, as I have said, in the woods, or sunk in the sea. At this time there were 30,000 sick—more than a third of the population. Still the death-rate increased. On December 10,808 small-pox dead were buried in the cemetery of Lagoa-funda, at least 75 in San Juan, and probably 150 in the woods and the sea—a total death record of over 1,000 in a single day—and this out of a population (now reduced) of only 75,000. The great plague at London reached this death-rate, but that was from a population of 300,000. After this the mortuary rate decreased, but only because the disease had nothing more to feed on. A certain per centage of a community are exempt from small-pox. A few, no doubt, were saved by vaccination. By the end of the year the death-rate had gone down to 200 per day. The entire number of deaths for the month was not far from 21,000. In all great epidemics, it is said, the people become indifferent to their danger. In Fortaleza this indifference was sufficiently astonishing. When I reached the place, on the 20th of December, the death rate was 400 per day; but business was going on much as usual, and hardly any body had been driven out of the city by the danger. . . I only know what has been—a province utterly ruined; a population of 900,000 reduced to 400,000, and those dying at an enormous rate. Probably there have been 300,000 deaths in the other drought-stricken provinces of which I have few notices. There is nothing in history that will compare with it. God grant that there never may be again!"

† The following is a complete list of the physicians who died:

Resident Physicians.
Avent, Dr. V. W.
Armstrong, Dr. A. J.
Beecher, Dr. P. D.
Clarke, Dr. S. R.
Dawson, Dr. S. R.
Dickerson, Dr. P. M.
Erskine, Dr. John H.
Hodges, Dr. W. R.
Hopson, Dr. H. R.
Ingalls, Dr.
Lowry, Dr. W. R.
Otey, Dr. Paul H.
Rogers, Dr. J. M.
Robbins, Dr. W. H.
Rogers, Dr. John C.
Watson, Dr. P. K.
Woodward, Dr. J. W.

Volunteer Physicians.
Bond, Dr. T. W., Brownsville, Tenn.
Bankson, Dr. J. S. Stevenson, Ala.
Bartholomew, Dr. O. D., Nashville, Tenn.
Burcham, Dr. R., Columbus, Ohio.
Chevis, Dr. L. A., Savannah, Ga.
Easley, Dr. E. T., Little Rock.
Force, Dr. F. H., Hot Springs, Ark.
Forbes, Dr. J. G., Round Rock, Texas.
Fort, R. B., Howard.
Gorrell, Dr. J. O. G., Ft. Wayne, Ind.
Harlan, Dr. L. B., Hot Springs, Ark.
Hicks, Dr, John B., Murfreesboro, Tenn.
Heady, Dr. Sherman, Texas.
Keating, Dr. M. T., New York.
Kim, Dr. N.
McKim, Dr. J. W., St. Louis.
McGregor, Dr. T. H., Tipton Co., Tenn.

nurses, proved unmanageable as patients. Even "with their eyes open" to the extreme dangers that resulted from fatigue, they rushed on to destruction. One of them, a volunteer from abroad, is recalled as a type of nearly all the rest. He was a man in middle life, small of stature, with a healthy mind and a healthy body, a trained thinker, and with some pretensions as a philosopher. His experience with yellow fever was as extensive as that of any of his brothers on duty. He had walked the wards of the charity hospital of New Orleans with the elder Stone, who, long before he died, had compassed and had lectured on all that is to-day known of yellow fever. He was proud of his profession, and practiced it skillfully, and with all the assurance of an adept. Broad and liberal in his views, he did not disdain the practice or experience of others in or out of the profession. He was anxious to save life, and counted his convalescents with an almost unspeakable joy. He visited every patient three times each day and carefully noted the changes from the first diagnosis. He went into the sick-room with an air that re-assured the sufferers, and gave hope and imparted courage to desponding friends. He was diligent and earnest, and drawing from a rich store of experiences in the old as in the new world, made for himself a place in the hearts of all who have survived him. He went deliberately to his death. So, too, did the priests of the Roman Catholic Church. The fever has always been to them singularly fatal. Only two escaped. This doctor was called to see one, the last of eleven—a man whose excessive nervous constitution forbade even the faintest hope of his recovery. He determined to save him. He did so at the cost of his own life. For 65 hours he remained by the bedside of this priest. When he emerged from the sick-room he was exhausted. His clothes stained with black vomit, his blood was poisoned beyond the power of any neutralizer. He was taken with the fever in a day or two, and after a few hours of "life in death," passed away, a "type of his Order." Another case, a type of the home physician, is recalled. He was a man of large mold. Physically he was perfect. Very tall, very stout, he was the picture of health. His handsome face was lighted by a perpetual smile. Good nature, good heart, and a cheerful soul were the convictions his manner carried to every beholder. He was a manly man. He had been a soldier, and he bore about him the evidences of gallant service. Nervous and eager, devoted and anxious, he went down to his grave the victim of overwork. He was an inspiration to his friends, an example of constancy, steadiness, unflinching courage, and unflagging zeal. To the sick-room he brought all these qualities, supplemented by an unusual experience, an inexhaustible stock of knowledge, and a sympathy as deep as the sad occasion. Tender as a woman, his heart ached at the recital of miseries he could not cure. Besides his duties as health officer, John Erskine was earnest in his attentions to patients, whose demands were incessant. For days before he succumbed, observant friends

Menes, Dr. T. W., Nashville.
Montgomery, Dr. R. B., Chattanooga.
Meade, Dr. W. C., Hopkinsville, Ky.
Nelson, Dr., St. Louis.
Nugent, Dr. P. C., St. Louis.
Pierce, Dr. Hiram M., Cincinnati.

Renner, Dr. J. G., Indianapolis.
Smith, Dr., druggist, Shreveport.
Tuerk, Dr. P., Cincinnati.
Tate, Dr. R. H., Cincinnati.
Williams, Dr. R. B., Woodburn, Ky.

felt that he must fall. He had tasked his powers far beyond endurance. His heart was, to the last, keenly sensitive to the sorrow about him. The mitigation of it was his anxiety. He chided himself because he could not do more for the people who loved him, and by whom he will ever be remembered; and, to the last, was questioning himself for a remedy for a disease that has so often conquered the ablest of a noble profession. No better man ever laid down his life in the cause of humanity. Old and young men vied with each other, and enthusiastically, not only in the infirmaries, in the hotels, and in houses of comfort and ease, but in the cabins of the negro, the absurd architecture and grotesque interiors of which were the comic settings of a deep and awful tragedy. Every call was obeyed, no matter when it came, or from whom. They made the most of time, and distributed their skill among as many as they could. While thus employed, every energy strained, they did not forget the cause of science. Observations were made and treasured, and nearly three hundred autopsies, at a greatly increased risk to health and life. They met every night to compare views and report results. These meetings were the light and life of each day. There they refreshed themselves in social intercourse, and gathered fresh hope for a struggle that seemed endless. Each day brought the same duties and similar experiences. Only one change was noticeable—the decrease of their numbers. And so it went on to the end.

I V.

The same earnestness and devotion characterized the priests, preachers, and nuns who committed themselves to good offices as ghostly counselors, and to all the tender solicitudes as nurses. As has already been said, the Roman Catholic priesthood suffered most severely.* Only two of the resident clergy escaped. One of these, Father Kelly, had survived an attack in 1873; the other, Luiselli, whose life was at one time despaired of, was preserved by the almost superhuman exertions of his physician. They were tireless in the administration of their sacred offices. They obeyed every call. These came every hour, accompanied by urgent appeals from the relatives of the dying, who stood appalled at the suddenness of dissolution. Absolution is, by all the members of the most ancient of the Christian sects, considered a prerequisite to an assurance of final happiness—hence the pleading demands upon the priests, who, in every instance, were found worthy of the sacred trust committed

---

* The following is a complete list of the Roman Catholic clergy who died: Rev. Martin Walsh, Pastor St. Bridget's Church, born in Ireland, 40 years of age; Rev. M. Meagher, Assistant Pastor, Tipperary County, Ireland; Rev. Father Asinus, Assistant Pastor, Germany, age unknown; Father Maternus, St. Mary's Church; Rev. J. R. McGarvey, a volunteer from Harrodsburg, Ky., aged 32; Rev. J. A. Bokel, from Baltimore, Md., aged 27; Rev. Van Troostenberg, from Kentucky, but originally from Belgium, aged 35; Rev. J. P. Scannell, a volunteer from Louisville, Ky., aged 27; the Very Rev. M. Riordan, Pastor, born in Ireland, aged 35; Father Marley.

to them. Every visit made by them was a step toward death—yet they went on. Every prayer for souls pluming for flight brought them nearer to the heavenly shores to which they sent confessing sinners. Overworked, their energies taxed beyond all that men under ordinary circumstances can endure, they fell easy victims to the disease, the poison of which they inhaled, in strongest infusion, with every act of shriving. In vain the best physicians were taxed for skillful treatment; in vain the best nurses watched every hour and every moment, every change. There was found no medicine in the whole range of the world's experience that could bring back health and life—they died as certainly as they were taken with the disease. So did the sisters of the Church, the nuns, who, as one, fell in the sacred work, were quick to volunteer, so that their saintly habit might not altogether pass away from the eyes of a world which had closed on so many forever. Their days and nights were devoted to the sick and dying. Their schools closed, there was nothing to distract them from what they loved as the most ennobling of duties. If they were to die (as they did, in numbers sufficient to give rise to the belief that they were specially marked by the destroyer), they would make their election sure. They were incessant in their visitations and attentions. They had no rest, no time for recuperation. Unlike the ordinary nurses, they never suspended to re-vitalize their wasted energies. What sleep they could get at brief intervals in the exercise of an occupation that more than ever required a sleepless vigilance, they considered a heaven-sent relief. This was not enough. Tired nature, wanting the sweet restorer, broke under the strain. They went down before the reaper like ripened grain. Theirs were not long to be beds of pain and anguish. A few hours of consuming fever, the pulse in the nineties, and the temperature as high as $106\frac{1}{2}°$, and death came mercifully to their release. Life ended, their tasks were done. But their mission was not completed. Other feet were already treading in the same path; other sweet and saintly lives were solemnly pledged to the same heroic sacrifice. The endless chain of events so sad as to shock the world beyond and summon from the remotest parts of the earth a benevolence that illumined the time with the blessed light of an abounding charity and hearty sympathy, still demanded that these brides of Christ should endure a long agony and literally bloody sweat before translation. They came and went willing sacrifices. No murmur escaped lips that had been sealed, save in prayer. Serenely, as to some feast, they went, bearing with them always the aroma of lives made precious by self-denial, and flooding the sick chamber with the glory of hearts wholly given to God.*

All members of the Christian Church are alike in their aspirations. They are inspired by the same hopes and restrained by the same fears. They pray, if not in the same language, in the same spirit. With or without ritual, with or without ceremony, they call upon the same name and build upon the same basis of faith.

---

* The following are the names of those who died: Alphonso, Mother, aged 34 years; Rose, Sister, aged 30 years; Josepha, Sister, aged 44 years; Bernardine, Sister Mary, aged 40 years; Dolora, Sister Mary, aged 24 years; Veronica, Sister Mary, aged 19 years; Wilhelmina, Sister, aged 30 years; Vincent, Sister, aged 22 years; Stanislaus, Sister, aged 21 years; Gertrude, Sister, aged 28 years; Winkelman, Sister, St. Louis.

To the sick, ministers or priests speak of heaven, urge repentance and preparation for death, and give absolution in the name of Him by whose commission they officiate, or repeat his assurances of pardon and eternal peace. Confronting the inevitable, doctrine and dogma almost wholly disappear. The terms of forgiveness and restoration to the Father's love are the same with all. What difference there is, to the sick does not appear. They have their thoughts fixed upon the end, and their vision is strained to see beyond. The Protestant pastors visit all who are distressed in mind, body, or estate, very much to the same purpose as their Roman Catholic brethren. They desire to lead souls to the solemn contemplation of death, and all that it involves, and smooth the way, so doubtful and so dark even to the best, with the assurance of Him who, in the agonies of dissolution, prayed to the Father, "If it be thy will, let this cup pass." Honest, earnest men, convinced of the truths they preach, they take with them on their mission of mercy not only hope for the dying, but compassion for the living, whom death most distresses. During the epidemic the demands upon them were in proportion to the "new cases" that every day developed. Men of family, they found themselves besieged at home, their hearts hedged round about with a profound anxiety for those whom nature asserted had first claims upon them. Sharing their faith, believing in their mission, their wives, no less courageous, sustained them and upheld their hands.*
But even thus fortified, they could not wholly dismiss the apprehensions of a situation horrible in the extreme. They, nevertheless, were true to their obligations. But few in number (a majority of their brethren having fled at the breaking out of the epidemic), they were in constant demand. A German, Rev. Mr. Thomas, was the first to die. He had been a diligent, faithful, earnest minister, a pastor to his people. Another of them, a Presbyterian, Rev. Dr. Daniels, fell early in the action, and did not regain his strength until the scourge had disappeared. Indeed, he has not regained it yet. Another, a Methodist, Rev. Dr. Slater, whose heart beat in unison with all who needed his counsel and advice, and who was universally beloved for an abounding charity and most amiable disposition, was borne to his grave after a few days' sickness, mourned by all in the city—still lamented by his people. Still another, a Baptist, Rev. Dr. Landrum, who differed widely from the preceding in, at least, what he considered one essential, after toilsome weeks, during which he officiated as a member of the Relief Committee, besides attending to pastoral calls, was arrested in his noble career, and, while in the throes of a sorrow beyond words to express—for the loss of sons whose promise was brighter than young men now often give—to the dismay of the then little band of heroes, was seized by the fever, and, with his wife—taken about the same time—made a

---

* The following are the names of those who died—men whose names are embalmed in the hearts of the people of Memphis as those of martyrs, as worthy of canonization as any on the long roll of mother church: Rev. Mr. Parsons, P. E. Church; Rev. Mr. Schuyler, P. E. Church; Rev. Mr. Thomas, German Reformed Church; Rev. Mr. Moody; Rev. A. F. Bailey (col.); Rev. E. C. Slater, Methodist; Rev. David R. S. Rosebrough, Methodist; Rev. P. T. Scruggs, Methodist; Rev. S. C. Arnold, wife and five children died; Rev. Victor Bath.

narrow escape. Yet another, a Presbyterian, Rev. Dr. Boggs, who was a worker with the Howards, and who had made the care of the orphans a special charge, and devoted himself to it in addition to his parish labors, fell when the force of the epidemic had expended itself, and, with his wife, too, survives, revered by men of every name. The Episcopal ministers were also severely tried. All who were residents when the fever broke out were attacked, and one died—Rev. C. C. Parsons. The circumstances of his life made his death felt as much, perhaps more than any that had preceded it. He had been an officer of great promise in the United States Army, and during the civil war had achieved distinction for discretion, skill, and bravery. After the war he continued in the service, for which he had been educated at the national military school, and rose to the rank of lieutenant colonel. His future was assured and held out to him a brilliant promise; but he voluntarily surrendered all to enter the ministry. Called to Memphis in 1875, he was not long in making for himself a place in the hearts of others than the people of his own faith. In manners he was gentle and unaffected. In his intercourse with his fellow-citizens these qualities, supported by his reputation as a brave soldier and his apparent culture, won upon them, so that his circle widened. His opportunities for good were thus unusual. The hopes formed of him were not disappointed. As a priest he was faithful, anxious, and earnest. When the epidemic was announced, he prepared for it as for a battle, and, as on a battle field soldiers love to fall, he fell at his post doing his duty. His place was taken by a brave young volunteer from the North, Rev. Mr. Schuyler, who entered gladly on his work, but who, in eight days after his arrival, was carried to his grave. Another volunteer, from Shreveport, Louisiana, Rev. Dr. Dalzell, who served as physician as well as priest, escaped, and fills to-day the place of the noble soldier-priest who died. Two of his brother clergy recovered—Rev. Dr. George White and Rev. Dr. George Harris—the former a venerable man, who has seen as many years in the ministry as most men live, survived his youngest son over whose remains he read the beautiful service which his church has appointed for the dead, he and his wife alone forming the funeral party. Few incidents, at a time when heart-breaking incidents abounded, so affected the public as this. It touched every heart and called out a sympathy of which the aged priest is the center to this day. The Sisters of St. Mary's (Episcopal), like those of the Roman Catholic Church, were active in works of mercy and benevolence. The mortality among them was sudden and severe,* an attestation of their devotion and of the malignity of the scourge they so heroically encountered. It would be impossible to speak in too high terms of laudation of these women. Educated and cultivated, they had dedicated themselves to a work much more agreeable and more in consonance with their tastes and their refinement and delicacy. They had made no provision for an emergency so dreadful, yet when it was announced they did not hesitate as to their duty. Some of their number were in the East, enjoying a brief vacation of repose

---

* Of seven who, from first to last, were engaged in the work, Sisters Constance, Thecla, Frances, and Ruth died.

upon the banks of the Hudson, the most beautiful of our rivers, when the fearful tidings of "yellow fever in Memphis" was flashed along the telegraph wires. They at once abandoned the comfort and ease of a delightful religious retreat, and, against the earnest entreaties of friends, made their way, as rapidly as steam could carry them, to the stricken city. They found work awaiting them. Their school building and convent was soon embraced in what, at the first of the epidemic, was known as the "infected district;" and several ministers as well as sisters were among the long list of the sick. In a few weeks many of them had gone over to the majority; and when the epidemic was declared at an end, it was found that they had suffered more and sustained heavier losses than any other of the relief organizations in the city, save the Roman Catholic priesthood and sisterhood. But they had won for their order an imperishable renown. They had proven that heroism and Christ-like self-denial are not the virtues of a particular sect. They had set an example worthy the sisterhood of apostolic times, and had silenced those of their creed whose Protestantism blinded them to the possibilities of an order whose vows are voluntary, and to be revoked at will. They had illumined the history of their sex, so rich in charity, by a religious zeal, softened and tempered by a sweet compassion; by unflinchingly encountering all that is terrible in one of the most loathsome of diseases; by braving death with the resignation of martyrs; by the outpouring of a sympathy as profound as the general sorrow, and by a pathos which could alone have its source in the faith of Him who has been painted for us—"A man of sorrows, acquainted with grief."*

---

* The Nashville *American*, in an article published while the epidemic was yet at its height, said of these devout and devoted women: "The Episcopal Church in Memphis has a large and flourishing school for girls and an orphanage, in charge of the Sisterhood of St. Mary. The bishop of the diocese (Rt. Rev. C. T. Quintard) began the work some eight years ago, and, in 1873, the ladies of the Sisterhood opened their school in the Episcopal residence, immediately after the epidemic of that year. Their faithful and devoted labors, during the yellow fever of 1873, had won them hosts of friends, and when the school was opened its patronage was abundant. When the epidemic of this summer began, the Sister Superior was absent, with Thecla, enjoying a much-needed rest, but at once returned on being informed that the fever had made its appearance in the city. Faithfully, constantly, unflinchingly, and with holy zeal, these faithful women administered to the sick and dying until they were themselves stricken down. Of six of the Sisters who were prostrated, four laid down their lives and wore the martyr's crown. Three additional Sisters from New York took up the work, but of the original Sisterhood only one remains. They have indeed *glorified* the cause for which they died. In a letter written the day before he himself was stricken by the fever, Rev. Charles Carroll Parsons wrote: 'The Sisters are doing a wonderful work. It is surprising to see how much these quiet, brave, unshrinking daughters of divine love can accomplish in efforts and results.' The following tribute has been forwarded to Bishop Quintard by the Bureau of Relief of Hartford, Connecticut:

"'IN MEMORIAM.

"'Having been brought into very pleasant relations with Sister Constance, Sister Superior of the Sisterhood of St. Mary, at Memphis, the ladies of the Bureau of Relief mourn her death. I desire to testify their deep sense of the loss which they and the whole church have sustained. Her noble labors among the poor and orphaned and in the schools, before the fatal pestilence of this summer broke out, are such as we

V.

The ministers and sisters of all the Christian sects were alike conspicuous for their zeal and fidelity. The absence of a few of the pastors, who fled at the outbreak of the fever, was all the more remarked upon. Indeed, no discordant incident of the epidemic gave rise to more general indignation or as bitter comment in the public press. They were denounced in unmeasured terms by the religious as well as irreligious. A few ill-conditioned zealots, taking advantage of this state of the public mind, made comparisons between the Protestant ministers and the Catholic priests, which the circumstances did not warrant, with a view to the injury of the Protestant churches. But this failed. It was admitted that there could not be a greater contrast; but while this was so, it was also true that most of the Protestant clergy walked in the footsteps of Him whose ministry was among those who were sick, who were heavy laden and needed rest; and that only the few had deserted their posts, and made no effort to repair the great wrong they inflicted upon themselves and the cause they were sworn to serve, above wife, children, and even life itself. It was claimed by those who most severely censured them, that, in dread of their lives, they had violated the most sacred pledges of their calling, and set an example of faithlessness which Christ himself has denounced. "If any man come to me," he says, "and hate not his father and mother, and wife and children, and brethren and sisters, yea, and his own life also, he can not be my disciple." It was also said that they forgot this assurance of the Master: "He that loveth his life shall lose it, and he that hateth his life in this world shall keep it unto life eternal." The broken-hearted

---

may well remember long with gratitude. But her heroic return to her post after the fever began to rage, in the face of such fearful danger, her unremitting toil for the sick, the dying, and the dead, amidst horrors which we, at this distance, can but faintly imagine, her care for the suffering and bereaved children, ministrations prolonged beyond her strength, even until stricken with unconsciousness, we feel are beyond the common words of praise. While we give thanks for the good example of our sister, for her beautiful life crowned by a martyr's death, we rejoice that her reward is on high, with the Divine Master, in whose footsteps she has so closely followed. To her—to Sisters Thecla, Frances, and Ruth, and to all who thus count not their lives dear unto them, while ministering to their suffering fellow-men in His name, we seem clearly to hear Him say: "Inasmuch as you have done it unto one of the least of these my brethren, ye have done it unto me."

"'*Resolved*, That we offer this loving tribute in memory of Sister Constance, to her late associates, to the mother superior of her order, to her pastor, Rev. Dr. Harris, and to Right Rev. Dr. Quintard, bishop of Tennessee, with our heartfelt sympathy and prayers.

MRS. F. D. HARRIMAN, *President.*
MRS. JOHN BROCKLESBY, *Vice-President.*
MRS. STEPHEN TERRY, *Corresponding Secretary.*
MRS. SARAH E. DAVIS, *Recording Secretary.*

"'HARTFORD, CONN., October 4, 1878.'"

A HISTORY OF THE YELLOW FEVER.

might be healed, but it would not be by their aid; they would preach the gospel, but not to the poor and afflicted. They would brave the condemnation they had so long hurled from the pulpit, and refuse to visit the sick. They would neither carry the cup of cold water, nor bear the bread of life to those who were stricken with the fever, and who called in vain for their ministrations. They could not even faintly imitate the compassion of Christ. They falsified their own teachings and inflicted an injury on the church that the work of their braver brethren could only in part repair.* The constancy and devotion of these strengthened the weak, imparted hope to the despondent, and inspired the despairing. They proved their faith by works, not a few of them sealing with their lives the faith which they thus so heroically illustrated. They knew that if there is ever a time when religion can bring peace and consolation, it is when panic, fear, and dread are aiding plague and pestilence in their work of wholesale destruction. They could not only minister to the sick, but they could be examples of that fearlessness and unselfishness which Jesus demanded of his disciples when he bade them take no thought of the morrow: to do their

---

* These attacks upon the ministers who sought safety in flight were not permitted to pass unnoticed. Many of their brave and heroic brethren, before they succumbed to the fever, or after they had recovered from attacks of it, made haste to defend what their own conduct and sufferings, to the popular mind, made more glaring and less excusable. They wrote long, and some of them able and manly vindications of a line of conduct they themselves could not, certainly did not, adopt, and by citations of Scripture, by arguments and precedents, sought to disabuse the people of what they deemed a prejudice. This they were not able to do. Whether just or unjust, the people everywhere regard it the duty of ministers, as well as priests, to visit the sick and carry consolation to the dying; that it is the most sacred part of their mission to prepare men and women for the passage through death to life, and that the greater the dangers and difficulties, the greater the triumphs for the church here, and for themselves hereafter. The laymen, who were in the midst of the fever, read these communications to the daily press with impatience, and insisted that such ministers as those were who remained, aids or helpers, should be the companions at least, of the Howard Visitor, or Citizens' Relief Committee. On the other hand, not a few agreed with Rev. C. K. Marshall, of Vicksburg, a gentleman whose religious zeal and broad humanitarian views were only equaled by his courage, earnestness, and efficiency in a life-long experience in yellow fever epidemics. He said—and the writer knows many influential and intelligent persons, both Catholic and Protestant, who agree with him—that, "were it not for the doctrine of extreme unction, deemed so essential by Catholics, the presence of clergymen and Sisters of Charity in sick-rooms, except as regular nurses, is the last thing I would permit were I a physician, *unless the patient, not his friends, were to express a desire for such ministrations.* I fully believe there are not a few lying asleep in the graveyard, whose end was hastened by the presence of clergymen and others, who, no matter of what denomination, have felt called upon to rush into sick-rooms to show their sympathy (?) and get the patient ready to die. Oh! will we never learn any thing higher and better than that? Everywhere this is the case. The ignorance of the dark ages still hangs in gloomy folds about us. Can five minutes' religious services over a poor fellow covered with blisters, choked with black vomit, and barely able to tell his nurse what he wants, probably not that, renovate a moral nature steeped in unbelief and sin for fifty years, blanch the blackness of a purely wicked life to snowy whiteness, and fit for angelic associates a man, who, if he were to recover, would laugh at the idea of wishing religious services at the time his death was deemed at hand?"

duty and leave the consequences with God. No incident of the epidemic is more to be regretted than the desertion of their charges by so many of the soldiers of the cross, mustered into an army pledged to special service in times of distress. It was not, it was said, so bad, but it was held to be akin to the desertion of wives and children by husbands and fathers, in whom fear, dread, panic, and personal safety dominated over love and duty, killing all sense of the sacred obligations which even the brutal savages sometime fulfill; and it was all the more remarkable, and, in view of the cause of religion, all the more to be deplored, that even outcast women, and men not so good in life or living, were jeopardizing their lives, and that some of them died in the performance of those offices which, it is held, are a part of the duty of the pastors and masters of the Christian Church.

Devotion in life, and heroism even to death, were not alone the products of religious life, though to Christianity must be given the credit of the humanity and charity of the age. The societies (of which the city has a large number) were conspicuous through their relief organizations; and the several nationalities made provision for their fellow-countrymen. The Free Masons,* the Odd-Fellows, the Knights of Pythias, Knights of Honor, the Hebrew Hospital Association, the Typographical, the Telegraphers, and many others, were remarkable for an active benevolence, a sleepless vigilance, and an intelligently directed energy worthy of all praise.† The members of the Hebrew Hospital Association were especially notable for ardor, for steadiness, for single-heartedness, and for unstinted charity. They were no respecter of persons. They went from house to house, asking but one question, "Is aid needed?" They made no distinction. The lessons of humanity which they had learned in the synagogue they illustrated by a heroism in nothing less than that which inspired their Christian fellow-workers. The printers‡ and telegraphers were also conspicuous for good works. The nature of their employment exposed them more than any other class, save the doctors and nurses, to the fever poison, which

---

*This body, which, like the Odd-Fellows, rests its claims to consideration upon love and charity, was conspicuous for good works through its members, one of whom, Ex-Past Grand Master Andrew J. Wheeler, was a noble example of what a Mason should be under circumstances so extraordinary. He had passed through the preceding epidemics unscathed, and would not be persuaded to abandon what he deemed his post of duty. He worked faithfully and energetically, notwithstanding he seemed to have a premonition of death. Masonry was his creed, and, according to the testimony of his brethren, he lived up to it as faithfully as man could. At a lodge of sorrow, held at Nashville, in January, 1879, and which was attended by the most distinguished Masons of the State, he was eulogized as a man of mark in an Order more illustrious than any other in the world, and as one whose memory should be embalmed for all time as that of a Mason worthy and well qualified for the higher honors of the heavenly Grand Lodge.

† The results of the labors of all these benevolent organizations will be found in the Appendix, at the close of this volume.

‡ The names of the printers who died will be found in the Appendix. The names of telegraphers who died are as follows: M. J. Keyer, Henry Mynatt, H. M. Goewey, E. W. Gibson, C. R. Langford, J. I. Connelly, Thomas Hood, J. W. McDonald, Howard Allen, J. R. Henrick, A. S. Hawkins.

at night, when they were at work, is thought to be most deadly. They fell very fast, and died so quick as to seem doomed to annihilation. Only one of all those employed by the telegraph company escaped, and of the proprietors, editors, compositors, and pressmen of the daily press, only one escaped of the *Ledger*, four of the *Avalanche*, and two of the *Appeal*. Their numbers thus so rapidly decreased, these heroic men continued not only to fulfill the duties expected of them by a public impatient for every fact and incident of the epidemic, but nursed their sick and buried their dead. Though often wearied to exhaustion, ready to fall for want of strength, they continued to send messages and print papers, and to succor those who had claims upon them. Their fidelity, courage, and humanity could not be surpassed; and their love and devotion for one another was as tender and solicitous as that of a mother for her child. They exhibited, from first to last, the noblest traits, and commanded the respect and admiration of the world. Something is also to be said for the bankers, who were necessary as the channels through which the money of the charitable and sympathizing people of the world reached those it was intended for. The cashiers of the four principal banks were attacked by the fever, but all fortunately recovered. The paying tellers of two, and the principal book-keeper of one, succumbed, and were numbered with the dead. These casualties only nerved the few whom panic and the fever had left to continue to deserve the commendation and confidence of the public. The Southern Express Company and all of the railroad companies were conspicuous for good deeds. Subjected to severe losses by the total suspension of business, they made ample provision for their employés, and continued their operations as common carriers, regardless of expenses, running trains, and bearing to the doomed city, free, the contributions of coffins, food, and clothing, sent from cities often thousands of miles away. They kept up their full estate of employés, and, with a generosity unparalleled, surrendered their machinery and all that they had to the public service. The Southern Express Company was especially conspicuous in this regard, and, of course, lost heavily. Its superintendent* and many of his subordinates sickened and died, and yet its work was continued as if it was merely part of the general machinery by which the city was governed and the sick and needy were provided for. There was no nobler exhibit of unselfishness than this of a corpora-

---

* Major W. A. Willis, superintendent of the Southern Express Company, was conspicuous as a member of the Citizens' Relief Committee. He was a noble example of true manhood. A man of fine address, of unsurpassed business qualifications, honest, earnest, and brave, he enjoyed the confidence of the public, and was looked to as a man for any emergency. At the most critical period of the epidemic he was entrusted by Gen. Wright with an important duty, which he entered upon with enthusiasm, performing it in such a manner as to confirm the prevalent opinion that he was a soldier in the best sense of the term. He died of the fever on Sunday, the 15th of September, and it is not saying too much, was mourned for by every man in the city. His services in behalf of the sick and needy can never be forgotten. Discreet in council, he was invaluable in the administration of the affairs of the committee which, organized to dispense food and clothing to the needy, gradually, as necessity compelled, absorbed all the functions of municipal government, and became the prop and stay of society.

tion that might have closed its doors without even a suspicion of seeming neglect. It might have done as the merchants did, and for the same reason; indeed it was urged to do so; but its officers chose to shoulder their share of the burden, let the result be what it might. The fatality which awaited them was appalling, yet their record was never dimmed—it was luminous to the last. They were worthy of the community, whose deplorable condition and intensified sufferings were the theme of every household in Christendom, exacting the tears of sinners and saints alike. The steamboat companies were also very generous; and the Western Union Telegraph Company placed no limit upon the gratuitous work it did—a work, the value of which is beyond any possible computation It surrendered its lines in the cause of humanity. The post-office was also administered by heroes. It was kept open every day, and the mails were regularly delivered, though at a very great cost of life. But it was not quick enough, and, owing to the detention of some mails, was not reliable enough. The telegraph became, therefore, more than ever, a necessity. It performed a service the postal department, worked ever so faithfully, could not. It linked Memphis with the great centers of political, financial, commercial, and literary activity, so that the momentary shocks of pain and anguish were felt simultaneously everywhere, even to the furthest parts of the continent, and appeals for help were heard almost as quick as uttered. Without the telegraph, the suffering must have been more severe than it was. There was nothing to intervene between it and the most rapid and satisfactory service. Those who were far removed from the epidemic could not object to its messages, as they did to the letters by mail, that they were tainted with yellow fever poison. They might have objected that, like the post-master* and his employés, the telegraphers were dying too fast, and that even so valuable a service was too dearly bought. But they did not. Dominating all other thoughts there was that one of interest in the thousands who were victims of the plague, and for whom these gallant men laid down their lives. "Duty" was thus exempli-

---

* Mr. R. A. Thompson, post-master, was also one of the editors and proprietors of the *Avalanche*. To these two positions he gave the closest attention, an attention that was redoubled as the epidemic increased in violence and his assistants died, as they did very rapidly. When taken with the disease he was promptly attended to. The city editor of the *Avalanche*, Mr. Herbert Landrum, took him to his home, and there he received all the nursing care that the best intelligence and the most friendly interest could inspire. He went through the crisis of the disease without much trouble, and was declared convalescing very nicely. But the second or third morning after he reached this stage, and contrary to the advice of Dr. Mitchell, who was attending him, he changed his pillow from the head to the foot of his bed, and changed his position correspondingly, in order to see better. Thus, as he thought, comfortably fixed, he indulged himself in a look through the morning papers, and perhaps some letters, partaking at the same time of some tea and toast. Little as this seems, it cost him his life. In sixteen hours after he was thus found by his doctor, he died, and in a few days was followed by his devoted friend young Landrum. Col. Knowlton, who succeeded him in the management of the post-office, also followed him very soon, as did Mr. Catron, the associated press agent, who assisted Landrum in performing the last sad offices of encoffining his remains and putting them away forever.

fied to be, as General Lee declared it, the best word in our language. The railroad companies, later on, when the fever had taken nearly every white person in the city—when there was no longer any food for it, and its decline was so perceptible as to encourage the beneficent organizations in the belief that they could turn their attention to the suffering communities near by— crowned all their previous liberality by placing daily hospital trains at the disposal of the Howard Association and Citizens' Relief Committee, on which were carried nurses, doctors, medical supplies, and food to places but lately invaded by the decimating disease. The dreadful visitation had thus its bright side. Humanity and benevolence enlisted the active coöperation of all sorts and conditions of men, and of corporations that, though suffering severe losses at that season of the year when they should have been making up for the dullness and deficiency of summer, spared no expense, counted no cost where a life could be saved and the charity of the world was to be dispensed to a sick and dependent people. Heroism was the rule in all the walks of life, neglect and desertion the exception. Forbearance, fidelity, and fortitude were qualities that were illustrated every day, and by persons widely separated by birth, education, habits, condition, and experience. This was most apparent in the beneficent organization known as the Citizens' Relief Committee, which, with the Howard Association, was looked to by all classes, not only for help and sustenance, but for protection. An organization better calculated for the purposes which called it into existence could not have been devised, nor could one have been more faithfully managed. It is not too much to say that but for its officers anarchy, confusion, robbery, arson, and murder would have prevailed to increase the burdens of a period, every hour of which was freighted with special horrors, and that perhaps the city would have been destroyed.* A clamorous and hungry mob, which did not hesitate to threaten, and support its threats, with a manifestation of disposition as cruel as its words, were prevented from carrying these threats into execution by the prompt and determined orders of the Citizens' Relief Committee, for

---

* Of this organization, but a few members survived the epidemic—these were Messrs. Luke E. Wright, Jas. S. Prestidge, C. F. Conn, W. W. Thatcher, D. F. Goodyear (acting Mayor), J. M. Keating, and D. T. Porter. Charles G. Fisher, so long the President of it, died of the fever. One of the first among the merchants of the city, he would not yield to the importunities of his relatives or friends. He helped to organize the association, and he would not desert his self-selected post. He was a tireless worker. Not content with the performance of the duties devolving upon him as president, he made a hospital of his residence, and there, while giving to the sick the hours he should have devoted to sleep and rest, he contracted the fever and died, after but a few days sickness. No more generous, warm-hearted man ever lived than Charles G. Fisher—no man, of all those who illustrated the best qualities of our race by self-sacrificing devotion to the cause of humanity, stood higher than he with his fellow-soldiers. Calm amid despair, self-contained and self-poised, he was prepared for any emergency, and when the summons came, met it with the resignation of a Christian. Beloved by his fellow-citizens, his death was a staggering blow to the few who survived him, and who had learned to know how strong, how reliable, how earnest, how truthful, honest, and good he was.

the suppression of a lawlessness, the dread of which, for a time, weighted the energies of all who were administering public affairs. With the police and fire departments reduced to a mere handful, it would not have been difficult for those so inclined to have pushed on to the consummation of the vilest purposes. With four or five thousand vacant houses, abandoned by their inmates, or by the death of the servants left to take care of them, hundreds of them filled with valuable family treasures, enough to excite the cupidity of the criminals who swarmed the unguarded streets, on which, sometimes, not a living thing was to be met with by night or day, it required more than the earnestness and determination of ordinary times to prevent the excesses so much dreaded by thinking men as the worst of the results of the epidemic. It was estimated, at one time, that not less than two hundred tramps and thieves invaded the stricken city, coming from no one could tell where, ultimately going no one could tell whither. They stole the badges of the nurses, and, representing themselves as Howard employés, gained entrance to homes where the fever had paralzyed all it had not killed. It was the operations of these vagabonds, under such circumstances, that first excited inquiry, and finally their expulsion. In a few days, owing to the measures for protection set on foot by the Citizens' Relief Committee, they disappeared, and with them went all fears for the safety of life or property. The police were instructed to arrest all persons, after nine o'clock at night, who could not give a satisfactory account of themselves—all who were not employed as nurses or doctors, or who were not employed by the telegraph company, or in the several newspaper offices. Two negro military companies were encamped opposite court-square; a train was held in readiness to bring in the Bluff City Grays,* then doing duty at Camp Joe Williams; and the Chickasaw Guards were recalled to Grand Junction, where they remained until the possible necessity for their aid had passed away. A company of one hundred and five citizens, at Raleigh, in the vicinity of the city, volunteered for service, and a like company in the southern part of the county, near the Mississippi line. An illustration of the apprehension then existing, furnished by the experience of Captain Mathes, editor of the *Ledger*, will satisfy skeptics, if any there be, that the information on which these preparations were based was not groundless. This gentleman had had the fever—a violent, and, for a time, it was feared, fatal attack of it—and was convalescing slowly; he had been, additionally, cursed by several sets of nurses, whose depth of depravity was only in part expressed by the robbery of his stable, his wife's wardrobe as well as his own, and the "cleaning out" of his well-stocked larder. Anxiety for him, as well as the condition in which she found herself—exposed to the vilest associations in the sick-room—prostrated his wife, and made her an easy prey for the fever, which she bravely fought, however, until her husband was out of danger. So soon

---

* This company, under the command of Captain John Cameron, who was also a valuable aid of the Relief Committee, lost the following-named members by the fever: Harvey, lieutenant; Ferguson, corporal; Wheatley, corporal; Goodwin, private; Haynes, W. D., private; Everett, private; Spiegel, private.

A HISTORY OF THE YELLOW FEVER. 131

as prudence would permit, he was on his feet—(this ought to be foot, since he left one of his legs on the field of Chickamauga). His presence at her bedside greatly aided in her recovery. Cheered and comforted by the knowledge that he was safe, she summoned all her strength and overcame the fever. She approached convalescence, but the indiscretion of a most attentive, kind, and gentle nurse, who had succeeded the vagabonds who had fled or been driven forth, induced a relapse, and in a few hours, in the house where joy prevailed, mourning had almost succeeded. The survivor of a dreadful civil war, and two previous epidemics, the husband nerved himself for the end, in all such cases deemed inevitable. While waiting for the call that was to announce to him the death of her who had proven herself worthy to be called wife—to whom he owed his own life—the nurse broke into his room, affrighted and nerveless, almost breathless; and in a suppressed tone of voice, called "Fire!" His thoughts were at once busy for his dying wife's safety. In a moment his mind pictured for her a fate that made him shudder. He thought, to use his own words, "that perhaps the thieves, by whom he had suffered so much, had begun their threatened work of wholesale crime." He hastened to his wife's room. She was sleeping tranquilly, her face indicating the blessed change from death to life. Noiselessly he pulled down the blinds of the windows, so as to exclude the glare of the light from the fire, which he then knew was near by—near enough even to endanger his home—and he turned on the gas, lighting all of the burners of the chandelier. If she should awake, the light of the room would hide that of the fire without, which, in spite of all he could do, found its way in. Leaving his wife to the nurse, with injunctions to keep from her what was passing beyond, he went out to find his garden filled with burning shingles, the air thick with smoke and sparks. To prevent the ignition of his own premises, he was kept busy for hours, and not until the fire died out, and the danger had passed away, did he think of his condition and a possible relapse. But he, as well as his wife, passed even that dreadful crisis. How great was his relief to learn from the papers of the next day that the fire, which had such terrors for him, was the only mishap of the kind in the previous twenty-four hours, and that the Citizens' Relief Committee had amply provided for a contingency, even the thought of which had blanched his cheek, and made him afraid indeed! To pass safely such a test is an ordeal that seldom occurs in the life of the most adventurous; but it was only one of many that followed in the train of the pestilence. Information of the military preparations, and the shooting of a ruffianly negro, who attempted to intimidate a colored soldier on guard at the commissary department, had the most happy effect. It proved to those who contemplated crime that, though few in numbers, the men who were managing affairs could not be trifled with, and that, at any hazard to themselves, they would enforce law and order. Ex-Attorney-General Luke E. Wright, who was an active and zealous member of the committee, and who was in the commissary building when the shot was fired, went quickly to the front, and in a tone of voice, distinctly heard above the wails of the terrified negro woman, thanked the sentry for his devotion to duty, complimented his company for its firmness, and assured all present that the shot, which was so well aimed, was merely the prelude to what would certainly follow if any attempt was made to violate the public peace, or interfere with the business of, or steal the goods entrusted to, the Relief Committee by the people of all the States. It was a perilous moment. The tide seemed for some days to have been with the evil-disposed. The quickly delivered shot of the negro guard, and the brave speech of General Wright turned it, and thereafter there was no trouble. The white man who incited the negro desperado, so summarily made an example of, was, it is said, soon after "lost." He has never been heard of since. Thus warned, the hitherto impudent thieves made their way from a city where they felt themselves besieged, and where they began to realize punishment swift and sure would be meted out to all of their number arrested for crime. Many citizens, and the press generally, hinted the necessity for a gallows. It was also suggested, by one of the papers, that, since there were no courts, the most summary process would be in order, as a certain means of insuring public safety. There was no time to dally with criminals, and but little disposition to bear with what was wholly inexcusable. No one suffered for food or clothing. Both were in abundant supply, and both were as regularly given as asked for, through the persons employed to see that there was no favoritism indulged in. A commissary department was organized, which took charge of all supplies that did not belong to the Howard Association. This department was admirably conducted. Order and precision characterized its management, notwithstanding the clerks died so fast, that for a time those who succeeded to their labors were compelled to work at night as well as by day. Rations were issued on requisitions supplied to the needy by ward committees. These requisitions were filed as vouchers, so that every pound and ounce of food, or bushel of fuel, or suit or part of a suit of clothes was accounted for.* Of course there were complaints. Out of these grew misrepresentations that were gross libels upon a committee whose usefulness and influence was thankfully and gratefully acknowledged by every class of the citizens of the ill-fated city. Human nature is weak, and every one is liable to err. But the administration of the Citizens' Relief Committee's affairs challenged the admiration of all who know what it is in ordinary times, when there is no epidemic to disorder the public mind, to minister to the poor. At one time, of all who at first gladly enrolled themselves members of it, only three remained, and of these one had recovered from a severe attack of fever. Its officers were constantly on duty. As they became known they were appealed to in the streets; but they unflinchingly adhered to the rules they had laid down for their own, and the guidance of those they employed. They had regular hours, during which they were to be found in their places. Between these hours—from nine A. M. to three P. M.—they indorsed all requisitions that came to them properly authenticated by the ward committees. By this system the bounty of the North, of the

---

* In the appendix part of the report of the Citizens' Relief Committee, there will be found a tabulated statement by the commissary, Captain J. C. Maccabe, in which every ration (its kind and weight) are given as they were taken from the books, which were kept with as unerring precision as those of any mercantile house in the country.

A HISTORY OF THE YELLOW FEVER. 133

South, and of Europe, found its way to the really needy, as was intended by the donors. There was no extravagance, no waste, no unnecessary delay; nothing that could be avoided, nothing that would needlessly intervene between those who needed the charity and those who gave it. Without money or price, these gentlemen, braving the epidemic, labored in the public behalf. They had no reward to expect other than that which is the recompense of every good action—the satisfaction of its performance. No honors awaited them. No government stood ready to decorate them as heroes. An approving conscience and the indorsement of those who knew what they were doing, how faithfully and honorably they did it, and with what largeness of sympathy for those to whom they were almoners they accompanied it—that was all. They preserved order and saved property from the touch of the thief and the house-breaker and the torch of the incendiary. They prevented, by a timely precaution, by an exhibit of determination, by an array of troops, the destruction, perhaps, of the city, and so saved the lives of thousands who, in the excitement of riot, would have perished on the streets, perhaps in the flames of their burning dwellings. It is no exaggeration to say that, had it not been for the firmness of this committee, chaos would have ensued upon the panic of August, and the most frightful excesses would have resulted. They enforced order and obedience to law, and reassured all who were engaged with the sick and the dead, that they could labor in peace, in absolute security, with none to make them afraid. With such an auxiliary, under the protection of such strength and firmness, the Howard Association felt free to prosecute its beneficent work without the dread, greater than that of death, which springs out of the existence of lawlessness, license, and disorder; could peacefully pursue its work and continue to stem the torrent of death and desolation. It could rely with certainty upon the will and resources of the Relief Committee, and rest secure that its beneficent and sacred task would not be interrupted or interfered with.

VI.

The Howard Association of Memphis, like its prototype of New Orleans, grew out of the necessities incident to an epidemic of yellow fever, which found the people of the city unprepared to cope with it. The first visitation of this disease, which occurred in 1855,[*] although it made a very profound impression upon the people of Memphis, was not of so serious a character as to call for or compel any thing like associated effort in behalf of those exposed to it. Memphis was then a small town of not more than twelve thousand five hundred inhabitants, and of these nearly all were personally known to each other, and were in the daily habit of those neighborly offices which distinguish the conduct of intimates and acquaintances. They, therefore, shared the bur-

---

[*] It is said to have prevailed epidemically in 1828 at Fort Pickering, now a suburb of Memphis.

dens of a calamity that claimed between sixty and seventy-five victims and brought, perhaps, two hundred and fifty persons under treatment. Besides, there was not then the dread of the fever which has since prevailed. Up to that time, and for as many years as the place had any existence, passengers from New Orleans were allowed to land without question at all seasons of the year, and persons who had contracted the fever in New Orleans, and in whom it only developed on their way up the river *en route* to their homes, were allowed to be landed and taken in vehicles through the streets to the hospital, or to private houses for treatment. The notion that prevailed throughout the country, and that still has hold on many otherwise well-informed persons, that there is a yellow fever zone, beyond the limits of which the dreaded disease can not flourish, had a great deal to do in the encouragement of a hardihood which, during 1878, cost Holly Springs and other places every life that was lost by yellow fever. The atmosphere and unclean conditions under which the disease is propagated did not exist, or the poison was not imported when they did exist until 1855, consequently, it was braved with reckless indifference, the almost yearly immunity strengthening the assumption of the zone theory and blinding the people to the possibilities of the plague that had swept New Orleans just two years before (in 1853) like a besom of destruction, costing her the lives of seven thousand nine hundred and seventy persons, and in the year following (1854), two thousand four hundred and twenty-three lives, and in that year (1855), two thousand six hundred and seventy lives. Intervening between the first and second visitations of yellow fever to Memphis came the civil war and the subsequent political trials, during which the impressions left by the epidemic of 1855 had passed from the minds of a population that had more than doubled, and whose very traditions had been swept away by the great tide of revolution. The problem of social and political life exclusively monopolized attention and consideration. The rehabilitation of homes and hearths, well nigh ruined, was of more importance to them than any other, or all the rest of the issues of life. Every thing was forgotten in the struggle for existence, aggravated, as it was, by the merciless attitude of the Northern States, the cunningly-devised agitation of political leaders, and by the shadow of the first of a series of commercial disasters by which Memphis suffered in common with all the other cities of the Union. Thus, sitting amid the ruins of the past, overwhelmed by the memories of a war, on the results of which all had been staked, by the gloom engendered by defeat, and by the foreshadowing clouds of a future, that proved worse than the most forlorn croakers could conjure, with an almost criminal neglect of the simplest sanitary laws, Memphis was for the second time, in September, 1867, visited by a plague, the origin of which is still a question, the progress of which is still in doubt, the best method of curing which is still debated, the sad results of which are alone apparent. It made its appearance late in the season, yet it lasted more than seventy days, the first two deaths occurring in the week ending September 29th, and the last three in the week ending December 1st. More than two hundred and fifty people died, and there was, perhaps, a total of fifteen hundred sick. The necessities of this dread emer-

A HISTORY OF THE YELLOW FEVER. 135

gency, unlooked for and unexpected, suggested the organization of the Howard Association, which took place on the twenty-ninth of September, 1867. A call which appeared in the city press was promptly responded to by the following named gentlemen : R. W. Ainslie, William Everett, H. Lonargan, John Heart, C. T. Geoghegan, J. K. Pritchard, A. D. Langstaff, J. B. Wasson, J. P. Gallagher, Jack Horn, E. J. Mansford, John Park, Rev. R. A. Simpson, Dr. P. P. Fraime, J. P. Robertson, T. C. McDonald, J. T. Collins, E. M. Levy, W. A. Strozzi, E. J. Corson, Dr. A. Sterling, A. A. Hyde, G. C. Wersch, W. S. Hamilton, A. H. Gresham, Fred Gutherz, W. J. B. Lonsdale, and J. G. Lonsdale, Sr. These, fully understanding and appreciating the work of the immortal philanthropist, John Howard, resolved to follow his example and devote themselves under his name to the succor of the sick, the relief of the suffering, and the burial of the dead.* After the officers were elected, on the 30th, announcement was made through the press that the Howard Association of Memphis was prepared to provide medical attendance, nurses, and medicines for the indigent sick. Physicians and ministers of religion were requested to coöperate and report all the fever cases coming to their attention which needed the help of the Association, which soon found its hands full. All the members were shortly employed, and before the end of the second week it became necessary to call for aid and assistance. This call was promptly responded to by the citizens of Memphis and the surrounding towns, so that the Association was at once enabled to employ skilled nurses, among them several from New Orleans. Great good was accomplished. The total amount of money subscribed was $4,996.56, all but $130 of which was expended, and the number of patients taken charge of and relieved was 244. The labors of the epidemic were not without sad and sorrowful results to the Association. Of the twenty-five who composed its membership, two died—laid down their lives that others might live. The beneficent experiences of 1867, and the high favor in which they were held by the public, determined the members to perpetuate the Association. They, therefore, applied to the legislature for, and obtained, a charter,† which gave

---

* R. W. Ainslie was elected President, John Heart, 1st Vice-President, C. T. Geoghegan, 2nd Vice-President, William Everett, Recording Secretary, H. Lonargan, Corresponding Secretary, and J. K. Pritchard, Treasurer.

† SECTION 1. Be it enacted by the General Assembly of the State of Tennessee, That John Park, R. A. Simpson, J. G. Lonsdale, Sr., John Heart, E. T. Geoghegan, R. W. Ainslie, J. P. Gallagher, T. E. McDonald, A. A. Hyde, and J. P. Robertson and their associates be, and they are hereby declared, a body politic and corporate, with ninety-nine years succession, by the name of the HOWARD ASSOCIATION OF MEMPHIS, whose object shall be to provide nurses and necessaries for those who may be taken sick, who are without means and without funds, and particularly during the prevalence of epidemics. Said Association, by this name, may contract and be contracted with, may sue and be sued in all courts, as other chartered corporations, in all matters whatsoever, and have full power to acquire, hold, possess, and enjoy, by gift, grant, or otherwise, and the same to sell and convey any or all such real, personal, or mixed estate, and invest and re-invest the same from time to time, as may be necessary for the benefit, support, and purposes of said HOWARD ASSOCIATION OF MEMPHIS, or which may be conveyed to the same for the security or payment of any debt or debts which may become due and owing to said Association, and may make, have, and use a common seal, and the same break, alter, or renew at pleasure; *Provided,* That the property, funds, and revenue of said HOWARD ASSOCIATION OF MEMPHIS shall not be used for any other than the purposes of said Association, and that all of said real, personal, or mixed estate shall be exempt from State, county, and corporation taxes and assessments, as the sole object of the Association is relief of the destitute.

SEC. 2. *Be it further enacted,* That the real and personal estate, property, and funds and revenues of said Association, and the administration of its affairs, shall be under the exclusive direction and control of the active members of said HOWARD ASSOCIATION OF MEMPHIS. That

it a status worthy of its name and the purposes had in view, and strengthened it in the respect and confidence of the public abroad, as well as at home. Thus constituted a body corporate, with powers adequate to any emergency of epidemics and the scope of their work, the Association was reorganized, with a greatly enlarged and influential membership. But the "changes and chances" of life in four years reduced their numbers. Some had removed from the city; others had died, so that, on the 14th of September, 1873, when the roll was called, in obedience to a summons to work, only eight responded: Messrs. J. G. Lonsdale, Sr., Dr. P. P. Fraime, A. D. Langstaff, W. J. B. Lonsdale, J. P. Robertson, E. J. Mansford, A. G. Raymond, and Fred'k Gutherz. On the 14th of September, two days after the Board of Health declared yellow fever epidemic, these gentlemen met and organized for a campaign, the dread results of which no one of them could then foresee. They found just $130 in the treasury, all that remained of the fund subscribed in 1867. They, therefore, made an appeal to their fellow-citizens of the other cities and States through a mass-meeting, held on the 16th of the same month, and the result was the almost immediate supply of a sum sufficient to enable them to begin work. A call was then made for recruits. This, too, was promptly responded to, and they were enabled to reorganize on as efficient a basis as the necessities of the occasion demanded. The new members, who thus swelled the list of the Association to something like the proportions necessary to grapple with the disease and prove successful almoners of a nation's bounty, were: J. J. Murphy, B. P. Anderson, J. G. Simpson, W. J. Smith, W. P. Wilson, G. W. Gordon, J. H. Smith, E. B. Foster, A. E. Frankland, W. S. Rogers, W. A. Holt, F. F. Bowen, J. F. Porter, R. T. Halstead, T. R. Waring, S. W. Rhode, W. J. Lemon, W. G. Barth, L. Seibeck, J. E. Lanphier, J. H. Edmondson, John Johnson (Attorney), J. W. Cooper, F. A. Tyler, Jr., C. A. Leffingwell, F. G. Connell, P. W. Semmes, D. E. Brettenum, and D. B. Graham. Strengthened by this company, many of whom, like Anderson and Smith, survived to win imperishable renown by their devotion and skill in 1878, the Association nobly and honorably illustrated what self-sacrificing philanthropy is through many weeks, during which they were subjected to weariness of soul, as well as body; to the anguish of heart inseparable from an overwhelming calamity, to mitigate which it seemed sometimes as if they

the parties named in the first section of this Act, or any five of them, may call the subscribers of said Association together, after having given five days' notice in some daily paper published in the city of Memphis, and proceed to organize the same, by electing a President, two Vice Presidents, Treasurer, Secretary, and six Directors, who shall constitute an Executive Committee, five of whom shall be a quorum, who shall conduct the affairs of the Association, and who shall continue in office until a new election is made. The regular election for officers shall be made on the first Monday in April, 1868, of which due notice shall be given in a daily paper published in Memphis. The members of said HOWARD ASSOCIATION OF MEMPHIS shall make such by-laws and regulations for the admission of members and the government of the Association as they may deem necessary; *Provided*, That no by-laws, rules, or regulations shall, in any wise, be contrary to the Constitution and laws of the State of Tennessee or the United States.

SEC. 3. *Be it further enacted*, That all the effects, real, personal and mixed, of every description, belonging to the said HOWARD ASSOCIATION, that may be remaining on hand at the expiration of this charter, shall be turned over to the Board of Mayor and Aldermen of the city of Memphis, or to whomsoever may be the representatives of the people of said city at that time, for the benefit of the poor and destitute people thereof.

SEC 10. *Be it further enacted*, That the foregoing Act shall take effect from and after its passage.
F. S. RICHARDS,
Speaker of the House of Representatives.
D. W. C. SENTER,
Speaker of Senate.

Passed January 23, 1869.

A HISTORY OF THE YELLOW FEVER.

worked in vain, and as if their heaven-appointed labors would prove barren of results. For more than two months they confronted death and bore witness, in their self-denial and devotion, that heroism did not die with the age of chivalry, that it still lives, purer and loftier, just as our age and time is purer and better than any that have preceded it. Many of them had had, on other occasions, some experience of the heart-rending scenes and sufferings that make up the horrors of an epidemic. Besides the eight old members that held together since 1867, who were the nucleus of the reorganization of an association, whose work is a monument of human love, some of the new had also encountered the fever elsewhere, and two of the eldest of them not only nursed in 1867, but also in 1855, when, as has been previously remarked, there was no organization, and the people had not learned how dreadful a scourge yellow fever is under conditions favoring its propagation and spread. These two members—one of them Major F. F. Bowen, advanced in years and well-spent in life, and the other, General W. J. Smith, a soldier of two wars—have survived attacks of the disease, passed through the last epidemic, and survive, to live, it is hoped, many years among the highest and noblest examples of constancy in labor, persistency in duty, and cool, calm courage in the face of danger. Butler P. Anderson, who, in 1878, immortalized himself and made for the Association a name far beyond the limits it set for itself, was also among the new members. A man of positive convictions, noble impulses, and the highest sense of honor, he entered enthusiastically upon the work, and so fearlessly and thoroughly performed every duty assigned him, that, before the close of the campaign of 1873, he was regarded by his fellow-soldiers as just the man to lead a forlorn hope like that of Grenada in 1878. They looked up to him as to a born leader, a man in whom they recognized all those qualities essential in a successful commander. They had been with him in the imminent and deadly breach, and saw how cool he could be, concerned only for those whom he had volunteered to succor and to save. They were proud of him; proud to be associated with a man so self-sacrificing, so indifferent to his own safety, so pure, not merely in intention, but in the entire dedication of self to a service whose recompenses were limited to an approving conscience. They were not surprised, therefore, when, in 1878, he volunteered with General W. J. Smith, and went down to almost certain death at Grenada.* This step was in

---

*The Memphis *Ledger*, of the 8th of April (1879), thus pays tribute to these worthies: " Butler P. Anderson was a martyr to his humane impulses and his sense of duty. He did not go to Grenada, as some have supposed, in a spirit of romance and adventure, but from a stern sense of duty, when others would not go. When the mayor of that stricken city sent an appeal to the Howards of Memphis for nurses, Gen. W. J. Smith and Col. Anderson and other Howards found it a difficult matter to find them at once. Several hours were spent in the effort, and, finally, ten were assembled at the depot to take the special train. They were inexperienced nurses, the most of them, and without a head would have been useless. The question arose as to who should go with them. One after another had reasons for saying, 'I pray thee, have me excused.' General Smith, as the first vice-president of the Howard Association, said he would go. No one else volunteered. It was a critical moment. At the last minute Col. Anderson stepped on the train and said: 'I will go myself.' After making the decision, he had

keeping with the promptings of a nature moved by the most humane impulses. It was in keeping with his life, part of the best years of which he devoted to the amelioration of the condition of the poor, the insane, the blind, the deaf and the dumb, and all whom affliction had made dependent upon public charity; to the cause of public education and the advancement especially of the negro, recently made free. He was a tower of strength to the Association, in whose well being he always took the liveliest interest. Physically a splendid type of the men of the south-west, he was as good and pure as he was handsome. Associated with him, besides Major Bowen and General Smith, there were many other old citizens of equal character and weight. Working day and night they found themselves unequal to the demands made upon them. They, therefore, called for help. Nurses, as well as money, clothes, and provisions, were at once sent by the other cities of the country, New Orleans and Mobile vieing with each other, and New York rivaling both. Dr. Luke P. Blackburn, of Kentucky, a gentleman, whose skill in the treatment of yellow fever had long before secured him preëminence among his profession at home and abroad, with Major W. P. Walthall, of Mobile, were put in charge of an infirmary, which was of great advantage to the Howards, as it secured prompt and proper treatment for a class of patients who already crowded the city hospital under Dr. Thornton, city physician and surgeon in charge of the Marine Hospital. Other societies and organizations aided in the work of cooling the fevered brow and closing the eyes of the dead. Conspicuous among them, the Odd-Fellows, the temperance lodges, the Free Masons, Knights of Pythias, Knights of Honor, and Christian Churches, the Hebrew Synagogues, the police and firemen, the telegraphers and typographers. The ministers of religion were, many of them, especially conspicuous, as much so as the physicians, in ministering to the wants of the sick and needy, relieving the widows and orphans, and carry-

---

only time to send a verbal message to his family. That was the last ever seen of him alive in Memphis.* He and General Smith found the city in the wildest confusion and fright. They went to work, forgetting themselves, and bent only on relieving the sick and dying. They often worked from early morning until long after midnight. The mayor fell the day after they arrived, and soon died. The six physicians of the place who remained all died. The mortality was appalling. They could not leave. The highest sense of duty and humanity impelled them to remain as they did, until one fell at his post and the other was brought away with the fever throbbing in every vein. And incidentally here we will say, that all the terrible trials and emergencies of the yellow fever period of 1878 did not develop a nobler, braver, and more unselfish man than General W. J. Smith. Of English birth and ideas, entertaining political opinions at variance with those of most Southern people, he had been the object of dislike and coolness. But when the occasion was presented, he went to the relief of those who, in a sense, might have been considered his enemies at the risk of his life. From this circumstance we may learn a lesson of forbearance and wisdom that should never be forgotten."

---

* The *Ledger* is mistaken in this. Col. Anderson returned to the city after some days of hard labor at Grenada, but only remained for twenty-four hours. He went back to his self-selected post, where as master of the situation, he continued, until the fever seized him, to administer to the necessities of the sick and the dying, acting as mayor and chief of all departments and societies.

ing consolation to all who were desolated and oppressed by the hand of the destroyer. All classes of the community suffered, and terror, dismay, and sorrow were universal. Heroes and heroines abounded in every rank of society. More than one outcast, more than one waif, who had strayed far from the admonitions and teachings of early life, vied with the religious pastors and masters in sacred ministrations. As death levels all, so in the presence of death all are leveled. The whole community stood face to face with, and in awe of, this King of Terrors, and there was no time to ask questions, there was no time to weigh the nice distinctions of social life. Whoever offered life a willing sacrifice on the altar of duty was hailed and treated as brother or sister. There was but one standard of justification — works. Those who gave the cup of water were mustered among the faithful; they were the lights that lighted up the gloom; they were the rich and blessed product of disease and death. Calm amid despair, brave in presence of a relentless foe, deliberate where Death himself was hurried, they practiced the sublimest lessons of Christian charity, and added fresh luster to the record of human endurance. In this campaign, the terrors and hardships of which were unparalleled by any then known experience in the annals of the Southwest, only five of the members of the Association contracted the fever, all of whom, it is pleasant to record, recovered. This amount of casualty out of a membership increased from eight to thirty-seven, by prompt responses to the calls for new members, was little less than miraculous. When the fact is recalled that out of a population estimated at not more than 15,000, half of the number negroes, more than 7,000 sickened, and more than 2,000 died, it was little less than miraculous—in view of the dangers of the pestilence, the lurking contagion in every stricken house, the suddenness of the fever's attack, the almost fiendish eagerness with which it prostrated, and the almost lightning speed with which it killed—it was little less than miraculous, that, returning to fever-haunted beds, after sometimes many nights and days spent in the sickroom, the nervous system all unstrung, their clothes loaded with the never-to-be-forgotten stench of the fever, and often stained from head to foot with black vomit, they did not all die, as warnings against a temerity that would risk life in what most regarded as a forlorn hope. But they were mercifully spared —spared for still more harrowing scenes, spared, many of them, to seal with their lives, during the greater calamity of 1878, their sublime devotion in 1873.

VII.

With this record, possessing the public confidence at home and abroad, the Association, on the fourteenth of August, 1878, was once more summoned to work, this time to face an ordeal, compared with which all previous epidemics were but a brief agony. Between that day and the fourth of November—nearly three months—they were to see 70 per cent. of a population of about 19,600 sicken of the fever, and of that number 5,150, or more than 25 per cent., die, the ratio of mortality among the whites being 70 per cent., and among the negroes 8 per cent. In 1873 they expended over $100,000, employed 825 nurses, and furnished doctors, nurses, medicines, and supplies to over 8,000 persons. In 1878 they were to expend over $500,000, employ 2,900 nurses, and furnished doctors, nurses, medicines, and supplies to more than 15,000 persons.* Taking no heed of their own safety, the members of the Association, placing themselves under the guidance and control of A. D. Langstaff, First Vice-President (who was President in 1873), prepared for the long siege during which they were to be tried as men have seldom been tried in this world. Visitors were at once appointed to the districts into which the city was mapped, and a census of the sick was taken, revealing a state of things that almost surpassed belief. By the end of the first week they found more than 1,500 sick, and the mortality averaged 10 each day; by the end of the second they found 3,000 sick, and the mortality had jumped to 50 per day. Consternation and panic increased the horrors of the situation, and the fear and dread that sat on every heart increased the difficulties of doctors and nurses in the treatment of the disease. The city hospital was full of poor patients, and the able, humane, and tender-hearted physician in charge, Dr Thornton, was already almost worked down. To relieve him, three infirmaries were established, but could not, for want of mechanics to fit them up, be made available earlier than the middle of September. A medical corps, under Dr. R. W. Mitchell, an experienced and able physician, was organized, and performed a work beyond all praise. With their aid, and such help as the other charitable organizations and benefit societies could give, the Association continued to battle with the pestilence, which, aggravated by other diseases, bid fair at one time to decimate the city. Toward the close of August it invaded their own ranks. The heroic General W. J. Smith was back from Grenada prostrate, as a difficult almost

---

* The work of the Howard Association was conducted systematically through Visitors appointed, two to each ward, whose duty it was to visit every house, and report, as promptly as discovered, every case of fever. They made their tours of duty in buggies, in which they carried a liberal supply of medical stores, such as are most needed in the incipient stages of the fever, and which they distributed as they found it necessary. When the cases were reported at the Medical Director's office, the physicians detailed for the ward in which they occurred were notified, and they gave them immediate attention, reporting at night, at the medical meeting, their whole number of cases, the new ones being particularized. All prescriptions for medicines by Howard physicians were filled at the expense of the Association, and all orders for medical supplies for the convalescents were filled at the depot of supplies, where, as well as the prescriptions at the drug-stores, all such orders were filed as vouchers, to be used in the final settlements which were made at the close of the epidemic. The Secretary received and receipted for all donations of money or supplies, and turned them over—the money to the Treasurer and the supplies to the officer in charge of the depot—taking their receipt therefor. All bills were made payable on the order of the President and Secretary, which orders, with bills accompanying, were the vouchers of the Treasurer. At the close of the epidemic these were examined by the auditing committee, who passed upon them and certified to their correctness, as will be seen in the Reports in the Appendix of this book.

hopeless case. The heroic Butler P. Anderson was on his bed, dying, a martyr to the cause of humanity. W. A. Finnie, W. A. Holt, and J. W. Cooper were down. John Forbes was dead. By this time dismay was visible on every face. It began to dawn on the minds of even the most sanguine, that the city was only on the verge of a fearful visitation. By the middle of September the death-rate averaged 200 per day, and there were fully 8,000 sick, perhaps 10,000. On the 14th of that month the mortality for that day was stated to be 127. It was more than 200. Nineteen Howards, including the president, were sick or dead. New members were called for. Out of a population greatly reduced, nearly all of whom were engaged in the benevolent work of nursing the sick or burying the dead, eleven responded, every one of them already doing good work as volunteer Howards. They brought an invaluable experience, a courage and sympathy to the work assigned them as members quite up to the reputation the Association enjoyed. Langstaff, who ultimately recovered, went down with the fever on the 12th of September. His place was taken by Ex-Mayor John Johnson, and afterward by General W. J. Smith, who had just recovered. The hero martyr, Butler P. Anderson, whose name is forever to be hallowed with the people of Memphis, died on the first. Edwin B. Foster died on the 15th, and Edward J. Mansford, one of the original members, and a hero of three epidemics, died on the 30th; A. M. Stoddard was taken on the 20th, but recovered; P. W. Semmes, taken on the 9th, recovered; A. F. C. Cook died on the 8th, Frederick Cole died on the 9th, and W. D. McCallum died on the 16th; Nathan D. Menken, the philanthropist, and an honor to the ancient race, whose good name he sustained by his life and living, died on the 2d;* D. G. Reahardt, taken on the 25th, recovered; John T. Moss, taken on the 15th, recovered; C. L. Staffer, taken on the 9th, recovered; Louis S. Frierson, taken on the 16th, recovered; Jesse W. Page, Jr., taken on the 18th, recovered; Charles Howard, taken on the 15th, recovered; James W. Heath died on the 17th, and W. S. Anderson was taken on the 28th and recovered. Of the honorary members, four in number, Rev. E. C. Slater, D. D., died on the 10th; Rev. S. Landrum, D. D., was taken on the 15th, in the midst of a deep affliction for the loss of

---

* Mr. Menken was in many respects a remarkable person. One of the wealthiest merchants of the city, a man of a very high order of talent and cultivation, and, although deeply devoted to his wife and children, he, long before the epidemic was officially declared to exist, resolved to give himself up to the good Samaritan work of the Howards. He so wrote to his wife in letters that were full of the purest and loftiest sentiments. Conscious of the risk he ran, he advised her of his last wishes, and, thus prepared, entered himself a willing worker in a cause he might have turned his back upon without any question as to his motives. Of a nervous temperament, like many others, he attempted too much, and fell an easy victim to the fever. At first, and for some weeks, he labored by himself, then with the Hebrew Hospital Association, and afterward with the Howard Association; all the time giving of his own bounty, his purse being as open as his heart. How many he relieved, how many griefs he assuaged, how many widows and orphans he comforted by ready help and a generous sympathy, is only known to the God he served so faithfully. His loss was a severe one, and his death was felt to be a public calamity, only overshadowed by the plague.

his two sons, but, happily, recovered; Rev. W. E. Boggs, D. D., was taken on the 26th, but recovered; and Chief of Police Athy was taken on the 31st of August, and recovered. The ranks of the Association were thus, in September, literally decimated. By the end of the first week in October, Vice-President Edmondson, John Johnson, Superintendent of Nurses, and J. H. Smith, Secretary, were, of all the officers, alone on duty. By that time the death-rate had declined to twenty-eight per day; yet the work was harder, and the demands upon the time of those who could work were greater than ever, their numbers considered. They were never off duty, save to sleep, and, of that, many of them were cut down to half the usual time. This induced exhaustion, and invited the plague. John G. Lonsdale, Sr., Treasurer of the Association, and a hero of four epidemics, died on the first of October, a few days after burying his youngest son and his wife; J. H. Smith, the Secretary, was taken on the 11th, but recovered; Samuel M. Jobe, conspicuous among the citizens of Memphis for an active benevolence and a pure and stainless life, died on the 4th; and W. J. B. Lonsdale, who had done good work in 1873, died on the 2d of November. This was the last death among the Howards, and the last case of fever. Those not thus mentioned escaped; they were—Vice-President J. H. Edmondson, who had the fever in the West Indies in 1865; Ex-Mayor John Johnson, who had the fever in 1873; Major F. F. Bowen, who had the fever in 1847; W. S. Rogers, who had the fever in 1873; T. R. Waring, who had the fever in the West Indies; Jacob Kohlberg, and Robert P. Waring, neither of whom ever had the fever. Thus, out of a total—including honorary members—of thirty-nine, only seven escaped, and, of these, only two of them had not had the fever during some of the preceding epidemics in this country or the West Indies. Twelve of the thirty-two attacked died. On the 7th of October, the fever having diminished to fifty-seven new cases and twenty-four deaths, and the labors of the Association having been correspondingly decreased, President Langstaff determined to answer the calls of the surrounding communities on a scale equal to their necessities, and, for that purpose, organized relief trains, to be run on the three principal railroads—the Memphis and Charleston, the Mississippi and Tennessee, and the Memphis and Louisville (or, as it is known abroad, the L., N. and Great Southern). The first of these trains went out on the 8th on the latter road, the second on the 9th on the first-named, and the third on the 13th on the Tennessee road. They carried provisions as well as medical and hospital supplies, medicines, physicians, and nurses, and, although it was late in the epidemic when they started, accomplished a great deal of good. Never were the good gifts of good hearts more heartily welcomed than were the comforts thus dispensed to their needy fellow-sufferers by the Memphis Howards. What the people of the small towns along the roads mentioned had endured was beyond belief. Death had in many cases taken nearly one hundred per cent., leaving only one or two to tell the awful tale. In vain the sublimest heroism was exhibited. In vain every suggestion of science was exhausted. The fever swept past every obstacle and carried all with it who could not withstand the shock—and they were few. From time to time the Memphis Howards had done what they could to relieve these sorely tried and bereaved people, but until the relief trains were organized, it was found impossible to do all that was necessary. For two weeks this most practical of the benevolences of the time continued, the trains being every-where hailed with gladness by the prostrate people, to whom they brought what money with them could not then purchase. Almost simultaneously from all the stricken towns, toward the close of October, the glad news went out to an impatient world that the fever was near its close. Its days were numbered. On the 29th the Memphis Board of Health declared the epidemic over. Many cases of fever existed, and some few occurred after that, but in epidemic form it had expended itself. The work of the Association was brought to a close. The relief trains ceased to run; the last of the nurses were called in and paid off; other help was discharged; the suburban agencies for the distribution of medicines and supplies were closed; the medical department was also closed, and the physicians were dismissed. This was gracefully accomplished at a banquet at the Peabody Hotel, whereat speeches were made and resolutions passed, expressive of the weight of obligation resting upon every citizen of Memphis, for services that were beyond any computation or value. Thus was brought to a close the third and hardest fought campaign of the Memphis Howard Association. The personal trials of its members had been severe. They had lost heavily, not only of their own members, but of physicians and nurses whom they had come to regard as of their number. Death dealt so severely with them that they were obliged to organize a burial corps, under a young Hebrew named Louis Daltroof, who deserves "special mention" for the courage and discretion with which, at such a time, he performed the last sad offices, generally alone and unaided. Some of the oldest and noblest of the original members had passed from human sight, and many who, though young in the cause, had brought to it the enthusiasm of natures ardent and eager to learn the sublime lesson of humanity. But as these fell the ranks were closed up, the step became firmer, the movement steadier, resolution stronger. So long as there was one case of disease and one Howard, so long there was need for the exhibition of all those qualities which, invaluable in the sick-room, were precious incentives to duty on future and similar occasions. Three times the Alabama Street depot was closed by the death of the agent. Whole families had perished in its vicinity. It was the hot-bed of the pestilence, yet every dead Howard was succeeded by a living one—the bridge of Lodi was held to the last. A painful incident of the epidemic, this illustrates the courage which braved all things to succor and save poor, helpless fellow-beings. Die they might, but die in the good cause to which they had devoted themselves the Howards would. The annals of war afford no higher evidence of courage, of unselfish devotion to duty, of a pure and lofty heroism; and it is doubtful if any other people than ours, trained to self-control in the school of personal liberty, could equal it. Theirs is a glorious record—of which their fellow-citizens are proud. It is a spotless record, free from all taint—a record that embraces all that is worthy of imitation in human goodness; it is a record that recalls the early ages of the Christian Church, when the zeal of the martyrs, inspired by a sublime hope, carried them through the fires of persecution, and enabled them to be an everlasting testimony to the faith, some of whose sublimest assurances are expressed in the texts: "Inasmuch as ye did it unto the least of these, my brethren, ye did it unto me." And, "Greater love hath no man than this, that a man lay down his life for his friend."

INCIDENTS OF THE EPIDEMIC.

The incidents of the epidemic in Memphis, 1878, which are here given, are, as nearly as possible, arranged in the order, according to dates, in which they were found in the daily papers, from which they are, for the most part, taken. They are given in the language of the time, and are believed to be faithful reports of facts as they occurred. As notes made and printed during the progress of the scourge, they serve the purpose here of proof, that what is stated in the preceding pages is not, in any sense, an exaggeration of the truth, but that the writer has kept quite within the limit of facts, verified by eye-witnesses of the scenes and participants in the labors incident to the dreadful visitation.

The mayor, by a proclamation, July 27th, declared a quarantine established, a competent physician, with medical stores, provisions, bedding, and all things needful, taking possession of the quarantine buildings, and preparing for a rigid enforcement of the laws. The Board of Health held two meetings on the 29th.

If there is any virtue in quarantine, Memphis ought to have felt secure against yellow fever this season, as Franklin, Louisiana, Natchez, Port Gibson, and other villages, in Mississippi, established quarantine against New Orleans as early as the 29th of July.

The so-called plague-stricken steam tow-boat, *John Porter*, passed up the river with her tow, at seven o'clock, on the evening of July 30th. Quite a crowd of citizens were on the bluff watching the boat. Dr. Erskine, health officer, boarded the *Porter* from a tug, and found but one man sick on board. The officers denied that any yellow fever had been or was on board. They stated that they lost four men from over-heating, or sunstroke. The men had been working around the furnaces and been drinking ice-water. The *Porter* was ordered not to stop on land, but to move on up the river.

In spite of the safeguards, with which the health board had surrounded the city, a few persons from New Orleans found their way here by railroad. One of these, who, for two weeks after his departure from New Orleans, had been up White River, arrived in the city on the night of the 1st of August, and, becoming sick, and being poor, was sent to the city hospital, where, after a few hours, the disease developed into a clear case of yellow fever. The health officer was at once notified, and had the sick man promptly removed to the quarantine hospital. When the unfortunate man was removed, the bed and bedclothes on which he slept, and the clothes he wore were burned, and the hospital was thoroughly disinfected. It was a clear case of development of disease contracted in New Orleans.

The man, William Warren, who slipped into the city from the yellow fever infected steamer *Golden Crown*, and who was sent to the quarantine hospital for yellow fever treatment, died, at quarantine, on Monday, August 5th.

The city was startled on Sunday, the 11th of August, by a series of telegrams from Grenada, Mississippi, confirming the suspicion that yellow fever, of a malignant type, had broken out in that city. The telegrams from officials and private citizens of Grenada created a sensation and somewhat of a panic among our citizens, which did not wear away before late last night. The Board of Health, Howard Association, Masons, Odd-Fellows, and Knights of Pythias, of the city, received telegrams of a most startling character, and up to the following day the telegraph office, on Madison Street, was crowded by visitors, all anxious to hear from Grenada.

The Howards assembled, on hearing the news, on Sunday, August 11th, and determined to aid the people of Grenada, in response to a telegram received by Mr. J. H. Smith, Secretary of the Association, asking for nurses. At half past seven o'clock, Sunday evening, a special train left for Grenada, carrying Colonel Butler P. Anderson and General W. J. Smith, of the Howard Association, seven experienced nurses, and Dr. R. F. Brown, secretary of the Board of Health, who concluded to go to the ground and inspect the sick, with a view to learn the character of the disease.

On Monday, August 12th, the Howard Association met at No. 16 Madison Street, and prepared to respond to the call for aid from Grenada. On the afternoon train, twenty-one experienced yellow-fever nurses were sent by the Howards, four by the Masons, and two by the Odd-Fellows, making thirty-four in all sent since the previous day.

A policeman, named McConnell, who had been sick for several days, died on the night of the 12th of August, his physician declaring his to have been a case of yellow fever. But other doctors disagreeing, it did not create much of a flurry.

On August 13th a clearly defined case of yellow fever appeared in this city, and was duly announced, according to promise, by the Board of Health.* The case was as follows: Mr. B. Bionda, wife and two children, lived at No. 212 Front Street, a few doors north of Adams Street. Mr. Bionda and wife kept an eating, or snack-house, principally frequented and patronized by river men, or people from the landing. They cleansed and cooked fish, meats, etc., in a room back of the snack-shop, where they fed their guests. They slept in a room over the snack-house and kitchen. Mr. and Mrs. Bionda were industrious, hard-working people. Their slops and refuse matter, from their snack-house, were thrown out into the street, or further out toward the river. Mrs. Kate Bionda was taken sick on August 9th, and was attended by Dr. Willett. Symptoms of yellow fever began to develop slowly but surely, and Dr. Willett became satisfied. He notified Dr. Saunders and Dr. Erskine, of the Board of Health, and Dr. Heber Jones, who visited the case. They at once pronounced it a well-marked case of yellow fever. Immediately Health Officer Erskine took charge of the building and vicinity. The rooms, house, and premises were thoroughly fumigated and disinfected with carbolic acid, copperas, etc. The sidewalk and street for half a square on Front Street, and the same distance back on Adams, were also disinfected. An obstruction or railing was placed across Adams Street at Center Alley, and the locality, No. 212, was fenced in around Front Street to the intersecting alley running east and west. Mrs. Kate Bionda died at eleven o'clock in the morning, and was buried at four o'clock on the afternoon of the 13th. The officers of the Board of Health are of the opinion that Mrs. Bionda contracted the disease from some guest who had come up the river from the infected district south. Not only was the building in which Mrs Bionda died disinfected and isolated, but all adjacent buildings in the block were likewise disinfected, and policemen were stationed to prevent people from visiting the particular locality.

---

* This was not, as was supposed at the time, the first case. See preceding pages of "Epidemic in Memphis in 1878" for the facts.

A HISTORY OF THE YELLOW FEVER. 147

When it was officially announced that there was an undoubted case of yellow fever in the city (Mrs. Bionda) considerable alarm was created. Many at once proposed to send their families away, and quite a number left the city before night. There was a feeling of alarm and uneasiness, but no panic or stampede.

The yellow fever developed, August 14th, to the extent of twenty-two new cases, but only two deaths were reported. The news found early and ready dissemination, and a panic was the result. The trains on the Charleston and Louisville Railroads, as a consequence, went out crowded, and every seat and berth was taken for the trains on both roads for the next two days. Business was in great part suspended, and every body that could left before the week ended. The Board of Health isolated the infected district, and literally saturated the buildings, streets, and alleys with disinfectants. Though the type of the disease was virulent, and did not readily yield to treatment, the sanitary officials were not without hope of mitigating its severity, if they did not overcome it.

The hegira from Memphis *via* the Louisville and Charleston Railroads, August 15th, was greater than ever. It was a regular panic and stampede.

By this time, many of the scenes and incidents in the infected district were of a sad and heart-rending character. Strong men and women and helpless little children lay sick and dying. The dead, the dying, and the sick in the same house—often in the same room, sometimes in the same bed—presenting a pitiful sight, one well calculated to affect the heart and soul of the most callous. Many of the poorer people who were sick were suffering for supplies and necessary attention. These were dreadful sights, not soon to be effaced from memory.

At the suggestion of Dr. Paul H. Otey, which was at once indorsed by Health Officer Erskine and others, a telegram was sent by the United States collector of internal revenue, and the postmaster of the city to Hon. G. W. McCreary, Secretary of War, to which an answer was received from the Secretary, ordering one thousand tents to be sent from Evansville, Indiana. Another telegram was sent by the same gentleman asking for rations. The idea is to send the poor people out of the city and form encampments at such eligible places as can be secured. The Bluff City Grays, a white militia company, volunteered to act as a guard for one of the camps (Joe Williams, so named after a physician who died during the epidemic of 1873). The McClellan Guards (colored) also volunteered. The services of both companies were accepted.

On August 16th quarantine was raised, people and freight being enabled to get to Memphis by rail or river, all restrictions having been removed. Those who were found sick on arrival were removed to the hospital.

A joke is told on Brownsville, which town had quarantined Memphis. The citizens refused to permit a barrel of gin and several barrels of carbolic acid, shipped from Memphis, to be delivered in town before they were thoroughly disinfected.

Hundreds of people now adopted the plan of leaving the city at sun-down, going out into the suburbs to sleep, and returning to business in the morning.

The outgoing railway trains continued to be crowded, and vehicles were in demand to carry people out the dirt roads to the country.

It is estimated that from 15,000 to 20,000 white people fled from this city by the 18th of August.

Mary Sloan, a white woman who had been nursing yellow fever patients, was arrested, and locked up at the station-house, on the charge of drunkenness. Soon after, she developed symptoms of fever, and was sent to the hospital. The mattresses in the cell were burned and the cell and surroundings disinfected.

In response to a telegram sent on Monday, August 20th, by Mayor Flippin and others, asking for rations for the poor, a response was received the following day from Geo. W. McCreary, Secretary of War, at Washington, stating that orders had been issued to send rations for 2,000 people for twenty days, upon the ground that the city was unable to secure relief for the sufferers from public charity.

Three persons were reported who had brought yellow fever upon themselves by indulging in drunkenness. After a drunk the stomach and entire system is out of order, which places the unfortunate inebriate in a too favorable condition to take the fever. Above all acts of imprudence, drunkenness should be avoided.

Cases of fever appeared in the southern portion of the city, on August 21st, at different places. The physicians believe that in these cases the disease was contracted in the infected districts.

President Langstaff, of the Howard Association, received the following on August 21st:—

"Husband is dead. Please send or come down, as I am in need. I do n't know how to get him buried. If you would help me, I could work for you all. Please do n't say you can't, if possible. Mrs. ——."

The Howards immediately made arrangements to have the dead husband buried, and responded with aid to the above appeal.

Captain Jno. C. Forbes died at the city hospital on the evening of August 22d, whither he had been taken a victim of the fever, with which during three visitations he had battled as a member of the St. Andrew's Society, and, lastly, of the Howard Association. While nursing Mr. Campbell and his wife, on Alabama Street, he also visited all the fever-stricken patients in that worst part of the infected district, and finally accepted the dangerous post of superintendent of the distribution depot of the Howard Association, the duties of which he had been discharging but a few days when the scourge seized him, and he died after three days' illness. All that was possible, and the care of one of our best physicians, was done for him, but to no purpose. Though a man of vigorous frame, he succumbed. To the last the work he had nearest to heart asserted itself in speech. A little girl of seven years of age—a fever patient—on being taken into the same ward, he gave minute directions as to her treatment, and when she died and was carried forth for burial, he said, "I have lost my life." This expression he repeated many times to those who visited him, and to whom he had endeared himself by many noble exhibitions of that quality of heart which Christ promised reward for in the words: "Forasmuch as ye have done it unto the least of these my brethren, ye have done it unto me." In view of his good Samaritan work and the hope of this text, we lose sight of the short-comings, the frailties, and infirmities of the man, and sorrow for one who bravely and unselfishly went about the Master's work, succoring the sick, and bringing aid and comfort to those who were in sickness and distress.

The Sisters of Charity could be found daily and nightly visiting the sick and afflicted.

But few magistrates could be found in the city by August 22d. They had taken a change of venue to other localities.

The telegraph operators were about worked down, so great was the additional amount of work which they already had to do.

On August 22d, the Board of Health passed a resolution urging all who could to leave the city, as the only hope of checking the spread of the fever was by depopulation.

Camp Joe Williams assumed the air and proportions of a military encampment. Men, women, and children enjoyed themselves, and were pleased with the prospect of being safe from yellow fever.

Avalanche, August 23d.—"The smile of nature beamed mockingly in the bright sunshine, and the gently-blowing winds breathed softly over this plague-stricken city. . . . Despite the dazzling light, the darkest of shadows enwrapped street and alley, highway and byway—the unseen shadow of disease and death. . . . The roll of stricken ran up alarmingly, and stout hearts began to shiver. . . . Brave men are fighting the plague with a heroism that can not be surpassed."

The colored citizens became alarmed over the fact that many of their race were down sick with the fever, they not being exempt from the ravages of the scourge. The colored people were cautioned that their houses and premises be kept clean and properly disinfected daily with carbolic acid; that they should also be more prudent in their diet; in fact, that they should observe all the rules of health which were observed by large numbers of white people.

John Roush, one of our leading mechanics, a man of great energy and skill in his business, succumbed to the fever, and died, August 23d. Mr. Roush served one term in the legislature, and had been for some years a very active politician, especially among his fellow-Germans. He came to Memphis immediately after the war, through which he served in the Federal army, and by industry and perseverance made himself an enviable place in the public esteem as an example of what integrity, united to industry, can accomplish.

The Board of Health, August 23d, declared the yellow fever epidemic in the city. The fever broke over the line on that day, and appeared at many points south of Madison Street. The circle of the infected district was thus extended.

The heavy medical report of August 24th, 106 new cases, caused hundreds of citizens to fly to the country. This was the last great panic and hegira.

The *Appeal*, of the morning of the 24th.—"Up to six o'clock yesterday evening, three hundred and six cases of yellow fever had been reported, and ninety-three deaths. . . . We all know the effect of fear upon those who, yielding to it, fled the city at the first announcement of yellow fever; how much more severe must be its effect upon those taken with the disease. They give up all heart and hope, and yielding to the fear inspired by the oft-repeated assertion that 'they all die,' make no effort to rally from the disease, and die as much from fright as from the plague. To what an alarming extent the fears of the people of Memphis have been excited it would be impossible to tell, and it would be equally impossible to say how much it has had to do in making the death-list and working the sorrow, the penury, want, and destitution which the Howard and other benevolent associations and the Citizens' Relief Committee have been and are trying to mitigate. . . . Instead of denying hope to ourselves, we should do every thing to inspire it, and, instead of asserting that all who take the fever have no chance of recovery, we should labor for it as if we had the assurance that in some remedies, in attentive and judicious nursing and skillful medical attendance, it can be found."

Two of the saddest cases of fever reported were those of Mrs. John Donovan and Mrs. Beno Hollenberg. The former, twelve hours after being taken, was delivered of a still-born babe, and the latter gave birth to a fine healthy child.

From the 1st of August to six o'clock on the 26th, 573 cases of yellow fever had been reported to the Board of Health, of which number 160 had died, and about forty had convalesced, leaving 373 still sick. Our only hope for an abatement of the disease lies in the ability of the city government to compel the people—white and black—who still remain to leave for the camps. We need more nurses and physicians. After dark, it was impossible to find, or, if found, to secure the services of a doctor. In addition to this, it was found almost impossible to get medicine after night-fall.

Among the new cases reported August 26th, were Sisters Veronica and Dominica, of La Salette Academy.

Little Jimmie Winters, aged six years, was found lying on a door-step at the corner of Exchange and Front Streets, on the morning of August 26th, suffering with the fever. His story was, that he came in from the camp looking for his brother, whom he did not find. He was carried to the hospital.

Mrs. Bennett and her daughter, of the family of Charles Bennett, the bricklayer, at No. 101 Robeson Street, was stricken with the fever on the 26th of August. Mr. Bennett and his son left home a few days prior, the latter saying they were going to Cincinnati, and had not been heard from since.

A colored woman declared herself insulted, one day late in August, because an item of the rations awarded her at the commissary depot was, as she termed it, "nasty, ole, greasy bacon." She said: "Dey 'se got some nice streak o' lean and streak o' fat dar, but dey gi me dat ole stuff, fat enough to kill a hog."

A citizen coming into the city, on Poplar Street, was nearly sickened by a nauseating stench proceeding from a building near the bayou bridge, west of the market-house. He went into the building from which the stench proceeded, and bursting in the door of a room, he discovered the dead body of its occupant lying on the bed, in a decomposed condition, where it had, evidently, been laying for four or five days. It was the body of a barber, who formerly occupied the lower floor as a barber-shop. The room presented a sickening sight. The remains were wrapped in a sheet, encoffined, and interred the same day.

The fate of the Donovan family occasioned much comment, in which Mr. Donovan, who was formerly held in high esteem and exercised considerable influence, politically and socially in this community, was severely censured for positively refusing to return to his family when notified that his wife and children were stricken down with the fever. Mrs. Donovan gave birth to a stillborn child, and, soon after, died herself; one of her children died the same day. Mr. Donovan was notified by telegraph, but coolly responded with instructions concerning the burial of the corpses, but still remained away. Another of the children died, but Mr. Donovan remained at Brownsville, fifty miles away.

Annie Cook, who kept the noted *demi-monde* establishment, the Mansionhouse, discharged all her female inmates, and taking yellow-fever patients in her elegantly furnished rooms—being herself an expert in the management of the disease—she personally superintended the nursing of all the patients.

Avalanche, August 28th.—"It is blue, very blue. The record of yesterday shows only a passage from bad to worse. . . . The plague is as great a gourmand as ever, and was only gorged by ninety-six new cases in the city. Total deaths in the city, thirty-two."

The *Appeal* of August 28th.—"Ninety-six new cases and thirty-two deaths from yellow fever are the appalling reports from the books of the Board of Health. . . . The close, damp, disagreeable weather is increasing its ravages, and the scarcity of nurses and physicians is leaving the cases entirely at the mercy of the disease. Several of the nurses have been stricken down already. It is blood-curdling to listen to the details of the heart-rending incidents encountered by the visiting nurses in various parts of the city. . . . To-day the nurses reported at the Board of Health office, two, three, and four corpses in one house, the undertakers not being able to bury them. . . . One of the remarkable features of the disease, as it prevails now, is, that whole families have been swept out of existence—father, mother, and children have followed each other in rapid succession to the grave, and in some instances several members of a family are lying dead at the same time, having died almost within the same hour. This was the case in several instances in what was known as the 'infected district.'"

The labors of Butler P. Anderson, at Grenada, were without a parallel in the history of epidemics. He not only nursed cases himself, but supervised all the philanthropic laborers, and, for a time, actually administered the affairs of the plague-stricken town. A hero among heroes, he carried hope and comfort to a people without either, and, from the chaos and confusion incident to so fearful a visitation, brought the order and system to which the few who survive the fever owe their lives. Like many another brave soldier, he was, at last, beaten by the enemy, and stricken with the fever.

Mr. Denie, by direction of the Board of Health, threw five hundred barrels of unslacked lime into the bayou, which he reported to be in a condition filthy beyond belief. He stated that the negro men he employed to do the work threatened to leave him, so horrible was the stench created by stirring up the foul water. He, however, prevailed upon them to keep on.

Of the 119 new cases of yellow fever reported in the twenty-four hours ending at six o'clock, August 28th, thirty were colored people, and yet negroes were to be seen at any and all hours of the day, in the alleys and back-ways, gorging themselves with watermelons and all sorts of unwholesome trash.

The absence of funeral processions, which contributed much to the horror of the epidemic of 1873, was noted. The dead were conveyed to the various burying places as quietly as possible, and the public were thus relieved of the one harrowing exhibition of sorrow.

The fever record of August 29th was one to make the stoutest heart quail. Briefly stated, it was 140 new cases—forty of them colored—and seventy deaths, twenty-four of them colored. This surpassed the worst of the terrible days of 1873, the deaths being fifteen in number more than was announced on the tenth of October, the worst day of that year. When it is remembered that the white population was less than that during the epidemic of 1873, by perhaps 5,000, and that at least 2,000 negroes had left the city, these figures became truly appalling.

Avalanche, August 30th, written midnight, 29th.—" We are doomed. It is hard, as we write in this dark, dismal night of death, not to realize the full meaning of that brief sentence. . . . Scarcely any are left, but those who are crowding down personal care, in the noble purposes of others' good. . . . To die for man is to imitate the greatest event in the history of our globe, it is to imitate the death of the Savior of the world. . . . Seventy dead and one hundred and forty new cases! God help us! If hope were not worn to a skeleton, if she had not taken herself to prayer, we might find a spark to kindle a weak glow of light in this impenetrable darkness, and expect that the heavy shower of to-day would wash from the air, from the gutter, and from the bayou a part of the foul pestilential air which is breeding death. The horrors of the hour can not be told, even if the heart did not sicken at the task!"

It is believed that the sudden breaking out of the fever in the jail was caused by the incarceration of infected prisoners, and not from any lack of attention to the rigid sanitary regulations which characterized the management of that institution.

Mrs. Newman, of 128 Washington Street, died August 30th, and willed all her worldly goods to the children of a friend, and was buried by the county undertaker, at her own request.

Great sympathy was expressed for General W. J. Smith, First Vice-President of the Howard Association, in the loss of his son, a bereavement which adds to his trials and makes his burden heavy indeed.

The illness of Chief of Police Athy, which occurred on the last day of August, was a severe blow in those critical times.

Among the number of shocking incidents of daily occurrence, that of the fate of Dr. K. P. Watson, was perhaps the most horrible. Dr. Watson was an efficient worker, both as physician and nurse, during the epidemic of 1873; and when the fever broke out in 1878, he entered the field again, and devoted himself and his talents to the work of staying the ravages of the disease. He made no boast of the work he was doing, nor stopped to discuss the nature of the pestilence, but wherever he found suffering he worked with all his energy to alleviate it. Finally he was missed, but it was thought that he had followed the spread of the disease into other quarters of the city. Sergeant McElroy, of the Signal Service, who worked like a Trojan, doing all in his power to help the sick and distressed, happened to be passing by No. 56½ Second Street, and was told that there was something wrong there; that in all probability a dead body lay in there. Without hesitation he kicked the door in, when he beheld a sickening sight. There lay the corpse of Dr. Watson, on an old mattress on the floor, no bedstead or other furniture except a single chair and a table. Being personally acquainted with Dr. Watson, he thought he recognized his features, and a closer examination confirmed his first impressions. Diligent inquiry in the neighborhood failed to elicit any information as to when or why he came there, how long ago, or any thing that could give a clue to his mysterious death. The condition of the corpse and surrounding circumstances told the story too truly. He had been seized with a violent attack of the fever, and during the attendant delirium, he had crept into the place, where he may have lingered for days, or it may have been only for hours, finally dying unattended by nurse or physician, not even a friend to smooth his dying pillow. His name appeared among the interments of August 31st.*

A man named Myers kept a second-hand clothing and dyeing establishment on Washington Street, between Main and Second Streets. Some one entered his place August 31st, and found him lying dead on the floor; no one could find out how long he had been in that condition. He bore evident marks of having died with the fever, without any attention whatever.

A poor woman was found on Main Street, near the Louisville Depot, in a miserable hut, sitting stiff, stark dead in a chair, with a dead child hanging by the nipple of her left breast on which it had closed its little gums as it breathed its last. Another child was lying in a pallet just breathing, and died a few moments after the entrance of the Howard visitor, who said the walls, floor and every thing in the room was covered with black vomit and excreta, the sight as well as smell being sickening in the extreme. Mother and children were buried in the same box.

On Poplar Street the remains of an old woman were found so far gone that they were gathered—putrid water and festering flesh—into the carpet on which they were lying, and so lifted into a box, in which she was buried in potter's field.

Another of the noble Howards was buried on Sunday, September 1st; Ed. Mansford, who, in 1873, and through the last epidemic, until two days before he died, was conspicuous for his untiring energy in a work but for which the poor would have no succor, passed away peacefully as Sunday morning dawned. His work was done. He had fought the good fight; henceforth there was for him the crown of martyrdom. He came out from the ranks of the people a

---

* This was subsequently contradicted, but the person who originally made the report adhered to it until he died. Sergeant McElroy, signal service officer at this station, was the person. A more honorable or faithful soldier never served his country. He nursed the sick and braved all the perils of the times, doing all that a man could to mitigate the sorrow and trouble that surrounded him. He fought, in the regular army, all through the civil war, had encountered the Indians on the plains many times, and passed through one epidemic of yellow fever in New Orleans, but his last campaign (the epidemic), he assured the writer, combined the horrors of them all.

mere private, he went to his grave acknowledged as a leader among those who were not afraid to die that others might live.

Avalanche, September 1st.—"The King of Terrors continues to snatch victims with fearful rapidity. . . . But three short weeks ago our city was active with business of all classes, our people were happy and prosperous. . . . Now our streets are deserted, our stores and residences empty, and out of a population of more than fifty thousand, barely five thousand remain, and of those nearly five hundred are in the grave, and perhaps double that number lie suffering with racking pains and burning fevers."

Appeal, September 1st.—"We believe the new cases of yesterday will reach two hundred (reported one hundred and fifty-two). The region of the city known as the 'infected district' is now so nearly depopulated by death and desertion, that but few cases are being reported from that quarter, but the great increase in numbers from the Ninth Ward (northern part of the city, called Chelsea) shows that the contagion has taken a firmer grasp in that locality. The Seventh Ward (south-east part) is also rolling up considerable numbers of new cases, as is also the Fifth Ward (north of the Seventh), where it is making frightful havoc among the colored people. There is still great need of physicians."

The name of N. D. Menkin, who passed away September 2d, will never be forgotten by the people of Memphis. He died at his post, a noble example of zeal and courage on a field where many brave men had fallen before him. He might, like many others of his class, have sought safety in flight, but he preferred to share the lot of the people to whom he was known as an honorable, enterprising merchant, whose money seconded every suggestion he ever made in the public interest. Early in the fight he saw that few of the public men or noted merchants would remain to lead the small company who proposed to do the good Samaritan work of nursing the sick, burying the dead, and caring for the impoverished; he therefore volunteered, and first, as the leader of a little band of his co-religionists, and afterward as a Howard, he went about, day and night, doing good, carrying comfort to sick-rooms, provisions to the destitute, and surpervising with all the energy of his nature the work of a district where the fever was raging at its worst.

A colored man was prostrated, September 2d, on the corner of Fifth and Saffarans Streets, in Chelsea. He was seen to fall by Captain A. T. Lacey, who went to him and found him insensible. Captain Lacey reported the case to the health office, and an ambulance was sent for him, but he was dead when it got there.

Innumerable complaints were made at the health office, September 2d, about corpses lying unburied, some of them having been dead thirty-six and forty-eight hours. Undertaker Walsh declared his inability to get material for coffins, or laborers to dig graves.

Avalanche, September 3d.—"The fever has spread rapidly to the southern part of the city. Fort Pickering is full of it. Chelsea (northern part) is covered with sick people. There is now no part of the corporate limits of the city not thoroughly infected with the fever poison. All of Sunday and yesterday hearses followed each other at a trot to the cemetery, unattended by any but the drivers. Even this was not fast enough, and corpses accumulated in various parts of the city, until the fearful stench became alarmingly offensive."

Rev. Dr. A. Thomas, pastor of the German Free Protestant Church, of this city, died, September 3d, of yellow fever, after a very short illness. Dr. Thomas was one of the noble army of martyrs, and since the breaking out of the fever had devoted himself entirely to the sick and afflicted of his parish. None were more earnest and self-denying than he, and his death was a severe loss to the city, as well as to the religious community of which he was the light and guide.

The death of Mr. R. A. Thompson, one of the editors and proprietors of the *Avalanche*, and postmaster of the city, occurred September 3d, and was the result of an attack of yellow fever. Mr. Thompson came to Memphis toward the close of the war, and was first engaged on the *Bulletin* as local, and subsequently as commercial, editor. In 1866, he was offered the position of commercial editor of the *Avalanche*, which he accepted, and has ever since been identified with the fortunes of that paper. In 1875, he became one of the proprietors, and, a few months before his death, was confirmed postmaster. He possessed and was guided by a great many of the intuitions which are prized by the true journalist, was useful in every branch of the profession, was a good business man, and fully justified the good opinion of a large circle of friends, by whom his death was regretted and his memory cherished.

Henry Stillman, at one time connected with the *Ledger* office, as engineer, was found dead in a residence on Broadway Street, in South Memphis, September 3d. He had probably been dead three or four days.

Butler Anderson's death was announced in the *Appeal* in these terms: No nobler spirit ever went out through death to life than that of Butler P. Anderson. He was of the stuff of which heroes are made. Large, open, generous, and self-sacrificing, intelligent as to the risks he ran, but counting them nothing when compared with the magnitude and character of the work to be done, he went down to Grenada when the call was first made upon us for help, and before we had even tasted of the sorrow with which our cup has been filled to overflowing many times since. He went cheerfully and willingly to the people of that once happy little town, and for them, during five weeks of almost unparalleled misery, he was as father and brother and husband, filling all places of relationship, and of social or political influence, the one dependence of a people dazed in presence of the awful fact of the yellow fever. His labors were incessant, but he performed them with an alacrity that was an inspiration to all those about him, and, while thus burdened, he went his rounds, carrying judicious advice for the sick, bearing cheering hope to the despondent, and inspiring those who, nerveless from despair, were giving way under the gloom which had settled over a once beautiful town. He was every thing to the Grenadians, and his must be to them the one specially cherished name above all others, bright and luminous as that of a hero who dies for his fellow-men. Here, where he was tried in 1873, and where he grew to proportions in the public esteem from which he never afterward fell away, we deeply deplore his loss.

The dead body of a negro woman was found at No. 13 Commerce Street, September 3d, her living babe trying to nurse from her putrid breast.

Visitor Anderson, of the Howards, September 4th, found J. Riviere in a dying condition at No. 81 Main Street. He was alone, stark naked, and literally covered with flies.

The *Ledger*, of September 4th, has the following: "We regret to learn that our brethren of the press of this city are sorely pressed for help. Our afternoon contemporary has been obliged to suspend altogether. Mr. J. M. Keating, assisted by Mr. W. S. Brooks, has all the labor and responsibility of running the *Appeal* on his own shoulders. Mr. Henry White has charge of the business department, as usual. Of the *Avalanche* editorial force only Captain W. L. Trask remains. He is assisted, at night, by Mr. R. R. Catron, the assiduous, accurate, and untiring agent of the Associated Press, who has likewise, in his spare moments, befriended the *Ledger* with his services. Mr. F. S. Nichols, one of the proprietors, looks after the business of the *Avalanche*. The typographical force of these papers is reduced correspondingly. These gentlemen are steady to their posts, with noble fidelity to duty and the public good."

Avalanche, September 5th.—"Great God! How his murderous work has increased! Those that are left are busy burying their dead; those that are left may be taken to-morrow. . . . Impotence lies at the feet of Omnipotence, and grovels there in the dust. Yesterday's record is run up, and in all its blackness lifts its death's head and defies the best plague that ever did a job of slaying among the children of men. . . . Who has the heart to use the multiplication table in the arithmetic of sorrow, and figure out the hearts broken, the lives embittered, the houses desolated? . . . Surely our cup of sorrow must be full. Black as the dead list is, to-day, in our city, it fails to represent all those ready for burial yesterday. The county undertaker has four furniture wagons busy all day. Upon each the coffins were piled as high as safety from falling would permit. These four great vehicles, doing the wholesale burial business, failed to take to the potter's field all of the indigent dead. At the time the officer made his report sixty bodies were awaiting interment. . . . The plague's course is surely and quickly toward the south. In the suburbs cases have appeared on every avenue almost, in many places deemed spots of perfect safety."

September 5th, Annie Cook, the keeper of a bagnio on Gayoso Street, who had most heroically devoted herself to the care of the sick since the fever set in, was down with a bad case of the fever.

September 5th, owing to the fact that Mrs. Brooks, wife of Mr. W. S. Brooks, of the *Appeal* editorial staff, had been taken down with the fever, Mr. J. M. Keating was alone on duty. Captain Fred. Brennan, city editor, was still lying in a precarious condition. All but one of the printers of the *Appeal* were absent or down with the fever. The one present was Mr. Henry Moode, who, besides setting type, had to assist Mr. Richard Smith in superintending the printers' infirmary, and was, consequently, absent a good deal during working hours.

September 5th, Mrs. Butler P. Anderson was taken down with fever. It had been hoped that she would have been spared to her children. The noble wife of a noble husband, she has the sympathies of the people of Memphis.

A man named Charles Gibson, who officiated as a nurse, was called to attend a family on Hernando Street, all stricken with the fever. The mother was found dying, with a babe at her breast, the father in a comatose condition, and three children sick, all in the same room. One child, being well, was sent to the orphan asylum. The father, mother, and two of the children, including the sucking babe, died during the day, and the third child it was expected would die during the night, having had the black vomit. The next morning Howard visitors came, and upon inquiry learned that the child was convalescing. The next day he got up, and recovered.

Dr. Pritchard was called upon to visit a negro in Fort Pickering, who was said to be very low. On reaching the dying man, he found him prone on the earthen floor of a mud cabin, in a comatose state, his extremities cold, and evidently in the last pangs of dissolution. His wife and mother were dead in the room, and it seemed almost inevitable that the husband and son must soon follow. The doctor, however, took hold of his case, and in three days he was out. He is now a roistering roustabout on the river.

While the largest proportion of those who died fell by disease, this was not the sole cause of the immense death rate. The constant nervous strain imposed, the uninterrupted labors to which the well were subjected, and the continued apprehension felt, were powerful causes in increasing the daily lists. To these can be added the negligence, inattention, and inebriety of nurses who were prompted in their labors by the hope of reward alone.

The body of a negro woman, name unknown, was found back of the *Appeal* office in an out-house, defaced beyond recognition, and half the body eaten by rats, hundreds of which were lying dead near by. The yellow fever proved too much for them, at least in that shape.

Avalanche, September 6th.—"New cases in the city, only thirty-six reported (several physicians not reporting). Deaths, ninety-two. The physicians have no time to make out lists of new cases, so the reporter has to search for himself. . . . Verbal reports show at least one hundred and fifty new cases not officially reported."

There were but five operators on duty at the telegraph office September 6th— the chief and one assistant by day, and the chief and two assistants by night.

September 5th, a singular-looking genius made his appearance on Main Street, dressed in a semi-Greek costume, with a large sponge tied about his neck. He kept to the middle of the street, and attracted the attention and excited the risibilities of the few bystanders.

A physician who died of fever, when first taken, called on a neighbor, on whose family he had waited like a brother, but the neighbor made no response, and the good doctor passed away, filled with mortification at the conduct of his one-time friend, who in a few days sickened and died, too.

The force was so small at the post-office, that some of the letter-carriers were called in.

Mr. W. S. Brooks, of the *Appeal* editorial corps, was taken down with the fever September 6th. He stood to his post to the last, doing all that he could to assist in getting out the paper. Enough can not be said in praise of his courage and devotion to duty.

Avalanche, September 7th.—"Total new cases reported in the city, ninety-five. Deaths, one hundred. These new cases were reported by eight physicians only. Verbal reports from twenty-three more (out of duty) reported three hundred cases. Dr. Mitchell (Medical Director) gave it as his opinion, at eleven o'clock last night, that the new cases would aggregate for yesterday (sick who had not seen a doctor before) fully six hundred. It is terribly dark, as the record reads to-day."

Avalanche, September 8th. — "Total new cases in the city, reports very meager. Deaths reported, ninety-seven. Another black leaf turned! Another chapter in our book of misery turned! As castaways on desert isle each day for occupation's sake enter up in their 'log' the monotonous record of the dreary day, so we sit down to our log-book to-night. . . . The day's record is horrible. The few new cases reported are not a tithe of those which have occurred. . . . The nurses in two more days can not attend one-half the sick."

Appeal, Sept. 8th.—Rev. C. C. Parsons, rector of Grace and St. Lazarus churches, died Sept. 7th, after six days of fever. From the first day of the epidemic he labored incessantly among his parishioners, knowing no rest so long as there was good to be done. Mr. Parsons was a graduate of West Point, and served during the war in the Federal army with distinction, rising to the rank of lieutenant-colonel of artillery, which he surrendered to take a place in the ranks of the ministry of the Episcopal Church. He was first settled in charge of a parish, we believe, in New Jersey, then in New York, whence he came to this city about three years ago. He was not long in making his way to the hearts of our people. All classes learned to love and confide in him, and to look to him as one of the most gentle of Christian ministers. He was chaplain of the Chickasaw Guards, and was beloved by his comrades as the unit of all that was strong, noble, manly, refined, and Christ-like. His loss was deeply deplored, not alone by the members of his own, but by those of other communions by whom he was beloved.

A HISTORY OF THE YELLOW FEVER. 157

Sister Alphonsa, Mother Superior of St. Agnes, died on September 6th. She was the seventh of her order that succumbed to the dreaded scourge.

Mrs. Butler P. Anderson died at Hernando, Mississippi, and Captain J. Harvey Mathes, editor of the *Ledger*, was taken down with the fever September 7th.

Most of the drug-stores were closed by September 7th, very much to the inconvenience of the doctors, and to the endangering of the lives of the sick. Druggists, like doctors, owe it to the public to stand to their posts at a time like that; but if they do not, they must expect to see others take their places.

A. J. Wheeler, past grand master of Masons of this State, and editor and proprietor of the *Masonic Jewel*, died September 7th, of yellow fever. Mr. Wheeler had devoted himself unflinchingly to the work of succoring the sick—not only of the craft, of which he was a distinguished light, but of all societies and conditions, and literally worked himself down.

Appeal, September 7th.—"To lose over 1,200 men, women, and children in twenty-seven days, out of a population of 19,000 white and black, and to be expending over $10,000 for 1,200 nurses and forty doctors, and for medicines and food, for more than 3,000 sick and 10,000 indigent, was a sad reality, enough to move even a Stoic to tears. But besides this there comes the tales of individual sorrow; of whole families swept away in a week, leaving not even one of the name; of nurses dying at their posts; of priests and ministers and good sisters following those they succored so fast as to appall the stoutest heart and 'give us pause' amid the general wreck and ruin. No pen can do these scenes and sights justice; no tongue exaggerate them. Lisping childhood, hoary and venerable old age, the vagrant and the merchant, the man of God and the unbeliever, all are taken, all are claimed alike by the awful pestilence. It thins all ranks, and brings sorrow to the mansion, the cottage and the cabin. The cry of the fatherless was heard every hour, claiming the pity, the sympathy, and the tears of the most hardened veteran. In this office, as we write, there are but two left of all who a month ago were employed in the editorial, counting, and composing-rooms, and our pressman is down with the fever. Strangers to the office, as to the business, are attending to our affairs, while the only editor left on duty alternates, through sixteen hours a day, between his desk and a case. This is our personal measure of the dreadful epidemic, and surely it is a sad one. It has moved us to tears many a time the past ten days, although we are not used to the melting mood. Our experience is one we will never forget, and it is a common one. The fifth epidemic we have passed through, this surpasses them all in the horrors it has uncovered. Men have dropped dead on the streets, while others have died neglected, only to be discovered by the death-spreading gases from their bodies. Little children clamoring for the food she could no longer give, have appealed to the dead mother, who gave up her spirit as she gave birth to her last, in an agony of the fever. Ministers of the gospel carrying messages of peace, hurrying from house to house, have had their weary feet arrested and their work stayed by the pestilence that walks in the noonday as at night. The priest, administering the extreme unction, and the bride of Christ, wiping the death-damp from the forehead of those whose friends and kinfolk are far away, are almost paralyzed in the sacred act, and die even before we know they are sick. The business of the hour is the succor of the sick, the burial of the dead, and the care of the needy living. The last words of those who are well, are at night farewells to the dead, and the first in the morning 'who lives, and who has died?' All day, and every hour of the day, this question is repeated and the heart sickens at the reports, and the soul grows weary over the repetition. And yet there is no relief nor any release. Worse and worse the epidemic has grown, until to-day it has capped the climax, and the hearts of the brave men who have stood in the breach are blanched with fear, with a dread that annihilation awaits us, and that we are destined to be blotted from the earth. Fear sits on every face and dread on every heart. We work, not in the shadow, but in the very face of death. We meet him on every hand and at every moment in the names of his victims and in the desolation he has spread about us. Hope, we have none. We despair of any relief, but we are nerved for the end. We pray blessings upon the generous who have helped us in all the States; we pray for the safety of those who have come among us to nurse the sick and minister to the dying, and we ask that the names of the women and the men who have laid down their lives for us shall be handed down forever as among the brightest and best of the earth."

September 8th, Dr. Willett, in medical charge of the Catholic La Salette Academy, reported as convalescent Sisters Dominica, Cecelia, Alberta, and Reginald. All these were reported dangerously ill at one time.

September 8th, another of the horrifying incidents, which startle people at home as well as abroad, and leave one dazed with amazement that human beings can be so cowardly, occurred on one of the streets of the originally infected district. A man and his wife and one child occupying a nice home, saw their little girl taken down with the fever, whereupon the wife, full of the heroism of which her sex had made so many displays during this epidemic, advised the husband to leave, which he did without delay, and from a house only across the street saw the bodies of his child and faithful wife carried by strangers for interment in Elmwood Cemetery.

At Camp Joe Williams a woman was taken sick, who, with her husband, had been occupying snug-looking quarters. When she was being taken to the hospital the physician remarked to the husband that he could follow to nurse her. He demurred, and repeatedly objected, when finally, all but overcome by the doctor's importunities, he, pointing to the dog, said: "No; if I goes, who takes care of my dog?" The brute should have been kicked out of camp right then. He is not fit to live.

September 8th, another sickening case of desertion came to light. A man named Townsley lost a child by fever, immediately after the funeral of which his wife and little daughter Florence, twelve years of age, were taken. In despair he told the neighbors he was going to make away with himself, and has not since been heard of. After he thus basely deserted his wife, she died and was buried, and his little Florence and his youngest child, a boy, were wards in the infirmary.

Mrs. Brooks, wife of W. S. Brooks, of the *Appeal*, was buried September 8th, Mr. J. M. Keating and Eugene Moore alone forming the funeral party.

John T. Moss, September 9th, found three little girls in a house sick with the fever, who had lost their parents two days before by the scourge. No one was in the house to assist the little ones, and Mr. Moss kindly procured food, medicines and a nurse for them.

Thomas Hood, a volunteer telegrapher, from Philadelphia, died Sept. 9th.

Appeal, September 9th.—Parents have deserted children, and children parents, husbands their wives, but not one wife a husband.

Appeal, September 9th.—Let it be recorded to their credit that the negro militia and policemen have discharged their duties zealously and with discretion. We are proud of them. They proved their title to the gratitude of the people of Memphis.

General Charles A. Adams, one of the ablest members of our bar, died on September 8th, of the prevailing epidemic, after a brief illness.

Mr. Jesse Page, who had been constantly on duty with the Howards, doing noble service, was taken with the fever September 10th. He buried his father and brother, who died of the same disease, only a few days before.

Appeal, September 10th.—Dr. Mitchell reports that 686 new cases of yellow fever have been reported to him by the physicians employed by the Howard Association for the forty eight hours embracing Sunday and Monday. If reported to him, why not to the Board of Health, charged with the duty of compiling statistics of the growth, as well as results, of the disease? The public demands that the names and residences of all new cases shall be given, and we have urged that duty upon all the physicians, Dr. Erskine, the health officer, threatening, by public advertisement, the full penalties of the law for every case of neglect to report. In the face of this, we have here a statement of 686 new cases for forty-eight hours, for which time the Board of Health reports only 137. This does not look well, to say the least of it. We appeal to Dr. Mitchell to see that the physicians under his directions make reports to the Board of Health promptly. We must all of us obey the law to the letter.

Appeal, September 10th.—Rev. E. C. Slater has gone to his reward as a faithful servant of Christ. He died yesterday. No man did more than he in behalf of the sick. He carried consolation to the afflicted, and bore the blessed assurance of Jesus to the dying. Night and day he traveled from one bedside to another, knowing no relief so long as there remained one unattended who needed his ministration. A faithful minister of the Methodist Church, he went wherever called, knowing no divisions among Christians; as he said himself many times, knowing "nothing but Christ, and him crucified." The years of his ministry in Memphis were full of grace to him and his people, though he passed with them through the epidemic of 1873, and so far through this. Endearing himself to all classes, the presiding elder of the district, yielding to a general desire, left him with us as one who had done, and was still capable of more good. Genial and full of sunshine; gentle, but strong in his religious convictions, he was at all times an example of the true Christian minister. No one ever knew him but to love him, and none can name him but to praise.

Avalanche, September 11th.—"A stricken city! Alas, fair Memphis! What sights meet the eye of those who yet remain in your midst! . . . On every side is met the bowed form of some citizen who has lost a relative or a friend. The small burnt piles of bedding that are seen on every street but tells the passer-by, 'A death has occurred here.' These blackened spots are growing in number daily. . . . During the day there is bustle and confusion. Doctors are hurrying by. The hearse is met on every square. . . . Each day brings its changes. The form that but yesterday was seen in the full vigor of manhood, to-night lies tossing upon a bed, aching with fever. . . . Who will be left to tell the tale to-morrow?"

Appeal, Sept. 12th.—Annie Cook, the woman who, after a long life of shame, ventured all she had of life and property for the sick, died Sept. 11th, of yellow fever, which she contracted while nursing her patients. If there was virtue in the faith of the woman who but touched the hem of the garment of the Divine Redeemer, surely the sins of this woman must have been forgiven her. Her faith hath made her whole—made her one with the loving Christ, whose example she followed in giving her life that others might live. Amid so much that was sorrowful to an agonizing degree, so much that illumined the graces of a common humanity, and so much that disgraced that humanity, the example of that brave woman stands by itself, singular but beautiful, sad but touching, the very expression of that hope the realization of which we have in the words, "Inasmuch as ye have done it unto the least of these my brethren, ye have done it unto me." Out of sin, the woman, in all the tenderness and true fullness of her womanhood, merged, transfigured and purified, to become the healer, and at last to come to the Healer of souls, with Him to rest forever. She is at peace.

President A. D. Langstaff, of the Howard Association, one of our foremost heroes, was taken with the fever on Wednesday morning, September 11th, about three o'clock, after the hardest day's work he had done during the epidemic. Perhaps it was the strain on his nervous system, consequent upon so much work, that brought on the fever. Any way he was down, very much to the sorrow of every body in the city, especially the Howard Association, to whom he was as a tower of strength, and by whose members he was considered equal to any work that might be devolved upon him.

Mr. Catron, local agent of the Western Associated Press, was taken with the fever September 11th.

Sister Vincent died, September 11th, of the fever. She has done her duty, and has gone to her reward.

Colonel Knowlton, the efficient assistant postmaster, who was appointed postmaster after the death of Mr. R. A. Thompson, was stricken with the fever, September 11th.

Avalanche, September 12th.—"The contest has been sharp and decisive. The battle-ground is strewn with dead bodies, and the Grim Monster still advances. The aged and the young, the rich and the poor, the high and the lowly, all share the same fate—death. What a sight will greet the absent ones when they return and count the little mounds that have been raised over the spot where the heroic garrison lie buried."

Dr. Avent, one of our best and oldest physicians, has paid the penalty of his devotion to duty. He died at his residence, 309 Vance Street, September 12th.

Judge Robert Hutchinson, who was a candidate on the Democratic ticket for Circuit Court Judge, died September 12th of the fever, at the residence of Judge Halsey, on the Poplar Street Boulevard.

Captain A. T. Lacey, at one time the most opulent merchant of Memphis, and always a well-to-do business man, died of yellow fever, September 12th, at his residence in Chelsea.

Appeal, September 13th. — Mr. Herbert Landrum, local editor of the *Avalanche*, died September 12th of the fever, at the residence of his parents. Like his father, the reverend pastor of the Central Baptist Church, he knew no fear where duty was to be performed. He stood to his post, and braved all the terrors of the epidemic, not only performing his own accustomed labors, but taking on cheerfully the load that others dropped as they died or fled from the plague. How tenderly and with what watchfulness he nursed the late Mr. Thompson, to whom he was very much attached, all who knew him are cognizant of. Falling from exhaustion when his brother editor died, he recuperated, and again took his place as the only one of the *Avalanche* staff left. There he staid, doing double duty until the fever took him. After a comparatively brief battle he succumbed, and is now numbered with those who fell with their faces to the foe. The most promising man in the profession, his triumphs were only limited by the demands which each day made upon him. Quick, witty, sparkling, and bright, he bade fair to outshine all his contemporaries as a paragraphist and chronicler of city affairs. He never knew a dull moment, and grasped as eagerly the points of others as he spontaneously made those of his own. Cut off in the bud and promise of a useful career in a profession to which he seemed to be born, it will be difficult to replace him. To the mental qualities and readiness of pen which distinguished him, he added diligence and sobriety. No man could be more earnest or more industrious. He knew what was valuable as news by instinct, and grasped it without delay. To the members of the profession he was always courteous, kind, and affable. They reciprocated fully his good feeling, and promptly as he won it, recognized his place in the profession. His death was deeply mourned, and all earnestly condoled with his parents upon the loss of a son who gave promise of a most useful and honorable career.

Some of the Howard physicians report finding the dead bodies of negroes in the fields in the suburbs of the city. One body, so found, was actually eaten to the bones in many places by carrion birds. These negroes, no doubt, when attacked by the fever, dropped, and, without the care of physician or nurse, died neglected and alone.

Avalanche, September 13th.—"In the city, 203 new cases reported, ninety-eight deaths. The cup of sorrow has been drained to the dregs. Now we are nerved to any fate. . . . Death has lost its terrors. It has been witnessed so often of late, so many dear friends have been stricken, no longer is felt the pain of the wounded and bleeding heart. The dart is embedded and the shaft protrudes, but the sense of feeling has gone. The eyes have wept until the fountain has gone dry. . . . The undertakers find it impossible to bury the dead fast enough. The keepers of cemeteries can not have graves dug in time to receive the coffins brought, and often it is that sorrowing friends must wait until the narrow tombs can be made which is to hold the form of the departed."

Major Stephenson, the oldest compositor in Memphis, and for nine years past engaged upon the *Appeal*, died, it is with regret said, at his residence, September 13th, of yellow fever, after but a few days' illness. His son was convalescing from the fever, and two of his daughters were very ill of it—one of them being insensible—a sad case, but one that had a hundred times been duplicated.

Colonel Knowlton, one of the best of men, who succeeded the late R. A. Thompson as postmaster, died at an early hour September 14th.

One of the saddest instances of family annihilation by the epidemic is that furnished by the Flack family. The widowed mother, two sons and four daughters, were swept away in a few days, the last to go being Miss Louisa, who died and was buried September 14th. Their names and ages are as follows: Mrs. Barbara Flack, 51 years; Mr. Tom Flack, 28 years; Mr. Willie Flack, 19 years; Miss Laura Flack, 24 years; Miss Louisa Flack, 22 years; Miss Jennie Flack, 20 years; Miss Clara Flack, 18 years. They resided at No. 11 Elliott Street, and were cared for and nursed by H. J. Buhler, the scenic painter at the theater.

The sexton of St. Patrick's Church reported a case where a man was shrouded and encoffined, but who, when the lid was about to be screwed down, opened his eyes and asked those performing the last offices for him, "What are you doing?" A little trepidated, if not consternated, they lifted him from his close confinement and put him into bed. Treatment was begun again, and, strange to say, he recovered. He was literally rescued from the grave.

A foul smell, September 14th, attracted attention to the Mosby & Hunt building, and the examination of the premises, made by George Hayden, a colored policeman, revealed the discovery, in room 22, of the dead and decomposed body of H. L. Waring, cotton buyer. The appearance of the body indicated that he had been dead two or three days.

General W. J. Smith, who divided the honors of heroism with Butler P. Anderson, at Grenada, completely recovered from perhaps one of the severest cases of fever known.

Mr. R. W. Blew, publisher of the *Western Methodist*, with his wife and three children, has paid the debt of nature. He died on Sunday, September 15th, of the fever. He was a quiet, modest, unassuming gentleman, a good citizen and a pious Christian.

"The need of nurses," writes the Louisville *Courier-Journal* correspondent, "was known to the country, and, as a distinguished physician put it, 'this fact brought upon us the scum of the nation—in fact, an invasion of cut-throats, thieves, and prostitutes, of as bad a type as ever trod the earth.' These people thrust themselves upon Memphis, and the suffering sick were at their mercy. 'Every thing depends upon nursing; a good attendant and a pail of water will accomplish more than all the medicines in the land,' says Dr. Woodward. The hope of pecuniary profit brought most of these many nurses to Memphis. This is an undeniable fact. Of their conduct in the sick-room I shall speak presently. Gathering at Memphis after the manner of the human vultures who follow the field of battle, robbing the dead or dying soldier, these villains swarmed by the hundreds into the heart of the yellow fever country. Some few came through noble motives. They were not many. The large majority having resolved to fatten their purses by pilfering the dead, they were not slow in seizing other opportunities to steal or swindle. This was managed by practicing frauds on the employers—the Howards—in spite of whose vigilant watching they made false returns and collected largely in excess of actual services rendered. How much fraud was perpetrated in this manner it is impossible to estimate, nor is there any disposition upon the part of interested parties to say much about it. The conduct of the leader of this brazen band after reaching Memphis was even more outrageous than before. *De mortuis nil nisi bonum* is all right in its way, but if I uncover any unpleasant odor I sincerely trust circumstances may justify. Sooner or later we meet our fate, and Mrs. ——— came by hers rather suddenly. She will be remembered as the female who wrote a card full of what seemed to be virtuous indignation over the *Courier-Journal's* truthful story. She would have jerked bald-headed the author of the publication, but the Lord—or, perhaps, the 'Lord-knows-who'—had set his eyes upon her, and she was set down for an early doom. This Mrs. ——— would have soared to the front. She wished all she could get, and a trifle additional. She got both, and the Lord—or the Lord-knows-who—got her. She was distantly related to Oliver Cromwell of yore, if the record of her deeds go for aught. Mrs. ——— was nursing in the family of a well-known judiciary officer. *Esse quam videri* is good enough in its way, but Mrs. ——— preferred to seem rather than to be. She had abundant opportunity to exercise any extraordinary avaricious inclination she might possess during the delirium of her patients; and having heard that the little busy bee improves each shining hour, she sought to profit by example and filled her trunk with valuables, such as jewelry and silverware. This trunk she sent to the express office to be shipped to ———. Before it had gone Mrs. ——— took the fever, or perhaps the fever took Mrs. ———. The Howards, being very naughty people, peeped into her trunk and discovered her stolen treasures. The relentless reaper, meanwhile, had set about harvesting Mrs. ———, and thus she escaped any punishment earth may have given her. 'One of the worst of my experiences with nurses,' said Dr. ——— to me, 'was in the case of a female patient. It took four to kill her. The first one stole her clothing and ran away; the second got drunk and neglected her; the third took sick and died; and the fourth, getting drunk, fell over on her bed with a wine bottle held high in one hand, dancing like an Indian in his intoxication. This scoundrel was arrested.' 'One man whom I wished especially to get well was deserted by his nurse at the most critical period,' remarked a physician to me, 'and other nurses I found drunk and their posts deserted. Some stole all they could, and many held drunken orgies in the rooms of patients.'"

The Church Orphans' Home, September 17th, was a hospital, with twenty sick children and one convalescent Sister of St. Mary's. Two of the good sisters

A HISTORY OF THE YELLOW FEVER. 163

died in the performance of their sacred duties, and two of the children. Under a happier condition of things the sisters were glad to give a welcome to all the orphan children that were sent them. As it was, they positively declined to receive any more until after the epidemic.

Major W. A. Willis, superintendent of the Southern Express Company, died on Sunday, September 15th, after nearly a week's battle with the fever. As a member of the Citizens' Relief Committee, he had been of great service to the city at a most critical juncture of the plague. A noble soul, type of the most chivalric heroism, his loss was mourned as that of a brother endeared by every tie.

The death of J. G. Lonsdale, Jr., treasurer of the Citizens' Relief Committee, was a shock to the community, on Sunday, September 15th. He had worked so earnestly and cheerfully, and enjoyed such unusual good health that it was believed and hoped he would pass the crisis and convalesce. God willed it otherwise.

September 17th, the proprietor of the *Evening Ledger*, Mr. Ed. Whitmore, conquered the fever and was pronounced convalescent. His pluck and energy, conjoined to the labor of Captain Mathes, kept the *Ledger* going.

One of the most distressing scenes witnessed since the epidemic commenced, was that reported by a neighbor of R. W. Blew's. The gentleman called at Mr. Blew's on Monday morning, September 16th, and there found four dead, and three very sick. The four deaths had occurred within twenty-four hours.

A lady from Memphis, Mrs. Evans, who lost her husband on August 30th, and who had had the fever, fainted and fell on the platform at Waverly Station, on the Chattanooga road. She had a sick child with her. The announcement of the fact stampeded the town, and the people fled to the mountains.

The Very Reverend M. Riordan, vicar-general of this diocese, and pastor of St. Patrick's Church, died, September 17th, after two weeks' illness, from yellow fever. Like those of his brethren of the priesthood, who preceded him, he fell at his post. He contracted the disease while in the discharge of the duties of his sacred office, and fell as the brave soldier of the cross loves to fall.

Dr. John Erskine, health officer, after a week's illness, died, September 17th. His death was a great loss to the city, and to the faculty of which he was one of the chief ornaments.

J. W. McDonald, the volunteer telegraph operator from Cincinnati, died, September 17th. Mr. McDonald was the sixth operator that succumbed to the fever. It was strange, but nevertheless true, that so far no telegrapher that had been attacked had recovered.

A very sudden death was that of Conrad Rasp, baker at the Peabody Hotel. He gave up work at nine o'clock, September 17th, and died at five in the afternoon. He had had the fever for several days, but refused to take to his bed.

Mrs. J. W. Clark, of Omaha, who volunteered to nurse the sick, fell a victim to the fever, and died September 18th. She was tenderly and lovingly prepared for the grave, and laid away by those who, knowing how noble her mission and how true she was to it, mourned for her as for a sister.

Dr. Hiram Pearce, of Cincinnati, Ohio, who volunteered and was assigned to duty by Dr. Mitchell, of the Howard Association, died September 18th, very much to the regret of the medical corps and all who had met him. His memory will ever be cherished by this people, as a noble example to the members of a profession whose ranks had been many times recruited and many times thinned since the epidemic began.

A gentleman, taken sick, was sent a nurse, who stole his horse and buggy and deserted him; another was sent, who took sick and died; a third was sent, who proved so worthless and inexperienced that he had to be sent away; and a fourth was sent, who got beastly drunk.

A cheeky nurse, but an incorrigible rascal and thief, who was sent to attend Captain Mathes, of the *Ledger*, stole his horse and buggy. September 18th, Captain Mathes received a postal card, mailed at Iuka, Mississippi, notifying him that as his ulster was inconvenient to carry he had left it at some point (name not remembered), and *my* horse could be found at Moscow.

Among the dead, of September 18th, was the name of Rev. Mr. Schuyler, of Hoboken, New Jersey, who came, a volunteer, to do what he could to help his brethren of the Episcopal Church. He was in Memphis but a few brief days when the pestilence claimed him for a victim, and he passed away to receive the reward which awaits the brave and the just. While on duty he was of great help, as Rev. Dr. White, of Calvary Church, and Rev. Dr. Dalzell, of Shreveport, were the only Episcopal clergymen to attend to the innumerable and every-day increasing wants of the members of the church. Rev. Mr. Harris, of St. Mary's, was still in the agonies of the fever, September 18th, and Rev. Mr. Parsons, of St. Lazarus and Grace Church parishes, had just been laid away to rest.

When the fever began there were four Episcopal ministers on duty—Rev. Dr. George White, rector of Calvary; Rev. George Harris, dean of St. Mary's Cathedral; Rev. C. C. Parsons, rector of the two parishes of St. Lazarus and Grace Church; and Rev. Mr. Gee, rector of the Church of the Good Shepherd. All of these gentlemen remained to share the fate of their people, only two of them escaping—Dr. White and Mr. Gee. Mr. Parsons died and Mr. Harris recovered after a long and serious illness. When the last two fell a prey to the epidemic, Rev. Mr. Schuyler, of Hoboken, New Jersey, and Rev. Dr. Dalzell, of Shreveport, Louisiana, volunteered. The former paid with his life for the noble act of heroism, and Dr. Dalzell was on duty in charge of St. Mary's parish.

Of the Methodist ministers, Rev. Messrs. Slater and Rosebrough devoted themselves to their people, with a singleness of purpose worthy the martyrs of the early church, laying down their lives as an attestation and seal of their faith and zeal as officers of the church.

Rev. Mr. Daniels, of the First Presbyterian Church, resided in the midst of what was originally the infected district, and fell early in the action, and found some difficulty in overcoming a severe attack of the fever.

Of the Baptist ministers Rev. Dr. Landrum alone remained. The witnesses of his zeal are as many as have died and lived. Even when the fever invaded his own household he was laboring in the streets, as a member of the Relief Committee, and in the homes of the people, carrying "the bread of life."

Of the German Protestant pastors, Mr. Thomas died from overwork, but Mr. Holmes was a tower of strength to his people. Their praises were spoken by every one.

The Catholic priesthood, for zeal, self-denial, and self-sacrifice stand unrivaled. The long roll of their dead attests this fact and challenges the admiration of all men, be their faith and nationality what it may. Upbearing the banner of the cross, symbol of faith and hope, Rev. Martin Walsh, pastor of St. Bridget's, fell, and with him his assistant, Rev. Mr. Meagher. The Rev. Father Asinus, of St. Mary's (German Franciscan) also gave up his life in his efforts for his parishioners. St. Peter's parish, under the care of the Dominicans, gave three martyrs, Rev. J. R. McGarvey, a volunteer from Harrodsburg, Ky., Rev. J. A. Bakel from Baltimore, Md., and the Rev. Mr. Van Troostenburg from Kentucky. St. Patrick's gave its pastor, the Vicar-General of the diocese, Rev. Martin Riordan, the Rev. M. McNamara, and the Rev. J. P. Scannell, a volunteer from Louisville, Ky. Only three priests remained on duty, Rev. Father Kelly, pastor of St. Peter's, Rev. Father Aloysius, of St. Mary's, Rev. Father Walsh, at St. Patrick's, and the Rev. Father Mooney,

A HISTORY OF THE YELLOW FEVER.

who volunteered and arrived a few days ago from Nashville. To the list of martyrs is also to be added the names of Father Scanlin, of St. Peter's, and Father Maternus, of St. Mary's (German) Franciscan Church.

Appeal, September 20th.—The following is a copy of a telegram sent to New York, to be read in Booth's Theater on the 21st: "Deaths to date, 2,250; number sick now, about 3,000; average deaths, sixty per cent. of the sick. We are feeding some 10,000 persons, sick and destitute, in camps and in the city. Our city is a hospital. Fifteen volunteer physicians have died; twenty others are sick. A great many nurses have died—many that had the fever before, and thought themselves proof. Fever abating some to-day, for want of material, perhaps, and things look a little more hopeful. We are praying for frost—it is our only hope. A thousand thanks to the generous people of New York."

Ledger, September 20th.—"One phase in the condition of the plague-smitten Southern cities is scarcely realized at the North, even with the daily descriptions given in the papers, of the distress prevailing there. All industries have ceased. The stores are closed, the factories are not running, wharves and depots are deserted, for boats and trains neither arrive nor depart, so that means for earning their daily bread is taken away from those who are not stricken with the fever. . . . Work is the panacea for many evils, and at such times as these if the head and hands are occupied the danger is diminished ten-fold; and besides the agony of brooding over the pestilence, hundreds and thousands of people have nothing to live upon. Their money is gone, and they can earn no more. Even if they could, the store of provisions is exhausted. Markets are closed, market wagons have ceased to come in from the country."

After two weeks or more of fever, Dr. S. R. Clarke, to the surprise of his physicians as well as friends, died September 20th, at his residence on Beale Street. The loss of his wife no doubt preyed upon his mind, and had much to do with the suddenness of his death. For several days he had been pronounced convalescent, and was supposed to be slowly but surely reaching that stage toward complete recovery when his doctors would be able to leave him to his own course, when, without premonition of the end, he died. His loss was deeply deplored. He had a wide circle of friends among the best of our people, and specially endeared himself to those who, like himself, had remained to brave the epidemic, by his devotion to the duties of the office he held as a member of the Citizens' Relief Committee. In all the relations of life he was a true man. His loss was mourned as one of the severest the epidemic had cost Memphis.

The figures of September 20th, as to the sick and dead by yellow fever, were most reassuring. The falling off in the number of both, from the average of the past ten days, afforded occasion for devout thanks.

September 22d, one by one the surviving employés of the *Appeal* returned to their posts. Mr. White, business manager, was at work on the 19th of September; Mr. Brooks, river and telegraph editor, on the 23d; and Mr. McGrann, foreman of the composing-room, Mr. Woodlock, foreman of the press-room, returned to duty on the 17th. Of the compositors, Mr. Schiller has been at work since September 16th, Mr. Hoskins since the 19th, for a few hours each day, and September 21st, Mr. Will Taylor tried his hand for a few hours. Mr. Fred Brennan, city editor, was still confined to his room, convalescing slowly, but surely.

September 22d the following postal card was received from George Francis Train:

MADISON SQUARE, P. E. 49.

Citizen J. M. Keating:

The fever is born of panic, based on gormandizing diseased animal food—fish, eggs, butter. Meat is the delirium tremens of flesh. All your remedies only make matters worse. Stop alcohol, tobacco, brandy, quinine, drugs. But, above all, keep in the open air. Abolish hearses, funerals, and the grave-yard horrors; they spread the pestilence. Commence at once cremating the dead. The disease is mental. It is not the yellow fever (that my father, mother, three sisters, nurse, doctor, and five servants died of in New Orleans in a few days when I was but four years old), 'tis the Asiatic plague, or consolidation of all the diseases through mental action or fear of death. Memphis knows me. If you have faith, I will stop the pestilence. Telegraph and I will come by express. Mayor and citizens' committee must sign the dispatch. My guarantee of good faith is that you will see me moving among the dying and dead.

G. F. T.

Appeal, Sept. 24th.—Mr. Robert R. Catron, agent of the Associated Press in this city, died last night of yellow fever, after four days' sickness. Every thing that the tenderest solicitude and the best medical skill could suggest and accomplish was made use of, but to no purpose. The disease invaded his brain, and he passed away peacefully in a semi-unconscious state. No man of his years and position did more or better work than he throughout the epidemic. When the editorial and reportorial staffs of the *Avalanche* and the *Ledger* were all down with the fever, some of them sick, and more dying, he volunteered, and for some days worked on both papers, besides doing what he could for immediate personal friends sick of the fever, and who, he thought, had paramount claims upon his time. Every moment of his waking hours was spent in doing good. Alive to the dreadful effects of the epidemic, and in full sympathy with the suffering people whom he knew so well, his dispatches were always within the limits of facts. He avoided sensationalizing as unworthy the occasion, and confined himself to the simplest statement of each day's sad history. What effect this had upon the public mind of every State in the Union, let the numberless active charities tell, which continue to pour their beneficence upon us. Modest and unassuming, his growth in the profession was due to his own worth and abilities, and not to any fictitious aids such as sometimes help to push men beyond their depth. He was equal to all the demands made upon him whether professional or friendly, and went to his grave followed by the regrets of all who knew him, especially those who saw how nobly he met death at his post.

Charley Brooks, the last member of the family of Mr. Will Brooks, of the *Appeal*, died September 23d.

The Gregg family were swept from the face of the earth. The father and six children had died, and, on September 24th, the mother died.

The brutality, barbarism, and indifference developed by this epidemic stand out in marked contrast with the heroisms which cost so many lives. Scarcely a day passed that the community, bowed in sorrow for so many weeks, was not shamed by one or other of these hideous phases of inhumanity; as if it were not enough that the experiences of the times developed cases of total neglect, which were brought to light when the sufferers were past hope and beyond the reach of human aid. But there were creatures, in the semblance of men, who, terrorized out of all reason, surrendered themselves to demoniacal passions, and expressed their fears in acts that were a disgrace to our race and blood.

A little child of, perhaps, three years was surrendered to the keeping of one of the noble volunteer doctors by a mother who now fills a nameless grave in the potter's field. She was an outcast—had thrown herself away because abandoned by her husband—and finding herself fast sinking, from the combined effects of the most loathsome of diseases and the yellow fever, gave her child to her physician, that it might find the home and care the cowardly father had denied to her and it. How shocking to every sense!

No man in Memphis had, during this epidemic, done more or better work than the Rev. Dr. Boggs, pastor of the Second Presbyterian Church. Night and day he was on the move, going anywhere and every-where he could do any good. Nothing came amiss to his hands. He prayed or nursed, counseled or consoled, as the time or place demanded; and he stood not for calls. He went about among his people and kept up with them. In the country or in the city, it was all the same to him. Poor or rich, they were all alike. He asked no questions. He saw what was to be done, and he did it. He was the messenger for the doctor, or the medicines, as often as any thing else, and yet he never lost a moment as guardian of the orphans of the Leath Asylum. His many anxieties concerning them were those of a father for his children, and when the fever made its appearance among them he was one of the first to fly to their succor and relief. He was vouchsafed just two days' duty with the poor children, when he and his wife were taken down. Of course, he had the best of nursing, care, and the first medical skill, besides which, he had a good constitution and a brave heart.

Dr. Augustus Kuehne, formerly of Ohio, at present of Memphis, paid the following tribute to his dead compatriots: "The physicians who died were Hiram B. Pearce, Cincinnati ; Robert Burchman, Columbus ; Dr. Tucrk, Cincinnati, and Dr. Tate (colored), also of Cincinnati. Dr. Tate was a friend of the suffering sick of his own race—a true and noble man. Without hesitancy, he worked, without rest, day and night. His own race caused him the greatest distress. Home physicians, with but very few exceptions, cared very little for the colored race. I have seen how colored men have placed their hands on Dr. Tate's coat collar, carrying him 'per force' (the doctor) to their wretched habitations. If a man had been cast of iron, he must, under such trying circumstances, have succumbed. Dr. Tate died in the house of a colored friend, Mr. Morgan, a dentist, residing on Beal Street. It is a fact that Dr. Tate's life could have been saved had he not been too brave. He left his bed, after four days' sickness, believing himself strong enough to return for duty. The sad result was a relapse of the fever, which cut him down within three days. Dr. Hiram B. Pearce, animated by the true sense of duty as a physician and a man who believed in our Savior—that friend beloved as he was to me—left Cincinnati in my company, notwithstanding he was surrounded by all the comforts and luxuries of life. No mercenary spirit tempted him to sacrifice his life in order to save the lives of others. Before our departure from Cincinnati, Dr. Pearce told me that he had received a letter from his father, threatening him with disinheritance should he leave for Memphis. Hold this up to the medical profession of Memphis, and, at least, let them speak a kind word of those who are slumbering now in Elmwood. Dr. Pearce was taken with fever in room 91 of the Peabody Hotel. Dr. Tate and your informant removed him to the Court Street Infirmary. Dr. Bryan, from Texas, had charge of the place. It is an old dilapidated building, and a terror crept over me as soon as I had placed my foot within it. *Misericorde*—how could valuable lives be preserved within such non-ventilated, but overheated, rooms like that? A long row of beds, and yellow fever pestilence every-where. Clouds of poisonous atmosphere were enshrouding the bedsteads of every individual patient. Dr. Bryan treated me with brusque discourtesy on the following morning. I desired to see my poor friend Dr. Pearce. He positively refused me 'as a physician,' entrance, stating that he had control over all his patients. I have no words to express my indignation over such unprofessional conduct. Dr. Pearce died. Dr. Robert Burchman was a graduate of Edinburgh, Scotland. I made his acquaintance in Cincinnati. Drs. Pearce, Burchman, and myself came to Memphis together. On the 17th of September, I was taken down, and while on my sick-bed I heard of his sickness, and in a few days of his subsequent death. Dr. Burchman was a brave and good man. Fearlessly he went to his work and discharged it faithfully. After midnight, Dr. Burchman and Dr. Tuerk came to my bedside, on the first day of my sickness, and rendered professional services. May his grave be kept green by some friendly hand in the Mississippi Valley. Dr. Tuerk was a graduate of Heidelberg, Germany. I do not know any thing of his previous history. However, I will say that he was one of the hardest workers in the First Ward. I valued his friendship, and never will I forget his memory. Dr. McFarland, Savannah, Ga., Hon. Milo Olin, Augusta, Ga., Dr. T. Grange Simmons, Charleston, Dr. Carswell, Americus, Ga., and Dr. De Graffenreid deserve special notice, and, in fact, a large number of the Southern Howard physicians will tell you what I do." Dr. Carswell indorsed the foregoing.

Major Pollard Trezevant, died September 25th, of fever, after an illness of only a few days. Since the epidemic began he had been working as a Howard, never thinking of himself, and only intent upon the good he might do. Major Trezevant, before and during the war, held high official positions, but since has been engaged in the real estate business. A member of one of our most honored families, he owed nothing to that fact. He made himself all that he was by his own efforts, and died, as he lived, an honest man.

"Mr. Charles G. Fisher, chairman of the Citizens Relief Committee, died and was buried yesterday (September 26, 1878)," says the *Appeal* of the 27th. "He had been sick of the fever only a few days, but having overtaxed himself in his efforts to keep up with all the demands upon his time, he had but little of his native vigor left with which to contend with so violent an enemy. His death was not any more the result of the yellow fever than of overwork. The position he occupied was one of more than ordinary care and responsibility, which, under brighter auspices, would task a very strong man to the uttermost. He might be said literally to be on duty every hour of the twenty-four, for though he had office hours, much of his business was transacted upon the streets, at his home, by the sick-bed, perhaps, of a friend, or wherever else the needy or the friends of the sick might find him. Kind and gentle, he was also firm and unswerving in the performance of his duty. He felt that to him and his associates the people of the whole country had given a sacred trust, the administration of which required more than ordinary care. He, therefore, scanned narrowly all claims for relief, and impressed on all about him the duty of so apportioning the money and food sent to us by the good people of all the States as to make their charity a beneficence and not a means of encouraging idleness. In this he succeeded only partially, but failure was due to circumstances he could not overcome, and which the citizens, though they have resolved time and again, have not yet been able to overcome. He was faithful to his trust, and zealous in the discharge of his duties. He was also energetic in behalf of the sick as well as suffering. His house was a home for many who were there nursed safely through the fever, and some who died, notwithstanding the greatest care. To them all he was full of consideration and kindness. He gave them what he could of his time, and nursed them to the neglect of himself. He was always equal to the occasion, equal to the demands made upon him, and proved himself throughout the epidemic a hero of heroic mold. Mr. Fisher was a member of one of our principal cotton firms, and had, with his partner, Mr. William Gage, built up a business within the past ten years that ranked second to that of no other house in the city. He was popular with the people, and was elected to represent the sixth ward in the Board of Councilmen for several terms. He was a native of Tipton County, a son of Dr. Fisher, of Covington, and served throughout the war in the Confederate army, making for himself a name as a brave soldier only second to that which he made within the past few weeks for a moral heroism and courage that crowned his life with martyrdom."

Avalanche, September 24th.—" New cases in the city, one hundred and fifty-six. Deaths, sixty-four. The hopes that had been raised in the hearts of the people that the fever was abating were rudely dispelled yesterday, when the reports of new cases began pouring in. All during the forenoon there was one continuous call for nurses, and many who were on the eve of departing home, thinking their services were no longer required, were placed on duty, and the demand was in excess of the supply. As the physicians extend their visits to the suburbs, many instances are discovered of whole families who are stricken, and have lain for days without any attention whatever."

There was a sad case out on Rayburn Avenue, just beyond the city limits. A family by the name of McNamee were severely afflicted. Two of their children died of the fever, the mother and the father were down some time, leaving the only remaining member of the family, a young girl, alone, well enough to administer to the wants of the others. September 25th she was stricken down, and three were left. Nurses were sent to them, and they were carefully attended to.

The most startling death since the epidemic was first announced, and one that conveyed a warning to convalescents, was that of Francis W. Schley, of 34 Winchester Avenue. It occurred September 27th, on Market Street, extended, between three and half past four o'clock—no one could tell exactly the moment, as he was alone, and no person seems to have traveled the street until about the latter hour—when Dr. Nuttal found the unfortunate man lying upon his back, quite dead, a basket containing a couple of bushels of potatoes beside him. He left his wife at three o'clock for the grocery, where he purchased the potatoes, and was on his way home and within, perhaps, a hundred yards of it when his strength, which he had overtaxed as a convalescent, gave out, and he fell, perhaps lay down, and died. He had had a very severe attack of the fever, but for two weeks had been convalescing, and was supposed to be beyond any danger. But so slender and tender is the cord of life, as the fever leaves it, that even the slight exertion of a short walk and the weight of a basket a little child might carry without strain, broke it, and he passed away alone, so near and yet so far from the touch of a tender hand and the kiss of affectionate lips.

Persons who were not in the city can never realize the sorrows and pressure of duties resting upon the few who remained during the epidemic. Let this case illustrate many, and indicate something of the condition. On September 26th the son of a pastor of one of the churches, numbering 400, was buried. The son himself had many friends. Who attended that funeral? The parents, themselves just from a yellow-fever bed, and two nurses of the son—one an Italian, and the other a negro. These *four* and no others. Not a member of that pastor's church, not a citizen could be spared for an hour to go with him and his heart-broken wife to the grave of their son. This was not from any want of friendship, sympathy, or affection on the part of thousands who knew the family; it simply shows into what fearful necessities and sorrows this "noisome" pestilence had brought them.

The Rev. W. P. Barton, of Greenville, Miss., assisted by one of our local physicians, a layman—Dr. C. W. Malone—ministers, and has been ministering, to the wants of the people of the Methodist Church since the epidemic began. Mr. Barton was on his way home and was compelled to remain when travel by the river was cut off. He at once volunteered his services, and was on duty for some weeks.

Nothing was so significant of the effect of the epidemic upon Memphis as the attendance at the Jewish Synagogue, corner of Exchange and Main Streets, September 27th. The occasion was one of the most interesting and sacred to the Hebrew race—the ushering in of the new year. When the fever was first announced there was a Jewish population of about three thousand. Of this number only eighteen were present at the solemn services, made more so by the surrounding sorrow and the evidence these few bore to the effect of the plague. Of the eighteen nine were fever convalescents, three were nurses from distant cities, the remaining six being those who alone escaped of all who remained to brave the disease. Mr. A. S. Meyers, acting president of the Masonic Relief Board, read the service, the scene being very affecting. There was not a dry eye among all those present, as they recalled the festival as it was observed in other and happier years, and remembered the brave and noble Menken, and many others who had passed away, the heroes of these times that try men's souls. It was a sad and mournful ushering in of the new year—a ceremony that will live in the hearts of all present to their latest hour.

One of the saddest cases that have come under our notice is that of the family of John Dawson, who died at Elmwood Cemetery. Mr. Dawson died September 17th, after an illness of three days' duration. His brave wife arose from her bed to administer to the wants of her four little girls. She went on bravely, doing her duty nursing her little ones, till, on the morning of the 23d, she succumbed to an attack of the fever. After four days of suffering she died peacefully, trusting in him who has promised to care for the fatherless. A friend was with her to receive her dying requests. As she has no relatives in America, her children were taken to the Church home, where, under the care of kind Sister Frances, they are assured a mother's tender, watchful guidance. Their ages are, respectively, eight, five, three, and one. Mr. Dawson came from England in 1872, and has been an employé of the cemetery company for the last six years. During the epidemic of 1873, he worked like the brave man he was. He did his duty nobly and well then, as always, and with his wife has gone to his reward. Till their English friends can be heard from the children will remain at the "home." It is hardly necessary to say that the children of a man who laid down his life in this sacred cause will be tenderly cared for till their relatives in England say what better can be done for them.

Dr. Paul Otey died of yellow fever at Mr. W. J. P. Doyle's residence, on Dunlap Street, at a late hour, September 28th. He had been sick for over a week, and it was hoped would rally from the effects of the disease he cured in others so often, but his strength was not equal to the task. Dr. Otey was the oldest son of the late Rt. Rev. James H. Otey, first Episcopal bishop of Tennessee, and was educated at Kenyon College, Ohio, President Hayes being among his classmates. Intended for the ministry, he preferred medicine, and studied for that profession with much of the ardor of a lover. As such, he followed it, attaining, both in the Confederate army, in which he served throughout the war, and here in Memphis, where he had lived since its close, an enviable distinction, although by his own preference his practice was limited. He was a man of strong mind but good heart. To him the people of Memphis were indebted for the camps which, while affording shelter and comfort to seven thousand refugees, insured them the health denied them at home. From the outbreak of the epidemic he was active in behalf of the nurses. His sympathies were fully aroused, and up to the hour when he lay down to die he never ceased to interest himself in behalf of the people.*

---

* St. Louis *Republican:* "This gentleman, who, on Saturday afternoon, 28th inst., in his fifty-fourth year, was added to the list of heroic Memphis martyrs, deserves a tribute to his memory. He was the eldest son of the late Right Rev. James Hervey Otey, bishop of the Protestant Episcopal Church for the diocese of Tennessee, and brother of Mrs. B. B. Minor, of St. Louis. After academic preparations in his native State, and chiefly under the auspices of his father (who was one of the greatest friends and promoters of Christian education that the West has ever had), he entered the Kenyon Col-

E. E. Furbish died September 27th at the Peabody. He was formerly in the employ of B. Lowenstein & Co., but had recently officiated in a clerical capacity at the Howard Association headquarters. He had been ailing for several days, but refused to acknowledge the presence of the prevailing fever. On the 27th, while walking in the hall of the hotel, he fainted and fell prostrate to the floor. He was conveyed to his room, and measures taken to produce a reaction, without avail, however, for he steadily sank and finally died as stated.

Mr. Eugene W. Moore appeared on the street safely convalescent September 27th. Mr. Moore was of invaluable service to the *Appeal*, acting business manager, city and commercial editor, mail clerk, office clerk, and wherever he could put in a hand for work.

Avalanche, October 28th.—" New cases in the city and suburbs, 117. Deaths, twenty-eight. The fever, although not abating in cases, is not as malignant as it was several days ago. It gradually, as the cool north wind greets us, becomes milder, and one can judge from the death rate, if correctly reported, that persons who take it from this time on, have at least two chances out of three of getting over it. . . . Our people have lost all appearance of panic, and are now coolly awaiting 'their turn,' as it were, like the soldier who goes out on picket, knowing not whether he will ever meet his comrades again."

Mr. R. B. Clarke, who succeeded John G. Lonsdale, Jr., as treasurer of the Citizens' Relief Committee, died of yellow fever, September 30th, after a week's sickness. Mr. Clarke, up to the time when he contracted the plague, was connected with the committee in a clerical capacity, and was so attentive to his duties as to commend himself to the officers of that organization as well fitted for the responsible position vacated by the death of Mr. Lonsdale. He accepted the trust, and proved, by his subsequent management of the duties of the office, the wisdom of the committee's choice. His death was deeply mourned by his associates and by a wide circle of friends, who esteemed him as a gentleman of the highest character, courteous and polite, and full of that moral courage of which heroes are made.

Mr. John M. Peabody, Superintendent of the Leath Orphan Asylum, died Tuesday evening, October 1st, of yellow fever. He had been in charge of the asylum for five years, and during his term of office made a faithful and

---

lege, Ohio. Thence he was drawn to Richmond, Va., by the residence there of his brother-in-law, and attended one full course of lectures in the Richmond College in the palmy days of Warner, Cullen, Bohannan, and Maupin. But he obtained his medical diploma from the Jefferson school in Philadelphia, where he continued his studies under the auspices and in the office of the distinguished Dr. Thos. H. Mutter. Though his preparation for his profession was so complete, he did not prosecute it long, but, having married quite early, he preferred the life of a planter, and opened a cotton plantation in a very fertile part of Phillips County, Arkansas. Here the late Confederate war found him in the immediate neighborhood of another brother-in-law, General Daniel C. Govan. They both entered unhesitatingly into the Confederate service, and Dr. Otey, resuming his profession, became known as a surgeon of no mean repute, and was as such quite intimately associated with his friend, Dr. Charles Michel, now of St. Louis. At the close of the war Dr. Otey settled in Memphis, to devote himself to his profession, and has done so ever since. He has remained faithful during two visitations from yellow fever, and one from cholera. A fearless sympathy with suffering, and a strong feeling of humanity, have combined with professional esprit to keep him at his post; and, no doubt, his experience, gained on former fields of duty and of danger, made him the more efficient until he was himself stricken down. Prepossessing in person, agreeable and easy in manners, and genial in disposition, he made many strong friends, who, while so deeply lamenting his death, will join with the whole community, whom he has so dauntlessly and ably served, in doing honor to his memory and spreading chaplets over his grave. He was suddenly and sadly made a widower soon after his last settlement in Memphis, and leaves an adopted daughter to bemoan her now redoubled orphanage."

efficient officer, ever sympathizing with the little ones under his charge, and doing all things to render their home an agreeable one. Mr. Peabody was an active member of the Masonic, Odd-Fellows, and Knights of Honor lodges of this city.

A man and his wife were living in rather an isolated locality. The husband was sick of the fever. The physician made his call about three o'clock in the afternoon, when he found him very low, but the wife, who had undertaken to nurse him, showed, up to that time, no symptoms of the fever. He called the next day, as usual, and found the man had been dead twelve hours, and his wife lay beside the corpse with a burning fever. She had been taken so suddenly and so severely that she was unable to summon assistance.

Mrs. Hood, a widow of some property, died and left two children. The undertakers were about to send her body to the potter's field, when Mr. Simmons, who had charge of the Howard nurses, interfered to prevent it. A telegram was sent to Mr. Barnum, of Werne & Barnum, Louisville, who telegraphed funds for proper sepulture. Two efforts had been made to take the body away during this interval, which had been frustrated; yet while Mr. Simmons was making arrangements necessary to the final disposition of the remains, the poor woman was carted off to the potter's field, or the trenches, and it would be utterly impossible at this day to tell where she is resting. This was caused by demands of the citizens made upon the undertakers. The laws required that bodies should be removed as soon as death had taken place, and the undertakers were several times arrested for the supposed violation of this rule.

A man named Donahoo was taken down with the fever. On the fourth day his reason was dethroned, and, invested with the strength born of insanity, he jumped from his bed, drove nurses out of doors, and, seizing a weapon that had been left in the house, attempted to murder his sister. Assistance came before he had accomplished the deed; he was overpowered, and was sent to the county-jail a raving maniac.

Avalanche, Oct. 2d.—"Louis Daltroof, the Howard undertaker, had the most terrible experience of any person who worked through the epidemic period. He has been alone, at midnight, with the rain falling, in the cemetery digging graves and burying the dead without assistance. One night, at twelve o'clock, while the patients were dying so fast at one of the hospitals, that from twenty to thirty corpses would accumulate in the dead-house between the trips of the wagons, he was handed a telegram from some one connected with the house of Menkin & Brother, requesting him to procure the body of a much-respected young Israelite, who had been in their employ, and died, also to bury the deceased in the Jewish cemetery. No time was to be lost if the wishes of the friends of the young man were to be respected. Daltroof repaired at once to the hospital charnel-house, where bodies were piled on top of each other, mattresses and all, just as they died. After working for an hour or more, and removing nine bodies in the last stages of putrefaction, he found the one he sought, and buried it according to instructions, digging the grave himself, and returned to headquarters for duty by four o'clock the same morning."

Avalanche, October 2d.—"New cases in the city and suburbs, ninety-nine. Deaths, thirty-three. The fever has spread until it has embraced within its death fold every residence within a radius of twelve miles, and the end is not yet. It has branched off and followed the line of railroads running out of the city until it has extended for fully fifty miles, to the north, east and south. Only the west has escaped, and not altogether, for there are several cases of fever in Hopefield."

Among the early victims of the epidemic was a man who, ten years ago, became a wreck. Coming to Memphis, where he was surrounded by kindly influences and encouraging friends, he reëstablished himself, and deserved and received the respect of all citizens. His name is unnecessary to the details of his fall, but he sleeps to-day amid the verdure of Elmwood, one of those men of heroic mold, who, like Anteus of old, renewed his strength with each defeat. At the time above stated he was a resident of New Orleans, in which city he mingled with men who are measured by their failings rather than the absence of them, and was identified with the fastest phases of a rapid life. He was engaged as a wholesale grocer on Tchoupitoulas Street, but outside expenses precipitated their unfailing sequel, and he suspended. For a time he was lost sight of, but at an unexpected period he came to the surface and involved himself in a conspiracy, in which the originator and director was a cotton factor and a former politician. The twain loaded a vessel with what was represented to be a cargo of cotton, but which was in fact moss, and cleared the venture for Liverpool. While in the Gulf the ship was mysteriously burned, the cargo reported lost, and a demand made on the companies which had written policies of insurance for an adjustment. The matter was investigated, the losses paid, and deceased disappeared. Soon after the true condition of affairs became known, and efforts were at once instituted for the apprehension of the alleged criminals. For a time the party referred to eluded arrest in the quiet of a side street in Chicago, but his retreat was discovered in the following manner: He cherished an affection for a beautiful Camelia, of New Orleans, who reciprocated, it is said, the feelings he manifested, and when he became a fugitive she was in the habit of posting him as to the situation of affairs in the Crescent City. This came to the knowledge of the Pinkerton Agency, who were upon his track, and their detectives closed in upon him, procured his arrest at the post-office in Chicago as he was receiving a letter from his New Orleans friend, and advised the companies he had defrauded. But he was not prosecuted; the companies recovered $275,000 of their loss, and ordered his discharge. As stated, he came to Memphis, where he built up for himself a redeemed reputation, and enjoyed the confidence of all who knew him. In the epidemic of 1873 he served as a humanitarian, and performed noble work. When the epidemic of 1878 came on, he sought the most exposed position, labored with the courage of a Spartan, sickened and died, and was buried among the first on the long list of heroes the terrible experience just closed gave birth to. Almost at the hour when he was laid away in his grave, Lelia Burton, the New Orleans friend of former days, fell in a faint at the bedside of a fever patient in that city she was nursing, and before aid could minister to her resuscitation she had crossed over the beautiful river, and was, it is to be hoped, in paradise.

There was truly a sad sight at the residence of the late Mike Cannon, a member of the old police force, who died early in the epidemic, after a ten hours' sickness. Three of his children, a girl just blooming into womanhood, a lad eleven or twelve years of age, and a little boy about nine years, lay dead in the house at one time, the mother being nearly prostrated with grief.

Through the kindness of Colonel M. Burke, Superintendent of the Memphis and Tennessee Railroad Company, a special train was, on October 7th, furnished Mr. J. H. Smith, Secretary of the Howard Association, to take nurses and supplies to the sick at Garner Station, twelve miles north of Grenada. Dr. T. L. Gelzer, of Mobile, was placed in charge as Howard physician. There were twelve cases, as follows: Dr. J. W. Payne, his wife, son, and grandson; three children of P. M. Robinson, Mrs. Dr. Combs, Mrs. H. L. Combs, Mrs. Broom, daughter of J. J. Slack, one colored woman and a colored boy. Dr. Payne and Mrs. H. L. Combs were very sick. The train was hailed and a physician inquired for at Courtland, to see Captain Knox, reported down with the fever.

The death of Dr. Nelson, the seven-footer, and of his entire family, was mentioned a few days ago. In the same connection it was mentioned that he was miserly, and possessed a large estate. Whether that be so or not, there is a little story connected with one Hamburger, who gets his comforts through the gratings of the Adams Street sation-house, that may develop something as to the true condition of the man's estate. Hamburger was one of the nurses, and very officiously performed the last sad rites at the demise of the only remaining member of the family, October 5th. A few days later Mr. Hamburger, in company with another of his kind, was seen taking unusual luxury in a hack in company with a couple of colored wenches. His conduct attracted the attention of the police to the extent that he and his party were pulled, during which there was a mysterious box, which was attempted to be concealed. This box contained a lot of valuable jewelry, which Hamburger claimed was given him by his uncle. He stuck to the "uncle" story until pressed to the last extremity, when he confessed that a daughter of Dr. Nelson had placed it in his keeping, with written instructions what to do with it. The instructions were in a book, somehow, that the police authorities had taken from him, and would not let him get hold of.

A sad sight might have been witnessed Sunday evening, October 6th, did not the laws which govern in this fearful epidemic forbid the keeping of late hours by those not engaged in caring for the sick. Mitchell Brown, son of the respected Dr. R. F. Brown, Secretary of the Board of Health, died just at sundown, under circumstances that necessitated the earliest possible interment. His friend, the companion of his childhood, Louis Frierson, was present, nearly heart-broken at the loss of his bosom friend. Appreciating the circumstances, with a stout heart and determined will he summoned three other persons, Mr. Wm. Lytle, Dr. Chandler, and Captain Harrison, in charge of the Charleston nurses, the four going on foot (no vehicle could be hired for love nor money) to the undertaker's establishment of Messrs. Flaherty & Sullivan, and procuring a suitable casket they carried it by the silver handles to the residence of Dr. Brown, on Madison Street, and carefully and tenderly placed the remains in it, closing it ready for the hearse early on the morning of the 7th. It was a sad sight to witness those four friends silently performing the last offices for the departed friend. But this is only one of the many equally as heart-touching events the present epidemic has produced.

Appeal, October 5th.—" A warning to refugees, in another column, will, we hope, have the attention it deserves from those for whom it is intended. To return now, or at any time before the epidemic is officially declared over, is to court almost certain death. A few of our citizens who did so, in defiance of good advice to the contrary, have paid the penalty of their temerity and are now numbered with the dead. Their fate should be a warning and serve to enforce the timely and urgent appeal of the Howard Association, to which we refer all readers of the *Appeal* at home or abroad."

Little Rock *Democrat*, October 5th.—" It is with a sad heart we announce the death of Dr. Easley. We have seen our friends dropping daily and dying rapidly. Of the many brave physicians and nurses our Howards have sent to Memphis, this day but a handful remains. Dr. Easley, one of the best surgeons in the United States, and an able physician, one of the first to risk his life in succoring the afflicted of our sister city, died this morning. We had hoped, as he held so tenaciously to life, that he would be spared, but relentless were the fates. He is dead. Mark his grave, ye Knights of Pythias, that in the future a monument may mark his last resting-place. Dr. Easley, we believe, was a native of Mississippi; a graduate of the Madison (Mississippi) College, a graduate in 1873 of the Louisville Medical College. He first practiced his profession in Dallas, Texas. He came to this city in 1875, and at the time of his departure for the fated city, he, with Dr. E. H. Skipwith, had joint offices in the *Gazette* building. The deceased was a star in his profession, about thirty years of age, and unmarried."

Dr. Hunter, of Kansas City, who has been one of the most devoted of the Howard physicians, returned from Masons, October 4th, where he had been sent to look after the sick of that place. The doctor says that he found a bad state of affairs there. True, there were not many citizens, the majority having fled into refuge on the first outbreak of the fever, but the few remaining, not sick, were much alarmed lest every one would be stricken down and the little place be desolated, as have been Grenada and many smaller places. The doctor tells a pleasing anecdote of his first adventure there. On arriving he met an aged darkey on the platform who was very communicative, and endeavored to tell of the suffering and privations; hadn't a mouthful to eat in forty-eight hours, and every body in town was either dead or down with the fever. "That is very bad, indeed," replied the doctor, " but how is it that the country people do not furnish supplies when there is so much destitution?" "Oh, sir," said the antiquated specimen of African anatomy, " dat's easy 'nough 'splained. You see, sir, dey *pontooned* agin every body, and dey quit comin' here, sir; dat's how dat come about, sir." The doctor has now a new subject for discussion before the Memphis Howard Medical Society as a preventive of the spread of yellow fever.

Appeal, October 5th.—"We took occasion, a few days ago, to speak of the faithful service and arduous labors of that good man, Colonel W. S. Pickett, who has charge of the office of the Howard Medical Directory. He is still on duty, as faithful and diligent as ever, and manages the affairs of the office in such manner as to have won the esteem of the entire corps of physicians. The old gentleman told a good joke on himself yesterday, which we feel compelled to print. A couple were married recently, the bridegroom comparatively a stranger, Colonel Pickett being one of the few of his acquaintances. The colonel thought it would be in order to extend congratulations in person, and, providing himself with an elegant bouquet, about nine o'clock at night, the hour when in the good old days of yore festivities on such occasions were 'red-hot," he called at the residence. The doors were closed, but he knocked once, twice, even thrice, before he could get a response. Finally the door was opened by an elderly lady, to whom he made known his mission. He told her that he had called to congratulate the newly-married couple and salute the bride, 'Bless your dear heart,' said the lady, 'they retired two hours ago.' '*What!*' exclaimed the colonel, with an emphasis that startled the old lady, but then, checking himself, he handed her the bouquet, asking her to please preserve it till morning and then present it to the bride with his compliments. Colonel Pickett says they don't do things now like they did when he was a boy."

The *Appeal*, October 5th.—"Camp Joe Williams, by the Hernando Road, is between five and six miles from the city. Under the same command, and in the immediate vicinity of 'Camp Joe,' are Camp Smith, Camp Griffin, Camp Wade, and the camps of the Bluff City Grays, and Captain Glass's colored company. The hills upon which these camps are situated are covered with fine forests, and Captain Cameron states that every one is apparently well satisfied with camp life and rations. Eight hundred and nine persons are receiving rations, they being *bona fide* residents of the camps; no individual can receive rations that is not registered at one of the camps. From Dr. Nall we learn that there are six cases of yellow fever and nine cases of malarial fever in the hospital and camps. Three of the 'Bluffs' are down with the malarial. Dr. Sample, from Austin, Mississippi, who acted as assistant physician, died yesterday (Monday) morning. Dr. Nall has had six assistants, all of whom have died or left the camp, and the doctor is alone to attend not only the camps, but also all the sick within a radius of four miles. The disease has been of a very mild type, and in most cases easily handled. Jennie McClain, during the illness of Wade Hampton, was in charge of the hospital; but Wade having recovered will soon return to duty. On the road to 'Camp Joe,' after passing the Poston place, there are small camps of two and three tents at every mile, the inhabitants of which appear to enjoy camp life to the utmost. The number of women and children around these camps, their merry shouts of laughter, and their hurried rush to the roadside to bid us good-bye as we whirled along in our buggy, soon made it apparent that we had left 'Yellow Jack' miles in the rear of us."

Appeal, October 5th.—"On Sunday last, a number of heart-stricken citizens repaired to Elmwood Cemetery for the purpose of visiting the fresh-made graves of their loved and lost, and spreading flowers on the earth-hillocks that marked those sacred spots. But to their horror and dismay, the graves of the dead could not be found, notwithstanding the long and patient search made by the mourners and by the employés of the cemetery. This is a horrible fact to have to disclose, because it is well calculated to awaken the deepest alarm in the minds of hundreds of citizens who had their loved ones interred at Elmwood. It will be well to remember how the dead daily encumbered the graveyard, and how a hundred coffins lay around Elmwood daily awaiting interment, which had to be postponed for days, sometimes, owing to the scarcity of gravediggers, the terrible death-rate, and the sickness of those in charge of the cemetery during the gloomy days of September, when the fever-pest gathered in two hundred victims a day. Those who died during those days, and whose relatives had not lots to bury their dead, purchased private graves in that part of the cemetery known as Chapel Hill. The dead were taken out, and the coffins, boxes, etc., were laid down on the rank grass, which locations, according to the then superintendent of the cemetery and those having charge of the interments, were the exact spots designated as lots number so-and-so. The graves could not be dug until the next day, and the relatives and friends of the dead could not, of course, wait to see their dead interred. It now turns out that in these days but little attention was paid to the manner of interments. Long trenches were dug and the coffins were placed therein, side by side, regardless of the fact that, in many instances, private graves with regular numbers were purchased and promised to be furnished. How can the living now find their dead? Can they feel certain (unless an exhumation takes place) that beneath the sod on which they kneel and pray and spread *immortelles* rests their own beloved dead? Certainly not. On Sunday last, it would make one's heart ache to have seen a gentleman searching for the lost grave of his wife at Elmwood Cemetery. He had purchased a private grave, but it can not be found, and the horrible belief that his wife had been buried in the trench or ditch haunted the unfortunate man as he wandered around, searching and weeping. He had flowers to strew on the grave, but he searched in vain. The employés of the grave-yard searched in vain. The grave was lost. A lady, at the same time, was searching for a private grave on Chapel Hill, but that grave was also lost, and the treacherous ditches near by the place suggested the fate of the loved one who died. The present employés at Elmwood are new people, who were not there during the dark death days of September, and they know nothing of the past. Many of the old employés have died, others are absent. As one of the present employés said: "In September, every thing was in a horrible condition here; there was no order nor system followed as to burying the dead, and many of those entitled to private graves were put in the trenches." The negro grave-diggers tell tales as to how the dead were buried in these days, tales not well calculated to assure the living that their dead were buried in accordance with directions, or in such graves as had been specially purchased for such purposes. There is no one to blame, probably, but the horrible fact exists nevertheless."

Avalanche, October 5th.—" New cases in the city and suburbs, 139. Deaths, thirty-five. The Citizens' Relief Committee are establishing depots in the suburbs and country adjacent. A depot has already been established in the eighteenth civil district (eastward), that includes also the fifth and fourteenth. Depots are to be opened on next Monday. Also, one in North Memphis, another in South Memphis, and one in the fifteenth civil district (north-east of the city). In addition, there is Camp Joe Williams, with 600 residents, and 200 others near by, who are receiving relief; also, Camp Father Mathew, with 400 residents, and 100 near by; Camp Benjes, with 200. When rations are issued to the different camps, they are delivered to responsible parties in charge, who take good care that the rations go to the proper persons."

Appeal October 5th.—" We published yesterday, from the London *Standard* and the New York *Times*, extracts from editorials eulogistic of the courage and endurance of the people of the South during this epidemic. Both have attracted very general attention, and both have found a place, with more or less of commendation and indorsement, in the leading papers of the Union, north and south. To us who share in this generous measure of approbation of the performance of an unusually perilous duty, the words of our contemporaries— the one a leading northern Republican journal, and the other the steadfast admirer and friend of the South—come laden with a strength to sustain and encourage that only those can appreciate who have watched the weary, heavy-footed hours pass away, bearing with them our bravest and our best. The strain and tension of mind in the contemplation of the awful facts of sixty-five days, during which 4,800 men, women, and children have died of the fever, out of a population at no time within that limit more than 19,000, would have been more than the stoutest heart among us could have withstood, were it not for such warm and heartfelt messages of sympathy as those we refer to. These kindly words have opened hearts that were steeling themselves in despair, and tears of relief have flowed freely, attesting the consolation of sympathy and the power of speech even from across the sea. During this awful harvest-time of death our churches have been closed and all business has been suspended, and the only relief or release from mental strain was found in fitful sleep, snatched in the intervals of calls that no one could disobey. It was death in the morning, at noon, and at night. But it was not to dwell upon the wearying acts of a dreary tragedy not yet closed, still less to plume ourselves as upon a victory not yet won, that we commenced this article. Our purpose was the more pleasing one of suggesting to the *Standard* that, while all that it says is true of the pluck and endurance of the southern people under the provocations of war, pestilence, and famine, there is something to be said for our brethren of the North, whose constancy, steadiness, and devotion to their cause, bravery and persistence in battle, and endurance in a prolonged contest that taxed all their energies and a skill and resources unequaled, have few parallels in history. To no other people could we of the South have surrendered. Magnanimous on the field so fiercely contested, despite the hazards of political disputes, they have many times since April, 1865, extended us the right hand of fellowship, full up and flowing over with good gifts, tendered with a manly spirit that robbed the generous tender of the humiliations of charity. The same men who led the armies of the North, the same journalists who inspired those armies, and the same religious teachers, and the same noble, heroic women who originated and sustained amid the heat of battle, and the excitement of sometimes perilous popular commotions, the grandest beneficence ever conceived of for the relief of soldiers in the field, have been foremost in the heaven-sent work of our relief in weeks that are the dreariest in our calendar Unwearied in their tasks, as did Joseph with his brethren, they have filled our sacks to overflowing, many, many times, and yet they are not done. From far Oregon and Montana to Vermont, from villages, towns, and cities of all the busy northern States, from the miners' camp, the newsboys' home, from the banker and the farmer, the professor and the mechanic, from all classes of that section of our country where American ingenuity has found its largest field of conquest, and whose industries challenge the world in vain for a comparison—from this seat of a great industrial population unmatched by any other on the earth, the gifts of an intelligent help and a touching sympathy have come, saving many thousands of our stricken ones from death, and lighting our dreary pathway with the light of an enduring brotherly love. 'Blood is thicker than water.' Of the same race, speaking the same tongue, the heirs of the same liberties, and citizens of the same glorious country, no memories of sectional divisions, of political animosities, or of civil war, have been allowed to stay the steady flow of the bounteous stream that has brought us, with all else, the assurance that we are one people in fact as well as in name, and that beyond the froth and fuss of politics, and the deceits and dangers of demagogues, the popular heart is safe, yielding only of its fullness when challenged in the cause of humanity and brothers' lives are at stake."

One of the most modest and best of our citizens engaged in the blessed task of nursing the sick and caring for the indigent was Mr. M. S. Jobe, who died October 6th, of a second attack of the yellow fever. Though he had just convalesced from what was deemed a light attack, and was hardly equal to the task, he promptly sent in his name when the Howard Association called for members, and was gladly accepted, and at once assigned to duty. Five weeks of most difficult labor in the eighth ward proved too much for him, and he at last gave way, notwithstanding he was sustained by the best medical skill and the most faithful nursing.

The wife of Mr. Abadie, a French citizen, died at Fort Pickering. Mr. Abadie and his children were stricken with the fever. Dr. Luppo was called to attend them, and all became nearly convalescent. Mr. Abadie continually brooded on the loss of his wife, but steadily grew better every day. On Saturday, October 5th, the physician called, and found all so far recovered as to report them convalescent. The next day, however, he was called to see Mr. Abadie, but, on arriving at his house, found him dead. The children said when the doctor called last on Saturday, and went away, their father dismissed the nurse, and made them bring him several bottles, which, on examination, were found to have contained respectively, laudanum, ergot, and paregoric, but which were nearly empty. The conclusion arrived at was, that Abadie, in deep grief at the loss of his wife, had taken the poisonous potions with the determination of ending his distress by death. Four children were thus left fatherless and motherless.

Sheriff J. W. Anderson died October 8th, after a brief illness, of yellow fever. He had been very active during the epidemic as a member of several relief committees, and in attendance upon the duties of his office, and had, like many others, gone to his bed broken down. He was a good citizen, and enjoyed the esteem of a wide circle of friends.

Mr. J. M. Tomeny died of yellow fever October 8th, after but three days' illness. The death of a lovely daughter and of his wife, whom he buried a few days previously, preyed upon his mind to an extent undermining his strength, so that he fell an easy prey to the scourge that has taken so many.

Avalanche, October 8th.—"It is with much regret we announce the death of that good man and useful citizen, Mr. John A. Holt, paying-teller of the Bank of Commerce of Memphis. Mr. Holt, when nearly all his associates fled the city, remained at his post, knowing full well the importance of his trust and the good work he could accomplish through his bank in aid of suffering humanity. Early and late he could be found at his place, and many a want was relieved through his kind offices. 'Death loves a shining mark,' and no brighter object could have attracted the attention of the grim visitor than John A. Holt. He was born on these bluffs in 1829, a son of that old respected citizen, Neal B. Holt. He leaves a wife and a helpless family of children, the mother at present an invalid."

Appeal, October 8th.—" The steamer *John M. Chambers*, loaded at St. Louis, at the suggestion of ex-Governor Alex. Shepherd, of Washington, with medical and other supplies and clothing, for the people of the fever-stricken towns on the Mississippi River, tied up at the landing yesterday for a couple of hours, during which two of the doctors on board came up town and interviewed our authorities. She visited Hickman on Sunday, and will stop at every town and landing between this city and Vicksburg, distributing supplies where needed. As we said a few days ago, this is a practical benevolence of which the people of Washington and St. Louis, and all who contributed toward it, may well feel proud. Governor Shepherd has linked his name with it indissolubly, and will always be remembered by the people of the Mississippi valley."

Appeal, October 8th.—" Major W. T. Walthall, of the Can't-Get-Away Club, of Mobile, left the city yesterday for his home, near Mississippi City, where his family is closely besieged by the plague. Since his arrival here the major has done good work among the sick, and has increased the list of friends he made when, in 1873, in the same heroic spirit, he came to our help. We part with him with a deep regret, as deep as that he felt in leaving the scene of his God-appointed labors, well knowing that nothing but the imperative calls from his home, which no man is at liberty to disobey, could take him from us until the epidemic had been declared over. He carries with him the best wishes of all classes of our people, coupled with earnest prayers for the safety of his wife and children. His devotion to the cause of humanity ought to be their shield at such a time, and so, we trust, when he reaches home, he will find it."

Appeal, October 8th.—" From almost every town of Louisiana and Mississippi, and our own State, affected by the fever, we get news of its rapid spread in the surrounding country. Removed from the centers, where the benevolence of the Union has collected medical assistance and supplies, the sufferings and deaths among the planters, in proportion to cases, must be a great increase over what we have mourned over the past nine weeks. We hope, therefore, that the Howard Associations of New Orleans and Vicksburg, as ours has done, will organize railroad relief trains, and, as near as possible, bring their multiplied blessings to every suffering home. There is no time to lose. The planters and their hands should be cared for to the utmost of the ability of New Orleans, Vicksburg, and Memphis, which, if they have not funds and supplies enough, can make a fresh appeal to the country, which has never turned a deaf ear, but has always held out full and willing hands."

Avalanche, October 8th.—" Yesterday there was one continuous call for nurses, and the demand was in excess of the supply. In addition to the request for nurses in the suburbs, appeals for physicians, nurses, and supplies were received from Brownsville (fifty-seven miles), Masons (thirty miles), Galloway's (forty miles), Paris (one hundred and fifty miles), on Louisville Railroad; Collierville (twenty-two miles), Moscow (forty miles), Tuscumbia (one hundred and thirty-seven miles), on Memphis and Charleston Railroad, and Garner (seventy-five miles), south, on Mississippi and Tennessee Railroad. Reports from these and other points where the fever has made its appearance, is truly startling. The cry of distress which we were forced to give utterance to six weeks ago, is now being echoed on every breeze that comes wafted to us from the small towns along the line of the Louisville, Memphis and Charleston, and Mississippi and Tennessee Railroads. Deplorable as may be our condition, theirs is exceedingly so. With us, a hundred or more brave hearts banded together and fought to the death the plague, until at last a gleam of hope beamed upon us, by still leaving a few of that band unscathed. In the country, one case of fever generally causes a stampede of the entire community, and it is left to the Howards and Citizens' Relief Committee (of Memphis) to succor the sick and distressed of those towns where the fever has appeared. If the present spell of warm weather continues for ten days longer, not a single village or hamlet along the railroads will escape."

A man and his wife came here from New Orleans, both entering the Howard service as nurses. Both were sent to nurse the same family. Several days after he made report at the Howards that the female nurse assisting him was continually drunk and worthless as a nurse, asking that she be discharged. She was discharged, he continuing in the service. It was subsequently discovered that she was his wife.

Probably the most pitiable case was that of the McKinley family on Brinckley Avenue, all of whom died. Their appeal sent to the Howards was, "For God's sake come to us, we are all dying!" The Howard visitor who was sent to them found one of the children, who had been dead three days, so far in decomposition that its abdomen had broken open and maggots were crawling from it. Another child had been dead a day, and all of the family were sick without any attendance whatever. The Howard visitor and physician, who first entered the house, describe it as the most dreadful that came under their notice during the epidemic.

Captain Rodgers, who lived on Tennessee Street, was nursed by two negroes, sent by the Masons. When he died some of his friends ordered the nurses to lay him out in his Mason's regalia, telling them they would find it in the wardrobe. The nurses, in their ignorance, found a grotesque suit of clothes which the poor gentleman had worn at Mardi-Gras the previous year, and he was buried in them before the mistake was discovered.

Susan Cunningham, residing on Carroll Avenue, had black vomit two different times in four days. Her attending physician reduced her temperature from 104° to 96°, but it went up again to 105°. It was again reduced to 97°, but went up again to 106°, from which it was reduced again to 97°, and yet she recovered.

The Rev. Mr. Schuyler, an Episcopal minister from Hoboken, N. J., came to Memphis, says the correspondent of the Louisville *Courier-Journal*, to supply the place of the Rev. Dr. Harris, who was stricken with the fever. He labored earnestly and incessantly for four days, during which he accomplished great good, converting among others an infidel who had long before been given up as lost by the clergy of Memphis. At the end of the fourth day Mr. Schuyler was taken with the fever at the house of Dr. Harris, who had not yet recovered. Dr. Dalzell, of Louisiana, and Dr. Green, of Memphis, were in the house at the time. They advised his removal to an infirmary set apart for physicians and nurses taken down. Mr. Schuyler was averse to complying, but announced himself willing to trust his life with the physician who advised his removal. He was accordingly taken to the Court Street Infirmary, Dr. Harris having expressed himself willing to permit his friend to remain if he desired. This infirmary was in charge of a physician from Texas. It is said that he honestly believed it best to remove a patient whose death was assured from the room of the living, than to permit him or her to remain, because the shock of a death always left its impression upon the living. *The charge is that Mr. Schuyler, who is said to have bore his illness with great fortitude, upon this ground was removed to what is known as the dead-room eighteen hours before he expired,* his faithful nurse following and remaining with him until death parted them. This story was related to me by an eye-witness. Malicious persons, desiring to injure Dr. Harris, spread the report that he had ordered the removal of Mr. Schuyler from his house. This story is entirely untrue and utterly uncalled for. Dr. Harris had not heard of it until mentioned to him by myself, when he addressed me the following letter:—

St. Mary's Cathedral, Memphis, November, 1878.

My Dear Sir: Complying with your request to furnish information relative to the illness and death of the late Rev. Louis S. Schuyler, volunteer priest from Hoboken, N. J., I beg to say that Mr. Schuyler arrived in Memphis on Sunday the eighth day of September, the Rev. Dr. Dalzell, of Shreveport, having arrived the day before. Both were assigned to the Peabody Hotel, there being no bed in my house not occupied already by a fever patient. Only Dr. Dalzell, however, went to the hotel, Mr. Schuyler preferring extemporized accommodation in the parlor. The four days during which he was able to stand up at all were days of great activity and usefulness. He was frequently in my room, and reported from time to time his acts. On Wednesday, the 11th, he came in and found visiting me Drs. Dalzell and Green, both physicians. Complaining of an uncomfortable feeling, he was examined by Dr. Dalzell, who pronounced him already sick with fever, and directed that he go with him at once in his buggy to the infirmary, where he could be better cared for than was possible at my house. He expressed a preference to remain at my house even under the discomforts of it, but, yielding to the advice of the physician, he joined Dr. Dalzell in his buggy, and was taken to the infirmary. Being myself ill, I was unable to see him afterward, and can not give you any of the incidents of those last days of a devoted life. Very respectfully, Geo. C! Harris.

Another letter in the same regard reads:

Dear Dr. Harris: When I was first told that Rev. Mr. Schuyler was ill, I asked permission to have him brought here to St. Mary's, for, although I was myself ill at the time, and there was no Sister here who could nurse him, I thought he would be happier, being somewhat under our care. The doctor told me not to propose this, as he would really be better cared for at the Physicians' Infirmary. I sent constantly to inquire concerning him, and was always answered that he had every thing he could need, and that he had a splendid nurse. Very sincerely, Sister Hughetta, S. S. M.

Mr. T. P. Holland, for several years foreman of the Evening *Ledger*, died Saturday morning, October 12th, after a short illness, of the prevailing fever. He was highly esteemed by all who knew him, especially his fellow-craftsmen. He left a large and almost helpless family.

Dr. Mitchell, in an address delivered before the Howard Medical Society, Wednesday evening, October 9th, said "that the society should recommend to boards of health the necessity of refusing aid from physicians or nurses who have never had the yellow fever. The fearful record of sacrificed lives that Memphis could show was a terrible warning, which should not go unheeded in the future. He knew the danger, and had not accepted the proffered service of any physician without first having warned him of the peril he underwent by remaining."

Mr. Phillips, superintendent of Elmwood Cemetery, replies to a local article in the *Appeal*, and says: "I forgot to say there was more to blame in the undertakers or their assistants than at Elmwood. While I worked the cemetery, up to September 10th, many orders came to me from them for single graves, when I knew the people owned lots, or had relatives who would have them buried in their lots, rather than single graves. So I buried them in the lots, and paid no attention to the undertakers' orders. The new men could not know this, and went by the orders from town. Give every one justice."

At half past one o'clock, October 17th, Dr. T. M. Keating, of New York, breathed his last. Not one of all the volunteer physicians more endeared himself to the people of Memphis, and his untimely death cast a shadow over a community bowed down with the weight of woe.

Avalanche, 17th.—"To-night we write with hope filling our breast. The death record in the city is the smallest since the fever was declared epidemic on the 23d of August last. At last we can see the beginning of the end. Every thing looks favorable. A heavy rain, which began falling at 9 o'clock, still continues, with indications of the weather turning cold, and bringing the frost that will end our present woes. The absentees can not watch with greater anxiety the progress of the fever, than do we who are here in the very midst of death; and every favorable turn of the epidemic is to us the knowledge that we will soon be joined by loving friends. Their return will be hailed with joy and gladness, but in the happiness of the meeting many a familiar face will be missing. Elmwood, that 'silent city of the dead,' contains the loved forms of hundreds who, in their devotion to the cause of suffering humanity, paid with their lives the love they bore their fellow-man. Their noble sacrifice may perhaps be rewarded in the Great Beyond. They fell martyrs, and their memories should ever be revered by the living, for whom they died."

In the death of Mr. John G. Lonsdale, Sr., which sad event occurred on the 2d of October, Memphis lost one of her oldest and most reputable citizens. For thirty years he had been engaged in the fire insurance business, and during that time had maintained a high character for capacity and integrity. He was a member of the Howard Association, and from the beginning of the epidemic had labored with a devotion worthy a much younger and stronger man, in behalf of the sick and destitute.

One of the terrible results of the epidemic was the large number of demented people developing from the effects of the yellow fever.

Of the entire police force of forty-eight men and officers, there were only thirty-one who remained on duty when the fever broke out. Of this number, ten died, fifteen had the fever and convalesced, and five escaped altogether. Of those who resigned and left the city, two took the fever and died in their place of refuge.

W J. B. Lonsdale, the last of the family of the late lamented John G. Lonsdale, Sr., died on the night of November 3d, after a comparatively short attack of the fever. He returned to the city before it was officially announced that it was safe to do so, and paid the penalty of such imprudence with his life.

"Let sweet-voiced Mercy plead for her, who calmly sleeps beneath the sod; nor erring man in pride usurp the promise of her judge, her God." This is a beautiful sentiment, the inspiration of one who fell with "his face to the enemy" during the epidemic of 1873. The tombstone on which it is engraved marks the burial place of a fallen woman, but one whose charities and good deeds far outnumbered her sins. The author, whose charity for that woman's sins was thus worded, died during the epidemic just past. Hundreds knew him and hundreds mourn his loss.

Ira Trout, of 192 Poplar, a working Howard, while in the heat of fever, in the absence of the nurse, got out of his bed and crawled on his hands and knees to a washbowl of ice-water and drank over a quart and finished off with a half bottle of port wine, and yet he recovered.

J. Kirchener, a shoemaker, well known in Memphis, after nursing several of his family, who died, took the fever, but did not take off his clothes until he recovered. He nursed himself and refused the attendance of a doctor or nurses. He cooked his own food, although suffering from a severe attack, and ate it when and in what quantities he chose, and yet recovered.

Dr. McGregor, of Covington, Tenn., against the remonstrances of his nurses, and perfectly sane, went into the yard to a pump and drank heavily of water, but died very suddenly from the effects of his indiscretion.

Mr. Fred. Brennan, local editor of the *Appeal*, was in bed ten weeks, perhaps the worst case of yellow fever on record. He had black vomit three times and the hiccoughs twice—once for twenty-four hours and once for eight hours—and yet recovered. A vigorous constitution and a will that nothing could break down brought him through.

Miss Clay, residing on Washington Street, who had the yellow fever in 1873, attended with black vomit, also had a severe attack of the fever in 1878, with black vomit and hiccoughs for thirty-six hours, yet she recovered.

Maria Hayden, residing on Alabama Street, while her temperature was 104°, went to the pump and drank freely of water, ate ice, pound cake, and drank condensed milk out of the original package, also drank champagne and porter. It was impossible to keep the clothes on her, or prevent her from getting up while the fever was at its height, and yet she recovered.

Miss Mary Sandberg, of Winchester Avenue, had a severe attack of fever, and, as her nurse describes, small pimples resembling small-pox covered her entire person. Her father bled her, yet she recovered. Her father, an old sailor, who had seen yellow fever in the West Indies, believed in blood-letting, and in operating on himself with a razor cut the jugular vein and died in fifteen minutes.

A little son of Mr. Goldsmith (broker) had black vomit and hemorrhage for three days and recovered.

John Latsch, whose kidneys were in an abnormal condition—creating an entire suppression of urine—was treated with poultice of onions on abdomen, and after three days of this treatment, and walking him up and down the room, the secretions were started, but too late for his recovery. He died while on one of his pedestrian tours.

James Duffey, 12 Alabama Street, after having black vomit six hours, got up from his bed, washed himself, changed his underclothing, dressed himself, and went down town. The next day he did the same thing, taking a body bath, and went on the Raleigh Road a half mile, vomiting black vomit all the way. He died a few minutes after his return home from his last trip.

In the middle of August, many people pawned watches, diamonds, and even silver spoons to raise money enough to get away from the city. Many small depositors drew their respective accounts from bank and departed. Persons went away with as little as ten or fifteen dollars, as their total worldly possessions.

Lengthy, populous streets in Memphis were left without a dozen families residing thereon. The occupants disappeared as if by magic. Some streets were wholly deserted by their white inhabitants, only colored servants—not deemed liable to the disease—remaining.

A doctor called to attend an Irishman, residing in Fort Pickering, about a mile from Court square, found his patient far advanced in the convalescent stage and disposed to be humorous. He told the doctor, also an Irishman, that he was very mad the day he was taken with the fever. He said that on that day the last of three of his friends had died, and he called in a negro man and gave him ten dollars to wash and dress the corpse. This he did satisfactorily. Having been paid and dismissed, the narrator bethought him that his dead friend had expressed a desire to be laid out and buried in the regalia of the society he belonged to. He, therefore, ran after the negro, overhauled him, told him what he wanted, promising him five dollars additional for its performance. When they got back to the house, he told the negro to look in the wardrobe and he would find the regalia, which, he said, must be put on immediately, as in a few minutes the hearse would be there. The colored man went to the wardrobe, took out what he supposed was the regalia, put it on, and reported the performance of his task. When the undertaker arrived and was about to screw down the lid of the coffin, he looked and saw a very laughable sight. He called the friend of the dead man, who said to the doctor, "What d'ye suppose I saw? The bloody ould stupid naggur had put a harlequin costume on me friend, the one he wore last Mardi-Gras." "And did you bury him in it?" asked the doctor. "Begorra, we did. The undertaker didn't have time to wait for the change to be made, and I didn't want to make the change if he had, and so Dennis wint to glory all colors and spangles."

Two little children, Sallie and Lulu Lester, were left by their father at the Citizens' Relief Committee's headquarters, and immediately the father disappeared. The little girls were taken in charge and carried to Camp Joe Williams, where they were made wards of the Bluff City Grays—"Daughters of the Regiment."

A visitor of the Howard Association encountered a horrible scene upon entering a house on Commerce Street, Sunday, August 25th. Upon a bed lay the living and the dead—a husband cold and stiff, a wife in the agony of dissolution. On the floor, tossing in delirium, were two children of this pair, and beside them their cousins, two little girls, themselves sick. To complete the repulsiveness of the scene, and give it a touch of disgusting horror, a drunken man and a drunken woman, parents of two of the little fever-baked girls, were reeling and cursing, and stumbling over the dying and the dead.

A sick man's lady friend wrote: "Please let me come." When his friends thought the die was cast, they consented to his summoning her. Boldly she laid aside her hat, pushed back her hair, and forcing a smile to her lips, entered the room. Some of his male friends stood outside on the door steps and inquired "how the dear old boy was getting along."

"I remember," says Mr. H. I. Simmons, a Howard, "one sight we visited in the neighborhood of the Louisville depot. The air was horribly soaked with the sickening odor of dead bodies. We went into one house where six persons had already been reported down. A new case was reported here, and we called to remove it, as our rules were to take every body to the infirmary when sick less than twenty-four hours, and, after that, to the hospital, if their condition would permit. This poor devil had been lying on the floor thirty-six hours. We put him in an ambulance and drove away, but had not gone far when he called to us to 'Stop, for God's sake, stop!' I made the driver halt. The sick man gasped a little, and said, 'I am going, sir; stop the driver here, for I will soon die.' In seven minutes he was dead."

One night in August, one of those beautiful nights when the harvest moon shone with a brilliancy peculiar to the tropics, a Howard visitor was making his way through the deserted and gloomy streets on an errand of mercy to receive the last messages of a dying colleague. While walking along in an aimless, mechanical sort of a way, his ears were saluted with the voice of a woman singing a melody which had lulled him to rest in his mother's arms during infancy. He halted in his tracks, and was so impressed by the singular occurrence that he determined to follow it up and ascertain from whom it proceeded. Guided by the voice, he reached a neat cottage en route to his destination, and, peering through the open window, saw a middle-aged woman caressing a child, and pacing the floor as she sang. Prompted by some irresistible impulse, he turned the door-knob, and, entering the room, accosted the inmate. She paid no attention to his salutation, and then he observed by her peculiar manner, her wandering eye, and general appearance, that she was crazed. Hurrying out into the street, he procured the assistance of a negro woman and returned to the house of sorrow. After some delay she was quieted temporarily, and being relieved of that which she held in her arms, it was found to be an infant a few months old, dead, and in a condition of decomposition. The mother was coaxed out of the room after a prolonged effort, and her child prepared for burial. She is now said to be a confirmed lunatic, and in the retreat to which she has been committed she paces the ward with a bundle in her arms crooning a lullaby to what she imagines is her living babe. Her husband had died a few days previous to this occurrence, her family had one by one been carried out to the "trenches," and, her last hope dying with her last born, her mind, already shattered, became a hopeless wreck.

Numerous instances are recited where the dying and sick were measured for grave-clothes and coffins from ten to twelve hours before dissolution, the patients being fully conscious of all that was taking place.

The poor and many of the middle classes often died unattended. Some breathed their last in the streets, and others in their own houses, where the stench arising from their dead bodies and the fermenting of medicines or other preventives they had taken made the first discovery of their deaths. A feeling of extreme terror existed in the breasts of every body, and it was always regarded that whom Æsculapius, Hippocrates, or Galen, were they living, might pronounce in good health at sunrise, might be dead at sunset. Instances were related where the Howard visitor, on following a street to discover a dead person, found that the moment a door leading to it was open the body would burst. A dead Chinaman, when discovered, was much eaten by rats. Revolting as these cases may be, they form their part in the horrible history of the plague at Memphis.

A scene behind a door at No. 32 St. Martin Street, illustrated the manner in which many negroes neglected the sick of their race. A dead negro boy lay upon the floor, and a tottering, fever-burned victim was handing a dipper of water to a delirious man lying on an old ragged quilt. Negroes, well men, lived in scores of houses around, but not one could be prevailed upon to enter the place. A brave white lady, disgusted with so much inhumanity, herself entered the house, taking oil and mustard. This, however, was no rare case.

Those who were buried in the trenches were all coffined, and these were packed as close to each other as possible. It would not be possible to identify or disinter the remains of any particular person who sleeps in these pits. Mounds have been shaped over the trenches, which give all the external appearance of the regular mode of burial, but there will average about three subjects to every two mounds.

A printer was allowed to die by the nurse in attendance, also a patient in Hopefield, Ark., who was obliged to leave a sick bed and compel the flight of a drunken nurse at the muzzle of a gun. Such instances were not numerous, but the Howards used every precaution to prevent their repetition, and finally succeeded in weeding out the unreliable and incompetent nurses the epidemic brought forth.

C. G. Fisher, President of the Relief Committee, labored incessantly night and day in the discharge of his official duties, as did Lonsdale, the Treasurer, and Clark, the Secretary. The consequence was that, when stricken, their systems were too exhausted to sustain the shock, and they died before a favorable reaction could be produced.

"There was no factor in the sum of elements that contributed more nobly and effectually to sustain the fading hopes of this people than the press," wrote the correspondent of the Chicago *Tribune*, "and to the editors of the daily journals, more than to any other personal efforts, is the city under obligations for the absence of riot, rapine, bloodshed, and chaos. These brave men stood to their posts when death stalked amid their ranks and took their choicest spirits."

Mr. Langstaff, Mr. Johnson, Louis Daltroof, Messrs. Simmons, Hargrove, and several other members of the Howard Association, accompanied the writer [a correspondent of the Louisville *Courier-Journal*] on a visit to the beautiful Elmwood Cemetery. The drive from the Peabody Hotel to the graves is about four miles. Almost every house along the route had its melancholy history, and many brief and sad incidents were related as we passed the desolated mansions of the wealthy, the dwellings of the prosperous merchants, the homes of the mechanic and the cottages of the laboring men. Each had presented a different and peculiarly touching scene, which was vividly recalled by members of the party as we rode along. The character of these scenes and incidents may be learned by a few which were jotted down by one of the party for me at random:

"There lived Mr. ——, who became delirious, jumped out of that second-story window, and killed himself. His wife died the same night, and they were both buried the next day."

"Three persons died in that little cottage."

"Nine persons were taken to the potters' field, all in one load, from that dwelling across the way."

"In that neat little dwelling, surrounded by flowers and shrubbery, lived a happy family, consisting of father, mother, and four children—they are now all in the cemetery."

"That store is the one in which there died four clerks who had succeeded each other rapidly in that capacity. After the death of the fourth one, none could be found to accept the place."

"Five corpses were taken out of that old shanty one night after 12 o'clock."

And so on in a similar strain to the end of the trip.

Four dead bodies were found, on the 2d of September, at various places within the city, all doubtless of persons who died without attendance of any kind. One was found in the rear of a residence, his face partly consumed by rats. Two others were lying in the old library building, on Jefferson Street, and another in a house on Union Street.

A man by the name of Townsley deserted his wife and child, while sick at 27 Main Street. President Langstaff, of the Howards, took the child in his arms, put the mother in an ambulance, and saw the pair comfortably located at the infirmary.

A kind-hearted lady was going to see a sick friend when she heard her name called. Turning, she saw a slender girl, dressed in mourning, advancing toward her. As the child came nearer, she recognized in her the daughter of a neighbor who had died the day before near the city. The little girl threw her arms about the lady, and, sobbing, cried: "You aren't afraid of me, are you?" "No, my dear," was the soothing response. "Every body else is," said the poor child. "They won't come near me because papa died of the fever, and we were with him, I and mamma." The little girl's heart was stung by the chilling repulsion which came to her in so deep a sorrow.

Seven men employed in one store were stricken down in one day, and the establishment closed.

The giant Death struck heavily when he took Mr. Ed. Worsham, who departed this life on Sunday, September 15th. None stood more manfully to their posts than he. He was a prominent Mason, and was active and untiring in behalf of the poor, the sick, the destitute, and the dying.

A man by the name of Callahan—a widower—a carpenter, who had borne a good character here, left his children at the beginning of the epidemic, went to Louisville, married again, and sent back, like several others, "Take care of my children." Those children were all dead or dying, but the cautious parent took good care not to put in a personal appearance.

On the 17th of September, died J. W. Heath, an active member of the Howard Association, who was conspicuous for his untiring labors in the cause of suffering humanity; also Vincent Baccigaluppo, one of our leading Italian citizens, and long a resident of this city.

"Last of all in this sad drama of death, of whom I have to speak," wrote the correspondent of the Louisville *Courier-Journal*, "is the undertaker, he who carried corpses to potter's field, and buried many in Elmwood. John Walsh, at No. 341 Second Street, Memphis, next door to the post-office, had the contract for burying paupers in Memphis and Shelby County, and had charge of all interments of that class during the fever. An interview with him disclosed the fact that very many persons of means and high social positions were handed to him for the potter's field, merely because there were no living friends of the deceased at hand to have them 'put away' in a different manner. Immediately after any death the whole neighborhood became clamorous for the instant removal of the corpse, and it was owing to this constant urging that many were hurried to an humble grave, who, under a different state of affairs, would have slept in choice lots at Elmwood. As many cases of the above description exist, I give the particulars of a few of the most prominent, as related by Mr. Walsh: Dr. Nelson, a man of considerable wealth, Thos. F. McCall, a merchant of some prominence, and Mr. Kinney, a cotton planter and speculator, who resided a part of the year at Memphis, and spent the other portion at some point in Arkansas, all died of fever, and now sleep in unknown potter's fields. A cotton broker, named Flack, and his whole family, consisting of seven persons, are dead and in the potter's field, except one child, which was buried in Elmwood Cemetery. In the family of Rev. Mr. Arnold, a Methodist minister, were five persons, all of whom died, and four of whom were put in paupers' graves; the other, a child, was sent to some one of the graveyards and placed in a marked grave. Nine-tenths of those who are buried in the potter's field sleep in unknown graves. Those which are known were marked by friends who were present when the bodies were brought out, and simply wrote the name on a piece of plank and placed it at the head of the grave for future identification. There were no trenches dug at the potter's field, but every body taken there was placed in a separate grave, which was dug five feet deep. The largest number of pauper funerals in one day was one hundred and nine. Mr. Walsh buried in all, as pauper undertaker, from August 15, 1878, to October 1, 1878, two thousand bodies. During this period he also attended to five hundred calls on private contract. The establishment employed, during the period above given, about one hundred and thirty hands. They paid their grave-diggers two dollars per day, and twenty cents per hour extra for night-work. They lost by fever fourteen grave-diggers, one coffin-trimmer, one stable-man, and two coffin-makers."

A physician in his daily rounds was called upon to visit a negro residing in a portion of the city known as "Fort Pickering." Upon interrogating the patient as to his symptoms, he replied that "there was great indignation of pain in his head." Pursuing his inquiries further, he was informed, with all the gravity of sincerity, that to promote his convalescence his colored nibs must be furnished with a piano!

John Thomas and Miss Beatrice Johnson met each other during the epidemic; while both were engaged in the noble mission of tending the unfortunate sick and distressed, fell in love at first sight, got married, and are living happily and contented.

In this great drama of death, those who played prominent parts were nurse, physician, and undertaker. Let us consider them separately. The nurse, I shall first speak of. The largest number on duty at any time by authority of the Howards was a trifle over four thousand. They came from all sections, included nearly all nationalities, and were good, bad, and indifferent. Between black and white, there was but little difference in efficiency, except the intelligence of the one over the other. Certainly, so far as the record goes, there was less rascality among the blacks than the whites. The colored nurses realized that any bad behavior would cause their death. Lamp-posts were their dread, and had any of them been guilty of outrage or theft their speedy doom would have been settled. The whites were bolder; and in their ranks were some of as vicious vultures as ever disgraced humanity or robbed the dead. The colored nurses made up in faithful attention all they lacked in intelligence, and their record is one to be justly proud of. The best nurses are said to have come from Savannah, Ga., and Port Royal, S. C. A Miss D. Murdock is said to have proven a most excellent nurse. She comes from a good family in Louisiana, and when the fever broke out was teaching school in Milwaukee. Gentle, good, and kind, a woman whose greatest happiness was in soothing the dying or seeking to save the sick, Miss Murdock went through the entire epidemic, drawing nothing for her services—one in many thousands whose presence in the chamber of death was not caused by the hope of pecuniary benefit. The Catholic and Episcopal sisters renewed their history of the past, gloriously following in the footsteps of their noble predecessors. The mortality among the sisters, priests, and brothers, President Lanstaff related to me, was terrible in the extreme. Every volunteer to lend a helping hand was propelled by some motive to Memphis, either noble or vicious. The Catholic and Episcopal sisters were sincere in their professions, and so were some others. There were those persons who, by grief or adversity, sought "surcease from sorrow." Women whose husbands had forsaken them, men whose wives were not what they seemed to be; this class composed a large element of the nurses whose names did not find their way on the "black list." "If there were evidences of the fellow-feeling which makes the whole world kin developed," continues the heroic correspondent of the Chicago *Tribune*, "there were also cases of inhumanity equally pronounced and unprecedentedly brutal. Your readers are familiar with the cases of wealthy men who left the city, and in places of safety mocked at the calamities of their fellows; of the wealthy lawyer who left his help to be supplied by the Relief Committee; of the landowner who ordered his employés' salaries to be cut down; of Donovan, and others. But I have heard of their counterparts. The owner of a cotton-gin, a bachelor and a man of wealth, sporting diamonds and fast horses, was among the first to flee. He left three sisters and an aged father, without means, and subject to the fever. When the epidemic was at its height, and one of the sisters had died, those remaining wrote to him for means to enable them to leave the city. He wrote them a cowardly letter, inclosing $5 and an order on Flaherty & Sullivan, undertakers, for a coffin. After some trouble, the father was sent out of the city on money borrowed from friends, and the sisters were left to take care of themselves."

At 62 Madison Street, September 20th, the remains of a colored woman were found, who had evidently been dead for four or five days. The rats had nearly devoured the corpse. Reports were numerous of corpses lying unburied for two or three days.

Madam Vincent, the wife of Vincent Baccigaluppo, who had died a few days previously, was buried on Sunday, September 22d. She was highly esteemed in Memphis, where, by industry and economy, she had accumulated a large fortune.

Sister Frances, of the Episcopal Church, who had charge of the Church Home, was buried on the 4th of October. She was one of the noblest women who ever faced death. No truer heart ever beat.

The remains of a white man were found, early on the morning of October 9th, at A. J. Vaughn's residence. He had been left in charge of the dwelling, and when found had been dead some hours.

But one outrage of a most serious nature is related, and it remains for this to be proven true. In this instance the patient was a lady, the nurse a man. Her fever was at its most critical point. The man drank until intoxicated. The woman's delirium coming on, she kicked the covering and clothing from her person. The drunken nurse, with champagne bottle in hand, was found, unconscious from the effects of drink, stretched across the body of the woman, who died before others came in. The early decomposition which follows death by yellow fever, and the fact that but a few days before the woman had given birth to a child, prevented ascertaining by outward signs satisfactory evidence that crime had been committed by the nurse, yet he was arrested and was held upon the charge of rape. Investigation afterward proved that he was innocent.

Said a nurse: "I came from Shreveport on Sunday, got here Monday, went to work Tuesday, Wednesday my patient was beautiful, Thursday he was tolerable, Thursday night he was restless, Friday he was dead, and Saturday he was in hell, for all that I know. Oh, I tell you, them was times when they went to heaven and the other place by telegraph, and not over the wires either—no, indeed."

"The medical hero of the great epidemic was Dr. J. W. Mitchell, the Medical Director of the Howard Association. Although sorely pressed, Dr. Mitchell gave me," says the correspondent of the Louisville *Courier-Journal*, "an hour of his time, and to his valuable fund of information is due much of the contents of this letter. Dr. Mitchell has not made up his mind as to the first case, and will say nothing yet as to the best treatment to pursue. 'Doctor, can you give me any idea of the mortality here in the present year from fever?' 'From the reports of my physicians, of whom at one time there were sixty on duty, who were required to keep accounts of all cases, deaths, and persons remaining, I judge and am convinced that the estimate is very nearly correct that 16,000 persons remained in Memphis for the fever to feed upon.' 'And the mortality among these?' 'Was simply terrible; the Howard physicians, including many brave volunteers, took a census of all persons in the different wards, camps, and suburbs. Upon the report of one physician, who worked in a section where less cases occurred than in the other, the number taken with the fever is reckoned at 89.2 per cent. This is where the fever made its last invasion. In the section where it was first felt the per cent. of persons taken down is reckoned at ninety-nine per cent. of those remaining.' 'How about negroes?' 'They were especially imprudent. If they had not been so imprudent, I think they wouldn't have had six deaths in a hundred cases.' 'Then it would be a good thing to be a negro in such epidemics?' 'Yes,' laughed the physician, 'if you could get over a colored man's love for champagne. That is what killed this class. The moment they were convalescent they began work on the champagne, and never knew when to quit. Indeed, there are instances where they came from the country and ran the risk of taking the fever to get champagne. Even poor white people caused their own deaths by wanting it when convalescent, and I at one time prevented its distribution, except when orders were indorsed by myself and a few trusted physicians in my lot.'"

A trading-boat, the *George O. Baker*, for some time lying up at Hen-and-Chickens' Island, came down, on the night of October 10th, to the foot of Market Street, with all sick on board. When the boat arrived at the levee, and word had passed to the Howards, instant succor was rendered. There were six persons on the boat, all sick. One of them, a beautiful young lady, had the black vomit.

"In regard to the large number of good deeds done in the flesh, I may say," writes the correspondent of the Chicago *Tribune*, "that they were not confined to those representing the upper walks of life, and many of the heroes who perished in their Samaritan work were gathered in from the slums of society. Gamblers, outcasts, and outlaws among the males, with those among the females who were marked with the scarlet letter, felt as keen sympathies, labored as heroically, nursed as tenderly, and died as bravely as those who, in the garb of purple and fine linen, forgot caste, station, and all the attractions of social superiority, to lend their efforts and presence to encourage the afflicted, with a self-denial characteristic of the times. *The Tribune* readers are familiar with the facts concerning Annie Cook, whose grave, strewn with flowers, is among the prominent features of the Howards' lot in Elmwood. She did the best she could, and, after a troubled life, the prayers of hundreds throughout this broad land go up this bright morning to the Throne, that she sleeps in peace:

> "Let sweet-voiced Mercy plead for her
> Who silent lies beneath the sod;
> Nor let proud, erring man assume
> The province of her Judge, her God.

"Another case, similar in many respects, came under my observation, the details of which may not be uninteresting. Lorena Mead is the name of a Louisiana girl of rare personal attractions and accomplishments, whom the war left bankrupt and helpless. She went down the Jericho road, and when the epidemic raised its hideous head, instead of consulting safety in flight, she remained to aid in its destruction. And a veritable ministering angel has she proven herself to be. There are bodies rotting in the potter's field she dressed for their narrow home, and there are convalescents walking the streets to-day, who speak her name with gratitude and veneration. She has gone home to renew her life of virtue, and, amid the scenes of her childhood, attempt to redeem herself from a bondage unutterably wretched. 'The trials through which I've passed, and the suffering I've witnessed and participated in, have made a Christian of me,' she says, 'and my future life, so far as I can make it, will be devoted to redemption and reformation.'"

"How do you account for all this?" remarked the correspondent of the Louisville *Courier-Journal* to a physician. "Champagne did it; this wine was the most demoralizing agent in the epidemic. Many a colored fellow risked the plague to taste, and, when convalescent, lost his life trying to get hold of it." "Had I had twenty-five acclimated nurses when the fever came," said Dr. Mitchell, "I could have done more good than a whole State full of such nurses as invaded Memphis."

Instances are related where watches and all manner of valuables were stolen by nurses. The boldest of yarns were brazenly told to cover up rascality. The general story was the valuables shown had been "given" by patients. Drunkenness and desertion were every-hour occurrences, and theft was extremely common.

There were many remarkable cases reported, which not only defied the physician's skill, but all precedent. One of these was that of H. E. Crandell, a printer, who suffered from the black vomit three times, and was given up for dead by his physician. But his nurse, a Mrs. Smith, from New Orleans, refused to be governed by this opinion, and labored on him with such good results that he is to-day well and at work.

Jefferson Davis, Jr., died at five o'clock, on the evening of October 16th, at Buntyn Station, near Memphis. He was a noble boy, inheriting the talents and genius of his illustrious father. His funeral took place the day following, at Elmwood Cemetery, and was attended by fifteen persons, which was the largest throng that had congregated at any one burial since the beginning of the epidemic.

An almost inexplainable fact in regard to the great scourge was the abject fear of all the residents of the cities, villages, and country generally. Men stood in Memphis, day by day, caring for the sick, shrouding and burying the dead victims of the plague, but the country and suburban mind was so stricken with fear that their victims, too, had, in most instances, to be cared for by Memphian hands. The Howard special relief trains passed out daily on all the railroads from Memphis, affording frequent illustrations of the fearful condition of mind prevailing in the country.

A heavy black frost was the pleasing spectacle that gladdened the sight of the many who were on the lookout for it, on the morning of October 19th. This harbinger of returning health to Memphis caused unalloyed joy.

Two little bootblacks lived in Memphis before the fever, and when it was declared epidemic one of the two was numbered among the early cases. The other would not leave him, but insisted on nursing his companion, until he himself was stricken, and was removed to another street. One recovered, and was told that his friend was dead. He believed this until, at the close of the epidemic, the two met unexpectedly, near Court Square. A thrill of sentiment, almost to the verge of weeping, went through the dozen spectators who had their attention drawn to the two little fellows, who, despite the crowd, despite the dust of the street, the jingle of the street-car bells, the hum and confusion incident to reviving Memphis, embraced each other, their joy finding utterance in the shedding of copious tears.

Of the Rev. Louis S. Schuyler, rector of the Church of the Holy Innocents, who volunteered and came to Memphis to assist his brethren of the Episcopal ministry during the plague, the New York *World* says: "Mr. Schuyler was the son of Rev. Dr. Montgomery Schuyler, the rector of Christ Church, St. Louis. After graduating at Hobart College, Geneva, he entered the ministry. He was for some time an assistant to Bishop Doane, at St. Peter's Church, Albany. He went to England in 1867, and joined the Episcopal Brotherhood of St. John the Evangelist, at Cowley, Oxford. Soon after his return to this country, last winter, he was called to assist in the Church of the Holy Innocents. On the first of July he took charge of the House of Prayer, in Newark, in the absence of the rector, Dr. Goodwin, and had entered on his duties at the Church of the Holy Innocents only a few days when the call from Memphis came. It had been proposed to Mr. Sword by the members of his congregation, mostly people in moderate circumstances, to present Mr. Schuyler with a testimonial on his return. His brother, M. Roosevelt Schuyler, left for the South on hearing of his illness."

This incident illustrates the romantic side of the epidemic: Dr. W. F. Besancny, a young physician, hailing from Jonestown, Mississippi, offered his services to Medical Director Mitchell. His credentials were perfect, and coming at a time when physicians were most needed, were readily accepted. Just as all the preliminaries had been settled satisfactorily, a messenger entered the office in great haste, in search of a physician to attend Miss D. P. Rutter, a young lady who had been stricken with the fever at her residence on Adams Street. Dr. Mitchell turned to the gallant young physician, and remarked that he could immediately be placed on duty, if he so felt disposed. Dr. Besancny unhesitatingly accepted the call, and at once accompanied the messenger to the young lady's residence, where he found her prostrate with a bad case of the fever. It is unnecessary to go through the details of the lingering illness, suffice it to say that the young doctor's attention was close and faithful, finally resulting in the young lady's recovery. Soon afterward the doctor was stricken down. True to the instincts of her womanly nature, doubly intensified by her self-acknowledged indebtedness to him for having saved her life, she went to his bedside, and there remained, giving such attentions as only a woman can bestow upon the sick, until the glad tidings was announced that he

13

had passed the crisis, and bid fair to recover. He passed through the tedious hours of convalescence, until entirely recovered. Nothing more was known or thought of the matter by the few intimate friends of the young lady until yesterday afternoon, when the doctor, accompanied by Esquire Quigley and a few friends, drove up to the residence, and in less time than it takes us to write this paragraph, the two were joined together in the holy bonds of wedlock. Such a union, consummated under such circumstances, can not fail to abound with happiness.

Savannah *News*.—" We regret deeply to announce the death, from yellow fever, in Memphis, of Dr. Langdon A. Cheves, of this city, who was one of the first to respond to the call of distress from the afflicted city. The information of this sad event was received through a private telegram sent by Dr. McFarland, and is also given in our associated press dispatches. Dr. Cheves entered the Virginia Military Institute, Lexington, Virginia, in the summer of 1869, and graduated with distinction in July, 1873. His high moral character, elevated sense of honor, and gentlemanly courtesy commanded the respect and affection of the faculty and of his fellow-cadets. He was exceedingly modest and quiet in his demeanor, of strong will and marked characteristics, which were strengthened and confirmed by his military education. On his return to Savannah, he studied medicine in the office of Dr. T. J. Charlton for several years, and then left for Baltimore city, where he entered the medical college, and graduated with honor in March last, and subsequently took an extra course of lectures in that city. On returning again to Savannah, he at once entered upon his profession, with the promise of a brilliant future, when the summons for assistance from the plague-stricken city of Memphis induced him to abandon his own interest and hasten to the relief of distressed humanity, in which noble cause he has fallen a martyr. Dr. Cheves was about twenty-four years of age, was a grandson of Hon. Langdon Cheves, president of the United States Bank, and son of Colonel Langdon Cheves, who was killed at Battery Wagner, Morris Island, in 1863. His father was a large and successful rice planter and a civil engineer of considerable note. He leaves a mother and two sisters—Mrs. Charles N. West, now residing in Baltimore, and Mrs. Gilbert A. Wilkins. He was first cousin of Judge Haskell, of the Supreme Court of South Carolina, and of Captain J. C. Haskell, of Savannah, and a relative by marriage of Governor Magrath, who married his aunt. He was in Savannah during the epidemic of 1876, and rendered efficient and zealous service during that terrible period, being himself stricken down in the midst of his good work. In the formation of his individual character he seemed to keep constantly in mind the supreme law of truth and probity, and was in every respect a high toned, honorable gentleman, useful citizen, a physician of rare promise, and a devoted son. His sad death will be deeply lamented by a large circle of friends and relatives."

Jackson (Tenn.) *Tribune and Sun*.—" Young Howlett, aged ten years, a grandson of Mr. Pledge, the hotel man of Grand Junction, passed up to Milan, a few days ago, where his grandfather was staying. Being from an infected town, although having stayed in it only a few hours, he could not remain in Milan. His grandfather, therefore, rented an isolated cabin, some mile or more from town, and hired a negro woman to take the boy and stay with him until the days of his quarantine were completed. The first night the poor boy attempted to stay in the cabin was a terrible one in his experience. A few persons, whom fear and cowardice had made brutes, went to the cabin at night, brickbatted it, shot into it, and ran the poor little boy out into the darkness, and fired shot after shot at him as he fled in wild terror. The little fellow, frightened almost out of his life, remained all night in the woods, wandering and hiding in terror, shivering in the pitiless cold, and almost crazed with a sense of loneliness and danger, and expecting every moment to be murdered. Next morning, he crept into Milan, and his grandfather took the terrified child to a place of safety. Now, we respect quarantine, we respect the fears of the people in these terrible times, but such treatment as this little boy received is simply inhuman, and damns the authors, brutes and cowards. We know that the respectable people of Milan condemn the acts denounced by us fully as much as we do, and we further know that the Milan authorities and quarantine officers are guiltless of any connection with the perpetrators, but they should hunt down the guilty and see that they are punished. They are evidently worthless and low-down characters, and no community is safe that holds them. For the facts upon which our remarks are based we have responsible authors."

Memphis Appeal.—"There was the case of the fever-stricken man in a railroad car, which was uncoupled and left on a side-track, near the National Cemetery, where, but for the ministrations of a brave friend and timely assistance from Memphis, he would have died, as the poor fellow did who, left in a box-car, near Stevenson, was beset by a cowardly mob, possessed of only one idea, that of self-preservation. Then we had the cases of the negro men, poor fellows, driven forth by a few inhuman persons, some of whom have since died of the fever they thus inhumanly sought to fight off. The three victims of their cowardice died miserably by the wayside, giving evidence, by the contortions of their bodies, that they passed away in nameless agonies. Horrible to think of, such an incident six weeks ago would have been scouted as impossible by the very persons who participated in it. Then there is the case of a poor negro woman who, dying of the fever, was rolled in a blanket and unceremoniously dumped into a hog-hole, by her terror-stricken husband and kinsfolks. Bad enough that those who died within the limits so well served by the Howard Association and Citizens' Relief Committee should some days ago, on account of the want of laborers and coffins, have had to lie for two and three days, poisoning the air with a nameless stench, and sending forth countless billions of spores to feed on the vitals of the faithful few who have done such noble service in battling with the scourge; bad enough that these horrors should exist, to appall the living, and help to increase the awful mortality, but when to them we add the wanton inhumanity of stoning and shooting at a defenseless boy of only ten years, driving helpless fever-stricken patients from the only shelter they have, and shaming our common humanity by leaving bodies in hog-holes, food for the hogs, we are overcome with shame for a brave people, a generous and noble people, who, after enduring all the trials of a great war, and attesting both their moral and physical courage, should have their fair escutcheon soiled by a brutalism without parallel. We have already referred to the cases—alas! too many—where fathers have deserted their families, and have called attention to the callous neglect of each other by near relatives, who, before the epidemic came to test the strength and sincerity of their affections, would have scorned the possibility of conduct that has secured some few a longer lease of life, at the cost of a desertion that hastened the death of others. Only a few days ago we saw a little child of, perhaps, three years, that had been surrendered to the keeping of one of our noble volunteer doctors by a mother who now fills a nameless grave in potter's field. She was an outcast—had thrown herself away because abandoned by her husband— and finding herself fast sinking from the combined effects of the most loathsome disease and the yellow fever, gave her child to her physician, that it might find the home and care the cowardly father had denied to her and it. How shocking to every sense. Hearing such things, one wonders if our civilization is really a failure, and we are going back to the days of the London plague, when all the bonds of society were loosened, and besides the disease, which carried away so many thousands, the people of the great capital were the prey of an epidemic of moral cowardice. Were it not for the thousands of cases of heroism, almost divine in their self-sacrifice, which we witness every day, such a conclusion would be irresistible. Another case, and we close for the present. Mr. Ben K. Pullen, an old and honored citizen, who is held in the highest esteem as an upright, honorable man, on Monday last went out to Elmwood Cemetery—loveliest of the cities of the dead—to perform the sad duty of burying his wife, who had died of the fever. It was late, past five o'clock in the evening, when the carriage and the hearse arrived at the cemetery. There was still three-quarters of an hour to pass before the hour arrived when funeral parties are refused admittance and the laborers suspend work. The man in charge of the cemetery (named Flynn or Edwards—it is not known which) came to the spot where the grave was to be dug, with a party of negroes, whom he informed that they would not receive any extra pay for work done after six o'clock, thus trying to prevent them from the work they were there to perform. The negroes, more humane than he, and indignant at such an exhibition of brutality before the husband and children, standing beside all that remained to them of a good wife and mother, replied that sometimes they worked for friendship. They dug the grave, lowered the casket, and had covered it out of sight, having almost completed their work, when the same cold-blooded creature, in the hearing of the mourning family, and almost in their faces, said : 'You have worked after six o'clock, and you shall receive no pay for it. Hereafter no work shall be done after that hour, matter how many d—d carcasses are brought here.' Powerless to resent an outrage so gross, the father and children passed out and on to their homes, their grief intensified by an insult that all men must share until it is punished as it should be." Subsequently the facts were investigated by the cemetery authorities, and the man was discharged. He left the city immediately.

METEOROLOGICAL TABLES.

Comparison of Mean Daily Barometer, Thermometer, Prevailing Direction of Wind, State of Weather, Mean Daily Humidity and Daily Rain-Fall of August, September, October, and November, 1878, in Memphis, as recorded by Dr. Thornton, Surgeon in charge of City Hospital, and assistants, with corresponding months of 1873.

DATE.	Barometer. 1873.	Barometer. 1878.	Thermometer. 1873.	Thermometer. 1878.	Prevailing Direction of Wind. 1873.	Prevailing Direction of Wind. 1878.	Condition of Weather. 1873.	Condition of Weather. 1878.	Mean Humidity. 1873.	Mean Humidity. 1878.	Rain-Fall. 1873.	Rain-Fall. 1878.
August 1	30,067	30,000	75	88.2	south	south-west	cloudy	clear	83.3	59.3	2.94	0
" 2	30,030	29,942	79	81.2	south-west	south	fair	fair	80.0	77.0	0	.21
" 3	30,090	29,872	75	80.2	north	westerly	fair	cloudy	78.0	77.0	.05	.02
" 4	30,170	29,881	72	78.2	north-east	northerly	clear	fair	63.7	69.3	0	.02
" 5	30,160	29,875	75	84.2	north-east	north-west	clear	clear	62.7	65.7	0	0
" 6	30,092	29,917	78	85.7	south-east	north-west	fair	clear	69.3	61.3	0	0
" 7	30,020	29,953	75	86.2	east	south-west	fair	clear	80.7	63.0	0	0
" 8	30,012	29,943	77	85.7	southerly	westerly	fair	clear	69.7	59.7	0	0
" 9	30,062	29,899	81	86.2	north-west	south-west	fair	clear	74.3	57.0	.03	.13
" 10	30,072	29,899	83	81.7	north-west	south-west	clear	cloudy	74.7	72.7	.23	.12
" 11	30,022	29,960	85	78.2	north	north	clear	cloudy	72.7	82.3	0	.33
" 12	29,978	29,737	84	75.5	west	north-east	cloudy	cloudy	68.0	81.7	0	0
" 13	29,967	29,897	79	78.7	westerly	north-east	fair	fair	80.0	72.0	1.09	.07
" 14	29,980	29,927	78	81.2	north-east	northerly	clear	clear	65.7	62.7	0	0
" 15	29,895	29,997	79	82.5	westerly	south-west	clear	clear	65.3	65.0	0	0
" 16	29,945	30,040	75	84.2	north-west	west	cloudy	clear	85.7	63.0	0	0
" 17	29,997	30,061	76	86.2	north-west	south	fair	clear	76.8	64.7	0	0
" 18	30,037	30,079	73	87.0	north	south-west	clear	clear	60.3	62.7	0	0
" 19	30,032	29,994	76	88.2	north	south-west	fair	clear	61.6	63.7	0	0
" 20	29,972	29,889	76	87.0	northerly	south-west	fair	fair	61.0	67.7	0	0
" 21	29,990	29,898	79	84.0	north-east	north-west	fair	fair	71.0	73.3	0	.02
" 22	30,042	29,965	77	81.7	easterly	north-east	fair	clear	70.6	68.3	0	0
" 23	30,095	30,006	81	81.5	east	north-west	fair	clear	66.0	55.0	0	0

DATE	Barometer 1873	Barometer 1878	Thermometer 1873	Thermometer 1878	Prevailing Direction of Wind 1873	Prevailing Direction of Wind 1878	Condition of Weather 1873	Condition of Weather 1878	Mean Humidity 1873	Mean Humidity 1878	Rain-Fall 1873	Rain-Fall 1878
August 24	30,100	29,989	83	84.5	easterly	westerly	clear	clear	65.6	54.0	0	0
" 25	29,997	29,898	84	80.7	south-west	westerly	clear	cloudy	67.6	76.3	0	.05
" 26	29,960	29,866	85	78.2	south-west	north-west	clear	cloudy	66.0	80.3	0	0
" 27	29,950	29,873	79	80.5	westerly	north-east	fair	cloudy	70.0	70.7	.19	0
" 28	30,022	29,914	79	82.0	north-west	north-west	fair	fair	70.6	61.3	0	0
" 29	30,110	29,958	79	73.2	north-west	north-west	fair	cloudy	65.6	81.0	0	.73
" 30	30,105	29,942	86	71.7	north	north	clear	fair	65.0	81.3	0	.02
" 31	30,067	29,995	84	78.2	south-west	south-west	clear	clear	64.0	69.0	0	0
Means	30,035	29,915	79	82.2	south-west	south-west			70	68.7	4.53	1.72
September 1	30,012	30,090	84	77.7	south-west	south-west	fair	clear	62.0	72.0	0	0
" 2	30,925	30,061	78	80.2	north-west	south-west	•fair	clear	77.0	65.6	.40	0
" 3	29,995	29,991	76	82.5	south	south-west	fair	clear	85.6	61.6	.48	0
" 4	29,987	29,978	82	83.5	south-west	north-west	fair	clear	68.0	61.0	0	0
" 5	30,132	30,000	79	77.2	south-west	north-east	fair	clear	75.3	57.3	0	0
" 6	30,190	30,005	76	78.2	north-east	north-east	clear	clear	57.3	56.0	0	0
" 7	30,010	30,014	68	80.5	northerly	northerly	fair	fair	70.3	61.3	0	0
" 8	30,225	29,989	67	80.7	north-east	south-east	fair	fair	65.3	61.6	0	0
" 9	30,100	28,965	74	79.2	north-east	northerly	fair	cloudy	65.3	70.0	0	.85
" 10	30,080	30,041	76	63.7	south-east	north	fair	cloudy	69.6	92.3	0	1.62
" 11	30,050	30,157	78	62.0	west	north	fair	fair	66.0	54.6	0	0
" 12	29,980	30,100	79	58.1	south-west	north-west	fair	clear	62.0	55.3	0	0
" 13	30,097	30,129	63	60.7	north	north-west	fair	clear	68.0	59.0	0	0
" 14	30,150	30,197	59	65.5	north	easterly	clear	clear	61.3	61.6	.10	0
" 15	30,105	30,184	65	69.7	westerly	north-east	clear	clear	58.6	53.6	0	0
" 16	30,120	30,139	72	70.2	north-west	south	clear	clear	62.3	63.3	0	0
" 17	29,985	30,169	76	71.7	west	south-west	clear	clear	61.0	60.3	0	0

A HISTORY OF THE YELLOW FEVER 197

DATE.	Barometer.		Thermometer.		Prevailing Direction of Wind.		Condition of Weather.		Mean Humidity.		Rain-Fall.	
	1873.	1878.	1873.	1878.	1873.	1878.	1873.	1878.	1873.	1878.	1873.	1878.
September 18.....	29,917	30,167	76	76.2	north-west	south-west	fair	clear	66.6	61.6	0	0
" 19.....	30,010	30,008	61	76.5	north	south	fair	clear	54.3	61.6	0	0
" 20.....	30,097	29,993	59	69.2	north-east	southerly	cloudy	cloudy	62.6	83.0	0	0
" 21.....	30,077	30,159	66	58.7	north-east	north	cloudy	clear	57.6	65.6	0	0
" 22.....	30,035	30,077	66	67.2	northerly	north-east	fair	fair	59.3	59.3	0	0
" 23.....	29,990	30,038	61	71.5	north	fair	fair	76.0	76.3	.31	0
" 24.....	29,875	30,093	66	74.2	south-east	easterly	fair	fair	73.3	70.3	0	.04
" 25.....	29,990	30,047	73	78.2	northerly	southerly	clear	clear	79.6	69.6	0	0
" 26.....	29,992	30,277	78	60.7	south	south	fair	cloudy	86.0	86.0	0	.08
" 27.....	30,052	30,146	76	65.2	north-east	north-east	clear	fair	67.3	73.6	.82	0
" 28.....	29,945	30,059	76	71.5	southerly	southerly	cloudy	fair	84.0	82.3	.24	0
" 29.....	30,085	30,011	64	74.7	north-west	south-east	fair	fair	78.3	75.6	1.18	0
" 30.....	30,152	29,953	58	75.7	north	south-east	clear	clear	66.6	69.3	0	0
Means......	30,048	30,073	71	72	northerly	north			68.0	66.6	2.53	2.59
October 1.....	30,090	29,927	63	76.2	north-east	south	fair	clear	66.3	66.3	0	0
" 2.....	30,100	30,043	67	70.2	north-east	north	fair	fair	64.6	73.3	0	.04
" 3.....	30,018	30,062	70	70.0	south-west	north	fair	clear	70.3	60.6	0	0
" 4.....	30,018	30,054	69	70.5	north-west	north-west	fair	clear	74.6	57.6	0	0
" 5.....	29,945	30,103	69	63.0	south-west	north-west	fair	cloudy	69.6	76.0	0	0
" 6.....	29,875	30,065	49	63.2	north	north	cloudy	fair	58.6	73.3	.04	0
" 7.....	30,165	30,070	51	69.2	north	north-west	fair	clear	58.6	80.0	0	0
" 8.....	30,132	30,025	57	69.0	north-west	south-west	clear	clear	42.3	71.6	0	0
" 9.....	30,115	30,037	62	70.0	south-west	south-east	clear	cloudy	63.0	90.0	0	.02
" 10.....	30,132	29,918	64	67.7	south-west	east	clear	fair	73.3	90.6	0	1.11
" 11.....	30,167	30,028	67	65.7	westerly	north	fair	cloudy	72.6	72.6	0	0
" 12.....	30,216	30,174	55	59.2	north-west	north-east	clear	clear	53.0	54.6	0	0

DATE.	Barometer. 1873.	Barometer. 1878.	Thermometer. 1873.	Thermometer. 1878.	Prevailing Direction of Wind. 1873.	Prevailing Direction of Wind. 1878.	Condition of Weather. 1873.	Condition of Weather. 1878.	Mean Humidity. 1873.	Mean Humidity. 1878.	Rain-Fall. 1873.	Rain-Fall. 1878.
October 13.....	30,181	30,076	56.6	62.2	westerly	south	clear	clear	59.0	65.0	0	0
" 14.....	30,241	30,044	56.6	69.7	east	south	clear	clear	55.0	72.0	0	0
" 15.....	30,290	29,900	66.6	74.2	south-east	south	fair	fair	65.3	66.6	0	0
" 16.....	30,274	29,888	72.6	72.2	south	south	fair	cloudy	70.3	79.6	0	1.04
" 17.....	30,069	30,125	72.0	56.5	south-west	north-west	cloudy	fair	64.6	55.3	17.6	0
" 18.....	30,084	30,216	55.0	66.6	north	north-west	cloudy	clear	88.6	52.3	0	0
" 19.....	30,176	30,190	50.0	49.0	north-west	east	clear	clear	62.3	64.0	0	0
" 20.....	30,099	30,024	48.0	55.0	north-west	south-east	clear	fair	61.6	55.0	0	0
" 21.....	29,913	29,938	52.6	64.0	west	south	clear	fair	57.0	60.3	.07	.43
" 22.....	29,919	30,115	64.6	49.5	south	north-west	cloudy	clear	77.6	57.6	2.14	0
" 23.....	30,283	30,067	39.0	54.5	north	south	fair	clear	86.6	63.3	0	0
" 24.....	30,325	30,103	45.0	61.5	north-east	south	fair	clear	71.6	53.6	0	0
" 25.....	30,253	30,179	49.0	66.2	east	south-west	cloudy	clear	92.0	69.3	0	0
" 26.....	29,835	30,225	60.0	61.2	south	south-west	rainy	cloudy	93.6	68.6	1.94	.18
" 27.....	29,959	30,438	49.0	40.5	north-west	north	fair	fair	61.0	71.3	0	0
" 28.....	30,393	30,211	36.0	41.2	north-west	north-east	clear	fair	58.3	58.6	0	0
" 29.....	30,343	29,950	40.5	48.7	south	northerly	clear	cloudy	54.0	85.0	0	0
" 30.....	30,116	30,125	49.0	53.7	south-west	north-west	fair	fair	54.6	58.0	0	0
" 31.....	30,368	30,435	39.0	39.0	north-west	north-west	clear	clear	52.3	44.0	0	0
Means.....	30,130	30,098	56	60.8	north-west	north-west			66	66.4	5.95	2.82
Novemb'r 1.....	30,394	30,288	44.5	45.5	south-east	south	clear	clear	49.0	49.0	0	0
" 2.....	30,218	30,260	50.0	54.0	easterly	south-west	cloudy	clear	66.0	53.3	0	0
" 3.....	30,218	30,360	47.0	57.2	north-east	north	fair	clear	67.0	34.0	0	0
" 4.....	30,185	30,307	50.5	52.2	north-east	south-east	cloudy	fair	87.3	49.0	.27	0
" 5.....	30,115	30,163	57.5	60.0	north-east	south-east	cloudy	fair	87.0	47.3	0	0
" 6.....	30,038	29,988	57.0	59.7	northerly	south-west	fair	clear	71.3	59.0	0	0

DATE.	Barometer. 1873.	Barometer. 1878.	Thermometer. 1873.	Thermometer. 1878.	Prevailing Direction of Wind. 1873.	Prevailing Direction of Wind. 1878.	Condition of Weather. 1873.	Condition of Weather. 1878.	Mean Humidity. 1873.	Mean Humidity. 1878.	Rain-Fall. 1873.	Rain-Fall. 1878.
November 7	29,975	30,083	57.0	64.7	south-west	south-west	fair	fair	68.0	68.0	0	.02
" 8	30,192	30,251	55.5	51.2	westerly	north	clear	clear	55.3	46.0	0	0
" 9	30,182	30,174	57.0	52.2	south-west	east	clear	clear	54.3	50.3	0	0
" 10	30,026	20,905	61.0	61.2	south-west	south	clear	fair	55.3	52.0	0	.01
" 11	29,863	29,922	63.0	54.0	south-west	north-west	clear	cloudy	32.0	56.0	0	0
" 12	30,169	30,059	43.0	52.0	north-west	north-west	cloudy	clear	47.0	49.6	0	0
" 13	30,140	30,095	42.0	53.5	west	south-west	clear	clear	42.6	48.0	0	0
" 14	30,136	30,142	48.0	55.7	westerly	north-east	clear	fair	45.6	43.3	0	0
" 15	30,039	29,952	62.0	52.0	south-west	east	fair	cloudy	67.3	90.0	.22	.96
" 16	29,714	30,089	60.0	50.5	south-west	south-west	fair	fair	63.0	90.6	0	.02
" 17	29,466	30,198	53.0	49.2	westerly	north-west	fair	fair	48.6	88.6	0	0
" 18	29,868	30,085	39.0	51.2	north-west	north-east	fair	clear	42.6	65.0	0	0
" 19	30,189	29,892	32.0	52.7	north-west	westerly	clear	clear	58.0	62.6	0	.14
" 20	30,216	29,932	39.0	49.0	south	westerly	clear	cloudy	55.6	65.6	0	.02
" 21	30,217	29,998	49.5	49.2	south-west	west	foggy	fair	63.0	66.3	0	0
" 22	30,028	29,904	50.0	52.7	easterly	west	rainy	clear	89.6	46.6	1.80	0
" 23	29,825	29,772	54.0	57.5	south-east	south	cloudy	clear	95.3	46.3	1.50	0
" 24	29,987	29,880	44.0	53.7	north-west	south	fair	cloudy	80.6	67.3	.07	.19
" 25	30,077	30,097	46.0	44.0	north-west	north	clear	cloudy	40.6	84.3	0	.22
" 26	29,932	29,849	49.0	42.2	south	north	fair	rainy	57.3	94.0	0	.38
" 27	30,040	29,010	46.0	41.2	north	west	fair	fair	47.6	72.3	0	.48
" 28	30,402	30,201	37.0	43.7	north-east	south-west	clear	clear	31.6	58.6	0	0
" 29	30,037	30,209	41.0	48.7	north-east	south-east	fair	clear	40.6	58.0	0	0
" 30	30,320	30,057	52.2	52.2	south-east	south-east	fair	cloudy	75.0	58.6	0	0
Means	30,087	30,069	40.	57.8	south-west	south-west			61	61.8	3.86	2.41

It will be seen from the preceding tables that the thermometer ranged very much higher during the epidemic months of 1878 than those of 1873, and that the humidity for August and September was two degrees less, while in October and November it was about the same as during the same months in 1873. The barometrical range is about an average for the same months of both years, as is the prevailing direction of the wind. The rain-fall for August of 1878 was 1.72 inches compared with 4.53 for the same month of 1873; 2.59 for September, 1878, as compared with 2.53 for the same month of 1873; 2.82 for October, 1878, as compared with 5.95 for the corresponding month of 1873; and 2.41 for November of 1878 as compared with 3.86 for the corresponding month of 1873. In August, 1878, there were 16 clear days, 7 fair, and 8 cloudy; and in August, 1873, there were 12 clear days, 16 fair, and 3 cloudy. In September, 1878, there were 18 clear days, 8 fair, and 4 cloudy; and in September, 1873, there were 7 clear days, 18 fair days, and 5 cloudy. In October, 1878, there were 14 clear days, 11 fair, and 6 cloudy; in October, 1873, there were 13 clear days, 13 fair, 4 cloudy, and 1 rainy. In November, 1878, there were 14 clear days, 9 fair, 6 cloudy, and 1 rainy; and in November, 1873, there were 11 clear, 12 fair, 5 cloudy, 1 foggy, and 1 rainy. The absence, in 1878, of the rain and humidity upon which many writers declare the propagation of yellow fever to depend is remarkable. In the tropics the rainy season is generally the most sickly, and some of the best authorities agree in assigning to heat there preventive and healthful properties. From this has grown the belief that heavy and continuous rains precede epidemics of yellow fever. This has not generally been the case in the United States. The summer of 1878 was for some weeks intensely hot. In St. Louis the number of cases of sun-stroke were so many as to amount to an epidemic, alarming the people to such an extent that many, if not most of them, suspended work, dreading the least exertion as they did death itself. In one week the mortality from this cause alone amounted to nearly 300. In 1837 the same intense heat prevailed and preceded an epidemic of unusual violence. In 1853, the year of greatest mortality from yellow fever, and the year of its greatest spread throughout the South, in June, July, and August, reports from ninety meteorological stations, from Canada to Florida and Texas, show that in the fourth week of June the maximum heat from New York to Savannah gave an average of 95°; and in New Orleans during August, September, and October of that year the thermometer ranged from 82° to 91°. A wave of heat moved across the country in that as in the year 1878; indeed there were two such waves, one in June and another in August. Blodgett says the first wave made itself manifest on the 29th and 30th of June. The extreme was central in the latitude of Washington and was limited at Savannah on the south and Burlington, Vermont, on the north, attaining 96° to 98° in Tennessee, Kentucky, and Southern Ohio, and 99.5° to 102° at Washington and in Eastern Virginia and North Carolina. In August the second wave made itself felt, beginning earlier at the west. The maximum in Illinois and the adjacent States was 90° to 94° from the 8th to the 13th, in Ohio and Kentucky nearly the same, and passing eastward the district of greatest excess was central New York. The mortality from this great heat was frightful. In June the yellow fever showed itself in New Orleans, the week ending on the 30th of the month, giving as the average of maxima 92° in that city. On comparing July and August, the two great epidemic months in New Orleans in 1853, Dowler says there was nothing peculiar—nothing that can account for the epidemic in regard to the quantity of rain, which was in some places greater or less than in regions free from the fever, and sometimes similar. The summer of 1699, when the fever prevailed severely in Philadelphia, was so intensely hot that men died while harvesting in the fields, and all business was suspended in the city. In 1762 it prevailed after a very hot and dry summer. In 1793 there was no rain from the 25th of August to the 15th of October—the crops failed and the springs dried. In 1794 the disease again prevailed, modified, Rush says, by occasional showers of rain. In 1797 the summer was hot and dry, and in 1798, when yellow fever made fearful havoc, the summer was characterized by extreme dryness, in consequence of which whole fields were burnt up by the sun, and the crops were seriously injured. In 1801 the fever broke out in Philadelphia after a drought of some duration. In 1805 the summer set in in June with great severity. The heat was unusually intense from thence to the end of August. This was accompanied by a severe drought, which commenced on the 28th of June and continued, without any intermission, except a very few sprinklings of rain, that barely moistened the surface of the earth, till the close of August. During this period, not only the rains failed, but even the dews ceased to descend, and the earth became parched. La Roche declares that neither heat nor moisture, when acting separately, can be productive of yellow and kindred fevers, and that equally objectionable is the belief that the disease arises from the combined influence of those two agencies, either unassisted by another cause of a more efficient kind and peculiar character, or with the aid of some agent, calculated only to render the system more prone to the impress of the other. Neither can we admit the propriety of referring the efficient cause of yellow and kindred fevers to the difference of temperature between day and night, or to mere atmospheric vicissitudes—the succession of cool or cold nights to hot days; nor to the sudden exposure of the body, at any period of the twenty-four hours, to a low degree of temperature after it has been placed for a greater or less extent of time under the influence of a high degree. Vicissitudes, if really the efficient cause of yellow fever, appear to be whimsical in their operations. The meteorological tables, published in the account of the voyage of D'Urville to the South Pole and Oceanica, show conclusively that the minimum degrees of nychthemeron oscillations occur in hot latitudes, the difference between the maxima and minima amounting only to a very few degrees. In temperate and cold climates, these oscillations are much more marked; and yet the yellow fever is a disease of hot climates. There it occurs frequently—in some parts almost annually; while in temperate climates, where the vicissitudes in question are constant, the fever only occasionally, and in many places never, shows itself. In hot climates themselves, places subject to considerable oscillations are free from the disease, while others, where the changes are unimportant, are not unfrequently visited by it. At Caraccas, where yellow fever has seldom, if ever, prevailed, the temperature is continually changing, while at Martinique, where yellow fever is of frequent occurrence, the oscillations are very trifling." As to the effect of wind, the same authority declares that the yellow fever occurs in different countries under the influence of different winds. In the greater portion of the West Indies, it would seem to be brought on through the agency of, or to be attended with, the prevalence of south winds, while in Havana this wind is comparatively inocuous, and the east and west winds exercise injurious effects. In some parts of this country it has appeared after and during the prevalence of south winds, sometimes during the occurrence of west winds. In other localities it has required an east or a north wind. Nor is the same difference less strikingly noticed elsewhere. In Leghorn it occurred under the influence of south winds; in Barcelona, of north-east and south-west winds; while in Andalusia and Gibraltar it has been almost invariably in some way connected with the prevalence of the east, or Levant wind, and was never produced by or associated with a south wind. From the diversity of results arising from the same wind, and the sameness of effect resulting from currents of different character, we derive the proof that no particular wind can be said, with any show of reason, to constitute by itself the necessary and efficient cause of the disease, and that whenever any of them exercise an agency, as regards the origin or diffusion of the fever, it derives that power, not from the fact of its coming from any particular quarter, but from the temperature and hygrometrical conditions of the moving column of air, and more especially, perhaps, from the injurious effluvia it raises from the localities over which it passes, and which are carried along with it. Treating of atmospheric pressure, La Roche says, that "all that can be said on the subject is, that a comparison of the state of the atmospheric pressure here and elsewhere during sickly seasons, with the results of observations made at periods when the disease does not show itself, does not lend much assistance to the belief in the reality of any such connection, so far, at least, as relates to the production of the efficient cause." He does not deny the influence which a difference of pressure of the atmosphere exercises on the system in health and disease, nor does he deny the fact that an undue increase of it produces unpleasant effects and leads even to diseased manifestations, and that other results of an equally deleterious effect attend an extreme in the opposite condition of the air; but there is nothing in all this calculated to induce the belief that it can do more than place the system in such a condition as will predispose it to the deleterious impression of some more efficient cause, especially when we find that the same condition of the barometer exists, as well when the yellow fever prevails as when it does not. The same may be said of the deficiency or excess of electricity. In Memphis in 1873, as well as in 1878, but especially the latter year, the absence of thunder-storms was so remarkable as to give rise to the belief that to this cause, above all others, was due the almost spontaneity and the malignancy of the fever. It was held by some that the atmosphere was deficient in ozone, and many expedients were resorted to to supply it in the belief that since it destroys the miasm from decaying animal matter it would be found efficient in the sick-rooms, in hospitals, and infirmaries in destroying the poison or germs of yellow fever. Some trials were made with an apparatus sent out by a leading physician of Buffalo, and by the more simple medical formula so well known, but the fever made such havoc with those who attempted these tests that satisfactory results were not reached. This is to be regretted, as a definite result would have gone far to settle another of the disputes of the faculty. Some doctors declare that an excess of electricity is a considerable agency in the promotion, if not the production, of yellow fever, while others hold that the deficiency is. Writers on the fever in the West Indies ascribe to electricity great power as an exciting and predisposing cause in epidemics of yellow fever. Dr. Clarke, of Dominica, attributed the fever, on the contrary, to a deficiency of thunder, as did Dr. Lallemant, of Rio Janeiro. Such was the case, La Roche says, in New York in the fever of 1795 and 1822, in New Haven and New London in 1798, in Savannah in 1820, in Charleston in 1817, and in Philadelphia in the fatal year of 1798. During the forty-four years of exemption from the disease enjoyed by Charleston from 1748, there was a frequent recurrence of showers and thunder gusts. After 1792 these were less frequent, and the fever was more common. In 1815 a hurricane which swept over Jamaica is said, by Dr. Arnold, to have had a wonderful effect in purifying the atmosphere and mitigating the effects of the fever. Dr. Caldwell, of Philadelphia, remarks that "during several of the yellow fever calamities in Philadelphia and the other Atlantic cities, electrical phenomena were unusually irregular. Shooting stars were at times abundant and brilliant in a degree far beyond what is common. Throughout some seasons, especially the summer of 1793, scarcely a gleam of lightning was to be seen, while in others, thunder-storms were inordinately frequent and severe. In 1799 the shooting stars were most abundant." Other authorities ascribe to astral influences a direct and exciting agency for this as well as other diseases. In the Middle Ages this was the conviction of physicians and learned men, and there are not wanting some who, in our own time, boldly declare their belief that to planetary movements are we indebted for the decimating diseases which, under the name of the black plague, cholera, and yellow fever, sweep so many thousands from the earth, stop the wheels of commerce, and paralyze the energies of whole nations. Professor Jenkins, of England, in a recent article in the Pall Mall *Gazette*, not only avows his belief in the potency of the planets in controlling epidemics, but gives the calculations which he has made through a series of years, and which are the reasons assigned for a belief which the prejudice against astrology does not prevent him from giving to the world. He writes: "About eight years ago I spent many months accumulating information on cholera throughout the world, from 1816 to 1871. I tabulated my results, threw them into the form of a curve, and was surprised to find that there had occurred a great outbreak about every seventeen years, and that these outbreaks took place alternately at maxima and minima of sun-spots. Certainly the sun-spots could not have produced the cholera, for there was a great outbreak when the spots were very plentiful, and the next when they were very few.

But that there was a connection I felt convinced, and also, that they were both in the nature of effects. I suggested it, in a paper on the subject which I read before the Royal Historical Society, that the cause would probably be found in the influence of the planets, and in their approach to the sun. There were minor outbreaks which I could not explain; but I felt sufficient confidence in my results to state (see *Nature*, May, 1872,) that, as there had been great outbreaks in 1816–17, 1832–4, 1848–50, 1865–7, we might confidently expect the next in 1883–4. I left the subject for seven years. Meanwhile I worked at the subject of sun-spots, and was rewarded by finding that the average period for these phenomena, for magnetic storms and for auroræ period was 11.9 years, the period of Jupiter's anomalistic year, and that these phenomena were always least when Jupiter was nearest to the sun. I then turned to terrestrial magnetism, and found that the needle of the compass, which at London was moving east up to 1580, and west till 1816, and east ever since, follows the movements of a strong magnetic pole, which Sir James Ross found in 1830 in Boothia, but which has now, I hold, traveled west to Prince Albert Land, and has moved at such a rate that it will complete its revolution round the pole of the earth in about 500 years. On examining the accumulated evidence in regard to the dip of the needle, I found that the magnetic pole must be in the atmosphere over the place where it appears to be in the earth. In the midst of this work a little incident occurred which induced me to write to the registrar-general for the number of deaths in England for the last forty years, which he kindly sent me. I immediately found that what I suspected was true—that the number of deaths in England was greatest, on an average over the whole period, every six years. I threw the numbers into the form of a curve, and under it placed the curve represented by Jupiter's orbit during the same period, and found that whenever Jupiter was at two points equally distant from his nearest point to the sun (corresponding to our September and March) the deaths in England were greatest. (A short paper on the subject will appear in the next number of the proceedings of the Statistical Society.) If this is true for England, it should be true for the death-rate of the world. On examining the curve for cholera over the world, from 1816 to 1871, which I drew out seven years ago, I found that this held good. I am at present engaged in examining the death-rate of the world for the last forty years, as far as possible. The outbreak of plague directed my attention to that subject. I examined a magnetic chart of the world, and found that the lines of no declination (*i. e.*, the lines which indicate where the needle points to true North, and therefore the lines in which the greatest magnetic power is manifested) are advancing west, at the average rate of about one-seventh of a degree annually over the regions which are the present epidemic-stricken quarters of the globe—Russia, Persia, United States, Brazil, and Western China. As the magnetic poles advance these lines advance, and epidemics on man and beast accompany them. On calculating back, I find that the line which is now passing across Russia must have passed over that region 500 years ago. This will take us back to the middle of the fourteenth century; and with similar magnetic conditions we have the same epidemic—the Black

Death. We know that plague devastated Europe more or less for the next two centuries, culminating in the great plague of London in 1665, and curiously enough just at the time when a line of no declination was advancing over England. It occurred to me that Neptune might be the cause of the movement of the magnetic pole. On examining the movements of the planet in its orbit, I found that those of the needle varied in accordance with those of that planet while it makes three revolutions. The magnetic poles make an eccentric circle round the pole of the earth; this eccentricity I found was due to some influence at a maximum of about eighty years. On examining the movements and position of Uranus, I found that they were such as to account for the anomaly. I have fully detailed the subject in a paper I sent to the Royal Astronomical Society; they have announced it; whether they will have the courage to have it read is another matter. In conclusion, I would say that within the next seven years there will happen that which has not happened for hundreds of years: all the planets at or near their nearest point to the sun about the same time. It is true of the earth that its magnetic intensity is greatest about the time when it is near the sun; the same is probably true of all the planets; therefore, we may expect extraordinary magnetic phenomena during the next seven years, and great plagues, which will manifest themselves in all their intensity when Jupiter is about three years from his perihelion—that is, in 1883."

La Roche admits that "electricity may, and no doubt does, act as an exciting cause by its excess, and as a predisposing one sometimes, by this excess, and more frequently by its deficiency and modifications. In a word, electricity may, by its excess or deficiency, operate on the system in a twofold manner—as an exciting and as a predisposing agent; and may, besides, under particular circumstances, promote the development of the efficient cause of the disease which an excess tends to neutralize. To all this no one can object. But when we find medical writers, while rejecting the idea of recognizing the existence of a separate and distinct poison for the several exanthemata, for influenza, for cholera, for each of the different kinds of fever, for whooping-cough, mumps, etc., and while maintaining that an etiology so manifold can not be true, refer all these different and dissimilar diseases to various modifications of a single principle—electricity; when we find that fluid accused of producing, in some occasions, scarlet fever, or small-pox, or measles, or typhoid, typhus, remittent, bilious, or yellow fever, or influenza, and at other times ordinary phlegmasiæ—the only reason of the difference being diversity of predispositions 'arising from a variety of circumstances existing in countless combinations and involving whole communities, or affecting individuals only'—we must pause. The idea of referring scarlet fever, small-pox, and yellow fever to a little more or less electricity, can scarcely be acceptable to sound pathologists. Whatever may be the case with respect to other zymotic diseases, the idea of looking to electricity for the remote or effective cause of the yellow fever is not tenable. . . . The disease is always the same, and must be produced every-where by the same cause. It is different from other diseases and must be produced by causes different from those which give rise to these. It can not, therefore, be the product of a morbific agent, which can by no possibility produce it artificially, and which, supposing the assertion of the advocates of its agency to be correct, produces diseases of a dissimilar kind. Add to this, that this agent is always associated with modifications of heat, humidity, etc., each of which is entitled to the regard in estimating the degree of influence of febriferous causes."

THE DEAD OF 1878.

THE DEAD OF 1878.*

I.

TENNESSEE—MEMPHIS.†

Aug. 16. Ashe, Rosa, w, Second St.
16. Allen, Eliza, w, Saffarans St.
21. Anderson, child of Frank, w, 97 Commerce St.
21. Adonis, Morris, w.
23. Anderson, August, w, 147½ Poplar St.
24. Alexander, A., c, City Hospital.
26. Anderson, John, c, 237 Dunlap St.
27. Able, R. H., w, City Hospital.
28. Anderson, Willie, w, 148 Poplar St
28. Alexander, Margaret, c, 188 Court St.
28. Alexander, Mrs. M., c, Court St.
29. Aaron, William. 147 Washington St.
30. Atkinson, Matilda, c.
31. Allison, M. A., w, Orleans St.
31. Allen, James, c, Central Hotel.
31. Atkinson, Geo., w, rear Cochran Hall.
Sept. 2. Anderson, Lynus.
2. Ames, Lewis D., w, Walker Ave.
2. Anderson, Butler P., w, Grenada, Miss.
2. Allen, Mary, w, 109 Madison St.
2. Anderson, H., w, Poplar St.
2. Able, Gabriel, Louisville, Ky.
3. Ames, Willie J., w, Walker Ave.
3. Allen, Mary, c, cor. Fifth & Looney Sts.
4. Austin, Mrs. Ann, w, 58½ Jefferson St.
5. Arsilli, E.
5. Amandus, Brother, w, Market St.
5. Archie, Andrew, c, cor. Second & Keel Sts.
5. Aiken, Mrs., w, 466 Main St.
5. Anderson, Ed., c, 209 Hernando St.
5. Alphonsa, Mother, w, LaSalette Academy.
6. Arneiga, Louis.
6. Arthur, Fred , 29 Old Madison St.
6. Austin, Wm. M., 58½ Jefferson St.
6. Armom, Martin, c, 386 Linden St.
7. Atchinson, Joseph H., w.
7. Anderson, John, w, Pontotoc St.
7. Anderson, Martha, c, 276 Third St.
7. Atkinson, John, w, cor. Shelby & South Sts.
7. Armstrong, John, w, 317 Union St.
8. Anderson, J. A., w, cor. Poplar & Hupert Sts.
8. Armstrong, Mrs. E. J.
8. Armstin, J. A. G., w.
8. Austin. Gracie, w.
9. Atkins, Harry, c, Clay St.
9. Ashe, Eliza, c, 65 Elliott St.
9. Arnold, Mr., w, 563 Main St.
9. Anderson, Rachel, c, Georgia St.
9. Avery, Allen G., w, Market St. Infirmary
10. Adams, Hon. C. W., w, Union St.
10. Anderson, Sarah N., w, Walker Ave.
10. Anderson, Richard, Rayburn Ave.
10. Allegins, P., cor. Third & Exchange Sts
10. Alexander, E. G.
10. Aaron, M.
10. Allie, son of Mrs., 283 South St.
11. Amonett, J. J., w, Adams St.
11. Amonett, Katie, w, Adams St.
11. App, Katie, w, Jefferson St.
11. Adare, Avery, Poplar St.
11. Acklin, Samuel.

Sept. 12. Avant, Dr. B. W., w, Vance St.
12. Anderson, L. B.. c, Shelby County.
12. Arnott, Katie, w, Adams St.
13. Anderson, Mrs. Butler P., w, Hernando St.
13. Austin, Jack, c, 191 Linden St.
13. Auer, A., w.
13. Avery, c, Fourth St,
14. Adams, Mr., Vance St.
14. Arnold, Mrs., w, 563 Main St.
14. Arnold, Bessie, w, 563 Main St.
14. Aaron, Mrs. C. J.
15. Anderson, Henrietta, w.
15. App, Matilda, w, Second St.
15. Auguste, City Hospital.
15. Anthony, Laura, 317 Union St.
15. Armstrong, Luna, w, Union St.
15. Adams, Mr., w, Vance St.
16. Allen, D. A., w, Madison St.
16. Adams, R. R., w, Hernando St.
16. Allensworth (child).
16. Ayers, Thomas, w, 431 Shelby St.
16. Allen, Fred., w, City Hospital.
16. Arnold, Lee, w, 563 Main St.
16. Arnold, Willie, w, 563 Main St.
16. Arnold, Maud, w, 563 Main St.
16. Arnold, Liddie, w, 563 Main St.
16. Atkins, Jerry, w.
16. Arnold, Bessie. w, 563 Main St,
17. Anderson, Callie, c, cor. Keel & Front Sts.
17. Achmann, Emma, w, cor. Fourth & Greenlaw Sts.
17. Armstrong, Sarah, w, Fort Pickering.
18. Ames, Mrs. Daniel, w, Walker Ave.
18. Aaron, C. J.
18. Archie, c, 113 Pontotoc St.
19. Ames, Miss Mollie, w, Walker Ave.
19. Acklin, Mrs., w, Rayburn Ave.
20. Amonett, J. I , w, Adams St.
20. Abberdie, Maggie, w.
20. Adams, Franklin, w, Market St. Infirm'ry.
20. Armstrong, Alfred, c, 379 Beale St.
21. Armstrong, Dr. W. J., w, Alabama St.
21. Allen, Laura, w, Church Home.
21. Arft, Louis, w. cor. Main & Carolina Sts.
21. Adams, Geo. H., c, Adams St.
22. Allen, J. H.
22. Anderson, Virgil, c, Lane Ave.
23. Anderson, Daniel, c, Rayburn Ave.
23. Anderson, Oscar, w, 102 Linden St.
23. Armstrong, W., w, City Hospital.
25. Anderson, William.
26. Amus, Mrs. A. A., w, Jackson St.
26. Allingham, J. S., w, Market St. Infirmary.
26. Anderson, Charles.
26. Atkinson, Martha, c, Union St.
29. Arnold, Mollie, w, Main St.
Oct. 1. Atkinson, H. J., w, Leath Orphan Asylum.
1. Allen, Henry, c, Beale St.
1. Anderson, Martin, w, County Jail.
3. Ashe, Wm., w, near Church Home.
5 Adams, Mrs. Lu.y, w, Hernando Road.
6. Allen, L M , w, Trigg Ave.
8. Anderson, J. W. (sheriff), w, Wright Ave.
10. Atkinson, Wm., w, Leath Orphan Asylum.

*Under this head there will be found authenticated lists of all who died of yellow fever during the epidemic of 1878.
† w. stands for white and c. for colored.

A HISTORY OF THE YELLOW FEVER.

Oct. 12. Adams, Annie, w, McLean Ave.
13. Armstrong, Bertha, c, cor. Main & Georgia Sts.
14. Avery, Major, w, Cane Creek, Shelby Co.
14. Allen, W. H., w, Boulevard, Shelby Co.
15. Allen, Ellen, w, Poplar St.
17. Allen, Mr., w, Poplar St.
18. Arata, Mrs. Laura, w, Lee Ave.
21. Adams, Geo., w, country.
24. Alston, F. I. F., c, Fort Pickering.
25. Allen, Mrs., w, Poplar St.
26. Austin, Ran., w, Boulevard.
26. Adams, Ben., w, Clay St.
Nov. 5. Anderson, Hannah.
8. Adams, Aaron, c, Exchange St.
18. Arzeno, Mrs. Eliza, w, Mulberry St.
19. Arzeno, Alexander, w, Mulberry St.
26. Arzeno, Nellie, w, Mulberry St.
Aug. 13. Bionda, Kate, w, Front St *
15. Bergman, Geo., w, Poplar St.
17. Blum, M.
17. Bailey, 242 Monroe St.
17. Bergshicker, J., w, Main St.
18. Bernhardt, Mrs., w, 158 Poplar St.
19. Banksmith, Minor, w, 3 Howard's Row.
19. Burke, Thomas, w.
19. Burks, Homan, cor. Beale St. & Charleston R. R.
19. Brown, Ada, w, 158 Washington St.
20. Bloomfield, Morris, w, cor. Poplar & High Sts.
20. Bullow, Julia N.
20. Bullock, Ellen, Watson Pl., Shelby Co.
22. Ballou, Johnnie, Woods Ave.
22. Baxter, Mollie, w, Madison St.
22. Berger, Doc., c, 11 Alabama St.
22. Burton, Philip, c.
23. Breman, John, w, 132½ Main St.
23. Byrne, J. W., w, Georgia St.
23. Burges, Maggie, w, Alabama St.
24. Brown, Dixie J., w, Fifth St., Fort Pickering.
24. Bannon, John, w, 132 Main St.
25. Berry, Mrs. S. E., w, City Hospital.
26. Beale, August, w, 186 Poplar St.
26. Barton, Ada, w, Raleigh Road.
26. Bell, Mary Bettie, w, 38 Johnson Ave.
27. Bell, Mrs. Annie, w, Adams St.
27. Brew, Mike, w, Overton St.
27. Bitterman, Mrs., w, 123 Exchange St.
27. Bergman, Miss Mary, w, 29 Beale St.
27. Bronson, James, Orleans St.
28. Bitterman, Mrs. H., w, 123 Exchange St.
28. Barnett, C. M.
28. Burchert, J., w, Main St.
28. Borg, James J., w, High St.
28. Bell, Maria, Adams St.
28. Burchett, Mrs., w, Manassas St.
29. Badinella, Antoine, w, 21 Goslee St.
29. Bitterman, Isaac, w, 123 Exchange St.
29. Bailey, Mary, w, Third St.
29. Brennan, Mrs. Katie, w, Auction St.
29. Bokel, Rev. John A., Jr., w, St. Peter's.
29. Barbee, Mollie, w, 80 Main St.
29. Baker, Charles, w, Vance St.
29. Banks, David, City Hospital.
29. Bowles, Maggie, c, Humphrey St.
29. Bantley, George, County Poor House.
29. Baker, William, 133 South St.
30. Borg, Katie, w.
30. Barker, J. B., w, 69 Jefferson St.
30. Bostwick, J. L., w, Brinkley Ave.
30. Bedford, George J., w, Carroll Ave.
30. Berry, James, City Hospital.
30. Brown, Tom, City Hospital.
30. Bohen, William, 135 South St.
30. Bradley, P. O., w, cor. Auction St. and Raleigh Road.
30. Brady, Mrs. Martha, w, cor. Auction and Seventh Sts.
31. Burks, Bill, c, alley, bet. Winchester & Third Sts
31. Brautner, John, w, 28 Third St.
Sept. 1. Bassea, Peter, Gayoso House.
1. Boyce, Josephine.
1. Birding, Goodman, c, Commerce St.
2. Buehl, John, w, Bass Ave.

Sept. 2. Brinkley, Mary, c, 102 Front St.
2. Burns Oscar.
2. Bassey, Mollie, 3 North Jackson St.
2. Butler, W. T., w, City Hospital.
2. Brennan, John, City Hospital.
2. Bernard, E. H, w, 22 Avery St.
2. Bornadin, Sister, w, La Salette Academy.
2. Bisman, Henry, Poplar St. Boulevard.
2. Barnes, Wm. C., w. Fifth St.
3. Barron, Ellen, w, Winchester St.
3. Barnes, Sarah, w, Monroe St.
3. Bock, Isadore, w, City Hospital.
3. Brown, Wash, 64 Johnson Ave.
3. Bruns, Robert, w, 14 Adams St.
4. Brown, G. W., 64 Johnson Ave.
4. Borner, Carrie, w, 161 Pontotoc St.
4. Burnes, Thomas, w, Main St.
4. Bruns, Mrs. Rebecca, w, Adams St.
4. Barton, Joseph, c, 166 Moseby St.
4. Barron, Maggie, Winchester St.
4. Broker, Mrs., 39 Jones Ave.
4. Bailey, Robert, w, 35 Third St.
4. Bailey, 61 Concord St.
4. Bowles, Jennie, c, 40 Causey St.
4 Brown, Lucy, c, City Hospital.
4. Barber, I., w. Market St. Infirmary.
4. Bruns, Mrs. Rebecca, w, 14 Adams St.
5. Beardon, Wm., City Hospital.
5. Bruns, Mike, w, City Hospital.
5. Bund, Planter, Mill St.
5. Beauford, Miss, c, De Soto St.
5. Boyd, Jack, City Hospital.
5. Bedin, Addie, cor. Beale & Hernando Sts.
5. Byrd, Mike, w, Market St. Infirmary.
5. Brown, E. A., c, 112 Jefferson St.
5. Biggers, W. L., w, City Hospital.
5. Beachmont, Pierre, w, Madison St.
5. Borner, John, w, Pontotoc St.
5. Bronson, Charles, c. Madison St.
5. Barnes, Corinne.
5. Bowman, B. F., Ft. Pickering.
5. Briggs, W. L., City Hospital.
5. Baum, Elenora, w, Poplar St.
6. Burke, Thomas, w, 61 Exchange St., extended.
6. Brignidello, Angelo, w, Navy Yard.
6. Bennett, Charles, w, Robeson St.
6. Burns. J. A., c, Short Third St.
6. Bender, Fred., w, 77 Jackson St.
6. Black, Katie. 15 St. Martin St.
6. Burke, Mr. Wm., w, 61 Exchange St., extended.
6. Burke, Margaret, w, 61 Exchange St., extended.
6. Beardon, William. City Hospital.
6. Boyd, Jack, City Hospital.
6. Burke, Mike, w, Causey St.
6. Brady, Thos., w, Poplar St.
7. Bowen, Nannie, Horn Lake Road.
7. Burns, Melinda, Short Third St.
7. Bowden, Harvey, w, flat-boat (Wolf River).
7. Brocher, Ernest, w, Market St. Infirmary.
7. Brame, J. R., City Hospital.
7. Bell, Mr.. 17 Hernando St.
7. Beavers, M. J., w, Moseby Ave.
7. Burns, Julin, Short Third St.
8. Brown, Emma, w.
8. Bear, Angus, 129 Dunlap St.
8. Boyd, Joe, w, 1 Beale St.
8. Bell, Mrs. M. E., w, 178½ Front St.
8. Bows, Caroline, 99 Third St.
8. Balomeney, Mike, w, cor. Orleans and Lauderdale Sts.
8. Balfour, John, w, City Hospital.
8. Byman, William, c, 259 Union St.
8. Bay, Mitchell, Front St.
8. Brooks, Mrs. Maria L., w.
8. Biggs, Mrs. E. C., cor. Beale & Second Sts.
9. Biauz. Clarence, w, Linden St.
9. Boss, Peter G., w, Beale St.
9. Boselman, E., w, Adams St.
9. Blackburne, Rob't, c, 4 Winchester St.
9. Balger, James, w, cor. Market & Main Sts.
9. Brown, Andrew, c, 144 De Soto St.
9. Bradford, Mrs., w. 703 Main St.
9. Boyd, Gus. B., w.

* This was the first case reported to or by the Board of Health.

A HISTORY OF THE YELLOW FEVER. 211

Sept. 9. Barnes, Caroline, c, Third St.
9. Bracie, James, w.
9. Burrows, Dr., w, 133 Main St.
10. Burke, Mrs. L. L.
10. Batty, Austin, Third St.
10. Bird, John, w. Market St. Infirmary.
10. Boyd, M., 231 Vance St.
10. Bradford, R. B., w, 703 Main St.
10. Bosji, Peter, w, 22 Bass Ave.
10. Bryson, Thos., w, 170 Main St.
10. Boylan, Mary, Walker Ave.
10. Boyd, Fred., c, 191 Elliott St.
10. Blair, Hattie. c, rear 14 Main St.
10. Brawner, J. H., w, Second St.
10. Burnes, Adolph.
10. Bostwick, Willie.
10. Brandon. 250 Second St.
10. Bolton, Thos. C., w, Camp Burke.
11. Burk, Emma, 199 Alabama St.
11. Brit, Mary, c, Hupert Ave.
11. Bennett, Mrs. D. Gray, w, cor. Second & Mill Sts.
11. Burk, Matilda, Bradford St.
11. Bradford, Blanche, 703 Main St.
11. Bevins, Fannie M., Moseby St.
11. Burk, Jeff., w.
11 Boja, Daisy, c, Monroe St.
11. Bushey, H. L., w, Market St. Infirmary.
12. Boss, L., c, 44 Causey St.
12. Broadnax, Bishop, cor. Auction and Fourth Sts.
12. Bush, Wm., c. 344 Second St.
12. Baccigaluppo, Joseph, w, Beale St.
12. Bradford, Geo., w, 703 Main St.
12. Brawner, Rob't, w, Second St.
12. Brown, Mrs. J., w, Dunlap St.
12. Banning, C. E.
12. Barber, Matilda, c, Broadway St.
12. Brown, Phil.
12. Best, Thos., w, Olympic Park.
12. Bader, Wm., c, City Hospital.
12. Burkins, Arthur, c, Third St.
13. Burk, Jackson.
13. Barnes, A., w, Monroe St.
13. Burnes, Pat.
13. Brown, Margaret D. L., w, Chelsea.
13. Bosji, Maggie, w, 22 Bass Ave.
13. Burns, Davy, c, Short Third St.
13. Bailey (child), c, 76 North Jackson St.
13. Baker. Wm., City Hosp'tal.
13. Bell, Jacob, Randolph Road.
13. Buckner, Alice.
13. Buckner, Hannah.
14. Benning, Francis, cor. Tennessee and Vance Sts.
14. Burr, Henry, c, 175 Madison St.
14. Boystic, Isaac, w, Market St. Infirmary.
14. Burtinner, Chas.,w, Market St. Infirmary.
14. Brown, Henry, w, Market St. Infirmary.
14. Brithney, H. S., w, Market St. Infirmary.
14. Black, Chas., City Hospital.
14. Barker, Mrs. L., w, Hernando Road.
14. Burton, Silas, c, cor. Main & Linden Sts.
14. Boyle, A. W..w, 22 Bass Ave.
14. Brinkley, Maria.
14. Badenella, Celesta, w, 182 Beale St.
14. Bailey. Charles.
14. Belte, Jacob.
14 Burgner, Fred., w. 39 Madison St.
14. Buckel, H. W., w. 39 Madison St.
14. Ballinger, C., w. Walnut St.
14. Bailey, Valentine.
14. Bostwick. J. M.
14. Brown, Mrs. P. P., w, 69½ Beale St.
14. Beck, G. H., w.
14. Bowen, W. G., w.
14. Brown, Bob, c, Ruth St.
15. Becker, G. H., Jr., w.
15. Brooks, Wm., w. factory lot, Chelsea.
15. Butler, Ed., w, Gholson St.
15. Brown, Sam., w, City Hospital.
15. Berrgin, Annie, w, 410 Beale St.
15. Burnes, Albert, w, Monroe St.
15. Butler, Ed.
15. Blew, R W., w, cor. Wellington & Vance Sts.
15. Blackmore, L. W., w.
15. Belford, Hannah, w.
15. Burgess, Annie, w, 410 Beale St.

Sept. 16. Briggs, H. H., w, Kerr Ave.
16. Bullock, Mrs. C.
16. Barlow, J. W.
16. Bond, Dr. T. W., w, Court St. Infirmary.
16. Ballena, Henry, Ft. Pickering.
16. Bell, Cow Island Road, Shelby County.
16. Bond, Henry, w, Randolph Road.
16. Barnes, Charles, w.
16. Ballard (child of Jim).
16. Bacher, w, La Salette Academy.
16. Burke, Andrew, w, City Hospital.
16. Bolen Andrew, w, foot of Jackson St.
16. Buckner, Wm., w, factory lot, Second St.
16. Brennen, Ellis, 206 Elliott St.
16. Bergen, Frank, w, 410 Beale St.
16. Blew, Robert, w. cor. Wellington and Vance Sts.
16. Blew, Mrs. R. W., w, cor. Wellington and Vance Sts.
16. Blew, Willie, w, cor. Wellington and Vance Sts.
16. Blew, Zilla, w, cor.Wellington and Vance Sts.
16. Bernandine, Sister, w.
16. Brown, Ellis, w.
17. Brautz, Henry, w, City Hospital.
17. Barnes, A., w, City Hospital.
17. Brown, Katie, c, near brick church (Chelsea).
17. Berkin, Caroline, c, Hernando and Beale Sts.
17. Brown, Hattie,c,cor.Beale & Divorce Ave.
17. Bliss, Mrs. Mary K., 151 Broadway.
17. Brown, Lewis, w, Wellington St.
17. Baker, Martha.
17. Burnes, Lewis, w, Henry Ave.
17. Bridgeford, Nancy, w, cor. Echols and Vance Sts.
17. Baccigaluppo, Vincent.
17. Banksmith, Dr. R. H., w, Court St.
17. Barton, J. W., w. Front St.
18. Brooks, Mrs. R. E., w, Rayburn Ave.
18. Barsman, Sallie.
18. Bankson, Dr. J. S.,w. Court St. Infirmary.
18. Brooks,Epp.,cor.Dubois Ave. & Middle St.
18. Barlew, Anna, City Hospital.
18. Breles, Robert, c, 13 Mulberry St.
18. Buddinella, G. A., 162 Beale St.
18. Blew, James,cor.Wellington & Vance Sts.
18. Burke, Thomas, w, Charleston Railroad.
18. Badiknelli, David, w, 12 Goslee St.
18. Brown, Fannie.
18. Ballie, Mrs. Frederika, w, Adams St.
18. Brown, Henry, c, Causey St.
18. Brown, Daniel, c, Causey St.
18 Brown, E., c, Central Point.
19. Brown, Hilliard, w, Carolina St.
19. Banks, Matilda, South St.
19. Brown, Col. A. S., w, Dunlap St.
19. Brooks, Mat., c, Linden St. Infirmary.
19. Brooks, Susan, c, cor. Mulberry and Hulingst.
19. Brown, Henry, c, Carolina St.
19. Breckenridge, W., w, cor. Hernando and Elliott Sts.
19. Bant, Ti'da, c, South St.
19. Barker, Hattie, w, 260 Second St.
19. Belford (child of Maggie), c. Court St.
20. Bush, John, c, cor. Poplar & Waldron Sts.
20. Beavers, Nora, w, Moseby Ave.
20. Byrd, William, c, City Hospital.
20. Barnes, Thomas, w, City Hospital.
20. Bowht, Rescord, Market St. Infirmary.
20. Black, R. E., w, Poplar St.
20. Brown, John, 73 De Soto St.
20. Bernard, Henry, w, Beale St.
20. Barnes, son of R.W., w, New Raleigh R'd.
20. Bohne, Rishora, w, cor. Houston and Tennessee Sts.
20. Brown, Mrs. Annie, c, Gayoso St.
21. Brown, Lucien, w.
21. Badger, Mrs. Caroline, w.
21. Beattie. John, w, Union Ave.
21. Bacon, Thomas, w, Union Ave.
22. Burnes, A. W., w, South St.
22. Bacigaluppo,Mrs.Vincent,w,Union Ave.
22. Blinso. J. H., w. Market St. Infirmary.
22. Bass, T. C., w, Market St. Infirmary.

A HISTORY OF THE YELLOW FEVER.

Sept. 22. Blanche,c,Brinkley's Woods,Raleigh R'd.
22. Borden, Annie Lou., w.
23. Brooks, Charles C., w.
23. Burrell, c, 144 Vance St.
24. Boisseau, J. C.
24. Booth, Mrs. Sarah.
24. Bernard, Henry, Jr., w, Beale St.
24. Baccigaluppo, Mary A., w, Union Ave.
24. Burke, A. A., w, Jackson St.
24. Burcham, Dr. R., w, Main St.
24. Brown, Lewis, c, 59 Elliott St.
24. Bernard, H. H., w, 187 Beale St.
24. Boisseau, D. E., w, Shelby St.
24. Borden, Luther, w.
25. Beard, J. H., Cleveland, Ohio.
25. Bans, Lettie, 234 South St.
25. Brown, Mary, Randolph Road.
25. Britton, Robert, Jr., w, Waldron Ave.
25. Britton, Robert, Sr., w, Waldron Ave.
25. Borden, Willie Webb, w.
26. Bowers, Nancy, w, Beale St.
26. Briggs, James T.
26. Barringer (child of I).
26. Bluhm, Julius.
26. Ballinger, Mrs. C., w, Walker Ave.
26. Bowers, Nancy, 447 Beale St.
26. Bradford, Ellen, w, City Hospital.
26. Blackwell, Frank, w, Spring St.
26. Baker, Auguste,w, 5 mile toll-gate,Shelby County.
26. Blakemore, W. J., w, Elliott St.
27. Burton, John.
27. Biggs, G. L., Court St. Infirmary.
27. Benevito, A.
27. Brass, Frank,w, cor.Walker & Second Sts.
27. Brown, D.
27. Brass, Annie,w, cor.Walker & Second Sts.
27. Brass, Fannie,w, cor. Fourth and Georgia Sts.
28. Barton, G. W.
28. Bennett, M., w, cor. Broadway and Second Sts.
28. Boyd, Charles, w, City Hospital.
29. Burke, A. A., Jr, w, Jackson St.
29. Botts, Mrs. Teddie, w, Union Ave.
29. Birdie, c, Henry Ave.
29. Blew, Maggie, w, cor. Wellington and Vance Sts.
29. Bernstein, A.
29. Butler, George, w, cor. Gayoso and De-Soto Sts.
29. Burke, H. M., Court St. Infirmary.
30. Butler, William.
30. Bailey, Alice.
30. Balkin, John C.
30. Burke, Kate, w, cor. Fifth & Gholson Sts.
30. Bossicke, Mrs. Sallie.
30. Brady, Mary, w, Shelby County.
30. Bailey, Africa, c, Carolina St.
Oct. 1. Bair, Bullette.
1. Brass, George, w, Second St.
1. Brown, Mrs. Jacob, w.
1. Brown, Emma, c, Union Ave.
1. Brown, Aggie, c, 394 De Soto St.
1. Brown, Jacob, w, 107 Wellington St.
2. Brinkman, Minnie, w, Jackson St.
2. Byrne, John C., w, Market St. Infirmary.
2. Burns, Edward, w, Hernando Road.
3. Brown, Charles M., w, Valentine Ave.
3. Blake, N., c, 217 Hernando St.
3. Blautz, John, Market St. Infirmary.
4. Booth, James, w, Walker Ave.
4. Bullick, B., c, Pop'ar St.
4. Briggs, Robert, w, Second St.
4. Borden, Elma Wood, w.
5. Briggs, Mr., w, Carolina St.
6. Brown, E., c, cor. Fourth & Jackson Sts.
6. Burne, Annie, w, Georgia St.
6. Buchignani, T., w, Raleigh Road.
7. Brown, P. M., w, Madison St.
7. Burleson, Mrs. M. J., w, State Female College.
8. Boyle, son of Henry, w, Vance St.
8. Burke, Michael, w, Manassas St.
8. Barton, Geo., c, Fourth St.
8. Bartholomew,Dr.O.D.,w, Hernando Road.
9. Brock, Mrs. A., w, Poplar St.
9. Brown, Nettie, c, City Hospital.
9. Barker, Mrs. S. L., w, 105 Robinson St.

Oct. 9. Barnard, A., w.
10. Bennett, Mary, w, Vance St.
10. Britton, Mrs. Robert, w, Waldron Ave.
10. Brearton, James, w, Jones Ave.
10. Brearton, Katie, w, Jones Ave.
10. Billar, Jasper, w, Country.
11. Brooks, Byron, w, Chelsea.
11. Belcher, La Rose St.
11. Bacon, Liddie, w. Quinby St.
11. Brock, A., w, Poplar St.
11. Brochvogel, Wm., w, Fifth St.
12. Bandy, J. F., w, Horn Lake Road.
12. Barnett, Betsey, c, Carr Ave.
12. Blankenburg, Wm., w, Central Ave.
12. Bowen, Alexander, w, Mosoby St.
13. Brennan, Thomas, w, No. 1 Engine.
13. Brown, Millie, c, Broadway St.
14. Baker, Charles, c, Old Raleigh Road.
14. Buck, Mrs. Caroline, w, Poplar St.
14. Burke, Mary E., w, South Jackson St.
15. Brochvogel, Wm., w, Georgia St.
15. Body, Van, w, Union Ave.
15. Ball, Mary Lee, w, Fort Pickering.
15. Burke, Mrs. C., w, Manassas St.
16. Behuns, George, w, Breedlove Ave.
16. Brown, Jeff., c, Erbs' Pl., Hernando Road.
16. Brown, child of Francis, c, 115 Butler St.
16. Bethney. Jim, w, County Jail.
17. Boyd, Willie, c, State Female College.
18. Bailey, Mrs. Kate, w, Horn Lake Road.
19. Brown, A. W., c, Georgia St.
20. Brock, Arthur, w, City Hospital.
21. Brown, Henry, w, Central Ave.
21. Burns, Willie, w, Overton Point.
21. Bisman, Charles, w, Huppers Ave.
22. Brooks, C. B., w, cor. Keel & Fifth Sts.
23. Black, Henry, w. State Female College.
23. Ball, Willie, c, Front St.
24. Buckhalter, Julia, w, Chelsea.
24. Berry, Mrs. C. J., w, Boulevard.
24. Bodell, Mr., w, Elmwood.
25. Burke, B., w, City Hospital.
25. Barr, C. H., w, Hernando St.
25. Beehn, Kate L., w, Country.
26. Buhn, Katie Leonora.
26. Brock, Bessie E., w, St. Peter's Orphan Asylum.
28. Bender, L., w, Braden Station.
30. Belle, child of Annie, c, cor. Georgia & Shelby Sts.
30. Botto, John V., w, Vance St.
Nov. 2. Brizzolara, James, w, Beale St.
2. Brown, Irwin, c, Front St
3. Busch, Mary F., w, Moseby St.
3. Bofiza, Adolph, w, City Hospital.
3. Burk, Michael, w, Front St.
4. Breen, Maggie, w, Union Ave.
4. Bolton, Bennie, w, Main St.
9. Buchignani, Mrs. M., w, Beale St.
9. Bingham, Mary D., w, Dunlap St.
10. Bammel, Geo., w, Marley Ave.
14. Brunner. Alice, w, Leath Orphan Asylum.
17. Burnes, Jane, c.
Aug. 12. Clarke, son of G. B., 210 Front St.
13. Coleman, Gustave A., w.
13. Crohn, Hattie, w.
15. Cairns, J. G.
16. Cook, Mrs. C. H., w, Pontotoc St.
19. Caruthers, Cheney, c.
19. Cohn, Jacob, City Hospital.
20. Clarke, Mrs. Margaret, Poplar St.
20. Craig, Sam., c.
20. Cheek, Philip M., w.
21. Clayton, Joe, 167 Fourth St.
22. Craig, Sam., w, 102 Front St.
22. Cloyd, Thomas S., w.
22. Cannon, Mike, w, Front St.
22. Cole, Mrs. Rachel, w, 113 Market St.
22. Clemmons, H. S., w, 25 Alabama St.
23. Cunningham, M. J., w, Alabama St.
23. Conner, Ben., c, Looney Switch.
25. Conlin, John, w, City Hospital.
25. Child, 101 Second St.
25. Cook, Eddie, c, Stewart Ave.
25. Cunepo, Mrs. Mary.
25. Clarke, Henry, w, Charleston Ave.
25. Cole, Gertrude, w, 115 Market St.
25. Cleary, Lucy, 34 St. Martin St.
25. Cleary, Mrs.

A HISTORY OF THE YELLOW FEVER. 213

Aug. 27. Church, C. H., w, Robinson St.
28. Campbell, Willie.
28. Cummings, Maggie, w, Causey St.
28. Conlin, Maggie, w, City Hospital.
28. Carey, James, w, 36 Bradford St.
28. Cummings, Mrs. Mary, 39½ Causey St.
28. Campbell, William, c, 156 Beale St.
28. Cooper, Amelia, c, 124 Washington St.
28. Cole, Stella, w, 115 Market St.
28. Crane, Charles, w, Market Square.
28. Crisbon, Eliza, c, Linden St.
29. Crocker, Fritz, 35 Jones Ave.
29. Clarke, Eliza.
29. Cuney, James, w, Dunlap St.
29. Cobb, Eli, c, 77 Hill St.
29. Cole, R., w, 113 Market St.
29. Connelly, Tim., 137 Dunlap St.
29. Cook, Peyton, 130 Madison St.
29. Calhoun, N. A., 133 Exchange St.
29. Clemens, Henry.
29. Chandler, J. F., w, Monroe St.
31. Coyle, Mrs. Mary, w, Madison St.
31. Connelly, Jane, 137 Dunlap St.
31. Calhoun, Mrs.
31. Chambers, Sallie, c, 16½ Causey St.
Sept. 1. Congrela, Bowman, Poplar St.
1. Cook, Adam, c, 55 Marshal Ave.
1. Clarke, Annie, Beale St.
1. Chapman, Mrs. B. N., w, Poplar St.
1. Cicella, Paul, w, cor. Main & Washington Sts.
1. Curat, Celia.
1. Cain, J. E., w, Memphis & Charleston R. R.
1. Caulfeld, Roman, w, Poplar St.
1. Carr, J. E., City Hospital.
1. Comba, F., w, Camp Father Mathew.
2. Consadine, John, w, Valentine Ave.
2. Cleveland, P. W., w ,Poplar St.
2. Cairns, Julia R., w.
2. Chalmers, Verona.
2. Clarke, Anna.
2. Connelly, Kate, 137 Dunlap St.
2. Carr, Ann.
2. Cummings, J. J.
2. Cook, Ellen, c, 14 Adams St.
2. Collar, Miss, 172 Poplar St.
2. Conchela, T. J., City Hospital.
2. Conrad, 150 Madison St.
2. Cook, Ellen, 14 Adams St.
2. Cleaverton, W. T., 92 Poplar St.
2. Cane, F., w, City Hospital.
3. Cinnetta, Cerelia, w, 233 Washington St.
3. Cooler, Harriet, 55 Winchester St.
3. Crocker, Mrs. w, 43 Jones Ave.
3. Chinaman, cor. Main & Poplar Sts.
3. Cole, Harriet, Winchester St.
3. Cook, Michael, w, 4 High St.
3. Coleman, Cullen, 369 Pontotoc St.
3. Cenles, Dennis, Dunlap St.
3. Cicalla, Mrs. N., w, Shelby St.
3. Cairns, Mary D., w, 125 Alabama St.
3. Cainevern, Alice, w, Vance St.
3. Callahan, John, w, Second St.
3. Collins, Miss, w, Poplar St.
4. Carlisle, Elizabeth, w, 217 Alabama St.
4. Connelly, Dennis, w, 137 Dunlap St.
4. Clarke, Barney, w, City Hospital.
4. Crossette, C. C., w, City Hospital.
4. Corrigan, Mike, w, City Hospital.
4. Crogan, D., w, Second St.
4. Callahan, Sister Rose, w, La Salette Academy.
5. Causey, Laura, Alabama St.
5. Coyle, P. J , w, City Hospital.
5. Carleston, Chas., City Hospital.
5. Cook, David, Jackson St.
5. Cunesse, John.
5. Crook, G. W. L., w, Adams St.
6. Cummins, Alex., w, Market St.
6. Cronin, John, w, Georgia St.
6. Cummins, Capt. John, w, 178 Robinson St.
6. Conners, Mike, 61 Exchange St.
6. Crittenden, Mrs. J. A., Whitehaven, Shelby County.
6. Clogston, A., Second St., Ft. Pickering.
6. Causey, Laura, cor. Second and Alabama Sts.
6. Childress, John, c, 76 Vance St.
6. Crawford, Sallie, c, 208 Dunlap St.

Sept. 6. Comba, John, w, Camp Father Mathew.
7. Chalmers, Charity, c, 33 Avery St.
7. Clarke, Charley, c, Chelsea St.
7. Cruikshank, James, w.
7. Carter, Gracie.
7. Cronin, John, w, Georgia St.
7. Cummins, Alex., w, Market St.
8. Cathey, Bettie, c, 37½ Commerce St.
8. Connelly, Mary, w. Poplar St.
8. Cleary, Mike, cor.Third & Van Buren Sts.
8. Cleary (child of Mike).
8. Calloway, Elsie, c.
9. Cook, A. F. C., w, Orleans St.
9. Castillo, Mike C., w, Court St.
9. Constance, Sister, w.
9. Cleary, Conn, Ft. Pickering.
9. Cook, Mrs. W., w, 170 South St.
9. Camp, William, c, 186 Commerce St.
9. Cole, Alice, Hatchie River Bridge, Second St.
9. Coleman, S., w.
9. Crefiril, J., w.
9. Cernes, H., c.
10. Conners, Pat , w, Front St.
10. Crowin, Tom, w, 448 Poplar St.
10. Carrie, Mrs., 18 Avery St.
10. Crutchen, Rubina, c, 89 Gayoso St.
10. Countess, Beckie, c, cor. Mill & Main Sts.
10. Cobb, Henry.
10. Coleman, Benj.
10. Canepo, Jennie, w, 41 Causey St.
10. Cook, S. D., w, Shelby St.
10. Cole, Frederick, w, 69 Adams St.
10. Chandler, William, w, Main St.
10. Connelly, John J., w, Madison St.
11. Comstock, C. M.
11. Cleary, Mike.
11. Cunningham, Lavina, c, cor. Jackson & Main Sts.
11. Crosby, Mahala, c, 372 Union St.
11. Carlisle, 23 Rayburn Ave.
11. Cricks, Kitty, c, Poplar St.
11. Cassenella, Miss, cor. Seventh & Alabama Sts., Ft. Pickering.
11. Cox, William, Bass Ave.
11. Cruse, S. P., 242 Old Raleigh Road.
11. Carr, James, 375 Linden St.
11. Conner, James.
11. Cardoll, John, Taylor St.
11. Cook, Annie, Mansion House.
11. Conner, Mrs. C., w, Beale St.
11. Curry, Dan., c, City Hospital.
11. Croto, A.
12. Cobb, George, 249 Union St.
12. Crissie, 44 Allen Ave.
12. Carson, Peter, w, 9 Memphis & Charleston R. R.
12. Crowder, Miss, Navy Yard.
12. Carr, T. J., w, Market St. Infirmary.
12. Cahope, Ed.
12. Cutting, B. N., w, Main St.
12. Clements, T. F. O., w, Hernando St.
12. Crowder (child of Mrs.), w, Navy Yard.
12. Coleman, E., c, Union St.
12. Coleman, Cally, c, Pontotoc St.
12. Coe, L. H., w, Linden St.
13. Clary, Joe, w, Gayoso St.
13. Clary, Mike, w, factory lot, South Mill St.
13. Charles, c, Mill St.
13. Cummins, Yansey, c.
13. Crawford Stephen, c.
14. Cheek, G. A., w, 46½ North Court St.
14. Carmichael, Mrs., w, 260 Second St.
14. Cody, Alex., c, cor. Hernando & Vance Sts.
14. Cole, George, City Hospital.
14. Castillo, Belinda, near Elmwood.
14. Conntee, Ike, c, cor. Mill & Main Sts.
14. Cooper, Thos , c, 20 Orleans St.
14. Celite, Johoe, w, Randolph Road.
15. Cleary, M., w, Carolina St.
15. Cleaves, E. L., w.
15. Clarke, H., w.
15. Casterilli, Joseph, w, cor. Seventh and Alabama Sts.
15. Cutter, John, w, Peabody Hotel.
15. Corey, W. H., w, Market St. Infirmary.
15. Coates, Almon, w, Woolen Mills, Fort Pickering.

A HISTORY OF THE YELLOW FEVER.

Sept. 15. Carter, Jackson, w, 131 Beale St.
15. Colton, Pat., 17 Jackson St.
15. Callahan, Lizzie, cor. Second & Bickford Sts.
15. Crawford, Cynthia.
15. Conner, Lonny, w.
15. Conner, Maggie, w.
15. Colter, Mary, w.
16. Chalmette. George.
16. Campbell, Frank, w, Pigeon Roost Road.
16. Conners, Frank. w.
16. Callahan, Maggie, w, Hernando Road.
16. Conner, J. W.
16. Courts, Angie, w, 205 Tennessee St.
16. Clarke, Mrs. E. W., w, 289 Beale St.
16. Callahan, Mrs. M., w, Hernando Road.
16. Chabrust, George, w.
16. Chensey, John W., w.
16. Clancey, Maggie, w.
16. Clarke, Mrs. Mollie, w, 273 Main St.
17. Cunningham, Mr., w.
17. Clapham, George E.
17. Cox, A., c, Short Third St.
17. Catleman, B. D., w, City Hospital.
17. Chandler, James, c, Rayburn Ave.
17. Calhoun, Mrs., w, 466 Main St.
18. Collins, Thomas, Cynthia St.
18. Clarke, Walter.
18. Clarke, G. W., Market St.
18. Crouch, Mary.
18. Conrad, Mrs. J F., w.
18. Crisman, Randolph, w, Brewery.
18. Callahan, Frank, w, Hernando Road.
18. Cook, Richard, w, 170 South St.
18. Cain, Matthew.
18. Cuffey, D. E., w, City Hospital.
19. Coe, Mrs. M. J., w, McGee Station.
19. Capehut, Mr., w, Orleans St.
19. Castello, Mr., w, near Elmwood.
19. Cleaves, Charles, 358 Beale St.
19. Chapple, Simon, c.
19. Comba, Richard, w, Camp Father Mathew.
20. Clarke, S. R., 259 Beale St.
20. Calhoun, R. F., w, City Hospital.
20. Cole, Hayden, c, cor. Dunlap St. & Bass Ave.
20. Cox, Mrs. E. A.
20. Cook, John, w, Hernando Road.
20. Cleary, John D., w, De Soto St.
20. Cold, Waller, c, Stewart Ave.
21. Carson, John, w, Monroe St.
21. Connell, Eliza, w, cor. Walnut & Tate Sts.
21. Cole, Emily, c, Broadway St.
21. Crutchen, Stephen, c, Pontotoc St.
21. Cobb, Rhoda, c, 217 South St.
21. Conners, Frank, w, 78 Wellington St.
22. Champlain, George, w, Henry Ave.
22. Chinn, Walter, w, Pontotoc St.
22. Cordano, Antonio.
22. Cronlus, c, Linden St.
23. Cox, William, c, Shelby St.
23. Cox, Sarah, w, 160 Gayoso St.
23. Cook, Mrs. George, w, cor. Jackson & Third Sts.
23. Carroll, Sidney, w, cor. Coffee & Second Sts.
23. Cook, John, w, cor. Jackson & Third Sts.
23. Coleman, Jessie, c, cor. Second & Bigelow Sts.
23. Carter, Mary, c, Beale St.
23. Cornellia, Eliza, c, 232 Linden St.
23. Countee, D., c, Dean Ave.
24. Catron, R. R., w, Peabody Hotel.
24. Connell, Annie, w, Walnut St.
24. Cox, Mrs., w.
25. Collins, James, w, Trigg Ave.
25. Caskall, Ellen, w, Georgia St.
25. Conrad, Monroe, c, Poplar St.
25. Carroll, Mrs. Ellen, w, cor. Georgia & Seventh Sts.
25. Cartney, Lucinda, w, 149 Vance St.
25. Coleman, Adam, w, cor. Broadway & Fifth Sts.
25. Cox, Thornton, Hernando Road.
26. Cunningham, Richard.
26. Cass, Abe.
26. Corson, Edward E.
26. Cromwell, Mrs.

Sept. 26. Canapole, Antonio.
26. Connell, Pat , w, Court St.
26. Campbell, Dolly, w, Second St.
26. Cheves, Dr C. L., w, Peabody Hotel.
26. Carroll. Edward, w, Madison St.
27. Cartman, Henry, foot of Jackson St.
27. Cooper, George, c, 108 Fourth St., Chelsea.
27. Croupra, Norman, w, Market St. Infirm'ry.
27. Cowtwill, Henry, foot of Jackson St.
28. Castmill. Henry, c, foot of Jackson St.
28. Clay, Mrs. Ann, w, Market St. Infirmary.
28. Carteon, J. E., w, City Hospital.
28. Cleary, Mary. w, Fort Pickering.
28. Cavanaugh. Martin, w, Memphis & Little Rock R. R.
28. Cables, Elder. c.
28. Cleary, John D., w, 138 De Soto St.
29. Courts, Lucy, Tennessee St.
29. Clapham, Thomas.
30. Clarke, Willie W.
30. Coe, Walter, c, 25 Stewart Ave.
30. Coe, Mrs. Alice E., w, Linden St.
30. Czapsky, Louis, w, State Female College.
30. Cooley, Mr., Memphis & Little Rock R. R.
30. Clarke, R. B., w, Shelby St.
Oct. 1. Cooper, Katie B., w, Ross Ave.
1. Carr, Joseph, c, Third St.
1. Carter, Miss Dora, c, cor. Beale & Turley Sts.
1. Coleman, child of J. M., Raleigh Road.
1. Carr, Luella, w, Main St.
1. Culley, R., w, Market St. Infirmary.
2. Connell, Miss Emma, w, Walnut St.
2. Clarke, R., c, Wolf River Ferry.
2. Christonson, Peter, w, Randolph Road.
2. Collins, George, c, Purtle St.
3. Cotton, Austin, c, Causey St.
3. Calson, John, w, Gayoso House.
3. Chambers, Vernon, c, Lauderdale St.
4. Clece, Jackson St.
4. Cannon, Francis, w, Front St.
4. Cannon, Bridget, Front St.
4. Carline, Katie, w, Poplar St.
4. Curtis, Lucy, w, City Hospital.
5. Carline, Mrs. A., w, Poplar St.
5. Cornelius, George, c.
5. Carter, Henry, c, cor. Carolina & Fifth Sts.
5. Cannon, James E., w, Front St.
5. Caldwell, Alex., w, Chapin Ave.
5. Crabb, John G., w, Lauderdale St.
5. Cannon, James, w, Walker Ave.
6. Cline, Miss, w, Raleigh.
6. Cook, Katie, w, Country.
6. Caldwell, Tennie, c, cor. Rayburn & Walker Aves.
6. Cazaretta, Christine, w, cor. Seventh & Alabama Sts.
6. Clarke, Annie, w, near Oil Works.
6. Clayton, Belle, c, Shelby County.
6. Clara. Mrs., w. Kerr Ave.
6. Coe, J. L., w, Vance St.
6. Cicalla, Paul, Sr., w, Shelby St.
6. Couch, Mrs. H. H., w, Kerr Ave.
6. Clere, W. P., w, Raleigh.
7. Carver, Mrs., w, Cooper Ave.
7. Clarke, Francis.
7. Clere, W. P., Raleigh.
7. Capeheart W. N., w, Orleans.
7. Cannon, Ples., c., Overton Point.
7. Clarke, Jane, c, Wolf River Ferry.
8. Crowder, Nancy, w, Navy Yard.
8. Cazaretta. Peter, w, cor. Seventh & Alabama Sts.
8. Cook, George, w, Jones Ave.
10. Crowell, daughter of Henry H., w, Country.
10. Caldwell, Fannie, c, cor. Rayburn & Walker Aves.
10. Carey, Albert, w, Pontotoc St.
10. Cohn, Harris, w, Trigg Ave.
11. Caroline, Frank, w, Poplar St.
11. Clark, Wm. Gwyn, w, Raleigh.
12. Cruse, John, w, Country.
12. Carr, Richmond, c, 20 Orleans St.
12. Cook, M. A., w, Georgia St.
12. Canapo, child of John, w. 41 Causey St.
12. Cook, A., w, Lauderdale St.
13. Connell, Thomas, w, Walnut St.
13. Chandler, Willie, c, Calvary Cemetery.

A HISTORY OF THE YELLOW FEVER. 215

Oct. 13. Cleburne, Adeline, c, cor. Third & Alabama Sts.
14. Carter, James, County Poor House.
14. Cappedonico, L., w, Beale St.
15. Carraway, Mrs., w, Randolph Road.
15. Carraway, Wm., w, Randolph Road.
16. Canali, P. D., w, Kerr Ave.
16. Cockrell, Richard, w, Boulevard.
16. Cockrell, B. F., w, Boulevard.
16. Clockton, child of Josephine, c, cor. Walnut & Spring Sts.
16. Cain, Mary, w, Second St.
16. Cohn, infant of Mr., w, Trigg Ave.
18. Clarke, Eddie, w, Calvary Cemetery.
18. Christonson, N. P., w, Randolph Road.
18. Carpenter, Chas., c., Linden St.
19. Clere, Mrs. W. P., w, Raleigh.
19. Clarke. Smith, c.
19. Cohn, Mrs H., w, Trigg Ave.
20. Clarke, child of Lucy, c, cor. St. Martin & Elliott Sts.
20. Campbell, James, w, City Hospital.
21. Crumpeci, Miss E., w, Horn Lake Road.
21. Clarke, Thaddeus, w, Country.
24. Carver, Thomas, w, Cooper Ave.
24. Coleman, Edward, w, Raleigh.
24. Cross, Jacob, w.
25. Cargill, John F., w, Washington St.
28. Condon, Mary, w. Gayoso St.
29. Cullen, Thomas, w, Jackson St.
Nov. 1. Growder, George, w, U. S. Survey Boat.
3. Cobb, Mrs. E. D., w, Madison St.
3. Costillo, Michael, w, Dunlap St.
4. Cockrell, Mrs. J., w. Boulevard.
4. Connelly, Pete., w, Union Ave.
10. Cameron. Mrs. J., w, Posten Ave.
13. Cocke, Mrs. S., w, Union St.
13. Creighton, Samuel Cook, w.
13. Cooper, W. L., w, Linden St.
16. Chase, Ruth W., w, Third St.
17. Costen, Mrs.
28. Campbell. Mary, c, Pigeon Roost Road.
28. Cohupe, Leon, w, Kerr Ave.
Aug. 14. Davenport, Darby.
14. Decker, Theodore, w, Alabama St.
16. Davis, Josephine.
17. Decker, Henry. 34 Alabama St.
18. Decker, Mrs., 34 Alabama St.
19. Drury. Mattie, w, Poplar St. Boulevard.
20. Dessauer, Fannie, w.
20. Donnelly, George L., w.
21. Duffey, James V., w, Alabama St.
21. Davis, child of Mrs. Mary, 144 Poplar St.
22. Davis, Sam., w, 131 Poplar St.
22. Dolan, Andy, w, 199 Main St.
24. Devey, Frank, C ty Hospital.
24. Davis, Florence, w, 144 Poplar St.
25. Dugan, Daniel, w, Linden St.
25. Donnovan, Mrs. John, w, Washington St.
26. Donnovan, John, Jr., w, Washington St.
26. Donnelly, Thomas H., w, Hospital.
27. Duffey, Dan., w, 12 Alabama St.
28. Dalston, Charles, w, City Hospital.
28. Dalston, Frank, w. City Hospital.
28. Dewey, Ellen, w, 63 Commerce St.
28. Douglass,Rosa,c,cor.Jackson & Front Sts.
28. Dolan, Thos. Francis.
28. Driser, Reinhardt.
29. Donnelly, Mina, w, 18 St. Martin St.
29. Dunlap, Amelia, c.
29. Davis, George, cor. Court and Front Sts.
29. Dow, Robert, 214 Washington St.
30. Davis, George.
30. Dennison, W. L., w, Caswell Ave.
30. Dalton, Elizabeth, w, Madison St.
31. Dowell, Mrs. M. C., 144 Poplar St.
31. Davey, T. J., w, Fifth St.
31. Dreyfus, Samuel.
Sept. 1. Davis (infant of Griffin),c, cor. Tennessee and Vance Sts.
2. Demmons, Thomas, w, Mill St.
2. Davis (child of Lou.), c.
2. Dawson, John.
2. Davis, Wm., c, Jefferson St.
3. Davis, E. O., 350 Beale St.
3. Daley, Mary, w, cor. Payton Ave. and Sycamore St.
3. Dunlap, Howard, 14 Front St.
4. Darby, Mrs. Jenny, w, 177 Second St.

Sept. 4. Dalton, Miss M., w, Jackson St.
4. Donohue, Ellen, w, Mulberry St.
4. Dau, Chas., w, Main St.
4. Daley,P.,w,cor. Peyton Ave. & Dunlap St.
4. Dunlap, H., 14 Front St.
4. Dorsey, Fannie, w, 36 Market St.
4. Davis, John, w, City Hospital.
4. Davis, Dolly, c.
4. Dalton, Mrs. Maggie, Jackson St.
5. Dowell, Frank T., w, Front St.
5. Dugan, Louisa, City Hospital.
5. Dawson, Chas., w, 36 Market St.
5. Dawson, Annie, w, 36 Market St.
5. Dunn, Ed., 102½ Linden St.
5. Dalton, H. G., w, Third St.
5. Donnelly, Dennis, w, 137 Dunlap St.
6. Dolara, Sister, w, La Salette Academy.
6. Dickerson, Dr. P. M., w, Peyton Ave.
6. Duty, Mary, c, 378 Second St.
6. Davis, Mary L., cor. Fifth & Safferans Sts.
6. Dugan, O. J., 449 Hernando St.
6. Davy,Mary L.,w,cor.Fifth & Safferans Sts.
7. Douglass, John, c, Vance St.
7. Dolan, Mike, w, cor. Fourth and Washington Sts.
7. Dalton, York, c, Exchange St.
8. Douglass, Mollie.
8. Davis, C. C., w, Market St. Infirmary.
8. Delaney, Wm., w.
8. Delaney, Mrs., w.
9. Duvall, Joseph.
9. Dewar, Norman, w, Main St.
9. Duncan, C. E., w.
9. Dullman, John, w, Gayoso House.
9. Davis, H., w, 201½ Linden St.
9. Dell, Catherine B., w.
10. Davis, Carrie, w, Market St. Infirmary.
10. Donehiff, F. A., w, Market St. Infirmary.
10. Downs, Mrs., w, Old Raleigh Road.
10. Dukes, Robert, c, Seventh St., Chelsea.
11. Dunaki, Lewis.
11. Devoto, D., w, 7 Causey St.
11. Devoto, A., w, 7 Causey St.
11. Daisey, c, rear of 133 Main St.
11. Davis, Charity, c, Short Third St.
11. Donaldson (child of Sarah), Stewart Ave.
11. Dwyer, Martin, cor. Alabama & Front Sts.
11. Dohertey, Mary C., cor. De Soto and Gayoso Sts,
11. Duncan, Robt., Pigeon Roost Road.
11. Dea, Michael, w, South St.
12. Daniels, Elvira, c, Broadway St.
12. Dunlap, Sam.
12. Davis, Byron, 240 Monroe St.
12. Dolan, Mike, w, river bank.
12. Davis, B., 42 Jackson St.
12. Downs, Mrs., w, Raleigh Road.
13. Donahue, Maggie, Beale St.
13. Davis, Minnie, c, Carolina St.
13. Dooley, Mike, w, City Hospital.
14. Dawson, Mrs. Amelia, w, 74 Greenlaw St.
14. Dawson, J. G.
14. Davis, Robert, c, 249 Union St.
14. Donaldson, Caroline, w, 10 Beale St.
14. Dillard, Mike, 40 Mulberry St.
14. Dillard,Jim,c,61 Exchange St., extended
14. Downs, James, w, Shelby County.
14. Davis, Mary, w, 391 Main St.
14. Davis, John, c, 99 Wellington St.
14. Duncan, Annie B., w, Hernando St.
15. Dreyfus, M., w, Raleigh Road.
15. Dodson, James, c, cor. Carolina and Eighth Sts.
15. Davis, James, c, 440 Shelby St.
15. Dunneway, Harriet, c, cor. Talbot and St. Martin Sts.
16. Dickerson, Dennis, c, 375 Beale St.
16. Davis, Ella B., w.
16. Dorgs, Fred.,w,cor.Clay & Tennessee Sts.
16. Derges, May.
16. Dolan, Ellen.
16. Doereicht, A., w, Ruth St.
16. Dickerson, J. W.
17. Dawson, John, w.
17. Dyer, Margaret B., w, Wellington St.
17. Dickens (child).
17. Dick, Albert, Court St. Infirmary.
17. Devoto, Davy, w, 24 Causey St.
18. Dickerson, Isaac.

216 A HISTORY OF THE YELLOW FEVER.

Sept. 18. Dodson (Infant of Lou.), c, Gayoso House.
18. Dreyfus, Lee.
18. Dodson, Lou., c, Gayoso House.
19. Dukes, W. C., 129 Causey St.
20. Dickerson, W. P., w, Peyton Ave.
20. Dargis, Joe, w, cor. Tennessee & Clay Sts.
20. Dorms, Sim., c, Poplar St.
20. Demans, F., c, Second St.
21. Davis. W. J., w.
21. Dickerson, H. N., w, Rayburn Ave.
22. Dargis.
23. Day, Owen, w, Vance St.
23. Doulan, Peter, 231 Georgia St.
23. Dyke, Mrs., cor. Jackson and Third Sts., Ft Pickering.
24. Dawson, Dr.
24. Donnelly, Mrs. T. H.
24. Dawson, Annie, c, Linden St. Infirmary.
24. Dashiell, Mrs. Tate E., w, Pigeon Roost R'd.
25. Duffey, P. J., w, McLemore Ave.
25. Davis, Josephine, w, Henry Ave.
26. Dashiell, Frank P., w, Pigeon Roost Road.
26. Dawson, Mr., w, Elmwood.
26. Duncan, Mrs. A. L., 449 Hernando St.
26. Dunn, Marian.
26. Dickson, Mrs., 14 Front St.
27. Doherty, C., c, City Hospital.
27. Dance (child of Belle), c, cor. Webster & De Soto Sts.
27. Donahue, John, w, Union St.
27. Decker, Mary, w, Shelby St.
27. Dupuy, P., w, Horn Lake Road.
28. Driver, Mrs. V., c, Beale St.
29. Dawson (child of P.), c, cor. Dunlap and Union Sts.
29. Dempsey, Charles, Market St. Infirmary.
29. Dink, Reverdy, w, Market St. Iufirmary.
29. Davis, Mrs. Mary F., Valentine Ave.
29. Dolan, Maggie, w, Fifth St.
29. Dreyfus, Samuel.
Oct. 1. Davis, E. A., w, Walnut Ave.
1. Doulan, John, cor. Georgia & Wright Ave.
1. Devlin, B. F., Shelby County.
1. Doravoid, Charley, w, cor. Third and Jackson Sts.
2. Dawson, Mary, w, Raleigh Road.
2. Damstadter, Mrs. J., w, Randolph Road.
3. Davis, Thad., c, Jackson St.
5. Dent, Giles, w, Memphis and Charleston Railroad.
5. Dink, George, c, factory lot, Chelsea.
5. Dyches, Mrs. Bettie, w, McLemore Ave.
6. Davis, Emma B , w, Suzette St.
7. Dunn, W. S , w, Broadway St.
7. Doyle, James, w, Marley Ave.
7. Daniel, George, c, Madison St.
8. Damstadter, J., w. Randolph Road.
8. Dotson, Mary, c, 217 South St.
8. Duffey, Simon B., w, Hernando Road.
9. Davis, Charles J., w, Suzette St.
9. De Donoto, Ruf., w, county jail.
9. Dunn, Anderson, w, Gill's Station.
10. Duffey, Alice, w, Alabama St.
10. Dodd, A. F., w, Poplar St.
10. Davis, George, c, Lauderdale St.
10. Donnelly, Thomas, w, Leath Orphan Asylum.
11. Dupree, Annie, c, 220 South St.
11. Donerty, Thomas L., w. Walker Ave.
11. Debruhl, Mrs. E., w, Jackson St.
11. Dreyfus, Ben., w, Raleigh Road.
12. Daucey, Thomas, C., c, 13 Stewart Ave.
12. Daucey, Thomas, c, 13 Stewart Ave.
13. Dominic, Mr., w. Union St.
14. Durke, Oscar, w, Memphis and Charleston Railroad.
15. Dzmiski, Charles, w. Shelby St.
15. Delaney, W. J., w, Boulevard.
15. Dalton, Ambrose G., w, Clay St.
16. Davis, Jeff., Jr., w, Buntyn's Station.
17. Deano, George, w, City Hospital.
18. Dwyer, Lizzie, w, Looney St.
18. Dunn, Mrs. Mary, w, Georgia St.
18. Diggins, George, c, Clay St.
18. Douglass, Mattie, c. Elliott St.
20. Dume, Paul, w, State Female College.
20. Duke, Eddie, w.
20. Dolan, James, w, Wolf River.
22. Downey, Joseph, w, Union St.

Oct. 22. Dowdy, F. H., w, Raleigh Road.
24. Davis, S. B.
25. Dies, Mrs. Lizzie, w, Central Ave.
28. Dries, Elizabeth, w, Union St.
28. Dagire, Mr., Pigeon Roost Road.
28. Davenport, Pattie, w, Madison St.
Nov. 8. Dickey, George, c. Clay St.
10. Donnelly, Mary E., w, Concord St.
12. Davis, Maria.
14. Davis, Mary F., w, Vance St.
21. Davis, S. W.
Aug. 21. Early, John, w.
23. Ewins, Lizzie, c, Selden Building.
25. Elliott, Capt. John D., w, Adams St.
26. Ewing, Frank, c, City Hospital.
29. Ellis, Richard, Winchester St.
31. Edmondson, J. H., c.
31. Egan, Thomas, w, 98½ Front St.
31. Erasmus, Brother, w, Market St.
Sept. 1. Early, W. F., w, 138 Washington St.
1. Eilert, Lizzie, w, Henry Ave.
3. Epplett, Thomas, w, LaSalette Academy.
3. Ebberhardt, Ellen, w, Union St.
4. Eldridge, Amos, c, City Hospital.
5. Eyke, Mrs. M., w, Madison St.
5. Egan, Nancy.
6. Egan, Mrs., w, 466 Main St.
6. Ellen, c. cor. Hawley & Manassas Sts.
6. Evans, Allen, 106 N. Winchester St.
6. Elliott, Joseph H., w, Second St.
6. Edwards, C. W., w, Georgia St.
6. Edmondson (son of H. B.), w, Gill's Station.
7. Evans, Cora, c, Carr Ave.
9. Edmondson, Henry B., w, Gill's Station.
10. Engels, Peter, w, Market St. Infirmary.
10. Edington, Charley. 40 Causey St.
11. Eyke, Martin, w, Madison St.
11. Elliott, Mrs., c, Richmond Ave,
12. Egberts, David.
12. Erb, John, w, Hernando St.
12. Elliott, Capt. Wm., w, Jefferson St.
12. Edmondson, Mrs. H. B., w, Gill's Station.
13. Eisler, B. A., w.
13. Erskine, Alice, c. 140 Union St.
13. Eliert, Louis.
13. Eliert, Fannie, Henry Ave.
13. Elliott, George B., w, Jackson St.
13. Eler, Elizabeth.
13. Earley, Rev. J. T., c, 280 Hernando St.
13. Erb, Philip, w, cor. Hernando & Orleans Sts.
14. Edmonds, Joe, c, 294 Poplar St.
14. Edington, Gus., w, 40 Causey St.
15. Erek. Chris.
15. Euchkins, Eliza, cor. Henry & Second Sts.
15. Everheart, Henry, w, Union St.
16. Edwards, Wm., cor. Elliott & South Sts.
16. Ebler, E., w, Gates' Place.
16. Evans, Melon, w, 9 Winchester St.
16. Eberle, V., w, City Hospital.
16. Earley, Angeline. c, 77 Adams St.
17. Ennis, John, w, Bagley Place.
17. Erskine, Dr. J. H., w, Wellington St.
18. Eceffey, D., City Hospital.
18. Epps, Wyatt, Walker St.
18. Ellis, Jennie, c, Beale St.
20. Edwards, Wm., c, 246 Elliott St.
22. Exom, Jeff., c, cor. Safferans & Fifth Sts.
22. Endsley, Eddie, c, Front St.
25. Erlich, A., w.
26. Ebler, Virginia, w.
26. Edwards, Mrs. E., Deans Ave.
26. Ellis, J., c, South Alabama St.
29. Edwards, Robert, w, 354 Deans Ave.
30. Easley, Dr. E. S., w, Union St. Hospital.
Oct. 2. Elliott, Annie E., c, South Jackson St.
8. Everett, W. E., w, Rozelle Station.
9. Enwright, Patrick, w, Hernando Road.
9. Edwards, Mrs., w, Main St.
10. Erskine, George, w, Randolph Road.
12. Erick, Albert, w, Market St. Infirmary.
14. Etchevarue, G., w, Horn Lake Road.
14. Enley, John, w, Country.
16. Egan, M. J., w, Elliott St.
24. Erby, W. E., 32 Promenade St.
24. Eddy, w, State Line Road.
25. Esch, Mrs. Emma, w, Country.

A HISTORY OF THE YELLOW FEVER. 217

Oct. 25. Edmondson, Miss Joanna H. w, Pigeon Roost Road.
Nov. 4. Ewell, Dr, w, Posten Ave.
5. Engle, Mrs Mary, w, Fifth St.
Aug. 15. Fuchs, Victor D. Jr. w.
15. Farrar, Willie.
18. Fuchs, Mrs. S., w, Johnson Ave.
21. Farrow, Mollie, Rocco's Alley
21. Farrell, Mary, w, Third St.
23. Forbes, John C., w, City Hospital.
24. Fealey, Mrs. Sarah, w, 57 Exchange St.
25. Forrester, Tom, w, City Hospital.
25. Froese, R.
26. Farris, E., c, Adams St.
28. Foley, Thomas, w, Memphis & Charleston R. R.
28. Fifer, William S., w, Raleigh Road.
28. Foster, T. J., w, Madison St.
29. Fischer, Mrs. C., w, Main St.
29. Fritz, Lucy E., w, Moseby St.
30. Frank, Sol., w, Poplar St.
30. Fritz, Henry, c, 156 Main St.
30. Foley, Annie, 155 Linden St.
30. Fullerton, Mollie, w, Whitemore House.
30. Felkins, Eliza, cor. Fifth & Looney Sts.
30. Fullerton, Ed.
31. Froese, Mrs. Mary, 50 Second St.
31. Friedman, child of, w, 10 Commerce St.
31. Farrell, Pat., w, City Hospital.
31. Fullerton, Mrs. Catherine, w, Whitemore House.
31. Flynn, D. P., w, 107 Vance St.
Sept. 1. Friedman, Mrs., w, Commerce St.
1. Fieldman, Mary, 76 North Jackson St.
1. Fritz, John, w, Moseby St.
2. Flaherty, Miss G., w. Vance St.
2. Fink, Gustave, 147 Main St.
2. Flannagan, M., w, 17 Causey St.
3. Fullerton, Eddie, Whitemore House.
3. Falls, Lizzie, c, 253 Washington St.
3. Franklin, Mary, 13 Commerce St.
3. Friedman, Louis, w, 10 Commerce St.
3. Friedman, Josephine, w, 10 Commerce St.
3. Featherstone, W. S., w, Springdale Ave.
3. Fowler, Mrs. J. J., w, 137 Moseby St.
4. Flowers, Jeff., c, 47 Commerce St.
4. Friedman, Henry, w, 10 Commerce St.
4. Friedman, Lulu, w, 10 Commerce St.
4. Foley, Mary, 13 Commerce St.
4. Field, Cora, c, 173 Madison St.
4. France, Henry L., 39 Poplar St.
4. Fricke, George, Front St.
5. Fricke, Philip G.
5. Fields, Dora, c, 255 Madison St.
5. Fields, Henry, c, City Hospital.
5. Frank, 104 Linden St.
5. Foley, Bate., Shelby County.
5. Frank, Frank, City Hospital.
6. Flannagan, Katie, w, 17 Causey St.
6. Flack, Jennie, w, 111 Elliott St.
6. Funck, Miss R., w, 83 Front St.
7. Fenwick, Effie L., w, Fifth St.
7. Fuller, B. F.
7. Foley, Edward, w, Second St.
7. Franck, Miss, w, 83 Fourth St., Chelsea.
7. Flynn, Ben., c, cor. Hawley & Dunlap Sts.
7. Finney, Mike, w, City Hospital.
7. Fields (infant of Harry), c, cor. Madison St. & Marshall Ave.
7. Fahey, Edward, w, Chelsea St.
8. Frazier, Ruth, c, 82 Pontotoc St.
8. Fisher, Baville, w, 33 Monroe St.
8. Fitch, w.
8. Ford, Willie Lee, w, Yates Lake.
9. Fraviga, Lizzie, w.
9. Ferrin, A., c.
9. Fairchild, w, Tennessee St.
9. Flannagan, Ed., w, Market St. Infirmary.
9. Fuller, B. F., w.
9. Folk, Amanda, c.
10. Frazier, Rudolph.
10. Franklin, Hattie, Hernando St.
10. Fannie, Hernando St. curve.
10. Flack, Clara, w, 111 Elliott St.
10. Flack, Mrs. B, w, 111 Elliott St.
10. Farris, J. B., w, Cooper Place.
10. Fisher, Patrick, w, Linden St.
10. Ferguson, Harry W., w, Camp Joe Williams.

Sept. 11. Firth, Robert F., w, Echols St.
11. Falls, Rachel, c, Vance St.
11. Foreman, William, w, 271 Main St.
11. Flack, W. J., w, 111 Elliott St.
11. Flack, L. B., w, 111 Elliott St.
11. Flack, T. J., w, 111 Elliott St.
11. Ford, Harriet.
11. Fensley, Susie, w, Echols St.
12. Fransiola, Frank, c, Elliott St.
12. Fithian, H. E., w, Alabama St.
12. Fabin, John W., Market St. Infirmary.
12. Farrels, Hugh, 436 Main St.
12. Freeman, Henry, 127 Beale St.
12. Francis, E. S., w, Moseby Ave.
12. Flannery, Mike, w, City Hospital.
13. Farrell, Nellie, Market St. Infirmary.
13. Fulsom, Charles, 252 Hernando St.
13. Fliggin, Harvey, c, Brinkley Ave.
13. Feuster, Simon, w.
13. Finley, Ennis, w, 98 Front St.
13. Fackler, John.
13. Fenwick, F. M., w, Fifth St.
13. Fenwick, Mrs. L. D., w, Fifth St.
14. Frinster, Caroline, w.
14. Flack, Miss Laura, w, 111 Elliott St.
14. Frazee, Kate, 18 Winchester St.
14. Fause, V., w, Market St Infirmary.
15. Franklin, Ben.
15. Franklin, Frank, c, cor. Center Alley & Commerce St.
15. Foster, E. B., w, Orleans St.
15. Firth, W. S., w.
16. Finster, Jacob, w.
16. Fenwick, Alice A., w, Fifth St.
16. Fisher, J. F., w, Orleans St.
16. Folger, Joe, c, City Hospital.
16. Flynn, Fred. W., w, Louisville & Nashville R. R.
16. Ford, Elizabeth, c, cor. North St. & Ross Ave.
17. Frary, Peter, c, cor. Sixth St. & Broadway.
18. Firth, R. N., w, Echols St.
18. Frederick, E., Union St.
19. Figgerd, Joseph.
19. Fox, Alf., c, 286 Third St.
19. Frank, c, cor. Main & Georgia Sts.
19. Felton, Fort, c, cor. Broadway & Hernando Sts.
20. Foster, Annie, w, cor. Third & Walker Sts.
20. Field, Mrs. Mary, w, Springdale.
20. Fields, Dick, cor. Elliott & South Sts.
21. Fannin, Francis, c, factory lot, Chelsea.
22. Frank, James.
22. Fowler, Jerry, Post-and-Rail Ave.
22. Fay, John.
22. Fields, Ida.
23. Foster, Ida, w, cor. Third St. & Walker Ave.
23. Firth, Ella, c, Echols St.
24. Forbes, Dr. James A, w, Chambers House.
24. Fenwick, Mrs. S. F., w.
25. Franklin, Ben.
25. Francis (child), w, Church Home.
25. Flynn, w, Elmwood.
26. Forrest, Mrs. C. G., w, Rayburn Ave.
26. Fisher, Charles G., w, Linden St.
26. Foster, Clara, w, cor. Walker Ave. and Third St.
26. Foster, Charles, w, cor. Walker Ave. and Third St.
27. Ferrett, M. E., w, 29 Echols St.
28. Fleming, Will., c, 37 Allen Ave.
28. Fisher, Wesley, c, Monroe St.
29. Foster, William, 286 De Soto St.
29. Farris, Ed, w, Chelsea.
29. Fields, Robert, Shelby County.
29. Flynn, Robert Emmet, w, 107 Vance St.
29. Fowler, Mrs. D. F.
29. Forney (infant), City Hospital.
29. Flynn, Robert Emmet, 107 Vance St.
29. Furbish, E. E.
Oct. 1. French, Martha, c, Greenlaw St.
1. Finnan, Kate, w, Washington St.
2. Franklin, Miles, w, 484 Pontotoc St.
2. Folks, Julia.
2. Fay, Mrs.
3. Fletcher, Miss Mary, w, Orphan Home.
3. Flynn, Eliza, w, Elmwood.
4. Frances, Sister, w, Church Home.

218 A HISTORY OF THE YELLOW FEVER.

Oct. 5. Frethy, Michael, Rayburn Ave.
5. Folks. Julia, c, Stewart Ave.
6. Ficklin, Laura Young, w, Cooper Ave.
8. Finacy, M., w. cor. Fourth & Division Sts.
10. Fox (child of Tom).
10. Fison, Nick, c, Exchange St.
12. Farrell, Ellen, w, Union St.
12. Force, Dr. F. H., w.
12. Fisher, R., w, Chelsea.
13. Fazzi, L., w, Second St.
14. Feesser, Charles, w, County Jail.
16. Farrell, Mike, w, 162 De Soto St.
18. Fort, Mary E., w, State Female College.
18. Finney, Miss W., w, Wellington St.
21. Fisher, Dave. c, New Raleigh Road.
21. Fitzpatrick, Mary Eliza, w, Market St.
23. Foy, E. A., w, City Hospital.
25. Fitzgibbon, John, w, Main St.
27. Falz, Theodore, w, Louisville, Ky.
28. Faltz, F.
28. Froman, Wm., w, Spring St.
Nov. 4. Fleming, Miss J., w, Layton Ave.
22. Finn, Lucy, w, Winchester St.
Aug. 14. Goldsmith, Cora, w.
15. Goodman, A. H., w, Main St.
25. Glautzer, Mrs. Mary, w, Third St.
25. Gray, Robert. c.
27. Glautzer, Wm., w, Third St.
28. Gillen, A. K., w, Shelby St.
28. Gribe, Ann, c, Allen Ave.
28. Gooding, John, w, City Hospital.
28. Gribe, Anna, c, Allen Ave.
28. Gibbs, George, 30 Third St.
28. Gusmanny, Jennie, w, Poplar St.
28. Gummer, Mattie, w, Poplar St.
29. Gray, Eli, c.
29. Grimes, Larry, w, Jefferson St.
29. Gauze, Frank, w.
29. Gilmore, John, w, City Hospital.
29. Glesse, Mary A., w, City Hospital.
29. Gribe, Fred., Allen Ave.
29. Grant, Jennie, 106 Market St.
29. Goss, Frank, 86 Third St.
29. Goslin, Mrs., Poplar St.
29. Grouse, Frank.
29. Goslin, Mary Ann, Poplar St.
29. Gummer, Mr., w, Poplar St.
31. Griffin, William, w, Winchester St.
31. Green, James, c, Dunlap St.
31. Grant, Mrs. L. S., w.
31. Gane, Frank, w
Sept. 1. Garney, Henry, 250 Poplar St.
1. Grant, George M., w, Poplar.
1. Gummer, Frederick, w, Poplar St.
1. Guriey, Henry, w, 250 Poplar St.
1. Goldsmith, Mrs, M., w. Alabama St.
2. Gleason, Archie, w, Main St.
2. Gotchlich, Amelia, w, Winchester St.
2. Gwynn, Indiana, c, 36 Winchester St.
2. Gable, Bo., 152 Poplar St.
2. Goodman, L., c, City Hosp'tal.
2. Gurney, Henry, w, Poplar St.
2. Grant, Inez, c, Raleigh Road.
3. Gunderson, Mrs. Andrew.
3. Grant, Lewis, Raleigh Road.
3. Gabers, B., w, 48 Poplar St.
3. Gotchlich, Mrs. M.,w, 161 Winchester St.
3. Grant, L. S., cor. Seventh & Auction Sts.
3. Gorman. Simon, 14 Alabama St.
3. Galley, Robert, 152 Poplar St.
3. Galley, Auguste, 142 Main St.
3. Green, Ellen, c, Auction St.
3. Grigsby, Mary, c, 154 Monroe St.
4. Griffin, John, w, Winchester St.
4. Grant, Robert, w, Auction St.
4. Groves, 88 Hernando St.
4. Gruber, Fred., w, 90 Hernando St.
4. Grant, Margaret, w, Seventh St.
4. Greenpur, Fred , w, 92 Hernando St.
4. Graham, Mattie, w. Washington St.
5. Guinea, J. L., w. City Hospital.
5. Green. Mrs., w, foot Vance St.
5. Gray, Mrs. w, Poplar St.
5. Grehen, William, w, Berlin Ave.
5. Green, Mrs. Margaret, w, Third St.
5. Gross, J. A., w, 111 Market St.
6. Grady, Thomas.
6. Gates, Frank.
6. Gaines, Mrs., w, Manassas St.

Sept. 6. Gross, James.
6. Grady, Thomas, w, 309 Poplar St.
6. Givin, R. G., w, Randolph Road.
7. Gorman, Joseph, 12 Dunlap St.
7. Goodrich, William, c, 354 Madison St.
7. Garland, Joseph, c, Dunlap St.
7. Goetz, Leno, w, Main St.
7. Griffin (infant of Tillie), c, Tennessee St.
7. Gray, Anna, c, Lauderdale.
8. Gray, Walker, w, Main St.
8. Garvey, Mary E., w, Madison St.
8. Gorman, Patrick, w. City Hospital.
8. Gordon, Missouri, c, 358 Beale St.
8. Gaut, Joseph, Fifth St.
8. Gwinn, Wm., c, 83 Front St.
8. Griswold, Mrs. C. A., w.
8. Getchell, Miss, w, Brinkley Ave.
8. Gay, Lucius, c.
9. Green, Jennie, w, 80 De Soto St.
9. Getchell, Mr., w, cor. Brinkley Ave. and Raleigh Road.
9. Getchell, Mrs., w, cor. Brinkley Ave. and Raleigh Road.
9. Gates, Mrs. Sam., Raleigh Road.
9. Garvey, Bridget, w, Madison St.
9. Gibson, Nathan, w, Wellington St.
9. Gray, W. W., w, Sycamore St.
9. Gates, Victoria, c.
9. Griswold, C. A., w, Mill St.
10. Green, W. H., c. Auction St.
10. Gleason, Mrs. M. J., w, Main St.
10. Gates, Mrs. S. M., w, Raleigh Road.
10. Granning, Mrs. William, w, Linden St.
10. Gatlin, G. W., Hernando Road.
10. Gummer, John, 448 Poplar St.
10. Gatlin, Johnson, w. Shelby County.
10. Gardner, H. E., 260 Hernando St.
10. Gills, child of Gilbert, Richmond Ave.
10. Going, Col. S. B., w, Main St.
10. Garagnon, Henry, Greenlaw St.
10. Goodman, Robert, 28 Causey St.
10. Gist, R. C., w, Market St. Infirmary.
10. Goodrich, Carrie, c, Avery St.
11. Gary, John W.
11. Gilbert, G., c, Gayoso St.
11. Gardner, H. C., Hernando St.
12. Garrison, Frank, w, Mulberry St.
12. Goenner, Mrs. Clara.
12. Grogun, Edward, w, St. Peter's Cemetery.
12. Garland, Charles, Dunlap St.
12. Giese, A. D., 10 Beale St.
12. Grant, G. H., Jr., w, Sixth St.
12. Getta, Asa, 62 Poplar St.
13. Green, Pink.
13. Gill, Annie, w, 135 Beale St.
13. Gates, Moses, c, cor. Raleigh Road and Brinkley Ave.
13. Gates, Aaron, cor. Coffee St. and Horn Lake Road.
13. Gates, Ripley, w.
13. Gawray, H. M., w, Madison St.
13. Gertrude, Sister, w, cor. Third and Market Sts.
14. Griffin, Austin, w, Market St. Infirmary.
14. Gee. Joseph C.
14. Griffin, Antonio, w, 78 First St.
15. Graham, Virgil.
15. Gray, Mrs., w, Poplar St.
15. Gillen, Friday, c, 66 St. Martin St.
15. Gibson, E. W., w, 90 Main St.
15. Glancey, Maggie, w, Boulevard.
15. Garrett, John, w, Chelsea.
15. Grove, Ada, c, 18 Butler St.
15. Garner, Fred., c, cor. Fourth and Madison Sts.
15. Gray, Nervy, c, Georgia St.
17. Gilman, M.
17. Green, Lizzie, w, 79 Front St.
17. Goodrich, David, w, cor. Fourth and Safferans Sts.
18. Garey, John, w.
18. Green, C., c, Dunlap St.
18. Grant, Claiborne, c, cor. Keel & Sixth Sts.
18. Garden, Robert, 50 Causey St.
18. Gatlin, Johnson.
18. Gurdici, A.
18. Gatlin, Mrs.
18. Groney, William, 104 Linden St.
18. Gregg, J. C., 64 Peyton Ave.

A HISTORY OF THE YELLOW FEVER. 219

Sept. 18. Gregg, Mrs. Jennie, 64 Peyton Ave.
18. Goodman, Mrs. D., c, Shelby St.
18. Glarkman, W. J., c, Elliott St.
19. Green, Eila, c, 415 Wellington St.
19. Gable, Sophy, w, 229 Madison St.
19. Green, Joe, c, Dunlap St.
20. Griffin, John, w, Market St. Infirmary.
20. Gallaher, James.
20. Gay, Iola.
21. Gregg, Miss Sallie, w, Peyton Ave.
21. Glass, Matt. A., w, Trigg Ave.
21. Gorrell, Dr. J. G. O., w, Court St. Infirm'ry.
21. Gordon, John, c, Walker Ave.
22. Griffin, Mr., w.
22. Gray, Susie, c, Jessamine St.
22. Gwyn, Miss M. Eliza, w, Raleigh.
24. Gregg, Willie, 64 Peyton Ave.
24. Griffin, Mary E., c.
24. Gabler, Elizabeth, w, Old Raleigh Road.
24. Gordon, Albert, c, cor. Hernando and Walker Ave.
25. Gilmore, William, w, Church Home.
25. Grigsby, Samuel, c, 172 Vance St.
26. Gorin, Eugene.
26. Grempe, Charles, w, Market St. Infirmary.
26. Gain, Eugene, w, Market St. Infirmary.
26. Genoke, Caroline, w, Poplar St.
26. Garrison, William.
27. Goodman. A., w.
27. Garrett, C., w, Chelsea.
27. Gordon, Millie, c, Hernando St. & Walker Ave.
27. Gatzen, Eliza, c, cor. Webster & De Soto Sts.
27. Garesche, Eugene, w.
27. Graham, Mrs. Martindale.
28. Gerlack, Franz, Sr., w, Shelby St.
28. Gerlack, Mary, w, Shelby St.
28. Goebel, Fred., w, Elmwood.
28. Gerlack, Franz, Jr., w, Shelby St.
29. Green, Mamie, w, 138 Beale St.
29. Gordon, Annie, Hernando Road.
29. Gath, James B., w, 27 Beale St.
29. Griggs, Mrs.
29. Green, Martin, c, Georgia St.
Oct. 1. Green, Capt. Nat., w, Gill's Station.
1. Green, Mrs. Elizabeth, w, Gill's Station.
1. Gordon, Charlotte, c, cor. Hernando St. and Walker Ave.
2. Gumbel, Francis, Buntyn's Station.
2. Gordon, Isaac.
2. Goodwin, child of E. B., w, Chelsea.
4. Grayson, Steve., c, 3 Butler St.
5. Goodman, George, c, Gas Works.
7. Garvin, Mike, w, City Hospital.
8. Gladden, Alfred, c, Overton Point.
9. Gustave, Fondam, w, City Hospital.
9. Goodwyn, E. B., w, Thomas Ave.
9. Griffin, Mrs. H., c, Tennessee St.
9. Griffin, Charles, c.
10. Galling, Mrs. John.
10. Gossett, Eliza, w, Market St.
12. Gear, Miss Docia, w, Raleigh Road.
13. Goebel, Theodore, w, Elmwood.
13. Galloway, Mary A., w, Cooper Ave.
13. Goldstein, Fannie, w, Raleigh Road.
16. Gill, Henry, w, Walker Ave.
17. Glass, Mrs. R., w, Trigg Ave.
19. Givers, Lewis, c, 88 Main St.
19. Gillem, child of Lena, c, McLemore Ave.
24. Gregor, Thomas, Elmwood.
25. Garnon, Fred., w, Country.
30. Gift, Sarah J., w, Rozelle Station.
30. Grant, Martha, 106 Market St.
30. Garvin, Sarah.
Nov. 6. Gregory, Isam, c, Huppers Ave.
9. Guigel, John H., w, Main St.
12. Galloway, M. E., w, Cooper Ave.
15. Griffin, R. S., w, McLemore Ave.
Aug. 14. Hill, Albert.
16. Hay, infant of Levi.
17. Hendricks, Mrs. F. C.
19. Houns, Ben. B.
20. Hahn, Moses. w, 2 Jackson St.
20. Haskell, Rachel, w, 159 Poplar St.
22. Hooges, Will am H., w, City Hospital.
22. Hill, E. J., w, Worsham House.
23. Hupert, M., w, Poplar St.
22. Heffener, Jerry, w, Exchange St.

Aug. 24. Hill, Mrs. E. J., w, Worsham House.
24. Haissig, Daniel S., w.
24. Hall, infant of Lulu, 101 Second St.
22. Haissig, Henry. w.
26. Halstead, W. H., w, 487 Pontotoc St.
26. Hollenberg, Mrs. Carrie, w.
26. Harrington, H. S., w, 242 Monroe St.
27. Holley, Luke, w, Breedlove Ave.
27. Holland, R. C., w, City Hospital.
27. Henry, John C.
27. Hunter, Sallie, Winchester St.
27. Haskell, Benjamin, Louisville, Ky.
28. Haynes, Nannie, w, cor. Exchange and Third Sts.
28. Hutchins, Thomas A.
28. Hesse, Hester.
28. Halliday, A., w, City Hospital.
28. Hall, James, w, Hernando Road.
28. Henery, Henry, c, Second St.
29. Harder, Henry, w, Market St.
29. Herman, Lizzie, w, Hill St.
29. Hewitt, Peter, w, Monroe St.
29. Harris, Jordan, Quinby St.
29. Hughes, James, City Hospital.
29. Hunt, Tilda, 37 Commerce St.
29. Hanson, William.
29. Hall, John.
29. Hissic, Catherine.
30. Heyman, Howard, w, Poplar St.
30. Heyman, Morris, w, Poplar St.
30. Hill, George. 60 Third St.
31. Hightower, Daniel, w, 84 Second St.
31. Hesson, Henry, w, 45 Beale St.
31. Hays, Mary, c, 42 Allen Ave.
31. Hill, Austin, c, 60 Third St.
31. Haley, Daniel, w, Main St.
31. Hackett, Mary, w, Hernando Road.
31. Hudson, James, c.
Sept. 1. Hutchinson, Emma, w, Front St.
1. Hurt, Otto, w, Dunlap St.
1. Houston, Charles, City Hospital.
1. Hall, Esther, c, Orleans St.
1. Hampton, Eli, c, 111 Court St.
1. Henderson, Jim, c, 42 Jackson St.
1. Hendricks, Dennis, South St.
1. Hopkins, c, 22 Main St.
1. Hardway, Goodman, 37 Commerce St.
1. Holt, Neil B., w, 359 Poplar St.
1. Holst, George A., w, Court St.
1. Hudson (child of John), c.
1. Hackett, Mary, w.
2. Hyman, Mrs. M., w.
2. Hargan, Mildred.
2. Hill, Tom, c, Monroe St.
2. Hosmar. Chris., w, 108 Vance St.
2. Hicks, George, c, City Hospital.
2. Henderson, Robert, c, 1 Suzette St.
2. Huber, J. J., w, Robinson St.
2. Hanson, Julia, w, Robinson St.
2. Hopper, James, w, Exchange St.
2. Hightower, Willie, w, Second St.
2. Heidaw (infant of John), cor. Third and Auction Sts.
2. Harman, Wm. N., w, South Jackson St.
2. Hustin, A.
3. Hardin, Monroe, 18 Washington St.
3. Holmes, Henry, c, 169 Jefferson St.
3. Hite, Henry, 197 Jefferson St.
3. Hamilton, Charles, w, Charleston Ave.
3. Holmes, Henry, Exposition Building.
3. Hollingsworth, Monroe, c, 86 Washington St.
3. Hill, Sam., c, 96 Adams St.
3. Hawkins, Florence, c. 11 Turley St.
3. Hoo, Lang, 34 Poplar St.
3. Howard, Willis, 6 Turley St.
3. Haber, Emily.
3. Hurst, Henry, c, Jefferson St.
3. Houston, Chas., c, City Hospital.
3. Harper, James, w, Exchange St.
4. Healey, Mary Ann, Winchester St.
4. Hodges, Dr. W. R., w, Fifth St., Chelsea.
4. Harrison, M. J., w, Robinson St.
4. Hohlin, Amelia, w, 172 Alabama St.
4. Hope, John, w, Second St.
5. Hoffman, Jacob, w, Second St.
5. Haggerty, James, w, 73 Railroad Ave.
5. Heins, Augustine, c, South St.
5. Hertz (infant of L.), w, Bull Run.

A HISTORY OF THE YELLOW FEVER.

Sept. 5. Hanson, M. J., w, Robinson St.
5. Hurnder, Millie, c, Pontotoc St.
6. Habaron, 120 Gayoso St.
6. Haggerty, N , Ohio R. R.
6. Hunter, Ida, 32 Ross Ave.
6. Hood, Miss, w, 59 Ross Ave.
6. Hagge, John C., w, Broadway St.
6. Hannegan, John, w, 18 De Soto St.
6. Hagge, Lewis, w, Broadway St.
6. Hadish, S., w, Chelsca.
6. Hood, Mrs., w, Ross Ave.
7. Harrington, Mary, w, Beale St.
7. Hose, Thomas, Ross Ave.
7. Hobson, Jesse, c, 255 Monroe St.
7. Hall, William, c, cor alley & Fifth St.
7. Horn, Maggie, w, 233 Main St.
7. Hays, Tobin, 209 Dunlap St.
7. Hays, Gabriel, c, Ross Ave.
8. Hanenburg, James, w, 244 Front St.
8. Hupper, Mrs., w, Second St.
8. Haggerty, Annie, w, Gill's Station.
8. Horn, Mrs. Maggie, w, Union St.
8. Hicks, George, w, Shelby St.
8. Hughes, Mary, Gayoso St.
9. Hewitt, Henry.
9. Hardin, Henry, w, 54 Jackson St.
9. Harris, Matt., 46 Allen Ave.
9. Higgins, William, w, Market St. Infirmary.
9. Hall, Rosa, w, cor. Fifth & Broadway Sts.
9. Ham nerstein, Laura, w, 83 Second St.
9. Hughes, Miss, w, Dunlap St.
9. Heath, Thos., w.
10. Hood, Thomas B., w, Madison St.
10. Hope, George, w, Commerce St.
10. Holt, Herman, w, Market St. Infirmary.
10. Harris, J., 44 Pontotoc St.
10. Hubert, w, Second St.
10. Hammerson, Pauline, w, 334 Third St.
10. Hyde, John, 19 Hernando St.
10. Hammerstein, Mrs., Greenlaw St.
10. Hicks, Erasmus, 55 Charleston Ave.
10. Harris, Mamie, 62½ Front St.
10. Humes, A. R., w, Main St.
10. Hoffmaster, Joanna, Louisville, Ky.
11. Hardy, John, 125 Union St.
11. Hallenhead, S. B.
11. Hickerson, Simon, 252 Elliott St.
11. Hayes, James, w, Market St.
11. Hammerstein, Emily, w, 83 Second St.
11. Hunter, Willie, w, 269 Union St.
11. Hurt, Henry, 2 Turley St.
11. Hodges, Mrs. E., w, Lauderdale St.
11. Hunter, George, 269 Union St
11. Hammerstein, Mrs., cor. Mill & Greenlaw Sts.
12. Hickerson, Simon, c, 252 Elliott St.
12. Harris, Willie, w, Gayoso House.
12. Hardy, John, 121 Beale St.
12. Holt, Mrs., w, 417 Main St.
12. Hutchins, R.
12. Hinds, Mrs. Ellen.
12. Hemmerly, John, w.
13. Harris, Ed., c, Poplar St.
13. Hodges, B. M., w, 416 Lauderdale St.
13. Hardin, Lucy, c, 11 North St.
13. Hudson, William, w, 374 Main St.
13. Hare, Henry, w, 136 Orleans St.
13. Haynes, Richard V., w, 364 Union St.
13. Harvey (child), c, 59½ Front St.
13. Hill, William A., Posten Ave.
14. Hanna, Tisha, c, St. Martin St.
14. Hamilton, J., c, Linden St.
14. Hallam, Sallie, c, Georgia St.
14. Hightower, Francis, w, cor. Third and Adams Sts
14. Hayden, James, w, Market St. Infirmary.
14. Hallam, Mollie, Front St.
14. Hameron, James V., 25 Vance St.
14. Hitzfield, William, w, 233 Second St.
14. Herman, Max, w, 39 Madison St.
14. Hutchinson, Mrs. Jennie, 81 Adams St.
14. Holcomb, Mollie, c, Ninth St.
14. Haynes, Richard V., w, 364 Union St.
15. Hampton, C., c.
15. Hope, Mrs. Tim., w.
15. Healey, Pat.
15. Holman, Harry, Hernando St.
15. House, Lee, c, 130 Beale St.
15. Hilton, Margaret, 182 Rayburn Ave.

Sept. 15. Hall, Georgiana, w, 135 Beale St.
15. Horsley, Nellie, w, City Hospital.
16. Hawley, Pat., c, South St.
16. Horton, Henrietta, c, Clinton St.
16. Hemple, Eliza, w. foot of Market St.
16. Henry, Lulu, w, foot of Auction St.
16. Hewitt, Mike, w, 298 Second St.
16. Hubert, George.
16. Hulah, William, w, Church Home.
16. Horasley (child of J.)
16. Harris, Miss Rosa, w, cor. Exchange and Third Sts.
16. Hausman, Fred. R., w, Market St. Infirmary.
16. Hicks, Willie, w.
17. Hinkle, M. W., w, Walnut St.
17. Hollensbud, C. B.
17. Hitchcock, Thomas.
17. Heath, J. W., w, 82 Fifth St.
17. Hope, Tim., w.
17. Hill, W. P.
17. Hanley, Margaret. w, Walnut St.
17. Hogg, Mrs., w, Fort Pickering.
17. Hogg (child of Mrs.), w, Fort Pickering.
17. Hinkle, M. W., cor. Georgia & Walnut Sts.
17. Henderson, Minnie, c, Linden St.
17. Higgins, H. C., w, Market St. Infirmary.
17. Haldron, John, 289 Linden St.
17. Hamilton, J. W., w, Front St. Ft. Pickering.
17. Hammock, R. L., w, Madison St.
17. Hoggin, Mrs., c, Alabama St.
17. Hicks, Dr. J. B., w, Court St. Infirmary.
17. Hays, Tim., w, 61 Commerce St.
18. Hardin, Ben., c, cor. Jones Avenue and North St.
18. Harris, Miss Jesse, 229½ Second St.
18. Hope, Mrs. Rachael.
18. Harris, Angeline R.
18. Higgerson, Fannie.
18. Hafron, John, w, Linden St.
18. Hotchkiss, Thomas (of Shreveport), Market St. Infirmary.
19. Harris, Lewis, cor. Hernando & Elliott Sts.
19. Heidson, Mrs., w, 83 Second St.
19. Hammerstein, Julia, 83 Second St.
19. Hicklin, Wm., c, Horn Lake Road.
19. Hellvig, Rudolph, Louisville, Ky.
20. Howard, Henry, City Hospital.
20. Hasten, V., w, City Hospital.
20. Hays, Thomas, c, 48 Ross Ave.
20. Horan, Mary.
20. Hunt, Fannie T., w, Hernando Road.
20. Herman, w, Adams St. Station-house.
20. Hays, Cynda, c, 42 Allen Ave.
20. Herring, Mary, c, Exchange St.
22. Hogge, John, c, Broadway St.
22. Hammerstein, J., w, Second St.
22. Houston, Alice.
22. Hendey, Dr. T. J., w, Market St. Infirmary.
22. High, Mansfield, w, Shelby County.
23. Hinds, Jackson, c, Overton St.
23. Horton, W. N.
23. Holtz, T. W.
23. Harris, Adolph.
23. Henderson, Virgey, c, cor. Lane Ave. & Ayers St.
23. Haggie, John, w, Broadway St.
24. Horton, C., w, Market St. Infirmary.
24. Hought, G., w, Market St. Infirmary.
24. Harris, c, Poplar St.
24. Horsley, T. T.
25. Hallows, Eveline, w. Pierson Place.
25. Haggerty, J. F., w, Orleans St.
26. Hightower, Lewis, c, cor. Tennessee and Clay Sts.
26. Hightower, Lewis.
26. Harmon, Capt. Wm.
26. Hendey, Mrs. Francis, w, Market St. Infirmary.
26. Horsley, Benton.
26. Hill, Alfred C.
28. Hays, child of Mrs., c, 209 Dunlap St.
20. Hunt, Wm. Wm., w, 450 Hernando St.
28. Heidelberg, Louis, Louisville, Ky.
29. Hughes, Christopher, c, cor. Tennessee and Clay Sts.
29. Hordon, c, 65 Elliott St.

A HISTORY OF THE YELLOW FEVER.

Sept. 29. Haggerty, Annie, w, Orleans St.
29. Higgins, Mr., w, Memphis and Little Rock R. R.
30. Haley, Mrs., w, Father Mathew Camp.
30. Hemple, Willie, w, Market St.
30. Higgins, Albert, c, cor. Vance and Walnut Sts.
Oct. 1. Harrison, James, c, cor. Third and Coffee Sts., Ft. Pickering.
1. Hollenberg, C. B., w, Market St Infirm'ry.
1. Highland, Jno. N., w, Market St. Infirm'ry.
2. Henderson, W., c, 430 Linden St.
2. Hickman, E., w, Georgia St.
2. Hatcher, J. S., w, Main St.
2. Holly, Joseph, w, Moseby Ave.
3. Hunt, Ellen V., c, Washington St.
3. Hereford, Harriet, c, Union St.
3. Hyman, William, w, City Hospital.
3. Heomig, I. M., w, Market St. Infirmary.
3. Hill, Lewis, Broadway St.
3. Harris, James, c, cor. Main and Beale Sts.
4. Henricle, J. R., w. Madison St.
4. Harris, Davey, c. Short Third St.
4. Hill, Lewis, c, 38 Jackson St.
4. Hunter, Carl, Shelby County.
4. Hewitt, Thomas, w, Main St.
5. Howard, Mrs. C. W., w, Posten Ave.
5. Hanley, Peter, w, Suzette St.
5. Holt, John A., w, 350 Poplar St.
6. Harris, Ruth, c, Linden St.
6. Hinkle, L., w, Georgia St.
6. Harrington, A., w, Horn Lake Road.
7. Hanley, Edward, w, Vance St.
7. Hack, Miss M., w, Marley Ave.
7. Hawley, Isaac H., w, Market St. Infirm'ry.
7. Hawkins, Mr., w, McLemore Ave.
8. Holmes, Maria, c, Poplar St.
8. Hewitt, Mrs. Jesse, w, Causey St.
8. Hewitt, child of Dr., w.
8. Howard, Frank, c, Waldron Ave.
9. Hardeman, Eva, c, near Elmwood.
10. Harvey, W. W., w, Camp Joe Williams.
11. Hawkins, A. S., w, Madison St.
11. Hawkins, Pres., c, New Gas Works.
12. Holland, T. P., w, Union St.
12. Holston, Martha, c, Trigg Ave.
14. Heffey, C., w, Wright Ave.
16. Henniger, Otto, w, Breedlove Ave.
17. Hainer, Mrs., w, Raleigh.
18. Heidel, Robert B., w.
18. Harrington, A., w, Market St.
19. Hollywood, Mrs. J., w, Camp Father Mathew.
19. Hollywood, L., w, Camp Father Mathew.
21. Henniger, Fred., w, Breedlove Ave.
22. Hellman, Fred., w, Dunlap St.
24. Henniger, Miss A., w, Breedlove Ave.
26. Harris, Mrs. M., w, Central Ave.
27. Haynes, W. B., w, Elliott St.
30. Horn, Mary A., w, Boulevard.
30. Henniger, Rosa, w, Breedlove Ave.
31. Henderson, infant of Mrs.
31. Hanna, Noah, w, Pigeon Roost Road.
Nov. 1. Hightower, James, w.
4. Hanley, Mrs. E. P., w, Ruth St.
11. Hug, Peter, w, Jackson St.
12. Henderson, Virginia, c, Walnut St.
21. Hartlege, Mollie, w, Alabama St.
30. Harris, W. H.
Aug. 12. Isaacs, Mattie L., w.
12. Ivery, Turner, c.
12. Ivery, Turner, cor. Sixth St. & Broadway.
15. Isaacs, E., w.
23. Isaacs, Isaac.
Sept. 7. Irby, Amanda D.. Main St.
7. Ingalls, Dr., w, 430 Main St.
12. Irwin, Lottie, 167 De Soto St.
12. Irwin, Peter.
13. Irwin, Emma N., w, Jones Ave.
14. Ida, w, Thomas Ave.
17. Ike, Ben., c, De Soto St.
18. Isdell, Carrie.
19. Idley, Jack, c, Huling St.
20. Isaac, cor. Carolina and Main Sts.
23. Infant child, City Hospital.
Oct. 5. Irving, Mrs. John, w, Poplar St.
Nov. 6. Isbell, Daniel, Madison St.
Aug. 12. Jones, Roger.
12. Jackson, M., City Hospital.

Aug. 12. Johnson, Ben., c., Turley St.
12. Jones, Rachael, 158 Poplar St.
14. Johl, Maxey.
15. Johl, Henrich.
15. Jenkins, Mrs. E.
18. Jones, Daniel, c, Robinson St.
21. Johnson, Henry, c, 9½ Johnson Ave.
23. Johnson, William, c, cor. Alabama and Quinby Sts.
24. Johnson, Henry, c, City Hospital.
24. Jones, Catherine, c, Worsham House.
25. Jones, Caroline C., w.
26. Jones, I. H., 242 Monroe St.
26. Johl, w, Commerce St.
26. Jackson, Colden, w, City Hospital.
27. Johnson, Cyrus, w, Poplar St.
27. Johl, Mrs. Z., w, Commerce St.
28. Jones, Anderson, c, Poplar St.
28. Jenkins, William, w, 17 Second St.
28. Johnson, Nannie, Cane Creek, Shelby Co.
28. Joslin, Mrs., 176 Poplar St.
30. Joyce, Patrick, w. Washington St.
30. Johnson, Ed., 37 Commerce St.
30. Jones, Robert, 222 Monroe St.
30. Jacobs, Joe., 39 Front St.
30. James, Robert, 242 Monroe St.
30. John, alias Chicago John, alley, between Main and Front Sts.
30. Johnson, Maria, c, St. Martin St.
31. Jones, Littleton, c, Market St.
31. Jackson, Minerva, c, 313 Union St.
31. Jones, Mollie, c, 11 Jackson St.
Sept. 1. Johnson, Mattie. 39 Adams St.
1. Jackson, R. J., w, 126 Johnson Ave.
2. Jackson, Mrs., Raleigh Road.
2. Jepson, Sarah, 18 Winchester St.
3. Jackson, James, c, cor. Front and Sycamore Sts.
3. Johnson, Mary, c, 71 Front St.
3. Jones, Mrs., 33 Third St.
3. Jones, Monroe, c, Huling St.
3. Johnson, Mary Jane, Jackson St.
3. Jackson, Anderson, c, 17 Poplar St.
3. Jones, Lavina, c, cor. Concord and Second Sts.
3. Jackson, Anderson, 17 Poplar St.
3. Jessen, Jerrold, c, Winchester St.
3. Jackson, Mary, c.
4. Jerome, Mrs. E. L, w, Worsham House.
4. Jacobs, Roberta, c, South Jackson St.
5. Jones, Albert, c, 32½ Causey St.
5. Johnson, Annie, c. Commerce St.
6. Jones, Manda, 216 Front St.
6. Jones, Henry A.. 216 Front St.
6. Johnson, Henry, c, Second St.
6. Jones, Nellie, c, 62 Promenade St.
6. Jefferson, Louis, c.
6. Josepha, Sister, w, La Salette Academy.
7. Jenny, F. W., w, Beale St.
7. James, Alice J., w, Georgia St.
7. Joete, Joseph, 800 Main St.
7. Jacobs, Dennis, c, 182 Georgia St., Ft. Pickering.
7. Joyce, Jennie, 110 Gayoso St.
7. Junkerman, Mr.
8. Johnson, Gus.
8. Jones, Monroe, De Soto St. Engine House.
8. Judah, Charles, w, City Hospital.
8. Jackson, Robt. L.
8. Jeffrey, Amanda, w.
9. James, Eddie.
9. Jobe, Jacob, c.
9. Jenkins, Henry, c.
10. Jones, Charles, c, Union St.
10. Johnson, Edward, w, Market St Infirmary.
10. Jones, Charles, c, 314 Union St.
10. Jackson, Mrs., w, Sycamore St.
10. Jackson, Andrew, c, foot of McCall St.
10. Jones, John, cor. Jackson & Seventh Sts.
10. Jones, C., c, 192 Robinson St.
10. Jackson, H., c, 8 Lauderdale St.
10. Jones, John, Monroe St.
11. Jones, Matilda, c, Monroe St., extended.
11. Jones, Lena, 192 Robinson St.
11. Johnson, William, c, 19 Winchester St.
11. Jackson, Phil., c, City Hospital.
12. Johnson, Ben., 257 Washington St.
12. Jones, Hailey, 47 Main St.
13. Johnson, John, w, cor. Second & Keel Sts.

Sept. 13. Jones, Melessa, w, Jackson St.
13. Johnson, Edward, c, 198 Elliott St.
13. James, Tucker, c, Broadway.
13. Jackson, Sol., c, De Soto St.
13. Jessie, c, cor. Adams and Manassas Sts.
13. Jackson, Al., c, De Soto St.
14. Joiner, Parker, c.
14. Jones, Richard, c, 65 Elliott St.
14. Johnson, Sallie, c, 99 Market St.
14. Judge, Theodore, w, 18 Exchange St.
14. Johnson, Annie N., w.
14. Johnson, Sallie, c, cor. Madison and De Soto Sts.
15. Jackson, John, c, Short Third St.
15. Jacobi, J. C., w.
15. Jarvis, w, Court St.
16. Joiner, Mary, c.
16. Johnson, Virginia, c, 75 Pontotoc St.
17. Johl, Mamie, cor. Seventh & Jackson Sts.
17. Johnson, Tom, w, 44 Causey St.
17. Johnson, Annie, c, De Soto St.
17. Jones, George, c, Spring St.
17. Jennings, Matthew, w, Church Home.
18. Johl, Mrs. Mary, w.
18. Johnson, Mrs. M., w, 245 Safferans St.
18. Johnson, Eliza, c, Broadway.
18. Jones, Walter, w, Bluff.
18. Jennie, c, 62 Madison St.
18. Jackson, Lou., c, Marlin Ave.
18. Johnson, Courtney.
19 Jukes, W. C., c, 129 Causey St.
19. Jones, Robert N., Raleigh Road.
19. Jones, Mrs. H., c, Court St.
20. Jordan, Henry, c, Echols St.
20. Joiner, Calvin, cor. Alabama & Seventh Sts.
20. Jones, Daisy, w, cor. Georgia & Fourth Sts.
20. Johnson, Fred., c, Tennessee Railroad.
20. Joiner, Calvin, c, cor. Safferans and Seventh Sts.
22. Jackson, John, c, Third St.
22. Johnson, Edmund, w, 245 Safferans Sts.
22. Jackson (child), c, Central Point.
22. Jackson, Mrs., w, cor. Third & Jackson Sts.
23. Jones, Alfred, c, cor. Linden & Walnut Sts.
23. Jones, Bettie, c, cor. Tennessee & Clay Sts.
24. Jones, Miss M.
25. Jefferson, Miss B., c, Poplar St.
25. Johnson, Mrs., w, Orleans St.
25. Jackson, Clara, c, Carolina St.
25. Johnson (child of Jennie), c, 915 Georgia St.
25. Josephine, c, Second St.
25 Johnson, Mrs. F., c, Spring St.
26. Johnson, J., Jr.
26. Jones, John, w, City Hospital.
27. Jones, Calvin, c, cor. Main and Mill Sts.
27. Johnson, Caroline, c, 139 Georgia St.
27. Jackson, Sarah, c, Waldron Ave.
27. Johnson, Jennie, 915 Georgia St.
27. Jones (child).
28. Jackson, George.
28. Jones, Hannah, w, Fourth & Georgia Sts.
28. Jamieson, Wm., w, Hernando Road.
29. Jefferson, Thomas, c, cor. Linden and Hernando Sts.
30. Johnson, Charles.
30. Johnson, Handy, c, Mill St.
30. Johl, Edward, w, Brinkley Ave.
Oct. 1. Johnson (child of Lizzie), 13 Market St.
1. Johnson, Charles, w, Hernando St.
2. Jones, Eliza, c, Chapin Ave.
2. Johnson, Sarah, c, foot of Beale St.
2. Jackson (infant of Julia), Carolina and Second Sts.
2. Joanna, w, 67 Jefferson St.
2. Johnson, Robert, c, City Hospital.
2. Jackson, Ella, c, Carolina St.
3. Jones, Mary E.
5. Jobe, S. M., w, Court St.
5. Johnson, Sidney, c, Hernando St.
5. Jones, Preston, c, Walnut St.
6. Jones, Susan, c, cor. Jackson & Allen Ave.
6. Jones, Lewis, c, Third St.
6. Jones, H., c, Union St.
6. Jackson, A., c, Walker Ave.
7. Jones, Clara, c, Shelby County.
8. Johnson, T. N., w, Hernando Road.
8. Johnson, J. S., w, Poplar St.
9. Jacobs, Mrs. J. C., w, Memphis and Charleston Railroad.

Oct. 9. Johnson (child of Pierce).
9. Jake, south gate, Elmwood.
9. Jacobi, J. C., w, Memphis and Charleston Railroad.
10. Jones, John, w, Union St.
10. John, c, 42 Second St.
10. Jones, Frank, c, 70 Auction St.
11. Johnson, Henry, c, Carr Ave.
12. Johnson, Miss, w, foot of Market St.
12. Johnson, Cora L., w, Market St.
14. Just, M. B., w, Gill's Station.
16. Jones, w.
30. Jones. Irene, c.
31. Johnson, Fayette.
Nov. 2. Jones, Daniel, w, Moseby Ave.
3. Jones, J. C., w, Fourth St.
4. Jackson. Cora, c, Madison St.
Dec. 10. Joyner, William, w, cor. Alabama St. and Jones Ave.
Aug. 12. Kearns, John W.
12. Kinney, M. W., w, Adams St.
14. Kuhn, Arthur.
17. Ketterman, C. F.
18. Kelley, James, 22 Alabama St.
19. Klostermeyer, Bertha, w.
20. Kearns, Mrs., 83 Winchester St.
21. Kounds, B. B., w, 179 Second St.
25. Kleiner, John R., w.
26. Kleiner, John.
26. Klaffki, Andrew, w.
26. Klein, John, w, North Court St.
27. Kesillen, A., w, Shelby St.
28. Kealhoffer, George, w, North Court St.
28. Kirkland, Harry, w, Monroe St.
28. Kenry, James C., w, Bradford St.
30. Kelly, John, w.
31. Kennerly, Martin, w, City Hospital.
31. Kallaher, C., w, City Hospital.
31. Kearn, Arthur, w, Washington St.
31. Kallaher, Sarah, w, Jefferson St.
31. Kleiner, Joseph, w, Jefferson St.
Sept. 1. Kinston, Auguste.
1. Keiston, Thomas, 40 Exchange St.
1. Knight, Anna, 59 Mosebey Ave.
1. Kelley, Jennie, c, Second St.
1. Kershaw, Thos., Exchange St.
1. Krutcher, Chas., c.
2. Kohler, Amelia, 172 Alabama St.
2. Kaufman (infant), w, City Hospital.
2. Knight, Mrs., 49 Second St.
2. Ketler, B. F., 147 Madison St.
2. Kaufman, Louis.
2. Keeley, Annie.
2. Kelley, Hugh.
3. Keef, Annie, w.
4. Keef, w, Causey St.
4. Knight, Andy, c, 69 Second St.
5. Kadish, S., w.
5. Keyer, Martin J., w.
5. Kennedy, Mrs., w, cor. Mill & Third Sts.
5. Keff, R., 48 Front St.
5. Knox, Florence, w, Jefferson St.
6. Kallaher, Mike, w, Market St. Infirmary.
6. Kadish, Mrs., w.
6. Keyer, M. J., w, Monroe St.
7. Kernell, Mamie E.
7. Kassava, Adolph, w, Market St. Infirmary.
7. Kearney, Martin, w, 18 Market St.
7. Kenzler, Louis, w, Jefferson St.
7. Keefaber, A. W., w, Market St.
8. Kearns. Frank.
8. Kraft, P., 148 Washington St.
8. Kelley, Michael, w, Ross Ave.
8. Kipper, Morris S., 82 Greenlaw St.
8. Kifferel, Joseph, cor. Poplar & Manassas Sts.
8. Kearns, Henry, 35 Main St.
8. Kelley, Lucy, 95 De Soto St.
8. Kernell, Lizzie, c, 26 St. Martin St.
8. Kelly, Luckaby, w.
9. Kerr, A. W.
9. Kauffman. Henry.
9. Kauffman, Henry.
9. Kallaher, John, w, Jefferson St.
9. Kenney, Mr., w, Walker Ave.
9. Kite, Mrs., c, 22 Allen Ave.
9 Koser, James, Shelby County.
9. Kerr, J. M., w, Madison St.
10. Kilpatrick, L.

A HISTORY OF THE YELLOW FEVER.   223

Sept. 10. Kelley, Jane.
10. Kohlieldt, Irwin, w, Poplar St.
10. Kilpatrick, L., c, Toll-gate.
10. Kelley, George, c, County Jail.
10. Kitchens, H., c, 94 Pontotoc St.
10. Kofford, Mollie, cor. Poplar & Manassas Sts.
10. Kelley, Mrs. Hannah.
11. Kadish.
11. Kumpf, William.
11. Koch, William, Jr., w, 170 South St.
12. Kindal, Katie, w, 159 Second St.
12. Kuhn, Paul. w, Market St. Infirmary.
12. Kumpf, Matilda.
12. Kester, Susie, w, City Hospital.
13. Klearheart, John, w, Shelby County.
13. Kind, Bridget, w. Vance St.
13. King, Lewis, c, City Hospital.
13. Kelher, John, Hernando St.
13. Keeley, Cornelius, c, cor. Front & Jackson Sts.
14. Kennedy, Miss.
14. Kates, John S., c, cor. Linden & Shelby Sts.
15. Knowlton, L. S., w, South Alabama St.
15. Kelley, Tillie, Old Hen Island.
16. Kilbourne, Henry, w, 77 Beale St.
16. Kinney, James, w, City Hospital.
16. Keyser, A., w, Butler St.
17. Kamera, Louis, w, Brinkley Ave.
17. Kirwin, Davie, w, Union St.
17. Kines, Joseph, Shelby County.
17. Krinn, John, Madison St., extended.
18. Kennedy, W. A., State Female College.
22. Kane, John, w, Poplar St.
24. Kanfieldt, E., Poplar St.
24. Kanfieldt, Ephraim.
24. Kerchner Alice, w, Clay St.
25. Kircheval, E., w, Spring St.
25. Kinney, John M., w, Carolina St.
26. Kelley, F., c, cor. Gaines & First Sts.
26. Krinn, Mrs. J.
26. Kim, Louis.
27. Kaufman, Charles, w, Leath Orphan Asylum.
28. Kaufman, Samuel, w.
30. Kendall, Peter, w, Carolina St.
Oct. 1. King, H. S., w, Magnolia Block.
3. Koch, William, w, 170 South St.
3. Kathasena, Emma, w, Hernando Road.
3. Kerr, Wm., w, Moseby Ave.
3. Kendall, Robert, w, Randolph Road.
3. King, Margaret, w, Georgia St.
3. Klarutz, John, w, Market St. Infirmary.
3. Koenig, J. M., w, Market St. Infirmary.
4. Kerr, Mrs. J. H., w, Moseby Ave.
4. Kofford, Thomas, w, Raleigh Road.
5. Kraus, William, w, Horn Lake Road.
6. Kimball, Ida, c, Carolina St.
6. Kutsch, Theodore, w, Ft. Pickering.
8. Kutsch, Katie, w, Ft. Pickering.
8. Kerr, Mollie, w, Moseby Ave.
8. Kerr, John, w Moseby Ave.
9. Knox, Miss Charlotte, w, Breedlove Ave.
9. Krause, Carlotta, w, Lewis Ave.
10. Kney, Charlotte, w.
10. Kincaid, Emma, c, Butler St.
10. Kane, James, w, Market St. Infirmary.
12. Kinman, Thomas, w, Raleigh Road.
12. Kerr, Charles, w, 87 Moseby Ave.
14. Kelley, James, w, Shelby County.
14. Kraus, Mrs. B., w, Vance St.
16. Kaufman, Mrs. L., w, Trigg Ave.
16. Kennedy, Florence, w, State Female College.
16. Kamera, Miss E., w, Olympic Park.
17. Kraus, George, w, Vance St.
18. Keating, Dr. M. T., w, Peabody Hotel.
18. Kerger, Mrs R., w, Broadway St.
18. Kutsch, George, w, Walker Ave.
23. Kutsch, John, w, Walker Ave.
23. Kraus, Jacob, w. Vance St.
Nov. 2. Kilpatrick, c, City Hospital.
6. Keating, Miss Katie, w, Elliott St.
7. Kirk, Sam., w. Elliott St.
Aug. 14. Lusher, Charlie, w, Madison St.
15. Lowenhardt, Wm.
16. Lowenhardt, Mrs. Katie, 168 Poplar St.
17. Lavegna, Frank, w.

Aug. 17. Landigan, Richard, w.
17. Lang, Miss Augusta, w.
17. Latch, Miss Louisa, w.
17. Latch, Miss Amelia, w.
21. Levarts, Fannie, w, 158 Poplar St.
21. Lochneyer, Wm., City Hospital.
21. Large, Jack, w.
22. Lochmeyer, A., 9 Washington St.
25. Lemon, Nellie J., w, 450 Poplar St.
26. Lester, Mollie, 26 Winchester St.
26. Lynch, Mrs. Mary, 12 Alabama St.
26. Lynch, Mary, w, 12 Adams St.
27. Latsch, John, w, Robinson St.
27. Louis, Louisa, w, Main St
27. Lohman, Katie. w, South Alabama St.
28. Lee, James, w, 97 Commerce St.
28. Lee, Bennie, cor. Jackson & Front Sts.
28. Livingston, Henry, w, Poplar St.
29. Livingston, Fannie.
29. Lutz, Jacob, Sr., w, Winchester St.
29. Lynch, Mrs., w, 68 Commerce St.
29. Lannagan, Maggie, City Hospital.
29. Lynch, James, 12 Alabama St.
30. Louis, F. W., w, 187 Main St.
30. Lavallen, Catherine, w, 4 High St.
30. Lowe, Esther, c, Fifth St.
30. Lasalle, Mrs., w, 111 Poplar St.
30. Lemon, Tom, Jefferson St.
30. Lucas, Robert, c.
30. Lemon, George W., w, Poplar St.
30. Lulkenie, Joseph.
31. Lutz, Jacob, w, Winchester St.
31. Le Guerre, Julia H., w, Washington St.
31. Logan, Catherine, w, Linden St.
31. Lindsay, Charles, c, City Hospital.
31. Loranz, L. M., w, City Hospital.
31. Lemoy, Alexander, c, 141 Washington St.
31. Luster, Bettie, c, Pontotoc St.
Sept. 1. Lynd, Mike, 78 Commerce St.
1. Lacey, Mrs. C., w, Chelsea.
1. Lihnbenner, Gus., 518 Shelby St.
1. Loranz, James.
1. Lynch, Mike, w, Commerce St.
1. Lytus, Dick, c.
2. Lynch, James, w, 3 North Jackson St.
2. Lindhilen, Gus., w, 518 Shelby St.
2. Lane, H. B., w. City Hospital.
2. Lindsay, Charles, w, City Hospital.
2. Lanigham, Bridget, City Hospital.
2. Lindsay, Belle, w, Hernando St.
2. Looney, R. H. A., w, Adams St.
3. Locke, Robert, 176 Vance St.
3. Lott, Robert, 156 Union St.
3. Lowell, Carrie, c, Madison St.
4. Littig, Willie, w, Chelsea.
4. Le Guerre, Julia E., w, Washington St.
5. Lutherty, Kate, w, camp, Shelby County.
5. Lohman, George, cor. South Alabama and Second Sts.
5. Lohman, Mrs., w, Alabama St.
5 Le France, Henry, 39 Poplar St.
5. Lehman, Leo, w, South Alabama St.
6. Lee, Bennett, c, cor. Sycamore & Chelsea Sts.
6. Lohman, Ida, 982 Alabama St.
6. Leary, Mrs. Joanna, w, Second St.
6. Loop, Annie, w, Ladies' Mission.
7. Look, Err, w, Adams St.
7. Letcher, Fannie, 31 Ruth St.
8. Laverson, Mrs. C., w, Jackson St.
8 Lastin, Miss A., w, Auction St.
8. Lilly, W., c.
9. Loeb, Jacob, w.
9. Lindey, Miles, c, cor. Vance & Tennessee Sts.
9. Louffle. Charley, w, 63 Causey St.
9. Langster, Lucuis, cor.Echols & Vance Sts.
10. Love, Alice, w, South St.
10. Lannegan, Morris, c. 3 Overton St.
10. Lane, George, w, North Court St.
11. Leopold, Isaac.
11. Lieben, Edward.
11. Laws, L.,c, cor. Manassas & Robinson Sts.
11. Lindsay,W.T.,w,cor.Walnut & Vance Sts.
11. Lamb, L., 36 St. Paul St.
11. Legorini, Lewis, w, Beale St.
12. Ling, Lucy, w, Market St. Infirmary.
12. Lirch, Mrs. Rosini, w, Shelby St.
12. Lovely, Eveline, c.

Sept. 12. Landrum, Herbert S., w, Wellington St.
12. Lacey, A. T., w, cor. Fifth & Greenlaw Sts.
12. Long, A., c, Second St.
13. Lane, Jesse, c, 2.0 South St.
13. Leverre, Mrs. R. S., c, Washington St.
13. Larkin, Dan., 53 Bradford St.
14. Lego, Charles, w, 313 Union St.
14. Lewis, John, c, cor. Seventh St. and Walker Ave.
14. Lundy, Tom, c, cor. Seventh & Alabama Sts.
14. Lea, Berry, c, Humboldt Park.
14. Lane, Ira. c, De Soto St.
14. Lucas, M. A.
14. Lingner, Lizzie, w, Henry Ave.
15. Leman, William, w, Sycamore St.
15. Lay, John, w, City Hospital.
15. Lunn, Miss Reno, w, Vance St.
15. Lonsdale, J. G., Jr., w, Belleview Ave.
15. Lyons, Larry, 166 Gayoso St.
15. Linn, Rosa, w.
15. Lasse, Mrs., w.
16. Lidwell, F. M.
16. Linsey. Jack.
16. Lieben, Miss Amelia, w, 217 De Soto St.
16. Lunn, Thomas, w, Vance St.
16. Lunn, Phil. H., w, Vance St.
16. Lunn, William, Jr., w, Vance St.
16. Lair, J. N., w, St. Martin St.
17. Lunster, Fred., w, 17 Causey St.
17 Linkhause, Jacob.
17. Larry, J. N.
17. Leath, Hamilton, w, Manassas St.
17. Lee, Charles, w.
18. Lewis, Thomas, Pontotoc St.
18. Loeffle, E., w, 96 Alabama St.
19. Love, Buddy, w, north gate, Elmwood.
19. Love, Robert, w, Elmwood.
19. Lyons, Lizzie, Brinkley Ave.
19. Love, Charley, w, Hernando & South Sts.
19. Lane, Adolphus, w, De Soto St.
20. Lynch, Bernard, Third St.
20. Lucarani, J. F., w.
20. Lertura, Miss Louise, w, Boulevard.
20. Lonsdale, Mrs.J. G., Sr.,w, Belleview Ave.
20. Littlejohn, Lewis, w, Linden St.
20. Latham, Tillie, c, Rayburn Ave.
21. Linsey, Joseph, c, Manassas St.
21. Love, Annie, c, 237 Monroe St.
21. Lonfield, Mrs. W. W.
21. Lawton, R. H., Louisville, Ky.
21. Lewellyn, J. C., c, Walker Ave.
23. Lewis, John, w, Second St.
23. Lewis, Noel, c, 98 Pontotoc St.
25. Lyman, H. J., w, Beale St.
25. Landrum, George, w, Rayburn Ave.
25. Lawson, Fred., c, 70 Causey St.
25. Lonsford, Jno. T.
26. Love, Rosa, w, cor. Jackson and Fifth Sts.
26. Lewis, Mary, c,cor. Walker & Seventh Sts.
26. Latson, B., c, Bond's building, Ft. Pickering.
27. Lonsford (child of Jno. T.).
27. Lewellyn, Mary, c, Hernando Road.
29. Leach, John, w, Market St. Infirmary.
29. Luetke, Lewis, w, Broadway.
29. Layden, Margaret, w, Front St.
30. Leman, Henry, w, 7 Sycamore St.
30. Langford, C. R., w, Madison St.
30. Lane, Ed.
Oct. 1. Lonsdale, John G., Sr., w, Shelby St
1. Lanham, E. W.. w, Chelsea.
2. Locke, Susie, c, Sixth St.
2. Luala, West, 555 Main St.
2. Locke, Phœbe, c, Sixth St.
3. Ludy, Mrs.
3. Ludy, Lewis.
3. Lynch, Amelia, w, Washington St.
3. Lewis, Henry, c, City Hospital.
3. Locke, Phœbe, cor. Sixth & Jackson Sts.
3. Lake, Peter, c, Webster St.
4. Loranz, Sister, w, St. Peter's Orphan Asylum.
4. Lake, Miss Flora. w, Walnut St.
4. Lolinski, L, w, Market St. Infirmary.
5. Lee, Susan, c, 48 Sixth St.
5. Lane, Crawford, c, Broadway St.
5. Lewis, Mason. c, Marley St.
6. Lake, Wm. H., w, Walnut St.

Oct. 6. Labadie, Mrs., w, Horn Lake Road.
6. Lehman,Willie,w, cor. Front & Sycamore Sts.
6. L'Homme, Leon P., w, Market St. Infirmary.
7. Lightmore, Pope, c, South Jackson St.
7. Leon, Market St. Infirmary.
7. Lake, Robert, w, Walnut St.
7. Lowery, Dr. James, w, Georgia St.
7. Ludlow, F. W., w, Market St. Infirmary.
8. Lavaza, Emma, Shelby County.
8. Lamb, Edward, w, Overton Point.
8. Labesque, Mrs. J. M.,w,Horn Lake Road,
8. Lawhorn, Jack, c, Carolina St.
9. Lindenburg, Chas., w.
9. Lupkin, w, Walnut St.
10. Lany, Louisa, c, Country.
10. Lewis, George, c, 430 Hernando St.
10. Lubrella, Major, w, Anderson Ave.
11. Lee. Tish. c, Overton Point.
11. Love, Richard, c, St. Martin St.
11. Lane, Richard, c, Elliott St.
14. Lumb, Annie, w, City Hospital.
14. Lucas, Miss Lou., c, College St.
14. Lippold, Wiley, w, Washington St.
15. Leibing, John, w, Front St.
15. Lewis, Clara,c.cor.Jackson & La Rose Sts.
15. Lindenburg, Mrs. Annie, w, S. E. cor. Elmwood.
18. Lonsford (child of W. W.), w, Gas Works.
21. Lillie, Joe, c, 209 Gayoso St.
21. Lawrence, Jennie, w, City Hospital.
21. Lake, Daniel, w, Jackson St.
23. Lewis, Adeline, w, Walker Ave.
23. Lindon, Charles, w, Elmwood.
25. Lawrence, C., w, Richmond Ave.
25. Lott, c.
25. Lehman, Y., w, Raleigh.
26. Lucas, William, w, Boulevard.
27. Lagoria, A., w, Country.
28. Lee, Bettie, c, County Jail.
29. Leydon, Margaret, 61 Front St.
Nov. 3. Lonsdale, W. J. B., w, Dunlap St.
4. Lehman (infant of Y.).
11. Levy, Ephraim.
15. Loop, E. Rush, w, Manassas St.
16. Lutz, Mis. S. E., w, Exchange St.
Aug. 12. Mitchell, George, c.
12. McConnell, James, w, 448 Poplar St.
12. McCombs, R. H.
13. Monnegan, M. E., w, Alabama St.
13. Miller, John H., w, Adams St.
15. Miller, Ida G.
16. Macbeth, Mabel.
17. Miller, Irwin.
17 McGregor, 162½ Poplar St.
17. Meyers, Adolph, cor. Main and Washington Sts.
17. McMahon, Joseph, w. Commerce St.
19 Metcalf, Sam., w, Chelsea.
20. Mason, Philip, Johnson Ave.
20. McMahon. Mrs. Ann, w, Alabama St.
22. Madison, John, w, City Hospital.
22. Morgan, Henry, w, 65 De Soto St.
23 Metcalf, Emmons, w, Shelby County.
25. McKenna, Mr., w, City Hospital.
25. Mitchell, R. W., c.
26. Murphy, Frank, w, Commerce St.
26. Malone, Robert, Monroe St.
26. Miller, R. B., w, Fifth St.
26. McKeon, James, w, Poplar St.
27. Mac. Pat., w, City Hospital.
27. Mitchell, S., c, City Hospital.
27. McCall, Henry, cor. Walnut and Pontotoc Sts.
27. Mitchell, Charley, 155 Main St.
27. Miller, Joe. w, City Hospital.
27. McKinn, Mrs. Mary, w, Poplar St.
27. Morris, Mrs. Alice, w, Poplar St.
27. McKinn. Raleigh.
27. Melvin, Robert, Monroe St.
28. McIlvaine, Mrs. Mary, Brinkley Ave.
28. Muller, Albert, w, Poplar St.
28. Miller, S. B., w, Alabama St.
28. Moffat, John.
28. McGiveney, Thomas, w. Carroll Ave.
28. Montgomery, Wm., w, Exchange St.
28. Michaels, Gus., w, City Hospital.
28. Morris, James, w, 144 Moseby Ave.

A HISTORY OF THE YELLOW FEVER.   225

Aug. 28. Maginus, Anetta, w, Market Square.
28. Malone, Josie, c, Monroe St.
28. McKain, Mrs. John, 35 Johnson Ave.
28. Many, James, Louisville, Ky.
29. McKain, 166 Washington St.
29. Martha, City Hospital.
29. Mary Ann, foot of Exchange St.
29. Morse, David, Alabama St.
29. Morris, James, 144 Moseby Ave.
29. Moreall, child, alley, between Main and Front Sts.
29. Miller, Auguste, w, Hupert St.
29. McGarvey, John R., w, St. Peter's Orphan Asylum.
29. Miner, T. F., w, Central Ave.
30. McKay, Catherine, Poplar St.
30. Miller, Mrs. S. B.
30. McMillan, Mrs. M., w, Winchester St.
30. Murphy, Olissa, w, Front St.
30. Melton, Thomas, 173 Jefferson St.
31. Magee, Susan, c, Elliott St.
31. Meyers, Ado'ph, w, Washington St.
31. Moore, W. W., w, Second St
31. McConley, James B., w, Hernando St.
31. Manly, Maggie Ellen, w, Winchester St.
31. McWilliams, C., w, County Jail.
Sept. 1. Macklin, A.
1. Mansford, E. J., w, Second St.
1. Morgan, Walter, w, Johnson Ave.
1. Merritt, George R., w, Orleans St.
1. Miller, J. W., w, Marshall Ave.
1. McElroy, W. N., w, Second St.
1. Morrill, R. R., w, 43 Poplar St.
1. Malone, Mike, w, 79½ Concord St.
1. McDonald, Mrs., w, Poplar St.
2. Meadows, Jane.
2. Madden, Wm., w, cor. Mulberry and Linden Sts.
2. Malone, Maria, c, cor. Third and Concord Sts.
2. Malone, Albert, cor. Safferans & Fifth Sts.
2. Molton, Uriah, w, Main St.
2. Morgan, John, w, Johnson Ave.
2. Meadows, Jane.
2. Menken, Nathan D., w, Peabody Hotel.
2. Madden, J. J., w, Yates Lake.
2. Miller, Mrs. John G., 224 Hernando St.
3. Morgan, Delia, c, Greenlaw St.
3. McCullough, Mrs. Ben., w.
3. McCullough, son of Ben., w.
3. Mullaney, Peter, w, Dunlap St.
3. McGirk, A., c, Lauderdale St.
3. Mitchell, Mrs. R. W., w, Fort Pickering.
3. Morgan, Delia, cor. Sixth and Greenlaw Sts.
3. McCullough, Mrs. Ben , w, Old Raleigh Road.
3. McCullough, Ben., w, Old Raleigh Road.
3. Mullaven, Orphan Asylum.
3. Murphy, John, w, City Hospital.
3. Mason, 243 Monroe St.
3. Murphy, Eliza. 9 Front St.
4. Mitche, Mrs. Mollie, Main St.
4. Mulligan, Richard, w, Monroe St.
4. Mackenzie, w, cor. South & Tennessee Sts.
4. McCauley, John, w, cor. De Soto & Beale Sts.
4. Maher, Mike, w. City Hospital.
4. Mud, John G., w, 224 Hernando St.
5. Moore, Edward, w, 199 Main St.
5. Moran, Mike, City Hospital.
5. Maddox, Robert O., w, City Hospital.
5. Moch, Millie, c, 129 De Soto St.
5. McCormick, John, w, Winchester St.
5. Moore, Virgil V., w, Pontotoc St.
5. McClellan, Millie, c.
5. McLane, John W., w, 319 Main St.
5. Maloney, Peter, w, Dunlap St.
5. McGorks, Alabama, w, Lauderdale St.
6. MacDougal, Chas. H., w, Gayoso St.
6. McDowell, Mrs.
6. Mitchell, Slater, c, Dunlap St.
6. Macelfresh, James, w, Peabody Hotel.
6. McLean, John, w, 319 Adams St.
6. Marshall, Henry, c. 248 Third St.
6. Moran, Mike, w, City Hospital.
6. McDew, c, 274 Washington St.
6. Moore, Miles, c, cor. Safferans & Looney Sts.

Sept. 7. McGhee, Tony, c, cor. Shelby & Vance Sts.
7. Moore, Miller. c, cor. Sycamore & Looney Sts.
7. McKinley, Mrs. E., w, Poplar St.
7. McDonald, Rosa, w, City Hospital.
7. Motley, Ike, c, Broadway.
7. Macnamara, John, 17 South St.
7. Meil, Michael C., w, Vance St.
7. Mead, Dr. W. C., w, Peabody Hotel.
7. Martin, J. R.
7. Malsi, Conrad.
7. Morton, Lewis, 66 De Soto St.
7. Moore, Miles.
7. McCracken, Miss M., w.
8. Macklin. Eliza, c.
8. Mazedye, Jeanetta, Van Buren St.
8. Mynatt, Lizzie, w, Alabama St.
8. Mynatt, Thos. B., w, Alabama St.
8. Manley, Theresa, w, Moseby Ave.
8. Marooney, David, 101 Pontotoc St.
8. McBride, Emma, cor. De Soto and Gayoso Sts.
8. McBindley, Ed., on Lamb Place.
8. Murphy, Mollie, w, 9 Front St.
8. McConnell, A., w, 147 Robinson St.
8. Mitchell, Josephine. c, cor. Overton and Promenade Sts.
8. Miller, Ferd. A., w, Brownsville.
8. Maucher, A., w.
8. Manley, Y. R., w.
9. Mackenzie, Mrs. S. A., w, cor. South and Tennessee Sts.
9. Mazetta, Annie, w, 188 Beale St.
9. Meek, Miss Sallie, w. Walker Ave.
9. Mitchell, Mollie, w, 95 De Soto St.
9. McMichaels, Thos., Market St. Infirmary.
9. Macether, A., Medical College, Union St.
9. Mackenzie (child of Ed.), w, Merriweather Ave.
9. Mack, Charles, 307 Fifth St.
9. Mathews, Mrs. F., w, Shelby St.
9. Mead, James.
9. Morrissey, Peter.
9. Mackenzie, E. S., cor. South and Tennessee Sts.
9. Mures, J., c, Pontotoc St.
9. Milenus, Father, w, Main St.
9. McArnish, Promenade St.
10. McGilvrey, Mrs. J. G.
10. McCauley, J. W.
10. Milden, Jennie.
10. McFall, Mollie E., 40 Cau ey St.
10. Morrissey, Peter, w, Third St.
10. Malone, Louis, c, cor. Third and Overton Sts.
10. Mulvahill, P. J., w, Market St. Infirmary.
10. McCloy, G. W., w, Market St. Infirmary.
10. Morris, James P., Louisville, Ky.
10. McKinley, child of., Boulevard.
10. Moore, Ernest, 45 Mulberry St.
11. Miller, D., c, 133 Monroe St.
11. McConnell, Tom, w, 147 Robinson St.
11. Mitchell, Moses, 334 Jefferson St.
11. Merrill, Wm., c, Valentine Ave.
11. Mary, c, Carolina St.
11. Mathews, F. A., w, Shelby St.
11. McGowen, Michael.
11. Mullen, George.
11. McPartland, 323 Madison St.
11. Madsley, John.
11. Murphy, Jane, c, Main St.
11. Mitchell, Joe, c, City Hospital.
12. Morrison, Channing M., w, Main St.
12. McClellan. c, Causey St.
12. McGraw, Nellie, w, Vance St.
12. Mahoney, Hannah, w, Second St.
12. Moore, C. G., w, Walnut St.
12. Meyers, Frances, w, Linden St.
12. Morgan, John, w, Orleans St.
12. Malone, Ned., c, 192 Beale St.
12. Madley, Frank, 28 Winchester St.
12. Moore, Charles, w, cor. Walnut and Tate Sts.
12. McBride, Margaret, Chelsea.
12. Murphy, Sam., Linden St. Infirmary.
12. McLemore, Jordan, c, 161 Gayoso St.
12. McLaughlin, Florence, w, City Hospital.
12. Maron, Reuben, c.
13. McSheve, John, 274 Second St.

Sept. 13. McKee, Sallie, c, Walker Ave.
13. Mary, c, Short Turley St.
13. McKinley, Mrs., w, Lamb Place.
13. MacDonald, c, 62 Spring St.
13. Morton, Bettie, c, Central Point.
13. McGee, Charles, w, Beale St.
13. Mynatt, Henry, w, 235 Alabama St.
13 Miller, William, w, Dunlap St.
13. Massey, Joseph, w, 10 Howard's Row.
13. Madhardt, Elizabeth, w, Hernando St.
13. Mirty, Tennie, w, Shelby St.
13. Miller, George S., w, Market St.
13. McShean, John, w, Seventh St.
13. Marks, M., c, Madison St.
14. Malone, Mrs. Wesley, McLemore Ave.
14. Miles, H.
14. Mayo, Samuel, w, cor. Madison and De Soto Sts.
14. McIlvaine, Mrs., c, cor. Linden and Wellington Sts.
14. McCall, Henry, w, cor. Pontotoc and Walnut Sts.
14. McCalf, Zac., City Hospital.
14. Murphey, Margaret, City Hospital.
14. McCurley, Thomas, w, Market St. Infirmary.
14. McRendle, Edmonds, w, Market St. Infirmary.
14. Murdock, Lottie, w, Beale St.
14. Miller, Laura.
14. McClann, John, w, cor. Vance & Walnut Sts.
14. McCadden, Mary Ann, c.
14. McCall, Henry, cor. Walnut & Pontotoc Sts.
14. Manning, George, w.
14. Mulligan, Tom. w, Winchester St.
14. McElroy, E., w, Waldron Place.
14. Mayes, Sam., c, 23 Madison St.
15. Marks, George, cor Seventh & Jackson Sts.
15. McGregor, Dr. T. H., w, Linden St.
15. McCallister, J., c.
15. Major, T. W. J.
15. Mahaffey, H. J., w.
15. McDowell, J. W., w, Madison & Second Sts.
15. Maag, George, w, Walker Ave.
15. Morrison, Florence, c, Georgia St.
15. McCullock, S. J., w, Market St. Infirmary.
15. McKinley, Mr., w, 148 Beale St.
15. McLemore, Belle, c, 161 Gayoso St.
15. Martin, Mrs. Maria, w, Market St.
15. Mulligan, F., w, McGhee's Station.
15. McLane, Morgan, 430 Linden St.
15. Massar, J. N., w.
16. Maag, Mrs. George, w, Walker Ave.
16. Marshall, E. C., w, Peabody Hotel.
16. McCain, George, w, 69 Fifth St.
16. McDonald, Peter, w, City Hospital.
16. Moses, Albert, c, City Hospital.
16. McDonald, Charles, c, 176 Spring St.
16. McFreeley, William, w, 177 Second St.
16. Marks, Mrs., w. cor. Sixth St. & Walker Ave.
16. Miller, Granville, c, Seventh St.
16. Moss, Major, c, Thomas Ave.
16. Manierre, Dr. Thos. W., w, Court St. Infirmary.
16. McCallum, W. D., w, 19 Madison St.
16. Moffat, Wm., w, Wright Ave.
16. Miller, Andrew, c, cor. Clay and Main Sts.
16. McManus, Sam'l W., w, Woodlawn.
17. McCullough, Bill, cor. Third & Overton Sts.
17. Mathews, Ferdie, w, cor. High and Washington Sts.
17. Moeller, Louis, cor. Main and Washington Sts.
17. Mofford, Wm.
17. McMunson, A. H.
17. Merriman, Georgia, 449 Hernando St.
17. Mason, Jane.
17. Mike, w, cor. Gayoso and Hernando Sts.
17. May, W. B.
17. McNamara, Mrs., w, Shelby St.
17. Marion, George, w, 449 Hernando St.
17. Madison, H., w, City Hospital.
17. Martin, Mary, w, City Hospital.
17. Manches, Gus., w, Medical College.
17. Moon (child of Alice), c, Causey St.
17. McMann, A. H., w, Rayburn Ave.
17. Mason, Jane, c, Ruth St.
17. McManus, A. S., w, Howard Infirmary.

Sept. 18. Mays, C., c, City Hospital.
18. McCullock, Wm., c, 58 Third St.
18. Moore, Mrs., w, cor. Maxwell and Safferans Sts.
18. Moon, W. J., Jr,, w.
18. Morti, Gus. A., w, cor. Shelby & South Sts.
18. Mogrige, Lottie.
18. Miller, Wm., cor. Looney & Manassas Sts.
18. McClellan, Wiley.
18. McCullom, W. D.
18. Meagher, Patrick.
18. Mitchell, J. H., w, Court St. Infirmary.
18. Mullett, Massy.
18. Mitchell, Mrs. Jno. H., w, Mill St.
18. McNeil, Mrs.
18. McDonald, J. W., Fifth St.
18. Meaher, Annie. w, 41 Fifth St.
19. Monier, C. V. S., w, Beale St.
19. Meyers, William, w, Ft. Pickering.
19. McCormick, W., w, Market St. Infirmary.
19. Maltese, Mrs., w, 23 Echols St.
20. Moseby, Mary, cor. Linden & Walnut Sts.
20. Mackenzie. H., c, City Hospital.
20. McGregor, Robert, w, 3 Wicks Ave.
20. Martin, Cornelius, cor. Third and Washington Sts.
20. McNamara, L.
20. Malone, C. C., w. McLemore Ave.
20. Morris, Frank, c, Second St.
20. Moody, Mary, c, cor. Linden & Walnut Sts.
21. McMenema, Francis J., w, Rayburn Ave.
21. Montgomery, J. D.
21. Marsh, Robbie, w, Pontotoc St.
21. Michel, Miss Annie.
21. Meyers, John, w, 300 Front St.
21. Morrow, J. S., w, Hernando Road.
21. McCoy, Miss Minnie, w, Pigeon Roost R'd.
21. Mhoon, R. B., w, Poplar St.
21. Mathews, Mrs. F., c, Mackelroy Ave.
21. McCrea, Mr., w, Second St.
21. Morton, William, c, cor. Walnut and Spring Sts.
21. Mathews, John, c., De Soto St.
22. McConnell, Alex., w, 59 Ross Ave.
23. Morgan, Mrs., w. Henry Ave.
23. McNeil, Willie, c, Short Third St.
23. Monteverdi, Miss K., w, Boulevard.
23. McGilvrey, David, w, Poplar St.
23. Morton, Miss Lizzie, w, Hernando Road.
23. McNeil, Annie, w.
23. Moseby, Emily, Mill St.
24. Montgomery (child of J. D.).
24. Moore, Jessie, 504 Rayburn Ave.
24. McDonald, Susie.
24. Marks, F.
24. Milton, Frank, w, 280 Second St.
24. McCall, F. F., w, 10 Jefferson St.
24. Moseby, Emily, c. Carolina St.
24. Mumford, w, Canfield Asylum.
25. McKinney, John, cor. Carolina & Fifth Sts.
25. Mullen, George, w. Market St. Infirmary.
25. Mullen, Mrs. Willie, w, Market St. Infirmary.
25. Monteverdi, Mary, w, Boulevard.
25. Meath, John, w, De Soto St.
25. McNulty, Robt., Jones Ave.
25. Marshall (child of Sam.), 110 Winchester St.
25. Moss, Mrs. A., c, Second St.
26. McCoy, Sallie.
26. Mitchell, Jno. H., w, Mill St.
26. McDonald, Wm. R.
26. Moore, G. W., 54 Jackson St.
26. Maurie, Annie.
26. Maunord (child of B.), c, cor. St. Martin and South Sts.
26. Meath, Thomas, w, De Soto St.
26. Miller, W. W. C., w, 448 Main St.
26. Merritt, Jane, c. 278 Linden St.
26. McNamara (child of John), w, 139 Main St.
27. Mordinn, Jno. H., w, Market St. Infirmary.
27. Mooney, Rev. Father, w, Camp Father Mathew.
27. McClannahan, Mrs. H., w, Main St.
27. McDowell, Carrie, w, Walker Ave.
27. Massa, Mary A., Poplar St.
27. McKitchen, J. N., White Haven.
27. Moreney, Mrs. M.
27. McDonald, Mrs. J. W., w, cor. Georgia & Fifth Sts.

A HISTORY OF THE YELLOW FEVER. 227

Sept. 28. Milburne Ed., Walnut St.
28. McKay, Mack, c, near Elmwood.
28. Marks, Jacob, w.
28. Massa, Mrs., w, Poplar St.
28. Mahoney (child of Mrs.), w, Dunlap St.
28. Maloney, Eliza, w, Pontotoc St.
29. Mallon, Green, c, Georgia St.
29. Millican, C. R., w, McGhee's Station.
29. Mead, Francis, w, Cherry Ave.
29. Moran, W. F., 353 Main St.
30. Miller, Caroline, cor. Central Ave. and Trezevant St.
30. McCall, Robert, w, Pontotoc St.
30. McDowell, Henry, w, Walker Ave.
30. Meredith, Bettie, c, Walker Ave.
30. Miller, w, Market St, Infirmary.
Oct. 1. Martley, Wm. P., c, Fort Pickering.
1. Mhoon W. J., w, Poplar St.
1. Michot, Minnie, w, Horn Lake Road.
1. Michels, N., w, Walker Ave.
1. Mann, Sallie.
1. McKenna, Mrs. Annie, Louisville, Ky.
1. McDonald, J. W., w, De Soto St.
1. Maur, Tillie, w, Raleigh Road.
1. Moran, John, w.
2. Moran, John.
2. Moore, W. H., w, Georgia St.
2. Mueller, G. W., w, Carolina St.
2. Michot, Eugene, w, Horn Lake Road.
2. Mack, Mike, w, Georgia St.
3. Marks, H.
3. Mhoon, Miss M. S., w, Poplar St.
3. McClure. Mrs. M.
4. Mason, Jack, c, Ruth St.
4. Murphy, Louisa, c, 440 Shelby St.
4. Murray, Henry, c, Linden St. Infirmary.
5. Mack, Ann, w, City Hospital.
5. McGregor, James, Hernando St.
5. Morrow, Miss Jennie, w, Hernando St.
5. Morrow, Mrs. Julia, w, Hernando St.
5. Manning, Pat., w, Center Alley.
5. Moffat, Edward, Shelby County.
5. Miller, Jos. E., w, Market St. Infirmary.
5. Moseby, Charlie.
5. Munter, Carl, w, Springdale.
5. McGregor, Jos., w.
6. Moseby, Mrs., w, Boulevard.
6. Morris, John, w, New Raleigh Road.
6. Michot, Lady, w, Horn Lake Road.
6. Mhoon, J. G., w, Poplar St.
7. Miller, John E., Market St. Infirmary.
7. Michot, Miss Eliza, w, Horn Lake Road.
7. Mitchell, Avery, Shelby County.
7. McNeil, Charles, w, Memphis & Charleston R. R.
8. McGowen, Jane.
8. McMillen, William, w, Jackson St.
8. McMillen, E. J., w, Jackson St.
8. McGowen, Charlie, c, Ft. Pickering.
8. McGowen, James, w, Shelby County.
9. Meyers, Pete., w, City Hospital.
9. McClure, George, c, City Hospital.
9. Martin, T., w, City Hospital.
9. Mallory. A. H., w, David Ave.
9. Meyer, Caroline, w, Ft. Pickering.
9. Massengale, A. S., w, country.
9. Maloney, Edward, w, Raleigh Road.
9. Monnegan, Mrs. Ellen, w, Poplar St.
9. Maley, Mary A., w, Main St.
9. Mallory, L. H., w, David Ave.
10. McNeil, James, w, Memphis & Charleston R. R.
10. Morean, E., w.
10. Madison, c, cor. Hernando & Walnut Sts.
11. McCartney, Mrs. M., w. Calvary Cemetery.
11. Meyer, Rest., Alabama St.
11. McDonald, Kate, w, Calvary Cemetery.
12. Maloney, Miss Maggie, M, Raleigh Road.
12. Maurer, Phil., w, Poplar St.
13. McDonald, Cornelius, w, Jones Ave.
13. Morris, Mary, w, cor. Manassas St. and Lane Ave.
14. Murphy, Jeremiah, w, 38 Front St.
14. Mann, Eddie, w, cor. Union St. & Waldron Ave.
14. Manuel, R. C., w, Adams St.
14. Meyer, William, w, Ft. Pickering.
14. Martin, Sam., c, Linden St. Infirmary.
14. Meyers, Ed., c, foot of Jackson St.

Oct. 14. Moore, Robert, c, City Hospital.
14. Martin, Joseph, w, City Hospital.
15. Maloney, Gracie, c, cor. Georgia and Seventh St.
15. Mayhew (infant of Wm.), w, Carolina St.
16. Morris, John, w, cor. Manassas St. and Lane Ave.
16. Morris, Mrs., w, cor. Manassas St. and Lane Ave.
16. Morris (son of John), w, cor. Manassas St. & Lane Ave.
16. Maddox, Charles, w, Thomas Ave.
16. McKay, D. L., w, Nesbit Station.
17. Michot, E. L., w, Horn Lake Road.
18. Marsden, John, w, 73 De Soto St.
18. McCoy, R. J., w, Poplar St.
18. Morton, Albert, w, Hernando St.
19. Monsuratt, Oscar, w, Valentine Ave.
19. McCrowell, Mrs.
19. McElroy, Patrick, w, Boulevard.
19. Martingley, M. A., w, Chrisman Place.
20. McLemore, John, c, cor. Tennessee and Linden Sts.
20. Maher, Wm., w, Turley St.
20. Mead, Sarah A., w, Peyton Ave.
21. Messick, Mr., w, Raleigh Road.
22. McAnelly, W. T., w, Main St.
23. Marks, Moses, w, Raleigh Road.
24. Mahaffey, L. W., w, Wellington St.
24. Mathews, William, c, McLemore Ave.
24. Mayo, Martha.
24. Malsi, Miss Caroline, w, Poplar St.
26. Meyers, Linda, c, Jackson St.
28. Mahon, Miss H., w, Pigeon Roost Road.
28. Mason, I. B., w.
31. Miller Phœbe, 111 Exchange St.
Nov. 4. McCabe, James, w, Henry Ave.
4. Martin, Michael, w, Davis Ave.
5. Martin, V. B., w, country.
5. Miller, Lucy, c.
9. McKeon, M., w.
11. May, Mrs. Mintie, w, Wilson Station.
13. McBride, Mary, w, Commerce St.
16. McGee, Martha, c.
17. Moore, Emma T., w, Gholson St.
21. Mowbry, R. A.
25. Mason, c, Alabama St.
25. Martin, John, c.
Aug. 12. Neighbors, Katie, c, Madison St.
17. Nelson, Susan H.
17. Nelson, Samuel.
20. Natchtbrand, J., Hupert St.
24. Nolan, Mary, w, City Hospital.
24. Noel, Emma, w, Vance St.
25. Norris, Mary E., w, City Hospital.
26. Nicholson, Robert.
26. Nelson, Mollie, w.
28. Napier, A., c, 7 Dunlap St.
28. Novitzky, Annie, w, Bradford St.
29. Nelms, Thomas, 173 Jefferson St.
30. Newman, Mrs. Mary, 128 Washington St.
30. Noonar, John.
31. Newman, James, De Soto St.
31. Newsom, Ida, w, Overton St.
Sept. 1. Norment, Tom, 256 Washington St.
1. Norment, Joseph, c.
3. Norris, Mrs., City Hospital.
4. Noble, Mary, City Hospital.
6. Nelson, Andrew, c, Poplar St.
6. Norris, John, w, 77 Front St.
7. Nelson, David, w, Monroe St.
8. Neeley, Frederick, c.
8. Neeley, Ed., c, cor. Orleans & Jefferson Sts.
9. Nelson, Dr. W. W., w, Trigg Ave.
10. Nelson, Martha, c, Exchange St.
10. Nichols, W. L., w, High St.
10. Noel, T., w, Vance St.
10. Noun, Ernest, County Jail.
10. Nelson, Mrs. 55 Exchange St.
10. Newhouse, Miss A. M., Market St. Infirmary.
11. Noel, Mrs., w, Vance St.
12. Nelding, N., w, Market St. Infirmary.
12. Nicolati, F., w, City Hospital.
14. Nelson, Albert, c, Gaines St.
14. Nolton, Eugenia, W., w.
15. Nilton, Margaret, w.
15. Nelson, Otto, w, 518 Shelby St.
15. Nelson, Albert, c, Woolen Mill.

228   A HISTORY OF THE YELLOW FEVER.

Sept. 15. Nugent, Dr. P. C., w, Court St. Infirmary.
18. Noble, Robert, w, Market St. Infirmary.
18. Noeler, Louis, w, cor. Main & Washington Sts.
19. Nail, John W., w, Elmwood.
20. Nelson, Romeo, c.
20. Nance, Spencer, c, Poplar St.
20. Nelson, Samuel, c, Linden St. Infirmary.
20. Neil, Mrs. M. C., w, near Elmwood.
21. Norman, Mrs. A. A., w.
21. Noah, Ellen, c, Gholson St.
21. Nelson, Mrs., w, Carolina St.
21. Nicholson, S. B.
23. Niewmann, W., w, Poplar St.
25. Nash, w, Manassas St.
25. Nutall, M. K., w, Market St. Infirmary.
29. Norman, Lewis, cor. Butler & Shelby Sts.
29. Noonan, Mary, w, Vance St.
30. Noonan, Mrs., w, Vance St.
Oct. 1. Nelson, Victor, w, Trigg Ave.
2. Nagle, Mrs. T., w, Broadway St.
3. Norfolk. John Henry, w, 163 Chester St.
3. Nelm, William, c, Sixth St., Ft. Pickering.
3. Nelm, Mollie, c, Sixth St., Ft. Pickering.
4. Nelson, Miss Julia, w, Trigg Ave.
5. Nelson, Mrs., Dr. A. W., w, Trigg Ave.
8. Nichols, John B.
10. Nail, Mrs. Mary, w, Walker Ave.
10. Nichols, Wm. L., High St.
12. Nutting, G. A., w, Overton Point.
12. Northrup, Rachael E., w, Chester St.
15. Naylor, Samuel, c, Main St.
16. North, Nelson, w, 169 Orleans St.
21. Nicholson, S. B., w, Broadway St.
28. Norman, Willie F.
Aug. 17. O'Brien, Willie A.
18. O'Donnell, Bridget.
26. O'Brien, Mrs. Ann, w, Manassas St.
26. Overtel, H., w, 177 Adams St.
28. Owen, A. J., 213 Court St.
30. Oakley, Walter D., w, Union St.
30. Owen, Henry, c, 173 Adams St.
30. O'Gara, Mary, w, Brinkley Ave.
30. O'Hearn, Mary, w, Winchester St.
31. O'Hara, John D., w, Whitemore House.
31. Otey, George, c, 61 Linden St.
31. Otto, A., w, City Hospital.
Sept. 2. O'Leary, John, w, De Soto St.
2. Oslay, Helen, City Hospital.
2. O'Hara, James T., w.
3. O'Connor, John, Jr., w, 115 Main St.,
3. O'Connor, John, Sr., w, 115 Main St.
4. Otto, Geo., w, 46 Orleans St.
5. Owen, Minnie, c, Jones Ave.
5. Orselle, E., w, Hernando St.
6. O'Brien, M., w, Manassas St.
6. Owens, Dock, c, cor. Hill & Robinson Sts.
6. Oriega, Lewis, w, Linden St.
6. O'Leary, Mrs. J., Second St.
8. O'Brien, Willie, w.
8. O'Brien, Terrence, w.
8. Overton (child), Overton St.
8. Owens, Jane, c, 68 Causey St.
8. Owens, Pierce, 68 Causey St.
8. Owens, Mary, w, Gayoso House.
8. O lell, Mrs. C., w, South St.
8. O'Neill, M., w, Vance St
9. Owens, James, 68 Causey St.
9. O'Farrell, Hugh, w, Main St.
11. O'Barst, Catherine, w, Thomas Ave.
12. O'Connor, John, w, 115 Main St.
12. O'Donnell, Wm., w, City Hospital.
13. O'Connor, c, Spring St.
13 O'Connor, Mary, Market St. Infirmary.
13. O'Farrell, Annie, c, 155 Beale St.
13. Odell, Ellen, 183 South St.
13. O'Connell, Ellen, w.
13. O'Connell, John, c, Clay St.
14. Onetta, G.
15. O'Neil, James, w, cor. Seventh and Jackson Sts.
15. Offutt, Alfred N., 170 Burlington St.
16. O'Brien, Patrick, w, 17 Jackson St.
16. O'Neil, Mrs. Maggie, w, Hernando Road.
16. Ording, Gertrude, w. 539 Main St.
17. Oberst, Wm., w, Thomas Place.
17. Olloted, Fred., w, Market St. Infirmary.
17. O'Donnell, Mrs , w, Main St.
18. Owen, Julia.

Sept. 19. O'Brien, John, w, 42 Jefferson St.
20. O'Neil, Alice, w, Bradford St.
23. Oliver, Lou., c, cor. Hernando and Broadway.
24. Oliver, Z. P., 82 Gayoso St.
27 O'Maley, Mrs., w, Orleans St.
28. Otey, Dr. Paul H., w, Dunlap St.
28. Oehmer, Martin.
29. O'Brien, Jerry, w, Main St.
30. O'Brien, James, w, Main St.
30. O'Connor, Bridget, 182 Front St.
Oct. 3. O'Nealey, Patrick.
6. Owens, John, w, Market St. Infirmary.
7. O'Connell, Mrs. C., w, Auction Square.
7. Owens, Julia M., w, Kerr Ave.
8. Owens, Thos. J., w, Kerr Ave.
9. O'Hearn, Miss H., w, Walker Ave.
9. Onley, Miss Emma, w, Raleigh Road.
9. O'Maley, Mary Ann, w, Main St.
9. Obermeimer, Joe, w, Boulevard.
12. Oberst, Catherine, Thomas Ave.
12. Onley, John.
13. Oberst, Miss Julia, w, Thomas Ave.
14. Oskman, Henry, w, Estival Park.
16. Oates, W. J., w, McLemore Ave.
18. Owens, Emma.
23. O'Keefe, Mamie, w, Breedlove Ave.
Nov. 11. Oates, Miss Laura, w, McLemore Ave.
Aug. 13. Perkins, Jefferson, Monroe St.
15. Patterson, Laura B.
17. Pease, Miss Lucy.
17. Packer, C. A., w.
20. Payne, Mary, Fifth St.
20. Peoples, Jennie.
20. Porter, William.
20. Pease, Fannie, w, 177 Second St.
21. Penn, Maggie, c, Washington St.
21. Paynes, Mary, w.
21. Pullen, Minerva, w, Gill's Station.
21. Page, William, Main St.
22. Porter, William, w, 91 Commerce St.
24. Price, Edward, w.
25. Pagles, Charles, w, 105 Main St.
25. Pollock, Samuel, w, Fourth St.
25. Parish, Brooks, c, City Hospital.
28. Precomp, G. L., w, Allen Ave.
28. Pratt, Patsey, cor. Third and Jefferson Sts.
28. Pearsall, A.
29. Patton, E. S., 37 Robinson St.
30. Powers, Edward, w, Poplar St.
31. Payne, Mary, c, Bass Ave.
31. Pleasant. Dilly, c, 33 Robinson St.
31. Powell, Charley, c, Monroe St.
31. Power, Green, c.
Sept. 1. Plischke, Chas. H., w, Vance St.
1. Pohl, Annie, Orleans St.
1. Price, Edward, c, Pontotoc St.
2. Pohl, Theodore, w, Jefferson St.
2. Privett, Miles, w, White's Station.
2. Pearson, Eliza, 86 Washington St.
2. Pryor, James, cor. Looney and Fourth Sts.
2. Perotti, Vincent, w, cor. Union and De Soto Sts.
2. Pelequin, Rosamond.
3 Potter, John.
3. Pryor, Melinda, cor. Fourth and Safferans Sts.
3. Perkins, N. T., w, Orleans St.
3. Pagels, Amelia, w, Main St.
3. Palmer, Dennis, c, City Hospital.
3. Pryor, Green.
3. Price, Annie, w, 173 Third St.
4. Parker, G. A., c, 109 Madison St.
4. Penn, City Hospital.
4. Pagels, Otto, w, Main St.
5. Pocai, Henry, w, Hernando St.
5. Powers, John H., w, Madison St.
5. Patillo, Lucy J., w, Walker Ave.
5. Parker, Eli, c, 173 Jefferson St.
5. Parker, Charlotte, c, cor. Looney and Seventh Sts.
5. Pryor, Matilda, cor. Fourth and Safferans Sts.
5. Pad, John, w, City Hospital.
5. Plummer, Frank, w, De Soto St.
6. Pease, Mrs. Nancy, w, Second St.
6. Parsons, Rev. C. C., w, Poplar St.
6. Phillips, Wm., Chelsea.
6. Pandert, Annie, w, 16 Second St.

A HISTORY OF THE YELLOW FEVER. 229

Sept. 7. Philmot, Mrs. Annie, 388 Main St.
7. Picot, Victor, w, 192 Robinson St.
7. Powell, M. T., w, 7 West Court St.
8. Plummer. Miss, w.
8. Polk, Amanda, 208 Gayoso St.
8. Pharow, Phil.
8. Potter. Mrs., Market St Infirmary.
8. Polk, Maud, 208 Gayoso St.
8 Pryor, Mick, 31 Robinson St.
8. Pilch, 56 Second St.
8. Purdy. Chrissa, 121 Union St.
8. Paul, N. P., w, Jefferson St.
8. Patillo, R. F., w, Walnut St.
9. Prescott, Walter, w, Chelsea St.
9. Presh, Fred., w, 220 Main St.
9 Perkins, Henry, 97 De Soto St.
9. Petway, S., c, Beale St.
9. Perfect, Ernest, w, Market St. Infirmary.
9. Perodeau, B. D., w, 77 Main St.
9. Parker, S.
10. Piper, J. H., w.
11. Parker, James G., Market St. Infirmary.
11. Patchell, James, w, 699 Poplar St.
10. Peck, F. B., w, Raleigh Road.
10. Payne. Michael, w, Market St. Infirmary.
10. Park, James G., w, Market St.
10. Peters, Wm.. Hernando St.
10. Pharow, Phil., w, Ross Ave.
11. Pohl, Mrs. Theodore, w, Vance St.
11. Patillo. R. H.. w, Walnut St.
11. Page, G., c, 147 Causey St.
11. Preston, John, c, cor. Sixth & Georgia Sts.
11. Packer, James, 261 De Soto St.
11. Paschal, Henry, c, De Soto St.
11. Pendergrast, Bridget.
11. Patillo, Dr R. H , W, Walnut St.
11. Parish, Charity.
11. Page, G. E.. 151 Causey St.
12. Plummer, Margaret, 38 Linden St.
12. Pickens, James, c. 487 Shelby St.
12. Partlow, Mrs. F., w, Hernando St.
12 Peeples, Isaac, c, Winchester St.
13. Parks. Ida, c. 61 Clay St.
13. Payne, Narcissa, c. 11 North St.
13. Perkins, Archie, Short Third St.
13. Parks (child).
13. Pearsall, Clara.
13. Pearsall, Aline.
13. Page, Miss M. B., w, Dunlap St.
14. Price, Mrs. Susan.
14. Pardieu, Charles.
14. Piggins, Felix, 216 Beale St.
14. Perkins Randall, c, 222 Washington St.
14. Patchell, Mrs., w, Poplar St.
15. Phillips, Mary. w, 220 Elliott St.
15. Pucher, P. D., w. foot of Broadway.
15. Plummer, Mrs. B., w.
15. Plummer, Al., w.
16. Penn, Dr. J. E., w, Court St. Infirmary.
16. Perry, Leonora, w, South St.
16. Penders. Barbara, w, cor. Fourth and Keel Sts.
16. Paschal, Andrew, c, 155 De Soto St.
16. Powell, Andrew. c, 101 Fourth St.
16. Pellegran, Emile, w, cor, Poplar and Washington Sts.
16. Peter, Thomas, w, 217 Pontotoc St.
16. Polk, Bud, c, cor. Fifth and Carolina Sts.
16. Peter, cor. Sixth and Broadway Sts.
16. Pointer, Roxina, c. Walnut St.
16. Paine, Mary, c, 131 Main St.
16. Page, N., w, cor. Second & Washington Sts.
16. Plummer, B. F., w. De Soto St.
16. Payne, Mary, w, 133 Main St.
16. Pletz, F.
16. Pierce, Dr. Hiram M., w, Court St. Infirmary.
16. Powders, R. W., w. Gayoso House.
16. Patterson, R. A., 174 Union St.
16. Pope, Rachel.
16. Perry, Somers, w, South St.
16. Parker, Richard, c, cor. Fifth and Alabama Sts.
19. Pointer, John, c. Walnut St.
20. Pierce, Thomas, c, 36 Linden St.
21. Pfister. Jacob, w.
23. Patterson, Joseph, w, Market St.
23. Polk, Lizzie, c, Marlin Ave.
23. Powers, Mr. J. C., w, Gayoso House.

Sept. 23. Peabody, Geo. N., w, Leathe Orphan Asylum.
24. Pierce, Nellie, w, 19 Hernando St.
25. Phoebus, R. W. K.
25. Patterson, Willie, c, 175 La Rosa St.
26. Partee, C. L., w, McLemore Ave.
26. Price, Sarah A., c, Central Point.
26. Pryor, Nathan.
28. Pliske, Mrs.
28. Palmer, Mrs. Lucinda, w.
29. Palmer, Elizabeth, w.
29. Petty, Joseph, c, South St.
30. Pitman, Carrie A., 450 Hernando St.
30. Probert, George C., w.
30. Pucket, Mr.
30. Poyner, Mr., w, Walker Ave.
30. Pickens, Oliver, c, Short Third St.
Oct. 1. Palmer, Miss Ella, w, Jackson St.
1. Pugo, Mr., w, Rayburn Ave.
2. Patter, Charles, w, Orleans St.
2. Pomato, Henry, c, Broadway.
2. Penacchi, Louis, Moon Ave.
3. Peoples, Jesse, w, Market St. Infirmary.
3. Porter (infant), 157 Poplar St.
3. Peabody, Jno. M., w, Leath Orphan Asylum.
3. Pearl, Emma, w, Davis Ave.
3. Peebles, Dr. P., w, City Hospital.
4. Pritchett, Thos. T., w, State Female College.
4. Payne, Charles, c, City Hospital.
4. Penacchi, Louis, w, Moon Ave.
6. Putnama, S. G., County Jail.
6. Pope, Willie, w, Craig's Nursery.
7. Provenzale, Mike, w, Poplar St.
7. Philson, Eliza, w, McLemore Ave.
7. Pollard, J. E., w, Kerr Ave.
8. Piaggio, Victoria, w, 216 Beale St.
10. Phillips, Miss M., w, Walker Ave.
10. Plain, Katie, w, Gayoso St.
10. Palmer, H. L., w, South Jackson St.
11. Pritchett, Mrs. F., w, State Female College.
11. Parker, Isaac, c.
11. Prescott, O. F., w, Walker Ave.
14. Plain, Miss Carrie, w, Walnut St.
14. Pugg, W. T., w, Raleigh Road.
14. Pearson, Albert, w, Church Home.
14. Pride, Mrs.. c. St. Martin St.
17. Peterson, Martha, w, City Hospital.
17. Perk, Elvira, c, City Hospital.
17. Patton, Maggie, w. Front Row.
18. Phillips, Jennie, Old Raleigh Road.
19. Payne, Jennie, c, McLemore Ave.
19. Pollard, Nancy L., w, 352 Vance St.
21. Pugh, Mary Ann, w, Raleigh Road.
22. Peterson, John, w, Poplar St
22. Phelan (child of P. H.), w, Springdale.
25. Posey, H. J., w, Boulevard.
28. Perry, Georgiana, w, 40 St. Martin St.
Nov. 4. Patterson, Mrs., w, Rayburn Ave.
Dec. 10. Patterson, Mrs., w.
Sept. 13. Quinn, Mary, w, cor. Mill & Second Sts.
14. Quinlan, John C.
19. Quigley, Mary, w, Jessamine St.
Oct. 2. Quinn, Mike, w, Hernando St.
2. Quinlan, Eugene, w, Hernando Road.
Aug. 13. Ryan, James, w, Washington St.
15. Rehkopf, C.
15. Reiley, Martha Hughes.
17. Rosenstiel, Auguste.
17. Reagan, T., City Hospital.
18. Roberts, Hannah, w, Moseby Ave.
19. Russell, Maggie.
20. Russell, Birdie, w, 14 Allen Ave.
21. Rinker, Ann, County Poor House.
23. Roush, John A., w, Monroe St.
24. Rodgers, Dr. Jno. C., w, Adams St.
24. Rehkopf, Fred,, w, cor. Alabama and Winchester Sts.
25. Ryan, Elizabeth, w, Johnson Ave.
25. Richardson, S. A., c, alley bet. Monroe and Madison Sts.
26. Riley, Mrs., w, 79 Winchester St.
26. Reyder, Patrick, w, Commerce St.
26. Rengg, Auguste, w, Adams St.
26. Rooks, Ellen, De Soto St.
27. Ring, Maggie, w, City Hospital.

Aug. 27. Ring, Dan., w, City Hospital.
27. Ritter, Alice E., w, Louisville, Ky.
28. Rezzinocco, Mrs. C., w, Poplar St.
29. Reiley, Joe, 14 Washington St.
29. Rozelle, Louisa, c
29. Regnold. Lewis, w, Bass Ave.
29. Rummel, A., w, Huppert Ave.
29. Redders, Auguste, w, 107 Poplar St.
29. Robeson, Mary, c.
30. Record, W. H., w, 104 Exchange St.
30. Ringwald, Minnie, w.
30. Riggonica, L. N., w.
30. Ringwald. Miss, w, Bass Ave.
30. Ryan, Steven, w, Alabama St.
31. Rummel, Sophy, w, Huppert Ave.
31. Roice, Josephine, w, Main St.
31. Russell, Joseph E., w, Carolina St.
31. Reiley, Mike, w, City Hospital.
31. Rinn, Vincent, w. City Hospital.
31. Ruffin, Charley, w, 215 Alabama St.
31. Ricord, Annie. w, 104 Exchange St.
31. Riley, Dan.. c, Monroe St.
31. Robertson, Perry, c.
Sept. 1. Reinig, Moses, w.
1. Ringwald, Edward, w, Bass Ave.
1. Ring, Moses, w, Marshall Ave.
1. Runs, Oscar, c, Poplar St.
2. Rice, Annie, w, La Salette Academy.
2. Raggio, Mary R., w, cor. Causey and Beale Sts.
2. Raggio, Amelia.
2. Rogers, Dennis, c, cor. Carolina and Eighth Sts.
2. Roddy, Jane, Shelby County.
2. Redd, Austin, c, 92 Second St.
2. Rice, Billy, 176 Vance St.
2. Richardson, B. A., c, City Hospital.
2. Reinert, Wm., w, City Hospital.
2. Rodgers, Robt., c.
3. Radcliffe, Steven, Main St.
3. Roberts, Wm., 6 Turley St.
3. Ruffin, Wm. H., 153 Johnson Ave.
3. Rubenstein, Lena N., w, Jackson St.
3. Roberts, Ann Eliza, w, Madison St.
3. Reder, Gus., w, Danceyville.
4. Ravenall, Alfred, w, 14 North Third St.
4. Radt, Mr., w, 407 Main St.
4. Reveiley, J., w, 81 Main St.
4. Raverson, A., 14 Second St.
4. Ruffin, Wm., c, Johnson Ave.
4. Ryan, Ellen, w, 138 Alabama St.
4. Ravenos, A., w, 36 Second St.
4. Reed, Wm., c, 176 Vance St.
5. Rootes, Mrs. Harriet A., w.
5. Risk. E. F., w, Main St.
5. Redders, Fred., w, Poplar St.
6. Ramsey, Cleburne, w, Vance St.
6. Rogers, Capt. Joseph, w, Tennessee St.
6. Ranburg, John, w, 72 Winchester St.
7. Retwick, w, Market St. Infirmary.
7. Rawlings, Hennie, c.
7. Rean, J. B., w, City Hospital.
8. Restmeyer, Fred., w, Alabama St.
8. Read, George, w, Ross Ave.
8. Reardon, Cohn, w, Hernando St.
8. Rush, R. L., w, Waldron Ave.
8. Rudd, Wm. A., w.
8. Robinson, Percy, c.
8. Ryan, John, w, Market St. Infirmary.
8. Rusk, Charley, w. Shelby County.
8. Rudd, George, 5 Ross Ave.
9. Rogers, Emily, 252½ Third St.
9. Rudd, Mr., Cooper Place.
9. Roseborough, Rev. D. R. S., w, Shelby County.
9. Russell, Wm., w, Carolina St.
9. Read, E. P., w, Cooper Place.
10. Ringwald, S., w, Bass Ave.
10. Rich, Henry, c, Hernando St.
10. Ryan, Jennie.
10. Read, Mrs., cor. Carolina & Second Sts.
10. Ryan, Jennie, South St.
10. Robins, Dr.
10. Rogers, A.
10. Rogers, Emma, w, 230 Third St.
10. Ryan, James, w, Market St. Infirmary.
10. Raws, Mrs. Millie, Charleston Ave.
10. Raggio, John, w, Hernando St.
11. Robinson, Mary, c, 61 Carolina St.

Sept. 11. Radt, Mr., 407 Main St.
11. Rooch, Frank, c, cor. Dunlap St. and Huppert Ave.
11. Roach, Bill, 120 De Soto St.
11. Rainey, P.
11. Robinson, George, w, Third St.
11. Royster, F. W., Jr., w, Boulevard.
12. Robinson, M.
12. Ryan, Wm., 84 South St.
12. Ray, C. W., 442 Beale St.
12. Rhodes, Louis, c, foot of Exchange St.
13. Rounds, Belle.
13. Rubenstein, Pike, w.
13. Ross, Benjamin, c.
13. Rentz, John, w, 230 Main St.
13. Romango, John, w, 252 Safferans St.
13. Reiley, James, w, City Hospital.
13. Rodgers, w. cor. Sixth & Looney Sts.
13. Randolph, Hudson, c.
14. Randall. Rachael, c.
14. Ripley, Fred., w, Market St.
14. Robinson, Anderson, c, foot of Exchange St.
14. Richardson, Turner, c. 109 De Soto St.
14. Ryan, James, w, 138 Alabama St.
14. Robinson, Eliza, w, 300 Beale St.
15. Roberts, John, c.
15. Reinig, Mrs. C., w.
15. Robinson, Grandison, c, 469 Court St.
15. Rogers, Peter, c, Martin Ave.
16. Randall, Fred., w, Gayoso House.
16. Root, Erwin, w, City Hospital.
16. Richmond, George, c, 212 Alabama St.
16. Renner, Dr. J. E., w.
16. Reynolds, Fannie.
16. Ruby, Jackson.
16. Rilford, Hannah, c.
17. Robinson, Sophie, c, 354 Lauderdale St.
17. Reardon, Rev. Father, w, De Soto St.
17. Reiley, Sarah, w, Linden St.
17. Roper, Ann. w, Hernando Road.
17. Reynolds, Maggie, c, 543 Main St.
17. Robinson, Lawrence, c, 174 South St.
17. Riffi (child of Telfy), c, Dunlap St.
18. Robinson, William, Market St. Infirmary.
18. Reynolds. H. S., w.
18. Ross, C., Peabody Hotel.
18. Reynolds, Mrs. H. S.
18. Runge, Wm.
18. Robinson, Cheney, c.
18. Ruth, Sister, w.
18. Ruth, Jester, w, Dunlap St.
19. Ryan, Mrs., cor. St. Martin & South Sts.
19. Richardson, John, w, Donahue Place.
20. Ross, John, c, South St.
21. Rice, David, c, 388 Main St.
21. Rester, Jacob, 434 Vance St.
21. Ray, Miss Lizzie, w, 442 Beale St.
22. Roberts, Sarah, w, Church Home.
22. Rognett. Mrs. Mary, w, Old Raleigh R'd.
22. Reynolds, Mrs. Fannie, w, Posten Ave.
22. Reynolds, Frank. w, Posten Ave.
22. Ritter, John, w, 52 Clay St.
22. Robertson, J. D.
22. Redcourt (child).
22. Ransom, Mary, w, Vance & Walnut Sts.
23. Richardson, Lucy, c, Donahue Place.
23. Richardson, c, Memphis & Charleston R. R.
23. Rutter, John.
23. Roper, Miss Lizzie, w, Hernando Road.
25. Ranier, Martin, w. City Hospital.
25. Rogson, J. A., w, Horn Lake Road.
26. Roark, Katie.
27. Reilly, Katie, w, Beale St.
27. Rinders, John, w, cor. Tennessee and Turley Sts.
28. Roberts, C. S.. Court St. Infirmary.
28. Redford, M. W., w, Adams St.
28. Ross, Miss Fannie.
29. Roemheld, John, w, 15 Washington St.
29. Robinson, Nora, c, Shelby County.
29. Reid, Walter, w, Cooper Place.
29. Roberts (child), w, near brewery.
29. Rooch, George, c, Georgia St.
29. Reid, Susan, c, Madison St.
30. Rancoske, A., w, City Hospital.
Oct. 1. Robins. Miss A. M., w. Cooper Place.
3. Robinson, Jane, c, cor. Third St. and Walker Ave.

A HISTORY OF THE YELLOW FEVER.   231

Oct. 3. Robinson, Willis. c, Walnut St.
3. Rutter, Miss Annie, w.
3. Ruby, Mrs Owen, 74 Jackson St.
3. Rutter, Miss C., w, Clay St.
6. Reese, Mary, c, Georgia St.
6. Rayford, Thomas, Walker Ave.
8. Restmeyer, Frank, w, Alabama St.
8 Revoy, Laura, w, Washington St.
8. Ruffin, Freddie, w, Fort Pickering.
8. Ringer, Lafayette, w, 40 Exchange St.
8. Restinger, J., Fort Pickering.
9. Roberts, Susan, w, Fort Pickering.
9. Reston, Wm., w.
9. Randall (son of Henry), c.
9. Ruffin, Joe, w, Gayoso St.
9. Raid, Susan, c, Causey St.
9. Randolph, Taylor, c.
10. Raggio, Miss Lizzie, w, Raleigh Road.
11. Revoli. Mrs. Lou., w, Walker Ave.
11. Ryan, Jack, w, Georgia St.
11. Rounds, James, Jr., w, Walker Ave.
11. Restmeyer, Mrs. Fred., w, Alabama St.
12. Revoli, Lizzie, w, Walker Ave.
13. Rossi, John, w, Trigg Ave.
13. Ryan, James, w, Sycamore St.
13. Ruffin, J. B., w, Carolina St.
13. Reinhardt, Dr., w, Jefferson St.
14. Reed, Ross, c, Gaines St.
14. Richardson, John, c, Main St.
15. Rice, John, w, South Jackson St.
15. Ruffin, Marley, w, Carolina St.
15. Reed, Louisa.
16. Rustin, Mrs., w, Coffee St.
16. Rustin, Miss, w. Coffee St.
17. Robinson, Clarke, c, 108 Linden St.
19. Richardson, Mattie.
19. Richards, Mollie, w. Raleigh Road.
19. Reidel, Robert, w, Raleigh Road.
21. Redford, Geo. R., w, City Hospital.
22. Richardson, Jane, c, cor. Seventh and Broadway Sts.
22. Roper, James. w, Hernando Road.
22. Rooch, Miss Delia, w, Union St.
22. Rawlings, Lou., c, Monroe St.
24. Rawls, Willie.
25. Rooch, Miss Lena, w, Union St.
26. Roper, Mrs. M., w, Hernando Road.
26. Rapp, Miss A. R., w, Thomas Ave.
29. Reiley, Nancy, c, Vance St.
31. Reiney, Caroline J., w, Boulevard.
Nov. 1. Roe, Mrs., w.
5. Ransom, W. Z.
7. Rivers, Gussie, c, Allen Ave.
14. Reddick, W. L., w.
Aug. 13. Stewart, Ellen J., w.
13. Stewart, Eliza J., w, Frain's Island.
15. Savage, Rosa.
15. Sarner, Dr. F.
17. Schalscha, Ida, w, Washington St.
17. Sronce, Jake.
17. Smith, Mrs. Barbara, w.
19. Shelton, child of Caroline.
20. Schleimance, Henry.
21. Shepherd, Thomas, w, Pontotoc St.
21. Shefley, John, w, Moseby Ave.
21. Schultz, John, w.
22. Schneider, E., w, City Hospital.
22. Shultz, Henry, w.
22. Schwab, Anthony. w.
22. Saunders, Thos. B.
23. Schlemmer, C. H., w, 25 Alabama St.
23. Sauter, Charles, w, Moseby Ave.
23. Shute, Frank, w, City Hospital.
24. Schalscher, Fannie, w, Washington St.
24. Stanberg, Charles, 2 Ross Ave.
24. Strauberg. Ernest, w, Bass Ave.
25. Sledge, Caroline, c, 155 Main St.
25. Shehan, Alice, w.
25. Schalscha, Hannah, w, Washington St.
26. Sullivan, L. S.
26. Scales, George, c, cor. Auction and Second Sts.
26. Stanberg, Ed. A., w, 2 Ross Ave.
26. Shepherd Mr., F., w, Linden St.
27. Shepherd, Laura, Poplar St.
27. Smith, Ann, c, Allen Ave.
27. Speckernagle, Wm., w, Poplar St.
27. Scalley, M. E, Louisville, Ky.
28. Schafer, Herman, w, Front St.

Aug. 28. Scully, Agnes, w, Moseby Ave.
28. Smith, John, w, City Hospital.
28. Smith, Frank, c, 22 Johnson Ave.
28. Sales, Ellen, c, 86 Winchester St.
29. Stewart, Maggie.
29. Salzeger, H. G.
29. Smith, John, c, 129 Main St.
29. Seymour, Joseph, 90 Hill St.
29. Scott, George. 173 Jefferson St.
29. Sipp, Mary, Court St. extended.
29. Stalin, Mrs. Helen, w, Fifth St.
29. Spencer, Nora, w, Poplar St.
29. Smith, Mrs., w, Pigeon Roost Road.
30. Saunders, Miss Clara, w, Robinson St.
30. Stahlen, J. N., w, Fifth St.
30. Shelby, Matt., w, Pigeon Roost Road.
30. Sweeney, Ada, Greenlaw St.
30. Selden, Jim, w, 3 Johnson Ave.
30. Shipling, Martha, 7 Moseby Ave.
30. Seymour, Monroe, c, 31 Robinson St.
30. Steinell, John, City Hospital.
30. Solomon, E.
30. Schultz, Charles.
30. Smith, W. J., Jr., w, Elliott St.
30. Schafer, Alice O., Overton St.
30. Scully, Charles.
30. Shipley, Mathias.
31. Samons, Harriet, c, cor. Poplar and Echols Sts.
31. Sherry, Patrick, w, Winchester Ave.
31. Saunders, Jim, w, Railroad.
31. Stehle, Frank, w, Memphis and Charleston R. R.
31. Shea, Thomas, w, Hill St.
31. Stinette, John, w, City Hospital.
Sept. 1. Shuter, Miss Emma, w, Madison St.
1. Saunders, Clara, w. Main St.
1. Selest, John, c, 111 Poplar St.
1. Shearer, Mary, c, 76 Third St.
1. Sanberg, c, cor. Washington and Main Sts.
1. Sheridan, Mary, c, Jackson St.
2. Stevenson, M., City Hospital.
2. Stanford, Tom, c, 95 Madison St.
2. Smith, John, w, City Hospital.
2. Smith, Edward, c, cor. Orleans and St. Paul Sts.
2. Steinau, Joseph, w. City Hospital.
2. Oakaford, Charles, Union Ave.
2. Schneider, Jacob, w, Linden St.
2. Shepherd, Annie, c, Jefferson St.
2. Sterla, Frederick, w, Chelsea.
3. Sturdevant, Mrs., w, Poplar St.
3. Sullivan, M., w, Orphan Asylum.
3. Sohm, Margaret, w, Bass Ave.
3. Stillman, Henry, w, Broadway.
3. Strehl, Mollie, w, Bass Ave.
3. Sillivan, Mary, w, 161 Pontotoc St.
3. Steel, 505 Rayburn Ave.
3. Schrider, Mrs., 188 Linden St.
3. Stetson, Eddie, c, Winchester St.
3. Sturdevant, Mrs., w, 65 Poplar St.
4. Sneed, Laura, w, 47 Huling St.
4. Smith, cor. St. Paul and Orleans Sts.
4. Switzer, Mary, w, 108 Vance St.
4. Strong, w, cor. Hernando and Beale Sts.
4. Smith, Bob, Old Raleigh Road.
4. Sullivan, Mrs., w, City Hospital.
4. Schmuck, Peter, w, Greenwood Ave.
4. Starrett, Mrs. F. E., w, Jackson St.
4. Smith, Martha, c, Jefferson St.
5. Smith, John, City Hospital.
5. Stanley, Mike, City Hospital.
5. Stever, Joseph, 178 Front St.
5. Smith, Martin, 163 Jefferson St.
5. Slocum, Ed., c, 209 Hernando St.
5. Shanders, Mrs., w, 46 Orleans St.
5. Strauberg, Charles, w, 11 Charleston Ave.
5. Sussete, George, City Hospital.
5. Swearingen, E. F., w, City Hospital.
5. Sprausberger, Chas., w, 11 Charleston Ave.
5. Steel, J. M., w, M. & C. R. R.
5. Starrett, Eddie, w, Jackson St.
5. Stewart, Mrs. N. M., w, Country.
5. Slagle, Josephine.
5. Sellers, Theresa, w, Louisville, Ky.
5. Smith, Adeline, c, Monroe St.
5. Smith, Mary, c, Avery St.

Sept. 6. Schulze, A. F., w, Dunlap St.
6. Smith, L., w, Vance St.
6. Sullivan, Dennis, w, Gayoso St.
6. Strong, Nancy, 113 Beale St.
6. Simmons, Rebecca, c, Poplar St.
6. Swift, cor. Third and Monroe Sts.
6. Shaw, Fannie, c, 170 Vance St.
6. Sundies, Wm., cor. Vance & St. Martin Sts.
6. Spellman, Wm., 164 Beale St.
6. Styles, Lucretia, c, 86 Winchester St.
6. Susette, George, City Hospital.
6. Smith, John, City Hospital.
6. Stanley, Mike, City Hospital.
6. Spellman, P., Beale St.
6. Smith, Sally, c, Jefferson St.
6. Speed, Martin, c.
6. Sanbarg, John, Winchester St.
7. Sprigg, John, Navy Yard.
7. Schutz, A O., w, Jefferson St.
7. Speers, Mrs. Elizabeth, w, Alabama St.
7. Stanberg, Arthur, w. 11 Charleston Ave.
7. Seymour, Rebecca, c, 37 Robinson St.
7. Smith, Willis, 56 Main St.
7. Selden, David, c, 3 Johnson Ave.
7. Summers, C. H., w, 224 Hernando St.
7. Southey, William, 132 Beale St.
7. Stack, Mrs. Margaret, w, Hernando St.
8. Shepherd, B. E., w, Linden St.
8. Sterlie, Helen, w, Ross Ave.
8. Schuler, Mollie, w, Georgia St.
8. Sanona, Emma, w.
8. Smith, Emma, w.
8. Stewart, Calvin, w, Causey St.
8. Smith, Charles M., Madison St.
8. Stewart, Albert, c, Lauderdale St.
8. Scott, Emma, c, 164 Moseby Ave.
8. Shay, Ed., w, City Hospital.
8. Safferans, A., c, City Hospital.
8. Selsey, Ann, City Hospital.
8. Southern, W., w.
8. Severson, P. C., w.
9. Smith, Miss B., w, 276 Washington St.
9. Slugher, A. T., Market St. Infirmary.
9. Scharf, Mrs., w, Second St.
9. Scharf (infant), Second St.
9. Sarago, John, 68 Hernando St.
9. Shines, Bottie, c, Walnut Ave.
9. Stylor, Joseph, w, Beale St.
10. Sweeney, w, Third St.
10. Sweeney, J H., w, Greenlaw St.
10. Stinson, Reess.
10. Saltalamachi, Frank, w, Orleans St.
10. Simpson, John.
10. Sterrett, James.
10. Shafer, Fred. C., w, Chelsea.
10. Simmons, L., w, La Rosa St.
10. Saltalamachi, Frank, w, cor. Orleans and Vance Sts.
10. Stovall, Mollie, 94 De Soto St.
10. Selvin, John, Second St.
10. Surries, J. B., Cooper Place.
11. Siss, Julia, 103 De Soto St.
11. Spencer, Caroline.
11. Scherer, H.
11. Sullivan, James J., w, Union St.
11. Steele, C. L., w, Union St.
11. Staley, Charlie, w, 271 Main St.
11. Sutton, Fannie, c, 66 Rose St.
11. Satherley, James, Safferans St.
11. Small, Mary, 176 Spring St.
11. Shaw, A., c, Clay St.
11. Sullivan, Mary, Union Ave.
11. Spain, Lucy, Concord St.
11. Safferans, James, c, Chelsea St.
11. Simmons, Mrs., w, Lauderdale St.
11. Sutton, Thomas, La Rosa St.
12. Schneider, Kate.
12. Slack, Eliza, w, Madison St.
12. Shuttleworth, Alfred, w, Manassas St.
12. Sivan, Mollie.
12. Stanislaus, Sister. w, Market St.
12. Smith, John, w, Tennessee St.
12. Sullivan, Tom, w. 500 Main St.
12 Sheeley, Gallins, Dunlap St.
12. Scott, Wm., c, 51 St. Martin St.
12. Simoo, 86 Causey St.
12. Smith, H., c, City Hospital.
12. Snider, Katie, w, Navy Yard.
13. Stokes, John.

Sept. 13. Sorry, Mitchell, 138 Elliott St.
13. Stewart, C. Y., w.
13. Stewart, Sarah W., w, 103 Hernando St.
13. Smith, Tennie.
13. Stickney, James, w, Market St. Infirmary.
13. Scruggs, Amanda, c, 10 Howard Row.
13. Saunders, Sallie, w, cor. Seventh and Alabama Sts.
13. Sevier, R.
13. Stevenson, William G., w, Dunlap St.
13. Simmons, Julius A., w, Pontotoc St.
13. Shelby, Georgia, c.
14. Stewart, P. B., w, 103 Hernando St.
14. Sears, J. J., w.
14. Schiller, Josephine, 152 Causey St.
14. Schcarer, Thomas.
14. Scatter, John, cor. Shelby & Linden Sts.
14. Stevenson, Rufus, c, 19 Winchester St.
14. Saylor, Mary, w, Beale St.
14. Sutton, Mollie, w, cor. Madison and Orleans Sts.
14. Shright, Minnie, c, cor. Walnut and Vance Sts.
14. Scruggs, Bradford, c, cor. Tennessee and Linden Sts.
14. Smith, Hettie, w, Church Home.
14. Saunders, Hannah, c, 6 Dunlap St.
14. Strehl, Sarah R., w, Bass Ave.
14. Smith, M. F., w, Peyton Ave.
14. Schneider, Mrs., w, Linden St.
14. Steinkuhl, Henry, w, Boulevard.
15. Schneider, w, Linden St.
15. Schumaker, P., w, Shelby St.
15. Sunberry, Mrs., w, 407 Main St.
15. Selke, Charles, w, Market St. Infirmary.
15. Scott, Fannie, c, Webster St.
15. Schumaker, Peter, w, 414 Shelby St.
15. Sullivan, Jerry, Union Ave.
15. Shepherd, Eliza A., w.
15. Slick, Carl, w, 133 South St.
15. Shuttleworth, James, w.
15. Schumaker (child of Peter), w, 414 Shelby St.
15. Schumaker (child of Peter), w, 414 Shelby St.
16. Shuttleworth, Annie R., w, Manassas St.
16. Smith (child).
16. Seibert, Ferdinand, w, Humboldt Park.
16. Smith, Sam., w, Tennessee St.
16. Sims, c, 163 De Soto St.
16. Scott, Mr., w, cor. South St. and Rayburn Ave.
16. Stanton, Eliza, c, Marshall Ave.
16. Scepers, Joe, c, Horn Lake Road.
16. Saharfen, J., w, Raleigh Road.
16. Sims, Lizzie, c, 303 De Soto St.
16. Souhr, Josephine, w, Andrew Ave.
16. Sadler, Sarah, w.
16. Saidburn, Ellen C., c, Bass Ave.
17. Simmons, Mary, c, 82 Clay St.
17. Smith, Dave, w, steamer Cohoma.
17. Smith, w, City Hospital.
17. Stenson, Reese, c, 103 Pontotoc St.
17. Swan, Auguste, w, Church Home.
17. Schneider, Cora, w, Linden St.
17. Shaw, James A., w, Huling St.
17. Shelton, Mrs. M. A., w, Sixth St.
17. Schuyler, Rev.L.S.,w, Court St. Infirmary.
17. Steinkuhl, Margaret.
18. Shepherd, W. B., w.
18. Shortey, Clara Matilda,w. 62 Peyton Ave.
18. Smooks, Louis, Greenwood Ave.
18. Stevenson, Miss Mary T., 32 Dunlap St.
18. Smith, Charley.
18. Schlatter, Sam'l, w. City Hospital.
18. Stanton, Lucy A., c, cor. Fifth and Lauderdale Sts.
18. Saltalamachi, Frank, w, Louisville, Ky
19. Street, Fannie, w, Church Home.
19. Scannell, Father, w. St. Peter's Church.
19. Swint, Lizz e, c, 81 South St.
19. Strain, Mr., w, Buntyn Station.
19. Sledge, Henry, c, cor. Second St. and Henry Ave.
19. Schultz, Fred., Hernando Road.
19. Street, Nannie, w, Church Home.
19. Smith, Josie, w, Second St.
20. Shelley, Henry.
20. Sims, Andrew, c, Elliott St.

A HISTORY OF THE YELLOW FEVER. 233

Sept. 20. Scafe, Alex, w, Second St.
20. Shields, Peter, w, City Hospital.
20. Stein, Mary, w, Front St.
20. Salari, Toney, w, cor. Alabama and Seventh Sts.
20. Steele, Mrs. C. L., w, City Hospital.
21. Scully, James H., w, Winchester Ave.
21. Sassamon, Frank, w, Georgia St.
21. Shive, W. H., w, City Hospital.
21. Silari, cor. Maxwell and Safferans St.
21. Stevenson, Miss, w, Dunlap St.
21. Stevens, Julia Ann.
21. Schullary. Thomas.
21. Shaddy, Margaret, w, near Elmwood.
21. Sledge, Mrs., w, Jackson St.
22. Scarafiatta, Joseph, w, Wolf River.
22. Schumaker, Mrs. M. G., w, Marley Ave.
22. Schneider, Andrew, w, City Hospital.
22. Saunders, Willie, c, cor. Orleans and Court Sts.
23. Suggs, Mrs, c, 75 Clay St.
23. Smith, Burrell, c, Chelsea.
23. Spears, Mrs., Jackson St.
23. Settle, Annie, c, 66 La Rosa St.
23. Sherrod, Fred., w, foot of Jackson St.
23. Salari, P. M, w, cor. Safferans and Maxwell Sts.
23. Scherer, Mr., w, foot of Jackson St.
23. Scherrie, Mrs., w, Poplar St.
24. Smith, Patrick, c, cor. Seventh and Broadway Sts.
24. Sink, Mrs., w, 133 Court St.
24. Smith, J. J., w, cor. Hernando and Vance Sts.
34. Shelton, Mrs. R.W., w, National Cemetery.
24. Strong, Henry, c, Alabama St.
24. Shurts, Mrs., w, foot of Jackson St.
24. Steel (child), w, Echols St.
25. Stall, August, w, 9 Linden St.
25. Schilling, L., w, Georgia St.
25. Sanders, M., c, Central Ave.
26. Smith, H. G., w, Market St. Infirmary.
26. Sanders, Charley.
26. Smith, Aggie, c, cor. Van Buren and Washington Sts.
23. Schafer, Henry, w, Raleigh Road.
26. Stewart, Geo, c, Wolf River Ferry.
27. Shoemaker, Mr.
27. Slater, Miss Sallie, w, Boulevard.
27. Sauer, Miss Amelia, w.
27. Sabrelie, Mr., w, Anders Place.
27. Smith, Miss H , w, Vance St.
28. Schley, F., w, Winchester Ave.
28. Scruggs, Caroline S.
28. Smith, W. C.
29. Smith, Eliza, w, City Hospital.
29. Sauer, Philip Henry, w.
29. Schilling, Ferd. S., w, 12 Adams St.
29. Stokie, Mrs. Annie. w, Main St.
29. Shepher l, Daisy, 215 Poplar St.
30. Sauer, Louis.
30. Sutton, George W.
30. Stewart, Charles, c.

Oct. 1. Snigg, Edward, w, Madison St.
1. Schroeder, Caroline, w, Second St.
1. Shelton, R. W., w, National Cemetery.
1 Shehan, John, w, Hernando St.
1 Sauer, Ada, w, Jefferson St.
1. Strattman, Bernard, w, Carolina St.
1. Schneider, Mrs., w, Raleigh Road.
2. Schroeder, H. L., w. Second St.
2. Smith, Nellie, w, Broadway.
2. Smith (child), w, Thomas Ave.
2. Sullivan, Mrs., w, City Hospital.
2. Scullin, Jim, 65 Union St.
3. Saxson, George, w.
3. Sticker (child of T.\, c.
4. Stanley, Jno. R., w, McLemore Ave.
5. Slack, Jerry.
5. Shaw, Mrs. Katie, w, Huling St.
5. Strattman, A., w, Fifth St.
5. Swep, Taylor, c, Mulberry St.
6. Scott, Thomas, c. Chelsea.
6. Smith, Cornelius, c, Stewart Ave.
6. Spain, Mary Ann, w, Woolen Mills.
6. Scullin, Patrick, w, Library Building.
6. Smith, Charles.
6. Sauer, Mrs. Margaret, w, Jefferson St.
6. Strehl, Mrs. J. A., w, Breedlove Ave.

Oct. 6. Smith, Clara, w, Hernando St.
7. Sample, Dr., w, Camp Joe Williams.
7. Shepherd, Wm., w, Front St.
7. Stovall, Dinah, c, Trigg Ave.
7. Schneyer, Edward, w, Beale St.
7. Stewart, Thomas, w. Elmwood,
8. Settle, Louis, w, 65 La Rosa St.
8. Snelling, C., Jr., w, Winchester Ave.
9 Smith, Bob, c, Bass Ave.
9. Shepherd, Mrs. Minnie.
9. Sherwood, Miss Lena, w, Raleigh Road.
9. Spiegle, Mr., w, Bluff City Grays.
9. Smith, Philip, w, Vance St.
9. Smith, Augus, w, City Hospital.
9. Scypel, Miss Minnie, w, Wilson Station.
10. Sabrelle, Mary.
10. Sharpe. Doc.
11. Smith, Robt., c, Mhoon Ave.
11. Shine, Charlotte, c, Sixth St.
11. Strange, Netta, w, Hernando Road.
11. Sullivan. Jaspar.
12. Slater, Mrs. E. C., w, Boulevard.
12. Shultz, Wiliiam, w, Court St.
12. Shoemaker, L. M., w, Poplar St.
14. Stone, James, w, Old Raleigh Road.
14. Shoemaker, Morris, w, Marley Ave.
14. Smith, Emma, c.
15. Scales, Ellen, c, 38 Third St.
15. Slater, Miss Mollie, w, Poplar St.
15. Shroyer, W. P., w, Latham Ave.
15. Scales, Allie, c, 38 Third St.
15. Stowe, Mrs., w, Raleigh Road.
16. Shields. Viney, c, Selma Railroad.
16. Shields, Charity, c. Elmwood.
17. Sample, Susan, w, Valentine Ave.
17. Sanpe. Frank, w, Valentine Ave.
19. Scruggs, P. T., w. Goodlett Station.
20. Smith, Mrs. H. D., w, Shelby County.
20. Stone, Ida, w, Church Home.
20. Strange, Tom, c, Jackson St.
21. Schilling, W. H., w, Georgia St.
21. Strong, Mrs., c, Commerce St.
22. Stewart, Maud, w, Raleigh Road.
22. Stephenson, Nelson, c, City Hospital.
23. Shehan, Mrs. M., w, Lucy Ave.
24. Shroyer. Miss Margaret, w, Latham Ave.
24. Summers, Mrs. Margaret, w, Kerr Ave.
24. Spicer, Jennie, w, Kerr Ave.
24. Stanley, Mrs. P. M., w, Second St.
28. Shehan, Mrs, C., w, Rayburn Ave.
28. Saul, Jacob, w, Market St. Infirmary.
29. Smith, Dorcas.
29. Sumners. William, w.
29. Simms, Mrs. M. L., w, Rozelle Station.
30. Scott, David, cor. Hernando St. & Kerr Ave.

Nov. 1. Scales, James.
1. Smith, Albert, 126 Pontotoc St.
1. Snell, Albert, w, Beale St.
1. Smith, Alfred, w, Pontotoc St.
1. Sullivan, Nelson, c. City Hospital.
8. Stevenson, Jennie, w, Clay St.
8. Sims, Lewis, w, Kerr Ave.
11. Steinkuhl, C. D., w, Madison St.
11. Shehan, Kate, w, South St.
13. Sambusetta, Victoria.
14. Schmidt, Mrs. Susan, w, Seventh St.
Aug. 12. Tah, Jung Yung, w, Jefferson St.
12. Tindall, C. M.
14. Tillman, Rosa.
17. Trombly, Geo., w, Moseby Ave.
18. Taffer, Sophy, Madison St.
18. Thompson, Minerva.
19. Taylor, W. H., w, Mulberry St.
21. Tighe, Peter A , w, Poplar St.
21. Trigg, Allen, N., Front St.
24. Tracey, Miss Maggie, w, Hernando Road.
24. Taylor, John L., c, cor. Broadway and Sixth Sts.
26. Turner, Thomas, w, cor. Court and Orleans Sts.
27. Turney, Mrs., 4 High St.
27. Theveat, A., w, cor. Poplar St. & Carroll Ave.
27. Thorn, Lillie, w, Brinkley Ave.
27. Thomas, Henry, 26 Second St.
27. Taylor, B.

234   A HISTORY OF THE YELLOW FEVER.

27. Tweedy, Thomas.
27. Tullman, K. M.
29. Townsend, Candes, 203 Monroe St.
29. Turner, Dunlap St.
29. Tate, David.
29. Tally, Annie, c.
31. Turley, Mike, w, City Hospital.
31. Tiernay, Charles.
Sept. 1. Townsend, Aleck, c, 111 Poplar St.
1. Tilford, M. A.
1. Taggert, R. L., w, County Jailer.
1. Tate, Lucy A., w, Orleans St.
1. Tinman, Alice, w. Winchester St.
1. Tierson, Alex., c, Winchester St.
1. Turner, Philis., c.
2. Taylor, Jennie, c, Goslee St.
2. Thumel, Adolph, Poplar St.
3. Thomas, Rev. A., 79 Robeson St.
3. Thompson, R. A., w, Wellington St.
3. Trueheart, Susan, c, 5 Auction St.
4. Townsend, Willie, w. 27 Main St.
4. Turner. Vina, c, Pontotoc St.
5. Tighe, Peter A., Jr., w, Poplar St.
5. Thomas, Joe, c, Winchester St.
5. Tighe, James C., w, Poplar St.
6. Taylor, Mrs. Annie, w, Union St.
6. Tibbs, Johnson, St. Martin St.
6. Townsend, Miss, w, 27 Main St.
6. Thompson, Jerry, c, 73 Lauderdale St.
7. Thomas, Mrs. Caroline, St. Martin St.
7. Thayers, Adolph., w.
7. Thomas, Sallie, c, 93 Alabama St.
7. Turner, Henrietta, c, 38 St. Martin St.
7. Tighe, Samuel, w, Poplar St.
7. Thomas, Hatch.
7. Thrall, J. C., w, Adams St.
8. Tenfull, Mrs. Breton, w, Poplar St.
8. Thompson, Mrs. Mattie, w.
8. Thompson, Willie, w, Shelby County.
8. Taylor, Lou., w, cor. Second and Auction Sts.
9. Tershus, Patrick, Linden St.
9. Townsley, Sam., w, Market St. Infirmary.
9. Tugler, James.
9. Turner, Robert, 259 Union St.
9. Taylor, Nora, w, 13 Main St.
9. Theobus, T. V., w, Madison St.
9. Torrence, Hugh, w, Poplar St.
9. Towns, Earnest, County Jail.
9. Turner, Edna, w, 167 De Soto St.
11. Thomas, Free, 217 South St.
11. Taylor, Caroline.
11. Turner, Sallie, c, 299 Union St.
11. Thompson, Donnie.
11. Trigg, Marshall.
11. Tucker, Charles, w, City Hospital.
11. Toulson, Charles, w, Hernando St.
12. Theveat, Noble.
12. Thomas, Richard, 242 South St.
12. Tithian, Hester E., w, Alabama St.
12. Thorne, Ed.
12. Taylor, James, c.
13. Terry, Jesse, c, Short Third St.
13. Terry, Andy, c, Short Third St.
13. Thomas, Ida.
13. Theckler, Sister, w, Poplar St.
13. Theveuth, Robert, w, Ruth St.
13. Turner, A., c.
14. Thomas, Hattie.
14. Temps, Willie, w, 179 South St.
14. Theveat, Bernard, w, cor. Beale St. and Charleston R. R.
14. Thompson, W. B., w, 43 Poplar St.
14. Thompson, A. R., w, Court St.
15. Thixton. W. K., w, Belin Ave.
15. Taylor, Caroline, c, 1078 Alabama St.
15. Treadwell, Gertrude, c, 65, Clay St.
15. Thompson, Mrs. Joanna, w, cor. Orleans & Georgia Sts.
15. Thompson, Tansey, c, City Hospital.
15. Thomas, Viola.
16. Tobin, Mrs. Ellen, w, cor. Hernando & South Sts.
16. Thompson, West, c. Southern Oil Works.
16. Tilton, R., Plank Road.
16. Taylor, Joe, City Hospital.
17. Tenfull, Julius, w, 179 South St.
17. Taylor, Eliza, 291 Union St.
18. Taylor, Charles, \., 220 Washington St.

Sept. 18. Thomas (infant of Bettie), c, 86 De Soto St.
18. Tenfull, Bettie, w, 179 South St.
18. Thomas, Renie.
19. Thomas, Joe, c, Front St.
19. Tucker, Francis, w, Raleigh Road.
20. Train, Thomas, w, City Hospital.
21. Thompson, Ann Eliza, c.
22. Tighe, James, w, Poplar St.
23. Tenfull, Joseph, w, 179 South St.
24. Thompson, Mrs., w, City Hospital.
25. Thomas, John, c, Rayburn Ave.
25. Tomeney, Hale, w, Bass Ave.
25. Tobin, Mike, w, South St.
26. Trezevant, S. P.
26. Tufts, Peter T. E., w, 377 Orleans St.
27. Thomas, H., c, 151 St. Martin St.
28. Tobyn, Dennis, w, 238 South St.
28. Tomeney, Helen, w, Bass Ave.
28. Taylor, Miss M., c, Concord St.
29. Tate, Jesse M., w, Orleans St.
29. Tate, Wm., w, Poplar St.
29. Tuerk, Dr., w, 450 Main St.
30. Thixton, Mrs.
Oct. 1. Tines, Esther. w, Seventh St.
1. Taylor, John B., w. Main St.
1. Turnan, Kate, w, Washington St.
3. Taylor, Marshall, w, City Hospital.
3. Thompson, Aggie, w, City Hospital.
4. Taylor, Lucy, w, cor. Walnut & Vance Sts.
4. Towers, Joe, c, cor. Front & Van Buren Sts.
4. Thomas, Miss Pauline, w, Breedlove Ave.
4. Taylor, Ensley. c, Union St.
5. Taylor, Swift, 114 Mulberry St.
5. Tomeney, Mrs. J. M., w, Bass Ave.
5. Taylor, D. S., w, Central Ave.
5. Taylor. A. W., w, Union St.
5. Thomas, D., c.
6. Tillson, Elizabeth, w, Walker Ave.
7. Taylor, Park, w, Central Ave.
7. Thomas, Alma, w, Thomas Ave.
7. Turner, Selby, c, 72 Marshall Ave.
7. Thompson, D. H., w, Market St. Infirmary.
7. Tomeney, J. M., w, Bass Ave.
9. Tilson, Samuel, w, south gate, Elmwood.
9. Thorpe, Richard, c, South Jackson St.
11. Tyson, Nick, 40 Exchange St.
12. Tillson, F., w, City Hospital.
13. Thornton, Ellen E. W., c, Pigeon Roost Road.
15. Taylor, Jesse, c, Turley St.
18. Taylor, Dave, c, Clay St.
19. Taylor, Preston, w, Jackson St.
20. Townsend, Joseph, w, Randolph Point.
22. Thomas, Miss Charlotte, w, Breedlove Ave.
25. Turner, Thomas, w, Gill Station.
28. Thompson, Sam'l, w, City Hospital.
29. Townsend, Miss Mollie, w.
31. Taylor, Preston, c, Beale St.
Nov. 2. Tucker, Mrs. Sallie A., w, Third St., Ft. Pickering.
15. Taylor, Mary Ann.
15. Taylor, Mrs. Ann E., w, Central Ave.
17. Tuhell, Mrs. C., w, College St.
Aug. 16. Unknown, 163½ Poplar St.
17. Unknown man, foot of Trezevant St.
19. Unknown, Raleigh Road.
24. Unverzagt, Wm., w, Exchange St.
25. Unknown man, w, 105 Main St.
25. Unknown woman, alley bet. Monroe and Madison Sts.
26. Unknown man, Poplar St.
27. Upchurch, C. H., w. 188 Robinson St.
28. Upchurch, Mrs. C. H., w, 188 Robinson St.
30. Unknown, cor. Pontotoc and De Soto Sts.
31. Unknown, Concord St.
31. Unknown child, c, Court St., extended.
31. Unknown.
Sept. 1. Unknown, Old Raleigh Road.
1. Unknown man, 518 Shelby St.
2. Unknown man, c, 90 Fifth St.
2. Unknown man, c, Library Building.
2. Unknown, Union St.
2. Unknown, room 396 Gayoso Hotel.
2. Unknown, cor. Market and Main Sts.
2. Unknown woman, c, cor. De Soto and Madison Sts.
2. Unknown, 108 Vance St.
2. Unknown, City Hospital.

A HISTORY OF THE YELLOW FEVER.

Sept. 2. Unknown man, w. Broadway.
3. Unknown.
3. Unknown, 294½ Poplar St.
3. Unknown, 34 Poplar St.
4. Unknown woman, w. 188 Linden St.
4. Unknown child, 188 Vance St.
4. Unknown, 181 Main St.
4. Unknown child, South St.
4. Unknown man, c, cor. St. Paul and Orleans Sts.
5. Unknown boy, Exchange St., extended.
5. Unknown man, w, City Hospital.
5. Unknown.
5. Unknown man, w.
5. Unknown, City Hospital.
5. Unknown man, 169 Jefferson St.
5. Unknown, 173 Jefferson St.
5. Unknown man, c, 209 Hernando St.
5. Unknown 112 Jefferson St.
5. Unknown woman, 129 De Soto St.
5. Unknown man, c, 129 Hernando St.
5. Unknown, buried by James Allen.
6. Unknown, c, 118 Front St.
6. Unknown, c, 169 Second St.
6. Unknown, 10 Howard's Row.
6. Unknown man, w, 11 Charleston Railroad.
6. Unknown woman, c, 50 Marshall Ave.
6. Unknown, 449 Hernando Road.
6. Unknown, 83 Front St.
6. Unknown woman, c, cor. Jefferson and Main Sts.
6. Unknown man, c, cor. Hill and Robinson Sts.
6. Unknown woman, w, 173 South St.
6. Unknown man, bet. Dunlap and Manassas Sts.
6. Unknown, cor. South and Hernando Sts.
6. Unknown, Monroe St.
6. Unknown, cor. Georgia and Seventh Sts.
6. Unknown, City Hospital.
6. Unknown, 238 Manassas St.
7. Unknown, Chelsea St.
7. Unknown, 139 Madison St.
7. Unknown, City Hospital.
7. Unknown, foot of Carolina St.
7. Unknown man, hospital wagon.
8. Unknown child.
8. Unknown, 40 Overton St.
8. Unknown, Court St., extended.
8. Unknown (bee raiser), Raleigh Road.
8. Unknown man, c, Monroe St.
9. Unknown, 381 Beale St.
9. Unknown woman, cor. Vance and Allen Ave.
9. Unknown man, cor. Elliott St. and Allen Ave.
9. Unknown, 250 Washington St.
9. Unknown, cor. Hernando and Vance Sts.
9. Unknown, Dickinson's Place.
9. Unknown child, 170 South St.
9. Unknown, 133 Main St.
9. Unknown, 13 Mulberry St.
9. Unknown, 128 Causey St.
9. Unknown, Raleigh Road.
9. Unknown, 320 Main St.
10. Unknown (hostler), 68 Monroe St.
10. Unknown woman, McLemore Ave.
10. Unknown, 21 Beale St.
10. Unknown, 370 Vance St.
11. Unknown.
11. Unknown.
11. Unknown man, 111 Pontotoc St.
11. Unknown, Lauderdale St.
11. Unknown, 129 Dunlap St.
11. Unknown, Old Library Building.
11. Unknown, 166 De Soto St.
12. Unknown.
12. Unknown, Pop'ar St.
12. Unknown, 389 Shelby St.
12. Unknown woman, 110 Main St.
12. Unknown, 67 Jefferson St.
12. Unknown woman, 372 Union St.
12. Unknown man, 189 South St.
12. Unknown, Breedlove Ave.
12. Unknown, 75 Clay St.
13. Unknown.
13. Unknown, 125 Fifth St.
13. Unknown man (in cornfield), Randolph Road.

Sept. 13. Unknown man, 230 Main St.
13. Underwood, Giles, c.
14. Unknown.
14. Unknown.
14. Unknown, cor. Exchange and Alabama Sts.
14. Unknown, cor. Exchange and Alabama Sts.
14. Unknown child, Church Orphan Home.
14. Unknown, City Hospital.
14. Unknown, 324 Jefferson St.
14. Unknown man, 285 South St.
15. Unknown, Linden St. Infirmary.
15. Unknown, cor. Keel and Second Sts.
15. Uritti, G., w.
16. Unknown man, Hernando Road.
17. Unknown child, Canfield Asylum.
17. Unknown, 17 Gholson St.
17. Untram, Charles, w, 90 Hernando St.
17. Unknown.
18. Unknown, Johnson Avenue.
18. Unknown, cor. Walnut St. and Pigeon Roost Road.
20. Unknown child, Canfield Asylum.
20. Unknown, City Hospital.
21. Unknown, Bass Ave.
21. Unknown.
22. Unknown.
22. Unknown, Raleigh Road.
23. Unknown, City Hospital.
24. Unknown man, 554 Main St.
24. Unknown.
26. Unknown.
27. Unknown, County Jail.
28. Unknown, Dunlap St.
30. Unknown child, Canfield Asylum.
30. Unknown man, foot of Adams St.
Oct. 2. Unknown child, 67 Jefferson St.
2. Unknown child, Canfield Asylum.
9. Unknown, 240 Johnson Ave.
10. Unknown woman, cor. Broadway and South Sts.
10. Unknown child, cor. Broadway and South Sts.
14. Unknown, City Hospital.
16. Unknown child, cor. Mill & Second Sts.
16. Unknown child, Church Home.
Oct. 23. Unknown man, new gas works.
Nov. 1. Unknown female.
Aug. 13. Vaccaro, Mrs. Nicoletta.
26. Varner, John, 114 Front St.
28. Veronica, Sister, w. Third St.
29. Van Hook, John, City Hospital.
31. Visbber, John, City Hospital.
31. Vinston, Wesley, c, Adams St.
Sept. 3. Vincent, Sol., 220 Poplar St.
5. Van Walsh, Daniel, w, Linden St.
5. Vogeli, H. J., w, died at Bartlett.
6. Vogeli, Mrs. H. J., w, died at Bartlett.
7. Volger, Violet.
10. Venable, Joseph, w, Chelsea.
11. Vincentia, Sister, w, Union St.
14. Valier, Thomas, City Hospital.
16. Vanburg, John.
18. Van Hame, W. C., w, Market St. Infirmary.
18. Virgeson, M. W., w, Monroe St.
19. Vanhoostenberg, Father, w, cor. Third & Adams Sts.
22. Varley, Thomas, w, Broadway.
22. Violet, Thomas, w, 70 Broadway.
23. Vinn, Clara C, w.
23. Valkner, Fred., w, City Hospital.
25. Vankunze, C. A., w, Market St. Infirmary.
26. Venu, Mary L., w.
28. Valuner, Nicholas.
Oct. 1. Voorhees, C. V., w. Poplar St.
8. Vaccaro, Alonzo, w, 79 Tate St.
21. Vaughn, Manuel, c, Kerr Ave.
Aug. 12. White, Mrs. Jennie L.
12. Wood, John W.
12. Wilcox, Nancy, c, Washington St.
12. Winston, Lucy, c.
14. Wilkins, Sharp, De Soto St.
14. White, S. M.
16. Washer, Hattie.
16. Winters, Emmet, Raleigh.
16. Walker, Willie, c.
17. Williams, Marry, 57 Main St.

Aug. 17. Walker, William, Clay St.
18. Wood, Wright, 150 Main St.
19. Walker, Cady, Old Raleigh Road.
21. Wright, Robert A., w, 99 Commerce St.
23. Werdt, Charlotte, w, 145 Washington St.
23. White, Frank, City Hospital.
23. Washington, Pinkie, c, Beale St.
24. West (infant of Angeline), 161 Union St.
25. Wills, Walter C., w, Madison St.
25. Williams, Mrs, S. E., w, Poplar St.
25. Williams, Miss Maggie, w, Main St.
25. Winters, Thomas, Jr., w, Linden St.
26. Welch, Mary, w.
26. Weiler, Lillie, w, Washington St.
26. Walsh, Katie.
26. Walsh, Lillie.
26. Walter, C.
26. Wilson, John O., w, City Hospital.
26. Ward, Albert, City Hospital.
26. Welch, Mike, w, City Hospital.
26. Walsh, John, City Hospital.
26. Winters, Thomas.
26. Warner, Tom, c. Front St.
26. Wande, Albert, w, City Hospital.
27. Wild, Ed., City Hospital.
27. Winston, Charles, 2 Ross Ave.
27. Walton, C., w, Madison St.
28. White, Mollie A., Shelby County.
28. Whittleton, Ben., c, Worsham House.
28. Watson, Dr. K. P., w, Second St.
29. White, Georgianna.
29. Williams, Biddy, 30 Overton St.
29. Woodsworth, Mrs., 29 Bass Ave.
29. Williams, Katie, c, 129 Poplar St.
29. Walsh, Rev. Martin.
29. Wallace, Elizabeth.
30. Wagner, Mike, w, Poplar St.
30. Woodruff, W. C., w, Main St.
30. West, Jeanette, c, Quinby St.
30. Wood, Louis, c, 35 Main St.
30. Williamson, Fred., c, 35 Third St.
30. Willette, Eliza, Shelby County.
30. Williams, County Jail.
30. West, Anthony, c.
30. Williams, Caroline, c, 79 Poplar St.
31. Wells, Francis, 185 Front St.
31. Woodsworth, Mr., w, Bass Ave.
31. Woodsworth, Mrs., w, Bass Ave.
31. Williams, Nannie, c, 13 Alabama St.
31. Wildberger, John, w.
31. Woeller, L., w, country.
Sept. 1. Warren, Jennie, Main St.
1. Washington, Lucy, c, Hill St.
1. Woodward, Mr., Bass Ave.
1. Walker, Alfred, c, 6 Turley St.
1. Wright, Willie, 8 Third St.
1. Winford, Thos., Elliott St.
1. Wilson, Mrs. M. M., Poplar St.
2. Widrig, George J., w, Pigeon Roost Road.
2. Wilson, Mrs. M. M., w, Poplar St.
2. Williams, Ed., w, City Hospital.
2. Wilson, Miss Mollie, 118 Main St.
2. Washington, Charles, c, 303 Washington St.
2. Williams, Charles, c, 197 Jefferson St.
2. Watkins, Eliza, c, 77 Commerce St.
2. Woodward, A. B., w, 63 Adams St.
2. Walker, Mrs., 6 Third St.
2. Williams, Eddie, c, 15 Bradford St.
2. Watkins, Belle, w, City Hospital.
2. Wright, Poplar St.
2. Weidlan, John, 178 Alabama St.
3. Windling, Frank.
3. White, Bertie, w, Peyton Ave.
3. Wildberger, Stella, w, Hernando Road.
3. Wray, John H., w, 442 Benle St.
3. Wiley, W., w, Memphis & Charleston R. R.
3. Walls, Henry, Madison St.
3. Williams, Mollie. c, 2½ North Turley St.
3. Walker, Martha, c, cor. Washington and High Sts.
3. Whitter, Mary, 108 Vance St.
3. Walsh, John, Randolph Road.
3. Wales, Hannah, c. Madison St.
3. Wood, Lizzie, c, 662 Main St.
4. Walker, George, c, Vance St.
4. Watson, H. C.
4. Waldron, James, w, 160 Main St.
4. Watkins, Ed., c, 36 Second St.
4. Wallace, Minnie, c, 130 St. Martin St.

Sept. 4. Walker, George, c, cor. Tennessee and Vance Sts.
4. Wray, Mrs., w, La Salette Academy.
4. Wettstein, Josephine, w, Poplar St.
5. Waldron, Polly, c, Fourth St.
5. Wright, Tom, 21 Exchange St., extended.
5. Williams, Mollie, c, 36 Bradford St.
5. Williams, Walter, c, 191 Jefferson St.
5. Williams, Caroline, c, 10 Howard Row.
5. Wilson, Andrew, c. 148 Poplar St.
5. Williams, Dan., c, 152 Poplar St.
5. Weathers, Richard, c, 169 Jefferson St.
5. Williams, Lizzie, c, 260 Madison St.
6. Williams, Frank, c, 153 Main St.
6. Williams, Billy, c, cor. Jefferson and Third Sts.
6. Woods, Josephine, 44 Promenade St.
6. Williams, Louis, c, 138 Alabama St.
6. Williams, Margaret, alley, bet. Main and Front Sts.
6. White, Matilda, cor. Wellington and Union Sts.
6. Walker, Jim, 106 Winchester St.
6. Walker, Scott, c, 345 Court St., extended.
6. Walker, William, c, New Raleigh Road.
7. White, D. L., w, Second St.
7. Williams, Dr. R. B., w, Peabody Hotel.
7. White, Weston.
7. Williams, Edward, c.
7. Wheeler, A. J., w.
7. White, D. F., 192 Second St,
7. Watson, Hernando Road.
7. Windler, Frank, w, 178 Alabama St.
7. Windler, John, w, 178 Alabama St.
7. Wolf, Mrs. Anna, w, Carolina St.
7. Warnecke, Mrs., w, Jones Ave.
7. Wolf, Gus ave A., w, Carolina St.
7. Weirich (child of Mrs.), w, Dunlap St.
8. Willhart, Miss, w.
8. Winfred, Henry, w, Market St. Infirmary.
8. Wilson, Henry, 139 Vance St.
8. Wilson, N. H., w, City Hospital.
8. Withe, Mrs. W., w.
8. Woods, Mrs., w, City Hospital.
8. Woodran, Armistend, 22 De Soto St.
8. Wilson, David, c, Monroe St.
8. Walden, Jack, Monroe St.
9. Woods, Zinnie, c.
9. Webb, Thomas.
9. Ward, Lillie, w, Market St. Infirmary.
9. Williams, Annie, Clay St.
9. Williams, Henry, c, 80 De Soto St.
9. Walsh, Thomas, w. Dunlap St.
9. Warnecke, Caroline, w, Jones Ave
9. Windex, Andrew, w, cor. Main and Pontotoc Sts.
9. Westfield, A. G. H., w, Tennessee St.
9. Washington, Boswell, w, 257 Monroe St.
9. Wilson, Mrs., w, near Lemon's Place.
9. Wetherington, cor. Third and Madison Sts.
9. Watkins, Ida, c, cor. Main and Georgia Sts.
9. Williamson, Mr., c, 71 Madison St.
9. Wise, Minor, Saffcrans St.
9. Washington, G W., c, cor. Mill and Second Sts.
9. Wagoner, Second St.
9. Winant, M. , c.
10. White, Robert.
10. White, Lou., c, Wellington St.
10. White Mary S., w, South St.
10. Wilhelmina, Sister, w, Market St.
10. Walker, Beckie, w, Linden St.
10. White, Ellen.
10. Woodfall, Henry.
10. Wilder, Hattie, cor. Seventh St. and Broadway.
10. Winter (child), cor. Hernando and Vance Sts.
10. Wilder, Mr., 35 Second St.
10. Watkins, S., c, Monroe St., extended.
10. Watkins, John, c, Monroe St., extended.
10. Whitfield, Thomas, w, Steamer City of Augusta.
10. Williams, A., c, 519 Shelby St.
10. Winston, Laura, c, 148 Beale St.
10. Whitemore, William, c. Shelby County.
10. Winn, Fred., w, Louisville, Ky.

A HISTORY OF THE YELLOW FEVER. 237

Sept. 10. Worsham, Clifford, w, Louisville, Ky.
11. Willheit, E., w, Main St.
11. Ward, Theodore F., w, Beale St.
11. Williams, Nannie H , w, Main St.
11. Wimberly, A. H., w, Union St.
11. Wilson, Laura C.
11. Winters, Charley, c, Avery St.
11. Wilson, James.
11. Wisely, Julia, w, City Hospital.
11. Williams, George, c, City Hospital.
11. Webb, Nannie, City Hospital.
12. Woern, Louisa.
12. Wind, Charles, c, Winchester St.
12. White, Peyton Ave.
12. Wilson, Nancy.
12. Wilson, W. W., w, City Hospital.
12. Woods, Mary, 662 Main St.
12. Walsh, Bridget, w, 34 Mulberry St.
12. Warring, B., Market St. Infirmary.
12. White, Louisa, w, 113 Orleans St.
12. Williams, H., c, 173 De Soto St.
12. Wells, Alfred, 62 Georgia St.
12. Wright, Henry, w, 180 Johnson Ave.
12. Wadley, Frank, c, Winchester St.
12. Wasche, Henry, w.
13. Woodward, Dr. J. D., w.
13. Wardlaw, David A., w, Howard Infirmary.
13. Wishe, A., w, Jackson St.
13. Williams, w. cor. Seventh & Jackson Sts.
13. Warren, c, 59 Jackson St.
13. Wells, John, w, City Hospital.
13. Webb, Mattie, c, 66 Beale St.
13. Waechter, Charles E., 182 Main St.
14. Williams, Sarah, c, Walnut St.
14. Walsh, John, w, Madison St.
14. Williams, John, c, 85 South St.
14. Wealey, R., City Hospital.
14. Williams, Ben., c, cor. St. Martin and South Sts.
14. Warring, H. L., w, Hunt's Building.
14. White, Donny.
14. Ward, James C., w, 270 Beale St.
14. Wishe, Mrs. A., w, cor. Sixth and Jackson Sts.
14. Wiley (child of John).
14. Wasche, Mrs. Caroline, w.
15. Worsham, E. R. T., w.
15. Willis, William, w, North Court St.
15. Ward, Horatio J., w.
15. Walsh, Katie, w, Dunlap St.
15. Welsh, William, w.
15. Winter, Charles, w, Randolph Road.
15. Walker, Annie.
15. Wiley (child of John), c.
15. White, Mary, c, Hernando Road.
15. Wood, Mrs., w, Rocco Alley.
15. Whitemore, James, c, Shelby County.
15. West, J. M., w, Market St. Infirmary.
15. Ward, Mary, on bluff.
16. Waggoner, W. S., 572 Shelby St.
16. Williams, Fred., c, Risk & Johnson's Foundry.
16. Walker, Calvin, c, Cow Island Road.
16. Williams, Wash , c, 167 Second St.
16. Walsh, Andrew, w, 18 Stewart Ave.
16. Williams, Sam., c, 217 South St.
16. Whiteside, C., c, 321 Carolina St.
16. White, M., w, South St.
16 Weller, Henry Clay, w.
17. Willheit, Adolph, w, 235 Main St.
17. Washington, Millie, c, cor. Alabama St. and Jones Ave.
17. Williams, George, c, 378 Main St.
17. Whitelaw, James, 150 Broadway.
17. Waggoner, J. H., Sr., 252 Turley St.
17. Worsmick, Mrs., w, City Hospital.
17. Waffon, William, w, Rayburn Ave.
18. Wilson, Helen B., w, 392 Main St.
18. Walker, Isaac.
18. White, Mary, c, Front St.
18. Worth, H., w, Fifth St.
18. Weager, Annie, 41 Fifth St.
18. Williams, Robert E , w, 107 Vance St.
19. Winson, S., w, Randolph Road.
19. Walker, Laura, c, Georgia St.
19. Walker, Eddie, c. 172 Vance St.
19. Wilker, John, 42 Causey St.
19. Wilson, Nathan.
19. Ward, Clinton Halst., w.

Sept. 19. Winson, Mrs., Randolph Road.
20. Walker, George.
20. Witte, Wilhelm, w, Madison St.
20. Wilson, Wood, Georgia St.
20. Worsneck, Joseph, w, City Hospital.
20. Williams. Isabel, w, 33 Ruth St.
20. Ward, Virginia, c, Wellington St.
21. Williams, Nancy, c, Charleston Ave.
21. Williams, Hatch, c, Adams St.
22. Warnecke, Fritz, w, Jones Ave.
22. Wright, Mrs., w, Library Building.
22. Walker, S. F., w, Raleigh.
23. Ward, Lillie, w, Leath Orphan Asylum.
23. Williams, Sarah G., foot of Broadway.
24 Wright, King, c, Hernando St.
24. Williams, Bussey.
24. White, Gottlieb, w, Plietz's Garden.
24. White, Dr. J. M. S., w, Main St.
24. Ware, J. H., w, South St.
25. Walsh, Aggie, Gayoso House.
25. Wood, Jonathan, w, 311 Vance St.
25. Weston, Richard, c, Carolina St.
25. Wash, Looney Switch.
25. Whitford, Mrs. C. L., w, Huling St.
25. Walshe, Martin, w, City Hospital.
25. Walker, Mrs. M. B., w, 110 Linden St.
25. Wilcox, S. H., w, 79 Madison St.
25. Wood, John.
25. Wilson, John.
25. Walker, Delia.
25. Westmiller, Mrs.
25. Webb, George S.
25. Wright, Casper, w, 76 Clay St.
28. Williams, Davie, w, Market St. Infirmary.
28. Williams, Caroline, c, Shelby County.
28. Winchester, Floy, cor. Alabama and Robinson Sts.
28. Walshe, Dennis, w, Stewart Ave.
28. Wells, Mr., w, Hernando St.
28. Wilburne, Ned, c, Walnut St.
28. Williams, Mrs. E., c.
29. Wolfe, Mr., w.
29. Whitemore, Mr., Hernando Road.
29. Woods, Martha, c.
29. Wiley, William, Market St. Infirmary.
29. White, Mrs. Julia, c, Pontotoc St.
29. Wilson, Mary Ella, w, Hernando Road.
30. Woodfold, James, w, Wolf River Ferry.
30. Willard, M. E., w, Hernando Road.
30. Walshe, John, w, Stewart Ave.
30. Whit, Julia, c, 134 Pontotoc St.
Oct. 1. Warner, David E., w, Hernando Road.
2. Williams, James, c, cor. Jackson and Front Sts.
2. Will, c, Horn Lake Road.
2. Wilson, Mrs., w.
2. Woodfold, B., c, near Elmwood.
4. Whelan, Andrew, w, cor. South and Hernando Sts.
4. Wallace, B., c, 70 Poplar St.
4. Webb, William, c, 19 Madison St.
4. Woods, George W., w, Carolina St.
4. Waldron, Elmira.
4. Welch, Charles, w, Gayoso House.
4. Williams, Charles, c, Linden St.
5. Weheren, Annie.
5. Washington, Mrs. E. D., w, Raleigh Road.
5. Williams, Walker, c, Exchange St.
6. White, Mrs. E. A.
6. Whipple, Mrs. E. A., w, M. & C. R. R.
7. Wilburne, Jane, c, Jones Ave.
7. Woods, Mrs. W. S., Shelby County.
9. White, M., w, Vance St.
9. Warner, F., w, Valentine Ave.
9. Wright, Mrs. Jessie, w, Jackson St.
10. Winder, Francisa, w.
10. Williams, W. T , w, 206 Tennessee St.
10. Williams, Peter. w, President's Island.
10. White, Henderson. Carolina St.
11. Wells, Mrs. N, w, Hernando St.
11. Walker, Joshua, Jr., c, Central Point.
11. Woods, Massie, c, Gill's Station.
11. Whitesides, H., w, Carolina St.
12. White, Fannie, c, Union Ave.
12. Warrener, Philip, 205 Poplar St.
12. Warner, Carrie, w, Valentine Ave.
12. Wiggin, James, w, Jackson St.
12. Walsh, John, Jr., w, Winchester St.
13. Webb, Macon, w, Vance St.

238   A HISTORY OF THE YELLOW FEVER.

Oct. 13. Williams. Mrs., c, South Jackson St.
15. Wenderlin, Brother. w, Market St.
18. White, Martha, c, Calhoun St.
18. Wheatley, P. B., w, McLemore Ave.
18. Webber, Edward, w, Monroe St.
19. Wupperman, A., w, Poplar St.
19. Wright, A., c, Randolph Road.
20. Whitfield, Wm., w, Country.
22. Woodruff, Andrew, c, Horn Lake Road.
22. Williams, Jane.
22. Walsh, Patrick, w, Country.
22. Wellman, Carey, w, Exchange St.
23. Winchester, Louisa, w, Poplar St.
23. Whitemore, Charley, c, Jefferson St.
23. Wellman, M. C., w, Exchange St.
24. Williams, Chas., w, mouth of Wolf River.
24. Williams, M. W., w, mouth of Wolf River.
24. Williams, Jane, c, Short Third St.
24. Williams, Wallace, w, Court St.
25. Wellfonn, Scott, c, Court St.
26. Weatherby, William. w, Hernando Road.
28. Woods, Emma, w, 18½ Causey St.
29. Wood, Mattie C., w, Broadway St.
29. Wheatley, Hugh, w, McLemore Ave.
29. Weaver, Sam.
31. Wright, Hardin.
Nov. 1. Williams, Emma, w.
1. White, Raymond.
5. Ware, J. N, w, Orleans St.
17. Ward, S. J., w, Moseby Ave.
17. Williams, Addie, c, Turley St.

Nov. 18. Wasche, Louise, w.
20. Whitford, Mrs. A. S.. w, Horn Lake Road.
22. Wilson, John, Third St.
27. Walker, Melinda, c.
30. Wilson, Henrietta, c, Main St.
Sept. 4. Young, Ed., c, 124 Poplar St.
6. Young, Fannie, 17 Second St.
8. Yates, Frank, Raleigh Road.
9. Young, M., c, 65 De Soto St.
12. Younger, Addie, c, 65 Gayoso St.
13. Young, Annie, w, 135 Causey St.
13. Yancey, Lou., w, Madison St.
13. Young, Thomas, w, City Hospital.
13. Yates, Esther, c, 150 Gayoso St.
17. York, Will. Q., w, 3 Trezevant St.
22. York, F. P., w, 3 Trezevant St.
26. Young, Thomas, w, City Hospital.
29. Yearger, Walter.
Oct. 2. Yonkers, Mrs., w, Bass Ave.
5. Yeager, Tillie.
15. Young, John, w, Randolph Road.
21. Yegge, Louis, w, Front St.
28. Yerby, A. N , w, Horn Lake Road.
Aug. 15. Zanna, Mary E.
Sept. 6. Zoanne, Baptiste, w, Grant St.
15. Zimmerman, Sophy, w, Gayoso House.
15. Zimmerman, w, Gayoso House.
Oct. 5. Zoyer, Tillie, w, Marley Ave.
18. Zanona, Mary N.. Pigeon Roost Road.
27. Zehring (child of John), w, Shelby St.

CITIZENS OF MEMPHIS WHO DIED ABROAD.

The following list embraces the names of citizens of Memphis who died while refugees from home during the epidemic, the dates of whose death we have been unable to obtain:

Armstrong, J. S., Covington, Tenn.
Alexander, Mrs., Frayser's Station, Tenn.
Albert, Mr., River, Tenn.
Atkinson, A. C., Raleigh, Tenn.
Baker, Mrs. Mattie R., Capersville, Tenn.
Belcher, Crabtree. Tuscumbia, Ala.
Cunningham, James, Brownsville, Tenn.
Conrad, J. W., Somerville, Tenn.
Clayton, Ed., Cornersville, Tenn.
Campbell, D. C., Hernando. Miss.
Carter, Miss M A., Cedar Grove, Tenn.
Coleman, Willie, Raleigh, Tenn.
Coleman, Maggie, Raleigh, Tenn.
Callihan, Ned., County, Tenn.
Cunningham, Mrs. H., Brownsville, Tenn.
Clare, Posey, Raleigh, Tenn.
Clare, Mrs. Posey, Raleigh, Tenn.
Dixon, Hon. L. V., Abingdon, Va.
Drury, W. C., McKenzie, Tenn.
Dixon, James, Raleigh, Tenn.
Ford, J. B., Hernando, Miss.
Flaherty, James, Hernando, Miss.
Flaherty, Miss, Hernando, Miss.
Frayser (child of R. D.), Somerville, Tenn.
Feldstadt, John, Hernando, Miss.
Forbes, Charles, river.
Graham, Miss Blanche, Lookout Mountain.
Graham, Lora B., Cincinnati, O.
Groves, Robert, Humboldt, Tenn.
Green, John A., country.
Hickey, James, Raleigh, Tenn.
Harry, Capt., River, Tenn.
Hainer, Nancy C., Raleigh, Tenn.
Hallows, Joseph, Country, Tenn.
Henning, T., Wythe Depot, Tenn.
Hooks, Mrs. H. C., Brownsville, Tenn.
Hobson, Dr. H. R., Murfreesboro, Tenn.
Henning. E. K., Wythe Depot, Tenn.
Hill, W. P., Cherry Station, Tenn.
Harder, Miss Ellen, Hernando, Miss.
Harder, Miss Annie, Hernando, Miss.
Haack, Julius, Hernando, Miss.

Hays, A. J., Bailey's Station, Miss.
Haskell, Mr., Cincinnati, O.
Hutchinson, Mrs. Ida F., McKenzie, Tenn.
Iglauer, L., Cincinnati, O.
Jefferson, Mrs. M. S., Fayette Co., Tenn.
Kortrecht, Hon. Charles, Bartlett, Tenn.
Kenden, Mr., Raleigh, Tenn.
Lingreen, Mr., Raleigh, Tenn.
Leidy, Eugene, Jr., Holly Springs, Miss.
Lewis, John E., Hernando, Miss.
Loewenthall, L., Raleigh. Tenn.
Lowell, Sam., Raleigh, Tenn.
Maury. J., Louisville, Ky.
Moore, H. J., Germantown, Tenn.
Moon, Miss Mollie B., Lagrange, Tenn.
Moore, Lloyd, Hernando, Miss.
Maury, Miss Mary, Hernando, Miss.
McNees, Mrs. Sarah, Hernando, Miss.
Morris, Mrs. John, Rossville, Tenn.
Moon, Nelson, Horn Lake, Miss.
McKeon, John E., Raleigh, Tenn.
McClannahan, J., Raleigh, Tenn.
Moore, Ed., river.
Pleitz, William, Cincinnati, O.
Pettus, L. O., Brownsville, Tenn.
Pillow, Gen. Gideon J., Phillips County, Ark.
Ritter, Mrs. A. E., Louisville, Ky.
Reinig, Cæsar, Raleigh, Tenn.
Reinig, Mrs. C., Raleigh, Tenn.
Reed, Ben., Somerville, Tenn.
Ringwald, Stella, Cedar Grove. Tenn.
Ralston, Sarah A., Raleigh. Tenn.
Ralston, W. Walter, Raleigh, Tenn.
Resney, Owen, Raleigh, Tenn.
Stewart, C. Young, Hernando, Miss.
Stewart, Mrs S. M., Hernando, Miss.
Stewart, Butler P., Hernando, Miss.
Scully, R., Louisville, Ky.
Scudder, C. D., Iuka, Miss.
Siefker, Miss Mena, Hernando, Miss.
Sneed, Arthur, Buntyn, Tenn.
Scruggs, Hon. P. T., Buntyn, Tenn.

A HISTORY OF THE YELLOW FEVER. 239

Somerville, R. B., Mason, Tenn.
Sanderson, John, river.
Sullivan, Miss, Raleigh, Tenn.
Smith, Henry, Raleigh, Tenn.
Smith, Mrs, Raleigh, Tenn.
Taylor, Mary E., Raleigh, Tenn.
Williams, J. P., Grenada, Miss.
Wesson, Walter, Trezevant, Tenn.
Wiggs, Jesse P., Lagrange, Tenn.
Walston, John, Germantown, Tenn.
Weaver, J. B., Cedar Grove, Tenn.
Weaver, Mrs. J. B., Cedar Grove, Tenn.
Webb, Mrs., Somerville, Tenn.
White, James M., Leighton, Ala.
Willett, J. H., St. Louis, Mo.
Woodward, A., St. Louis, Mo.
Walker, W J., St. Louis, Mo.
White, M., Milan, Tenn.
Woods, J. K., Grenada, Miss.
Woods, Mrs. Carrie N, Hernando, Miss.
Walker, S. F., Raleigh, Tenn.
Winters, Emmet, Raleigh, Miss.
Vallentine, C. O., New Jersey.
Voudran, Peter, Hernando, Miss.
Vondran, Mrs. Peter, Hernando, Miss.

TENNESSEE.

Bartlett.
Ward, H. J.
Weaver, J. B.
Weaver, Mrs. J. B.
Carter, Miss.
Graves, Mrs. J.
Le Fere, P. A.
Sleidger, Fritz.
Cannon, Miss Hattie.
Hill, Nancy.
Williams, Fannie.
Voegele, Mrs. H. J.
Voegele, H. J.
Ringwald, Miss Stella.
Forgey, John W.
Wright, A. L.
King, James.
Duncan, Mr.
McGowan, Alfred.
Thomas, James.
Tate, Mary.

Bell's Depot.
Hunter, Dr. John.
Parker, John.

Bethel Springs.
Yarbo, J. J.

Bolivar.
Coleman, A. A.
Coleman, Lizzie.

Chattanooga.
Austin, J. A.
Adcock, Joe.
Ackerman, Miss Hattie.
Ancil, John.
Ancil, Mrs.
Butler, Mrs. Margaret.
Butler, Robert.
Butler, William.
Bisplinghoff, Chas.
Burke, James.
Burke, Mrs. James.
Bell, Mrs.
Bell, Miss W. M.
Bell, Wm. M.
Baird, Dr. E. M.
Barr, Dr. R. N.
Barr, G. N.
Burkhart, Rosa.
Bosley, Wm.
Brown, Mrs.
Brenner, Rev. G. H.
Bean, Annie.
Burge, Mrs. Mary.
Burge, Vincent.
Burge, Wm.
Curry, C. W.
Carlisle, Hon. Thos. J.
Conley, Mrs. Nancy.
Conley, Harry.
Cash, John.
Chamberlain, Mrs.Delia.
Chamberlain, Mrs. M. C.

Chamberlain, Miss Cora.
Corey, Joseph.
Corey, Mrs. S. H.
Connelly, Mrs.
Calder, Mrs. J.
Crandell, Mrs. Delia.
Carlin, D. B.
Drake, Miss Ethel.
Dietz, Mrs. Oswald.
Erwin, Wm.
Ewing, W. J.
Farmer, Miss Sallie.
Farmer, Miss Kate.
Flemming, Mrs. Pat.
Goldstein, S.
Goodwin, W. G.
Griffin, Arthur.
Gleason, Oscar.
Graham, Miss.
Gledhill, G. H.
Harder, Mrs. Mary.
Hartman, L.
Hartman, Margaret.
Hartman, John.
Hartman, Mrs. J.
Hartman, Thomas.
Hartman, J. H.
Henly, Mrs. Lena.
Haran, Mrs. Mary.
Hunnicutt, Mrs.
Hunnicutt, Walter.
Hall, Mrs. Sarah.
Hammel, Albert.
Harkness, C. D.
Jones, Ed. J.
Jones, E. L.
Jennings, J. B.
Kaufman, Mrs.
Kenny, Mrs. Julia.
Kenny, Jessie.
Kiesle, Charles.
Kiesle, Ed.
Legras, Edward.
Lumpkins, Thos.
Moyle, Mrs.
Matill, John.
McAfee, J. A.
McIntosh, R.
Marsh, Howard.
Miller, Jessie.
Merricke, Albert.
Morgan, W. T.
Morgan, Eliza.
Maloney, Pat.
McMillin, Daniel.
McMahon, John.
O'Donnell, Mrs.
O'Neal, John.
O'Neal, Mary.
Price, Mattie.
Price, Maggie.
Perryman, Reuben.
Parham, A. K.
Parker, John.
Ragsdale, B. F.
Ragsdale, Mrs. B. F.

Robinson, Ed. H.
Ryan, Father P.
Rose, Porter.
Rector, R. S.
Singleton, Thos.
Singleton, Harry.
Singleton, Mrs. Mary.
Singleton, Mrs. Thos.
Schneidman, Jacob.
Schneidman, Sue.
Schneidman, Louisa.
Salters, John.
Sweeney, Mary.
Schleissinger, E.
Schnee, Geo.
Stanfield (child).
Stanfield, Fannie.
Sullivan, John J.
Savage, Henry.
Scheveir, Henry.
Scheveir, Matt.
Swofford, Ed.
Stewart.
Stewart, Mrs. E.
Spencer, Mrs.
Schwatzenburg, Mrs.
Tabler, John.
Tally, Hugh.
Underhill, W. D.
Varillo, John.
Warren, Kate.
Warner, Andrew.
Weinnecate, Chas.
Weinaike, Andrew.
Wilkenson, Mrs. P. A.
Wiltze, Ralph.
Whites.................... 137
Colored................... 56
Total 193

Collierville.
Bowman, M. R.
Bowman, Mrs. M. R.
Mangum, S. D.
Mangum, Mrs. S. D.
Person, Jimmy.
Webb, Mrs. D. A.
Webb, Miss Willie.
Jones, Fannie.
Perkins, Dr. P. A.
Perkins, Mrs. P. A.
Madison, Charles.
Raymond, Charles.
McElwee, Charles.
McElwee, S. J.
Leon, Mrs.
Hayes, Mrs. G.
Hayes, Mr. G.
Scott, G. W.
Lake, Mrs. Sam'l.
Davis, Mayor G. H.
Estes, T. L.
Boyd, Mrs.
Holland, A. J.
Rogers, Harry.

Rogers, Miss Flora.
Johnson, Peter.
Harris, J. T.
Galvin, Mrs. John.

COLORED.
Branch, Oliver.
Hatch, Love.
Porter, L. A.
Zach.
Logan.
Bonner, Joseph.
Ross, Elbert.
Owens, Thomas.

Covington.
Wiseman, W. J.

Erin.
Bradley, Mrs. L.
Grigsby, Dr. J. P.
Humphrey, C. S.
Nichols, W. B.
Reynolds, J. H.
Rushing, R. W.
Stanfield, M. M.
Simpson, G. W.
Stanfield, Mrs. M. M.
Stanfield, Mrs.
Stanfield, Mr.
Stanfield, M. M.

Frayser's Station.
Alexander, Mrs.
Caraway, Miss.
Erskine, Geo.
Pipe, O. H.
Watkins, James.
Young, John.

Gadsden.
Cornatzar, Geo. M., Jr.
Finder, Wm. F.
Richardson, Capt.
Saunders, R. G.
Smith, Julia.

Galloway.
Amos, Mrs.
Greer, Nannie.
Hodges, J. W., Jr.
Hodges, Lovie.
Humblette, Mrs.
Moore, Mrs.
Perkins, Mrs.
Tarry, Dr. Thomas H.

Gardner's Station.
Scobey, Mrs.

Germantown.
Allen, Miss Nellie.
Buster, J. C.
Carpenter, Sidney.
Carpenter, Sidney, Jr.
Clark, S. C.

16

Clark, Mrs. S. C.
Edmonson, Ellen.
Gorman, James.
Gorman, Nellie.
Hurt, B. F.
Hurt, Mrs. B. F.
Hurt, W. S.
Hurt, Julian.
Hurt, Robert Lee.
Hurt, Thos.
Johnson, Jennie.
Kelly, Bettie.
Matlock, Mrs. Carrie V.
McKay, Dr. R. H.
Miller, Mrs. W. E.
Miller, Laura W.
Miller, V. R.
Moore, H. J.
Mooreman, Randall, col.
Neal's two children.
O'Neil, Wm.
O'Neil, Mary.
Rogers, J. H.
Rhodes, L. A.
Rhodes, Mrs. Cornelia.
Reneau, Sallie E.
Rainey, Lee B.
Roberts, J. S.
Robinson, America, col.
Shepard, Sallie B.
Spivey, Jack, col.
St. Clair, Dr.
Simmons, Rev. R. S.
Simmons, Mrs. R. S.
Simmons, Mattie Lou.
Walston, John C.
Walker, Sallie W.

Gill's Station.
Pullen, Mrs. Ben. K.

Grand Junction.
Boyd, Hilliard.
Ball, C. W.
Bellew, Mrs. R. W.
Bass, W. W.
Bledsoe, Mrs. Mary.
Brook, Sam.
Brook, Henry.
Beaty, Dr. J. H.
Culligan, Julia.
Clampett, Robert.
Clampett, Mrs. Mollie.
Clampett, Harris.
Clampett, Chalmer.
Campbell (child of Mrs.)
Flannery, Dennis.
Flannery, Mrs. Dennis.
Flannery, Mary.
Hewitt, Miss.
Hawkins, Frank.
Hagard, N. P.
Hayes, Bettie.
Handy, C. G.
Jenkins, Mrs. Susan.
Jones, F.
Jones, Thos. E.
Loyce, George.
Lavinder, Frank.
Lavinder, Harry.
Lavinder, Jasper.
Moore, Miss M. B.
Milam, R. P.
Netherland, James, Jr.
Netherland, Parvin.
Owens, N. J.
Owens, Mrs.
Owens, Mrs. N. J.
Patterson, N. S.
Patterson, Smith.
Patterson, Mrs. Virginia.
Prewitt, C. V.
Prewitt, Earnest.

Prewitt, Dr. N. W.
Prewitt, Miss Nannie.
Prewitt, Dr. J. H.
Prewitt, Mrs. J. H.
Prewitt, S. E., Jr.
Prewitt, Mrs. Mary.
Prewitt, May.
Stinson, Mrs. A.
Stinson, Miss Eugene.
Stinson, A. F.
Stinson, Samuel.
Stinson, Charles.
Smith, Mrs. M.
Smith, Beauregard.
Swann, Booker.
Tucker, Mary.
Tucker, Susie.
Thompson, Ella.
Thompson, Evan.
Thompson, Albert.
Woods, W. J.
Woods, Mollie.
Woods, Annie.
Woods, Willie.
Woods, Katie.
Woods, James.
Unknown, 3.

Huntingdon.
Simpson, Mrs. James R.

Jackson.
Hadaway, James.
Reardon, Mrs.
Wilson, Andrew.

Mason.
Brannon, Young.
Lannahan, John.
Nicholson, R. G.
Parish, Mrs.
Parish, Ella.
Pippen, Henry.
Pippen (child of).
Rice, Rev. Dr.
Spane, Thomas.
Somerville, Col. R. B.
Sturdevant, A. J.
Sturdevant, Mrs. Peter.
Sturdevant, Miss.
Sturdevant, N.
Unknown, 6 col.

McKenzie.
Branch, W. P.
Crutchfield, J. H.
Cartis, C.

Moscow.
Allen, Mrs. B.
Allen, Emma.
Allen, Bertha.
Cowan, John.
Cowan (infant of J. S. R.)
Calaway, Marshall.
DeAragon, Mrs. Dennie.
Epp, Mrs. Wm.
Epp, Mrs. E. A.
Epp, Fred.
Epp, Tealey.
Frenchman, A.
Goley, Fred.
Hazlewood, T. B.
Hill, Dr. J. S.
Kite, Mrs. Lucy, col.
Layton, Willie.
Layton, W. J.
Layton, Mrs M. C.
Marsh, Ed. (col. nurse).
Maas, Mrs. H.
McConnel, Mrs. C. W.
Morris, Edward, col.
Oharro.

O'Harel, Michael.
Smith, John.
Steger, Jack S.
Steger, Mrs. E. A.
Stover, Mrs. R. B.
Stover, Mattie.
Stover, Miss Donnie.
Simmons, Miss Nannie.
Simmons, Miss Annie.
Storm, Fritz.
Staun, Harry.
Sturm, James.
Smith, Dealey, infant, col.
Thomas, Geo.
Thompson, J., infant, col.
Wade, Sidney Y.
White, Mrs. R. B.
White, Mrs. K.
Wheeler, Dr. J. M.
Wright, Lucy.

Murfreesboro.
Hopson, Dr. H. R., of Memphis.
Hicks, Dr. at Memphis).

Nashville.
Atkins, Mrs.
Eastman, John U.
Haggard, Wm.
Laurent, Emile C.
Looney, Wm. Z.
Martin, Mrs. M. P.
Maurey, Edward.
McGaughey.
Sheetz, H. C.
Thompson, N. B.

Nubbin Ridge.
Walker, Thos. J.

Paris.
Arnold, Mr.
Beeler, J. H.
Carroll, Ed.
Chester, Price, col.
Ernest, Mrs.
Foley, Pat.
Kendall, Alf., col.
Lewis, W. J.
Layton.
Lawton, Mr.
Milam, Dr. E. E.
Nance, J. W.
Steed, W. H.
Tedro, Mrs., col.
Tedro, J. H., col.
Tedro (child of Mrs.), col.
Warren, E. F.
Williams, Emma, col.

Raleigh.
Cleere, Emma V.
Cleere, Mrs. W. P.
Goodman.
Gear, Dosca.
Heiner, Mrs.
King, Amanda.
Lemburg.
Newberg.
Ringwald, Jesse.
Ralston, James.
Ralston, Walter.
Shovenall, Mrs.
Shovenall, Miss Lena.
Taylor, Miss Mollie.

Rossville.
Gwynn, W. H.
Graves, Mrs. P.
Graves, Alonzo, Jr.
Graves, Mr. A. P.
Morris, Mrs. John.

Warr, Americus V., Jr.

Shelby Depot.
Stewart, J. R.
Sackett, Eddie.
Sackett, Walter.

Somerville.
Plummer, Capt. P. B.
Bowers, Mr.
Bowers, Miss Annie.
Weatherby, Wm.
Weatherby, James.
Webb, Mrs.
Small, F. T.
Gilliam, W. A.
Hobson, Dr.
Lattin, Miss.
Winva, Mrs.
Pulliam, Geo.
Olbrecht, Mrs.
Scruggs, Amy.
Etta, Mr.
Eartharn, E. J.
Cabeler, L. F.
Bowers, Mrs.
Conrad, Mr.
Plummer, Mrs. P. B.
Schwar, Rev. M.
Schwar (child of Rev. M)
Gilliam, Mr.
Bowles, Mr.
Lattin, Jno. T.
Freeman, Jno.
Privette, D. H.
Moore, Knox.
Cabeler, Mrs.
Howell, Rev. Mr.
Pulliam, Julius.
Greenway, W. W.
Ford, Dr. E. C.
Harris, Dr. E. W.

COLORED.
Humphreys, Eliza.
Jones, Robert.
Unknown boy.
Ross, Serena.
Jones (child of V.).
Jones (child of B.).
Halloway, Esther.
Williamson, Spencer.
Reed, Benj.
Herndon, Jno.
Reed, Jane.
Cloyd, Rose.
Fraser, Henry.
Shaw, Henry.
Williamson, Alice.
Taylor, Wash.
Berry, Mrs. Gus.
Cabeler, Zach.
Jackson, E.

Union City.
Curlin, Amos.

Williston.
Black, L. M.
Bryals, Thomas.
Crawfore, W. M.
Crawford, W. M.
Dobbins, Dr. A. M. C.
Garvin, Dr. Joe G.
Garvin, R. W.
Koonce, R. M.
Wilson, John, Sr.
Wilson, Joe.
Walker, Jake H.

Withe Depot.
League, W. H.

TENNESSEE.—BROWNSVILLE.

Owen, H.
Beard, Stephen, col.
McIntosh, Mrs.
Lee, Eldora.
Bailey, Ben., col.
Unknown white man.
Unknown col'd woman.
Hughes, Frank.
Doran (child of Mr.).
Pettus, L. O.
McIntosh, Mrs.
Gordon, James.
Bennett, Major W. K.
Williams, Mrs.
Young, Alex, Jr.
Young, Martha.
Hill, Mrs. J. E.
Miller, Ferdinand.
Bradford, Miles.
Reynick, A. C.
Logan, John.
Osbenchain, J. T.
Osley (boy), col.
Beard, Mrs., col.
Butts (child of A.).
Dunlap (child of Sue).
Caldwell, Mrs. John.
Scott, R. H.
Williams, Vina.
Wills, Dr. W. T.
Tomlin (child of G. M.).
Pleitz, Willie.
Pleitz, Mr.
Westbrook, Col. W. Ivie.
Walker, James, col.

Byrum, T. G.
Drennan, Mrs. E. C.
Turner, Elder.
Hilyer, Ed.
Martin, Thomas.
Martin, Mrs.
Martin, Miss Tillie.
Keatly, Mrs.
McBride, Charles.
Woods, Pat.
McFarland, Mrs.
Rayner, June.
Talbot, Willis.
Sevier, Peter.
Chandler, Mrs.
Hawkins, Miss Emeline.
Ware, Dr. John J.
Turner, Mrs. Harriet.
McBride. Mrs. S. F.
Turner, Miss Harriet.
Riley, John.
Wood, Emma.
Haskins, Gus., Jr.
Wood, Spencer R.
Haskins, Mrs. Gus.
Byars, Billy, col.
Guntlach, Mrs.
Wills, Alfred, col.
Warrington, W. H.
Whitelaw, Richard.
Ware, Miss Maria.
Edwards, B. F.
Jones, Jacob.
Caldwell, Miss Jessie.
McFarland, Miss Kate.

Moses (child of John).
*Grove, Cog.
Klice, A. J.
Selig, Simon.
Unknown col'd man.
Henderson, Julia.
Unknown col'd woman.
Oldham, Charles.
Cuthbert, E. B.
Bond, Jeff.
Dunlap, Eugene.
Jackson, Miss Florence.
Keeley, James.
Cunningham, Mrs. Anna.
Lane, J. W., col.
Thomas, Ed., col.
Townsley, Sam, col.
Winston, Ed., col.
Heathcock, Mrs.
McDonald, Carrie.
Beard, Henry, col.
Beard, Mr., col.
Ashe, John J.
Kendall, Anthony.
Calhoun, Jas. Dick.
Howell, Miss May Belle.
Mann, Mrs. Joel.
Pressly, Mr.
Goss, Horace.
Holbrook, M. V.
Bond, Hon. Lewis.
Moses, Nancy.
Lewlin Henry.
Mann, Eliza, col.
Willis, Wesley.

Beard (child of Stephen).
Graham, Chas.
German, Henry.
Boss, R. G.
Beard, Eliza.
Obenchain, Mrs. J. T.
McBride, Mrs.
Kinney, D. M.
Unknown col'd woman.
Taylor (child of Joe.).
Unknown col'd woman.
Unknown white man.
Aldridge (child of Mr.).
Young, Alex.
Unknown colored man.
Unknown col'd woman.
Sturdevant, Mrs.
Pearson, Reed.
Clark, George.
Rogers, Gid., col.
Starks, Henry.
Haskins (infant of Gus.).
Walker, Manson, col.
Plietz, Mrs. and son.
Guntlach, Dr.
Drennan, E. C.
Bond (child of Mira), col.
Hammons, Lewis, col.
Sherman, Dock.
Russell, Wm. C.
Reeves, (child of Mr.)
Logan, John.
Smith, J. C.
Aldrich (child of J. B.).

* In a delirium, after being deserted by his nurse, turned the lamp over, set the house on fire, and was himself burned to death.

242   A HISTORY OF THE YELLOW FEVER.

II.

MISSISSIPPI.—VICKSBURG.

Murphy, Thomas.
Bryan, Henry N.
McCallum, James.
Townsend, Franklin.
Stoltz, Paul.
Thompson, T. J.
Ratigan, Frances.
Levins, John.
Jones, Fanny.
Buurdo, Frank.
Sagona, Frank.
Arnold, Mr.
Conway, Mrs. Bridget.
Conway, Joseph.
Giovanini, Dominico
Burns, James.
Woman, unknown.
Shelby, Howard.
Murphy, Geo.
Conlan, Chas.
Baurdo, Mamie.
Schwink. L. T.
Stangel, Jas.
Gerard, Ellis.
Burdo, Mrs.
Gebhaur, Maggie.
Ellis, W. J.
Kuntz, Lowis.
Lynch, Mary.
Sagona, Peter.
Guy, Geo.
Marrian, J.
Conway, J.
Kaufman, A.
Man, unknown.
Allen, Minnie.
Fowler, G.
Pierce, Katie M.
Burd, G. M.
Stutz, Frank.
Delaney, Michael.
Behring, Chas.
Giovanini, Mrs.
Gibbs, C. H.
Fleming, W. S.
Honlehan, T.
Roshe, Lizzie.
Pelton, Mrs.
Russell, W. R.
Buurdo, Chas.
Burrell, Mattie.
Francis, Amelia.
Klein, Frank H.
Hayes, James.
Smoker, John.
Morrow, David.
Golden, Jas.
Winfield, Morris.
Downs, Rose.
Bertoni, A. A.
Brown, Annie.
Weyer, John.
Petro, Felice.
Kellar, Louis.
Wright, Anderson.
Welsh, Mrs. E. A.
Babb, Mary L.
Brooke, Frank T.
Schwink, Jacob L.
Savard, Chas.
Johnson, Mrs. J. E.
Dohler, C. E.
Russell, Mrs. J.
Johnson, Annie.
Russell, G. A.
Eggleston, Robt. E.
Foley, Margaret J.
Cooper, Belle.
Rivers, Mary.
Mullen, Nicholas.
Ryan, Mary.

Italian, unknown.
Fisher, Frank C.
Devlin, Chas.
Roberson, Bettie.
Thrift, Mrs. Elizabeth.
Voeinkle, Louisa.
Anter, Wm. M.
Roost, Caroline.
Bowen, J. J.
Kennedy, David P.
Allen, Thos.
Berry, Geo.
Guise, Thos.
Kendall, Thos.
Hundermonk, Alice V.
West, Mrs.
West, J. H.
West, M. C.
Green, Pompey.
Bodine, John.
North, W. V.
McManus, M.
Davis, Annie.
Porter, Wm.
McCoy. Mollie.
Barnett, Miss Addie.
Brown, M.
McKenna, Annie.
McKenna, Hugh.
Marona, Joseph.
Moltedo, Tarnatore.
Cross, Maliso.
Brown, Harry.
Stubble, A. M.
Schiller, M. M.
Frainor, Thos.
Gomes, Antoine.
Dixon, Lizzie.
Sims, Robt.
Gerard, Lummie.
Simons, A.
Duggan, C. F.
Hanley. Isaac.
McNamara, M.
Enlow, Clarence.
Haines, T.
Williams, Bettie.
Fegilno, Jos.
Fagans, Ike.
Tyler, Scott.
Methua, J. S.
Spengler, Willie.
Mason, Luke.
Coleman, Sam.
Haines, Willie.
Thornton, E.
Homan, Geo.
Kalmbach, E.
Meyer, Maurice.
Jones, Joe.
Ware, P. A.
Marchant, Daniel J.
Cooper, J. A.
Hardwick, Fred.
Huener, Ida S.
Rice, W H.
Middleton, A. H.
Middleton, Margaret.
White, Mrs.
Davis, Annie.
Tinney, J. T.
Manlove, A. B.
Salley, C.
Blanchard, J. S.
Harlan, Gustave.
Arther, Louisa.
Mathias, Maggie.
Fishback, Calvin.
Williams, Henry.
Walsh, R.
Davis, D.

Zimmerman, Jake.
Ferguson, J. F.
Whitehead, Dr. P. F.
Miles, Wm.
Ward, Martha.
Coleman, Frank.
Roach, John D.
Karney, John.
Horn, Miss Mary L.
Carter, Charles L.
Hundermark, Robt. A.
Anderson, R.
Graham, Hannah.
Langford, R.
Entel, Mary.
Duffner, Miss Lena.
Schmidt, Louisa.
Vincends, Arthur.
McClendon, Miss Mattie.
Leofold, Maggie M.
Hennesy, Chas.
Wheat, Susie.
Dunbar, Fay.
Whitehead, John.
Moon.
Parker, Annie.
Crawford, Miss Margaret.
Fitzpatrick, Miss Mary A.
McElroy, Miss Martha.
Wilson, Lucy.
Hubbard, Philip.
Carr, John.
Levié, J. R.
Pellrin, C.
McHenry, W.
Adams, Green.
Williams, Sarah.
McKenna, Louisa.
Stewart, Augustus.
Caldwell, Sarah.
Tindall, R.
Grant, Sister Mary Regis.
Burtz.
Fends, Mrs. Ann.
Ryan, Mrs. Edward.
Metzler, Thos., Jr.
Unknown.
Fitzpatrick, J. C.
Cullen, John.
Rose, Chas. M.
Guscio, Louisa M.
Carter, Fulton.
Clark, Emma.
Burns, Geo.
McCrady, W. L.
Hanes, Bettie S.
Fitzpatrick, Thos.
Parvangher, C.
Benson, R. C.
Carroll, Mary.
Edwards, Albert.
Roost, Jacob.
Murphy, Jerry.
Melvaney, E.
Brown, Dolly.
Walmsley, Francis P.
Jacobson, M.
Murray, Sister Mary Bernadine.
Fields, Sam.
Mosyel. E.
Potts, Mrs. S. C.
Robinson, Isaac.
Child.
Zucker, Mrs. Gussie.
Dardinnac, J. B. P.
Harrison, W. S.
Camillo, N.
McGinty, G. W.
Diggs, Robt.
Wallace, Mary.

Brown. Rev. Calvin.
Perry, Martha E.
Margueritz, E.
Glass, Nancy.
Burns, Peter.
Wilson, J. C.
Morton, Richard.
Orris, Mary F.
Lassell, Mrs. Minnie.
Guscio, Peter W.
Connors, E. F.
Rose, Walter C.
Brown, H. E.
Shorter, D.
Davis, Frank.
Shields, D. A.
Chambers, Royal.
Thornton, Luke.
Jones, Oscar.
Atwood, Lizzie.
McCann, John.
Smarr, J. W.
Crayton, Emma.
Miller, Fred.
Mason, Mary.
Moore, J.
McFichd, J.
Coleman, D.
Lavins, Wm. B.
Sally, C.
Conway, Jas.
Simpson, John.
Lowenberg, Abe.
Haining, S. M.
McCoy, Hugh.
Hudson, Justice.
Schuler, Rosa E.
Warrington, Jas.
Conklin, Mrs. C.
Ferrell, Wm.
French, Robt.
Brown, Minty.
Moore, Jas.
Hannelia, Antoine.
Lawrence, Henry.
Fousse, Carrie.
Auter, Josie.
Berg, Alfred.
Murphy, Letitia.
Frank, Eddie.
Duffner, Ella.
Dixie, Mollie.
Burke, A.
Delaney, Josephine.
Starks, H.
Maloy, Belle Lee.
Sappington, Dr.
Carter, E.
Porterfield, Jeff.
McGrath, Sister Mary Columba.
Frank, Matthew.
Johnson, Thomas.
Gallagher, Katie.
Harmon, Dave.
Wilson, R.
Dyke, John.
Hubbard, J. W.
Mitchell, James.
Donaldson, Sam.
Donaldson, Jim.
Johnson, Antonia.
McKenna, James.
Smitta, John.
O'Rourke, W. H.
Arnold, Maggie L.
Mahin, Joseph.
Johnson, Lucy.
Reynolds, James.
Kendall, Chas. T.
Dyke, Virginia.

A HISTORY OF THE YELLOW FEVER.

Graff, J. H.
Rebay, Mrs. E.
Maberry, Sarah.
Green, Ben.
Coleman, Laura.
French, Hiram.
Fishback, Josephine.
Wherman, Ott.)
Wherman, Lizzie.
Bridge, Geo.
Taffe, Chas. F.
O'Connor, Miss Mary.
Grinstead, Wm.
Stringer, Abe.
Harrison, Edward.
Geary, Mi s Mary.
Potts, Dr.
Blichfeldt, Dr.
Clowery, Primas.
Owens, Frankie.
Biling, Albert.
Yerger, Julia.
Walker, Thos. B.
McMellan, Miss Maggie.
Cully, D. A.
Wagner, I.
Plump, Mary.
Briscoe, Mary.
Grammer, Mrs. Ella.
Harris, John.
Saunders, Katie.
Carter, Phœbe.
Brown, John.
Rashell.
Ipolite, P.
Haining, Miss Minnie.
Holmes, Willie.
Dorwart, Florence Anna.
Sharp, Chas. P.
Moody, Eva B.
Rothschild. Eddie.
Auguste, Miss Virginia.
Duffner, Hattie.
Scott, Harriett.
Rankins, Orelia.
Arnold, Geo. W.
Wood, G. V.
Carr, C. M.
McClendon, Matt.
Graff, J. W.
Wilson, Robert.
Kellogg, C. W.
Jamison, J. D.
McGuire, E. E.
Jones, Thos. H.
Dyer, Oliver.
Edwards, Thomas.
Davis, Margaret.
Morris, Frank.
Doyle, Nellie.
Haining, Mrs.
Harrison, Mrs. C. B.
James, F. B.
Engle, Nat.
Johnson. W.
Thompkins, La Rue C.
Johnson, John.
Mulvihill, Miss Bridget.
Gannon, Wm.
Swafford, Le Grand.
Mullen, Miss Mattie.
E wards, Freeman.
Munroe, Daisy.
Walmsley, Julia A.
Dalley, Sister Mary Gonzaga.
Sterling, Sandy.
McMorrow, John.
Haining, Katie.
Shelliday, Sanford.
West, Clotilda.
Morrison, Eliza J.
Hossley, Josephine M.
O'Sullivan, D.
Hanes, Florence A.
Vitola, Rev. John.
Flowerree, Conway.
Gannon, Geo.
Marble, Robert.

Salley, Lelia.
McCabe, Miss Ella.
Thomas, G. M.
North, Geo. M.
Lewis, H. E., Jr.
Hoggatt, Philip.
Smith, Matilda.
Boswell, Mary E.
Ryan, Edward.
Blake, Anthony.
Anderson, James.
Chapman.
Rigby, Thos. H. W.
Green, Jim.
Porter, Calvin.
Vincents, Gramilla.
Brown, Jennie.
Augustine, John.
Russell, John.
Bolton, Henry.
Green, Charlotte L.
Haines, Lewis H.
Williams, Carter.
Credon, Mrs.
Bitterman, Miss Annie.
Rivinac, Pierre.
Rebay, George.
Snow, John.
Shaw, F. G.
Elrington, W. H.
Massengale, Ed.
Bridges, Mrs. M. A.
Marble, E. V.
Walmsley, Geo. S., Jr.
Jingles, A.
Beresford, James.
Bridges, A. L.
Cully, Mrs. M. A.
Mann, Lelia.
Drushell, Philip.
Smith, James.
Cox, James B.
Austin, Poladore.
Demarchi, Thomas.
Wood, Annie M.
Hasie, Chas.
Duffner, Lena.
Bonizio, Carminio.
Thompson, Rev. Jeff.
Jingles, Mary.
Mitchell, Frank.
Johnson, Stephen.
Geary.
Munroe, John W.
Jackson, Violet.
Golden, Mike.
Brady, Taylor.
Vandenburg, Mary A.
Geary, Morris.
Wolfe, Miss Mary J. F.
Jones, W. R.
Hammond, Wm.
Hunt, Norman.
Laughlin, Terrence.
Chatam, John.
Russell, W.
Allen, Mary.
Marcus, Violet.
Dennett, A. W.
Scott, Sam.
Shepp ird. Eliza.
Hauer, Ida W.
Lucett, Catherine.
Mendel, Herman.
Schendal, Marcus.
Bingham, Chas.
Cox, Susan.
Harris, Kate.
Schendal, Maurice.
Anderson, James.
Bacon, Mrs. Mattie E.
Drushell, Munie.
Blackman, Dr. M.
Hammett, E. H.
Bacon, Arthur N.
Williams. Sam.
Terrell, Henrietta.
Arnold, William Q.
Walker, Fred.

Kalmbach, R.
Powell, Bessie K.
Powell, Henry.
Dixon, Irwin.
Spengler, Charles C.
Grey, Lizzie.
Bogle, Barney.
Marks, Gus. E.
Woods, Mrs. Sophia W.
Mendel, Minnie.
Lewis, James.
Davenport, Isham.
Jackson, James R.
Fate, Houston.
Collins, Patrick.
Davison, E. B.
King, John.
King, Lafayette.
Weyer, Joseph.
Crecey, Julia.
Zollinger, Alois.
Hapholdt, Dr.
Worthey, B.
Minor, Betsy.
Floyd, Annie.
Raum, Augusta.
Jordan, B. N.
Owens, Charles.
Willingham, Ellen.
Bacon, Willis J.
Gray, Mrs. E. L.
Hassell, Samuel J.
Winbush, Lucelia.
Brackett, John W.
Haven, Sophia.
Feibleman, Joseph.
Latcher. Barbara E.
Schaffer, Louis.
Yerger, George S.
Jenney.
Porterfield, Floyd.
Snead, Horace H.
Cox, George C.
Cook, Levie.
Goldberg, Mrs. C.
Love, Frank E.
Benner, Lieut. H. H.
Tilitz, Helen.
Bobb, Antonia G.
Griffin, John.
Lacroix, Miss Carrie.
Dalton, J. M.
Laughlin, Mike.
Smith, Percy.
Graves, Louisa.
Hall, Will. H.
Curran, Julia.
Miles, Freddie B.
Augustus, Clayton.
Steele, Sam.
Dorsey, Delia.
Hill, R. J.
Hall, Edwin B.
Kidd, Virginia.
Cox, Mitchell.
Hoggatt, Stacey A.
Katzenmier, Jacob L.
Ransom.
Smith, Ida.
Gilland, Dr. Lewis.
Peale, Mary Belle.
Willis, Capt. E. B.
Edwards, G. W.
Lane, N. V., Jr.
O'Neal, Edward.
Meyer, Mary E.
Brown, Alex. V.
La Katzenmier, Mamie.
Jacobs, E.
Hammett, Bessie S.
Unknown white man.
Corkern, Major J. B.
Smith, Ada A.
Lahen, John.
Saaguinetti, Charles.
Wall, John M.
O'Hara, Clara J.
Richards, Andrew
Smith, Marshall.

Conway, Moses.
Corkern, Mrs. J. B.
Lawrence. Mrs. Mary E.
Hillyard, Mead.
Tucker, B. O.
Jones, Miss Henrietta.
Howard, Halsie.
Cunningham, James.
Fitzgerald, Mrs. Jennie N.
O'Neal (infant of M.).
Raney, James P.
Buckley, Sandy.
Kanard, Martin.
Alexson, C.
Smith, Tom.
Lewis, Frank.
Armstead, William.
Mossinger, Miss.
Carson, Nora
Kahn, Samuel.
Thomas, Belle.
Hughes, Mary.
Cooley, Mrs., and two children.
Fitzgerald, Clifton.
Mannell, John.
Heflinger, George.
Alerdice, Joseph.
Graff, Mary E.
Brown, Mrs. Fannie.
Tanner, Miss Sallie L.
Tanner, Miss Annie R.
Rivinac, Cornelia.
Owens, Bessie.
Snow, Robert.
Pintz, Wm.
Henegan, Patrick.
Martin, James.
Golden, Willie.
Spengler. Joseph.
English, James.
Duffner, Bernard.
Lambert, Mrs. Cyrille.
Leonard, Rose.
Ragan, Miss Rosanna.
Harris, Mrs. F. J.
Aiken, Mary.
Rigley, Bill.
Taylor, Henry.
Munroe, L.
Williams, Lewis.
Coleman, Emeline.
Smith, Mattie.
Cameron, Angus.
Riedell, Mrs.
Wadsworth, Miss Clara.
Goodrich, F. W.
Schuler, W. J.
McGinnis, Annie.
Watson.
McCabe, Miss Annie.
Lewis, Frank C.
Sutherland, Chas.
Fairchild, Wm. A.
Davidson, John A.
Duffey, Andrew.
Pierce, Fanny.
Rothschild, Albert.
Moorehead, Sandy.
Kezer, A. R.
Baggett, T. M.
Washington, Fannie.
Clark.
Kern, Mary C.
Mitchell, W.
Jackson, Henry.
Thomas, Mack.
Adams.
Unknown colored man.
Wertz, Mrs.
Fort, L.
Jenkins, Lucinda.
Henessy. Mary.
O'Neal, Patrick.
Young, John.
Matox, Thomas.
Cook, Henry W.
Flowers, Fred. L.
Hedrick, A. W.

Klein, Annie M.
King, Willie M.
Onsley, Melissa.
Frank, Rosa.
Hennessey, Maggie.
Russell, Thos. C.
Collins, Rosalie.
Toohey, Mary.
Morgan, Annie L.
Ross, Albert.
Turner, Louis.
Vandenberg, Minnie L.
Boswell, James J.
Meyer, Isadore.
Rockwood, Wm. M.
Reede, Chas.
Cook, Lucy W.
Potts, H.
Cameron, Mrs.
Roach, Dr. J. S.
Bennett.
Dugan, Albert.
Schlottman, Chas. B.
Augustine, Mrs.
Harris, Milton.
McClenon, Mattie.
Marcus, John.
Marcus, Hannah.
O'Brien, Benny.
Green, Minnie.
Weaver, Sister Agnes.
Kingspight.
Drushell, Philip.
Taylor, Bettie.
Mount, Stephen R.
Williams, Lou.
Kluch, John.
Neal, J. A.
Washington, G. C.
Schendal, Mrs.
Sagona, John.
Schendal, Minnie.
Hennessey, Kate.
Golden, John.
Dohler, Richard M.
Black, D. R.
Clark, Elisha.
Saddler, L.
Feelan, Wm. J.
Geary, Willie.
Fultz, Thos.
Stith, Oscar N.
Willingham, Matt.
Davenport, C. F.
Zollinger, Valentine.
Reynolds, Chas. M.
Brown, Marks.
Taylor, Zack.
Jingles, Robt.
Susman, Julius.
Ford, Miss Laura.
Puneky, Mrs. Mary M.
Mayer, Isadore.
Williams, Carrie.
Fox, James J.
McGinnis, James.
Butler, Alex. M.
Jordan, Mrs. M. L.
O'Leary, Ignatius.
Mendle, Israel.
McGinty, W. J.
Scannell, John M.
Flowers, Albert A.
Weatherly, Willie.
Dwight, C. W.
Smith, Mary A.
Schiller, Daniel.
Jones, Robert.
Schendal, Bertha.
Adams, Mrs. R. C.
O'Neal, N.
Moore, Maggie.
Wesche, Herman.
Evans, Mrs. M. A. R.
Russell, Mrs. Carrie T.
Miller, Henry A.
Gunella, Oscar F.
Peoples, W. H.
Alexander, A.

Sokolosky, Wolf.
Holmes, Joe.
Sutbrocker, Antoine.
Bowen, John.
Latcher, John.
Devlin, Chas.
Kauth, Michael.
Brown, Geo. F.
Duval, Emma.
French, Mrs. Fannie V.
Stevens, Samuel.
Walsh, Jas. J.
McNamara, Thos.
King, Alex. E.
Hirsh, Henry.
Marks, R.
Demarchi, Angelo.
Tucker, Lillie.
Walker, Jno.
Ryan, Sallie L.
Johnson, Frank.
Fox, Philip.
O'Brien, Tim.
Guntz, Peter.
Clary, Cecelia.
Schmidt, Adam.
Black, A.
Williams, R.
Travers, Katie.
McCabe, Michael.
Folz, Sam.
Allen, Mary.
Burrell, Mrs. M. A.
Robinson, J. A.
Spillaine, Jno.
Parlen, M. G.
Parker, Chas.
Jones, C. E.
Pieroni.
Ponito, Vito.
McEver, J. N.
Unknown man.
Bryant, Lewis.
Thomas, Stella.
Jones, C.
Elliott, Geo.
Moore, Daniel.
Dexter, Geo.
Walters, Mrs. Margaret.
Owens, Thos.
Brown, Bruce.
King, Albert.
Hayes, Mary E.
Little, Willie E.
Lamkin, Mary.
Neely, Rosa.
Smith, W. H.
Davis, Kate.
Schwartz, L.
Parker, Albert.
Miller, E. H.
Page, A.
Semple, Jas.
Conkley, Mary.
Thomas, S.
Williams, Mattie.
Tucker, Henry.
Gray, H.
Hardy, J.
Myers, Sallie.
Tafunin, Ida.
Booth, Dr. D. W.
Hutcheson, Geo. W., Jr.,
Searles, E. H.
Cambridge, R.
Rylie, M.
Wehrman, G.
Curtis, C.
White, Joseph.
Schumacher, Benj.
Whitehead, C.
Hill, M. M. C.
Dickson, Sallie.
Dent, Frank, Jr.
Wilson, M. A.
Kinney, Patrick.
Owen, H.
Winston, Jno.
Carter, Geo.

Gleeson, Jno.
Gordon, G.
Quinn, Thos. R.
Sneelan, W. F.
Strong, Wash.
Hassell, S.
Hirsch, Leon.
Barber, Dr. L. E.
Myers, H.
Jones, J.
Freeman, Lizzie B.
Wehrman, Mrs. M.
Noland, Thos.
Fisher, L.
Bradley, Patrick.
Ross, S.
Moore, Hattie.
Reynolds, Matt.
Hennegan, C. P.
Allen, J. P.
McGuire, Mollie.
Spengler, Albert.
Doyle, Bridget.
Ryan, Annie L.
Sperry, Henry.
Stringer, Jno.
Simpson, Alfred.
Walters, C.
Conners, M.
King, Henry E.
Murphy, Jerry.
Bottcher, Fred.
Eggleston, John F.
Toohey, P. J.
Keller, E.
Fitzpatrick, Annie E.
Miller, Jno.
Bursley, A. A.
Netherland, M. E.
Bowman, Mrs. R. H.
Clements, W. H.
Podesta, Angelo.
Neville, Mollie.
Watt, Helen.
Ransom, S.
Jenkins, Julia.
Huener, Wm. W.
Rouen, Pete.
Perry, Lizzie.
Mitchell, Robt.
Gant, E.
Winston, Brown.
Crump, David.
Nason, Henry.
Cash, Lit.
Rutley, Harry.
Tlieller, Cecelia.
Johnson, Mary.
Feno, Dr.
O'Donnell, Martin.
O'Brien, Jerry.
Travis, Mrs. Ann.
Lamb, Patrick.
McManus, Father J. H.
Haining, Louisa.
White, Maggie.
Bradley, Charles.
Parmer, Jno.
Box, i. P.
McKenna, Mrs. Delia.
Gillan, Hugh.
Morrow, Delia.
Nathan, C. H.
Burt, Maggie.
Jolley, J. W.
Alexander, Miss Jessie.
Doll, Joseph E.
Camillo, Mrs. B. C.
Woodruff, J. W.
Clark, Ellen.
Jordan, E.
Cooper, Milton.
Rice, Lee.
James, Henry.
Moore, Geo.
Roe, Philip.
Scott, Wm.
Jackson, Wm.
Scott, Clarinda.

Clayer, Chas.
Gray, Sarah.
Alvis, J. W.
Rosenthal, Ralph.
Cody, Honora.
Kyle, David.
Ellis, A. K.
Harris, Margaret D.
Butcher, Wm.
Boswell, C. S.
Methun, A.
Lafayette.
Caskey, A. B.
Gibson.
Baum, Bettie.
Dougherty, Mary E.
Russell, Calvin.
Peacock.
Box (infant of Mrs.).
Meny, Henry.
Roost, Caroline.
Lirgot, Jacob.
Kelly, Jno.
Roost, Rosaline.
Cass, Lewis.
Keary, Martin.
Daymond, Emma.
Read, Francis.
Rooks, Mamie.
Moore, W. G., Jr.
Tvargosky, Delia.
Carrington, H.
Wheat, Albert.
Mack, Charlotte.
Jackson, Wm.
Cash, Wm.
Roeshe, Chas.
McDonald, W.
Jones, Jim.
Brown, J. C.
Powder, S.
Geary, Jas. W.
Lewis, C.
Butler, Katie.
Mays, Robert.
Thomas, John.
Reid, Burrell.
Goldon, James.
Norris, Dr. J. B.
Colovan, Chas.
Knight, Mrs. C. C.

Warren County.

Collier, Miss Bettie.
Collier, James.
Collier, Miss Alice.
Trindle, Eola Maud.
Trindle, Wm. Geo.
Trindle, Margaret Belle.
Axelson, Miss Agnes.
Axelson, Cornelius.
Axelson, Henry P.
Standard, Mrs. Mary.
Standard, Mrs. Millie.
McHam, S. W.
McHam, G. B.
McHam, Mrs. S. H.
McHam, Miss H. G.
Ryan, Mrs.
Ryan.
Solomon, Morris.
Loyd, Wm.
Loyd, Sophie.
Loyd, Freddie.
Loyd, Miss Annie.
Loyd, Albert, Jr.
Warnaph, C. A.
Beall, Miss Bettie.
Gibson, Miss Katie.
Gibson, Miss Emma.
Wosterberg.
Kline, Mrs. Patience.
Nailor, Mrs. D. B.
Kline, Minion E., Jr.
Vickstron, Larson.
Holt, Lewis.
Oberg.
Monette, Mrs. Sallie.
Monette, Miss Annie K.

A HISTORY OF THE YELLOW FEVER. 245

Monette. Gibson.
Larson, C. A.
Pettit, Mrs. Sophia.
Monette, Dr. Wm. E.
Featherstun, Mrs. M. E.
Featherstun, Wesley.
Featherstun, Miss Laura
Featherstun, Abbie.
Featherstun, Willie.
Rundell, Miss A. A.
Cleland, W. B.
Cleland, Bobie.
Billingslea, Mrs. Sarah.
Bullock, Wm.
Wilkins, Jones.
Johnston, Joe.
Johnston, Mrs. Joe.
Johnston, Miss Annie.
Taylor, Dick.
Taylor, Eddie.
Tribble, George A.
Tribble, Mrs. George A.
Gotthelf, Dr B. H.
Gotthelf, Morris H.
Strealy, Miss.
Strealy, Jerry.
Davis, Ben.
Davis, Mrs. Ben.
Davis, Judge.
Keller, Sally.
Oatis, Jaurdie.
Oatis, Addison.
Oatis, Leslie.
Oatis, Warren.
Oatis, Laura.
Oatis, Amanda.
Oatis, Fannie.
Oatis, Willis.
Ferguson, Laura.
Obrien, Mr.
O'brien (son of Mr.).
Finch, Mrs. J. W.
Biglow, Milton.
Cimpel, Robert W.
Meyer, Isadore,
Cameron, A. C.
Cameron, Benny.
Fox, L. Cameron.
Roberts, Mrs.
McInnis, J. A.
McInnis, Mrs. Laura.
McInnis, Mary Belle.
Powell, Aleck B.
Powell, Clarence.
Newman, Augustus.
Newman, Mrs. Sallie.
Newman, Mrs. Dr. J. C.
Brabston, Mrs. C. N.
Birdsong, Dr. Geo. T.
Dart, Mrs. Ben.
Dart, Julius.
Cook, Maj. J. Reese.
Willis, Capt. E. Bryant.
Shannon, Louis N.
Marvin.
Nesmith, Dr. Wm. J.
Edwards, Miss Matilda.
Wall, S. B.
Spears, Willie.
Weaver, Mrs.
Lanier, Lawrence.
Brooks, Aaron C.
Holt (child of Mrs.).
Lorch, Adolph.
Baker, H.
King, L.
King, John.
Cushman, W. R.
Cushman, W. A.
Cushman, C. B.
Cushman, Mrs. M., and two children.
Kendall, Mrs. M. E., and child.
Cushman, Mrs. W. R., and child.
Clark, Mrs. D. W.
Four children of Mrs. James Higgins.

Jones, Mrs. J. C.
Ketzenmier, J. L.
Martz, Mr.
Martz, Mrs.
Wertz, Mr.. and two children.
Edwards, B. T.
Edwards, Miss Matilda.
Wahl, S. W.
Standard, Mrs. Jessie.
Jones, Henry.
Wilson.
Wilson, Mrs.
Johnson, Mrs. Margaret.
Hall, Henderson.
Hall, Thomas.
Hall, Mrs. M. A.
Brown, Mrs. A.
Ferriss, Dr.
Ferriss, Mrs. Dr.
Ferriss (son of Dr.).
Riddle, Charles V. D.
Riddle, Lottie Tuley.
Riddle, Thomas.
Hollman, Charles.
Jemerson, Mrs. J. C.
McCarty, Alex.
McCarty (infant of Mrs.).
Watts, James C., Sr.
German gardener.
Dye, James.
Brown, Mrs. Ada.
Snyder, Mrs. Lillie.
Snyder, Miss Sallie.
Wilson, Mrs.
Wilson, Miss Cora.
Wilson. Mollie.
Wilson, Willie.
Ferry, Mrs. Dr.
Ferry, Douglas.
Jones, H. T.
MacEver, Wm.

Holly Springs.

Downs. E. L.
Lake, Miss.
Goodrich, A. W.
Wilshire, A. T.
Mackin, Wm.
Tandler, Isaac.
Chism, James.
Brown (child of A. F.).
McCroskey, H. A.
Ganter, Frank.
McLain, Robert.
Fort, James.
Nuttall, Mrs. James.
Oliver, B. P.
Bateman's 2 children.
Knapp, Mrs. Stephen.
Hogan, Wm.
Thomas, Mrs E. A.
Smith, Gus.
Snider (child of H.).
Nabers, B. D.
Moore, A. F.
Leak, Mrs.
Todd, W. R.
Chenowith, John.
Abernathy, Sam.
Crockett, Sam.
Crump, B. S.
Bonner, Dr. Charles.
Walker, James.
Glassy, Chas.
Nuttall, James.
Bonner, Sam.
Watson, R. L.
Waite, Miss Julia.
Blank, Mrs.
Campbell, R. G.
Falconer, Thomas A.
Wing, George.
Lynch, Virginia.
Ross, U. H.
Crump, Wm.
Dougherty, Mrs. J. R.
Record, Miss Corilla.
Johnson, Hal.

Read, Clem.
Smith, Victor.
Marett. W. J.
Pryor, Mrs. S. H.
Wooten, Willie.
Chenowith, Charles.
Brinkley (child of E.T.).
Seyple, Alex.
Potter, J. C.
Fort, R. W.
Armstrong, A. A.
Davis, Clarissa.
Oberti, Father.
Schneider, Charles.
Featherston, W. S., Jr.
Daniel, Mrs. Richard.
Daniel, Richard.
Lynch, Minerva.
Read, Miss.
Epps, Henry.
Epps, Scott.
Brannon, Mr.
Brinkley (child of E. T.)
Upshaw, E. W.
Potter, Mrs. John.
Hasting, Mrs. R.
Kimball, Sam.
Kimball, George.
Casey, Ben.
McGuire, Pat.
Demmey, Laura.
Thompson, Lewis.
Dunn, Mr.
Kean, James M.
Quiggins (child of O.J.).
Kimball, Mrs. Geo.
Miller, Mrs. E D.
Watson, Mrs. R. L.
Webber, Peter.
Stewart, Miss Mary.
Featherston, Mrs. W. S.
Foreman, Mrs. John.
Webber, J. W.
Stone, J. H.
Knable, Mrs. Martin.
McGary, Jane.
Knapp, Stephen.
Thompson, Mrs. Louis.
Walter, Col. H. W.
Brinkley, E. T.
Fennell, Capt. John.
Manning, Dr.
Butler, Miss Lizzie.
Falconer, Howard.
Winburn, Hugh.
Stojowski, Julia.
Stanislaus, Sister.
Walter, Avant.
Larouche, John.
Leidy, Eugene, Jr.
Allen, Miss Liza.
Stone, Mrs.
Falconer, Maj. Kinloch.
Allen, Miss Darthula.
Allen, Miss Nancy.
Fennell, Dr. F. M.
Henderson (child of T.).
Glassy, Margaret.
McWilliams, Mrs. Cora.
Nellums, Tede.
McWilliams (twins of Mrs. R. A.).
Hebdon, Thos.
Gaitley (son of Mrs.).
Castello, Willie.
Fennell, Dr. J. W.
Power, John.
Stewart, Miss Annie.
Hutchinson, Mrs.
Harrington, Mrs.
Yancey (child of Wm.).
Wells, Jim.
Lewis, Mr.
Yancey, Mrs.
Hunt, James R. L.
Walter, Frank.
McGowen, Mrs. Jeff.
Walter, Jimmy.
Gouldon, Allen.

Stella, Sister.
Hempton (son of).
Lumpkins, J. M.
Johnston, Mr.
Fant, Glenn.
Banks, John.
Hastings, John.
Gholston, Mr.
O'Gray, Mrs. Kate.
Wells, Mrs. Jim.
Straws, Mrs. Archie.
Roxy, Cowan.
Wade, Thos.
McGhery, Mrs.
Hohenwart, Alex.
Saunders, Austin.
McGuire, Mrs. Crown.
Fort, Miss Lucy.
Margarette, Sister.
Thomas, Martin.
Virginia, Mollie.
Walker, Eli.
Featherston, George.
Walker, C. H.
McKinney, Dr. W. O.
McDermott, Mrs.
Unknown lady.
Unknown person.
Oliver, Dan.
Parish, L. P.
German, John.
Pearson, John.
Strauss (infant of).
Herr (infant of).
Carlson, Miss Christina.
Herr, Mrs. C. J.
Parish, Mrs.
Henderson, A. C.
Tiernan, Mike.
McKissack, Haywood.
Cowan, Henry.
Herr, Joseph.
Parish, Mrs.
Stineman, Peter.
Maughan (child of).
McKeugh, H. J.
Knable, Martin.
Webber (child of).
Bowman, Augustus.
Walker, Martha.
Roberts, Mrs. Julia.
Hess, Col. A. J.
Fant, Selden.
Myers, Mrs. B. A.
Daily, Mr.
Crump, E. H.
Malei, Miss Lizzie.
Henry, James V.
Victori, Sister.
Miller, Mr.
Diller, Mr.
Allen, Miss.
Malei, Jack.
Adams, Jas. G.
McHugh, Jas.
Parks, George.
Harris (child of Chas.).
Haley, Mrs.
Lorentia, Sister.
Miller, Mrs. James.
Thomas, G.
Krouse, Jacob.
Lane, Mrs.
Brim, Edward.
Skoesburg (son of).
Watson, Joshua.
Luckey, Joseph.
Lane, Dennis.
Calvin, James.
Connington, Burton.
Edwards, Willis.
Vandive. Henry.
Martin, Polly.
King, Robert.
Yowell, Squire.
Lesseur, Lulu.
Mooney, Mr.
Gealar (son of Peter).
Compton, Mrs.

A HISTORY OF THE YELLOW FEVER.

Dresler, Th.
Compton, Dr. Wm.
Kimbrough, John.
Tiernan, John.
Holland, W. J. L.
McKinney, Mrs. Dr.
Gheelan, Mrs. Peter.
Gutheries, Mrs.
Byers, Mrs.
Coffin, Mrs. Sam.
Armstead (child of Mrs. Henry).
Adams, Robert.
Cockran, Eugene.
Corinthia, Sister.

Dry Grove.
Stubbs, Mrs. Phœbe.
Callendar, Hiram.
Williams, Mr. Dan.
Williams, Walter.
Williams, Henry.
Stewart, Hugh.
Stewart, Jas. H.
Stewart, Nettie.
French, Geo. C.
Cherry, Frank.
Clowers, Mrs.
Coker, Miss Mary.
Caston, Miss Edith.
Caston, Charles.
Griffin, Calvin.
Johnson, Mrs. Mary.
Dickson, Dr. Geo.
Flewellen, Miss Jane.
Flewellen, Zella.
Morgan, Mrs.
Wall, Thomas.
Kyle, Miss.
Unknown printer.
Terry (two children of Augustus).
Stubbs, Jack.
Callendar, Lulu.
Williams, Mrs. Dan.
Williams, J. Calvin.
Stewart, Jas.
Horton, Miss Nellie.
Stewart, Arthur.
Douglass, Mrs. Sarah.
Douglass, Miss Netta.
Caston, Wm. T.
Coker, Miss Jennie.
Caston, Miss Bettie.
Caston, Wiggins.
Coker, Miss Bettie.
Johnson, Mrs. Amanda.
Johnson, Maggie.
O'Brien, Emmet.
Flewellen, Mrs. J. H.
Flewellen, Sarah.
Morgan, Charles.
Kyle, W. D.
Cook, Mrs.
Morgan, George.

Lebanon District, Hinds Co.
Jacobs, Joseph.
Jacobs, Mrs. J.
Harrison (child of A.).
Jacobs (infant of Ben.).
Ward.
Moses, Mrs.
O'Brien, Mrs.
O'Brien, Emmet.
Monell, Mrs.
McNair, Robert.
McNair, Eddie.
McNair, David.
McNair, L. D., Sr.
Hamilton, Mrs. Jas.
Allen, Mrs.
Edmondson, Mrs. E.
Jacobs, Ben.
Gibbes, A.
Ward.
Moses, J. M.
McNair, Miss Bettie.

Roberts, Miss Emma.
Jacobs, Joseph, Jr.
McNair, L. D., Jr.
Jacobs, Mrs. Ben.
Russell, Miss Essie.
McNair, Mrs. David.
McDermon, Pat.
Noble, Mrs. Fannie.

Yazoo City.
Littlejohn, Rev. W. B.
Harris, Mrs. S. C.
Harris, Capt. Hal. C.
Zenobia, Sister.
Corona, Sister.
Monton, Father J.
Kelly, James.
Lawrence, Sister Mary.

Water Valley.
Becton, J. E.
Pennington, L. M.
Gross, M. A.
Williams, Peter.
Bartlett, W. L.
Lees, Kenny.
Reems, Walter.
Gartine, N. U.
Jones, W. H.
McClure, John.
Murphey, A. B.
Walker, Tom.
Hall, James.
Donahue, D.
Howard, Jack.
Strong, G. W.
Townsend, Robt.
McMillen, Clay.
Crops, James M.
Holmes, Gus.
Goodwin, Wm.
Summers, C. E.
Fly, J. H.
Pate, Mark E.
Taylor, Mr. J. B.
Hendricks, J. O.
Buford, Mrs. A. G.
Gartine, Mrs.
Reed, Mrs.
Edstrom, Mrs.
Miller, Miss Jane.
Miller, Lige.
Miller, Jeff.
White, Wm.
Brewer, B. W.
Simmons, A. V.
Block, E.
Freeman, H. W.
Reese (child of H.).
Smith, Mrs. E. F.
Smith, Miss Mollie.
Thorns, A. C.
Trainer, Mrs. Tom.
Pennell, P. W.
Prophit, Mrs. Robt.
Reasons, Thomas.
Mattson, John.
Edstrom (child of Mrs.).
Long, R. A.

Canton.
Henry, Mrs. Rachael.
McKie, Dr. Nath. W.
Henry, Miss Elizabeth.
Henry, Miss Lizzie.
Garrett, Mrs. S. D.
Fulton, Mrs. D. M.
Steele, Miss Annie.
Fulton, Col. D. M.
Benthall, Miss Sallie.
Mann, Miss Minnie.
Mann, Ben. F.
Feldman, Dedrick.
Wickham, James.
Vance, Mary.
Conway, Mrs. C.
Conway, Edwin
Capurro, Peter.
Harter, Mike.

Demarchi, Fred.
Noe, Geo.
Botto, Louis.
Otto, Mrs. D. H.
Otto, Wylie.
Shaw, David H.
McMicken, Col. M. B.
Cogan, Father P.
McKie, Dr. M. J.
McKie, Miss Zoe,
Benthall, Josie.
Jeffries, St. Clair.
Welsh, Wm.
Reid, John.
Reid, Mrs. D. Wm.
Gouh, B. C.
Fitchett (child of J. V.).
Scales, Jennie Belle.
Peyton, Mrs. P.
Demarchi, Louisa.
Harter (child of Jake).
Mounohan, Mary.
Luckett, O. A., Jr.
McCoskey, Barney.
Lee, Mrs. A. S.
Leonard, James.
Jones, Wm.
Benthall, Daisy.
Kennedy, M., and child.
Scheifler (child of J. B.).
Catlett (child of).
Billings, Mrs.
Scheifler (son of Mrs.).
Collins, C. T.
Smith, Monti.
Stone, Perry S.
Montgomery, John.
Montgomery, Mrs. Jno.
Smith, Mrs. Jas. A.
Smith, Miss Mittie.
Joseph, Mrs. Mark.
Paul, Frank.
Van Buren, George.
Magruder, Dr. J. T.
Leitch, Mrs.
Peyton, Pat.
Morris, Robt.
Demarchi, Frank.
Arnold, August.
Johanna, Sister.
Leonard, Miss Mattie.
Leonard, Freddie.
Scales, Pinkey.
Hill, Miss Mary.
Capurro, Mrs. P.
Richards, Joe C.
Canalli, C.
Clavarri, Chas.
Coplin, Jas. A.
Cage, Dr. A. H.
Petty (child of Mr.).
Boersig, J.
Langley, W. A.
Kennedy, Miss Bridget.
Linderman, Mrs.
Smith, Eddie.
Benthall, Mrs. W. H.
Smith, Mrs.
Blanchard(child of Joe).
Duffey, James.
Durfey, R. W.
Young, Daisy.
Ford.
Ernest, Jno., Sr.
Campbell.
Chavivari, Guiseppe.
Alsworth, Mrs. Ben.
Thompson, Mrs. E. L.
Scheifler, Mrs.
Wilcox, Mrs.
Leonard, Mrs. Robt.
Green, Chas.
Peyton (two children of Tom).
Shackelford, Susie.
Gary, John.
Benwell, H. R. C.
Gary (child of John).
Leonard, Mrs. James.

Cassell, Willie.
Kelly, Mary.
Benwell(child of H R.C.)
Strohecker, Mrs. Lucy.
Logue, Edward.
Barnes, Mrs. B.
Chambers(child of Wm.)
Henry, John M.
Logue, B.
Leitch, D.
Fulton (son of David).
Latimer, Mark.
Semmes, Fitz.
Benthall, Mrs. Minerva.
Engle.
Wilson, Mrs. M. A.
Harter, Geo.

Greenville.
Mobray, Miss.
Perry.
Finnegan, Pat.
Marshall, Wm.
Byrne, E. J.
Simpson, John.
Brooks, D. E.
Morris, Mrs. D.
Pryor, Miss.
Perry, Fred.
——, Maria.
Bathke, C.
Brooks, Mrs. Fanny.
Perry, Mrs. James.
Chicsa, J. A.
Lee, Sow (Chinaman).
Scott (daughter of R.B.).
Fox, Josephine (child).
Mowbry, Mrs. Thos.
Stowell, Lyman.
Sanford, Mrs. Geo.
Ballard, Mrs. J. S.
Smith, Mrs. F. P.
Stream, George.
Shorey, Mrs.
Bird, George.
Ballard, Mrs K. A.
Pryor, Fred.
Stafford, Dr.
Aleck (butcher).
Caffall, Willie.
Pogle, Mrs. Julia.
Unknown blacksmith.
Maskey, Louisa.
Perry, Mrs. T. P.
Smith, Abe.
Wetherbee, Eva.
Dodge, Elliot.
Dorman, George.
Sutton, Steve.
Butler, Walter B.
McLean, Thomas.
Wagner, Frank.
Putnam, H. (boy).
Haycraft, W. A.
Shanahan, Mrs. D.
Morris, Mrs. M.
Barnett, Philip.
Scott, Miss Willie.
Jones, Milton.
Morgan, Col. C. E.
Perry (boy).
Cox, Mrs.
Perry, James.
Telfer, Wm.
Duvall, Emma.
Huntley, Charles.
Ratchlitz, Julius.
Walker, J.
McCullough, Richard.
Corney, James.
Young, Mrs.
Caffall, Edward.
Caffall, Louis.
Radjesky, Louis.
Beck, Mrs.
Fleischer, Mrs.
Trammel, Mrs.
Habicht, Theodore.
Wetherbee, Mrs. L. P.

A HISTORY OF THE YELLOW FEVER. 247

Hassberg, Mrs. B.
Quick, Walter.
Steinberg, E.
Platt, Mrs.
Ehler (boy).
Putnam, H. B.
Enler, Mrs.
Alexander, Dr. V. F. P.
Cooper, Robert.
McCann, James.
Marshall, Raphael.
Minzies, James.
Green, Rev. Duncan.
Forrester, Gus.
Gallagher, Frank.
Ballard (infant of John).
Radjesky, J.
Long Hou (Chinaman).
Diggs, Bennie.
Taylor, Wm.
Ballard, Mrs.
Boswick, Chas.
Buckner, J. H.
Davidson, James.
Green, Stephen.
Connell, James.
Kyle.
Pryor, Mrs. F.
Bathke, Mrs. Henrietta.
Badwick, Joe.
Bigelow (child).
Habicht, Mrs.
Laurens, Henry.
Phillips, Leonard.
Wall, Abe.
Manly, W. J.
Perry, T. P.
Sylvester, Tom.
Williams, Chas.
Diggs, Fanny.
Shanahan, Dan.
Barnhurst, Mrs. J. S.
Morris, Dave.
Duffy, Michael.
Wheeler, Albert.
Shaw, Mrs. T. B.
Small, Mrs.
Simphondorfer, John.
Wiesenfeldt, L.
Barnhurst, John.
Lockman, Julius.
Trammel, George.
McLean, James.
McAllister, Gus.
Morgan, L. E.
Byrnes, Pat.
French (child of W. J.)
Youcum, Sophia.
Brazicar, George.
Tilley, W., Jr.
Speaks, T. B.
Wiesenfeldt, Mrs. L.
Nelson, John H.
Kress, Eliza.
Shaw, Helena.
Wetherbee, Wes.
Langley, L. M.
Mitchell, Mrs.
Kleiber, Minnie.
Stafford, Mrs.
Page, Rev. T.
James, Harry.
Lumkin, Miss Annie.
Hammond, Sam.
Brown, Mrs. Sam.
Rivers, O. C.
Manatzer(infant of Mrs.)
Sievers, Mrs. M.
Patt, Anna.
Unknown man.
Coughler, Gus.
Finlay, Helen.
Smith, Frank P.
Freundt, Henry.
Polle, Mrs L.
Ehlers, Wm.
Porter, W. L.
Ballard, John S.
Waite, Willie B.

Warden, Nellie.
Ralph, John.
Nelson, N. J.
Morris, M.
Kretschmar, W. P.
Kintsler, J.
Trigg, A. B.
Yerger, Arthur R.
Berry, Anna.
Fleischer, Adolphe.
Wetherbee, L. P.
Kintsler, Amelia.
Vaughn, Harry.
Perry (child).
Kelly, Fanny.
Gossett, J.
Scott, Garrett.
Fleischer, A.
Elliott, Mrs. G. W.
Manifold, John.
Hamburger, Abe.
Pryor (child).
Meisner, C. F.
Radjesky, Ruchael.
Ward, Mrs. A.
Herman, Lena.
Byers, Jake.
McCall, Dr.
Johnson, M. W.
Berry, Walter S.
James, Mrs. Mattie.
Elliott, G. W.
Archer, Dr.
Wetherbee, Mabel.
Morris (child of Dave).
Greenfield, Mrs. E. C.
Meyer, Wm.
Clarke, George R.
Hamilton, John.
Cottrell, John.
Childs, Emma.
Ah Ways (Chinaman).
Gernelle, Adeline.
Burdette, Marsh.
Crockett, Sam.
Brown, Katie.
Coburn, J.
Mathers, Mrs.

Neighborhood of Greenville.

Monk, Henry.
Lemler, Henry.
Snowberger, Blanche.
Morzinski (child).
Morzinski, M. J.
Hartman, Mrs. Marcella.
Winter, Jack.
McAllister, C. K.
Brashear, Watt.
Montgomery, Mrs. Wm.
Winter, Shirley.
Stone, D. L.
Gerdine, Dr. A. S.
Gaddis, Dr.
Kleiber, Mr.
Winter, Mrs. C. A.
McCune, Pat.
McLean, Mrs. Felix.
McAllister, Mrs. C.
Montgomery, Wm.
Everett, J. E.
Kirby, Dr.
Johnson, Fred.
Johnson, Thomas.
Griffin, Dr.
Winter, T. E.
Crockett.

Jackson.

Sayle, Joseph.
Swett, Wm. H.
McCallum, Wm.
Granberry, Junius.
Granberry, Geo. C.
Ledbetter, J. H.
Reinhemier, Lewis.
Taylor, Wm.
Brunson, Alonzo L.

Cusmani, C.
Granberry, Geo.
Johnson, Mrs. W. H.
Wilson, Andrew.
Granberry, Miss Ida.
Barrett, Wm.
Cusmani, Mrs.
McCallum, Mrs.
Muller, Wm.
Ewing, Wm.
Eschelman, Daniel.
McInnis, Fannie.
Eschelman, Henry.
Clark, Matt.
Parker, Wm. L.
Black, Robert.
Clancy, Daniel.
Watterson, P. M.
McDonald, Tony.
Pierce, Harvey.
Clancy, Mrs.
Bailey, Edward.
Muller, Joseph.
Marion, Mrs. Thomas.
Divine, Bettie.
Bayol, John F.
Barrett, Minnie.
O'Leary, Patrick.
Sizer, Henry E.
Johnson, C. Eva.
Daughtry, Mrs. P. C.
Roach, P. J.
Taylor, Miss Louise.
Kolb, P.
Glennon, Ben. F.
Ryan, Mrs. Phil.

Grenada.

Feild, Mrs.
Feild, Harry.
Feild, Thomas.
Feild, Mattie.
Sheppard, Katie.
Wilson, Mrs.
Davidson, Mrs.
Bakewell, Mrs. Irene.
Doak, Mrs.
Doak, Miss Lulu.
Beauchamp, W. T.
McMillian, Mrs.
French, Mrs. L.
Peacock, T. E.
Peacock, Miss Mamie.
Dejarnett, Mr.
Dejarnett, Sallie.
Cromwell, Geo.
Cromwell, John.
Mole, Miss Maria.
Lake, Geo. W.
Lake, Mrs. Geo. W.
Lake, Miss Annie.
Lake, Delia.
Sadler, Mrs.
Sadler, Miss Rosa.
Sadler, Walter.
Sadler, Jos. E.
Sadler, Amos.
Sadler, Robt.
Ayres, A. W.
Ayres, W. I.
Ayres, Miss Jennie.
Ayres, Miss Lizzie.
Hughes, Dr. E. W.
Hughes, Mrs.
Hughes, Mrs. J. E.
Coffman, Mrs.
Coffman, Mrs. R.
Coffman, Chas.
Coffman, Miss Kate.
Derrick, H. S.
Derrick, Mrs. H. S.
Huffington, Miss M.
Huffington, Miss S.
Huffington, Miss M.
Huffington, Miss M.
Lacock, Miss M.
Lacock, Miss Alice.
Bishop, Miss Addie.

Bishop, Miss Belle.
Bishop, Eugene.
Bishop, Mrs. J. M.
Shankle, Mrs. E.
Kirby, Mrs. Pete.
Kirby, Pete.
Shankle, Wm.
Shankle, Robt.
McLenn, Mrs.
McLean, Miss Lulu.
Bristol, D. C.
Bristol, Miss Emma.
Clark, Miss Kate.
Conley, M.
Carl, Price.
Carl, Ella.
German carpenter.
Wilkings, Dr. J. R.
Irwin, Mrs. R. A.
Young, Robt. A.
Young, Mrs. Robt. A.
Kendrick, Miss Lulu.
Mayhew, Bob.
Angevine, S. S.
Angevine, Miss M.
Poitevent, Jacob.
Poitevent, Miss M.
Poitevent, Miss J.
Redding, Wyatt M.
Marshall, Tom F.
Leedy, Miss Sallie.
Kettle, Mrs., and child.
Hall, Charlie.
Rafalsky, Alex.
Morrison, Mrs. J. A.
Gillespie, Dr.
Irwin, R. A.
Knox, J. M.
Kendall, Samuel.
Marshall, Sammie.
Eason, John P.
Campbell, G. W.
Mitchell, Frank.
Wolfork, Dr.
Fenner, Fred.
Bowles, R. S.
Scanlin, Mrs.
Ringgold, Mrs. Dr.
Beauchamp, J. W.
McMillian, Mr.
Coffman, Mrs. Chas.
McDonald, Mrs.
Virson, E. E.
Newell, Chas.
Williams, J. A.
Phillips, Tom.
Wolfe, Mrs.
Cole, W. T.
Cole, Mrs. W. T.
Davis, Clayton.
Hughes, Miss Mary.
Gillespie, Mrs.
Postell, Mattie.
Ringgold, Dr.
Armstrong, Colman.
Lacock, Miss Helen.
Doak, Johnnie.
Mitchell, John.
Lehman, Mr.
Applegate, Mr.
Garner, Arch.
Anderson, B. P.
Heshburg, Herman.
Housman, Chas (Sardis).
Powell, Thos.
Haddick, Rev. H. T.
Hall, Dr. W. W.
Hall, Mrs. W. W.
Hall, Rev. J. G.
Hall, Mrs. J. G.
Stokes, Mrs. J. C.
Stokes, James.
Stokes, John.
Gray, Judge J. C.
Gray, Mrs. J. C.
Gray, J. N.
Gray, Ed.
Ingram, Mrs.
Ingram, Eugene.

Ingram, Miss Florence.
Welsh, Prof.
Welsh, Miss Sidney.
Wile, M.
Strang, Mr.
Wile, Emanuel.
Eskridge, W. C.
Eskridge (child of W. C.).
Eskridge, Walter.
Eskridge, Fox.
May, Mrs. W. B.
May, Dr. W. B.
Hankins, Dr.
Hankins, Mrs.
Peeples, Miss Fannie.
Rafalsky, Henry.
Rollins, O. B.
Rollins, Marshall.
Gage, Ben.
Gage (2 children of Dr.).
Doak, B. M.
Hooks, Mrs.
Hooks, David.
Burke, James.
Scanlin (child of Mrs.).
Chandler, Wm.
Collins, R. A.
Irby, Tom.
Moore, Dave.
Rivers, Mr.
Milton, Dr. J. L.
Morrow, John.
Rose, Barry.
Hall, F. K.
Graham, Hugh.
Sherman (inft. of H. B.).
Stevenson, Robt.
Hart, Harry.
Barnes, T. P.
Thomas, John.
Jones, H. M.
Williams, R. Sr.
Moore, John T.
Morrison, Joseph A.
Gerard, A.
Signaigo, Mrs. Alice.
Walton, Judge Tom.
Kendall, Thomas.
Flippin, Samuel.
Davis, Hugh R.
Downs, S. L.
Davis, Cally.
Parker, Mrs. I. S.
Satterfield, Miss Jennie.
Friedman, M. (N. O.).
Smith, Mrs.
Wood, I. K.
McCampbell, Rev. J.
Marshall, Samuel.
Cary, Mr.
Sanders, A. P.
Weigert, Chas.
Belew, Mrs. W. A.
Holly, Frank.
Armstrong, Rev. J. K.
Hummel, Ludwig.
Cawein (child).
Shaw, Mr.
Bailey, Mrs.
Yates, Chas.
Lacock, Mary.
Coon, G. T.
Telair, Mrs. Sallie.
Flippin, Sam.
Flippin, Mrs., and child.
Beck, Willie.
Miller, Sallie.
Turner, Mrs. Aleck.
Sanders, O. P.
Sanders, Mrs. O. P.
Wright (child of John).
Nowell, Mrs.
Mitchell, Mary.
Mitchell, Chas.
Boatright, Mr.
Meador, James.
Burt, Miss K.
Thompson, E. F.
Barnes, Sallie.

Collins, George.
Williams, Isaac.
Long, Mrs. W. E.
Shankle, W. F.
Crowder, R. D.
Eli, E. G.
Eli, Mrs. Eliza.
Latham, Wm.
Wright, Mack.
Hosbin, Martha.
Rosser, Ida.
Fitzgerald, Dr. P. F.
Sanders, Mollie.
Spencer, Mrs.
Rush, Mrs. Mollie.
Nowell, Joseph.
Mitchell, James.
Rosser, Hattie.
Beasly, Mrs.
Burt, Henry.
Shankle, Robt.

Port Gibson.

Barrot, C. L.
Barrot, Mrs. Paul.
Barrot, Paul.
Burnet, Miss Sallie.
Bertron, Rev. S. R.
Boughton, John.
Broughton, Jimmy.
Bertron, Mrs. J. C.
Brumley, Dr.
Crowley, John.
Daugherty, Wm.
Dempsey, Andy.
Daugherty, Mary.
Daugherty, May.
Day, Willie.
Day, Joseph.
Day, Charlie.
Disheroon, Miss Alice.
Disheroon, William.
Evans, Lindsey R.
Evans, Mrs. L. R.
Faust, Mr.
Faust, Mrs.
Fairly, Maj. J. D.
Fife, Butler.
Fife (child of Wm.).
Fife, Eliza.
Fife, Wm.
Gordon, W. R. (son of R. F. Gordon.)
Green, Miss Lizzie.
Green, Miss Gayoza.
Griffing, Emma.
Green (daughter of W. A.).
Guess (child of Wm.).
Greer Estelle.
Green, Joseph.
Greer, Mrs. Mary.
Gilchrist, Malcomb.
Greer, Lavinia.
Greer, Eugenia.
Harris, Simon.
Hall, Rev. Geo.
Huber, Mrs.
Healey, Mrs. T. C., and two children.
Hawkins (infant of T.S.).
Hawkins, Tommy.
Humphreys, Eva.
Humphreys, Ben.
Humphreys, Mrs. D. B.
Haeley, Jacob.
Henderson, John.
Ingram, Mrs John, and child.
Jones, T. E.
Jones, Eliza.
Johnson, Miss Fannie.
Kilcrease, Dorsey.
Kelly, Thomas.
Kavanaugh, Mrs. Thos.
Kirkbride, Mrs. S. M.
Louder, And. J.
Little, Samuel.
Leisher, Geo.

Leisher, Frank.
Mackey, Mrs. Samuel.
Leisher, John.
Leisher (infant of E. E.).
Lynch, Mrs. Mary M.
Leonard, Janie.
Lee, Johnnie.
Lilly, Tyre.
McCann, Billy.
McClinton, R. H.
Mason, Miss Jennie.
Martin, W. H.
Moore, Dr. Wm.
Moore, Ella.
Moore, Duncan.
Murphey, James.
McClure, Simpson.
Newman, Mrs. L. T.
Newman, Bernard.
Newman, Sidney.
Newman, Corinne.
Nolan, Patrick.
Nance, James, Jr.
O'Day, Mike.
O'Connell, Katie.
O'Connell, Mrs Dan.
Purnell, Bertron.
Patton, Mrs. R. S.
Patton. R. S., Jr.
Price, Joseph.
Price, Robert J.
Price, Mrs. Eliza.
Price, J. A.
Price.
Peoples, Mrs. John.
Sammelson, Aug.
Simonson, Mrs. H. J.
Strowbridge, Mrs. Dr. J. G.
Shreve, Chas., Sr.
Shreve, Chas., Jr.
Shreve, Mrs. Chas.
Strowbridge, Dr. J. G.
Stewart, T. N.
Scharff, Geo.
Scharff, Mrs. Geo.
Snodgrass, Dr. H. C.
Shafer, A. K., Jr.
Sprott, Dr. W. D.
Sylvester, Philip.
Thaler, Adolph.
Thaler, Mrs. Adolph.
Thaler, Rudolph.
Thaler, Tobias.
Thaler, John.
Thrasher, Judge John B.
Trevellian, Mrs. T. C.
Thomas, Casey.
Tucker, Mrs.
Ungerer, Fritz.
Vertner (infant of Gen. J. D.
Wheeless, Miss Mary.
Wheeless, Capt. H. S.
Woods, John.
Weeks, Charlie.
Weeks, Jimmy.
Walker (infant of N. S.).
Young, Dr. Thomas.
Hasie (child of Major).

Meridian.

Ethridge, John.
Preston, Wm. A.
Taggart, Mrs. John.
McCluster, R. H.
Owens, Mrs. Mary.
Lipscomb, Mrs. M. J.
Sadler, Wm. L.
Sinklair, Robt.
McLean, Chas. T.
Tucker, Edward.
Vail, B. M.
Bragg, Mrs. Ellen.
Raney, Miss Ella.
Lawrence, Albert.
Jones, Josiah.
Tallichet, E. H.

Pulham, Doshia.
Marshall, Nancy.
Theilgaard, S. C.
Freank, J. C.
Williams, Mrs. Ben.
Williams, R. T.
White, George.
Prestridge, Mrs. J. M.
Habercorn, L. F.
Miller, Mrs. M. E.
Peters, J. C.
Lawrence, Mrs. Albert.
Terry, T. J.
Tarver, Wm. S.
Laughton, J. G.
Terrell, James.
Mosley, Robt. J.
Ward, John.
Taft, Miss Mattie.
McLean, Wm. T.
Riley, Miss Mary.
Owens, Wm. Henry.
Owens, Lela Lovetta.
Habercorn, Edward.
Raney, Wm. V.
Tarver, Mrs. S. J.
Gould, Mrs. Dr. L.
Mosley, Benj. Frank.
Robinson, Emma.
Rogers, Thos.
Easly, Capt. E. V.
Currie, A. A.
Henderson, John.
Hoffer, Wm.
Sinclair, Lutie.
Broach, Mrs. W. P.
Enslen, Henry.
Ethridge, Mark.
Smith, Erla May.

Rocky Springs.

Cessna, Love.
Goosehorn, Tom.
Goosehorn, Sallie.
Ely, Nannie.
Duvall, Mrs.
Duvall, Mahala.
Emerick, Lilly.
Emerick, Aleck.
Wallace, Mollie.
Goza, George.
McLean, George H.
Haring, Ellen.
Harper, Emily.
Lum, Ed. O.
McLemore, Laman.
Henderson, Susan.
Goza, Mrs. George.
Thompson, Mrs. Mary.
Boggs, Mrs. Mary.
Harper, J. J.
Brock, W. W.
Parker, Rev. D. A. J.
Parker, Mrs. D. A. J.
Foster, Alice.
Harper, Mattie.
Harper, Mrs. O. B.
Emerick, Dan.
Wright, James.
Wright, Mrs. M. M.
Flowers, A. E.

Hernando.

West, Mrs. R. R.
Hildebrand, Mrs.
McNeese, Mrs. S. P.
Hickling, R.
Deinheart, Mrs. Adam.
Pullin, Miss Ruth W.
Connelly, Michael.
Vondran, E. J.
Avera, Col. J. C.
Reid, Mrs. S. I.
Gore, Robert.
Waller, Mrs. A.
Swartz, Mrs.
Johnson, Mrs. Bertha.
Powell, Dr. J. W.
Hickling, Mrs. R.

A HISTORY OF THE YELLOW FEVER. 249

Deinheart, Eddie.
Pullin, Miss Ella.
Connelly, Mrs. Michael.
Vondran, Mrs. E. J.
Kellogg, O. M.
Giddion, D. P.
Niles, Mrs.

COLORED.
Thompson, A. D.
Legan, Pat.
Taylor, Mrs. Henry.
Wise, Bob.
Washington, Mary.
Taylor, Henry.
Walker, Robert.
Coghill, Jackson.

MEMPHIS REFUGEES.
Campbell, D. C.
Vondran, Peter.
Flaherty, James,
Haack, Julius.
Soelfker, Miss Mena.
Harder, Miss Annie.
Feldstadt, John.
Anderson, Mrs. B. P.
Vondran, Mrs. Peter.
Flaherty, Miss.
Murray, Miss Mary.
Harder, Miss Ella.
Ford, John B.
Wood, Mrs.

Bay St. Louis.
Arnold, Alice.
Adams, Julian.
Breath, Charles.
Barthe, Henry.
Barnard, Frazier.
Campe (child of).
Combel, Wilfred.
Cameron, Hubbard.
Doyle, Mrs.
Doyle (daughter of Mrs.).
DeWolf, Miss.
Davis, Eliza.
Dore, Mrs.
Dore (daughter of Mrs.).
Estapa, Alphonsine.
Estapa, Francis.
Estapa, Josephine.
Etiena, Sister, St. Joseph Convent.
Fischer, Lena.
Frederick, Bernedina.
Frederic, Barbara.
Foster, Mary.
Foster, Susie.
Fairchild, Harry B.
Fairchild, Ella.
Franklin, Stephen.
Gonzales, Joseph.
Henderson, Malcomb.
Howell, Henry.
Henderson, John, col.
Johnston, Sallie.
Johnston, James.
Krost, Mrs. E.
Klein, Mr.
L'st, W. B.
Lawler, Ellen.
Lawler, Emma.
Lawler, Dan.
Lissa (adopted daughter of Sim m),
Lamourant, Philman.
Lassabe, Victor.
Lassabe, Delphine.
Lassabe, Bertrand.
Lawlor, Miss.
Mayo, George.
Mudge, Ephraim C.
Muller (child of).
Mayfield, Helen G.
May, G. S.
Maggiore, Antoine.
Mittenberger, Odile.
Nicaise, Abel.

Nicaise, Rebecca.
Prestel, Caroline.
Prestel, Nicholas.
Pierre, Antonio.
Suarez, Mrs. Helen.
Suarez, Regina M.
Sylvester, Walter.
Sancier, John J.
Taylor, Capt. I. L.
Taconi, Alfred.
Taconi, Jules.
Tarrant. Salvador.
Terzia, Steffano.
Vassali, P.
Vassali.
Valconar, Francois.
Vicelli.
Vicelli.
Vicelli.
White, Mrs.
Walters, Stella.
Williams, George, col.
Wolff, Annie S. D.
Nine unknown.

Mississippi City.
Brockatt, Mrs. W. B.
Brockatt (child of).
Carter, Col. M. A.
Mayer, Fred.
Mayer, Albert.
Rowland, Mrs.

Morgan City.
Clare, Samuel.
Farrell, Miss.
Hennessy, James.
Martin (daughter of Wm.)
Warchiell, Daniel W.

Cardiff Landing.
Thompson, Alice.
Ross, Miss Elizabeth.
Ross, Jesse S.
Wiley, Minerva.
Ross, Melissa.
Ross, W. N.
Murchant, Mrs. Amy.
Mathews, Mrs. Nancy.

Bolton.
Shields, Peter.
Myrick, Mrs. R. A.
Myrick, E. K.
Walton, Miss Annie.
McKay, Miss Ida.
Alexander, Mrs. Dr.
Peebles, Mrs. Ida.
Peebles, Clifton.
Schwartz, M.
Walton, George.
Wells, Henry.and child.
Sholner, W. E.
Powell, Mrs. Allie.
Fitzgerald, Mrs. Jennie.
Pepper, G. C.
Pepper, Mrs. Mattie S.

Friar's Point.
Alcorn, Geo. R.
Alcorn, Mrs. Geo. R.
Dwyer, J. W.
Rucks, Judge Jas.
Maynard, Jos.
Wood, Mr., Col.

Handsboro.
Andrews, Daniel.
Bailey, Matilda.
Blacklidge, John G.
Cleary, Mary Ann.
Cullivan, John.
Cullivan, Walter.
Hempstead, Edward.
Lyon, Dr. J. E.
Murphy, Mrs. J.
McBey, Alex.
McBey, Mrs. D.

McBey, Mrs. E.
Odom, Charles.
Poleicho, M.
Vierling, Georgia.
Waycott, Monica.
Zundt, Joseph.

Senatobia.
Creager. C. W.
Davis, Mrs. Mira.
Dean, Mrs. D. L,
Dickey, Dabney.
Dickey, Mattie.
Dickey, George.
McGehee, Margaret.
Parker, Mrs. Cora.
Sanders, Mrs. A. V.

Stevenson's Plantation.
Stevenson (child of J. A., Jr.).
Vinson, Mr.

Summit.
Griffin.
Griffin.
Griffin.
Willhoft, Mr.

Sulphur Springs.
Caldwell, Wells.
Frentil, John.
Jones, Louisa.
Kennedy. M.
Schaeffer.

Sunflower.
Badford, A. V. (sheriff).
Bookout, Capt. Ben. C.

Bovina.
Bigelow, Mrs. W. H.
Cameron, D. A.
Chappell, R. W.
Featherstone, Laura W.
Fox, Mrs. Joseph J.
Gray, Mis. J. W
McInnis, John.
Powell, J. W.
Smith, Mary E.
Shannon, S. W.
Wilkins, Capt John.
Wurman, John.
Powell(children of J.N.).

Ricohoc.
Marlose, S.

Smith's Station.
Brooks, Aaron.
Jewel, Mrs.

Stoneville.
Brown, Ida.
Byrne, Jno.
Burdett, Walsh.
Burdett, Miss.
Burdett, Nathan.
Crockett, Sam.
Dawkens, Geo.
Davis(three children of).
Evenittz, J. E.
Foley. B. F.
Gerdine, Dr. A. S.
Gaddis, Dr. Thos.
Griffin, Dr.
Hill, J. W.
Hartman, M.
Jones, Henry.
Kirby, Dr.
Kleiber, Jacob, Jr.
Kleiber, Jacob, Sr.
Kamsler, Adolph.
Lemler, Henry
Lamkin. Mrs. Nancy.
Monk. Henry.
Moozinski, M. J.
Moozinski (child of).

McAlister, C. K.
McAlister, Mrs. A. W.
Montgomery, Mrs. Wm.
Montgomery, Dr. Wm.
McLean, Phil.
Melvin, Mrs. Rebecca.
McKeon, Pat.
McDonald, Andy.
Oden, Dr.
O'Brien, Thos.
Olson, Dan.
Priest, Sr.
Priest, Jr.
Quinn, Pat.
Steverson, James.
Stone, D. L.
Snowberger, Blanche.
Spears.
Shannahan, Dan.
Walker (son of J. B.).
Winters, Eddie.
Winters (child of).
Winters, Jack.
Winters, Mr. C. A.
Wingfield, Willie.
Wingfield, Walter.

Horn Lake.
Collins, Wm.

Terry.
Grayson, Lisa, col.
Grayson, Jane.
Godman. Dr. H. R.
Samson, Joe, col.
One unknown.

Osyka.
Addison, Mrs. John.
Baramon (child of).
Bullion (daughter of).
Bardalis, Jennie.
Bonds, Martin.
Bonds, Mrs. Martin.
Borus, Frank.
Borus, Edward.
Butcher, Willie.
Cortney, Mrs.
Cain, Adolph.
Cutrer (child of).
Cerf, Isaac.
Cerf, Manuel.
Donois, Wm.
Dreyfus, Lehman.
Eastman, Mr.
Feithen, Mrs.
Ford (four sons of Dr.).
Human, Isaac.
Hart, Mrs. Hyman.
Jones, Willie.
Keating, Henry.
Loeb, Mrs.
Miller, Margaret.
Ott, J. A.
Rehorst, Henry.
Rehorst, Joe.
Ricks, Bill.
Redmond, Charles.
Raoul, Griffin.
Sipple, Margaret.
Schnider, Caroline.
Schnider, Tom.
Smithner, Jacob.
Vernado, T.
Vernado (son of).
Weil, Charles.
Weihs, Augustus.
Wolf, Meyer.
Wolf, Henry.
Wales, Ben.

Ocean Springs.
Charles, Father.
Ryan, Joseph.
Strout, Col.

Pearlington.
Carre, R. B.
Graves, Polena.

A HISTORY OF THE YELLOW FEVER.

Lake.
Crowson, Mrs. Amanda.
Crowson, W. E.
Tate, Frank.
Scott, Lee C.
McCallum, Dr. Geo. C.
Evers, Wm. H.
McFarland, Hugh G.
Tate, Dr. J. J.
Wilkins, Leroy B.
Clay, John.
Crosby, Willie J.
Davison, Robt.
Tate, Simpson.
Young, Mathew.
Hoskins, Mrs. W. S.
Lowry, Mrs.
Lowry, Geo. F.
Yarbrough, J. S.
Rhea, Mrs. Tom.
Evers, Miss Mamie.
Snead, Mrs. J. P.
Couch, John.
Yarbrough, Mrs. J. S.
Evers, Miss Carrie.
Lowry, Miss Lulu.
Evers, Mrs. W. H.
McFarland (child of Charlie).
McCallum (child of Mary).
Kennedy, S. D.
Couch, Jas. M.
Crosby, Jno. H.
Long, Jesse.
Burge, Mrs. Sarah.
McFarland, Mrs. Bessie
Saunders, P.
McCallum, Mrs. M.
Saunders, Mrs. M. P.
Saunders, Miss Fannie.

Kennedy, Mrs. S. D.
Tate, Miss Bena.
McFarland (child of Mary).
Evans (infant of Mrs.).
Shackleford, J. N.
Burge, Miss Ella.
Scott, Mrs. Kittie.
Long, Oscar.
Hoskins(infant of Robt.).
Weaver, Willie.
Adams, Miss Lyda.
Ritter, L.
Ray, R. A.
Burge, Rachael.
Long, A.
Weaver, Jno. R.
McGraty, Barney.
Adams, W. J.
McCallum, Miss Kate.
Burge, Richard.
Stewart, Mrs. James.
Wells, Mrs. Sarah.
McCallum, Charley.
Weaver, Lafayette.
Stewart(daughter of Mrs. James).
Weaver, Tommie.
Tate, Bob.
Nichols, Wm.
Burge, Miss Stelle.
Burge, Miss Nettie.
Burge, Richard, Jr.
Wells, Jno. D.
Burge, Miss Julia.
Tate, Miss Ann.
Lee, Mrs.
Burge, Miss Pinkie.

Biloxi.
Dunn, Miss.

Gregory, John Henry.
Gerson, Reuben.
Guillotte, Ed. J.
Hogan, Margaret.
Lambricki, Dimitry
Murphy, Mrs.
Weingart John.

Beachland.
Bullock, Wm.
Biblingstene, Mrs.
Brodsing, Dr.
Featherstone, Laura.
Featherstone, W. W.
Featherstone, Mrs.
Featherstone (gr'dchild of).
Finch, John W.
Flowers, E.
Fox. Mrs. L.
Gotthelf, B. N. (Rabbi).
Holt, Mrs.
Johnson, Mrs. Jos.
Johnson, Mrs. J. B.
Johnson, Mrs. M.
Leach, H.
Lorch, Adolph.
Meyer, Isadore.
McEnnis, J. N.
McEnnis, Mrs. L.
Newman, Gus.
Powell, Clarence.
Powell, Alexander.
20 M. E. of Vicksburg.

Winona.
Blackston, Benj.
Campbell, Wm.
Harris, Francis, col.
Kittrell, Jo. C.
McGeure.

Mingo, col.
Onry, Geo.
Oury, Lyle.
Reese, Mrs.

Valley Home.
Black, Mrs.
Berry, Sam.
Grose, Mr.
Murphy, Smith.
Marither, M.
Montgomery, Lena.
Montgomery, H.
Payne, Wm.
Payne, Geo.
Russell, Mrs.
Thompson, John.
Thompson, Mrs. John.
Thompson, A. J.
Thompson, Bettie.
Turnipseed, Dr.
White, Mr.

Winterville.
McAllister, A. W.
McAllister, C. K.
McKeon, Pat.
Montgomery, Dr. Wm.
Montgomery, Mrs. Dr. Wm.
Shannahan, Mrs. Dan.
Winters, Jack.
Winter, Sam.

Carrollton.
Liddle, J. M., Jr.

Cayuga.
Griffin, Gen. T. M.
Griffin, Mrs. Tom.
Hack, Mr.
One colored.

III.

ARKANSAS.

Augusta.
Freeman.
Hendricks, Mrs.
Johnson, Wm.
Mulready.
Plummer, Wm., col.

Golden Lake.
No report.

Haynes' Bluff.
Ferry (son of Dr. R. H.).
Ross, Jessie.

Snyder (two daughters).

Helena.
Miller, J. B.
Withers, Gertrude.

Hopefield.
Bailey, Mrs., col.
Bailey (boy of, col.
Bruce, Mrs.
Burrie, Mrs., col.
Carpenter, John.
Connelly, Mrs.

Costello, Austin.
Drake, Archie, col.
Everett, W. E.
Guthrie, Michael.
Guthrie, Jerry.
Hawkins, Mrs.
Leonard, Mrs.
Munne, Mrs. Sarah.
Quinlan, Thomas.
Stack, Jerry.
Stack, Mrs.
Stuart, Bill, col.
Unknown man.

Terrene.
Abraham (two children of).
Cohn, Johnny
Keely, John.
Loeb, Louie.
Mayson, Dr.
Shelby, John, col.
Zadeck (child of Ben.).
Zadeck, Mrs. Ben.
Zadeck (child of).
Zadeck, Ben.

IV.

ALABAMA.

Athens.
Rodgers, Alexander.
Rodgers, Elizabeth.

Courtland.
Newsom, A.

Decatur.
Ayers, Mr.
Cramer (son of).

Edwards.
Fennell, Miss Sallie.
Gill, Mrs. D.
Gilson, Mr.
Henry, J.
Houk, R.
Houk, Mrs. A.
Heavitson, Mr.
Howard, Mrs. M. J.
Johnson, Thomas.

McCarty, Mrs.
McCarty, Miss.
Polk, Mrs. G.
Williams, Mrs. J., col.
Whitten, Rev. Joel.

Florence.
Brown, James.
Bernhard, Mr.
Cox, James.

Cox, Joseph.
Crow, Josie.
Cain, Jane.
Grob, Mr.
Lambert, M:s.
Price, J. H.
Perry, T. M.
Pelty, Johnnie.
Pelty, Mrs.
Pelty (two children of).

A HISTORY OF THE YELLOW FEVER. 251

Rodgers, Thomas.
Ragsdale, John.
Ragsdale, Claudia.
Rice, Will H.
Rice, Miss Nora.
Reid, John S.
Timbeck, Mr.
Wade A. C., child.
Twenty-six colored.

Huntsville.

Brock, John.
Brodie, Mrs. Jno.
Booth, T. J.
Clark, W. A.
Edwards, Ida.
Edwards, Frank.
Engering, Frank.

Fisher, Jonathan.
Gohen, Fannie.
Gohen, Margaret.
Reagin, W. R.
Solomons, Pauline.
Yonkha, Margaret.
Zolenka, Maggie.

Mobile.

Both, Rev. Victor.
Fort, R. B.
Marley, Father.
Unknown woman, col.

Stevenson.

Rose, Porter.
Welch, T. J.

Child from Germantown.

Tuscumbia.

Williams, Charles.
Jones, Miss B.
Stamps, Mr. & Mrs.
Maunch, Mr. & Mrs.
Belcher, C.
Rather, Geo.
Jones, Mrs.
Ross, Mrs.
Christian, Miss C.
Warren, Mervin.
Duprez, Dr.
King, Mr.
Downs, Miss Bettie.
Young, Mr.

Unknown German.
Prout, Edward.
Smoot, Mrs.
Smoot, Miss.
Gilbert, Mrs.
Clark, Mrs.
Moulton, Thomas.
Osborne, Sandy.
Entress, Ella.
Unknown boy.

Tuscaloosa.

Rhinehart, Alex.
Rhinehart, Sidney.

Whistler.

Marley, Rev. Father.

V.

KENTUCKY.

Bowling Green.

Cough, Mrs. Jack.
Curren, Mr.
Fitzpatrick, Joseph.
Hespin, John.
Hogan, John.
Houghton, Mrs. M.
McCarty, Mrs. Tim.
Murphy, Wm.
Palmer, John.
Ritter, L. R.
Sullivan, Ellen.
Schafer, Mrs. H.
Weaver, Wm.
Williamson, C. M.

Danville.

Craft, John Young.

Fulton.

Bennett, Mrs. Sam.
Wooldridge, Amanda.
Boaz, Dr. C. D.

Hickman.

Amberg, Miss Irene.
Amberg, Joseph.
Amberg, Miss Vic.
Anderson, Dr. J. M.
Anderson, Miss Belle.
Bearger, Herman.
Bearger, John.
Bearger, Miss.
Bearger, Mrs. John.
Brevard, W. A.
Baltzer, Philip.
Bailey, Edward.
Buckner, W. T., Jr.
Blanton, Dr. C.
Buncho, Andy.
Buncho, Mrs. Andy.
Black, Joseph.
Bright, David F.
Barnes, Doc.
Barnes, T. D.
Barnes, Will.
Beaster, W. H.
Bondurant, Mrs. J. J. C.
Bondurant, Miss Jennie.
Bondurant (child of).
Betts, Wm.
Buck, T. C.
Barry, Mrs. John.
Coffey, Wm.
Catlett, Dr. H. C.
Cole, Miss Lotta.
Cobb, Chas. S.
Corbett, Dr. W. D.
Corbett, Mrs. W. D.
Cook, Dr. J. L.

Dozier, Thomas C.
Donevant, Geo.
Davis, Miss Lulu.
Davis, Gus.
Dodds, Robert.
Dale (son of Wm.).
Echard, Eliza.
Echert, Miss Lou.
Farris, Tom.
Fortune, B. W.
Frenz, W. J.
Funk, Fred.
Farris, Dr. J. W.
Gleason, T. E.
Gleason, Burt.
Gleason, Hallie.
Gardner, Mrs. C.
Gardner, W. H.
Gardner, Meta.
Greenup, John.
Gibb, Frank.
Glaser, R.
Glaser, Joseph.
Hendricks, Mrs.
Hendricks, Miss Louisa.
Hendricks, Miss Anna.
Hendricks, John.
Hendricks(2 children of).
Heatherly, Mac.
Hertweck, Max.
Hertweck, Mrs. Max.
Harness, N. P.
Holt, R. D.
Holman, Mrs.
Hancock, W. W.
Hallyburton, Mrs. Cora.
Hallyburton (son of).
Jones, Thomas M.
Kingman, A. D., Jr.
Kingman, Katie.
Kingman, Muff.
Kreiger, Miss.
Kreiger, Mrs.
Kreiger(two children of).
Kitchison.
Kesterson, C. H.
Kirger, Mrs.
Keistner, M.
Karcher, Miss Mary.
Karcher, Miss Josie.
Karcher, Miss Eva.
Luttrell, Miss Cappie.
Luttrell, John.
Luttrell, Mrs.
Lacy, Miss.
Lane, T. J.
McCain, Wm.
Morrow, Lutha.
Metheny, Robbie.
Manuel (a baker).
Monroe, Lewis.

Mangle, Ed.
Mangle, Mrs. Ed.
Miller, Frank.
Miller, Mrs. Frank.
Miller, Joseph.
Millett, John.
Muse, Miss Annie.
Maggie (at hotel).
McConnel, James.
Mason, Charles.
Nelson, N. L.
Nelson, Mrs. N. L.
Neal, Michael.
O'Neal, Mike.
Overton, Mary J.
Overton, Maggie.
Prather, Dr. R. C.
Prather, Dr. Hugh L.
Prather, G. B. (mayor.)
Pollard, Ed. M.
Parham Miss.
Puckett, Geo. W.
Pohm, Mrs.
Person (child of).
Person, Louisa.
Ray.
Reasoner, Wm.
Roulhac, George G.
Reid, R. J., Jr.
Simons, John.
Sherron, Thomas.
Sherron, Joseph.
Sherron, John.
Smith, O. P.
Seagrist, Frank.
Seagrist, Mrs. Frank.
Seagrist, Otto.
Seagrist (son of).
Stoner, Kate.
Stoner, Fred.
Shoemaker, John.
Shoemaker, A.
Sohm, Miss Eureka.
Sohm, Willie.
Sohm, John.
Sohm (child).
Stone, John.
Scherbe, Emil.
Simse, S.
Samse, Mrs. Ida.
Samse, F.
Samse, Chas.
Samse, Mrs. F.
Simse, Henry.
Scharfe, Emil.
Sampree, Ida.
Stephens, Mrs. E.
Sollis, Henry.
Sollis, Mary.
Titus, Nelson.
Thomas, Miss Sallie.

Thomas, J. C.
Thomas, T. W.
Thomas, Thad. N.
Thomas, Margaret.

Jordan Station.

Alexander, Miss Belle.
Prather, Dr. Hugh.

Louisville.

Able, Gabriel.
Berryman, Eddie.
Coleman, Sam.
Casey, Mike.
Croghan, David.
Coffee, Patrick.
Connell, J. B. M.
Davis, H. R.
Dryfus, Samuel.
Ernest, Geo. M.
Ernest, Mrs. Geo. M.
Fisher, Charles.
Flynn, Meta.
Gary.
Gallenher, N. G.
Hollahan, Mary.
Heidelburg, Louis.
Haskill, Ben.
Haffmeister, Johanna.
Hellrig, Rudolph.
Howard, John.
Jones, Sebastian.
Laurie, Mary A.
Leake, W. L.
Lawton, W. F.
Lutz.
Moore, Richard.
McKenna, Mrs. Annie.
Maney, James.
Morriss, James P.
Mudd, Nathaniel.
Plunkett, Charles.
Ryan, Mrs. Mary.
Ritter, Alice R.
Rawes, Mrs. Geo.
Shaw, Wm.
Samuels, Henry B.
Shannahan, Maggie.
Scalley, M. E.
Sellar, John.
Sellar, Therese.
Saltalamachie, Frank.
Tedro, Mrs. Annie.
Winn, Fred.
Worsham, Clifford.
Voss, Ann.
Voss, Ernest.
Two colored.

Trenton.

Hord, C. C.

VI.

LOUISIANA.—NEW ORLEANS.

Arberies, Giovani.
Antonio, Marzd.
Admirall, Isabella.
Antonio, Mary.
Ambers, Daniel.
Ackerman, Joseph.
Archidell, Antonio.
Adams, L.
Adams, James.
Arms, Harry.
Antoine, Maie d'.
Aschenbrenner, O.
Anten, Anna A.
Amendt, Flor.
Anderson, Christian.
Anderson, Ida.
Avery, James.
Anderson, F. B.
Aborg, Mrs.
Augor, L. E.
Aubin, George S.
Adams, Jeanie.
Artigne, Fred.
Anastapiades, A.
Adams, Louis.
Adams, George.
Adams, H. D.
Arnold, E.
Armstrong, E. L.
Anthony, F. M.
Alonzo, A.
Arnbult, Peter.
Alderman, E. J.
Auer, Julia W.
Allen, Lebean V.
Augbecker, Aug.
Adams, W. N.
Augustin, J. A.
Adams, Flor. G.
Aikens, John W.
Ahern, Patrick.
Antonia, H. L.
Alber, J. N.
Apffel, Gab.
Ahlburn, Henry.
Adler, Wm. S.
Assanti, J. DeP.
Allen, Mary J.
Appley, Blanche.
Augustine, Joseph.
Anderson, Martin.
Ayrand, Bascal.
Adams, Teresa.
Adams, Aleck.
Ames, Laura.
Alexander, F. G.
Ault, Alvis.
Adele, Aloysius.
Andry, Charles J.
Allen, Nich.
Astrado, Antoniette.
Antelny, Leonce.
Artus, Marid.
Abram J. J.
Allen, W. D.
Abtte, Johanna S.
Abbot, Clara.
Ansbery, Hugh.
Arnett, F. C.
Archaffenberg, F.
Armas, D'Anna.
Argentum, A. G.
Abner, E. D.
Anseman, Ernest V.
Arcott, Lizzie.
Armstrong, S. H.
Arin, Benedicto.
Anderson, Charles W.
Arthurs, Wm. E.
Arnault, Genel.
Apken, Joseph.

Alito, Francisco.
Adelton, Wm.
Andrieu, Jules.
Albers, John A.
Anthony, Francois M.
Alonzo, Antonie.
Amauit, Peter.
Arnold, Edward.
Armstrong, Ellen L.
Acker, Zavier.
Avaril, Camille.
Abadie, Henry.
Adler, Jennie.
Adamzig, Jacob
Ankar, Bessie.
Albert, Sister Josephine.
Aranes, John P.
Avery, James.
Andrews, Eli.
Arnato, Corneto.
Anderson, Augustine.
Antonio, Andre.
Arastase, Mrs. Alex.
Adams, Mrs. Eliza.
Andeek, Joseph.
Arnold, Mrs. J. N.
Adlier, Albert.
Apply, Blanche.
Augustins, Joseph.
Allen, Richard.
Aycock, Joseph.
Allen, Charles.
Angela.
Allen, John.
Audrette, John.
Abadie, Warie.
Amitt, Mr.
Abrahams, Elias.
Addicks, Matt.
Arbogas, Jacques.
Auguste, Mrs.
Antonini, Adolph.
Aitken, Elizabeth B.
Anderson, Christine.
Anderson, Sarah.
Anderson, Martha.
Argenton, Antonie G.
Apps, Henrietta.
Abodie, Jean L.
Anthony, Michael.
Aufdemot, Mary.
Benedits, Salvadore.
Bruchert, A.
Bird John.
Benton, Rosalie.
Burke, Jack.
Bibren, Charles.
Bugge, Diddenka.
Brady, Mary.
Bokenfohr, F.
Becker, Mary L.
Bruguiere, L.
Brennan, Joseph.
Brummer, T.
Barlow, Mary.
Benning, C. A.
Bussa, Fred.
Balancia, Paul.
Brown, Miss Kate.
Betzer, Henry.
Baer, Joseph.
Brown, Joseph.
Bruneau, J. M.
Bercier, Al. M. L.
Broyer, L. A.
Betancourt, J.
Brady, James.
Behla, Anna.
Bonge, Wm.
Bainsfather, J. C.
Berges, Laurent.

Brady, Theresa.
Bueler, Josephine.
Bouisse, Odillie.
Bellalmel, Ernan.
Barry, Mary L.
Burns, Robert.
Bernardo, Louisa.
Becker, Paul.
Basil, Joe.
Bernauer, Charles.
Begarrie, Jean.
Butts, Warren S.
Brown, L.
Bradley, Wm.
Biri, Henry.
Brady.
Bundy, Louis F.
Bergmann, Wm.
Baldwin, Charles.
Bringgold, R.
Baushey, Sam.
Britton, Annie.
Braig, James.
Blein, Juliet.
Burns, L. L.
Bradford, C. E.
Bathe, Mrs. Berth.
Bridge, Wm. B.
Brady, Andrew.
Baker, George L.
Bell, Laura.
Baker, Eli.
Bemar, Louis.
Bernier, E. M.
Beauman, C.
Brecht, J. E.
Burner, Margaret.
Burns, Edward.
Bersier, Paul.
Bickman, H. F.
Blake, Richard J.
Bailey, Agnes.
Bonnecarrere, M.
Bussani, A.
Boshaus, Wm.
Boyarella, Jos.
Bourgoyne, H. V.
Bruns, Otto.
Burkhardt, Geo.
Barnes, J. D.
Barnes, Robert.
Beauchere, C. K.
Bailey, Kate.
Boyle, Ada.
Bardin, Joseph.
Boreau, Mrs. D.
Bergeret, Jean M.
Boigelle, Mrs.
Byrnes, Chas.
Bruns, Wm. H.
Braudel, Louisa.
Balles, Bernard.
Battu, James T.
Balds, Isadori.
Beweruug, Fred.
Beratina, Antonio.
Brunnert, August.
Boehm, John.
Budey, George.
Barbe, John.
Brown, Thomas.
Berlin, R. Alice.
Berry, H D.
Bottick, Charles.
Berley, John.
Buchman, Gotria.
Bruct, Eugene.
Bounier, Jean.
Bartel, Henry.
Bacher, Marie L. J.
Bercher, Fred.

Buffler, Auguste.
Bourgeois, H.
Batemore, George.
Baciagalopi, J.
Baratine, B.
Bonneau, Henry.
Boucher, Charles.
Brewster, Mrs. M.
Bander, Anna.
Bauman, Rev. G.
Braraton, Anna.
Baumstark, L.
Bruce, Marie.
Bower, Elizabeth.
Bessier, Marie.
Breen, Aleck.
Barnes, W.
Benton, Charles.
Byrne, Dr. J. G.
Bruccolori, Rosalie.
Berry, Ellen.
Bantz, Catherine.
Bretz, John B.
Barret, Patrick.
Brady, James.
Bencoks, A.
Behune, Bern. J.
Barrett, John.
Becocque, John.
Bonhager, Fred.
Browne, Mrs. E.
Burns, Elizabeth.
Braus, Perre.
Bruns, Rosalie.
Bence, Charles.
Bowers, G. B.
Bowman, Mrs. Anna S.
Brodel, Bernard.
Brown, Mary B.
Burns, Robert, C.
Bugge, W.
Barnett, John.
Boe, Louis.
Bache, Katie.
Birchman, Katie.
Benza, Richard.
Bofill, Paul H.
Bond, James W.
Brickel, Philip.
Batheiny, F. J.
Blank, Charles T.
Bogart, Francisco.
Beuz, Nellie.
Bermheim, J.
Bashounse, F. V.
Broker, Louisa.
Bauder, George.
Bobo, B. A.
Bruno, Joseph.
Bailey, Kate.
Barnes, Sister.
Berno, D. F.
Beck, Fred.
Block, Gabe.
Bertrand, Aug.
Buogacre, Ed.
Blanchard, W.
Babb, W. T.
Behreus, Henry.
Bauman, John.
Baker, C. L.
Bergery, James P.
Burkman, Julius.
Brindamour, V.
Bernard, Maria.
Barber, Charles.
Bronges, Celina.
Boutinaro, Peter.
Berna, A.
Burk, Elizabeth.

A HISTORY OF THE YELLOW FEVER. 253

Baudard, Sim. J.
Benulier, Will.
Bernard, Philip.
Benclaire, Charles.
Billiski, Wilhoit.
Bache, Anna.
Brady, Charles
Bobilote, Mary J.
Bachman, Joseph.
Bloemeyer, C. H.
Bernias, William.
Babbit, A. D.
Buckhart, Bertha.
Benzel, Alice.
Biedinger, Josephine.
Bruse, Julius.
Borgas, Albert.
Berner, Teresa.
Bervan, C. A.
Brigetta, Sister Mary.
Berricks, John.
Burns, Franklin.
Bridges, Abram B.
Baker, R. J. H.
Brady, F. W.
Banzano, Blank.
Burke, Fritz.
Burst, Augustus.
Brown, Sophia C.
Blanco, Catherena.
Buffler, Augusti.
Bourgoin, H.
Bercier, Oscar L. F. L.
Bercher, Fred.
Biringman, John.
Barnes, Robert.
Barnes, Jeff. D.
Buckhart, George.
Boyle, Ada.
Beauchare, Charles K.
Bousleaur, William.
Burgoyne, Henrietta B.
Burns, Otto.
Busana, Antionette.
Bogaretta, Joseph.
Brady, Andrew.
Baker, George M.
Burg, Catherine.
Brens, Ida.
Bamatto, John.
Black, J. W.
Bullet, William.
Boline, Dora H.
Bloodgood, C. B.
Birch, John.
Beret, Marie.
Bird, Annie.
Buckley, Mary D.
Bettison, Agnes S.
Bourny, Mary F.
Banas, Mary W.
Bares, Willie.
Black, Edmund.
Berthand, Mary A.
Benecke, A.
Bourg, Philip.
Bastino, John.
Burgone, John D.
Bullit, Louisa.
Baldwin, Culbert S.
Biza, Adam.
Bertucei, S.
Buhl, Fred.
Bluemenson, Ig.
Beverly, Reed.
Bise, Cleavely.
Behrens, William.
Bathelar, Mary E.
Block, Blanche.
Blessey, Florence A.
Block, Alice.
Brown, Augusta.
Bieblizka, Anna.
Britten, Edward.
Block, Lucy.
Boufette, Charles.
Bassett, Nicholas.
Bawman, Aleck.
Baldwin, Mrs. Ella W.

Bonnetts. Mary.
Blanca, Jean Marie.
Bancourt, Lucene.
Benson, C. L.
Bell, George.
Bloman, Henry.
Bacas, Marie.
Bender, Andrew K.
Bamford H.
Bonich, Mrs. Rosa.
Bonich, Victoria.
Beacoudray, Aug.
Bruguins, John.
Bell, Frank.
Blocher, Herman.
Berg, Charles.
Blume, Charles.
Burgniens, James.
Bernhardt, John F.
Boyle, P. J.
Breman, Edward.
Benz, Mary E.
Brennan, Willie.
Braun, Matilda.
Begue, Peter.
Bennedettode, G.
Basby, Mrs. Sallie.
Balla, Cu-mus.
Blasini, Elizabeth.
Brun, Patrick.
Bryant, Anna.
Burns, Mary A.
Brown, W. J.
Berniol, Aleck.
Braselman, Guy.
Boyne, Hubert B.
Brewster, Annie S.
Bordeware, Pierre.
Beaudeuas, Didie F.
Balla, Mrs. Rosa.
Brickmann, Herman.
Barr, Albert.
Burke, Mary.
Bossant, Edgar.
Butler, Walter, J.
Bardsell, Henry.
Brimstone, Alex.
Berry, J. A.
Barr, James E.
Bernhardt, Pauline.
Bremmer, H.
Buck, M. J.
Barnett, Fred.
Beecher, Rev. J. C.
Benton, Charles.
Byrne, Dr. J. G.
Bruccolori, Rosalie.
Berry, Ellen.
Bentz, Catherine.
Bietry, John B.
Barrett, Patrick.
Brady, James.
Barnes, Edmund W.
Brock, Anna M.
Brion, Henry De.
Rocker, Peter.
Boyle, Charles.
Bruno, Marie.
Boraseo, Dominico.
Bremond, Hilarian.
Briffa, Benedetto.
Bissom, Andreas.
Brown, Malone.
Baler, John.
Brady, James.
Britton, John.
Bundy, Mrs. L. F.
Balsamo, Leo.
Belon, Louise.
Bush, Samuel.
Bender, H.
Brown, Edward J.
Braun, Louis.
Brady, Thomas J.
Bordernu, A.
Blapes, Charles.
Bradley, Robert L.
Belaire, L. H.
Bluhm, Louis.

Bannon, Andrew.
Bauman, Henrich.
Bretano, Adolph.
Battle, William.
Baily, Mary.
Brown, Gregory.
Barnes, Robert.
Bell, Joseph.
Benson, Alfred.
Brown, Edward.
Brandt, Christina.
Bagale, Mrs. G.
Bacher, Joseph.
Barthelmy, L. H.
Brown, Anna M.
Brady, E.
Behrena, C.
Brennan, Edward.
Belt, Charles R.
Berzie, Mary J.
Babcock, Orson S.
Buchler, Rudolph.
Bayst, August.
Beryans, Joseph.
Beaumount, Samuel.
Buono, Salvador.
Barnes, Miss Harriet.
Brughien, Amedee.
Bauman, Fred.
Burns, Thomas.
Beroni, Lena.
Byers, Edward M.
Bohne, Henry.
Burns, Mr.
Bauman, Sophie.
Baltz, Alexander.
Benzie, B. M.
Billard, Lucie.
Barnes, Matilda J.
Bertrand, Henry.
Baurmann, John.
Baker, C. M.
Barkman, Julius.
Buell, Jimmy.
Bonner, Jeff.
Blake, James.
Baratinni, Maria.
Butler, Sister T. C.
Birkenroad, Julius.
Berkel, Fred. W.
Bordes, Mary.
Biggie, Paul.
Brouc, Jean.
Baur, Theodore.
Barry, James.
Catania, George.
Cruchent, Mrs. A.
Cloney, Miles.
Connelly, John.
Constantine.
Cullen, Mary Ann.
Cunningham, Wm.
Cruchent, Jose.
Clark, Walter.
Connor, Michael.
Clairal, Felicie.
Cochran, James.
Camella, Salvador.
Cordes, Mrs.
Comfort, Wm.
Botogniro, Anthony.
Curtis, James.
Coughlan, Richard.
Christopher, John.
Conners, James.
Cazzella, Santina.
Chapsky, Hugo.
Cullen, Alice F.
Carran, Mrs. O. J.
Carriere, Frank N.
Coates, Mrs. S. A.
Camienski, F.
Camille, Gustave.
Conroy, Fred.
Cabariol, Mrs. Rosa L.
Chietta, Pietro.
Cartel, Leon.
Cleaver, Henry.
Conners.

Carnovan, Carlo.
Cosenana, Maria.
Cazoux, Bernard.
Collins, Mary.
Canepa, Rosalie.
Croix, Dela.
Chapman, Henry.
Christy, Henry.
Camila, Crestina
Clain, August.
Cundiff, Jas. B.
Christinna, An.
Casio, Geronimo.
Clamous, John.
Claude, Mrs. M.
Clement, Louis.
Campbell, Sarah.
Casey, Mary.
Cazeres, Wm.
Carbini, Nicola.
Church, John.
Catalana, Rileta.
Checapelia, Philip.
Cashell, Emma J.
Cornelius, Philip.
Callery, Cecelia.
Catalona, A.
Craft, Charles.
Charles, Henry.
Conrad, Lena.
Campbell, E. E.
Clark, Maggie.
Caldwell, M. F.
Casey, Hugh W.
Charlton, Wm.
Crammond, J. E.
Coffrey. F. D.
Curia, Dominico.
Canius, G. A.
Camo, Lizzie.
Clavich, Mateo.
Cullen, John M.
Cohen, Rebecca.
Coppersmith, Henry.
Carrallina, Louisa.
Connolly, Maggie.
Cazant, Alexander.
Connel, Dan. R.
Curry, Terrence.
Clental, Paschal.
Collins, Francis.
Clifford, Mary.
Cazale, Adelaide.
Copps, J. P.
Cleary, Mary E.
Converse, Daisy.
Chew, J. D.
Covington, N.
Couneis, Mrs.
Casteretto, J. B.
Chandler, D. R.
Cottam, R. A.
Collery, Michael.
Canos, Rosa.
Clouzet, Rosette.
Chacorcau, Louis.
Clemments, John.
Camache, Jonathan.
Calleja, Joseph.
Cazeaux, Emile.
Canela, Antonio.
Clark, Sarah J.
Chapman, J. F.
Connigan, Mary.
Cochran. Mary A.
Crawford, J. A.
Chalan, Julius C.
Calvert, Mrs. M. A.
Corry, Arthur.
Caleb, Rosa.
Cashell, Eugene.
Connelly, James.
Cohman, Mary.
Chalin, Fred.
Carlisle, Edward.
Cashell, Joseph.
Coltraro, Callora.
Cohen, Nidam.
Clark, Elizabeth.

Cutter, Ella J.
Comstock, C. B.
Cook, Wallis.
Charles, S.
Curien, Armauld.
Corull, James.
Conget, L. A.
Cunfe, Fran.
Canan, Philip.
Clark, James.
Curtis, Truman.
Carmille, Mrs. A.
Court, Atrica.
Cowperthwaite, Henry.
Charton, J. N.
Compter, S. A.
Cox, James K.
Campbell, M.
Calligan, N.
Charto, Jacinuo.
Cabero, M. C.
Catola, Jean.
Capus, Henry.
Cook, Thomas N.
Chavurgny, Louise.
Cable, George B.
Chibnall, Wm.
Caruso, Luca.
Cady, Jacob.
Canella, John.
Conte, Pierre.
Crews, George.
Conry, Fannie.
Cuilte, Emile.
Casaubor, Alex.
Cahill, James.
Corbin, John H.
Conrad, Emma.
Cavanaugh, Martin.
Cook, John Lewis.
Clarae, Joseph.
Coughlin, James.
Chopen, Anna.
Carbos, P. G.
Caster, Camille.
Condon, Richard.
Clayton, Joseph.
Chew, J. D.
Converse, Daisy.
Christ, George.
Chardon, Wm.
Cramond, J. Emily.
Caffrey, F. Demoret.
Capo, Prosper.
Clarke, Maggie.
Conrad, Lena.
Callery, Cecelia.
Campbell, Esther E.
Catalana, Antonio.
Charles, Henry.
Carey, Hugh W.
Chambora, John.
Comes, Blaise.
Carambat, E. D.
Coates, Maud A.
Cox, Teresa A.
Clark, Sarah J.
Chapman, John T.
Cundiff, Virg. T.
Cazaloote, Bertrand
Colegoro, Dimetry.
Clesta, Antonio.
Corisse, Pierre.
Casson, Widow.
Colome, Henry.
Chantelou, Edward.
Cassady Emanuel.
Charlton, Eva L.
Castopper, Antonie.
Case, George.
Capuano, Julia.
Cooper, James.
Carroll, Timothy.
Colozero, Annieall.
Conovan, John.
Couway, Michael.
Coyne, Thomas.
Coffee, George B.
Chaery, Bertha.

Close, David.
Christina, Leonarda.
Cioccio, Giachin.
Capriana, Aug.
Castaing, Cath.
Connell, R.
Costello, Miles.
Canto, Gabriel.
Comanda, Goetano.
Collins, J.
Cohen, Joseph H.
Cohen, Solomon J.
Camash, Robert.
Connelly, Andrew.
Calamara, Antoni.
Clark, Sarah S.
Carbo, Tony.
Coggshall, S. W.
Cahubley, Theo.
Cohen, Lena.
Coffin, Francis.
Cribbins, Joseph.
Casey, John W.
Ceres, Gabriel.
Chapsky, Albert.
Conolly, Joseph.
Colinsky, Earnest.
Coockmeyer, Louisa.
Caw, Herbert.
Ceres, Marie.
Chabretto, John.
Creelambon, L.
Cardenas, Andrew.
Clorezette, Rosette.
Chacoreau, Louis.
Clements, John.
Camach, Jonathan.
Callija, Joseph.
Cazeaux, Omile.
Canela, Antonio.
Chadwick, Joseph.
Conley, Mary.
Craren, Margareth.
Camilla, Anna.
Cohen, Henry S.
Champagne, Louis.
Chiaca, Theo.
Corrers, Concetta G.
Corrers, Concetta.
Coleman, Ella.
Caldovora, Angelina.
Caufield, Martin.
Croze, Camille de Bres.
Chevreau, Marie.
Chadwick, Winfred.
Converse, W. H.
Clars, Bridget.
Carney, Wm.
Cicero, Salvador La.
Chartonez, John.
Coulan, James.
Campbell, Anna.
Chiappetta, Antonio.
Cramond, Henry A.
Cheehan, Laurence.
Cherrowillett, Cezar.
Conrad, James.
Cefalu, Concheta.
Cousins, Mary E.
Cahill, Patrick.
Catral, John.
Clark, Margaret.
Clary, Joseph M.
Crabe, Perric.
Collings, Joseph W.
Clarke, Myra May.
Costley, T. W.
Croll, Anna M.
Connors, Thomas.
Clement, Charles.
Czarwick, Anton.
Caffrey, Patrick.
Charlton, Ida L.
Carter, Mary.
Colica, Gisvan.
Capus, Henri.
Chuvigny, Louise.
Cooke, Thomas F.
Carey, Joseph R.

Carbarini, Anna.
Collier, Genevive C.
Cleary, Mary E,
Cyrmis, R. A. St.
Camille.
Clark, Helen C.
Calamar, Dominico.
Capley, Albert R.
Camblong. Bevnara.
Coleman, Wood.
Calderaro, Manuel.
Dunn, Louisa.
Duer, Michael.
Druillott, Joseph.
Doufforg, Alexandre.
DePasquali, Marie.
Duthilth, Mrs. A.
Dousse, Henry.
Divincenzo, Antonio.
Dulsheimer, Stella B.
Deyleman, John.
Dotto, Antonio.
D Heremberg, Mrs. A.
Duprey, Francois.
Dietrich, Barbara.
Dillman, Mrs. Della.
Denny, Michael.
Dohoney, Michael.
Depke, Fred. H.
Diedrich, Aleves.
Dreenerding, Phil.
Despow, Marie.
Duffy, James.
Dedelot, Marie.
Doane, Albert C.
Daverede, Pierre.
Doran, John.
Desforges, Louis B.
Dantin, Eugene.
Daudous, Mary.
Daley, Patrick.
DeBlanc, Mary L.
Doran, Michael.
Delaney, Michael.
Dupreux, Mrs. Julia.
Davis, Louis.
Duc, John.
Dermody, James A.
Doueys, Mrs. Bernan.
Derr, Henry W.
Dicks, Eva.
Dibetta, Philomene.
Doyle, James W.
Dietrick, W. A. L.
Dertel, Louise.
Dupont, Gabriel.
Della, Magdalena.
Dietrick, E. B. G.
Donahoe, Julia.
Daray, Jeanne.
Duboler, Charles.
Dutilh, August.
Dantoni, Maria.
Durgin, Daniel.
Dauterive, B. B.
Dasiagne, A.
Deneausse, F.
Drury, Ellen M.
Desuda, Marco.
Donnelly, James.
Deneur, J.
Dorenberger, L.
Dusuan, Gustave.
Dautignan, M.
Defess, Marie.
Dolan, Frank.
Dawson, James.
DeLancy, James.
Dansoni, Maria.
Devere, Kate F.
Doyle, Wm.
Denerling, G.
Dupuy, Chas.
Dwyer, Wm.
Durring, Lavinia.
Dayeson, Pierre.
Dobbs, Mary.
Doyle. Thomas.
Drouett, C. M.

Dutrey, Marie.
Dominique, Mrs J.
Dixel, George.
Dubret, Martha.
Daly, Mary A.
DeForest, James S.
Delarno, Angelo.
Davis, H. W.
Dufour, J. B.
Davis, S. A.
Dwyer, Theresa.
Desdunes, M'lde.
Duchin, Victor.
Dautrive, Marie J.
Denn, James.,
Dilkenkopier, W.
Denice, Mabel.
Durward, G. H.
Donnolly, Mary J.
Duprat, Aleck.
Davenport, Sam.
Dupont, J. M.
Doughty, C. F.
Duba, J. S.
Duffy, Owen.
Daggeu, Wm.
Deal, John E.
Dowie, Robert.
Donagan, Mary.
Druck, Henry.
Drop, N.
Deshane. H.
Doaul, Owen E.
Duer, Jacob.
Dummermath, John.
Daily, Thomas.
DeLa, Renos M.
Daborg, Raymond.
Depke, Aug.
Dowlling, Wm.
Davis, Oliver.
Dilaruza, Rosa.
Dixon, Mary.
Damilo, L. S.
Demerque, J.
Dupuls, Louis.
Dupuls, Marie.
Downeys, Jean.
Dorson, Robert.
Davis, Felicia.
Duzere, Jean N.
Dubois, Michael.
Degat, John.
Daly, Michael.
Deering, H. F. T.
Dejan, Gaston E.
Doudle, Chas.
Demuth. Maggie L.
Duboretti, John.
Drier, M.
Daly, John.
Dawson, H. E.
Dugerre, Pierre.
Dargle, Julia.
Doherty, C. C.
Davis, Jo.
Deitrick. Aug.
Duffy, Willie.
Daubitz, Paul.
Doane, A. C.
Deltoz, Miss B.
Degan, Laurence.
Doune. Susan.
DeBodlin, T.
Durby, Joseph.
Disbia, Oscar M.
Delary, Aug.
Daniels, Joseph.
DeLate, Edward.
Diermann, John.
Ditton, James A.
Doyle, Mary.
Diermann, Barb.
Donehue, Michael.
Doyle, Margaret.
Delgad, B. H.
Decan, Geo. R.
Darlin, Thos. A.

A HISTORY OF THE YELLOW FEVER.

Duco, Armand.
Duncan, Thos. F.
Deferes, Marie.
Daley, Mary.
Ditz, Constance.
Dicket, Philip.
Doughty, Charles.
Duffy, Owen.
Dargin, Wm.
Dufour, Jean B.
Dwyer, Teresa.
Davis, Lina A.
Dennis, Harry Wm.
Deering, Lavinia.
Dietz, Joseph.
Davizan, Pierre.
Donnelly, Joanna.
Danhauer, E.
Decker, Katie.
Delacroix, M. A.
Dabat. Paul W.
Detham, Augustine.
Dennagro, S.
Diermann, Val.
Danorelle, John.
Dionias, Marie.
Doussau, Marie.
Deveness, L. H. H.
Divestin, M. M.
Dietz, Joseph.
Dovel, D. E.
Dertilo.
Davis, Jerry.
Defestus, E. C.
Dumerges, John.
Deroche, Rosa.
Devlin, Jack.
Doyle, Agnes.
Dietz, Rosanna.
Demerest, George.
Dennuzio, Natale.
Davidson, Rev. A.
Duff, Maggie.
Day, Thos. O.
Drewry, James.
Dooley, M.
Donolly, James.
Donaldson, Mioma K.
Davine, Mary Ann.
Delay, J. H.
Davis, L.
D'Amico, Victor.
Drum, Mary I.
Doyle, George.
Douley, John.
Durand, A.
Delancy, John.
Duncan, John.
Doyle, Mary.
Dupuy, Blanche.
Doerr, Lewis.
Dambelli, Jo.
Dedon, Annie.
Daoley, Mrs. Jane.
Davenport, Thos. F.
Davies, Mary.
Dufreshon, Lewis.
Donnelly, Pat.
Davis, Mary J.
Dielman, M.
Dissac, Eugene.
Dahl, Charles.
Dana, Caleb R.
D'Mega, Hen. Estelle.
Darzie, Kate.
Despommiers, Auguste.
Desham, H.
Doaul, Owen E.
Duer, Jacob.
Dummermuth, John.
Dailey, Thos.
Dourin, Marie.
Dillon, Melanie.
Davis, Joseph.
Davis, Theresa.
Daubauer, Geo.
Exterstein, Aug. W.
Edmondson, Rebecca.
Eiger, George.

Elder, A. M.
Escoude, Josie.
Everett, George.
Edler, Louis.
Edwards, T. B.
Elernburg, George.
Eagan, James.
Erne, Caroline.
Erdsmandorff, Maria.
Effinger. Marie.
Ebner, Mrs.
Eudeffries, E.
Estrado, John.
Earse, John A.
Every, Luciana.
Eagan. Kate.
Elerman, Joseph.
Elliott, George.
Encus, Mary.
Eucel, John.
Eciner, Frank.
Emanuel, Mary.
Effinger, Lucie.
Evers, H. M.
Ewing, Emma.
Escat, Alice.
Emerlein, H. John.
Eeveran, Benedict.
Elgere, Ed.
Elsenson, N.
Elder, Alfred.
Elsinger, C.
Eploriam, Sister Mary.
Evans, B. F.
Estebenet, F.
Eustace, M.
Ecklott, Bro. Sylvanus.
Escaaz, Jean E.
Ellison, Laura.
Eagen, Mrs. Ann.
Escudi, Vincent.
Eaton, Joseph.
Esteberal, Francois.
Edwards, James W.
Escuref, Jo. M.
Estrado, Raymond.
Eubanks, Jennie.
Escobedo, Jo. A.
Eurich, Alice.
Eagan, Anthony J.
Evans, Fred. J.
Eustace, Joseph.
Eyrich, Adolphe.
Estrado, Paulino.
Eggers, William.
Erlicher, John.
Eutriken, Samuel.
Eupel, Barbara.
Effinger, Lucie.
Ehrenberger, Amelia.
Eaves, Alfred.
Eberhardt, Mrs. M. M.
Edler, Alfred.
Elsenoolin, Nicholas.
Erlinger, Caroline.
Elgire, Edward.
Elms, James.
Escudi, Theophill.
Forest, John J.
Fitzmuarance, Michael.
Fitzpatrick, Mary.
Fitzpatrick, Kate.
Fenney, Denny.
Forest, Annie.
Frank, A.
Fitzpatrick, William.
Ford, John.
Flourade, Florence.
Frederick, Charles.
Fitzpatrick, Jule.
Ferrer, Catellina.
Fitzpatrick, Camelia.
Fulner. Auton.
Ford, Mrs. Annie E.
Fitzgibbons, Mrs. E.
Fernon. John.
Flynn, Annie E.
Foster, Edgar.
Francis, Marie.

Fox, Thomas.
Fenero, Andrew.
Fitzgibbon, And.
Foriassil, Marie.
Frederick, Frank.
Fernandez, Margaret.
Franz, Anna.
Ferguson, A.
Flannagan, T. (Bro. C.).
Farina, Muncio.
Freenor, Charles.
Ford, Hannah.
Ford, Alice.
Flack, George F.
Flinch, Joseph.
Faust, H. Ludwig.
Fisher, Louisa P. G.
Fahrner, Annie.
Finnegan, C. A.
Flake, Catherine.
Fry, Violet.
Fallar, Hogan.
Fix, Mina.
Ferguson, E. G.
Flemming, William.
Flannaghan, John.
Fonvirgue, R.
Fitzgerald, G.
Fourney, Louis.
Fritsche, Robert.
Fort, Mary C.
Fitzgerald, A. J.
Ferrette, Roza.
Foester, Paul.
Flynn, Margaret.
Fust, Mary.
Fisher, Antonio.
Felin, Lizette.
Flack, Annie M.
Ferrand, Cozamar.
Foisher, Louisa.
Fust, Mrs. Kate.
Feguata, Joseph.
Funk, F.
Furguson, Louise.
Franze, Ida.
Fisher, Louis.
Francis, J.
Ferrand, J. J.
Florimon, Frank.
Ferran, Salvino.
Friend, Victor.
Faure, Jean Paul.
Flannegan, Joseph.
Freted, Nicolena.
Fisher, Elizabeth.
Funk, F.
Fold, Henry.
Foley, John.
Foster. Rev. Tipp.
Fortoricla, A.
Price, Sophia.
Fischer, L.
Fisher, Daniel.
Fable, Charles.
Floureade. Catherine.
Freney, Lillian.
Faure, Jeanna.
Fourot, A. Frances.
Fishel, Mrs. Lewis.
Ford, Michael.
Ferana, D.
Foster. Charles.
Favelora, Angelo.
Fulton, Miss A. M.
Fallon, John.
Frenderberg, George.
Flynn, Kate E.
Foerster, Fred.
Freitag, Fred.
Francisco, Jo. H.
Ferina, Peter.
Fletcher, Henry.
Fitte, Louisa.
Frederico, Guiseppe.
Frennara, Ignazio.
Ferguson, Mary. L.
Feahney, Kate.
Faller, John.

Fix, Minor.
Ferguson, Ellen G.
Fuchs, John.
Falche, Dominico.
Fazello, Rose.
Ferina, Joseph.
Fedelio, Vicenzo.
Franco, Nicols.
Florentine, D.
Frege, Emile.
Fitzgerald, Eugene.
Faber, Philip.
Ferry, Joseph.
Fozzin, Elizabeth F.
Ferrar, Macali.
Fritz, Emile.
Flori, Stephano.
Fuero, Laciano.
Fazelli, Philippi.
Foucou, Oval.
Fine, Henry E.
Francis, Eddie.
Fahey, J. L.
Foley, Edmund J.
Francis, Mrs. G.
Fernandez. A.
Frelling, Henry.
Florrinon, Francois.
Fernandez, Anna M.
Foster, Zella E.
Ferris, Mrs. A. M.
Formaris, Eugene.
Fitz, William.
Ferguson, Eliza.
Ferrier, Gabrille.
Flynn, James.
Fritz, John D.
Fitze, Joseph R.
Frichette, Jane.
Fischer, Daniel.
Freret, Armand.
Ferring, James.
Freek, John.
Frank, George.
Fonvergue, Raoul.
Flemming, William.
Flanagan, John.
Fourcade, Cath.
Freudenthal, Albert.
Foley, William.
Foster, Rev. T.
Fitzgerald, Katie.
Funck, George.
Field. Clara.
Fiedmann, William.
Fearson, Lula A.
Forter, Arthur B.
Graham, John.
Gallagher, Morris.
Gernou, Julia.
Gilmore, Louis J. B.
Griffith, Grace.
Gorman, John.
Goryis, E.
Gerlinger. Lewis.
Geheeb, Charge.
Guerchaux, E. D.
Gover, George W.
Graham, L. R.
Gibbons, Pat.
Griffin, John.
Gerard, A.
Graney, James.
Gurt, Marin.
Gatte, Carman.
Gross, Mrs. K F.
Gauche, Viola.
Gaunall, B. R.
Guirrin, Mrs.
Gardner, Wm. R.
Graham, John F.
Gray, Minerva.
Girard, Ulger.
Groch. Fred.
Gerard, Caroline.
Gull, E. A.
Ghee Chow Ah.
Gavlina, Antonie.

17

Graumann, A.
Gallagher, P.
Gaviane, G.
Goser, Henrietta.
Gorman, J.
Gillare, Edward.
Gregory, Thomas.
Grisbaim, Nora.
Goal, Mrs.
Gallaway, Wm.
Gleason, John.
Gleeny, Andrew.
Gay, Charles.
Gilman, W. S.
Gerachi, Natalie.
Gardon, Matilda.
Gast, John.
Galle, Josephine.
Garees, Joseph.
Gage, Marie.
Gladinger, W. S.
Gunther, Joseph.
Gazara, Pasq.
Giller, Eli C.
Gannon, Steven.
Garritty, Daniel P.
Glass, Henry.
Garcissi, Anna.
Guenault, Oscar.
Gamotis, Miss A.
Graffe, John, Jr.
Gutenberg, R.
Gateman, A.
Guerin, C.
Giligman, Mary.
Guerins, Stefano.
Gally, Mary.
Green, Margaret.
Gites Wm. F.
Gourgoi, J.
Gascisi, Maria.
Gammon, Thomas.
Geneva, Adesio O.
Goushoff, C. R.
Gilbert, Otto.
Gallagher, J. P.
Geraley, Louise.
Gary, Bridget.
Ghavearo, Mattie.
Graves, H. F.
Gebauer, G.
Gardner, K.
Ghaviano, L.
Gillartin, America.
Givens, Mary V.
Groom, L. A.
Gregory, Maggie.
Gormley, Ala.
Gillis, K. H.
Gaston, Paul.
Grauzin, Carrie.
Gerard, George W.
Goldsmith, Wm.
Golmisno, S.
Garcissi, Joseph.
Grauna, Antonio.
Gordere, Louis.
Greatna, G. H.
Gearday, Mrs. Bazil.
Geale, John.
Glacer, Louis.
Gallagher, Dr. C.
Grossweiler, E. G.
Gerday, Pauline.
Gregeris, Demetry.
Guthrie. Joseph.
Giargi, Joseph.
Garaufio, Paulini L.
Goldsmith, Henry.
Gallagher, Thomas J.
Gadol, Jean Emile.
Graude, Antonio.
Gillen, J. J.
Gibbons, Mrs.
Grafenheim, Jacob.
Gillespie, Michael.
Glenn, W. L.
Geuder, Andre.
Guiseppe, Giacommo.

Glenn, Philip.
Garcia, Julia.
Garcia, Anna.
Grauel, Karl.
Gorman, Joseph.
Gouffier, Francois.
Gloetten, Barbara.
German, Lize.
Golden, Bernard A.
Gell, Edward.
Gunseead, Oscar.
Gudenan, Peter.
Gregory, Michael.
Gocke, Anna.
Gannon, Stephen.
Garrity, Daniel P.
Glass, Henry.
Gardner, J. P.
Gibbons, Maggie.
Girardano, Antonio.
Grant, Mary L.
Grebe, Louis.
Gorman, James.
Guderain, Maggie.
Graff, Dillon.
Glass, Mrs.
Glass, Edward.
Gauman, John M.
Gueitas, Colombau.
Gugel, Henry.
Geehan, Laurence.
Gneble, Rene.
Gebhard, John.
Guinshorn, F. J.
Garrity, Mary E.
Garrera, Antonio.
Gossweiler, Emile.
Gaillardo, Gaetano.
Gleason, John A.
Griffin, G. W.
Geretz, F.
Gunnell, Florida.
Gardere, Jennie.
Gunnell, Sarah.
Gaillardia, Angelina.
Gibbons, Edward.
Gadd, James.
Gordon, Henry.
Gormly, Ala.
Gillis, R. H.
Gregory, Miss Mag. H. C.
Gaston, Paul.
Griffin, Eliz.
Gay, Edward J.
Grayburn, Mrs. Minnie.
Gillis, Elizabeth.
Guerin, Isabella.
Gross, N.
Gaillardanno, Alice.
Garcissi, Joe.
Grunewald, Henry A.
Green, Barnes.
Goelsenleuchter, L.
Gas, Jennie D.
Gregory, Joseph.
Grefer, Henry.
Gliss, Lizetta.
Gannon, Frank.
Gilmore, Robert.
Gruber, Jacob.
Guillot, Albertine.
Guinault, Oscar.
Garcissi, Anna.
Gatts, John.
Gardy, Eliza.
Granna, Anna.
Gurniot, Heloise.
Gernon, Robert K.
Garbini, G.
Graurin, Paul.
Goetz, J. A. E.
Haser, Magdalena.
Hartell, Samuel.
Hernandes, Paschal G.
Hammond, Sarah.
Hughes, Delia.
Hageman, M.
Henry, Fannie M.
Herbeline, Blanche.

Harris, Annie.
Hauton, Sopiria M.
Harran, Wm.
Hughes, James.
Howes, Chas. J.
Healy, John.
Hirme, Edward.
Healy, Thomas.
Henderson, Viola.
Hett, Julianna.
Hilbert, Henry.
Hyland. Michael.
Henry, O. H. P.
Hilborn, Manetta.
Hunter, O. B.
Henry, Wm.
Healey, Pat.
Head, John.
Herndon, Dr. C. L.
Hunt, Wm. B.
Heap, Joseph.
Holich, W. P.
Heissel, Joanna.
Hamilton, Sam.
Hess, John L.
Hunson, Thos. J.
Hagan, Mary.
Heels, Willie.
Hackey, James.
Harrison, Caroline.
Henry, Mary A.
Hughes, Joe E.
Herbert Charles.
Hurschman, M.
Hamilton, C.
Hutchinson, H.
Healy, M. H.
Howe, R. A.
Huge, Louisa.
Hamilton, Robert.
Hogan, M.
Hardoustette, E. L.
Hausler, Kate.
Hotard, James E.
Howgueltas, F.
Hartnutt, E. J.
Hausche, Robert.
Henis, A.
Harrigan, Patrick.
Hasta, Antonio.
Held, Gerhard.
Held, Frank A.
Hart, John.
Hubert, Peter.
Hubbes, Christian.
Holabeiser, Jo.
Higginbotham, Helen A.
Hamblet, Henry.
Hennessy, M.
Hans, John.
Huhner, George.
Hashern, L. A.
Hughes, R. G.
Herron, Mrs.
Holland, Emily.
Hogan, Vincent.
Hahn, Henry.
Hollerbach, Ella.
Hayes, Henry.
Hauslaner, Christian.
Hill, Harry.
Holahan, Mary.
Harrison, E. W. B.
Hughes, Granger.
Haymi, Geo.
Hearn, Joseph O.
Hauy, Victor.
Hassan, A.
Hasse, Robert.
Hussey, A W.
Harrison, Geo. H.
Highly, Mrs. Harriet.
Huff, Jacob.
Hansburg, Thos.
Hemard, W. J.
Herman, F.
Hansen, John F.
Hinton, Fred.
Hendricks, Mrs. Sophia.

Hubbert, Mrs. Cath.
Hartnett, M.
Holmes, S.
Hughes, M. E.
Hudson, Annie.
Harris, Louis.
Harvey, Willie.
Huss, Alphonse.
Heimke, F. W.
Hahn, Wm.
Hawly, Ellen.
Hargan, Mary L.
Hupp, Wm.
Howe, Mrs. O. M.
Houder, John.
Hayes, Charlie.
Hare, James M.
Himes, Wm. E.
Houla, Rhoda.
Humbert, Jean.
Haskin, L. M.
Hammozed, Ed.
Howe, Isabel.
Hamel, Eliz.
Harder, Emile.
Haul, Mrs. Alfred.
Heck, Mrs. John.
Haas, Adolphus.
Haney, Albert O. C.
Hunt, H. H.
Hart, John.
Heryeg, S.
Harsey, Henry.
Hern, A. S. J.
Hofft, L. L.
Hestler, Maria.
Heyn. Margaret.
Horteriche, Master.
Hupp, Rosa.
Hauharlt, Oscar.
Herriman, A.
Harden, Wm.
Hall, Albert J.
Herris, A.
Hussey, G. A. C.
Hacker, Edward.
Harrison, Stella.
Harden, Fanny.
Hoskins, Ezekiel.
Hogan, Hattie.
Huss, Charles.
Horn, Wm.
Hall, J. R.
Hauck, Nicholas.
Hausell, Maggie M.
Hart, John.
Harris, L.
Hardy, Geo. W.
Haywood. Carrie.
Hatch, Emile H.
Herring. C. Marie.
Hoffer, Mrs. Josephine.
Hart, Charlotte C.
Heitt, J. W.
Howard, Geo. W.
Hoffman, Frooich.
Hauton, Geo. A. J.
Holzer, Kate.
Hofer, Anna.
Holland, John H.
Hahn, Wm.
Hess, Edward.
Hall, Geo. F
Hamilton, Eliz.
Hodge, Mrs. E. K.
Houston, Mary.
Holger, Fritz.
Hagan, Mrs. M. A.
Heiman, Moritz.
Haberg, Louis.
Hien, Otto.
Hudson, Anna.
Hogan, Callom.
Hines, John.
Heisch, Catherine.
Harrison, Claudia.
Harrison, Loretta.
Hartner, Margaret.
Hauk, Louis.

A HISTORY OF THE YELLOW FEVER. 257

Hall, Thomas.
Heider, John.
Heidenreich, Rev. John.
Haar, Peter.
Holgern, L. H.
Holland, Emily.
Hogan, Vincent.
Hahn, Henry.
Hollenbach, Emma.
Hayes, Henry.
Hill, Harry.
Hollahan, Mary.
Harris, Iola A.
Harrison, E. W. B.
Hughes, Granger.
Holsen, Elias.
Hagan, Pat.
Hinish, Marie.
Hilari, Pierre.
Hahl, Jacob.
Hodgins, John M.
Heffner, Frances M.
Hustead, Louisa.
Hart, A. M.
Hanneman, Julius.
Harrington, Patrick.
Heath, J. M.
Harris, Joseph.
Heaton, Nath. E.
Havenae, E. D.
Hundy, Mrs. Alice.
Henchel, Louis.
Harrison, M. A. V.
Haber, Lena.
Harris, Richard O.
Haley, Timothy.
Huber, Rosie.
Huber, Theresa.
Holler, Adam.
Hoehn, Sophie M.
Heidengsfelder, H.
Hagan, Patrick.
Hervinean, Mrs. Marie.
Hailinger, A. J.
Huff, Fred. C.
Handy, Thomas H.
Helmke, Wilhel.
Harper, Wm.
Hawkins, Henry.
Hughes, M. H.
Hoffmeister, Lydia.
Hemard, Mary.
Hirsch, Eugene.
Heissel, Michael.
Hupp, Wm.
Hines, W. E.
Howe, Mrs. Olympe M.
Honlay, Rody.
Hayes, Charlie.
Humbert, Jeannie.
Haskins, Charles M.
Hare, James M.
Hogan, Arthur S.
Heino, Victor.
Hagan, Mary C.
Henrich, Emile.
Hagen, Henry.
Haly, Charles.
Haibthorne, Ida.
Hosrey, Catherine.
Heino, Victor, Sr.
Hallor, Henry C.
Honold, C. A. G.
Harper, Robert L.
Hayes, Patrick.
Hurley, John.
Hall, Albert J.
Hilliard, Jane.
Houlihan, Patrick.
Howard, John.
Hodges, George.
Howe, Mary I. J.
Hertzer, John.
Hestler, Marie.
Hufft, Lenra Lee.
Hussey, Geo. H. C.
Haieslaur, Ch.
Irvine, Hugh.
Israel, Estelle.

Ingersol, Merona B. G.
Ittman, Rosa.
Irby, Sanders.
Icolina, Nicola.
Imbau, Hortaise.
Inwood, Harold.
Isler, F.
Itro, John.
Ireevy, P. W. J.
Ingraham, J.
Irwin, D. C.
Isaacs, Samuel.
Icolina, Arcola.
Irby, V. R.
Inman, Gabriel J.
Irwin, Charles T.
Johnson, Elizabeth H.
Joyce, John.
Jones, Mrs Annie.
Johnson, Christopher.
Jahn, John.
Jacobs, Lewis, col.
Jones, Mary.
Johnson, M. A.
Jeffries, Anna.
Jeffer, M. J.
Johnson, Nadim.
Jackson, Sam. H.
Jac, Placide.
Jones, Mary.
Johnson, Andro.
Jeakle, Samuel.
James, Wm.
Jeness, Helen.
Johnson, Mrs. Carrie.
Josephine.
Johnson, Isaac.
Johnston, Wesley.
Johnson, John.
James, Frederick.
Jensen, Fred.
Jacobs, Edwin A.
Jeannorut, John.
Jacornett, Mrs. Lucie.
James, Elvira.
Jones, Joseph.
Jones, Louis.
Jones, George.
Jonca, William John.
Jacolin, Nicola.
Jensen, Lizzie.
Johnson, Oscar.
James, Levi C.
Jordan, Charles.
Julius, M. C.
Jett, Carrie L.
Johnson, J. B.
Jordan, John B.
Johnson, Cecil.
Johnes, J. J.
Jackson, Louis.
Jacobson, Louis.
Jacobs, Esther.
Jones, Charles.
Justus, Dorothia.
Johausenbach, A.
Joint, Sarah Ann.
Jones, Mary.
Jacob, Henry.
Joubert, Emma.
Johnson, Katie.
Jackson, John.
Jackson, Joseph.
Jincenor, Lejohn.
Jacobson, A.
Jaomed, Gaetano.
Jonan, Alex.
John, Leon T.
Johnson, D M.
Juergen, H, Jr.
Jones, D. W.
Johnson, Charles E.
Johlisant, Edna.
Jay, Arthur.
Jeffries, Anna.
Johnson, George.
Juary, Guiseppe.
James, A. K.
Kearney, Evaline.

Killian, R. J.
Kuntz, A. G.
Keir, A. J.
Keever, M.
Khiup, John.
Klein, Rosa.
Knoblock, Charles.
Kiefer, Emile Mary.
Kirkham, Dora E.
Kelz, Louisa.
Karll, Emile.
Kenny, Pat.
Kienemann, George.
Kampman, E. T.
Koswig, Albert.
Knechel, Aug.
Kottelli, Nicholas.
Kuhn, Laura.
Killenea, Thomas J.
Kiutz Teresa.
Kieneman, Charles.
Kennedy, Mary A.
Kerzey, A.
Krail, Viola.
Kampman, F.
Kelly, Henry.
King, Lizzie.
Kennedy, Edward.
Kisser, John.
Kattman, Clara.
Kinney, Thomas.
Korke, Ken.
Kilbride, Nora.
Keys, William.
Keene, Mary B.
Keutsgel, Joseph.
Kessel, Kath.
Kelly, William.
Krail, Mary J.
Kringer, Carl.
Kaughman, R. C.
Kern, William A.
Kenner, Peter.
Kruse, William.
Kutz, Frank J.
Kelly, Ida.
Kieler, Sophia W.
Krumpelmann, E.
Kersalich, Sam.
King, Maria A.
Keith, Robert.
Keller, William.
Keaghey, Mary D.
Kelly, Mary.
Kohhause, H. E.
Kochler, Maggie.
Kennedy, Thomas.
Keen, Theodore.
Kern, J. E.
Kozenser, Johanna.
Kelting, John H.
Kelting, Louis.
Kronopsky, Francis.
Kearny, Lawrence.
Kliempeter, W. B.
Krentle, F.
Klinger, David.
Kennedy, John.
Kiernan, Francis E.
Kupfer, Edward.
Kister, Emile.
Kennedy, Peter.
Keegan, Mary.
Keegan, Sister Mary.
Kavaney, John.
Kearney, J. Watts.
Kenney, Edward S.
Krumplemann, Theo.
Kiernan, Kate.
Killum, George.
Keller, William.
Kuetenmacher, F. A.
Keeves, Margaret.
Kelly, Mrs. Ann.
Krucker, John.
Kaiser, John.
Kilelia, Annie.
Kuhner, Joseph.
Knooys, Marie L.

Kerny, Jacob S.
Kroeper, J. G.
Keith, J. H.
Klein, Joseph.
Kremer, Paul M.
Kent, S. J.
Kappes, William.
Kenney, John B.
King, Ellen.
Kenny, James.
Kerwin, M.
Kaninski, Joseph.
Knatz, Joseph.
Koehler, Ferdinand.
Kiernan, Edward.
Keenan, Edward.
Kaufman, William.
Kay, C. H. D.
Kratz, John.
Kroggman, H. C.
Kilbride, Nora.
Kenney, James.
Koike, Benjamin.
Knatz, Ferdinand.
Kraft, Anna.
Kern, William.
Kavenaugh, Cath.
Kohl, Theo. H.
Kreeger, Rosa A.
Kauffman, D. C.
Kerr, W. E.
Kenner, Peter.
Kretz, John.
Kenney, Marion.
Lee, George W.
Lauiza, Nicholas.
Lehsoy, Maria.
Londen, Edgar G.
Locquet, Ida.
Lerath, Mary.
LaGlaise, D.
Larkin, D. W.
Llalin, Nicolina.
Letannier, E.
Lindner, Aug.
Levi, Charles.
Latino, Rosario.
Landwehr, F. W.
Lewis, M. P.
Loewer, Mrs. M. E.
Levi, Mark.
Lichtentein, C.
Lichtenfield, E. B.
Long, Sarah J.
Lewis, Mrs. Ann.
Liebman, Paul.
Lewis, John.
Link, Louisa.
Lespominet, J.
Labadi, Peter.
Leuschner, R.
Lee, Mrs. Mollie.
Lorch, Henry.
Levi, Caroline.
Latena, R.
Long, Edwin.
Laville, Miss M.
Labre, John R.
Lederz, Constant.
Lascascio, Antonio.
Lenfant, Eugene.
Laroude, John.
Langaballe, R. P.
Latina, Nicola.
Latove, Mrs. C.
Lasmar, Robert.
Lanero, G.
Levy, Sam. J.
Landreaux, M.
Lavedon, Pierre.
Lyons, Robert A.
Lochert, M.
Lochert, Regina.
Laine, Eva C.
Lafon, Joseph L.
Lutersbacher, B. A.
Lafosse, J. B.
Liebel, Martin.

Liebel, Theresa.
Lorie, Mrs. F.
Lala, Margaret.
Lewis, Mary A.
Leveniah, Emilie.
Lohman, Henry.
Lacoume, Eulabc.
Lala, John.
Lethiegae, Henry.
Lever, Catherine.
Lewis, John J.
Lohr, Rose H.
Luke, Peter.
Landwehr, M.
Lacassagne, L.
Logan, M. E.
Lippo, M.
Lorch, R. P.
Larque, Jules.
Levy, Moses.
Luluhardt, C. L.
Landrum, May E.
Luke, Elizabeth.
Lateno, John.
Lange, Mrs.
Levy, Arthur.
Langboles, E.
Logier, Marie C.
Lopez, Mrs.
Lots. Henry J.
Louis, George F.
Lawry, Frank B.
Lacourage, Benoit.
Lyskle, Wm.
Leippert, Geo. W.
Lusca, Mateo.
Lavallee, Barbara.
Lavallee, Caroline.
Lacaze, Emily T.
Lacaze, Michael.
Loutan, Ernest.
Lawraver. A. Rose.
Lochert, Mrs.
Laforte, Jean.
Lambert, A. J.
Louis, Miss E.
Lebar, Wm.
Leone, Gossip.
Lenagran, Lawrence.
Longreen. Peter.
Latcher, Henry G.
Lathroy, Lyman.
Loeb, Henry L.
Lafoze, Rosalie.
Lafuett, Mary.
Lahey, Charles.
Lacey, Patrick.
Layne, Enos T.
Lempasion, Anton.
Large, G.
Lafourch. E. B.
Ludlow, Blanche.
Lundy, Chas. S.
Lyre, Thomas.
Lopez, Philip.
Lina, B. F.
Leclerc, Augusta.
Lee, Wm.
Lord, Chas. H.
Lochert, Sebastian.
Labour, J. B.
Landrake, Wm.
Lewis, H.
Lacassagne, L.
Lavallee, Barbara.
Leglaize, Catherine.
Leglaize, Elizabeth.
Lang, Martin.
Leone, Mary.
Lynch, Katie.
Lippseheatz, Theo.
Levy, A.
Lembo, Luigi.
Lambert, Alice H.
Leche, Milson A.
Leary, Bridget.
Loos, Julius.
Lowry, Lezina.
Leblanc, John.

Lardner, Thos. R.
Lowry, Wm.
Levy, Jacob.
Lestere, Donald.
Lochni, Minnie.
Labrousseau, Julio.
Lebetgern, Eugene.
Labarbe, Gustave.
Lambert, James.
Lacaze, Julius.
Lebaneri, Chas.
Lenton, James.
Lee, Mary Ellie.
Lusse.
Lantine, Sarah.
Lyons, James.
Lawler, Sister Loyola.
Levellier, Emma.
Loiseau, Hyacinthe.
Lawler, Henry T., Jr.
Lamy, Rev. John.
Lacaze, Edward.
Lesassier, B. B.
Lascar, Jennie.
Lefranc, Lorenn.
Lungo, Francisco.
Lehbeher, John.
Lewis, John.
Leslie, Thomas.
Long, Jane.
Lopez, Emily.
L'Esponde, Pierre.
Lennis, Moses.
Latemier, Julie.
Leducs, Alice.
Lapon, Jean.
Lyle, John.
Ledig, Walter A.
Lehmann, M. W.
Lattien, Julia.
Lenae, Louisa.
Lunn, Mary E.
Lehmann, Dr. Isadore.
Lambardi, Emile.
Lala, Francisco.
Lohmann, Gertrude.
Levy, M. C.
Lerm. John.
Lee, Henry.
Lacour, Mary De.
Lalemana, Mrs.
Lynch, Mary.
Laughton, John C.
Lawson, Addison.
Lemants, C.
Lchleitner, Willie.
Leon, Theo.
Lambert, Urban.
Lopez, Victor.
Lowe, John.
Link, Alois.
Lear, John N.
Latine, Razada.
Lannanna, Antonio.
Long, Edwin.
Longaret, James.
Long, Luther.
Long, John.
Lopcz, Margaret.
Lamm.
Longrois, Louis.
Lotz, Susan A.
Lala, Francisco.
Levingston, Roy B.
Lawton, John.
Lank, Rosa.
Lacosta, Jean.
Levellier, Joseph.
Levy, Mary.
Lowe, John.
Lowden, Lawrence D.
Lebatice, Louisa.
Levy, Solomon.
Lapelsronx, Francis.
Larsen, Julius.
Lowinsohn, Louis.
Lagenbecker, Leonora.
Latugo, Mag.
Loechner, Anna.

Larsen, P. W.
Loubert, Clarence.
Lesko, Rev.
Lyons, Robert A.
Lochert, Regina.
Lochert, Michael.
Leslie, Charles.
Locassie, Rosalie.
Loeb, Adelbert.
Luduke, Joseph.
Lanasa, Guiseppe.
Levenson, Frederick.
Luizza, Antonio.
Ladd, Charles C.
Lerouge, Anthony F.
Masson, Mrs. Matilda.
McStea, Terrence.
McDonald, Michael.
McCammon, Moses.
Malasguiva, Luigi.
McNamara, Mary.
Moser, May.
Maniouloux, Eugene.
Marks, Calhoun.
Murphy, Mrs. Mary.
Mazounave, Pierre.
McGovern, John.
Mailhes, Marie.
Merriam, Wm.
Madison, J. H., col.
Moffett, Charles J.
McQuirk, John D.
Mahoney, Mary Jane.
Miller, Leonora.
Maiting, Miss Nina.
Moody, Fred.
Monalxen, Wm.
Martello, Gaetano.
Moses, Jacob
Musseys, Adeline.
Moneth, Peale.
McConville, Peter.
McNeal, Mattie.
McSweeney, Deborah.
Maher, James.
Mary, Sister.
Masson, D. B.
McCormick, Charles.
Mehrents, Gertrude.
McLaughlin, Mrs. Ann.
Meinke, Mrs. Joseph.
McCauley, Mary.
Manaby, Joseph.
McKinnay, Maggie.
Mulder, Daniel.
Moncusa, Mary T.
Manning, Regina.
Mancoosa, Rosalie.
McGuire, Kate.
Mahler, Edward.
Murphy, Lawrence
McCormick, Anna T.
Mann, Henry C.
McDermott, Frank.
Manala, Mrs.
McDonald, John.
Manala, Para.
Metzler, Frank.
Meyer, Charles.
Maaendinu, Antonio.
Mohr, Jacob.
McCall, Mrs. Ellen.
Meyer, Theresa.
Maloney, Laurent.
Mount, John.
McKenzie, Mary C.
McNeal.
McArthur, Daniel.
Magdeline, Julius.
Murphy, James.
Mentel, Mrs. Mary.
Mesritz, Alex.
Moser, Charles.
McEven, Samuel.
Mayor, John.
Morten, Harry.
Miller. Ruby.
Maguire, Winfred.
Meyer, Henry.

Manuel, Mrs. L.
Martella, Rosalie.
Murray, Lillie.
Miller, Ella.
Martin, Madame.
Moses, Mrs. Max.
Maari, B. A. A.
McClain, Wm.
McCain, John.
McLennan, Frank.
Meyer, John.
Moore, Eugene W.
Montedonico, John.
Miller, Charles.
Murphy, Geo. A.
McNamara, L. W.
Millet, Rev. J. M.
Malloy. Mary E.
Mohr, Caroline H.
McEnery, Margareth.
Miller, Rosalie.
Miller, Louis S.
Mickler, Conrad.
Moran, Eugene M.
McConnell, Mrs.
Monroe, Ella.
McGuin, Patrick.
McBride, Mary C.
McDona'd, James L.
Mundz, Mary.
Moore, Thomas E.
McCove, Geo. P.
Moriarty, James.
Murphy, Philip.
McGarvy, Mary.
Manyon, Andrew.
Monette, Mrs. G. N.
Mather, John.
Mayne, Mary.
Munson, Louisa.
McStay, Francis.
Mouledous, George.
Maley, Charles.
Murphy, John.
Miller, Louis.
Munson, Louis.
Miller, Anthony.
Majorin, Angelo.
McManus, John.
Majorana, Rosa.
McManus, Emma.
Moreldchouse, Josie.
Moran, Mary.
Mitchell, Peter.
Morris, Bridget.
Milhot, Louis.
Marks, Adelaide.
Murphy, John.
Meadeloon, Em.
McMert, Lizzie.
Martinay, Mary G
Makin, Patrick.
Makin, Julia.
Mitchell, R. D.
Mack, James.
Monosterio, J. B. R.
Morris, Edward T.
McArthur, Wm.
Manne, Joseph.
Mattel, Charles.
Mazeron, Mrs.
Mozlet, Frank.
Magenta, Santa.
Markey, Josephine.
McGuire, Willis.
Miller, Joseph C.
Meyer, Charles A.
Moncref, Mrs. E. A.
McCune, James.
Morrissey, Patrick.
Manale, Anna.
Murray, George.
Morris, Henry.
Maneisso, D. J.
Madison, M.
McBride, Patrick.
McClane, John.
Marningues, Rev. J.
Montizin, Jean M.

A HISTORY OF THE YELLOW FEVER. 259

Meunier, E J.
Morrow, John B.
Mackae, Geo. L J.
McGraw, Martin.
McCarthy, Eugene.
Monroe, Mary C.
Mohr, Edwin.
Mains, Fred.
Morouey, John C.
McGuirk, Kate G.
Mellies, Theresa.
Morere, Wm.
Mitchell, Jack.
Meyer, Barbara.
Mason, Fred. M.
Maloney, James.
McManus, John.
Marino, Salvatore.
Morell, Robert.
Miller, Fred. W.
Martin, Michael.
Mararour, Henry.
Manning, Dennis.
Myhan, Mary.
Meyer, Henry.
Molaison. Maria.
Metlige, Mulita.
Maurin, Joseph C.
Mauroner, Louisa E
McHenry, George.
Magendre, Oscar.
Murphy, John.
Marigny, Blavebe.
Murphy, John.
McDermott, J. J.
McQuinlan, Joseph T.
Marsh, Ernestine.
Monneaux, Francis.
McEwan, John.
Miles, Virginia E.
Miller, Wm. H.
McGain, Sam.
Marigny, Miss B.
Mailho, Charles.
McGill, Daniel.
Michand, Paul.
McMannus, Thomas.
Marcello, Vincent.
Musachiar, Rosella.
Meyer, J. J.
Mendolsohn, J.
Mendolsohn, Mrs. J.
Morante, Mattie.
Melville, John.
Menzies, Caspar.
McLashtin, Mary.
Muller, Francis.
McNamara, M. J.
Munro, Martha.
Mosset, Mathilda.
Magoranna, Sarah.
McClintock, Aleck.
Mossett, Ernam C.
Morganstein, A.
Miroy, K. Eugene.
Murray, Thomas.
Marcault, Maria A.
Maumus, A. M.
Mailes, Pauline C.
Marchand, Victoria.
Moore, John F.
Morris, H. N.
Mankin, H.
Mild, Jacques.
Marshall, J. A.
Moore, E.
Michaelis, Ern.
Manassas, Simon.
Morley, Dr. Thomas.
Mustachia, Joseph.
Macazo, Francisco.
Morton, A. W.
McGloin, Charles.
Manfree, Tony.
McKay, Mary.
Murphy, Mary E.
Momgae, Ettiene.
McGrath, John.
McMahon, Mrs. C.

Meyer, Otto.
Mathews, Robert.
Mulhenru, Hugh.
Morris, Margaret A.
Moriggo, Mary.
McTique,Sister Augusta.
Mitchell, Carrie.
Moran, Joseph.
Murphy, Wm. J.
Mathers, Henry.
Monier, Henry D.
Melbourne, Lou.
Monier, Frank.
McManus, Miss A.
Michalls, Catherine.
McManus, David.
Mirable, Nich. J.
McQuillon, John.
McMullen, Chris.
Martin, Geo. M.
Michaelis, Clara.
Merendina, G.
Marinino, P.
Murphy, Rev. T.
Murray, Daniel.
Morey, Mrs. D. B.
Murphy, Patrick.
Moony, Bridget.
McArthur, Hugh.
McConnell, James.
Morris, Miss Betsy.
Mannion, Lawrence.
Malone, Patrick.
Moore, Mary.
McCabb, Eliz.
Miller, Maggie.
Malony, Michael.
Murphy, Sarah Ann.
Margee, Mary C.
McQuaid, Lizzie.
Mentel, Bosanna L.
McSweeny, Pat.
Mathews, Louis.
Mausen, Charles.
Meumier, Jule.
Mullholland, David.
Meh, John.
McDonald, Mrs.
McIntyre, Wm.
McDonald, R. G.
McClaffry, Peter.
Milet, Marcellin.
Mahoney, Thomas.
McDonald, R. A.
Mathen, Wm.
Mignon, Philomena.
McClure, Mrs. Mary.
Moxon, Fred. B.
McMurray, Mary E.
Medelfreche, P.
Madary, Wm.
Mulvey, Jane A.
Mosfeld, F. L.
Martha, Mary A.
Masser, Teresa.
Moore, John.
McClosky, Kate Ann.
Morris, Robert.
Miller, Geo.
Miret, N.
McClosky, Geo.
Mond, Labeire.
Morton, John.
Murphy, John.
Momus, Mary L.
Marino, Salvatrie.
Murphy, R. P.
Matas, Joseph.
Mousohur, J. D.
Morris, James.
Mears, Fred.
Morris, Mrs. M.
Moses, Isaac.
McDonald, Wm.
McCardell, Thomas.
McDermott, James J.
Mayer, Bernard.
McCorneal, Wm.
Murphy, M. G.

Mortept, Jean W.
McTique, August.
Mastalseh, Matt.
Mills, Mollie.
Meush, Fred.
Meza, J. J. D.
McIntosh, James.
Moses, Alice.
Murray, John.
Maugriocia, Mary.
Maugriocia, Jena.
Moran, Emile G.
Moore, Edward.
McGuire, James.
McKenly. J.
Maya, Fred.
McCoy, Charles.
Martin, Rose.
Maniornioux, F.
Muir, T. B.
Miller, Alice G.
Michaeis, Anette.
Meeke, T.
McDonald, Alec.
Malony, Thos.
Mager, Mary.
Meyers, Thos.
Mayner, Joseph E.
Mohl, F.
Michramers, John.
McCormick, Mary.
Mathewsen, C. C.
Minges, B.
McKay, Daniel.
Moore, Henry.
Meyer, George.
McGuire, M.
McGibbons, M. J.
Malverhill, P. R.
Martin, John.
Moody, Wm. A.
Macon, Fred. M.
Myer, Barbara.
Marrion, S.
Maloney, James.
McMannus, John.
Morrell, Robert.
Miller, F. W.
Miller, Wm. C.
Martin, Philip.
McGoey, Mary.
Mitchell, Sarah.
Meyer, Robert A.
Mandell, Anna.
Meyer, John F.
Munster, Fred. F.
Moore, Susan.
McGrath, Charles P.
Mortequi, Marguerite.
McWhirter, Wm.
McCorneal, Tony.
Munster, Joseph E.
McCullough, Ellen.
Muritzen, Otto.
Merichen, Henry.
Moses, Jane.
Mitchell, Harry.
McCormick, Andrew.
Miller, Louis.
McNamara, Eliz.
Mendelsohn, C.
McArdle, Joseph P.
Meyer, Samuel.
Mayer, Karl.
McGuire, Mrs. B.
Martin, Joseph.
Mavorans, J. M.
McQuillon, Mary.
McDonald, Andrew.
McArey, Michael.
Meyer, Anton.
Moltzgay, V.
Muller, Kath.
McCarthey, Dan.
Miedner, Mich.
Newbauer, Henrietta.
Negrotto, Mrs. D.
Nolting, Eliz.

Nuberg, Leon.
Norton, Ann.
Noble, Kath.
Neal, John.
Nicholvick, Peter.
Neumiller, J.
Nelson, Mary.
Ney, L.
Nussbaum, J.
Nicholls, H. S.
Newhouse, Josephine.
Noble, Sam. W. H.
Nessaus. Jules.
Noe, Arbogast.
Narf, Emma E.
Nosley, Mary.
Noyer, Sophia.
Newhouse, Lee.
Nicolaud, Rev. B.
Newall, Wm.
Nelson, Mary.
Norwood, Eliza.
Noble, Edward.
Nauty, Extreme F.
Ninut, Joseph.
Nicholson, Mary C.
Noisseaux, Joseph.
Nobles. Charles E.
Norvell, Reed.
Norvell. Clement R.
Nagle, Henry.
Nolan, John.
Nobin, Pat.
Nies, Charles.
Norvell, Mrs. Mattie.
Narbon, Michael.
Newman, Albert.
Novaille, Charles.
Newhouse, Leopold.
Niedel, Michael.
Nugent, James.
Naumburg, Benj.
Neumann, Theo.
Ney, Henry F.
Nelson, Mary.
Ney, L.
Norcross, Albert.
Navaret, Louis.
Netzer, Ernest.
Neailly, Joseph.
Nuss, Anna W.
Norden, Anthony.
Notari, Rosalin.
Natali, Charles.
Navailes, Joseph.
Noble, Anna L.
Obrey, Sidney.
O'Keefe. Anna.
Oneill, W. J.
Obhoff, Joseph.
O'Connell, Henry.
O'Connell, Mary.
O'Connell, Anna.
O'Connors, John F.
Oppenheimer, S. W.
O'Mally, Sister F.
Oppenheimer, J.
O'Conner, Thos.
Ogden, Lizzie H.
Ochesie. John.
O'Connell, Thos.
Opferknck, Mary.
Owens, Wm.
Oletio, Francisco.
O'Bryan, Mary.
Oster, Charles.
Osborn, J. T.
O'Neal, Owen.
Olin, Heder.
O'Donnell. A.
Orpheus, Wm.
Owens, Owen.
O'Hara, Michael
O'Rourke, Michael.
O'Bryan, Mary M.
O'Neal, Thos.
Obers, Kate.
Oliver, Louis.
Ohlenschlager, G.

260 A HISTORY OF THE YELLOW FEVER.

Oberts, Sarah.
Oliva, Helena.
Osterman, Giovani.
O'Brien, Delia.
O'Connell, Henry.
Olin, Amanda.
O'Brien, Marian.
Oliviera, Bridget.
Oswald, Mary J.
Ortepp, August.
Orkus, John.
O'Brien, Edward.
Oppenheimer, Henrietta
O'Brien, Mrs. Mary Ann.
Pendergrast, James.
Peterson, Charles.
Pyckard, Lucine.
Pettet, Clancy J.
Pernett, James E.
Pendergrast, Mary.
Paul, Andrew.
Pinttsmier, Anna.
Poschell, Louis J. C.
Pfannkucker, H.
Pequi, Francois.
Puches, Charles.
Patten, Amos.
Pernal, Joseph Y.
Peix, Frederick.
Poltharst, Christian.
Ponge, Albert.
Polleino, V. M.
Poporny, A.
Phillips, Jules A.
Ponjade, Henry.
Pezold, Emil L.
Pablo, John.
Pitro, Antonio.
Prince, Alfred.
Porteous, John P.
Price, R. B.
Phillips, John.
Petriman, William.
Pope, Henry.
Pavice, Picena.
Packert, Dedrick.
Perry, Thomas.
Planket, Mary.
Phillips, Elizabeth.
Pratt, Charles B.
Peterson, O.
Petzetsky, Joseph.
Poretto, S.
Place, Paul.
Pickens, Charles.
Pogue, Victor.
Palmasino, D.
Poulsen, James.
Piez, Joseph.
Pastor, Mary.
Palthon, M.
Philbert, Philip.
Prilleaux, Adolph.
Pohlman, John.
Pepper, John P.
Pettetory, Louisa E. E.
Place, Mary C.
Pupor, Josephine.
Pericapa, John.
Paderner, Jean.
Pohnfich, F.
Potfork, Samuel.
Pedro, Josie.
Payenne, Jean M.
Pinda, Philip.
Pope, Edmund.
Philip, Archy.
Pascoe, Agnes.
Pettis, Louisa.
Protine, Jean W.
Paschke, Otto.
Poole, William.
Powers, Mary.
Petralia, Antonio.
Peters, E. W. W.
Parker, James C.
Pike, Z. M.
Peters, Samuel J.
Philipin, Theo.

Peterson, John C.
Paysse, Jean M.
Pellip, Peaton W.
Pujo, Marie.
Peters, Margaret.
Pheffer, E. W.
Pelletier, Paul R.
Peres, Pierre.
Polk, John.
Pradella, Cath.
Paillet, Francois.
Pefer, Cora.
Perez, Santo.
Porello, L.
Penser, Joseph.
Perriland, Remy.
Perault, F.
Place, Gervais.
Potts, R. M.
Ponder, Mary.
Porticq, Antonio.
Perez, John B.
Pearson, L.
Purdon, James S.
Price, William.
Palezzini, Andrew.
Pastorius, John.
Palmer, John.
Paysse, Andre.
Pitard, Henry.
Pritchara, E. J.
Patterson, Mrs.
Ponder, John.
Perkins, Mary J.
Peetz, John.
Phillips, F. A.
Phelan, Charles R.
Pyott, James.
Palmer, George N.
Perone, Francisco.
Pounds, John.
Pascal, Macrez.
Pellegrims, Simone.
Pourdan, Felix G.
Pelissier, Martin.
Peilert, Charles.
Panellees, Manuel.
Paretti, Jean.
Perregat, Paul.
Peterson, Antoine.
Pond, Gertrude.
Pool, Annie.
Prestice, Dominica.
Pontico, Marie S.
Planchard, John J.
Payne, Henry.
Pettit, Louis.
Pons, Lawrence.
Payzale, Jean B.
Peniston, John J.
Pepper, Joseph P.
Patterson, Jones.
Pena, Lelia M. S. Dela.
Paulian, C. F.
Pavane, Antonio.
Pys, Joseph.
Pednour, N. E. J.
Quinlan, D. O. C.
Quigley, H. W.
Quinn, John.
Quinn, Thomas.
Quane, John.
Reynard, Barth.
Rothass, William.
Rothass, George J.
Rheiffer, Charles.
Ritzmann, George.
Reiley, Timothy.
Runy, Mary E.
Rice, John A.
Russo, Giovani.
Reeves, James J.
Riley, Mary.
Rose, Blanche G.
Robertson, Lentman F.
Reynolds, James H.
Rowell, Mrs. H.
Reyff, Joseph.
Reid, Albert.

Richards, William.
Rerch, M. J.
Ritzens, Willie.
Reichert, Mrs. Bettle.
Roehrs, Louise S. M.
Robertson, John.
Rintte, Julia.
Roberts, William Y.
Ritchie, James M.
Reynolds, Emma P.
Rabeneck, Richard.
Roth, John G.
Rosa, Franco.
Ruffy, Frank.
Raunch, Henry.
Reyner, Mary A.
Redwood, Gustave.
Reinhardt, Jacques.
Rourk, Jane.
Roach, John.
Roebecker, John.
Robertson, Mildred.
Resegnet, Louis.
Roubillac, Ellen P.
Robinson, Elizabeth.
Rollin, Joseph.
Rocker, August.
Rousseau, Edith M.
Rogers, Anna.
Reinerth.
Ross, M. B.
Rodriguez, Arthur.
Ratine, Josephine.
Raymond, Maggie.
Raback, F.
Roubillac, Alph.
Rickett, Joseph.
Riley, Mary.
Riard, Nettie.
Richlemann, George.
Rossie, Jobe.
Riley, Louise.
Robinson, Eliza J.
Riddell, Holma P.
Restine, Joseph.
Roth, Gustave.
Revel, Henry.
Robinson, Josephine.
Richard, Percy C.
Rempp, Joseph.
Romer, Valentine.
Rachore, Mrs. Pierre.
Rummel, William.
Ruf, Frank.
Rogers, James.
Rauer, Marie.
Rosche, J. H.
Rosenbaum, C.
Richardson, M. S.
Rottenberry, H. W. A.
Raurind, E.
Rokbein, Wm.
Relleux, George.
Roux, J. D.
Robathoenk, H.
Randle, George.
Ross, Edward.
Rudolph, T.
Reinhardt, H.
Redon, Leon S.
Redon, Leon S., Jr.
Rioeler, Ida J.
Rohr, N.
Reidehufer, George.
Ruffier, James.
Roehlet, Otto H.
Ruleef, H. H.
Richardson, G.
Rickerty, Lizzie.
Rechner, Anna.
Ryan, George.
Regende, R. R.
Rennyson, L. A.
Richardson, Mrs. Sarah.
Raymond, Mary C.
Rank, Mrs. P.
Roust, Alice C.
Reems, Elizabeth.
Ryan, Elizabeth.

Rous, Spencer.
Roche, John H.
Randon, Carl.
Rosa, Mary.
Rhodes, Miss E.
Rank, Willie.
Ray, Mary M.
Ricks, Tena.
Rive, Julius.
Roney, Pat. H.
Reinhardt, John N.
Rommel, Fred.
Regend, Leonie O.
Robinson, George.
Reel, Henry.
Reinhardt, Fred.
Rowerty, Frank.
Randall, Joseph.
Rodites, Salvador.
Ridley, Mrs. James.
Riley, Simon.
Ragouso, Joseph.
Rem, George.
Reynolds, J. S.
Rossarth, John.
Reffly, Hubert.
Rosseau, S.
Richards, Grace H.
Rowell, W. Irvine.
Rogers, John.
Redman, Margarette.
Roibenack, E.
Roland, Francis.
Remington, George W.
Reuder, Michael.
Rossi, Mrs. Julie.
Reif, Sophia.
Riley, Genevieve.
Ruppel, John.
Reid, John.
Rice, John.
Ranesua, C.
Romer, Adolph.
Ringer, Mrs.
Roussel, Frank.
Robinson, Thomas.
Richards, Chester.
Reynolds, R. B.
Rogers, Rebecca.
Reinhardt, Oscar.
Roesseler, Louis.
Rosone, Antonie.
Roblet, Ed. Paul.
Rigon, Mary E.
Rugge, Victor.
Robinson, P. C.
Rochet, Joseph.
Ray, Ben. A.
Reeder, U. S.
Raymond, Fred.
Rademacher. J.
Ryan, James.
Rogers, Anna.
Rudenbery, Ada.
Roche, Geo. W.
Rampurty, John.
Rapp, Fred.
Roche, Laura.
Rous, Mary A.
Richardson, M.
Revilla, Angelo.
Rowanes, B.
Rino, Paul.
Rosenbaum, Mrs.
Reamer, Bella.
Robins, Louisa.
Roella, Joseph.
Remech, S. K.
Roth, Jacob.
Robertson, Rozelle.
Rosenbaum, G.
Renandin, John.
Reeder, Joseph.
Ruzza, G.
Rumples, George.
Rodigne, Paul.
Raymer, Henry.
Rivere, Frank E.
Ratzwell, Louis.

A HISTORY OF THE YELLOW FEVER.

Reynolds, W. L.
Robinson, Ellen.
Rando, Joseph.
Riley, Thomas.
Raymond, John.
Relf, D. O.
Rettel, Louise.
Roth, Gustave.
Rieule, Simon.
Ryan, Edward.
Robinson, George P.
Rative, Henry.
Reist, Gustave.
Ryan, Mary E.
Raffaci, A.
Red, Aug.
Reidling, Rosa.
Rousset, Blanche.
Stann, Rosa.
Schunaman, Aug.
Smith, Georgiana.
Stahl, Jacob.
Sampoon, C.
Schaeffer, Frank.
Scherf, Albert.
Stewart, Thomas H.
Scott, Geo. R.
Smith, John.
Slater, Oliver, H.
Spana, Joseph.
Schluter, A. F.
Stewart, F.
Saltanichia, F.
Straus, Morris.
Steth, Wm. B.
Sherlock, James.
Scanlin, Francis.
Schriever, J. G.
Stark, W. N.
Smith, Bella.
Salles, Gabriel.
Sanden, Matthew.
Shepperd, S. K.
Singer, Christina.
Sabat, Peter.
Solomon, Fannie.
Salvato, Francisco.
Seeber, John.
Seebolt, Frank.
Spinito, Cæsar.
Sampson, Hannah.
Stegman, Joseph.
Stern, Sophia.
Silverstein, M.
Schefiel, Mrs. E.
Schweitzer, George.
Scarbonie, Luc.
Schreiner, Fred.
Stepprich, M. D.
Siegel, Fred. H.
Salman, Estelle.
Stehaing, Rebettie.
Sebastian, Louise.
Stern, M.
Smith, John.
Saradet, H.
Schumacher, E.
Sadevia, Salvador.
Smith, E. H.
Squan, Victor.
Spliedt, C. F.
Sillman, Bertha.
Smith, Mrs. C.
Schaul, L. H.
Sweetman, C.
Schlunberg, M.
Stevens, Florence.
Scheimoner, Peter.
Schildnedt, C.
Spahm, S.
Swift, James.
Schlichte, Edmin.
Smith, Fred.
Smith, Robert.
Smith, John E.
Schroeder, John.
Seeler, Simon.
Saylor, Thomas E.
Shifferstein, V.

Schomillar, M.
Schere, John.
Sullivan, P. J.
Schultz, Emile.
Schwaner, J.
Shawhan, J. N.
Singer, Wm.
Smith, C. A.
Scheoudorff, P.
Squire, Mrs. Joseph.
Smith, Mary.
Smith, Henry.
Senoeuski, A.
Sabadi, George.
Schoff, Joseph.
Sabathe, Mary.
Stein, Mary M.
Schillaght, J.
Sullivan, Samuel.
Schummer, Frank.
Stafford, Elizabeth J.
Smith, Henry.
Schummer, Henrich.
Seifer, M. M.
Schenrer, Jacob.
Schenrer, Mary.
Strother, Ira B.
Steele, Leda, J.
Simonds, Mrs. D.
Spreen, Fred.
Sheridan, Maggie.
Sheridan, James A.
Spess, Robert G.
Stanter, N.
Smith, C.
Sweetmon, Millie.
Shepley, Martha.
Spence, W. F.
Sims, John H.
Sterenberg, L.
Smith, Teresa.
Soners, Charlie.
Shallack, Anna.
Steprick, M. D.
Schnechen, Berge.
Stephenson, T. F.
Smith, Wm. M.
Saunden, Charles.
Shumaker, Millie.
Schibe, Alice.
Schwennelien, J.
Stumpf, C. A.
Schalumbrecht, J. L.
Saxton, Robert John.
Schillect, J.
Soubil, Jean.
Smith, John A.
Smith, Joseph.
Schloeser, Joseph.
Swyier, James.
Sherry, M. L.
Stafford, R B.
Saxe, Philip.
Schultzele, Margaret.
Steefiel, George.
Smith, Mary R.
Smith, Sarah.
Smith, Henry.
Solares, Romain.
Schiff, Mrs. Joseph.
Schwarz, Edna.
Scharff, John P.
Soumeillans, H.
Schott, John.
Sancier, Leela.
Sullivan, John.
Silberstein, David.
Simmone, Felix D.
Small, M. Louisa.
S nders, James M.
Scally, John.
Stortz, Henry.
Shakeiort, William.
Schwarze, Karl.
Schroeder, Mary.
Selerin, Jean P.
Schmidt, Louis.
Samuels, Ruth M.
Smith, Charles.

Searcy, Nella.
Stanley, May.
Stanton, Mrs. Julia.
Shardy, Octave.
Sneck, Louis.
Sherlock, Annie.
Suarez, Maximo.
Smith, William.
Schroeder, Henry.
Seng, Charles.
Schoen, Jacob.
Springman, Louis.
Stevenson, Mrs M. B.
Southmayd, G. F.
Starke, Charles E.
Sipido, Albert.
Smith, Charles.
Stouder, John.
Scanlan, Patrick.
Small, George.
Small, George S.
Snead, John.
Schaefer, Mary.
Shuto, Edward P.
Sommer, Julius.
Schrumpf, Arthur.
Smith, Celia.
Seibel, Daniel.
Sullivan, Patrick.
Sicollier, Alphonso.
Storz, John M.
Seenauder, Mary H.
Salorz, Lydia.
Schelles, John.
Salisa, Sister.
Schelin, Carl S.
Skire, Antonio.
Sullivan, Helen.
Scott, John.
Schuler, Robert R.
Saunders, Fred. M.
Sanford, William.
Steele, Francis P.
Schelmann, Eugene.
Salvant, Josephine.
Schaeffer, John.
Simmons, J. M.
Smith, Henry.
Sangerson, Mrs. B,
Seerville, Henry.
Shneiper, Ida.
Soniat, E. E.
Sage, J. E.
Schmidt, L. E.
Soubrier, A.
Schneckler, John.
Scanlan, Thomas.
Sailes, Mrs. Mary.
St. Clair, Henry S.
Stack, Patrick.
Stephens, Joseph D.
Sanderson, William.
Sanderson, Mrs. Wm.
Sullivan, James.
Soniat, Louise E.
Smith, Annie M.
Sontag, George.
St. Clair, Mary.
Searing, Robert B.
Schmaltz, Julia C.
Schahill, Mike.
Sancas, Henri.
Schoen, Theodore.
Staub, Oswald.
Silverstein, Lena.
Schmitt, Mrs. C.
Sprague, Daniel R.
Scheler, Joseph.
Schiro, Antonio.
Sparks, Florence H.
Sansoucy, Aug. P.
Sansoucy, Madame.
Sinnier, Jean B.
Schmidt, Julius.
Shearer, Oliver W.
Seigel, Emilie.
Shannon, Michael.
Stine, Martin.
Sansoucy, Alfred.

Steinhardt, Sarah.
Smith, Wm.
Smith, John H.
Shannon, Annie.
Smith, Lawrence.
Schuling, Henry.
Smith, Edward.
Schaefer, Aug.
Scott, John.
Schuldt, William.
Scheurmann, Charles.
Schneider, Henry.
Seynanoski, E. Van.
Schneider, Aug.
Sullivan, Thomas.
Smith, Margaret.
Simmons, Mrs. H.
Sweetman, Nich.
Simon, Adolphus.
Schumaker, Henry.
Shermann, Simon.
Schmidt, C.
Souberville, Louis.
Serre, Kate.
Shannon, Melinda.
Sanders, Monie J.
Scott, William.
Sill, Henry.
Serwinski, Aaron.
Smith, Henry.
Saladino, J.
Schmidt, Sophie.
Smith, Eva.
Sutera, Christiana.
Schneider, William.
Sullivan, Joseph.
Silver, Manuel.
Schevantz, Hermann.
Smith, Maggie M.
Stonehouse, Emanuel.
Singer, Rosa.
Sarvatori, Major.
Sabala, Mary Ann.
Sturgess, W. A.
Smith, John H.
Stringer, Alfred D.
Tainter, H. W.
Traylor, Alber.
Tarrant, Walter.
Toll, John.
Thibaut, Christian.
Tredger, John.
Taylor, Ashton.
Turner, Gus. H.
Thanes, Orillo.
Trark, Anna.
Tortorice, Peter.
Taylor, Mary E.
Tammie, William.
Toussaint, M.
Thompson, Charles.
Thirrcat, William.
Trawick, Rev. M. T.
Toelhe, Mary, A.
Toka, Frank.
Thomas, Ann.
Topse, Gernard.
Tebalt, John.
Totto, Vincenzo.
Tony, Charles H.
Teutsch, J.
Taylor, Ada.
Tourtable, Lucien.
Toby, James J.
Trichanard, C.
Trichanard, A. C.
Tyler, Charles.
Taleisouer, Mrs. C.
Tnaffee, E. R.
Taylor, Dr. J. Theus.
Thompson, D.
Tansen, Louis.
Trenchard, V.
Thenram, Aleck.
Tarle, Samuel H.
Tashey, E. E.
Thomas, Charles M.
Turney, H. M.
Turney, C. R.

Tran, V. Alex.
Thomas, Maud.
Taylor, J. W.
Trelforde, R. N.
Tierney, M. M.
Tierney, Thomas J.
Tonman, Hubert.
Trampalore, Cologers.
Tucker, Mary L.
Thompson, Bertha E.
Talbot, Charles.
Tamporella, Mich.
Trombly, Aug.
Todd, James.
Tertrou, Jules.
Tscleppert, Robert.
Theresa, Sister Mary.
Troully, Hubert.
Toujet, Margaret.
Terry, Mary.
Timmons, Edward.
Traub, August.
Trois, John.
Turpin, John.
Tracy, John P.
Tamme, Emily.
Twitchell, Grace.
Tonmilla, Jean.
Turner, James.
Tournier, J. J.
Thoman, Johannes.
Taylor, John.
Teiglchueter, Cath.
Tolland, D. W.
Tromanovich, S.
Touce, Mary.
Twomey, Ello.
Thomas, Ignatius.
Troessard, Geo. A.
Thompson, Ida.
Taylor, Eugenia.
Tujague, Bernard.
Thilberger, Fred.
Thorpe, Adelaide.
Templet, Josephine.
Taylor, Howell L.
Treil, L. Nado.
Trauth, Mrs. Caroline.
Tolivar, Pauline.
Turpin, John.
Tocca, Emma.
Tape, Gerhard.
Touzan, Emile.
Thuer, John K.
Urdgis, Catherine.
Ulard, Gustave.
Up, Fanny.
Ubee, Richard.
Urger, Lena.
Vaccari, Vin.
Voiscult, Louis.
Vicha, Catherine.
Vergez, J. Ed.
Vonwesterhayen, T. R.
Voslon, Michael.
Vicknar, Marie.
Vincent, Edward.
Veasey, Ellen.
Vogl, G.
Vulcon, Henry.
Vermis, P. D.
Verhoff, Charles.
Vaccaro, Maria.
Vanier, Mrs.
Vincent, G.
Vas, Joseph.
Vanderhooder, F.
Veuta, J.
Volte, Francisco.
Verges, Charles.
Vinne, Sister M. N.
Van Hooven, A.
Valencia, Viel.
Van Hoove.
Vagelsaengo, J. G.
Vivar, Mary S.
Verdichizzi, Jo.
Van Ostern, Eva M.
Vilter, Max.

Vogeley, Charles.
Venus, Charles F.
Voconowich, C.
Vidoo, Amedee.
Vogel, Mrs. Martha.
Vaccaro, Antonio.
Verlander, Georgiana.
Vosbergh, John R.
Vaccaro, Antonio.
Vigard, George.
Vanier, A.
Volois, Henry.
Valnote, Poblo.
Vessein, Mrs. Julia.
Vocheran, Claude.
Vamote, Joseph.
Voss, Mattie A.
Verges, Jean P.
Veavant, Fred. S.
Vilter, Bertha.
Verges, John.
Viendahaar, Lewis.
Vanderheiden, F. A.
Voight, Frantz.
Vitruno, Maria.
Voight, Mrs. Clara.
Vincent, J. B. P.
Veaux, Pierre.
Willet, Henry.
Williams, S.
Wyrth, Henry J.
Williams, R. E.
Wagner, John.
Walsh, James.
Winstein, A.
Whall, Aug.
Woodsen, Philip.
Wardwell, D. W.
Waltz, Char.es.
Wolff, Eva.
Witt, Albert C.
Wermeal, Mrs. L.
Wilkins, Louis.
Wasserman, A.
Wighthert, Gareana.
Work, Chas. A.
Wendling, Geo.
Walter, Augusta.
Williams, W. H.
Waugh, Henry.
Wolfert, Fred.
Weisch, Jennie.
Wolf, Willie.
Walter, Nicholas.
Wright, Mary A.
Walds, Ad. J. A.
Walsh, Amelia.
Wambaugh, R.
Woods, Joseph.
Wernett, Joseph.
Wilber, H. W.
Walther, Henry L.
Warner, Leo.
Waterman, M. G.
Wiseman, Catherine.
Walther, Charles T.
Williamson, Warren.
Williams, Mrs. Annie.
Welch, Patrick.
Wall, Henry.
Warfield, John.
Welsh, Thomas W.
Wheeler, Wm. J.
White, George.
Walheng, John.
Walsh, John L.
Wheeler, Mary A.
Wood, W. C.
Wachenfield, Mary.
Williams, Alfred.
Weiner, Emilie.
Walker, Mary.
Ward, John.
Worth, Pauline.
Williams, Pinckney.
Wright, Robert.
Wilson, Cora A.
Wright, Ruth J.
Werner, Mary E.

Williams, Annie M.
Warner, Geo.
Wilson, George H.
Wilson, Thomas.
Woods, Rosina.
Worthberg, Mrs. Nuevia.
Williams, Sam. E.
Watts, Harriet.
Williams, Henry.
Wahl, Dorothea.
Winterberger, Mary.
Wain, Wm.
Whitaker, John F.
Wise, Wm.
Weinang, Fritz.
Wilkins, Mary E.
Wyley, Wm. T.
Wolcott, Rosa.
Wagner, Elenora.
Wallace, Margueretta.
Wright, Mr.
Weltense, Louis.
Wilkinson, Thos. C.
Williams, Michael.
Williams, Maggie.
Welch, John.
Welsh, Minnie W.
Wertz, Wm. H.
Welman, Mrs. C.
Waters, Sam.
Webmeyer, F.
Walker, Ed.
West, Henry.
Woodworth, Mabel.
Wellpool, John.
Watenlifer, K.
Weinzentied, Chas.
Wunder, M. L.
Welsh, Jennie.
Wuernasa, Mic. A.
Williams, Lillie.
Wuaranara, S.
Wolff, John W.
Wight, John.
Warle, C. H.
Walter, Herman.
Weathers, Joseph.
Wight, Charles.
Webel, Emma C.
Wight, Frank.
Walsh, Mary E.
Weisenberg, Joseph.
Wick, Mrs. Sarah W.
Wischer, Bernard.
Watson, C.
Werner, George.
Williams, Eugene.
Weiss, John K.
Williamson, F. E.
Williams, Alice.
Williams, Annie.
Willbrath, Aug.
Wiggins, Eliz. R.
Wall, Wm. E.
Ward, John J.
Welling, Jonas.
Welsh, Mrs. Bridget.
Winstead, T. H.
Walin, Jacques A.
Wockerborth, Adolph.
Wahl, Fred.
Welsh, Wm.
Wilhelmine, Eliz.
Wangenheim, Albert.
Weigel, Charles.
Wilson, Dr Norvell W.
Woolf, Willis K.
Wall, Alice.
Walker, Charles.
Walsh, Wm.
Wassern, Henry.
White, Nicholas.
Wilson, William.
Welsh, Johanna.
White, James.
Warheit, N.
Wichmann, Jacques.
Wiltenmuth, John.
Wood, Charlotte M.

Wiggering, John.
Wernick, O. O.
Wansch, Helena.
Williams, Alice.
Weimers, Rev. C. J.
Wizohski, Henry.
Wogan, Louis G.
Wekman, Margaret.
Williams, John.
Williamson, Frank E.
Weaver, John.
Williams, Joseph.
Wild, Am.
Wuerpel, Ada O.
Wylie, Patrick.
Wessenberger, Martin.
Young, Wm.
Young, Anna.
Young, Peter.
Yuille. Mrs. Kittie.
York, John.
Young, Louise.
Yob, Henry.
Yung, Magdalena.
Young, Wm.
Young, Charles.
Youngblut, E. J.
Young, Annie R.
Yaegan, John.
Youngz, Agnes.
Zerega, Maud A.
Zlidel, Franz.
Zoeller, Mrs. Mina.
Zerega, Alber.
Zaconi, Gaeltane.
Zamanta, M.
Zetlmann, Andrew.
Zerega, Charles.
Zichici, G.
Zemmer, Theo.
Zill, Annie V.
Zappa, Henry.
Zable, Ernest.
Zellman, Isawm.
Zella, Coniconda.
Zenzer, Dr. W.

Delhi.

Blakie, Dan.
Neathery, Miss Mattie.
Hedrick, John.
Merritt, Mrs. Jane.
Williams, Mrs. Fanny.
Bishop, Lillie.
Bishop, Lizzie.
Hogan, Thomas.
Lilley, Mrs. Rosa.
Colbert, John.
Berry, James D.
Meagher, Charley W.
Fontaine, Bennie.
Mazelin, George.
Moss, Philip.
Lilley, Dr. T. W.
Kincaid, Spencer.
Colbert, Mrs.
Dixon, John.
Ardoin, Henry.
Montgomery, Spencer.
Lilley, Wright.
Montgomery, Mrs. Jenny.
Gibson, Mr.
Isaacs, John.
Schnackle, Rembrandt.
Gammel, John.

Delta.

Felt, Burney.
Neillson, August.
Short, Wm. P.
McIntosh, Wm. H.
Clemens, Hale.
Clemens, Mary.
Larkin, E. J.
Marteen, Julius.
Van Epps, Harry.
Johnson, Henry.
Lindenstein, Chas.
Burton, Martin.

A HISTORY OF THE YELLOW FEVER.

Wilkerson, Mrs. J.
Wallace, Wm.
Unknown man.
Floyd, Annie.
Porterfield, Floyd.
Cook, Spottswell.
Kaiser, Eldie.
Feibleman, Jos.
Branch, Edward.
Blackshire, Luke.
Cobb, Mr.
Gray, Ellen.
Unknown man.
Gilland, Dr. L. W.
Cramer, Capt. E. M.
Brown, Capt. A. V.
Pryor, Bobt.
Pryor, Mrs.
Reed (child of John B.).
Welsh (child of Mrs.).
Williams, Mrs. Ed.
Corkern, Maj. J. B.
Corkern, Mrs. J. F.
Conway (child of Mrs.).
Lawrence, Mrs. Ella.
Oben, Mrs. Emma.
Smith, Nellie.
Cassman, Chas.
Eugene, John.
Cassman, Mrs. Chas.
Ray, Frederick.
Cuhn, Sam.
Hardy, N. L.
Oben, Lulu Maude.
Goldsburg, Mrs. Caroline.
Hoggatt, Stacey, Mounds.
Griffin, T. P., Milliken's Bend.
Pierce, J. G., Cooper Place.
Farrar, Howard, Kilarney Place.
Dangerfield, Garnett J., Dalmatia Place.

Dunboyne Plantation.

Edwards, Miss.
Hubbard, Major.
Hubbard (wife of).
Hubbard (mother-in-law of).
Williamson, Dr. W. B.

Gretna.

Goodlet, James R., Jr.
Gale.
Mathews.
Sutton.
Walker.

Harrisonburg.

Knight, Mr.

Henderson, Goodrich. Omega and Raleigh Landings.

Rhoton, Albert C.
Hays, Dr. R. T. D.
Denson, Thomas.
Craig, James A.
Frazier, Wm.
Weeden, Frederick.
Mayer, Caroline.
Mayer, Marcus.
Block, Moses.
Kleinhaus, Catherine.
Lincoln, George.
Bowling, Joseph.
McDonald, John A.
Bernd, Oscar.
Bledsoe, W. F.
Powell, Mr.
Powell, Mrs.
Powell, Robert.
Langham, Mrs. Chas., & baby.
Vickers, Miss Sarah.
Barham, Mrs., & baby.

Graves, Eugene.
Armstead, Willie.
Dunlap, M. A., died in flatboat on Steven's bar, opposite Carolina Landing, Oct. 10.

Lagonda.

Broussard, Fucay.
Cringer, Frank.
Clark, Oliver.
Edgar, wife and daughter.

Lafourche Crossing.

Adams, August (child).
Ballard, Miss Jennie.
Bourgeois, Nolbert, and three children.
Bourgeois, Alic.
Cantrale, Miss.
Cauvin, Alc. (child).
Guidray, Miss Aurelien.
Guitlian, Mr. (child of).
Gabert, George.
Henry, J. H.
Henry, Joseph.
Lefort, Mrs. Wallace.
LeBlanc, Robert.
Longerpie, Mr. Y. (child of).
Leoron, James.
Ledet, Mr. Sylver.
Leffal, Wallace.

Pecan Grove.

Baker, Frank.
Creophor, E. T.

Tallulah.

Fell, Harry F.
Askew, Mrs. S. A.
Griffin, Thomas P.

White Haven.

Rains, Dr.

Baton Rouge.

Anderson, Annie.
Acosta, Julia.
Acosta (child of Mrs).
Allain, Mary Lulu.
Aldrich, Jennie.
Amos, Scott.
Arbour, Jos. Stacy.
Amiss, Wm. Duchien.
Burns, John.
Bard, Sam. Gov.
Burns, John.
Brady, John.
Bareyre, Marie L.
Bonche, John A.
Brower, Lilly Belle.
Bott, Augusta.
Broussard, Annie.
Bertram, Gustave.
Berghality, Augustus.
Bumgard, Christian.
Bolkman (son of Tony).
Benjamin, Lulu.
Benjamin, Henry.
Benjamin, Mary.
Baum, Charles.
Bell (child of Emily).
Birch, John.
Boyd, Alfred, col.
Bareyre, Anna M.
Beliocq, Laurinza.
Balsineur, Louis S.
Bresenham, Adele.
Beizron, John.
Baum, Mrs. Mary.
Bernhard (daughter of Mrs.).
Bryan, Anne H.
Bartlet, S.
Bogan, Lorena.
Brooks, A. R.

Cade, Robert.
Cain, Dempsey.
Cronan (child of John).
Capdevielle, Cornelia M.
Capdevielle, Lindsey.
Clark, James.
Conner, Julia.
Comeaux, James.
Comeaux, James.
Cramer, Martin.
Collins, Scott.
Cooper, Thos.
Collins, Jack.
Cox, J. J.
Curry, Trevanion.
Carter, Margaret.
Clavery, John.
Cade, Robert.
Curry, Sarah.
Cheatham, Oliver.
Cooper, Ida C.
Cairo, Jim.
Ducros (child of Mr.).
Doiron, A. F.
Doiron, Elise.
Dubroca, Corinne.
Daigre, J. D.
Daigre, Delmar.
Duralde, J. V., Jr.
Dupwis, Melanie.
Duralde, Mrs. Jos. V.
Duralde, Jos. V.
Doison, Annatone.
Doison, Mrs. Elise.
Dubroca, Caroline.
Daigre, Delmar.
Dubroca, Jules V.
Doyle, Emma L.
Defondellas, Clarina.
Darling (child of).
Davergne, Octave.
Excememan, M.
Fairbanks, Ella.
Funke, Doretta.
Fairie, Robert J., Jr.
Fair, Ida Isabelle.
Fonlien, G. G.
Favrot, Sidney Joseph.
Femoreau, Vallery.
Favrot, Claude J.
Frank, David.
Frank, Sophia.
Fields, Charles.
Froescher, John G.
Fremont, Vallery.
Gallagher, John.
Garig, Wm.
Gass, Gertrude.
Grand, George L.
Gray, Willie.
Gray, Daniel.
Gerlock, Frederic.
Grady, William.
Gailey, Jane.
Grice, Charles E.
Gunot, Victor H.
Howard, Geo., col.
Hereford, R., col.
Hereford, Mrs. L. S.
Hilden, Nancy, col.
Herst, Louis.
Hebert, Cecelia C.
Harlt, William.
Hare, Walter F.
Hare, Maude C.
Hays, Emily M.
Hearse, Wilson.
Hoit, Joseph.
Jones, Ben., col.
Jefferson (child of).
Jolly, R. Emmett.
Jolly, Lawrence.
Jones, Charles.
Jolly, Eva Louise.
Johnson (child of).
Jones, Caroline.
Jones, Nellie.
Johnson, Fannie.
Jolly, Charles E.

Jolly, Andrew H.
Jackson, Susan.
Jones, Regina G.
Jones, George.
Jackson, A. S.
Jones, Mack.
Jodd, Michael.
Jodd, Bernard P.
Knox, Lily, col.
Kain, Joseph.
Kraus, N.
Kearn, James.
Knox (child of).
Kleinburry, Louis F.
Kennedy, Ellen.
Kinchen, Philip.
Knox, Louis.
Louis, Camille.
LeBlanc, Villeneuve.
Levy, Charles.
Lacrampe, Antoine.
Latchford, Alvin C.
Lafargne, Henry.
Lamon, William R.
Lamon, John H., Jr.
Larkin, Michael.
LeBlanc, Paul H.
Legendre, Louise.
Levi, Mina.
Levi, Charles.
Lee, Martha.
Lee, William.
Lee, Cora, col.
Levi, Charles.
Marks, Jacob.
McCloskey, Mary Ann.
Mulcahey, Sophie.
McNamara, Michael.
Marker, Louis.
Muschrous, Ignatius.
Molaison, Pauline.
Martiney, Mrs. M.
Murphy, John.
Morrison, Alton.
Martin, Theodore.
Martin, Bertha.
McMain, Edith.
Miller, Julius.
Miles, Benj. F.
Moore, Caroline.
Martinez, William.
Miranda, Beatrice.
Macdon, Mary Estelle.
Morgan, Ophelia.
Miller, Henry.
Mendelssohn, Leon.
Mayer, Isadore.
Marks, Jacob.
Marks, Isaac.
May, Job.
May, Wm. Harrison.
McWhorter, W. J.
Nodler, Emile.
O'Connor, David.
Pierce, Granville M.
Pino, Leonie.
Pope, Edward.
Pope, James.
Ponsylrain, Francois.
Potts, Martha M.
Potter, Willie.
Pujol, Anna Louise.
Power, James Silas.
Pinckney (child of).
Phillips, J. H.
Pettit, Wm. D.
Ross. Charles H.
Rodrigney, Emile.
Richardson, Wm. R.
Remeres, Lavinia.
Richardson, Jane.
Reynaud, Albert G.
Robbins, S. M.
Rowley, William.
Stephens, C. A.
Saachez, Dora.
Strauss, Charles.
Scott.
Skolfield, Pearl.

Stewart, George.
Stewart, Mrs. George.
Scott, Louisa.
Skolfield, Killian S.
Sanchey, Isabella.
Smith, Thomas.
Scott (son of Louis).
Smith.
Scarborough, Effie.
Sanders, Lirey.
Scully, John.
Terpinitz, Edward J.
Thomas, Laura.
Thompson, Georgiana.
Thibodeaux, Edgar.
Thomas, Henry.
Thomas, Henry.
Thomas, Bertha.
Thornton, Cal.
Vining, Rosa.
Voivodich, John.
Vienn t, Anne E.
Vernier, Charles.
Verdue, Emile.
Wolf, Leon.
Williams (child of T.).
Wilson, Mary.
Wiseman, Robert.
Wunsch, Josephine.
Wolff, Lizzie.
Widney, Charles.
Wilkinson, Benj.
Woods, Ann Emily.
Widney, Mary A.
Williams, Mary Ella.
Wax, Francis N.
Williams, Josephine G.
Willis, Douglas.
Wilson, Trevel.
Woods, John H.
Williams, Julius Wilson.
Young (son of Henry).
Zahn, George A.

Bayou Goula.

A stranger.
Blanchard (child of L.).
Fitzenreiter (child of).
Lawe (child of James.)

Brule Sacramento.

Albarado, Sebastian.
Albarado, Domingo.
Albarex, Perique.
Ayrand Amelia.
Denoux, Tauvier (son)
Denoux, Henri.
Denoux, Owen.
Dugas, Alece.
Dugas, Luce.
Dugas, Jerome.
Dugas, J.
Dille, James.
Falcon, Hilaire.
Falcon, Louisa.
Falcon, Antoine.
Gomez, Mrs. Sebastian.
Gonzalles, Mrs. Perique.
Gonzalles, Joseph.
LeBlanc.
Monticino, Emanuel.
Monticino, Mrs. Eman.
Ourso.

Clinton.

Butler, John S.
Camrer, J. I.
Cafert, J. J.
Dixon, Mrs. Lucas.
Dupnes, Abraham.
Drehr, Richard.
Drehr, Miss.
De Grey, James.
De Grey, James (child).
Depues, H.
Hernon, Mrs.
Marston, Geo.
Marston, David.
Marston, David.

Marston, Miss.
Mahoney, Mr.
Mandou, Geo.
Newson, James (child).
Neson, Mrs. Libby.
Neson, Miss Libby.
Neson, Mr. Libby.
Reily, Miss Mary.
Reily, Rev. John A.
Reily, Geo.
Reily, Willie.
Rutherford, Dr. (nurse).

Donaldsonville.

Antonio, Mr.
Alford, Mattie, col.
Boudereaux, Adele.
Bosco, Carl.
Boronca, Ouida.
Brand, Emile.
Bergerson, Mathilde.
Bergerson, Paul.
Cheevers, Ed.
Cocorillo, Francis.
Carlo, Charles.
Carlo, Calisse.
Cambre, Camille.
Drach, Ed.
Duke, Evelina.
Duffel, Clarence F.
Domingo, F.
Fucich, Joseph A.
Folse, Joe, col.
Faillomisea, Joe.
Falcon, Louisa, col.
Faillouzea, Jos.
Gue iry, Leontia.
Gauthreaux, Mrs. G.
Gauthreaux, Leonce.
Gauthreaux, George.
Greggs, Wm.
Genazzine, Austide.
Gona, Victor.
Gentil, George.
Guedry, Mrs. Paul.
Genevieve, Mrs. P.
Gallata, Vincent.
Gomez, Frenzel.
Gaire, Alexandre.
Green, Wm.
Goodloe, G., col.
Hick, Emilie.
Hiss, Louisa.
Hiss, Willic.
Hiss, Rosa.
Harris, Leon.
Harp, Mrs. Anna.
Hilton, Maud.
Hether, Fred.
Hutton, Thos.
Herron, Cecil.
Hether, Joseph.
Ilsley, Chas.
Israel, C. B.
Israel, Henry L.
Joseph, Leon.
Johnson, Julia, col.
Jardel, H. L.
Kennedy, Jack.
Kenner, John.
Keating, Jesse, col.
Krause, Frank.
Krause, Lulu.
Kraus, Wilhelmina.
Kline, Frank.
Kruse, H. C.
Little, Wm. S.
Loeb, Alex.
Loeb, Henry.
Loeb, Emanuel.
Lafargue, Emma.
Lafargue, Raoul.
LeBlanc, Rene.
LeBlanc, Ed.
LeBlanc, Lawrence
LeBlanc, Emilie.
LeBlanc, Alba.
Landry, Stella.
Landry, Julia.

Landry, Mederic.
Landry, Uloze.
Landry, Julia.
Landry, Augustine.
Landry, Mrs. Eupheamia,
Mollere, Louis.
Maher, Joe.
Melrusse, M.
Muneaster, I.
Maurin, Walter.
Melancon, Ada.
Michel, Eliziphord, col.
Mayse, Henry.
McDermott, Mr.
Naive, Jean.
O'Connor, Chas.
Proffitt, Annic.
Perez, Letitia.
Pope, Joe.
Pfortzmeiner, L.
Pinch, Xavier.
Propar, Salvador.
Pyliski, James H.
Profichel, Anne.
Rodrigue, Celestine.
Rodrigue, Victorine.
Rodrigue, Klebert.
Rodelilior, Alice.
Sommerville, Mary.
Sommerville, Allen.
Solares, Anthony.
Stranger, A.
Smythe, Augusta.
Savadras, Mrs. Vic.
Smith, A.
Shewmaker, H. C.
Stucker, Wm.
Terrio, Octava.
Unknown.
Varinnani, Marie.
Vite, Deserve.
Varinnani, Celestine.
Wilson, Irene.
Weil, Sam.
Wiggins, Jackson.
Willis, Mrs. P. C.
Willis, Clara A.

Pattersonville.

Bernard, Mrs. Louisa.
Bernard, George.
Bernard, Charlie.
Bourke, Clare.
Bourke, Alidin.
Broussard, Alice.
Baker, Frank.
Cox, Lelia.
Cropper, Ernest T.
Corndy, Amelius.
Consienne, Adrian.
Clarke, Oliver.
Dowdall, Mrs. Sidney.
Dauphin (niece).
Duffy, M. E.
Davies, R. G.
Edgar, Irwin.
Edgar, Mrs. Irwin.
Edgar, Miss.
Felterman, Mrs
Gross, Mrs.
Gomaux, J. L.
Hayes, Willie.
Holland, James.
Hall, Henry, Sr.
Innerarity, Catherine.
Kellar, Richardson.
Knight, Rev. Mrs. Jos.
LeBlanc, C. O.
Martin, R. R.
Mayloz, T. W.

Plaquemine.

Altimus, J. F.
Alexander, James.
Biehler, Leontine.
Barker, Fabian Alchus.
Banzau (child).
Barker, Mary E. a.
Brusle, Ophelia.

Brunet, Pierre.
Bouvy, N. C.
Barker, C. O. D.
Billings, Frank.
Bell (daughter).
Burnes, Patrick.
Burnes, James S.
Brown, Edward.
Bergeson, Z. R.
Bartel, Charles.
Bruce, Adelaide.
Blouin, Sidney.
Barbay, Mary.
Barton, Joseph.
Bartel, M.
Barthel, Dominique.
Babin, Alphonse.
Brown, Arthur.
Brown, Aristide.
Brown (infant).
Blanchard, Laura.
Broissac, Charles.
Blouin, R. M.
Brown, Joseph.
Coomes, Camille.
Chastant, Sidney.

Pass Christian.

Babin, V., col.
Berry, C.
Chandler, Mary T.
Champlin, Lou.
Cary, Mrs.
Courteney, T.
Cezerin, Beajio.
Doran, J.
French, Bennie.
Fulger, Joseph.
Gibson, John, Jr.
Gibson, Frank T.
Hart, Lena.
Hart (child of Junius).
Hiern, Mrs. Finley B.
Holley (child of N.).
Jeffries, Prof. J. S. B
Jeffries, Mrs. M. R.
Jeffries, Miss.
Jeffries, B. L.
Maloney, Miss.
Pecante, Madame John.

Point-a-la-Hache.

Berret (son of Joe).
Landry (two children of d.).
Merrill, Dr. De.

Port Barrow.

Hohensee, Andrew J.
Jackson, Mollie.
Philip, John.
Rodrigue, Anna.
Rodrigue, Miss H.
Soires, Raphael.
Vinette, Emanuel.

St. James' Parish.

Chanvin (child of P.).
Sarrazin (child of).

Southwest Pass.

Flynn, Mrs. M. E.
Flynn, Jessie Louisa.
Flynn, Mary Elizabeth.

Tangipahoa.

Barrow, Mrs. Alex.
Barrow, Wm.
Butler, Tom., col.
Carter, Dr. W. N.
Cutrer, Rachael, col.
Daley, John.
Daley, Mrs John.
Daley, Harriet.
Daley, Lizzie.
Fisher, Martha.
Fairchild, Wm.
Frogg, Peter.
Harvey, Clark.

A HISTORY OF THE YELLOW FEVER.

Hodges, Noel.
Hodges, Eugene.
Hodges, Jennie.
Hyde, Serena.
Hyde, Willie.
Hall, Mrs.
Jones, Mrs. Serena B.
Jones, Hattie.
Jackson, C., col.
Knoff, Capt. L.
Kohlhaas, Jos.
Kohlhaas, Mrs.
Kennon, Dr. C. E.
Kennon, C. R.
Kennon, Hubert.
Lewis, Mrs. Mary.
Losey, Charlie.
McDaniel, John.
McGehee, F. D.
McGehee, Harriet, col.
Nelson, C., col.
Prince, Annie.
Ricks, J. D.
Russell, Fred.
Russell, Johnnie.
Suasey, Dr. H. A.
Suasey, Ida A.
Simmons, Wm.
Simmons, Jennie.
Smith, Nelson, col.
Teatons, Mr.
Varnardo, Sammie.
Waller, Mrs. Green.
Waller, Jessie.
Waller (child of Jessie).
Waller, Penn.
Waller, Alcina.
Wall, Abe.
Wall, Dempsey K.
Wolf, Rosalie.
Weathers, Geo., col.
Wheat, Peter, col.

Terre Aux Boeuf.

Bolton. •
Myrick, M. A.
Peeples, Mrs.
Peeples (child of Mrs.).

Thibodaux.

Aubort, M. T. C.
Agatha, Sister.
Ancoin, Numa.
Alberti, Thomas
Adam, Robt.
Ayot, Vilfried.
Aubort, W. C.

Alteman, Martine.
Boudreaux, Theodrule.
Boudreaux, Philomene.
Boudreaux, Menville.
Boudreaux, Joseph.
Boudreaux, Azelia.
Boudreaux, Wel.
Boudreaux, Edgard.
Boudreaux, Eulalie.
Boudreaux, Wm. Louis.
Boudreaux, Charles.
Boudreaux, Jules.
Boudreaux, Mrs.
Boudreaux, Hebert.
Boudreaux, Oscar.
Brown, John.
Bourgeois, L. N.
Bourgeois, Mathilde.
Bardreaux, L.
Bourgeois, Sarah.
Bourgeois, Mrs. Justinian
Blanchard, Robt.
Badeaux, Allen, Jr.
Baricleux, Eugene.
Brockhoft, Louis.
Brockhoft, Oscar.
Brockhoft, Louise.
Blanchard, E. N.
Blanchard, T. L.
Bussow, Henry.
Ballard, Eugene.
Bourgeois, N., Jr.
Bourgeois, Alcesti.
Bourgeois, Young.
Bourgeois, N., Sr.
Bourgeois, Cecile.
Chol, E., Jr.
Curtis, Jolive.
Callarie, Eugenia.
Champagne, Abel.
Champagne, Francis.
Cogan, John.
Clement, Mrs. Joseph.
Clement, Mrs. U.
Clement, Clevnille.
Clement, Theophile.
Cantrale, Josephine.
Castro, Nevville.
Chamin, Dertha.
Cancienne, Villier.
Cluasson, Octave.
Concannon, James.
Durgan, Thomas.
Dionne, Theresa.
Dionne, Louis.
Damereau, Dr. P.
Dugas, Joseph.

Doucet, Alphonsine.
Doucet, Mathilda.
Davidson, Eva.
Dias, Ed.
Duhamel, Calixte.
Dupre, Nenville.
Estivan, Marcelin.
Erskine, Mrs. John.
Erskine, John.
Erskine, Polexanie.
Feta, Valmon.
Forest, Celestine.
Forest, Cyprien.
Forest, Felicien.
Fanestine, Sister.
Fulford, Anna.
Guillot, Mrs A.
Guillot, Mrs. Loui
Gros, I.
Gros, Zephir.
Ganbert, Lem.
Guidry, Julia.
Guidry (child of Ad.).
Gros, H.
Gros, L.
Gantreaux, Orvile.
Hargis, Marie.
Heber, Thomas.
Hebert, Arthur.
Hendricks, Dennis.
Hoffman, Sam.
Hawk, Robt.
Hebert, Theresa.
Hebret, Alfred.
Henry, Joseph.
Iteibs, Anna.
Josephine, Sister.
Jules, Charles.
Knoblock, Bertha.
Loiseaux, Joseph.
Legendre, Louis.
Legendre, Emile.
Legendre, Adolphine.
Legendre, Gustave.
Lefort, Mrs. W.
Lafond, Mrs. Josephine.
Lagarde, Frank J.
Lagarde, Dalilab.
Lagrdo, John.
Leleim, Robt.
Ledet, Silver.
Ledet, Mrs. Amedec.
Lirette (child of).
Leron, Joseph.
Leron's (child at).
Leblave, Robt.
Leblave, A.

Lovia, Ida.
Movant, Ulysses (child).
Morris, Charles.
Moluison, Onezippe.
Martin, Anna.
Martin, Eulalic.
Mure, T. K.
Marouge, Onezippe.
Murray, Willie.
Murray, Mollie.
Naguin, Joseph.
Naguin, Mrs.
Naguin, Arthur.
Naguin, Louise.
Nicholls, Madge.
Pochon, Jean.
Patterson, Harrison.
Perrin, Adolph.
Pichon, Alice.
Rogers, Emile.
Richard, Charles.
Richard, Marie.
Ragan, Ella.
Ribet, J. M.
Robertson, Adam.
Roth, Angelina.
Robert, Henri.
Sevin, Mrs. Joseph.
Sevin, Josephine.
Sevin, Mrs. Onezipp
Schiffersteine, Marie.
Sabourin, Dr. C.
Saunders, Ralph.
Two Chinamen.
Toups, Mrs. Overstile.
Toups, Clebert.
Toups, Marie.
Turner, Charles.
Troselair, Ida.
Troselair, Joseph.
Taylor, Daniel.
Taylor, Charles.
Thibodaux, Mrs. C.
Thibodaux, L.
Thibodaux, Georgina.
Thibodaux, Mrs. H.
Thibodaux, Elder.
Thibodaux, Angelc.
Tarcliff, Oliver
Tarcliff, Mrs. Victor.
Temple, Horace.
Turgeon, T. D.
Uhrman, Martin.
Walch, James.
Wade, Thruston.
Weill, Gus.

VII.

Ohio.—Cincinnati.

Bleets, H. W.
Colored man.
Davis, Mrs.
Hackett, Harris.
Heines, Wm.
Iglauer, Mr.
Lewis, Rev.

Lewis, S. (servant).
Lewison, Mr.
Lock, Jasper.
Muller, Chris.
Offner, Blanche.
Roback, H.

Gallipolis.

Brown, Mrs.
Brothers, Clodius.
Buck, Wm.
Degelman, Chas.
Hall, Wm.

Knoedler, Wm.
Porter, Joseph.
Plymede, Hugh.
Unknown woman.
Walker, Wm.
Walker, Loring.
Walker, Alice.

VIII.

Missouri.—St. Louis.

Benner, H.
Brown, George.
Boehn, August.
Bunton, Wm.
Byrne, E. R
Colden, Henry.
Clark, Lee.
Decker, Eddie.

Daniels, T. O.
Effert, Jake.
Fortes, C. H.
Gilmore, C.
Hendricks, J. O.
Jennings, J.
Langley, S. J.
Lepere, Emma.

Malen, F.
Mahler, Louisa.
Morgan, Pat.
Nelson, C. H.
Nelson, W. O.
Payton, James.
Possati, Peter.

Pittman, Scott.
Parsons, C. M.
Runolds, M.
Stephani, G.
Vaggart, W.
Walker, W. J.
Woodward, A.

IX.

Other Points.

Philadelphia, Pa.
Tate, Mark.

Dalton, Ga.
Bohannon, Mrs.
Hogan, Mary.

Abingdon, Va.
Dickson, Judge L. V.

New York.
Lindley, Dr. N. A.

Reilley, Wm.
Sheetz, Wm.

Delaware Breakwater.
Barrett, A.

Warrington, Isaac H.
Seven sailors.

Fernandina, Fla.
One mate.
One seaman.

X.

Memphis Railroad Companies.

Memphis and Charleston R. R.
Allen, J. D.
Biggers, W. L.
Cloyd, T. S.
Clark, W. A.
Cain, J. E.
Carlson, Charley.
Coe, Lafayette.
Delaney, Wm.
Grady, Thos.
Grimes, Larry.
Gray, Walter.
Gamble, Frank.
Gregg, J. C.
Jackson, R. J.
Kelly, M.
Kallaher, M.
Moran, M.
McCorshin, Frank.
Merritt, G. R.
Mitchell, Moses.
Moss, David.
Moffatt, John.
Nicholls, Wm.
Otto, A. G.
Pearsall, A.
Paul, Major.
Roberts, John.
Smith, F. J.
Thompson, Jerry.

Thompson, Wm.
Wiley, W. H.
Williams, Wallace.
Wehle, Stephen.

Mississippi & Tennessee R. R.
Burk, A. A.
Brown, Thomas.
Berry, A.
Bolton, Thos. C.
Eason, John P.
Kendall, Peter.
Kirby, William.
Kirby, Mrs. Wm.
Lewis, George E.
Hallows, Joseph.
Hallows, Miss.
McNamara, John.
McNamara, Mrs. John.
Moore, G. W.
McCormick, M.
Mister, Thomas.
McManus, Samuel.
North, Nelson.
O'Neal, James.
O'Neal, Maurice.
Petty, Joe.
Ratcliff, S.
Ryan, Dennis.
Ryan, Miss Mary,

Reding, W. M.
Rousseau, Monroe.
Shinkle, Robert.
Wood, J. K.
Wood, Mrs. J. K.

Louisville & Nashville R. R.
Arnold, T. J.
Anderson, F.
Brew, Mike.
Burrell, Ed.
Becler, J. H.
Bugg, Phil.
Bronson, Charles.
Bons, W. G. N.
Cully, R. R.
Crawford, N.
Curtis, C.
Carroll, Ed.
Chester, Price.
Connelly, J. B. W.
Coleman, S.
Daley, Patsey.
Ernest, G. W.
Ernest, Mrs. G. W.
Featherstone, W. T.
Finch, J. W.
Griffin, D. T.
Goodwin, E. B.
Garrett, Kenneth, Jr.

Harris, Jordan.
Hannon, James.
Johns, Conrad.
Kendall, Alfred.
Kayhn, John.
Kanovan, M.
Lindenwood, F.
Lane, H. B.
Lawton, Eugene.
McClanahan, Thos.
McCormick, Isaac.
Matthews, A. J.
Murray, Ed.
Noble, Robert.
Nicholson, J. G.
Owen, H.
Pickle, V.
Pope, Emmet.
Pedro, Joe.
Rummagio, John
Riley, Mike.
Ritter, L. F.
Rosen, F. J.
Stewart, P. B.
Schuler, Martin.
Steel, W. H.
Smith, Ed.
Sheetz, H. C.
Samuels, H. B.
Teague, W. H.
Williams, E.
Winn, Charles.

XI.

Telegraph Operators who Died in Memphis.

Allen, J. H.
Connelly, John I.
Goewey, H. M.

Gibson, E. W.
Hood, Thos.
Henrickle, J. R.

Hawkins, A. S.
Keyes, M. J.
Langford, C. R.

Mynatt, W. H.
McDonald, J. W.
Walsh, Daniel.

QUARANTINE AND SANITATION.

QUARANTINE AND SANITATION.

I.

QUARANTINE, from the Italian word *quarantina* (a space of forty days), a police regulation for the exclusion of contagious diseases from a city, state, or nation. This regulation prescribes the interdiction of communication with individuals, ships, steam-ships, steam-boats, railroad cars, and by cargoes of goods supposed or suspected of being tainted by certain diseases—such as the cholera, black plague, or yellow fever—prevailing at the place where such passengers, vessels, or vehicles for intercommunication hail from at their time of sailing or departure. All the civilized nations of the world have and enforce such regulations. The United States as well as the several States, and nearly all the cities in the Union of more than 20,000 people, and many of the smaller towns, have adopted, and, when necessary, enforce quarantine.* In Europe an international code, adopted in 1874, has taken the place of the barbarous system which grew out of the Mosaic law, set forth at length in the Book of Leviticus, from the eleventh to the fifteenth chapters inclusive. Moses therein prescribes the most stringent precautionary measures to prevent the spread of disease. Leprosy is described in its various stages, and the leper is ordered to be set apart from the people without the camp for a certain number of days. The treatment for his

---

* In 1878 the cities and towns of Mississippi, Texas, Arkansas, and Tennessee, situated on rivers and railroads, enforced quarantine by companies of hastily improvised police armed with double-barreled shot-guns; and Dowler, writing in 1853, says that in that year, "as yellow fever appeared in New Orleans at an unusually early period of the season, and long before its invasion of other towns in the southern slope of the Mississippi Valley, the town authorities, in many cases, imposed quarantine laws for their own protection early in August, as Natchez, Baton Rouge, etc. No exemption, great mortality, neglect of the sick, and other evils followed, some of which grew directly out of quarantine itself, and were by no means creditable to humanity. While experience shows that quarantine does not prevent yellow fever, it does prevent free intercourse with the sick, nursing attendance, and the physical comforts, by which alone the disease can be combated with the greatest success. Fortunately, however, humanity is usually stronger than quarantine, in practice. Non-intercourse, seclusion, and abandonment, which quarantine directs, or necessity implies, are too revolting to common sense to be practiced toward friends, neighbors, and relatives; and, consequently, in yellow fever, these not being carried out in practice, quarantine will always be violated, until morality and charity be extinguished." And yet some happy results may be cited for these restrictive measures. Several towns in Mississippi, Tennessee, and Arkansas owe their exemption from the yellow fever in 1878 to their shot-gun quarantines, and, so far, the spread of the plague in Russia this year has been prevented by military cordons such as in 1831-2 prevented the spread of the cholera in the same country and in Palestine and Arabia.

recovery is given, and instructions how he is to purify himself; and even after purification, and when he has been allowed to return to the camp, how long he is to remain apart from the people. He also gives instructions as to the cleansing of the leper's clothes, and, finally, as to the burning of them ; and also the burning of his house where the case is of a malignant type. In modern times we first hear of quarantine in connection with the Eastern Empire, for its protection from the plague; and in Venice, where, in 1127, it was enforced against merchants and others arriving from the Levant, where leprosy and the plague then prevailed. A house for persons thus detained was established on a small island some distance from the city where they were held as in a prison for the full term of forty days. This was known as the House of St. Lazarus—hence the term *lazaretto*, which was afterward given to all the quarantine houses of refuge in Europe, some of which, almost as forbidding as the black-hole of Calcutta, were continued to our own time. The regulations thus established, which also required the production of bills of health, clean or foul as the case might be, remained in force for many years,—Florence and a few of the cities of England copying them as early as 1348. But it was not until the code of Viscount Bernabo was promulgated and enforced on the 17th of January, 1374, that quarantine was permanently established. This was based, as will be seen, upon the law of Moses. He ordered that every plague patient should be taken out of the city into the fields, there to die or recover. The persons who attended upon a plague patient were required to remain apart for ten days before they again associated with any one. The priests were directed to examine the diseased, and point out to special commissioners the persons infected, under penalty of being burned alive. The goods of any one importing the plague were confiscated. Finally, none except those appointed for the purpose were to attend upon a person affected with the plague, on penalty of death and confiscation of goods. In 1388 he forbade the admission of people from infected places into the Venetian dominions, on pain of death. These rigorous and severe rules were copied by all the commercial cities of the Mediterranean, and the consequence was that for a time they were closed to navigators. In 1448, the Venetian Senate enacted quarantine laws which required all ships and individuals arriving from places suspected of being infected with contagious diseases to undergo a term of probation before entering port and discharging cargo. In 1453 the first *lazaretto*, or pest-house, was permanently organized on the island of Sardinia. Another, erected in 1468, was called the new *lazaretto*, and was the place whence those who were cured of the plague were sent to spend the prescribed probation of forty days. A board or council of health was about this time established, which, in 1504, was invested with the powers of life and death. In 1603 the municipal ordinances enforcing quarantine which, up to that time, had prevailed in England, gave way to a specific code adopted by the privy council of James I., on the 30th of July of that year. This code required persons living in infected houses, whether in town or country, to be shut up for six weeks under penalty of being "punished as vagabonds by whipping," and provided that "any person going abroad with the disease upon him shall be deemed guilty of felony."* In 1636, bills of health were first made obligatory in England. They have been enforced in Italy ever since 1527. They were then, as they are now, passports for vessels given by the magistrate of the port from which a vessel sails, or by the consul or commercial agent residing there who represents the nation whose flag a vessel sails under. They were distinguished as clean or foul, according to the condition of the place where they were given.

---

* This brutal code was supplemented and made more cruel in 1665, when the plague having continued to recur, houses were required to be closed an additional month after all the family were dead or recovered; and a guard was placed in front day and night to keep out visitors, and a large red cross, with the words, "Lord have mercy upon us!" painted on the door. Defoe, in his history of the plague in London, in 1665, shows that the horrors of quarantine were worse than the plague itself. "A whole family was shut up and locked in because the maid-servant was taken sick; these people obtained no liberty to stir, neither for aid nor exercise for forty days; want of air, fear, anger, vexation, and all the other griefs attending such an injurious treatment cast the mistress of the family into a fever, and visitors came into the house and said it was plague, though the physician said it was not. However, the family were obliged to begin their quarantine anew, on the report of the visitor or examiner, though their former quarantine wanted but a few days of being finished. This oppressed them so with anger and grief and, as before, straitened them also so much as to room and for want of free air, that most of the family fell sick—one of one distemper, one of another, chiefly scorbutic ailments—one of a violent colic—until, after several prolongations of their confinement, some or other of those that came in with the visitors to inspect the persons that were ill, in hopes of releasing them, brought the distemper along with them, and infected the whole house; and all or most of them died, not of the plague as really upon them before, but of the plague that those people brought them who should have been careful to have protected them from it. And this was a thing which frequently happened, and was indeed one of the worst consequences of shutting up houses. Watchmen were stationed at the doors of the sick to prevent escape, and the passer-by shuddered when he looked up and saw the fatal mark of isolation on the door." "This merciless imprisonment," says Dr. A. N. Bell, the sanitarian, "was pursued with a heartless obduracy, engendered by the belief that it was the only means of averting death to those who inflicted it." Defoe also records the noble deeds of some of the health officers, and some country people who constantly sought out the suffering, and procured and carried them food; and such persons "very seldom got any harm from it," and were therefore deemed to have been miraculously preserved, while hundreds and thousands of those who fled died in their flight. "They had the taint of the disease in their vitals, and after their spirits were so diseased they could never escape it." Thus prevailed the quarantine epidemic of Viscount Bernabo, with its attendant symptoms of terror, starvation, and suicidal mania, "until," in the words of Defoe, "it was impossible to beat any thing into their heads; they gave way to the impetuosity of their temper, full of outcries and lamentations when taken sick; and madly careless of themselves, foolhardy and obstinate while they were well." France, Holland, Spain, Portugal, indeed all the commercial States and seaports of Europe, followed the example of Venice; and plague reigned. Quarantines, which took no cognizance of municipal or domestic filth were not only powerless, but were promotive of the diseases against which they were enforced. Insomuch that at the beginning of the eighteenth century M. Aubert Roche estimated that for the three centuries next preceding the general establishment of lazarettos, there were 105 epidemics; for the three centuries next after, 143. The more effectual suppression of the plague since the beginning of the eighteenth century he rightly attributed to the general progress of civilization under the auspices of public hygiene.

A foul bill is delivered in a port where cholera, the black plague, or yellow fever exist; a clean bill where none of these exist. At first forty days was exactingly enforced, but now the extent of the probation is determined by the health bill, at the option of the quarantine authorities. In 1700, after the yellow fever visitation of 1699, in Philadelphia, the General Assembly of the colony of Pennsylvania, enacted the first quarantine law in this country, imposing a fine of one hundred pounds upon every unhealthy vessel that landed. In 1701, a health law providing for quarantine was enacted in Massachusetts. In 1710, the English Parliament passed an act establishing quarantine throughout the kingdom, in preparation for the plague which then prevailed along the shores of the Baltic. In a few years after, another act was passed "to enable His Majesty more effectually to prohibit commerce, for the space of one year, with any country that is or shall be infected with the plague." In France no regular system was instituted until after the great plague in Marseilles, in 1720-21. A general system was then adopted, and made applicable to all the French ports on the Mediterranean for the exclusion and sequestration of all vessels and persons from infected places, and where plague prevailed of all infected houses and their occupants, under extremely rigid restrictions and heavy penalties.* In 1720, while plague was prevailing at Marseilles, the celebrated Dr. Richard Mead was requested by the English government to furnish necessary regulations for the occasion. He advised a continuance of the forty days' lazaretto system of Bernabo, the separation of the sick from the well, and the sinking of infected goods and vessels in the sea. In 1721, it was further enacted by Parliament that infected persons escaping from quarantine, and well persons not liable to quarantine, but who, having entered, escaped therefrom, should suffer death.† The inhumanity of these acts soon

---

* "But," as Dr. A. N. Bell, in his article on quarantine, says, "on a return of the disease to Marseilles some time after, the restrictions having proven to be exceedingly vexatious, the Chamber of Commerce opposed their further execution as being unnecessarily oppressive, without any corresponding benefit, and prejudicial to the commercial world. This opposition of the merchants was soon after followed by special administration under officers known as Intendents of Health, who, after certain sanitary precautions, admitted vessels to *pratique* from infected places. The independence of Marseilles and Toulon of the general ordinances was, at the first, severely criticised by the other ports, and much discontent created. Marseilles especially was accused of inviting plague. But her independent sanitary administration gained ground. By a succession of royal edicts she was sustained in her efforts to render quarantine less oppressive to commerce, and confirmed in her independence."

† An evidence of the extremes to which quarantinists, in modern times, are forced to go to maintain their theory is furnished by the late Dr. Townsend, who was a consistent, honest, and able quarantinist, and who says, in his book on the yellow fever in New York, as it appeared in 1822, that all intercourse with the West Indies (and why not with New Orleans ?) should be prohibited for five months in every year, beginning with June, in order to prevent the importation of yellow fever. He says, that "unless an unbroken line of lazarettos be established along the whole coast, to guard against the pestilence, we can not ever hope to be entirely secure. What will avail the most efficient system of quarantine laws, established here and there in a few cities on the coast, if all the intermediate towns, with which a constant intercourse is going on, freely admit vessels? etc."

after caused their repeal. But in 1728 another was passed, limited to three years, declaring any person escaping or violating quarantine guilty of felony, and forfeiting ship and goods. This act was revived, and, with but slight modification, kept in force until 1753, when the system was improved by adding floating lazarettos, for the purpose of unloading and aerating merchandise, at a distance from the shore in Standish Creek, instead of requiring an almost interminable detention of vessels off the Scilly Islands, as previously practiced. The first port physician in what is now the United States was appointed by the council of Philadelphia, in 1720. The first actual enforcement of quarantine laws in the American colonies took place at Philadelphia, in 1728, from which time on the various ports in the other colonies gradually adopted the same system with various degrees of severity, and captains and owners were forced to observe them from fear of heavy penalties. In 1738, pilots were ordered not to bring a vessel with passengers nearer the city than one mile, until she had been boarded and examined by a physician appointed for that purpose. In 1743, a regular quarantine establishment was built on Fisher's (now State) Island, at the junction of the Delaware and Schuylkill rivers. In 1758, New York enacted her first quarantine laws. In 1776, Pennsylvania fixed a penalty of one hundred pounds for bringing a passenger vessel, or one from a sickly port, nearer to Philadelphia than Mud Island, or Fort Mifflin, without a permit from a health officer. A fine of one hundred pounds was also exacted for concealing a sick passenger. In 1780, in England, the number of quarantine stations was increased to thirteen; seven in England, four in Scotland, and two in Jersey and Guernsey. These regulations remained unchanged until a comparatively recent period. The Congress of the United States passed an act in 1799, "respecting quarantine and health laws," which still stands upon the statute books. In 1817, New Orleans first enforced quarantine. In 1818 the law was repealed, but was re-enacted in 1819. In 1821,* it was strengthened

* Dowler, in the fourth, twelfth, and fourteenth chapters of his pamphlet, treating of the yellow fever as to the quarantine established and enforced in New Orleans in 1821, says: "The quarantine laws passed by the Legislature in February, 1821, creating a Board of Health, with the most plenary powers, legislative, judicial, executive, pecuniary, and sanitary, modeled after codes the most rigid, and enforced by the heaviest penalties, were carried into effect in March of the same year. The quarantine ground established at the English Turn, including incidental expenses, cost over twenty-two thousand dollars. The year proved salubrious—a result attributed to the strict quarantine. The Governor, in January, 1822, congratulated the Legislature upon the good fortune of New Orleans, as being 'the healthiest city' in the Union. But, at the close of August, the yellow fever appeared; it augmented throughout September, but did not reach its culminating point until October—the month of greatest mortality—having amounted to 665, exceeding the preceding month by eighty-three. Governor Robertson's next message breathed sorrow and despair. "It is," says he, "an idle waste of time for me to inquire into the causes, origin, and nature of this dreadful malady. . . . The State resorted to quarantine, under the expectation that it would add to the chances of escape from this dreadful visitation. If this hope be fallacious, if no good effect has been produced, if even a procrastination of its appearance has not resulted from this measure, then should it be abandoned, and our commerce be relieved from the expense and inconvenience which it occasions." The Legislature declared that the city was perfectly healthy until the month of September,

and was continued five years, during which two epidemics occurred; and in other years it prevailed in sporadic forms. In 1825 quarantine was abandoned and the Board of Health said until the close of August, when the Lynch family, having arrived from Pensacola, communicated the disease to the inhabitants of Bienville Street, and thence to the inhabitants of the whole city. This same Board of Health, the previous year, in an official manifesto, dated September 4th, gave a very different account of the origin of this epidemic, charging the disease to the sun, the weather, and fatigue, and never so much as hinting that the poor Lynches had introduced contagion into the city, which latter, saving five yellow fever deaths, " never was more healthy." The Board testified to the " strictness of the measures " (quarantine then existing) to check its progress. "This document," says the inexorable Dowler, " is a melancholy proof of the inconsistent and contradictory opinions and actions of men unwilling to relinquish power, who resort to the sun, etc., to account for the origin of the fever ; then fly to contagion ; now misleading the public, by stating that there are but five cases having the usual symptoms, and then saying that their strict measures will check its progress, thereby jeopardizing the lives of a whole city, upon the supposition of the contagiousness of the disease. What can be more criminal in a Board of Health, whether its members believe in the contagious or local origin of the yellow fever, than the suppression of truth, except it be the promulgation of falsehood ? Seclusion in the one case, if contagion be true, and flight in the other, if the fever be of local origin, might have saved hundreds of lives, if adopted early enough." The late Dr. Townsend, of New York, a consistent contagionist, in a work on yellow fever, published in 1823, avers that facts known in that city " show that the disease actually prevailed in New Orleans at least a month anterior to this meeting of the Board of Health." He says, "that from information derived from various sources, which may be fully relied on, yellow fever broke out in New Orleans as early as the beginning of or middle of July." " While the facts, arguments, and quarantine operations were still fresh," says Dowler again, " the public felt convinced of the evil of this system of yellow fever prevention, and determined to petition the Legislature to abolish the quarantine laws. Accordingly, on the 23d of January, 1823, a large public meeting took place, in which it was moved and carried, ' that the late epidemic had tested the total inefficiency of the quarantine laws and regulations; we consider them not only useless, but in the highest degree oppressive and injurious to the commerce of this city, and that application ought to be made to the Legislature for the purpose of having them annulled.' A memorial was addressed to the Legislature accordingly for that purpose. The quarantine had been tried for three years, and yet two epidemics had occurred. The contagionists began to waver, and the joint committee of both houses of the Legislature, disagreeing on quarantine, were discharged from the consideration of the same on the last day of November, 1824. Experience, which is ever opposed to false theory, convinced the public that quarantine was not only useless, but supremely mischievous, in a city so exclusively commercial, that a free, untrammeled trade, with freedom of ingress, egress, and progress is not only simply useful, but a social necessity, involving the question of subsistence or starvation. Accordingly, on the 19th of February, 1825, the Legislature repealed the quarantine laws which it had enacted just four years previously; at the same time the quarantine grounds were ordered to be sold. During the eight years that followed, without quarantine, the yellow fever diminished. It never equaled that which took place under the strict quarantine of 1822, when, according to some authorities, 2,000 died of that malady, although the records, which I have examined, show only 808, a number sufficiently appalling in the comparatively small population then resident in the city, especially during the hot season; the whole reported mortality for the three months, ending with October, being 1,362. The ratio of mortality in the Charity Hospital was enormous—out of 349 admissions, 239 deaths, and only ninety-eight cures took place. The maximum mortality upon one day rose to 80—of yellow fever to 60."

not resumed until 1855, since which time four epidemics have occurred, and it has appeared sporadically every year up to 1872, and since then, epidemically. The triumphant march of cholera in Europe and this country, in 1831-2, when it passed through the most crucial tests of quarantine, first induced a change in the enactments above recited. Confidence in quarantine was every-where shaken. It was found to be no barrier to the spread of the plague to cities whose unsanitary condition invited it, and that it hampered, hindered, and prevented commerce, without affording the equivalent of safety. It was, therefore, resolved by many French scientists to try and effect a change or modification of the quarantine enactments that would relieve commerce and yet afford the surveillance necessary to adequate protection. A report upon quarantines, from the Academy of Medicine, of Paris, concurred in the propriety of a complete reform; and, on August 18, 1847, a royal ordinance of France declared the first recognition of truths based upon the opinions of medical men, that many of the restrictions of quarantine were unnecessarily burdensome, and therefore abolished. Still other reforms were decreed in France, in 1849-50. But the eminent sanitarians of France were not satisfied by the reforms accomplished in their own country. This was only the beginning of the work they had in view. They proposed to show that it was in accordance with science, and for the interests of the commerce of all other nations, to accept the reforms which they had effected in France. Accordingly, Dupeyron suggested to the ministers of commerce the idea of a Sanitary Congress,* which was adopted, and delegates to it from all the principal countries of Europe, by invitation of the French government, met in Paris, in 1851. This congress adopted a quarantine code, which was afterward ratified by the nations represented. In 1865, on the approach of the cholera, the French government called an international sanitary conference, to meet at Constantinople, where a further modification of the quarantine restrictions was had. The yellow fever having prevailed epidemically in 1855, in Norfolk, Virginia, and in 1856, in Bay Ridge and at Fort Hamilton, New York, in spite of the most stringent

---

* The sanitary reform, which began in England about the same time, under the provisions of the new poor-law, attacked no less vigorously the ancient fallacies of quarantine in that country. The General Board of Health, instituted by act of Parliament, in 1848, persisted in repeated efforts against the quarantine regulations for plague, yellow fever, and cholera; protesting that protection from pestilential diseases does not consist in quarantine regulations alone, but more in internal sanitary measures—measures which have for their object the suppression and prevention of conditions without which the diseases regarded as quarantinable would not exist. The measures proposed by the General Board of Health were the destruction of all the sources of infection in town and country; sanitary improvement of habitations; a full supply of wholesome food and wholesome water, extending to the persons and materials employed in commerce; and, finally, if in spite of these precautions, pestilence manifests itself in any place, abandonment of the locality, until the cause of the pestilence is found out and eradicated. In its enthusiastic war on the local causes of diseases, it includes among them quarantines, and by resolution declared, in their report of 1849, "that quarantine, instead of guarding against and preventing disease, fosters and concentrates it, and places it under conditions the most favorable that can be desired for its general extension."

quarantine restrictions, and as many, with good reason believed, in consequence of them, Dr. A. N. Bell, in Hunt's *Merchants' Magazine*, advocated free pratique to all well persons, under whatever circumstances, and asserted that "things and not persons cause and propagate disease."* Dr. Wilson Jewell, of the Philadelphia Board of Health, in November, 1856, secured the passage of a resolution by that body, providing for a quarantine and sanitary convention—the first ever held in America. It met on the 13th of May, 1857, was in session three days, nine States being represented. It adopted resolutions favoring quarantine of persons sick of small-pox, and, under certain circumstances, typhus fever, cholera, and yellow fever; and of infected vessels and cargoes. At the second annual meeting of the convention, in Baltimore, in April, 1858, committees were appointed on external hygiene, or quarantine, and internal hygiene, or the sanitary arrangements of cities. These reported at the third annual meeting, held in New York, in April, 1859. The subject most discussed at this meeting was the contagious or non-contagious nature of yellow fever. This followed upon the introduction, by Dr. W. H. Stevens, of a resolution declaring "that in the absence of any evidence establishing the conclusion that yellow fever has ever been conveyed by one person to another, it is the opinion of this convention that personal quarantine of cases of yellow fever may be safely abolished." This was adopted by a vote of eighty-five to six.

"In the summer of 1858," says Dr. A. N. Bell, "there being a fleet of vessels detained in New York quarantine, and a number of cases of yellow fever in the hospitals, excitement ran so high that, on the night of September 1st, a mob, estimated at a thousand strong, removed the sick from the hospitals and burned the buildings. Subsequent to this act, and until the law of 1863 was carried into effect, the quarantine in New York was extemporized. In 1862 the writer was physician-in-chief of the floating hospital in the lower bay, for the special care of yellow fever. On the conclusion of that service, in his report to the Commissioners of Quarantine, he especially recommended the shoals of West Bank in the lower bay as the most suitable place for rebuilding the establishment. Shortly thereafter, at the instance of Hon. H. C. Murphy, of the State Senate, he drew the law known as the law of 1863 (which is still in force), deducing its main provisions from the report submitted at the Fourth Annual Quarantine Convention, and designated West Bank as the situation for the structures." Many members of the Legislature, however,

---

* So it proved in the great epidemic at Norfolk, Virginia, in 1858. A large number of refugees to Baltimore and Wilmington, N. C., sickened and died in those cities, but none of the inhabitants contracted the disease. Again, cases of yellow fever were introduced in New Orleans in 1870, '71, '72, '73, and '76, but no epidemic ensued. The conditions were not favorable to the propagation of the special cause. The epidemic in Shreveport, of 1873, was occasioned by persons going from New Orleans, who had been exposed to cases brought there on board the brig *Valparaiso*, and not less than 250 cases appeared in the vicinity of where the vessel was moored, but no epidemic took place. The atmosphere of New Orleans was not in the condition favorable to the propagation of the organisms to the extent of an epidemic; but that of Shreveport was pre-eminently so, the fever proving peculiarly fatal.

deeming the erection of suitable structures on West Bank impracticable, that clause was stricken out for the time, and the bill passed, excluding all other places. It took three years more, the arrival of cholera in 1865, and the effectual resistance of various devices and attempts to possess other localities, to convince those who conducted quarantine for the time, and the Legislature, of the propriety of reinstating the provision for West Bank. Dr. John Swinburne, health officer at that time, on careful investigation of the subject, secured the needful amendment of the law in 1866, which has resulted in the erection of the most effectual and the least oppressive quarantine establishment in the world.* In the same year of this enabling act for the completion of the New York quarantine, owing to the prevalence of cholera, a second European conference convened at Constantinople, and, in 1874, an International Sanitary Convention at Vienna. These were attended by representatives of the highest standing from the various governments of Europe, from Egypt, and Persia. The latter of these conventions, after a thorough review of the former, and an animated discussion of a programme comprehending twenty-six stated questions on the nature of cholera, adopted the following rules, as the sense of the conference:

1. Vessels from infected ports must undergo observations which, according

* Under and by virtue of this act, the quarantine establishment for the port of New York consists of warehouses, docks and wharves, anchorage for vessels, a floating hospital, boarding-station, burying-ground, and residences for officers and men. Merchants are afforded facilities for overhauling and refitting vessels while in quarantine. Connected with the warehouses are apartments with appliances for special disinfection by forced ventilation, refrigeration, high steam, dry heat, and chemical disinfection. The boarding-stations for suspected vessels, arriving between the 1st day of April and the 1st day of November, is in the lower bay, below the Narrows. Vessels are boarded as soon as practicable after their arrival—between sunrise and sunset. The anchorage for vessels under quarantine is in the lower bay, two miles from shore, and within an area designated by buoys. Quarantine applies against yellow fever, cholera, typhus or ship fever, and small-pox, and any new disease of a contagious, infectious, or pestilential nature. The floating hospital, with a capacity sufficient to accommodate 100 patients, is anchored in the lower bay from the 1st of May to the 1st of November; at other times it is anchored in some more secure place. The hospital at West Bank, when so required, is used exclusively for yellow fever and cholera patients. The buildings on Hoffman Island are used as a place of reception and temporary detention of persons who have been exposed to contagious or infectious diseases, but who are not actually sick. The health officer is the custodian of the quarantine establishment; his jurisdiction extends within the limits of the city and county of New York. In ascertaining the sanitary condition of a vessel, he is authorized to examine, under oath, the captain, crew, and passengers, and to inspect the bill of health, manifest, log-book, cargo, etc. Vessels liable to quarantine are required to discharge in quarantine, and be detained long enough thereafter for disinfection and aeration, such detention not to exceed ten days, unless the disease occurs or re-appears during that interval, in which event the time is extended ten days. But no vessel or cargo, which has been in quarantine, is allowed to proceed to New York or Brooklyn without the approval of the mayor or Board of Health of those cities respectively. Filthy or unhealthy vessels are subject to quarantine for purification, not exceeding ten days. On infected or suspected vessels, all clothing, personal baggage, cotton, hemp, rags, paper, hides, skins, feathers, hair, woolens, and other articles of animal origin,

to circumstances, may last from one to seven days. In the eastern parts of Europe and elsewhere, though only in certain exceptional cases, the surveillance may be prolonged to ten days.

2. When the Board of Health have sufficient proof that during the voyage no case of cholera, or of any other suspected disease, has occurred on board, the observation is to last three to seven days, reckoned from the medical inspection. If, under these circumstances, the voyage has lasted at least seven days, the surveillance is to be limited to twenty-four hours, to give time for the examination and disinfection considered as necessary. In cases under this category the observation may be held on board, as long as no case of cholera or suspicious circumstance occurs, and when the hygienic condition of the ship allows. In these cases the unloading of the ship for disinfection is not necessary.

3. When, during the passage, or after the ship's arrival, cases of cholera or other suspected diseases occur, the surveillance for those who are not ill is to last seven full days, beginning from their isolation in a hospital, or whatever place is assigned to them. The sick will be disembarked and properly attended to in a place separated from the persons under surveillance. The ship and all objects belonging to it are to undergo a thorough disinfection, after which persons obliged to remain on board will be subjected to surveillance for seven days.

4. Vessels from suspected ports—that is, such as lie near places or ports where cholera prevails, and are in intercourse with them—may be subjected to observation lasting, at most, five days, provided that no suspicious cases of disease have occurred on board.

5. The quarantine of emigrant and pilgrim ships, and, in general, all vessels whose condition is deemed especially dangerous to the public health, shall be carried out under particular regulations, which the Board of Health shall decide.

6. When the conditions of a place do not allow the presented regulations to

---

are subjected to an obligatory quarantine and purification. Molasses, sugar, and live and healthy cattle are subjected to quarantine at the option of the health officer. All other merchandise is exempted from quarantine and admitted without delay. The effects of persons who die in quarantine are taken in charge by the health officer, and if not claimed by the rightful heir in three months, are delivered to the public administrator of the city of New York. All persons who have died are interred, without delay, in the quarantine burying-ground, at Seguin's Point. A vessel has the right to put to sea before breaking bulk, in preference to going into quarantine; but the health officer in such case indorses on her bill of health the circumstances under which she leaves port, the length of her detention, and her actual condition, and sends to the quarantine hospital such sick as may desire to remain. All passengers on board of vessels under quarantine are provided for by the master of the vessel. Any person violating the quarantine regulations, or who shall oppose or obstruct the health officer, or any of his employés, in the performance of their duties, is guilty of misdemeanor, and punishable by a fine of not less than $100, or by imprisonment not less than three nor more than six months, or by both such fine and imprisonment. Any person aggrieved by any decision of the health officer may appeal therefrom to the commissioners of quarantine, who constitute a board of appeal.

be carried out, the inspected ship is to be dispatched to the nearest hospital, after it has received all the assistance that its condition may require.

7. Ships coming from infected ports, which have touched at a port en route, and have left it without undergoing quarantine, will be treated as ships coming from an infected harbor.

8. In cases of mere suspicion the sanitary board may order special disinfection regulations.

9. In ports where cholera is epidemic full quarantine is not to be kept, but means of disinfection are to be strictly applied.

In 1874, also, the minister of agriculture of France appointed a commission, to report upon the sanitary laws in force at the various ports and other maritime towns of France, and to suggest the changes which the development of international communications by the introduction of steam seemed to render necessary. The result of their labors, as decreed by the President of the Republic, was: For the future, cholera, yellow fever, and the plague will be the only foreign epidemics to guard against. A permanent embargo will be placed upon all vessels arriving from countries where they prevail. Typhus fever and small-pox will be made merely the object of exceptional precautions, and even in these cases the measures taken will apply solely to vessels upon which there is some sign of disease. Vessels which are entirely free from disease will be exempt from quarantine after inspection by the officers of health. . . . The presentation of a bill of health, upon arriving in a French port, will only be compulsory for vessels coming from the eastern shores of Turkey in Europe, from the Black Sea, and from all countries beyond Europe . . . The merchandise arriving by any vessels which can show that there have been no deaths or contagious diseases on board will be exempt from all detention, and be allowed on shore at once, with the exception of leather, hair, and other animal debris. The coast line has been divided into eleven circumscriptions, each to be provided with a sanitary officer, whose duty it will be to see that the regulations are carried out in his own district.

The United States laws on quarantine make those of each State supreme, and United States vessels, in common with all others, are obliged to submit, The national quarantine law which was enacted by Congress last year [1878] provides: That whenever any infectious or contagious disease shall appear in any foreign port or country, and whenever any vessel shall leave any infected foreign port, or having on board goods or passengers coming from any place or district infected with cholera or yellow fever, shall leave any foreign port, bound for any port in the United States, the consular officer, or other representative of the United States, at or near such port, shall immediately give information thereof to the supervising surgeon-general of the marine hospital service, and shall report to him the name, the date of departure, and the port of destination of such vessel; and shall also make the same report to the health officer of the port of destination in the United States; and the consular officers of the United States shall make weekly reports to him of the sanitary condition of the ports at which they are respectively stationed; and the said surgeon-general of the marine hospital service shall, under the direction of the secretary of the treasury, be charged with the execution of the provisions of this act, and shall frame all needful rules and regulations for that purpose, which rules and regulations shall be subject to the approval of the president; but such rules and regulations shall not conflict with or impair any sanitary or quarantine laws or regulations of any State or municipal authorities now existing, or which may hereafter be enacted. That it shall be the duty of the medical officers of the marine hospital service, and of custom officers, to aid in the enforcement of the national quarantine rules and regulations established under the preceding section; but no additional compensation shall be allowed said officers by reason of such services as they may be required to perform under this act, except actual and necessary traveling expenses. That the surgeon-general of the marine hospital service shall, upon receipt of information of the departure of any vessel, goods, or passengers from infected places to any port in the United States, immediately notify the proper State or municipal and United States officer or officers at the threatened port of destination of the vessel, and shall prepare and transmit to the medical officers of the marine hospital service, to collectors of customs, and to the State and municipal health authorities in the United States, weekly abstracts of the consular sanitary reports and other pertinent information received by him. That wherever, at any port of the United States, any State or municipal quarantine system may now or may hereafter exist, the officers or agents of such system shall, upon the application of the respective State or municipal authorities, be authorized and empowered to act as officers of the national quarantine system, and shall be clothed with all the powers of the United States officers for quarantine purposes, but shall receive no pay or emoluments from the United States. At all other ports where, in the opinion of the secretary of the treasury, it shall be deemed necessary to establish quarantine, the medical officers or other agents of the marine hospital service shall perform such duties in the enforcement of the quarantine rules and regulations as may be assigned them by the surgeon-general of that service, under this act: *Provided*, that there shall be no interference in any manner with any quarantine laws or regulations as they now exist, or may hereafter be adopted, under State laws.

The legislature of Tennessee, at the session which closed on the 1st of April, 1879, adopted amendments to the act of the preceding legislature, providing for a State Board of Health, as follows :

1. That the State Board of Health be, and they are hereby, empowered to declare quarantine, whenever in their judgment the welfare of the public require it, and to prescribe such rules and regulations as they may deem proper for the prevention of the introduction of yellow fever, cholera, and other epidemic diseases into the State of Tennessee; and whenever the yellow fever, cholera, small-pox, or other epidemic diseases appear in any locality within the State, and information thereof is brought to the knowledge of said State Board of Health, they shall prepare and carry into effect such rules and regulations as in their judgment will, with the least inconvenience to commercial travel, prevent the spread of the disease; they shall select suitable localities for establishing quarantine stations, and may erect necessary temporary build-

A HISTORY OF THE YELLOW FEVER. 281

ings for the disinfection of passengers, baggage, cargoes, and other matters believed to convey the contagious principle of yellow fever, cholera, small-pox, and other epidemic diseases, and may enforce such transhipment of passengers as they may deem necessary, and shall assign to the charge of each station a competent physician and necessary assistants, who shall receive such compensation as the said Board of Health may deem reasonable and just; and the members of said board shall be allowed a per diem compensation of not more than ten dollars, with traveling and other necessary expenses, for each and every day while actively employed in the business of said board.

2. That any person or persons who shall willfully disregard or evade such quarantine as said Board of Health may declare, or violate any rule or regulation they shall make in attempting to prevent the spread of any epidemic disease, shall be guilty of a misdemeanor, and, upon conviction, shall be fined not less than fifty dollars nor more than five hundred, or imprisoned in the county jail for a period of three months, or both, at the discretion of the court.

3. That for the purpose of enabling the State Board of Health to accomplish the end for which it was created, the sum of three thousand dollars per annum is hereby appropriated, which amount the comptroller of the treasury is hereby directed to issue his warrant for, or any part thereof, first having the sum duly certified by said board.

4. That the governor shall have power, and it is hereby made his duty, to appoint two additional members of said board connected with the commerce and transportation of the country.

In addition to the above enactment, Memphis, under the act repealing her city charter and creating the Taxing-district government, will also enjoy all the benefits likely to flow from the enforcement of an ordinance providing for a local Board of Health, and declaring the law of quarantine. This ordinance, which is almost identical with that in force in New York city, confers upon the health officer almost absolute powers. It is made his duty to "carry out all the orders of the Board of Health and the laws of the State and ordinances of the district in relation to the sanitary regulations of the district; to proceed, from time to time, to make a thorough and systematic examination of the district, and cause all nuisances to be abated with all reasonable promptness. And for the purpose of carrying out the foregoing requirements, he shall be permitted, at all times, from the rising to the setting of the sun, to enter into any house, store, stable, or other building, and to cause the floors to be raised, if he shall deem necessary, in order to a thorough examination of cellars, vaults, sinks, or drains; to enter upon all lots or grounds, and to cause all stagnant waters to be drained off, the pools, sinks, vaults, drains, or low grounds to be cleansed, filled up, or otherwise improved or amended; to cause all privies to be cleansed and kept in good condition, and to cause all dead animals or other nauseous or unwholesome things or substances to be buried or removed beyond the limits of the district." It is also made his duty "to visit and examine all sick persons who shall be reported to him as laboring, or supposed to be laboring, under any yellow or ship fever, small-pox, cholera, or any infectious or pestilential disease, and, under the advice of the president of the Board of Health, cause all such infected persons to be removed to the cholera, small-pox, or other hospitals, or such other safe and proper place as he may think proper, or as shall be directed by the said president, not exceeding four miles from said district, and cause them to be provided with suitable nurses and medical attendance, at their own expense, if they are able to pay for the same, but, if not, then at the expense of the county, as provided in sections 1729 and 1730 of the Code of Tennessee." This act also declares that no other officer or board within the said district, except the Board of Health and its proper officers, shall sign, grant, or deliver any certificate or bill of health. It also confers upon the Board of Health a direct oversight over medicines or poisons, construction of buildings, ventilation; over boarding-houses, public halls, assembly rooms, theaters, jails or prisons, water-closets, sinks, privies, vaults, cisterns, and wells; also over sidewalks, streets and gutters, sewers, drains and pipes, plumbing, food, unwholesome fruits or vegetables, milk, cheese and butter, hydrants and the water supply, cattle and horses, slaughtering and slaughter-houses; also over dogs, pounds, stables, offensive odors, places, and liquids, and over public vehicles and street-cars—every thing, in fact, that can nearly or remotely affect the public health. This ordinance, so all-embracing, can be enforced by penalties, the penal clause providing, "that every person who knowingly omits or refuses to comply with, or who resists or willfully violates any of the provisions of this ordinance, or any of the rules, orders, sanitary regulations, or ordinances established or declared by the Board of Health in carrying out the provisions of this ordinance, or the execution of any order or special regulation of the Board of Health, made for that purpose, is hereby declared to be guilty of a misdemeanor, and, on arrest and conviction before the president of the Board of Fire and Police Commissioners, he shall be fined for each offense in any sum not less than one nor more than fifty dollars, to be collected as other fines are collected." In addition to this, by Article V of the ordinances it is made a nuisance—

1. To do, or cause to be done, any of the following acts, and any person convicted thereof shall be fined not less than five nor more than fifty dollars:

2. To build, construct, or keep a slaughter-pen or house within the taxing-district, or within one-half mile thereof.

3. To construct a vault or privy less than fifteen feet deep, or less than four feet distant from the line of any street or public place, or from the property of others, without the consent of the owner.

4. To have a vault or privy on the land owned or occupied by one's self, the contents of which escape therefrom or overflow.

5. To cause, create, or permit within the taxing-district, or within one mile thereof, any nuisance on one's premises; and each day such nuisance is permitted to remain shall constitute a separate offense.

6. To throw or put into any street or public place any dead animal, or fail to remove and bury without the taxing-district limits the carcass of any dead animal owned by him, her, or them.

7. To throw into the street or other public place any filth or noxious sub-

stance, or to permit the same to flow from one's premises into any street or public place, or on the property of others.

8. To haul dirt through the streets in carts without sufficient tail-boards to prevent it from falling out upon the streets.

9. To throw any water or other substance from the windows of any house into the streets or public places, or on the premises of others.

10. To keep any horses, mules, oxen, or cows within the taxing-district, and fail to remove without the taxing-district, at least twice a week, all dung, filth, and litter.

The Forty-Fifth Congress, which adjourned *sine die*, on the 4th of March of this year (1879), passed an act creating a National Board of Health, which provides:

1. That there shall be established a National Board of Health, to consist of seven members, to be appointed by the President, by and with the advice and consent of the Senate, not more than one of whom shall be appointed from any one State, whose compensation, during the time when actually engaged in the performance of their duties under this act, shall be ten dollars per diem each, and reasonable expenses, and of one medical officer of the Army, one medical officer of the Navy, one medical officer of the Marine Hospital Service, and one officer from the department of justice, to be detailed by the secretaries of the several departments and the attorney-general, respectively, and the officers so detailed shall receive no compensation. Said board shall meet in Washington within thirty days after the passage of this act, and in Washington or elsewhere from time to time, upon notice from the president of the board, who is to be chosen by the members thereof, or upon its own adjournments, and shall frame all rules and regulations authorized or required by this act, and shall make, or cause to be made, such special examinations and investigations at any place or places within the United States or at foreign ports, as they may deem best, to aid in the execution of this act and the promotion of its objects.

2. The duties of the National Board of Health shall be to obtain information upon all matters affecting the public health, to advise the several departments of the government, the executives of the several States, and the Commissioners of the District of Columbia, on all questions submitted by them, or whenever, in the opinion of the board, such advice may tend to the preservation and improvement of the public health.

3. That the Board of Health, with the assistance of the Academy of Science, which is hereby requested and directed to co-operate with them for that purpose, shall report to Congress, at its next session, a full statement of its transactions, together with a plan for a national public health organization, which plan shall be prepared after consultation with the principal sanitary organizations and the sanitarians of the several states of the United States, special attention being given to the subject of quarantine, both maritime and inland, and especially as to regulations which should be established between State or local systems of quarantine and a national quarantine system.

4. The sum of fifty thousand dollars, or so much thereof as may be neces-

sary, is hereby appropriated to pay the salaries and expenses of said board to carry out the purposes of this act.

Congress has now (May, 1879) under consideration, at the called session of the Forty-Sixth Congress, a bill introduced by Hon. Casey Young, of the Tenth District of Tennessee, and which, by the efforts of Senator Harris, of Tennessee, passed the Senate before the close of the second session of the Forty-Fifth Congress. It is entitled an act "to prevent the introduction of infectious or contagious diseases into the United States, and to establish a Board of Health." It provides:

1. That it shall be unlawful for any vessel engaged in the transportation of goods or persons from any foreign port to and into the United States, to enter any port of the United States, except in accordance with the provisions of this act, and all rules and regulations made in pursuance thereof; and any such vessel which shall enter, or attempt to enter, a port of the United States in violation thereof, shall forfeit to the United States a sum, to be awarded in the discretion of the court, not exceeding five thousand dollars, which shall be a lien upon said vessel, to be recovered by proceedings in admiralty in the proper district court of the United States.

2. That all such vessels shall be required to obtain from the consul, vice-consul, or other consular officer of the United States at the port of departure, or from the medical officer, where such officer has been detailed by the President for that purpose, a certificate, in duplicate, setting forth the sanitary history of said vessel, and that it has in all respects complied with the rules and regulations in such cases prescribed, and herein authorized, for securing the best possible sanitary condition of the said vessel, its cargo, passengers, and crew; and said consular officer is required, before granting such certificate, to be satisfied that the matters and things therein stated are true; and for his services in that behalf shall be entitled to demand and receive such fees as shall by lawful regulation be allowed, to be accounted for as is required in other cases. That upon the request of the National Board of Health, the President is authorized to detail a medical officer to serve in the office of the consul at a foreign port for the purpose of making the inspection and giving the certificates hereinbefore mentioned: *Provided*, That the number of officers so detailed shall not exceed, at any one time, six: *Provided further*, That any vessel sailing from any such port without such certificate of said medical officer, entering any port of the United States, shall forfeit to the United States the sum of five hundred dollars, which shall be a lien on the same, to be recovered by proceedings in admiralty in the proper district court of the United States.

3. That the National Board of Health shall make all needful rules and regulations authorized by the laws of the United States for the prevention of the introduction and spread within the United States of contagious or infectious diseases, which shall be uniform and subject to approval by the President, and shall be charged with the execution of the same, and of the provisions of this act and all other laws of the United States for the prevention of the introduction and spread of contagious or infectious diseases, and all quarantine regulations established under the authority of said laws in respect to all vessels and

vehicles engaged in commerce with foreign nations and among the respective States, whether by land or water.

4. That the Board of Health shall also be charged with the duty of obtaining information of the sanitary condition of foreign ports and places from which contagious or infectious diseases are or may be imported into the United States; and to this end the consular officers of the United States, at all ports and places, shall make to the National Board of Health weekly reports of the sanitary condition of the ports and places at which they are respectively stationed, according to such forms as said Board of Health may prescribe; and the Board of Health shall also obtain, through all sources accessible, including State and municipal health authorities throughout the United States, weekly reports of the sanitary condition of ports and places within the United States; and the Board of Health shall prepare, publish, and transmit to the medical officers of the marine hospital service, to collectors of customs, and to State and municipal health officers and authorities, weekly abstracts of the consular sanitary reports, and other pertinent information received by said board; and said Board of Health shall also, as far as it may be able, by means of voluntary co-operation of State and municipal authorities, of public associations and private persons, procure information relating to the climatic and other conditions affecting the public health; and the Board of Health shall make, to the Secretary of the Treasury, an annual report of its operations, for transmission to Congress, with such recommendations as it may deem important to the public interests; and said report, if ordered to be published by Congress, shall be published under the direction of the board.

5. That the National Board of Health shall, from time to time, issue to the consular officers of the United States, and to the medical officers serving at foreign ports, and otherwise make publicly known, the rules and regulations made by it and approved by the President, to be used and complied with by vessels in foreign ports, for securing the best possible sanitary condition of such vessels, their cargoes, passengers, and crew, before their departure for any port in the United States, and in the course of the voyage; and also such other rules and regulations as shall be observed in the inspection of the same on the arrival thereof at any quarantine station at the port of destination, and for the disinfection and isolation of the same, and the treatment of cargo and persons on board, so as to prevent the spread of cholera, yellow fever, or other contagious or infectious diseases; and it shall not be lawful for any vessel to enter said port to discharge its cargo or land its passengers, except upon a permit from the health officer at such quarantine station, certifying that said rules and regulations have in all respects been observed and complied with, as well on his part as on the part of the said vessel and its master, in respect to the same, and to its cargo, passengers, and crew; and the master of every such vessel shall produce and deliver to the collector of customs at said port of entry, together with the other papers of the vessel, the said certificates required to be obtained at the port of departure and the permit and certificate herein required to be obtained from the health officer at the port of entry.

6. That rules and regulations made and approved as herein authorized shall

be promulgated, so that when cholera, yellow fever, and other contagious or infectious diseases shall be ascertained by the Board of Health to exist in any port or place within the United States in such form as threatens its spread, the communication of the same to other ports and places within other States by means of vessels and vehicles engaged in the transportation of goods or passengers between two or more States shall, as far as practicable, be prevented; and in that case the Board of Health shall select suitable localities for establishing stations on rivers and other lines of inter-State commerce and travel by railroads, and may cause to be erected necessary temporary buildings for the disinfection of passengers, baggage, cargoes, vessels, and vehicles, and may enforce such rules and regulations relating thereto as may have been prescribed therefor.

7. That it shall be the duty of the National Board of Health, so far as it lawfully may, in the execution of the powers conferred upon it by law, to invite the co-operation of, and to correspond and co-operate with, local sanitary officers, boards, and authorities acting under the laws of the States in sanitary measures, to prevent the introduction and spread of contagious and infectious diseases from foreign countries into the United States, and from one State into any other State, by means of commercial intercourse, upon and along the lines of inter-State trade and travel; and to that end it shall be lawful for said Board of Health to confer upon any such local officer or board within or near the locality where his or its authority is exercised power also to enforce the provisions of this act, and all rules and regulations made in pursuance thereof. And in case such local officer or board shall refuse to execute and enforce the laws of the United States, and the rules and regulations of the National Board of Health, made in pursuance thereof, for the inspection, disinfection, and treatment of vehicles and vessels, their cargoes, passengers, and crews, or, in the opinion of the National Board of Health, shall neglect or fail to do so, it shall be the duty of the President, upon the application of the National Board of Health, to detail from the medical staff of the Army or Navy or the marine hospital service a suitable officer to execute or enforce said laws, rules, and regulations, or to appoint some suitable person for that purpose. (And it shall be the duty of the National Board of Health to report the facts to the governor of such State, with such sanitary advice as the board may think proper in the premises.)

8. That to pay the necessary expenses of placing vessels in proper sanitary condition under the provisions of this act, the Secretary of the Treasury be, and he hereby is, authorized and required to make the necessary rules and regulations, fixing the amount of fees to be paid by vessels for such service, and the manner of collecting the same.

9. That the National Board of Health is hereby directed to make, or cause to be made, an investigation into the contagious or infectious diseases of domestic animals in the United States, and especially such as tend to interfere with the supply of wholesome food, and into the best means of controlling or preventing such diseases, and to report the result of its investigations at the next session of Congress.

10. That the National Board of Health is also directed to cause a thorough inspection to be made of all animals arriving at, or exported from, the different shipping ports of the United States, and to cause the owners or shippers of such cattle to be promptly notified of the results of such inspections, with such recommendations as may be proper in each case. It shall also notify State and local sanitary authorities of the existence of such diseases of domestic animals as it deems proper to bring to their notice, with such recommendations as may be deemed expedient in each case.

11. That the President is authorized, when requested by the National Board of Health, to detail officers from the several departments of the government for temporary duty, to act under the direction of said board, to carry out the provisions of this act; and such officers shall receive no additional compensation except for actual and necessary expenses incurred in the performance of such duties.

12. That to meet the expenses to be incurred in carrying out the provisions of this act, the sum of six hundred and fifty thousand dollars is hereby appropriated, to be disbursed under the direction of the National Board of Health, which shall make to the Secretary of the Treasury a full and accurate report of its operations under this act, and of all expenditures connected therewith, to be by him reported to Congress.

13. That nothing in this act shall be so construed as to supersede or impair any sanitary or quarantine law of any State.

II.

The question of yellow fever quarantine is a very vexed one. Many of the best physicians, those most searching in their investigations, most studious and scholarly, of the largest experience and most enlightened views, have opposed it. In support of their position they adduce very strong arguments, fortified by undeniable facts. Some of these the reader is already acquainted with. They are to be found in the origin and prevalence of the disease, in epidemic form, at interior points remote from, and having no communication with, sea-ports to which the yellow fever might be brought in ships; its origin in New Orleans and other places, as attested by commissions organized to investigate for the fact of its origin, and by reputable and able physicians who could have no object in a purposed misrepresentation, that, in view of possible after results, would be criminally cruel; in the admission by the homeopathic as well as allopathic commissions of 1878, of the possibility of the germs being perpetuated through the winter months, to break forth so soon as the intense heats of summer come to recuperate them, and enable them to breed and multiply; in the general admission that the filth of cities is a necessary factor in its propagation, and that, without a system of thorough sanitation, no city can claim exemption from it; in the fact that frost has not always killed it, and that cases of fever have originated and proven fatal in the coldest months of winter several weeks after ice has formed, and the thermometer has been many degrees below the freezing-point; in the fact that it runs its course within ninety days regardless of conditions, whether of weather, sanitation, or population; that its degrees of latitude are as far apart as the European settlements on this continent and that of South America; and that it is no respecter of nationalities, of color, of sex, of age, of acclimated or unacclimated persons,* of high or low lands, mountains or swamps; that it is unknown as to its cause; that science has not discovered either a preventive or a cure for it, and the best medical skill can only mitigate and not prevent its cruelties, can only assist to arrest its progress short of decimation. No question has been more ably argued, more vehemently opposed or defended. "At the beginning of the present century," says Dowler, "and for some years after, the yellow fever element was so mingled with the great concerns of humanity, that it excited the public mind to an unexampled degree; in the cabinet and in the field, in the legislative halls and in the medical schools, both at home and abroad, and in the colonial governments. It had long been the conqueror of armies and navies, and at one time it threatened to desolate the peninsula of Europe. Its contagiousness was a leading topic, on which reports, pamphlets, and books went forth raging like the epidemic itself. Neutrality was scarcely possible in a matter so deeply involving the interests, passions, and transactions of humanity. Opinions founded on mere hypothesis concerning the cause of this malady, which remains to this day unknown, were not for that reason less, but even more, positive and dogmatic. Affidavits and affronts, certificates and satires, logic and duels, personal contagion and personal invective, bad air and worse legislation, divided the professional and non-professional public on this subject. The non-contagionists, however, greatly outnumbered their opponents. They, for the most part, controlled the legislation of the States of the Union by their efforts or their arguments. But no sooner were they off their guard than the contagionists appealed to the fears of the people, and urged the legislature to do something for the protection of the people by making laws against the importation of yellow fever, whereupon new

---

Dr. Francis, of New York, on the contrary, upon the authority of Judge Andrews, Mr. Delespine, and Colonel Forbes, says that the yellow fever which devastated St. Augustine, in Florida, chiefly during the month of October, 1821, "did not affect a single individual from the West Indies, nor a native of the country, nor any one who had previously suffered from yellow fever. Forty or fifty deaths occurred among newly arrived immigrants before the alarm became general. Eleven deaths happened in one day. About 200 were exposed to the influence of the disease. Of this aggregate 140 were attacked, of which 132 died, including three blacks. Forty deaths took place in the garrison, in a body of 120 soldiers." The official army report asserts that this epidemic was "entirely confined to strangers, that is, all persons not inured to the atmosphere of the city by nativity or a residence of a long series of years. Spaniards or natives resident in the country, who had the temerity to venture into the city during its prevalence, were liable to its attack, though in a milder degree than immigrants."

---

*All which has been disproved by subsequent experiences, notably those in Memphis in 1873 and 1878, when the fever proved itself no respecter of persons, sparing neither age, sex. color, the acclimated, the unacclimated, the sober, the drunkard, the chaste or the unchaste, the sinner or the saint.

laws were often enacted with no effect in this behalf. The anti-contagionists, like Sicyphus, must roll the stones perpetually—then, now, evermore. Contagionists have, during this, as well as during all former epidemics, collected facts to prove their theory. A peddler, from an infected district, arrives in a town, his pack is opened, he, the family, and many of the villagers die of yellow fever. Exactly the same occurrence (a mere coincidence) takes place a hundred times, where there has been no peddler, no box of goods opened, no travelers from an infected district. In one town, a crate of crocks, from New Orleans, is said to have been the means of transmitting contagion to the village, but at the very time nearly all the other towns, for 500 miles around, were falling under the malign influence of the epidemic. It would be most extraordinary if crates, boxes, passengers, and pestilence should never happen to get together—not as causes and effect, but as coincidence, necessary in the ordinary course of business. If the pestilence got into town before the arrival of a bale of goods, the former did not cause the arrival of the latter. If the man who opens the goods dies of black vomit, together with all his family, a hundred other families take the disease without any such apparent exposure, and die in like manner. A planter fences up his ground and secludes himself, family, and slaves, and all escape; another does the same thing and all are attacked. The great majority of the learned, in Europe, attribute the black plague to the conjunction of Saturn, Jupiter, and Mars, on the 24th of March, 1345; just as many now attribute the late epidemic (1853) to events that happen to coincide in time and place. Those not irrevocably wedded to contagion, might find it useful to study the events which have passed before their eyes within the last seven years. The last Mexican war furnishes the most complete refutation of the contagiousness of yellow fever, in the absence of quarantine, so far as negative evidence can go. If the United States government had tried to devise an experiment, on a vast scale, to ascertain whether the yellow fever could be propagated by ships and armies, it could not have achieved its purpose more effectually. In 1846, 1847, and 1848, this malady existed in Tampico and Vera Cruz, and was very severe in New Orleans in 1847. The troops and material of the army, leaving New Orleans for Vera Cruz, and Vera Cruz for the interior of Mexico, did not suffer themselves from yellow fever, nor spread contagion through the towns and country. In 1848, thousands of the returning soldiers passed through Vera Cruz, in June, where yellow fever existed, and, on reaching New Orleans, in July and August, a few died, out of 15,000 who remained in the city and its environs some time, without communicating any disease to the city, by means of their goods, army materials, and selves. Thousands thus, without having been quarantined, remained in the city for a time, and quitted it for their homes, in other towns and places, without having communicated the disease to any one.* After the

---

* The Jamaica report, drawn up by some of the ablest medical men England has produced, and by very able civilians who knew what they were talking about, says: "Epidemics of fever in this island are often confined to certain districts, showing that the local causes are then and there in one force. Thus, at this very time severe fevers are prevalent at

reduction of Vera Cruz, yellow fever appeared, and many invalids and sick persons were sent to New Orleans and other places for treatment, in the transports which carried out the troops, yet they did not propagate the disease anywhere. Thus at least fifty thousand experiments made in Tampico, Vera Cruz, and New Orleans, not to name other places, produced no personal or other kind of contagion, though in both the first named places yellow fever prevailed moderately among residents not acclimated. The Board of Health of New Orleans, in an official document, announced for the month beginning with the 26th of November, 1853, that 6,707 passengers from foreign ports, chiefly emigrants, had arrived at our wharves in forty-seven sea-going vessels, by the river route. Now, if we add the num-

---

St. Thomas in the east and St. Thomas in the vale, places wide apart and unconnected; at other times the cause is more general, and it rages over the whole; months and years sometimes pass without the disease occurring, either in a sporadic or epidemic form, and then suddenly it bursts out with all its force. These fevers are common to all classes; some, however, deny that the black race can suffer from yellow fever; instances, however, do occur, though rarely. The prevalent opinion that one attack of yellow fever defends the person from another is decidedly fallacious." In another part of the report the Board of Health of Jamaica say: "Not one single epidemic witnessed by the health officers there could be attributed to importation." . . . "Yellow fever patients constantly arrive at Kingston, and for the last twenty-five years have never been put into quarantine." At Gibraltar, in 1828, great numbers of the British troops were attacked who could not possibly have come in contact with any infected individual. Of 282 women and children of the 12th regiment, who were not allowed to enter the fortress, but remained in the camp, not one had the fever, though several of them slept in the same beds with their husbands laboring under the epidemic (which they had caught while on duty in the fortress), and continued, with their children, to use the same bedding after their husbands were removed into the hospital." M. Amiel says: "Where the wife in the same bed came in contact with the patient, scorched by febrile heat, or bedewed with copious perspiration, when she inhaled, under the same tent, the effluvia of his breath, how could the air sufficiently interpose to prevent the process of contagion and its fatal consequences?" In 1804, while yellow fever was devastating Leghorn, 6,000 persons left Leghorn for Pisa. The French army moved at the same time to the same place, taking with them 180 men with the disease; yet there was no propagation of the disease at Pisa. Dr. Blair, one of the latest and one of the ablest writers on yellow fever, says of British Guiana: "There was no difference of opinion to excite discussion here, for there was not a single person, professional or non-professional, in the length and breadth of the colony, who, in 1838, after the first alarm had subsided, had the least suspicion of contagion in our yellow fever. During the epidemic the yellow fever cases, in their worst form, were never separated from other patients in our hospital wards. Such a thing was not deemed necessary and never thought of. They were classified with acute diseases. Our hospital nurses never got infected, although in the closest connection with the sick, and often smeared with their ejections; and these nurses were chiefly German and Portuguese immigrants." Dr. Bell, of Louisville, a distinguished physician and a recognized authority in all that relates to the yellow fever, reinforces the above evidence by his own experience. He says: "I have seen and attended in this city some of the severest forms of yellow fever that have been described in the tropics. I have walked through the quarantine grounds at Staten Island and conversed with the yellow fever patients; I was in the yellow fever haunts below Brooklyn Heights in 1856; I was in the yellow fever district of Philadelphia while the fever was prevailing there, and I never had the least fear of catching it."

ber which had previously arrived to the number which has since arrived from sea, the aggregate will scarcely fall below 10,000, while by other routes, chiefly by the river, the emigrants, absentees, and other unacclimated persons (as the steamboat population coming to the city in September, October, November, and December), 40,000 may be added, making 50,000 living experiments against possible contagion—50,000 exposures to all the possible sources of contagion—the houses, goods, etc., of persons recently dead, including emanations from the sick and dying, during the decline of the epidemic, and during the whole of this period, all proving harmless. If the yellow fever be contagious or transportable, why has it not been carried beyond the tropic of Capricorn during centuries of active intercommunication? Why did it appear only north of the equator, with two or three exceptions, always near the line, until 1850, when it traveled for the first time to Rio Janeiro, which, however, is within the tropic? Such vast, yet significant, experiments quite overthrow those few cases where the opening of a box or a bale of goods is followed by yellow fever—mere coincidents, not causes. There is not the least reason to think that the world, combined for the purpose, could create an epidemic yellow fever, or even a single case, in any city, street, or house upon the globe. The enlightened governments of Europe, whose intertropical possessions enable them to judge from large experimental intercourse, have not only gradually lost confidence in quarantine as a preventive of yellow fever, but they oppose it as altogether mischievous—at least such is the case in Great Britain. Quarantine in our own country is nominal, illusory, and never comes up to the theory of real quarantinists. The deception is, therefore, less mischievous than an honest enforcement would be. The provisional assumptions of contagion, seclusion, and quarantine in yellow fever, once altogether proper and wise, anterior to experimental tests, are now no longer such. In the hour of despair and ignorance, the theory that the building of a large city in a country where earthquakes and volcanoes prevailed, would prevent them, might be tolerated until after a fair trial. But, if experience prove that earthquakes continue as before, the building of cities for this purpose should not continue. If faith is but proved by works, the contagiousness of yellow fever in New Orleans falls to the ground, because, in practice, it is disregarded both by the acclimated and the unacclimated, inasmuch as doctors, nurses, and neighbors visit the sick in the freest and most fearless way, and with equal impunity with those who keep at a distance from the sick.* Experience shows, both in

---

* A New Orleans correspondent of the New York *Times*, who wrote intelligently, and like a man of experience, in one of his letters asked: "Is there any danger in visiting the sick-room?" And he answers, "I do not believe there is, other than that the close air of the room is prejudicial, and may derange the system, in slight degree. This is my own view, based upon the fact that there are hundreds of unacclimated persons in this city who are attendant upon the sick, and who exhibit no more tendency to contract the disease than do those who avoid even the passing of an infected house when practicable. In fact, yellow fever seems to be caused by a morbid principle entirely different in its characteristics than any which excite or produce other epidemic diseases. Every day experience here shows that it can not be communicated from person to person, but that it is

hospital and private practice, that proximity to the sick does not enhance the danger to one living in the "infected district." In the rural districts, and in the towns where fear was great and experimental knowledge of the fever little, the people adopted a different line of conduct—the principle of seclusion and non-intercourse. The traveler, denied the hospitalities of the house because he had merely passed through an "infected district" or village, wandered along the road, seeking shelter in vain for the night. Towns suffered for want of provisions, because their rural neighbors feared to approach the sick. Sometimes depots were established near these self-beleaguered towns, where the sick and their attendants and families went for supplies, and thereby escaped starvation. The artillery placed at the landings and wharves, threatened to send grape and cannister shot into boats and vessels that dared to approach from infected districts.[*] Individuals as well as towns carried out the principle of seclusion, and were alike unsuccessful. Although the quarantine party is, to a great extent, composed of men of the highest integrity, talent, patriotism, and disinterestedness, yet it is feared that some who profess quarantine loudest are, at heart, infidels; if they are sincere they are not consistent. By what code of morality can they justify themselves in dispensing with quarantine in any case like the following example, taken from the *Daily Delta*, of September 13th, 1853? Captain Baxter's statement, as given by the editor: "Captain Baxter left here (New Orleans) with the *Cherokee*, on the 12th of August last, when the epidemic was at its height, with 169 passengers, the majority of whom were unacclimated, and liable to the yellow fever. During the voyage, there were ten of the crew down with the fever, and on the arrival of the *Cherokee* in New York, there being two still sick, they were ordered into the hospital, where one of them died; the other recovered." Were the crew and passengers (without mentioning the ship and cargo) kept forty days in the lazaretto undergoing fumigation? Not at all. Captain Baxter adds: "They were all permitted to land in New York, after eighteen hours, and the sick members of the crew were alone compelled

---

strictly individual in its attack." And Dr. Westmoreland, of Atlanta, Georgia, scouts the idea of contagion, and sustains his position by his own personal experience in 1878. He says: "I nursed the case of young Brand, in Atlanta. I felt that if yellow fever was contagious, after all I had said—if I had actually been deceiving the people—that I deserved to catch it, and ought to die. I therefore determined to give it a full trial. I staid in the room with my patient all day. I even slept in the room with him all night, with the black vomit all around me, and the room thoroughly impregnated. I unpacked his clothes, and handled them freely; I touched the patient, nursed him, and waited on him, till he was dead. I had two nurses who went through the same ordeal with me, and they both came out unscathed. Dr. Johnson went through even worse than that. He was with us all the time, and held the patient's head while he was vomiting. He is now in perfect health. If there is any thing that is absolutely demonstrated, it is that yellow fever is not contagious."

[*] Exactly as in 1878, when panic prevailed from New Orleans to Chicago, by river and railroad, and from the Mississippi as far as Knoxville, in the mountains. And many, indeed most of the towns so quarantining escaped the fever, the people being thus confirmed in their faith in quarantine as their only safeguard against the pest.

to go into hospital detention. Such a quarantine is but a kaleidoscopic illusion. If the New York authorities entertained the belief that yellow fever is contagious, they would not, in this strongest possible case of importation, have willfully exposed the lives of half a million of people, unless they are worse than pirates themselves.* Their acts, more than their words, show that they have no belief in quarantine as a preventive of yellow fever. The same infidelity is obvious in the actions of the few contagionists in New Orleans. They no more avoid yellow fever patients than they do rheumatic patients, or charity. They are better than their doctrine." Continuing his logical disquisition on the cruelty to persons, the cost to commerce, and the injury quarantine inflicts upon those who are the prey of it, Dr. Dowler says: "If New Orleans contagionists succeed in getting the city and State governments to establish the contagiousness of yellow fever, by a special act, let the same act forbid the exportation of cotton, even to our enemies in time of war. In time of peace, it would be more unjust to send infected cotton to the subjects of her Britannic Majesty, or to the subjects of the Emperor of the French. It would be still more criminal to export cotton and contagion to Philadelphia, New York, Boston, and other cities, as a return for their opulent donations to yellow fever sufferers during the late epidemic.† It may be said that a contagionist, how sincere soever he may be, is not bound to care for his neighbors' interests and health, but honesty requires him to care for both. It is doubtful whether the English Minister was strictly moral when he declared that he 'cared for England and English interests alone.' The same dubiety hangs over Commodore Bainbridge's toast, 'My country, if right, but my country, right or wrong.' If yellow fever be contagious and transportable, quarantine ought to be enforced by grape and cannister, gibbets, and fines, though commerce should perish altogether. If quarantine is to reign in New Orleans, let it be as rigid as in the Levant, for no Eastern mummery can be more absurd than that practiced at the quarantine stations of the United States at the present time. The strictness of the East has both consistency and reason in its favor (admitting the doctrine of contagion), which can not be urged in favor of the West. A doctor of some Atlantic city of the Union goes on board of a ship from New Orleans—the plague-stricken city—he looks at the cotton bales, and the passengers, and he straightway ignores his own theory, his oath, and the law; for in a few minutes or hours after the vessel is admitted, no one being able to

---

* The authorities of New York now enforce a rigid quarantine. In 1878, every case of yellow fever that found its way to that city was at once sent to the quarantine hospital for treatment; and that is the declared policy for the future, not only of New York, but of every other city in the Union.

† During and after the epidemic of 1878, persons residing in cities competing with Memphis for trade in Arkansas, Mississippi, as well as West Tennessee, made no scruple of declaring their belief in the contagion theory, so far as the dry goods, woollen goods, furniture, and even certain kinds of groceries, that Memphis offered for sale, were concerned, but when it came to their receiving either bales of cotton or wool from, or passing through, Memphis or other infected points, they closed their ears to the contagion theory, and not only willingly became the agents for the sale of such cotton or wool, but eagerly solicited the sale of it.

know how he could possibly have ascertained, by a look, whether contagion was or was not in the vessel. If yellow fever quarantine be well founded, such conduct is murder by the thousand. If the laws of the land and of nature have established the fact of the importability of yellow fever, by means of persons and merchandise, and if quarantine be necessary to prevent this importation, then quarantine can never be dispensed with by a look or a whim; that is, the laws of nature can not be changed in this way. If importation be the antecedent of yellow fever in New Orleans, let quarantine against it be not only strict, but eternal. If the act of the Legislature of Louisiana, in the winter of 1817, establishing a code of quarantine laws was wise, the repeal of those laws in 1818 was foolish. But it may be said that these laws had failed to prevent an epidemic during the summer of 1817. True, but why has the same course been pursued since, and why pursue it again, as is intended now? The experiment has been often repeated in various countries, and with like results—results mischievous, demoralizing, repulsive to humanity, and tending to increase the mortality of yellow fever during an epidemic. If the people of New Orleans could be brought to believe in the contagiousness* of this disease, benevolent as they are known to be, the rich would be secluded; intercourse would be so restricted that many would perish from neglect." This testimony against yellow fever quarantine by Dr. Dowler, fortifies Dr. Dupuy De Chambrey, of New Orleans, who, in his historical sketch of yellow fever, as it appeared in that city in 1819, says:

---

* "Contagion in its most literal and restricted sense" is defined by Dowler to "imply the actual contact of a well person with a dead, or sick person, or his apparel, by which a specific poison is transmitted from one to the other, reproducing a similar disease, as in small-pox, cow-pox, itch, etc. In a more enlarged sense this term includes invisible emanations from the sick, consisting of specific poison, doubtless dissolved or suspended in the air, and capable of reproducing a similar disease in any indefinite number of persons who come near the patient, of which small-pox again affords the most complete typical illustration. Here the fundamental idea of contact is, perhaps, real, though unseen. Another type or criterion of contagion is this: it can not act except within a very circumscribed space, in any season, latitude or climate; it may be limited by isolation from, or non-intercourse with, the healthy; its extension probably might reach from pole to pole, if all could be brought in proximity with a single sick individual, although the emanations from his body, at a few feet from the same, mixing with the atmospheric ocean, become harmless, not epidemic. The word INFECTION, generally used as synonymous with the word contagion, has too often played a conspicuous, if not a satisfactory, role in the vague and inconclusive disputations of yellow fever quarantinists. If the word infection means an emanation of a specific aerial poison from the sick, giving rise to a similar malady in the well, it must be precisely the same as contagion; but if it means an impure air arising from an animal or vegetable source, or from both combined, then it is but another word for miasma, malaria, or bad air. The labored attempts to explain this word—the bad faith in which it has been used—at one time for contagion, at another for the bad air of a sick room, a sick city, a vile scent, or paludian exhalation, go to show that it is a most perfidious word, the shiboleth of dialecticians— a word pregnant with mental reservations. It is the limbo of countless pamphlets, books, and laws upon yellow fever quarantine, the lumber of the last and present centuries. If infection be used to denote the contamination of the atmosphere of a room, or

"I formerly believed the yellow fever to be contagious, but since I have been in the midst of it, my numerous practical observations have never been able to furnish me with a proof of this much dreaded attribute. Indeed the result has been quite the reverse; and I am now convinced that the disease is permanently fixed to the spot, and within the limits of the place which has created it. Not one case occurred beyond the limits of the city, during its prevalence in the years 1817 and 1819, that could be traced to the innumerable patients, although daily intercourse was kept up between the people of the neighboring estates and plantations. A great number of our inhabitants who carried the seeds of the disorder abroad, seeking refuge from the danger at a distance, suffered an attack of the fever and died, but in no instance was it communicated to their friends. Fifty times have I had my hands and face besmeared with the putrid blood, black vomit, or fœtid, slimy matter of perspiration. Fifty times have I been immersed in the effluvia issuing from a dead or living subject, and never been infected by the disease.* From extensive observations, I infer that the yellow fever of this place is a disease *sui generis*, the product of local causes, and neither contagious nor exportable. Flight from the infected spot is the only preservative." Governor Villere, of Louisiana, in 1820, in his message to the legislature, a firm advocate of contagion and for quarantine, says: " All the medical faculty appear definitely to have adopted the opinion that the yellow fever which, during the last year (1819), has plunged us once more into mourning and desolation, is not contagious." But he argues: " During the months of August, September, and October, there has been almost constantly in the prison of this distressed city a great number of prisoners, and not a single one among them has been affected with the disorder."†
Quoting this, Dowler asks: " If the yellow fever were natural to our climate, how has it happened that among such a number of persons heaped together in so small a space as the prison of the city, not a single one should have been attacked?" Dr. T. H. Bache, of Philadelphia, writing in 1820, also furnished Dowler with non-contagion evidence of a valuable character. He stated that " the number of cases of yellow fever admitted into the Pennsylvania Hospital had been twenty-three ; of these fourteen had died, seven recovered, and two still remain [October 6th]. These cases were placed in the common wards, without any attempt to separate them from, or prevent intercourse between

---

of an urban district or focus, with or without offensive scent, an emanation from vegeto-animal decomposition, not an emanation of a specific nature from a sick man, which in any climate, season, and latitude produces similar malady in the well, then the word becomes intelligible. Such contamination however, does not originate a strictly contagious disease, though it may, and often does, aggravate the latter. Seclusion from sick persons does not insure exemption, while the individual lives in the infected district. The locality, not the person, is dangerous.

* The young man, Louis Daltroof, employed in 1878 by the Memphis Howard Association to bury their members and employés, faithfully performed that duty, and escaped the fever, though he had as offensive an experience as De Chambrey.

† The same was true as to the prisoners confined in the Memphis jail in 1873 ; but in 1878 it proved the reverse. The prisoners were attacked ; some died, and the rest had to be removed to a place of safety.

them and the other patients, but in no instance had the disease been communicated to the latter!" Dr. Reese, in 1820, in his *Medical Gazette*, affords Dowler additional evidence. He said: "How strange that the antiquated fable of contagion* should still haunt the popular creed, and be made the hobby-horse on which so many flippant political doctors ride into places of profit, under that silly relic of barbarism known as the 'quarantine regulations,' which are as powerless in keeping out yellow fever from the cities in which it is generated by local sources of effluvia, as they would be in imposing restrictions against the waves of Old Ocean rising in her wrath. Even here, in Philadelphia, where a few score of cases have occurred in a district infected by an old and filthy common sewer, we find certain medical savants hunting for its cause in an old ship, guiltless of all but bilge-water; and this with an obvious source of yellow fever under their noses. When will this ghost of contagion and importation be exorcised?" Dr. Brickell, a practitioner of high repute in New Orleans, sustains Dowler, and, in a recently written letter to Senator Lamar, a member of the congressional committee to investigate the origin, causes, and means of prevention of yellow fever, states that he believes that the fever has become naturalized in New Orleans, and originates there. He concludes:

1. I have seen and treated the disease—yellow fever—from the epidemic of 1848 to that of 1878, inclusive, and in city and country.

2. I believe that the disease can be, and has been, imported.

3. I believe that the disease is transmissible, and that it is not—that is, that when carried from one point to another, it must find the conditions or surroundings necessary to its propagation, or it will not spread. Therefore, the disease has at times been brought to New Orleans, and to other places, and has not spread. In illustration of this point, I cited the case I carried to Cooper's Well, in 1853 (not willfully), the case that bought its way through General Butler's boasted military quarantine, in September, 1862, and the case carried from Memphis or Shreveport into New York city, by rail, in September, 1873; as well as cases known to have been carried into New York, by rail, during the past summer—1878.

4. In view of the foregoing, it is difficult to establish the *fact* that a given ship or person spreads yellow fever. Yet all the probabilities of the ship or person having done so may be strong, and even satisfactory, to many minds.

5. I believe that it is most probable that yellow fever was originally brought to New Orleans; but I also believe that it has long ago become engrafted on us, and that it has appeared here in summers, and will appear again, independent of importation from abroad. I am satisfied that I saw the first case

---

* Illustrating the absurdity of the doctrine of contagion, Dowler mentions that Carlos, King of Spain, by proclamation, in 1805, conferred on Don Cabanellas and his two children an annuity of $1,200, making the Don physician to the royal household, bestowing other privileges on him, for having slept one night with his children in the bed whereon yellow fever victims had died in the lazaretto. A number of galley convicts, in chains, who voluntarily accompanied the Don for the night, had one year's punishment remitted from their penalties. The party consisted of fifty persons, who suffered no harm. Great was the astonishment of His Catholic Majesty and his doctors.

that appeared here in 1867—the young English servant man of Mr. J. O. Nixon, living on St. Charles Street, between Julia and Girod, the central and granite-paved portion of our city. The most careful inquiry revealed no conection of this man with any ship, or passengers of a ship; the city was perfectly healthy at the time, and I only saw the patient after the fever had passed off. I predicted an epidemic on the strength of the case, and it came speedily.

The late Dr. Stone, of New Orleans, does not believe in the contagion theory. He also sustains Dowler. He said, in his Bellevue Hospital lecture, delivered in 1867, after the epidemic of that year: "If the disease were contagious once, it would always be so, for it is the same disease in all places. It is a specific disease, and the same person has it but once. Acclimation is perpetual, but it is very hard to convince the human understanding of that. There are, however, exceptions to these rules, as to every rule, and as there is to the rule governing small pox, for instance. I have observed, honestly at least, if not closely, and the result of my observations has led me to believe yellow fever non-contagious. In 1833 I arrived in New Orleans, and went into the Charity Hospital on duty. The hospital became full, and as there was great scarcity of help, it became filthy. The passages (halls) were often filled with bed-sacks covered with excrement and black vomit, so that a sort of typhoid fever was generated, yet the persons employed there escaped yellow fever, and I did not have it myself until late in the season, after these conditions had been remedied. In 1853, I had an infirmary in which there were 300 cases of yellow fever, treated by ten or twelve sisters of charity, all of whom were unacclimated, yet the atmospheric influence did not prevail where the hospital was situated. In 1847, in 1853, in 1854, and in 1859, my experience had been substantially the same. In 1859, some forty cases of yellow fever were placed in the Charity Hospital, among a number of other patients, who were unacclimated, and although a large number of the forty died, not a solitary new case occurred in the house. Cases were constantly occurring of persons who went into infected districts, took the disease, were taken to uninfected districts, treated and nursed, and yet no one took the disease from them. In 1856 and 1857, yellow fever of a severe character prevailed in New Orleans, but was strictly confined to six squares. No intercourse with vessels had taken place, and it was evident the disease had originated there. In the country, I made diligent inquiries, with the same result. It did not spread from person to person. It was quite possible that a quantity of the poisoned atmosphere might be conveyed in the hold of a ship to distant places, and that persons breathing that atmosphere might have disease, but they could not impart it to others. Just how much air would suffice to render the fever portable, it was impossible to ascertain. The question of its contagiousness is of great importance, and ought to be settled, both for the interest of sufferers from the disease, and as a guidance in the matter of quarantine. I am perfectly convinced, beyond all doubt or hesitation, that personally it is not contagious; *I know that it is not!*"

The late Dr. L. Shanks, a physician long resident in Memphis, and well known as one of the ablest members of his profession in the Mississippi Valley, utterly scouted the theory of contagion. Giving his experience of yellow fever up to 1855, he says: "Previous to the late epidemic [1855], Memphis has been regarded as being above the yellow fever region in the Mississippi Valley, and secure against its origin and development as an epidemic from any cause. Memphis has heretofore occupied a position on the Mississippi River above the region in which cases of the yellow fever have originated, and though exempt from the disease, the citizens, and especially the physicians, have been familiarized with it, by the number of cases on the boats passing up the river, when it has prevailed as an epidemic in New Orleans, Natchez, Vicksburg, and at other places below. The boats coming from the infected places always landed here, and were freely visited by the citizens and physicians, when either business or the professional call of the physician required it. In this way the sick passengers upon the boats were not only frequently seen and administered to, but, when they desired it, were occasionally removed from the boats to the hotels and boarding-houses in the city, to be better attended to in the way of nursing and having medical aid. No fear ever existed here of the propagation of the disease by cases thus brought from the infected boats on the river into the city; and no instance has occurred in which a single case of the yellow fever has thus been produced here by contact with the sick, the dying, or the dead from the boats. The non-contagiousness of the disease has not only been demonstrated here in that way for many years, but it has been still more largely confirmed by the results at the Memphis Charity Hospital. When the yellow fever has prevailed as an epidemic in New Orleans, there has always been cases occurring on the boats after leaving that city, before their arrival at this port. Many of these cases have been put off at the landing here, and sent through the city to the hospital, in former years. In 1853, about sixty cases; in 1854, forty cases; and, in 1855, forty-two cases were thus sent from the boats to the hospital. Of these cases a large proportion died, as they were sent out at an advanced period of the attack; but not a single instance has ever occurred of a nurse, or other patients, or persons in or about the hospital taking the yellow fever from these cases." Dr. W. R. Milner, of New Orleans, writes as positively against contagion and quarantine as Dowler. He says: "The specific action of our common swamp malaria, which produces ordinary chill and fever, is upon the red corpuscles of the blood. It is attracted to these with as uniform certainty as the needle to the pole. This fact is known to every intelligent physician. It is the cause of the anæmic condition which universally follows prostrated intermittents; and this destruction of the red blood is slow or rapid, according to the mildness or severity of the attack. Now I have observed that the same specific destruction of the red-blood corpuscles takes place not only in intermittents, but in remittents, in pernicious fever, in congestive chills, in purpura hæmorrhagica, in malarial hæmaturia, and in yellow fever. In 1867 I was called to see a boy, the patient of another doctor, who had had the yellow fever for some days, and was then slowly bleeding to death from the gum of a decayed tooth. The red corpuscles had been nearly consumed by the poison, and nothing could stop the hemorrhage; he died. Now, if there is a point of specific agreement, uniform, identical, and typical between yellow fever and all other forms of malarial diseases, are we not forced to the logical conclusion that the specific nature of yellow fever is identical with that of our common intermittents? Most assuredly. Then, if it be intrinsically the same, is it not of the utmost importance to commerce and to humanity that the fact be known and obeyed? Does not the wide-spread panic of the present, with its train of evils, not to mention the equally damaging effects of quarantine of past years, appeal to the common sense of an enlightened people to take this question up and compel its solution? If I have stated a fact, and not an hypothesis, as to the specific and typical quality in the behavior of all of these diseases, what use of quarantine? Certainly none. Is there any intelligent observer of malarial diseases who can deny the fact? Why is quinine, the known specific of common swamp fevers, the specific and prophylactic of yellow fever also, if my premise be not true?* Will the advocates of the importation theory explain? Nay, they can't. We have two great evils to contend with, one is natural, and the other is artificial; one is yellow fever, and the other is quarantine. Shall we keep both? Has quarantine ever prevented yellow fever? Tell me where, and when. Let the next legislature abolish the quarantine laws, and I tell you, sir, we shall have less yellow fever than we have ever had. Why? Because attention being thus drawn off from quarantine as a prevention, the useless expenditures of time and money in that direction will cease, and time and money will be utilized by concentration upon the only means of prevention—that of thorough drainage and cleanliness. And the work commenced in such good earnest would pay so well that in a few years success would be a demonstrated fact. The fires of enterprise would burn out the poisons of our swamps. A salubrious atmosphere would bless the city and State, invigorating and purifying the body, mind, and soul of the people; emigration would flow in; our lands would be taken and cultivated by God's noblest yeomanry, and soon Louisiana would become the example and the garden spot of the world."

The position against quarantine, so strongly taken by Dowler, and the physicians quoted to sustain him, was indorsed by the convention of the Boards of Health, held in New York on April 27–30, 1859. Early in the session Prof. A. H. Stevens, M. D., submitted the following resolution:

Resolved, That in the absence of any evidence establishing the conclusion that yellow fever has ever been conveyed by one person to another, it is the opinion of this convention that personal quarantine of cases of yellow fever may be safely abolished.

This resolution elicited discussion by many members, and some of them the most profound students of this disease that had ever met in debate: such were Drs. R. La Roche and George B. Wood, of Philadelphia; Drs. A. H. Stevens and John W. Francis, of New York; Drs. John Jeffries and D. H. Storer, of

---

* The doctor is unfortunate in this question, so far as the experience of 1878 goes. Quinine proved then to be any thing but a specific or prophylactic for yellow fever. In most instances it was a positive aggravation of the disease.

Boston; and several younger men, who appeared as living witnesses of modern epidemics. Finally, Dr. Stevens' resolution was amended by A. N. Bell, M. D., by the addition of a proviso, "that fomites of every kind be rigidly restricted," and passed by eighty-five affirmative votes to six negative; two physicians only voting in the negative. Before adjournment a committee was appointed to report at the next convention "specific recommendations of principles and measures of quarantine, as severally applicable to yellow fever, cholera, typhus fever, and small-pox, having reference also to the variations which different localities require." The committee consisted of Drs. A. N. Bell, Elisha Harris, Wilson Jewell, Isaac A. Nichols, and D. B. Reid. At the fourth annual convention, in Boston, June 14, 1860, this committee reported a "Code of Marine Hygiene," introduced by the following declarations:

1. Every organized government has the right of protecting itself against the introduction of infectious diseases, and of putting any country, place, or thing in quarantine which would introduce infectious diseases; provided, however, that no sanitary measures shall go so far as to exclude or drive from port a vessel, whatever be her condition.

2. The only diseases at present known, against the introduction of which general quarantine regulations should be enforced, are plague, yellow fever, cholera, small-pox, and typhus fever. As regards plague, the European Congress at Paris had the right to settle the question for the nations there represented; and inasmuch as they and the other nations of the Eastern Continent have reason to subject the plague to quarantine restrictions, the States of America yield implicit obedience to that convention.

3. All quarantine regulations, of any place whatever, should bear with equal force against the toleration or propagation of disease as against its introduction; and authority to prevent the introduction of disease in any place should be equally applicable against its exportation.

4. All quarantinable diseases are chiefly introduced by the *material* of commerce; and it is therefore against it that quarantine restrictions should be instituted, and not against the *personnel*; excepting, however, persons with no evidence of vaccination, and known to have been exposed to small-pox; such persons shall be vaccinated as soon as possible, and detained until the vaccina shall have taken effect; otherwise they may be detained fourteen days from the time of the known exposure.

5. The application of quarantine shall be regulated by the official declaration of the constituted sanitary authority at the port of departure where the malady exists. The cessation of these measures shall be determined by a like declaration that the malady has ceased after, however, the expiration of a fixed delay of thirty days for the plague, fifteen days for yellow fever, and ten days for cholera.

6. It is obligatory on all vessels to have a bill of health; this shall consist of two kinds only—a clean bill and a gross bill—the first for the attested absence of disease, and the second for the attested presence of disease. The bill shall state the hygienic state of the vessel; and a vessel in a bad condition,

even with a clean bill of health, shall be regarded as a vessel having a gross bill, and shall be submitted to the same regime.

7. The plague, yellow fever, and cholera being the only maladies that entail general measures, and place in quarantine those places whence they proceed, the restrictions enforced against these diseases shall not be applied to any other suspected or diseased vessel.

8. The power of applying the general principles of this code, and of acceding to its provisions, is expressly reserved to those nations and governments who consent to accept the obligations which it imposes; and all the administrative measures proceeding from it shall be determined by international sanitary regulations, or by a convention of the representatives of the governments which have adopted it.

9. This code shall continue in force and vigor among the governments adopting it for five years; and it shall be the duty of any party wishing to withdraw from its observance at the end of that time to officially declare his intention six months before the time expires; if there be no such notice the code shall be regarded as in force one year longer; and thus it shall continue year after year with all the governments accepting it, until after due notice six months before withdrawal. Then follow the provisions in detail: (1) Measures relating to departure; (2) Sanitary measures during the voyage; (3) Sanitary measures on arrival; (4) Executive arrangements; (5) Sanitary authorities.

This code was accepted by the unanimous vote of the convention, and recommitted to the committee, with instructions to secure its adoption by different governments.

Dr. Dowell, of Galveston, in the chapter on "quarantine" in his "Yellow Fever," says: "I have stated quarantine, to be effective, must be complete, both as to person and goods. But I do not think this either practicable or possible at the present time in most cities of the United States, as a man may take the seeds of the disease in Rio Janeiro, South America, and come to Galveston and pass its quarantine sound and well, and yet have the disease, and infect the whole city, for I have seen such cases—as the revenue cutter *Delaware*, at Galveston, in 1867, where four men came to the city, and eighteen and twenty days afterward these four had the disease, which shows, conclusively, that at least twenty days may intervene before the stage of incubation is over. So you see one may go almost around the world before he would have the disease. Hence I contend for quarantine, for cleanliness, and not for prohibition of ingress and egress, and that we must rely on sanitary means and sanitary measures almost exclusively for our protection from yellow fever. All animal filth should be removed—no open privies should be allowed in any town or city where yellow fever can prevail. All low streets or under-houses should be filled up. Better do it in summer than not at all; but best to be done in winter. For the further discussion of quarantine, we quote from an address by Prof. J. M. Calloway, M. D., before the Galveston Historical Society, which was written at my suggestion, and all of which I indorse, except that part where he says personal contagion can not take place. This I have fully argued above, and think, if I am wrong, it is at least safest to believe in it,* and in all cases avoid personal contact with any one after the fever rises and until the fever ceases, and all discharges and clothing have been removed. and the room well and completely ventilated or frozen out, and this must be for at least, seven consecutive days—below zero; as it will be seen, from reports, that persons have returned to the city several weeks after a frost, and slept in rooms where it has been, and taken the disease and died. No one should return who leaves, until at least four weeks after the last case, or after a seven days' freeze, the thermometer being below zero, centigrade, at least.† New York was, among the first of the States of the Union to establish quarantine. She suffered four epidemics of the yellow fever before, and ten since, its establishment, and had an interval of twenty-two years without yellow fever and without quarantine. Philadelphia had quarantine restrictions during all her epidemics. Boston, though the most favored city on the Atlantic coast, in the United States, regarding yellow fever epidemics, has had the most lax quarantine laws of any city of its size. The quarantine convention of Philadelphia, in 1857, one of the most able and intelligent bodies ever convened on the American continent, announce the opinion that "yellow fever can not become epidemic or endemic, unless there exists in the community the circumstances which are calculated to produce such diseases, independent of the importation." Dr. Gaillard, of Louisville, Kentucky, is of the same opinion. In a paper on the yellow fever, published during the epidemic of 1878, he says: "That New Orleans should, up to a certain time, have been absolutely free from yellow fever, that a fruit-vessel should land some of her crew sick with this disease, that the fever should at once spread, that it

---

* Mr. E. M. Avery, a respectable and reliable citizen of Memphis, states, in confirmation of the contagion theory, and as part of his experience in 1878, as follows: I was refugeed for exactly eight weeks, at White Haven, a station on the Mississippi and Tennessee Railroad, just eight miles south of our city. During that time there were three deaths by yellow fever in my immediate neighborhood—the first was that of Dr. Raines, who had visited the sick at Camp Joe Williams, contracted the fever, and died at his home, about a mile from White Haven station: the second was the case of young Bolton, at Camp Burke, located about a quarter of a mile south of the station; he had been exposed to the malaria of the city, and died after a few days' sickness. The third case, and which proves, most conclusively, the contagious nature of the late epidemic, was that of a young girl by the name of Colhouer, ten years of age, a resident with her parents at the station, who had not been away from home in many months, who was living in a pure and healthy atmosphere, but who contracted the disease by sleeping one night with a Mrs. Nicholson, whose husband had died of the fever in Memphis, and whom she had nursed. The little girl died of yellow fever; her mother took the disease the day after the child died, but recovered.

† In opposition to this advice we have the fact that the fever runs its course, and absolutely dies out without the killing effects of frost. This is the case, not only in Rio Janeiro, Vera Cruz, Havana, Kingston, Jamaica, but in all points in the United States. The fever, in 1878, was declared no longer epidemic in Memphis on the 29th of October, when the thermometer stood at 48.7, falling to 39.0 on the 31st, which was its lowest decline until December; so that there was no heavy black frost, as was declared by some, and the fever died out in its own good time.

should infect first those in immediate proximity to it, and subsequently those in remote communication with it, is simply a repetition of the old record. A further addition to the testimony which for generations has demonstrated the fact, clear and indisputable, that yellow fever will exist always in its well-known zone; that it will not originate out of this zone; that carried beyond it, and introduced into foul municipal air—its favorite, if not essential, nidus —it will spread and decimate; will bring ruin and desolation in its train. Norfolk and Mobile, and Philadelphia and Quebec, and Marshall, Texas, and St. Louis, and Montgomery, Alabama, and many other places which could be named, have climates and surroundings in every respect different from each other, but they have all been desolated by yellow fever, whenever the germs of the disease have been carried there. The alleged causes of yellow fever are often active in these cities, but the disease prevails only when it is manifestly transported there. The great authorities in all civilized lands believe yellow fever and malarial fevers to be essentially and totally different, while they believe the yellow fever poison to be essentially transportable, and, therefore, communicable; for its communicability is the logical evidence of its transportability. The great writers and teachers warn all of the communicability of this terrible plague; and the list is an imposing one—Hosack, Blane, Wistar, Townsend, Dickson, Hartshorne, George Gregory, Flint, Copland, Stevens, and J. W. Monette, Pym, Fellows, Audouard, Lining, Ramsay, Strobel, and a host of distinguished worthies." Hænisch writes thus: "The disease has been carried and has appeared at elevations of 2,000, and even 4,000, feet above the level of the sea," a fact attributed by Hænisch and Hirsch solely to the transportability and communicability of the disease.

Dr. Joseph Holt, of New Orleans, in a paper read before the congressional commission of 1878, says:

1. I believe that yellow fever is due to a specific poison, the existence of which is known only as manifested in man. Intangible, imponderable, unrecognizable to any of the senses, we have no positive knowledge of the essential nature of this poison. Every effort to prevent its appearance and to limit its spread must, therefore, be purely experimental.

2. The virus, if not indigenous, was imported at an early period in the history of New Orleans, and is ever present with us, requiring only a concurrence of certain conditions to call it forth, all of which conditions or factors are not known.

3. That the climate of New Orleans is sufficiently tropical to call into activity the virus of yellow fever without importation, and that New Orleans is allied to the cities of Havana and Vera Cruz in the power of developing the poison at certain seasons; which powers depend upon the fact that these cities are within the geographical area of development of this particular contagion. Why it is not developed at all times in places apparently under the same conditions, is unknown, because we are not acquainted with all of the essential factors of its development.

4. To prevail as an epidemic, there must exist certain favorable conditions. Such states or conditions of fitness prevailing, the early importation of the

virus will insure an epidemic, the magnitude of which will be determined by the number of persons unacclimated.

5. The specific virus of yellow fever, whether pre-existing as a dormant germ, or even as a germ at all, requires, among factors of its development, a certain geographical area of the earth, a long-continued high temperature, and the congregation in dense community of a large number of people, as in large towns and cities.

6. That it is not the simple fact of people living together in large numbers which furnishes this last factor, but the violation of hygienic law likely to result from such massing of humanity in the accumulation of their filth.

7. The contagion is readily transplanted through fomites, as in the garments of the sick, as well as in the recognized methods along the highways of commerce by ships and other carriers of merchandise. In regard to the transmission of yellow fever, it is almost impossible to determine the boundary line, in some instances, between infection strictly speaking and contagion.

8. Quarantine established with such vigor as to assure absolute non-intercourse with infected ports, can furnish the only crucial test of its own efficacy. Two formidable difficulties stand in the way. Evasion, that is, running the blockade—a performance at one time so common in the face of the artillery of the whole United States navy—and the established fact that ships once infected, and after that subjected to repeated cleansings, and even changing the crews, years afterward, coming into the yellow fever regions, have developed the disease, even on the high seas, without having touched at a tropical port.* In the history of New Orleans, quarantine has failed utterly to afford protection against yellow fever. We can only hope that its value may be discovered in its thoroughness.

9. The greatest good which may be reasonably expected of quarantine is in the prevention of the early introduction of the specific poison. Inasmuch as long-continued heat is required for its spontaneous manifestation, the disease is likely, therefore, to appear very late in the warm season, at a time when the cold weather may easily overtake it and prevent epidemic prevalence. That the specific poison, however, which has given rise to our great epidemics has invariably been imported, is by no means proven. In regard to some of them there is abundant evidence to the contrary.

10. Another great benefit which may be derived from quarantine, is probably in the fact that unless New Orleans shows a determined effort to furnish a guarantee to all inland and coast cities and towns by endeavoring to prevent the importation of the yellow fever poison, the whole country will be ready, upon the slightest provocation or idle rumor, to establish a shot-gun quarantine against New Orleans.

Dr. Southwood Smith, of the London Fever Hospital, in a "Treatise on Fever," published at London, in 1829, in a chapter on the causes of fever, explains clearly that under known conditions the yellow fever, like other

---

* As in the case of the United States steamship *Plymouth*, an account of which is given at length on pp. 97 and 98 of the chronology of yellow fever in this book.

fevers, may originate spontaneously in any place, and the immediate or exciting cause may become the predisposing cause, the fever being thus propagated to the extent of an epidemic. He says: "The immediate, or the exciting cause of fever, is a poison formed by the corruption or the decomposition of organic matter. Vegetable and animal matter, during the process of putrefaction, give off a principle, or give origin to a new compound, which, when applied to the human body, produces the phenomena constituting fever. What this principle or compound is, whether it be one of the constituent substances which enter into the composition of organized matter, or whether the primary elements of organized matter, as they are disengaged in the process of putrefaction, enter into some new combination, and thus generate a new product, we are wholly ignorant. Of the composition of the poison, of the laws which regulate its formation, and of its properties when generated, we know nothing beyond its power to strike the human being with sickness or death. We know that, under certain circumstances, vegetable and animal substances will putrefy; we know that a poison capable of producing fever will result from this putrefactive process, and we know nothing more. Of the conditions which are ascertained to be essential to the putrefactive process of dead organic substance, whether vegetable or animal, those of heat and moisture are the most certain, and as far as we yet know, the most powerful. Accordingly, in every situation in which circumstances concur to produce great moisture, while the heat is maintained with some steadiness within a certain range, there the febrile poison is invariably generated in large quantity, and in great potency. Wherever generated, we have no means of ascertaining its existence but by the effects it produces on the human body. Now and then circumstances arise which illustrate these effects in an exceedingly striking manner. This is the case when large numbers of men, previously in a state of sound health, are simultaneously exposed to it. Examples of such occurrences, as numerous and as complete as can be desired, were long since recorded. The suddenness with which fever sometimes attacks individuals on board a ship, or even an entire ship's crew, on the approach of the vessel to a shore where this poison is generated in large quantity, and in a high state of concentration, illustrates its operation, perhaps, in a still more striking manner. Dr. McCulloch, who has labored with great ability and zeal to recall attention to the most important and long-forgotten subject of malaria, relates an instance of some men on board a ship, who were seized, while the vessel was five miles from shore, with fatal cholera, the very instant the land smell first became perceptible. Several of these men, who were unavoidably employed on deck, died of the disease in a few hours. The armorer of the ship, who, before he could protect himself from the noxious blast, was accidently delayed on deck a few minutes to clear an obstruction in the chain cable, was seized with the malady while in that act, and was dead in a few hours. Dr. Potter states* that he witnessed the rise of a most malignant yellow

---

* See a Memoir on Contagion, more especially as it respects the yellow fever, etc., by N. Potter, M. D., Baltimore.

fever, in a valley in Pennsylvania, which contained numerous ponds of fresh water, and which, from the heat and dryness of the season, emitted a most offensive smell; that the fever prevailed most, and with the greatest degree of malignity, among the people who lived nearest these ponds; and adds an exceedingly instructive case, illustrative of the generation and operation of the cause of fever, recorded by Major Prior, in his account of a fever which attacked the army of the United States, at Gallipolis [1796]. The source of the malady was clearly traced to a large pond near the cantonment. When the disease was most severe, it assumed the continued form, and was accompanied with yellowness of the skin; when proper means were taken to destroy the pond, the fever immediately lost its continued form, and became first remittent, then intermittent, and ultimately disappeared. 'The fever,' says this intelligent officer, 'was, I think, justly charged to a large pond near the cantonment. An attempt had been made two or three years before to fill it up, by felling a number of large trees that grew on and near its margin, and by covering the wood thus fallen with earth. This intention had not been fulfilled. In August, the weather was extremely hot, and uncommonly dry; the water had evaporated considerably, leaving a great quantity of muddy water, with a thick, slimy mixture of putrefying vegetables, which emitted a stench almost intolerable. The inhabitants of the village, principally French, and very poor, as well as filthy in their mode of living, began to suffer first, and died so rapidly, that a general consternation seized the whole settlement. The garrison continued healthy for some days, and we began to console ourselves with the hope that we should escape altogether; we were, however, soon undeceived, and the reason of our exemption heretofore was soon discovered. The wind had blown the air arising from the pond from the camp; but as soon as it shifted to the reverse point, the soldiers began to sicken; in five days, half the garrison were on the sick list, and in ten, half of them were dead. They were generally seized with a chill, followed by headache, pains in the back and limbs, red eyes, constant sickness at stomach, or vomiting, and generally, just before death, with a vomiting of matter like coffee-grounds. They were often yellow before, but almost always after death. The sick died generally on the seventh, ninth, and eleventh days, though sometimes on the fifth, and on the third. As some decisive measures became necessary to save the remainder of the troops, I first thought of changing my quarters, but as the station was in every respect more eligible than any other, and had been made so by much labor and expense, I determined to try the experiment of changing the condition of the pond, from which the disease was believed to have arisen. A ditch was accordingly cut; what little water remained was conveyed off, and the whole surface covered with fresh earth. The effects of this scheme were soon obvious. Not a man was seized with the worst form of the fever after the work was finished, and the sick were not a little benefited, for they generally recovered, though slowly, because the fever became a common remitent, or gradually assumed the intermitting form. A few cases of remitting and intermitting fever occurred occasionally, till frost put an end to it in every form. As soon as the contents of the pond were changed, by cutting the ditch, the cause, whatever it was, seems to have been rendered incapable of communicating the disease in its worst form. Dr. Potter further states that, on one occasion, he saw a lady, who had been confined three days only, and whom he found in the agonies of death, with the skin of a deep orange color, the eyes red and prominent, the pulse intermittent, and ejecting copiously from the stomach every eight or ten minutes the secretion now known by the name of the black vomit; that she expired in a convulsion while he sat at her side; that petechiæ appeared immediately after death, and that putrefaction succeeded so rapidly, that it was necessary to order immediate interment; that, shortly afterward, he was called to a gentleman, who had been ill five days, and who, having expired in an hour or two after his visit, was removed into the coffin with the utmost difficulty, the flesh literally dropping from the bones; that, in one family, residing in a house which stood on a level piece of ground, apparently beyond the reach of noxious exhalation, there being no stagnant water, as was supposed, within a mile of it, he found the mother laboring under a bilious remitting fever, which had continued eleven days, the daughter, seventeen years of age, suffering from a similar fever; two sons, the one between eight and nine, and the other six, ill with dysentery; and the father on the brink of the grave from a most malignant fever. There being no apparent cause for the condition of this afflicted family, the immediate neighborhood of the house being free from the ordinary sources of malaria, and the adjacent country being not unhealthy, the condition of the house itself was minutely investigated. The cause of the evil was manifest. It appeared that the present family had resided in the house only about five weeks; that immediately preceding their occupation of it a man had died suddenly in it; that he, himself (Dr. Potter), was seized with nausea and general lassitude immediately on leaving the house after his first visit; and that a fever, as he supposes, was arrested by a strong dose of tartarized antimony, which operated violently by vomiting and purging. On examining the premises, it was found that the cellar contained water about two feet deep, which had remained there from the first week in June, the country having been then inundated by torrents of rain. The cellar being useless, the door had been closed, and the only vent for the pestiferous gases was through the floor, which was open in several places. The family being immediately removed, all the sick became convalescent from the time they ceased to breathe the air of the place. The owner of the house hired two men to empty the cellar. These men having ripped up the floor, and placed a pump in the deepest part of the water, evacuated the cellar to the dregs in one day. On the second day after the execution of this task one of these men was seized with a chillness, succeeded by an ardent fever, which terminated with the usual symptoms of yellow fever; namely, hæmorrhages, yellow skin and petechiæ, and proved fatal on the third day from the attack; the day following the seizure of the first, the second man was attacked with similar symptoms, and died on the seventh day of the disease, with the black vomit, in addition to the ordinary symptoms of the yellow fever. These examples may suffice to illustrate the operation of that febrile poison which arises chiefly from the decomposition of vegetable matter. The poison derived from the putrefaction of animal matter is still more pernicious;

its effects are more powerful in degree, and worse in character; it operates more intensely on the nervous system, and less on the vascular; and the fevers it produces are invariably of the typhoid type, and of the continued form. Without doubt, a febrile poison, purely of animal origin, in a high degree of concentration, would kill instantaneously; and when not intense enough to strike with instantaneous death, it would produce a continued fever with the typhoid characters, in the greatest possible degree of completeness and perfection. And this appears to afford the true solution of the origin of the plague. The more closely the localities are examined of every situation in which the plague prevails, the more abundant the sources of putrefying animal matter will appear, and the more manifest it will become, not only that such matter must be present, but that it must abound. In assigning the reason why Grand Cairo, in Egypt, is [was] the birth-place and the cradle of the plague, Mead states that that city is crowded with vast numbers of inhabitants, who live not only poorly, but nastily; that the streets are narrow and close; that the city itself is situated in a sandy plain, at the foot of a mountain, which keeps off the winds that might refresh the air; that consequently the heat is rendered extremely stifling; that a great canal passes through the midst of the city, which, at the overflowing of the Nile, is filled with water; that on the decrease of the river, this canal is gradually dried up, and the people throw into it all manner of filth, carrion, offal, and so on; that the stench which arises from this, and the mud together, is intolerably offensive; and that, from this source, the plague constantly springing up every year, preys upon the inhabitants, and is stopped only by the return of the Nile, the overflowing of which washes away this load of filth; that in Ethiopia the swarms of locusts are so prodigious that they sometimes cause a famine, by devouring the fruits of the earth, and when they die create a pestilence by the putrefaction of their bodies; that this putrefaction is greatly increased by the dampness of the climate, which, during the sultry heats of July and August, is often excessive; that the effluvia which arise from this immense quantity of putrefying animal substance, combined with so much heat and moisture, continually generate the plague in its intensest form; and that the Egyptians of old were so sensible how much the putrefaction of dead animals contributed toward breeding the plague, that they worshiped the bird Ibis, from the services it did in devouring great numbers of serpents, which they observed injured by their stench when dead, as much as by their bite when alive. Nothing can be more striking than the cases recorded by Pringle, and which daily occurred to him of the production of fever, exquisitely typhoid (according to the language of that day, jail and hospital fever), and of the sudden transition of intermittent and remittent into the continued and typhoid type, from the presence of a poison clearly and certainly of animal origin. Whenever wounded soldiers, with malignant sores, or mortified limbs, were crowded together, or whenever only a few of such diseased persons were placed in a room with the sick from other diseases, with those laboring under intermittent and remittent, for example, a severe and mortal typhus immediately arose; nay, whenever men, previously in a state of sound health, were too much crowded together for any considerable time, typhus (jail or hospital fever) was sure to be produced. The instances of such occurrences that are detailed are too numerous to be cited, but they are so clearly stated, and so striking, that they well deserve to be consulted by whoever is desirous of clearly tracing the operation of this great cause of fever. But by far the most potent febrile poison, derived from an animal origin, is that which is formed by exhalations given off from the living bodies of those who are affected with fever, especially when such exhalations are pent up in a close and confined apartment. The room of a fever-patient, in a small and heated apartment in London, with no perflation of fresh air, is perfectly analogous to a stagnant pool in Ethiopia, full of the bodies of dead locusts. The poison generated in both cases is the same; the difference is merely in the degree of its potency. Nature, with her burning sun, her still and pent-up wind, her stagnant and teeming marsh, manufactures plague on a large and fearful scale: poverty in her hut, covered with her rags, surrounded with her filth, striving with all her might to keep out the pure air, and to increase the heat, imitates nature but too successfully; the process and the product are the same, the only difference is in the magnitude of the result. Penury and ignorance can thus at any time, and in any place, create a mortal plague. And of this no one has ever doubted. Of the power of the living body, even when in sound health, much more when in disease, and, above all, when that disease is fever, to produce a poison capable of generating fever, no one disputes, and the fact has never been called in question. Thus far the agreement among all medical men, of all sects, and of all ages, is perfect. But it happens that there is another form of animal matter capable of producing fever; namely, a matter secreted by the living body, constituting not only a poison, but a peculiar and specific poison. This specific poison produces not merely fever, but fever with a specific train of symptoms. In the acknowledgment of this fact, also, the agreement among all medical men is equally perfect. But some contend that the poison generated in the first case, and that generated in the second, may both be properly called contagious; others maintain that the application of the same term to two cases so specifically different, destroys a distinction which it is useful to preserve, and that it would be more correct, as well as more conducive to clearness of conception, to call the poison generated in the first case an infection, and to restrict the term contagion to designate the poison generated in the latter. Vast and immeasurable as the difference appears to be between the contagionists and the anti-contagionists, if regard be had merely to their language, yet if attention be paid only to their ideas, to this, and to this only, narrow as the compass is, the whole controversy is reduced. It resolves itself wholly into the question, whether one word shall be used to express two cases which differ from each other in some important circumstances, or whether it may not be more convenient to employ two terms, and strictly to appropriate each to designate its own specific class. It must be manifest that, since both sects are perfectly agreed about the facts, the dispute can be only verbal. If the one would consent to restrict their use of the term contagious, for which there is the best authority and ancient custom, to those diseases which arise from a specific contagion, and would call those which arise from every other poison infectious, there would be an end to this apparently interminable, and, in many respects, mischievous controversy. Is the febrile poison, whether of vegetable or animal origin, or whether composed of both, capable of adhering to clothes, apparel, and other substances, in such a manner as truly to infect them, so that when applied to the bodies of the healthy, at any distance of place, and at some distance of time, the specific effects of the poison are produced? That such substances may be so imbued with the poison of the small-pox, all admit: that the evidence should not be as complete relative to the power, or the inability of such substances to convey and communicate the poison of ordinary continued fever, is alike disgraceful to the state of our science, and injurious to the cause of humanity. There is no reason why the question should not be settled with absolute certainty; there is no manner of difficulty in determining it. Experiments the most direct, complete, and decisive, might be performed, which, if observed, during their progress, by competent witnesses, and duly authenticated, might ascertain the point, with sufficient clearness and certainty, to satisfy not only the present age, but future generations. Of all predisposing causes, the most powerful is the continued presence and the slow operation of the immediate or exciting cause. It is a matter of constant observation, that the febrile poison may be present in sufficient intensity to affect the health, without being sufficiently potent to produce fever. In this case, the energy of the action of the organs is diminished, their functions are languidly performed, the entire system is weakened, and this increases, until at length the power of resistance is less than the power of the poison. Whenever this happens, fever is induced; not that the power of the poison may be at all increased; but the condition of the system is changed, in consequence of which, it is capable of offering to the noxious agent that asssails it less resistance. Dr. Potter performed some experiments, to show that the continual presence of the exciting cause not only operates upon the general system, but actually produces a morbid change in the blood before it induces fever. During the prevalence of an epidemic, it was observed that, in all the cases in which the patients were bled, the general appearance of the blood was precisely the same; that the coagulum was either of a yellow or of a deep orange color, and that a portion of the red particles was invariably precipitated. It occurred to Dr. Potter that if the cause of the disease were contained in the common atmosphere, the blood of those who had inhaled it a certain time would exhibit similar phenomena; and that should this be the case, it would prove that the cause, before actually producing the disease, brought about a state of the system which predisposed it to be affected by the poison. To ascertain the appearances of the blood in persons who were exposed to the febrile poison, but who still remained apparently in perfect health, he drew a quantity of blood from five persons who had lived during the whole epidemic season in the most infected parts of the city. To external appearance and inward feeling, each of these persons was in sound health. Their blood could in no respect be distinguished from the blood of those who labored under the most intense forms of the prevailing fever. As it was necessary to the conclusiveness of the experiment that their blood should be compared with the blood of those who lived in an atmosphere unquestionably pure, Dr. Potter selected an equal number of persons who dwelt on the hills, in Baltimore County, and drew from each of them ten ounces of blood. The contrast was most manifest. The serum was neither of a yellow nor of an orange color; there was no red precipitate; the appearances were such as are found in the blood of persons in perfect health. A young gentleman having returned to the city from the western part of Pennsylvania, on the 10th of September, in a state of sound health, Dr. Potter drew a few ounces of blood from a vein on the day of his arrival; it exhibited no deviation from that of a healthy person. He remained in the family until the 26th of the month, that is, sixteen days. On the sixteenth day the bleeding was repeated. The serum had assumed a deep yellow hue, and a copious precipitation of red globules had likewise fallen to the bottom of the vessel. In these experiments, the blood in six persons indicated the operation of the morbid cause, while each remained in a state of apparent health. Of these six persons, four were actually seized with yellow fever during the prevalence of the epidemic; and the other two, though they escaped any formal attack, did not escape indisposition. They were affected with headache, nausea, and other indications of disease, like hundreds besides, who were never absolutely confined to the house, and who never took any medicine, but who still experienced, in nausea, giddiness, headache, pain in the extremities, and so on, abundant intimations of the presence of the poison. These examples may suffice to show how the exciting may itself become a most powerful predisposing cause. The predisposition to subsequent attacks, after the system has once suffered from the disease, is very remarkable; that predisposition remains for a considerable period after convalescence and apparent recovery. Of this, striking examples continually occur, both with regard to intermittent and to continued fever. In fact, the disposition to relapse remains until the constitution has recovered its previous strength and vigor, however distant that period may be. The influence of cold, moisture, fatigue, intemperance, constipation, anxiety, fear, and all the depressing passions, are likewise extremely powerful predisposing causes. They enable a less dose of the poison to produce fever, and they increase the intensity of the fever when it is established. They all act by weakening the resisting power inherent in the constitution, that is, by enfeebling the powers of life."

Dr. Drake, of Nashville, thus formulates his views as to quarantine:

1. The danger of attacks from yellow fever is in proportion to the amount of the poison taken into the system.

2. There is a systemic toleration of the poison varying with the vital resistance of each individual, and zymotic action is mainly concerned in the process of sporulation and fructification without the body, and not within, until the line of vital resistance is broken down, when this process may come into active operation as in other effete matter without the body; otherwise it would seem impossible for a single human being to escape.*

---

* In Coleridge's "Table Talk," under date of April 7, 1832, and the heading "Epidemic Diseases—Quarantine" the following views are expressed: "Quarantine can

3. In the midst of an epidemic, depopulation of rooms and avoidance of confined areas of stagnant air afford the safest personal prophylaxis.

4. Quarantine of the ordinary landing of vessels, cars, and other vehicles, and of the baggage and clothing of travelers from infected districts, should be rigidly enforced until disinfection is thoroughly consummated. Cities and towns should quarantine against infected districts, but the open country need not be put under restriction, as the facts in the case of the refugee camp near Memphis abundantly prove. Camps of refuge should be provided at convenient distances from a city or town infected, and the entire population exposed to danger should abandon all inclosures, and live in the open air.

The Homeopathic Commission, whose investigation was thorough, and whose recommendations are of the most sensible and practical character, in relation to quarantine, recommend the erection of a permanent sanitary commission, ably constituted, well salaried, and invested by the government with large powers, to be composed of medical men, yellow fever experts, and of professed scientists; which sanitary commission shall devote itself exclusively to matters of public hygiene. The measures they recommend to prevent the importation and spread of yellow fever are the following:

1. An intelligent oversight of all the tropical ports during the summer months. The sanitary commission should have agents in all those ports con-

---

not keep out an atmospheric disease, but it can, and does always, increase the predisposing causes of its reception." And this: "There are two grand divisions under which all contagious diseases may be classed, 1st. Those which spring from organized living beings, and from the life in them, and which enter, as it were, into the life of those in whom they reproduce themselves—such as small-pox and measles. These become so domesticated with the habit and system that they are rarely received twice. 2d. Those which spring from dead, organized, or unorganized, matter, and which may be comprehended under the wide term, malaria. You may have passed a stagnant pond a hundred times without injury, you happen to pass it again, in low spirits and chilled, precisely at the moment of the explosion of the gas, the malaria strikes on the cutaneous or veno-glandular system and drives the blood from the surface, the shivering fit comes on, till the musculo-arterial irritability reacts, and then the hot fit succeeds, and, unless bark or arsenic—particularly bark, because it is bitter as well as tonic—be applied to strengthen the veno-glandular, and to moderate the musculo-arterial system, a man may have the ague for thirty years together. But if, instead of being exposed to the solitary malaria of a pond, a man, traveling through the Pontine marshes, permits his animal energies to play, and surrenders himself to the drowsiness which generally attacks him, then blast upon blast strikes upon the cutaneous system, and passes through it to the musculo-arterial, and so completely overpowers the latter that it can not react, and the man dies at once, instead of only catching an ague. There are three factors of the operation of an epidemic, or atmospheric disease. The first and principal one is the predisposed state of the body. Secondly, the specific virus in the atmosphere; and, thirdly, the accidental circumstances of weather, locality, food, occupation, etc. Against the second of these we are powerless; its nature, causes, and sympathies are too subtle for our senses to find data to go upon. Against the first, medicine may act profitably; against the third, a wise and sagacious medical police ought to be adopted; but, above all, let every man act like a Christian, in all charity and love, and brotherly kindness, and sincere reliance on God's merciful providence."

nected either with our consulates or with responsible commercial houses. It should be their business to keep the commission regularly and frequently advised of the sanitary condition of every locality, to report the appearance and progress of the fever, the sailing of every suspicious or infected vessel, and to furnish all information the commission may require.

2. The declaration of a discriminating quarantine only against ports notoriously infected, regulated in character and duration by the actual facts obtained by the commission.

3. The thorough cleansing, disinfecting, and refrigeration of every vessel arriving from yellow fever ports during the summer months. The character, mode, and extent of the disinfection will be determined by the studies and experiments of the commission in that special direction. We call attention to the refrigeration of vessels suggested to us by Dr. Bushrod W. James, of Philadelphia. From the recent inventions and improvements in the way of fitting up refrigerating rooms and ice-making machines, he is convinced that all difficulties can be easily overcome, and the hold, cargoes, and passengers of vessels can be subjected for two or three days to a low temperature, say ten or fifteen degrees below the freezing-point—a temperature quite destructive of the yellow fever germ, but entirely compatible with human comfort.

4. The sanitary surveillance for thirty days after landing of all persons coming from tropical ports and remaining in the city. Physicians should be compelled, under heavy penalties, to report the slightest sickness among such passengers, and as soon as yellow fever is diagnosed by experts, measures for the immediate suppression of the disease should be adopted.

Dr. A. N. Bell, editor of the *Sanitarian*, perhaps the highest authority in this country on quarantine and sanitation, concluding a very able article on this subject in the number of his magazine for February of this year (1879), says, in regard to yellow fever: "This epidemic, more than any other, concerns the commercial prosperity of the southern ports of the United States. It is of little consequence whether it was originally indigenous or exotic. It is a disease of communities, rarely or never originating or spreading in a scattered population. It has been common to the cities of the Gulf coast of America, and in the West Indies, as far back as we have any authentic history of their diseases, and has recurred sufficiently often to maintain a potential activity whenever favored by local conditions and protracted periods of prevailing high temperature. But every place where yellow fever arises spontaneously, is epidemic, or is capable of being introduced, must have, in addition to localizing causes, a prevailing temperature for several weeks above 75°, a condition comparatively rare in our sea-ports north of Charleston. It is apparent, therefore, that quarantine restrictions necessary to southern ports may be unnecessarily oppressive to northern ones, that a low temperature is ordinarily an effectual quarantine against the introduction of yellow fever. The portability of yellow fever is a settled question; but no matter what the differences of opinion in regard to the essential nature of the cause of the disease, the relations of yellow fever to commerce, wherever brought in contact with it, have shown that vessels are liable to become infected, and to convey it from port to port in proportion to their over-crowded state, want of cleanliness, and want of ventilation. And no measures are more imperatively necessary for the prevention of the spread of yellow fever and other epidemics by commerce than those which will effectually enforce room, *cleanliness*, and *ventilation* in the naval, mercantile marine, lake, and river services. Finally, no quarantine can ever be made successful without coördinate internal sanitary measures for both ports and vessels of every class. The remarks of John Simon, in his Report to the Commissioners of Sewers of London, 1854, in regard to cholera, are equally applicable to yellow fever: 'The specific migrating power, whatever its nature, has the faculty of infecting districts in a manner detrimental to life *only when their atmosphere is fraught with certain products susceptible, under its influence, of undergoing poisonous transformation.* . . . Through the unpolluted atmosphere of cleanly districts it migrates silently, without a blow; that which it can kindle into poison lies not there. To the foul, damp breath of low-lying cities it comes like a spark to powder. Here is contained that which it can quickly make destructive—soaked into soil, stagnant in water, grimming the pavement, tainting the air—the slow rottenness of unremoved excrement, to which the first contact of this foreign ferment brings the occasion of changing into new and more deadly combinations.'"

III.

Disagreeing upon nearly every other point, the doctors are almost a unit as to the necessity for thorough sanitation, in order to ward off or mitigate attacks of yellow fever. They all declare that filth, especially decaying animal matter and human excrement, is a prime, if not the potent, cause of the severity of the attacks of this curse to the people of the Mississippi Valley. The specific poison may be in the air, but its propagation depends upon conditions, the destruction of which are within the reach of all classes in the South. Dr. Joseph Holt, in a paper read before the Congressional Yellow Fever Commission of 1878, while sitting in New Orleans, declares that, "while we can not trace a direct causative relation between the filth of a city, town, or ship[*] and the first appearance of this disease, it invariably develops itself,

---

[*] A writer, in the Nashville *Banner*, of the 19th of March, 1879, gives the filth attendant upon the Middle Passage as the source and origin of this disease, which, like a direful retribution, he thinks, continues to plague all the slave-cursed countries of North and South America. He paints the horrifying picture graphically. He says: "As for the origin and birth-place of the yellow fever, there can be but little doubt, no matter how much ink has been used on the subject. It is ocean born. I have seen more sides of the world than one, and spent more than one Saturday night at 'sea,' in the forecastle of a

primarily associated with a bad sanitary condition of the community. In certain cities—Philadelphia and New York especially—formerly devastated by this pestilence, the scourge has ceased coincidently with an improved sanitary system.

---

ship, among seamen of all nations, hearing them tell of all their voyages and the voyages of their fathers, in plain, unmistakable language. The horrors of the Middle Passage, sometimes called High Latitudes, have been related by some bronzed fellow, an eye-witness from the Gulf of Guinea, a deadhead, in such language as none other dare to use or could use. That fever about which there has been, and still is, much discussion and difference of opinion among landsmen and philanthropists, is the fruit of this Middle Passage, in my belief. Here hundreds, sometimes a thousand, human beings, torn from their rude yet happy homes, were huddled together between the upper and lower decks of a floating hell, commanded by a demon in human shape, and managed by the offscouring of God's earth, to be carried to a Christian land and sold, 'slaves for life.' My God! could you be with them—mad, naked, hopeless, forlorn!—as a squall strikes the ship and hurls to leeward a raving mass, you would see what the Middle Passage means. Could you hear them in a dead calm, not even a cat's paw of wind on the rolling deep, the thermometer 110° Fahrenheit, the pitch boiling from the seams in the black sides of the ship, the white deck so hot with a vertical sun that you could not tread on it with a bare foot, and then hear the wild anguish beneath you, and smell! Could you stand on that deck, again, of a dark, murky night—a night of the tropic—and feel it rain in torrents, such as you never saw, decks full of port-sills, a heavy ground-swell on, ship rolling and tumbling about, her unfilled sails slashing, and dashing, and crashing against the mast with a noise like thunder, the deck load of water hurled from side to side, while beneath is untold misery for want of some of that dashing water, you would see the origin of the dread pestilence. Wait for the morning after such a night, look at your mast boats, your canon, your hatchways, your lower mast, your pumps; they are all covered with a lead-colored, silver-looking coat, and large drops of black dew. This is the emanation—the poison gas from the catacomb beneath you. Dreadful! Ain't it dreadful? Hark! The bell strikes one; 'tis death! The gratings are off, and from that dark, concentrated misery below is passed up thirty or more nude forms. Their white, blearing eyes, their open mouths, their fallen chins, their bluish-looking skin, wrinkled and parboiled with the heat of the damp ship, and their last agonies—ain't it dreadful! Then they are tumbled into the sea, food for the sharks, with a Coast of Guineaman's prayer, 'D—n the niggers; what ails them? There is thirty more gone.' Ain't it dreadful? Gentlemen, here is the birth-place and cause of our scourge, the yellow fever. It was not known among the Caribbean Islands, nor at Brazil, nor on the western Continent, until the curse of slavery came there. It is a creature of the Middle Passage—the high latitudes of misery, nakedness, want, and filth. Gentlemen, you have heard of these things, but have never seen them. You have heard of a slave-ship, but she has never come with all her horrors before you. It is from her we receive this dread curse; it is not of western birth—not indigenous. Its footsteps come up from mid-ocean. Why is it thus? In 1825, I was in Liverpool. The barque *Mollie*, from Fernando Po, Gulf of Guinea, was brought into dock, a condemned slaver. She was 'eighty years old,' had been in the west coast of Africa trade most of that time; was a low, black craft with a short shark's head above her cut-water, a smoky black, looked as if she had been below. I heard her history from an old sailor. I have given you part of that history. Her name should be changed to Aceldama. Every look about her told a tale of horror, yet her owner bowed at the name of Jesus. The officers and crews of these slave-ships slept above the slave-decks in the poop or top-gallant forecastle, where the air was pure, were well fed and kept clean, and thus, in most cases, escaped the contagion. But for this no voyage could have been safely made. Gentlemen, keep clean, stir around out of doors, let the wind feel your skin, and, above all,

Sanitary negligence in India is punished with cholera; in the Orient, with plague and leprosy; in Europe, the British Islands, and the Northern United States, with typhus, typhoid, diphtheria, and scarlatina, in their malignant and epidemic forms; in the West Indies and tropical and semi-tropical Americas with yellow fever. For the disobedience of sanitary law these are among the prices paid by the human race according to its distribution upon the earth." The Board of Health of New Orleans adopting these views of Dr. Holt, in a report to the general council of that city, say that "One duty paramount to all others confronts the people of New Orleans—that they shall perfect the sanitary condition of our city. This can only be done in accordance with a system of the most liberal and enlightened sanitary engineering, and in an absolute obedience to all the laws relating to the public health. By the enforcement of wisely-appointed sanitary measures, we will accomplish a double reformation, the crowning necessity of our time—we will improve by it the health and prosperity of our people, and in equal measure diminish the miseries of our poor." The report of the Board of Health of England,* on quarantine and yellow fever, presented to both houses of Parliament, in April, 1852, says: "The means of protection from yellow fever is not in quarantine restrictions and sanitary cordons, but in sanitary works and operations. . . . We believe there is a general belief in the conclusion that the substitution of sanitary hygienic measures for quarantine isolation and restriction would afford more certain and effectual protection." Dr. Louis A. Falligant, who differed on many points from his colleagues of the Allopathic Commission, appointed by the congressional committee, holds the view that yellow fever may be developed by indigenous as well as by imported poison, and that local hygiene is of equal importance with quarantine in checking the spread of the imported fever, and of absolute necessity in the prevention of that of domestic origin. He says, clearly and forcibly, "I can not overlook the fact that, whilst fire will explode powder, the fire may be produced in one locality by electricity, in another by

---

don't hide dirt. Better let the hot sun lick its poison up, and the winds scatter it, than to turn it into badly-covered sewers, to creep along and ripen, and then cast its breath out with the dews of night through thousands of little openings. There is more safety in this than in all your quarantine, inland. Quarantine ships and foreign travelers as much as you please, but when they have introduced the evil, cleanliness is the best and surest remedy I have seen yet."

* This commission, composed of Lord Shaftsbury and Drs. Edwin Chadwick and I. Southwood Smith, in their report to that government, declare "that the conditions which influence the localization of yellow fever are known, definite, and, to a great extent, removable, and are substantially the same as the localizing causes of cholera and all other epidemic diseases. That, as in the case of all other epidemic diseases, in proportion as there localizing causes are removed or diminished, yellow fever ceases to appear, or recurs at more distant intervals, and in milder forms. That there is no evidence to prove that yellow fever has ever been imported. That consequently the means of protection from yellow fever, are not quarantine restrictions and sanitary cordons, but sanitary works and operations, having for their object the removal and prevention of the several localizing conditions, and when such permanent works are impracticable [as they can not be in cities] the temporary removal, as far as may be possible, of the population from the infected districts.

the collision of flint and steel, and in still another by striking a match." Dr. Holt, as sanitary inspector for the fourth district, in his report to the New Orleans Board of Health, calls attention to the fact that it " has by no means been satisfactorily proven that putrefying animal matter and the filth of great communities of human beings has not its position as a factor in the production or first appearance of yellow fever poison. No instance has yet been adduced of yellow fever appearing *de novo*, except as associated with large communities in a filthy condition, or on ship-board, where the same unsanitary condition exists in a concentrated form. There are precisely the same reasons for declaring yellow fever to be *ab initio* the product of human filth, as malaria

But so clear a statement of cause and effect, a judgment delivered after the most careful examination, has not been allowed to pass unchallenged. Even so respectable a body as the State Medical Society of Tennessee has declared against it—against this so deliberately stated experience. At its last session, and on the 3d of April, 1879, that body resolved: "That we recommend to those in authority a quarantine in its most judicious shape—national, State, and local—as the *only* means yet known by which this terrible scourge can be even partially stayed and controlled; and that all measures now pending in Congress or in any State legislature looking to this end have the hearty indorsement of this body." And this in the face of the testimony of the most experienced yellow fever physicians, who declare that filth in every form—from the offal of the slaughter-house to human excreta—is the nidus on which yellow fever feeds and propagates, and by which it is sustained and perpetuated. Quarantine may be *one*, but it is not "*the only*" means of prevention of the spread of this awful scourge. As Dr. McDonald says: "Whatever physical conditions, such as an increase of temperature, moisture, and subsequent evaporation, or the common decompositions of cess-pools, or the effluvia evolved in bad drainage, may be operative on shore, yet, when once communicated to a man-of-war vessel, and isolated on her voyage by far removal from all local land influences, the phenomena are very striking and suggestive. Under such circumstances it is difficult to witness the spread of the disease from one individual to another, and its virulence becoming more intensified by the unavoidable crowding of the sick, without recognizing the important part that the emanations and excretions of the human body must take in the matter. It may be objected that all the most potent of the terrestrial or atmospheric conditions alluded to are fulfilled in the bilge-effluvia of the vessel, but it must be apparent to the close observer that the human element far outweighs all other suppositions, although bilge-water and all other foulnesses in the vessel may form a *nidus* for the further development of the disease and its spread. But when the disease is again landed at some new port, this bilge-water is not brought on shore, although it may be communicated to foul docks. The clothing and effects of the dead, and of the survivors, and even of those who have not been sick, but which have been long exposed to the emanations of the sick, are then brought on shore and taken to near or distant points in the unfortunate town. The more crowded and the more filthy the houses into which these infected things are brought, the greater will be the danger of an outbreak. It is believed that the specific yellow fever poison can not be conveyed directly from the sick to the healthy, but must first be deposited in decomposing animal and vegetable matter. Still, however this may be, it is certainly a portable disease, which can be conveyed from one locality to another by means of clothing, foul merchandise, and in the holds of vessels. If filth is necessary to its propagation, where is that most easily met with but in the unwashed bodies and clothes of the dirty poor, and in their foul rooms, kitchens, privies, yards, streets, gutters, sewers, etc., and even in the houses of the slovenly and careless rich—for not every rich person is a clean person in every part of his house and belongings."

to be the product of the marsh or swamp. Emanating from a more deadly and pestilential source than mere rotting leaves and a wet soil, the virus is possessed of special qualities in keeping with the foul source of its origin. It gives no warning of its coming,* it is limited geographically; it is transmissible in fomites, and is, of all specific poisons, perhaps, the most intensely infectious; the disease runs its course quickly and ceases, one attack usually giving immunity from a second. Typhus, typhoid, diphtheria, the plague, and yellow fever are only such products as we might reasonably expect from effete animal matter under certain conditions of special foulness. Their specific nature, transmissibility, and power of spreading, independently of the conditions of their origin, are no proofs against their having such an origin." Substantiating these views, Dr. Holt gives this sickening description of the source, as he suggests, of yellow fever in New Orleans. He says: "It is not asserting too much to declare that our privies are the most dangerous enemies of our lives and happiness. There is hardly one in New Orleans but whose contents have free access to the soil, to saturate the ground with liquid ordure. Thousands of them were originally huge boxes or wooden tanks, but are now only common sinks or pits in the ground, with hardly a vestige of the woodwork left. The most mischievous parts of their contents soak into the earth, and so contaminate the soil under our feet that specimens

---

* "While Esculapians have no special gift of foretelling which will, and which will not, be an epidemic year," says Dowler, in 1853, " history furnishes presumptions, analogies, and deductions more or less favorable to the future in New Orleans, even though the next few years should be as insalubrious as the past. Epidemics have not only a limited period of increment and decrement in any one year, but they usually have more prolonged periods of increment and decrement through series of years, often constituting what may be called a cycle of variable duration, after which they generally cease. So it was with the plague in Europe; so it was with the fever in the Spanish peninsula ; so it was with the fever in the cities of the United States, in the North, as in Boston, New York, Philadelphia, Baltimore, and other places. Its invasion of the southern tropic, at Rio, so recent and severe, together with its decline in the north temperate zone, may be the precursors of its northern declination and southern advance, so that both Charleston, Mobile, New Orleans, and other southern towns and districts have now, at the least, the same probabilities in favor of approaching exemption that many other cities further north had more than half a century ago, before yellow fever appeared on the banks of the Mississippi. New Orleans is now, and has long been, near the northern border of the yellow fever zone. If yellow fever has, as may be the case, reached its culminating case in this city, its history elsewhere in the temperate zone indicates a progressive decline. Charleston, desolated at the close of the seventeenth century, was nearly exempt from yellow fever in the first quarter, and in the two last quarters, of the eighteenth century. New York was exempt for forty years, ending in the last decimal period of the same century—a period longer than the exemption of which the present forms a part—the prolongation of which may be suddenly arrested, for any thing that human foresight or science can show to the contrary. The history of the past affords no guarantee that its scenes shall ever be repeated. It is as idle to deny as to predict this lamentable contingency. It is consolatory to reflect, however, that the plague, as well as the yellow fever, has almost entirely left Europe, and that the latter disease is scarcely known in the Atlantic States of the Republic. No thanks to quarantine! If any visible causes can be assigned for this exemption, the most probable are the extensions of knowledge in hygiene, physiology, and physical or sanitary improvements. Thanks to science!"

of subsoil water, taken from different depths, as low as ninety-five feet, and from different parts of the city, have been carefully analyzed by Professor Joseph Jones, and have yielded a large percentage of urea and organic matters, the products of animal excretion, fully fifty-three grains to every gallon. 'It is evident,' Jones says, 'that these waters are suitable neither for drinking nor for washing, nor for cooking. In fact, they are as bad as, if not worse than, the drainings of graveyards'—which he proves by comparison with certain English analyses. During wet weather, these vaults or sinks quickly fill with water, and overflow, flooding yards and gutters with ordure. Under a sun almost tropical one-half the year, this ferments, and emits a most abominable stench, which, of all others, must be a fruitful source of disease, operating directly in its production, and indirectly in lowering the vital stamina of the inhabitants. While in wet seasons these vaults are flooded, in dry weather, as before stated, they are largely emptied by their fluid contents soaking into the ground, thus saturating the soil upon which we live with human excrement. In this respect it may be properly stated that the people have a huge privy in common, and that the inhabitants of New Orleans live upon a dung-heap. Is it possible to imagine a sanitary condition more deplorably bad? That epidemic diseases should sweep at times as a fire is no marvel. It is a righteous retribution for violated law. The excellent health which we usually enjoy is more greatly to be wondered at. However, so long as this flagrant disobedience of sanitary law exists, so long must we surely pay the price, as we paid it last summer." And this picture, so repugnant to every sense of decency, as well as violative of the simplest laws of life, will serve not only for New Orleans, but for every city of the South, of the West, or of the North, where adequate provision is not made for the washing away or carting away of offal, refuse, ashes, and human excreta. This may be said, too, of many cities that boast of a sewerage system, supposed to be effective, but that is really defective—that leaks its noxious emissions into the soil in the form of seepage, or gases more subtle and deadly. Memphis, so much more highly favored as to situation, could not, and never has been in a condition so disgraceful as this which Holt paints for New Orleans, and which we can well believe to be true. With unsurpassed surface drainage, and bayous, that send their branches far beyond the confines of the city, and into the country to sources that well up from springs of pure, good water—with these, Memphis is well drained and dry, and it might be supposed is beyond the contamination, which, after one hundred and fifty years has made of the site of New Orleans, as Holt says, a mere "dung-heap." But a careful examination reveals the fact that this is not altogether the case.[*] The privies, many of them in Memphis, are so deep as to reach the sand substratum on which rests the great clay bank known as the Chickasaw Bluffs.

---

[*] Mr. James B. Cook, an accomplished architect and sanitary engineer, who has resided in Memphis for many years, while the plague was in progress, in 1878, gave his testimony as to the origin of the epidemic, in a letter for the press, of which the following is an extract: "The predominating cause of disease, is filth. So largely recognized is this—that filth is the origin and promoter of disease—that special legislation

Through this sand the water of the river finds its way at every great rise, so is enacted by the governments of the civilized nations to prevent its accumulation, for proper and effective means to carry off the same, and the creation of Boards of Health, with such laws and regulations for the proper supervision of towns and cities in all that relates to sanitary affairs; and so effective have these sanitary boards been in the work of reducing filth diseases to a minimum, that diseases of an epidemic form, which formerly were so well known to large cities, such as London, Paris, Berlin, Boston, New York, and Philadelphia, are now rarely known, and, if known, are confined to small localities. The creation of sanitary boards and the enactments of laws governing cities, in a sanitary point of view, has given rise to a new profession, co-ordinate with that of the civil engineer, viz., the sanitary engineer; and it is to the sanitary engineer we must look for the proper arrangement of the machinery for the workings of a city, and to him alone must be confided a city's drainage and water supply, for no city can be healthy without a proper system of drainage and a pure water supply. Without these we engender filth and fevers. Have we, in this city, these two conditions so essential to health? I answer most positively, we have not, and to these two causes may be attributed the present plague. As an example of what the excreta from defective drainage may do, I will call attention to the fact, that in one of the healthiest towns in England—Over Darwen—a man contracted a disease from some other town and went to that place to die; after his arrival, and within a very short period, 2,035 people were attacked with filth fever, out of which 104 died. A thorough examination, as to the cause of this disease and the terrible mortality, showed that the excreta of this first patient passed itself through channels used for the irrigation of a neighboring field. The water-main of the town passed through this field, and, although special precautions had been taken to prevent any infiltration of sewerage into the main, it had been found the concrete had sprung a leak and allowed the contents of the drain to be sucked freely into the water-pipe; thus the poisonous excreta was regularly thrown down the drain, and as regularly passed into the town. After this discovery, the authorities went to work and removed the cause; the sway of the filth devil was arrested, and the town once again assumed its healthy condition. I cite this case to show what defective drainage can do in an hitherto healthy town, and with the thermometer at a low temperature. Turn to our own city, with its ten thousand odors assailing one's nostrils at every turn, and at every street corner, with the cellars of stores reeking in the accumulation of filth of years, others with stinking and contaminated bilge-water, bayous contaminated with the excreta of many privies, bayous with sewers emptying into them by the express permission of the city authorities, also with the drainage from the woolen mill in Fort Pickering, being the stinking washings of dirty wool and other refuse matter; these and a thousand others, any one of which is enough, in this latitude, to produce death to a community. We have nothing to complain of in the atmosphere of Memphis; it is as salubrious and as fine as can be found anywhere, and for general healthfulness, excepting at filth-disease times, is rated high. So far as I am concerned, and I have traveled far on the earth's surface, I have never been in a healthier locality. What, then, have we to complain of? We have to complain of filth and its results, brought about by the negligence of those in authority. To filth and the filthy condition of the city I attribute the present experience, and had this filth never been allowed to accumulate, we never should have been visited by this present plague. 1855 taught a lesson, we failed to profit by it. 1867 taught another lesson. 1873 taught a fearful one, but we failed to profit by it. Scientists recognize the cause of disease to be filth. Remove the cause, then the effect will disappear. The recollection of the fever, in the fall of 1873, has had much to do with intensifying the disease of the present time. Fear is playing its part, together with the absurd rumors on the streets, the wild teachings of fanatics, and last, though not least, the headings to some of the local articles on the fever in the daily press. Fear has played its part, and to these two agencies—fear and filth—we are indebted for our unhappy and deplorable condition."

that in many places the gradual advance of the Mississippi may be actually gauged by the rise of the excreta which, when the river falls, is drawn after the water through the soil, the gases formed by its assimilation finding a passage, no doubt, to the atmosphere above, to become the means of propagating the deadly poison of yellow fever. In the early days of Memphis, privy vaults were purposely, and are yet, made deep enough to reach this sand, as a sure means of dispensing with the labor of the night-soiler. When the population was small, as in 1855, when the yellow fever first visited the city epidemically, this was not felt to be the evil it now is, when perhaps 12,000 families are increasing the capital of this bank of death by not less than 1,000 barrels of excreta every day, and by at least 4,000 barrels of offal and other refuse. The accumulations of filth are more rapid than is generally imagined possible. If the amount of animal and other food consumed by 50,000 or more persons per day is recalled, some estimate may be formed of the amount of refuse which accumulates each year in a city without a scavenger system, and the people of which have not been educated up to the standard of even a half-way system of hygiene.* In such a condition, there can not fail to be a gradual deterioration of human health and strength, especially when the human filth poison is supplemented by the equally deadly malaria of the swamp. In his message to the city council, on the 11th of September, 1824, Mayor J. Roffignac stated that the primary cause of the insalubrity of New Orleans was due to two causes, one of them internal, the other external. He said: "The internal causes are: 1st. The filth created by a populous city. 2d. The low grounds and pools where stagnant water lies, the wooden gutters [equal to the Nicholson pavement, now decaying in Memphis] constantly wet and fermenting under the rays of a torrid sun. 3d. The want of privies in most of the populous districts, which renders it necessary to recur to the disgusting and dangerous use of tubs. The external causes are the marshes lying north and west of the city, uncovered but undrained, and deprived, by the cutting down of trees, of the shelter formerly afforded to them by the shade of a luxuriant vegetation, for which the very miasms that now spread death and desolation among us were a source of life and vigor. 2d. To the south and east the Mississippi, which in its periodical retreat, at the hottest season of the year, leaves in its tracks a great portion of the filth which has been thrown into the current, but is brought back by eddies. 3d. The winds, which at the moment we feel most secure, may, as was the case in 1822, convey to us the deadly effluvia of the dangerous spots which they sweep in their course." Dowler refers to the excavation of the original basin of Canal Carondelet, in 1796, and also that of the basin for the same canal in 1853, as coincidents of the epidemics of those years, and he urges that the crowding of filth, a want of ventilation, incomplete drainage, and humidity must be injurious to the health and detrimental to the physical comforts of the citizens—healthy or sick, pure air being vital to both. He

---

* The government of Memphis has recently been changed, and very much for the better. One, and the greatest result of this change, is the enforcement of sanitary regulations, that bid fair, in time, to completely reverse this unsanitary condition.

then describes the homes of New Orleans, as follows: "About ninety in every hundred houses, even in the richer portion of the city, are constructed in a manner that must be condemned in any climate, but in none so much as in this city, depressed as it is below the high-water mark of the river, almost every-where, and in the rear nearly on the sea-level. The lower floor, in a great majority of the houses, especially the stores, rests on the humid soil, sometimes at a lower level than the streets, no air being admitted underneath. The fresh water *newer pliocene* being largely mixed with decaying animal and vegetable matter, moistened by rains and infiltrations from the river, gutters, and swamps, generates perennial crops of algæ, fungi, infusoria, blight, mildew, mould, etc., which abound in, under, and around the lower story of these unventilated houses, where, indeed, crops of mushrooms would flourish, were they not repressed by the tread of the tenant. Hence goods rust and spot; delicate colors are discharged; health, too, is deteriorated, from moist and unsalubrious exhalations during the day, and at night—as many persons sleep on these decaying, humid floors. Physicians, in visiting the poor, especially in depressed portions of the city, must have often found the flooring of houses floating, and sometimes, after rains, quite covered with water too filthy and offensive for description—laboratories for generating carbonic and other deadly gases, predisposing to disease, and rendering recovery from any kind of sickness tedious, too often impossible. What drug can supply the place of pure air, pure water, and dry sleeping?" These conditions, he thinks, "with the warm season of the year, with unacclimated constitutions, and with aggregations of people," is all that is needed to produce yellow fever in epidemic form, and bring death—speedy, yellow, bloody, repulsive, and hideous death—to thousands of unsuspecting households. "Much may be done," says Dowell, "in the way of preventive, by sanitary measures. No animal matter should be allowed to decay in the city limits. Bones, heads of fish, dead chickens, slops from the kitchen, should be removed; all low places, where there are worms, bugs, or snails, should be filled up or covered with sand until no smell would arise after night, or after a rain. This would, no doubt, prevent the spreading of yellow fever to so great an extent, and would make persons living in the district better prepared to stand the disease when attacked. New York, Philadelphia, Baltimore, Savannah, Charleston, and other cities have been wholly or to a great extent relieved from this scourge, by being better drained and better sewered than when it prevailed in them. New Orleans has been greatly improved by its water-works, and but for its shipping, I doubt if it would spread there now. Its mortality has been greatly reduced since 1853,* though the inhabitants have increased." Within the last fifty years land-draining, town-sewering, and stringent laws regulating

---

* This is true. The total number of deaths in New Orleans, in 1878, was something under 4,000, the population of the city during the epidemic being not less than 220,000; while in Memphis, the total of deaths was 5,150 out of a total population of 20,000, of which 14,000 were negroes and only 6,000 were whites—the proportion of deaths according to color, being 946 colored to 4,204 whites, out of a total of 15,000, sick.

the deposit and final disposition of garbage, ashes, offal, excreta, and debris of every kind, have largely contributed to the saving and prolonging of human life. The plague, the cholera, the small-pox, and other diseases are no longer dreaded in Europe, or in our own country. The conditions under which they once prevailed epidemically are not allowed to exist. The result is a vast improvement, not only in the health of the people, but in their strength and will to resist disease in any form. In England, in towns where, before 1845, the average annual mortality was as forty-four in one thousand, it has been reduced to twenty-seven, and where it was thirty it has been reduced to fifteen. In our own country—so far in advance of all others in its general average of happiness, peace, content, cleanliness, and good food, and plenty of it—the average of life is a special wonder to European vital statisticians. But much yet remains to be done to reach the standard possible to a people who desire to reach the highest limit of perfect sanitation. A national, the State and the municipal Boards of Health must be clothed with almost absolute powers. The enforcement of national, State, and local quarantine must be committed to them. To them, too, must be given the oversight and selection of street-pavements, the construction of sewers, the soil-pipe connections, and plumbing and gas-fitting, the sweeping of streets, collection of garbage, and disposition of the same, establishment of slaughter-houses, chemical and other manufactories, so as to prevent the poisoning of the waters of our rivers, which should be sources of life, not death. They should, in a word, have oversight, control, and direction of every thing calculated to preserve the public health and advance the average of human life, and for that purpose should be sustained by penalties, both of fine and imprisonment, equal to the magnitude of the trusts reposed in them. Heretofore legislation has been largely devoted to the material prosperity of the people. Let us now legislate to protect and save life. Until this is done we can not hope for that immunity from epidemic diseases which quarantine it has been supposed could insure. We must cease to rely upon the doctrine of chance as it is illustrated at our quarantine stations, and if we can not have an international system of quarantine, let us have the next thing to it—a quarantine that will defend every mile of our coast on the Pacific as well as the Atlantic side of the continent, a quarantine that enforced by the national government will cover the full period of forty days in every case, as less than that may let in persons or goods already having the seeds of yellow fever, and therefore the seeds of a possibly and probably malignant epidemic. The country thus sealed to persons from infected places, quarantine would have a fair trial, and the theorists who oppose it would be silenced by its success, or be assured a triumph by its failure. Prophylaxis, fires, gun-firing, disinfectants, all have proved unavailing. Quarantine has sometimes (very often), as we have seen, totally failed. If sanitation, enforced as above suggested, fail too, then there is nothing between the people and death, but flight. They must emigrate in a body from the places threatened. In case this becomes necessary, on the appearance of yellow fever it should be enforced by the establishment of the one-man-power, under a fearless, vigorous, and vigilant man, whose example of energy would become contagious, and whose measures would likely be such as would inspire confidence in his intelligence, sagacity, and will. The example furnished by Count Gregory Orloff, sent by the Empress Catherine, in September, 1771, to stamp out the plague,* then ravaging Moscow, is a case in point. The city had been, for months, in a condition of chaos. Murder was rife, and the incendiary was plying his torch. The archbishop had been killed at the very horns of the altar. The city, thus delivered to confusion and anarchy, hailed Orloff's arrival with acclamation, and he deserved to be, for he attacked the plague with such vigor that he overcame it. Drawing a number of sanitary cordons round Moscow, he maintained so strict a quarantine that even the dogs which ran across his lines and the crows which flew over them were shot. All popular gatherings were prohibited; no burials were allowed within the city; and the faithful were even prevented from entering the churches, being obliged to listen to divine service from without. Before Count Orloff's arrival, the common people had shown a decided aversion toward the hospitals, in which they were roughly treated and badly fed by coarse and ignorant medical practitioners. Orloff inspected the buildings set apart for the sufferers, visited them frequently, and soon brought about a change greatly for the better in the treatment of the patients. The number of daily deaths soon fell to 300, and then became smaller and smaller until the plague was stayed. Count Orloff was enabled, on November 28th (O. S.), to leave Moscow rejoicing over a clean bill of health. Such an example as this should not be lost sight of. Had Memphis been governed by one such man in 1878, the mortality might not have been half so appalling as it was; and it is due to the energy and determination of the Citizens' Relief Committee that it was not greater. That

---

*Dr. E. D. Dickson, at present physician to the British Embassy at Constantinople, in a recently prepared paper on the plague which again recently afflicted Russia, says, "that it began to appear in the autumn, continued through the winter, and reached its acme of intensity in the spring, and died out suddenly during the summer season. During the prevalence of the plague the thermometer ranged between five and thirty degrees, and as the thermometer increased from thirty to forty-five the epidemic began to diminish. The symptoms —its glandular swellings, attacks of carbuncles, sanguineous diarrhœa, convulsive shakes —were described in detail, and in regard to its treatment it was pointed out that there was no instance on record of plague having been cut short by the administration of sulphate of quinine. With regard to the contagion, Cabiadis who had had much personal experience, held that the atmosphere which surrounded a person affected with the disease was the true medium of transmission. With regard to the etiology of the plague, Dr. Dickson acknowledged that the origin of plague, and the causes that brought it into activity, were utterly unknown, and he disputed the idea that marsh-miasm might be the exciting cause of it. The proximate cause which predisposed an attack of plague during an epidemic outbreak was poverty, and it was styled *miseride morbus*. The wealthy were hardly ever attacked. The prophylactic measures to be taken were the isolation of the sick, the destruction by fire of their clothes, the whitewashing with lime, and the free ventilation of their domiciles. The *cordon sanitaires* were regarded as valuable in checking the extension of the outbreak of the plague; but the practice adopted in Bagdad of shutting up persons smitten in their houses was condemned as leading to concealment, and helping to intensify and propagate the evil it was intended to mitigate.

body, which gradually dwindled with the progress of the epidemic until it was governed by only two of the survivors, made provision for the camps to which so many owe their lives, policed the city, maintained the military organizations, and sustained the city government, which was reduced to the mayor or acting mayor and comptroller. Only heroic measures will do in such an emergency, and only by the most arbitrary will, guided by the best intelligence can it override the fear and dread that sits on every heart; only a supreme power can bring order out of chaos and compel obedience by the citizen to laws which are enforced for his own safety. But better than this terrible necessity, this last resort, is the ounce of prevention that may kill the causes and so prevent an epidemic of yellow fever. This will be found in the active intervention, as has already been stated, of national, State, and local boards of health, composed of sanitarians* who have experience in all that concerns human life in large cities. As the Homeopathic Commission suggests, they " would enforce the frequent emptying and disinfection of water closets, sewers, and all places containing putrescent matters, vegetable or animal. They would see that no sacks of decaying coffee, or chaff in rice pits, or dead animals, or any offensive matter was left exposed, so as to poison the atmosphere. They would prevent, so far as possible, the destruction of trees, and in every way encourage their planting and growth. Above all, they would forbid the upturning of the soil during the spring and summer months, as epidemics of yellow fever have followed such upturning at New Orleans, Natchez, and Vicksburg, in such a manner as very strongly to suggest that the relation of cause and effect existed between this exposure of the earth and the development of the disease." They would see that cities were properly drained, that the gutters were regularly flushed with fresh water, that the water-works system itself was a prime source of health, and, that the ashes, garbage, vegetable

---

* Dr. J. P. Drake, of Nashville, a distinguished homeopathist, in this connection, suggests that: "What the people of this age and country desire, is not the aggrandizement of any set, sect, or school of medical men, but such a knowledge of the yellow fever and of Asiatic cholera, and other destructive epidemic diseases, as may enable them to prevent their visitations, orovercome their attacks, by any means, orthodox or heterodox, new or old, in the hands of physician, nurse, or friend. Since the grocer-boy and afterward philanthropist, John Howard, and not a titled and arrogant doctor of medicine, inaugurated the great prison-reform of the world; and since the gentle Florence Nightingale, and not an epauletted surgeon-general, led the greatest of all improvements in the sanitary arrangements of army life; and since our own Miss Dix, and not a titled medical superintendent, revolutionized the management of asylums for the insane, every worker among sanitary facts, whether titled or untitled, 'regular or irregular,' man or woman, must have a recognition and a voice in the health and life-saving efforts of the public. The arrogance and exclusiveness, hitherto displayed by army surgeons and the American Public Health Association, are not in keeping with the beneficial and scientfic character of the work proposed, nor at all calculated to inspire confidence in what they may say or do. When they enter the arena where stricken humanity struggles with the pestilence, laying aside all prejudice and all sectarian hatreds, ready to gather facts from all experiences, new or old, and to render praise where praise is due, to this preventive measure or that, this remedy or that, then will their coming be hailed with joy and their efforts be crowned with some degree of success."

debris, sweepings of stores and factories, excreta, and offal of whatever nature, was cremated, and so placed beyond the possibility of injury. "Quarantine," says the Homeopathic Commission, "is a delusive security; home prevention is the great desideratum. Aggregation of human beings is one of the factors of yellow fever. Yellow fever germs always exist in New Orleans, and other cities in a feeble and latent state, waiting to be aroused into activity by some fortuitous combination of some or all the factors necessary to its vitalization. New Orleans is notably the point of its development, and the center of its radiating violence. Keep New Orleans in a perfect sanitary condition, and the great valley of the Mississippi is safe. Let it lie in its present state for another generation, and it will become a hot-bed of pestilence, which will dart its baneful influence along the lines of rapid transit, and repeat in St. Louis and Chicago the horrors which befell New York and Philadelphia in the last century."

APPENDIX.

THANKS TO ALL.

Resolved, That the Howard Association of Memphis, speaking for the dead as well as the survivors of the epidemic of 1878, with hearts overflowing with gratitude, thanks all, every one, who contributed in any way to the relief of our fever-stricken people, thanks the people of the whole world who, with a generosity unsurpassed, relieved our necessities, and, with a sympathy that never flagged, sustained us in our work.

Unanimously adopted, January 6, 1879.

APPENDIX.

APPENDED are the Reports of the President, Secretary and Treasurer, Medical Director, and Superintendent of the Nurse Department, of the Memphis Howard Association, and of the survivor of the two members of the Association—Gen. W. J. Smith—who went down to Grenada and labored there until nearly the close of the epidemic, their work being continued by Messrs. Bragga and Cohen until the end. In presenting these reports, in justice to them, as well as for the information of the public, the names of the members and officers of the Howard Association,* who served through the epidemic of 1878, are given as follows:

A. D. Langstaff, *President.*
W. J. Smith, 1st *Vice-Pres.;* J. H. Edmondson, 2d *Vice-Pres.;* J. H. Smith, *Secretary;* John Johnson, *Treasurer.*

---

* It is deemed proper here to append a synopsis of the report of the work done and receipts and disbursements of the Howard Association of New Orleans during the epidemic of 1878. The report of the Howard Association, prepared and published in the New Orleans *Democrat* by the Secretary, Mr. F. B. Southmayd, is a simple, straightforward, business-like account of their work, receipts, and expenditures during the yellow fever epidemic of the past autumn, but it forms a striking record of the dire plague's rapid spread and fatal work, and of the boundless generosity that poured into the hands of the Howards great sums of money for their noble work. But if the response to their demands was munificent, their own deeds proved them worthy executors of such a trust. They labored with a zeal and utter forgetfulness of self that is almost unparalleled in the history of epidemics, yet they are able to show, with all the clearness of a banker's balance-sheet, to what use they put the money confided to their care. The hope that the fever would be mild and of short duration was abandoned on the 15th of August, and on the morning of the 17th the New Orleans newspapers published the Howards' appeal for help to begin their work. The same morning their doors were open for the relief of the destitute sick, though they had not then a dollar in the treasury. But their appeal was quickly answered, and, as the fever spread, funds began to pour in from outside the city and, as days passed, from the whole North and South. Railroads and telegraph lines and steamboats were placed at their free disposition; and their numbers were increased by new members anxious to join the work. The city of New Orleans was divided into 20 districts, and slates were hung up at convenient points whereon applications from the destitute sick were written. Including members and physicians, the working force of the association was 125 men, whose time was entirely devoted to the sick and suffering. The total number of patients cared for by the Howards in New Orleans during the 71 days of the fever's rage, from Aug. 17 to Oct. 26, was 22,244; of these 5,132 were blacks and 16,112 whites. It should be understood that this does not include all the cases occurring in the city, but only those cared for by the Howards. As some members only reported the first cases in many families where there were several cases, the total probably did not fall short of 24,000. Mr. Southmayd's report covers also the country towns and villages of a wide section of territory around New Orleans, where assistance was rendered by the Howards. Thus, at Grenada they cared for 600 cases, at Holly Springs for 900, at Plaquemine and Donaldsonville 1,000 each, and at nearly 50 other places for numbers ranging from 10 to 850. The total cases attended outside the city were 11,750, making the grand total of patients cared for by the New Orleans Howards, 35,750. Not the sick only, but the suffering appealed to their humanity. Fully 60,000 destitute people were provided for by them during the prevalence of the fever. Let the following table, showing the receipts of the Howards of New Orleans, and the sources of the donations, tell the eloquent story of the unstinted giving that equipped them for their work:

New York	$82,637 01	Pittsburg, Penn	$2,925 00	Galveston, Texas	$1,050 00
Philadelphia	29,862 40	Milwaukee, Wis	2,148 45	Richmond, Va	1,035 90
Boston	26,704 29	Indianapolis, Ind	2,400 00	Charleston, S. C	503 48
Chicago	23,024 80	Washington, D. C	2,101 50	Baltimore, Md	460 00
New Orleans	22,220 60	Hartford, Conn	1,861 50	Other parts of our country	117,807 52
San Francisco	20,675 00	Cincinnati	1,513 50	Liverpool and London	7,875 00
St. Louis	7,463 45	Savannah, Ga	1,500 00	Paris and France	4,780 96
Brooklyn	3,816 00	Buffalo, N. Y	1,500 00	Havana	1,009 13
Providence	3,025 00	Albany, N. Y	1,500 00		
Springfield, Mass	3,050 00	Columbus, Ga	1,362 10	Total	$383,449 93
Memphis	2,716 94	Louisville, Ky	1,275 00		
Portland, Oregon	2,500 00	Mobile, Ala	1,146 30		

The full table of disbursements given by Secretary Southmayd includes all moneys and supplies used in the city and sent to points outside. The following condensed table shows the amount of these expenditures:

Receipts to date...$383,449 93

APPENDIX.

Executive Committee.—A. D. Langstaff, W. J. Smith, J. H. Edmondson, J. H. Smith, John Johnson, W. A. Holt, P. W. Semmes, A. M. Stoddard, F. F. Bowen, T. R. Waring, J. Kohlberg.

Auditing Committee.—F. F. Bowen, W. J. Smith, J. T. Moss.

Active Members.—A. D. Langstaff,† W. J. Smith,† J. H. Edmondson, J. H. Smith,† John Johnson, A. M. Stoddard,† J. W. Cooper,† B. P. Anderson,* W. D. McCallum,* Louis Frierson,† D. G. Reahardt,† W. S. Rogers, F. F. Bowen, J. G. Lonsdale,* E. B. Mansford,* N. D. Menken,* J. T. Moss,† S. M. Jobe,* R. P. Waring, J. Kohlberg, Charles Howard,† J. W. Page,† T. R. Waring, P. W. Semmes,† W. A. Holt,† E. B. Foster,* J. W. Heath,* Fred'k Cole,* A. F. C. Cook,* W. S. Anderson,† C. L. Staffer,† Wm. Finnie.†

Honorary Members.—Dr. Luke P. Blackburn, Louisville, Ky.; Major W. T. Walthall, Mobile, Ala.; P. A. Ralston, Richmond, Va.; S. F. Cameron, Baltimore, Md.; Rev. W. E. Boggs, D. D.,† Rev. S. Landrum, D. D.,† Rev. E. C. Slater, D. D.,* Capt. P. R. Athey,† J. J. Busby, Memphis, Tenn.

PRESIDENT A. D. LANGSTAFF'S REPORT.

MEMPHIS, *January 6th*, 1879.

To the Members of the Howard Association, Memphis, Tenn.:

GENTLEMEN,—Since our last quarterly meeting this Association has again been called into active service, to relieve the distressed and fever-stricken people of this city and of the surrounding country. The labors that the members performed during this term of service is well known to us who have survived. In justice, however, to the memory of our brothers who died, and for the information of those who may hereafter become members of our Association, I submit to you the following brief report.

On Sunday morning, August 11th, our city was startled by a series of telegrams from Grenada, Miss., announcing that yellow fever had broken out there in a malignant form. A telegram to our secretary, from the mayor of Grenada, asking for assistance, met with a ready response. He immediately advised with several of our members.

True to the purposes of our Association, true to their records as Howards in the epidemic of 1873, W. J. Smith and Butler P. Anderson promptly volunteered to answer in person this cry of distress. They went by special train, taking with them several nurses and accompanied by Dr. R. F. Brown, Secretary of the Memphis Board of Health. The telegram that was received from them soon after their arrival in Grenada read as follows: "Yellow fever, and no mistake: sixty cases and five deaths to-day." This intelligence confirmed the report of the morning.

EXPENDITURES.

Howard Association, New Orleans		$278,850 15
Other associations, New Orleans		8,481 22
Country points:		
Doctors	$20,018 50	
Nurses	31,871 95	
Money and supplies	40,964 01	
		92,854 46

BALANCES.

Pittsburg orphan fund	$1,800 00	
Chicago special fund	800 00	
Reserved for claims in suits, printing report, etc	664 10	
		3,264 10
Total		$383,449 93

The amount received up to September 12th, and advices of further sums to come were so numerous, that the Association judged it wise to send out notice that they were amply supplied, and that no more contributions would be needed. The rapid and unexpected spread of the disease after that date, however, compelled other appeals for help. The call was answered in such a manner as to leave them unfettered for their work, and to allow of their distributing a certain sum among the physicians who had aided them without fee thus far. With a word of reply to some unmanly calumnies upon the Association, equally false and malicious, and against which they need no defense here at the North, Mr. Southmayd closes his report by expressing the gratitude of the Howards for the divinely inspired charity which enabled them to carry on their work.

* Died of yellow fever during the epidemic of 1878.
† Members who had the fever, during the epidemic of 1878, and recovered.

Monday morning brought more telegrams from Grenada, all telling us the painful news that the disease was spreading rapidly, and asking for more nurses, medical supplies, and disinfectants, which were forwarded at once. Our Association met the same day and took such action as was necessary to render further aid to Grenada, if called for, and to provide ways and means to assist any of our own citizens who might be attacked by the disease, a visitation of which was becoming hour by hour more inevitable. While that first meeting was progressing dispatches were received from Smith and Anderson of a still more alarming character than those previously received. Anderson had tried by public speech to quiet the people of Grenada, who were fleeing from their homes as if pursued by a monster ready to devour them. Aided by a few who remained, he and Smith began operations. For a complete report of their operations I refer you to the report of W. J. Smith. How nobly they fulfilled the mission of mercy and charity which they had entered upon, how calmly and earnestly they acted in that trying ordeal, is a very prominent part of the history of the epidemic of 1878. They labored until attacked by the disease. Well do we remember the night when W. J. Smith returned to us on his bed, before rising from which he almost died. Butler P. Anderson continued at Grenada until he too had to succumb to the disease. As he could not be brought home, we hour by hour waited for information as to his condition. In a few days, although attended by his wife and receiving every attention to promote his recovery, he yielded up his spirit to the God who gave it.

This Association may well be proud of having such members to represent them. While they were battling with the pestilence in Grenada, we at home were allowed to be at rest. At our first meeting, August 13th, the following members answered to the roll-call: J. G. Lonsdale, Sr., Edw'd Mansford, E. B. Foster, A. M. Stoddard, W. S. Rogers, W. A. Holt, P. M. Semmes, T. R. Waring, J. H. Smith, J. H. Edmondson, F. F. Bowen, J. W. Cooper, and A. D. Langstaff. The following members were elected afterwards, during the epidemic, and assigned to duty: N. D. Menken, W. D. McCallum, A. F. C. Cook, S. M. Jobe, J. M. Heath, Fred'k Cole, J. W. Page, Wm. Finnie, C. L. Staffer, D. G. Reahardt, J. Kohlberg, Charles Howard, John T. Moss, R. P. Waring, Lewis S. Frierson, and W. S. Anderson. At our meeting August 14th, John Johnson, who had, since 1873, been an honorary member, was elected an active member and superintendent of the nurse department. The wisdom of our choice was shown afterward by the faithful performance of the very responsible duties of that department.

On August 13th the President of the Board of Health published the first case of yellow fever, the victim being Mrs. Bionda. All hopes that our city would be spared from the disease was banished by us, and all things necessary for active service were provided as rapidly as possible. Our people, like those of Grenada, became panicstricken, and fled from the city as rapidly as possible. Future events prove that had they gone less promptly our Association would have been paralyzed in endeavoring to nurse them, and all of us would have died. On August 15th the first nurse was placed on duty; then began what afterwards culminated in the most terrible and deadly epidemic that our Association has been called upon to combat. All business, save that pertaining to the relief of the distressed, soon ceased. Pleasant carriages and merchants' drays were replaced on our streets by funeral carriages and hearses. The fever, from which none then seemed to recover, invaded the homes of all. Death, with rapid strides, marched through our streets, leaving victims everywhere. He was, indeed, the king.

On August 19th two physicians were employed by the Association, which number was increased on the 20th to five. On August 27th the Howard Medical Corps was established, with R. W. Mitchell as Medical Director, who at once proceeded to organize his department, to promptly provide medical attention to the stricken.

To him, personally, and to the physicians, both abroad and at home, who were members of the Howard Medical Corps, is great praise and honor due from us, and from the citizens of Memphis. Many of them sacrificed their lives in the discharge of their duties. For a full report of this department I refer you to the report of the Medical Director, herewith submitted. By a vote of your executive committee, J. G. Lonsdale, Jno. Johnson, and J. H. Edmondson, were appointed, on August 15th, a committee to confer with the city authorities relative to sending our patients to the City Hospital. The arrangement was perfected. Within five days other hospitals had to be provided. By direction of the executive committee I obtained possession of Market-street Schoolhouse, and at once had seats and desks removed, and, with the assistance of Major W. T. Walthall and others, had it ready for the reception of patients. In three days it was filled. Other hospitals or infirmaries were immediately opened. I respectfully call your special attention to that part of the report of the Medical Director referring to the organization of a National Howard Association, for the purposes set forth therein. Little did we anticipate, in the early days of the epidemic, that it would assume the proportions that it afterwards did assume: that citizens would die at the rate of five and six score per day; that instead of providing two hundred or three hundred persons with nurses and assistance, we would provide for twice as many thousands; that our expenses would be ten thousand instead of five hundred dollars per day; nor did we anticipate that the surrounding towns would be stricken with the fever, that our Association would be called upon to distribute to them, by donations of money and provisions, by supplying them with physicians and nurses, and by having relief trains on the several railroads leading out of Memphis. Relief was furnished to the neighboring towns to the amount of about forty thousand dollars. More would have been furnished them, to have enabled them to fully pay all their indebtedness, but they did not advise us of the amounts needed, although asked to do so in several instances, until we had notified the world not to send us further funds, and not until our own funds had become nearly exhausted. To enable us to meet all these expenditures, amounting to more than $500,000, a generous people furnished the means. From every hamlet in our land, from countries separated from us by thousands of miles of ocean, from the orphan and the widow, from rich and poor, from white and black, came the aid to help us. Let us not forget, brother Howards, that our Association has not, during this epidemic, made an appeal for aid: it came to us without the necessity of an appeal. We ought to, and do feel gratified that an appreciative people had not forgotten our previous record. Wherever the name of our Association is known, that it is respected and honored. There is no organization, so far as known, that is as purely charitable as ours. All applicants for aid are the same to us, whether rich or poor, white or black, saint or sinner. If I had to choose between ours and any other association, I would prefer to be a Howard. Remembering the many kind words that have been said to us, and of us, for our efforts in relieving the distressed since August 12th, we have reason to feel that said efforts have been appreciated. Our hearts are sad, however, for we must at all times, and particularly when gathered together on such occasions as the present, remember our absent brothers, who have given their lives, and who are now sleeping in the tomb. I here record their names: Butler P. Anderson, John G. Lonsdale, Sr., Edward B. Foster, Edward J. Mansford, J. W. Heath, W. D. McCallum, Nathan D. Menken, Samuel M. Jobe, A. F. C. Cook, Fred Cole. But a few days ago they were with us, and were ever ready to assist the distressed. They more than fulfilled God's command "Love thy neighbor as thyself," for they proved, day after day, that they loved their neighbor more than themselves. The records of our Association show that I am the only survivor of the little band that organized this Association, for work in 1867, who now belongs to it. All are dead, except three. These dead brothers well knew, before they entered upon the field of duty, that they went with their lives in their hands. They faced greater danger than the soldier on the field of battle. They did not thus endanger their lives either for their own glory, or for the glory of any church or nation. Their hearts were moved with a sympathy and pity, the depth of which all people appreciate, yet few personally understand, for their suffering fellow-beings who had become the victims of the fever. That their good deeds may not be forgotten, but serve to inspire those for whom they labored so well to do likewise, I respectfully suggest that a committee be appointed to solicit subscriptions, from the citizens of Memphis, for the erection of a suitable monument to their memory, in the Howard lot, in Elmwood Cemetery, where they are buried. I must not forget here to remember the worthy actions of several of our honorary members, who labored by our sides with a devotion second to none of us. To Rev. W. E. Boggs, in particular, who was more closely identified with us, and acting under our orders, am I pleased to make mention. I desire also to record the organization, by Gov. Alex. Shepherd, of Washington, of the relief boat "Chambers,"* which left our sister city, St. Louis, early in October, laden with supplies for the yellow fever sufferers along the Mississippi River. When a commander was needed for this expedition, Lieut. H. H. Benner, of the United States Army, promptly volunteered, as did also Lieut. Chas. S. Hall, of the 13th U. S. Infantry, and H. M. Keys, assistant surgeon of the same army, to accompany him. The officers and others, who with them formed the officers and crew of the Steamer *Chambers*, are worthy of the most lasting remembrance for their unselfish devotion to

---

* The National Relief-boat Chambers, sent out by the Relief Committee of Washington, of which ex-Gov. Alex. Shepherd was President, steamed from St. Louis, where it was fitted up, with a cargo consisting of about one hundred and fifty tons of ice, between two and three hundred tons of provisions, clothing, and medical stores. As the crew of this steamer was composed of what may be designated a little band of heroes on a journey into the jaws of death, it is deemed appropriate to give their names, which are appended as follows: Lieutenants Benner and Hall, in charge of the expedition; Surgeon Keys, United States Army, lately in charge of the Marine Hospital, Vicksburg, in charge of the medical stores; Dr. Frank W. Reilly, representing the Chicago Relief Committee; Charles S. Snyder, St. Louis telegraph operator; Captain V. M. Yore, master of the steamer; L. A. Haines, clerk; Thomas Wetzell, mate; Charles Duffy and George Langell, pilots; Wm. Shepard, first, and John Williams, second engineers. Besides there were twelve deck-hands and cabin-boys. W. S. Kessler, druggist; Horace L. Hyde, newspaper correspondent; H. Mulford, carpenter; Robert J. Matchman, steward; J. M. Dalton, watchman. There was a total of forty souls on board.—J. M. K.]

suffering humanity. They visited our city, as they descended the river, and offered us assistance; we, however, did not need it, and they continued their journey. All along the river where assistance was needed they gave it. While lying in front of Vicksburg, Lieut. Benner, the commander, and one of the engineers were attacked by the fever and died, thus adding two more names to the already long list of those who had given their lives in their efforts to save the lives of their fellow-men. Whether or not the names of H. H. Benner and the engineer be written on shafts of marble or storied urn, they will not be forgotten by the people of the South, or by the world.

Towards the close of September repeated and urgent calls came to us for physicians, nurses, and medicines, from the towns along the railroads, and who therefore had until then felt secure against a visitation of the fever. To many of these we promptly responded. While going to Brownsville, early in October, I made inquiries at the several depots at which we stopped, and learned that the fever had broken out in nearly all of them, and that persons were dying—had died, and remained unburied—to whom, in some instances, no assistance had been rendered. The physicians in these and other country towns, with a few exceptions, remained at their post of duty, and many of them died while attending to their duties. Then it was I saw the necessity of establishing relief trains, which might leave Memphis each morning with physicians, nurses, medicines, etc., which trains would stop at each depot long enough to enable the physicians to visit the afflicted and leave with them nurses and supplies. The following telegram to Mr. H. A. Montgomery, Superintendent of the Louisville and Memphis Railroad—

"People sick, suffering, and dying, at almost every depot between here and Memphis, for want of physicians and medicine. Can give them attention promptly, and probably save lives, if you can furnish our Association with locomotive and baggage-car, which, leaving Memphis in the morning with physicians, etc., shall stop—say one or two hours—on side track to attend to wants of sick at each depot, which we can not furnish without your assistance. The life of your agent at Withe and Mason might have been saved by attention. If necessary to pay, please state amount per day. Fever will continue to frost—say fifteen (15) days. We all appreciate your past generosity. Answer here. A. D. LANGSTAFF, Pres't Memphis Howard Association"—

met with this prompt and favorable response:

"*To* A. D. LANGSTAFF, *Pres't Howard Association, Brownsville, Tenn.:*

"Yes, sir, we will furnish you an engine and coach and express-car at any time, and as often as desired, to bring out medical assistance and supplies, free of cost. Will you not please extend trips as far north as Paris and Erin? Much suffering at these two points, and especially at Paris. We will gladly give you any assistance in our power. Please answer, and when you will want to leave Memphis on first trip.
"JAMES MONTGOMERY."

In a few days the first train left Memphis. Similar trains were furnished with equal promptness by Sup't John A. Grant, of the Memphis and Charleston Railroad, and by Sup't Burke, of the Mississippi and Tennessee Railroad. In organizing and running these trains, which were of great benefit, I was very ably assisted by W. J. Smith, 1st Vice-President; J. H. Edmondson, 2d Vice-President; P. W. Semmes, William Finnie, and others: and to the physicians accompanying the trains, to the officers and employés of the railroads throughout the whole land, to the steamboat, express, and telegraph companies, and to their employés particularly; and last, but not by any means least, to the press of our city, and to the press everywhere, are we under the most weighty obligations. I would respectfully suggest that a committee be appointed for the purpose of expressing by resolutions the gratitude of the Association to all outside of its ranks who, by deed, word, or work, aided or assisted us in the performance of our sacred mission. For particulars as to receipts and expenditures I refer you to the reports of the Secretary and Treasurer, and for particulars in regard to the nurse department I refer you to the superintendent of that department, which reports are herewith submitted.

In conclusion, brothers, I desire to sincerely thank you for your cheerful readiness in assisting me throughout the recent epidemic. I will always remember how devoted you have been to your principles as Howards, how kind and generous you have been to me. Very respectfully,

A. D. LANGSTAFF, *President, Memphis Howard Association.*

APPENDIX.

SECRETARY'S REPORT FOR 1878.

To the President, Directors, and Members of the Howard Association of Memphis, Tenn.:

BRETHREN,—I submit for your consideration the following as my report of the late epidemic, together with such collateral observations as seemed pertinent under the circumstances: and for whatever deficiencies may appear therein, either in manner or matter, I appeal to the same kind indulgence that has characterized your action toward me heretofore, asking you to remember the present pressure of my other and unavoidable obligations.

It is a melancholy duty to review the work and events of the last few months, and to contemplate the scenes and trials through which we were called to pass. The prevalence of the late pestilence constitutes the most mournful and thrilling period of our city's history—a period so tragic and awful that its memory now seems like a strange troubled dream. None, save those who witnessed it, can for a moment realize the dreadful power and fatal swiftness of the plague of 1878. It was the herald of danger, the carnival of suffering, and the triumph of death. No language however graphic and no imagination however fertile can give any adequate description of the terror of its presence, the cruelty of its destruction. Its appearance spread consternation, like a tempest, and its touch diffused suffering, like a deadly poison. The young and the old, the weak and the strong, the evil and the good, the beautiful and the brave, all alike went down beneath the fatal breath of the unseen destroyer. It seemed as if the very genius of desolation was in our midst, and with no formidable power to stay his mighty havoc. But relying upon the succor and pity of divine Providence, and armed with the assistance rendered us by the generous people of our entire country, we made (with all humility) the best and bravest fight we could. And now that the battle is over and our dead buried, thanks be to God that it *is* over, and for our preservation amid the perils of the conflict. And though we emerge from the struggle weary with toil, torn with trials and sore with sorrow, we can but rejoice in the freedom from pestilence, in the blessing of health, in the comfort of hope, in the association of friends returned, and in the pleasing consciousness of duty done.

The first call upon our Association came by telegraph, August 11th, 1878, from the mayor of Grenada, Miss., appealing for immediate help. On receipt of this information I at once sought our 1st Vice-President, Gen. W. J. Smith (our President then being absent from the city), and he and I, with the assistance of our late beloved brethren, Butler P. Anderson and Edwin B. Foster, in a few hours collected seven of our nurses of 1873, and had every thing in readiness for immediate departure, when, thanks to the kindness of Col. Burke, Sup't of the M. & T. R. R., a train was soon speeding its way to that stricken city with nurses and general supplies. Gen. Smith and Maj. Anderson volunteered to go to the relief of that people, now already panic-stricken and flying for safety.

On the following day numerous telegrams were received from that place, telling us of the malignancy of the fever and the needs of the stricken. Additional nurses and supplies were daily forwarded as their wants required. Our Association had in the meantime convened, and commenced preparing to meet the terrible ordeal which all felt assured we would soon be called to encounter at home. As rapidly as possible every thing was put in readiness for the expected issue. Locations for hospitals were selected; a nurse department was organized, and the Hon. John Johnson, an honorary member of 1873, was elected an active member, and made superintendent of this department, which, under his able and efficient management, was soon in an active and good working condition. And for full information in this department, reference is made to the report of its superintendent, herewith filed.

Our Board of Health established a rigid quarantine against New Orleans and Grenada; but it was stealthily evaded, and parties from the infected localities made their way into the city, and it was soon announced that yellow fever was in our midst. This announcement spread terror throughout the community. Fear and despair were written in the face of men. The people became panic-stricken, and rushed, by thousands, to the various railway depots to escape the dread destroyer. Here the wildest and most unreasonable excitement prevailed—women wept and begged, and men cursed and fought, in their efforts to be first. Every inch of available room in the cars would be occupied, and, as the train moved out, ordinary dangers seemed to have no terror; and men would leap upon the platform, or cling, swinging, to whatever offered a hand-hold. In this, the hour of their dread, many abandoned their homes without preparation, some their baggage, and others forgot that they had any at all. Friend forgot friend, and kindred forgot kindred, in their wild struggle for self-preservation. The scenes at these depots, for some days, defy description; while people on foot and in every character of vehicle could be seen flying to the country in all directions. May a recurrence of such a calamity, of such heart-rending scenes, never again be witnessed here! It is estimated that more than thirty-five thousand of our people fled, seeking safety in all parts of the country.

The entire force of our Association was at once called into active duty, and all who remained to share *your* fate, will bear testimony to the faithful manner in which you thought, felt, and labored for others both by day and night, in storm and sunshine, and without complaint. The membership of our Association being so inadequate to the demands of the sick, a call was made for volunteers, and was promptly responded to by the following noble-hearted men: Nathan D. Menken, W. D. McCallum, A. F. C. Cook, D. G. Reahart, C. L. Staffer, Jno. T. Moss, Fred. Cole, Samuel M. Jobe, Lewis S. Frierson, J. W. Heath, J. W. Page, Chas. Howard, W. S. Anderson, Jacob Kohlberg, Wm. Finnie, and R. P. Waring, Jr., who were elected active members, and at once assigned to duty. The Rev. Drs. W. E. Boggs, S. Landrum, and E. C. Slater, also Phil. R. Athey, were elected honorary members, and did most noble and efficient work until themselves were stricken down. Out of a maximum membership of thirty-two, during the contagion, twenty-six were stricken down, and of that number ten of our best and bravest died. The heart grows sad and the eye dim as we contemplate the deeds and fate of these noble heroes. They did their duty and they did it well. They perished in the great cause of humanity, going down in a voluntary struggle with death while fighting him at the bed-side of others. "Greater love than this hath *no* man, that he lay down his life for another." But a full history of their brave deeds and noble self-sacrifice I leave to abler and worthier hands than mine. Peace to their shades, honor to their memories!

I here present a complete roll of our membership, showing those who had the fever, those who recovered, those who died, and those who escaped entirely:

A. D. Langstaff, President, had fever in 1867, taken again Sept. 12th, recovered.
W. J. Smith, 1st Vice-President, taken at Grenada, Aug. 22d, recovered.
J. H. Edmondson, 2d Vice-President, escaped, had fever in 1865.
J. H. Smith, Secretary, had fever in 1867, taken again Oct. 11th, recovered.
J. G. Lonsdale, Sr., Treasurer, died with fever at Memphis, Oct. 1st.
John Johnson, Superintendent of Nurses, escaped, had fever in 1873.
Butler P. Anderson, died with fever at Grenada, Sept. 1st.
Edwin B. Foster, died with fever at Memphis, Sept. 15th.
Edward J. Mansford, died with fever at Memphis, Sept. 1st.
F. F. Bowen, escaped, had fever in 1847.
A. M. Stoddard, taken at Raleigh, Sept. 20th, recovered.
P. W. Semmes, taken at Memphis, Sept. 9th, recovered.
W. H. Holt, taken at Memphis, Aug. 31st, recovered.
W. S. Rogers, escaped, had fever in 1873.
J. W. Cooper, taken Aug. 27th, at Memphis, recovered.
T. R. Waring, escaped.
N. D. Menken, died at Memphis, Sept. 2d.
W. D. McCallum, died at Memphis, Sept. 16th.
A. F. C. Cook, died at Memphis, Sept. 8th.
Fred. Cole, died at Memphis, Sept. 9th.
S. M. Jobe, died at Memphis, Oct. 4th.
J. W. Heath, died at Memphis, Sept. 17th.
Jno. T. Moss, taken at Memphis, Sept. 15th, recovered.
D. G. Reahart, taken at Memphis, Sept. 25th, recovered.
C L. Staffer, taken at Memphis, Sept. 9th, recovered.
L. S. Frierson, taken at Memphis, Sept. 16th, recovered.
J W. Page, taken at Memphis, Sept. 18th, recovered.
Chas. Howard, taken at Memphis, Sept. 15th, recovered.
Wm. Finnie, taken at Memphis, Aug. 22d, recovered.
W. S. Anderson, taken at Memphis, Sept. 28th, recovered.
Jacob Kohlberg, escaped.
R. P. Waring, escaped.

APPENDIX.

Honorary Members:

Rev. W. E. Boggs, D. D., taken Sept. 26th, recovered.
Rev. S. Landrum, D. D., taken Sept. 15th, recovered.
Rev. E. C. Slater, D. D., died Sept. 10th, at Memphis.
Chief of Police P. R. Athey, taken Aug. 31st, recovered.

From the foregoing statement you will see that near one third of our entire number died at their posts. The language of eulogy can not exaggerate the calm courage, splendid energy, and noble service of these brave men in behalf of this afflicted people. The Rev. Dr. Slater was added to the list of martyrs, and now sleeps with his fathers, while his memory grows brighter and more beautiful with the praise and blessings of those he loved, and those who loved him.

A medical department was organized by our Association early in the epidemic, and Dr. R. W. Mitchell, with whose conspicuous service the whole country is already familiar, was elected medical director. And for a full report of the services of the gallant, untiring, and self-sacrificing men composing this department, reference is made to the report of Dr. Mitchell, herewith filed. On behalf of our Association, I would here return our heartfelt thanks to the medical department for countless courtesies shown, and for their prompt compliance with every call, by day or night, made upon it by us in behalf of the sick and distressed. And I can not forget, here, to offer my personal and profoundest thanks to that learned and accomplished gentleman, Dr. J. T. McFarland, of Savannah, Georgia, to whose skill and attention I feel that I chiefly owe my own recovery from an attack of the fever.

Supply stores were established as promptly as practicable in different parts of the city, as the wants of the people demanded, and at which every thing necessary for either the sick or destitute was furnished upon proper requisitions of the members or physicians. The great benefit, indeed the indispensability of these, was soon apparent, for in a few days almost every business establishment in the city was closed, and the people, consequently, were left dependent, in a great degree, on the Howard stores for necessary supplies of all kinds. I regret that I am unable to give a full and perfectly accurate report of all the supplies sent us by kind and sympathizing friends from all parts of the country. Owing to the fact that the force in my office was so reduced by the fever, it was impossible to keep closely up with the receipts. At one time, out of a force of seven, I had but two left on duty. I endeavored earnestly to keep a true and correct record of every donation received. Yet I fear, owing to the sickness of myself and assistants, and to the immense amount of work daily to be done, some errors or omissions may appear in the account; and should our friends discover any, we will thank them to point them out and we will take pleasure in making the correction. I would gladly give the name of each donor, and article of supplies, but it would encumber the report of donations to an indefinite length, as they are numbered by hundreds. I think that special mention is due to S. Lester Taylor, Esq., Treasurer of Cincinnati Southern Relief Committee, and J. H. Lindenberger, Chairman of Louisville Clearing House Committee, for their prompt kindness in filling all requisitions drawn upon them, and often even anticipating our wants. I herewith hand you report of donations of money received, to which I refer you for full particulars. I also present herewith my report of expenditures, showing amount paid for nurses, physicians, supplies, etc., to which your attention is especially invited.

I have also prepared, with much labor, a complete list of the names, as far as could be ascertained, of all our citizens who died during the late epidemic.

And now, before closing, I desire to return thanks to the officers of the Southern Express Company, to the officers of the Western Union Telegraph Company, to the officers of the Memphis and Louisville, the Memphis and Charleston, and Mississippi and Tennessee Railroads, for many and great favors shown us, and especially to Col. M. Burke of the latter road.

And to you, brethren, I make my acknowledgments for many acts of courtesy and kindness to me while in the discharge of the duties of my office, and especially to Gen. W. J. Smith, 1st Vice-Pres., who took charge of my office during my sickness. I would also return my special thanks to Messrs. J. R. Ray, Thos. F. Sneed, C. H. Haight, J. R. Miller, W. S. McCloy, Ira Trout, D. W. Coan (clerks), for the faithful manner in which they conducted themselves through the ordeal that "tried men's souls." May a happy life and fair fortunes be theirs.

And now, to the generous people (God bless them!) of this entire country, and to the good and charitable of the Old World, who did not forget us, for their timely succor in the dark hour of our affliction, we tender, in the spirit of sacred sincerity and brotherly love, our unspeakable thanks and everlasting gratitude.

Yours truly,

J. H. SMITH, *Secretary.*

DONATIONS.

ARKANSAS.

Aug. 27—Citizens of Searcy	$113	50
29—Col'd Masons' Lodge,No.2,Lit.Rock	25	00
29—Howard Association, Little Rock	75	00
30—Maj. Jno. D. Adams, Little Rock	100	00
30—E. L. Watson, Jacksonport	20	00
31—Citizens of Hopefield	28	60
31—Citizens of Fulton	32	50
31—Citizens of Augusta	112	35
Sept. 1—Howard Ass'n,thro'L.W.Cox,Cas'r.	500	00
2—Citizens of Osceola, for Grenada	37	65
2—Batesville Chapter, R. A. M	74	50
2—Citizens of Mariana	71	00
3—C. M. Neal, Pine Bluff	100	00
4—J. A. Matthews, Ozark	10	00
4—Citizens of Alma	55	00
4—Citizens of Clarksville	140	00
4—Howard Association, Little Rock	300	00
4—J. Merrill, Pine Bluff	50	00
6—Citizens of Dardanelle	23	00
6—Citizens of Washington	31	60
6—P. Irwin, Des Arc	50	00
6—Citizens of Carlisle	61	50
6—Cit zens of Prescott	12	50
6—Spring St. M. E. Ch., Little Rock	7	00
6—Citizens of Van Buren	170	00
9—Ladies & children of Jacksonport.	60	00
9—Bell Point Lodge, F. & A. M	80	00
10—Citizens of Arkadelphia	16	00
10—M. E. Church, South Dardanelle	50	00
10—Howard Association, Little Rock	350	00
10—Cave Hill Masonic L'dge,Boonsboro	50	00
11—Guest of G. C. Hotel, Hot Springs	25	00
11—Citizens of Atkins	126	00
11—Citizens of Conway	72	65
11—Miss Irene Bocage, Pine Bluff	5	50
12—Proceeds of Festival, Augusta	168	00
13—Howard Association, Little Rock	300	00
13—E. J. McGaroe, Pecan Point	100	00
13—Proceeds of Festival, Fort Smith	204	35
13—Citizens of Hot Springs	200	00
16—Citizens of Pine Bluff	100	00
16—H. H. Hunn, Pine Bluff	100	00
16—Ozark Methodist Sunday School	14	50
16—Union Prayer Meeting, Camden	78	00
16—Crystal Lodge, K. of H., Hot Spr'gs.	25	00
16—Citizens of Russellville	68	00
16—Howard Association, Little Rock	75	00
16—Ladies of Hope	115	33
17—Citizens of Ozark	17	00
17—Citizens of Prescott	53	00
17—Cotton Blossom Minstrels, of Hope	35	00
18—Kyle & Cassidy, Prescott	50	00
18—James A. Payne, Jacksonport	20	00
18—Baptist Church, Forrest City	20	00
19—St. James Church, Prescott	6	55
20—H. H. Hunn, Cashier, Pine Bluff	316	00
20—U. Bros. Friendship, Pine Bluff	10	00
20—M. E. Church of Little Rock	30	00
20—8 little girls of Searcy	40	00
21—Citizens of Monticello	78	00
21—Presbyterian S. S., Dardanelle	8	50
21—Citizens of Batesville	100	00
23—Citizens of Conway	55	50
23—Young ladies of Pine Bluff	197	00
23—John O'Connell, Pine Bluff	.	
23—Little girls of Fayetteville	15	50
23—Cit zens of Bentonville	45	55
24—Presbyterian Church of Camden	61	25
24—M. M. Maguire, Dardanelle	15	00
24—Colored citizens of Augusta	10	00

Sept. 25—Order Royal Arcanum, Hot Sp'gs	$25	00
25—Howard Association, Little Rock	100	00
25—Union Sabbath School, Ozark	17	00
26—Musical Club of Fayetteville	75	00
27—Annie May and playmates, L. Rock	2	50
27—Trinity Sabbath School,Van Buren	15	00
27—Colored Temperance Union. "	10	00
28—Episcopal Sab. School, Van Buren	5	00
28—Citizens of Bradley County	150	00
28—Citizens of Quitman	14	10
28—Relief Committee of Dover	35	80
29—Colored citizens of Fort Smith	11	05
29—J. W. White, Dardanelle	7	55
Oct. 1—Colored Sab. School, Pine Bluff	5	20
1—W. S. Walker, Cincinnati	10	00
3—Citizens of Clarendon	10	00
3—Citizens of Locksburg	44	00
4—Howard Association. Little Rock	100	00
5—D. B. Elliott & Co., Hot Springs	112	75
7—Presbyterian Sab. S., Pine Bluff	10	00
7—Children's Pub. School, Bell Grove	5	00
10—Sympathizers, Little Rock	2	10
10—Union Sab. School of Malvern	20	00
22—Relief Committee of Warren	38	95
29—Citizens of Mineral Springs	21	00
Dec. 12—Dr. G. B. Malone, Indian Bay	10	00
12—Wm. H Boyce, Indian Bay	5	00
12—H. L. Silverman & Co., Indian Bay	10	00
Total	$6,690	37

ARIZONA.

Nov. 11—Mrs. G. H. Wicks, Prescott Barracks $5 00

ALABAMA.

Aug. 24—Citizens of Huntsville, Madison I. O. O. F.	$90	00
24—Citizens of Huntsville, Madison, I. O. O. F., for Grenada	30	00
26—Cant-get-away Club, Mobile	300	00
26—Citizens of Decatur	40	45
26—Citizens of Stephenson	15	15
26—Citizens of Selma, for Grenada	100	00
27—J. Neil & Bro., Huntsville	25	00
28—Citizens of Florence	81	45
28—Citizens of Florence, for Canton	20	00
28—Citizens of Opelika	96	00
28—Citizens of Opelika, for Grenada	30	00
29—Visitors & citizens of Blount Spr'gs	100	00
29—Jno. P. Tanner, Athens	25	00
31—Corporation of Florence	200	00
31—Citizens of Florence, for Canton	48	55
31—Citizens of Athens	100	00
31—Citizens of Athens	10	00
31—J.H.Pitts & Co.,Tuscaloosa	50	00
31—J.H.Pitts & Co., " for Vicksburg	50	00
31—J.H.Pitts & Co., " for Grenada	50	00
Sept. 1—Proceeds of concert at Selma	50	00
2—Employés of L. & N. R. R., Birmingham	33	00
2—Employés and Officers of Insane Asylum. Tuscaloosa	57	00
2—Mobile & Mont. R. R., Montgomery	86	30
2—Citizens of Wheeler	58	00
2—Proc. of bale of cotton,Tuscumbia	150	00
3—Presbyterian Church, Athens	10	00

338 APPENDIX.

Sept.	3—J. M. Hamette & Co., Huntsville	$ 5 00
	3—Montgomery Fire Department	25 00
	3—Dan'l Pratt Gin Co., Prattsville	200 00
	6—A. G. Henry, Guntersville	25 00
	6—Citizens of Marion	35 00
	10—Citizens of Tuscaloosa	25 00
	11—R. H. Brogen, Auburn	6 82
	11—Can't-get-away Club, Mobile	369 00
	12—Citizens of Opelika	44 50
	12—Citizens of Madison	17 30
	13—Hebrew Relief Association, Troy	45 00
	13—Spring Creek Church	5 70
	13—Relief Committee, Montgomery	500 00
	13—R. M. Schwartz, Hamburg	10 35
	13—Citizens of Planton and Verbena	25 00
	14—Brass band of Scotsboro	35 70
	14—Citizens of Monterallo	80 00
	15—Citizens of Opelika	76 00
	15—Citizens of Oxmoor	120 80
	16—Miss Evelyn Randolph, Montgom'ry	1 00
	17—White citizens of Uniontown	75 00
	17—Col'd Bap. and S. S., Uniontown	40 00
	17—Citizens of Evergreen	55 00
	17—Baptist Sab. School, Union Springs	4 56
	17—Citizens of Union Springs	57 65
	17—Sabbath School, Birmingham	2 25
	17—L. H. Bowles, Troy	125 00
	19—Mite Meeting, Coosa Station	100 00
	20—Citizens of Marion	192 20
	20—Citizens of Columbiana	55 00
	20—Citizens of Greensboro	58 25
	20—Citizens of Crawford	13 50
	20—Citizens of Greenville	200 00
	21—Meth.,Bap., and Pres Chs.,Opelika	58 70
	21—Citizens of Athens	47 00
	21—Citizens of Prattsville	24 65
	21—M. E. Church, Spring Valley	2 50
	21—Colored M. E. Ch., Greensboro	8 00
	21—Colored Bap. Ch., Greensboro	17 00
	21—Citizens of Oxford	49 10
	22—David Coleman, Huntsville	10 00
	22—Baptist Association, Tuscaloosa	21 25
	22—Citizens of Tuscaloosa	41 40
	23—Literary Society, Selma	75 00
	24—Citizens of Richmond	50 00
	25—Citizens of Courtland	10 00
	25—Miss Zila Russell, Athens	2 50
	25—Can't-get-away Club, Mobile	500 00
	25—Church of Marion	40 00
	28—Sabbath School of Hebena	25 25
	29—Citizens of Weaver Sta. & vicinity	36 60
	29—Citizens of Mooresville	168 00
Oct.	2—Citizens of Monterallo	23 10
	4—O. C. Wiley, Troy	52 00
	5—Misses Kerr and Price, N.Harmony	38 65
	7—Churches of Gadsden	8 10
	7—Citizens of Bolling	80 00
	9—School-girls of Opelika	63 00
	10—Citizens of Cussetta	53 90
	11—T. J. Williamson, Oak Bowery	10 00
	13—G. H. Prinz, Cullman	18 00
	16—Wood & Powell, Childersburg	38 00
	16—J. M. Hawkins, Huntingdon	50 00
	17—Relief Committee, Montgomery	12 75
	18—Citizens of Vienna	58 20
	22—O. C. Wiley, Troy	4 10
	22—Citizens of Andalusia	18 00
	23—Bruce Harris, Columbiana	7 15
	26—Jno. Dixon, Childersburg	42 30
	29—J. H. Fitts & Co., Tuscaloosa	45 75
	Total	$6,281 43

CONNECTICUT.

Sept.	4—1st Presbyterian Church, Bristol	$ 13 56
	10—Governor Jewell, Hartford	200 00
	13—Citizens of Hartford	500 00
	17—Citizens of Hartford	200 00
	18—Citizens of Hartford	250 00
	18—Citizens of New Haven	500 00
	18—Y. M. C. A., Hartford	200 00
	20—Citizens of Norwalk	300 00
	21—Citizens of Stamford	250 00
	21—Citizens of Greenville	8 15
	23—Citizens of Hartford	400 00
	28—Citizens of New Britain	500 00

Sept.	29—Relief Committee, New Haven	$600 00
Nov.	6—Citizens of New Haven—W.F.Day	478 57
	23—Citizens of Meriden,per H.W.Lines	500 00
Dec.	3—Citizens of Meriden,per "	125 00
	16—Citizens of Meriden,per " "	50 00
	Total	$5,070 28

COLORADO.

Sept.	3—Citizens of Denver	$500 00
	16—Citizens of Suisan City	113 00
	16—Citizens of Denver	200 00
	19—Proc. of Festival at Central City	300 00
	19—Citizens of Central City	358 50
	21—M. E. Ch. and S. S., Cañon City	100 00
	21—St. James M. E. S. S., Central City	21 50
	24—1st National Bank, Boulder	335 00
	27—Warren Camp, No. 2, K. of N. W., Central City	85 00
	28—Presbyterian S. S. of Georgetown	80 00
	28—Citizens of Golden	240 70
	28—Citizens of Colton	35 00
	29—Sunday School of Russell Gulch	35 00
Oct.	2—Winnemick Mine, Leadville	200 00
	2—Citizens of Nederland	40 00
	7—Relief fund of Golden	85 75
	9—H. P. Cowenhovan, Black Hawk	30 00
	9—Ladies of Stockton	540 00
	9—Ladies of Pueblo	301 70
	10—Mite box at Central City	6 65
	16—H. C. Greer, Rock Ridge	5 00
	21—Relief Committee, Denver, thro' J. T. Wellborn	283 87
	29—O. G. Buckingham, Boulder	150 00
Nov.	4—A. J. Vandeier, Boulder	4 28
	Total	$3,950 95

CALIFORNIA.

Aug.	24—C. C. Clay, San Francisco	$300 00
	24—C. C. Clay, " for Grenada	200 00
	31—Citizen's Com., by J. C. Patrick	1,500 00
Sept.	3—Leonora M. Filkins, Los Angeles	80 00
	6—Citizens of San Francisco, thro' J. C. Patrick	1,500 00
	8—Citizens of Los Angeles, thro' J. R. Dunkelberger	50 00
	9—Wells, Fargo & Co., thro' Valentine, Sup't	1,000 00
	9—Citizens of Santa Barbara	500 00
	9—Citizens of Puebla	152 30
	10—Citizens of Watsonville	120 00
	12—Citizens of California,thro'Anglo-California Bank	1,500 00
	14—Citizens of San Francisco, thro' Anglo-California Bank	1,500 00
	14—Citizens of Los Angeles, thro' J. R. Dunkelberger	150 00
	14—Mrs. P. P. McGee and daughter, Watsonville	226 50
	16—Wells, F. & Co., thro' Valentine	1,000 00
	18—Citizens of San Francisco	3,500 00
	18—Citizens of Tulare County	27 00
	18—Citizens of Modesta	700 00
	24—Citizens of San Francisco	5.000 00
	24—Wells, F. & Co.,thro' E.K.Wright	9,000 00
	26—Christian Muller, San Francisco	20 00
Oct.	1—Anglo-Cal. Bank, San Francisco	400 00
	2—Clark, Dixon & Pedlock, Fresno	127 50
	3—Citizens of Santa Barbara	105 00
	9—Sabbath School near Riversdale	81 00
	31—Citizens of Santa Barbara, thro' A. Lincoln	83 00
Nov.	6—J. K. Alsup, San Francisco	10 00
	6—Wells, F. & Co., San Francisco	255 00
	Total	$29,047 30

DAKOTA TERRITORY.

Sept.	14—Entertainment, Whitney Opera House, Bismark	$25 00

APPENDIX. 339

Sept. 18—Citizens of Deadwood.................$132 50
22—Citizens of B.smark................ 136 00
22—Colored Citizens of B.ack Hills..... 134 00
Oct. 5—Officers & soldiers, U.S.A., Ft.Rice.. 75 00
7—Officers, " & citizens,Ft.Buford 78 00
7—Citizens of Lead City................ 150 00
9—Citizens of Spearfish................ 22 50
10—Citizens of Lead City.............. 30 50

Total.......................$663 50

DELAWARE.

Sept. 18—Citizens of New Castle........... $21 02
29—Citizens of New Castle............ 20 00

Total............................. $41 02

FLORIDA.

Sept. 20—Citizens of Lake City............$ 12 00
21—Proc. of bale of cotton, Mariana.... 100 00
21—Mrs.W.H.Sebring & chil'n,Bronson 5 00
22—Citizens of Quincy................ 100 00
22—Nickly Club of Quincy............ 31 42
24—Citizens & young ladies, Palatka... 85 00
24—Knowles & Brent, Pensacola........ 356 30
25—Citizens' Aid Com., Tallahassee... 257 61
25—Citizens of Live Oak. 63 00
29—Citizens of St. Augustine............ 100 05
29—St. Barnabas P. E. Mission.......... 6 20
29—Germania Fire Co , Pensacola....... 200 00
Oct. 3—Proc. of bale of cotton, Mariana.... 102 75
4 -E. T. Lane, Crystal Lake............ 21 00
9 –Citizens of Fort Reid................ 45 00
23—" Sun and Press." Jacksonville.... 20 00
Nov. 2—Crescent City, thro' C. S.Williams.. 11 50

Total.......................$1,516 83

GEORGIA.

Aug. 26—J. E. Jones, Macon, for Grenada...$100 00
30 Citizens of Washington............ 34 80
Sept. 2—J. E. Jones, Macon Relief Com...... 220 00
2—Citizens of Decatur,perW.R.Patello 26 35
2—Banks & Bro., Gainesville.......... 5 00
4—Concordia Association, Atlanta..... 33 05
5—Citizens of Greenville............. 53 35
6—Citizens of Griffin................ 45 90
6—Citizens of Tunnel Hill 13 25
6—Citizens of Augusta, per Dr.Wright 215 50
6—Citizens of Augusta,per J.P.Garvin 220 00
6—Citizens of Washington 58 20
6—Unknown, Gainesville.............. 2 00
7—J. G. Meyer, Augusta.............. 25 00
9—Relief Com., Atlanta,thro' A. Fox. 50 00
9—Citizens of Augusta, thro' J. P. Garvin, for Grenada................ 100 00
9—Concordia Association,Atlanta, for Grenada 33 05
9—Relief Ass'n,Macon, thro'J.E.Jones 100 00
9—City Council of Hawkinsville..... 100 00
12—Children of M.E.S.S., East Point... 2 00
12—Citizens of Lumber City............ 10 00
13—R. J. Brown, Augusta.............. 5 00
13—R. J. Brown, Augusta.............. 12 35
13—Mord Society, No. 1, Augusta...... 15 25
13—J. G. Meyer, Mayor of Augusta..... 46 00
13—Relief Committee, Atlanta........ 200 00
13—Ladies of National Hotel, Dalton.. 50 00
13—Methodist Sab. School Congress... 5 00
13—Smyrna Sab. School, Rockdale..... 5 55
13—Presbyterian Church Congress..... 13 95
14—G. P. Hanks (Chairman), Dalton.. 71 00
14—M. H. Hellburn, Warrenton........ 32 00
14—G. C. Terry, Dublin.............. 13 60
14—Piedmont Aid Ass'n,Gainesville... 50 00
14—Citizens of Athens................ 140 00
15—Citizens of Thomasville.......... 374 75
15—Y. M. C. A., Rome................ 75 00
16—P. Callaway, West Point........... 1 00
16—Cornet band, Marietta............ 248 35

Sept. 16—Corgill & Co., Marietta........... $ 48 00
16—J. D. Waddell, Marietta........... 6 00
16—J. Spillman, Marietta 5 00
16—G. W. Woodruff, Columbus......... 100 00
16—S. Gardner, Augusta.............. 3 00
16—Relief Committee, Savannah....... 500 00
16—Citizens of Macon................ 100 00
17—J. C. Fargo, Augusta............. 35 00
17—Harmony Church, Augusta......... 6 60
17—Citizens of Greensboro........... 100 25
17—Proc. of an entertainment, Atlanta 310 25
17—Relief Committee, Macon......... 200 00
19—Citizens of Albany............... 84 00
19—Baptist Church, Pine Bluff........ 6 00
19—J. G. Meyer, Augusta............. 8 50
19—Citizens of Gainesville........... 13 00
19—Rossini Musical Club, Atlanta.... 184 25
19—E. S. Grigg, Marietta............ 10 00
19—Baptist Church of Canton......... 9 25
20—Relief Committee of Atlanta..... 380 00
20—Conference of Augusta, through J. T. Jarvis...................... 500 00
20—J. G. Meyer, Augusta............. 19 65
20—Miss Nora Faw, Madison.......... 11 50
20—Churches of Cave Springs......... 41 05
21—Citizens of Maxwell.............. 45 00
21—Citizens of Washington........... 20 15
21—Citizens of Columbus............ 123 75
21—J. G. Meyer, Augusta............. 5 00
21—St.Luke's Episcopal Ch.,Columbus 29 00
21—Relief Committee of Warrenton... 12 80
21—Citizens of Cartersville......... 51 50
21—Citizens of Rome................ 75 00
21—Citizens of Macon................ 200 00
22—Citizens of Guyton............... 20 00
22—Employés of Central R.R.,Augusta 77 00
22—Irving & Neal, Thomasson........ 23 05
23—Citizens of Atlanta.............. 98 00
23—Citizens of Augusta.............. 74 75
23—Colored Church of Augusta....... 6 95
23—Citizens of Columbus............ 34 00
23—Citizens of Greensboro........... 4 05
23—Brass band of Greensboro........ 26 00
23—A lady of Columbus.............. 1 50
23—Citizen's Relief Com., Augusta...1,701 26
23—Conc'rt,res.M.G.Whitlock,Marietta 50 00
24—Citizens of Warrenton............ 10 25
25—Burns' Silver Cornet Band,Athens. 306 50
25—Mrs. E. Glass, Hopkinsville...... 10 00
25—J. G. Meyer, Augusta............. 28 05
25—J. G. Meyer, Augusta............. 10 00
25—J. G. Meyer, Augusta............. 91 50
26—J. G. Meyer, Augusta............. 54 50
27—Citizens of Thomasville.......... 21 25
27—Unknown friend, Cuthbert........ 1 63
29—J. G. Meyer, Augusta............. 88 00
29—J. G. Meyer, Augusta............. 20 00
29—W. Bronson, Perry................ 91 00
29—Baptist Church of Cobb County.... 19 00
29—Relief Association, Macon........ 600 00
29—B'rd of Trustees & Masons,Augusta 75 00
29—Rev. W. D. Anderson, Cedartown. 37 00
29—Colored Baptist Ch. of Marietta.. 10 40
29—Citizens of Columbus............ 26 00
29—Colored ladies of Columbus...... 36 00
29—Citizens of Columbus............ 67 00
30—Mite box, Albany................ 5 50
30—Rossini Musical Club, Bainbridge. 33 00
Oct. 1—M. L. Dunlap, Cedartown........ 1 00
2—Citizens of Newman.............. 50 00
2—Presbyterian Sab. Sch., Eulaulee.. 30 00
2—Ladies of Louisville............ 142 00
2—Baptist Church of Hickory Head... 15 15
3—Citizens of Cairo................ 22 80
3—Citizens of Quitman.............. 41 32
3—J. G. Meyer, Augusta 50 00
3—Masonic L'dge & M.E.S.S.,Hamilt'n 33 00
3—Citizens of Buena Vista.......... 12 15
4—Presbyterian Sab. School, Griffin.. 44 55
4—McIntosh Union S. S., McIntosh .. 2 50
4—Citizens of Pike County.......... 20 00
4—Sundry collect'ne of J.M.Brawner. 4 50
5—J. G. Meyer, Augusta............. 20 00
5—Baptist Church near Valdosta..... 24 30
5—Citizens of Jefferson............ 42 00
7—Benevolent Association, Albany... 100 00
7—Citizens of Guysboro............. 36 00
7—Ladies' Ass'n, Cave Springs...... 11 10
9—A friend in Centre Village....... 1 00

APPENDIX.

Oct. 10—Relief Committee, Augusta	$458	63
13—W. T. Remmian, Brunswick	25	00
13—J. G. Meyer, Augusta	34	67
13—J. G. Meyer, Augusta	5	00
13—S. D. Brodwell, McIntosh	24	00
19—Colored Church of Thomasson	4	00
21—Church at Clark's Station	16	50
Nov. 4—Citizens'Relief Com.,Augusta,thro' Jno. L. Maxwell	100	85
Dec. 12—Golden Fleece Lodge, No. 6, F. & A. M , Covington	10	00
20—Columbus Manf'g Co., Columbus, thro' Howard Ass'n,New Orleans	33	33
Total	$11,415	34

ILLINOIS.

Aug. 15—Potter Palmer, Chicago	$ 50	00
23—Various contribut'ns, St.Clair Co., through J. H. Knox	200	00
23—Various contribut'ns, St.Clair Co., for Grenada	100	00
23—Freeman Huling,Mayor,Kankakee	100	00
27—T. J. Robertson, Edwardsville	50	00
27—Centennial Lodge, I.O.G.T., Freeport	25	00
28—Citizens of Freeport	100	00
28—Citizens of Leroy	26	00
28—Citizens of Springfield	25	10
28—Allan Pinkerton, Chicago	20	00
28—Frank Trimble, Paris	10	00
28—J. W. McCoy & Son, Golconda	10	00
29—R. B. Lewis, Quincy	50	00
30—Presbyterian Ch., Bloomington	61	00
30—Citizens of Tishkilwa	61	00
30—Factory hands of Chicago	8	25
30—Samuel Wernech, Quincy	10	00
31—W. D. A. Matthews, Sup't Prison, Chicago	21	00
31—Officers U. S. Snag Boat, DeRussy, Mound City	40	00
31—Employés M. & St. P. R. R., thro' J. H. Barber	51	25
31—Humboldt Lodge, No. 61, Quincy	25	00
31—Citizens of Cayuga	5	00
31—P. S. Schnable, Mayor of Geneseo	100	00
31—Base Ball players, Peoria	22	50
Sept. 2—S. E. Leger, Quincy	200	00
2—Proc. of entertainment, Urbana	112	25
2—Officers and employés Asylum for feeble-minded chil., Springfield	40	00
2—A friend at Chenoa	1	00
2—Citizens of Cairo	100	00
2—Murray Nelson,Chairm'n,Chicago	1,000	00
3—Proc. of concert at Metropolis	113	25
3—James H. Gilbert, Chicago	151	75
3—J. L. Atwood, DeKalb	100	00
4—Citizens of Galesburg	200	00
4—A friend at Carbondale	10	00
4—Potter Palmer, Chicago	50	00
4—Citizens & Y. M. C. A., Mt. Carmel	101	35
4—J. N. Arthur, Quincy	5	00
4—Citizens of Mattoon	51	45
4—Citizens of Gibson City	130	00
4—J. T. Stewart, Plano	2	00
4—Cole, Bro. & Co., Chester	211	00
5—Citizens of Cobden	100	00
5—Citizens of Oden	50	75
5—Citizens of Champaign	100	00
5—2d Pres. Sab. School, Freeport	13	20
5—Friends, thro' H.H.Black,Chicago	24	25
5—Citizens of Grand Tower	118	00
6—Ladies of Nashville	50	00
6—Citizens of Carmi	185	50
6—Citizens of Edwardsville	255	00
6—Peter Svinoe, Vice-Con. to Sweden, Chicago	5	00
6—1st Baptist Ch., Mount Carroll	25	35
6—1st Baptist S. S., Mount Carroll	5	00
6—Relief Committe, Rock Island	200	00
6—Citizens of Ottumwa	150	00
6—Citizens of Lexington	30	40
6—Proc.entertainm't " for Grenada	18	00
6—Citizens of Windsor Station	65	55
6—Old John Robinson's Circus, Quincy	200	00
Sept. 6—Murray Nelson, Chairman, Chicago, for Canton	$250	00
6—Murray Nelson, Chairman, Chicago, for Holly Springs	250	00
7—Ladies' Relief Ass'n, Streetor	109	31
7—Citizens of Alton	400	00
7—Citizens of Alton, for Grenada	146	80
7—I. O. O. F., No. 38, Carlyle	25	00
7—Citizens of Williams	68	00
7—S. A. Litteray, Barry, Pike Co	15	00
7—Citizens & City Council,Bushnell	179	65
7—Citizens of Joliet	338	48
7—Union Band, Freeport	135	00
7—Citizens of El Paso	112	00
7—Commandery 8, K. T., Galesburg	25	00
7—Board of Trade, Peoria	280	00
9—Citizens of Elgin	83	55
9—Citizens of Plainfield	24	40
9—Stapp's Chapel,M.E.Ch., Decatur	45	00
9—Good Templars of Decatur	45	00
9—Gennesee Lorgue, Monmouth	5	00
9—Citizens of Griggsville	34	50
9—Proceeds of concert, Springfield	253	65
9—Citizens of Murphysboro	103	70
9—Merchants' Nat. Bank, Chicago, for Grenada	400	00
9—3 young ladies of Golconda	33	75
9—Murray Nelson,Chairm'n,Chicago	2,000	00
9—P. B. Updike, Litchfield	150	00
10—Citizens of Bunker Hill	250	00
10—Mrs. Peck, Petersburg	5	00
10—Citizens of Alton	248	10
10—Officers and guards, State Prison, Springfield	168	65
10—Citizens of Springfield	345	53
11—Ladies of Keithsburg	20	00
11—Pres. Cong. Ch. S. S., Charleston	30	00
11—Bap. Cong. Ch. S. S., Charleston	2	31
11—Citizens of Charleston	83	25
11—Citizens of Durant	36	00
11—Congregational Church, Alton	38	20
11—Hope Hose Co., Alton	15	00
11—F. Huling, Mayor, Kankakee	66	60
12—Citizens of Carrollton	590	00
12—Literary Society, Mendota	30	00
12—Citizens of Mendota	102	25
12—Ladies' Literary Ass'n,Kankakee	26	00
12—Union of all churches,Kirkwood	25	11
12—Employés of Peniten'ry,Springf'd	17	00
12—Citizens of Aledo	57	50
12—Citizens of Rock Island	183	95
12—Olmsted Lodge, I.O.G.T.,Olmsted	19	45
12—Citizens of St. Joseph	23	28
12—Citizens of Astoria	65	50
12—Citizens of Douglas	75	00
12—Citizens of Arcola	50	00
12—A. Amman & E. Flaherty, Springfield	16	65
13—Citizens of Sandoval	13	50
13—Citizens of Warsaw	157	05
13—Citizens of Perry	96	35
13—Unknown friend, Chicago	5	00
13—Citizens of Waverly	28	10
13—M. E. Church, South Evanston	17	18
13—M. E. Ch. S. S., South Evanston	3	41
13—Proceeds of Base Ball, Peoria	31	85
13—Edgar Co.Agricult'l Board, Paris	59	00
13—Citizens of Sterling	400	00
13—Citizens of Carlinville	250	00
13—Citizens of Henry	114	00
13—R. Conc, Hennepin	137	40
12—A. J. Alexander, Gillman	5	00
13—Citizens of Maywood	60	00
13—Citizens of Clinton	106	20
13—Citizens of Monmouth	100	00
13—Citizens of Neponset	50	00
14—W. H. Platt, Grand Island	165	00
14—Waukegan Methodist Society	13	00
14—Citizens of Waukegan	150	00
14—Citizens of Fairfield	205	50
14—Citizens of Eureka	200	00
14—Chapter 46, R.A.M., Galesburg	15	00
14—E. L. Phillips	15	00
14—Union Baptist Church, Aurora	82	00
14—Board of Trade, Elgin	55	00
14—Citizens of Aurora	201	25
14—Proc. concert, Choral Soc , Lima	70	00
14—A. Phillips, Red Bird	5	00
14—Young ladies of Shawneetown	143	41

APPENDIX. 341

Sept. 14—Proceeds of lecture by Right Rev. Spaulding, Peoria	$100 00
14—Congregational Church, Peoria...	117 18
14—Edward Mullin, Graysville	7 25
14—Proc. ent'm't, A O.U.W.,Carthage	56 25
14—Citizens of Macomb	280 00
14—Citizens of Mendota	25 00
14—Citizens of Salem	70 43
14—Collections by churches, Polo	51 27
15—Citizens of Sparta	100 00
15—Citizens' Relief Ass'n, Lemont	250 00
15—Murray Nelson,Chairm'n,Chicago	3,000 00
16—Employés C. & I. R.R.,Rochelle...	75 00
16—Citizens of Virginia	100 00
16—Citizens of Belleville	300 00
16—Citizens of Carbondale	190 00
16—Murray Nelson, Chicago	2,000 00
16—Nat. Ch. T. Union, Hamburg	93 00
16—Relief Association, Bethallo	27 00
16—Citizens of Princeton	200 00
16—St. Mary's Cath. Ch., Joliet	42 00
16—Concert at Galesburg	200 00
16—Concert at Galesburg,for Grenada	81 55
16—Masons at Galesburg	50 00
16—Citizens of Warrensburg	20 00
17—German M. E. Ch., Aurora	8 00
17—L. E. Conover, Glendale	25 00
17—Citizens' Relief Com.,Washington	110 40
17—Citizens of Olney	437 55
17—Citizens of Warrensburg	10 65
17—Altha Lodge, Galesburg	20 00
17—Citizens of Champaign	33 00
17—Citizens of Xenia	50 00
17—Board of Supervisors,Tazewell Co.	70 00
17—Murray Nelson, Chairman, Chicago, from the Owl Club	1,000 00
17—Murray Nelson, Ch'm'n, Chicago, for Brownsville	1,000 00
18—Citizens of McLeansboro	65 00
18—Knights of Honor, McLeansboro..	22 00
18—H. P. Tracy, Elmwood	61 00
18—Various sources, Kirkwood	23 70
18—Entertainment at Elmwood	61 00
18— " by young men,Goleonda	39 00
18—Employés Watch Co., Elgin	292 30
18—Paxton Choral Society, Paxton	50 00
18—S. L. Wissner, Anna	4 70
18—Citizens of Galesburg	137 50
18—Mayor's office, Chicago	114 00
18—Murray Nelson, Chairm'n,Chicago	3,100 00
19—Citizens of Arcola	60 00
19—Silver Lodge, K. of H., Carlinville	131 25
19—Citizens of Carlinville	86 30
19—Ladies of Forreston	84 46
19—Citizens of Newton	50 35
19—Citizens of Willow Hill	4 45
19—Committee of Eureka	149 60
19—Citizens of Charleston	44 94
19—Citizens of Vandalia	126 30
19—Presbyterian Ch., Du Quoin	15 55
19—Citizens of Whitehall	375 00
19—Benevolent Ass'n, Mason City	27 60
19—Citizens of Decatur	447 78
19—Congregational Ch., Lockport	28 00
19—A butcher of Nokomis	6 70
19—H. C. Hawenhauer, Peru	400 00
19—Citizens of Lincoln	95 00
19—Citizens of Pekin	311 30
19—Citizens of Pluto	47 00
19—Citizens of Oakland	23 00
19—Sabbath Schools of Diggsville	52 00
19—J. P. Forsythe, Onarga	128 00
19—Employés Crane Bros., Chicago...	74 75
19—Citizens of Mount Carmel	41 10
19—Employés Insane Hospital,Elgin..	101 50
19—Congregational Ch., Providence...	19 15
20—Citizens of Litchfield	200 00
20—Citizens of Farmington	151 60
20—U. P. Congregation, Sparta	28 90
20—Randle School, Sparta	23 40
20—Citizens of Blandinsville	100 00
20—Citizens of Alton	50 00
20—Citizens of Owance	33 45
20—Citizens of Centralia	62 00
20—Citizens of Mount Vernon	42 75
20—Citizens of Belleville	300 00
20—Citizens of Hardin	26 00
20—Citizens of Collinsville	162 55
20—Citizens of Vienna	54 35
Sept. 20—Citizens of Williamstown	$ 22 00
20—Citizens of Havana	114 40
20—A. B. Sawyer, Fremont	22 25
20—Benevolent Association, Pekin	116 00
20—Relief fund, Jacksonville	500 00
20—Citizens of Eaglewood	100 00
20—Citizens of Mount Sterling	75 05
21—E. K. Stone, Quincy	22 25
21—Employés Rolling Mill,N.Chicago	400 00
21—Citizens of Carrollton	29 00
21—Trinity Epis. Church. Aurora	17 25
21—Churches of Kirkwood	38 07
21—Citizens of La Harpe	78 00
21—Free Cong. Society,Bloomington..	14 06
21—Citizens of Springfield	147 00
21—Citizens of Rock Island	43 09
21—C.tizens of Franklin	16 00
21—7 little girls of Aurora	85 42
22—Baptist Church. Chicago	119 85
22—Citizens of Chicago	47 35
22—Citizens of Fairfield	10 00
22—Citizens of Payson	46 40
22—Snp'ts& Cont'rsof Prison,Joliet...	169 00
22—Citizens of Waverly	26 09
22—Congregational Church, Seward...	12 00
22—Citizens of Carmi	22 70
22—Relief Committee, Du Quoin	314 71
22—Miners of Coal Co., McLean Co...	32 10
22—Citizens of Shannon	84 45
22—M. E. Sab. School, Belmont	5 25
22—Citizens of Bradford	72 00
22—Citizens of Minooka	107 00
22—A. B. L. Society, Paxton	25 00
22—City and county officials,Chicago.	1,500 00
22—J. T. Evans, Clay City	6 00
23—Pres. Ch. and S. S., Carrollton	15 00
23—Union Lodge,K.of H.,1033,Virden	71 75
23—Citizens of Lockport	11 00
23—Congregational Ch.,Griggsville...	87 50
23—Murray Nelson,Chairm'n.Chicago	5,000 00
24—Relief Committee, Belknap	62 75
24—Citizens of Pekin	158 05
24—Citizens of Butler	81 60
24—13 little girls of Englewood	26 00
24—Citizens' Relief Com., Paris	100 00
24—Y. M. C. A , Chicago	7 00
25—Citizens of Vermont	120 00
25—Citizens of Danville	200 00
23—Presbyterian.O. G., Henderson....	14 52
25—Germania Ass'n, Freeport	42 85
25—J. Barnsack, Troy	61 55
25—Murray Nelson,Chairm'n.Chicago	3,000 00
25—Union Sabbath School, Carbon..	12 00
25—Citizens of Ivesdale	55 05
25—Catholic Church, Ivesdale	38 15
25—Citizens of Warrensburg	12 00
25—Irving Literary Soc., Chicago	5 00
25—A. O. U. W. of Roseville	12 70
25—U. P. Congregation, Bethel	10 00
25—Citizens of Vermillion Co	500 00
25—Citizens of Danville	274 55
25—Citizens of Chillicothe	50 00
25—Jno. H. Adams, Cedarville	20 00
25—Geo. H. Tuck, Plymouth	10 00
25—Citizens of Charleston	6 76
25—Thos. H. Clark, Golconda	12 15
25—H. Carson, Hennepin	52 50
25—Relief Committee, Chicago	100 00
25—Crane Bros. M'f'g Co., Chicago...	8 75
25—Presbyterian Ch., Grand Ridge...	26 00
25—Baptist Church, Effingham	3 00
25—Christian Gels, Arlingt'n Heights	200 00
25—Presbyterian Ch., Plum Creek...	16 05
5—Citizens of Rood House	59 55
25—J. Ulrich, Decatur	11 40
25—Board of Trade, Peoria	15 60
25—Charles Fensburgh, Cayuga	1 00
28—Citizens' Relief Com., Sterling....	259 75
28—E. R. Brown, Elmwood	45
28—Citizens' Relief Com., Englewood	100 00
28—Citizens' Relief Com., Blue Island and vicinity	313 67
28—Rev. Thos. Dooley, Grand Ridge.	4 00
28—Citizens of Channahow	27 00
28—W. T. Rogers, Mayor, Quincy	127 65
28—Children of Reform Ch. Bushnell.	2 00
29—R. E. Moreland, Belle Fower	45 00
29—Congregation of Ivesdale	9 00
29—Home Nat. Bank, Chicago	5 00

APPENDIX

Sept 29—Rev. J. W. Long, Salem	$	5 00
Oct. 2—Citizens of Bennett		33 26
2—J. Taylor Smith, Springfield		97 27
2—A. T. Hemmingway, Chicago		9 65
2—Mayor's office, Chicago		81 00
2—Citizens of Edwardsville		25 00
2—Baptist Church of Barry		9 10
3—Red Sch. House Sub. S. of Du Page		15 00
3—County Fair, Fairfield		11 50
3—Citizens of Orian		37 10
4—Shiloh Church, Huntsville		6 00
4—Camp Creek Pres. Ch., Macomb		13 15
4—Milton McClure, Carlinville		10 50
4—Citizens of Rattan		1 30
5—Citizens of Burnside		12 00
5—E S. Frey, Carmi		5 00
5—Citizens of Mount Morris		10 00
5—Wm. Gascoigne, Plainfield		10 50
7—City Council, Danville		100 00
7—E. M. Eaton, Marion		78 45
9—Entertainment at Eugenie		5 35
9—Church at Wine Hill		3 33
10—Citizens of Mount Carmel		27 75
10—Ladies of Grand Tower		43 00
10—J. T. Swan, Bethallo		7 75
10—Zinc City Fire Co., Lasalle		66 00
10—Lyford & Sprague, Sheffield		5 00
13—Citizens of Verona and vicinity		26 83
13—Citizens of Jacksonville		75 00
13—Citizens of " for Decatur, Ala.		75 00
16—Rev. J. Montgomery, Walnut Grove		9 00
16—J. R. Jewett, Harrison		7 00
16—Citizens of Bushnell		11 25
16—Citizens of Fulton		113 80
16—Citizens of Arlington Heights		200 00
16—Congregational Church, Wyanet		46 75
16—Temperance Union, Atlanta		6 25
16—Bethlehem C. P. Church, Decatur		4 54
25—W. H. Gest, Rock Island		5 00
25—German Banking Co., Peoria		3 00
25—Citizens of Roberts, through T. M. Hubbard		20 00
25—W. H. Orrington, 50 Randolph St., Chicago		2 00
25—Elgin Club, through E. D. Waldron, Chicago		48 00
25—Jas. L. Metz, Perry		27 00
25—W. A. Riel (Treas,) Monmouth		102 37
Nov. 6—W. B. Bonnefield, Ottumwa		59 25
6—F. Huling, Mayor, Kankakee		38 60
7—C. S. Conger, Carmi		23 70
7—Citizens of Cambridge		113 55
15—D. B. Smith, Jacksonville		100 00
Total		$52,307 00

INDIANA

Aug. 22—Woodburn Wheel Co., Ind'apolis	$	100 00
22—Lawyers of Indianapolis		376 65
24—Hebrew Ladies' Benevolent Society, Plymouth, for Grenada		100 00
27—Fletcher & Sharpe, Indianapolis		300 00
29—Brownell. Granville & Co., Evansv'le		25 00
29—Y. M. C. A., Michigan City		173 80
31—Ft. Wayne Lodge, No. 14, I.O.O.F., Ft. Wayne		25 00
Sept. 2—Hebrew Congregation, Ft. Wayne		23 00
2—Citizens of New Albany		250 00
2—Citizens of " for Grenada		100 00
2—Y. M. Association, Laporte		200 00
2—Mitchell & Reed, Jeffersonville		147 55
2—Doric Lodge, A.O.U.W., New Alb'y		50 00
4—E. & T. H. R. R. Co., Evansville		170 00
4—J. M. Hutton & Co., Richmond		70 00
5—Universalist Church of Aurora		77 00
5—J. M. Wilder, Terre Haute		600 00
5—Citizens of State Centre		31 00
5—Y. M. C. A., Greensburg		33 00
6—Ladies of Pres. Ch., Greencastle		10 00
6—Entert'm't by citizens of Madison		120 75
6—Citizens of Madison		100 00
6—Employés and stockholders Gaar, Scott & Co., Richmond		228 25
6—Proceeds of concert, Lawrenceburg		76 60
6—Citizens of Indianapolis		300 00
6—Mission Sab. School, Vincennes		2 36
Sept. 6—Jno. L. Hatfield, Knightstown		$10 00
6—Citizens of Bloomington		50 00
6—Citizens of Kokomo		55 00
6—Public Schools, Evansville		266 00
8—C. W. Gabbert, for ladies of Rockport		145 00
8—Wabash Relief Com., Ind'apolis		333 56
9—Red Ribbon Club of Orleans		25 55
9—Grace M. E. Church of Richmond		70 00
9—Hamilton Bank, Ft. Wayne		137 18
9—McKim, Madison		100 00
10—1st National Bank, Richmond		400 00
11—Brass band of Paoli		7 00
11—Graves Sab. School, Terre Haute		8 25
12—Citizens of New Albany		45 00
12—Citizens of " for Holly Sp'gs		36 25
12—Citizens of Greenville		10 25
12—Citizens of Louisville		26 00
12—Citizens of Madison		100 00
12—Concord Leiderkranz, Mt. Vernon		102 50
12—M. E. Church, Kingston		15 37
12—Timothy Wilson, Springland		8 00
12—G. W. Burton, Mitchell		16 00
12—Sweetser Bank, Marion		102 50
12—Citizens of Madison		115 00
13—Woolen Mills, Seymour		50 00
13—Mayor of Seymour		48 00
13—German M. E. Church, Madison		31 00
13—Chair-makers' Union, Tell City		25 00
13—Barbers & hair-dressers, Madison		19 05
13—Citizens of Worthington		14 60
13—Citizens of Greencastle		200 00
13—Citizens of Rockville		250 00
13—Citizens of Indianapolis		1,000 00
14—Y. M. C. A., Laporte		150 00
14—Citizens of Huntingdon		210 00
14—Citizens of Vincennes		351 00
14—Proceeds of concert at Orleans		30 00
14—Citizens of South Bend		250 00
14—Rapier Commandery, Ind'apolis		75 00
15—Charity Lodge, F. & A. M., Washington		50 00
15—W. Trow & Co., Madison		25 00
16—Citizens of Seymour		20 25
16—Citizens of Shelbyville		160 00
16—Citizens of Evansville		90 00
16—Citizens of Queensville		28 00
17—Hanover College, Hanover		54 50
17—J. M. Nash, Lafayette		200 00
17—Citizens & Gesang Verein, Crown Point		133 00
17—Relief Committee, Logansport		200 00
17—Citizens of Edwardsport		20 00
17—Vawtor, Reichele, Davis, Dickinson, and Smith, North Vernon		20 00
18—Printers of Indianapolis		41 80
18—Citizens of Oxford		67 85
18—Citizens of Vevay		50 00
18—Citizens of Rochester		73 57
18—Citizens of Rochester		73 58
18—Citizens of Worthington		6 40
18—Citizens of Edinburgh		150 00
18—G. W. Hartley, Goodland		50 00
19—Proceeds of concert, Vevay		111 35
19—Citizens of Zionsville		13 00
20—Citizens of Shelbyville		5 00
20—1st Presbyterian Ch., Madison		40 00
20—U. P. Church, Madison		15 41
20—Citizens of Cloverdale		22 57
20—Congregational S. S., Cresco		5 00
20—Presbyterian S. S., Rushville		12 10
20—Citizens of Marion		75 00
20—Citizens of New Albany		91 25
21—Christian Church of Bedford		29 00
21—Citizens of Bedford		71 00
21—Citizens of Logansport		235 75
21—Ladies of Clayton		23 28
22—Citizens of Whitestown		12 10
22—Citizens of Manckport		10 00
22—Citizens of Lawrenceburg		228 45
22—Citizens of Attica		73 00
22—Hebrew Benev. Society of Ladies, Plymouth		25 00
23—Citizens of Indianapolis		500 00
23—Citizens of Rockville		20 00
23—F. & A. M. Lodge, 687, Bean Blossom		10 00
24—Hebrew Congregation, Ft. Wayne		9 00
25—Ladies of Anderson		100 00

APPENDIX. 343

Sept. 25—Jesse Wagoner, Stony Point	$ 5 00	
26—Citizens of Peru	18 00	
26—Friends' Sab. School, Spiceland	6 00	
27—Edwin C. Watson, Vincennes	12 74	
27—E. W. Sherk, Tipton	32 66	
27—Citizens of Bloomington	20 16	
27—Citizens of Logansport	123 48	
27—Citizens of Bourbon	52 43	
28—Typos of Lafayette	30 00	
28—Masonic Fraternity, Worthington	5 52	
29—Christian Church of Mishawaka	11 15	
29—Citizens of Vincennes	103 67	
29—Citizens of Logansport	45 10	
Oct. 1—Citizens of Union City	178 17	
3—Mite box, Vincennes	6 00	
4—Friends' Sab. School, Spiceland	2 00	
4—Citizens of South Bend	150 00	
5—Citizens of Decatur	37 00	
10—Relief Association, Tell City	37 50	
10—A church of Shelbyville	16 00	
10—Relief Committee of Plymouth	61 00	
16—N. C. Follett. Michigan City	50 00	
16—Dramatic Club of Hagerstown	23 60	
16—Mary O'Hara, Anderson	122 00	
19—Citizens of Rochester	73 58	
21—Citizens of Washington	102 00	
26—C. R. & S. R. R., Rockport, through C. W. Gilbert	24 75	
26—J. M. Wildy, Mayor, Terre Haute	41 95	
Nov. 6—Irving W. Smith, Anadusko	5 00	
Dec. 18—Combs, Hartman & Co., Tell City	62 50	
20—Citizens of Indianapolis, through Howard Ass'n, New Orleans	200 00	
20—Relief Association, Aurora, thro' Howard Ass'n, New Orleans	250 00	
30—South Western Furniture Association, Tell City	50 00	
Total	$13,787 69	

IOWA.

Aug. 25—J. B. Carpenter, Marshall	$ 31 00	
27—Hebrew Congregat'n, Des Moines	100 00	
30—W. S. Moore, Keokuk	35 00	
31—Thos Brook, Des Moines	10 00	
31—Plymouth Church, Des Moines	71 00	
31—1st Baptist Sab. Sch., Des Moines	6 00	
31—Citizens of Council Bluffs	2 00	
31—Citizens of De Witt	10 00	
Sept. 2—Officer & Pussey, Council Bluffs	200 00	
2—Citizens of Sigourney	22 90	
2—Tootle, Livingston & Co., Sioux City	20 00	
2—D. Pingrey, Durant	9 75	
2—Citizens of Davenport	84 00	
3—Unknown, thro' Nat. State Bank	10 00	
3—Citizens of Davenport	186 00	
3—Citizens of Boone	57 50	
5—Pres. Church and S. S., Waterford	52 07	
6—Carter, Hussy & Culry, Des Moines	3 25	
6—Children's concert, Des Moines	6 00	
6—Citizens of Mason City	32 00	
6—Citizens of Marshalltown	128 75	
6—Congregational Ch., McGregor	17 00	
6—Citizens of Lyons	175 00	
7—W. A. McHenry, Dennison	22 13	
7—Citizens of Mechanicsville	101 65	
9—Citizens of Lansing	50 00	
9—Citizens of Belle Plain	77 60	
9—Citizens of Glenwood	66 75	
10—Citizens of Lyons	50 00	
10—Citizens of Davenport	131 00	
12—Presbyterian Church, Boone	28 10	
13—Congregational Ch., Charles City	34 00	
13—Citizens of Charles City	19 05	
13—Presbyterian Ch., Garden Grove	4 20	
13—Citizens of Fort Madison	250 00	
13—Citizens of Sabula	47 21	
13—Methodist Church, Sabula	4 65	
13—Congregational S. S., Sabula	6 25	
13—George Canfield	16 79	
13—Citizens of Russell	15 25	
13—Pres. Church & S. S., Mt. Vernon	23 00	
13—Citizens of Burlington	150 00	
14—Jno. Knebs, Grinnell	10 00	
14—Citizens of Fort Madison	28 00	
Sept. 14—Citizens of Clarinda	$161 75	
14—Citizens of Sibley	12 50	
14—Citizens of Alkader	40 10	
15—Citizens of Dexter	106 50	
15—Citizens of Blue Glass	20 00	
15—Citizens of Vail	10 00	
16—Citizens of Cherokee	22 25	
16—Congregational Ch., Keosauqua	30 00	
16—Cong. Pres. Church, Oskaloosa	30 47	
16—Baldwin Bros., Oskaloosa	26 65	
16—M. A. Blanchard, Newton	131 00	
17—Citizens of Sigourney	62 60	
18—Cit'zens of Red Oak	100 00	
18—Little girls' parlor entertainment, Des Moines	16 50	
18—Citizens of Anamosa	100 00	
18—Lillie Day & Jno. R. Hays, Nevada	10 00	
19—Bakers of Des Moines	25 00	
19—Presbyterian Church, Adel	23 50	
19—Baptist Church, Cascade	21 50	
19—Pres Church & S. S., Ft. Madison	23 00	
19—O. H. Miller, Tama City	47 45	
19—Citizens of Council Bluffs	18 00	
19—M. E. Sab. School, Muscatine	9 65	
19—Proceeds of concert, Atlantic	15 00	
19—Citizens of Bonaparte	159 20	
20—Liquor dealers of Keokuk	100 00	
20—Nickel box, McGregor	4 48	
20—Asleway Sab. School, Des Moines	40 41	
20—1st Baptist Church, Clinton	24 25	
21—Concord Sab. School, Garner	10 72	
21—Baptist Sab. School, Riverton	10 00	
21—Chas. Plaline, Oskaloosa	20 00	
21—E. M. Davies, Clinton	12 80	
22—"Burlington Hawkeye," Burl'ton	21 41	
22—Churches of Rowley & Pine Creek	41 00	
22—Sunday-school, Columbus Junct	6 53	
22—Citizens of Morning Sun	70 00	
22—Citizens of Pella	223 45	
22—Lodge No. 13, A.O.U.W, Wilcott	13 25	
22—Relief Association, Navarre	37 80	
23—Board of Trade canvassers, Muscatine	245 30	
23—Miss Kate Finnick & others, Muscatine	72 50	
23—German Ch's & S. S's, Muscatine	28 55	
23—1st Baptist Sab School, Muscatine	19 00	
23—9th St. Mission S. S., Muscatine	12 00	
13—Old School Pres. Church, Clarinda	16 00	
23—Executive Committee, Creston	124 15	
23—Young ladies of Oskaloosa	78 26	
24—Sunday-schools of Iowa, through S. Merril, Des Moines	219 60	
24—Congregational Ch. of Kellogg	8 00	
24—M. E. Church of Nevada	4 88	
24—Presbyterian Sab. School, Nevada	3 86	
25—Sunday-school, Eldorado	2 25	
25—A Friend, Sioux City	1 00	
25—Congregational S. S., Des Moines	18 26	
25—Young People's C. A., Waterloo	10 00	
25—M. E. Sunday-school, Knoxville	10 00	
25—Chones Club, Ames	58 00	
26—Evangelical Lutheran Ch., Lisbon	10 00	
26—Lodge No. 79, I.O.O.F., Boonsboro	10 00	
26—Meth. & Cong Ch's, Leeds Grove	23 75	
27—W. A. McHenry, Denison	5 00	
27—H C. Brown, Cedar Rapids	2 00	
27—Land Dep't, C. B. & Q. R. R., Burlington	50 00	
27—E. S. Ormsby, Emmetsburg	10 83	
27—Nickel boxes, Council Bluffs	7 39	
27—Citizens of Lisbon	63 46	
28—Entertainment by L. B. Jackson, Sioux City	5 60	
28—Lennox Collegi. Inst., Hopkinton	14 00	
28—Citizens of Oskaloosa	23 56	
28—Unknown Friend, Bedford	7 00	
29—Citizens of Sioux City	52 60	
29—Citizens' Meeting, Sabula	15 75	
29—M. E. Church, Mt. Vernon	40 75	
29—Children's Band of Hope, Clarinda	9 00	
29—1st Congregational Church, Exira	6 00	
29—1st Congregational Ch., Joust City	1 26	
Oct. 2—Lodge No. 76, Centerville	5 00	
2—Ladies' Relief Ass'n, Indianola	120 75	
4—Cong. Church, College Springs	3 50	
4—J. V. Hookson, Creston	18 40	
4—M. E. Sab. School, Kellogg	10 00	
5—A. N. Higley & others, Allentown	15 50	

APPENDIX.

Oct.	7—Soldiers' Reunion, Muscatine	$ 26 11
	10—Relief Com. Pres. Ch., Page Co.	11 00
	10—Citizens of Marshalltown	33 45
	10—Employés Ft. D. & D. R. R., Des Moines	77 50
	10—Rev. F. Edwards, Centerville	7 04
	11—Howard Ass'n, Council Bluffs	25 10
	11—Citizens of Waverley	132 00
	11—Citizens of Davenport	100 00
	13—U. P. Congregations of Washington and Crawfordville	72 10
	18—Ladies' Reading Club, Muscatine	5 00
	19—Citizens of Cedar Falls	28 00
	21—Buena Vista S. S., Jasper Co.	9 70
	24—Citizens of Davenport, through Jno. W. Thompson	100 00
	27—Proceeds of concert at Kellogg, through D. L. Lawson	17 00
	29—Mite box at Earlville	5 00
	30—High Prairie M. E. Ch., Muscatine	8 50
Nov.	6—F. M. Loomis, Jefferson	2 00
	6—A. Downing, Boone	3 95
	Total	$6,407 58

INDIAN TERRITORY.

Sept.	22—An Unknown Friend at Ft. Reno	$5 00

KANSAS.

Aug.	25—L. B. Terrill, Wichita	$300 00
	28—Israelites of Leavenworth	25 00
	29—E. Richardson, Kansas City	85 00
	31—A. B. Haas, Leavenworth	25 00
Sept.	2—Hebrew males, Atchison	46 00
	2—Hebrew Ladies' Society, Atchison	25 00
	6—M. H. Case, Mayor of Topeka	300 00
	7—Atchison Liederkranz, Atchison	25 00
	9—Citizens of Dodge City	120 00
	9—Employés Q. M. Dep't, Leavenw'h	204 00
	10—Bertha Helfingler, Leavenworth	12 00
	11—Sam'l Taylor, Mayor of Newton	114 00
	11—Howard Association, Holton	100 00
	11—G. E. Morgan, Osage City	1 00
	11—J. W. Crance, Ch'm'n, Leavenw'h	400 00
	11—Wm. Crowell, Paoli	90 00
	12—Citizens of Parsons	100 00
	12—L. U. B., Wyandotte	1 00
	12—M. E. Church and S. S., Les Cygne	28 75
	13—Turn-Verein, Topeka	54 00
	14—Citizens of Atchison, thro' C. Rohr	609 00
	14—Citizens of Hutchison	163 35
	16—G. W. Batker, Les Cygne	15 00
	17—Citizens of Burlingham	100 00
	17—Officers and soldiers of Ft. Hayes	45 50
	17—Citizens of Oskaloosa	35 00
	17—Contribution boxes & donations, Lawrence	46 50
	18—Presbyterian Church, Topeka	11 00
	18—U. S. Army officers, Ft. Hayes	13 70
	18—Officers Mil. Prison, Leavenworth	140 00
	18—B. J. Purcell, Girard	35 25
	18—Citizens of Ft. Scott	100 00
	19—Harmony F're Co., Junction City	25 00
	20—U. P. S. S., Winchester	3 00
	20—Citizens of Wichita	7 50
	21—Citizens of Holton	47 77
	22—Citizens of Wyandotte	220 00
	21—Officers, soldiers, and citizens, Ft. Wallace	118 26
	21—National Bank, Burlington	147 00
	22—Citizens of Wichita	144 35
	23—Citizens and Centennial Lodge, I. O. O. F., 138, McPherson	31 70
	23—Officers & soldiers, Ft. McPherson	42 00
	25—Young girls of Junction City	85 00
	25—M. E. Society. Council Grove	8 50
	26—Citizens of Wanego	41 00
	26—Plymouth Cong. Ch., Lawrence	71 43
	26—Ladies of Garnett	70 85
	26—Emmett Benev. Soc., Leavenw'h	50 00
	27—E. W. Spencer, Council Grove	5 00
	27—Pupils of City Scho'ls, Humboldt	4 95
	28—Ladies of Olathe	75 56

Sept.	28—Union Sab. School, Cherokee	$ 5 80
	29—Citizens of Ottawa	36 50
	29—Citizens of Leavenworth	802 80
	30—Country Sab. Sch. near Holton	4 17
Oct.	1—S. T. Marsh, Newton	10 00
	1—Citizens of Lawrence	314 00
	2—Citizens of Coffeeville	76 25
	3—Citizens of Edgarton	12 00
	3—Proceeds of entertainm't. Olathe	18 00
	3—Unknown Friend, Osborne	2 91
	3—Concert by Liederkanz, Salina	404 00
	5—J. B. Ives, Douglass	5 95
	5—P. G. O'Meara, J. B. Grub, and R. C. & W. K. Benton, Effingham	27 00
	7—Proceeds of concert, Lawrence	56 53
	7—U. P. Church & S. S., Nortonville	8 05
	7—Webster Literary Soc., Manhattan	15 00
	10—Citizens of Clyde Station	26 69
	11—Unknown, La Crosse	4 50
	13—German Ch. & Banner S.S., Holton	8 70
	16—Mite box, "Eagle" Office, Wichita	9 45
	18—R. B. Foster, Osborne	1 00
	20—Citizens of Atchison	50 15
	20—Citizens of St. Marys	5 00
	21—Citizens of Augusta	57 80
Nov.	7—E. J. Arnold, Raymond	9 00
Dec.	13—Citizens of Atchison	9 00
	Total	$6,559 67

KENTUCKY.

Aug.	22—Pres. Congregation, Huber Stat'n	$ 9 00
	23—Erskine & Erskine, Louisville	25 00
	28—Mrs. L. P. Corwine, Maysville	2 00
	28—J. W. Knightly, Lonisville	25 00
	29—Citizens of Caseyville	26 00
	29—Louisville Clearing House, Louisville	400 00
	29—James H. Buffington, Covington	100 00
	30—S. H. Dunscomb, Russellville	25 00
	30—Citizens of Glasgow	85 00
	30—L. L. Carpenter, Louisville	1 00
	30—Friends in Covington, through Rebecca Swope	30 00
	31—Jno. Wandling, Owensboro	150 00
	31—Jno. Wandling, " for Grenada	100 00
	31—Citizens of Henderson	400 00
	31—Citizens of Elkton	53 20
	31—A Friend at Cadiz	2 00
Sept.	1—Jewish Relief Fund	100 00
	2—Passengers and employés P. & D. R. R., Paducah	30 00
	2—S. Levy, Allanville	20 00
	2—Royal Insurance Ag'y, Louisville	100 00
	2—Mutual Lodge, No. 1, A. O. U. W., Lexington	25 00
	2—Centennial Lodge, 40, A. O. U. W., Lexington	10 00
	2—Phantom Lodge, No. 15, K. of P., Lexington	10 00
	2—Citizens of Carlisle	25 00
	3—Jno. W. Howe & Son, Carrollton	250 00
	3—Jno. H. Buffington, Covington	100 00
	3—Butchers of Paducah	36 50
	3—Misses Barziza and Alexander, South Carrollton	26 25
	3—Young ladies' concert, Glasgow	54 60
	5—Christian Church, Georgetown	67 43
	5—Board of Education, Newport	50 00
	5—M. C. Johnson, Lexington	300 00
	5—Honor Lodge, 559, K. of H., Paris	25 00
	5—Relief Committee, Franklin	50 00
	6—Broadway St. Christian Church, Lexington	40 45
	6—A. O. U. W, 53, Hopkinsville	16 05
	6—Colored Benev. Ass'n. Hopkinsv'e	25 00
	7—Meth. Colored Ch., Hopkinsville	10 00
	7—Citizens of Pembroke	40 00
	8—Evergreen Lodge, No. 28, K. of P., Hopkinsville	68 00
	8—Green and Barren River Nav. Co., Bowling Green	100 00
	8—M. T. Brashy, Georgetown	204 85
	9—Relief Committee, Hadensville	382 00
	9—L., C. & L. R. R. Co., Louisville	200 00
	9—Citizens of Cadiz	51 00

APPENDIX. 345

Sept.			Sept.		
9—Relief Association, Wingo	$30	45	3—1 tierce hams, 1 cask bacon	$127	40
9—T. J. Brogan, Louisville	5	00	3—25 bbls. potatoes	32	50
10—J. M. Gleen, Carlisle	25	00	3—3 cases corn beef	11	10
11—Grant Green, Frankfort, for Holly Springs	100	00	3—1 case sago, 1 case tapioca	25	09
11—Blanton Duncan, Louisville	25	00	3—5 bbls. crackers	11	90
11—Relief Association, Nicholasville and Jassamin	275	50	9—300 lbs. roasted coffee	57	10
12—Citizens of Trenton	75	50	9—4000 paper bags	11	20
12—Christian Church S. S., Newport	12	25	9—6 doz. brandy	36	00
12—Cane Run, Burgen	30	00	9—2 bbls. white sugar, 1 box tea	69	63
12—Antioch Church, Franklin	23	65	9—2 casks Scotch ale, 3 doz. ext. beef.	53	00
13—Southern Relief Association, Paris	250	00	9—10 bbls crackers	33	02
13—Southern Relief Association, Paris, for Holly Springs	150	00	9—10 bbls. corn meal, 10 bbls. grits	54	00
13—Citizens of Winchester	111	50	9—2 tierces hams	93	84
13—Sally Morris, Glasgow	10	85	9—5 bbls. beef, 3 tierces breakfast bacon	134	40
13—Proceeds concert, Pewee Valley	78	50	9—150 jugs Seltzer water	18	75
13—Citizens of Flemingsburg	100	00	12—300 lbs. roasted coffee, 50 lbs. mustard, 1 bbl. mustard meal	89	24
13—Relief Ass'n, Bowling Green	150	00	12—12 doz. brandy	56	00
14—Citizens of Henderson	212	20	12—2 casks Scotch ale	34	50
14—Citizens of Cedar Bluff College, Woodburn	15	65	12—12 bbls. crackers	37	35
14—Entertainment at Dayton	100	00	12—146 cans corn beef	84	70
14—J. V. Morrow, Wingo	6	25	12—5 bbls. ham sausage	76	36
14—Citizens of Warsaw	51	00	12—24 doz. cans tomatoes	22	80
14—Broadwell Union S. S., Lairs Sta'n.	25	00	12—10 bbls. beef	115	00
14—Citizens of Lexington	23	25	12—9 doz. extract beef	35	75
14—Baptist S. S., Elkton	50	00	13—90 bbls. potatoes	126	00
14—Citizens of Bowling Green	52	00	13—480 bags flour	150	00
15—Christian Church, Glasgow	27	55	18—4 doz. Boneset tonic	28	00
16—Miss S. Allen, Lexington	78	00	18—60 coffins and dressed lumber	315	00
16—Relief Soc. and W. C. A., Louisville	50	00	18—40 coffins and caskets	259	95
16—Main Street S. S., Lexington	12	25	18—25 oz. quinine	95	00
16—Masons of Newport	200	00	18—50 clinical thermometers, 1 bbl. buchu leaf	104	65
16—Rescue Fire Co., Paris	31	25	Oct. 3—Fresh fruit	8	07
17—Colored Baptist Ch., Hopkinsville.	10	60			
17—Citizens of Lairs Station	13	25	Total (Clearing-house)	$2,582	84
17—Cynthiana	23	50	Total Donations	8,810	52
17—Proceeds calico hop, Cynthiana	76	00			
17—Congregational Church, Paducah.	25	00	Grand Total	$11,393	36
17—Western Fin. Corp., Louisville	500	00			
18—Old Jassamin Church, Lexington	12	00	**LOUISIANA.**		
18—Employés post-office, Shelbyville.	7	20			
18—Methodist S. S., Cynthiana	15	00	Aug. 28—American Cotton Tie Association of New Orleans	$1,000	00
19—Confed. Relief Com., Louisville	100	00	31—Unknown, Hammond	5	00
19—Good Templars of McHenry	10	00	Sept. 6—Clem. St. James	10	00
19—Citizens of McHenry	24	75	14—Henry Kindsman, Monroe	10	00
19—Miss Aula Moore, Franklin	10	00	17—Shreveport Ward Committee	320	15
10 Colored Citizens of Henderson	50	00	22—E. & B. Jacobs, Shreveport	25	00
20—Relief Committee, Elkton	20	00	Oct. 22—Proceeds of raffle by Miss Templeman of Shreveport	25	00
20—Citizens of North Middleton	54	65	20—St. Paul's Colored Church, Shreveport, through Howard Association, New Orleans	22	00
20—Citizens of Carlisle	25	00	20—F. Gautier & Sons, W. Pascagoula, through Howard Association, New Orleans	10	00
20—W. W. Mester, Mayfield	8	50			
20—Hunter Wood, Hopkinsville	25	00	Total	$1,427	15
20—M. E. Church, Sardis	7	85			
21—S. P. Read, thro' Northern Bank of Kentucky, Louisville	200	00	**MARYLAND.**		
21—Citizens of Marion	45	00			
21—Citizens of Petersburgh	123	53	Aug. 4—Ira P. Pleasants & Son, Baltimore.	$50	00
21—Nicholasville & Jassamine Southern Relief Committee	120	70	Sept. 2—Mite box, Adams Exp. Co., " ..	80	00
21—South'n Relief Fund, Caldwell Co.	25	00	6—Wilson Burns & Co., Baltimore	150	00
22—Church at Big Clifty	5	00	19—Wm. Warburg, Baltimore	25	00
22—Rev. J. Bey, Pleasanton	26	00	20—Citizens of Chestertown	50	00
24—Relief Committee, Harrodsburg	150	00	23—Hon. F. C. Latrobe, Baltimore	47	23
25—B. F. Cabell, Woodburn	1	00	24—Deaf and Dumb Inst., Baltimore..	5	00
25—Valley Lodge, 58, A. O. U. W., Covington	100	00	24—Citizens of Oakland	86	75
26—Citizens of Louisville	195	00	Nov. 4—J. J. Nicholson & Sons, Baltimore	2	00
26—L. Schepp, Louisville	100	00			
27—Northern Bank of Lexington	172	76	Total	$495	98
27—Citizens of Warsaw	60	00			
28—James Jackman, Greelyboro	5	00	**MAINE.**		
29—W. W. Ballard, Penhope	20	00			
Oct. 1—Citizens of Maysville	149	55	Sept. 7—Citizens of Portland	$500	00
3—Robert Pfeiffer, Paris	5	00	16—Citizens of Bath	200	00
4—R. Y. Pendleton, Pembroke	12	00	20—Norwich Com., South Portland	50	00
11—C tizens of Ghent	62	00	27—Citizens of Waterville	67	00
11—Mrs. J. K. Schooler's two sons, Shelbyville	2	00			
16—Citizens of Dixon	49	65	Total	$817	00
Nov. 6—Mess. Wheats & Co., Maysville	25	00			

LOUISVILLE CLEARING-HOUSE.

Sept. 8—320 bags flour............................ 100 00
3—1 bbl. rice, 1 bbl. sugar, 1 bag coffee,
1 box tea, 1 case baked beans......... 85 54

APPENDIX.

MASSACHUSETTS.

Sept.	1—Idlewild House, Cambridge	$ 15 00
	2—H. L. Pierce, mayor, Boston	100 00
	9—Citizens' Relief Com., Lynn	1,000 00
	11—Executive Com., Lowell, through J. S. Ludson	200 00
	14—Churches, Shelburne Falls	90 00
	16—Relief Committee, Salem	250 00
	17—Employés Brewster, Henry & Co., Brookfield	20 20
	20—Citizens of North Attleboro	321 00
	20—Citizens of Barnardstown	67 81
	23—St. Patrick's T. Association, South Hadley Falls	25 00
	24—Citizens of Newburyport	1,000 00
	25—Relief Committee, Salem	500 00
	27—1st Cong. Society, Greenfield	16 50
	27—Citizens' Com. of Greenfield	21 47
	28—J. Rogers, Lowell	300 00
Oct.	1—St. John's Episcopal Ch., Farmingham	19 30
	1—Cong. Church, Coleraine	13 00
	1—Unknown friend, Quincy	5 00
	Total	$3,964 28

MINNESOTA.

Sept.	4—J. & J, Mankato	$10 00
	8—Business men of Northfield	67 66
	10—Cataract Engine Co., Red Wing	25 00
	11—Citizens of Winona	24 85
	13—Locomotive Brotherhood, St. Paul Div., 150, St. Paul	25 00
	15—1st Pres. Church, Minneapolis	25 00
	16—Spaulding Cong. S. S., Northfield	30 00
	16—Town L'ne S. S., Northfield	20 00
	16—C. & G.W. Scott, Minneapolis	25 00
	16—Collections State Fair, St. Paul	118 00
	18—City Council, Stillwater	100 00
	18—Citizens of Winona	26 85
	18—J., P. O. Box 1145, Mankato	10 00
	20—Presbyterian and Congregational Churches, Winona	73 32
	20—Citizens of Farmington	16 00
	20—Citizens of Belle Plaine	36 50
	20—C. M. Hooper, Belle Plaine	5 00
	20—W. W. Thompson, Belle Plaine	1 00
	20—E. Zimmerman, Belle Plaine	1 00
	20—Jno. Schlitz, Belle Plaine	3 00
	20—Citizens of Belle Plaine	25 50
	21—Churches of Winebago City	20 00
	22—4 little girls, Minneapolis	10 28
	23—Cong. Church & Soc., Alexandria	11 00
	25—Presbyterian S. S. of St. Cloud	10 15
	25—H. A. Parkes, Red Wing	50 00
	29—Citizens of Fairbault	100 00
	30—Police Department, Minneapolis	600 00
Oct.	2—D. H. Williams, mayor, Rochester	388 42
	3—Citizens of Northfield	42 49
	3—Citizens of Minnesota, thro' Gov. Pillsbury, St. Paul	500 00
	7—Citizens of St. Paul	80 00
	7—Union Sunday School, Pilot Grove	6 00
	10—Proceeds horse trot, Minneapolis	119 75
	10—D. H. Williams, mayor, Rochester	46 00
	Total	$2,651 77

MONTANA.

Sept.	21—Masons of Montana, through Nat. Bank, St. Louis	$200 00
	22—Citizens of Montana	200 00
	29—E. M. Govern, Virginia City	5 00
Oct.	15—Maj. A. L. Clupton, 2d Infantry, at Fort Missouli	10 00
	15—Ass't Surgeon S. O. Robinson, Ft. Missouli	5 00
	15—Arthur Williams, 2d lieutenant, Ft. Missouli	5 00
	15—Citizens of Fort Benton	562 00
	Total	$987 00

MICHIGAN.

Aug.	31—Detroit " Free Press," Detroit	$100 00
Sept.	4—Citizens of Grand Rapids	500 00
	5—Citizens of Kalamazoo	400 00
	5—A. J. Hadseil, Hartford	5 00
	6—Citizens of Lansing	75 00
	6—Gymnasium Club, Grand Rapids	100 00
	6—Red Ribbon Reform Club, Ann Arbor	73 15
	6—Nathan Church, Grand Rapids	50 00
	7—Citizens of Monroe	38 00
	7—A. P. Baldwin, treasurer, Detroit	500 00
	8—Employés custom house, Port Huron	39 00
	8—Women's Christian Temp. Union, Dexter	10 00
	9—Citizens of Lansing	25 00
	9—Citizens of Detroit, thro' "Free Press"	60 00
	9—Citizens of Bay City, through Hon. Geo. Lord	250 00
	9—Citizens of Blissfield	32 00
	9—Second National Bank, Detroit, for Grenada	300 00
	9—Citizens of Muskegon, through Mayor Holt	200 00
	11—Citizens of Lansing	125 00
	11—Citizens of Jackson, through C. C. Bloomfield	200 00
	11—Citizens of Detroit, thro' "Free Press"	183 00
	11—Citizens of Hastings	116 25
	13—1st Pres. Church, East Saginaw	23 62
	13—Citizens of Novi	25 00
	13—Citizens of Portland	101 00
	13—Cong. Church, Ann Arbor	31 25
	13—Palmer Lodge, K. of P., 20, St. Clair	28 00
	13—Mrs. A. M. Meeks, St. Clair	7 59
	13—Citizens of St. Clair	99 19
	13—Citizens of St. Clair	95 78
	15—Entertainm't Ladies' Relief Soc., St. Joseph	105 00
	15—Cong. Church, Rochester	18 00
	16—Citizens of Port Huron	100 00
	16—Citizens of Coldwater	100 00
	16—Employés and boarders, Dudley House, Mason	18 00
	16—Citizens of Detroit, thro' "Free Press"	250 00
	16—Citizens of Detroit, through H. P. Baldwin	1,200 00
	16—Citizens of Dexter	75 00
	16—Fire Company, St. Joe	54 80
	16—Citizens of Henderson	200 00
	17—Citizens of Wilmington	51 00
	17—Citizens of Decatur	83 00
	17—Citizens of Romeo	131 00
	17—Citizens of Hartford	50 00
	17—Citizens of Chelsea	159 00
	19—Firemen at Quincy	50 00
	19—Old Soldiers' and Sailors' Club, Ishpenning	106 40
	19—Old Soldiers' and Sailors' Club, Ishpenning	10 00
	19—Masonic fraternity, Flint	100 00
	19—Citizens of Detroit	1,200 00
	19—Ref. Dutch Church, Kalamazoo	31 00
	21—E. G. Raymond, Hersey	2 10
	21—Cong. Church, Rochester	10 00
	21—Citizens of Hersey	25 00
	21—Citizens of Grenville	100 00
	21—Citizens of Detroit, thro' "Free Press"	100 00
	22—H. J. Price, Marshall	15 00
	22—Capt. Hawlett, Grand Haven	5 00
	22—Jno. McTie, Grand Haven	2 00
	22—H. W. Busucie, Grand Haven	2 00
	22—Jno. Hopkins, Grand Haven	3 00
	22—Churches at Holland	221 58
	22—Proceeds of dance, Cutler House, Grand Haven	24 75
	22—Michigan State Fire Association, Quincy	43 79
	22—C. C. Lat, Mackinac	10 00
	22—School children of L. Anse	23 00
	22—Citizens of Marshall	131 94
	22—Citizens of Zilwaukee	40 00

APPENDIX. 347

Sept. 22—Citizens' Relief Com., Flint $190 00
23—Relief Com. at Reed City 15 00
24—C P. Dibble, Marshall 10 00
24—Citizens of Grand Rapids 250 00
25—Citizens of Grand Rapids 43 51
25—Citizens of Lansing 60 00
25—Citizens of Marquette 125 40
25—M. E. Church of Hanover 13 00
25—Citizens of Monroe 20 97
25—Prisoners, Michigan State Prison, Jackson 10 00
27—Cong. Church at Alamo 9 50
27—Red Ribbon Club, Grand Blanc 18 00
27—Citizens of Big Rapids 21 00
27—G. W. Mathews, Paw Paw 2 30
29—Citizens of Allegan 110 00
29—Citizens of Detroit, thro' "Free Press" 76 00
29—Citizens of Muskegon 79 90
Oct. 2—1st Pres. Church, Sault Ste. Marie 35 00
2—J. F. Cessaner, Zilwaukee 21 15
2—A. D. Sayler (Treas.), Ann Arbor 24 00
2—Red Ribbon Club, Ann Arbor 9 00
3—W. B. Johnson, Rockford 2 40
4—D. B. Dennis, Coldwater 150 00
7—South Jackson S. S., Jackson 20 77
7—Citizens of Romeo 33 25
7—Reformed Church, Amanda 10 60
7—Ref. Church and S. S. of Niesland 85 41
11—German Aid Society, Manistee 100 00
13—Detroit "Free Press," Detroit 100 00
22—Citizens of Detroit 700 00
Nov. 6—Citizens of Detroit, from H. P. Baldwin 250 00
7—Citizens of Otsego 9 90

Total $11,200 43

MISSOURI.

Aug. 22—Watkins & Gilliland, St. Louis $100 00
23—Hebrew Y. M. Lit. Soc., St. Louis 250 00
24—Merchants' Exchange, St. Louis 250 00
27—E. Fairbanks, Sedalia 5 00
27—Merchants' Exchange, St. Louis .. 1,000 00
30—C B. Frank, St. Joseph 100 00
30—Citizens of Cape Girardeau 200 00
30—Merchants' Exchange, St. Louis 500 00
31—Bant m Lodge I.O.O.F., St. Louis 25 00
Sept. 1—Citizens of Otterville 55 00
2—Citizens of Chamois 51 00
2—Citizens of Montrose 52 70
2—Citizens of Monticello 10 00
2—Friends of Shelbina 3 00
2—Citizens of Palmyra 133 75
3—Avery Wolfolk & Co., Moberly 266 00
3—Mayor of Sedalia 250 00
3—Citizens of Appleton City 50 00
3—Merchants' Exchange, St. Louis 400 00
4—J. M. Halmet, Huntsville 39 00
4—W. McDonald, Carrollton 100 00
4—Relief Committee St. Joe, Mo., through Joe Olds 200 00
5—Collec. by Misses Foster, Filche, and Greenfield, through Merchants' Exchange, St. Louis 50 00
5—Citizens of Fayette 80 00
5—Citizens of Sturgeon 43 55
6—Citizens of New Madrid 21 30
6—Citizens of Lexington 65 00
6—Citizens of Mexico 200 00
6—J. F. Gruelich, mayor, Booneville ... 500 00
6—Citizens of Monsterratt 32 75
6—Citizens of Clarksville 34 17
6—Citizens of Commerce 21 00
6—Citizens of Cambridge 34 50
7—Citizens of Hyattville 30 00
7—Merchants' Exchange, St. Louis, through G. H. Morgan 250 00
7—Employés "Globe Democrat," St. Louis 6 85
7—M. F. Royle (Treas.), Lexington 50 00
9—M. F. Royle (Treas.), Lexington 104 50
9—Citizens of Craig 100 00
9—Citizens of Maysville 22 65
9—Citizens of Charleston 100 00

Sept. 9—Brunswick, Mo., thro' Merchants' Exchange, St. Louis $53 25
9—Windsor, Mo., thro' Merchants' Exchange, St. Louis 60 00
9—Pleasant Hill,Mo.,thro' Merch'ts' Exchange, St. Louis 10 00
9—Avery Wolfolk, Moberly 120 00
10—A. M. Haswell, Springfield 50 00
11—Appleton.Noyes & Maude,St.Louis 50 00
11—Citizens of Memphis 61 00
11—W H. Stearne, Neoshonie 180 00
11—Mehts' Ex.Relief Com., St. Louis, 500 00
11—Citizens of Jefferson 139 00
12—Basket-meeting, M. E. Ch., Chillicothe 6 60
13—Citizens of Monroe City 66 93
13—Citizens of Plattsburg 125 00
13—M. E. Church, Trenton 5 06
13—Citizens of Columbia 428 65
13—Relief Ass'n, St. Joseph 400 00
13—Relief Ass'n, " for Grenada. 100 00
14—Fire Co. of Mexico 15 00
14—C. H. Loseley, Shelbina 75 00
14—Lodge 185, F. & A. M., Ligonier ... 45 00
14—Jno. J. Miller, Warrensburg 5 28
14—J. F. Covington, Butler 3 76
14—Citizens of Rockport 26 65
14—Dramatic Ass'n, Edina 34 85
14—Presbyterian Church, Edina 31 15
14—Citizens of Princeton 70 50
15—Presbyterian Church, Weston 60 00
16—Presbyterian Church, Carrollton.. 20 00
16—G. W. McKinstry, St. Louis 5 00
17—Relief Committee, Lexington 80 00
17—Citizens of Independence 256 40
17—Citizens of Jefferson City 194 70
17—Citizens of Booneville 850 00
17—Relief Committee, St. Louis 1,515 00
17—Appleton Lodge, K.P.,Hannibal.. 25 00
17—W. A. McCause, Mt Vernon 15 00
17—R. A. Gerstman (rabbi·, St.Joseph 19 17
17—Citizens of Kirksville 210 73
18—M. E. Church, Holden 12 50
19—Needham Sikes, Sikeston 25 00
20—J. M. Marmaduke, Mexico 14 05
20—M. E. S. S., Trenton 6 56
20—Citizens of Palmyra 104 95
20—Citizens of Warrenton 65 05
20—Citizens of Modoc 5 00
20—Citizens of Lamar 65 50
20—Citizens of Warsaw 50 00
20—Citizens of Fulton 67 55
20—Citizens of Joplin 220 85
20—Citizens of Higginsville 70 00
20—Citizens of Mt. Vernon 15 00
20—Citizens of Potosi 100 00
21—Citizens of Aullville 30 40
21—Church Birmingham, thro' A. L. Shotwell, St. Louis 23 36
21—West Ely Lodge, St. of T.,Hannibal 15 00
21—Citizens of Marysville 238 75
21—Citizens of St. Louis 400 00
21—Relief fund, St. Louis 200 00
22—Miss Sue V. Crane, Palmyra 1 00
22—J. Van Dyke, Marshall 14 70
22—Citizens of Princeton 19 35
22—Citizens of Unionville 42 42
22—Jno. Page, Page City 33 00
24—Citizens of Cape Girardeau 100 00
24—Citizens of Kirksville 39 40
25—Relief Committee, Lexington 100 00
25—J. S. Wallace, Brunswick 10 15
25—M. F. Spaulding, B·unswick 36 50
25—A. M. Haswell, Springfield 35 70
25—Citizens of Lancaster 40 00
26—Salt Pond Bap. Ch., Marshall 16 58
27—Citizens of Plattsburg 29 75
27—Christian S. S., Edina 10 00
27—Good Templars of Breckenridge.. 13 00
27—German Ass'n, Kansas City 107 00
27—Citizens of Columbia 110 78
28—Sabbath School of Platte City 6 75
28—Benj. Wood, Kansas City 29 71
28—M. E. Church, Mecklin 5 00
29—Board of Trade, Kansas City 40 00
29—Relief fund of Weston 40 00
29—Cong. Ch. & S. S., Somer Hill 40 00
29—Citizens of Liberty 212 00
29—Employés of Glasgow Bridge 120 00

348   APPENDIX.

Sept. 29—Southern Relief Ass'n, St. Joseph	$300 00	
29—Southern Relief Ass'n, St. Joseph, for Greenville	200 00	
30—Baptist Church, Independence	20 50	
40—Southern Relief Com., Lexington	68 70	
30—Unknown friend, Sedalia	5 00	
Oct. 5—Citizens of Gunn City	67 75	
10—Union Christian Aid Ass'n, Lee's Summit	25 00	
10—Ohio & Miss. River employés, thro' A. Donaldson, St. Louis	633 81	
10—Citizens of Burton	17 50	
10—Unknown friend, St. Louis	1 00	
13—Country adjoining Independence	12 75	
13—S.S , S. of T.,& citizens of Palmyra	86 50	
16—Colored citizens of Kirkwood	15 55	
16—Fabius Fair Ass'n, Palmyra	332 85	
16—Gymnastic Ass'n, St. Louis	200 00	
30—Relief Com., St. Joseph	76 80	
30—Relief Com., " for Brownsville	100 00	
30—J. A. Piner, mayor of St. Joseph	308 15	
Nov. 11—M. F. Royle, Lexington	6 50	
19—Great Western Glass Co.,St. Louis	50 00	
27—A lady of Marshall	50	
Total	$16,891 37	

MISSISSIPPI.

Aug. 23—Unknown friend, Oxford	$ 1 00	
26—J. J. Thornton, Coldwater	50 00	
31—Citizens of Horn Lake, for Grenada	73 20	
Sept. 2—Milton Blocker, Olive Branch	5 00	
5—Citizens of Friar's Point	75 00	
6—Dr. A. J. Foster, Bennett's Land'g.	20 00	
7—Citizens of Como	23 00	
17—Phœnix Ins. Co , Natchez	50 00	
18—Contribution by Rev. Honeycutt, Phœnix	10 00	
18—Jno. Clark, Clarksdale	10 00	
18—Anderson & Sandridge,Coldwater.	100 00	
21—Citizens of Oxford	20 00	
21—Misses Effie Small & Mary Adams, Corinth	7 00	
22—Citizens of Columbus	100 00	
24—Miss Kate E. May & others,Charlestown	10 25	
24—J. L. Jones, Como	5 00	
24—Sabbath School, Courtland	5 00	
Oct. 2—Miss Clara Conway, Friar's Point.	5 00	
12—Citizens of Oxford	50 20	
16—Citizens of Coldwater	8 00	
Nov. 22—W. Y. Eckels, Senatobia	100 00	
Total	$727 65	

MISCELLANEOUS.

Aug. 30—Liverpool,Eng.,thro' J. B. Laffitte & Co. New Orleans	$500 00	
Sept. 1—Liverpool,Eng., thro' J. B. Laffitte & Co., New Orleans	250 00	
15—Liverpool,Eng.,thro' U.& P.Bank, Memphis	729 75	
Oct. 17—Liverpool,Eng., thro' J. B. Laffitte & Co., New Orleans,for Grenada	500 00	
17—Citizens of Liverpool. Eng., thro' J. B. Laffitte & Co., New Orleans	1,458 00	
Sept. 11—Brown,Shipley & Co.,London,Eng	243 25	
6—Mrs. Newburg, Prov. of Ontario	1 00	
11—Chas. A. Hester, Shulenberg, Ont.	30 00	
Oct. 3—Citizens of Shulenberg, Ontario	228 66	
22—Citizens of St. Thomas, Ontario	12 75	
22—Pres. Ch., St. Thomas, Ontario	55 00	
15—D. B. Warren, U. S. Consul, St. John, New Brunswick	150 00	
29—G. B. Cushing, St. John, N. B	103 00	
Sept. 6—Stones River Nat. Bank	34 55	
13—Proc. concert pupils German Ch., thro' Prof.C.H.Lachmund	20 50	
14—Unknown	2 00	
17—Unknown	1 00	
18—Dr. S. A. Reeves, Orangeburg	4 75	
18—Winchester Mus.Club.Winchester	27 45	

Sept. 20—A. J. Fuzer, Clermont, by W. A. Kendall	$ 6 50	
21—Du West Church, by H. M. Young	53 00	
21—Mrs. Carrie A. Moffet	1 25	
21—Entertainment by musical club	3 75	
21—Misses E. Barton & Helen Carloss	12 25	
23—Unknown	5 00	
25—Valley Mills & Searsville Bap.Ch., through A. Launa	61 25	
25—Unknown lady	1 00	
25—Germ Bass Club, Effingham	73 00	
28—Unknown	5 00	
26—Locust Grove Church, thro' M. A. Garrott	11 25	
27—Unknown	2 00	
28—Citizens of Greenbush	220 25	
27—Ladies' Relief As'sn,thro' Am.Ex.	188 00	
29—Unknown	38 50	
Oct. 2—Unknown	2 00	
4—H. W Scheidmantle, Grapeland	14 75	
7—J. H. King, Stillman Valley	151 60	
9—Unknown	7 40	
9—Unknown, thro' S. M. Jones	36 67	
11—Employés Wabash R. R. Machine Shops	7 00	
13—Relief Committee, Russellville	46 00	
15—Unknown	1 00	
15—Unknown	1 00	
16—E. L. Marlin, Reidenville	8 25	
16—W. A. Stettin, St. Simon's Mills, Jno. Johnson	75 00	
17—F. J. Thorp, Rocky Mount	22 62	
29—Geo. Kennedy, Pattisonville	95 70	
31—Free Sons of Israel	35 00	
Sept. 19—Entert'm'nt Spring Bank Hotel, St. Catherine's, Ontario	60 00	
19—Citizens of Lynch's Station, L. & D. R. R	15 70	
19—E. W. Porter, St.Thomas, Ontario	2 00	
Total	$5,617 95	
Unknown, different sources	3,989 23	
Grand total	$9,607 18	

NEW HAMPSHIRE.

Sept 17—Relief Committee, Manchester	$500 00	
21—Citizens of Portsmouth, by Hon.F. James	500 00	
23—Citizens' Relief Com., Manchester.	600 00	
Oct. 3—Citizens of Milton Mills	5 50	
Nov. 6—Joseph Dow, Hampton	2 00	
Total	$1,607 50	

NEW MEXICO.

Oct. 2—Ladies of Sante Fe	$75 00	
15—Proc. entertainment, Sante Fe	69 30	
Total	$134 30	

NEVADA.

Sept. 18—Employés Va. & Truckee R. R., Virginia City	$408 00	
19—F. & A. M., Eureka	44 94	
20—Mayor Belknap, Virginia City	25 00	
20—Good Templars, Virginia City	113 00	
25—Parker Lodge, I.O.O.F.,Gold Hill.	50 00	
25—Ladies of Central City	402 00	
26—Officers & soldiers, Ft. McPherson.	50 00	
Oct. 10—Ladies of Gold Hill	150 00	
18—Chapter 5, R. A. M., Eureka	50 00	
23—H. L. Tickault, Carson	82 00	
Total	$1,374 94	

NEBRASKA.

Aug. 27—Conductors' Brotherhood,Omaha.	$ 25 00	

APPENDIX. 349

Aug. 28—R. H. Wilbur, mayor, Omaha	$100	00
29—Relief Committee, North Platte	250	00
29—Mr.& Mrs.S.M.Benedict,Lincoln	5	00
30—R. H. Wilbur, mayor, Omaha	1,000	00
Sept. 5—Citizens of Plattsmouth	250	00
6—G. A. Acken, Humboldt	5	00
8—Brass and string bands of North Platte	110	00
8—Citizens of Fremont, thro' Davidson & Sheridan	221	25
9—Cit'zens of B'air	88	80
9—H. C. Ties, Lincoln	1	00
9—Contributions from Lincoln	90	00
9—R. H. Wilbur, mayor, Omaha	350	00
12—City of Ashland	23	35
12—Sidney bank of Nebraska	42	00
16—Citizens of Brownsville	151	00
16—50 citizens of Elk Horn Valley	90	00
16—Citizens of Lincoln, by W. J.Quinlan	100	00
16—W. J. Quinlan, for Lincoln	38	43
18—J. R. Moore, Omaha	150	00
19—Union Sabbath School, Fairfield	50	00
19—Chairman Ex. Com., Beatrice	128	00
20—Citizens of Pawnee City	101	75
20—R. H. Wilbur, mayor, Omaha	350	00
22—Presbyterian Church, Teckmah	5	67
22—Union Sabbath School, Teckmah	3	40
22—Rev. W. G. O., Teckmah		93
22—Miss Mary Wright, Pawnee City	5	00
23—Citizens of Plattsmouth	90	00
23—St. Luke's Epis.Ch.,Plattsmouth	10	00
24—Citizens of Crete	14	00
27—Crete Dramatic Club & M. E. Ch.	80	00
27—Citizens of Nebraska City	380	00
29—Indian children of Omaha Mission	5	00
Oct. 2—Mrs. Mary A. George, Clarksville	33	21
7—L. E. Zimmerman, Beatrice	61	50
15—Mite box, Meth. Ch., Pawnee City	2	97
19—Citizens of Fremont	21	00
29—W. W. Cline, Hastings	5	00
Nov. 6—Citizens of Fairmont, thro' H. S. Gordon	71	15
Total	$4,509	41

NEW JERSEY.

Aug. 31—Trinity Church, Elizabeth	$10	00
31—B.ble class, 1st Ref. S. S., Bayonne	9	00
Sept. 6—Citizens of Red Bank	84	50
9—St. John's Church, Somerville,for Grenada	40	00
10—D. B. Bodine, mayor, Trenton	180	00
10—Prospect St. Pres. Ch., Trenton	170	00
11—Citizens of Orange	300	00
13—Citizens of Trenton	150	00
14—Baptist Church, New Market	16	00
14—Jas. D. Hall, Trenton	50	00
17—D. B. Bodine, mayor, Trenton	100	00
18—1st Baptist Ch.,thro' 1st Nat.Bank, Memphis	104	00
18—Y. M. C. A., Plainfield	124	00
18—J. Van Winkle, Patterson	10	00
20—J. D. Hall, Trenton	150	00
20—Citizens of Red Bank	120	00
20—D. B Bodine, mayor, Trenton	100	00
21—Relief fund,Trenton,thro'J.D.Hall	125	00
21—Citizens of " thro' J. D.Hall	50	00
22—Employés Courtland Wagon Manufacturing Co	40	00
24—Committee of Monmouth June	50	00
25—G. G. Green, Woodbury	25	00
25—T. B. Stephens, Hoboken	15	00
26—H. B. Sherman, Newark	10	00
Oct. 1—Rev. J. D. Hall, Trenton	350	00
2—Citizens of Red Bank	23	00
5—Mayor Yates of Newark	1,000	00
13—J. S. Long, Freehold	20	00
16—E L. Joy, Newark	200	00
17—Citizens of Trenton	64	89
18—Citizens of Orange	210	00
19—Citizens of Hightstown	45	50
23—E. D. Ell, Trenton	3	00
Nov. 11—Ladies of Montclair	34	78
Total	$3,983	67

NEW YORK.

Aug. 21—R. B. Gardner, New York	$310	00
22—W. A. Camp, manager, New York	250	00
22—W. A. Camp, manager, New York	250	00
22—W. A. Camp, manager, New York, for Grenada	100	00
24—D. J. Garth, Son & Co., New York	15	00
27—Chamber of Com., from Drexel, Morgan & Co	500	00
27—Chamber of Com., from Drexel, Morgan & Co	1,000	00
28—J. L. McCauley, treas., Cotton Exchange, New York	800	00
28—Rice, Lowenstein, S. and others, New York	1,000	00
29—J. Cunningham, Son & Co., Rochester	100	00
29—Chamber of Com.. thro' Drexel, Morgan & Co., New York	1,750	00
29—Hon. S. Campbell, Utica	20	00
30—O. Lanfer & Co., New York	25	00
30—Exchange Relief Fund, thro' A. E. Orr, New York	500	00
30—Jackson & O'Hara, Church street, New York	25	00
31—W. A. Camp, manager, New York	250	00
Sept. 2—Allen & B., Astor House, New York	100	00
2—J. P. Morgan, treas., New York	2,000	00
2—Jno. H. Rochester, Rochester	200	00
2—C. C. Hyne, New York	77	50
2—New York "Herald," New York.	684	80
3—M. Vassar, Jr., Poughkeepsie	5	00
4—J. S. Warren & Co., New York	25	00
4—J. P. Morgan, treas., New York	1,000	00
4—Mrs. E. A. Hopkins, Catskill	25	00
4—New York "Herald," New York.	62	10
5—Israelites of Syracuse, by Drexel, Morgan & Co	100	00
6—New York Stock Exchange, thro' W. H. Smith	1,125	00
6—New York "Herald," New York.	122	80
6—W. A. Camp, manager, New York	150	00
6—Citizens of Troy, through Drexel, Morgan & Co	500	00
6—Drexel, M. & Co., for Brownsville	700	00
6—Drexel, M. & Co., New York	1,500	00
6—Citizens of Brooklyn, thro' Ripley Roper	1,000	00
7—Jno. H. Rochester, Rochester	200	00
7—Cotton Exchange, through J. L. McCauley, New York	500	00
8—New York "Herald," New York	89	30
9—Dan'l Krouse & Sons, Utica	10	00
10—Drexel, Morgan & Co., New York.	1,500	00
10—"Insurance Monitor," New York	53	00
11—T. W. Devoe, New York	50	00
11—Jno. Arnot, Elmira	100	00
11—C. Lindsay, Elmira	200	00
11—Israelites of Syracuse	150	00
11—Drexel, Morgan & Co., New York,	2,000	00
11—"New York Herald," New York..	52	60
12—Salance & Grosyear, New York	50	00
12—Mayor Ely, New York	1,412	74
13—J. H. Rochester, Rochester	200	00
13—Randolph Ballard, Leroy	12	70
13—Combined fraternities of Harlem	200	00
14—Charles Osman Rose, New York	5	00
14—L. P. Hawes, New York	100	00
14—Citizens of Brooklyn, thro' Ripley Roper	1,000	00
14—Drexel, Morgan & Co., New York,	3,000	00
14—Drexel, Morgan & Co., New York, for Holly Springs	1,000	00
14—Churches of Homer	22	83
14—New York Stock Exchange, thro' W. H. Smith	479	00
15—Citizens of Jamestown	30	52
15—Citizens of Avon, through Jno. Rochester	270	00
15—Citizens of Poughkeepsie	200	00
16—Citizens of Cazenovia	47	44
16—Citizens of Amsterdam	31	60
16—Security Lodge, 164, Rochester	105	26
17—Friendly Sons of St. Patrick, Williamsburg	200	00
18—Pres. Church, Freemansburg	89	00
18—Mayor Ely, New York	590	85

APPENDIX.

Sept. 18—New York "Herald," New York..	$166 00	
18—Bap. Church of Freemansburg.....	26 00	
18—Relief Committee, Lockport.........	300 00	
18—Relief Committee, White Plains..	350 00	
18—Jno. H. Rochester, Rochester	350 00	
20—Citizens of Medina....................	50 00	
20—Citizens of Frewsburg................	42 57	
20—Citizens of Afton......................	5 85	
20—Citizens of Fredonia.................	171 50	
20—Pres. Church of Westfield............	124 35	
20—New York Exchange, thro' A. E. Orr. New York......................	750 00	
21—Charles Butler, Birmingham.......	56 53	
21—Universalist Church of Gaines.....	70 00	
21—Presbyterian S. S. of Gainesville..	21 00	
21—Geo. S. Hutchinson, Gainesville..	9 00	
21—Relief Committee, Lockport.......	200 00	
21—Citizens of Spencerport.............	11 87	
21—Pres. Church, Spencerport..........	45 00	
21—Cong. Church, Spencerport.........	41 25	
21—M. E. Church, Spencerport.........	13 01	
21—Citizens of O.ean.....................	220 00	
21—Goldsmith & Plant, New York....	25 00	
21—Strauss & Arenstein, New York...	25 00	
21—Union & Bay State Manuf'g Co...	50 00	
21—St. John's Epis. Ch. of Mt. Morris	117 56	
21—Augustus Keep, Lockport...........	34 00	
21—Drexel, Morgan & Co , New York.	2,100 00	
21—J. M. Tinker, New York............	250 00	
21—A. B. Farquahar, treas., New York	100 00	
22—Petit Jury (Sept. term), Binghamton..............................	11 00	
22—Combined fraternities, Harlem....	200 00	
23—Citizens of Troy	86 70	
23—Presbyterian Church, Newark....	31 73	
23—M. Nash, Martinsburgh.............	5 00	
23—Citizens of Hudson	210 (0	
23—Episcopal Church, Lockport.......	90 00	
23—Citizens of Syracuse..................	500 00	
24—Citizens of West Troy................	193 00	
24—Mayor Ely, New York...............	1,159 96	
24—Democratic County Convention, Binghamton...................	25 50	
24—Cong. Church, Rochester............	39 76	
24—New York Chamber of Com., thro' J. P. Morgan, New York..........	2,500 00	
24—Citizens of Jamestown	27 25	
24—Charles Ipsom, Jamestown........	28 00	
24—Ludlow & Co., New York	103 25	
24—Chas. T. White & Co.. New York..	50 00	
25—Employés of H. B. Claflin & Co., New York...........................	2,000 00	
25—"The Christian at Work " (newspaper), New York	37 50	
25—Citizens of Bath......................	73 00	
25—Citizens of Poughkeepsie...........	159 50	
25—New York Stock Exchange, thro' W. H. Smith, New York..........	350 00	
25—New York Stock Exchange, thro' W. H. Smith, New York..........	50 00	
25—Christian Church, through Stock Exchange, New York	81 72	
25—Jno. Susden, through Stock Exchange, New York.................	100 00	
26—"Morning Herald and Gazette," Utica.............................	235 00	
26—4th National Bank, New York ,...	85 00	
26—Mrs. Van Zandt, 2d Ave. and 14th Street, New York................	35 00	
26—Citizens of Little Falls...............	388 00	
26—Citizens of Jamestown..............	300 00	
26—1st Pres. Ch. & Soc., Binghamton.	111 80	
27—C. S. Hussey, Rochester.............	5 00	
27—Union Temperance. Windsor......	17 00	
28—Old gentleman of Lima.............	50 00	
28—Cong. Society of Kinstone..........	6 00	
28—Co. F, 48th Regiment, Oswego....	150 00	
29—Churches of Fairport................	156 00	
29—Citizens of Albany...................	10 00	
29—C. D. Chase, Fairport................	1 00	
30—Citizens of Brooklyn................	475 93	
30—Combined fraternities of Harlem	200 00	
30—Citizens of New York, thro' New York "Times"	500 00	
30—German Evang Soc., Binghamton	18 00	
Oct. 1—Stationers' Board of Trade, New York	200 00	
1—New York Stock Exchange, thro' W. H. Smith..........................	5 75	

Oct. 1—Citizens of Poughkeepsie............	$100 00	
2—Ludlow & Co., New York..........	103 25	
2—J.P. Morgan, New York (currency)	3,300 00	
2—C. S. Stowits, Westfield.............	20 63	
2—J. P. Morgan, New York (silver)...	200 00	
3—Mite box at Half Moon..............	2 25	
4—1st Pres. Church, Bath...............	50 00	
4—Proc. concert by colored citizens, New York........................	125 00	
5—Citizens of Long Island.............	500 00	
7—Ladies of Albion......................	66 12	
8—Drexel, Morgan & Co., New York, for Lagrange......................	300 00	
9—C. Butler, mayor, Binghamton ..	10 00	
10—Rev. W. H. Granger, Long Island	24 15	
10—Citizens of Weedsport................	35 13	
10—Mite box, Jamestown................	17 50	
11—Pupils public schools, Brooklyn...	105 75	
12—Relief fund, Amsterdam...........	4 30	
12—Drexel, Morgan & Co., New York, for Holly Springs.................	250 00	
13—Drexel, Morgan & Co., New York, for Water Valley.................	500 00	
13—Drexel, Morgan & Co., New York, for Tuscumbia....................	500 00	
16—Lyman Carr, Mount Morris........	5 00	
17—J. J. Higginson, New York	25 00	
18—Proceeds concert by Blumenthal & S., Rochester....................	72 02	
18—A. J. Hineman, New York........	10 00	
22—Citizens' Relief Com., Brooklyn...	500 00	
22—Citizens of Fredonia.................	21 73	
22—Cong. Church, New Haven........	23 47	
23—David Cady, Amsterdam	5 10	
27—Citizens of Brooklyn, through R. Roper.............................	250 00	
29—E. Hill, cashier, New York	14 40	
29—W. B. Brady, New York.............	66 50	
29—Thomas F. Olmstead, treasurer, Genesco, Livingston Co..........	127 00	
Nov. 4—Citizens of Brooklyn, through R. Roper.............................	1,000 00	
11—Thomas F. Olmstead, treasurer, Genesco, Livingston Co	9 06	
11—Smith Ely, mayor, New York......	767 49	
11—Citizens of Troy....................	13 33	
Sept. 2—Moore, Tingue & Co., New York, through Menken Bros...............	50 00	
Oct. 28—J. P. Morgan, treasurer, for Holly Springs..........................	500 00	
Dec. 3—Condensed Milk Co., New York, through J. W. Oliver................	100 00	
Total	$56,804 16	

NORTH CAROLINA.

Aug. 31—Hebrew Union, Raleigh..............	$67 50
Sept. 2—L. Overman, Raleigh	9 00
2—J. Rosenbaum. Raleigh.............	17 50
2—Mite box, South'n Exp.Co.,Raleigh	5 00
2—T. O. Troy Co. Shops, Troy	9 50
2—Mayor of Manly	35 10
5—Citizens of Halesville...............	70 15
6—Mayor of Asheville...................	100 00
6—Mayor of Asheville for Grenada...	50 00
8—G. K. Walker, Wilmington.........	838 00
8—Dr. W. J. Hawkins, Ridgeway.....	20 00
12—Colored Cong. Church, Raleigh....	5 00
12—Ladies' Relief Association, Raleigh	500 00
13—Citizens of Pineville..................	15 00
13—H. P. Pruden, mayor, Edenton....	31 22
16—Presbyterian Ch., Hamfield and Melanville.........................	52 30
16—J. C. & D. G. Cooper, Henderson...	25 00
16—J. E. Patillo, Henderson............	5 00
16—Citizens of Kingston..................	26 18
17—Citizens of Charlotte.................	15 00
17—Hon. B. T. Moore, Raleigh.........	25 00
17—Citizens of Halifax...................	70 20
17—I. O. O. F. of Oxford.................	12 50
17—Citizens of Oxford....................	53 70
17—Mite box at Raleigh..................	5 50
17—Ladies' Aid Ass'n, Charlotte........	275 00
17—Citizens of Windsor..................	21 00
17—Citizens & students, Wake Forrest.	11 57
17—A citizen of Charlotte................	100 00

APPENDIX. 351

Sept. 17—Citizens of Saulsbury	$300 00
17—Baptist Church, Lisleville	7 00
17—Contributions thro' G. W. Kidder, Wilmington	213 00
18—Citizens of Hillsboro	137 00
18—Colored citizens of Raleigh	93 66
19—Colored citizens of Wilmington	272 93
20—Citizens of Greensboro	163 59
20—Buffalo Church of Greensboro	4 30
20—Pres. Church, Lawrenceburg	40 50
20—Meth., Pres., and M. E. Churches, Monroe	55 10
20—G. W. Kidder, Wilmington	250 00
21—T. D. Crawford & Co., Oxford	5 00
21—Great Falls Manufacturing Co., Rockingham	10 00
21—Citizens of Warrenton	170 61
21—R. Chambers and employés, Charlotte	20 30
21—Presbyterian Church, Hillsboro	4 25
22—Citizens of Rockingham	125 90
21—Speights Chapel S. S. of Whitakers	16 17
21—Scotland Neck Lodge, 68	25 00
21—Citizens of Thomasville	19 05
22—Ladies of Concord	55 00
22—Citizens of Wentworth	61 06
22—Co ored citizens of Wentworth	6 84
23—South. Relief Fund, Clinton	13 85
23—Citizens of Henderson	166 85
23—Citizens of Statesville	264 08
24—Baptist Church of Forrestville	13 48
25—Citizens of Hendersonville	67 40
25—Junaluskee Lodge, A. F. & A. M., Franklin	33 00
28—Sunday School Class of J. H. Robinson, Oxford	1 00
29—Ladies of Newbern	361 50
29—M. E. Church of Concord	5 15
29—Citizens of Wilmington	276 67
29—Citizens of Roxboro	43 75
29—Citizens of Graham	14 50
29—Ladies of Jonesborough	23 11
29—S. M. McGregor, Halifax	10 00
29—Citizens of Bristol	66 00
29—R. W. Floyd, Saulsbury	16 00
29—Hill Chapel Lodge, Charlotte	10 00
30—Presbyterian Church, Charlotte	13 75
Oct. 2—Proceeds of a hop at Faulkland	15 00
2—Ladies of Marion	31 00
2—Jordan Womble, Raleigh	17 65
2—Citizens of Graham	100 00
3—Rev. H. Blvarris, Whitesville	45 33
3—Citizens of Wilmington	110 95
4—Arlvlee Church, through Jordan Womble, Raleigh	11 23
4—Ely City Church	10 00
4—Colored M. E. Ch. of Henderson	5 20
4—Citizens of Newbern	24 00
4—Citizens of Dallas	4 25
7—Academy of Medicine, Raleigh	17 00
7—Citizens of Ashboro	32 47
7—Citizens of Morrisville	12 60
7—Members Mil. Inst., Charlotteville	15 00
9—Jordan Womble and others, Deanville	9 00
9—Congregation Chapel, Black Run	13 00
10—Ladies of Weldon	37 28
10—Ladies of Snow Hill	39 00
13—W. A. Louden, Jr., Moncure	62 58
13—W. E. Anderson, Raleigh	104 50
13—Cannon, Fitser & Wadsworth, Concord	43 30
13—J. Allen Brown, Saulsbury	14 25
13—Jordan Womble, Jr., Raleigh	10 00
15—John Ledbetter, Rockingham	5 00
18—Ladies of Durham	101 00
19—R. Burwell, Raleigh	22 50
19—Employés Lidell & Co., Charlotte	25 85
21—Hoover & Love, Concord	15 00
21—South'n Relief Ass'n, Wilmington	54 45
21—Centre Church, Mount Monroe	15 00
21—Ladies' festival, St. Louisberg	109 10
21—Ladies' festival, St. Louisberg	75 00
26—J. R. Holland & Co., Charlotte	25 80
26—J. Y. Morrison, Concord	4 00
30—Pres. Church, Mecklenburg	13 20
Nov. 4—W. D. Pruden, mayor, Edenton	13 00
Total	$7,190 76

OHIO.

Aug. 22—Chas. Kahn, Jr., Cincinnati	100 00
22—Evans, Lippincott & Cunningham, Cincinnati	100 00
23—Beckel House, Dayton	130 00
23—Friends at Cleveland	6 38
23—Friend, thro' Panoli Oil Works, Cincinnati	9 50
23—Dr. R B. Ironside, Cincinnati	5 00
23—J. Heitman. mayor, Columbus	300 00
29—Citizens of Newark	75 00
29—Citizens of Newark, for New Orleans	50 00
29—Citizens of Newark, for Vicksburg	50 00
29—Citizens of Newark, for Grenada	25 00
29—Citizens of Dayton	116 50
29—Guests and Props Phillips House, Dayton	100 00
29—Free Sons of Israel, Cleveland	25 00
30—Martin's Ferry, for Canton	57 00
30—Episcopal Church of the Advent, Cincinnati	29 45
30—F. Lukenheimer, Cincinnati	10 00
30—Citizens of Mount Vernon	300 00
31—W. H. Wilson, mayor, Sandusky	100 00
31—Jas. Leffel & Co., Springfield	100 00
31—Relief Committee, Steubenville	256 16
31—Disabled Vol. Soldiers, Dayton	66 00
31—Citizens of Dayton	75 65
Sept. 2—W. H. Davis, Newark	50 00
2—Citizens of Zanesville	242 00
2—3d Pres. Church, Cincinnati	50 60
2—Isaac Johnston, Wooster	1 00
4—W. H. Davis, Newark	50 00
4—Citizens of Springfield	200 00
4—Employés of Davis, Gould & Co., Cincinnati	43 00
4—Citizens of Coshocton	152 00
4—Citizens of Hanoverton	7 00
4—Members Disciple Ch., Coshocton	3 00
4—Pres. Church, Hanoverton	9 45
4—Citizens of Chillicothe	700 00
5—St. James Epis. Ch., Painesville	100 00
5—Relief Committee, Steubenville	256 16
5—Relief Committee, Cleveland	1,000 00
5—Merchants Nat. Bank, Dayton	25 00
5—Chas. E. Silobre, Hamilton	3 50
5—Citizens of Xenia	230 75
6—Citizens of Findlay	250 00
6—Champion Machine Co., Springfield	50 00
6—Citizens of Toledo	400 00
7—Citizens' Relief Com., Columbus	300 00
7—Ladies' Sewing Soc., Kelly Island	50 00
7—G. T. Robinson, mayor, Ravenna	53 61
7—Relief Association, Wilmington	200 00
8—Temperance Union, Beverly	15 35
8—Citizens of Dayton, through J. H. Winter	200 00
8—Firemans Insurance Co., Dayton	25 00
8—Citizens of Mount Gilead	30 00
8—Entertainment by home talent, Coshocton	106 30
9—Concert by Zeigler and Sisters and Misses Sleiman and Rogers, thro' L. C. Weir, Cincinnati	220 15
9—Proceeds entertainment by Helen D'Este Troupe, Zanesville	280 40
9—South. Relief Ass'n, Cincinnati	196 17
9—Episcopal Society, London	26 85
9—Dramatic Club, Marysville	71 60
9—Welsh Cong. Church, Cincinnati, for Grenada	16 35
9—M. H. Brooks, Logan	110 00
9—Relief Com. Cincinnati, by Lester Taylor	1,000 00
9—Mendelssohn Quartette Club of Dayton	325 00
9—Citizens of New Philadelphia	100 00
9—Citizens of New Philadelphia, for Grenada	100 00
9—Citizens of New Philadelphia, for Vicksburg	100 00
10—M. H. Hayes, mayor, Troy	200 00
10—Golden Rule Lodge, I. O. O. F., Steubenville	20 00
10—Equitable Loan and Savings Association, Dayton	8 00

23

APPENDIX.

Sept. 10—Citiz'ns of Painesville, thro' E. K. Wright	$170 00
11—Postmaster, Ironton	2 19
11—L. M. Kenton, of Kenton	167 00
12—Citizens of Kansas	25 00
12—Cong. Church, Marietta	60 00
12—Mrs. Wallace McGrath, Chillicothe	5 00
12—U. P. Church, Millersburg	35 00
12—Citizens of Carrollton	200 00
12—Citizens of Weston	34 00
12—Furniture dealers and employés, Cincinnati	400 00
12—Entertain'nt, ladies, Youngstown	300 00
12—Members of Christ Ch., Warren	40 00
12—J. H. Stanley, Cuyahoga Falls	225 00
12—German citizens of Xenia	56 30
12—G. T. Robinson, mayor, Ravenna	23 00
13—U. P. Congregation, Wooster	50 00
13—Citizens of Belleville	41 53
13—Cong. Church of Ironton	28 00
13—Ice cream festival, Powhattan	78 02
13—Relief Committee, Marion	515 00
13—C. S. Deyarman, mayor of Loudonville	100 00
13—J. D. McCormack, Lancaster	450 00
14—M. E. Sunday School, Arcadia	12 00
14—Proceeds excursion, C., S. & C. R. R., Sandusky	154 95
14—Entertainment by Murdoch Club, Loveland	22 15
14—Citizens of Massillon	143 00
14—J. C. Klaw, Massillon	30 00
14—Soldiers' Relief Union Fund, Marietta	156 27
14—Citizens of Upper Sandusky	301 75
14—Presbyterian S. S., Cumberland	15 00
14—C. P. Evans, Irondale	10 00
14—Letter 87, Urbana	6 60
15—Citizens of Genesee or Geneva, thro' J. L. Morgan	100 00
15—Citizens of Norwalk	5 80
15—Citizens of Canton, for Canton, Mississippi	100 00
15—Citizens of Canton, for Vicksburg	100 00
15—Citizens of Canton, for Memphis	100 00
15—C., C., C. & I. R. R., Galion	25 50
15—Dramatic Society, Versailles	14 50
16—Citizens of Bucyrus	191 65
16—Citizens of Middletown	100 00
16—Citizens of London	45 10
16—Jno. Moore, Cadiz	200 00
16—Citizens of St. Marys	148 00
16—Geo. T. Holman, Ravenna	18 24
16—Jno. H. Thomas, Springfield	500 00
16—Jay & Silvermail, Fostoria	9 56
16—Citizens of Fostoria	52 75
17—German Relief Soc., Canton	21 50
17—Citizens of Bellaire	261 03
17—Citizens of Madisonville	25 25
18—1st National Bank, Painesville	55 00
18—Sabbath School, Marysville	12 00
18—Murphy Temperance Congregation, Leesburg	18 94
18—M. E. Sunday School, Leesburg	3 76
18—Citizens of West Jefferson	40 00
18—Citizens of Zanesville	425 80
18—M. G. Harry, Cincinnati	50 00
19—Little ones of Ottawa	1 16
19—School children of Ottawa	5 00
19—Citizens of Ottawa	115 65
19—Citizens of North Fairfield	23 23
19—Jno. T. Bourgun, Lima	57 00
19—T. C. McKahm, Norwalk	6 31
19—Bap. & Cong. Chs., Ashtabula	23 62
19—Citizens of Paulding	15 00
19—Citizens of Crestline	100 00
19—Cong. Church, Kelly's Island	27 46
19—Cit'zens of Kenton	100 00
19—H. C. Dramatic Club, Sardrina	21 00
19—Presbyterian Church, Sardrina	4 37
20—Relief, P. S. S., Rushsylvania	6 00
20—Citizens of Massillon, thro' Geo. Hirsh	200 00
20—Greentown Academy, Perryville	15 00
20—Citizens of Perryville	40 50
20—Italian citizens of Cincinnati	200 50
20—Citizens of Dresden	111 50
20—Citizens' Relief Com., Toledo	340 00
20—W. H. Foster, Urichsville	50 00
Sept. 20—G. M. Neville, Xenia	17 25
20—G. M. Neville, Xenia	20 00
21—Ladies of Ironton	331 78
21—Citizens of Defiance	261 00
21—U. P. Church of Thornville and Rushcreek	35 60
21—Reformed Church, Salem	16 40
21—Citizens of Coshocton	15 00
21—M. E. Sunday School of Tarlton	15 00
21—Citizens of New Lexington	40 00
21—Citizens of Four Corners	23 25
21—W. Anderson, White Cottage	1 00
21—Citizens of Waktonica Cross Roads	7 75
21—Citizens of New Castle	11 67
21—Citizens of Beach City	23 48
21—Citizens of Bluffton	33 00
21—Sunday Schools of Bluffton	23 00
21—German Benev. Ass'n, Massillon	10 00
21—Pres. Church, Worthington	24 00
21—Citizens of Somerset	166 42
21—U. P. Church, Jamestown	18 00
22—Tymochitee Tribe, 1, Cardington	13 00
22—Sunday Schools of Ashland	51 60
22—Citizens of Bellaire	71 80
22—Presbyterian Church, Savannah	33 16
22—Methodist Church, Savannah	11 49
22—Union prayer meeting, Savannah	14 36
22—Presbyterian S. S., Savannah	5 00
22—Post-office, Savannah	6 99
22—Wayne Pres. Ch., Congress City	56 00
22—Citizens of Congress City	14 00
22—4th Street Pres. Church, Marietta	30 28
23—James Withrow, Newport	10 55
23—Cong. Church, Belpre	18 54
23—Citizens of Logan	9 00
24—Quakers of Mount Pleasant	40 00
24—Relief Committee, Cincinnati	2,000 00
25—Home talent, Cincinnati	60 00
25—1st Pres. Church, Warren	156 94
25—Relief Ass'n, West Middlebury	13 75
25—Relief Association, Wilmingham, through Telfair	100 00
25—Citizens of Smithville	27 85
26—D. Lilienthal. Cincinnati	5 00
26—Citizens of Eaton	157 65
26—Joseph Getz, Bench City	2 00
26—Lutheran Ch., New Comerstown	3 46
26—Jefferson Pres. Church, Warsaw	10 00
27—Citizens' Committee, Mt. Vernon	111 79
27—Citizens of New Lisbon	121 34
27—Union Church, Norwalk	9 90
27—Citizens of Clyde	81 50
27—1st Pres. Church, Alliance	27 69
27—Citizens of Dunkirk, thro' Misses Wood and M	10 00
27—Citizens of Coalville	17 00
28—Citizens of New Castle	13 15
28—Citizens of Freedonia	52 33
28—Citizens of Ironton	67 04
28—Relief Committee of Dayton	1,000 00
28—Ref. Presbyterian Church, Uniontown and Waranochs	26 20
28—C. S. Hawkins, Kellogsville	5 00
28—Royer Wheel Co., Cincinnati	25 00
28—Citizens of Canal Fulton	25 00
29—C tizens of Shannon	76 00
29—1st Pres. Church of Wooster	76 50
29—Harmonic Ass'n of Akron	50 00
29—Isaac Smith, Mooresville	08 00
29—Citizens of New Bremen	182 53
29—Presbyterian Ch. and S. S., Rome	10 70
30—Southern Relief Fund of Canal Dover	53 00
30—Citizens of Urichsville	34 40
30—Congregation of Millersburg	7 50
Oct. 1—Citizens of Geneva	81 50
1—Sand Hill S. S., Quaker City	8 00
2—Citizens of Mantua	44 00
3—Young ladies of Athens	50 00
3—Township of Lawrence	8 40
3—C. O. Tannehill, Perrysville	4 94
4—U. P. Congregation, Savannah	18 33
4—Bellmont U. P. Church. Bellaire	24 55
4—Daniel P. Eels, treas., Cleveland	1,000 00
7—Soldiers' Reunion, Marietta	12 00
7—Citizens of Bellaire	42 85
9—Buffalo Pres. Ch., Cumberland	26 73
9—Singing Choir, Gnadenhutten	4 00
10—Guests of Hayes House, Fostoria	2 12

APPENDIX. 353

Oct. 10—Citizens of Findlay	$ 9 43
11—Citizens of Carrollton	85 70
11—Presbyterian Church, Del Roy	19 25
11—M. E. Church, Harlem Springs	20 60
11—Unknown, Mount Pleasant	2 00
12—Presbyterian Church, West Salem	19 00
13—German Bap. Soc., Sugar Creek	30 00
13—G. F. Robinson, Ravenna	6 00
13—Citizens of Crawford Co	9 00
16—Mrs. Wallace McGrath, Chillicothe	5 00
18—Miss Mattie Gibson, Summerfield	20 15
18—Postmaster of West Alexandria	50
18—Relief Committee, Ashland	51 60
21—Citizens of Chillicothe	421 37
21—Mess. Case, Mills, Gricks, and Fay, Milan, Erie Co	18 25
25—Relief Association, Urbana, thro' L. Hervey	50 00
29—Mrs. Neil Mitchell, London	40 00
Nov. 7—Rev. F. Eddy, for Pres. Ch. Cong	10 00
7—Cong. Society, Burton	15 29
11—Cong. Ch., Huntsburg, thro' Lucy A. Barnes	12 00
19—C. Haywood, Conneaut	60 00
Dec. 13—Furniture Trade, Cincinnati, thro' G. Horshman and others, for the orphans	214 12
Total	$26,029 72

CINCINNATI SOUTHERN RELIEF COMMITTEE.

Aug. 27—100 sheets, 50 Excelsior mattresses, 50 cots, 50 pillows	$195 83
Sept. 5—300 suits of children's clothing	1,000 00
5—Paid fares physicians and nurses to Memphis	200 00
5—100 sheets, 50 mattresses, 50 cots, 50 pillows	205 83
10—300 sheets, 150 cots, 150 pillows, 150 mattresses, sent. by direction, to Peabody & Court St Infrm'ries	633 09
10—25 clinical thermometers	52 50
14—50 cases corned beef, 1 bbl dried beef	204 32
19—25 bbls crackers, 15 doz cans beef, 10 doz cans beans, 10 doz cans pigs' feet, 1 bbl dried beef, 5 bxs cheese, 20 doz cans cove oysters.	231 46
Oct. 5—10 top buggies	825 00
16—20 boxes lemons	150 00
Total	$3,698 03
Total Donations	26,029 72
Grand Total	$29,727 75

OREGON.

Sept. 9—Citizens of Portland, thro' N.Y.	$2,000 00
22—Citizens of Portland	500 00
26—Rev. A.O. Parker, Astoria, for W.C. McCracken	7 00
26—Rev. A. O. Parker, Astoria, for G. C. Harris	7 00
Total	$2,514 00

PENNSYLVANIA.

Aug. —Relief Committee, Pittsburgh, for Grenada	$300 00
22—Two ladies thro' D. Leet Wilson, Pittsburgh, for Grenada	25 00
22—Rook & O'Neil, Pittsburgh	104 00
22—Henry H. Houston, Philadelphia	200 00
25—Citizens of Oil City	100 00
29—Cin. & St. L. R. R. Co., Pittsburgh	250 00
29—Citizens of York	100 00
29—E.C. Backus, Petrolia, for Grenada	50 00
29—1st Presbyterian Ch., Washington	20 00
29—Citizens of Washington	27 00
29—Citizens of Foxburg	105 00
29—Publ'hers "Dispatch," Pittsburgh	160 00
31—Citizens of Emlenton	61 50
Sept. 2—Emp. Nat. Tube W'ks., McKeesport	200 00

Sept. 2—H.R. Fullerton, mayor, Parker City	$164 00
2—Delameter & Co., Meadville	100 00
4—Presbyterian S. Sch., Morristown	26 00
5—Oil Exchange, Oil City	150 00
5—Citizens of York	100 00
5—Citizens of Altoona	22 50
6—Citizens' Relief Com., Meadville	100 00
6—Ladies of Kittanning	324 00
6—Churches & citizens, St. Petersburg	156 20
7—Presbyterian Church of Lebanon	30 00
7—Rook & O'Neil, Pittsburgh	150 00
8—Lawyers of Altoona	65 00
8—Employés of A. & G. W. R. R., Meadville	300 00
9—P. R. Fullerton, Parker City	13 00
9—Dr. E. G. Crawford, Edinburg	50 00
10—Citizens of Altoona	288 88
11—Relief Committee, Pittsburgh	500 00
11—A. Wiley, Chief Eng. Fire Dept., Franklin	60 00
12—L. Hefling & others, Mercer	15 00
13—Relief Committee, Pittsburgh	1,000 00
13—East Buffalo Pres. Ch., Washington	8 22
13—2d Presbyterian Ch., Washington	29 60
13—Hopewell Lodge, I.O.O.F., Washington	10 00
13—Citizens of Washington	32 00
13—Citizens of Millerstown	37 45
13—K. of H., Millerstown	15 00
13—I.O.O.F., Millerstown	15 00
14—C. Gregor, Tyrone	100 00
14—W. B. Blizell, Dallsburg	15 00
14—Citizens of Beaver Falls	300 00
14—Citizens of Beaver Falls, for Grenada	200 00
14—Citizens of Beaver Falls, for Port Gibson	100 00
15—S. S. of U. P. Church, Greenville	21 34
15—James A. Linen, Scranton	400 00
15—Citizens of Easton	500 00
16—Grace Episcopal Ch., Miles Grove	16 08
16—Relief Committee, Pittsburgh	1,000 00
17—1st Presbyterian S. School, Tyrone	22 53
17—African M. E. Church, Titusville	15 50
17—Citizens of Washington	225 22
17—Unknown Friend, Pittsburgh	10 00
17—Citizens of Pottsville	100 00
17—Citizens of Queenstown	100 00
17—Citizens of Williamsburg	195 00
18—Citizens of McKeesport	223 13
18—Citizens of Bellefonte	260 00
18—Southern Relief Fund, Altoona	425 70
18—Southern Relief Fund, Reading	1,000 00
18—Churches of York	100 00
18—Neighboring towns to Oil City, through H. D. Hancock	162 00
20—Citizens of Selin's Grove	110 00
20—Relief Committee, Pittsburgh	1,000 00
21—Employés of A. & G. W. R. R., Meadville	250 00
21—Presbyterian Ch., Cannonsburg	46 18
21—Chartier's Pres. Ch., Cannonsburg	17 10
21—Chartier's Pres. " W. Alexandria	62 50
21—Chartier's Pres. " Mt. Pleasant	12 00
21—Disciples Church, Line Run	4 71
21—Citizens of Washington	46 25
21—Citizens' Committee, Altoona	217 02
21—G. H. Trabert, Lebanon	52 50
21—G. B. Maloney, Pres. Fire Ins. Co., Franklin	70 00
22—Relief Committee, Franklin	100 00
22—Relief Committee, Beaver Falls	291 54
23—Employés of Morrison, Bare & Caps, Roaring Springs	57 50
25—Citizens of Johnstown & vicinity	300 00
25—Citizens of Sharon	380 75
25—Citizens of Tryburgh	12 00
25—Citizens & churches of Baldwin	261 27
26—Citizens of New Castle	192 90
27—Citizens of Girard	50 96
28—Presbyterian Church, Frankfort	19 00
28—Zone Baptist Church, Hillsville	10 00
28—Relief Committee, Pittsburgh	2,000 00
29—Various churches, thro' H. Hazlett, Washington	113 32
29—G. W. Kennedy, Pottsville	171 97
29—Citizens of Macungie	40 00
Oct. 5—Citizens of Greensburg	15 55
8—Unknown, Lansford	1 00

354 APPENDIX.

Oct.	9—C. B. North, Selin's Grove	$ 2 50
	11—Citizens of Altoona	20 00
	18—Delameter & Co., Meadville	50 00
	23—G. H. Barclay, Williamsport	30 50
	29—M. A. Foltz, Chambersburg	40 57
	31—Jacob Heyser, Chambersburg	18 07
Nov.	7—Relief Committee, Washington, through H. Hazlett	223 17
	29—Teachers & students Lake Shore Seminary, North East	1 25
Dec.	20—Johnson Lodge, I.O.B.B., Pittsburgh, thro' Howard Ass'n, New Orleans	100 00
	Total	**$17,770 33**

RHODE ISLAND.

Sept.	18—Mayor of Providence	$1,000 00
	18—Citizens of Dover	735 03
	20—Commodore Baldwin & D. King, Newport	8 00
	24—Mayor of Providence	2,000 00
	24—Citizens of Bristol	270 00
	27—Providence Board of Trade	1,000 00
	27—Providence Board of Trade, for Grenada	500 00
	29—Providence Board of Trade	1,000 00
	Total	**$6,513 00**

SOUTH CAROLINA.

Aug.	31—T'wn Council Marion, for Grenada	$20 00
	31—T'wn Council " Vicksburg	15 00
	31—T'wn Council " Canton	15 00
Sept.	2—City of Anderson	62 50
	12—City of Unionville and vicinity	147 12
	12—Christ Church, Greenville	34 00
	12—Christ Church, " for Vicksburg	34 00
	13—Riordan & Dawson, Charleston, from city	500 00
	13—Citizens of Port Royal	34 50
	14—Ladies'Col.R'lief Ass'n,Greenville	85 91
	14—Citizens of Rock Hill	53 15
	14—J. R. Minten, Sedalia	3 00
	16—Ladies of Newberg	72 10
	16—M. E. Church, South Cheraw	22 95
	16—Citizens of Liberty Hill	13 00
	16—Citizens of Langley	42 00
	16—Employés Newspapers, Langley	29 50
	17—Baptist & M. E. Ch., Bennettsville	108 00
	17—Town Council, Bennettsville	25 00
	17—Ladies of Greenwood	30 25
	17—City of Greenville	73 00
	17—Col. Ladies' R'lief Ass'n, Greenville	40 00
	17—"News and Courier," Charleston	300 00
	18—Citizens of Anderson	78 15
	18—Baptist Church, Seneca City	2 20
	19—Citizens of Greenville	55 95
	19—Baptist Church, Greenville	68 30
	19—Citizens of Horea Path	42 08
	20—Citizens of Port Royal	35 00
	21—C. T. Scaife, Union S. School	5 00
	21—Moise Guards, Rock Hill	15 45
	21—Citizens of Rock Hill	37 55
	21—Employés So. Ex. Co., Columbia	20 17
	21—Employés So Ex. Co., Columbia, for Grenada	20 50
	21—Citizens of Edgefield	95 65
	21—Ladies of Greenville	200 30
	22—Citizens of Greenville	70 45
	22—C. T. Scaife, Union S. School	5 00
	22—Christians of Cokesburg	18 10
	23—Citizens of Florence	12 25
	23—All Saints' Parish, Waccaniwa	30 00
	24—Citizens of Laurens	58 00
	25—Citizens of vicinity of Columbia	168 50
	28—Ebenezer M. E. Church, Chester	8 00
	28—Church, Pleasant Grove	2 20
	29—Citizens of Townsville	12 00
	30—Methodist Church, Mount Bethel	8 35
Oct.	1—F. Jacobs & M. E. Church,Laurens	18 60
	2—Misses Simpson & Knox, Spartanburg	23 00

Oct.	2—Belle Lodge, No. 22, I.O.G.T., Edgefield	$ 5 00
	2—Citizens of Wainsboro'	101 25
	2—Citizens of Columbia	136 76
	3—T.D.Gillespie,Exp.Agt.,Columbia	52 84
	5—Citizens of Winnsboro'	4 15
	5—Pleasant Grove Church, Chester	20 00
	7—U. Presbyterian Ch., Pawnee City	21 35
	7—Lebanon Pres. Ch., Winnsboro'	37 00
	7—Good Hope Pres. Ch., Anderson	13 65
	7—Unit'd Cong.Ref P.Ch.,Lewisville	40 00
	10—Citizens of Rock Hill	52 40
	13—Musical Club, Laurens	13 60
	13—Citizens of Gastoria	15 00
	13—T. D. Gillespie, Columbia	65 10
	19—G.A. Ref. Pres. Church, Anderson	7 50
	21—Roberts P. Ch. & Divine Readings	12 76
	24—Riordan & Dawson, "News and Courier," Charleston	400 00
	24—E. W. Seibels, Columbia, for Senatobia	75 00
	29—City Council, Charleston	1,000 00
	29—Citizens of Charleston	498 91
	29—Academy of Music, Charleston	477 00
	30—Citizens of Bancroft	28 51
Nov.	4—W. H. Anderson, Laurens C. H	9 40
	4—T. D. Gillespie, Columbia	59 35
	7—J. M. Ivey, mayor of Rockville	12 40
	Total	**$6,039 66**

TENNESSEE.

Aug.	15—J. T. Trezevant, of Memphis	$ 5 00
	22—J. G. Lonsdale, from a lady of Memphis	50 00
	22—J. P. Gentry, from citizens of Collierville	50 00
	22—D. Eisman, from a young man, New York	10 00
	22—Employers L. & N. R. R. shops, Memphis, for Grenada	57 00
	22—Jerry O'Brien, Memphis, for Grenada	10 00
	22—Kahn & Freiburg, Memphis	10 00
	22—W. T. Cooper, Nashville	100 00
	23—J. Lowenhaupt, Covington	10 00
	23—Hon. C. W. Adams, Memphis	10 00
	24—B. Douglass, Nashville	100 00
	24—B. Douglass, " for Grenada	30 00
	24—B. Douglass, " for Canton	20 00
	24—S. W. Coan, Brownsville	6 00
	24—Relief Committee, Chattanooga	100 00
	26—William Roosart, Memphis	25 00
	26—C. Thomas, Memphis	5 00
	26—Employés Car Wheel Co., Knoxville	27 00
	26—Joyner, Lemon & Gale, Memphis	50 00
	26—Hebrew Congregation, Knoxville	25 00
	27—P. B. Plummer, Somerville	20 00
	27—Citizens of Macon Depot	50 00
	27—Citizens of " " for Grenada	27 70
	27—Citizens of Bolivar	40 50
	27—J. S. Carpenter, Memphis	10 00
	28—J. B. & W. A. Faires, Memphis	10 00
	28—McMinnville juvenile boarders at Warren House, McMinnville	16 85
	28—G. A. Dickell & Co., Nashville	25 00
	28—Employés E. T. Va. & G. R. R., Knoxville	133 50
	28—Merchants of Jackson, one-half proceeds bale cotton	185 00
	28—Nora Duke, Memphis	1 00
	28—E. S. Molloy, of G.W. Jones & Co., Memphis	25 00
	28—W. H. Wood, Memphis	100 00
	28—W. A. Bickford, Memphis	25 00
	28—Tullahoma, Tenn., through G. W. Davidson	137 50
	28—Jennie Ridley, a nurse	1 50
	29—L. B. Horigan, Memphis	10 00
	29—A. M. Scarborough, Memphis	50 00
	29—Randle, Heath & Co., Memphis	30 00
	29—Nashville, thro' J. D. Anderson	200 00
	29—Daisey Johnson, coll., Clarksville	53 25
	29—C. C. Davis, Gadsden	6 00
	29—Unknown friend, Athens	1 00

APPENDIX. 355

Aug. 30—J. P. Johnson, Nashville, for Grenada	$ 25 00
31—A friend, through W. H. Carroll, Nashville	500 00
31—Churches & citizens of Gallatin	111 35
31—Knoxville Iron Co., Knoxville	25 00
31—R. T. Tompkins, Mur:reesboro.	50 00
31—Colored Benev. Soc., Brownsville	25 00
31—Mrs. Belle Wright, Memphis	50 00
31—Father Mathew Ass'n, Memphis.	75 00
Sept. 2—John M. Lee, N.ishville	100 00
2—City of Murfreesboro	200 00
2—Woodruff & Co., Memphis	25 00
2—Henry Krobs. Covington	5 00
3—A. J. White, President Relief Association, Cleveland	100 00
3—Business Department Nashville "Banner," Nashville	7 00
3—Mrs. M. L. Shelton, Memphis	2 00
4—A. L. Elliott, Memphis	5 00
4—John M. Lee, Nashville	100 00
4—Jasper, Tenn	65 95
4—John H. Savage, Nashville	100 00
4—Relief Committee, Columbia	150 00
4—Goodlett & Co., Memphis	100 00
4—C. M. Taylor, Beershcba	25 00
5—Wythe Depot	55 00
5—Memphis refugees, Bartlett	57 55
5—Methodist Church, Alamo	20 00
5—Citizens of Humboldt	72 35
5—Postmaster, Grand Junction	2 00
5—A friend, Memphis	10 00
6—Tom Holman, Memphis	10 00
6—Mrs. R. M. McClain, Memphis	5 00
6—Sternberg & Lee, Memphis. ,	25 00
6—Presbyterian Church, Trenton	38 00
6—Capt. C. B. Church, Memphis	40 00
6—H. B. Shanks, Memphis	5 00
6—Proc. lecture by Rev. Geo. White	50 00
6—Thos. H. Allen & Co., Memphis.	100 00
6—Citizens of Pulaski	222 40
6—Citizens of Athens	200 00
7—Colored Relief Ass'n, Bolivar	10 00
7—Citizens of Ralston	16 30
7—Merchants of Henderson, Tenn., & Louisville, Ky.	256 48
8—Thos. Williams, thro' Mr. Griffin.	100 00
8—John M. Lee, Nashville	250 00
9—Citizens' Board of Relief,Lebanon	100 00
9—J. T. Williams, Columbia	100 00
9—Young ladies of Winchester	43 05
9—Citizens meeting, Franklin	289 05
9—Citizens, through Mollie J. Stone, Falcon	30 00
9—Students, Cailawha Institute	6 50
9—A little boy, who hadn't much to give, Clarksville	2 00
9—Benton Co. Aid Ass'n, Camden	48 00
9—Kind-hearted lady, through Daisy Johnson, Clarksville	2 00
9—Citizens of Falcon	30 00
9—Tobacco Board of Trade, Clarksville	222 50
9—Lagrange Warehouse Association, Clarksville	100 00
9—Mrs. A. S. Marks, Winchester	25 00
9—M. E. Church South, Winchester.	20 35
10—F & A M.. Lodge,No. 208,Danville	10 00
10—City Oil Works, Memphis	100 00
10—Citizens of Rodgersville	25 75
10—A. T. M., Columbia	10 00
11—Annie Thompson & M. L. Bailey, Clarksville	10 00
11—Citizens' Committee, Gallatin	91 50
11—Cit:zens of Bell Buckle	40 00
11—Citizens of Clarksville	101 75
11—Citizens of Pulaski	59 65
11—J. W. Cochran, Memphis	50 00
12—Colored citizens of Jackson	20 60
12—Citizens & visitors of Kingston Springs	39 00
12—Citizens of Lewisburg	100 00
12—Mrs. G. L. Laws, Huntington	5 00
12—Citizens of Dandridge	19 25
13—J. D. Richardson, Murfreesboro.	18 00
13—John Anderson, thro' S. P. Read, Memphis	10 00
13—J. N. Falls, through S. P. Read, Memphis	50 00
Sept. 13—John Overton, Jr., Memphis	$200 00
13—Citizens of Whiteville	17 71
13—Citizens of Newport	34 00
13—Citizens of Spring Hill	16 00
13—J. J. Galbreath, Henderson	22 10
13—J. J. Galbreath, " for Grenada	10 00
13—A. E. Scott, Ralston	9 20
14—A. J. Vienna, Memphis	100 00
14—S. H. Alexander, Jasper	23 18
14—S. L Finley, Benton	5 00
14—W. E. Butler, Jackson	20 00
14—T. M. White, Gainesville	50 00
15—Morning Sun Council, No. 258, Fisherville	26 50
16—Employés Eagle Machine Co.	65 00
16—C. W. Goyer & Co., Memphis	100 00
16—A. A. Patten & Co., Men phis	100 00
16—J. D. Richardson, Murfreesboro.	17 00
16—Citizens of Unionville	34 65
16—Citizens 1st District of Pulaski	42 65
16—Citizens of Tullahoma	18 00
17—Proc. of bale cotton, Lagrange	435 00
17—Concordia, Knox County, S. S.	102 80
17—Midway Sunday-school	10 00
17—Oakland Sunday-school	1 10
17—Cedar Springs Sunday-school	1 00
17—Union Sunday-school	1 10
17—Mrs. D. M. Rabb, Gallatin	3 00
18—Citizens of Stewart Creek	19 40
18—Hebrew Hospital Ass'n, through Rice, Stix & Co., Memphis	50 00
18—Y. M. C. A., Cleveland	100 00
18—Citizens of Cleveland	62 00
18—2d Pres. S. S., Chattanooga	3 47
18—Methodist S. S., Kenton	10 00
18—N. G. Ingleheart, thro' S. P. Read, Memphis	153 50
19—Olio Club & Musical Soc., Pulaski	144 50
19—Proc. lec. T. H. White, Nashville.	50 00
19—Young people of McMinnville.	40 25
19—Citizens' Relief Board, Lebanon.	100 00
19—Cumberland Pres. Ch., Pulaski.	3 25
19—Mt. Moriah Pres. Ch., Giles Co.	10 50
19—District No. 20. Giles Co	12 65
19—Bethel Lodge, No. 194, F. & A. M., Pulaski	30 00
19—A. B. Hamm, Rammer	5 00
19—Citizens of Farmington	62 00
20—Relief Committee, Chattanooga.	200 00
20—Citizens of Christiana	10 05
20—Citizens of Walton Hill	40 00
20—4 contribu'ns thro' W. A. Douglass, Murfreesboro	2 70
20—Citizens of Carboni	20 00
20—Ladies' Tabernacle, thro' W. B. Ross	56 70
20—James Warren, Falcon	5 00
20— City Relief Ccmmittee, Ottuwah.	12 25
20—Lizzie Bryan, thro' T. R. Waring.	5 00
21—John Gaston, Memphis	200 10
21—Joyner, Lemon & Gale, Memphis	100 00
21—Linden St. Christ'n Ch., Memphis	50 00
21—1st Col'd Baptist Ch., Memphis.	18 10
21—Maury Co. Lodge, I. O. G. T., No. 423, Columbia	5 00
21—Relief Committee, Lewisburg	50 00
21—J. H. Clark, Collierville	5 00
21—A few friends, Cowan	50 00
21—First National Bank, Columbia.	10 00
22—Rev. A. W. Mangum and others, Chapel Hill	32 00
25—Valentino & Co., Nashville	5 00
25—C. F. Vance, Memphis	100 00
25—Chickasaw Guards, Memphis	512 95
25—Citizens of Franklin	123 00
25—Relief Association, Lewisburg	65 00
25—Citizens of Clarksville	282 00
26—Miss Sue B. Gunnaway, Murfreesboro	14 25
26—D. A. Townsend, Winchester	12 00
26—Burwinkle & Strawing, Memphis	50 00
26—Citizens' Relief Com.. Nashville.	500 00
26—R. W Brown, Nashville	50 00
26—Lide Merriwether, Memphis	40 00
27—R. L. C. White, for Collierville, Lebanon	50 00
27—Colored Relief Society, Bolivar.	7 60
27—Jas. D. Richardson, Murfreesboro	11 20
27—Roll Ellen Aid Soc., Dyer Station	36 00

APPENDIX.

Sept. 29—Freedmans' S. S., Concord	$5 00	
29—Bell's Depot Minstrels, Bell's Depot	17 00	
29—W. H. Deety, Loudon	79 10	
29—Rehobath Church, Dyer Station	30 00	
Oct. 1—Citizens of Dyersburg, for Brownsville	83 85	
2—J. B. Pond, Limestone	30	
2—Relief Com., Serieville, thro' Miss A. Carnes	32 00	
3—Young ladies of Carbondale	31 30	
3—Unknown, thro' Colly & Graves, White Pine	2 00	
4—Goshen Church, Cowan	18 00	
7—Citizens of Center Point	19 85	
7—Major Wm. Messick, Memphis	35 00	
9—Little Annie May, Clarksville	2 50	
9—Isham G. Harris, Memphis	50 00	
10—J. W. Page, Memphis	2 00	
10—Citizens of Franklin	46 95	
10—W. D. Highlander, Memphis	3 50	
10—Relief fund, Chattanooga	177 13	
10—J. E. Johnston, Wythe	50 00	
10—Louis Hughes and wife, Memphis	5 00	
10—Punkett, Isom & Co., by T. H. Allen, Memphis	19 00	
10—J. W. Clapp, Memphis	50 00	
10—Mrs. E. C. James, Bristol	10 00	
10—George Gill, Brownsville	34 00	
10—J. H. Moore, Memphis	10 00	
10—J. L. Lee, Fulton	50 00	
10—Flaherty & Sullivan, Memphis	100 00	
10—Aid Society, Roll Ellen	36 00	
10—Citizens of Dyersburg	25 90	
Aug. 24—Rev. J. N. Waddell, Memphis	10 00	
28—W. E. Smith, Memphis	10 00	
Sept. 6—J. T. Pickitt, Memphis	1 00	
19—Jas. S. Robinson, Memphis	100 00	
22—Andrew Renkert, Memphis	100 00	
27—Horace E. Anderson, Memphis	40 00	
27—W.W. Etler. Memphis	25 00	
27—S. C. Toof & Co., Memphis	20 00	
Nov. 7—Olio Club, Pulaski	64 50	
11—J. R. Flippin, mayor, Memphis	10,00 00	
11—Porter, Taylor & Co., Memphis	50 00	
29—Citizens of Lebanon, thro' R. L. C. White	50 00	
Dec. 18—W. & S. Jack & Co., Memphis	100 00	
18—Sundry coll., by Dr.R.W.Mitchell, Memphis	88 13	
Total	**$23,847 97**	

TEXAS.

Aug. 28—Citizens of Huntingdon	$70 00	
30—Vorwarts Society, Dennison	50 00	
31—Citizens of Galveston	500 00	
31—Lumber dealers, Fort Worth	100 00	
Sept. 2—Merchants of Rockville	50 00	
4—Christian Church, Fort Worth	32 00	
4—Citizens of Weimar	25 00	
4—Citizens of Victoria	150 00	
4—R. A. Chapter, Dennison, for Grenada	70 00	
6—Amateur Concert, Dennison	124 50	
6—Drs. Swearengen & Manning, Austin	500 00	
7—City of Houston	200 00	
7—City of Gainesville	50 00	
8—City of Sherman	100 00	
8—Paoli Lodge, No. 28, I.O W.M	21 00	
8—B. Saunders, Round Rock	80 00	
9—Citizens of Dallas	300 00	
9—Sam Houston Fire Co., No. 1, Sherman	25 00	
9—Exchange Bank, Dallas	55 70	
10—E. A. Sturges, Waco	45 00	
11—City of San Antonio	500 00	
12—T. J. Harrison & Co., Longview	31 50	
13—E. A. Sturges, mayor, Waco	20 50	
14—Proceeds concert, Austin	144 50	
16—Citizens' Rel.Ass'n, Flatinia, thro' S. H. Kimball	194 00	
16—M. E. Church & S. Sch, Houston	54 40	
16—Minneola Lodge, No. 511, K. of H., Minneola	20 00	

Oct. 17—Citizens of Rusk	$82 00	
17—Masonic Fraternity, Austin	50 00	
17—Masonic Fraternity, Austin, for Holly Springs	50 00	
17—Citizens of Weatherford	42 50	
17—Relief Ass'n, Paris	300 00	
17—City of Bastrop	65 00	
17—Mayor of Weimar	60 50	
18—Citizens of Henderson	100 00	
18—J. Yerdel, Dennison	25 00	
18—Citizens of Brennan	735 00	
18—Citizens of Galveston	600 00	
18—Rev. B. J. Cunningham, Waco	10 20	
20—A widow, Palestine	1 00	
20—Methodist S. School, Douglasville	39 00	
20—Citizens of McKinney	100 00	
20—Citizens of Huntsville	75 00	
21—Social Club, Orange	53 20	
21—Citizens of Seguin	65 15	
21—Moulton Chapter, Platinia	20 00	
21—Moulton Lodge, Platinia	14 00	
21—Citizens Western Texas, through State Nat. Bank, New Orleans	400 00	
21—Employés Street R. R., Houston	23 00	
21—Young Men's Aid Soc., Beaumont	14 00	
21—Citizens of Texarkana	100 00	
22—Heard, Allen & Rainer, Clebourne	22 70	
22—Colorado Commandery, No. 4, for Memphis Masons	100 00	
22—Paris Commandery, No. 9, for Memphis Masons	50 00	
22—Prairie Grove S. School, Mexia	15 00	
22—M. E. Sunday School, Bastrop	26 00	
22—Employés H.& T C.R.R., Houston	150 00	
24—Baptist Sunday School, Longview	13 50	
24—Colored M. E. Church, Brennan	25 45	
24—Citizens of San Saba	140 00	
24—Mark, Lallimer & Co., Ennis	21 00	
24—Citizens of Houston	500 00	
24—Dr. S. E. Clements, Paris	10 00	
24—Machinists of Int. & Gt. N. R. R., Palestine	222 00	
25—Baptist Church, Casqueville	18 00	
25—Baptist & Christian Ch.,Longview	19 00	
25—Citizens of Millican	33 50	
25—Citizens of Brownwood	54 25	
25—Citizens of Breckenridge	18 00	
26—Citizens of Washa	10 15	
26—Citizens of Clarksville	15 00	
27—Dramatic Club, Benham	55 00	
27—Christ's Church, Pilot Point	51 00	
27—Ladies of Belton	156 30	
27—Forest Glade Church, Mexia	47 40	
27—Ladies of Hempstead	142 00	
27—Christian Church, Waxahatchie	13 00	
27—Cumberland Ch., Waxahatchie	7 45	
28—Church near Terrell	6 90	
28—Colored M. E. Church, Henderson	5 70	
28—Methodist E. Church, Palestine	25 00	
28—Citizens' concert	12 65	
28—Capt. Caraher & Co. F, 8th Cav., Fort McIntosh	31 00	
28—Lieut. Eldridge & Co. D, 10th Inf., Fort McIntosh	32 50	
28—Lieut. Wyman & Co. E, 24th Inf. (col.), Fort McIntosh	31 75	
28—Co. D, 24th Inf. (col.), Fort McIntosh	21 50	
28—Capt. Gilman & Co. H, 24th Inf. (col.), Fort McIntosh	30 00	
28—Maj. W. R. Price, commanding 8th Cavalry	10 00	
29—Churches of Gainesville	25 00	
29—Churches of Palestine	11 35	
29—Churches of Crockett	43 80	
29—Churches of Wellburn	4 55	
29—Citizens of Stephensville	44 75	
29—Congregation of Granbury	15 00	
30—White and col. citizens of Seguin	140 00	
30—Citizens of Carthage	35 00	
30—Baptist Church, Mexia	20 05	
30—Baptist Church, Caldwell	40 00	
30—Citizens of Valley View	13 50	
30—Citizens of Rockdale	45 00	
32—Citizens of Laredo	284 00	
Oct. 1—Citizens of Howard	73 05	
1—Citizens of Courtney	39 15	
1—Citizens of New Bronfelds	30 25	
2—M. E. Church, Greenville	34 80	

APPENDIX. 357

Oct. 3—Citizens of Mongolia	$38 50	
3—Maj. E. E. Sellers, Fort McIntosh	5 00	
3—Lieut. Duggan, 10th Inf., Fort McIntosh	5 00	
3—Lieut. Maretilloi, 24th Inf., Fort McIntosh	10 00	
4—Citizens of Matagorda	51 50	
4—Churches of Cotton Gin	13 30	
4—City refugees	99 50	
4—Hickory Grove Church	3 15	
4—Dr. C. C. Burke	8 70	
4—H. Richards Willis	14 25	
5—L. Cartwright, San Augustine	100 00	
5—Ladies of Calvert	206 95	
5—Presbyterian Church, Windham	6 50	
5—Citizens of Denton	49 90	
5—W. B. McClellan & Son, Ledbetter	13 00	
7—Relief Committee, Hearne	50 00	
7—Baptist Church, Post Oak Grove	16 50	
7—Citizens of Oenaville, Bell Co.	7 15	
7—Citizens of Troy	37 30	
7—M.E.Church & S. School, Cameron	56 60	
7—Citizens' Committee, Cold Springs	45 00	
7—Citizens' Committee, Bellville	71 00	
9—Citizens of Cieres & DeWitt Cos.	101 00	
9—Citizens of Terrell & Kaufman	20 35	
10—Relief Committee, Luling	24 40	
10—Churches of Luling	8 40	
10—Dixie Minstrels, Luling	20 00	
10—Citizens of Honey Grove	21 00	
11—Citizens of Pittsburg	12 15	
13—Osage Church, Weimar	17 60	
13—Fire Department, Austin	204 00	
13—Citizens of Longview	14 00	
13—James B. Young, Clarksville	15 50	
15—Concert by Cornet Band, Columbia	19 20	
15—Little girls of Waco	23 50	
23—Leyene Lodge, A. F. M., Dallas Co.	10 00	
29—Little Elm Grange, Harrisville, Bell Co.	21 00	
Nov. 2—Jno. B. Leduc, Weathersford	2 00	
4—San Gabriel Lodge, 89, A. F. & A. M., Georgetown	10 00	
Oct. 29—Citizens of Corsicana	90 00	
Dec. 20—Citizens of Jefferson, thro' Howard Ass'n, New Orleans	150 00	
20—Citizens of Fort Worth, through Howard Ass'n, New Orleans	20 00	
20—Churches of Tyler, through Howard Ass'n, New Orleans	140 00	
20—Churches of Waxahatchie, thro' Howard Ass'n, New Orleans	24 80	
Total	$11,400 30	

UTAH.

Sept. 15—Citizens of Ogden	$414 00
19—Ladies' Relief Ass'n, Salt Lake	184 35
19—Pro. game base ball, Salt Lake	415 00
19—Lecture, Rev. Van Horn, Salt Lake	41 00
19—Subs'n of Capt. Codman, Salt Lake	25 00
19—Ladies' Relief Ass'n, Salt Lake	116 00
19—Henry Clay Soc	46 50
19—Miners of Frisco	220 00
19—Miners of Wild Dutchman Camp	36 50
26—Mayor of Salt Lake City, from R. J. Cone	841 95
26—Mayor of Salt Lake City	214 50
27—Park City Mining Camp	133 90
29—Miners of Stockton	86 00
Total	$2,774 70

VIRGINIA.

Aug. 28—W. R. Quarles, Richmond	$100 00
28—Citizens of Alexandria	109 00
29—Richmond & P. R. R	25 00
29—W. R. Quarles, Richmond	250 00
29—Howard Ass'n, Norfolk	300 00
29—Howard Ass'n, " for Grenada	200 00
29—T. H. Arnold, Bufordsville	5 00
29—J. W. Arnold, Bufordsville	5 00
29—Lodge No. 13, Staunton	25 00
Aug. 29—W. L. Balthes, mayor, Staunton	$150 00
29—W. R. Quarles, Richmond	400 00
Sept. 2—City of Alexandria	59 75
2—City of Alexandria, for Grenada	50 00
2—City of Lynchburg	100 00
2—City of Tazewell C. H., for Grenada	7 00
2—Guests and propr's White Sulphur Springs	100 00
2—R. W. Newsom, Mont White Sulphur Springs	25 00
4—City of Abington	51 30
4—City of Abington, for Vicksburg	51 00
4—City of Abington, for New Orleans	51 00
4—City of Abington, for Grenada	51 00
6—W. G. Venable, Falmouth	80 00
6—W. G. Venable, " for Grenada	40 00
6—W. G. Venable, " " Vicksburg	40 00
7—2d Pres. Ch., Bristol	29 10
7—Citizens of Charlottesville	282 00
8—Fairfield C. H., thro' M H. Wells	50 35
9—Disbursing Com., Fredericksburg	166 00
9—City of Staunton	56 80
9—Stonewall brigade band, Staunton	65 00
10—City of Harrisonburg, thro' C. C. Strayer	100 00
10—A lady of Leed's Ch., Fauquier Co., thro' C. C. Strayer, for Grenada	46 75
10—Citizens of Alexandria	111 25
10—Citizens of Glade Springs	36 75
10—Citizens of Christiansburg	63 00
11—Miss Maggie B. Jones, Danville	236 00
11—W. R. Quarles, Richmond	200 00
13—City of Lexington	250 00
13—Pro. Ent'mt Mont White Sulphur Springs	100 00
13—J. Eichberg, for Hebrew Society, Alexandria	25 00
14—W. R. Quarles, Richmond	250 00
17—A few Masonic friends, Matthews C. H.	10 00
17—Howard Ass'n, Norfolk	700 00
17—Lt. C. Chase, U. S. A., Norfolk	55 00
17—St. Stephen's Epis. Ch., Culpepper, for Holly Springs	55 00
18—Stonewall brigade band, Staunton	108 50
18—Thos. J. Goodwyn, Fincastle	50 00
18—Citizens of Salem	50 00
19—Citizens of Covington	70 00
19—W. R. Quarles, Richmond	200 00
20—Ladies' Aid Society, Liberty	10 00
20—Baptist Sunday-school, Liberty	16 00
20—W. L. Balthes, Staunton	55 75
20—South Side Masonic Lodge, 191, Pampalia City	11 75
20—W. R. Quarles, Richmond	100 00
21—Knights of the Crescent, Danville	25 00
21—Citizens of Nottaway County	72 74
21—Y. M. C. A., Norfolk	185 00
21—Citizens of Rockingham Co., thro' C. C. Strayer	148 39
22—G. W. Carroll, Lynchburg	100 00
22—Mansfield & Loyd, Lynchburg	25 00
22—Citizens of Lynchburg	75 00
22—Citizens of Rappahannock Station	29 00
23—White and col'd citizens of Alexandria	55 50
23—W. R. Quarles, Richmond, for Moscow	100 00
23—W. R. Quarles, Richmond, for Williston	100 00
23—W. R. Quarles, Richmond, for Grand Junction	100 00
24—Catholic Ch., Lynchburg	93 00
24—Citizens of Lynchburg	11 25
25—John Gardner, Christiansburg	16 43
25—Citizens of Fairfax	20 00
26—Methodist E. Ch., Danville	76 39
26—P. B. Gravelly, Danville	25 00
27—Dr. W. E. Hoge, Bland C. H.	5 00
28—Good Templars, Fairfax C. H.	26 67
28—Rev. A. P. Gray, Lynchburg	19 78
28—Lafayette Lodge, 137, F. & A. M., Lauray	44 10
28—W. R. Quarles, Richmond	200 00
29—Church at Sulphur Springs	5 85
29—Musical club, Danville	117 45
29—Presbyterian Ch., Danville	238 40
29—Citizens of Alexandria	176 50
29—Citizens of Warrenton Junction	30 00

APPENDIX.

Sept. 29—Citizens of Gordonsville	$66 00
29—W. L. Balthes, mayor, Staunton	10 38
Oct. 1—Good Templars, Fairfax	23 75
2—Citizens of Leesburg	100 00
2—J. H. Dash, Dublin	26 15
2—St. Luke's Church, Pedlar Mills	4 77
2—Rev. P. H. Pischer	1 10
2—K. Kemper, Alexandria	151 45
2—Conway, Gordon & Garnett, Fredericksburg	58 68
2—Sunday-school of Cappahosic	5 25
5—Proceeds concert, Tazewell C. H.	59 75
5—F. G. McMillan, Mouth of Wilson	35
7—Citizens of Orange C. H	102 71
7—Y. M. C. A., Salem	36 00
9—Citizens and churches of Salem	26 55
9—Colored citizens of Salem	5 85
10—Citizens of New Market, thro' A. Henkle	25 00
11—Citizens of Harrisonburg	62 50
15—Citizens of Nottoway County	20 28
16—W. G. Venable & Bro., Farmville	57 45
23—Lodge No. 119, Sidney	5 00
23—A. St. Clair, Bluestone	5 00
29—W. L. Balthe, mayor, Staunton	44 32
31—Citizens of New Market	16 00
Nov. 15—C. C. Strayer, Harrisonburg	24 75
15—K. Kemper, mayor, Alexandria	180 00
16—Pierce Sab. School, Fincastle	11 75
Dec. 11—Citizens of Rockbridge Co., thro' C. M. Tiggatt, Lexington	132 00
13—Emanuel P. E. Ch., Dublin	6 45
20—Old Chapel, Clark Co., thro' Howard Ass'n, New Orleans	31 81
20—Citizens of Winchester, thro' Howard Ass'n. New Orleans	200 00
20—Little Girls Bazar, Winchester, thro' Howard Ass n, New Orleans	27 00
20—Citizens of Clark Co., thro' Howard Ass'n, New Orleans	50 00
Total	$9,524 55

VERMONT.

Sept. 21—Ladies of Burlington	$723 81
21—Citizens of North Bennington	75 00
25—Mrs. E. M. Barnes, Bakersfield	10 00
29—Cong. Sunday-school, Woodstock	20 50
Total	$829 31

WASHINGTON, D. C.

Sept. 6—United States Treasury	$300 00
6—United States Treasury	700 00
6—"Evening Star" newspaper, and employés	79 75
6—Government printing office, and employés	80 00
9—C. H. McAlister, Chairman	67 00
13—G. M. Lockwood, Int. Dep't	113 05
14—East Washington Relief Ass'n	75 00
18—Whiting and Moses (racers)	105 50
18—Unknown Washingtonian	5 00
18—Citizens of Washington	200 00
18—Citizens' Relief Committee, East Washington	50 00
Total	$1,775 30

WEST VIRGINIA.

Aug. 27—J. H. Hobbs, Brockermier & Co., Wheeling	$200 00
Sept. 5—Citizens of Wellsburg	50 00
6—Lutheran S S., Wheeling	8 94
6—Mrs. E. Burt & Lizzie Burt, Wheeling	5 00
9—Citizens of Hinton	14 00
9—John H. Russell, Huntington	380 00
10—Hebrew ladies of Charleston	51 00
12—City of Point Pleasant	107 00
Sept. 13—City of Guyandotte	$53 50
13—Citizens of Parkersburg	150 00
19—Citizens of Piedmont	10 85
20—Employés La Belle Iron Works, Wheeling	119 55
20—Citizens of Martinsburg	308 00
22—Hail City Boat Club, Wheeling	100 00
24—Ladies of St. Albans	24 20
28—Citizens of Piedmont	116 05
30—Ladies' Relief Ass'n, Fairmount	110 00
Oct. 1—P. B. Regleter, Bob Town	100 00
1—Relief Committee, Wheeling	700 00
1—Citizens of Moundsville	248 76
2—R. M. Stinkler, Philippi	1 00
8—Citizens of Parkersburg	50 00
Nov. 6—Collection at election polls, Fairview, thro' Plattenburg	55 00
11—Employés of Raymond Coal Co	28 00
Total	$2,990 55

WISCONSIN.

Aug. 22—D. Ferguson, Milwaukee	$500 00
25—Joseph Schlitz Brewing Co., Milwaukee	500 00
26—Guests of Draper Hall, Oconomowac	100 00
27—State officers & employés, Madison	150 00
28—Jewett & Sherman, Milwaukee	75 00
28—Jewett & Sherman, Milwaukee	25 00
31—Edward Vain, Kenosha	100 00
Sept. 2—Citizens of Watertown	100 00
2—Ladies' Benev. Ass'n, Stephens Pt	153 50
2—Shaurette Lodge, No. 92, I.O.O.F., Stephens Pt	10 00
3—City of Prairie Du Chien	40 00
4—Musical & Southside Relief Ass'n, Milwaukee	145 00
5—Citizens of Evansville	200 00
6—M. E. Church, Prairie Du Chien	6 30
6—City of Janesville and Temple of Honor	575 58
8—City of Racine	300 00
9—Baptist Church, Waukegan	10 82
9—Employés "Sentinel," Milwaukee	100 00
9—City of Burlington	84 00
10—City of Boscobel	100 00
10—Presbyterian S. S., Stephens Pt	4 00
11—"State Journal," Madison	50 00
11—R. Eberts, Fond du Lac	10 00
11—Congregational Ch., Whitewater	281 81
11—T. Z. Throwig, Plattsville	6 87
13—Citizens of Pactogue	81 00
13—Ladies' Committee, Milwaukee	27 75
13—Citizens of Jefferson	20 00
13—Citizens' Ass'n, Manitoowoc	370 00
14—Citizens of Mazomanie	76 80
14—Citizens of Beloit	83 00
14—Citizens of Elkhorn	83 00
14—Musical Entertainment, A. O. U. W., Atkinson	62 75
16—Citizens of Jefferson	50 00
16—Relief Committee, Darlington	193 15
17—Employés T. H. Chapman & Co., Milwaukee	50 00
17—R.W. Bonnee & C.J. Little, Mexico	20 00
18—Citizens of Tomah	62 00
18—Citizens of Sheboygan	200 00
18—Citizens of Ashland	70 40
18—Wauwatosa Relief Ass'n, by T. W. Hunt	160 00
19—Relief Committee, Monroe	100 00
19—Citizens of Watertown	100 00
19—Citizens of Appleton	1,000 00
19—M'ch'ts & M'f'g Ass'n, Pt. Washington	152 65
19—Citizens of Delafield	25 00
19—Mayor of Menasha	395 00
20—Volunteer Fire Co., Waukesha	75 00
20—Citizens' Relief Com., Racine	200 00
20—Dramatic Club, Geneva Lake	92 50
20—Citizens of Two Rivers	160 00
20—Citizens of Prescott	112 00
21—John B. Clark, mayor, Milwaukee	200 00
21—Choir 1st Pres. Ch., Green Bay	205 35
21—Citizens of Waukegan	100 00

APPENDIX. 359

Sept.	21—Citizens of Plattsville	$129 00	Oct.	2—Citizens of Burlington		$ 10 00
	22—Citizens of Plymouth	40 00		5—J. Hewitt & P. Jacobs, Mineral Pt.		5 50
	22—James O. Pierce, Horicon	10 00		9—P. A. Orton, Darlington		24 25
	22—Public schools, Green Bay	10 08		12—Concert, by G.W. Pratt, River Falls		104 00
	22—Citizens of Whitewater	14 75		13—J. H. Cameron. Pewaukee		10 00
	22—Citizens of Elkhorn	19 00		13—J. Dawson, Pewaukee		5 50
	22—Citizens of Plymouth	60 00		17—Wm. Hoar, Mineral Pt		1 00
	23—Proc. of Concert, Sheboygan Falls	68 40		17—Miss Eliza Fink, Mineral Pt		1 00
	25—H. G. Truman, Green Bay	1 25		23—J. H. Hewitt, Mineral Pt		2 00
	25—J. Ross, Chippewa Falls	10 85		23—Citizens of Appleton		429 00
	25—Citizens of Columbus	49 50		23—Citizens of Watertown		204 09
	25—Citizens of Oshkosh	400 00	Nov.	23—Citizens of Chippewa Falls		20 00
	25—Ogema Temple of Honor, Stephen's Point	25 00		Total		$10,592 77
	25—Citizens of La Crosse	150 00				
	25—Ladies of Schofield Mills	15 00				
	26—Son & daughter of John Arneal, Washington	5 25		**WYOMING TERRITORY.**		
	26—Citizens' Relief Com., Waukesha	346 58				
	27—G. W. Black, Lake Mills	5 00	Aug.	31—Officers U. S. Army, at Cheyenne.		$ 90 00
	27—German M. E. Church, Jefferson.	15 00	Sept.	1—Citizens of Cheyenne		168 50
	27—Fairwater Baptist Church, Ripon.	6 91		22—Proc. game of base-ball, at Ft. A. D. Russell		94 75
	28—Citizens' Relief Com., Waukesha.	8 10		27—Citizens of Laramie City		400 00
	28—Citizens of Janesville	20 35		29—M. H. Foote, Easton		122 50
	28—Citizens of Monroe	81 50				
	30—Temple of Honor, No. 82, De Pere	41 00		Total		$875 75
Oct.	1—Citizens of Bennington	70 68				

SUPPLEMENTAL REPORT OF DONATIONS RECEIVED SINCE JANUARY 1, 1879.

Jan. 20—J.H.Milliken,Weatherford,Texas, proceeds bale of cotton, sold by Kirtland, Humphreys & Mitchell, of St. Louis, Mo., in damaged condition .... $ 18 34
Feb. 15—W. O. Cox, Springfield, Mo., from children of First Baptist Church and Sunday-school..................... 3 90
21—Florence L. Royal, Big Creek,Va. 2 63
Mar. 7—J. D. Scully,treasurer, Pittsburgh. P.a., to be given to those made orphans by the epidemic of 1878. 100 00
Thos. French & Son. publishers, of New York, in September last, gave Mr. F. S. Davis, of Memphis, Tenn., one hundred dollars in cash. which, on a telegram from Dr. R. W. Mitchell, Medical Director, he invested in Leibig's Extract of Beef, and shipped same to Howard Ass'n, was received and used by them.
Mar. 11—Y. M. C. A , Newberry, S. C......... $ 7 15
11—Sam'l P. Read, Memphis, Tenn... 100 00
Brown & Brother, Winston, N. C., received October 21, and by mistake included in unknown. 202 50

APPENDIX.

CONTRIBUTIONS OF FOOD, CLOTHING, AND MEDICAL SUPPLIES.

The following is a detailed statement of the contributions of food, clothing, and medical supplies sent to the people of Memphis by the citizens of the Union, through the Howard Association:

Aug. 15—Wills & Wildberger. Memphis, stationery.
19—Clark, Johnson & Co., Memphis, 2 bbls flour.
19—Jno. H. Brand & Co., Louisville, Ky., 1 bbl and 1 bx mustard.
21—R. G. Latting, Memphis, all the soap we want.
21—Edward Allges, Shelby Co., 1 bbl apples.
21—W. J. Chase & Co., Memphis, 2 bbls meal, 2 bbls flour.
23—Citizens of Mason's Depot and vicinity, 2 bbls flour, 2 shoulders bacon, 2 bbls potatoes, 1 jug honey, 2 bbls meal, 2 lambs, 20 chickens.
23—E. H. Wathan, Caseyville, Ky., 2 bbls flour.
24—Bejac & Co., Memphis, 1 bx fans.
24—J. C. Baker, Memphis, 5 bxs tomatoes.
24—Lea & Cowan, Brownsville, Tenn., 2 bbls flour.
24—Citizens of McKenzie, Tenn., 2 bbls flour.
24—W. A. White, Covington, Tenn., 50 doz eggs.
24—A widow, Memphis, 1 lb tea.
24—Citizens' Relief Committee, Memphis, 5 doz chickens.
25—Dozier, Weyl & Co., St. Louis, Mo., 10 bxs crackers.
26—Valentine Meat Juice Works, Richmond, Va., 3 doz meat juice.
26—Wm. S. Kene & Co., Louisville, Ky., 5 bbls carbolic acid.
26—J. H. Winkleman, Memphis, 2 bbls flour, 2 bbls meal.
26—Washington Ice Co., Chicago, Ill., 1 car ice.
26—R. G. Craig & Co., Memphis, bouquets and watermelon seed.
26—Schoolfield, Hanauer & Co., Memphis, 10 bxs crackers.
26—Simon N. Jones, Louisville, Ky., 1 doz Crab Orchard salts.
26—Mrs. M. C. Blaine, Brunswick, Ga., 1 bx wines and sundries.
26—Dr. J. J. Hoskins, St. Paul, Minn., 1 bx medicines.

Sept. 1—Paul Mohr, Cincinnati, O., 3 bxs bitters.
2—R. G. Latting & Co., Memphis, 5 bxs soap.
2—Ladies of Bloomington, Ind., 1 bbl supplies.
2—Blake, Walker & Co, Chicago, Ill., 25 bxs crackers.
2—Dr. G. S. Coleman, Dallas, Tex., 1 case sulphur water.
2—Rollins, Whitcher & Co., Norfolk, Va., 1 car ice.
3—M. L. Meacham & Co., Memphis, sugar and tea.
3—E. G. Whires & Co., Metropolis, Ill., 2 bbls flour.
4—Lewis Gage & Co., Louisville, Ky., 2 sacks watermelon seed.
4—Chicago Bakery Co., 10 bbls crackers.
4—Holding & Anderson, Columbia, Tenn., 400 lbs flour.
4—From Detroit, Mich., through Toof & Co., 2 cases champagne.
5—Thos. Gibson, Wood Lawn Mills, Tenn., 8 sacks flour.

Sept. 5—Mrs. W. H. Campbell, Cincinnati, O., 1 bx clothing.
5—Dr. J. O. Hurley, Cincinnati, O., 6 medicated cloaks.
5—Ladies of Presbyterian Church, Birmingham, Ala., 1 bx preserves and fruit.
5—Louisville Coffin Co., Louisville, Ky., 60 coffins.
5—Hall & Eddy and Saw Mill Co., Louisville, Ky., 4,000 feet lumber.
6—Wm Zinsser & Co., New York City, salicylic acid.
6—Jno. Hilt & Co., Laporte, Ind., 1 car load ice.
6—Mrs. Hattie Brewster, Memphis, 8 lbs. butter.
6—J. T. Caple, Memphis, meat and potatoes.
6—Citizens of Morristown, Tenn., 58 sacks flour.
6—Ladies' Relief Ass'n, Brunswick, Ga., 1 bx supplies.
6—W. I. Walker, Chicago, Ill., 6 doz pints blue sulphur water.
6—Merchants' Exchange, St. Louis, Mo., 50 cots, 100 beds, 100 moss pillows, 200 sheets, 200 pillow slips.
6—Lovely Mount P. O., Montgomery Co., 8 bbls flour, 1 bx bacon.
8—Mrs. Nellie Balch, Golconda, Ill., 1 bx clothing.
8—Talmage Lake Ice Co., Louisville, Ky., 1 car ice.
8—Belleville Minstrels, Bell's Depot, Tenn., 2 coops chickens, 1 bbl potatoes, 1 bx eggs.
8—Chamber of Commerce, New York, 5 cases condensed milk.
8—Citizens of Mount Vernon, N. Y., 1 bx provisions.
9—Ladies of Wilmington, Del., 1 bx sheets.
9—C. C. Graham, Memphis, Tenn., 5 bbls flour.
9—Citizens' Relief Committee, Memphis, Tenn., 4 coops chickens.
9—Hance Bros. & White, Philadelphia, 5 bbls phenoline.
9—J. L. Parks, Franklin, Tenn., 4 bbls flour, 2 pkgs coffee, 9 sacks flour, 2 pkgs meat.
9—S. Levy, Allenville, Ky., 1 bbl flour, 1 bx meat.
10—Citizens of St. Joseph, Mo., 1 bx clothing.
10—Clark Bros., Detroit, Mich., 3 bbls crackers.
10—Talley & Eaton, Lynchburg, Tenn., 1 bbl apple brandy.
10—Lewis McKinnie, Alexandria, Va., 1 case brandy.
10—Citizens' Relief Committee, Memphis, Tenn., 1 coop chickens.
10—Peabody Association, St. Louis, Mo., 1 car provisions.
10—S. Levy, Allenville, Ky., 1 bbl flour, 1 bx meal.
10—Terchheimer Bros., Detroit, Mich., 1 case champagne.
10—Kentucky Distillery Co., Louisville, Ky., 2 bbls whisky.

APPENDIX. 361

Sept. 10—W. H. McCutchem, Waverly, Tenn., 18 sacks flour. 4 bbls potatoes.
10—Young men and citizens of Bell's, Tenn., 80 chickens, 95 doz eggs, 1 bbl potatoes.
10—Doolittle, Webster & Co., 2 cases wine.
13—Citizens of Courtland, Ala., 5 galls wine, 50 lbs flour, 2 coops chickens, 1 coop turkeys.
13—A. E. Scott, Ralston, Tenn., 6 sacks flour and meal, 1 sack bacon.
14—Citizens of Courtland, Ala., 10 cattle, 1 mutton, 6 sacks flour.
14—P. M. Patterson, Trezevant, Tenn., 7 coops chickens.
14—Salem Church, Atoka, Tenn., 4 bbls meal, 1 bx eggs, 1 bbl flour, 1 coop chickens, 1 bbl potatoes, 2 sacks flour and meal.
17—Sabbath School, Concord, Tenn., 105 bags flour, 35 sacks potatoes, 1 bbl potatoes, 1 sack peas, 6 sacks bacon, 5 sacks beans, 1 bx beans, 34 bags meal, 26 bags dried fruit, 24 bags onions, 1 keg onions, 3 cans butter, 3 coops chickens, 4 bbls potatoes.
18—Staunton, Va., 22 bbls flour, 3 bags potatoes, 10 pieces bacon, 3 pieces dried fruit, 3 pkgs tea, 1 jar preserves.
18—Millbrook, Va., 2 bbls flour.
18—De Paince, Va., 12 bbls flour, 1 bbl potatoes, 1 bag soap, 2 pieces meat.
18—Mount Sidway, Va., 2 bbls potatoes, 2 bbls flour, 1 bx bacon.
18—Stephen's Cave, Va., 4 bbls flour, 1 bx bacon.
18—Mount Crawford, Va., 7 bbls flour.
18—Harrisonburg, Va., 13 bbls flour, 1 bbl potatoes, 1 pkg tea.
18—Linville, Va., 19 bbls flour, 1 bbl potatoes, 8 bags potatoes, 1 piece bacon, 3 crocks butter.
18—Broadway, Va., 17 bbls flour, 1 bag meal, 1 bag onions, 6 bxs jellies, 1 bag potatoes, clothing.
18—Timberville, Va., 15 bbls flour, ½ bbl flour, 1 bbl bacon, 7 bags pota'oes, 1 bx potatoes.
18—Forrest, Va., ½ bbl flour, 4 bbls potatoes, 1 bag bacon.
18—Edinburg, Va., 22 bbls flour, 1 bbl potatoes, 1 bbl onions, 8 bags potatoes, 1 bx jellies, 1 tub lard.
18—Strasburg, Va., 12 bbls flour, 3 bxs, 2 sacks sundries.
18—Cedar Creek, Va., 13 bbls flour.
18—Newtown, Va., 2 bbls flour, 1 bbl and 1 bag potatoes.
18—Methodist Relief Association, Newtown, Va., 2 bbls flour, 1 bbl potatoes, 1 piece bacon, 1 bag onions, 6 bags potatoes.
18—Kenton, Va., 1 bx tea.
18—Mount Jackson, Va., 35 bbls flour, 11 bags potatoes, 3 bbls potatoes, 2 bxs potatoes, bacon & apple-butter.
18—Middleton, Va., 6 bbls flour, 1 keg flour, 1 ham, 1 bx sundries, 4 bags onions & potatoes.
18—Winchester, Va, 26 bbls flour, 2 bxs & 1 bbl for New Orleans.
18—Stephenson, Va., 1 bbl flour, 1 piece bacon.
18—Halltown, Va., 4 bxs supplies.
18—Summit Point, Va., 18 bbls flour, 1 bx groceries, 1 bbl sundries, 2 bbl cakes, 2 pkgs clothing, 1 bx bacon, 2 bxs eggs, 1 bx sundries, 1 bx flour, 1 bx clothing.
18—Summit Point, Va., for Grenada, 1 bx cheese, 1 pkg clothing, 1 bx potatoes, 1 sack meat.
18—Statesville, Va., 9 bbls flour.
18—Charleston, Va., 106 bbls flour, 1 bx tea.
19—Allensville, Ky., 7 bbls flour, ½ bbl lard, 1 sack bacon, 1 sack potatoes, 1 bx bacon, 1 bx eggs.
19—John L. Moore, Quincy, Ill., 1 bbl wine.
20—Elkton Relief Committee, Elkton, Ky., 1 bx flour, 1 bx bacon, 1 bx potatoes.
20—Ladies of Wilmington, Del., 1 bx clothing.
21—A. M. Connett, Lebanon, Ky., 6 mattresses and pillows.

Sept. 22—Relief Com., Marion Co., Ky., through L. A. Spaulding, of Lebanon, Ky., 4 bbls potatoes, 7 bbls flour, 2 bbls meal.
22—Ladies of Elgin, Ill., through C.R.Collins, 1 spread. 26 skirts, 13 aprons, 15 nightdresses, 83 dresses, 11 waists and sacques. 19 chemisettes, 30 pr stockings, 1 overcoat, 11 coats, 15 vests, 12 pants, 19 drawers, 4 towels, 53 shirts, 8 pr hose, boots and shoes, 23 sheets, 31 pillowslips, 2 comforts.
22—Friends of Memphis, at White Pine, Tenn., 7 sacks flour, 3 sacks potatoes, 1 sack bacon.
22—Citizens of Peoria, Ill., through Mayor Warner, 161 bu potatoes, 132 bu onions, 7 bbls beans, 475 sacks flour, 240 sacks meal, 9 bxs bacon.
22—Relief Com., Will's Point, Texas, through T. D. Stearn, 11 sacks flour, 90 half sacks flour.
22—Ladies of Peckskill,N.Y.,through Eliza N. Ferr.s, 1 bx clothing.
22—Citizens of Fond du Lac, Wis., 82 bbls flour.
22—Citizens of Hollow Rock, Tenn., 2 coops chickens.
23—Ladies of Easton, Pa., 41 mattresses, 7 bxs supplies. Mrs. Sam'l & S. P. Way, 1 bx provisions, wine, jellies & clothing. Bonsack & Kiser, Bonsack, Va., 64 bbls flour. Coffin M'f'g Co., Richmond, Ind., 4 burial cases.
24—Citizens of Garrettsville, O., 2 bxs clothing.
24—Citizens of Dallas, Texas, 220 half sacks flour.
25—Citizens of Franklin, Tenn., 24 pkgs flour and meat.
26—W. L. Cabell, Dallas,Tex.. 20,000 lbs flour.
26—W. J. Walker, Chicago, Ill., 1 bbl Blue Sulphur Water.
26—Mrs. A. B. Fitch, 1 bx clothing.
26—Wm.Woodruff,London, Ont., 45 blankets.
26—Miss Marland, Cleveland, O., 1 bx provisions.
26—L. Caillet, Creston, Iowa, 1 bx clothing & supplies.
26 W. H. Donset, St. Louis, 5 cans oatmeal, 1 keg farina, 10 cans peaches, 50 bxs crackers,4 bxs shoulders, 10 bxs canned beef, 13 bbls flour, 30 bbls potatoes, 20 bbls onions, 5 bbls grits.
27—Citizens of Indianapolis,Ind.,27 bbls flour, 5 bbls meal, 8 bbls crackers, 4 bbls beans, 2 bbls potatoes, 2 bbls salt, 2 bags dried apples, 2 half chests tea, 6 bags potatoes, 4 hams, 6 bbls pork, 1 bbl bacon, 1 bx bacon, 1 kit fish, 1 bag flour, 7 bbls bread.
27—Citizens of Elmo, Texas, 62 half sacks flour, 9 sacks flour.
27—Guild of St. Luke's Church, Plattsmouth, Neb., 1 bx bed clothing.
27—Citizens of Bangs, Va., 20 bbls flour.
27—Southern Relief Com., through W. H. Purse (no city named), 20,000 lbs cornmeal, 500 lbs flour, 2 kits mackerel, 3 pkgs dried fruits.
28—Ladies of Battle Creek, Mich., 1 bx delicacies
28—Scientific Ass'n,Atlanta, Ga., 1 bx honey, 1 bx wine, 1 dem wine, 1 bbl crackers, 2 bbl flour, 12 sacks flour, 2 bxs drugs & clothing.
29—H. K. Thurbur, New York, 12 ca cs port wine.
29—Committee at Newport, Tenn., 4 sacks flour, 2 sacks meal, 2 sacks fruit, 2 half flour, 1 sack onions, 1 bbl potatoes, 2 bags peaches.
29—Order of the Eastern Star, and ladies of Mt. Vernon, Ind., 15 bxs fruit, 3 bxs clothing, 1 bbl potatoes, 12 bbls grits, 1 bbl flour, 4 bbls crackers.
29—A lady of Marshall, Mich., 1 pkge.
30—Ladies of Petersburgh,Va., 1 bx clothing.
30—Mrs. Jas. E. W. Wallace, Albany, N. Y., 1 bx sundries.

APPENDIX.

Oct. 1—Citizens of Glade Springs, Va., 500 lbs supplies.
1—Citizens of Greeley, Col., 200 sacks flour.
1—Congregations of Friends, Philadelphia, 1 bx clothing.
1—Ladies of Paterson, N.J., 11 cases clothing.
2—Ladies of Goldsboro, N.C., 2 bxs clothing.
2—Dallas and Lancaster, Texas, 20,000 lbs flour.
3—Wm. Woodruff, London, Ontario, 50 pair blankets.
3—Citizens of Greeley, Col., 1 car-load flour.
3—Citizens of Westfield, N. Y., 1 bx clothing and supplies.
3—Elizabethtown, East Tenn., 800 lbs flour, 4 bbls potatoes.
3—Relief Com., Leetsville, Iowa, 1 car-load supplies, for country towns around Memphis.
4—Citizens of Wauseon, Ohio, clothing and bedding.
5—Citizens of Big Lick, Va., 29 sacks flour.
5—Sabbath School, Pierceville, Ala., 100 sacks flour, 1 bx bacon.
7—E. D. Willett, 1 case clothing.
7—Citizens of Poughkeepsie, N. Y., 2 bbls clothing.
7—Ladies of Haledon, N. J., 1 bx sundries.
7—W. H. Huntington, Waterloo, Ill., 10 bbls flour.
7—Relief Association, Richmond, Ind., 92 pkgs coffins.
9—German Church, Hazleton, Ill., 8 bbls flour, 2 bbls apples.
9—Green Allen, Wolf Creek, Tenn., 100 lbs bacon, 2 bbls potatoes, 2 sacks flour.
9—J. K. Bambo, Rural Retreat, Va., 2 bbls flour, 1 sack flour, 2 pieces bacon.
10—Relief Committee, Charlottesville, Va., 20 lbs tea, 6 tins beef, 1 doz chocolate, 4 doz corn starch, 1 case wine, 7 bbls cocoa, 1 case mustard, 4 lbs mustard, 6 bbls flour.
10—J. H. Baxter, Cartersville, Ga., 2 bxs supplies.
12—Citizens of Kentland, Ind., 14 bbls flour, 4 bbls meal, 2 bbls hams, 1 bbl mess pork, 1 bbl beans, 1 case peaches, 1 case canned beef.
12—Ladies of Quincy, Ill., 2 bxs clothing.
12—Citizens of Monroe, Mich., 4 cases clothing, 1 bx smoked beef, 4 bbls crackers, 1 bbl potatoes.
13—M. B. Sadler, Centralia, Ill., 6 bbls flour.
15—From unknown, 1 bx clothing.
15—Peter Hilton, Lumbertown, N. C., 1 bx clothing.
17—Urbana, O, Wine Co., 5 cases champagne.

Oct. 17—W. L. Caball, Dallas, Tex., 60 half sacks flour.
17—Trinity University and citizens of Tehauncana, Tex., and citizens of Dallas, 45 sacks flour.
18—Albert Fischer & Co., Cincinnati, O., 7 cases canned peaches, 6 cases jellies.
18—Geo. Hofer, Cincinnati, O., 1 bbl clothing.
18—Leath Orphan Asylum, Cincinnati, O., 1 bbl clothing.
18—Sallie McGraw, Braden, Tenn., 1 coop chickens.
21—Ladies of New London, Conn., 2 bxs clothes.
22—Two ladies and two little girls, Newberry, S. C., 1 pkg clothing.
24—W. B. England, Lebanon, Ky., 1 bbl flour.
25—Geo. Hofer, Cincinnati, O., 2 bbls flour, 1 bbl pork, 1 bx sundries.
25—T. J. Seixas, South Bend, Ind., 9 bbls meal, 7 bbls and 50 lbs flour.
Nov. 6—Soda Bottling Co., Indianapolis, Ind., 1 doz bitters.
23—Laurel Band Class, Geneva Lake, Wis., 1 bx clothing.
29—Citizens of Rogersville, 6 sacks flour, 7 half sacks flour, 2 sacks meal, 1 can lard, 2 sacks potatoes, 1 sack sundries, 1 ham, 2 bbls potatoes.
29—Teachers and students Lake Shore Seminary, North East, Pa., 1 bx clothing.

CLEARING-HOUSE COMMITTEE, LOUISVILLE, KY.

Sept. 3—320 bags flour, 1 bbl rice, 1 bbl sugar, 1 tierce hams, 25 bbls potatoes, 1 case sago, 1 case tapioca, 1 bag coffee, 1 bx tea, 1 case baked beans, 1 cask bacon, 3 cases corn beef, 5 bbls crackers.
9—300 lbs roasted coffee, 4,000 paper bags, 6 doz brandy, 2 bbls white sugar, 10 bbls corn meal, 10 bbls grits, 3 tierces bacon, 1 bx tea, 2 casks Scotch ale, 3 doz extract of beef, 10 bbls crackers, 2 tierces hams, 5 bbls mess beef, 150 jugs seltzer water.
12—300 lbs roasted coffee, 50 lbs mustard, 1 bbl mustard meal, 146 cans corn beef, 5 bbls ham sausage, 9 doz extract beef, 12 doz brandy, 2 cases Scotch ale, 12 bbls crackers, 24 doz cans tomatoes, 10 bbls mess beef.
13—90 bbls potatoes, 480 bags flour.
18—4 doz boneset tonic, 60 coffins and dressed lumber, 40 coffins and caskets, 25 oz quinine, 50 clinical thermometers, 1 bbl buchu leaves.
Oct. 5—Fresh fruit.

APPENDIX. 363

SUMMARY.*

TOTAL DONATIONS RECEIVED BY STATES, AS PER DETAILED STATEMENT.

Arkansas	$ 6,690 37	Maine	$ 817 00	Oregon	$ 2,514 00
Arizona	5 00	Maryland	495 98	Pennsylvania	11,770 33
Alabama	6,281 43	Massachusetts	3,964 28	Rhode Island	6,513 00
California	29,047 30	Minnesota	2,651 77	South Carolina	6,039 66
Colorado	3,950 95	Mississippi	727 65	Texas	11,400 30
Connecticut	5,070 28	Missouri	16,891 37	Tennessee	23,847 97
Dakota	663 50	Michigan	11,200 43	Utah Territory	2,774 70
Delaware	41 02	Montana	987 00	Virginia	9,521 55
Florida	1,516 83	Miscellaneous	9,607 18	Vermont	829 31
Georgia	11,414 34	Nebraska	4,509 41	Washington, D. C.	1,775 50
Illinois	52,307 60	Nevada	1,374 94	West Virginia	2,990 55
Indiana	13,787 69	New Hampshire	1,607 50	Wisconsin	10,592 77
Indian Territory	5 00	New Jersey	3,983 67	Wyoming	875 75
Iowa	6,407 58	New Mexico	134 30		
Kansas	6,559 67	New York	56,804 16	Total	$400,412 54
Kentucky	8,810 52	North Carolina	7,190 76		
Louisiana	1,427 15	Ohio	26,029 72		

CASH RECEIPTS AND DISBURSEMENTS.

1878.		1878.	
April 1—To am't in Secretary's hands.	$ 22 50	Dec. 31—To interest on bonds	$ 1,211 00
Aug. 31—To proceeds sale of $15,000 U.S. bonds	15,890 62	31—To donations, per exhibit "A"	400,412 54
		Total	$417,536 66

CREDITS.

1878.		1878.	
Dec. 31—By amount paid to nurses	$185,666 52	Dec. 31—By expense account	$ 14,636 88
31 By amount paid for supplies	74,432 01	31 By transportation and livery account	10,265 12
31—By amount paid for drugs and medicines	39,233 95	31—By burial account	10,520 50
31—By amount paid to physicians	39,225 80	31—By infirmary account	4,220 50
31—By donations to other points	19,457 05		
31—By amount paid, board, physicians, and nurses	18,131 30	Total	$415,790 53
		Balance on hand	$1,746 13

MEMPHIS, TENN., *December* 31, 1878.

J. H. SMITH, *Secretary.*
JOHN JOHNSON, *Treasurer.*

*The following statement is as near correct as is possible. The world at large contributed for the people of all the stricken States of the South, during the prevalence of the epidemic of 1878, $4,548,703 as follows:

Alabama	$68,920	Indian Territory	$ 916	New Hampshire	$ 6,920	West Virginia	$13,912
Alaska	375	Iowa	48,120	New Jersey	36,988	Wisconsin	46,163
Arizona	4,750	Kansas	22,535	New Mexico	1,175	Wyoming	2,859
Arkansas	37,446	Kentucky	169,052	New York	679,340	Canada	11,126
California	132,118	Louisiana	189,639	North Carolina	33,727	Foreign countries	164,811
Colorado	21,186	Maine	19,621	Ohio	196,298	U.S. Government	100,0.0
Connecticut	40,275	Maryland	86,022	Oregon	11,041	Miscellaneous	5,015
Dakota	15,332	Massachusetts	149,256	Pennsylvania	248,090	R. R. transportation, free	285,000
Delaware	28,936	Michigan	40,671	Rhode Island	14,845	Express Companies, free	255,000
Dist. of Columbia	39,981	Minnesota	28,235	South Carolina	60,242	W. U. Telegraph Co., free	44,000
Florida	25,615	Mississippi	119,675	Tennessee	145,882		
Georgia	113,684	Missouri	199,353	Texas	139,529	Grand total	$4,548,703
Idaho	1,050	Montana	2,611	Utah	5,522		
Illinois	192,845	Nebraska	15,191	Virginia	80,145		
Indiana	117,826	Nevada	9,681	Vermont	11,125		

AUDITING COMMITTEE'S REPORT.

To the President, Directors, and Members of the Howard Association of Memphis, Tenn.:

GENTLEMEN,—Your auditing committee beg leave to present herewith their report for the six months commencing July 1st and ending December 31st, 1878.

Your committee would state that the reason that no audited accounts were rendered at our quarterly meeting, October 1st, was on account of the prevalence of the yellow fever, and the utter impossibility to spare the time from the afflicted to investigate and audit accounts.

Your committee examined very carefully the books of the Secretary and Treasurer. We noted carefully the receipts, and compared the disbursements with the vouchers; and when it is considered that there are more than eight thousand vouchers for nurses alone, you, gentlemen, can form some idea of the magnitude of the work.

Your committee was surprised to find so few clerical errors in the accounts, when it is remembered that the Secretary and Treasurer received over four hundred thousand dollars in less than three months, from all parts of the United States and Europe, in sums ranging from fifty cents to one thousand dollars, and paid it out in the same manner.

Your committee very carefully examined to see if the proper credits had been given, and from what source received, and find, with but few exceptions, that they have been credited to the States from which received. There were hundreds of dollars received from individuals who were either too modest or who forgot to give their names, all of which appear in the miscellaneous receipts. Of the disbursements, we find vouchers to correspond with each amount disbursed. Your committee consider it wonderful that accounts balanced so well, when it is remembered that the Treasurer died at his post of duty October 1st, and the Secretary was struck down October 11th, and others had to fill their places.

Your committee take great pleasure in testifying to the correct condition in which they found the books of the Association, when we consider the amount of labor required, the amount of money handled, and the amount of business generally transacted by the officers of the Association in such a short space of time.

The Auditing Committee think proper to state, to those not familiar with the magnitude of the work done by the Association during the past year, that we have had in our employ over two thousand nine hundred nurses, and have furnished supplies to more than fifteen thousand persons.

Your committee would report the financial condition of the Association as follows, to-wit:

1878.
```
July  1—Cash in hand of Secretary..................................$      22 50
      1—U. S. bonds.................................................   38,200 00
Aug. 31—Premium and interest on $15,000 bonds sold..........          890 62
Dec. 31—Interest on bonds.........................................    1,211 00
         Donations received.......................................  400,412 54

         Total...................................................$440,736 66
         Expenditures as per Secretary and Treasurer's account....$415,790 53

         Balance.................................................  $24,946 13
         Which consists of cash on hand..........................$ 1,746 13
         U. S. bonds.............................................  23,200 00

                      Total......................................  $24,946 13
```

Your committee find the account of J. H. Smith, Secretary, and John Johnson, Treasurer, as follows:

SECRETARY AND TREASURER'S REPORT.

1878.
July 1—Balance in hand of Secretary..................$ 22 50
Aug. 31—To proceeds of sale of $15,000 U. S. bonds....   15,890 62
Dec. 31—To interest on bonds..........................   1,211 00
        To donations as per Exhibit A................. 400,412 54

Total...$417,536 66

CREDITS.

1878.
Dec. 31—By amount paid to nurses......................$185,666 52
        By amount paid for supplies...................   74,432 91
        By amount paid for drugs and medicines........   39,233 95
        By amount paid to physicians..................   39,225 80
        By amount paid donations to other points......   19,457 05
        By amount paid board physicians and nurses....   18,131 30
        By amount paid expense account................   14,636 88
        By amount paid transportation and livery......   10,265 12
        By amount paid burial account.................   10,520 50
        By amount paid infirmary account..............   4,220 50

Total...$415,790 53

Balance in hand....................................... $1,746 13

Your committee would report that the difference between our report of the financial condition and the Secretary and Treasurer's report, arises from the fact that the $38,200 in U. S. bonds was in charge of bond committee, and safely deposited at the German National Bank. Fifteen thousand dollars of bonds being sold, the proceeds thereof went into his accounts, the remaining $23,200 being still in charge of the bond committee and deposited at the German National Bank.

All of which is respectfully submitted.

F. F. BOWEN, }
W. J. SMITH, } *Committee.*
JNO. T. MOSS, }

REPORT OF DR. R. W. MITCHELL,

MEDICAL DIRECTOR OF THE HOWARD ASSOCIATION.

A. D. Langstaff, President Howard Association of Memphis:

SIR,—When notified of my election to the position of Medical Director of the Howard Association, I immediately commenced the organization of a Howard Medical Corps, by securing the coöperation of most of the local physicians, in a systematic effort to supply medical attention to those sick with yellow fever.

I soon saw from the rapid progress of the disease that, unaided, we could not give the requisite attention, and requested you to call on Southern cities to assist us by sending here acclimated physicians. By acclimated I mean those who have had yellow fever. This call was promptly responded to by medical men from all parts of the United States. On reporting to me after their arrival, I was surprised to find that a majority of them had never been exposed to yellow fever.

I immediately apprised them of the great danger they incurred, and advised the unacclimated to leave the city. Less than ten took my advice and left. When they told me they were fully aware of the risk they incurred, and were determined to stay, I assigned them to duty where they were most needed.

My plan of directing their labors was to have a certain number of them to report to the local physician in a ward, and to have this subdivided into small districts, each physician being assigned to a sub-district. As the disease invaded new districts, I would re-assign those on duty with the new-comers, and in this way endeavored to keep pace with the epidemic.

My advice to every unacclimated physician who reported to me, was to put himself in the best possible condition for recovery if attacked; to accomplish all the work he could between the hours of sunrise and nightfall; to get eight hours' uninterrupted rest, and to commit no excesses of any kind. I knew that to be stricken down when exhausted mentally and physically was to insure death.

For a time I experienced great difficulty in obtaining conveyances for the use of volunteer physicians, and had to rely upon express wagons. There was one advantage in this, for the drivers were familiar with the city, and could readily take the physicians wherever they wished to go. The physicians were supplied with rubber coats and umbrellas to protect them from the weather.

Blank books were furnished to each physician employed by the Association, and he was requested to keep his book in such shape as would enable me to utilize it when we were relieved by additional assistance.

Many physicians resided in distant parts of the city, and I could not require them, after a hard day's work, to come to my office to report, and I knew they had no means of sending a report. But when the physicians fell, their records were lost sight of. My estimates, therefore, are necessarily approximations to the truth, for it was utterly impossible for me to obtain complete reports. Those who were with me can readily appreciate why, but the world can never realize our condition.

I endeavored in the beginning of our organization to obtain blank forms for reports, but before they could be issued all the printing establishments closed.

So rapidly did the disease spread that for some weeks not more than one-half the sick were seen by a physician at all, and I could not relax in my own personal attentions to the sick. Had I, however, remained to listen to all the personal appeals for help, I would not at night have moved a step from the spot I stood upon in the morning.

Mr. W. S. Pickett, who acted as my Secretary, had his whole time occupied in directing applicants where to leave messages for Howard physicians (calls were to be left at the different drug-stores in each ward). For his efficient services and ceaseless attention to all demands made upon him, I am greatly indebted.

Soon all the market-houses were deserted, and the question of nourishment for the sick became a grave one. At my request, his Excellency Governor James D. Porter sent me daily a supply of fresh beef. The continued hot weather soon made it necessary to procure live stock instead, and then a great difficulty followed in finding a butcher. To my call for one, Mr. George Whitsett responded, and I take this occasion to acknowledge his invaluable services to the public until the close of the epidemic.

The meat was cut into two-pound pieces, and supplies sent to every Howard depot. In this shape it furnished material to make broth for the sick, and also answered as food for the nurses, and was supplied on every requisition made for the sick.

All the beef and mutton which could be bought within a distance of twenty miles from the city was purchased.

Another serious difficulty encountered was the supply of medicines. All our wholesale drug-houses closed, and most of the retail houses were compelled to do the same thing on account of sickness, death, or absence of proprietors and employés. The few that remained open ran short of supplies.

I was then compelled to obtain, for a time, drugs from St. Louis, Louisville, and Nashville. Afterward, on representing the condition of affairs to Mr. W. N. Wilkerson, of the firm of Wilkerson & Co., he turned over the keys of his large drug establishment to me. Mr. C. L. Clay, of Fernandino, Florida, with four assistants, was placed in charge, and from this time there was no scarcity of medicines. All requisitions for drugs from physicians throughout the country, who were in the habit of procuring their supplies from the city, were filled. To him and his assistants are we indebted beyond measure.

As the fever extended along the line of railroads leading from Memphis, I was called upon to send physicians to other towns and villages to counsel and advise with their physicians, who were unacquainted with the fever. These calls were all responded to; and where a community was without medical aid, a physician was detailed to remain with it as long as his services were required.

After the Associated Press agent, at my request, had announced that the mortality among unacclimated physicians was so great that I would not put them on duty, they still continued to report to me.

Under these circumstances, I urged them invariably to leave the city. Even then some would go into the outskirts and work. Whenever such information was brought to me, I would send for and assign them to regular duty. I am happy to state that of those who came here in this way, though all sickened, none died.

When an epidemic becomes general in a community, the demoralization is great. Fear renders men helpless and irrational, and, in many instances, heartless.

In this epidemic, while examples of generosity, heroism, and unselfishness were abundant, yet, on the other hand, there were many instances of ties of kindred and friendship broken—friend deserted friend, parents deserted children, and husband deserted wife.

And again, when you called upon the country for help, while many excellent and worthy nurses came, others also came whose only purpose seemed to be plunder and the gratification of alcoholic thirst, and whose presence here was scarcely less destructive to human life than the plague itself.

In Southern seaboard cities, where yellow fever frequently prevails, a large proportion of the people are protected by previous attacks, and can well care for the sick; but with us the population was wholly unprotected, and consequently at the mercy of hundreds of uninformed and incompetent nurses. Under such circumstances the mortality must necessarily be great.

In New Orleans, because of the acclimation of so large a per centage of her population, while there will be six or eight out of ten to nurse their own sick, with us nineteen out of twenty were unprotected.

With all these obstacles and disadvantages, it is not to be wondered that our ratio of attack and mortality was so great. When the epidemic began to abate, I first relieved those members of the Medical Corps who had access to their homes, retaining those who could not return because of local quarantine; and when their services were no longer required, they were invited to remain as guests of the Howard Association until the removal of quarantine restrictions.

It is with pleasure I here acknowledge my grateful appreciation of the kind consideration shown me at all times, personally and officially, by the members of the Medical Corps. To their unselfish and hearty coöperation in every measure adopted, and to their intelligent and ready discharge of every duty imposed, are we indebted for whatever good results may have attended the organization and conduct of this department of the Howard Association. So noble, exalted, and single seemed to be their purpose for the general good, that all personal disappointments and discomforts were ignored, and not an incident of which I am aware was permitted to disturb the harmonious and cordial relations existing between myself and them.

In this connection, also, I am sadly reminded of those who fell by our sides in the darkest moments of our dreadful and deadly strife. They have passed beyond the reach of temporal praise or gratitude. They have gone to their reward, higher, more priceless and imperishable than man can bestow; and yet they have not gone beyond the reach of our recollection and love. Their good deeds and names survive them; their sublime lives and glorious sacrifices still live in our hearts and memories, as to which

"Time will but the impression deeper make,
As streams their channels deeper wear."

ROLL OF THE HOWARD MEDICAL CORPS

ON DUTY IN OR ASSIGNED FROM MEMPHIS DURING THE YELLOW FEVER EPIDEMIC, 1878.

1. Abercrombie, J. B., Memphis.
2. Armstrong, W.J., Memphis, died Sept. 20.
3. Bankson, J. S., Stevenson, Ala., died Sept. 16.
4. Bartholomew, O. D., Nashville, Tenn., died Oct. 8.
5. Baskerville, Chas., Horn Lake, Miss.
6. Besancny, W. F., Jonestown, Miss.
7. Bobo, B. A., Thomasville, Ga.
8. Bond, T. W., Brownsville, Tenn., died Sept. 16.
9. Boyle, Samuel, Baltimore, Md.

APPENDIX.

10. Burcham, Robt., Columbus, Ohio, died Sept. 25.
11. Brown, S. H., Memphis.
12. Bryan, L. A., Houston, Texas.
13. Bradford, G. D., Longpoint, Texas.
14. Cavanagh, W. C., Memphis, Tenn.
15. Carswell, W. A., Americus, Ga.
16. Chevis, L. A., Savannah, Ga., died Sept. 25.
17. Childs, L. B., Fisherville, Ky.
18. Coleman, W. L., San Antonio, Texas.
19. Collins, S. H., Cincinnati, Ohio.
20. Dawson, G. R., Memphis, died Sept. 24.
21. Davis, J. G., Lincoln, Nebraska.
22. Dale, J. R., Arkadelphia, Ark.
23. De Graffenried, E. F., Columbus, Ga.
24. De Saussure, P. G., Charleston, S. C.
25. De Hulin, Gordon, New York.
26. Duncan, Wm., Savannah, Ga.
27. Dowell, Greenville, Galveston, Texas.
28. Easton, Thos., New York.
29. Ess, H., Memphis.
30. Fogarty, N. J., Columbus, Ga.
31. Force, H. F., Hot Springs, Ark., died Oct. 13.
32. Forbes, J. G., Round Rock, Texas, died Sept. 24.
33. Gilzer, T. L., Mobile.
34. Gordon, John, Memphis.
35. Green, H. J., Shelby Co., Tenn.
36. Green, S. P., Memphis.
37. Gray, G. H., Dennison, Texas.
38. Gorrell, J. G. O., Ft. Wayne, Ind., died Sept. 20.
39. Hall, R. P., Mobile, Alabama.
40. Harlan, L. B., Hot Springs, Ark., died Sept. 16.
41. Hicks, J. B., Murfreesboro, Tenn., died Sept. 17.
42. Hodges, W. R., Memphis, Tenn., died Sept. 4.
43. Hunter, R. R., Kansas City, Mo.
44. Jones, Heber, Memphis.
45. Jones, P. S., Memphis.
46. Kenhue, Aug., Dayton, Ohio.
47. Keating, M. T., New York, died Sept. 17.
48. Kimbro, A. L., Memphis.
49. Laurence, A. A., Memphis.
50. Legare, J. Cecil, New Orleans.
51. Lowry, H. T., Cincinnati, Ohio.
52. Lowry, W R., Memphis, died.
53. Luppo, J., Los Angelos, Cal.
54. Meade, W. C., Hopefield, Ark., died Sept. 7.
55. Menees, T. W., Nashville, died Sept. 16.
56. Marable, J. T., Memphis.
57. Montgomery, B. R., Chattanooga, Tenn., died Oct. 9.
58. McCormick, S. H., Terre Haute, Ind.
59. McCully, W. A., Independence, Kansas.
60. McGregor, T. H., Tipton Co., Tenn., died Sept. 15.
61. McKim, J. W., St. Louis, Mo., died Sept. 9.
62. McFarland, J. T, Savannah, Ga.
63. McMillan, E. W., Memphis.
64. Nugent, P. C., St. Louis, Mo., died Sept. 14.
65. Nuttall, J. H., Memphis.
66. Orr, J. G., Cincinnati, Ohio.
67. Overall, G. W., Murfreesboro, Tenn.
68. Palmer, J. D., Fernanda, Florida.
69. Pearce, H. M., Cin., O., died Sept. 18.
70. Pittman, John, Memphis.
71. Pritchard, Maurice, Virginia City, Mo.
72. Purnell, H. W., Memphis.
73. Renner, J. G., Indianapolis, Ind., died Sept. 14.
74. Roberts, C. S., Sulphur Springs, Ky., died Sept. 28.
75. Robins, W. H., Memphis.
76. Rogers, W. E., Memphis.
77. Sample, G. F., Austin, Miss., died Sept. 6.
78. Sauvé, H. C., Hot Springs, Ark.
79. Sheftall, Benj., Savannah, Ga.
80. Sim, F. L., Memphis.
81. Simons, T. G., Charleston, S. C.
82. Smith, T. M., Rockport, Ind.
83. Snyder, S. C., Memphis.
84. Somers, T. O., Nashville.
85. Spencer, A. K., Charleston, S. C.
86. St. Clair, T. C., Vaiden, Miss., died Oct. 7.
87. Tate, R. H., Cin., O., died Sept. 21.
88. Tryon, W. A., Houston, Texas.
89. Tuerke, P., Cin., O., died Sept. 29.
90. Tucker, G. W., Dallas, Texas.
91. Webb, A., Colliersville, Tenn.
92. Wendall, A. G., Minneapolis, Minn.
93. Westbrook, J. L., Newborn, Tenn.
94. White, E. A., Memphis.
95. White, E. P., Detroit, Mich.
96. Willett, E. Miles, Memphis.
97. Winn, W. B., Memphis.
98. Williams, R. B., Woodburn, Ky., died Sept. 7.
99. Williams, T. E., Sherman, Texas.
100. Wilks, A. B., Lebanon, Tenn.
101. Woolfolk, R. F., Orange Co., Va.
102. Yates, J., Charleston, S. C.
103. Young, S. O., Houston, Texas.
104. Younge, Easton, Savannah, Ga.
105. Easley, E. T., Little Rock, Ark., died Sept. 30.
106. Heady, F., Sherman, Texas.
107. Manning, T. D., Austin, Texas.
108. McGrew, J. E., Terre Haute, Ind.
109. Logan, J. C., New Orleans.
110. White, J M., Atlanta, Ga.
111. Wise, Julius, Memphis.

APPENDIX. 369

ROLL OF VOLUNTEER HOWARD DRUGGISTS.

1. Clay, J. L., Florida, Superintendent.
2. Dieck, Albert, Cincinnati, O., died.
3. Hotchkiss, R. G., Savannah, Ga.
4. Hunter, S. W., Virginia.
5. Rollman, Otto G., Cincinnati, O.

SAMARITANS AND PHILANTHROPISTS
WHO CO-OPERATED WITH THE HOWARD MEDICAL CORPS.

1. Rev. W. T. Dalzell, M.D., D.D., Shreveport, La.
2. Judge W. Milo Olin, Augusta, Ga.

LIST OF UNACCLIMATED VOLUNTEER PHYSICIANS
IN MEMPHIS DURING YELLOW FEVER EPIDEMIC OF 1878.

NAME.	RESIDENCE.	Date of Arrival.	Date of Attack.	Period of Incubation.	Result.	Remarks.
Armstrong, W. J	Memphis		Sept. 16		Died Sept. 20	
Bankson, J. S	Stevenson, Ala	Sept. 5	Sept. 12	7 days	" Sept. 16	
Bartholomew, O. D	Nashville	Sept. 2	Sept. 16	14 days	" Oct. 8	fr.rel'pse.
Bond, T. W	Brownsville	Sept. 2	Sept. 12	10 days	" Sept. 16	
Burcham, Robt	Columbus, O	Sept. 5	Sept. 21	16 days	" Sept. 25	
Chevis, L. A	Savannah, Ga	Sept. 6	Sept. 20	14 days	" Sept. 25	
Dawson, G. R	Memphis		Sept. 14		" Sept. 24	
Easley, E. T	Little Rock	Aug. 31	Sept. 20	21 days	" Sept. 30	
Forbes, J. G	Round Rock, Tex.	Sept. 13	Sept. 20	7 days	" Sept. 24	
Force, H. F	Hot Springs	Sept. 4	Sept. 19	15 days	" Oct. 13	fr.rel'pse.
Gorrell, J. G. O	Ft. Wayne, Ind	Sept. 7	Sept. 16	9 days	" Sept. 20	
Harlan, L. B	Hot Springs	Sept. 4	Sept. 11	7 days	" Sept. 16	
Hicks, J. B	Murfreesboro	Sept. 8	Sept. 14	6 days	" Sept. 17	
Heady, F	Sherman, Tex	Sept. 7	Sept. 21	14 days	" Sept. 22	
Hodges, W. R	Memphis		Sept. 1		" Sept. 4	
Keating, M. T	New York	Sept. 21	Oct. 14	23 days	" Sept. 17	
Meade, W. C	Hopefield, Ark	Aug. 30	Sept. 1	2 days	" Sept. 7	
Menees, T. W	Nashville	Sept. 8	Sept. 12	4 days	" Sept. 16	
Manning, T. D	Austin, Tex	Sept. 5	Sept. 18	13 days	" Sept. 20	
Montgomery, B.R	Chattanooga	Sept. 12	Sept. 13	1 day	" Oct. 9	fr.rel'pse.
Lowry, W. R	Memphis					
McGregor, T. H	Tipton Co., Tenn	Sept. 5	Sept. 10	5 days	" Sept. 15	
McKim, J. W	St. Louis	Sept. 2	Sept. 5	3 days	" Sept. 9	
Nugent, P. C	St. Louis	Sept. 2	Sept. 10	8 days	" Sept. 14	
Pearce, H. M	Cincinnati, O	Sept. 5	Sept. 14	9 days	" Sept. 18	
Renner, J. G	St. Louis	Sept. 2	Sept. 10	8 days	" Sept. 14	
Robins, W. H	Memphis					
Sample, G. F	Austin, Miss	Aug. 18	Aug. 30	12 days	" Sept. 6	
St. Clair, T. C	Vaiden, Miss	Sept. 27	Oct. 3	6 days	" Oct. 7	
Tate, R. H	Cincinnati, O	Sept. 3	Sept. 16	13 days	" Sept. 21	
Tuerke, P	Cincinnati, O	Sept. 1	Sept. 26	25 days	" Sept. 29	
Williams, R. B	Woodburn, Ky	Aug. 29	Sept. 1	2 days	" Sept. 7	
White, J. M	Atlanta, Ga	Sept. 13	Sept. 26	13 days	" Sept. 30	

APPENDIX.

LIST OF UNACCLIMATED VOLUNTEER PHYSICIANS.—Continued.

NAME.	RESIDENCE.	Date of Arrival.	Date of Attack.	Period of Incubation.	Result.
Abercrombie, J. B	Memphis		Aug. 30		recovered.
Brown, S. H	Memphis				
Besancny, W. F					
Cavanagh, W. C	Memphis		Sept. 25		"
Childs, L. B	Louisville	Sept. 11	Sept. 17	6 days	"
Collins, S. H	Cincinnati, O	Aug. 31	Sept. 11	11 days	"
Dale, J. R	Little Rock	Sept. 15	Sept. 28	13 days	"
Green, H. J	Shelby Co	Sept. 2	Sept. 11	9 days	"
Green, S. P	Memphis				
Hunter, R. R	Kansas City	Sept. 2	Sept. 10	8 days	"
Kenhue, Aug	Dayton, O	Sept. 3	Sept. 17	14 days	"
Lowry, H. T	Cincinnati, O	Sept. 6	Sept. 15	9 days	"
McCormick, S. H	Saline City, Ind	Aug. 31	Sept. 7	7 days	"
Luppo, J	Los Angelos, Cal	Sept. 14	Sept. 19	5 days	"
Orr, J. G	Cincinnati, O	Sept. 8	Sept. 22	14 days	"
Overall, G. W	Murfreesboro	Sept. 2			
Pritchard, Maurice	Virginia City, Mo	Sept. 13	Oct. 4	21 days	"
Westbrook, J. L	Newborn, Tenn	Sept. 6	Sept. 13	7 days	"
White, E. P	Detroit, Mich	Sept. 20	Oct. 1	10 days	"
Woolfolk, R. F	Orange Co., Va	Sept. 26	Oct. 9	14 days	"
Winn, W. B	Memphis		Aug. 27		"

Total No. sick, 54.
Total No. died, 33, or.................... 61.11%   Shortest period incubation............ 1 day
Total No. recovered, 20, or............ 37.04%   Longest period incubation..............25 days
Total No. escaped, 1, or................. 1.85%   Average period incubation............10 days

Total.......................................100.00%

Only one physician (Dr. Keating, of New York) who reported to me as previously having had the fever died during the epidemic. No other was sick.

Only one unacclimated physician (Dr. G. W. Overall, of Murfreesboro, Tenn.) went through without contracting the fever.

My experience and observation has satisfied me of the absolute necessity of so organizing your Association as that it will be ready promptly to call into action and efficient operation all of its agencies and powers, without having to rely upon the exigencies of the moment when the plague is present doing its deadly work. Since it is probable that many years must elapse before a thorough system of sanitation can be adopted which will prevent the occurrence of yellow fever, I would recommend, as a means of saving human life, the adoption of the following measures:

1. The calling of a convention of representatives from every Howard organization in the country.

2. Organization of a permanent medical corps of physicians who have had yellow fever.

3. Enrollment of a permanent corps of nurses possessing the proper mental and moral qualifications.

4. Local Howard organizations will have their nurses enrolled with them.

5. Whenever a call for help is heard from any city in the country, each organization will be required to supply a certain number of trained physicians and nurses, and to increase this number if necessity demands it.

My report to you would be incomplete and my feelings unsatisfied if I did not, in the conclusion of our official relations, give free and sincere expression to the good will entertained by myself to the general membership of your organization, and especially to my kind and warm affection for you its president.

At all times my hands have been upheld and my plans and suggestions have found a ready adoption. It is with exceeding gratification and pride that I am enabled to

APPENDIX. 371

record the fidelity and promptness which characterized the conduct of yourself and all others in the compliance with my wishes and directions. This department of your Association, as we all know, was created in the very midst of the epidemic, and in the emergency of the occasion it was necessarily difficult to establish and conduct it as a perfect organization, and yet, with all of its embarrassments and difficulties, I am happy to say that I found you and your members ready, willing, and active in every thing to aid and support me. A fraternal feeling between us has thus been engendered. Created as it was, in the midst of affliction and danger, I trust it may long survive even the recollection of its sorrowful origin.

Respectfully, R. W. MITCHELL, M. D.

REPORT OF THE SUPERINTENDENT OF NURSES.

A. D. LANGSTAFF, President Howard Association:

DEAR SIR,—I herewith hand you a brief statement of the Nurse Department of the Howard Association, to which I was assigned as Superintendent during the late epidemic. The whole number of nurses employed, as shown by the register, was 2,995. Of these 529 were volunteers from points outside of the city of Memphis. I append a statement showing the residence and sex of all the nurses from abroad, who reported to me as such, with a list of their names.

NUMBER OF NURSES FROM OTHER STATES AND CITIES.

	Males.	Females.		Males.	Females.
Augusta, Georgia	6		Knoxville, Tennessee	1	3
Austin, Texas	2	2	Kentucky	1	
Arkadelphia, Arkansas	1		Louisville, Kentucky	13	2
Brunswick, Georgia	1		Little Rock, Arkansas	32	6
Brenham, Texas	7		Mobile, Alabama	13	30
Brownsboro, Alabama	1		Marshall, Texas	5	
Baldwin County, Alabama	1		Macon, Georgia	2	
Bowling Green, Kentucky	1		Macomb City, Mississippi	...	1
Baltimore, Maryland	1		Milwaukee, Wisconsin	...	1
Charleston, South Carolina	15	24	New Orleans, Louisiana	25	20
Cairo, Illinois	1		Nashville, Tennessee	10	6
Cobb County, Georgia	1		New York City, New York	5	2
Cincinnati, Ohio	9	1	Newark, Ohio	1	
Columbus, Texas	1		Norfolk, Virginia	16	2
Chicago, Illinois	5	1	Natchez, Mississippi	1	
Cleveland, Tennessee	1		Newport, Arkansas	2	
Corpus Christi, Texas	1		New Haven, Kentucky	1	
Chillicothe, Ohio	1		New Brunswick, New Jersey	1	
Collierville, Tennessee	2		Ohio	1	
Cleveland, Ohio	1		Omaha, Nebraska	...	1
Covington, Kentucky	1		Portsmouth, Virginia	1	
Charlotte, North Carolina	1		Port Royal, South Carolina	3	4
Dallas, Texas	8	5	Pittsburgh, Pennsylvania	1	
Dennison, Texas	1		Paducah, Kentucky	1	
Dayton, Ohio	1		Pine Bluff, Arkansas	1	1
Detroit, Michigan	1		Paris, Texas	2	
Fort Worth, Texas	6	1	Richmond, Virginia	1	
Fernandina, Florida	9		Round Rock, Texas	5	1
Franklin, Tennessee	1	1	Roswood, Indiana	1	
Galveston, Texas	2	1	Savannah, Georgia	15	14
Grand Junction, Mississippi	...	1	St. Louis, Missouri	16	9
Hot Springs, Arkansas	16	2	Shreveport, Louisiana	31	5
Houston, Texas	14	9	Sherman, Texas	2	1
Hamilton, Ohio	1		San Francisco, California	1	
Helena, Arkansas	1	1	San Antonio, Texas	2	
Horn Lake, Mississippi	1		Terre Haute, Indiana	...	1
Hartford, Connecticut	1		Tuskegee, Alabama	1	
Hopkinsville, Kentucky	1		Vicksburg, Mississippi	3	
Indianapolis, Indiana	1		Victoria, Texas	1	
Jackson, Mississippi	4		Washington, District of Columbia	9	7
Jackson, Tennessee	1		Wilmington, North Carolina	3	
Jackson, Michigan	1				
Jacksonville, Florida	...	1	Total	362	167

NAMES OF NURSES FROM OTHER STATES AND CITIES.

Augusta, Ga.
Blair, Peter.
Bunch, John M.
Hitchcock, Ed.
Jones, William.
Jones, James.

Austin, Tex.
Davis, Mrs. Kate.
Ford, Mrs. Emily.
Ford, J.
Jones, Emanuel.

Arkadelphia, Ark.
Thomasson, C. R.

Brunswick, Ga.
Wallace, J. W.

Brenham, Tex.
Carpenter, Charles.
Estes, B. F.
Gaylord, G. G.
Jodon, F. D.
Jackson, W. J.
McIntyre, Frank.
McIntyre, Willie.

Brownsboro, Ala.
Williams, Andy.

Baldwin Co., Ala.
Booth, Thomas J.

Bowling Green, Ky.
Govin, Eugenie.

Baltimore, Md.
Phoebus, J. W.

Charleston, S. C.
Bull, Miss J. D.
Boniface, Mrs. C.
Burrows, Mary.
Daly, Mrs. Mary.
Doran, Mrs. Mary.
Dawson, Miss Mary.
Hayes, Mrs. Mary.
Myatt, Mrs. M. J.
McArn, Mrs. Mary.
Ryan, Mrs. Mary.
Sayres, Mrs. Ann.
Silvery, Mrs. Sarah.
Thrower, Miss Sarah.
Forrestine, Mrs. Sarah.
Brown, Matilda.
Walsh, Kate.
Lewis, Nancy.
Johnson, Henrietta.
Harman, Mrs. M.
Forrestine, Mrs. Sarah A.

Johnson, Mrs. Margaret.
Murdock, Miss Daisy.
Campbell, Mrs. J. C.
O'Donnell, Mrs. B.
Boyce, J. C.
Boniface, Lewis.
Ancrum, John.
Donaue, J. B.
Daly, Ely.
Green, Henry.
Habbinett, A.
Halsey, M. P.
Myatt, Lewis.
Montgomery, E.
Tobias, Arthur W.
Mathews, J. C.
Hare, T. S.
Eberhardt, C. H.
Johnson, Benj.

Cairo, Ill.
Hare, Filo S.

Cobb Co., Ga.
Proudfoot, J. R.

Cincinnati, O.
Mendelson, Phœbe.
Uphoof, John.
Deike, Albert.
Seager, William.
Weiter, Fred.
Graham, Wm. H.
Orr, J. G.
Ahern, Michael.
Woodington, E. J.

Columbus, Tex.
Kautzer, F.

Chicago, Ill.
Ainslie, Mrs.
LeVin, L. J.
Van Hame, W. C.
Heidelberg, Louis.
Shelden, N. E.
Biggs, Geo. L.

Cleveland, Tenn.
Beard, John H.

Corpus Christi, Tex.
Clark, W. S.

Chillicothe, Ohio.
Howard, James.

Collierville, Tenn.
Hill, W. H.

Cleveland, Ohio.
McCavesy, F.
Wright, A. D.

Covington, Ky.
Pillman, W. A.

Charlotte, N. C.
Waring, R. P., Jr.

Dallas, Tex.
Yarborough, Harriet.
Booth, Mrs. S. J.
Henry, Mrs. S. F.
Albertson, Mrs. L.
Ridley, Mrs. M. J.
Hock, William.
McGoupf, Beverley.
Marcusy, E.
Solomon, Nicholas.
Page, E.
Marchant, C.
Fox, John.
Sweeney, W. J.

Dennison, Tex.
Flynn, John R.

Dayton, Ohio.
Huesman, F. R.

Detroit, Mich.
Sheridan, W. H.

Fort Worth, Tex.
Mann, Mrs. J. B.
Booth, J. W.
Ibeck, Julius.
Verschoyle, Charles H.
McClellan, W. H.
Wiskerman, W. C.

Fernandina, Fla.
Dupree, Bristow.
Williams, Henry G.
Stafford, Perry.
Mann, Charles G.
Robinson, Bart.
Ballard, George.
Clay, John L.
Stiles, Julian.
Day, John L.

Franklin, Tenn.
Foys, Mrs.
Foys, Mr.

Galveston, Tex.
O'Bryan, Mrs. O.
Parker, G. G.
Breedlove, J. W.

APPENDIX. 373

GRAND JUNCTION, MISS.
Davis, Mrs. C. E.

HOT SPRINGS, ARK.
Donnelly, Mrs. Hattie.
Harcourt, Mrs. M. A.
Jones, S. M.
Lee, Charles E.
Collins, Tom.
Reinhardt, John.
Burch, Stephen.
Scully, Patrick.
Buniff, B. F.
Mannings, Richard.
Cook, Major F.
Mukes, Mark.
Rollins, Dan.
Madison, H. M.
Johnson, J. H.
Gaines, Charles.
Hudson, James.
Richardson, G. L.

HOUSTON, TEX.
Wright, Mrs. Mary.
Heckle, Mrs. E. K.
Burt, Mrs. Mary L.
Warren, Mrs. Maria.
McCloskey, Mrs. M. D.
Bliss, Mrs. M. E.
Smith, Mrs. C. A.
DePelchin, Mrs. K.
McDonald, Mrs. M.
Wright, W. H.
Salm, J.
Owen, Thomas.
Bohm, R. H.
Brenner, John.
Bookmeyer, H.
Bertallot, A.
Bradford, A.
Eberle, George.
Jenore, Augustus.
Laertz, Herman.
Miller, John E.
Schwartz, C. T.
White, John.

HAMILTON, OHIO.
Riley, James.

HELENA, ARK.
Cleaveland, Mrs. L. J.
Cleaveland, W. C.

HORN LAKE, MISS.
Lane, A. C.

HARTFORD, CONN.
Brooks, H. W.

HOPKINSVILLE, KY.
Hamill, W. E.

INDIANAPOLIS, IND.
Evans, Charles.

JACKSON, MISS.
Burnes, John.
Wood, L. H.
Sheffield, T. J.
Donnell, George S.

JACKSON, TENN.
White, Z. T.

JACKSON, MICH.
Bernard, B. W.

JACKSONVILLE, FLA.
McClure, Miss M. L.

KNOXVILLE, TENN.
Stone, Melinda.
Payne, Mary.
Levere, Mrs. Rosetta.
Gilbert, Tom.

KENTUCKY.
Putnam, S. G.

LOUISVILLE, KY.
Carelton, Mrs.
Ames, Mrs. M.
Adams, Franklin R.
Roberts, C. S.
Smith, B. P.
Winters, J.
Schmidt, John.
Humphreys, Warren.
Lindo, W. H.
Byrd, J. Edgar.
Hood, E.
Kelley, James P.
Patterson, J. A.
Smeck, Jackson.
Traynor, Thomas.

LITTLE ROCK, ARK.
Jones, Mrs. Emma L.
Baer, Mrs. A. A.
Smith, Mrs. Amelia.
Jones, Mrs. Rossi.
Munn, Mrs.
McCleary, Mrs. M. J.
Baer, A. A.
Taylor, C. L.
Fabin, John W.
Bungener, Ferd.
Schmidt, Louis.
Reéd, A. F.
Boush, William.
Hunt, John.
White, A. L.
Rhodes, A. T.
Going, Sam. B.
Benner, F.
Breding, Charles.
Carr, T. J.
Dickinson, J. W.
Egan, Joe.
Forbish, E. E.
West, John M.

Hoit, Gustav.
Vogel, Abe.
Kruner, Martin.
Vogel, Moses.
Mead, John W.
Taylor, E. D.
Manning, T. M.
Trigg, J. M.
Moseby, Henry.
Thompson, Charles.
Richardson, John.
Schmelig, H.
Robinson, John.
Bort, Phil.

MOBILE, ALA.
Bass, Mrs. Sophie.
McWhorter, Mrs.
Cassimere, Miss Jennie.
McGonnegal, Mrs. E.
McDonald, Mrs.
Ward, Mrs. C. M.
James, Mrs. Amelia.
Ballondi, Mrs.
Hicks, Mrs. N. M.
Stone, Mrs. Agnes.
Hamilton, Miss E. M.
Bell, Mrs. Annie.
Ford, Mrs. Mary.
Brady, Mrs. Ellen.
Roesler, Mrs. Theresa.
Myer, Mrs. F.
Horton, Mrs. S.
Boyle, Mrs. R.
Fallon, Mrs. M.
McLain, Mrs. C.
Brown, Mrs. E.
Campbell, Mrs. R.
Makin, Mrs. C.
Stringer, Mrs. Mary.
Garvin, Mrs. Mary.
Moore, Mrs. Mary.
Weed, Mrs. H. M.
Connor, Mrs.
Miles, Mrs.
Pallo, Mrs. Mary.
Hicks, N. M.
Bowman, R. H.
Wyman, L. W.
Burke, H. M.
Crawford, R.
Conroy, Thomas.
Gibbons, William.
Heppler, G. A.
Myers, F.
Reeves, R.
Watson, G. S.
Walthall, Major W. T.
Walthall, W. T., Jr.

MARSHALL, TEX.
Pendleton, Ed.
Baker, Ezra.
Bevins, Lee.
Curry, Harry.
Pounder, Frank.

APPENDIX.

Macon, Ga.
Foster, C. W.
Jones, H. V.

Macomb City, Miss.
Drury, Mrs. M.

Milwaukee, Wis.
Sely, Mrs. Charles.

New Orleans, La.
Edwards, Mrs.
Murphy, Mrs. R.
Cearney, Mrs. Alice.
Clark, Mrs. Kate.
Simpson, Mrs. E. A.
West, Mrs. Sarah.
Roosevelt, Mrs. M. E.
Beakley, Mrs.
Hamilton, Mrs.
Harrison, Mrs. Alabama.
Polonio, Mrs. L.
Dolhonde, Mrs. C.
Dolhonde, Mrs. Annette.
Kelley, Mrs.
Portonic, Eroga.
Hill, Mrs. Mary S.
King, Mrs. Mary.
Mead, Mrs. Lorena.
Lovell, Mrs. Nellie.
Shepperd, Mrs.
Wild, Jacob.
Picot, J. T.
Dwyer, James.
Getty, J. H.
Luddy, John.
Wilson, E.
Negle, John.
Hunter, J. C.
Scully, Pat.
Brady, John.
Cuff, M. J.
Romhelt, George.
Welsh, F.
Altmeyer, J. L.
Tumblety, Dennis F.
Schultz, William.
Sullivan, Pat.
Williams, John.
Lashley, L. C.
Maudeville, G. A.
West, Charles.
Heider, Fred.
Fields, C. H.
Stearns, John E.
Grosjean, Henry.

Nashville, Tenn.
Cole, Miss Emma.
Davis, Mrs. C
Hughes, Clara.
Knight, Priscilla.
Mulvin, Mrs.
Dismukes, Mrs. E.
Miller, John.

Ralston, Thomas.
Hearn, Michael A.
Meyers, Fred.
Perry, John H.
Williams, R. H.
Leonard, Martin.
Jones, B. P.
Butler, John.
Jarvis, W. J.

New York City.
Haldrum, Miss Annie.
Bocking, Mrs. Mary.
Malmont, August.
Blakesly, Robert.
Hildermandt, B.
Ludlow, T. W.
Urban, T.

Newark, O.
Probert, Geo. C.

Natchez, Miss.
Ashby, Robert,

Norfolk, Va.
Graves, Mrs. L.
Garris, Mrs.
Mordecai, P. M.
Parker, James.
Dickson, W. H.
Allendorf, Geo.
Herbert, J. L.
Elliot, Thos.
Tomkins, J. J.
Dashields, F. S.
Berry, N. W.
Hunter, G. W.
Merton, C.
Webb, Geo.
Cuthrell, Wm.
Harrison, H. C.
Roche, James.
Hustmell, W.

Newport, Ark.
Ballauf, Edward.
Reudel, Fred.

New Haven, Ky.
Blincoe, J. H.

New Brunswick, N. J.
Mitchell, George H.

Ohio.
Gimo, Lorenz.

Omaha, Neb.
Clark, Mrs. J. W.

Portsmouth, Va.
Kiesele, Charles,

Pittsburgh, Pa.
Aler, P.

Port Royal, S. C.
Southmate, Mrs. Sarah.
Stickley, John.
Alston, Maria.
Jackson, Sarah.
Harrison, G. S.
Akins, Adelia.
Gaillard, J.

Paducah, Ky.
Dixon, Lu.

Pine Bluff, Ark.
Ward, H. S.
Ward, Mrs. H. S.

Paris, Tex.
Grimes, M.
Fields, Robert.

Richmond, Va.
Russell, T. L.

Round Rock, Tex.
Saloi, Mrs. P.
Saloi, Capt. P.
Gilbert, G. T. A.
Clifton, H.
Hart, Stephen.
Williams, John.

Roswood, Ind.
Woods, John.

Savannah, Ga.
Morehouse, Miss Anna.
Keenan, Mrs. Sarah.
Rankin, Mrs. L.
Miller, Jane.
Habersham, Matilda.
Jones, Sarah.
Gillison, Silva.
Fields, Lizzie.
McDonald, Celia.
Brown, Ella.
Brownfield, Rachel.
Barron, James A.
Tant, James C.
Fareman, William.
Baufferet, William.
Adams, James.
Burke, Sam.
Smith, Charles.
Haines, Smart.
Gaudrey, Vincent E.
Rankin, C. C.
Lynch, Mary.
Thompson, Celia.
Burton, Mrs.
Redman, M. J.
Hancock, G. W.
Cohen, D. L.
Ruhl, E. J.
Gomaz, Louis.

APPENDIX. 375

St. Louis, Mo.
Hughes, Mrs. Jane.
Sister Mary Alphonsa.
Sister Cornelia.
Sister Engelberta.
Sister Melania.
Baldenwick, Mrs.
Craffey, Mrs.
Curran, Mrs. J.
Hays, Miss Belle.
Drake, L. H.
Redwood, R. G.
Strach, Joe.
Wong, Chin Foo.
Baer, A.
Curran, J.
Alston, Henry.
Hogey, Jesse.
Brown, Jesse.
Emanuel, J. M.
Heggia, Jesse.
Jamison, E. S.
Rollman, Otto G.
Throols, T.
Vaudry, J.
Wilkins, F. G.

Shreveport, La.
Curtis, Mrs. O. L.
Pierce, Mrs. K.
Blackstone, Mrs. A.
Benton, Carrie.
Allen, Rose.
Murray, John.
Hargrove, H. H.
Blackman, A. O.
Bryson, Thomas.
Hotchkiss, Thomas E.

Smith, C. J.
Downs, Wiley.
Abbert, Augustus.
Newman, M.
Maguire, J. E.
Lyttle, N. B.
Gibilant, Philip.
Logan, John.
Logan, J. W.
Williams, J. R.
Stewart, S. A.
Muller, John.
Brown, William.
Nivoche, M. E.
Williams, Frank.
Feeney, M. A.
Cowart, W. W.
Dittmer, H.
Hotchkiss, R. E.
Dewing, W. T.
Heaton, J. K.
Kunter, J. K. C.
Pierce, K.
Schmidt, C. J.
Smith, G. G.
Stewart, S. A.

Sherman, Tex.
Rost, Mrs. Louisa.
Allingham, John S.
Bass, Thomas C.

San Francisco, Cal.
Lathrop, M.

San Antonio, Tex.
Kendall, G. A.
Sheldon, W. J.

Terre Haute, Ind.
Flannagan, Miss E. M.

Tuskegee, Ala.
Douglass, N. E.

Vicksburg, Miss.
Hays, J. B.
Bowman, Robert.
O'Flaherty, Dennis.

Victoria, Tex.
Sharkey, W. L.

Washington, D. C.
Cromwell, Mrs. N.
Elder, Mrs.
Davidson, Mrs.
Silvey, Mrs. Louisa.
Beasley, Mrs.
Dorsey, Mrs.
Wallace, Miss.
Rebstock, L.
Lowe, O.
Thompson, W. B.
Oxe, Charles,
Woodwen, D.
Babette, Charles.
Barbour, George W.
Uzell, J. D.
Davison, Mr.

Wilmington, N. C.
Bowman, J. C.
Poppe, Geo. A. A.
McCallum, James A.

I also append a statement showing the number of cases, or heads of families, registered daily, amounting to 6,041; but, as in most cases, one registration represented a whole family, I estimate the whole number of persons sick and nursed by the nurses of the Howard Association at fully 15,000.

NUMBER OF HEADS OF FAMILIES REGISTERED DAILY.

1878.		1878.		1878.		1878.	
Aug. 13	7	Sept. 3	128	Sept. 24	121	Oct. 14	41
14	4	4	113	25	95	15	42
15	28	5	148	26	79	16	52
16	32	6	159	27	78	17	33
17	29	7	198	28	102	18	41
18	32	8	127	29	82	19	21
19	25	9	109	30	103	20	58
20	16	10	99	Oct. 1	97	21	34
21	37	11	105	2	85	22	24
22	42	12	177	3	85	23	20
23	63	13	157	4	70	24	12
24	69	14	126	5	68	25	14
25	79	15	119	6	62	26	12
26	70	16	162	7	91	27	7
27	134	17	108	8	85	28	8
28	86	18	119	9	91	29	12
29	82	19	106	10	37	30	11
30	130	20	65	11	46	31	5
31	158	21	96	12	58		
Sept. 1	102	22	101	13	60	Total	6,041
2	136	23	116				

RECAPITULATION.

August..1,123
September..3,536
October..1,382

Total..6,041

APPENDIX.

The majority of the nurses and workers in my department, both those from abroad and those resident in our city, served with remarkable zeal and efficiency, displaying, under the most trying and discouraging circumstances, a heroism and fidelity to the cause of humanity unsurpassed in the history of epidemics. Many individuals, with utter disregard of personal safety, hastened to our succor from northern, eastern, and western cities. A large number of these, as well as nurses from all parts of the South, fell victims to the scourge. There were times, during the prevalence of the epidemic, when contact with the disease seemed to foreshadow almost certain death; but instances were most rare where any nurse in my department failed to respond promptly to the call of duty. Where so many fulfilled their mission so nobly and faithfully, it would be invidious, if not next to impossible, for me to designate particular individuals. I feel called upon, however, to particularly mention the following persons, with whom I came in frequent personal contact, and whose services, and the positions they filled with so much faithfulness and ability in my department, require special notice from me.

To Major W. T. Walthall, in charge of the forty-three well-trained nurses sent to our relief by the "Can't-Get-Away-Club" of Mobile, Ala., and especially to his son, a boy but sixteen years of age, for their valuable assistance in managing this corps of nurses, and other timely aid and advice, I would return my sincere thanks.

To Captain John Murray, of Shreveport, La., placed by me in charge of the nurses from Shreveport, Northern Louisiana, and Texas, numbering between fifty and sixty, for the faithful and efficient manner in which, during the whole time, he assisted me at all hours caring for our sick and suffering people (to many of whom his name will long remain a household word), and in looking after the large number of nurses under his charge, seeing that they were employed and doing good service, and at the same time ever alert for their personal comfort, is due our warmest gratitude and highest meed of praise.

Captain James A. Barron, and his assistant, James Taut, in charge of the splendid corps of nurses from Savannah, Ga.—and, indeed, their entire force of nurses—are entitled to the warmest encomiums for their uniform good nursing and general good conduct.

Mr. J. Edgar Byrd, of Louisville, Ky., detailed in charge of nurses at Collierville, Tenn.; Mr. R. A. Peebles, of Tennessee, detailed in charge of nurses at Brownsville, Tenn.; Mr. H. C. Harrison, of Norfolk, Va., placed in charge of the Norfolk nurses, are, I think, worthy of most honorable mention for their able services rendered at their respective posts.

Of the gentlemen in the different departments of my office, Major F. F. Bowen, the oldest member of the Howard Association, merits special recognition for his efficient and unremitting services, in charge of one of the most important desks, during the entire period of the epidemic.

I also desire to mention, and to return my kindest personal thanks, to Mr. H. I. Simmons, my principal clerk; to Captain Joseph Spears and Sim L. Barinds, of Memphis; to H. H. Hargrove, of Shreveport, La.; to R. P. Waring, of Charlotte, N. C.; and L. J. LeVin, of Chicago, Ill., for their most valuable assistance, rendered in the most difficult of positions, under the most trying circumstances, keeping up the records of sick cases, and aiding in assigning and placing nurses on duty at all hours of the day and night, thereby constantly exposing themselves to the most malignant cases of the dreadful disease; and to Mr. Louis Daltroof, in charge of the burial of physicians and nurses, for the prompt and satisfactory manner in which he executed this most dangerous and disagreeable labor.

It is also my duty to recognize the valuable services of W. B. Shepherd, who aided in opening and organizing the supply-store, but who soon fell a martyr to his devotion to the dangerous duty, dying after an illness of but three days, on September 17th. Also to return thanks to his successor, Mr. Alex. Gunn, of ————, Canada; Mr. Frank Frierson, F. G. Watkins, and Edward Shaw, for their arduous and unremitting labors in disbursing and taking care of the immense quantities of supplies furnished at the Main and Court Street store, under my charge; and to Mrs. Sarah H. Thompson, matron in charge of the nurses' sleeping-rooms over the Main and Court Street offices, for her uniform courtesy and good management, under the immediate supervision of Second Vice-President J. H. Edmondson, to whom I am specially indebted for much valuable assistance in my department.

To the members of the Howard Association, one and all, for their courtesy and kindness to me personally, in aiding me to discharge this, the most trying and difficult labor of my life, I beg to return my sincere thanks.

JOHN JOHNSON, *Superintendent Nurse Department.*

APPENDIX. 377

W. J. SMITH'S REPORT OF OPERATIONS AT GRENADA.

A. D. Langstaff, Esq., President of the Howard Association of Memphis, Tennessee.

SIR:—I respectfully submit for your information the following report of my experience and observations of the late pestilence at Grenada, Miss.

On Sunday, August 11, 1878, I attended Grace Church to hear the Rev. Dr. Parsons. Soon after reaching my home from church, a dispatch was brought me by the hand of the late beloved and lamented John G. Lonsdale, Jr., Esq. It was addressed "President Howard Association." Our worthy President, General G. W. Gordon, was then absent from the city recuperating his shattered health, and I being the senior officer of the Association in the city, opened the dispatch. It was from the mayor of Grenada. It announced the presence of the yellow fever in that city, and called for nurses and other assistance. I immediately had a consultation with Colonel Butler P. Anderson, and Hon. J. H. Smith, the Secretary of our Association. We hurried up town and informed all the Howards we could find of the dispatch. All were unanimous that we should furnish immediate assistance. It was now four o'clock P. M. Having obtained carriages, we searched the city to find as many as possible of our old nurses of the pestilence of 1873. Meantime some of us had met that kind-hearted and obliging superintendent of the Mississippi and Tennessee Railroad, Major M. Burke, who, with characteristic promptness, on being informed of the situation at Grenada and our purpose, promised that a special train should be ready for us to start at half-past seven o'clock P. M. By seven P. M. we had gathered at the depot seven of our old nurses who had consented to go. I deemed it my duty as an officer, and as a representative of the Howards, to go to the assistance of the stricken people, and had agreed to accompay the nurses and share their fate. Of our Association there were at the depot, soon after seven P. N., the following: Col. J. H. Edmondson, J. H. Smith, Secretary; Col. Butler P. Anderson, A. M. Stoddard, E. D. Foster, and myself. Just as the train was about to start, Col. Anderson volunteered to go with me. I told him I had not expected him to go, but that I would be rejoiced to have his company.

We reached Grenada a little before twelve that night. We soon learned from citizens we met at the hotel and on the public square that there was a fearful panic, and the people were rushing out of the fated place by every possible conveyance.

A malignant fever had broken out in Grenada the previous week. The yellow fever having never visited the place, it was not recognized as such until on the Sunday we left Memphis. Dr. R. F. Brown, the secretary of the Memphis Board of Health, in response to a telegram, had reached Grenada Saturday at midnight, and his investigations the following morning satisfied him that it was none else than the yellow fever, and that of the most virulent type.

The first death had occurred on August 9th. None attacked had recovered—it was sweeping all before it. The terror it had very naturally awakened can not be described nor adequately conceived. All that could hurried away. Nearly one-tenth of the whites who remained were already prostrated with the fever. The sick were unvisited and uncared for, except by the physicians and, occasionally, by their nearest kindred. The destitution of every thing needed for the sick was fearful. The dead were left unburied. As Dr. Brown reported, on his return to Memphis, "the situation was appalling;" and, as Col. Anderson telegraphed, "it was worse than in Memphis in 1873."

On the night of our arrival, we placed three of our nurses on duty. The following morning we visited the sick, placed the remainder of our nurses on duty, and telegraphed to New Orleans and to Memphis for more, and for supplies. We urged all who could to flee, and endeavored to arouse the citizens who remained to exert themselves for their own protection. We secured the organization of burial parties, who were not very efficient, but who buried a portion of the dead. We hired as many of the frightened colored people as we could to wait on the sick.

When the citizens learned that some of the Memphis Howards, who had safely passed through the fevers of 1867 and 1873, were among them, and expected to remain with them, they regained some confidence. The fever, however, spread with great rapidity. None recovered. The home physicians did all in their power, and acted their part bravely and nobly, but the fatality of the disease destroyed the confidence of the people in them. We were sent for to examine every new case. It was useless for us to disclaim being physicians, we had to go. Such was the pressure upon us that neither Colonel Anderson nor myself ever worked less than eighteen hours out of every twenty-four.

In response to our telegrams, nurses arrived on August 13th from both Memphis and New Orleans, and doctors, also, from the latter place. Needed supplies reached us almost daily from Memphis. On August 14th we issued the following circular:

CIRCULAR.

The nurses of the Howard Association of Memphis will receive three dollars per day for their services. They are required to give constant attention to the sick under their charge, and obey promptly all orders and directions of the physician in charge. Any dereliction of duty will cause the instant discharge of the guilty party.

Persons who have nurses in their houses are urgently requested to report any dereliction of duty to the undersigned, at the Chamberlain House.

It is our request that the nurses will be supplied with food, and that some one will report to us a correct account of the time each nurse is employed. Nurses are directed to report all deaths to us promptly. This rule must be rigidly observed.

The nurses from New Orleans are also under our charge, and will obey the above rules.

W. J. SMITH, } Howard Association.
B. P. ANDERSON,

We now had with us Dr. J. H. Beatty, of the Can't-Get-Away Club of Mobile, and Doctors W. R. Mandeville and H. A. Veazie, sent by the New Orleans Howard Association. They rendered noble service, but still the people died under their care as under that of the home physicians. All worked devotedly to save life, but such was the virulence of the disease all medical aid seemed in vain.

From our arrival we had endeavored to secure organization among the citizens for the relief and care of the sick and burial of the dead. Col. Anderson and I urged the formation of a relief committee, and the establishment of a hospital. But as the fever spread with such fearful rapidity, and as there were none recovering, a very natural demoralization prevailed. This was heightened by the cutting off of the place from communication by rail with the outside world. The trains on the Mississippi Central Railroad ceased to stop on August 14th. Ever after they rushed by, blowing the whistle and giving a scream like the despairing cry of the lost.

Many were paralyzed by the horrible situation and general distress. The result was that we had very little coöperation. Every thing was left to us to attend to. Our suggestions fell unheeded. Col. Anderson and I felt discouraged, and after a full consultation, I decided to return to Memphis, and report to you that we thought we could accomplish little at Grenada, compared with what ought to be done, for want of that activity on the part of her citizens which we had a right to expect. This was on the morning of August 15th. Our determination was made known. At ten o'clock A. M. the town-bell was rung lustily. A meeting of the citizens was held in the courthouse. A citizens' relief committee, consisting of Col. John Powell, Robert Mullin, Esq., and Gen. Thomas Watson, was appointed. This committee was authorized to appeal for help, and directed to coöperate with us in the establishment of a hospital for both white and colored. As I was busy visiting the sick, Col. Anderson addressed the citizens' day meeting. At eight o'clock that night I attended their evening meeting, and was handed the following paper by Judge Thomas Watson, of their relief committee:

GRENADA, MISS., *August* 15, 1878.

Gen. Smith and Col. Anderson:

DEAR SIRS:—Having heard that there is a probability of your being called to Memphis, we feel that it is our duty to the afflicted people of this town to entreat you to remain with us as long as you see things in the deplorable condition they are now. You have seen how inefficient have been the responses of communities away from here for the relief of those who are sick in our midst. You see that we are largely dependent on the generous benevolence of the Howard Association of Memphis to prevent men and women from dying here without having a single hand to administer even a glass of water to them in their misery. Memphis has thus far already overwhelmed us with the use of her generous charity, and we beg not to be deprived of the aid of what has proven thus far to be our best stay and our best friend. We trust, therefore, that you, as representatives of the power and influence of your Association, will continue with us.

JOHN POWELL, }
ROBERT MULLIN, } *Committee.*
THOMAS WATSON, }

After reading this I told them that we had no wish to leave them if we could see and feel that we were having the coöperation from them which we had a right to expect

We had come to serve them and to do them good, and if they would act with us and second our efforts, we could assure them of two thousand dollars from the Memphis Howards to pay nurses and other expenses if citizens of other places did not respond. I told them I would stay with them to bury the last man if it became necessary, and I was not stricken down myself. This appeared to give general satisfaction, and on the next day we began to prepare and to furnish the court-house for a hospital. On the 16th this was filled with patients. The gathering of the sick in a hospital relieved the doctors and visitors of much labor, and insured more watchful care and effective work on the part of the nurses. About this time Colonel Anderson became uneasy about his family in Memphis. His wife frequently telegraphed him of the spread of the fever, and the general alarm. He became so uneasy that he excused himself from duty for three days and went to Memphis. He there laid the situation at Grenada fully before our Association, and after removing his family to Hernando, returned to duty.

Up to this time those attacked had been among the wealthiest and best citizens. Mrs. Fields, Mrs. Davidson, Mrs. Shankle, Wm. McMillan and wife, the Huffington, the Peacock, the Ingram, the Crowell, the Crowder, the Coffman, the Eskridge, the Judge Gray, the Deadrick, the Lake, the Highgate, the Hughes, and the Bishop families had suffered.

On August 16th, only one week after the first death, there were seventeen deaths among the remnant of the people left in the place. J. B. Townsend on that day telegraphed to the *Avalanche:* "Mortality fearful; not a single case recovered. The town is almost depopulated. We need help in every form."

I hope I may be spared from ever again witnessing such scenes of distress and despair. Whole families, family after family, were swept away. It looked as though no one would be left. Our nurses now began to take the fever, and we had not enough to care for all the sick. Judge Thomas Watton, on August 18th, telegraphed: "People dying to-day without an attendant."

The fever swept on as virulent as ever; the appalling rate of mortality held its own; and on August 19th we telegraphed the following report to the Howard Association of Memphis:

"As your representatives sent here for the purpose, we have looked carefully into the situation of every thing connected with the yellow fever in Grenada. The epidemic, considering the size of the town, appears to be the most malignant and fatal that has ever been known in the country, and this after only nine days. The fever is unabated and unchecked. The great need is for nurses, and for money to pay them. There have been persons here sick for long periods without a single attendant. At present the contributions amount to not more than one-half of what seems to be necessary. The funds are certainly managed by the relief committee with a rigorous economy, and with judgment, and the men who handle them are known to the business men of the south-west as a certain guarantee for their faithful application to the purposes for which they are intended. We hope the liberal and generous contributions made up to this time will not cease. The appeal to the charitable has no equal in the sad history of this disease.
"WILLIAM J. SMITH,
"BUTLER P. ANDERSON."

The above dispatch was published throughout the country with the following endorsement:

The Howard Association of Memphis indorse the appeal of their associate members now on duty at Grenada. Messrs. Smith and Anderson, who have labored among the sick there for nine days past, are fully posted as to the exact condition, and are gentlemen in every way worthy of public confidence.
Signed, A. D. LANGSTAFF, *Vice-Pres.*
J. H. SMITH, *Secretary.*

In response to this telegram of our Association, contributions from the charitable all over the land flowed into Grenada. After this became available there was no want of funds.

Previously Grenada had been entirely dependent upon the Howard Association of Memphis for all supplies for the sick. The trains from Memphis were run only to bring our supplies. The pay of all nurses, including those from Mobile and New Orleans, had been guaranteed by us. Your representatives had entire charge of the distribution of supplies and of the nursing of the sick. Every thing in the power of Colonel Anderson and myself, backed as we were by the liberality of the Howards of Memphis, was done to relieve the general distress; yet in the terror and demoralization which prevailed, and the fewness of the well who could be relied upon for assistance, there were doubtless many cases of death without any attention or succor whatever.

I might add that the Memphis Howards were virtually in charge of Grenada. The mayor, Hon. J. R. Milton, had fallen an early victim of the fever. There were no civil officers—state, county, or municipal—in the town. All were dead or had fled. All the functions of civil society that were left were concentrated in the care of the sick.

On August 21st I telegraphed as follows: "The death rate not so large to-day, but the fever continues to spread. There have been not less than seventy-five taken down in the last twenty-four hours. We have twelve, colored, in the hospital, where they are equally well cared for with the whites. This is the most malignant type of fever I have ever seen. It is a pestilence that will not yield to medicine. Both of our New Orleans doctors are dumbfounded at the malignity of the disease. Frequently after the seventh or eighth day, in spite of the utmost care, they die in a few hours. Our efforts are paralyzed for want of proper remedies. We are short of lemons, ice, beef-tea, and, in fact, all kinds of nourishment for the sick. Five per cent. of the whole population have now died. Money to pay nurses and care for the indigent sick is very much needed."

This call for supplies was immediately responded to, and after August 22d, as I am informed, there was no further scarcity.

On the morning of August 22d I was myself attacked with the fever, but I did not quit my work till late in the afternoon. I met with all the sympathy and kind attention that it was possible for friends to bestow upon any one. Colonel Anderson wanted me to go to bed. I declined to go to bed in Grenada. He became alarmed, and sent for Dr. J. H. Beatty, of Mobile, and Dr. Hall, resident physician, to advise with me and to prescribe. Dr. Beatty tested the temperature of my body, and pronounced it 104°, and both doctors advised that I should go to bed. I respectfully declined, however, to do so in Grenada. I then said to Colonel Anderson that if I was sick, as the doctors and himself made out, that he would oblige me by going to the telegraph office and telegraphing Major Burke to send me a special car. He said he would, and suited his action to the word.

The doctors assured me it would cost me my life to make the trip. Dr. Beatty very kindly offered to go to Memphis with me. I declined his generous offer.

To Major Burke I owe a lasting debt of gratitude for the promptness with which he sent a special engine and car. It arrived at about 7 P. M., and by 8 o'clock I was on the car for Memphis. I feel deeply indebted, too, to all the friends for the great care they manifested in seeing that every thing was done to make me comfortable and the ride easy. General Thomas Watson, the one man who took such a deep interest in every thing, after he accepted a place on the committee, and who put his buggy and driver at my service, was no less active when I was struck down. He ordered a mattress, blankets, sheets, and coverlid from the hotel to make me comfortable in the car. I had hoped to be able to take his friendly hand once more, but alas! he is gone "to that bourne from whence no traveler returns." Peace to his ashes. My acknowledgments are also due to the steward at the hotel, and my friend Mr. Wyatt M. Redding (who has since paid the penalty that we all must pay sooner or later), who rendered invaluable services in making me comfortable on the cars. When I arrived at Memphis I was met by yourself, Col. J. H. Edmondson, Second Vice-President, W. H. Holt, A. M. Stoddard, and a number of the members of the Association. All seemed to sympathize with me, and vie with each other to see which could do the most to make me comfortable. I was taken at my own request, to my office, not wishing to endanger the life of any of my family. I was carefully watched over the remainder of the night (having arrived at Memphis about midnight) by the president of the Association, and in thirteen days, through the kind attention of Doctors Sims and Quimby, and the tender nursing of kind friends, I was enabled to report for duty just in time to take the place of our worthy president when he was taken down.

On my sickness and return to Memphis, Captain D. W. Coan and Mr. Brogan volunteered to assist Colonel Anderson in his care of the sick at Grenada. Captain Coan remained to the last in the employ and as a representative of our Association. He did his duty nobly. Finally stricken down, he happily recovered.

As showing the fatality of this plague at Grenada, I may add that in a late visit to that place I was credibly informed that out of all the whites who remained during its rage only five survived.

It is befitting that I should mention some of the citizens of Grenada who were in those trying days conspicuous for their courage and humanity. First of all upon this roll of honor should be placed the names of that devoted band of home physicians, every one of whom perished in their zeal to relieve the sick and distressed. The following are their names: Drs. W. E. Hughes, W. W. Hall, —— Woolfolk, —— Gillespie, —— Hawkins, B. W. May, J. L. Milton, J. R. Wilkins, and —— Ringgold. The last was the health officer. Of the clergy, Rev. John McCampbell, Rev. Dr. J. G. Hall, Rev. J. K. Armstrong, and Rev. A. S. Haddick shared the fate of so many of their people. Rev. W. C. McCracken was throughout the pestilence always on duty, doing all in his

APPENDIX. 381

power to relieve the afflicted. Mr. Will. Ayers, of the Odd-Fellows, died working faithfully for the sick. Thos. F. Marshall, telegraph operator, was very kind and courteous. Wyatt C. Redding succeeded him, and worked every night till two o'clock in the morning. He was kind-hearted to the last degree. Mr. Wilshire, of Memphis, assisted in the telegraph office. All three died. Mr. R. A. Armstead, express agent, was exceedingly useful. The steward of the Chamberlain House, Mr. ———, remained at his post, and though attacked with the fever, kept that hotel open throughout the epidemic; had it not been for this there would have been no place where the doctors, the nurses, and the Howards could have been fed. The Relief Committee, consisting of Messrs. Robert Mullin, John Powell, and Judge Thos. Watson, rendered invaluable services. To their high integrity and excellent business qualities it was largely due that the overflowing charity, which relieved the sick and suffering of Grenada, was wisely and faithfully disbursed. Judge Watson has passed beyond the reach of my poor thanks, but I shall always gratefully remember his many kindnesses to me. General Walthall, who gave so generously, and labored so zealously to secure money for the relief of his people, can not be too warmly praised.

There were many noble examples of fortitude and endurance among the nurses, both those from Memphis and New Orleans. There were some whose fidelity can not be too highly praised. Among the best may be mentioned Mrs. Kelly, who nursed Mrs. Judge Gray and family; Robert Butcher, who nursed at Mrs. W. A. Cromwell's; Madam Bashorn, of New Orleans, who nursed at Mrs. George Lake's; Mrs. Angelina Wolf, who nursed at Mrs. Huffington's; and Mrs. Karr, who nursed at Mr. Ingraham's; Pat. Ford, who nursed at W. A. Dejarnett's, and others, and Thos. Watkins, who nursed at A. J. Gerard's. There were many others who deserve honorable mention, but whose names have slipped my memory.

There could have been no more devoted and faithful men than the doctors with us from New Orleans and Mobile, who have already been referred to.

It is but my duty to add that, notwithstanding the Memphis Howards were recognized as in charge at Grenada, the New Orleans Howards responded to our calls for doctors and nurses with the greatest promptitude and generosity.

My noble co-worker of the Memphis Howards, Colonel Butler P. Anderson, needs no praise from me. All know of the courage and devotion with which he met and worked through the pestilence of 1873. He volunteered to go to Grenada in the same philanthropic spirit, and there faced a plague many times more horrible than that of 1873, with the same steadfastness, and the same untiring zeal in relieving its terrible suffering and distress. He was a brave, tender, and great-hearted man. When forced to leave Grenada, I left him in that impenetrable gloom as valiant and cheerful as ever. In a few days he also was stricken, and died at the post of duty. I shall never cease to mourn his loss as that of a brother and a comrade in arms.

Respectfully submitted,
W. J. SMITH,
First Vice-Pres. Howard Association.

REPORT OF THE SUPERINTENDENT OF THE INFIRMARY.

NEAR BEAUVOIR STATION, HARRISON CO., MISS., }
April 19, 1879. }

A. D. Langstaff, President Howard Association of Memphis:

MY DEAR SIR,—In consequence of a misapprehension with regard to your request for an account of my observations and experience of the yellow fever epidemics of 1873 and 1878, at Memphis, its preparation has been postponed until actually, as I presume, the very last day at which it can be of any service to you. It must necessarily, therefore, be hurried and imperfect.

In both these years it fell to my lot to be on duty in Memphis, as representative of the "Can't-Get-Away Club" of Mobile, in charge of a band of nurses, selected and sent by that association. With regard to the operations of the former year, I avail myself of an incomplete report made to the Club soon after my return from Memphis.

1873.

This document, after a recital of the facts concerning the first appearance of the fever, about the latter part of August, 1873, the official announcement of its epidemic character by your Board of Health, on the 13th of September, etc., etc.—all of which, I presume, appears elsewhere in your narrative—proceeds as follows:

[*Extract from report to Can't-Get-Away Club of Mobile.*]

. . . .

The above outline of the incipient history of the epidemic has been given in order to a correct understanding of the subject-matter proper of this report; that is, our own action thereon. Accounts of the rapid progress and threatening aspect of the fever having reached us through telegraphic reports, and other sources of information, on the 17th of September, I was, as Secretary, instructed by the president of the Club to telegraph to the mayor of Memphis, offering our services in selecting and sending experienced and competent nurses, if desired. In anticipation of an immediate answer, a meeting of the Club was at the same time called for the next morning. No answer had been received, however, when the Club convened, nor was any thing heard from Memphis in reply until the afternoon of that day (the 18th), when the mayor of Mobile received a telegram from the "Howard Association" of Memphis, asking for ten nurses. Mayor Moulton promptly replied to this dispatch, referring the Howard Association to the Can't-Get-Away Club, which had already made a tender of its services in the matter. The final result was another dispatch from the Howard Association to the Club, received late in the evening of the 18th, asking for fifteen experienced female nurses—an increase from the number specified at an earlier hour of the same day, which was itself of some significance.

The president, on receipt of this last dispatch, notwithstanding the lateness of the hour, immediately ordered a meeting of the Club for the next morning, and at the same time published a call for nurses. The Club, as you are well aware, at its meeting on that day (the 19th of September) approved the action of the president and secretary by taking measures for the prompt engagement of nurses. They were carefully, and, as the result proved, most judiciously, selected by the Executive Committee, which went into permanent session for the day. This action was taken about ten o'clock of the morning, and at six o'clock of the afternoon of the same day, the full complement of fifteen nurses having been completed and got ready, they set off for Memphis, under charge of your senior secretary, who had tendered his services to the Club for that duty.

We arrived at Memphis near midnight of Saturday, the 20th of September. As you have already been informed, my own first impressions were those of surprise at the absence of the usual signs of the existence of a severe epidemic. Even at that late hour the streets, in that part of the city through which we passed, presented an appearance of animation altogether unlooked for. Lager beer saloons and other places of resort were still open, lighted as brilliantly as usual, and not by any means destitute of groups of persons in pursuit of pleasure or amusement. The next morning was Sunday, and business was, of course, to a great extent suspended, but there were no superficial indications of a public calamity or general distress. The churches and Sunday-schools were open; ladies, ladies' maids, and children were passing to and fro, or enjoying the lovely weather in the shades of the public parks; there were the familiar groups of loiterers about the hotels and news-stands, and the effect of the whole was an impression that the danger and distress had been much magnified by imagination. [Perhaps in my own mind this impression was deepened by pre-occupation with recollections of the great pestilence in Norfolk, and the contrast presented to the aspect of that city on my arrival there, when the ordinary avocations of life were entirely suspended—stores, shops, banks, newspaper offices, and even churches closed—not a lady, nor a child to be seen in the streets—and when a visible pall of funereal desolation enveloped the city like a shroud.] This favorable and cheerful impression was, however, but temporary. I had not yet seen the *infected district*.

The first place to be sought for, on Sunday morning, was the office of the Howard Association, in order to report my arrival with our nurses. This office I found in a small, semi-subterranean apartment in West Court Street. The Association, originally organized in 1867, had been virtually disbanded, or suspended. When reorganized, a few days before my arrival, there were only six or seven active members remaining. These had already set to work with great zeal and energy, to meet the emergency, though little aware at the time to what extent their labors and resources were to be called forth.

In company with Mr. Langstaff, president of the Association, a great part of this first day (Sunday, September 21st) was spent in visiting the houses of the infected district—including "Happy Hollow"—and assigning our nurses to duty, where they

APPENDIX.

were most urgently needed. To one who has never seen the boundary lines of local infection as clearly and distinctly drawn as they were in Memphis, it would be impossible to communicate an adequate conception of the startling contrast presented by appearances within and without those limits. Some idea of their extent and location may be obtained by those familiar with the topography of Memphis, from the statement that the fever was at this time chiefly confined to that part of the city lying north of Poplar and west of Third or Fourth Streets. Beyond these boundaries there was then scarcely a case, or, at farthest, only a few scattered cases, of an origin clearly traceable to the infected region. It is wonderful, to anticipate a little, how long the disease lingered within these bounds. Intangible as they were, they seemed sufficient to repel the efforts of the fever to overleap them; or, rather, sated with the supply of victims within, the fever itself seemed comparatively indifferent as to further progress for days or weeks after spreading thus far. In fact, it *never did* obtain the same full control of the remainder of the city, and to the very last, even after it had spread into every nook and corner of Memphis, by far the greater part of the mortality occurred within the limits which have been described. Within these, no accounts that have been written have exaggerated the frightful realities. They embraced an extent of perhaps fifteen or twenty squares, most of them closely and compactly built. Some of the dwellings in certain parts of this area are of the better class, but it is largely occupied by small retail shops and groceries, drinking saloons, boarding-houses, and the crowded dwellings of the very poor. In these might be seen the sick, the dying, and the dead, huddled together sometimes in the same room. A cooking-stove would be steaming within a few feet of the mattress of some sufferer during the heat of the day, while at night the same patient would be exposed to the chilling influence of the north winds that whistled through the crevices of the dismal dwelling. Add to this the effects of the excessive terror inspired by the unwonted malignancy of the disease, paralyzing the energies, stupefying the intellect, and, in some instances, obliterating the domestic charities and humane impulses of those still in health. Remember, also, that many of the inhabitants of this district were isolated and homeless—boarding in the houses of persons bound to them by no ties of kindred or affection—and you may form some idea of the distress within the "infected district."

This distress was but partially known outside of its local boundaries; and for a long time the illusory, but not unnatural, hope was indulged, that the fever would spread no further, and that the worst was even then over. For more than a week after my arrival the suggestion of asking pecuniary contributions from abroad was hardly tolerated, and the rapid subsidence of the fever was confidently looked for by many.

The effect upon my own mind of that first day's observations was very different. It was obvious that the fever was one of unusual, perhaps unexampled, malignity, and that it would continue to advance with greater or less rapidity, unless it should falsify the precedents of all past experience, or unless the weather should become prematurely cold. It was evidently necessary that there should be an enlargement of means and appliances for meeting what was *coming*, as well as what was already existing. With this view, I urged upon the gentlemen of the Howard Association (as far as was proper in consideration of my merely advisory position) the importance of two measures—the enlargement of their membership, and the establishment of a temporary hospital or infirmary for the sick. Both of these objects were ultimately accomplished, the latter sooner than the former.

The subject of a hospital had been already under consideration, both by the Howard Association and by others, before my arrival in Memphis. The Board of Health had resigned their functions about that time, partly on account of failure to obtain sufficient support to carry into effect a proposition of that sort. The Israelites of the city, some of whom were among the very foremost in benevolent activity, from beginning to end of the affliction, had made arrangements for the establishment of one, but had been met both by injunctions at law and by threats of personal violence, and had abandoned the enterprise. The opposition to the very idea of a yellow fever hospital among the more ignorant and turbulent classes of the population, although utterly unreasonable, was intense and violent, to a degree which it is hard to comprehend, and which, I confess, *I* did not at all comprehend or realize at first. Under these circumstances, the Howard Association had been considering the feasibility of taking possession of a large, isolated, and unoccupied edifice—originally a warehouse, or something of that sort, but entirely destitute of the conveniences and comforts so necessary for the purpose intended. It was fortunate that this idea was not carried into execution.

In going through the "infected district" with Mr. Langstaff, I had been struck with the adaptation to the desired object of a large dwelling, originally erected by the United States Government as a residence for the commandant of the navy-yard, at the period when a navy-yard existed at Memphis. It had recently been occupied as a first-class boarding-house. Early in the epidemic, the proprietor and his wife—among the first cases, perhaps the very first outside of "Happy Hollow"—had both died of it. The other inmates had abandoned the house, and it was now entirely unoccupied. It had cisterns, kitchen, laundry, gas-burners, window-blinds, and, indeed, almost every requisite, except lack of sufficient room for the probable demand. Moreover, it was in the very midst of the infection. The sick, the dead, and the dying lay all around, except in front—for it fronted on a street that runs along the very brow of the bluff, with no dwellings between the bluff and the river. There could, as it seemed, be no possible opposition to the establishment of a hospital *there*, and it would be eminently convenient to the sufferers for whose accommodation it was designed.

So impressed was my mind with the necessity for this enterprise—regarding it, however, as probably only a beginning—that I offered to take personal charge of it, at all events until it was fairly on foot, provided the Mobile nurses were given me, or at least a sufficient number of them to perform the duty that would be required.

Mr. Langstaff concurred in these views, but feared it would be impracticable to obtain possession of the building. It is needless, however, to enter into further detail of the difficulties that were to be encountered. Let it suffice to say that they were all overcome, and the project of the Infirmary fully resolved upon in the course of a day or two.

There were further difficulties, however, before the design could be executed. One of the most serious of these was that of obtaining the requisite medical attention. The experienced physicians of the city were already fully occupied, and it was not desirable to entrust this important duty to one who was inexperienced. This difficulty was providentially and most happily solved by one of those seemingly fortuitous occurrences which sometimes settle difficulties for us when the best efforts of our own ingenuity have failed.

On the evening of the 23d of September, the third day after my arrival in Memphis, "happening" into the editorial office of the Memphis *Appeal*, in the hope of finding a Mobile newspaper, I there met Dr. Luke P. Blackburn, of Louisville, Ky., who had just arrived, having been deputed by a number of the merchants in that city to bestow his services upon the sufferers in Memphis, or wherever else they might be most needed or most desired. A very few minutes' conversation satisfied me that Dr. Blackburn was the very man, of all others, for the place to be filled. So prompt and so forcible was this impression, that I begged him to remain in the *Appeal* office until I could find President Langstaff of the Howard Association. Mr. Langstaff was found, accompanied me to the *Appeal* office, and the result was the engagement of Dr. Blackburn's services for our Infirmary—a most fortunate step, as it afterwards proved.

. . . .

THE INFIRMARY.

It would occupy too much of your space to continue in detail the narrative from which the foregoing extract is taken. I can but briefly condense the remainder of it.

Our Infirmary was opened on the 25th of September, and the first patient was received.* Meantime the opposition to the movement from a portion of the inhabitants of the vicinity had grown to a point which afforded a singular illustration of that peculiar frenzy, amounting to a species of insanity, which sometimes takes possession of the minds of the ignorant in time of public danger or calamity, and of which we read so much in the records of the plagues of former ages. To such persons, the establishment of a yellow fever hospital, instead of a measure for relief, appeared to present the idea of a measure for fixing, propagating, and perpetuating the pestilence in their vicinity. Dr. Blackburn and myself being both strangers, who had made our appearance in the bad company of the dreadful visitant, there were some wild ideas as to the sinister character of our objects. Intimations were made of a purpose to tear down the building, and the first few days of its occupancy was a period of some anxiety, requiring the performance of guard duty at night, as well as the care of the sick who were beginning to be brought in. The Hon. John Johnson, then mayor of the city, who took a warm and most efficient interest in every measure of relief, placed a detachment of armed police at my disposal, who were stationed within convenient distance for prompt service

---

* This first patient brought in was also the last taken out. He was a man somewhat advanced in life, known as "Major Buell," and said to have been an officer in the Federal army during the late war. He recovered of yellow fever, and became well enough to walk, but remained in the Infirmary, suffering from the *sequelæ*, or more probably from some constitutional infirmity, until the 1st of November—after the epidemic was over—when he died. He was brought in by W. J. B. Lonsdale, then a member of the Howard Association, who returned to Memphis about the close of the late epidemic (1878), after the death of his father, mother, and brother, and contracted the fever, and died, although he had been a frequent visitor to the Infirmary, and otherwise actively on duty and freely exposed to infection in 1873.

in case of necessity. These precautions, the failure of the malcontents to obtain any sympathy outside of their own very small circle, and the warm, hearty, and generous support extended us by all classes of the community, as soon as the facts became known, speedily and effectually suppressed this temporary and very limited opposition. After a futile effort to obtain a legal injunction against the Infirmary, it subsided altogether, and our work went on throughout the whole period of the prevalence of the fever, not only without molestation, but with the zealous approval and cordial coöperation of the whole community.

The Infirmary was soon filled to the utmost extent of its too limited capacity, and for several weeks the demand for accommodation was beyond our ability to meet it. From the 25th of September, when our doors were opened, to my departure from Memphis on the 28th of October, when they had been closed against new admissions—the fever being virtually at an end—the records of the Infirmary give the following results: Of 167 patients admitted, 76 had died; 70 had been discharged, cured; and there were 21 remaining, nearly all convalescent. Of those then remaining, from information subsequently received, it is believed that 3 died and 18 recovered. Of those admitted, 107 were males and 60 females. Of the deaths, there were 62 males and 17 females. Among the admissions were 20 children between the ages of 4 and 16 years, of whom 5 died and 15 recovered. Eight of whole number admitted were colored, of whom two died. The principal items may be tabulated as follows:

Admissions:—Males, 107; females, 60; total..................................167
Discharged:—Males, 45; females, 43; total............................88
Died:—Males, 62; females, 17; total..................................79

167

It is to be borne in mind that even to a greater extent than usual in hospital treatment, on account of the dread of the Infirmary at first prevailing among the more ignorant classes, a large proportion of the patients were not brought in until they were already in a moribund condition, many of them dying within a few hours—in one case within one hour—after their reception. Deducting those cases whose removal from their dwellings should never have been permitted, as they were already beyond hope of relief by human treatment, there can be no doubt that the total mortality (about 47 per centum) would have been reduced at least to an equality with that shown by the female patients (28 per centum), although many of these were in a like hopeless condition when received. These considerations, conjoined with that of the almost unprecedented malignity of the fever, leave us good ground for satisfaction with the degree of success attained by the operations of the Infirmary—a success which was fully recognized by a friendly and appreciative public opinion.

These results are mainly to be attributed to the incomparable skill and efficiency of Dr. Blackburn, with whom my relations were those of unbroken harmony throughout the whole prevalence of the epidemic. In this gentleman, professional knowledge and experience were combined with sound practical judgment, a diagnostic insight into disease which seemed to be intuitive, extraordinary capability of physical endurance, and a cheerfulness and kindliness of heart, which are better than medicine to the suffering patient. I had a corps of excellent nurses, whose fidelity deserves more than this passing notice. A rigorous discipline was maintained. My assistant, Mr. Parker, who volunteered his services soon after the Infirmary was opened, and continued in the faithful discharge of his duties to the close, merits a large degree of whatever credit may have been awarded to the institution. All would have been of no avail, however, but for the confidence bestowed upon the management and the cordial support rendered us by the Howard Association, under whose authority we were acting.

It is proper to state that accessions made from time to time to the number of nurses, furnished me by the Can't-Get-Away Club, made the whole number on duty, in Memphis, twenty-six—all females, except one. Only a part of these, however, were employed in the Infirmary, the others being engaged in nursing in private houses. Among all these there was only one decided case of yellow fever, and that not a fatal case.

1878.

But brief space remains for a response to that part of your request which relates to my personal experience of the great epidemic of last year, 1878. Its outbreak in Memphis found me at the place from which this communication is sent. At that time, although the fever had been prevailing for some weeks in New Orleans, this coast was entirely free from it, and continued so for a long time afterward.

On the 15th of August, having learned, from the newspapers, that my dear friend,

Col. Butler P. Anderson, of the Memphis Howard Association, had gone to Grenada, in company with General Smith, Vice-President of the same Association, on a mission of relief, I wrote to him to call upon me, if he thought my services there could be of any avail. At the same time I made a similar tender of service to the president of my own club (the Can't-Get-Away Club, of Mobile, from which city I was already excluded by a rigorous quarantine), in case it was contemplated to send any assistance abroad.

On the evening of the 23d of August I received a dispatch from Col. Anderson, urging me to proceed to Grenada as soon as possible. Before I could get off, however, another telegram was received from the President of the Can't-Get-Away Club, in Mobile, informing me that a number of nurses were on the eve of being dispatched for Memphis, and asking me, if possible, to proceed there at once and take charge of them. This latter request seemed to be the more imperative of the two, but I determined, at least, to stop on the way, at Grenada, for conference with Anderson.

Accompanied by my son, a youth of seventeen years, who had solicited permission to go with me, I left home on the morning of Sunday, August 25th, and proceeded, by way of New Orleans, to Grenada, where we arrived early the next morning. Col. Anderson was the first person to greet me. His appearance, as he sat on the threshold of the desolate hotel, en déshabilé, without his coat, and with a beard long unshaven—tokens of the hard work in which he was engaged—but full of calm courage and chastened cheerfulness, made an impression which can never be effaced from my remembrance. The day was spent with him in visiting the scenes of distress, which were then so rife in Grenada, and in consultation with the two surviving members of the resident Relief Committee. I was very reluctant to leave Grenada, and especially to leave Anderson and my friend Dr. Beatty, of Mobile (who was rendering admirable professional service to the sick), but, under the demands of what seemed to be a higher claim, I bade them farewell, in the evening of the same day, and proceeded by special train to Memphis. The impressions made on my arrival there (which was on the night of the 26th of August), are given in the following extract from a letter written a few days afterward:

"Entering Memphis at night, as at a similar stage of the great epidemic of 1873, the contrast was startling. On the former occasion there were no external signs or tokens of pestilence in the principal streets. Shops and saloons were open, people passing to and fro, groups gathered, as usual, about the hotels and bar-rooms, billiard tables in activity, and life presenting its ordinary aspects, except in the 'infected district,' to which it was then fondly hoped that the fever would be confined. Such was the case, in some degree, during the whole prevalence of the epidemic of that year. Now, on the contrary, the streets were dark, deserted, and silent. At the Peabody Hotel—the only hostelry open to the public—there were no loungers to relieve the solitude of the lonely clerk in the office. A solitary light shone from the door of a saloon in Monroe Street, and a few others twinkled from drug-stores here and there. The only place that presented a scene of activity was the office of the Howard Association, where I was greeted by a dozen true and tried comrades of a former campaign, now girded with full armor for another. Two or three have passed away during the lustrum that has elapsed since they were last on active duty, but most of them still remain, and are at their posts. As I write, however, *five* of them lie ill of the fever, brought on, most probably, by overwork and exposure. General Smith, First Vice-President of the Association, was prostrated in Grenada. Three of them, including the veteran Mansford, who was one of the original five that began the fight in 1873, have given way (here) since my arrival; and now comes to-day the painful news that the gallant and generous Anderson, who has been doing such splendid service for Grenada, is lying ill at that place."

"It is a singular fact that until now only three or four members of this Association have ever had yellow fever, although nearly all passed through it unscathed in 1873. The accounts of the distress here, which you have no doubt received from various sources (I speak conjecturally, having scarcely seen any other than the Memphis papers since my arrival), can scarcely have been exaggerated. The ravages of the fever have been aggravated by the unprecedented panic, the general destitution, the paralysis of business, the lack of nurses and physicians, the rapid spread of the epidemic, and the utter demoralization of the negroes. There is no trade or intercourse with the country. Some of the business houses are open for a few hours of the day, but many of them are entirely closed. With the exception of the nurses, a few sisters of religious orders, and the negresses, no female figure is seen in the streets. The depopulation of the city by flight and removal has done good in diminishing the material for disease, but has been accompanied by some incidental evils. The scarcity of physicians is a great evil, but that of skilled nurses is a greater. One of the most distressing things in daily experience is the necessity of turning a deaf ear to the piteous appeals for a doctor, a nurse, or other help. Several physicians arrived to-day, and others are expected. Nurses, also, are coming in almost daily, but far from fast enough to supply the increasing demand."

The day after my arrival (27th of August) I was requested by the Howard Association to organize and superintend the infirmary, or infirmaries, which they were about to establish. Readily consenting to this, I set to work at once, in conjunction with Dr. W. E. Rogers, physician in charge, to effect the proper organization. The public school buildings having been tendered for this use, that on Market Street was selected as combining the most advantages, and thoroughly fitted up. In consequence, however, of various annoying difficulties and delays, it was not opened for patients until the 3d of September. The school-house on Linden Street was fitted up for colored patients, but was always on the jut of prejudice or distrust with that class of the population, and was never more than partially occupied.

After fitting up the Market Street Infirmary, supplying it with a corps of nurses, a matron, and other requisites, I found, for reasons which it is not necessary to state, that there was no probability of further usefulness, on my part, in that particular duty, and finally, on the 12th of September, resigned the superintendency of infirmaries, and devoted my attention to other duties. At the earnest request, however, of Dr. Rogers, with whom it was always a pleasure to coöperate, on account of the complete accord and harmony of action between us, I fitted up the "Peabody" school building for use as a convalescent infirmary. It was never occupied as such, however, whether on account of the illness of Dr. Rogers, which occurred about that time, a decline in the demand for accommodation, or for some other reason, I am unable to say.

Before leaving altogether the subject of the infirmaries, with which, thenceforth I ceased to have any special connection, it is proper to bestow a slight tribute of recognition upon the merits of a lady, whose duties were of a sort that naturally escaped the observation of the public. This was Miss Mary S. Hill, matron of the Market Street Infirmary.

Having some knowledge of this lady, and of her admirable services rendered to Confederate soldiers during the late war, I had telegraphed for her immediately on being requested to take charge of the infirmaries of the Howard Association. Some necessary delay occurring with regard to her coming, the duty was kindly assumed for a few days by Miss Daisy Murdock, who afterwards resigned it into the hands of Miss Hill, on the arrival of the latter. Miss Hill's devotion to duty, her kindness of heart, and her excellent management of all the details of her department, are attested by all who had occasion to know her, and merit the highest recognition.

Having altogether forty-nine nurses of the Can't-Get-Away Club under my charge, besides many other duties in behalf of the sick, my time was fully occupied during the remainder of my stay in Memphis, which continued until the 25th of October, with the exception of about eight days spent in a visit to my family, then reported sick. During this period there were many incidents, which it would be interesting to record, if your space or my time would permit. As this, however, is impracticable, I must be content to close with the mere statement of two or three facts, or general deductions derived from facts.

Among the forty-nine Mobile nurses already mentioned as under my charge, to whom the addition of myself and my son would make fifty-one persons, there were four or five cases of yellow fever, only one of which was fatal. A comparison of this statement with the figures relative to unacclimated physicians, visitors, and nurses, which I presume you have ascertained from other sources, will be found to have striking significance.

As already stated, only one of my nurses in 1873 was a man. In 1878—as nearly as now remembered, without having their names before me—seven of them were male, and forty-two female. This is, in my opinion, about the proper relative proportion of the two sexes desirable for attendance on the sick in yellow fever epidemics. In 1878 there was an unusual and altogether unaccountable preference, in many cases, for male nurses. I can not but regard it as unfortunate that so large a proportion of those employed in Memphis were of the rougher sex. It is true this was partly from necessity, rather than choice, but provision should be made against a recurrence of such necessity in case of future visitations. Some men are admirable nurses, but, in general, except for delirious or otherwise unruly patients, women are far preferable. They are more attentive, more sympathetic, with readier instincts to discern what is wanted, and more capable of patient endurance.

The sad experience of the past year should impress upon us the importance of obtaining and having always in readiness a supply of competent, acclimated, and as far as practicable well-trained nurses, for service whenever an epidemic may appear. Your correspondent made an effort to interest the Public Health Association on this subject at its meeting held last November in Richmond, but it failed on account of the pre-occupation of that body with the one-absorbing question of quarantine. Quarantine is, indeed, a matter of vital moment, but the prospect of an entire exclusion of yellow fever is not promising enough to justify any neglect of the proper measures for meeting and resisting in case of failure to shut it out. Perhaps a general concert of action among the active benevolent associations of the country, especially of the South, might do something toward the accomplishment of the object.

In comparing the fevers of 1873 and 1878, in Memphis, it is often assumed that the latter was the more malignant of the two. As a close observer of both, I can not concur in this opinion, but rather incline to the contrary. Within the limits of the "infected district," the percentage of the disease to the population, and the percentage of mortality to the disease, were perhaps as great in the former year as they were anywhere in the latter, if not greater; the symptoms, I think, were in general more violent, and the cases (if an unprofessional observer may presume to judge) less manageable. The striking and most remarkable distinction between the phenomena of the two years was the confinement of the pestilence of 1873 within a limited area, beyond which there was scarcely any thing more than a sporadic extension during its whole duration, while in 1878 it spread through the whole city as a fire spreads through a dry prairie. Why this was so is one of the yellow fever mysteries for which no satisfactory solution has yet been suggested.

The yellow fever, which had broken out late in the season on this coast, continued to prevail with no little severity for some weeks after my return from Memphis, that is, until late in November. There were five or perhaps six cases in my own family, some of them severe, though happily none fatal. The most malignant and rapidly fatal case, however, that I saw anywhere during the whole season, occurred on this pure sand-beech, swept as it is by the breezes from the Gulf and free from all suspicion of malaria, in the dwelling of my nearest neighbor, not two hundred yards from my own.

But this is presumably beyond the scope of your inquiries, my answer to which has already been, perhaps, extended beyond the proper limits.

Very truly yours,

W. T. WALTHALL.

REPORT FROM THE CITY HOSPITAL.

From the official report of Dr. G. B. Thornton, physician in charge of the City Hospital in 1878, the following extract is, by his permission, made, showing the number of cases of yellow fever treated during the epidemic, the deaths, recoveries, and other important data:

Number of patients in hospital January, 1878	102
Number of patients admitted during 1878	1570
Number of patients treated during 1878	1672
Number of patients discharged during 1878	1176
Number of patients died	390
Number of patients remaining Dec. 31	106
Daily average for the year	86
Total percentage of deaths for the year	23.3

Of the above 460 were yellow fever patients. The first case was admitted August 2d, a steamboatman from New Orleans. This was the first case officially reported to the Board of Health. He was sent to quarantine hospital on the morning of the 3d, by order of Health Officer Erskine, where he died. The last case admitted was November 7. The 460 cases were divided as follows:

Number of whites	339
Number of blacks	121
Number of whites recovered	159
Per cent. of recovery	46.9
Number of whites died	180
Per cent. of deaths	53
Number of blacks recovered	47
Per cent. of recovery	61.1

APPENDIX. 389

Number of blacks died	47
Per cent. of deaths	38.8
Total recoveries from yellow fever	233
Total deaths from yellow fever	227
Per centage of deaths	49.3

Of the medical staff, which was increased by two assistants to the resident physician, Dr. Thornton, Drs. T. J. Lynn, of the city, and E. T. Easley, of Little Rock, all three had the disease; Dr. Lynn first, on September 19th, recovered, and subsequently resumed his duties, and served until the end of the epidemic. Dr. Easley second, September 20th, and died September 30th. Dr. Thornton was attacked on October 10th, was so prostrated by the disease as to be unable to resume his duties in the wards during the remainder of the epidemic. It is a fact of interest to the general reader and the profession, to note that this was a second attack, well defined. The first was equally well marked, and occurred in October of 1867, when the disease prevailed in Memphis. The second attack was doubtless modified by the first, but the same pathological changes existed.

Dr. Berlin Peeples, a young graduate in medicine, who went on duty as druggist of the hospital August 15th, was attacked September 27th, and died October 2d. Dr. H. C. Sauvé, of Hot Springs, Arkansas, on duty as a Howard physician in the city, who succeeded Drs. Lynn and Easley, escaped, and the only physician connected with the institution who did. He had previously had the disease in New Orleans.

There were four employés who escaped, who had never had the disease, two of whom were white men nurses, one from the North, who had lived in the South but a few months, consequently was wholly unacclimated; the other, a native of Mississippi, whose whole life had been spent in the South, but had never before been exposed to the disease. It may be of interest to mention that these two nurses served in wards of twenty-five beds each, which were filled the greater part of the time; that the duties they performed was very exciting, and consequently they could not have been more exposed to the contagious influence of the disease anywhere. The other two who escaped were negroes, employed as laborers about the institution.

Of those admitted a large number died a few hours after admission, in one or two instances death occurred while en route to the hospital, and instead of a living a dead body was taken from the ambulance. The hospital records show that the number for August and September who died within thirty-six hours after admission was ninety-six; for October and November, fifteen. Total who died within thirty-six hours, one hundred and eleven. Number for August and September who died within nine hours after admission, fifteen; for October who died within nine hours, one. Total number who died within nine hours, sixteen. Number for August and September who died within eighteen hours after admission, thirty-seven; for October and November, seven. Total within eighteen hours, forty-four.

The above list will show, or at least give some idea of the extreme condition of many on admission. They were really beyond the reach of any medication or nursing. This fact in regard to the admissions into this hospital should be noted. It being the public charity of the city, the regular hospital in contradistinction to the Howard Infirmaries, no cases were denied admission on account of condition or length of time sick. The order governing the admissions into the Howard Infirmaries was, that no case should be admitted that had been sick over twenty-four hours. The infirmaries were located in the city in charge of the Howard physicians; this hospital was about the center of the extreme eastern limit of the city at the terminus of Union Street.

THE CITIZENS' RELIEF COMMITTEE.

This organization, under the management of such gentlemen as Charles G. Fisher, Luke E. Wright, William Willis, and James S. Prestidge, accomplished a great deal of good. It provided food for the needy, camps of refuge for all who would avail themselves of them, insured safety of life and property by a thorough military supervision of the city, and gave courage by its constant, undeviating course. Its history is brief, but it is a record luminous with every thing that can redeem poor fallen humanity. As we find it in the daily papers, it is as follows:

On the 16th of August the following notice appeared in the daily papers:

CITIZENS' MEETING TO-DAY.

The undersigned citizens, who intend to remain in the city during the prevalence of the fever, invite all of our people similarly inclined to meet at the Greenlaw Opera House, at eleven o'clock, for consultation and action with regard to assisting each other through the scourge, and providing ways and means for removing from the city to a place of safety such of our people as are pecuniarily unable to do so without assistance. It is expected that answers to telegrams sent to President Hayes will be placed before the meeting.

C. G. Fisher,	R. A. Thompson,	C. P. Hunt,
E. C. Mosby,	N. M. Jones,	G. Falls & Co.,
H. Furstenheim,	J. S. Day,	S. C. Toof,
W. B. Galbreath,	Orgill Bros. & Co.,	R. C. Nicholson,
R. F. Patterson,	B. Babb,	John M. Peters,
S. M. Gates,	John S. Toof,	W. P. Proudfit,
J. M. Keating,	S. Mosby,	Fader, Jacobs & Co.,
W. H. Bates,	Alf. Tuther,	J. R. Goodwin, and others.
J. T. Pettit,	Porter, Taylor & Co.,	

In obedience to this call, on the next day a mass meeting was held at the place indicated, at which steps were taken to accomplish the purposes indicated in the call, and at which the Citizens' Relief Committee was organized, as follows: M. H. Riley and W. J. Chase, for the first ward; D. F. Goodyear and E. Marshall, second ward; W. P. Proudfit and J. C. Maccabee, third ward; John Beamish and Hugh L. Brinkley, fourth ward; Rev. Dr. Landrum, and Captain James Cleary, of the Fire Department, for the fifth ward; Luke E. Wright and Charles G. Fisher, for the sixth ward; John Lonsdale, Jr., and W. A. Wheatley, for the seventh ward; Henry Furstenheim and C. F. Conn, for the eighth ward; Gus. Reder and R. B. Miller, for the ninth ward; Butler P. Anderson and John A. Strehl, for the tenth ward; and for the city at large, Major John R. Flippin and L. D. Eisman. When this committee organized, a resolution to add one colored man for each ward to their number was unanimously adopted. At the same meeting it was resolved to ask the government for rations, through General R. F. Patterson, collector of internal revenue, and committees were appointed to select a site for a camp, and solicit subscriptions of food and money. On the following day, Saturday, the 18th, the committee on selection of a camping-ground reported in favor of the Webb Place, on the Memphis and Tennessee Railroad, about seven miles from the city, and Captain Cameron's company, the Bluff City Grays, was selected to assist in policing it. Charles G. Fisher was elected permanent chairman; John G. Lonsdale, Jr., treasurer; W. A. Wheatley, secretary; and J. C. Maccabee, commissary. The following-named colored men were added to the committee: Aaron Stephenson, for the first ward; F. B. Davis, second; Thomas A. Grigsby, third; Coleman Thomas, fourth; Townsend Jackson, fifth; J. A. Thompson, sixth; Vernon Chalmers, seventh; James Glass, eighth; James Lott. ninth; Jesse Wood, tenth. At the meeting on Monday, many subscriptions of money and provisions, and other help, were received and gratefully acknowledged. Camp Joe Williams

APPENDIX. 301

was announced as ready for the people, who were urged to take refuge in it without delay. The tents for it were supplied by the government, which also, through secretary of war McCreary—who, with the President, acted very promptly and nobly—supplied 40,000 rations, to be drawn as needed. Superintendent Willis, of the Southern Express Company, Dr. D. T. Porter, and Mr. Thomas B. Turley were added to the committee. Captain A. T. Lacey, John Consadine, and John J. Duffy were elected to fill vacancies by resignation. Camp Wright was established on the 21st, located on the Cuba road. Camp Smith, Camp Griffin, Camp Wade, Camp Father Mathew, and Camp Duffy were established about this time. Father Mathew Camp was independent of the committee, but all the others were under its supervision. At the meeting of the 21st, the people were again appealed to to remove from the city, and provision was made for the support of the families of the McClellan (colored) Guards and Brown's (colored) Zouaves, both of which companies were mustered into permanent service. At a meeting on the 24th of August, Hon. Casey Young, member of Congress, and Rev. Dr. Slater were added to the committee; J. A. Thompson, colored, was also added to the committee. On the same day the colored people held a mass meeting, and appointed committees to co-operate with the Citizens' Relief Committee in the maintenance of law and order. At a meeting on the 27th, the chief of police was empowered to fill all vacancies on the police, the committee becoming responsible for their pay. General Luke E. Wright reported all the camps doing well, and that Camp Morris Henderson had been established a quarter of a mile from Camp Joe Williams—the McClellan guards to police it. There were no more meetings of the committee up to the 1st of September. Thoroughly organized and equipped, there was no need for any. On that day an appeal for aid was made, which was signed by Charles G. Fisher, chairman; J. G. Lonsdale, Jr., treasurer, who also acted as secretary; by Luke E. Wright, C. F. Conn, William Willis, D. F. Goodyear, and S. M. Jobe. A meeting of the committee was held on the 5th of September, at which Hon. Casey Young presided, but it was devoted to the distribution of supplies, which, with money, continued to pour in from all parts of the country. At a public meeting held on the 10th of September, the people were urged to go to the camps. The committee were still at work, though very much diminished in numbers. A great many had left the city, and many had died. Those who remained were doing an almost exhaustive work every day. On the 26th of September the committee sent the following, addressed

To the People of the United States, and the World at Large:

Your generous contributions for the relief of the sufferers by the yellow fever in Memphis, especially within the past few days, and what is now on the way to us, has placed us beyond the reach of immediate or probable want in the future. We have enough, not only for our own needs, but to enable us to assist the people of our county, and of the villages of this and the adjoining States. With hearts overflowing with gratitude for your aid and sympathy, and prayers for your welfare, we are,

Your grateful servants,

A. D. LANGSTAFF, Pres. Howard Association,
LUKE E. WRIGHT, Acting Pres. Citizens' Relief Com.,
D. F. GOODYEAR, Acting Mayor,
J. M. KEATING, Editor Memphis *Appeal*,
W. W. THATCHER, Cashier, First National Bank,
Committee on Address, Citizens' Relief Committee.

On the 30th of October a meeting of the Citizens' Relief Committee was held, of which J. M. Keating was chairman, and James S. Prestidge, (treasurer since the death of John G. Lonsdale, Jr.) was secretary. Upon motion of Dr. D. T. Porter, it was

Resolved, That all commissary stores now on hand be at once turned over to the mayor, and his receipt taken therefor.

Upon motion of General Luke E. Wright it was

Resolved, That a committee of five be appointed by the chair, and same empowered to distribute among the orphans in this city, *pro rata*, any balance of funds that may remain on hand after all the liabilities of this committee are discharged; and that the treasurer be instructed to turn over to said committee said balance when ascertained. General Wright declining to serve on said committee of five, the chairman appointed Dr. D. T. Porter, James S. Prestidge, W. W. Thatcher, C. F. Conn, and Dr. D. F. Goodyear, and, upon motion, the chairman, Mr. J. M. Keating, was added to said committee.

At a meeting held December 7th, the committee appointed by the Citizens' Relief Committee, on the 30th of October, 1878, to distribute among the different orphan asylums in this city the balance remaining on hand after paying all the liabilities of said committee, there were present—Dr. D. T. Porter, chairman; James S. Prestidge, W. W. Thatcher, and Dr. D. F. Goodyear (Messrs. C. F. Conn and J. M. Keating being absent). James S. Prestidge was appointed secretary, and the following proceedings were had:

The treasurer made his report, showing a balance on hand, in cash, of $7,253.29, and county warrants (of Shelby County), received in settlement with John Walsh, of $1,208.80. Upon motion, it was

Resolved, That the county warrants on hand, $1,208.80, be deposited in the hands of a committee, composed of Hon. John Johnson and Dr. D. F. Goodyear, to be given to the Colored Orphan Asylum of this city, when its organization is completed and legalized; and in the event such organization is not completed so as to entitle said asylum to said fund, under this resolution, within twelve months from this date, then said committee is authorized, and hereby directed, to distribute said amount, *pro rata*, to the orphan asylums in the same manner, and in the same ratio, as the general fund is hereinafter divided.

Resolved, That the Treasurer of the Citizens' Relief Committee be instructed to divide among the several orphan asylums of this city the sum now on hand, on the following basis:

St. Peter's, 126 orphans	$2,986 64
Leath, 70 orphans	1,659 25
St. Mary, 70 orphans	1,659 25
Hebrew, 40 orphans	948 15
Total	$7,253 29

And the receipt of the treasurers of the said several asylums shall be his voucher for the payment of the same.

TREASURER'S REPORT OF CITIZENS' RELIEF COMMITTEE FROM AUGUST 16 TO DECEMBER 13, 1878.

Receipts by John G. Lonsdale, Jr. (died), from Aug. 16 to Sept. 10, 1878	$42,186 40
Receipts by R. B. Clarke (died), from 11th to 23d Sept., 1878	39,529 30
Receipts by James S. Prestidge, from Sept. 24 to Dec. 13, 1878	19,451 70
Total	$101,167 40
Aggregate disbursements during above period, including distribution among orphans	$93,914 11
Balance	7,253 29
	$101,167 40

REPORT OF THE COMMISSARY DEPARTMENT.

The following tabulated statement shows the number of rations issued to the sick and poor, during the months of August, September, and up to the 25th of October. It was carefully copied from the books of the Commissary, Captain J. C. Maccabee, who, it is proper to say here, was complimented not only by the officers of the Citizens' Relief Committee, but by the press of the city. His administration of his department was both just, fair, and reasonable. Five of his book-keepers succumbed to the fever and died. Undismayed, he stood to his post and closed his books and wound up the affairs of the Commissary as coolly as if he was settling the affairs of a great public trust in ordinary times.

APPENDIX.

Article.	August.	September.	October.	Total.	Article.	August.	September.	October.	Total.
Oysters, cans		36	25	61	Soap, lbs	798	1409½	6,394	8,001½
Fish, lbs		789	2,368	3,157	Salt, lbs	667	1,362	4,722	6,751
Shoulders, lbs	579	19,612	8,352	28,543	Mustard, lbs	1	52	107½	160½
Bacon, lbs	15,048	68,650	206,605	290,303	Pepper, lbs	16	75.15	141.02	230.01
Hams, lbs	2,839	10,392	14,641	27,872	Preserves, number	1	132	220	353
Canned Beef, cans		170	310	480	Molasses, gal	232	87	171¾	490¾
Fresh Beef, lbs	1,756	3,639		5,395	Soda, lbs	11	112	1	124
Dried Beef, lbs			124	124	Lard, lbs	586	393½	1,612	2,591½
Mutton, lbs		2,565	4,172	6,737	Apples, lbs	1	13	536	670
Flour, bbls	146	705	1,491	2,342	Oats, bush	6		387½	393½
Flour, lbs	53	74	153	280	Ice, lbs	1,200	1,025		2,225
Cornmeal, bbls	22	258	843	1,123	Chickens, number	188	658	206	1,052
Cornmeal, lbs	15	51	140	206	Eggs, doz	60	264	113	437
Potatoes, bbls	111	404	531	1,046	Wine, bot	12	29	105	146
Potatoes, pecks	2½	4½		7	Hay, lbs	38,200	10,000	20,640	68,840
Onions, bbls	54	64	6	124	Butter, lbs	163	351	101	615
Onions, pecks	8	5½	7½	21	Yeast Powders, boxes	114	122	60	296
Hard Bread, lbs		1,288	8,760	10,048	Tobacco, lbs	31	49	10	90
Cheese, lbs			352	352	Cigars, number		100		100
Crackers, lbs	2,543	6,392	14,287	23,222	Hops, lbs		5		5
Soft Bread, loaves	3,076	1,657	3	5,636	Oranges, doz		3		3
Peas, lbs	140	212	137	489	Peaches, lbs		235	803	1,038
Beans, lbs	724	7,834	11,526	20,084	Lemons, doz	27	19	33	79
Rice, lbs	1,530	4,520	10,347	16,397	Corn, cans		55	168	223
Hominy, lbs	2	214	4	220	Tomatoes, cans	72	64	243	379
Grits, lbs	100		156	256	Beans, cans		63	206	269
Tea, lbs	59.07	304.03	1174.10	1628.04	Condensed Milk, cans		24	83	107
Grain Coffee, lbs	1,742	7,875	23,241	32,858	Pig's Feet, cans		2	158	160
Roasted Coffee, lbs	1130½	855		1,985½	Gin, gal		2		2
Sugar, lbs	5,380	16,084	37,407	58,870	Brandy, gal	6½		10½	17
Vinegar, gal	43	340	150½	533½	Whisky, gal	59½	47¼	94	200¾
Coal Oil, gal		15	114	129	Corn Starch, lbs	1	9	23	33
Candles, lbs	308	615¼	1,818	2,741¼	Lime, bbls	12	40		52

The total number of rations issued in August was 41,518; in September, 212,027; and, in October, 492,190. Total number issued, 745,735.

The beneficiaries in August numbered 4,042; in September, 22,871, and in October, 41,109; total, 68,022. In October a great many rations were supplied to persons beyond the city limits, and to persons who were not in either of the camps which were supplied by the Commissary.

REPORT OF THE SURGEON IN CHARGE OF CAMP JOE WILLIAMS.

On the appearance of the terrible scourge, in the city of Memphis, during the latter part of July, 1878, and the apprehension that a third visitation would, if in epidemic form, carry before it thousands of helpless human beings, with no apparent avenue of escape, a few of our more thoughtful fellow-citizens suggested the establishment of camps at points accessible to supplies, and beyond the supposed limits of infected atmosphere.

The government readily responded to a call for 1,000 tents, and upon their arrival, August 15th, Camp Joe Williams, four and one-half miles from the city, was established, under the direction of the Citizens' Committee. The sight was selected for its isolated position, altitude, shade, ample springs of superior water, perfect drainage, and accessibility to rail communication.

The sole fault in the selection was its proximity to the city, which rendered it impossible to prevent visitations to the infected districts by the inhabitants, who, despite rigid rules, entered the jaws of almost certain death, rather than forego the pleasure of a drunken debauch, plunder, or the like.

The camp was laid out upon the crests of three swells of ground, stretching one-half mile. The tents were arranged in avenues, having two sides, faced inward, and along the edges of slopes, whose crests ranged from fifty to one hundred and fifty feet in width. The tents were planted five feet apart, and numbered by shipping tags.

The rows were designated by name, such as Fisher Row, Otey Row, Wright Row, etc., the number ending with each row or street.

Each swell of ground was laid off separately, with the same regularity, and designated by a different name, such as Camp Willis, Camp Retreat, etc.

Two adults, or a family with one child were assigned to each tent; single men were quartered in separate rows.

A complete register of names and locality made, cooking utensils, straw and ration-ticket furnished the instant of assignment, when the inmates set about arranging their households.

It being observed that the current of air at evening ranged invariably east of north, and from the south-west, a Palilisic hospital was fitted up at the extreme north end of the encampment. The military and medical headquarters were set up at easy distance from this point. This was deemed necessary, as the printed regulations required that all residents, when pronounced stricken of the plague, should be, per force if needs be, removed on litters to the hospital. It was deemed best that those in authority should set an example of indifference to attack, in order to appease, as far as possible, the constant anxiety of the population.

The camp was governed by a flexible military discipline. Two military companies—the Bluff City Grays (white) and the McClellan Guards (colored)—were quartered in the heart of the encampment, to enforce the published regulations hereto appended, to wit:

CAMP JOE WILLIAMS, *August* 24, 1878.

GENERAL RULES NO. 1.

The following Regulations are issued for the government of this Camp, with which every soul within its jurisdiction must cheerfully comply, or be driven from its limits:

Reveille will sound at 5 A. M.
Labor Call, 6½ A. M., when the roll of paid labor will be called, and duty begin.
Surgeon's Call will sound at 7 A. M., when all requiring medical treatment will report to Medical Headquarters.
Police Call will sound at 9 A. M.
Dinner Call will sound at 12 M.
Police Call will sound at 2 P. M.
Tattoo will sound at 9 P. M.
Taps will sound at 10 P. M.

At Police Call the details will fall in and be verified by the bosses, who will then march them to portions of the Camp requiring duty.

At Police Call the inhabitants are required to ventilate tents, clear ditches, sun straw and bedding, and police round about their quarters, kitchens, and parade.

Families having no male adults present must police their tents and immediate surroundings. The police gangs, on application, will attend to their wants.

The inhabitants are required to make use of the kitchen pits, into which all waste water and kitchen waste must be thrown. The sinks must be used by the inhabitants in answer to all calls of nature. A violation of this rule will subject the offender to expulsion from Camp.

The officer of the day will make the rounds at 10 A. M, and enforce these regulations. He will report to the commandant the tenant guilty of neglect.

All able-bodied men are required to do police duty. They will be divided into gangs, or reliefs; be assigned to duty in turn, and for no longer than one-half of each day, between Reveille and Retreat.

The orderly sergeants, the quartermaster and commissary, bosses of labor gangs, and the surgeon in charge will make a daily report of all officers, men and women doing duty under them, and to whom ration stores and medicines are issued. The surgeon will also report number of prescriptions, number of inhabitants sick and in hospital, and all deaths and births occurring within each twenty-four hours. These reports will be filed at headquarters by 12 M of each day.

A condensed daily report, in printed form, will be issued and forwarded to the Citizens' Committee at 12 M.

A weekly report of refugees and citizens employed as laborers and mechanics will be furnished the Citizens' Committee by the quartermaster, after receiving the signature of the commanding officer.

The senior officer of each department will confine himself, to his respective duties, and will report to the commanding officer only for instructions, details and orders pertaining thereto.

By order,

JOHN F. CAMERON, *Commander*.

The staff consisted of one commander, two surgeons, one commissary and quartermaster. The subaltern force, three bakers, one butcher, one carpenter, one wagon-master, and one drug clerk; also, to the hospital, one head cook, one steward or head nurse, to which were added, from the inhabitants, such additional force as needs required. Four stretcher-hands and four grave-diggers were also added to the hospital force. The duties of the former were to remove the sick, destroy or disinfect the tenement of the sick, and erect new tents where needs required. Wood and water was distributed daily to the inmates, and every want supplied. All infractions of the rules were punished, and no excuses allowed in mitigation of offenses.

Ten days' rations were stored in the general warehouse, from which issues were made every other day. The inhabitants presented themselves at the call, with buckets and sacks in hand, and took position by file, the women having precedence. As each ticket was presented, the same was checked off on the register, rations furnished, and so on. The meat was cut by experts in rations, and issued without delay ; so with sugar, coffee, etc. It required not exceeding two hours to supply one thousand people in detail of say three hundred separate tickets.

We baked our bread, purchased and slaughtered our beef, which was issued half fresh and half salt. The commissary was supplied with tea, coffee, sugar, rice, beans, candles, soap, vinegar, molasses, crackers, flour, bread, meal, and soda. The inhabitants drew shoes and blankets when necessary. The camp was inhabited by the lower classes, and from the districts where the plague was most violent. Many had been employed on public works, and readily accommodated themselves to camp life. I am not sure, but the general health was attributable to this fact, and that the season was excessively dry, and well suited to outdoor life. Under different conditions, the mortality from other causes might have been alarming. The camp broke up October 31, 1878.

R. B. NALL, M. D., *Surgeon in charge of Camp Joe Williams.*

The following list embraces the names of those who died at Camp Joe Williams, six miles south of the city, as furnished by Dr. R. B. Nall, surgeon in charge :

Berry, Isaac.
Brady, Mrs.
Berry, A.
Brady, Ellen.
Brown, F.
Calere, Mrs. J.
Cannon, Mrs.
Clinton, James.
Calere, T. C.
Carson, Mrs.
Coe, Wm.
Dirosy, Wm.
Dannion, Wm.
Easterbrook, Frank.
Gilbert, J.
Garrison, Mrs. Bruce.
Grecco, Angelo.
Freeland, Wm.
Jones, J. W.
Johnson, A. J.
Kirk, Fannie.
Karrigan, Thos.
Kelly, Mr.
Lee, Mrs.
Laurence, Mrs. & 3 children.
Lanigan, Joseph.
Lutz, Martha.
Limburger, Albert.
McDonald, Mary.
Manton, John.
Miles, Mike.
McQuillan, Wm.
Murphy, E. K.
Murphy, Owen.
Murphy, J. P.
Merrill, Mrs. M. A.
Powers, Wm.
Peterson, John.
Pinder, Sarah.
Ringer, Wm.
Ryan, Wm.
Ruhle, Mrs. Geo.
Richardson, Stella.
Sculderhoff, C.
Taylor, Dr.
Webber, Mrs.
Wright, Mary.
Woods, W. E.
Williams, S. W.
Lady, unknown.
Frenchman, unknown.
Colored man, unknown.

CAMP DUFFY.

Camp Duffy was called after our fellow citizen, John J. Duffy, and was situated in Raleigh and vicinity, and comprised about fifty families, refugees from Memphis. They drew weekly rations from the commission, composed of Messrs. Duffy, Meyers, and Stoddard. Some of the families occupied tents furnished by the Citizens' Relief Committee. During the latter part of September and first of October, the fever broke out in the camp. Having no physician but Dr. Duncan, whose time was principally taken up at the Poor House, the Howards sent to their relief Drs. Wilkes, Fogarty, and Spencer. The deaths numbered from forty to fifty, the names of which are embraced in the general death-list of the Howard Association.

REPORT OF THE FATHER MATHEW CAMP.

In giving to the public this list of contributions, I feel that a word of preface, explanatory of what has been done by means of the generous aid sent me, is very desirable, especially as I have received many letters of inquiry as to what I have been enabled to do to relieve the miseries which, during the past three months, have been caused here, by the yellow fever plague, and as to why I would not publish the contributions sent me. In answer to all these inquiries, in some instances complaints, I have to plead *want of time.* The many letters of sympathy sent me have not been forgotten. In the midst of most gloomy scenes, they afforded me, very frequently, the relief of consolation.

APPENDIX.

When the yellow fever plague was *imported* here, early last August, it was not difficult to anticipate its scourging ravages. I was assistant priest at St. Patrick's Church, and honorary President of the Father Mathew Society here. It was attached to the Irish Catholic Benevolent Union and to the Catholic Total Abstinence Union of America. We had a meeting of our society on the Sunday after the plague had made its appearance. Forty-five members were present. Many were unaware of the great calamity which was imminent, and some were anxious, in the event of the fever becoming epidemic, to have the society organize, from among its members, a corps of nurses or others to assist the families of the members who might be stricken down, and, as far as they might be able, other afflicted families—without distinction, as I apprehended, of race, creed, or color. Knowing full well that our society did not contain the class of men who would be enabled to effectually carry out this grand idea, I suggested that the members save themselves and families by timely flight, and establish, in quarters considered safe, a camp, which might be made a SOURCE of refuge and relief. This suggestion met with an unanimous approval. I assured them that I would provide the funds and look after every interest. An unanimous resolution was then passed to leave the treasury and powers of board, in fact, all the rules of the society, in the hands of a committee of five members, with me as chairman. On the next day I issued an appeal for aid, to the societies comprising the two great National Unions to which our society was attached. I was anxious, as I wrote, "to show to the world the great power that might be wielded by the co-operative efforts of our Unions, and to convince Catholic societies of some of the great benefits of membership in these Unions."

It has enabled us to be a source of charity and benevolence among the needy, the dying, and the dead, irrespective of creed, race, or color, during nearly three months of a most trying ordeal—an ordeal which made our fair city a city of the dying and dead. Out of its population of 45,000 or 50,000 inhabitants, 35,000 or 40,000 had fled for their lives when the plague broke out; of the 8,000 or 10,000 who remained, over 7,000 are reported as having been stricken down by the fever. The county undertaker has a registry of 2,500 burials by him alone.

The bravest and the noblest of every rank were being daily stricken down, and their remains hurriedly carried away to the cemeteries or the potter's field.

Those of us whom God was pleased to spare, in order to minister to the wants of the sick, the needy, and the dead, had to witness scenes which pen can not well describe, and to undergo labors which, on some occasions at least, might be considered superhuman.

Among our sisters and priests the fever made great havoc. Almost a score of sisters died. Of the priests who were in the city when the fever broke out, only three of us escaped without having to submit to the treatment of physicians and nurses, who, as yet, know no specific remedy for yellow fever patients. It is a fact that wherever the disease was directly attacked by the powers of medicine, the life of the patient was directly attacked.

Since the 29th of August, ten of our priests have been laid down "to sleep" in Calvary Cemetery, making, in all, fifteen priests—five in 1873 and ten in 1878—who have died here of yellow fever! Fifteen who have died on the field of battle, to which the call of their ministry summoned them. This great mortality among priests is not to be wondered at, when it is taken into consideration that every dying Catholic needs his priest; that the priest has to sit and kneel beside the bed of the plague-stricken patient, and, whilst hearing the confession of years of sin, to lean over the patient, inhaling his poisonous breath; and he has very often to draw out, from beside his person, the hands that are stiffening in death, in order to anoint them with the holy oils of the dying. Thus, humanly speaking, it was almost impossible for a priest on duty here to have escaped the plague.

On the day that I gave my appeal to the printer, Mr. Consadine, our very worthy and self-sacrificing vice-president, and myself set out to select a suitable place on which to erect our Father Mathew Camp of Refuge. The idea was somewhat novel. The undertaking was considered very arduous, and some of our best friends warned us that the labor would be herculean. Yet we were determined to carry out our project. Few, if any, could have anticipated our wonderful success.

The inhabitants of the country districts were scared of any who came from the city. Panic was every-where around us. The managing committee of our Citizens' Relief had to call upon the military to force its way to the camping-ground selected for the Joe Williams Camp.

We *quietly* found out an eligible site, of about 200 acres of land. There was a boiling spring in the midst, and groves of forest trees on each side of the crystal stream, to which the spring was a main tributary. We ascertained that the tract was unoccupied, and that it belonged to Messrs. Hill, Fontaine & Co., distinguished merchants of our city. Before we could make arrangements with them, we, next day, had five sentries on the tract, to take possession of it. By the same evening we had a number of tents on the ground and

APPENDIX. 397

the camp established. We published and posted around the tract our rules and regulations, among which it was declared that "no one under the influence of intoxicating liquor would be allowed to enter the grounds, and that, without special permit, no intoxicating liquor would be allowed."

We established, on one side of the grounds, a quarantine department. There we detained, for a number of days, every one with permit seeking admission to the camp. They, as far as we could make them, worked in grading their portion of the streets in the main camp, into which, after fifteen days, they were admitted. This precaution against introducing the plague into the camp, was very desirable, and it worked most admirably. The dangers of a panic, which might disperse the camp, were thus obviated. Every one felt the more secure, and the elements of harmony and peace were strengthened.

Of course, we did not entirely depend upon human precaution to protect us. The most of those admitted to our camp were Catholics; hence, one of the first buildings erected on the grounds was a little church. It was on wheels, and located at one end of our main, or Father Mathew Avenue, beneath the shades of a forest tree. It was dedicated in honor of the Sacred Heart of our Divine Lord, and we all looked upon it as the Ark of our safety. There, during the plague, I celebrated mass almost every morning, and recited the rosary and gave benediction of the most blessed sacrament every night, when, after the day's labor in the plague-stricken city, I returned to rest at the camp, and be consoled by the prayerful greetings of our poor, faithful people, who daily feared that I would be stricken down. These esteemed greetings afforded me many a relieving joy amidst the most gloomy days of the awful plague.

In a very few days we had a commissary and drug-store, a kitchen and commodious dining-hall erected, until every thing was so admirably arranged, that a friend, coming from a distance, suggested that we should call the place NEW MEMPHIS.

For a few weeks we reserved the main avenue and the camp for the members of our society and for their families. *They did not all avail themselves of the opportunities thus afforded them.* Of those who did do so, none of themselves or their families died, except one good woman, who, having gone to the city, contracted the disease there, and died in a few days after returning to the camp.

Within a very few weeks after the camp was established, we had any number of applicants for admission. We issued permits, to be distributed, by responsible parties, among those alone who were in need of our protection, of good morals, and prepared to submit to our rules and regulations. Without one of these permits no one was admitted beyond the lines of the sentries. Thus it was that we were enabled to keep out of the camp those who might become elements of discord or vice, and to maintain it, for ten long weeks, in HARMONY and VIRTUE.

The plague raged every-where through the country districts around us. Its victims, from even the very confines of the camp, were being daily carried to their graves. Out of our population of about 400, we had *only* ten deaths from fever. In each case the fever was *contracted* in the city. It did not spread in the camp. In fact we had not one certain case, of a fatal or unfavorable result, contracted in our camp: Providence must have assisted us.

In writing of the health of our camp, I must make mention of our devoted physician, Dr. W. C. Cavanagh. He was ever untiring in his efforts to assist us, by his wise counsel and medical skill, until he was stricken down at the post of duty. His devoted wife, *without the aid of a physician*, successfully nursed him through a severe attack, and, in a few weeks, he was able to revisit our camp, to inspire once more renewed confidence for the safety of our poor people.

After we had been about a month in the camp, we rented commodious adjacent buildings, and established a school for the children. Three of the Sisters of St. Joseph took charge of it, and, for the time, made their home with us, and rendered invaluable assistance, in ministering to a variety of necessities among our poor people. Thus, by the generous aid we sent, we were enabled to provide for the every necessity of our community, and not only that, but to disburse, for a period of ninety days, an average of $150 a day in general charities outside of the camp. I disbursed this much, and much more, I am sure, through the Sisters of St. Joseph, and through responsible parties, whom I found going about doing good, my invaluable instruction being: "Relieve all you can, and call on me for more." Thus, as fast as I received money, I put it at once into circulation among the needy.

The Howard Association, *for awhile,* honored my requisitions for nourishment for those sick of the *fever in the city.*

The Citizens' Relief here gave us hard rations for about one-fifth of our people, and, during the last three weeks of its existence, it paid for our fresh meats, firewood, and some lumber to set up back kitchens in the camp. It also gave us a few boxes of ill-assorted clothing, and two small supplies of delicacies for the sickly. If we did not get more of our necessities supplied by this excellent relief committee, it was not the fault of its untiring and self-sacrificing chairman, General Luke Wright, who, from the beginning, recognized us a public benefactor, and who, when we had a complaint to make to him, assured us, that by "O. K.-ing" bills to him, he would have supplied to us "every thing that *I* deemed necessary for our people." This assurance was made during the waning weeks of the plague, and in order to carry it out, General Wright interested himself *personally* in our behalf, when our orders on the commissary were being, from day to day, left unfilled. To him, and to the Citizens' Relief here in general, we are thankful. Being *independent* in the management of our camp, we only called for such assistance as we needed for those *alone* who *in no way* were connected with our society, or with the family of any of its members. I must say that among the Citizens' Relief Committee and Howard Association a very grand spirit of catholic or universal charity was manifested. I met their representatives almost every-where—even in the negro hospital that I was wont to visit. *The plague here did develop the grandest attributes of our common humanity.* A common feeling took possession of all. Catholic charity was the bond which made a grand confraternity of almost all of us who were spared being stricken down.

At the end of October, the long-wished-for visitor arrived. Frost made its appearance, and "Yellow Jack" was slain for the *present*. We had reason to thank God. I proclaimed in the camp a three days preparation for thanksgiving. All were permitted to enter the city and arrange their household effects during the day. At night we had devotions at the camp.

On All-Hallows Day, we determined on moving HOME in solemn procession. I celebrated a thanksgiving mass, and administered holy communion to a vast number of men, women, and children, who had flocked around us, with those in the camp, to return thanks to God for our wonderful preservation. The scene was inspiringly grand. I thought it worthy of being preserved, and, in consequence, had on hand, by the assistance of my energetic society friend, W. N. Webb, of Louisville, Kentucky, a first-class artist. He photographed the mass of thanksgiving and the scene after it, when, in joy, all prepared to "pick up stakes," and march in solemn procession to the church, where benediction of the most blessed sacrament was given, and the te deum solemnly chanted. The scene is one which I shall never forget. We all had reason to thank God, but more especially I, the most youthful among my comrade priests, who now sleep in death, but all of whom marked me out, as the first victim for the plague!

On examining the bank-book of the Father Mathew Camp, I found, to-day, to its credit, $1269.21. Of this amount over $900 is still due to the undertakers. The balance, for the most part is due on relief bills issued to grocery stores, to relieve those in their vicinities. Thus, it is that I have endeavored to disburse every thing, to the best advantage which was sent me.

I have to thank especially the Citizens' Relief of Philadelphia, Pittsburgh, Worcester, and Newark, Ohio, for recognizing the claim of our necessities. Outside of our comrade Catholic societies, our priests and bishops, those alone, assisted us.

Our most special thanks are due to Martin I. J. Griffin, Secretary of the I. C. B. U., who has proved himself to be our BEST friend, and who declined to accept of personal expenses. He was the FIRST and the LAST to send us contributions.

In our list there must be many mistakes. We have done our best to prevent them. All telegrams for cash were sent back for collection. Of those I have not been enabled to keep a regular registry. But for Brother Maurelian and his comrade Christian brothers I could not keep a registry, for I was engaged almost day and night in ministering to the dying.

No words can sufficiently express my gratitude to all who in any way have aided me. Perhaps there was never a grander response to the appeal of a *private* and unknown individual! It brought into my hands about $29,000! I could not have anticipated such a grand response. My thanks, and the thanks of our community, are, therefore, the more sincere. As such our friends will, therefore, the more readily accept them.

Miseries consequent on the plague still surround me. *The condition in which I am placed as rector of this church is embarrassing.* The effects of the plague shall long remain. But, whilst I am enabled to offer up, at the altar, the holy sacrifice of the mass, I shall ever remember *there* our generous sympathizers.

WILLIAM WALSH, *Rector of St. Bridget's Church.*

MEMPHIS, TENN., *December* 5, 1878.

APPENDIX.

CONTRIBUTIONS.

Location.	Received Through.	Society.	Union.	Amt.
Adrian, Mich	James J. Carey, Sec	St. Patrick's Ben. Soc	No. 274, I.C.B.U	$25 00
Atchison, Kansas	Rt. Rev. Albert Wolfe	Catholic Ben. Irish Soc	" 220, "	35 00
" "	"	Collected in church		13 00
Anderson, Ind	H. F. Brenan, Sec	Irish Ben. Soc	No. 16, I.C.B.U	15 00
" "	Rev. John B. Crawley	Collected from congregation		22 00
Ashton, R. I	Edw'd Hanlon, Cor. Sec.	St. Joseph's T. A. Soc	No. 445, C.T.A.U. of A.	10 00
Allentown, Pa	Patrick Reynolds, Sec	St. Patrick's Soc	" 185, I.C.B.U	5 00
Ansonia, Conn	T. O. Sullivan, Sec	F. M. T. A. Soc	" 342, C.T.A.U. of A.	20 00
" "	Rev. H. T. Brady	Collected from congregation		228 78
Austin, Minn	Patrick Geraghty, Tr	F. M. T. A. Soc	No. 166, C.T.A.U. of A.	18 00
Anot, Pa	Richard Purcell, Sec	F. M. Soc	" 386	5 00
" "		Subscribed by sundry persons		50
Akron, Ohio	Rev. F. M. Mahoney	St.Vincent de Paul Brother'd		15 00
" "	" " "	Subscribed by sundry persons		13 00
" "	" " "	F. M. Soc	No. 8, C.T.A.U. of A.	27 00
Aurora, Ill	Garrett Quin, V. P	F. M. T. A. and B. Soc	" 487, " "	20 00
Ayer, Mass	Martin I. J. Griffin	Irish Ben. Soc	" 218, I.C.B.U.	25 00
Alleghany City, Pa	Rev. M. Carroll, per V. Rev. Aug. Bossonies.	Temperance Soc	No. 277, C.T.A.U. of A.	20 00
Appleton, Wis	Thos. J. McCann, Sec	St. Patrick's T. A. B. Soc		10 00
Bristol, R. I	Thos. Duffy, Tr	St. Mary's T. A. B. Soc	No. 117, C.T.A.U. of A.	21 50
Baltimore, Md	A. J. Berger, Sec	St. John Ev. Temp. Soc	" 40, I.C.B.U	25 00
" "	Rev. E. A. McGurk, S. J.	St. Ignatius B. Soc	" 77, "	100 00
" "	Most Rev. Jas. Gibbons	Collections		450 00
Boston, Mass	Rev. Jas. N. Supple	St. Augustine's T. A. & M. B. S.	No. 447, C.T.A.U. of A.	25 00
" "	Rev. Jas. McCullough	St. Stephen's T. A. Soc	" 252, " "	25 00
" "	Rev. H. R. O'Donnell	Cathedral T. A. B. Soc	" 364, " "	50 00
" "	"	Sts. Peter & Paul T. A. B. Soc.		50 00
" "		F. M. No. 2 of St. James		15 00
" "		St. James Society		25 00
" "		F. M. No. 2, Sts. Peter & Paul.		25 00
Bowling Green, Ky	W. F. Konenberg, Pres	St. Joseph's Ben. Soc	No. 177, I.C.B.U	25 00
Brooklyn, N. Y	Rt. Rev. John Loughlin.	St. James' T. A. Soc	No. 214, C.T.A.U. of A.	100 00
" E. D., N.Y.	Rev. S. Malone	Sts. Peter and Paul Church	Collection	10 00
Bridgewater, Mass	Michael Cashin, Rec.Sec.	F. M. T. Soc	" 244, I.C.B.U	105 38
Butler, Pa	H. J. Berg, Jr	Proceeds Festival Cath. Socs.	No. 602, C.T.A.U. of A.	25 00
Blackstone, Mass	Rev. W. A. Power	St. Paul's T. A. Soc	" 428, "	5 00
Blossburgh. Pa	Michael Ely, Pres	C. T. A. Soc		22 00
Buffalo, N. Y	William Franklin, Pres.	F. M. T. A. & B. Soc	No. 373, I.C.B.U	20 00
" "	John Shea, Rec. Sec	St. John Baptist B. Soc	" 429, C.T.A.U. of A.	47 00
" "	Timothy Cochrane	St. Joseph's T. A. B. Soc	" 562, " "	50 00
Bridgeport, Conn	Patrick Kane, Tr	F. M. Y. M. T. A. and B. Soc.	" 351, I.C.B.U	10 00
Blairsville, Pa	J. M. Harvey, Sec	Sts. Simon and Jude B. Soc	" 215, C.T.A.U. of A.	15 00
Bloomington, Ill	P. F. Bell, V. P	St. Patrick's T. A. and B. Soc.	" 58, I.C.B.U	100 00
Brandywine, Del	John Doran, Pres	St. Joseph's B. Soc		10 00
Bordentown, N. J	C		No. 222, C.T.A.U. of A.	31 00
" "	James Powell, Sec	Hib. T. A. B. Soc	" 160, " "	10 00
Barclay, Pa	John Sweeny, Pres	St. Patrick's T. A. and B. Soc.	" 45, " "	50 00
Bay City, Mich	Rev. T. Rafter, Pastor	St. James' R. C. T. A. & B. S.	" 438, " "	50 00
Binghampton, N. Y.	M. C. Madden, Tr	St. Patrick's T. A. & B. Soc		1 00
Bernardsville, N. J	Hugh Sheriden	F. M. T. A. Soc	No. 416	20 00
Belle Creek, Minn	Jas. O'Reilly, Pres	St. Malachy's T. A. & B. Soc.	C.T.A.U. of A.	40 00
Benson, Minn	Rev. H. R. O'Donnell	St. John's T. A. & B. Soc	" 188, " "	10 00
Bangor, Me	Michael Crowley, Pres	Catholic Ben. Soc	" 283, I.C.B.U	30 00
Brunswick, Ga	Rev. H. Schlenke	St. Patrick's Soc	" 458, C.T.A.U. of A.	10 00
Bellows Falls, Vt	Henry B. Fitzsimmons, Cor. Se.			
Cairo, Ill	D. J. Foley, Sec	Knights F. M. C. T. A. Soc		35 65
" "		St. Patrick's Ben. Soc	No. 243, I.C.B.U	30 00
Champaign, Ill	Patrick Lynch	United Sons of Erin	" 17, "	22 35
Cleveland, Ohio	John J. L'Estrange	St. Patrick's Society	" 300, "	20 00
" "	P. O'Brien, Pres	Knights St. Joseph	" 340, "	10 00
" "	J. F. Gallagher	Knights of Erin	" 255, "	25 00
" "	Rev. Wm. McMahon			48 00
" "	Wm. J. Fitzgerald	St. Malachy's T. A. & M. R. S.	No. 67, C.T.A.U. of A.	26 50
" "	Rev. J. Kuhn	Holy Family Church		50 00
Chattanooga, Tenn	Rev. P. Ryan, Pastor			100 00
Clarkesville, Tenn	Rev. P. J. Gleason			165 00
Clinton, Iowa	James Furlong, Cor. Sec.	R. C. T. A. Soc	No. 324, C.T.A.U. of A.	30 25
" Mass		Cash by express		109 66
Chester, Pa	Rev. R. J. Patterson	St. John's Church		58 00
" "	J. Bradley, Sec., per M. I. J. Griffin	St. Michael's B. Soc	No. 30, I.C.B.U	20 00
" "	Wm. Fennell	Im. Heart Soc	" 239, "	25 00
Central Falls. R. I	James Mulligan, Pres	Sac. Heart T. A. Soc	" 307, C.T.A.U. of A.	75 22
Cambridge, Mass	Michael Corcoran	St. Peter's T. Soc	" 550, " "	25 00
" "	Rev. R. H. O'Donnell	St. Paul's T. A. Soc		25 00
" "	"	F. M. Society of St. John's		73 00
Corry, Pa	James Carney, Sec	St. Thomas' B. Society	No. 203, I C.B.U	5 15
Connellsville, Pa	Chas. Malloy	T. A. and B. Soc	"	44 25
Charleston, S. C	Jas. F. Redding, Pres	St. Joseph's T. A. and B. Soc.	" 109, C.T.A.U. of A.	270 75
" "	Simon Fogarty, Tr	Irish Volunteers		55 00
Columbus, Ohio	Rev. A. A. Gallagher	St. Patrick's Church		155 00
" Ga	Louis Wells	Y. M. C. Union		25 00
" "	Matt. O'Brien, Agt			25 00
Cape Girardeau, Mo	Rev. J. W. Hickey, Pres.			60 00
Centralia, Pa	Wm. J. Nash, Sec	St. Ignatius T. A. and B. Soc	No. 604, C.T.A.U. of A.	25 00
Chicago, Ky	Rev. E. Downey, per W. N. Webb	St. Francis Church		28 00
" "	W. Neh. Webb	St. Francis C. T. A. Soc	No. 95	12 00

26

APPENDIX

LOCATION.	RECEIVED THROUGH.	SOCIETY.	UNION.	AMT.
Chicago, Ill...............	Very Rev. J. D. Riordan, per Bp. Feehan......	T. A. Societies................		$249 25
" "	John Carey, Sec............	K. I. P........................		50 00
" "	Rev. H. R. O'Donnell....	Societies of the C. T. A. U.....		254 10
		Young Men's	$17 00	
		St. James.....................	62 60	
		All Saints	20 00	
		National	11 50	
		Holy Family...................	59 50	
		Sacred Heart..................	60 00	
		Catholic Young Men's.........	25 00	
		Less expenses.................	$255 60 1 50	
				$254 10
Cohoes, N. Y...............	Pat. Doyle.....................	St. Bernard's T. A. B. Soc.....	No. 506, C.T.A.U. of A.	25 00
Council Bluffs, Iowa..	Officers and Persey.........			50 00
Champaign, Ill...........	Patrick Lynch...............	United Sons of Erin............	No. 37, I.C.B.U.............	22 35
Carleton, N. B............	Very Rev. T. Connolly...	Temp. Soc.....................	" 30..........................	60 00
Charlotte, Iowa...........	B. J. Monoghan, Sec........	T. C. T. A. B. S. of St. Mary's, of Deep Creek..................		50 00
Connersville, Ind......	John Garrity..................	St. Patrick's B. Soc............	No. 44, I.C.B.U..............	54 00
Camden, N. J...............	Martin I. J. Griffin.........	St. Joseph's B. Soc............	" 293, "	50 00
Dover, N. H.................	Dan'l D. Mahoney, Pres..	St. Mary's C. T. A. Soc........	" 546..........................	25 00
Danbury, Conn.............	John J. Stone, Pres.........	St. Vin. de Paul T. A. B. Soc..	" 559, C.T.A.U. of A.	10 00
Detroit, Mich..............	P. Blake.......................	Hib. Ben. Soc.................	" 1............................	100 00
Dennison, Ohio...........	John Jordan, Sec............	St. Patrick's Soc..............	" 353, I.C.B.U..............	25 00
De Pere, Wis...............	Dr. J. L. Cleary, Pres......	T. A. and B. Soc..............	" 22, C.T A.U. of A.	20 00
Denver, Col.................	A. Renouard, Cor. Sec....	St. Joseph's C. T. A. B. Soc...		30 00
" "	A. Manely, Jr................	C. T. B. Soc...................		30 00
Dubuque, Iowa............	Dan. Riordan, Pres	C. B. Soc......................	No. 98, I.C.B.U.............	100 00
Drifton, Pa..................	P. M. Boyle, Sec.............	St. Anne's T. A. and B. Soc...	" 454, C.T.A.U. of A.	5 00
	Thos. A. Buckley, Pres...	St. Patrick's B. Soc...........	" 103, I.C.B.U.............	10 00
Davenport, Iowa	J. P. Kerrigan, per Bp. Feehan........................	St. Patrick's B. Soc...........	" 19, "	100 00
" "	Rev. H. Flavin, per Bp. Feehan........................	St. Mary's Church T. A. B. S.		60 00
" "	John N. Dolan, per Bp. Feehan........................	Hib. Ben. Soc.................	" 18, I.C.B.U..............	50 00
" "	John N. Dolan, per Bp. Feehan........................	St. Margaret's T. A. Soc.....	" 630, C.T.A.U. of A.	40 00
Elmira, Pa...................	Nicholas Baker, Tr.........	F. M. T. A. Soc...............	" 350, "	10 00
Edenberg, Pa...............	Rev. H. Mullen..............	Subscribed by Jones Bros.....		5 00
Erie, Pa.......................	Florence Lynch, Sec........	I. A. B. A. Soc................	No. 295, I.C.B.U............	25 00
	Rev. Thos. A. Casey........			102 30
East Saginaw, Mich...	M. W. Madigan, Sec........	St. Joseph's C. T. A. Soc......	No. 382, I.C.B.U............	9 65
Earlham, Iowa............	John C. Regan...............			12 30
Essex Ferry, N. Y.......	John Brenneck, Pres.......	St. John's Society.............		20 00
E. Cambridge, Mass...	Rev. H. R. O'Donnell.....	F. M. T. A. Soc...............	No. 457, C.T.A.U. of A.	24 55
El Paso, Ill..................	Patrick O'Conner...........	C. T. A. Soc...................	" 326, "	13 00
Elkador, Iowa.............	Rev. J. J. Quigley............	St. Joseph's Ben Soc...........	" 251, I.C.B.U.............	10 00
Elyria, Ohio.................	John C. Wagner.............	Cath. Hib. B. Soc.............	" 379, "	50 00
Evansville, Ind..........	Eug. McGrath, Fin. Sec..	St. Bernard's B. Soc..........	" 188, "	50 00
Easton, Pa...................				50 00
Frankfort, Ky..............	R. L. Young, Pastor........	St. Joseph's C. B. Soc.........	No. 229, I.C.B.U............	50 00
Frostburg, Md.............	Daniel F. Cain, Sec.........	St. Joseph's B. Soc............	" 276, "	20 00
Fisherville, N. H.........	John C. Linehan, Sec......	St. John's C. T. A. Soc........	" 219, C.T.A.U. of A.	56 25
Fairbury, Ill................	Rev. John A. Fanning.....			68 00
Fond du Lac, Wis........	A. A. Kelly, Pres............	St. Patrick's Ben. Soc........		81 00
Fair Haven, Conn.......	John J. Doohan, Sec........	St. Francis T. A. B. Soc......	No. 346, C.T.A.U. of A.	11 70
Fort Ellis, M. T............	Sergt. T. Monaghan, V.P.	St. Mary's Soc.................	Seventh Infantry...........	15 00
Fort Wayne, Ind.........	Rt. Rev. Bishop Dwenger.			100 00
Gloucester City, N. J.	Michael M. Mullin, Sec...	Y. M. C. B. Soc...............	No. 314, I.C.B.U............	25 00
" "	Michael Cavanagh..........	St. Mary's Soc.................	" 339, "	25 00
Germantown, Pa.........	Robt. J. Foster...............	St. Vin. de Paul T. A. B. Soc..	" 182, C.T.A.U. of A.	25 00
Grafton, W. Va............	John L. Hezlmer.............	Hib. Ben. Soc.................	" 228, I.C.B.U.............	11 00
Greenville, Ohio.........	B. Blattman, Sec............	St...............................	" 343, "	15 00
Galveston, Texas.........	Rev. L. Glenn................			60 00
Geneva, N. Y...............	Very Rev. J. T. Winans..			75 10
Honesdale, Pa.............	M. P. Coyne, Cor. Sec.....	F. M. T. A. Soc...............	No. 566, C.T.A.U. of A.	15 00
Huntington, W. Va.....	J. V. Werlander, Sec.......	C. Aid Soc.....................	" 357, I.C.B.U.............	31 00
Hopkinsville, Ky........	B. Dinneen....................	Subscribed by sundry persons.		13 75
Hancock, Md...............	D. T. Baxter, Sec............	St. Peter's T. and B. Soc.....	No. 337, I.C.B.U............	10 00
Havre de Grace, Md..	Rev. J. L. Barry, Pres.....	St. John the Baptist Soc......	" 319, "	20 00
Houghton Co., Mich...	Michael Finnegan..........			25 00
Hoosac Falls, N. Y.....	Rev. J. D. Waldran, O.S.A.	F. M. T. A. and B. Soc.......	No. 571.......................	51 00
Helena, M. T...............	Terrence O'Donnell, Pres.	St. Patrick's C. B. T. A. Soc..	" 504, C.T.A.U. of A.	50 00
Houston, Texas...........	R. A. Girand, Pres.........	St. Joseph's T. A. B. Soc.....		10 00
Hudson, Ohio..............	Rev. P. H. O'Mara, per Rev. Wm. McMahon.....			
Holmesburg, Pa..........	Martin I. J. Griffin.........	St. Dominic's T. A. B. Soc...	No. 191, C.T.A.U. of A.	20 00
		St. Dominic's Ben. Soc.......	" 172, I.C.B.U.............	25 00
Hartford, Conn............	Daniel Smith, Cor. Sec....	St. Peter's T. A. and B. Soc..		50 00
				9 25
Indianapolis, Ind.......	Rev. D. O'Donaghue......	Subscribed by a member of St. John's Church...........		50 00
" "	Very Rev. A. Bessonies..	St. Patrick's T. A. B. Soc.....	No. 318, C.T.A.U. of A.	25 00
		Collections....................		296 00
Indianola, Texas.........	H. Runge & Co...............	Temperance Friends..........		53 00
Ishpening, Mich..........	Edward McGinty............	St. Patrick's C. B. Soc........	No. 325, I.C.B.U............	25 00
Irvington, N. Y...........	Rev. P. J. Halzacker......	Pastor...........................		25 00

APPENDIX. 401

LOCATION.	RECEIVED THROUGH.	SOCIETY.	UNION.	AMT.
Jersey City, N. J	Michael Nevin, Pres.	St. Bridget's T. A. B. Soc	No. 53, C.T.A.U. of A.	$20 00
" "	Patrick McCabe	St. Michael's T. A. B. Soc	" 2, " "	60 00
Joliet, Ill	Peter Collins, Pres.	F. M. T. A. and B. Soc	" 131, " "	25 00
" "		St. Patrick's B. Soc	" 322, I.C.B.U.	25 00
Jeffersonville, Ind		St. Augustine's B. Soc	" 227, "	25 00
Jackson, Tenn	Rev. F. Doyle	Collections		100 00
" "	H. D. Purnell	Cath. M. B. Soc	No. 367, I.C.B.U.	25 00
Kellyville, Pa	Wm. F. Deally, Sec	St. Charles T. A. B. Soc	No. 145, C.T.A.U. of A.	16 00
" "	James Jordan	St. Mary's B. Soc	" 112, I.C.B.U.	13 00
" "	Martin I. J. Griffin	St. Mary's B. Soc	" 112, "	2 25
Kingston, N. Y	Ira Morrell, Sec	St. Joseph's T. A. and B. Suc.	" 472, C.T.A.U. of A.	30 00
Keene, N. H	Cornelius Sullivan,	St. Bernard's T. A. Soc	" 217, I.C.B.U.	40 00
Kansas City, Mo	Jeremiah Dorva, Pres.	I. C. B. Soc	" 330, "	50 00
" "	Rev. James A. Dunn	Collections		100 25
Kokomo, Ind	Rev. Francis Lordeman.	F. M. T. A. and B. Soc	No. 614, C.T.A.U. of A.	7 60
Knottsville, Ky	W. Neh. Webb	St. Lawrence C. T. A. Soc	" 197, "	75 62
" "	" "	St. Lawrence C. T. A. Soc	" 197, "	13 12
Kent, Ohio		St. Vincent de Paul Soc	" 375, I.C.B.U.	25 00
Louisville, Ky	C N. Jacques, Sec	St. Patrick's T. A. Soc	No. 206, C.T.A.U. of A.	12 00
" "	W. Neh. Webb	St. Alphonsus T. A. Soc	" 404, " "	14 84
" "	" "	St. Francis T. A. Soc		1 00
" "	Rev. Farber Demy	Collections per W. N. Webb.		14 35
" "	Hon. John W. Kearney.	Per W. N. Webb		5 00
" "	Gran. W. Smith			25 00
" "	John Kerberg	St. Cecelia's B. Soc	No. 308, I.C.B.U.	47 00
La Salle, Ill	Thos. Rafter, Sec	St. Patrick's Ben. Soc	" 301, "	25 00
" "	Thos. Cahill, Pres	St. Patrick's T. A. B. Soc		50 00
Leetonia, Ohio	A. Clarke, Pres	St. Patrick's Soc	" 257, I.C.B.U.	25 00
Leavenworth, Kansas	Rev. James Reilly			61 00
" "	Rt. Rev. Bishop Fink			15 50
Lancaster, Penn	D. A. Altrick	St. Bernard's Ben. Soc	No. 111, I.C.B.U.	50 00
Le Roy, N. Y	John Brown	St. Patrick's Soc	" 527, C.T.A.U. of A.	15 00
Lawrence, Mass	Mark Doherty	St. Mary's Ass'n of Prayer		206 75
Lowell, Mass	Rev. M. O'Brien, Pastor.	St. Patrick's Church		15 00
Lostant, Ill	T. Drew	F. M. T. Soc		20 00
Lynchburg, Va	J. M. McLaughlin, Treas.	St. J. B. Soc	No. 236, I.C.B.U.	50 00
" "	James McGowan, Sec	St. Patrick's B. Soc		
Lafayette, Ind	Rev. M. Carroll, per Very Rev. Aug. Bossonies...	St. Michael's T. A. B. Soc	No. 549, C.T.A.U. of A.	15 00
Lemont, Ill	Garrett Finvin, Cor. Sec.	F. M. T. A. Soc	" 401, " "	10 00
Lincoln, Ill	E. Lynch, V. P		" 140, " "	21 45
Mount Savage, Md	Jas. G. Smith, Sec	St. Patrick's B. Soc	No. 341, I.C.B.U.	10 00
Morris Run, Pa	Wm. Hayes, Sec	St. Joseph's T. A. B. Soc	" 442, C.T.A.U. of A.	5 00
Martinsburgh, W. Va.	W. D. Sullivan, Sec	St. Patrick's Soc	" 371, I.C.B.U.	5 00
" "	E. V. Little, Sec	St. Joseph's Soc	" 197, "	5 00
Media, Pa	Rev. H. L. Wright,			35 00
Milbury Mass	P. H. Keefe, Sec	F. M. T. A. and B, Soc		25 00
" "	Rev. N. J. Dougherty			56 00
Mahanoy Plane, Pa...	Wm. Wright, Pres	St. Patrick's T. A. B. Soc	No. 90, C.T.A.U. of A.	12 00
Meriden, Conn	Michael Moroney, Pres.	S. Rose's T. A. B. Soc	" 531, " "	10 00
" "		Subscribed by sundry persons.		10 25
" "		St. Patrick's M. R. Soc	No. 138, I.C.B.U.	15 00
Mendota, Ill,	John Kane, Pres	I. C. B. Soc	" 369, "	26 50
" "	Dan Keefe, Sec	I. C. B. Soc	" 369, "	25 00
Manayunk, Pa	Patrick J. Curran	St. John Baptist T. A. B. Soc.	" 383, C.T.A.U. of A.	32 50
" "	M. F. Wilhere, V. P	St. Patrick's Soc	" 197, I.C.B.U.	25 00
" "				25 00
" "	Jos. McNamee, Sec	St. Patrick's B. Soc	No. 197, I.C.B.U.	50 00
" "	M. F. Wilhere	Rev. David Mulholland, Soc.	" 109, "	25 00
" "				10 00
Mansfield Valley	Jas. Ford, Sec. and Treas.	Cath. Mut. Aid Soc	No. 312, I.C.B.U.	25 00
Muscatine, Iowa	Dennis Ryan, Pres	St. Mary's T. A. Soc	" 550, C.T.A.U. of A.	10 00
Moosic, Pa	John King, Sec	St. Mary's R. C. B. Soc	" 204, I.C.B.U.	10 00
Mt. Carmel, Pa	A. J. Malone, Sec	St. Patrick's T. A. B. Soc	" 435, C.T.A.U. of A.	10 00
Mystic Bridge, Conn.	J. Fleming	Proceeds Raffle Lady's Scarf.		21 50
Montgomery Ala	Mrs. A. O. Knap	Party		23 00
" "	Estelle Club	Cake Raffle		3 05
" "	Miss Mary A. Simpson	Pin-cush on Raffle		3 55
" "	Miss Mellie Stowe			144 10
Marysville, Ky	Rev. John Glorieux	Congregation		25 00
McKeesport, Pa	Jos. A. Skelly, Sec	St. Joseph's Ben. Soc	" 318, I.C.B.U.	25 00
" "	Rev. Jas. Nolan, Pastor.			77 50
Moberly, Mo	Wm. O'Leary, Pres	Irish Catholic Ben. Soc	" 299, I.C.B.U.	50 00
Milwaukee, Wis	B. F. Cook, Treas	I. Catholics		50 00
" "		Hibernian B. Soc	No. 320, I.C.B.U.	20 00
Massillon, Ohio	H. L. Leahy, Sec	St. Jno. C. T. A. & M. R. Soc.	" 256, "	28 70
Manchester, N. H		St. Paul's C. T. A. Soc	" 567, C.T.A.U. of A.	20 00
" "	P. A. Devine	T. A. Soc	" 220, "	20 00
Minneapolis, Miss	Rev. James McGolrick..	Father Mathew Soc	" 417, "	25 00
" "	Rev. H. R. O'Donnell		" 93, "	67 50
Mahanoy City, Pa	M. Lavelle, Pres	St. Joseph's T. A. Soc	" 332, I.C.B.U.	10 00
Macon, Ga	John Ingalls, Pres	St. Vincent de Paul B. Soc	" 304, "	20 00
Mt. Vernon, Ohio	S. J. Brent. Sec	St. Vincent de Paul B. Soc	" 204, "	25 00
Middletown, Ohio	Martin I. J. Griffin	St. Patrick's B. Soc		2 50
Middletown, Conn	John Barrett			10 00
Memphis, Tenn	James Reilly			25 00
" "	Tom Keely	Hibernian Aid Soc	No. 365, I.C.B.U.	10 00
Michigamme, Mich	Nicholas King, Sec			25 00
New York, N. Y	Michael O'Keeffe, Treas.	Irish Brigade Officer's Ass'n		50 00
" "	Alex. Patton	Transfiguration R. C.T.A.B.S.	No. 1, C.T.A.U. of A.	5 00
" "		Temp. Soc. Ch. Holy Innoc...		100 00
" "	Rev. J.W. Larkin, Pastor.			30 55
" "	Philip Meredith, Sec	St. Michael's R. C. T. A. B. S.	No. 60, C.T.A.U. of A.	50 50

APPENDIX.

LOCATION.	RECEIVED THROUGH.	SOCIETY.	UNION.	AMT.
New York, N. Y.	Very Rev. T. C. Preston.	Subscribed by a lady		$25 00
" "	St. Vincent de Paul Soc. through Bp. Feehan			
Nashville, Tenn	Rt. Rev. P. A. Feehan.	Contributions		200 00
" "	J. J. O'Rorke, Sec	St. Joseph's T. A. B. Soc.	No. 35, C.T.A.U. of A.	3:90 75
" "	Ch. Power, Pres	Hibernian Soc	49, I.C.B.U	100 00
N. Hampton Jun., N. J.	John Kerr, Sec	F. M. T. A. and B. Soc		100 00
Nashua, N. H.		St. Mary's Soc		10 00
National Milit. Home, Dayton, Ohio	F. J. O'Sullivan, Rec.Sec.	Hibernian B. Soc	No. 354, I.C.B.U	25 00
Northampton, Mass.	John H. Sullivan, Sec	F. M. T. A. and B. Soc	" 538, C.T.A.U. of A.	100 00
Nth. Brockfield, Mass.	John Rusk, Tr	American Soc. of Hibernians.	" 358, I.C.B.U	15 00
New Bethlehem, Pa.	Rev. B. Magreny	T. A. B. Soc	" 509, C.T.A.U. of A.	10 00
Norwood, Mass	M. J. Fahy			74 35
Negaunee, Mich	Nicholas McLaughlin, Tr	St. Patrick's B. Soc	" 199, I.C.B.U	27 00
New Castle, Del	Alex. McGee	C. T. A. Soc	" 124, "	10 00
New London, Conn.	Walter Fitzmaurice	Star of the Sea T. A. B. Soc	" 618, C.T.A.U. of A.	30 55
" "	Timothy Sugure, Cor.Sec.	St. John's B. Soc	" 245, I.C.B.U	50 00
Newark, N. J.	Rev. Jos. M. Flynn	St. Patrick's Cathedral		50 00
" "		St. John's Church		150 00
" "	Rev. John McKenna			80 00
Ohio	John McCarthy	Citizens' Relief Fund		80 50
North Adams, Mass.	C. P. Manning, Sec	F. M. T. A. Soc	No. 544, C.T.A.U. of A.	100 00
New Albany, Ind	John Byrne, Sec	St. Patrick's B. Soc	" 165, I.C.B.U	10 90
Norfolk, Va	J. C. Carroll			50 00
New Haven, Ky.	Rev. A. Viala	St. Catherine's T.A.B.S.& C.		31 00
Nelson Co., Ky	Rev. Father Demy, per W. N. Webb	St. Vincent's Church		57 00
Natchez, Miss	Britton Kormtz			7 60
				35 00
Oconto, Wis	J. A. D. Levy, Pres.	St. John's C. T. A. & B. Soc	No. 394, C.T.A.U. of A.	50 00
Ottawa, Ill	M. H. Crowley, Pres.	F. M. T. A. Soc	" 173, " "	20 00
"	Anonymous			*10 00
Orange, N. J.		St. John's T. A. Soc	No. 577, C.T.A.U. of A.	50 00
Owensboro, Ky.	A. Manheim, Pres	St. Stephen's T. A. Soc	" 270, " "	8 00
Oil City, Pa.	T. S. McGuinn, Pres.	St. Joseph's T. Soc	" 260, " "	26 00
Oconomowoc, Wis.	Wm. E. Ennessy, Sec.	St. Jerome T. A. and B. Soc		40 00
Oshkosh, Wis.	Rev. Jas. O'Malley	St. Peter's Church		20 00
"	Pres.	St. Peter's T. A. Soc	No. 265, C.T.A.U. of A.	15 00
Philadelphia, Pa.	Martin I. J. Griffin	Daniel Carroll B. Soc	No. 131, I C.B.U	50 00
" "	" " " "	Father Barbelin B. Soc		50 00
" "	" " " "	St. Elizabeth B. Soc		31 00
" "	" " " "	Father Mark Crane B. Soc	No. 104, I.C.B.U	50 00
" "	" " " "	Contribution		4 00
" "	" " " "	St. Agnes Female B. Soc		50 00
" "	" " " "	A member of the Bishop Wood B. Soc	I.C.B.U No. 130, I.C.B.U	10 00 75 00
" "	" " " "	Our Lady of Lourdes B. Soc		10 00
" "	" " " "	St. Edward's B. Soc	No. 303, I.C.B.U	100 00
" "	" " " "	National Catholic B. Soc	" 90, "	100 00
" "	" " " "	Phila. Nat. Catholic B. Soc	" 155, "	165 00
" "	" " " "	Kensington Cath. Soc		25 00
" "	" " " "	Phila. Citizens' Relief Com.		1700 00
" "	" " " "	St. Cecelia's Ben. Soc	No. 355, I.C.B.U	50 00
" "	" " " "	St. Michael's T. A. B. Soc	" 485, C.T.A.U. of A.	100 00
" "	" " " "	Rev. Thomas Fox Ben. Soc., Falls of Schuylkill	" 234, I.C.B.U	50 00
" "	" " " "	Delegates to Worcester I. C. B. U. Convention		40 00
" "	" " " "	Very Rev. Ed. McMahon B.S.		25 00
" "	" " " "	John Lee Carroll B. Soc	No. 350, I.C.B.U	20 00
" "	" " " "	Waterman's B. Soc		75 00
" "	" " " "	Father Burke B. Soc	No. 217, I.C.B.U	35 00
" "	" " " "	Archbishop Carroll B Soc	" 240, "	71 25
" "	" " " "	Archbishop MacHale B. Soc	" 364, "	10 00
" "	" " " "	Jas. D. Howley B. Soc	" 313, "	50 00
" "	" " " "	Pius IX. B. Soc	" 260, "	60 00
" "	" " " "	St. Monica Fem. B. Soc		60 00
" "	Most Rev. Archb'p Wood.	Contributions		1700 00
" "	Michael Hughes, Pres.	Im. Con. T. B. B. Soc	No. 229, C.T.A.U. of A.	50 00
" "	Philip Heneberry, Pres.	St. Charles T. A. Soc		50 00
" "	James Mehan, Tr	Sac. Heart T. A. B. Soc	" 189, " "	25 00
" "	C. Jas. Dacy, Pres.	St. Cecelia's T. A. B. Soc		17 00
" "	Jas. C. Hassett, Pres.	St. Philip Neri T. A. B. Soc	No. 273, C.T.A.U. of A.	29 00
" "	Danl. Gallagher, Fin.Sec.	St. Paul's T. A. B. Soc	" 144, " "	68 00
" "		St. Paul's Pioneer Corps		20 00
" "	Philip McManus	Keystone M. and F. B. Soc		25 00
" "	Thos. Greene, Sec	Dr. Moriarity B. Soc	No. 120, I.C.B.U	32 00
" "	And. J. Springer	Annunciation C. T. A. Soc		10 00
" "	Y. G			20 00
" "	A. Westenberg, per M. I. J. Griffin			2 00
" "	F. J. Liebherr			10 00
" "	Bernard J. Brady	Ancient O. Hib., Div. No. 1		50 00
" "	Patrick Gallagher	Ancient O. Hib., Div. No. 7		30 00
Pittsburg, Pa.	Martin Foley, Pres.	T. A. and B. Soc		10 00
" "	Jas. T. Tabany	St. Agnes T. A. and B. Soc	No. 368, C.T.A.U. of A.	
" "	M. A. Byrne, Tr	Emerald B. Soc		100 00
" "	J. D. Scully	Pittsburg Relief Committee.		320 00
" "	Wm. McLaughlin, Sec.	St. Bridget's T. A. and B. Soc.	No. 302, C.T.A.U. of A.	37 00
Providence, R. I.	Rev. A. A. Lambig	Brother'd of St. Mary of Con.	" 123, I.C.B.U	35 50
" "	Patrick Bosler	Sts. Peter & Paul Conference.	" 107, C.T.A.U. of A.	25 00
" "	Miss Ellen Hefferna			10 00
" "	Anonymous			5 00
" "	Rev. C. Hughes, Pastor.	St. Patrick's Church		12 00
" Pa	David P. Roche	St. Thaddeus F. M. T. A. B. S.	No. 92, C.T.A.U. of A.	26 00

APPENDIX. 403

LOCATION.	RECEIVED THROUGH.	SOCIETY.	UNION.	AMT.
Pittsfield, Mass......	Rich. V. Walsh............	St. Joseph's C. U.............	....	$188 55
" "	" "	F. M. T. A. Soc...............	No. 502, C.T.A.U. of A.	22 00
Patter on, N. J.........	" "	St. Patrick's T. A. B. Soc...	" 11, " "	50 00
" "	James O'Brien............	F. M. T. A. B. Soc............	" 237, " "	50 00
Pawtucket. R. I......	Edward McCaug ey...	S. Joseph's T. A. and B. Soc..	" 419. " "	25 00
" "	Rev. F. H. Kern in.......	" "	....	10 00
" "	B rnard Cusin, Tr.......	St. Mary's T. A. and B. Soc...	No. 113, C.T.A.U. of A.	95 00
Portland, Or.............	Rev. A. G. Glorieux......	F. M. T. A. and B. Soc........	" 221, " "	100 00
" "	" "	" "	....	47 25
Port Deposit, Md.....	Thos. E. Duke, Sec......	St. Joseph's B. Soc............	No. 105, I.C.B.U.............	28 00
Ph.en.xville, Pa......	Henry McGuckin........	St. Mary and St. Joseph Soc..	Nos. 126 & 131, I.C.B.U.	31 75
Petersburg, Va........	Rev. Thos. J. Wilson....	St. Joseph's C. B. Soc........	No. 404, I.C.B.U.............	52 00
Plattsburg, Mo........	J. W. O'Connor, Pres....	St. Mary's C. T. A. Soc......	....	20 00
Peoria, Ill.................	Rev. M. Hurley, Pastor..	St. Patrick's Church........	....	25 00
Plainfield, N. J.........	Patrick Keely, Pres......	A. O. Hib., Div. No. 4........	....	25 00
" "	J. W. Moynihan, Pres...	St. Mary's C. T. A. & B. Soc...	No. 320, C.T.A.U. of A.	25 00
Poughkeepsie, N. Y...	Rev. Jas. Nilan............	St. Peter's T. A. B. Soc......	" 63, " "	31 00
Paris, Ky..................	Jas. Flannigan, Pres.....	St. Patrick's B. Soc...........	" 259, I.C.B.U...............	25 00
Pulaski, Tenn...........	J. D. Lewis, Pres..........	J. J. Sullivan....................	....	10 00
Plymouth, Pa...........	B. O'Keefe, Cor. Sec.....	St.Vincent T. A. B. Soc......	No. 81, C.T.A.U. of A.	25 00
Pittston, Pa..............	John A. Collier, Pres....	F. M. Soc.........................	" 82, " "	100 00
Piqua, Ohio..............	" "	St. Patrick's B. Soc...........	" 3, I.C.B.U..................	25 00
Parkersburg, W. Va..	P. Flaherty, Sec...........	St. Patrick's M. R. Soc......	" 253, "	10 00
Port Hudson, Mich....	Very Rev. P. Hannart, per Bp. Feehan...........	St. Patrick's Soc...............	....	100 00
Portsmouth, Va........	Rev. Thos. J. Brady, per Bp. Feehan.................	St. Patrick's B. Soc...........	No. 192, I.C.B.U.............	50 00
Quincy, Mass...........	Rev. F. A. Zignsticker...	St. John's T. Soc...............	" 620, C.T.A.U. of A.	15 00
Ripon, Wis...............	R. J. Keenan, Sec.........	St. Patrick's C. T. A. B. Soc...	" 616, " "	21 80
Renova, Pa...............	D. J. Connor, Sec.........	St. Joseph's B. Soc............	" 127, I.C.B.U...............	10 00
Richmond, Va..........	A.M.Kelly, Pres.I.C.B.U.	" "	....	10 00
" "	Rt. Rev. John J. Keane..	" "	....	121 00
" "	Thomas Cox, Pres........	St. Peter's T. A. B. Soc.......	No. 151, C.T.A.U. of A.	20 00
" "	Daniel Hannigan.........	Catholic Ben. Soc.............	" 132, " "	100 00
Rochester, N. Y........	Rev. M. Magher...........	" "	....	150 00
" "	Thos. Howe, Pres.........	St. Patrick's B. Soc...........	No. 321, I.C.B.U.............	50 00
Rushville, Ind..........	Patrick Lenagh, Sec.....	Im. Conception T. A. Soc....	" 475, C.T.A.U. of A.	5 60
" "	" "	Subscribed by sundry persons	....	5 00
" "	M. J. Curran...............	" "	....	12 00
Ravenna, Ohio.........	Rev. J. D. Bowles.........	C. T. A. and B. Soc............	....	72 00
" "	" "	Collected from congregation..	....	10 00
Rock Island, Ill........	Thomas Devine, Sec....	St. Patrick's B. Soc...........	No. 281, I.C.B.U.............	28 00
Rockville, Conn........	John E. Davis, Sec......	F. M. T. A. B. Soc.............	" 26, C.T.A.U. of A.	5 00
Raleigh, N. C............	J. P. Hayes, Pres..........	St. John's B. Soc...............	" 361, I.C.B.U...............	31 00
St. Louis, Mo............	Rev. John J. Hennessy..	Im. Concep. T. A. B. Soc. of Iron Mountain...............	No. 368, I.C.B.U.............	40 00
" "	" "	" "	....	25 00
" "	Benziger Bros.............	" "	....	50 00
" "	Ed. Quinlan, Pres.........	Hibernian B. Soc..............	No. 71, I.C.B.U...............	300 00
" "	Rt. Rev. P. J. Ryan......	" "	....	100 00
" "	E. K. Brennan, Fin. Sec.	Knights F. M...................	....	20 00
" "	James O'Neil, Pres.......	U. C. St. Vincent de Paul Soc.	....	400 00
St. Paul, Minn..........	Rt. Rev. Thos. Grace....	" "	....	17 00
" "	Rev. J. Shanley............	" "	....	14 00
" "	" "	F. M. T. A. Soc................	No. 126, C.T.A.U. of A.	50 00
" "	" "	Cathedral B. Soc...............	....	25 00
Springfield, Ohio......	W. H. Sidley...............	Friendly Sons Soc.............	No. 12, I.C.B.U...............	50 00
" "	" "	Knights of St. Patrick.......	" 374, "	13 00
" "	" "	" "	....	50 00
" Ill.........	James M. Burke, Tr.....	Y. M. Hib. Soc.................	No. 13, I.C.B.U...............	25 00
" "	Dan. Hallahan, Pres....	F. M. T. A. B. Soc.............	....	30 00
Shelbyville, Ky........	Rev. Chas. E. Burke.....	Temp. Soc., Sac. Heart......	....	50 00
" "	Wm. Cotter, Sec...........	" "	....	
" "	Martin I. J. Griffin......	Cath. M. A. Soc................	No. 352, I.C.B.U.............	20 00
" "	Pat O'Connor, per M. I. J. Griffin......................	" "	....	3 00
St. John's N. B.........	R. H. Rochester............	St. Malachy's T. A. R. Soc..	....	65 00
St. Joseph, Mo..........	Rt. Rev. Bishop Hogan..	" "	....	100 00
Seymour, Ind...........	John J. Shiel, Pres.......	St. Ambrose B. Soc...........	No. 344, I.C.B.U.............	20 00
Stempton, Pa...........	Thomas Quin, Sec........	Workingmen's B. Soc........	" 163, " "	5 00
" "	Martin I. J. Griffin......	" "	" 163, " "	5 00
Staunton, Va............	D. Crimmens, Rec. Sec...	C. Hibernian B. Soc..........	" 252, " "	15 00
Stamford, Conn........	Wm. H. Rogers............	St. Patrick's T. A. Soc.......	" 316, C.T.A.U. of A.	10 00
Southington, Conn...	Maurice Cronin, Cor. Sec.	St. Thomas' T. A. B. Soc....	" 444, " "	30 00
South Bend, Ind.......	L. G. Tong, Pres...........	St. Joseph's T. A. B. Soc.....	" 405, " "	29 00
Sedalia, Mo...............	Ed. Hurley, Pres..........	Catholic B. Soc.................	No. 222, I.C.B.U.............	71 00
Seneca Falls, N. Y.....	John McBride..............	F. M. T. A. Soc................	" 300, "	5 00
Stillwater, Minn.......	J. F. Burke..................	" "	" 631, C.T.A.U. of A.	25 00
" "	" "	Crusaders' Soc..................	" 578, " "	15 00
South Bethlehem, Pa.	John M. Enright, Sec....	Catholic Ben. Soc.............	" 250, C.T.A.U. of A.	15 00
Stevens' Point, Wis...	Matt. Collins, Sec.........	" "	....	125 00
Stockton, Cal...........	Wells, Fargo & Co........	St. Mary's T. Soc..............	....	75 00
" "	" "	Irish Am. B. Soc...............	....	10 00
" Wis........	Jas. Dineen, Sec., per Bp. Feehan......................	St. John's T. A. Soc...........	No. 586, C.T.A.U. of A.	10 00
Salmon Falls, N. H...	Hugh Cunningham.......	St. Mary's C. T. A. B. Soc...	" 170, " "	23 20
Scranton, Pa.............	P. M. Walsh, Rec. Sec...	F. M. T. A. B. Soc.............	" 272, I.C.B.U...............	20 00
Santa Cruz, Cal........	Rev. J. Adams.............	T. A. B. Soc......................	....	74 00
" "	" "	Congregation....................	....	12 50
San Francisco, Cal....	Martin O'Brien, Sec.....	St. Joseph's T. A. B. & L. Soc.	No. 286, C.T.A.U. of A.	5 00
Salem, N. J...............	Rev. James McKernan..	St. Mary's Church.............	....	30 00
Sharon, Pa................	Wm. McNally, Cor. Sec.	F. M. T. A. & B. Soc..........	No. 251, I.C.B.U.............	34 00
Swarthmore, Pa.......	Thos. J. Dolphin, Pres...	F. M. B. Soc.....................	" "	20 00
Savannah, Ga...........	Wm. Hussey, Pres........	St. Patr ck's T. A. B. Soc....	No. 9, C.T.A.U. of A.	40 00
Summit, N. J............	Rev. J. A. Vassalo.........	C. T. A. Soc......................	....	

APPENDIX.

Location.	Received Through.	Society.	Union.	Amt.
Trenton, N. J.	Rev. James Curran	St. John's Church		$76 00
" "	S. D. Johnson, Sec.	Red Stocking Assembly		10 00
" "	F. D. Lane, Sec.	Y. M. League C. T. A.	No. 23, C.T.A.U. of A.	10 00
" "	D. F. Laun			10 00
Toledo, Ohio	Rev. J. O'Reiley	St. Vincent de Paul Soc.		25 00
"	Rev.Pat.O'Brien, Pastor.	Collection		38 73
Topeka, Kansas	Michael Heely, Pres.	Catholic B. Soc.	No. 220, I.C.B.U.	36 80
Terre Haute, Ind.	Dan. Lynch, Pres.	Hibernian C. B. Soc.	" 20, "	25 00
" "	" "	St. Joseph's Soc.	" 421, C.T.A.U. of A.	26 00
" "	" "	Knights F. M.		
Tiffin, Ohio	Frank Kellar, Sec.	St. Patrick's T. A. and B. Soc.	No. 340, C.T.A.U. of A.	15 50
Taunton, Mass.	Rev. E. J. Sheridan	Contribution		18 00
"	David Mahoney	Catholic Ben. Soc.	No. 180, I.C.B.U	100 00
Triadelphia, W. Va.	John Rinkers, Pres.	St. Mary's Y. A. B. Soc.	" 333, "	25 00
				10 00
Urbana, Ohio	J. C. Edmondson, Pres.	United Sons of Hib. Soc.	No. 9, I.C.B.U.	20 00
Vincennes, Ind	Rt. Rev. Bp. Chatard, per Very Rev. A. Bessonies.			200 00
Worcester, Mass.	T. H. Murphy, Pres.	I. C. B. Soc.	No. 114, I.C.B.U	56 00
" "	Rev. T. J. Conaty	F. M. T. Soc.	" 37, C.T.A.U. of A.	54 00
" "	"	St. John's Church		33 00
Wilmington, Del.	Rev. Thomas Griffin	Citizens' Relief Committee		500 00
" "	Very Rev. P. Reilly	St. Mary's B. Soc.	No. 28, I.C.B.U	50 00
" "	P. F McCullough, Pres.	St. Peter's B. Soc.	" 26, "	41 00
Westernport, Md.	Rev. D. C. DeWulf	St. Michael's B. Soc.	" 72, "	25 00
"		St. Peter's T. A. B. Soc.		25 00
Wilkesbarre, Pa.	John O'Donnel, Sec.	F. M. Y. M. Soc.	No. 505, C.T.A.U. of A.	22 45
" "	Martin F. Krowan, Tr.	F. M. T. A. B. Soc.	" 588, "	10 00
Williamsport, Pa.	C. Callahan, Se.		" 137, "	10 00
" "	M. J. O'Brien, Sec.	F. M. C. T. A. Soc.	" 130, "	15 00
Waltham, Mass.	Mrs. C. M. T.	St. Patrick's B. Soc.	" 284, I.C.B.U.	20 00
Whitewater, Wis	James Casserly, Sec.	St. Patrick's C. T. A. Soc.	No. 382, C.T.A.U. of A.	10 00
Winona, Minn.	James O'Brien, Sec.	F. M. T. A. Soc.	" 126, "	48 50
" "	Rev. J. B. Cotter	St. Thomas' Church.		15 00
Wenona, Ill	Denis O'Connor, Sec.	F. M. T. A. Soc.	No. 353, C.T.A.U. of A.	67 25
Willimantic, Conn.	James E. Manery	St. Joseph's T. Soc.	" 27, "	13 50
West Quincy, Mass.	Wm. F. Shea, Pres.	St. Mary's C. T. A. & M. R. S.		10 00
West Chester, Pa.	N. S. Bowen, Pres.	St. Agnes' T. A. B. Soc.	No. 194, C.T.A.U. of A.	10 00
West Winstead,Conn.	D. Maxwell			30 00
Wabash, Ind.	Rev. E. C. Wechmann.	S.P., D.R., St. P.T. A. & B.S.		15 00
Woonsocket, R. I.	Rev. P. O'Reilly, Sec.	F. M. T. A. Soc.	No. 585, C.T.A.U. of A.	35 00
Whiteville, Ky.	G. P. Howard	St. Mary's T. A. Soc.	" 497, "	50 00
Washington, D. C.	Cornelius Ryan	Hibernian Ben. Soc.	No. 63, I.C.B.U	5 00
West Troy, N. Y.	P. McCallen, Pres.	St. P. F. M. T. A. B. Soc.	" 327, C.T.A.U. of A.	125 00
Westbrookfield,Mass	Rev. H. R. O'Donnell	T. A. B. Soc.		50 00
				20 00
Xenia, Ohio.	Rev. Thos. Blake	Pastor		10 00
Youngstown, Ohio.	Thos. P. Coyne, Sec.	St. Anne's T. A. Soc.	No. 6, C.T.A.U. of A.	20 00
	Rev. D. Mears, Pastor.	St. Columba's Church		56 00
Yonkers, N. Y.	Cornelius Coghlen	Im. Concep. T. A. Soc.	No. 102, C.T.A.U. of A.	55 67
York, Pa.	John Mayer, Pres.		" 100, I.C.B.U.	50 00
Zanesville, Ohio.	Thos. S. McCornick.	St. Thomas' B. A. Soc	No. 52, I.C.B.U.	10 00
" "	James F. Ryan, Tr.	St. Patrick's B. Soc.	No. 14, "	20 00
" "	" "	F. M. T. A. Soc.	" 387, C.T.A.U. of A.	20 00

CLOTHING, ETC.

Location.	Received Through.	Articles.
Atlanta, Ga.	John Ryan	1 Box Clothing.
Cleveland, Ohio.	J. F. Gallagher	1 Box Blankets, etc.
Camden, N. J.	Sisters, per M. I. J. Griffin	Sundries.
Indianapolis, Ind.	Very Rev. Aug. Bessonies	1 Box Comforters.
New London, Conn.		1 Box Sundries.
Philadelphia, Pa.	Martin I. J. Griffin	1 Trunk Clothing.
" "		1 Overcoat.
" "	Jas. Carroll, per M. I. J. Griffin.	1 Box Medicine.
" "	Meyers & Co.	1 Package Merchandise.
" "		1 Keg Detergent.
" "	Frank J. Liebherr.	1 Bottle Medicine.
" "	Martin I. J. Griffin	1 Box Blankets.
" "	Mrs. Rockafeller, per M. I. J. Griffin	1 Box Clothing.
" "	Father Kelly's mother, per M. I. J. Griffin	1 Box Clothing.
Paducah, Ky.	Mrs. J. R. McKenna, per M. I. J. Griffin	Clothing.
Springfield, Ohio.	Per Rev. Fr. Feehan, O. C. C	Clothing.
Wilmington, Del.	John Brennan	1 Box Provisions.
"		1 Box Sundries.
"	St. Peter's Fem. B. Soc., per J. J. Smith	2 Boxes Clothing.

APPENDIX.   405

REPORTS OF OTHER ORGANIZATIONS.

The following embraces the reports of the religious societies, beneficiary orders, and individuals who coöperated with the Howard Association and the Citizens' Relief Committee, in attending to and providing for the sick and the needy during the epidemic of 1878, in Memphis and the vicinity:

REPORT OF MEMPHIS MASONIC RELIEF BOARD.

MEMPHIS, TENN., *Nov.* 6, 1878.

To the President and Members of the Masonic Board of Relief of Memphis:

BRETHREN,—I submit herewith a brief and condensed report of the action of the Board of Relief, during the terrible epidemic of yellow fever through which we have just passed. I regret exceedingly that my private business had been so pressing as to prevent my making a more lengthy report, detailing the work of each day or week, and making mention of the noble martyrs who so heroically yielded their lives upon the altar of humanity. But as I anticipate this will be done by an abler pen than mine, I ask from you a charitable indulgence and consideration for this. We are greatly indebted to Brother John D. Huhn, W. M., of Park Avenue Lodge, for compiling the list of those who came under the care and supervision of the Relief Board, which makes the greater part of this report. Fraternally and respectfully,

JOHN W. WAYNESBURG, *Acting Secretary.*

MEMPHIS, TENN., *Nov.* 3, 1878.

BRETHREN,—Appended is a list of cases of yellow fever which came under the supervision of the Masonic Relief Board of Memphis, Tennessee. Summarizing the same, we find that the fever struck the families of 120 brethren, classed as follows:

Affiliated in city of Memphis.. 91
Affiliated elsewhere.. 14
Non-affiliates 15

Total... 120

Total number of cases.. 317

Total number of deaths.. 136
Total number of recoveries... 181

317

M. M. affiliated dead.. 47
M. M. non-affiliates dead.. 11
F. C... 3

Total.. 61

Although this list has been compiled from the books and papers of the Relief Board with great care, it can not be considered as absolutely accurate. Nor will it be wondered at that errors should creep into the record, when it is remembered that *three times* the force of the brethren on duty were changed—death and sickness making vacancies, which were filled by new and inexperienced brethren. Of those connected more or less intimately with the duties of the Board, nine were forced to suspend their work by yellow fever; and of the nine, five brethren were called from labor by the Grand Master of all, and now rest in Elmwood. The list gives but an incomplete view of the work of the Board. Afflicted families were supplied with food, or with means of removing their desolate and mourning living beyond the reach of contagion. Nurses in actual employ were stricken at their posts and were cared for as Masons, although not belonging to the order. In some instances whole families were down at the same time, and not only was it necessary to furnish physicians and nurses, but a brother had to be placed in charge, and the necessary servants and supplies furnished to sustain the family which had thus, through the dispensation of Providence, found their quiet home transformed into a pest hospital. Nor does the list give accurately the actual Masonic death-loss of our city. Many Masons fled, with their families, to places of fancied security, into the country and to stations along our lines of railway, and many of these were there stricken with the fever and died beyond our purview. Some brethren remaining in the city were ill, and were nursed by their families, or by others, without our knowledge. Only the detailed reports of several lodges can give the actual loss to our fraternity. The malignancy of the epidemic of 1878 is plainly shown by this record. One-half the cases resulted in death; and this despite the best care and attention that relatives and trained skill of experienced nurses, supervised closely by the fraternity, could give.

BRETHREN AIDED BY RELIEF BOARD, 1878.

SOUTH MEMPHIS LODGE, 118.

NAMES.	Died.	Recovered.	Total.
G. Salen, self and child	...	2	2
J. B. Campbell, self and wife	1	1	2
A. J. Wheeler, P. G. M., P. G. H. P., etc., self and wife	1	1	2
Wm. W. White, self	1	...	1
Fred. Brennan, self	...	1	1
J. Fenwick, wife and four children	3	2	5
J. Harvey Mathes, self and wife	...	2	2
John Fritz, self, wife, and one child	...	3	3
S. F. Walker, S. W., self	1	...	1
W. S. Matthews, P. M., self	...	1	1
Theodore Holst, self	1	...	1
R. B. Clark, self	1	...	1
J. T. Bourne, child	...	1	1
John A. Holt, self	1	...	1
B. K. Pullen, wife	1	...	1
S. M. Jobe, self	1	...	1
J. M. Peabody, self	1	...	1
John Rosser, self	...	1	1
J. P. Trezevant, self	1	...	1
	14	15	29

ANGERONA LODGE, 168.

John Zent, ward, Emma Madox	...	1	1
A. L. Kimbro, nephew, sister-in-law, and family	2	4	6
Thos. E. Norvell, self and wife	...	2	2
Gus. Reder, self	1	...	1
J. W. Heath, self, wife, and daughter	2	1	3
J. B. Cook, self	...	1	1
J. C. Zehring, self, wife, and child	1	2	3
Jos. Specht, self	...	1	1
J. W. Anderson, self and child	1	1	2
—— McNeal, self, wife, and four children	4	2	6
J. J. Lovin, self	...	1	1
M. Jones, self and five children	...	6	6
S. Foltz, self	1	...	1
John A. Roush, F. C., self	1	...	1
C. W. Mosby, mother and three children	4	...	4
Wm. McElroy, self	1	...	1
	18	22	40

APPENDIX. 407

LEILA SCOTT LODGE, 289.

NAMES.	Died.	Recovered.	Total.
A. S. Myers, W. M., self, wife, and five children	...	7	7
H. Lemon, four children	2	2	4
Thos. Donnelly, self and two children	3	...	3
Robert Nicholson, self	1	...	1
H. G. Salzeiger, one child	1	...	1
John Edwards, self, wife, and four children	3	3	6
Martin Eyke, self and wife	2	...	2
Wm. Calhoun, self, wife, and one child	...	3	3
Geo. H. Holst, Treas., self	1	...	1
H. S. King, self	1	...	1
John L. Eichburg, self, wife, and two children	...	4	4
J. N. Keef, self	...	1	1
R. W. Mitchell, self and wife	2	...	2
M. Bloomfield, self	1	...	1
W. J. Hunt, F. C., self	1	...	1
	18	20	38

DE SOTO LODGE, 299.

NAMES.	Died.	Recovered.	Total.
E. R. T. Worsham, P. G. C., self	1	...	1
J. C. Scronce, wife and child	1	1	2
T. S. Cloyd, self	1	...	1
D. T. Porter, self	...	1	1
J. E. Russell, self, sister-in-law, and two children	3	1	4
R. C. Nicholson, self	1	...	1
J. C. Thrall, self	1	...	1
H. C. Daniels, mother and five sisters and brothers	...	6	6
W. H. Butts, self	...	1	1
V. H. McElroy, self, wife, and three children	3	2	5
Dr. W. R. Hodges, self	1	...	1
Jos. Rodgers, self	1	...	1
J. Kelly, self, wife, and child	3	...	3
C. Mundinger, self	...	1	1
N. W. Spears, Jr., self	...	1	1
Henry White, self	...	1	1
J. J. Sears, self and one child	2	...	2
Alex. Hunn, self	...	1	1
J. G. Lonsdale, Jr., Treas., self	1	...	1
J. N. Barlow, self	1	...	1
B. F. Price, W. M., uncle, brother in-law, and two children	...	3	3
M. Ragan, self	...	1	1
Frank Bras, self and three children	4	...	4
R. R. Catron, self	1	...	1
Ed. Corson, self	1	...	1
P. M. Stanley, wife and four children	3	2	5
Dr. S. Hinson, self	...	1	1
Dr. E. A. White, self, wife, and one child	...	3	3
I. D. Connoway, self	...	1	1
L. P. Judd, self	...	1	1
C. R. Pollard, self and father	1	1	2
J. Wilson, wife	...	1	1
Geo. Reed, self and mother-in-law	...	2	2
Rev. Geo. C. Harris, self	...	1	1
	30	33	63

KILWINNING LODGE, 341.

Names.	Died.	Recovered.	Total.
A Pearcall, self, and two daughters	3	...	3
C. Pearcall, self	...	1	1
Rev. S. Landrum, self, wife, and two sons	2	2	4
E. H. Lanham, wife	1	...	1
John B. Taylor, self	1	...	1
L. Chapski, self	1	...	1
J. W. Waynesburg, W. M., self, wife, mother, and son	...	4	4
Chas. N. Dare, self	1	...	1
H. S. Reynolds, self, and wife	2	...	2
T. M. McKee, self, wife, and three children	...	5	5
J. Wood, self	1	...	1
	12	12	24

PARK AVENUE LODGE, 362.

	Died.	Recovered.	Total.
John D. Huhn, self, and family	1	1	2
W. B. May, self, wife, and child	1	2	3
	2	3	5

AFFILIATED OUT OF STATE.

	Died.	Recovered.	Total.
B. T. Plummer, Washington Lodge, Alexandria, Va., self, wife, and six children	5	3	8
Geo. Kelhofer, self, Ark	1	...	1
Wm. Finnie, self, Scotland	...	1	1
J. W. McMillan, self, Brookhaven Lodge, 291, Miss	1	...	1
—— Wimberley, Baldwyne Lodge, 374, Allegheny Co., Pa	...	4	4
H. Schauer, Darage Lodge, 374, Allegheny, Pa	...	1	1
Geo. C. Probert, self, Norwalk, Ohio, Commandery	1	...	1
A. M. Munson, wife, Cayuga Falls	...	1	1
	8	10	18

NON-AFFILIATED.

	Died.	Recovered.	Total.
C. P. Oakley, Cyrene Commandery, wife, and son	1	1	2
B. Colmam, Cyrene Commandery, self, wife, and three children	1	5	6
L. Hawkins, Cyrene Commandery, self, and son	1	1	2
Rev. Geo. White, Cyrene Commandery, self, and son	1	1	2
Rev. D. C Slater, S. Elmo Commandery, self, wife, and two daughters	4	2	6
James Dixon, St. Elmo Commandery, self	...	1	1
Z. T. White, self, and wife	1	1	2
John Hall, self	1	...	1
J. W. McDonald, Peoria, Ill., self, wife, and child	3	...	3
R. M. Firth, self, and three children	4	...	4
Rev. N. Rosebrough, self	1	...	1
J. C. Jacoba, self	1	...	1
A. R. Redford, self, and two children	1	2	3
W. B. Waldron, self, and wife	...	2	2
R. W. Shelton, self, wife, mother-in-law, sister-in-law, and father-in-law	4	1	5
R. R. James, self	...	1	1
—— Burns, self, wife, and three children	2	3	5
A. C. Arnold, self, wife, and five children	7	...	7
Jack Wilson, self	...	1	1
Dr. Hughy, self, wife, and four children	1	5	6
	34	27	61

APPENDIX.

FUNDS RECEIVED BY THE MASONIC BOARD OF RELIEF FROM AUGUST 26 TO OCTOBER 31.

John Frizzell, G. S., Nashville	$12,827 80
John D. Vincil, G. S. St. Louis	1,211 00
Mrs. H. H. Higbee	25 00
Masons of Cacyville, Ky	22 00
A. B. Tredwell, Memphis	25 00
Franklin Lodge, 14, Troy, O	26 25
Covington Chapter, 35, Cov., Ky.	25 00
Butler Lodge, 272, Butler, Pa	7 50
Va. May Lodge, 233, Montgomery Co	20 00
Grand Chapter of Arkansas	50 00
Oostanaula Lodge, Rome, Ga	25 00
Masons of Sioux City, through D. A Magee	224 50
Grand Lodge of Arkansas	200 00
Masons of Leavenworth, Kan	76 00
Masons of Cynthiana Ky	46 00
J. D. Richardson, P. G. M	50 00
Masons of Adams' Station, Tenn.	13 00
Albert Pike, Washington, D. C.	100 00
Martin Collins, St. Louis	50 00
Grand Lodge of Kansas	150 00
Grand Lodge of Massachusetts	100 00
Masons of Fort Scott, Kan	50 00
H. P. Seavy, Secretary, Columbia, Tenn	50 00
G. H. Newbert, Wyandotte, Kan.	50 00
Berlin Lodge, 170, Saulsbury, Tenn	25 00
Hartwell Lodge, 101, Oxford, Ala.	25 00
Kenesaw Lodge, 33, Marietta, Ga.	15 00
Tyrlan Lodge and Chapter, Springfield, Ill	15 00
Masons of Jacksonville, Ill	75 00
Amity Lodge, 87, Newberry, S. C.	10 00
Centralia Lodge, 201, Centralia, Ill.	82 10
Osceola Lodge, 27, Osceola, Ark.	50 00
Vernon Lodge, 14, Georgetown, Ky	42 00
Masons of Oswego, Kan	105 00
Andrew Jackson Lodge, by Grand Master Warr	20 00
Wyandotte Chapter, 70, Huntingdon, W. Va	50 00
Richland Lodge, 39, Columbia, S. C.	25 00
Prospect Lodge, 456, Prospect, Tenn	25 00
Crescent Lodge, 25, Cedar Rapids.	10 00
Mount Hermon Lodge, 263, Cedar Rapids	10 00
St. John's Lodge, 20, Columbus, Ind	50 00
Madison Lodge, 329, Madison, Ala.	15 00
T. C. Park, Memphis	10 00
Masons of Austin, Ark	33 00
Golconda, Lodge, 131	25 00
Poagee Lodge, 325, Ashland, Ky.	40 50
Harmony Chapter, Sheboygan Falls, Wis	25 00
Ellwood Commandery, 6, Springfield, Ill	25 00
Mount Pleasant Lodge, 57	30 00
Gainsville Lodge, 375, Gainesville, O	$50 00
Fredonia Lodge, 225	35 00
Joseph K. Wheeler, G. S., Hartford, Conn	200 00
Masons of Jackson, Tenn	100 00
Adams Lodge, 246, Middleton, Tenn	25 00
Otawah Chapter, Kan	25 00
Franklin Lodge, 18, Otawah, Kan.	15 00
Marcus Lodge, 110, Fredericks town, Mo	25 00
Otawah Lodge. 7, Otahwah, Kan.	20 00
Masons, Montvale, Ala	10 00
Hess Lodge, 93, Dyersburg, Tenn.	20 00
Chatopa Lodge, 73, St. Louis, Mo.	20 00
H. G. Miller, Memphis	12 65
Citizens, Duwanda, Wis	20 00
Fellowship Lodge, 89, Marion, Ill.	20 00
Masons of Petersburg, Va	26 00
C. H. Johnson, G. M. of Ky	35 00
La Fayette Commandery, 3, La Fayette, Ind	50 00
W. H. Smythe, G. S., Indianapolis, Ind	182 40
Bay City Lodge, 129, Bay City, Mich	50 00
Ft. Worth Chapter, Ft. Worth, Tex.	50 00
Masons of Chicago, Ill	200 00
Masons of Pine Bluff, Ark	50 00
W. B. Isaacs, G. S., Richmond, Va.	150 00
W. S. Floyd, Baltimore, Md	10 00
Reno Lodge, 13, Reno, Nev	50 00
Munster Lodge,199,Ft.Monroe,Va.	50 00
St. John's Chapter, 57, Ft. Monroe, Va	50 00
Fort Worth Lodge, 148, Ft. Worth, Texas	50 00
Duquoin Lodge, 234, Duquoin, Ill.	25 00
Jacksonport Lodge, Jacksonport, Ark	100 00
Wyandotte Chapter, 6, Wyandotte, Kan	25 00
Mountain Lodge, 197, Sevierville, Tenn	25 00
Charlottesville Lodge, 55, Charlottesville, Va	25 00
Golden Rule Lodge, 345, Covington, Ky	25 00
Norfolk Lodge, 1, Norfolk, Va	25 00
Moriah Grove Lodge, 301, Stewart Co	20 00
Chapter, Henderson, Ky	50 00
King Solomon Lodge, 94, Gallatin.	25 00
Jerseyville Chapter, 140, Jerseyville, Ill	25 00
Grand Chapter of Arkansas	50 00
Masons of Louisville, Ky	200 00
Vesper Lodge, 223, Onawa, Iowa.	15 00
Brother of Ripley Lodge, 100	1 00
Masons of Ellenton, S. C	36 50
Dardanelle Chapter,64,Dardanelle, Ark	25 00

APPENDIX.

J. F. Hill Lodge, 270, Little Rock, Ark...	$10 00	Masons of Saraham, Ga...	$377 00
Hill City Lodge, 173, Lynchburg, Va...	50 00	F. M. Nelson, Memphis...	50 00
		The Ladies of Akron, O...	11 15
Masons of Columbus, Ga., through J. W. King...	60 00	Mount Moriah Lodge, 309, Fayette Co., Tenn...	10 00
Masons of Helena, Montana...	200 00	Mrs. Lemon, Mattoon, Ill...	50 00
Adairsville Lodge, Logan Co., Ky.	25 00	Caldwell Lodge, 273, Johnsonville, Tenn...	6 00
Masons of Griffin, Ga...	80 00	Masons of Virginia City, Nev...	182 00
J. W. Smith, Versailles, Ky...	25 00	Reynolds Chapter, 75, Carbondale, Ill...	25 00
Attica Lodge, 18, Attica, Ind...	50 00		
Ozark Lodge, 79, Ozark, Ark...	21 50	Astoria Lodge, 100, Astoria, Ill...	13 25
Herman Ruther, Pioneer City, Montana...	4 00	Tuscan Lodge, 143, La Gro, Ind...	10 00
		Masons of Tuscarora, Nev...	100 00
Reed Commandery, 6, Dayton, O..	50 00	Bright Star Lodge, 212, Dardanelle, Ark...	25 00
Masonic Relief Committee, Russellville, Ky...	36 70	Masons of Weston, N. C...	18 75
Grand Lodge of Arkansas...	200 00	Western Star Lodge, 2...	25 00
John H. Brown, G. S., Wyandotte, Kan...	17 70	From other sources...	802 05
J. W. Luke, St. Louis, Mo...	100 00	Total cash...	$21,196 30

DISBURSEMENTS.

Paid nurses...	$8,202 25
Paid burying the dead...	3,258 50
Paid physicians...	2,197 50
Paid supplies...	3,308 32
Paid relief of distressed Masons and their families...	1,612 35
Paid postage, advertising, porterage, etc...	101 05
	$18,679 97

Total Receipts...	$21,196 30
Total Disbursements...	18,679 97
Balance in Bank of Commerce...	$2,516 33

REPORT OF THE SPECIAL RELIEF COMMITTEE, I. O. O. F.

To E. G. Budd, Grand Master of the Right Worthy Grand Lodge, I. O. O. F., of the State of Tennessee, and to our Brothers of the United States and Territories and British Possessions:

In view of your unbounded acts of benevolence and generosity, we desire to give you a statement in regard to the action of your committee during the terrible scourge, which devastated by death our devoted city, this year of 1878.

During the latter part of the month of July, there were quite a number of undoubted cases of yellow fever; and as early as the 5th of August a resolution was offered in Chickasaw Lodge, No. 8, appointing a committee, consisting of the Noble Grand and Vice-Grand, to act with a similar committee from sister Lodges, to organize and be ready for efficient work. The resolution was adopted by all of the six Lodges in the city, and they each and all appointed their N. G. and V. G. as said committee, to organize a permanent one. This committee met in Odd-Fellows' Hall, August 13th. Every Lodge in the city was represented. Bro. J. W. X. Browne, N. G. of No. 6, was appointed chairman, and Bro. A. E. Kennedy, P. G. of No. 187, as secretary. A committee was appointed consisting of P. G. Jos. E. Russell, P. G. John Linkhauer, and V. G. H. M. Gage, to define the duties of the officers to be appointed.

On the following day the committee reported that a Board of Special Relief be appointed, which was carried into effect, the said Board to consist of a president, vice-president, treasurer, secretary, superintendent, and an executive committee of three; and an election was held with the following result:

John Linkhauer, P. G., president; H. M. Gage, V. G., vice-president; Wm. Henry, P. G., secretary; J. P. Hoffman, P. G., treasurer; Jos. E. Russell, P. G., superintendent of nurses.

APPENDIX.   411

The committee agreed to meet every morning. Also, that good and sufficient bonds be given by the treasurer, to the amount of $10,000, the secretary $2,500, and the superintendent $1,000. The bonds were given and approved.

Bros. Marcus Jones, P. G., G. W. L. Crook, P. G., and T. N. Johnston, V. G., were appointed an executive committee. It was ordered that they should act in conjunction with the Masonic Relief Committee as far as advisable.

The duties of your committee were defined and agreed to, which was to provide for the sick, the dying, and the dead, employ nurses, buy and furnish supplies, receive and disburse any donations, and order all authenticated accounts to be paid.

At the commencement of the fever, the funds in the hands of the treasurer—the balance of the epidemic fund of 1873—was $7,544 37. With the first acts of your committee, there was one donating the sum of $266 to our suffering brothers of Grenada, where the fever was raging with unheard-of malignity. On the 23d of August, the great increase of the fever over the city generally induced the Board of Health to proclaim the fever had become epidemic, and urged and advised the citizens to leave the city. The daily press also urged every person to do so. Many new cases of sickness were reported this day among the members and families of our Order, and it was becoming worse daily, but your committee, with sad hearts, continued to perform their duties with hope and courage. On motion, it was agreed that your committee be constituted a burial one, with authority to call upon any member of our Order to accompany them to funerals, if possible; it was further agreed, that a competent physician should be employed, and Dr. John Gordon be employed to attend to all cases of sickness when ordered to do so by the Board.

On the 26th day of August Bro. Wm. Henry, secretary, tendered his resignation as such, which was accepted by the committee. Bro. L. S. Burr, P. G., was nominated and elected to fill the office of secretary in his place, and gave his bond for $2,500, which was accepted, and he assumed the duties of the office.

Bro. J. E. Russell, superintendent of nurses, was taken sick with the fever on the 25th day of August, and Bro. John Linkhauer, in addition to the duties of his office, assumed the duties of the superintendent.

From the first organization of your committee to this time, August 30th, they have been in receipt of daily communications offering material aid and kind sympathy for our sufferers, which were answered with thanks, declining the proffered aid; but in view of the magnitude of the scourge, and the certain exhaustion of all means at their command in a very short time, your committee decided to accept such offers of aid as might be tendered. After due notice had been given by the Grand Master of this State at this time, Bro. C. M. Carroll, your committee soon commenced to receive funds from most every section of the country.

From this time, September 1st, for many weeks, the fever raged with fearful mortality, and took all the energy and courage of those who escaped it to perform their duty.

On the 31st day of August Bro. Jos. Russell died, being the first one of your committee that fell at the post of duty. He was a good man, and an efficient worker. Bro. E. F. Risk, Jr., was elected assistant secretary, and Bro. A. H. Leroy as assistant superintendent of nurses. This was necessitated by the daily increase of the fever. Bro. Geo. W. L. Crook, of your committee, was reported sick with the scourge on the 1st day of September, also Bro. E. F. Risk, Jr., who in a few days followed Bro. Russell to his everlasting home. He was an efficient young man, and his death regretted by all who knew him.

On the 2d of September, at a meeting of your committee, Bro. John Linkhauer resigned his position as president of the Board, and was elected general superintendent of nurses. Bro. Marcus Jones was then elected to the position of president of the Board. On motion it was ordered that a notice calling a meeting of brothers should be inserted in the morning papers, which was accordingly done, as follows:

"I.O.O.F.—All members of the different Lodges now in the city are most earnestly requested to meet at the Lodge room this (Tuesday) morning, 3d inst., at 10 o'clock, on important business. Brothers, your services are needed in behalf of the sick and dying."

There was no response to this call for help, and your committee considered it their duty to procure help, if possible, from persons not connected with our Order, when imperatively needed.

Bro. H. M. Gage tendered his resignation as vice-president of your committee, as his duties as president of the Knights of Honor required all his time. Bro. Geo. W. L. Crook, P. G., of your committee, died on the 5th day of September. He, too, was an active, energetic worker, and fell doing his duty for the benefit of his fellow-man. Bro. John P. Hoffman having left the city, there was but four of your original committee now on duty. Bro. Rev. E. C. Slater was appointed one of the Executive Committee, vacated by the death of Bro. Crook.

The great increase of sickness and death among our Order, and heavy increase of expenses, induced your committee to issue the following appeal to the Odd-Fellows, wheresoever dispersed:

"Brothers,—The Special Relief Committee of the six Lodges of the city of Memphis, Tenn., say to the members of our beloved Order in America, in answer to many inquiries, both by letter and telegram, that we are in the midst of a fearful epidemic, the end of which no one can foresee. More than one hundred of our brethren, including their families, have sickened and died. We need your sympathy, and God alone knows how soon your aid. In view of the heavy drain upon our resources, we have concluded to accept all donations that our brethren in their generosity may forward us."

This appeal was published, through the great kindness of the Associated Press, the 6th day of September, with good results, as it was soon responded to by our kind brothers throughout the land.

Bro. Rev. E. C. Slater met with your committee but once—on the 7th day of September. On the 8th he was taken sick with the fever, and on the 9th he too was numbered with our dead. No nobler soul ever went out through death to life than Bro. Dr. Slater. The soul of self-sacrifice and generosity, he died doing more than his duty for his fellow-man. His wife and two daughters soon followed him to that place of rest eternal, that land where all is love and truth, where there is no sickness or death.

The plague was at this time assuming frightful proportions, four to six hundred new cases and over one hundred deaths were reported in the city daily, and the proportion in the surrounding country was about the same. Bro. H. M. Gage was taken sick with the fever; his capacity and good work was sadly missed by the committee and the suffering brothers and their families he cared for. Bro. O. F. Prescott, P. G. M., was appointed assistant secretary September 8th. Bro. L. S. Burr, secretary, was taken sick September 10th, which only left three of your committee on duty. B. D. Castleman, P. G., and Irvine Root, assistants to your committee as clerks, were soon stricken with death.

At this time we found it almost impossible to care for the living and bury the dead within or near the city limits. In consequence, there was more suffering among our brothers and their families in the country, as we could not pay proper attention to their needs. The scenes of agony, despair, and desolation may be imagined, but can not be described. Your committee have had relatives and nurses come and implore them to have the dead removed from their houses, as they had lain much too long unburied. We could not help them, as the undertakers had much more to do than they could possibly attend to, and all had to be buried by turns, according to the time the application was made for that purpose. In many instances we were compelled to hire spring wagons, and carry the dead to the cemetery, as there were no hearses to be had. There were no funerals. The drivers of the hearses or wagons were the only ones, with the help of the grave-diggers at the cemetery, to assist at the burials. Your committee could scarcely attend to the sick, therefore the dead of our Order could not receive the attention we wished to give them.

One of the daily papers remarks: "There is now no part of the corporate limits of the city not thoroughly infected with the fever poison. One by one our remaining people fall, and since Saturday night's closing report, an appalling list of deaths have occurred. All of Sunday and yesterday, hearses followed each other at a trot, carrying a corpse to the grave unattended by any one but the hearse-driver. Even this was not fast enough, and the dead accumulated in various parts of the city until they became very offensive. The way it now looks, there will shortly be not enough here to bury the dead. Much confusion and disorder follows this state of affairs, but at the present time there seems to be no help for it until the fever abates, which, at present, it seems not inclined to do. So long as there is food for it, no relief can be expected. Woe, pestilence, and death seems to be our portion."

How unfortunate it was that our brothers and families with friends did not leave the city when advised to do so by the Board of Health and daily press. How many valuable lives might have been saved if the advice had been taken in time. Many left after too long a delay, after their systems had been infected with the poison of the dread disease. Many died uncared for, away from home, with no friend or nurse to care for their wants.

Bro. Marcus Jones, president of your committee, was taken sick with a severe case of the fever on the 20th day of September, which reduced your working committee to two members. We missed the president very much indeed, as he was never absent from a meeting of the Board, although five of his family, out of six, were sick with the fever.

Bro. T. N. Johnston being so much engaged with the business affairs of his employers that he could not attend to the meetings of the Board, Mr. Walter Jones, son of our president, was employed as an assistant to your committee, and with his marked capacity and energy, his services proved very valuable indeed.

APPENDIX.

Bro. A. H. Leroy, assistant superintendent of nurses, was reported sick on the 21st day of September, and Mr. Frank Jones was employed for the position.

The painful intelligence was reported that the fever was spreading to a great extent in the surrounding country, among our brothers and families who sought safety by leaving the city. It appears there is no refuge of safety for many miles from our plague-stricken place. At this time, September 22d, we were receiving donations from our kind brothers from every section of our country. We needed them, as our expenses were very heavy, and increasing.

Bro. T. N. Johnston, of your committee, was reported sick the 27th day of September, and in a few days he too was numbered with those that had gone before. With his capacity and tact he had made his mark as one of the best business men in the city. This leaving only one of the committee (who remained in the city), Bro. John Linkhauer, that escaped from having the scourge.

On or near the 2d day of October, the president being still sick, Bro. John Linkhauer ordered a telegram to be sent to the different Grand Lodges to forward more means, if possible, as our expenses and disbursements were largely on the increase. The appeal was answered with liberal donations. At this time there was some decrease of the sickness in the city generally, but among our Order it was on the increase.

On the 7th day of October, O. F. Prescott, P. G. M., assistant secretary, was taken sick with the fever, and in a few days he too passed away. How much his cheerful face and good work were missed. The very committee-room seemed infected with the fever poison, causing sickness and death. Out of eleven workers in it, seven have died. Perhaps the contact of so many nurses, just from the house of the sick and laying out the dead, made it worse off with us than it would have been otherwise.

Bro. L. S. Burr, secretary, reported for duty to-day, 8th of October, after four weeks' sickness. He was very welcome and added strength to our reduced committee.

On the 10th day of October we opened a commissary depot, which we filled with provisions and various other supplies, procured by donations and purchase, for the benefit of our brothers in distress, and their families. Bro. A. H. Leroy was appointed superintendent.

Bro. Marcus Jones, president, reported this day, October 17th, after four weeks' sickness with a dangerous case of the fever. He was gladly welcomed, and a meeting of Gayoso Encampment, No. 3, on the same day, he was elected a representative to the Grand Encampment of the State of Tennessee, which met at Nashville, Tenn., the 21st day of October, when he was elected Grand Patriarch of the State of Tennessee. On his return he at once assumed the duties of his office, where his assistance was greatly needed.

There appeared to be at that time a marked decrease of the fever generally; we had hopes the worst was passed; with us it must be so, as nearly all of our brothers and their families who remained in the city have been down with it. The great fear was that the absent ones would return too soon. The fearful number of deaths among our Order and city, shows the awful fatality of the plague which has so decimated our city and caused agony and suffering unspeakable. There is no place, except Grenada, Miss., that has suffered as we have. How terrible to think of, that four persons were found dead in the streets in one day, and several in houses, and two merchants in their offices, all dying without help to minister to their last moments.

Out of a population of about 20,000 remaining in the city and vicinity, over 4,250 died. Had the city of New Orleans been so afflicted, in proportion to her inhabitants, there would have been over 30,000 deaths in that city.

Your committee have employed 475 nurses, at an average cost of over $15 each. The number of brothers that have died is 95, and of their families 134, making the number of deaths 229. The convalescents amount to 214, making the number of cases of yellow fever 443. The number of widows is 54, and the orphans 150, that have been made so by the terrible scourge. The different Lodges of the city will now have to care for 109 widows and 196 orphans. This, indeed, tells a sad story of our calamities. Chickasaw Lodge, No. 8, lost all of their elective officers. There were only four of our brothers that remained in the city escaped having the fever. The first death reported was that of Bro. J. B. Campbell, August 2d; the last deaths were those of Bro. S. J. Ward, who died November 17th, and Bro. W. C. Coate, who died on the 27th. Both of the brothers named had been absent from the city all summer, and took the fever after their return, although there had been several heavy frosts. The labors of your committee are near ended; we have done the best we could under the circumstances surrounding us. More than one-half of the cases under our care died.

We find there are more worthy widows and orphans in distressed circumstances, whose husbands and fathers died owing to their Lodge small amounts on the first of the term. The laws of the Order being strict and imperative, no relief can be granted them, unless we make some provision for them, which we have done by including in our donation account, the sum of $2,323.36.

Our commissary department is still open, with supplies sufficient to last for some time, which we intend to distribute to the needy.

Your committee do not believe that the yellow fever is indigenous to this country, but that it is introduced from the West Indies or tropical ports through our southern ports, thence over the southern portion of our country. And we would most earnestly appeal to our brothers of the Order to recommend the establishment of a national quarantine, at such times as we may be threatened with its introduction from infected foreign ports, and that in no way but the interposition of our government in this matter will save us from the infliction of many repetitions of this terrible scourge.

We would call attention to the subjoined report of the Special Trustees of the Yellow Fever Fund of 1873.

REPORT OF RECEIPTS.

Arkansas	$341 00	Maine	$408 89
Alabama	309 00	Nebraska	136 00
British Columbia, (British Prov.)	50 00	New Hampshire	52 00
California	3,385 00	New Brunswick, (British Prov.)	337 00
Colorado	135 00	New Jersey	200 00
Connecticut	200 00	New York	825 00
Delaware	166 75	Nova Scotia, (British Province)	392 76
Dakota Territory	62 00	North Carolina	96 25
Georgia	685 00	Ohio	850 00
Iowa	222 25	Pennsylvania	532 00
Illinois	1,570 00	Rhode Island	130 00
Indiana	910 00	South Carolina	6 00
Kentucky	200 00	Tennessee	2,161 40
Kansas	344 48	Texas	731 50
Montana Territory	53 50	Utah Territory	125 00
Michigan	165 00	Virginia	130 00
Massachusetts	58 34	Wyoming Territory	290 60
Mississippi	25 00	Wisconsin	345 00
Minnesota	25 00	Unknown friends in the U. S	285 30
Maryland	619 00		
Missouri	500 00	Whole am't of cash rec'd to date..	$18,061 57

We have received from the General Relief Committee, I. O. O. F., of Cincinnati, a bounteous supply of provisions. Also from the Odd Fellows of Staunton, Va., Rutherford Station, Tenn., Knoxville, Tenn., the Citizens' Relief Committee, and Dr. D. F. Goodyear, acting mayor of this city. We are under very many obligations to the Howard and other associations, they, with great courtesy, having honored our orders for supplies, etc. Friends and brothers, accept our grateful thanks. The provisions sent from Cincinnati cost, there, $416.51.

REPORT OF DISBURSEMENTS.

For nurses	$7,143 31
For burial expenses	6,749 10
For physicians	2,195 50
For supplies	2,511 20
For expenses	2,677 80
Donations to sick and destitute Odd-Fellows and their families	4,836 81
Total disbursements	$26,113 72
Cash disbursed in excess of the receipts of 1878	8,052 15

The donation account includes money donated to Grenada, Miss., Chattanooga, Tenn., and Brownsville, Tenn. Supplies were also sent to our suffering brothers of Tuscumbia, Ala. Your committee wrote to the afflicted cities and towns of Mississippi and Tennessee, offering aid to our suffering brothers if needed.

The expense account is composed of the amounts paid for horses and vehicles for the superintendent of nurses in visiting the sick and in burying the dead, printing, postage hire of clerks, and secretary and superintendent of nurses, and incidental expenses.

The committee, excepting those mentioned above, received no compensation for their services.

A portion of the receipts per State of Tennessee, that were sent by Grand Secretary J. R. Harwell, from Nashville, was from different States.

APPENDIX. 415

Brothers, we say that you have done a brother's part; you have indeed lightened our burden; your letters of affection, with offers of assistance, were a tower of strength to your committee, and our hearts are overflowing with a full measure of gratitude and thanks for your kind sympathy, your brotherly love, and your noble generosity. We can trustingly say, and are certain, that such deeds as yours will meet their just reward, and will ever be cherished in the hearts of the widow and orphan, and your brothers. We hope you will receive our report with favor, and that you will never have occasion to exercise the great magnanimity and kindness you have in relieving your brothers and their families in another fatal epidemic, such as we have just passed through.

Respectfully submitted, in Friendship, Love, and Truth.
MARCUS JONES, President,
L. S. BURR, Secretary,
J. P. HOFFMAN, Treasurer,
JNO. LINKHAUER, Supt. Nurses.
} *I. O. O. F. Special Relief Committee.*

REPORT OF MEMPHIS TYPOGRAPHICAL UNION.

MEMPHIS, *February 1, 1879.*

To Memphis Union No. 11, and to the Typographical Unions of the United States and Canada:

The following is transmitted as the Report of Receipts and Disbursements by your Relief Committee, in behalf of the distressed members of Union No. 11, during the fearful plague of 1878. The report should have been furnished sister Unions at an earlier date, but the impracticability of closing up all accounts rendered it impossible, hence the circular of to-day. In answer to the appeal made by the Relief Committee, of date August 26, 1878, the following Receipts from sister Unions were entered:

New York Union	$200 00
Philadelphia Union	150 00
Courier-Journal Office, Louisville	110 40
Journal Office, Chicago	92 25
Employés Government Printing Office, Washington	80 00
Salt Lake Tribune, through Gallaway & Keating	71 50
New York Herald Office	61 00
St. Louis Globe-Democrat Office	50 00
S. K. Head	50 00
Washoe Union	50 00
Detroit Union	50 00
Baltimore Union	50 00
New York World Office	40 00
Printers St. John's, N. B., through J. M. Keating	40 00
Springfield (Ill.) Union	40 00
Chicago Union	38 00
Proceeds of Entertainment in New York, through H. Dalton	37 00
Rochester Union and Advertiser Office	36 00
Utica (N. Y.) Union	35 25
Richmond (Va.) Union	35 00
Printers of Lafayette, Ind	35 00
Columbus (Ohio) Union	34 00
Little Rock Union	33 30
Cincinnati Enquirer Office	30 50
Nashville Union	30 00
Printers of Erie, Pa	26 00
Detroit Union	25 00
Austin (Tex.) Union	25 00
Galveston (Tex.) Union	25 00
Cincinnati Union	24 00
New York Bulletin	23 50
People of Capleville, Tenn., through J. M. Keating	$22 65
Denver (Col.) Union	22 00
New York Herald compositors	20 00
Quincy (Ill.) Union	20 00
Unknown friend in Illinois, through J. M. Keating	20 00
Norwich (Conn.) Union	17 00
Cambridge Station, Boston	15 00
Trenton (N. J.) Union	15 00
Pittsburgh (Pa.) Union	15 00
Fort Wayne Union	10 00
St. Joseph (Mo.) Union, through Lou. Hardman	13 00
Oil City (Pa.) Union	10 00
W. H. Bates, through J. S. Toof	10 00
Toronto Union	10 00
New Haven (Conn.) Union	10 00
Pressman's Union, Washington	10 00
Buffalo (N. Y.) Union	10 00
Raleigh (N. C.) Union	10 00
Courier Printers, East Saginaw	10 00
Newark (N. J.) Union	10 00
Portland (Maine) Union	10 00
Toledo Union	10 00
Memphis Telegraph Aid Associat'n	8 35
Peoria (Ill.) Union	8 00
St. Louis Globe-Democrat	6 85
Macon (Ga.) Union	5 00
Columbia (S. C.) Union	5 00
Miss Johns, Capleville, Tenn., thro' J. M. Keating	4 00
Memphis Union, No. 11	1 75
Peter B. Lee (postage stamps)	21
Total	$1,966 51

The following disbursements in bulk is reported, the itemized accounts being on file with No. 11, and open to inspection from any Sister Union, or individual member, having doubt as to the appropriate use of all moneys collected. Considering the number dead and their burial, sick and destitute, the committee prides itself as having accomplished the greatest good out of the smallest amount contributed to any society of men in the city:

Undertakers' accounts	$531 50
Amount paid physicians	440 00
Outfitting of infirmary, including bedding and furniture, rent of rooms, and supplies	228 75
Amount paid for necessary supplies for convalescents, including liquors ordered by physicians	215 75
Amt. paid for nurses, porters, and errand boys, including board, etc.	213 90
Amount paid for conveyances for physicians, committee, and express purposes	125 75
Amount paid for medicines	93 50
Amount of cash paid to distressed families	125 00
Printing account, telegrams, postage, etc	43 80
Ice bill	16 10
Total	$2,034 05

In closing the preceding accounts the Relief Committee, in behalf of Union No. 11, desire to extend their warmest praise to the Unions responding, and would also state that but for the promptness characterized, the death and distress would have been much greater —perhaps total. They also desire to extend their heartfelt thanks to the Howard Association for assistance rendered, and to make special mention of A. D. Langstaff, J. M. Keating, Jesse Page, F. F. Bowen, Henry White, Sim. Barinds and Louis Daltroof, for their untiring energies in behalf of our sick and destitute.

Trusting that it may never again be our misfortune to present such a record of death and sickness as the above, and that it shall be our spirit to hold in kind and lasting remembrance the relief sent from abroad, we close our labors, with prayers for the future prosperity and health of all Unions throughout the States and dominion.

       Wm. G. Taylor, Chairman,
       Henry Moode, Secretary,
       R. S. Smith,
       J. P. Wheles,   *Committee.*
       T. P. Kavanaugh,
       H. W. Clayton,
       J. W. Chambers,

R. S. SMITH, *Secretary.*   W. G. TAYLOR, *President.*

NAMES OF THE DEAD.

L. M. Lorentz, August 30th.
John B. Barker, August 31st.
Benj. F. Fuller, September 7th.
Jas. Cruikshank, September 7th.
Chas. M. Smith, September 9th.
Jas. M. Kerr, September 9th.
Baxter N. Cutting, September 11th.
Wm. G. Stevenson, September 13th.

Edward J. Snigg, September 30th.
W. H. Blalock, October 11th.
T. P. Holland, October 12th.
Harry O. Bowden.
Thos. E. Hotchkiss.
Wm. H. Cummins.
R. R. Catron.
Wm. Spickernagle.

SICK AND RECOVERED MEMBERS.

Henry White.
H. E. Crandall.
Jno. B. Hoskins.
W. W. Stephenson.
T. D. Uzell, (transient.)
H. J. McGrann.
W. G. Taylor.
H. M. Crowell.
W. S. Brooks, (honorary.)
Ed. Schiller.

Frank Van Horn.
J. P. Wheles.
O. P. Bard.
George Bird.
Louis Rozelle.
L. H. Grant.
Joseph Crabb.
S. L. Reneau.
T. P. Kavanaugh.
Ed. R. Holland.

FAMILIES OF MEMBERS SICK.

Miss Sallie D. Stephenson.
Mrs. B. N. Cutting.
Mrs. Crowell and son.
Mrs. W. W. Stephenson and two children.
Mrs. Frank Van Horn and three children.
Miss Schiller.
Mrs. H. J. McGrann, son and niece.
Mrs. J. P. Wheles and child.
Five members of family of Joseph Crabb.
Mrs. W. H. Blalock and child.
Mrs. T. P. Holland and two daughters.
Three Misses Reneau and brother.

FAMILIES OF MEMBERS DEAD.

W. S. Brooks' mother, wife, and son.
H. M. Crowell's daughter.
H. J. McGrann's daughter.
George Bird's child.
Major W. G. Stephenson's two daughters.
Ed. Schiller's son.
Joseph Crabb's son.

REPORT OF THE HEBREW HOSPITAL ASSOCIATION.

To the Officers and Members of the Hebrew Hospital Association:

Although not a member of your organization, by force of circumstances I am necessarily compelled to submit to you the result of my labors during the late epidemic.

Hardly had we experienced the effects of the peace following the scourge of 1873, when we were compelled to listen to the trumpets from near and far calling to arms all able-bodied men and women to fight an enemy far more dangerous and destructive than any experienced in the annals of history—a battle where the implements used consisted not of musketry, but of knowledge. Although the highest attainment of such was reached, yet we felt the effects of the terrible scourge of 1878. Like an adder it came unseen, darting its poisonous fangs into nearly every house in the city and surrounding country, without respect to quality. The rich and poor, educated and uneducated, old and young, were all placed upon a level, each sharing the same danger. The timid who sought their hiding-place, and the brave man who had faced danger in time of war and feared not death, were also classed among the victims.

The suffering among our co-religionists was as great as any. The bulk of them were poor and destitute, and unable to reach places of safety. For the time being they thought themselves secure; but hardly had the fever reached its zenith before the surrounding country felt its deadly effects. To our utter dismay we found every avenue leading to the city densely packed with Jewish families, and with few exceptions did any escape the force of the fever.

To speak of the sights and sufferings witnessed would fill volumes; yet to show our co-religionists and others who donated to our cause, an item or so is not out of place. Picture yourself at home, living in luxury and good health, enjoying every comfort imaginable and receiving the caresses of your children; then, on the contrary, find yourself away from the busy walks of life, living in an old log cabin or corn-crib, far out in the woods, almost away from civilization, with starvation staring you and your family in the face, and lying on the floor, without bed or cover, and in constant dread of the disease reaching you; to see whole families down sick at one time, and in one room, with no relative or friend to even pass them a glass of water to quench the thirst caused by the burning fever. Then you will have but a partial insight to the effects of the scourge as has just been witnessed in the southern district. This was not only with the poor, but the rich (who were well able to travel to places of safety) shared the same. Living as they were in huts, stables, outhouses, and barn-yards, their riches were nothing to them so long as it was not convertible. They were so overcome with fear that they dared not visit the city to purchase the necessities of life—rather starvation than take the chances of an introduction to that fell destroyer.

No one knows what the consequences would have been had not the vigilant eyes of the workers of the Hebrew Hospital Association succeeded in ferreting out their abode and rendering them timely assistance—appearing before them as miraculously as an angel descending from heaven. Many were the prayers and praises received from parents with but aching hearts; many an embrace did I receive from the widowed mother and helpless orphans, who looked upon me as their preserver. "No one to help me, none to care for me and my dear children!" was the exclamation of many.

But receiving the assurance desired, which we gave with a willing hand, many a beating heart was soothed—many a tear was saved. The extent of the suffering during this fever will never be known. Father bereft of mother, mother bereft of children, brothers of brothers, and sisters of sisters. To listen to the lamentations of the sick, the moans and groans of the dying, and when the last and solemn rites were performed to the dead, the weeping and sorrow was almost unendurable. Such sights made us weep—such sights gave us courage. With renewed vigor and a stout heart we added extra exertions to continue our good work. When death closed the eyes of many mothers, we took the precious little ones in charge and gave them as comfortable a home as possible, cheering them up and drowning their sorrows. Notwithstanding our limited help every appeal made to us was answered promptly, whether in the city or miles in the country—rain or shine, day or night, we were always there. Nothing was left undone, nor money spared to relieve the wants of the suffering. Although the funds of the Association were low, no one wanted. As an active member of the Howard Association, and visitor of the Citizens' Relief Committee, I was enabled to procure such necessaries as money would not procure at that time.

My attention was not limited to the Israelites alone, but to all denominations, both white and black. Nor did I limit myself to alleviating solely their wants. As a prescriber for the cure of yellow fever, I made an unbounded success—a thing I am most proud of. Having treated, personally, over one hundred cases (many Yehudim), without the use of medicine, I have the extreme pleasure of saying that I have not lost one single case. I could furnish names of every one treated, but it would not be essential upon this occasion. Many families hailed my appearance with delight, and only regretted I did not appear sooner, so as to follow my advice.

The acts of heroism displayed by many are known, but not too well. Out of the officers comprising the Association, every one had left, leaving their duties and funds to outsiders. How well these men did the work we leave for you to determine. One thing I can say, a braver and nobler band never existed. Always in the worst of the storm, doing most heroic acts and sacrificing their lives for the sake of others. Is it not braver for one to risk his life for strangers than one of his own kin? A man may pay every attention to his own family, and there let his responsibility rest. But where one possessed of talent, highly educated and experienced—wealth, family, and all luxuries that can be possessed—lays down his life for the benefit of others, such a man must be a hero. When the name of Nathan D. Menken, the brave and noble martyr, was flashed across the wires upon that fatal day, September 2d, telling of his heroic death, what a blow it was to mankind! I can surmise the feeling abroad. But when those that stood by him in his hour of peril were compelled to look upon all that remained of him, it was heart-rending. Every one ceased from their daily labor and discussed the subject. If there ever was hard feeling against him, it was forgotten then. If ever tears were shed, it was then. Although gone to a better world, his presence is in the heart of every one. Who would die a nobler death? What a blow to me and all of us! Left, as I was, alone to follow my daily pursuits singly, for seven weeks, visiting the sick and burying the dead, his name came from more than one sick one that missed him. My hopes were almost blighted. But succor came in the way of one who has won a place in my bosom—that made a tie of friendship that can never be cut asunder except by death. Mr. M. Sartorius, who, after a struggle with the monster held the upper hand and came out victorious, relieved me for a few days when about to fall from nervous prostration. He proved himself capable of the trying work, and, with a firm resolution and a determined heart, has done heroic acts never to be forgotten. He was amongst the sick and well, and when death closed the eyes of the suffering he did not shrink from performing that delicate work.

Dr. Julius Wise, the only Jewish resident physician on active duty, did good and noble work. He labored with a zeal and earnestness that is claimed by many and earned by few. After a long attack with the fever, he is again on duty, with much more experience. Mr. Dave Eiseman remained with us part of the time. As treasurer, he did good and faithful service, receiving contributions and relieving the wants of the needy and securing all transportation to more congenial climes.

Mr. L. Iglauer, who recovered from an attack of the fever, produced by his untiring devotion to his partner, N. D. Menken, has left us to return no more. Contrary to the wishes of his physician and friends, he returned to his former home, to die amongst his relations. Among the others deserving mention are H. I. Simmons, David Thilman, Louis Daltroof, and Sim. L. Barinds.

To the contributors, Howard Association, Citizens' Relief Committee, Southern Express Company, Western Union Telegraph Company, and the press throughout the country, we owe a debt of gratitude long to be remembered.

APPENDIX. 419

RECAPITULATION.

Number of families sent away 144
Number of persons assisted 337
Number of persons sick 223
Number of persons died 85
Number of full orphans 32
Number of half orphans 46

JACOB KOHLBERG, *Acting President.*

RECEIPTS.

ALABAMA.
Aug. 30. Hebrew Benevolent Society, Mobile. $50 00
Sept. 23. Thro' M. Ulman, Montgomery 25 00
24. Ladies' Benevolent Society, Mobile... 50 00
24. Coll., Greenville 17 00
Oct. 3. Israelites, thro' H. Fox, Montvale...... 5 00
8.   "   "   " 6 00
8. Concordia Lodge, 152, Uniontown 71 75
24. Marengo Ldg.,283,I.O.B.B.,Demopolis. 50 00

Total $274 75

ARKANSAS.
Sept. 2. M. Isaacs, Forrest City $50 00
30. Jennie and Gertie Mook, Hot Springs 1 00
Oct. 5. Phœnix Lodge, 279, I. O. B. B., Pine Bluff 20 00
28. Citizens of Hot Springs 15 00

Total $86 00

CALIFORNIA.
Sept. 30. Thro' Dr. E. Cohen, San Francisco....$500 00
Oct. 14. Will of M. Reese, San Francisco 200 00

Total $700 00

NORTH CAROLINA.
Aug. 31. S. Hammonlough, Kingston $1 00
Sept. 26. Manhattan Lodge, 158, K. S. B., Wilmington 25 00
Oct. 9. Thro' Julius Ash, Goldsboro 15 20
24. Cong. Bnai Israel, Tarboro 15 00
27. North State Lodge, 222, I. O. B. B., Wilmington 35 00

Total $91 20

SOUTH CAROLINA.
Nov. 1. Dan Lodge, 93, I. O. B. B., Charleston. $50 00
Dec. 1. Cong. Beth Elohim, Charleston 111 25

Total $161 25

CONNECTICUT.
Oct. 11. Abraham Lodge, 89, I. O. B. B., Bridgeport $5 00

DISTRICT OF COLUMBIA.
Sept. 27. Capital Lodge, 131, K. S. B., Washington $25 00
Oct. 24. Grace Aguilar Lodge, 117, I. O. B. B., Washington 15 00

Total $40 00

GEORGIA.
Sept. 2. Hebrew Benevolent Soc., Savannah..$100 00
17. Cong. Beth Israel, Macon 50 00
19. Joseph Ldg., 76, I. O. B. B., Savannah. 40 00
21. Hebrew Benevolent Soc., Savannah.. 100 00
26. Georgia Ldg., 151, K. S. B., Savannah. 25 00
26. Sigmund Mendel, Savannah 20 00
30. Savannah Lodge, No. 317, I. O. B. B... 50 00
Oct. 3. Atlanta Benevolent Soc., Atlanta 15 00
6. Citizens, thro' M. Myer, Athens 70 00
11. Columbus Ldg., 77, I.O.B.B, Col'mb's. 10 00
11. Georgia Ldg., 207, I. O. B. B., Thomasville 15 00
24. Hebrew Congregation, Thomasville.. 10 00
24. Malachi Ldg., 146, I. O. B. B., Macon. 27 20
Nov. 2. Joseph Ldg.,76, I. O. B. B., Savannah. 25 00
5. Coll. thro' E. B. M. Browne, Atlanta. 50 00
Dec. 1. Micha Lodge, 147, I. O. B. B., Albany. 27 00

Total $634 20

ILLINOIS.
Aug. 27. H. Felsenthal, Aurora $100 00
31. J. Lesser, Quincy 165 00
31. Ladies of Springfield 25 50
Sept. 4. Ladies of Springfield 72 00
6. Illinois Ldg., 264, I. O. B. B., Chicago.. 25 00
10. Thro'Stettauer Bros., Chicago 185 00

Sept. 19. I. O. B. B., Chicago $200 00
23. Sisters of Peace, Chicago 100 00
Oct. 3. Mr. and Mrs. Frei, Kansas 5 00
3. Zion Society, Chicago 25 00
10. Thro' H. L. Frank, Chicago 309 25
15. Sinai Congregation, Chicago 400 00
17. Illinois Ldg., 264, I. O. B. B., Chicago. 40 00
21. Deborah Verein, Chicago 25 00

Total $1676 75

INDIANA.
Aug. 30. Thro' Mrs. S. Loeb. Ligonier $42 00
30. Thro' Max Frank, Fort Wayne 35 00
30. Rebecca Verein, Mt. Vernon 15 00
Sept. 23. Tree of Life Society, Indianapolis..... 75 00
25. B. Lowenhaupt, Mt. Vernon 25 00
27. C. Knefter, Indianapolis 3 50
27. Rebecca Verein, Mt. Vernon 18 00
Nov. 1. Barzillai Ldg., 111, I.O.B.B, Lafayette. 12 00
28. Aug. Brantann, Pres. K. S. B., Evansville 25 00

Total $250 50

KANSAS.
Aug. 31. W. B. Haas, Leavenworth $50 00
Oct. 15. S. Barnum & Co., Topeka 10 00

Total $60 00

KENTUCKY.
Sept. 17. Yellow Fever Committee, Louisville.$100 00
27. H. Herman, Louisville 10 00
Oct. 4. Thro' Bernheim & Co., Paducah 35 00
Nov. 1. Harmony Ldg., 149, I.O.B.B.,Paducah. 10 00

Total $155 00

LOUISIANA.
Sept. 11. La. Lodge, 107, I. O. B. B., Shreveport. $25 00
12. Thro' J. G. Devereux, Shreveport 100 00
Oct. 24. La. Lodge, 107, I. O. B. B., Shreveport. 25 00
24. Jordan Ldg., 102, O.K.S.B., Shrevep't. 25 00

Total $177 00

MARYLAND.
Sept. 27. Baltimore Heb. Ben. Soc., Baltimore.$500 00

MASSACHUSETTS.
Sept. 13. Mendelssohn Lodge, 25, I. O. B. B., Boston $20 00

MICHIGAN.
Sept. 30. Congrgation Beth El, Detroit $138 00
Oct. 11. Charity Ldg., 14, I. O. F. S. I., Detroit. 10 00

Total $148 00

MINNESOTA.
Aug. 26. R. Reis & Gumbach, Minneapolis $52 50

MISSISSIPPI.
Sept. 16. Citizens, thro' F. Harpman, Corinth.. $25 00
21. D. G. Lodge, 7, I.O.B.B., Natchez 75 00
27. Through E. Pfeifer, Brookhaven 10 00
27. Through S. Abrahms, Kosciusko 25 00
Oct. 1. D. G. Lodge, 7, I.O.B.B., Natchez 50 00
1. Ezra Lodge, 134, I.O.B.B., Natchez 50 00

Total $315 50

MISSOURI.
Sept. 11. St. Louis Lodges, St. Louis $100 00
26. Through B. Sinzer, St. Louis 200 00
27. Through B. Ford, Mineral Point 9 75
30. D. G. Lodge, 2, I.O.F.S.I., St. Louis..... 75 00
Oct. 3. St. Louis Lodges, St. Louis 50 00
3. Missouri Lodge, 25, I.O.F.S.I., St. Louis. 25 00

Total $459 75

APPENDIX.

NEW JERSEY.
Sept. 27. Young Men's Heb. Ass'n, Newark...... $50 00
Oct. 3. Noah Lodge, 186, I.O.B.B., Hoboken... 25 00

Total $75 00

NEW YORK.
Sept. 20. Through Henry Rice, New York.....$1875 00
20. Temple Emanuel, New York............... 212 00
20. Mt. Sinai Lodge, I.O.B.B., New York. 460 00
20. Young Ladies' Charitable Union, N.Y. 40 00
21. Yellow Fever Relief Com., N. Y......... 500 00
23. Yellow Fever Relief Com., N. Y......... 500 00
23. Mrs. S. Tuska, New York................... 5 00
25. Through Mrs. F. Cohen, Saugerties.... 33 50
25. Akiba Eger Lodge, 26, K.S.B., N. Y... 25 00
Oct. 6. Dr. M. Landsberg's Con., Rochester... 150 00
7. Ladies' Heb. Ben. Society, Troy......... 25 00
7. Through Menken Bros., New York... 19 40
Nov. 1. Union Lodge, 34, I.O.F.S.I., Brooklyn. 15 00

Total $3840 90

OHIO.
Aug. 23. Collections, Dayton........................... $80 00
23. Through Israelite and Deborah, Cin... 15 00
23. Through Seasongood & Sons, Cin...... 200 00
31. Grand Lodge, 2, I.O.B.B., Cincinnati. 100 00
Sept. 2. Dr. Aub, Cincinnati............................ 10 00
7. Grand Lodge, 2, I.O.B.B., Cincinnati. 100 00
14. Southern Relief Com., Cleveland 100 00
14. Through Israelite and Deborah, Cin... 100 00
16. Thro' Stix, Krouse & Co., Cincinnati.. 240 00
16. Thro' Dr. Lilienthal, Cincinnati........ 12 00
21. Southern Relief Com., Cincinnati...... 500 00
24. Thro, Israelite and Deborah, Cin...... 217 00
26. Thro' Dr. Lilienthal, Cincinnati......... 15 00
27. Southern Relief Com., Cincinnati...... 250 00
27. Hebrew Relief Com., Cleveland........ 100 00
27. Daughters of Israel, Cleveland. 100 00
Oct. 3. Lodges, thro' H. Janowitz, Cleveland. 50 00
3. Bertha Eberhard and others................ 50 00
3. Dist. Gr. Lodge, 2, I.O.B.B., Cin........ 100 00
3. King Solomon Lodge, 23, I.O.F.S.I., Cleveland... 5 00
6. Through Israelite and Deborah, Cin... 100 00
7. Citizens' Relief Com., Toledo............. 50 00
27. Through Israelite and Deborah, Cin... 100 00
Nov. 15. Gr. Lodge, 2, I.O.B.B., Cincinnati...... 41 20
22. Wolfgang Speyer, Cincinnati.............. 8 00

Total $2643 20

PENNSYLVANIA.
Aug. 31. German National Bank, Pittsburgh. $70 00
Sept. 11. Grand Lodge, K.S.B., Philadelphia... 50 00
13. I.O.K.S.B., Erie.................................... 103 25
20. Grand Lodge, K.S.B., Philadelphia.. 50 00
20. Jeshurun Lodge, 59, I.O.B.B., Phila.. 50 00
23. Thro' S. Vendig & G. H. Judah, Phila. 67 00
23. Franklin Lodge, K.S.B., 43, Phila...... 10 00
23. Rebecca Lodge, K.S.B., Phila............. 10 00
23. Through A. T. Jones, Phila.................. 19 00
23. Congregation Rodef Sholem, Phila... 36 25
23. Potsdamer & Co., Phila....................... 4 00
24. Covenant Lodge, 66, K.S.B., Phila.... 10 00
26. Congregation Mickve Israel, Phila... 50 00
26. D.G. Lodge, 6, I.O.B.B., Phila............ 200 00
26. Rodef Sholem Lodge, 129, I.O.B.B., Wilkesbarre..................................... 10 00
26. Montefoire Lodge, 108, K.S.B., Williamsport... 5 00

Sept. 30. I.O.F.S.I Lodges, 19, 13, 17, 4, Williamsport.. $55 00
30. Union Lodge, 124, I.O.B.B., Pottsville. 5 00
Oct. 1. Era Lodge, 7, I.O.F.S.I., Phila............. 10 00
1. Franklin Club, Phila.............................. 100 00
2. Franklin Lodge, 32, I.O.F.S.I., Phila.. 32 00
3. Cong. House Israel, Phila.................... 50 00
4. Cremeiux Lodge, 88, I.O.B.B., Phila... 10 00
4. Har Moriah Lodge, 10, I.O.B.B., Phila. 5 00
4. Part pro. Fair Jewish Temple, Phila. 25 00
4. Hebrew Sunday-school, Phila............. 14 37
4. Aushai Emeth Sabbath-school, Phila. 2 90
4. Leon Rosskam, Phila............................ 10 00
4. Leah Lodge, 3, F.D. of I. Phila........... 3 25
4. Sholem Lodge, 154, I.O.B.B., Alleah'y 5 00
10. Jericho Lodge, 44, I.O.B.B., Pittsb'gh 35 00
11. George Jacobs, Phila........................... 50 00
14. Isaac Nusbaum, Phila......................... 20 00
24. Har Nevoh Lodge, 12, I.O.B.B., Phila. 10 00
24. M. Lowenthal, Phila............................. 10 00
24. Wyoming Lodge, 16, I.O.F.S.I., Wilkesbarre.. 2 00
Nov. 1. Garrick Literary Ass'n, Phila............. 5 00
5. D. G. Lodge, 4, K.S.B., Phila............... 7 00
5. Mordecai Lodge, 3s, K.S.B. Phila....... 15 00
5. Hiram Lodge, 46, K.S.B., Phila........... 5 00
5. Etz Chaim Lodge, 205, I.O.B.B., Phila.. 5 00

Total $1221 00

TENNESSEE.
Sept. 4. Contribution, from Dyersburg. $50 00
17. Thro' A. Ochs, Chattanooga................. 27 75
19. Citizens' Relief Com., Memphis......... 500 00
21. Through Max Sax, Nashville.............. 400 00
21. Through J. Friedlob, Jackson............. 52 05
23. Howard Association, Memphis........... 500 00
25. Will of Charles Grupe, Memphis........ 29 00
30. S. Bejah, Moscow................................ 10 00
Oct. 14. Through Leo Jonas, Columbia........... 10 90
14. Collections from other sources.......... 92 25

Total $1678 95

TEXAS.
Sept. 2. M. Hockstadter, Fort Worth.............. $50 00
16. Ladies' Heb. Ben. Soc., Galveston...... 50 00
19. Hebrew Ben. Soc., Galveston............. 150 00
19. Heb. Ben. Soc. (Leon & Blum)........... 300 00
Oct. 24. Lone Star Lodge, 210, I.O.B.B., Houston.. 30 00

Total $580 00

VIRGINIA.
Sept. 17. Ladies' Heb. Ben. Ass'n, Richmond... $35 00
17. M. Millheiser, Richmond..................... 10 00
27. Cong. Rodef Sholem, Petersburg....... 34 00
Oct. 24. M. Millheiser. Richmond.................... 10 00
Nov. 1. Cong. Beth Ahaba, Richmond............ 24 00

Total $103 00

WISCONSIN.
Oct. 23. Ladies' Emanuel Soc., Milwaukee..... $81 21
Sept. 24. Thro' D. Adler & E. Friend, Milw'kee 100 00

Total $181 21

Grand Total $16,139 68

EXPENDITURES.

For supplies.. $1,005 60
For nurses... 508 05
For livery and wagons....................................... 409 50
For labor... 293 50
For physicians.. 1,108 00
For drugs.. 144 20
For funerals.. 1,293 00
For support and transportation of families..... 7,032 65
For donations to distressed families returned, and supplies for orphans... 1,556 30
For Hebrew Relief Association for distressed families........ 1,500 00
Due physicians, and sundries as per vouchers, unpaid...... 475 00
For sundries... 1,366 15

Total... 16,691 95
Balance for contingent fund.............................. $10,000 00

APPENDIX. 421

REPORT OF THE KNIGHTS OF HONOR CENTRAL RELIEF COMMITTEE.

MEMBERS.

From Memphis Lodge, No. 196—H. M. Gage, M. A. Telford (died Sept. 1), and J. H. Banks (absent, vacancy not filled).
From Unity Lodge, No. 217—Anthony Ross, Henry Clements (died Aug. 29), and T. B. Allen.
From Chelsea Lodge, No. 280—Geo. B. Elliott (died Sept. 12), P. G. Kennett, and J. P. Prescott.
From Fountain Lodge, No. 296—J. B. Aldrich, E. Frederick (died Sept. 18), Barney Hughes, J. M. Johnson (in place of E. Frederick).
From Germania Lodge, No. 369—Rev. A. Thomas (died Sept. 3), Max Herman (died Sept. 14), John Brenner, Chas. Meyers.
From Diamond Lodge, No. 583—L. B. Reubenstein, served a few days only.
Committee organized August 21, 1878, by electing H. M. Gage, President; Henry Clements, 1st Vice-President; J. B. Aldrich, 2d Vice-President (Aug. 29) ; Max Herman, 1st Secretary (died Sept. 14); C. F. Aaron, 2d Secretary, Sept. 7 to 12 (died Sept. 18); J. P. Prescott, 3d Secretary, Sept. 13 ; W. J. Berlin, 1st Treasurer (resigned Aug. 30); John A. Holt, 2d Treasurer, Aug. 31 (died Oct. 5); Rev. A. Thomas, 1st Supt. Nurses (died Sept. 3); Geo. B. Elliott, 2d Supt. Nurses (died Sept. 12); C. W. Hoffman, 3d Supt. Nurses, Sept. 15 to Oct. 5; C. V. Snell, 4th Supt. Nurses, Oct. 6 to 28 ; E, Frederick, Commissary, to Sept. 11 (died Sept. 18); J. M. Johnson, Commissary, from Sept. 12.

SICKNESS AND MORTALITY.

	Cases.	Recovered.	Died.
Members	153	47	106
Wives	66	46	20
Children	107	77	30
Relatives	20	13	7
Totals	346	183	163

EXPLANATION AS TO MEMBERS.

Number of members who were sick and died (one out of the city) on or before August 21, 1878.. 7
Number of members who died, attended by their own families or other persons, or by another society (twelve out of the city)... 44
Number of members who recovered, attended, one by own family, the other by a society... 2
Number of members who died after sickness of three days or longer, but committee notified only one day before death... 7
Number of members who died, and committee notified only two days before death... 7
Number of members who died, and committee notified three days or more before death, nursed and attended to by them... 42
Number of members who recovered, having been nursed and attended to by the committee... 44

Total, as above... 153

SUPPLIES CONTRIBUTED.

1878.
Sept. 11. From C. A. Robinson, Wm. Meyers, and W. H. Fariss, Relief Com., K. of H., Huntsville, Ala., 50 dozen eggs, 100 chickens.
13. From Limestone, No. 1132, Limestone, Tenn., 13 sacks flour, 50 pounds each.
16. From Gate City, No. 346, Atlanta, Ga., 2 cases Rhine wine, ½ doz. canned beef, 2 bushels meal, ½ dozen cans ox-tail soup, 1 barrel grits, 100 pounds flour, 1 pound tea, 4 pounds coffee, 11 pounds sugar, 10 pounds rice, 1 gallon whisky, 1 dozen jellies, 2 dozen cans tomatoes, 2 dozen lemons.
18. From Teutonia, No. 141, Knoxville, Tenn., 1 can butter, 1 case eggs.
18. From Lord Baltimore, No. 275, Baltimore, Md., 2 dozen cans peaches, 1 bale socks, 2 packages sugar, 2 dozen assorted jellies, ½ dozen packages ground coffee, 3 cans extract beef, 6 packages tea, 1 can fruit, 1 sack coffee, 1 box candy, 1 jug sherry wine (from R. T. Duncan).

422　　　　　　　　　　　　　APPENDIX.

Sept. 22. From Teutonia, No. 141, Knoxville, Tenn., 1 coop chickens, 1 barrel onions.
 22. From citizens of Scottsboro, Ala., through Bro. Snodgrass, 2 boxes eggs.
Oct. 8. From Success, No. 773, Warrior, Ala., 30 sacks flour.
 8. From Maryland, No. 1133, Baltimore, Md., 8 jars assorted jellies, 7 papers corn starch, 28 glasses assorted jellies, 1 paper gelatine.
 10. From Teutonia, No. 141, Knoxville, Tenn., 1 coop chickens, 1 case eggs.
 10. From Oriental, No. 532, Careyville, Tenn., 2 coops chickens.
 10. From L. K. Byers, Altoona, Ill., 1 keg wine.

RECEIPTS.

1878.
Aug. 21. Germania Lodge, 369, Memphis.......... $25 00
 21. Fountain Lodge, 296, Memphis............ 25 00
 22. Diamond Lodge, 583, Memphis............ 25 00
 23. Chelsea Lodge, 280, Memphis............ 25 00
 23. Unity Lodge, 217, Memphis............... 25 00
 23. Memphis Lodge, 196, Memphis............ 25 00
 24. Central, 253, Columbia, Tenn............. 60 00
 26. Lincoln, 430, St. Louis, Mo............... 10 00
 26. Martin Schmidt, of Corona, No. 537...... 5 00
 27. Fayetteville, 181, Fayetteville, Tenn..... 25 00
 27. N. L. Avery, of Unity, 217................. 2 00
 28. Rose City, 1099, Little Rock, Ark......... 25 00
 28. Germania, 910, Little Rock, Ark.......... 30 00
 28. Eureka, 643, Piedmont, W. Va............. 10 00
 29. Relief Com., K. of H., Cincinnati, O.,
   thro' L. Wilson, G. V. D. of Ohio.... 100 00
 29. Members W. B. Hoke, 177, Louisville,
   Ky... 31 75
 29. Citizens of Princeton, Ky. (of all religions), thro' J. S. Hawthorn, V. D.
   of 685....................................... 53 10
 29. Members Peerless, 493, Springfield, Ill. 20 00
 30. Little Rock, 454, Little Rock, Ark....... 100 00
 30. Central, 164, Louisville, Ky............... 10 00
 30. Relief Com., K. of H., Cincinnati, O.,
   thro' L. Wilson, G. V. D. of Ohio.... 60 00
 30. Monitor, 879, Columbus, Neb.............. 25 00
 31. Excelsior, 4, Louisville, Ky................. 20 00
 31. Mystic, 212, Louisville, Ky................. 20 00
 31. Toledo, 73, Toledo, O....................... 25 00
Sept. 2. A. L. Rieber, 679, Butler, Pa.............. 7 50
 2. Franklin, 320, Franklin, Ky................ 20 00
 2. Una, 518, Lexington, Ky.................... 25 00
 2. Glasgow, 263, Glasgow, Ky................ 25 00
 2. Crescent, 413, Tuscumbia, Ala............ 50 00
 2. Thos. Turley................................... 8 00
 2. D. F. Goodyear, Grand Treasurer........ 561 00
 2. Christian, 820, Hopkinsville, Ky......... 50 00
 2. Dixon, 569, Henderson, Ky................ 25 00
 2. North Star, 803, Kasson, Minn............ 25 00
 3. Jefferson, 5, Louisville, Ky................. 25 00
 3. Lee, 713, Marianna, Ark.................... 25 00
 5. Centennial, 200, Louisville, Ky........... 25 00
 6. Relief Com., K. of H., Cincinnati, O.... 100 00
 6. Alpha, 37, and Germania, 38, K. & L.
   of H., Cincinnati, O., thro' L. Wilson, G. V. D. of Ohio..................... 20 00
 6. Austin, 418, Austin, Texas.................. 50 00
 6. Cedartown, 273, Cedartown, Ga.......... 6 10
 6. Omaha, 829, Omaha, Neb................... 25 00
 6. Golden, 1, Louisville, Ky................... 25 00
 6. Boyle, 385, Danville, Ky.................... 25 00
 6. Brother Keneyld.............................. 5 00
 7. Plattsmouth, 1043, Plattsmouth, Neb. 25 00
 7. Fremont, 859, Fremont, Neb.............. 10 00
 9. D. F. Goodyear, Grand Treasurer....... 525 00
 10. Mystic, 212, Louisville, Ky................. 50 00
 10. Abraham Lincoln, 710, Detroit, Mich. 50 00
 10. Little Rock, 452, Little Rock, Ark...... 50 00
 10. Alpha, 424, Wheeling, W. Va.............. 25 00
 11. Georgia, 127, Atlanta, Ga................... 200 00
 11. Washington, 455, Paducah, Ky............ 50 00
 11. Schiller, 400, St. Louis, Mo................ 25 00
 11. R. E. Lee, 6, Louisville, Ky................. 12 50
 11. S. H. Shepard, G. D., Augusta, Ga...... 150 00
 11. Hardin, 249, Elizabethtown, Ky......... 98 40
 11. Nebraska City, 925, Neb. City, Neb.... 40 00
 12. Christian, 820, Hopkinsville, Ky........ 69 15
 12. Hero, 991, Effingham, Ill................... 17 25
 12. Keokuk, 544, Keokuk, Iowa................ 25 00
 12. Illinois, 268, East St. Louis, Ill........... 50 00

1878.
Sept. 12. Warren, 248, Bowling Green, Ky....... $10 00
 12. Marion, 601, Indianapolis, Ind........... 10 00
 13. D. F. Goodyear, Grand Treasurer....... 350 00
 14. Relief Com., K. of H., Cincinnati, O.... 90 00
 14. Jas. A. Mathews................................ 10 00
 14. Ely, 45, Corry, Pa............................. 25 00
 14. Iron Banks, 802, Columbus, Ky.......... 25 00
 14. Mizpah, 822, Springfield, Ky.............. 25 00
 14. S. H. Shepard, G. D., Augusta, Ga..... 100 00
 15. C. H. Cogswell, G.D.,Cedar Rapids, Ia. 15 00
 16. Adelphi, 1159, Little Rock. Ark.......... 50 00
 17. D. F. Goodyear, Grand Treasurer...... 500 00
 18. W. B. Hoke, 177, Louisville, Ky......... 13 15
 18. Muhlenberg, 108, Greenville, Ky....... 25 00
 18. Saunders, 974, Wahoo, Neb................ 11 00
 18. Centennial, 200, Louisville, Ky.......... 10 00
 18. S. L. Finley, Benton, Tenn................ 5 00
 19. S. H. Shepard, G. D., Augusta, Ga..... 150 00
 19. Lincoln, 430, St. Louis, Mo................ 25 00
 20. Crescent, 413, Tuscumbia. Ala........... 4 00
 20. North Star, 803, Kasson, Minn............ 25 00
 20. Mrs. A. W. Anthony, Kasson, Minn... 5 00
 20. Indianapolis, 14, Indianapolis, Ind.... 25 00
 20. Arminius, 7, Louisville, Ky................. 106 00
 20. C. H. Cogswell, G.D.,Cedar Rapids, Ia. 33 00
 21. W. L.Wood,G. Rep.,Indianapolis, Ind. 160 00
 21. D. F. Goodyear, Grand Treasurer...... 250 00
 23. "   "   "   "........ 500 00
 25. S. H. Shepard, G. D., Augusta, Ga..... 50 00
 26. D. F. Goodyear, Grand Treasurer...... 500 00
 26. Dayton, 23, Dayton, Ohio.................. 50 00
 27. D. F. Goodyear, Grand Treasurer...... 250 00
 28. "   "   "   "........ 82 60
 28. Amo, 274. Lagrange, Ky.................... 25 00
 30. St. Francis, 492, Forrest City, Ark..... 25 00
 30. D. F. Goodyear, Grand Treasurer...... 500 00
Oct. 1. "   "   "   "........ 500 00
 2. "   "   "   "........ 183 58
 2. C. M. Haywood, G. T., Oswego, N. Y. 100 00
 2. Centennial, 200, Louisville, Ky.......... 20 00
 3. D. F. Goodyear, Grand Treasurer...... 154 50
 7. "   "   "   "........ 311 25
 8. "   "   "   "........ 124 10
 8. Little Rock, 452, Little Rock, Ark..... 100 00
 9. D. F. Goodyear, Grand Treasurer...... 122 45
 11. "   "   "   "........ 250 00
 12. Riverside, 959, Camden, Ark............. 10 00
 12. Piedmont, 558, Statesville, N. C......... 25 00
 12. D. F. Goodyear, Grand Treasurer...... 268 50
 16. "   "   "   "........ 218 00
 18. S. H. Shepard, G. D., Augusta, Ga..... 60 00
 18. Crescent, 413, Tuscumbia, Ala........... 34 60
 19. D. F. Goodyear, Grand Treasurer...... 502 80
 20. C. M. Haywood, G. T., Oswego, N. Y. 100 00
 26. H. W. Robinson, for ladies of Bridgeport, Mich................................. 17 00
 26. Toledo, 73, Toledo, O....................... 25 00
 26. D. F. Goodyear, Grand Treasurer...... 672 15
 30. "   "   "   "........ 471 00
 30. Sales of rations................................ 64 40
Nov. 5. D. F. Goodyear, Grand Treasurer...... 112 35
Dec. 9. W. L.Wood, G.Rep.,Indianapolis,Ind. 21 80
 15. D. F. Goodyear, Grand Treasurer...... 465 70
 15. "   "   "   "........ 157 60
 21. "   "   "   "........ 408 50
 " "   "   "   "........ 707 00
1879.
Jan. 16. "   "   "   "........ 668 05
Feb. 5. C. H. Eaton, G. Rep.,'Boston, Mass... 10 00
 20. G. T. Smith, Newark, N. J.................. 50 00

RECAPITULATION.

From Memphis lodges.. $150 00
From other lodges and sources.. 3,617 00
From D. F. Goodyear, grand treasurer..................................... 10,415 53

Total $14,182 53

APPENDIX. 423

DISBURSEMENTS.

For nurses	$6,704 31
For burial expenses	667 50
For expenses	2,013 85
For supplies	2,066 02
For physicians	1,639 65
Remittances to other places for relief of K. of H.	850 00
Total	$13,941 33
Balance in hand	241 20

There still remains several physicians' bills unsettled (balances on some of them), the aggregate of which considerably exceed the amount remaining in the hands of the committee.

INDEPENDENT ORDER OF MUTUAL AID.

ORGANIZED AUGUST 18, 1878.

Wm. McElroy, Chairman.
H. Buttenberg, Sup't Nurses.
J. C. Thrall, Treasurer.

S. A. Taylor, Secretary.
J. C. Shehan, C. Hoffman, W. F. Sheppy, J. H. Sheppard, Asst. Sup't Nurses.

Whole number sick	206
Brothers of this order	98
Wives of members	36
Children and relatives	72

DEATHS.

Members	63
Wives of brothers	10
Children and relatives	21
Total number	94
Amount received and disbursed	$3,385 81

ADDRESS OF SUPREME PRESIDENT.

MEMPHIS, TENN., *November* 1, 1878.

To the Members of the I. O. M. A.:

BROTHERS,—As you are by this time well aware, a fearful pestilence has swept over a portion of our dominion, and carried with it many of our brethren.

(Names of members and other information concerning their death, as required, will be duly forwarded by the Supreme Secretary when the official returns are received in full.)

Some contracted the disease at its earliest incipiency, others yielded up their lives, noble martyrs, to the great cause of brotherly love and humanity. According to our laws, the families of the deceased are entitled to the mutual aid benefits which our order guarantees. This may appear to some an enormous amount, and beyond our ability to meet, yet by united efforts it may soon be accomplished.

Your Supreme President feels that it is not necessary to appeal to the honor and manhood of the I. O. M. A. to stand firm in this our hour of trial, believing it is only requisite to lay a plain statement of facts before you, feeling assured that your own consciences will dictate your duty in carrying out the obligations that bind us one and all in that great indissoluble bond, called brotherhood.

The fundamental principle of our institution is "Mutual Aid," and nowhere in the history of organizations, similar to ours, has an order been put to its test so early in its infancy.

Brothers, to falter now would not only be a death-blow to our organization, but would show to the world that beneficial societies are not to be trusted in times of epidemics and plagues.

The majority of those who enter societies such as ours are those in moderate circumstances, and do so from a sense of honor and duty to their families, feeling that they have made provision, in case of death, to secure their loved ones above immediate want. This is the case in nearly every instance among our deceased brothers; and now the widow's tear and orphan's cry come up to us, not for aid, charity, nor succor, but for their just and legal rights.

We promised the husband and father that his dear ones should receive two thousand dollars and accrued assessments upon his demise. We assured the brothers generally that their legal heirs, whoever they may be, the same. Shall we fail to fulfill that promise so faithfully made? The response comes from each and every heart, "No! they must and shall be paid." In order to meet these payments your Supreme President deems it advisable to make yellow fever assessments "special," and not to send out more than two each month, paying the beneficiaries in installments. Assessments for deaths from other causes will be issued regularly.

Feeling confident that the many words of encouragement that come to me from prominent members of our organization, and from lodges who have by resolutions resolved to stand by the order, that this reflects the sentiments of the brotherhood at large, I can continue the discharge of my official duties with renewed zeal, assured that I am surrounded by a band of brothers, who know no such word as fail.

Thankful to an all-wise Providence that the fever is over, and trusting that health and prosperity will abound with you all, I am Yours in M. A.,

Attest: A. J. KNAPP, *Supreme President.*
THOS. BALDWIN, *Supreme Secretary.*

ASSOCIATION FOR RELIEF OF FRENCH RESIDENTS.

Isadore Ozanne, Treasurer and Secretary.
Amount received and disbursed, $1760.25.
Number of dead, 37.

KNIGHTS OF PYTHIAS.

M. T. Williamson, B. P. Smith, and L. W. Allen, Committee.
Amount received, $4,289.67; amount disbursed, $4,039.67.
Number of dead, 22.

ANCIENT ORDER OF UNITED WORKMEN.

RELIEF COMMITTEE ORGANIZED AUGUST 16, 1878.

Saml. A. Payler, Chairman; Geo. E. Tate, Secretary; Henry Brown, Superintendent Nurses; W. C. Davis, Dr. Quimby, S. B. Robinson, J. A. Wells, Visiting Committee.
Amount received and disbursed, $2,402.15.
Number of deaths, 35. Number of nurses, 28.

REPORT OF THE MEMPHIS BRANCH OF THE LOUISVILLE AND NASHVILLE RAILROAD.

During the yellow fever epidemic this road, by night and day exertion on the part of the management, was kept open throughout, constituting the only avenue to the South during the dire visitation. The estimated loss from the interruption of traffic is $300,000; of pounds freight carried free for sufferers, 1,500,000 lbs.; of persons carried free and at reduced rates on account of epidemic, 20,000; money value of free transportation, $50,000; of employés who died of yellow fever, 71 (see list subjoined); attacked, 145 (see subjoined list); of persons thrown out of employment by decrease of traffic, 500; estimated loss to employés from interruption of employment, $110,000; contributions by officers and employés to sufferers, $2,000; number of officers and employés, 5,000. The road ran 1,550 miles of special trains, with nurses and supplies for relief of rural points. The company carefully nursed its own employés, employing doctors and a staff of nurses for the purpose; and it interred those who succumbed, at a cost of $5,000.

With barely an exception, all the employés stuck to their posts during the continuance of the epidemic, vieng with each other in their devotion to the company and ministering to the sick. Employés also in the non-affected districts of the road did not hesitate to take part in the affected districts.

General Superintendent Rowland, to whom we are indebted for the above figures, adds:

"So general was the manifestation of devotion on the part of the employés that it would be hard to give prominence to any particular case, but I do not think any one will grudge the singling out of Geo. W. Ernest and his wife, who were in charge of the company's hotel at Paris, Tennessee, and who both succumbed to the fatal destroyer in the midst of a heroic and devoted attention to the company's sick employés. It is a sad spot in a sad story. May such another visitation be far distant."

YELLOW FEVER VICTIMS.

Class of Employee.	No. sick.	Died.	Class of Employee.	No. sick.	Died.
Station agents	9	7	Laborers and porters	9	5
Clerks	16	9	Train dispatchers	1	0
Conductors	6	3	Telegraph operators	5	3
Baggage-masters	4	2	Messengers	2	1
Brakemen	13	8	Section men	3	2
Engineers	16	4	Mechanics	23	7
Firemen	19	7	Hotel superintendents	2	2
Master mechanics	1	1	Hotel waiters	1	1
Storekeeper	1	0	Hotel laundresses	1	1
Yardmasters	3	1	Nurses	1	1
Switchmen	2	1			
Watchmen	7	5	Total	145	71

Nearly all of these were on the division of road from Memphis to Paris, Tennessee.

REPORT OF THE HON. CASEY YOUNG.

Money received by Casey Young for the benefit of yellow fever sufferers in the South during the recent epidemic:

1878.
Aug. 23. L. C. Silvermail, M. D., Fostoria, Ohio $12 00
 26. Hon. Carter H. Harrison, Chicago, Ill 600 00
 31. Hon. R. M. Knapp, Jerseyville, Ill 200 00
Sept. 2. Hon. Spencer F. Baird, Washington, D. C. 40 00
 2. Peter D. Boyle, Washington, D. C., with direction to divide between Irish Literary Soc. and Citizens' Relief Ass'n.. 50 00
 2. Hon. Addison Oliver, Onona, Iowa 25 00
 4. Hon.Dan.M.Henry,Carlisle,Md 106 00
 5. Hon. Carter H. Harrison, Chicago, Ill 400 00
 6. Hon. D. M. Lockwood, Buffalo, N. Y. 100 00
 8. Hon. Thomas J. Henderson, Princeton, Ill 300 00
 8. Officer & Percy, Council Bluffs, Iowa, from Hon. W. F. Sopp 260 00
 10. Hon. Richard W. Townshend, Shawneetown, Ill 220 00
 11. Gorghee & Sell, Erie, Pa., proceeds of concert, Park Opera House 180 80

1878.
Sept. 11. Hon. Wm. Lathrop, Rockford, Ill.,contributed by the Rockford Rifles $103 02
 12. Hon.Wm.Lathrop,Rockford,Ill 100 00
 12. E. W. Stanton, Sec. Iowa Agricultural Society, Ames,Iowa 64 45
 16. Hon. A. H. Hamilton, Lavergne, Ind 40 00
 12. C. P. Huntington, through J. E. Gates 1,000 00
Oct. 16. William Dickson, Sec. Relief Com., Washington, D. C 400 00
 16. Col. S. Bassett French, Richmond, Va 5 00
 16 Geo. E. King, Rockford, Ill 209 40
 16. M. McKeogh, Orkney Springs, Va., contributed by guests and employés at Orkney Springs 104 50
 16. Hon. Frank Jones, Dover,N.H. 1,000 00
 16. Mrs. Sarah B. F. Mays, Elizabeth City,Md.,through Hon. F.B.Stanton,Washingt'n,D.C 25 00
 16. E. S. Wright, pastor Presbyterian Church, North East, Pa. 76 54
Nov. 5. Hon. Wm. Evarts, Secretary of State, Washington, D. C 1,000 00
 5. T. M. Hodges, Portsmouth, Va 100 00

Received by A. D. Langstaff, and distributed as advised by donors, the following sums:

Employés of Collins & Co., Hartford, Conn $113 60
Ames Iron Works, Oswego, N. Y. 50 00
Norton Iron Works, Ashland, Ky. 200 00
Miller & Eastmead, New York City 25 00

  Total $388 00

The above amounts were distributed, in Memphis and other places, in accordance with the directions which accompanied them when sent to me, except a portion which still remains in my hands, and which will be disposed of as directed by the donors. My vouchers, receipts, etc, are in Memphis, and I can not at present furnish a detailed statement of disbursements.
               CASEY YOUNG.
WASHINGTON, D. C., *March* 25, 1879.

Besides the foregoing there was perhaps $10,000 sent through other individuals who have not reported, besides over $70,000 sent to the mayor, making a total of fully $80,000 in money contributed for the relief of Memphis, exclusive of rations, which would amount in money to at least $20,000, making the grand total foot up $100,000.

REPORT OF THE TELEGRAPHERS.

Statement of receipts and expenses of the Telegraphers' Aid Association at Memphis, Tennessee, during the yellow fever epidemic of 1878.

RECEIPTS.

Cash from Jno. Van Horne, Chairman General Relief, N. Y.	$2,099	87
Cash from Memphis Employés	50	00
Cash from Jos. W. Fisher, Nashville, Tenn	200	00
Cash from R. G. Bradford, Marianna, Ark	5	00
Cash from A. D. Odell, Washington, Mo	5	00
Cash from W. Parker, Bonapart, Iowa		25
Cash from Manager, Pine Bluff, Ark	25	00
Cash from Manager, Senatobia, Miss	5	00
Cash from Manager, Duvall's Bluff, Ark	5	00
Cash from Manager, Helena, Ark	7	50
Cash from United States Signal Sergeant, Wm. McElroy	5	00
Cash from Sale of Infirmary effects	25	50
Total	$2,433	12

EXPENSES.

Voucher No. 1. Medical attention—				
Memphis, Tenn	$559	00		
Paris, Tenn	10	00		
McKenzie, Tenn	40	00		
			609	00
Voucher No. 2. Medicines—				
Memphis, Tenn	113	45		
Paris, Tenn	13	20		
Grenada, Miss	9	00		
Decatur, Ala	1	50		
McKenzie, Tenn	3	50		
			140	65
Voucher No. 3. Wines and liquors—				
Memphis, Tenn	110	15		
			110	15
Voucher No. 4. Provisions—				
Memphis, Tenn	65	73		
			65	73
Voucher No. 5. Infirmary—				
Memphis, Tenn	328	31		
McKenzie, Tenn	5	00		
			333	31
Voucher No. 6. Burials—				
McKenzie, Tenn	20	00		
Memphis, Tenn	846	00		
			866	00
Voucher No. 7. Miscellaneous—				
Memphis, Tenn	59	03		
Grenada, Miss	50	00		
Louisville, Ky	46	25		
Paris, Tenn	21	00		
McKenzie, Tenn	27	00		
Amount advanced G. M. Dugan, Jackson, Tenn., for distribution	100	00		
			303	28
Cash remitted to Jno. Van Horne, Chairman, New York.	5	00		
			5	00
			$2,433	12

The following persons were under the care of this Association at this point.

J. R. Henricle, volunteer, Pittsburgh, Pa., died.

A. S. Hawkins, volunteer, Pittsburgh, Pa., died.

H. M. Goewey, volunteer, Pittsburgh, Pa., died.

J. Howard Allen, volunteer, Chillicothe, O., died.

J. W. McDonald, volunteer, Cincinnati, O., died.

C. R. Langford, volunteer, Montgomery, Ala., died.

Thomas Hood, volunteer, Memphis, Tenn., died.

M. J. Keyer, volunteer, Louisville, Ky., died.

APPENDIX. 427

W. H. Mynatt, operator, Memphis, Tenn., died.
E. W. Gibson, operator, Memphis, Tenn., died.
Jno. I. Connelly, operator, Memphis, Tenn., died.
Daniel Walsh, clerk, Memphis, Tenn., died.
Jno. McFeely, messenger, Memphis, Tenn., died.
Mrs. E. Fowler, wife of J. J. Fowler, Memphis, Tenn., died.
Mrs. Clements, wife of F. T. O. Clements, Memphis, Tenn., died.
Lewis Klotz, volunteer, Mobile, Ala., recovered.
C. T. Smithson, volunteer, Guthrie, Ky., recovered.
B. Deklyn, volunteer, New York, recovered.
C. W. McReynolds, volunteer, Akron, O., recovered.
Jno. M. Mullins, delivery clerk, Memphis, Tenn., recovered.
H. Sigler, chief operator, Memphis, Tenn., recovered.
W. E. Mulford, operator, Memphis, Tenn., recovered.
Mrs. Julia E. Gibson, wife of E. W. Gibson, Memphis, Tenn., recovered.
Chas. Wright, messenger, Memphis, Tenn., recovered.
G. M. Baker, manager, Memphis, Tenn., recovered.
C. A. Gaston, receiving clerk, Memphis, Tenn., recovered.
H. E. Conly, repairer, Memphis, Tenn., recovered.

The only one of our original force who escaped the epidemic was George A. Putnam, and of the volunteers J. B. R. Spalding, of Baltimore, and N. S. Graves, of Houston, Texas, alone escaped.

This Association desire to express their thanks to Drs. Gelzier, Mobile, Ala., Easton Yonge, Savannah, Georgia, T. O. Summers, Nashville, Tenn., —— Simmons, Charleston, S. C., Major W. T. Walthall, Mobile, Ala., Judge Olin, Augusta, Ga., for their valuable assistance, so freely given among our sick, and to Manager A. C. Frey, Decatur, Ala., for liberal contributions of poultry, etc.

CHARLES A. GASTON, *Chairman.*
G. M. BAKER, *Treasurer.*

MISCELLANEOUS.

THE MILITARY.

Memphis *Appeal.*—Preliminary to the breaking up of Camp Joe Williams, which will take place Nov. 2d, the two companies of the city military struck tents, and returned to the city yesterday morning, and made quite a striking appearance as they passed up Main Street, escorted by the company which had been on duty in the city during the epidemic. The boys looked like veterans, and their appearance made the tears well up in many an old Confed's eyes, reminding them, as it did, of the times when knapsacks and haversacks looked like an elephant had stepped on them. The two companies—the Bluff City Grays, composed, rank and file, of some of our most promising young men, and the McClellan Guards, of the same class of our colored citizens—arrived by special train at the depot of the Mississippi and Tennessee Railway, where they were met by the Zouave Guards, Captain Brown. The three companies were formed into battalion, Captain John F. Cameron, of the Bluffs, taking command—the command of his company devolving upon First Lieutenant Herbert Rhett. Headed by the Bluff City Cornet Band, one of the best colored musical organizations in the country, the line of march was taken up Main Street to Court, down Court to Second, and to the Bluff City's armory, where, after a brief speech from Colonel Cameron, the companies were "mustered out of service," the gallant young soldiers returning to the arms of their friends and sweethearts.

Colonel John F. Cameron made the following remarks before disbanding:

"Fellow-soldiers (and I am most proud to so address you), we are now about to stack arms—not disband and lay aside, for we stand ready as ever to respond to the call of duty—but simply disband and return to our daily vocations. Citizen-soldiers, assembling as usual for weekly training, when you were called upon by the citizens to do military duty, you regarded it in the light of a compliment and an honor conferred, to which you heartily responded. For have you not long paraded these streets, clad in the habiliments of war, seeking servage? And did you not point out a field of duty? And you have well discharged it. You are of the organizations who believe that military companies were organized, equipped by the State, and sustained by this community, for the protection of life and property in the hour of civil commotion, pestilence, and famine, and you have simply done your duty. You have your reward in the plaudits of your fellow-citizens; the gracious smiles of fair women, which every manly fellow yearns to merit; added to which you carry with you the satisfaction which comes from the consciousness of having discharged your duty to the community in which you live, and in which you and your families receive your daily sustenance."

These companies went on duty at Camp Joe Williams on the 12th of August, when the movement to establish a camp of refuge there was threatened with violence by those living in the neighborhood. Their presence served to overawe those who would otherwise, perhaps, have interfered with what has proven to have been the wisest means of saving human life from the ravages of the terrible pestilence. Colonel Cameron took command of the two companies organized in battalion, and brought into requisition his well-known military genius and hard-earned experience, by which the camp was excellently guarded, and its citizens assured of safety from molestation from any quarter. It would have done those who have lost no opportunity to flaunt the bloody shirt in the face of the South good to have seen how harmoniously the white and colored troops served in the same organization, each ready to help the other in a soldierly way at the word. The fever made inroads into their ranks, however, and several of those gallant young spirits, who left their homes on the 12th of August, inspired by the same sense of duty as impels the patriot to take up arms in defense of his country, fell victims. Peace to their memories. Our limited space prevents a more extended report of the valuable duties performed by our gallant military. We append the rosters of both companies, with those who were sick and those who died, kindly furnished by members of each company.

BLUFF CITY GRAYS.

OFFICERS.

John F. Cameron, Captain.
Herbert Rhett, First Lieutenant.
W. W. Harvey, Second Lieutenant.
C H. Raine, Third Lieutenant.
W. B. Rogers, Surgeon.
W. W. Talbert, Orderly Sergeant.
J. M. Bradley, Ensign.

Robert Armour, Second Sergeant.
F. M. Irion, Third Sergeant.
Harry Ferguson, First Corporal.
E. Kelley, Second Corporal.
John Harbert, Third Corporal.
Walter Armour, Fourth Corporal.

PRIVATES.

H. S. Ashe,
C. Boisseau,
Arthur Clarke,
Fred. Fowler,
O. B. Haynes,
—— Ingram,
Ambrose Mayre,
Paul Spiegel,

Henry Bailey,
A. B. Carter,
Ed. Cobb,
William Graham,
W. D. Haynes,
James Jones,
Ed. Sayle,
—— Wildberger.

MEMBERS THAT WERE SICK.

Rhett, Lieutenant.
Harvey, Lieutenant.
Rogers, Surgeon.
Armour, Sergeant,
Ferguson, Corporal,
Ashe, Private.
Cobb, Private.
W. D. Haynes, Private.
Mayre, Private.

Spiegel, Private,
Goodwin, Private.
Boisseau, Private.
O. B. Haynes, Private.
Ingram, Private.
Sayle, Private.
Everett, Private.
Wheatley, Private.

MEMBERS THAT DIED.

Harvey, Lieutenant.
Ferguson, Corporal.
Wheatley, Corporal.
Goodwin, Private.

W. D. Haynes, Private.
Everett, Private.
Spiegel, Private.

McCLELLAN GUARDS.

OFFICERS.

J. S. Glass, Captain.
T. D. Jackson, Lieutenant.
Lorenzo Dow, Lieutenant.
B. Ick, Sergeant.

T. A. Grexby, Sergeant.
B. Dickinson, Sergeant.
H. Cobb, Sergeant.
Dick Smith, Sergeant.

PRIVATES.

Henry Davis,
Robert Johnson,
R. Hicks,
Richard Land.
Green Otey,
James Winn,
Albert Carey,
Isaac Simmons,
Haywood Bradshaw,
Gilbert Gill,
Jesse Simmons,
Pompey Yearger,
Robert Lyons,
Sam. Hilliard,
Henry Wilson,
Jim Gaston,

F. B. Davis,
W. M. Armistead,
C. W. Winland,
Tip Harris,
Cicero Nelson,
Charles Crutcher,
Vance P. Percell,
James Clark,
Nelson Wright,
Phil. Dickenson,
Carey White,
John Jefferson,
Fred. Thomas,
Henry White,
Charles Hart.

Peck, Sergeant,
Cobb, Sergeant,
Lane, Private,

MEMBERS WHO DIED.

Crutcher, Private,
Harris, Private,
Carey, Private.

BLUFF CITY CORNET BAND.

Thomas Marley, Leader,
Lance Robinson,
Eli Elliston,
Robert Finley,
James Norman,

James Harris,
Henry Andrews,
Stephen Brown,
James Mann,
Thomas Maxley.

ZOUAVE GUARDS.

Memphis *Appeal*.—We took occasion recently to speak of the two companies of our citizen military, which have been on duty at Camp Joe Williams. We have also a few words to say about the Zouave Guards, the second colored military organization in the city, who have rendered the public faithful service in various capacities in the city, and at the prison camp on President's Island during the epidemic. Too much praise can not be accorded both officers and privates for the excellent and trusty manner in which they performed their duty, coming to the rescue, as it were, at a time when threats were made to raid the citizens' relief commissary, by those to whom rations were not issued without regard to their condition of distress. We append the company muster-roll, together with the names of those who died during the service:

OFFICERS.

R. T. Brown, Captain.
C. V. Reed, First Lieutenant.
H. Clay, Third Lieutenant.
W. F. Morgan, Chaplain.
E. Gorgon, Orderly Sergeant.
R. R. Smith, Ensign.

John Walton, First Sergeant.
C. H. Thomas, Second Sergeant.
J. L. McNeal, First Corporal.
T. H. Burton, Second Corporal.
J. W. Gay, Third Corporal.
Dan. Fleming, Fourth Corporal.

PRIVATES.

J. Felton,
F. Talbot,
M. Donneally,
David Banks,
Danely Brown,
C. T. Drayton,
J. Ellington,
A. Jackson,
Joseph Walton,
Joseph Hall,
Douglas Burke,

M. G. Jones,
J. Robertson,
John Moore,
Wm. Stephenson,
R. Sneed,
W. Coleman,
John Banks,
Henry Martin,
R. G. Gerney,
H. Macklin,
E. Hooker,

Sam. Glenn,
Andrew Mann,
John White,
A. McCoy,
W. Overton,
Thos. Smith,
Ben. Smith,
F. Pierce,
James Crawford.

DIED.

Second Lieutenant, W. M. Hanson; Privates, A. W. Brown and Tom Lewis.

A squad of this company, under command of Lieutenant H. Clay, was placed on guard duty at the prison camp on President's Island, and are highly complimented by the authorities for their faithful services. On Tuesday this squad returned to the city with the prisoners. On arriving at the wharf they were met by that portion of the company on duty in the city, under command of Captain R. G. Brown, who escorted them to the jail. After delivering the prisoners safely over to the jailer, the company returned to their armory, where it was disbanded. Captain Brown delivered an appropriate address on the occasion. He congratulated the company on their safe arrival to their homes, and hoped that every man had performed his duty conscientiously. He advised that every man go about his business earnestly, honestly, and industriously, and endeavor to merit the good opinions of the public. That all should live in peace and harmony, and with malice toward none. The captain's remarks were received with three hearty cheers, when the company was properly mustered out of the service of the Citizens' Relief Committee, each member retiring peacefully to his home.

THE POST-OFFICE.

Memphis *Appeal*.—The employés of the Memphis post-office have done their whole duty during the epidemic just passed. The fever robbed them of both the post-master and his assistant, besides taking off some of the most valuable of their number, yet the business of the office has never been neglected; on the contrary, it has been conducted regularly, and in a manner which is a surprise to every one. When the lamented Thompson died, the management of the office fell upon the shoulders of Colonel Knowlton, who, soon after, had to succumb, and died after a short illness. Mr. W. J. Chase then took charge of the office, and continues to discharge the duties of post-master with a skill most creditable to his business tact and ability. No complaints have been made, and, notwithstanding the greatly reduced force, on account of sickness and death, every thing has moved like clock-work. Several of the carriers have recovered from their attacks of the fever, and have resumed their routes, and soon every thing about the post-office will be in working order as usual. Below we give the names of those who have died, convalesced, and now on duty:

DEAD.

R. A. Thompson, post-master.
C. S. Knowlton, ass't post-master.
J. O'Brien, clerk.
M. J. Cunningham, clerk.

I. P. Oliver, letter carrier.
W. A. Hill, Jr., letter carrier.
George Cooper, col'd, letter carrier.
Frank Reynolds, letter carrier.

CONVALESCENTS.

The following named had the fever, recovered, and are now on duty:

H. C. Bigelow, sup't of carriers.
Lafe Jennings, sup't of mails.
Charles Stewart, clerk.
W. J. Jones, clerk.
Douglas Muir, clerk.
Phil. J. Shide, clerk.
W. B. Hood, letter carrier.

Burt White, letter carrier.
Thad Plummer, col'd, letter carrier.
M. O'Reilly, letter carrier.
Levi McCoy, col'd, letter carrier.
C. W. Miller, col'd, letter carrier.
D. W. Washington, col'd, letter carrier.
Sam Fransciola, porter.

ON DUTY.

The following are the names of those who have not had the fever, and have been on duty throughout the epidemic:

W. J. Chase, post-master.
Frank Stewart, assistant.
Lee Trout, clerk,
Gus Ennis, clerk,
W. E. Douglas, clerk.

D. L. Stewart, clerk.
John Raquet, letter carrier.
W. R. Chandler, letter carrier.
J. P. Rogers, letter carrier.
F. T. Cage, col'd, letter carrier.

THE TELEGRAPHERS.

Memphis Appeal.—Of twenty-five employés of the telegraph office, eleven have died, nine have convalesced—only five escaping the disease. Of these five, two of the operators are new comers—Mr. Putman being alone entitled to the honors of having met the enemy and defeated him. We recall many nights when he was the solitary occupant of the operating-room, the click of the instruments, as they told the story of the busy world abroad, being the only accompaniments he had to feelings that must have been sad indeed, as he recalled the dead and speculated upon the chances for recovery of his sick comrades. Those were sad and solitary hours which required in the sentinel who kept his lonely vigil a more than brave heart, and a courage much cooler than that which impels the soldier to the cannon's mouth. The story of the telegraphers of Memphis is an honorable one. Like a band of brothers they stood by each other "in sickness and in health, till death did them part." As one was carried to his rest another took his place. The pulsations of the good hearts who, in distant northern and western cities, were sending us sympathy and succor, were carried to us along the wires without a moment's interruption. Kind messages, inquiries for loved ones, drafts of money, all came to us over the wires to which one or other of the brave band stood whose names we record to-day with pride and pleasure. Undismayed by the intelligence which every hour was flashed to and from us of the growing strength of the epidemic, and the increase of its victims, the telegraphers continued to interpret sad and joyful messages; to be the medium of death and life; the harbingers of hope or the messengers of despair. They stood to their posts like men, and did their duty like heroes indeed, in whom was united the broadest humanity and the tenderest sentiments of love for their fellow-men. The telegraph was to us a priceless boon during the reign of the plague. What the mails failed to do it did with the steadiness and rapidity of the days when health and peace were supreme. To us of the press, it has always been invaluable. It has been more so than ever the last ninety days. As the operators, the manager, and the clerks went down one by one, until there were but two clerks and one operator to do the more than usually large business, which pressed with more than usual eagerness, we shuddered to think what would be the result if that brave last man went down. For many days he was the interpreter of the hopes and fears of thousands, and the means of joy and happiness that was a compensation for all the sorrow that many of his messages bore. We rejoice that he was spared. The following list, complete, gives the names of all who died, convalesced, and escaped, together with the members of the several telegraphers' families who escaped:

DEAD.

M. J. Keyer,
Henry Mynatt,
H. M. Goewey,
E. W. Gibson,
C. R. Langford,
J. I. Connelly,

Thomas Hood,
J. W. McDonald,
Howard Allen,
J. R. Herricle,
A. Hawkins.

CONVALESCENTS.

G. M. Baker, manager,
Howell Sigler, chief operator,
Lewis Klotz, night chief operator,
C. A. Gaston, cashier,
C. McReynolds, operator,

B. Deklyn, operator,
W. E. Molford, operator,
J. M. Mullins, clerk,
H. E. Conley, repairer.

ESCAPED.

George A. Putnam, operator,
John B. R. Spalding, operator,
N. S. Graves, operator,

C. R. Newell, clerk,
Jesse B. Waggener, clerk.

AMONG THE FAMILIES.

DEAD.

Operator J. J. Fowler's wife.   Batteryman Clements' wife.

CONVALESCENT.

Chief operator H. Sigler's wife.   Operator E. W. Gibson's wife.

THE PRESS.

Memphis Appeal.—The awful facts of the yellow fever, now that the epidemic is over, come out one by one. In the statement of its havoc in the ranks of our police and firemen and the employés of our three principal railroads, which we have given from day to day, we have astonished even the closest scrutinizers of the course of the scourge. But soul harrowing as these figures were considered by the many correspondents who have written us concerning them, they are surpassed by those which we give below, as furnished by the *Appeal, Avalanche,* and *Ledger* offices. These lists embrace all, from the press-room to the editorial-room of each paper, together with accurate details of the ravages of the disease in the families of each one:

APPEAL OFFICE.

DEAD.

COUNTING-ROOM.

George W. Woods, temporary book-keeper.

COMPOSING-ROOM.

Maj. W. G. Stephenson,
J. B. Barker,
B. F. Fuller,
James F. Cummins,

B. N. Cutting,
L. M. Lorentz,
Charles M. Smith,
George Beamish.

APPENDIX.

Al. Plummer,
Frank Plummer,
Nick (porter),
A. S. Hollenshead,
Byron Brooks,

PRESS-ROOM.

John Kelly, Sr.,
John Kelly, Jr.,
James Kelly,
M. Virgeson,
Andy Harrington.

CONVALESCENTS.

COUNTING-ROOM.

Henry White,
John S. Fifer,

Frank Backus.

EDITORIAL-ROOM.

Fred. Brennan,
Eug. W. Moore,

W. S. Brooks.

COMPOSING-ROOM.

H. E. Crandall,
John B. Hoskins,
W. W. Stephenson,
T. D. Uzell,
H. J. McGrann (foreman),

W. G. Taylor,
H. M. Crowell,
Ed. Schiller,
Frank Beamish.

PRESS-ROOM.

Kinch Virgeson,
Louis Beckenbecker,
Darius Brooks,

Sam. Ellison,
Henry Moore,
H. P. Woodlock (foreman)

FAMILIES.

W. S. Brooks' mother, wife, and son dead.
Major Stephenson's two daughters dead and one convalescent.
B. N. Cutting's wife convalescent.
George W. Woods' wife convalescent.
H. M. Crowell's daughter dead and wife and son convalescent.
W. W. Stephenson's wife and two children convalescent.
Ed. Schiller's son dead and daughter convalescent.
H. J. McGrann's daughter dead, wife, son, and niece convalescent.
H. P. Woodlock's daughter convalescent.
Frank and Al. Plummer's father, mother, and two sisters dead, and brother and sister convalescent.
Darius Brooks' sister dead and mother convalescent.
Byron Brooks' son dead and wife convalescent.
Kinch Virgeson's wife convalescent.
Andy Harrington's wife dead.

ESCAPED.

J. M. Keating, editor,

Henry Moode, compositor.

RECAPITULATION.

Total employés dead 19
Total employés convalescent... 21
Total members of families dead... 15
Total members of families convalescent... 18

Total 73

AVALANCHE OFFICE.
DEAD.

R. A. Thompson, business manager.

EDITORIAL DEPARTMENT.

Herbert Landrum,

George Landrum.

COMPOSING-ROOM.

Ed. J. Snigg,
James M. Kerr,
James Cruikshank,

James M. Banksmith.
John Crabb.

434   APPENDIX.

PRESS-ROOM.

Augustus Anderson,   Charles Case.

PORTER.
Mike Corrigan.

CARRIERS.

John Myers,   James Hunter.

CONVALESCENTS.

COMPOSING-ROOM.

J. P. Wheles,   Joe Crabb,
O. P. Bard,   Denny Sullivan,
George Bird,   Ed. Case.
Louis Roselle,

COUNTING-ROOM.

J. C. Price,   L. W. Bruder.
M. W. Luff,

Of the families, Mr. Crabb has seven members convalescent; also Mr. Wheles' wife and child.

ESCAPED.

F. S. Nichols,   L. E. Royster,
H. W. Clayton,   Dallas Townley.
R. S. Smith,

RECAPITULATION.

Employés dead 13
Employés convalescent 10
Family members convalescent 9

Total 32

LEDGER OFFICE.

DEAD.

COMPOSING-ROOM.

T. P. Holland,   W. H. Blalock,
John S. Terry,   Henry Stillman, bill poster.

CONVALESCENTS.

EDITORIAL DEPARTMENT.
J. H. Mathes.

COUNTING-ROOM.
E. Whitmore.

JOB-ROOM.
Ed. R. Holland.

COMPOSING-ROOM.

S. L. Reneau,   T. P. Kavanaugh,
Russell Reneau,   John Burns.

PRESS-ROOM.

Larry Grehan,   Allen Avery (col.), engineer.

ESCAPED.
John R. Grehan.

FAMILIES CONVALESCENT.

J. H. Mathes' wife.
W. H. Blalock's wife and child.
John R. Grehan's wife.
Larry Grehan's wife and child.
T. P. Holland's wife and two daughters—Misses Idelle and Vernon.
S. L. Reneau's three daughters—Misses Lulu, Maggie, and Jane.

APPENDIX.

RECAPITULATION.

Employés dead... 4
Convalescent employés... 9
Family members convalescent.. 12

Total... 25

From the above it will be seen that of those employed on the *Evening Ledger* only one escaped, of the *Avalanche* four escaped, and of the *Appeal* only two. Of the *Ledger* employés four died, of the *Avalanche* thirteen, and of the *Appeal* nineteen. Of the *Ledger* employés nine convalesced to recovery, of the *Avalanche* ten, and of the *Appeal* twenty-one. These figures are eloquent of the ravages of the pestilence among the newspaper people, but when our readers study the statistics for themselves, they will see that when the wives and children who were dependent upon these employés and employers are taken into account, the story is intensified almost beyond belief. Take the *Appeal* office, for instance, where, out of seventy-five persons—men, women, and children—thirty-four were buried, thirty-nine convalesced, and only two escaped. Sad and sorrowful facts, they tell a story of endurance unparalleled in modern times, and of which we trust the world will forever be spared a repetition.

TRIBUTES TO SOUTHERN JOURNALISTS.

London *Standard*— * * It is this people, the flower and pride of the great English race, on whom a more terrible, more merciless enemy has now fallen. There can be now no division of sympathy, as there is no passion to excite and keep up the courage needed for the occasion. Yet the men and women of the South are true to the old tradition. Her youth volunteer to serve and die in the streets of plague-stricken citizens as rapidly as they went forth, boys, and gray-haired men, to meet the threatened surprise of Petersburg—as they volunteered to charge again and again the cannon-crowned hills of Gettysburg, and to enrich with their blood, and honor with the name of a new victory, every field around Richmond. Their sisters, mothers, wives, and daughters are doing and suffering now, as they suffered from famine, disease, incessant anxiety and alarm throughout the four years of the civil war. There may be among the various nations of the Aryan family one or two who would claim that they could have furnished troops like those which followed Lee and Johnston, Stuart and Stonewall Jackson, but we doubt whether there be one race beside our own that could send forth its children by hundreds to face, in towns desolated by yellow fever, the horrors of a nurse's life, and the imminent terms of a martyr's death.

New York *Times*—The South has borne herself bravely and nobly during the yellow fever scourge; no people could have behaved better. One class in particular has shown unflinching courage and the most generous humanity. Its members may not have done, probably they did not, any thing more than many others in the infected districts, but they have been conspicuous from their calling. These, the journalists of the South, meaning all who are occupied with getting, transmitting, or arranging news, have reflected credit on themselves and the profession by the resolute and fearless manner in which they have discharged to the fullest their highest duty. Hardly an instance can be given in which one of them has quitted his post. In New Orleans, Vicksburg, Memphis, and smaller towns, they have refused to go away, as they might, and as so many others, have done. They determined to face the danger—a very formidable one, since very few of them had had the fever, and a large number were new to the South—and to challenge death in order to render the service which they knew would be sadly needed. Scores of them have been down with the pestilence; many of them have died, but none have faltered or retreated. On some newspapers, only one or two journalists have been left, but the survivor or survivors have kept religiously at their work. Nor have they by any means restricted themselves to their business; they have distributed supplies—many belong to the Howards—attended to the sick and dying, and worked incessantly to relieve suffering, to help humanity in every way possible. They have seen death steadily approaching; they have looked him calmly in the face; they have felt they must be victims. But they have not blanched nor abated effort while they could lift voice or hand; and, as their fatal turn came, they have shown remarkable fortitude, fighting disease to the last, and, when forced to submit, yielding as dauntless men overcome, not as men conquered. The southern journalists deserve well of the nation. They have been fearfully tried, and their trial has brought out all their virtues. They have proved themselves to be men not less than journalists, and very manly men. They have defects neither few nor small; but, surely, lack of courage and want of humanity are not among them.

THE NATIONAL RELIEF BOAT JOHN M. CHAMBERS.

This boat, fitted out at St. Louis, under the direction of the National Relief Committee, of Washington, of which Ex-Governor Alexander Shepherd was chairman, on her return from her mission to all the points below Memphis needing supplies, medicines, ice, etc., stopped at Memphis for twenty-four hours on the 22d of October. The *Appeal* of the 23d mentions her arrival in the following article:

The national relief boat *John M. Chambers*, in command of Lieutenant Chas. M. Hall, Surgeon H. M. Keys in charge of medical department, arrived at this port last evening at seven o'clock, after a tedious journey from Vicksburg, having left that port last Friday evening at four o'clock. Though danger was anticipated by Surgeon Keys, on account of the infection caused on the boat by the sickness of Lieutenant H. H. Benner, who gave up his life in the noble cause of administering to the suffering people at points along the river where the malaria was most virulent, the health of all on board has been good, not a single case of illness having occurred throughout the return journey. Just before leaving Vicksburg, Lieutenant Hall received a note from the authorities of the hospital announcing the death of the night watchman of the boat, who was taken down a day after Lieutenant Benner was attacked, and immediately removed to the hospital, where he died last Friday morning of the fever. The two St. Louis pilots, who started out with the boat from that city, were advised that it would be imprudent for them to proceed up the river, as there were strong probabilities of another case of steamer *Porter*, with all her attendant horrors. This necessitated taking two other pilots who had gone through the fever, and Captain Robt. Bowman and Frank Marritia were secured, and though almost too weak from prostration to do full service, agreed to take the wheel and pilot the boat through to this port. The former not knowing the river above this point, the boat is delayed here, but will back out as soon as his place can be supplied. The Howard Association of Vicksburg kindly tendered two of their best nurses to the use of the boat, as a precautionary measure in case of sickness, and though the offer was accepted by Surgeon Keys, they were fortunately not needed, and will return to Vicksburg on the first train to-morrow. The relief boat made but one stoppage at any port on the up-trip, that at Terrene, at the mouth of White River, where the steamer replenished her coal supply. This town, too, has its story of woe, and though the scourge has not been wide-spread at that point, it has left but two out of a household of ten, the survivors being Mr. J. H. Zadeck, the post-master, and a babe of but two summers. On arriving at Terrene, Lieutenant Hall heard of the distress of Zadeck, and sent a note of sympathy, coupled with the announcement that it would be impossible to render assistance, as the relief boat was destitute of supplies. Mr. Zadeck sent back word that he was a prisoner in his own house, that the citizens of the town had his house guarded against his egress, and would permit no one to see him. In fact, he was in quarantine in his own home. He was not suffering for the necessaries of life and health, but was anxious to get away from the house of death, where wife, children, and relatives had slept their last sleep. In his letter he says that most of the dead were buried by himself, the people refusing to render assistance for fear of infection. Lieutenant Hall, of course, could render no assistance, as his orders were peremptory to reach St. Louis as soon as possible, and he had no jurisdiction in the case, though the cry for help sounded as pitiful as that of a drowning man. As soon as a Memphis and St. Louis pilot is secured, and Lieutenant Hall and Surgeon Keys have transacted official business by telegraph with District-Attorney Bliss, of St. Louis, and Governor Shepherd, of Washington, the boat will move up on her way home, followed by the blessings of many to whom it has ministered.

Memphis has furnished its hero in connection with the God's-errand of the national relief boat. Mr. George H. Mitchell, connected with the post-office of this city, volunteered to take out the mail for points on the Mississippi which had heard no word from us since the fever first struck the town. Though he had never made a trip down the river, he adapted himself to circumstances, and left every landing its missive of letters and papers except half a dozen or so, where shot-guns and quarantine laws prevented him from doing so. He took out ten tons of mail matter, the largest that has ever left this city on any route, and spent sleepless nights in the performance of his duty. That duty finished, he tendered his services as a nurse to Lieutenant Benner, and watched faithfully by his bedside to the last, giving the same aid which had signalized his success in that capacity in so many instances in this city. The distribution of that mail to the benighted denizens along the banks of the Mississippi, who had been virtually out of the world since the incipiency of the plague, was the crowning glory of the mission of the relief boat.

Appeal, October 8th.—The steamer *John M. Chambers*, a vessel chartered by citizens of Washington City and St. Louis, and loaded at the latter city with a complete cargo of supplies, passed this port yesterday, being the first incident in river circles worthy of note that has transpired within the past sixty days. In other words, river business would be completely dried up but for the great event of to-day, which will be hailed all along the river, as the *Chambers* passes down, with eager delight. No quarantine laws will be formidable enough to prevent the great carrier of help for the needy and distressed from landing at any and all ports. The freight consists of every thing needful for the sick, the convalescent, and the destitute, such as medicines, clothing, and general household supplies. It is a complete equipment, and has been gotten up in shape in a remarkably short space of time. The chartering of the boat, the purchase of the supplies, and all other expenses, will not fall short of twenty-five thousand dollars. It is one of the grandest single works of charity yet accomplished. The money to purchase the goods came from all over the country, so that it may be appropriately called a national offering. The boat is under charge of a United States officer, Lieutenant H. H. Benner, and the supplies were selected and purchased by General Beckwith and United States Assistant-Surgeon Wyman. The following is a list of those on board:

Officer in charge, Lieut. H. H. Benner, Eighteenth Infantry.
Lieut. Chas. S. Hall, Thirteenth Infantry.
H. M. Keys, assistant-surgeon United States Hospital Service.
F. T. Reily, assistant-physician.
H. S. Kessler, prescription clerk.
H. S. Hyde, correspondent.
Captain of the boat, Vincent M. Yore.
Clerk, Loyd A. Haynes.
Pilots, Geo. Longwell and Chas. Duffy.
First engineer, Wm. Shepherd.
Second engineer, Martin Williams.
Mate, Thomas Wetzell.
Carpenter, H. Mulford.
Watchman, J. M. Dalton.
Steward, Robert J. Matchman.

Besides these, there are twenty-five firemen, chambermaids, cooks, cabin-boys, roustabouts, and deck-hands, making a total of forty-one people. All seemed to be in good spirits, and all hope to come back safe. In noting the departure from that port of the *John M. Chambers*, the St. Louis *Evening Post*, of the 4th instant, says: "The two United States officers have been in the South, and believe themselves acclimated. Lieut. Benner yesterday received a draft for five hundred dollars, sent to him by the United States army officers stationed at New York city, with the request that he distribute it among the most deserving, wherever he should go. The boat will probably be gone twenty days, and may not go below Vicksburg. The first stopping-place will be Hickman, Kentucky. A good many articles of freight had not arrived, but Governor Shepherd thought it unwise to wait longer. Early this morning quite a crowd began to gather on the wharf about the *Chambers*. From her must-head floated a yellow streamer, with the words on it, "National Relief Boat," while on her left was a large canvas with the same inscription in heavy black letters. Both decks were crowded with boxes, barrels, and packages of all kinds, and every thing was hurry and bustle. At half-past nine o'clock Governor Shepherd, Mr. John T. Mitchell, General Beckwith, and Mr. W. H. Bliss came on board, and proceeded to make all final preparations for the final departure. One thousand dollars was delivered to Lieutenant Benner, to use as he saw best, and full instructions given to the officers. There was some delay, because the two surgeons were not on time. They arrived at half-past ten, and at fifteen minutes to eleven o'clock the bell rang for the last time, hasty and earnest farewells were said, and the *Chambers* slowly backed out into the great river. Governor Shepherd, Mr. Bliss, Mr. Mitchell, and Gen. Beckwith stood on the edge of the wharf-boat, and, along with hundreds of others whose hearts were full of sympathy, watched her until she turned her head down stream and began to steam away. She went with the good wishes of the whole nation, and a million prayers are going up for the safe return of the men on board. To go was something like walking into the jaws of death, for few have gone from the North into the plague-stricken land who lived to return. It is something like a bourne from which no traveler does return. But, whether they come back or not, their good work will be done, and the nation honored by a noble deed. Many a sufferer will be relieved, many a heart made glad, and many a life saved. It is such things that weld together the hearts of the North and the people of the South, and is another proof of the eloquent saying of the great and lamented Governor Yates, that the Mississippi was never made to run through a divided country. All honor to Governor A. R. Shepherd, the chairman of the National Relief Committee, and the man, above all others, who has contributed to the success of this great national undertaking; and great credit is due to Mr. W. H. Bliss for his untiring labors, and also to Mr. John T. Mitchell, of Washington."

BENNER RELIEF FUND.

Appeal, November 11.—At half-past two o'clock yesterday afternoon the Benner bale of cotton, contributed through Miss Clara Conway, for the benefit of the family of the late Lieutenant Benner, United States Army, who died at his post on board the government supply boat, near Vicksburg, on the Mississippi River, while relieving the wants of the yellow-fever sufferers, was sold at public auction in front of the cotton exchange by Mr. A. E. Frankland, auctioneer. The bale weighed 506 pounds, and classed middling fair. The bidding was lively, Mr. Simon W. Green starting it at fifty cents per pound, Major G. V. Rambaut bid ninety-five cents, Mr. Green called it ninety-eight cents, Major Rambaut $1.00, Mr. Green $1.01, and Major Rambaut $1.02, and it was knocked down at $1.02 a pound. The bale weighing 506 pounds, brought $516.12. The bale was sold by subscription under the direction of a committee of the cotton exchange, composed of Messrs. G. V. Rambaut, Simon W. Green, H. M. Neely, John K. Speed, and C. T. Curtis. On the sale being made auctioneer Frankland read the following notice:

"The members of the Memphis Cotton Exchange most respectfully donate the Benner bale of cotton to the cotton exchanges of New Orleans, Galveston, Mobile, Savannah, Charleston, and Richmond, Virginia, with the sincere request that each one pass it to the other after it has been sold, the proceeds to be forwarded to the Benner fund, care of the secretary of the treasury." The contributors to the fund are as follows:

We, the undersigned, hereby agree to pay the amounts hereto annexed and opposite our names, the same to be used in the purchase of a bale of cotton donated by Miss Clara Conway to the "Benner relief fund," the money subscribed for the said purchase to go to that fund: Hill & Mitchell, $10; Joyner, Lemmon & Gale, $10; W. S. Jack & Co., $10; Ferguson & Hampson, $10; Goodbar & Co., $10; Schwab & Co., $10; Rice, Stix & Co., $10; James S. Wilkins, $10; Mammoth cotton press, $10; Brown & Jones, $10; Union cotton compress association, $10; Johnson & Vance, $10; Bohlen, Huse & Co., $10; Oliver Finnie & Co., $10; B. Lowenstein & Bros., $5; Walker Brothers & Co., $5; Townsend, Woolly & Co., $5; Guy, Dillard & Coffin, $10; J. J. Freeman, $5; Felix Fransciola, $5; Porter, Taylor & Co., $10; Peter Trazey, $5; Joe Wetter, $5; G. H. Latham, $5; ——, Clark, $5; S. Mansfield, $5; W. B. Galbreath & Co., $10; J. T Pettit, $10; Goyer & Co., $15: A. M. Scarborough, $5; C. T. Curtis, $5; Ad. Storm, $5; J. S. Richardson & Co., $5; Horace E. Andrews, $5; J. M. James and Sons, $5; M. Gavin & Co., $5; Schoolfield, Hanauer & Co., $5; Cooper & Co., $5; Ashbrook & White, $5; Pearce, Suggs & Co., $5; Harris, Mallory & Co., $5; Bowles & Son., $10; J. H. Coffee & Co., $2; J. J. Busby & Co., $5; E. M. Apperson & Co., $10; Furstenheim & Wellford, $5; Hadder and Avery, $5; J. F. Frank & Co., $5; C. P. Hunt & Co., $5; Fader, Jacobs & Co., $5; Hill, Fontaine & Co., $5; C. B. Carter & Co., $5; Day & Proudfit, $5; W. H. Wood, $5; Orgill Bros. & Co., $5; Thos. H. Allen & Co., $5; A. Vacarro & Co., $5; John K. Speed, $5; M. L. Meacham & Co., $5; Estes, Doan Co., $5; Brooks, Neely & Co., $15; J. T. Fargason & Co., $15; J. W. Jefferson & Co., $5; G. Falls & Co., $10; Wm. M. Roots, $5; Cage & Fisher, $5; Wm. R. Moore, $5; W. S. Bruce & Co., $10; R. G. Craig, $2; Grubbs, Austin & Berry, $5; Wills & Wildberger, $2; Martin & Co., $5; Mitchell, Hoffman & Co., $5; F. S. Davis, $5; A. M. Agelasto, $5; R. V. Vredenburgh, $5; E. G. Barnaby, $1.

DISPOSITION OF FUNDS AND BALE.

Major Rambaut will send the check for the amount to Miss Clara Conway, who will transmit it to the secretary of the treasury of the United States. The bale of cotton will be sent, after being fixed up with bagging, ties, etc., to New Orleans, in accordance with the wish of the cotton exchange. It is not intended to permit the cotton bale to be taken or sent outside of the cotton States of the South.

Rev. C. K. Marshall, writing, on the 17th of October, to the Louisville *Courier-Journal*, gives the following account of the funeral of Lieutenant Benner, the brave soldier who perished at his post: "I have just participated in the most solemn and imposing funeral ceremony I ever witnessed here in nearly half a century. We have buried the commander of the national relief expedition. Lieutenant Benner sleeps to-night in the national cemetery, by the side of the majestic waters of the great river. The gallant Custer, fighting to his death in defense of and dying with his brave band of heroes, did not meet death more nobly than has this chivalrous and heroic young officer. He heard the Macedonian cry, and in its incarnation came to our relief. The hero martyr fell in the sacred performance of the highest obligation. We received him and his companions as an abridgment of the nation's sympathy, wept with joy at meeting such tender, noble, manly courage and solicitude. When he sickened, we trembled. When he died this morning, we all wept in sorrow for so great a loss. The burial brought into procession every movable article. It was over a mile in length, and thousands thronged the streets to pay their tribute of mourning for the public bereavement. All the military companies, fire companies, orders, and societies, colored and white, all the clergy of every denomination, Catholic and Protestant, all the convalescents able to stand, and weeping women and tender young people, turned out to testify their sense of the calamity. The officers of the Howard Association followed the hearse, next to Lieutenant Hall, and the mayor and aldermen of the city accompanied them. The Right Rev. Bishop Adams read the solemn service at the grave, as the setting sun was just passing from view, emblematic of our departed brother, and amidst the surrounding masses of real mourners, we laid his mortal remains to rest. May his name shine while the stars shine, and good men pay homage at his grave, while these waves of this inland sea glide to the distant ocean; and may the magnanimous and philanthropic people who have blessed us in this deepest distress never experience the necessities of our helpless, suffering, and desolate condition. We send our sympathies to, and offer our prayers for, the sorrowing family of the noble dead."

SERMON OF REV. DR. LANDRUM ON THE EPIDEMIC.

DELIVERED AT THE CENTRAL BAPTIST CHURCH ON SUNDAY, OCT. 26th, 1878.

The first services in ten weeks were held at the Central Baptist Church last Sunday. Rev. Dr. Landrum was in the pulpit, and the sermon which he preached, a report of which we give below, will be found a sermon for the times, a reminder of what we have passed through and of what we must do to be saved from similar afflictions in the future. Dr. Landrum, after the singing of hymn No. 5, gospel series, opened with the following

PRAYER:

O God, who didst create and redeem us, who dost permit us to call thee Father, to thee we confess our sins and acknowledge our dependence. We are unworthy the least of thy mercies. We thank thee so many of us have met together for praise, for forgiveness, for blessing. We thank thee for the Sabbath; for a desire to consecrate ourselves to thy service; for the gift of thy Son, our Savior, by whose death, resurrection, and ascension, life and immortality are brought to light in the gospel. May we seek life and strength through him, live unto him--ever ready for death, ever prepared for the life to come. We thank thee for this hope, for the home above, the glories that await us there. Help us, O Lord, to know more of thee, to understand thy word, to obey thy will. Revive thy work, O Lord, we beseech thee. Reveal, by thy Spirit, Christ Jesus unto us as the way, the truth, and the life. Draw now sensibly near unto us, that we may know that we are in the way of life; and minister unto us the consolations of the gospel, which the world knows not of, and can neither give nor take away, enabling us to cast our cares upon thee, who careth for us. We can not, would not, call our loved ones back again, but we thank thee we can go to them where all is peace, purity, and love, and no pain, no plague, no death, nor tears, nor partings. May we bear our cross patiently, humbly, faithfully, and, like good soldiers, stand firmly, bravely; following unflinchingly the Captain of our salvation, himself made perfect through sufferings. Bless us, O Lord, in our hearts, in our homes, in our church; bless our afflicted city, bless all with the wisdom and the fear and the love of God. Bless the absentees. May they come back from their chastening willingly, humbly, obediently to serve thee, the only true and living God. Bless our scourged land. Bless all those who have so generously ministered to our necessities and solaced us with words of comfort and sympathy. Reward them, O Lord, with thy mercies, and enlarge our hearts with grateful love toward them. We need every blessing—individuals, the family, the city, the nation—all need thy help. And may we honor these blessings by honoring thee. Hear us, O Lord, and thine shall be the praise. For Jesus' sake, amen.

Hymn No. 33, "Trusting Jesus every day," was then sung.

THE SERMON.

It is now ten weeks since we last assembled in this house. Within the past few days certain persons, and it is pleasure to say, mostly young men, have said to me, "Why not resume services? We are hungry for preaching." I therefore announced services this morning. The sudden change to inclement weather led me to expect only a few. I am gratified to see so many present. You have come to seek God and invoke the divine consolations. Great and sad changes have taken place since we last met, but it is better not to dwell on what is possibly uppermost in every mind—personal sufferings and bereavements. Let us rather try to learn a few lessons for future good. Text: "And he (Aaron) stood between the dead and the living, and the plague was stayed." Num. 16: 48. You, perhaps, have not, lately at least, looked into those Scriptures which declare pestilence to be God's curse upon the sin of disobedience. Let us read you a few of these texts: "If ye walk contrary to me, I will send the pestilence among you." Lev. 26: 21–26. Because of rebellion, Moses was told to speak thus to the children of Israel: "I will smite them with the pestilence, and disinherit them." Num. 14: 12. "Because of the wickedness of thy doings, the Lord shall make the pestilence cleave unto thee, until he has consumed thee from off the face of the land." Deut. 38: 21. "When they fast I will not hear them cry, and when they offer burnt offering and oblation I will not accept them, but I will consume them by the sword, and by the famine, and by the pestilence." Jer. 14: 12. The result of disobedience in the last times: "Nation shall rise against nation, and kingdom against kingdom; and there shall be famines and pestilences and earthquakes in divers places. All these are the beginning of sorrows." Matthew 24: 7, 8. If these be "the beginning," what must the continuance and the end of these sorrows be? Therefore, be ye also ready; for in such an hour as ye think not, the Son of man cometh, rewarding those that diligently seek him, and punishing the disobedient. His ways are shown to be "equal," and he "justifies" himself before the good and the bad. Of the twelve spies sent by Moses to Canaan, the ten who made a cowardly report, producing a rebellion, died in the wilderness with the thousands which were corrupted with them. Two, Caleb and Joshua, who "followed" God "fully," were brought into the land of promise. Num. 14. And so, in the cases of Nadab and Abihu, and of Korah and Dathan, you see the Lord emphasizing by example this great precept of obedience. Law is every-where. It is too often thought that the ten commandments comprise all of God's laws. A mistaken, short-sighted idea. There are spiritual and physical laws, with rewards and punishments. These laws must be obeyed if you would be happy. To obey them, you must know them; to know and understand them, you must study God's word by the light of his Spirit. "The plague was stayed." How? By Israel's priestly intercessor Aaron. Jesus is our High Priest and Intercessor. He is now standing between dead and perishing sinners and an offended God. He put himself in our stead. He lived, and suffered, and died, and rose again for us. Let us look to him to bear away from us and our children the plague of sin; and stay the just wrath of God, that we and they may not suffer the rightful penalty of our many misdoings. God's children are all intercessors. Abraham interceded for Sodom, Moses repeatedly for Israel, and Paul for his brethren according to the flesh. So let us plead with God, one for the other, and for our own erring brethren, in Jesus' name. He is our refuge and our strength.

THE PESTILENCE.

A remarkable feature of this pestilence is its malignity; the mortality, at one time, being one death in every two cases. Of my flock, who remained in the city, more than half have died. How wonderful this mortality! Nearly thirty-three per cent. elsewhere, nearly fifty per cent. here. What a terrible strain upon the minds and spirits and bodies of the living witnesses! Another remarkable feature: The wide extent of territory it has spread over. Norfolk, Savannah, New Orleans, and this city have repeatedly been scourged, and heretofore the plague has been confined to certain localities in these cities. Never before has it extended its baneful, blighting influence over so vast an area, and with a malignity as fatal in the country as in the city. How vast, how awful its death-dealing touch! It is terrible to contemplate. Another sad feature: It carried off so many little children, and swept the young men by scores and hundreds. It was far more destructive among these than any former epidemic. Look around you and see how many parents have been left, with the children all, or nearly all, gone. Many Rachels are weeping because her children are not; many Davids, in agony, cry out, "O my son Absalom! my son, my son Absalom! Would to God I had died for thee, O Absalom, my son, my son!" A few godly men, adopting David's language, after the death of his little child, say, "Now he is dead: wherefore should I fast? Can I bring him back again? I shall go to him, but he shall not return to me."

A FEW PRACTICAL LESSONS.

First Lesson.—It has been suggested that physical laws can not be violated with impunity; hence, the vital importance of due attention to the drainage and sewerage of the city. Cleanliness is a prerequisite of health, the best preventive of malarial epidemics. If indifferent to this virtue, you may expect only pestilence. If you would have exemption, look well to the cleanliness of your city. This virtue is classed in the inspired Word next to godliness. It is wiser to pay taxes in money than in the lives of your citizens, and the tears and sufferings of the widow and the orphan. These will not pave your streets, nor restore a dishonored credit, nor rebuild broken fortunes.

Second Lesson.—The moral developments under this trial have been always interesting, sometimes astounding. As in war, so in times of pestilence, there are remarkable revealments of character. Where you have counted on firmness, patience, self-sacrifice, you have been surprised with weakness, fear, and meanness. Where you have had little hope of noble deeds, you have found magnanimity, kindness, tenderness, love. You have seen the husband desert the wife, the mother her children, and children abandon parents. Then, you have seen the "stranger" come in, and, without fear of death or hope of reward, fill with touching tenderness these deserted places. This is really wonderful, inexplicable. The Lord alone can know the heart.

Third Lesson.—Religion is judged improperly, unjustly. Only "the few," who know from revelation and experience somewhat of God's will and ways, are competent to judge. The "many" are not qualified to say what a Christian's duty is.

One word for all: Refrain from a censorious spirit—judge not. To his Master the servant standeth or falleth. It is impossible for you to know the circumstances and the motives of your brother. Judge yourself, not another. Leave him to himself and to God.

One other remark: True religion, vital godliness, is a living, active, controlling power. It has been often manifested during this fiery ordeal—and sometimes when not expected, it has shown forth as a light in the darkness, a glorious reality. An illustration: My family physician sent for me. He said: "Oh, my pastor, I wanted to see you and tell you of the perfect peace within. Precious thoughts of Jesus and my sainted mother come to me. My longing desire is to join her in that blissful home. I try to sing; but too feeble now; but then I'll sing, I'll sing." Death was robbed of his sting, the grave of its victory. The religion of the Lord Jesus Christ can alone do this. It is indeed a triumphant, glorious power. One now from a sister's letter: "I have often wanted to write you since the death of my beloved husband. When death was seen to be inevitable, he called me to his side to repeat a few of God's promises. I asked: Can you trust him? 'Oh, yes, yes. I long for the rest of heaven.' I repeated these precious words of Jesus: 'I am the resurrection and the life; he that believeth in me, though he were dead (and my husband finished the passage), yet shall he live, and whosoever liveth and believeth in me shall never die.' The Lord, the good Savior, never seemed so close to him. To him I commit myself and my children; and, from my heart, say: 'Thy will be done.'" I repeat, brethren, the religion of Jesus is a power—a controlling, sustaining power. But that prayer, brethren. Its words are brief and simple—so easy to say, but how hard to pray it, to utter it from the heart, when that prayer alone is left to you. I have repeated it a thousand times without feeling it. When called to speak it from the heart, I found it no easy thing. This sister adds: "The everlasting arms are beneath me. It is sweet to lie passive in his hands." Is not this "religion," or "power?"

Another lesson. Let us prove ourselves an appreciative, grateful people. There could be no greater evidence of unworthiness than to forget our benefactors, our tried friends. All over the country, from the extreme east to the far distant west, the warmest, most practical sympathy has been shown. The United States are a nation, a grand national brotherhood, with one heart. May all purposes be as noble as the good deeds to us, and our destiny one. Words fail to tell of the sympathy, the prayers, and the acts of loving kindness that have come from every point of the compass. Of the many wonderful developments of this marvelous scourge, the lavish generosity displayed is one most worthy to be noted, one never to be forgotten. We are indeed one. It is more blessed to give than to receive. Especially is this true when the giving is so freely, cheerfully done that the receiver is saved the humiliation. Let us, therefore, remember this lesson of love with gratitude.

ONE FEAR.

Do you remember the pestilence of 1873? Can you recall the frivolities and the godlessness of the winter and spring following? Shall we, can we have a repetition? The masses, like the pendulum, go from one extreme to the other, from a state of affliction and humility to frivolous exhilaration and rebellious, and often blasphemous, wickedness. Hence, a great display of worldliness is to be feared. God forbid it. Many have pledged great reformation. Will they keep their vows? It is better not to vow than to vow and not pay. How has not God's house been avoided, his will disregarded, his word mocked, his Sabbath desecrated. Shall we do so again? If so, he will laugh at your calamity, and mock when your fear cometh again. Be not high-minded, but fear. "In all thy ways acknowledge him, and he shall direct thy paths." "Behold the fear of the Lord, that is wisdom; and to depart from evil, that is understanding." Let us hold forth the word of life, stand up for the truth, exemplify the truth in our lives; and seek the blessing of God upon ourselves, our homes, our city, our country, our whole country. As did Joshua, so let each for himself resolve: "As for me and my house, we will serve the Lord." Oh, what a happy city, what a prosperous country, if every family "was a household of faith," as was Joshua's.

A closing word: We can not call back the dead. But there are two things we have been taught:

1. To cultivate a sympathetic, helping disposition toward all men, especially the humble and the needy. Yesterday a widow, not of my flock, sent for me. She said: "I wanted to talk to one who had suffered; I, therefore, sent for you." In this way, my fellow sufferers, you may find compensation for the things you have suffered.

2. These bereavements weaken the ties of earth. We are the more easily attracted toward heaven. When all the cords are cut the balloon rises above the clouds that shut out the sunlight. So when affliction has severed the natural bonds that bind us to this life, our spiritual desires increase; our tendency is more and more heavenward; our purposes more and more single to the glory of God; and, finally, by an unseen process, we are brought to the consecrated faith of Paul: "I am crucified with Christ: nevertheless, I live; yet not I, but Christ liveth in me; and the life which I now live in the flesh I live by the faith of the Son of God, who loved me, and gave himself for me." It is sweet to go home with the consciousness of duty done. It is sweeter far to contemplate the home beyond the skies, to anticipate the joys of the blessed, to enjoy a foretaste of the rest that remains for the people of God. Then the reunion there! Heaven is not a world of strangers. We shall sit down at our Elder Brother's table with the loved ones who have gone before—gone only for a short while before. They wait our coming. They beckon us onward, upward. Let us follow on, patiently, unmurmuringly, cheerfully, thankfully onward. We shall have larger capacities there; more knowledge, more love, more happiness there; no uncongenial spirits there; no plague, no pestilence there. The grave, on this side, is death; on the other side, birth to an immortal existence. "For God hath not appointed us to wrath, but to obtain salvation by our Lord Jesus Christ, who died for us, that, whether we wake or sleep, we should live together with him." 1 Thessalonians v: 9, 10. "I would not have you to be ignorant, brethren, concerning them which are asleep, that ye sorrow not, even as others who have no hope. For if we believe that Jesus died and rose again, even so them also which sleep in Jesus will God bring with him." 1 Thessalonians iv: 13, 14. "And to you who are troubled, rest with us, when the Lord Jesus shall be revealed from heaven with his mighty angels, in flaming fire taking vengeance on them that know not God, and that obey not the gospel of our Lord Jesus Christ." 2 Thessalonians i: 7, 8. Fear not; believe only.

After prayer, and the singing of the hymn, "In the Sweet By-and-By," the benediction was pronounced.

DR. LANDRUM ON PASTORS AND EPIDEMICS.

Editor Reflector.—I see that in several papers there are articles on the relation of ministers to epidemics. I think it would be better to narrow the question to the real issue; the relation of pastors to epidemics. I think it is true that most of the correspondents on this subject are inexperienced, never having been in real yellow fever epidemics. Some things affirmed sound strangely to those who have borne the heat and burden of the day. For instance, that a minister is reduced to a mere nurse, and that any hireling can do as well as he can. This is wonderful to me! My experience is that in the matter of nursing, the intelligence and sympathy of a pastor is worth, to the sick and their families, more than forty nurses. There are not assemblies of congregations in epidemics, but there is no want of opportunities for preaching. Jesus preached to one woman at the well in Samaria, and he wept with two sisters at the grave of Lazarus. There are hourly openings in the time of pestilence for following the Savior in this work. I am sure I have never had more reason to believe that I accomplished so much work, effective *gospel* work, in the same length of time as during the fever of 1878. If one wanted a congregation the camps Joe Williams and Wright were open every day

APPENDIX. 443

with six or eight hundred people to the herald of the cross. It is a great mistake to hold that there is no place for a minister's special work in such a time, and that for this reason he may go away. Then, for the pastor's own flock there is no one in the world so much needed. If his people ever need him it is in time of trouble. Nothing so quiets and encourages the sick as the presence of a trusted and loved pastor. It is not true that all the members of a church go away, and that on this account the pastor may flee also. We can not depopulate a city in this country. To do so you need a government that can make provision for all the people elsewhere, and then possessing power to compel all to leave, while the government protects the property or burns it up. Russia can do this, but the United States can not, except partially. The colored population, and many others, will not leave the city. If the pastor's flock left here, how is it that the churches have reported from ten to fifty of their members victims of yellow fever? The special charities sent to ministers, who remained, enabled them to keep their members, and those of absentee pastors also, from a burial in the potter's field, and to support or to send to their friends many widows and orphans during the present winter. Had all left, this work could not have been done. The outside world did not commit their charities to the absent pastors, but to those who remained with the afflicted of the city. There is no fixed rule in the matter of a minister's leaving. There are ministers who are not pastors; there are editors, business men, or teachers, they can go. There are *exceptional* cases among pastors, as where a family is in such a condition that they can not remain, and the husband is obliged to be with them. The general rule, however, is that *pastors must remain with their people in epidemics.* This should be considered in becoming a pastor. If the Master would not shun the cross, nor the apostles martyrdom for the cause of Christianity, their followers should not run from danger. To do so results in great loss of influence and respect. They are representatives of religion, and when they flee the cause of Christ suffers. We preach much about our protection under God, and the blessedness of heaven. Let not our conduct defeat our teaching. On all sides let there be charity, so that we may walk together in peace and helpfulness.

The statement has gone abroad that Protestants did not volunteer to take the places of those who fell in the yellow fever in this city and elsewhere. I remember well that Bro. A. D. Phillips proposed coming, and he has expressed regret that I did not accept his offer. Also two ministerial students at Mossy Creek College wrote, asking me to accept their services. I am sure that if I had consented, they would have come at once. I have not their names by me, but I wish to keep them in remembrance.

S. LANDRUM.

March 26, 1879.

NAME INDEX 447

A

Aaron
  C. F., 421
  C. J., 209
  C. J. (Mrs.), 209
  M., 209
  William, 209
Abadie
  Henry, 252
  Warie, 252
  ____ (Mrs.), 178
  ____, 178
Abberdie, Maggie, 209
Abbert, Augustus, 375
Abbot, Clara, 252
Abercrombie, J. B., 367, 370
Abernathie, Sam, 245
Able
  Gabriel, 209, 251
  R. H., 209
Abner, E. D., 252
Abodie, Jean L., 252
Aborg, ____ (Mrs.), 252
Abraham, ____, 250
Abrahams, Elias, 252
Abrahms, S., 419
Abram, J. J., 252
Abtte, Johanna S., 252
Achmann, Emma, 209
Acken, G. A., 349
Acker, Zavier, 252
Ackerman
  Hattie, 239
  Joseph, 252
Acklin
  Samuel, 209
  ____ (Mrs.), 209
Acosta
  Julia, 263
  ____ (Mrs.), 263
  ____, 263
Adam, Robert, 265
Adams
  Aaron, 210
  Aleck, 252
  Annie, 210
  August, 263
  Ben, 210
  C. W., 209, 354
  Charles A., 158
  Eliza (Mrs.), 252
  Flor. G., 252
  Franklin, 209
  Franklin R., 373
  George, 210, 252
  George H., 209
  Green, 242
  H. D., 252
  J., 403
  James, 252, 374
  James G., 245
  Jeanie, 252
  John D., 337
  John H., 341
  Julian, 249
  L., 252
  Louis, 252
  Lucy (Mrs.), 209
  Lyda, 250
  Mary, 348
  R. C. (Mrs.), 244
  R. R., 209
  Robert, 246
  Teresa, 252
  W. J., 250
  W. N., 252
  ____ (Right Rev. Bishop), 439
  ____, 209, 243
Adamzig, Jacob, 252
Adare, Avery, 209
Adcock, Joe, 239
Addicks, Matt, 252
Addison, John (Mrs.), 249
Adele, Aloysius, 252
Adelton, William, 252
Adler
  D., 420
  Jennie, 252
  William S., 252
Adlier, Albert, 252
Admirall, Isabella, 252
Adonis, Morris, 209
Aesculapius, 14, 72, 185
Agatha (Sister), 265
Agelasto, A. M., 438
Ah Ways, 247
Ahern
  Michael, 372
  Patrick, 252
Ahlburn, Henry, 252
Aiken
  Mary, 243
  ____ (Mrs.), 209
Aikens, John W., 252
Ainolie
  R. W., 135
  ____ (Mrs.), 372
Aitken, Elizabeth B., 252
Akins, Adelia, 374
Albarado
  Domingo, 264
  Sebastian, 264
Albarex, Perique, 264
Alber, J. N., 252
Albers, John A., 252
Albert
  Josephine (Sister), 252
  ____, 238
Alberta (Sister), 158
Albertin, Thomas, 265
Albertson, L. (Mrs.), 372
Alcorn
  George R., 249
  George R. (Mrs.), 249
Alderman, E. J., 252
Aldrich
  J. B., 241, 421
  Jennie, 263
  ____, 241
Aldridge, ____, 241
Aler, P., 374
Alerdice, Joseph, 243
Alexander
  A., 209, 244
  A. J., 340
  Belle, 251
  E. G., 209
  F. G., 252
  James, 264
  Jessie, 244
  M. (Mrs.), 209
  Margaret, 209
  S., 68
  S. H., 355
  V. F. P., 247
  ____ (Miss), 344
  ____ (Mrs.), 238, 239
  ____ (Mrs. Dr.), 249
Alexson, C., 243
Alford, Mattie, 264
Alito, Francisco, 252
Allain, Mary Lulu, 263
Allegins, P., 209
Allen
  B. (Mrs.), 240
  Bertha, 240
  Charles, 252
  D. A., 209
  Darthula, 245
  Eliza, 209
  Ellen, 210
  Emma, 240
  Frederick, 209
  Green, 362
  Henry, 209
  Howard, 126, 432
  J. D., 266
  J. H., 209, 266
  J. Howard, 426
  J. P., 244
  James, 209
  John, 252
  L. M., 209
  L. W., 424
  Laura, 209
  Lebean V., 252
  Liza, 245
  Mary, 209, 243, 244
  Mary J., 252
  Minnie, 242
  Nancy, 245
  Nellie, 239
  Nicholas, 252
  Richard, 252
  Rose, 375
  S., 345
  T. B., 421
  T. H., 356
  Thomas, 247
  W. D., 252
  W. H., 210
  ____ (Mrs.), 210, 246
  ____, 210, 245
Allendorf, George, 374
Allensworth, ____, 209
Allges, Edward, 360
Allie
  ____ (Mrs.), 209, 210, 246
  ____, 209
Allingham
  J. S., 209
  John S., 375
Allison
  M. A., 209
  M. M., 112
Alonzo,
  A., 252
  Antonie, 252
Aloysius (Father), 164
Alphonsa (Mother), 209
Alphonsa (Sister), 157
Alphonso (Mother), 120
Alston
  F. I. F., 210
  Henry, 375
  Maria, 374
Alsup, J. K., 338
Alsworth, Ben (Mrs.), 246
Alteman, Martine, 265
Altimus, J. F., 264
Altmeyer, J. L., 374
Altrick, D. A., 401
Alvis, J. W., 244
Amandus (Brother), 209
Amault, Peter, 252
Amberg
  Irene, 251
  Joseph, 251
  Vic, 251
Ambers, Daniel, 252
Amendt, Flor, 252
Ames
  Daniel (Mrs.), 209
  Laura, 252
  Lewis D., 209
  M. (Mrs.), 373
  Mullie, 200
  Willie J., 209
Amiel, ____, 290
Amiss, William Duchien, 263
Amitt, ____, 252
Amman, A., 340
Amonette
  J. I., 209
  J. J., 209
  Katie, 209
Amos
  Scott, 263
  ____ (Mrs.), 239
Amus, A. A. (Mrs.), 209
Anastapiades, A., 252
Anbort
  M. T. C., 265
  W. C., 265
Ancil
  John, 239
  ____ (Mrs.), 239
Ancoin, Numa, 265
Ancrum, John, 372

Andeek, Joseph, 252
Anderson
  Annie, 263
  August, 209
  Augustine, 252
  Augustus, 434
  Belle, 251
  Butler P., 106, 136, 137, 138, 141, 146, 151, 154, 161, 209, 247, 330, 331, 332, 334, 335, 377, 378, 379, 380, 381, 386, 390
  Butler P. (Mrs.), 155, 157, 209, 249, 379
  Callie, 209
  Charles, 209
  Charles W., 252
  Christian, 252
  Christine, 252
  Daniel, 209
  Ed, 209
  F., 266
  F. B., 252
  Frank, 209
  H., 209
  Hannah, 210
  Henrietta, 209
  Horace E., 356
  Ida, 252
  J. A., 209
  J. D., 354
  J. M., 251
  J. W., 178, 209, 406
  James, 243
  John, 209, 355
  L. B., 209
  Lynus, 209
  Martha, 209, 252
  Martin, 209, 252
  Oscar, 209
  R., 242
  Rachel, 209
  Richard, 209
  Sarah, 252
  Sarah N., 209
  Virgil, 209
  W., 352
  W. D., 339
  W. E., 351
  W. H., 354
  W. S., 141, 330, 331, 335
  William, 209
  Willie, 209
  _____, 154, 209, 406
Andrette, John, 252
Andrews
  Daniel, 249
  Eli, 252
  Henry, 430
  Horace E., 438
  _____ (Judge), 288
Andrien, Jules, 252
Andry, Charles J., 252

Angevine
  M. (Miss), 247
  S. S., 247
Ankar, Bessie, 252
Ansbery, Hugh, 252
Anse, L., 346
Anseman, Ernest V., 252
Antelny, Leonce, 252
Anten, Anna A., 252
Anter, William M., 242
Anteus, 173
Anthony
  A. W. (Mrs.), 422
  F. M., 252
  Francois M., 252
  Laura, 209
  Michael, 252
Antoine, Maie d', 252
Antonia, H. L., 252
Antonini, Adolph, 252
Antonio
  Andre, 252
  Mary, 252
  _____, 264
Marzd, 252
Apffel, Gab., 252
Apken, Joseph, 252
App
  Katie, 209
  Matilda, 209
Applegate, _____, 247
Appley [Apply], Blanche, 252
Apps, Henrietta, 252
Aranes, John P., 252
Arastase, Alex (Mrs.), 252
Arata, Laura (Mrs.), 210
Arberies, Giovani, 252
Arbogas, Jacques, 252
Arbour, Joseph Stacy, 263
Archaffenberg, F., 252
Archidell, Antonio, 252
Archer, _____ (Dr.), 247
Archie
  Arnold, 209
  _____, 209
Arcott, Lizzie, 252
Ardoin, Henry, 262
Arft, Louis, 209
Argenton, Antonie G., 252
Argentum, A. G., 252
Arin, Benedicto, 252
Armas, D'Anna, 252
Armistead [Armstead]
  Henry (Mrs.), 246
  R. A., 381
  W. M., 429
  William, 243
  Willie, 263
  _____, 246
Armom, Martin, 209
Armour
  Robert, 429
  Walter, 429
Arms, Harry, 252
Armstin, J. A. G., 209

Armstrong
  A. A., 245
  A. J., 117
  Alfred, 209
  Bertha, 210
  Colman, 247
  E. J. (Mrs.), 209
  E. L., 252
  Ellen L., 252
  J. K., 248, 380
  J. S., 238
  John, 209
  Luna, 209
  S. H., 252
  Sarah, 209
  W., 209
  W. J., 47, 209, 367, 369
Arnato, Corneto, 252
Arnault, Genel, 252
Arnbult, Peter, 252
Arneal
  John, 359
  _____, 359
Arneiga, Louis, 209
Arnett, F. C., 252
Arnold
  A. C., 408
  A. C. (Mrs.), 408
  Alice, 249
  August, 246
  Bessie, 209
  E., 252
  E. J., 344
  Edward, 252
  George W., 243
  J. N. (Mrs.), 252
  J. W., 357
  Lee, 209
  Liddie, 209
  Maggie L., 242
  Maud, 209
  Mollie, 209
  S. C., 121
  S. C. (Mrs.), 121
  T. H., 357
  T. J., 266
  William Q., 243
  Willie, 209
  _____ (Dr.), 203
  _____ (Mrs.), 209
  _____ (Rev. Mr.), 187
  _____, 121, 209, 240, 242, 408
Arnot [Arnott]
  John, 349
  Katie, 209
Arsilli, E., 209
Arthur [Arther, Arthurs]
  Fred, 209
  J. N., 340
  Louisa, 242
  William E., 252
Artigne, Fred, 252
Artus, Marid, 252
Arzeno
  Alexander, 210

Eliza (Mrs.), 210
  Nellie, 210
Aschenbrenner, O., 252
Ashby, Robert, 374
Ashe [Ash]
  Eliza, 209
  H. S., 429
  John J., 241
  Julius, 419
  Rosa, 209
  William, 209
Asinus, _____ (Rev. Father), 119, 164
Askew, S. A. (Mrs.), 263
Assanti, J. DeP., 252
Astrado, Antoniette, 252
Atchinson, Joseph H., 209
Athey [Athy]
  P. R., 330, 336
  Phil. R., 335
  _____, 142, 151
Atkins
  Harry, 209
  Jerry, 209
  _____ (Mrs.), 240
Atkinson
  A. C., 238
  George, 209
  John, 209
  Martha, 209
  Matilda, 209
  W. J., 209
  William, 209
Atwood
  J. L., 340
  Lizzie, 242
Aub, _____ (Dr.), 420
Aubin, George S., 252
Audouard, _____, 303
Auer
  A., 209
  Julia W., 252
Aufdemot, Mary, 252
Augbecker, Aug., 252
Augor, L. E., 252
Auguste
  Virginia, 243
  _____ (Mrs.), 252
  _____, 209
Augustine [Augustin, Augustins]
  J. A., 252
  John, 243
  Joseph, 252
  _____ (Mrs.), 244
Augustus, Clayton, 243
Ault, Alvis, 252
Austin
  Ann (Mrs.), 209
  Gracie, 209
  J. A., 239
  Jack, 209
  Poladore, 243
  Ran., 210
  William M., 209
Auter, Josie, 242

NAME INDEX 449

Avant, B. W., 209
Avaril, Camille, 252
Avent
  V. W., 117
  ___ (Dr.), 160
Avera, J. C., 248
Avery
  Allen, 434
  Allen G., 209
  E. M., 302
  James, 252
  N. L., 422
  ___ (Maj.), 210
  ___, 209
Avicenna, 14
Axelson
  Agnes, 244
  Cornelius, 244
  Henry P., 244
Aycock, Joseph, 252
Ayers [Ayres]
  A. W., 247
  Jennie, 247
  Lizzie, 247
  Thomas, 209
  W. I., 247
  William, 381
  ___, 250
Ayot, Vilfried, 265
Ayrand
  Amelia, 264
  Bascal, 252

B

Babb
  B., 390
  Mary L., 242
  W. T., 252
Babbit, A. D., 253
Babcock, Orson S., 253
Babette, Charles, 375
Babin
  Alphonse, 264
  V., 264
Bacas, Marie, 253
Baccigaluppo
  Joseph, 211
  Mary A., 212
  Vincent, 186, 188, 211
  Vincent (Madam,
    Mrs.), 188, 211
Bache
  Anna, 253
  Katie, 252
  T. H., 295
Bacher
  Joseph, 253
  Marie L. J., 252
  ___, 211
Bachman, Joseph, 253
Baciagalopi, J. C., 252
Backus
  E. C., 353
  Frank, 433
Bacon
  Arthur N., 243

Liddie, 212
Mattie E. (Mrs.), 243
Thomas, 211
Willis J., 243
Badeaux, Allen Jr., 265
Badenella [Badinella]
  Antoine, 210
  Celesta, 211
Bader, William, 211
Badford, A. V., 249
Badger, Caroline (Mrs.), 211
Badiknelli, David, 211
Badinella, Antoine, 210
Badwick, Joe, 247
Baer
  A., 375
  A. A., 373
  A. A. (Mrs.), 373
  Joseph, 252
Bagale, G. (Mrs.), 253
Baggett, T. M., 243
Bahl, Fred, 253
Baier, John, 253
Bailey [Baily]
  A. F., 121
  Africa, 212
  Agnes, 252
  Alice, 212
  Ben., 241
  Charles, 211
  Edward, 247, 251
  Henry, 429
  Kate, 252
  Kate (Mrs.), 212
  M. L., 355
  Mary, 210, 253
  Matilda, 249
  Robert, 210
  Valentine, 211
  ___ (Mrs.), 248, 250
  ___, 210, 211, 250
Bainbridge ___
  (Commo.), 293
Bainsfather, J. C., 252
Bair, Ballette, 212
Baird
  E. M., 239
  Spencer F., 425
Bakel, J. A., 164
Baker
  Auguste, 212
  C. L., 252
  C. M., 253
  Charles, 210, 212
  Eli, 252
  Ezra, 373
  Frank, 263, 264
  G. M., 427, 432
  George L., 252
  George M., 253
  H., 245
  J. C., 360
  Martha, 211
  Mattie R. (Mrs.), 238
  Nicholas, 400

R. J. H., 253
William, 210, 211
Bakewell, Irene (Mrs.), 247
Balancia, Paul, 252
Balch, Nellie (Mrs.), 360
Baldenwick, ___ (Mrs.), 375
Balds, Isadori, 252
Baldwin
  A. P., 346
  Charles, 252
  Culbert S., 253
  Ella W. (Mrs.), 253
  H. P., 346, 347
  Thomas, 424
  ___ (Commo.), 354
Balew, ___, 211
Balfour, John, 210
Balger, James, 210
Balkin, John C., 212
Ball
  C. W., 240
  Mary Lee, 212
  Willie, 212
Balla
  Cusmus, 253
  Rosa (Mrs.), 253
Ballard
  Eugene, 265
  George, 372
  J. S. (Mrs.), 246
  Jennie, 263
  Jim, 211
  John, 247
  John S., 247
  K. A., 246
  Randolph, 349
  W. W., 345
  ___ (Mrs.), 247
  ___, 211, 247
Ballauf, Edward, 374
Ballena, Henry, 211
Balles, Bernard, 252
Ballick, B., 212
Ballie, Frederika (Mrs.), 211
Ballinger
  C., 211
  C. (Mrs.), 212
Ballondi, ___ (Mrs.), 373
Ballou, Johnnie, 210
Ballow, Julia N., 210
Balomeney, Mike, 210
Balsamo, Leo, 253
Balsineur, Louis S., 263
Balthes, W. L., 357, 358
Baltz, Alexander, 253
Baltzer, Philip, 251
Bamatto, John, 253
Bambo, J. K., 362
Bamford, H., 253
Bammel, George, 212
Banas, Mary W., 253
Bancourt, Lucene, 253
Bancroft, ___, 25
Bander, Anna, 252
Bandy, J. F., 212

Banks
  David, 210, 430
  J. H., 421
  John, 245, 430
  Matilda, 211
Banksmith
  James M., 433
  Minor, 210
  R. H., 211
Bankson, J. S., 117, 211, 367, 369
Banning, C. E., 211
Bannon
  Andrew, 253
  John, 210
Bans, Lettie, 212
Bant, Tilda, 211
Bantley, George, 210
Bantz, Catherine, 252
Banzano, Blank, 253
Baramon, ___, 249
Baratine, B., 252
Baratinni, Maria, 253
Barbay, Mary, 264
Barbe, John, 252
Barbee, Mollie, 210
Barber [Barbour]
  Charles, 252
  George W., 375
  I., 210
  J. H., 340
  John, 252
  L. E., 244
  Matilda, 211
Barclay, G. H., 354
Bard
  O. P., 416, 434
  Sam. Gov., 263
Bardalis, Jennie, 249
Bardin, Joseph, 252
Barding, Goodman, 210
Bardreaux, L., 265
Bardsell, Henry, 253
Baies, Willie, 253
Bareyre
  Anna M., 263
  Marie L., 263
Bargone, John D., 253
Barham
  ___ (Mrs.), 263
  ___, 263
Baricleux, Eugene, 265
Barinds
  Sim., 416
  Sim. L., 376, 418
Barke, A. A. Jr., 212
Barker
  C. O. D., 264
  Fabian Alchus, 264
  Hattie, 211
  J. B., 210, 432
  John B., 416
  L. (Mrs.), 211
  Mary E. A., 264
  S. L. (Mrs.), 212
Barkman, Julius, 253

Barlow
  J. N., 407
  J. W., 211
  Mary, 252
Barnaby, E. G., 438
Barnard
  A., 212
  Frazier, 249
Barnes [Barns]
  A., 211
  Anna, 211
  B. (Mrs.), 246
  Caroline, 211
  Charles, 211
  Corinne, 210
  Doc, 251
  E. M. (Mrs.), 358
  Edward, 212
  Edmund W., 253
  Harriet, 253
  J. D., 252
  Jeff. D., 253
  Lucy A., 353
  Matilda J., 253
  R. W., 211
  Robert, 252, 253
  Sallie, 248
  Sarah, 210
  T. D., 251
  T. P., 248
  Thomas, 211
  W., 252
  Will, 251
  William C., 210
  _____, 211
Barnes (Sister), 252
Barnett [Barnet]
  Addie, 242
  Betsey, 212
  C. M., 210
  Fred, 253
  John, 252
  Philip, 246
Barnhurst
  J. S. (Mrs.), 247
  John, 247
Barns, Edward, 212
Barnsack, J., 341
Barnum, _____, 172
Barr
  Albert, 253
  C. H., 212
  G. N., 239
  James E., 253
  R. N., 239
Barrett [Barret]
  A., 266
  John, 252, 401
  Minnie, 247
  Patrick, 252, 253
  William, 247
Barringer
  I., 212
  _____, 212
Barron
  Ellen, 210

James A., 374, 376
Maggie, 210
Barrot
  C. L., 248
  Paul, 248
  Paul (Mrs.), 248
Barrow
  Alex (Mrs.), 264
  William, 264
Barry
  J. L., 400
  James, 253
  John (Mrs.), 251
  Mary L., 252
Barsman, Sallie, 211
Bartel
  Charles, 264
  Henry, 252
  M., 264
Barth, W. G., 136
Barthe, Henry, 249
Barthel, Dominique, 264
Barthelmy, L. H., 253
Bartholomew, O. D., 117, 212, 367, 369
Bartlett [Bartlet]
  S., 263
  W. L., 246
Barton
  Ada, 210
  E., 348
  Edward H., 88
  G. W., 212
  George, 212
  J. W., 211
  Joseph, 210, 264
  W. P., 169
  _____ (Dr.), 109
Barziza, _____ (Miss), 344
Basby, Sallie (Mrs.), 253
Bashorn, _____ (Madame), 381
Bashounse, F. V., 252
Basil, Joe, 252
Baskerville, Charles, 367
Bass
  Sophie (Mrs.), 373
  T. C., 247
  Thomas C., 375
  W. W., 240
Bassea, Peter, 210
Bassett, Nicholas, 253
Bassey, Mollie, 210
Bastino, John, 253
Bateman, _____, 245
Batemore, George, 252
Bates, W. H., 390, 415
Bath [Bathe]
  Berth. (Mrs.), 252
  Victor, 121
Batheiny, F. J., 252
Bathelar, Mary E., 253
Bathke
  C., 246
  Henrietta (Mrs.), 247
Batker, G. W., 344
Battle, William, 253

Battu, James T., 252
Batty, Austin, 211
Baudard, Sim J., 253
Bauder, George, 252
Baufferet, William, 374
Baum
  Bettie, 244
  Charles, 263
  Elenora, 210
  Mary (Mrs.), 263
Bauman
  Fred, 253
  G., 252
  Henrich, 253
  John, 252
  Sophie, 253
Baumstark, L., 252
Baur, Theodore, 253
Baurdo
  Charles, 242
  Frank, 242
  Mamie, 242
  _____ (Mrs.), 242
Baurmann, John, 253
Bausney, Sam, 252
Bauzau, _____, 264
Bawman, Aleck, 253
Baxter
  D. T., 400
  J. H., 362
  Mollie, 210
  _____ (Capt.), 292
Bay, Mitchell, 210
Bayol, John F., 247
Bayst, August, 253
Beachmont, Pierre, 210
Beacondray, Aug., 253
Beakley, _____ (Mrs.), 374
Beale, August, 210
Beall, Bettie, 244
Beamish
  Frank, 433
  George, 432
  John, 390
Bean, Annie, 239
Bear, Angus, 210
Beard
  Eliza, 241
  Henry, 241
  J. H., 212
  John H., 372
  Stephen, 241
  _____ (Mrs.), 241
  _____, 241
Beardon, William, 210
Bearger
  Herman, 251
  John, 251
  John (Mrs.), 251
  _____ (Miss), 251
Beasley [Beasly]
  _____ (Mrs.), 248, 375
Beaster, W. H., 251
Beatty [Beattie, Beaty]
  Austin, 112
  J. H., 240, 378, 380

John, 211
_____ (Dr.), 386
Beauchamp
  J. W., 247
  W. T., 247
Beauchare [Beauchere]
  C. K., 252
  Charles K., 253
Beaudeuas, Didie F., 253
Beauford, _____ (Miss), 210
Beauman, C., 252
Beaumont, Samuel, 253
Beavers
  M. J., 210
  Nora, 211
Beck
  Fred, 252
  G. H., 211
  Willie, 248
  _____ (Mrs.), 246
Beckenbecker, Louis, 433
Becker
  G. H. Jr., 211
  Mary L., 252
  Paul, 252
Becton, J. E., 246
Beckwith, _____ (Gen.), 437
Becocque, John, 252
Bedford, George J., 210
Bedin, Addie, 210
Beecher
  J. C., 253
  P. D., 117
Beehn, Kate L., 212
Beeler, J. H., 240, 266
Begarrie, Jean, 252
Begue, Peter, 253
Behla, Anna, 252
Behrena, C., 253
Behrens, William, 253
Behreus, Henry, 252
Behring, Charles, 242
Behune, Bern. J., 252
Behuns, George, 212
Beizron, John, 263
Bejah, S., 420
Belaire, L. H., 253
Belcher
  C., 251
  Crabtree, 238
  _____, 212
Belew, W. A. (Mrs.), 248
Belford
  Hannah, 211
  Maggie, 211
  _____, 211
Beling, Albert, 243
Beliocq, Laurinza, 263
Belknap, _____ (Mayor), 348
Bell
  A. N., 15, 16, 271, 272, 276, 290, 300, 313
  Annie (Mrs.), 210, 373
  Emily, 263
  Frank, 253

NAME INDEX 451

George, 253
Jacob, 211
Joseph, 253
Laura, 252
M. E. (Mrs.), 210
Maria, 210
Mary Bettie, 210
P. F., 399
W. M., 239
William M., 239
——— (Mrs.), 239
———, 210, 211, 263, 264
Bellalmel, Ernan, 252
Bellew, R. W. (Mrs.), 240
Belon, Louise, 253
Belot, Charles, 71
Belt [Belte]
  Charles R., 253
  Jacob, 211
Bemar, Louis, 252
Bemiss, S. M., 27
Bence, Charles, 252
Benclaire, Charles, 253
Bender
  Andrew K., 253
  Fred, 210
  H., 253
  L., 212
Benecke, A., 253
Benecks, A., 252
Benedict
  S. M., 349
  S. M. (Mrs.), 349
Benedits, Salvadore, 252
Benevita, A., 212
Benjamin
  Henry, 263
  Lulu, 263
  Mary, 263
Bennedettodo, G., 253
Benner
  F., 373
  H., 265
  H. H., 243, 332, 333, 436, 437, 438
Bennett
  Charles, 150, 210
  Charles (Mrs.), 150
  De Gray (Mrs.), 211
  M., 212
  Mary, 212
  Sam (Mrs.), 251
  W. K., 241
  ———, 150, 244
Benning
  C. A., 252
  Francis, 211
Benson
  Alfred, 253
  C. L., 253
  R. C., 242
Benthall
  Daisy, 246
  Josie, 246
  Minerva (Mrs.), 246

Sallie, 246
W. H. (Mrs.), 246
Benton
  Carrie, 375
  Charles, 252, 253
  R. C., 344
  Rosalie, 252
  W. K., 344
Bentz, Catherine, 253
Benulier, Will, 253
Benwell
  H. R. C., 246
  ———, 246
Benz, Mary E., 253
Benza, Richard, 252
Benzel, Alice, 253
Benzger, ———, 403
Benzie, B. M., 253
Beratina, Antonio, 252
Bercher, Fred, 252, 253
Bercier
  Al. M. L., 252
  Oscar L. F. L., 253
Berderau, A., 253
Beresford, James, 243
Beret, Marie, 253
Berg
  Alfred, 242
  Charles, 253
  H. J. Jr., 399
Bergen, Frank, 211
Berger
  A. J., 399
  ———, Doc, 210
Bergeret, Jean M., 252
Bergerson
  Mathilde, 264
  Paul, 264
Bergory, James P., 252
Berges, Laurent, 252
Bergeson, Z. R., 264
Berghality, Augustus, 263
Bergman [Bergmann]
  George, 210
  Mary, 210
  William, 252
Bergshicker, J., 210
Berkel, Frederick W., 253
Berkin, Caroline, 211
Berley, John, 252
Berlin
  R. Alice, 252
  W. J., 421
Berlocher, W. J., 38
Berman, Edward, 253
Bermheim, J., 252
Berna, A., 252
Bernabo, ——— (Viscount), 270, 271, 272
Bernandine (Sister), 211
Bernard
  B. W., 373
  Charlie, 264
  E. H., 210
  George, 264
  H. H., 212
  Henry, 211

Henry Jr., 212
Louisa (Mrs.), 264
Maria, 252
Philip, 253
——— (Mrs.), 263
———, 263
Bernardo, Louisa, 252
Bernauer, Charles, 252
Bernd, Oscar, 263
Berner, Teresa, 253
Bernhard, ———, 250
Bernhardt
  John F., 253
  Pauline, 253
  ——— (Mrs.), 210
Bernias, William, 253
Bernier, E. M., 252
Berniol, Aleck, 253
Berno, D. F., 252
Bernstein, A., 212
Beroni, Lena, 253
Berret
  Joe, 264
  ———, 264
Berrgin, Annie, 211
Berricks, John, 253
Berry
  A., 266, 395
  Anna, 247
  C., 264
  C. J. (Mrs.), 212
  Ellen, 252, 253
  George, 242
  Gus (Mrs.), 240
  H. D., 252
  Isaac, 395
  J. A., 253
  James, 210
  James D., 262
  N. W., 374
  S. E. (Mrs.), 210
  Sam, 250
  Walter S., 247
Berryman, Eddie, 251
Bersier, Paul, 252
Bertallot, A., 373
Berthand, Mary A., 253
Bertoni, A. A., 242
Bertram, Gustave, 263
Bertrand
  Aug., 252
  Henry, 253
Bertron
  J. C. (Mrs.), 248
  S. R., 248
Bertucei, S., 253
Bervan, C. A., 253
Beryans, Joseph, 253
Berzie, Mary J., 253
Besancny [Besancy], W. F., 191, 367, 370
Bessier, Marie, 252
Bessonies [Bossonies]
  A., 400, 404
  Aug., 399, 401, 404
Best, Thomas, 211
Betancourt, J., 252

Bethney, Jim, 212
Bettison, Agnes S., 253
Betts, William, 251
Betzer, Henry, 252
Beuz, Nellie, 252
Beverly, Reed, 253
Bevins
  Fannie M., 211
  Lee, 373
Bewerung, Fred, 252
Bey, J., 345
Biblingstene, ——— (Mrs.), 250
Bibren, Charles, 252
Bickerstaff, John, 95
Bickford, W. A., 354
Bickman, H. F., 252
Bieblizka, Anna, 253
Biedinger, Josephine, 253
Biehler, Leontine, 264
Bietry, John B., 253
Bigelow [Biglow]
  H. C., 431
  Milton, 245
  W. H. (Mrs.), 249
  ———, 247
Biggers, W. L., 210, 266
Biggie, Paul, 253
Biggs
  E. C. (Mrs.), 210
  G. L., 212
  George L., 372
Billar,
  Jasper, 212
Billard, Lucie, 253
Billings
  Frank, 264
  ——— (Mrs.), 246
Billingslea, Sarah (Mrs.), 245
Billiski, Wilhoit, 253
Bingham
  Charles, 243
  Mary D., 212
Bionda
  B., 146
  Kate, 210
  Kate (Mrs.), 107, 146, 147, 331
  ———, 146
Birch, John, 253, 263
Birchman, Katie, 252
Bird
  Annie, 253
  George, 246, 416, 417, 434
  John, 211, 252
  ———, 417
Birdsong, George T., 245
Biri, Henry, 252
Biringman, John, 253
Birkenroad, Julius, 253
Bise, Cleavely, 253
Bishop
  Addie, 247
  Belle, 247
  Eugene, 247

J. M. (Mrs.), 247
Lillie, 262
Lizzie, 262
———, 379
Bisman
　Charles, 212
　Henry, 210
Bisplinghoff, Charles, 239
Bissorn, Andreas, 253
Bitterman
　Annie, 243
　H. (Mrs.), 210
　Isaac, 210
　——— (Mrs.), 210
Biza, Adam, 253
Black
　A., 244
　Charles, 211
　D. R., 244
　Edmund, 253
　G. W., 359
　H. H., 340
　Henry, 212
　J. W., 253
　Joseph, 251
　Katie, 210
　L. M., 240
　R. E., 211
　Robert, 247
　——— (Mrs.), 250
Blackburn [Blackburne]
　Luke P., 31, 48, 56,
　　138, 330, 384, 385
　Robert, 210
Blacklidge, John G., 249
Blackman
　A. O., 375
　M., 243
Blackmore, L. W., 211
Blackshire, Luke, 263
Blackston, Benjamin, 250
Blackstone, A. (Mrs.), 375
Blackwell, Frank, 212
Blaine [Blane]
　M. C. (Mrs.), 360
　———, 303
Blair
　Hattie, 211
　Peter, 372
　——— (Dr.), 290
　———, 48
Blake
　Anthony, 243
　James, 253
　N., 212
　P., 400
　Richard J., 252
　Thomas, 404
Blakemore, W. J., 212
Blakesley, Robert, 374
Blakie, Dan, 262
Blalock
　W. H., 416, 434
　W. H. (Mrs.), 417, 434
　———, 417, 434
Blanca, Jean Marie, 253

Blanchard
　E. N., 265
　J. S., 242
　Joe, 246
　L., 264
　Laura, 264
　M. A., 343
　Robert, 265
　T. L., 265
　W., 252
　———, 246, 264
Blanco, Catherena, 253
Blane, see Blaine
Blank
　Charles T., 252
　——— (Mrs.), 245
Blankenburg, William, 212
Blanton, C., 251
Blapes, Charles, 253
Blasini, Elizabeth, 253
Blattman, B., 400
Blautz, John, 212
Blauz, Clarence, 210
Bledsoe
　Mary (Mrs.), 240
　W. F., 263
Bleets, H. W., 265
Blein, Juliet, 252
Blessey, Florence A., 253
Blew
　James, 211
　Maggie, 212
　R. W., 161, 163, 211
　R. W. (Mrs.), 161, 211
　Robert, 211
　Willie, 211
　Zilla, 211
　———, 161
Blichfeldt, ——— (Dr.), 243
Blincoe, J. H., 374
Blinso, J. H., 211
Bliss
　M. E. (Mrs.), 373
　Mary K. (Mrs.), 211
　W. H., 437
　——— (Dist. Atty.), 436
Blizell, W. B., 353
Blocher, Herman, 253
Block
　Alice, 253
　Blanche, 253
　E., 246
　Gabe, 252
　Lucy, 253
　Moses, 263
Blocker, Milton, 348
Blodgett, ———, 200
Bloemeyer, C. H., 253
Bloman, Henry, 253
Bloodgood, C. B., 253
Bloomfield
　C. C., 346
　M., 407
　Morris, 210
Blouin
　R. M., 264
　Sidney, 264

Bluemenson, Ig., 253
Bluhm
　Julius, 212
　Louis, 253
Blum, M., 210
Blume, Charles, 253
Blyarris, H., 351
Boas, W. G. N., 266
Boatright, ———, 248
Boaz, C. D., 251
Bobb, Antonia G., 243
Bobilote, Mary J., 253
Bobo, B. A., 252, 367
Bocage, Irene, 337
Bock, Isadore, 210
Bocking, Mary (Mrs.), 374
Bodell, ———, 212
Boden, Emile, 252
Bodine
　D. B., 349
　John, 242
Body, Van, 212
Boe, William, 252
Boehm, John, 252
Boehn, August, 265
Boersig, J., 246
Bofill, Paul H., 252
Bofiza, Adolph, 212
Bogan, Lorena, 263
Bogarett, Joseph, 253
Bogart, Francisco, 252
Boggs
　Mary (Mrs.), 248
　W. E., 122, 142, 167,
　　330, 332, 335, 336
　——— (Mrs.), 122, 167
Bogle, Barney, 243
Bohannon [Bohannan]
　——— (Mrs.), 266
　———, 171
Bohen, William, 210
Bohm, R. H., 373
Bohne
　Henry, 253
　Rishora, 211
Boigelle, ——— (Mrs.), 252
Boisseau
　C., 429
　D. E., 212
　J. C., 212
Boja, Daisy, 211
Bokel
　J. A., 119
　John A. Jr., 210
Bokenfohr, F., 252
Bolen, Andrew, 211
Boline, Dora H., 253
Bolkman
　Tony, 263
　———, 263
Bolton
　Bennie, 212
　Henry, 243
　Thomas C., 211, 266
　———, 265
Bonche, John A., 263

Bond
　Henry, 211
　James W., 252
　Jeff., 241
　Lewis, 241
　Mira, 241
　T. W., 117, 211, 367,
　　369
　———, 241
Bondreaux
　Azelia, 265
　Charles, 265
　Edgard, 265
　Eulalie, 265
　Hebert, 265
　Joseph, 265
　Jules, 265
　Menville, 265
　Oscar, 265
　Philomene, 265
　Theodrule, 265
　Wel., 265
　William Louis, 265
　——— (Mrs.), 265
Bonds
　Martin, 249
　Martin (Mrs.), 249
Bondurant
　J. J. C. (Mrs.), 251
　Jennie, 251
　———, 251
Bonge, William, 252
Bonhager, Fred, 252
Bonich
　Rosa (Mrs.), 253
　Victoria, 253
Boniface
　C. (Mrs.), 372
　Lewis, 372
Bonizio, Carminio, 243
Bonneau, Henry, 252
Bonnecarrere, M., 252
Bonnee, R. W., 358
Bonnefield, W. B., 342
Bonner
　Charles, 245
　Jeff, 253
　Joseph, 239
　Sam, 245
Bonnetts, Mary, 253
Bonset, W. H., 361
Bonvy, N. C., 264
Bookmeyer, H., 373
Bookout, Benjamin C., 249
Booth
　D. W., 244
　J. W., 372
　James, 212
　S. J. (Mrs.), 372
　Sarah (Mrs.), 212
　T. J., 251
　Thomas J., 372
Boraseo, Dominico, 253
Borden
　Annie Lou., 212
　Elma Wood, 212

NAME INDEX

Luther, 212
Willie Webb, 212
Bordes, Mary, 253
Bordeware, Pierre, 253
Boreau, D. (Mrs.), 252
Borg
  James J., 210
  Katie, 210
Borgas, Albert, 253
Bornadine (Sister), 210
Borner
  Carrie, 210
  John, 210
Boronca, Ouida, 264
Bort, Phil, 373
Borus
  Edward, 249
  Frank, 249
Bosco, Carl, 264
Bosder, Patrick, 402
Boselman, E., 210
Boshaus, William, 252
Bosji
  Maggie, 211
  Peter, 211
Bosley, William, 239
Boss
  L., 211
  Peter G., 210
  R. G., 241
Bossant, Edgar, 253
Bossicke, Sallie (Mrs.), 212
Bossonies, see *Bessonies*
Bostwick
  J. L., 210
  J. M., 211
  Willie, 211
Boswell
  C. S., 244
  James J., 244
  Mary E., 243
Boswick, Charles, 247
Both, Victor, 251
Botogniro, Anthony, 253
Bott, Augusta, 264
Bottcher, Fred, 244
Bottick, Charles, 252
Botto
  John V., 212
  Louis, 246
Botts, Teddie (Mrs.), 212
Boucher, Charles, 252
Boudereaux, Adele, 264
Boufette, Charles, 253
Bouisse, Odillie, 252
Bounier, Jean, 252
Bourg, Philip, 253
Bourgeois [Bourgeouis]
  Alic., 263
  Alcesti, 265
  Cecile, 265
  H., 252
  Justinian (Mrs.), 265
  L. N., 265
  Mathilde, 265
  N. Jr., 265
  N. Sr., 265

Nolbert, 263
Sarah, 265
Young, 265
____, 263
Bourgoyne [Bourgoin]
  H., 253
  H. V., 252
Bourgun, John T., 352
Bourke
  Alidia, 264
  Clare, 264
Bourne, J. T., 406
Bourny, Mary F., 253
Boush, William, 373
Bousleaur, William, 253
Boutinaro, Peter, 252
Bowden
  Harry O., 416
  Harvey, 210
Bowen
  Alexander, 212
  F. F., 136, 137, 138, 142, 330, 331, 335, 365, 376, 416
  J. J., 242
  John, 244
  N. S., 404
  Nannie, 210
  W. G., 211
Bower, Elizabeth, 252
Bowers
  Annie, 240
  G. B., 252
  Nancy, 212
  ____ (Mrs.), 240
  ____, 240
Bowht, Rescord, 211
Bowles
  J. D., 403
  Jennie, 210
  L. H., 338
  Maggie, 210
  R. S., 247
  ____, 240
Bowling, Joseph, 263
Bowman
  Anna S. (Mrs.), 252
  Augustus, 245
  B. F., 210
  J. C., 375
  M. R., 239
  M. R. (Mrs.), 239
  R. H., 373
  R. H. (Mrs.), 244
  Robert, 375, 436
Bows, Caroline, 210
Box
  I. P., 244
  ____ (Mrs.), 244
  ____, 244
Boyarella, Jos., 252
Boyce
  J. C., 372
  Josephine, 210
  William H., 337
Boyd
  Alfred, 263

Charles, 212
Frederick, 211
Gus B., 210
Hilliard, 240
Jack, 210
Joe, 210
M., 211
Willie, 212
____ (Mrs.), 239
Boylan, Mary, 211
Boyle
  A. W., 211
  Ada, 252, 253
  Charles, 253
  Henry, 212
  P. J., 253
  P. M., 400
  Peter D., 425
  R. (Mrs.), 373
  Samuel, 367
  ____, 212
Boyne, Hubert B., 253
Boystic, Isaac, 211
Brabston, C. N., 245
Bracie, James, 211
Brackett, John W., 243
Bradford
  A., 373
  Blanche, 211
  C. E., 252
  Ellen, 212
  G. D., 368
  George, 211
  Miles, 241
  R. B., 211
  R. G., 426
  ____ (Mrs.), 210
Bradley
  Charles, 244
  J., 399
  J. M., 429
  L. (Mrs.), 239
  M. T., 344
  P, O., 210
  Patrick, 244
  Robert L., 253
  William, 252
Bradshaw, Haywood, 429
Brady
  Andrew, 252, 253
  Bernard J., 402
  Charles, 253
  E., 253
  Ellen, 395
  Ellen (Mrs.), 373
  F. W., 253
  H. T., 399
  James, 252, 253
  John, 263, 374
  Martha (Mrs.), 210
  Mary, 212, 252
  Taylor, 243
  Theresa, 252
  Thomas, 210
  Thomas J., 253, 403
  W. B., 350

____ (Mrs.), 395
____, 252
Bragg, Ellen (Mrs.), 248
Bragga, ____, 329
Braig, James, 252
Brame, J. R., 210
Branch
  Edward, 263
  Oliver, 239
  W. P., 240
Brand
  Emile, 264
  ____, 292
Brandon, ____, 211
Brandt, Christina, 253
Brannon
  Young, 240
  ____, 245
Brantann, Aug., 419
Braraton, Anna, 252
Bras
  Frank, 407
  ____, 407
Brase, Julius, 253
Braselman, Guy, 253
Brashear, Watt, 247
Brass
  Annie, 212
  Fannie, 212
  Frank, 212
  George, 212
Braudel, Louisa, 252
Braun
  Louis, 253
  Matilda, 253
Braus, Perre, 252
Brautner, John, 210
Brautz, Henry, 211
Brawner
  J. H., 211
  J. M., 339
  Robert, 211
Braziner, George, 247
Brearton
  James, 212
  Katie, 212
Breath, Charles, 249
Brecht, J. E., 252
Breckenridge, W., 211
Breding, Charles, 373
Breedlove, J. W., 372
Breen
  Aleck, 252
  Maggie, 212
Breles, Robert, 211
Breman
  Edward, 253
  John, 210
Bremmer, H., 253
Bremond, Hilarian, 253
Brennan [Brenan, Brennen]
  E. K., 403
  Edward, 253
  Ellis, 211
  Fred, 155, 165, 183, 406, 433

H. F., 399
John, 210, 404
Joseph, 252
Kate (Mrs.), 210
Thomas, 112, 212
Willie, 253
Brenneck, John, 400
Brenner
  G. H., 239
  John, 373, 421
Brens, Ida, 253
Brent, S. J., 401
Bresenham, Adele, 263
Bretano, Adolph, 253
Breton, ____, 13
Brettenum, D. E., 136
Bretz, John B., 252
Brevard, W. A., 251
Brew, Mike, 210, 266
Brewer, B. W., 246
Brewster
  Annie S., 253
  Hattie (Mrs.), 360
  M. (Mrs.), 252
Breyfogle, W. L., 29
Brickel, Philip, 252
Brickell, ____ (Dr.), 296
Brickmann, Herman, 253
Bridge
  George, 243
  William B., 252
Bridgeford, Nancy, 211
Bridges
  A. L., 243
  Abram B., 253
  M. A. (Mrs.), 243
Briffa, Benedetto, 253
Briggs
  H. H., 211
  James T., 212
  Robert, 212
  W. L., 210
  ____, 212
Bright, David F., 251
Brignidello, Angelo, 210
Brim, Edward, 245
Brimstone, Alex, 253
Brindamour, V., 252
Bringgold, R., 252
Brinkley
  E. T., 245
  Hugh L., 390
  Maria, 211
  Mary, 210
  ____, 245
Brinkman, Minnie, 212
Brion, Henry De., 253
Briscoe, Mary, 243
Bristol
  D. C., 247
  Emma, 247
Brit, Mary, 211
Brithney, H. S., 211
Britten, Edward, 253
Britton
  Annie, 252
  John, 253

Robert Jr., 212
Robert (Mrs.), 212
Robert Sr., 212
Brizzolara, James, 212
Broach, W. P. (Mrs.), 248
Broadnax, Bishop, 211
Broadwell, S. D., 340
Brocher, Ernest, 210
Brochvogel, William, 212
Brock
  A., 212
  A. (Mrs.), 212
  Anna M., 253
  Arthur, 212
  Bessie E., 212
  John, 251
  W. W., 248
Brockatt
  W. B. (Mrs.), 249
  ____, 249
Brockhoft
  Louis, 265
  Louise, 265
  Oscar, 265
Brocklesby, John (Mrs.), 124
Brodel, Bernard, 252
Brodie, John (Mrs.), 251
Brodsing, ____ (Dr.), 250
Brogan
  T. J., 345
  ____, 380
Brogen, R. H., 338
Broissac, Charles, 264
Broker
  Louisa, 252
  ____ (Mrs.), 210
Bronges, Celina, 252
Bronson
  Charles, 210, 266
  James, 210
  W., 339
Brook [Brooke]
  Frank T., 242
  Henry, 240
  Sam., 240
  Thomas, 343
Brooks
  A. R., 263
  Aaron, 249
  Aaron C., 245
  Byron, 212, 433
  Byron (Mrs.), 433
  C. B., 212
  Charles C., 212
  Charley, 166
  D. E., 246
  Darius, 433
  Epp., 211
  Fanny (Mrs.), 246
  H. W., 373
  Joseph, 37
  Joseph (Mrs.), 37
  M. H., 351
  Maria L. (Mrs.), 210
  Mat., 211
  R. E. (Mrs.), 211

Susan, 211
W. S., 154, 155, 156, 158, 416, 417, 433
W. S. (Mrs.), 155, 158, 417, 433
Will, 166
William, 211
____ (Mrs.), 433
____, 165, 417, 433
Broom, ____ (Mrs.), 173
Brothers, Clodius, 265
Brouc, Jean, 253
Broughton
  Jimmy, 248
  John, 248
Broussard
  Alice, 264
  Annie, 263
  Facay, 263
Brower, Lilly Belle, 263
Brown [Browne]
  A. E., 245
  A. (Mrs.), 245
  A. S., 211
  A. V., 263
  A. W., 113, 212, 430
  Ada, 210
  Ada (Mrs.), 245
  Aggie, 212
  Alexander V., 243
  Andrew, 210
  Anna M., 253
  Annie, 242
  Annie (Mrs.), 211
  Aristide, 264
  Arthur, 264
  Augusta, 253
  Bob, 211
  Bruce, 244
  Calvin, 242
  Charles M., 212
  D., 212
  Danely, 430
  Daniel, 211
  Dixie J., 210
  Dolly, 242
  E., 211, 212
  E. A., 210
  E. B. M., 419
  E. (Mrs.), 252, 373
  E. R., 341
  Edward, 253, 264
  Edward J., 253
  Ella, 374
  Ellis, 211
  Emma, 210, 212
  F., 395
  Fannie, 211
  Fannie (Mrs.), 243
  Francis, 212
  G. W., 210
  George, 265
  George F., 244
  Gregory, 253
  H. C., 343
  H. E., 242
  Harry, 242

Harvey E., 20
Hattie, 211
Henry, 211, 212, 424
Hilliard, 211
Ida, 249
Irwin, 212
J. (Mrs.), 211
J. Allen, 351
J. C., 244
J. W. X., 410
Jacob, 212
Jacob (Mrs.), 212
James, 250
Jeff., 212
Jennie, 243
Jesse, 375
John, 211, 243, 265, 401
John H., 410
Joseph, 252, 264
Kate, 252
Katie, 211, 247
L., 252
Lewis, 211, 212
Lucien, 211
Lucy, 210
M., 242
Malone, 253
Margaret D. L., 211
Marks, 244
Mary, 212
Mary B., 252
Matilda, 372
Millie, 212
Minty, 242
Mitchell, 174
Nettie, 212
P. M., 212
P. P. (Mrs.), 211
Phil., 211
R. F., 146, 174, 330, 377
R. G., 430
R. J., 339
R. T., 430
R. W., 355
S. H., 368, 370
Sam (Mrs.), 247
Samuel, 211
Sophia C., 253
Stephen, 430
Thomas, 252, 266
Tom, 210
W. J., 253
Wash, 210
William, 375
____ (Capt.), 428
____ (Mrs.), 239, 265
____, 212, 245, 264
Brownfield, Rachel, 374
Broyer, L. A., 252
Bruccolori, Rosalie, 252, 253
Bruce
  Adelaide, 264
  Marie, 252
  ____ (Mrs.), 250

NAME INDEX

Bruchert, A., 252
Bruder, L. W., 434
Bruet, Eugene, 252
Brugiere, L., 252
Brugnien, Amedee, 253
Bruguins, John, 253
Brumley, ____ (Dr.), 248
Brummer, T., 252
Brun, Patrick, 253
Bruneau, J. M., 252
Brunet, Pierre, 264
Brunner, Alice, 212
Brunnert, August, 252
Bruno
  Joseph, 252
  Marie, 253
Bruns
  Mike, 210
  Otto, 252
  Rebecca (Mrs.), 210
  Robert, 210
  Rosalie, 252
  William H., 252
Brunson, Alonzo L., 247
Brusle, Ophelia, 264
Bryals, Thomas, 240
Bryan
  Anne H., 263
  Henry N., 242
  L. A., 368
  Lizzie, 355
  ____ (Dr.), 167
Bryant
  Anna, 253
  Lewis, 244
Bryson
  Thomas, 211, 375
  ____ (Dr.), 25, 28
Buchignani
  M. (Mrs.), 212
  T., 212
Buchler, Rudolph, 253
Buchman, Gotria, 252
Buck
  Caroline, 212
  M. J., 253
  T. C., 251
  William, 265
  ____, 95
Buckel, H. W., 211
Buckhalter, Julia, 212
Buckhart
  Bertha, 253
  George, 253
Buckingham, O. G., 338
Buckley
  Mary D., 253
  Sandy, 243
  Thomas A., 400
Buckner
  Alice, 211
  Hannah, 211
  J. H., 247
  W. T. Jr., 251
  William, 211
Budd, E. G., 410
Buddinella, G. A., 211

Budey, George, 252
Buehl, John, 210
Bueler, Josephine, 252
Buell
  Jimmy, 253
  ____ (Maj.), 384
Buffier
  Auguste, 252
  Augusti, 253
Buffington
  James H., 344
  John H., 344
Buford, A. G. (Mrs.), 246
Bugg [Bugge]
  Diddenka, 252
  Phil, 266
  W., 252
Buhler, H. J., 161
Buhn, Katie Leonora, 212
Bull, J. D., 372
Bullet [Bullit]
  Louisa, 253
  William, 253
Bullion, ____, 249
Bullock
  C. (Mrs.), 211
  Ellen, 210
  William, 245, 250
Bumgard, Christian, 263
Bunch, John M., 372
Buncho
  Andy, 251
  Andy (Mrs.), 251
Bund, Planter, 210
Bundy
  L. F. (Mrs.), 253
  Louis F., 252
Bungener, Ferd., 373
Buniff, B. F., 373
Bunton, William, 265
Buogacre, Ed, 252
Buono, Salvador, 253
Buras, Mary A., 253
Burch, Stephen, 373
Burcham
  R., 117, 212
  Robert, 368, 369
Burchert, J., 210
Burchett, ____ (Mrs.), 210
Burchman, Robert, 167, 168
Burd, G. M., 242
Burdett [Burdette]
  Marsh, 247
  Nathan, 249
  Walsh, 249
  ____ (Miss), 249
Burge [Burg]
  Catherine, 253
  Ella, 250
  Julia, 250
  Mary (Mrs.), 239
  Nettie, 250
  Pinkie, 250
  Rachael, 250
  Richard, 250
  Richard Jr., 250

  Sarah (Mrs.), 250
  Stelle, 250
  Vincent, 239
  William, 239
Burges, Maggie, 210
Burgess, Annie, 211
Burgner, Frederick, 211
Burgniens, James, 253
Burgoyne, Henrietta B., 253
Burke [Burk]
  A., 242
  A. A., 212, 266
  Andrew, 211
  B., 212
  C. C., 357
  C. (Mrs.), 212
  Charles E., 403
  Douglas, 430
  Elizabeth, 252
  Emma, 211
  Fritz, 253
  H. M., 212, 373
  J. F., 403
  Jack, 252
  Jackson, 211
  James, 239, 248
  James (Mrs.), 239
  James M., 403
  Jeff., 211
  Kate, 212
  L. L. (Mrs.), 211
  M., 173, 333, 334, 336, 377
  Margaret, 210
  Mary, 253
  Mary E., 212
  Matilda, 211
  Michael, 212
  Mike, 210
  Sam, 374
  Thomas, 210, 211
  William, 210
  ____ (Col.), 334
  ____ (Maj.), 380
  ____ (Mrs.), 211
  ____, 95
Burkhardt, George, 252
Burkhart, Rosa, 239
Burkins, Arthur, 211
Burkman, Julius, 252
Burks
  Bill, 210
  Homan, 210
Burleson, M. J. (Mrs.), 212
Burne, Annie, 212
Burner, Margaret, 252
Burnet, Sallie, 248
Burns [Burnes]
  Adoph, 211
  Albert, 211
  Davy, 211
  Edward, 252
  Elizabeth, 252
  Franklin, 253
  George, 242
  J. A., 210

  James, 242
  James S., 264
  Jane, 212
  John, 263, 373, 434
  Julia, 210
  L. L., 252
  Lewis, 211
  Melinda, 210
  Oscar, 210
  Otto, 253
  Pat, 211
  Patrick, 264
  Peter, 242
  Robert, 252
  Robert C., 252
  Thomas, 210, 253
  Willie, 212
  ____ (Mrs.), 408
  ____, 253, 408
Burr
  Henry, 211
  L. S., 411, 412, 413, 415
Burrell
  Ed, 266
  M. A. (Mrs.), 244
  Mattie, 242
  ____, 212
Burrie, ____ (Mrs.), 250
Burrows
  Mary, 372
  ____ (Dr.), 211
Bursley, A. A., 244
Burst, Augustus, 253
Burt
  E. (Mrs.), 358
  Henry, 248
  K., 248
  Lizzie, 358
  Maggie, 244
  Mary L. (Mrs.), 373
Burtinner, Charles, 211
Burton
  G. W., 342
  John, 212
  Lelia, 173
  Martin, 262
  Philip, 210
  Silas, 211
  T. H., 430
  ____ (Mrs.), 374
Burtz, ____, 242
Burus, Davy, 211
Burwell, R., 351
Busany, Antoinette, 253
Busby, J. J., 330
Busch, Mary F., 212
Bush
  John, 211
  Samuel, 253
  William, 211
Bushey, H. L., 211
Bussa, Fred, 252
Bussani, A., 252
Bussow, Henry, 265
Buster, J. C., 239
Busucie, H. W., 346

Butcher
  Robert, 381
  William, 244
  Willie, 249
Butler
  Alexander M., 244
  C., 350
  Charles, 350
  Ed., 211
  George, 212
  John, 374
  John S., 264
  Katie, 244
  Lizzie, 245
  Margaret (Mrs.), 239
  Robert, 239
  T. C. (Sister), 253
  Tom, 264
  W. E., 355
  W. T., 210
  Walter B., 246
  Walter J., 253
  William, 212, 239
  ____ (Gen.), 296
Buttenberg. H., 423
Butts
  A., 241
  W. H., 407
  Warren S., 252
  ____, 241
Byers [Byars]
  Billy, 241
  Edward M., 253
  Jake, 247
  L. K., 422
  ____ (Mrs.), 246
Byman, William, 210
Byrd
  J. Edgar, 373, 376
  Mike, 210
  William, 211
Byrne
  E. J., 246
  E. R., 265
  J. G., 252, 253
  J. W., 210
  John, 249, 402
  John C., 212
  M. A., 402
Byrnes
  James, 252
  Pat, 247
Byrum, T. G., 241

C

Cabanellas, ____, 296
Cabariol, Rosa L. (Mrs.), 253
Cabeler
  L. F., 240
  Zach, 240
  ____ (Mrs.), 240
Cabell [Caball]
  B. F., 345
  W. L., 361, 362
Cabero, M. C., 254

Cabiadis, ____, 324
Cable, George B., 254
Cables, Elder, 214
Cade, Robert, 263
Cady
  David, 350
  Jacob, 254
Cafert, J. J., 264
Caffall
  Edward, 246
  Louis, 246
  Willie, 246
Caffrey
  F. Demoret, 254
  Patrick, 254
Cage
  A. H., 246
  F. T., 431
Cahill
  James, 254
  Patrick, 254
  Thomas, 401
Cahn
  Adolph, 249
  Sam, 263
Cahnbley, Theodore, 254
Cahope, Ed., 213
Caillet, L., 361
Cain [Cane]
  Daniel F., 400
  Dempsey, 263
  F., 213
  J. E., 213, 266
  Jane, 250
  Mary, 215
  Matthew, 214
Cainevern, Alice, 213
Cairns
  J. G., 212
  Julia R., 213
  Mary D., 213
Cairo, Jim, 263
Calamar, Dominico, 254
Calamara, Antoni, 254
Calaway, Marshall, 240
Calder, J. (Mrs.), 239
Calderaro
  J. (Mrs.), 239
  Manuel, 254
Caldovora, Angelina, 254
Caldwell
  Alex, 214
  Fannie, 214
  Jessie, 241
  John (Mrs.), 241
  M. F., 253
  Sarah, 242
  Tennie, 214
  Wells, 249
  ____ (Dr.), 203
Caleb, Rosa, 253
Calere
  J. (Mrs.), 395
  T. C., 395
Calhoun
  James Dick, 241
  N. A., 213

R. F., 214
William, 407
William (Mrs.), 407
____ (Mrs.), 213, 214
____, 407
Callahan
  C., 404
  Frank, 214
  John, 213
  Lizzie, 214
  M. (Mrs.), 214
  Maggie, 214
  Rose (Sister), 213
  ____, 186
Callarie, Eugenia, 265
Callaway, P., 339
Calleja [Callija[, Joseph, 238, 253
Callendar
  Hiram, 246
  Lulu, 246
Callery, Cecelia, 253, 254
Calligan, N., 254
Callihan, Ned., 238
Calloway
  Elsie, 213
  J. M., 301
Calson, John, 214
Calvert, M. A. (Mrs.), 253
Calvin, James, 245
Camach, Jonathan, 254
Camache, Jonathan, 253
Camash, Robert, 254
Camblong, Bevnara, 254
Cambre, Camille, 264
Cambridge, R., 244
Camella, Salvador, 253
Cameron
  A. C., 245
  Angus, 243
  Benny, 245
  D. A., 249
  Hubbard, 249
  J. H., 359
  J. (Mrs.), 215
  John, 130
  John F., 394, 428, 429
  S. F., 330
  ____ (Capt.), 175, 390
  ____ (Mrs.), 244
Camienski, F., 253
Camilla [Camila]
  Anna, 254
  Crestina, 253
Camille, Gustave, 253
Camillo
  B. C. (Mrs.), 244
  N., 242
Camo, Lizzie, 253
Camp
  W. A., 349
  William, 213
Campbell
  Anna, 254
  D. C., 238, 249
  Dolly, 214
  E. E., 253

  Esther E., 254
  Frank, 214
  G. W., 247
  J. B., 406, 413
  J. B. (Mrs.), 406
  J. C. (Mrs.), 372
  James, 215
  John, 107
  M., 254
  Mary, 215
  R. G., 245
  R. (Mrs.), 373
  S., 349
  Sarah, 253
  W. H. (Mrs.), 360
  William, 213, 250
  Willie, 213
  ____ (Mrs.), 148, 240
  ____, 148, 240, 246
Campe, ____, 249
Camrer, J. I., 264
Canalli [Canali]
  C., 246
  P. D., 215
Canan, Philip, 254
Canapo
  John, 214
  ____, 214
Canapole, Antonio, 214
Cancienne, Villier, 265
Cane, see Cain
Canella [Canela]
  Antonio, 253, 254
  John, 254
Canepa, Rosalie, 253
Canepo, Jennie, 213
Canfield
  George, 343
  Martin, 254
Canius, G. A., 253
Cannon
  Bridget, 214
  Francis, 214
  Hattie, 239
  James, 214
  James E., 214
  M., 112
  Mike, 173, 212
  Mike (Mrs.), 173
  Ples., 214
  ____ (Mrs.), 395
  ____, 173
Canos, Rosa, 253
Canto, Gabriel, 254
Cantrale
  Josephine, 265
  ____ (Miss), 263
Capdevielle
  Cornelia M., 263
  Lindsey, 263
Capeheart, W. N., 214
Capehut, ____, 214
Caple, J. T., 360
Capley, Albert R., 254
Capo, Prosper, 254
Cappedonico, L., 215
Capriana, Aug., 254

NAME INDEX

Capuano, Julia, 254
Capurro
  P. (Mrs.), 246
  Peter, 246
Capus
  Henri, 254
  Henry, 254
Caraher, ____ (Capt.), 356
Carambat, E. D., 254
Caraway, ____ (Miss), 239
Carbarini, Anna, 254
Carbini, Nicola, 253
Carbo, Tony, 254
Carbos, P. G., 254
Cardell, John, 213
Cardenas, Andrew, 254
Carelton, ____ (Mrs.), 373
Carey [Cary]
  Albert, 214, 429
  Hugh W., 254
  James, 213
  James J., 399
  John, 400
  Joseph R., 254
  Nellie, 44
  S. E., 44, 45
  ____ (Mrs.), 264
  ____ (Pvt.), 113, 429
Cargill, John F., 215
Carl
  Ella, 247
  Price, 247
Carleston, Charles, 213
Carlin, D. B., 239
Carline
  A. (Mrs.), 214
  Katie, 214
Carlisle
  Edward, 253
  Elizabeth, 213
  Thomas J., 239
  ____, 213
Carlo
  Calisse, 264
  Charles, 264
Carlos, King of Spain, 296
Carloss, Helen, 348
Carlson
  Charley, 266
  Christina, 245
Carmichael, ____ (Mrs.), 213
Carmille, A. (Mrs.), 254
Carnes, A., 356
Carney
  James, 399
  Martin, 112
  William, 254
Carnovan, Cario, 253
Caroline, Frank, 214
Carondelet, de, (Baron) (Gov.), 42, 69
Carpenter
  Charles, 215, 372
  J. B., 343
  J. S., 354
  John, 250

L. L., 344
Sidney, 239
Sidney Jr., 239
Carr
  Ann, 213
  C. M., 243
  J. E., 213
  James, 213
  John, 242
  Joseph, 214
  Luella, 214
  Lyman, 350
  Richmond, 214
  T. J., 213, 373
  ____ (Dr.), 95, 96
Carrallina, Louisa, 253
Carran, O. J. (Mrs.), 253
Carraway
  William, 215
  ____ (Mrs.), 215
Carre, R. B., 249
Carrie, ____ (Mrs.), 213
Carriere, Frank N., 253
Carrington, H., 244
Carroll
  C. M., 411
  Ed., 240, 266
  Edward, 214
  Ellen (Mrs.), 214
  Fondy, 95
  G. W., 357
  J. C., 402
  James, 404
  M., 399, 401
  Mary, 242
  Sidney, 214
  Timothy, 254
  W. H., 355
Carson
  H., 341
  John, 214
  Nora, 243
  Peter, 213
  ____ (Mrs.), 395
Carswell
  W. A., 368
  ____ (Dr.), 168
Cartel, Leon, 253
Carteon, J. E., 214
Carter
  A. B., 429
  Charles L., 242
  Dora, 214
  E., 242
  Fulton, 242
  George, 244
  Gracie, 213
  Henry, 214
  Jackson, 214
  James, 215
  M. A., 238, 249
  Margaret, 363
  Mary, 214
  Phoebe, 243
  W. N., 264
  ____ (Miss), 239
Cartis, C., 240

Cartman, Henry, 214
Cartney, Lucinda, 214
Cartwright
  L., 357
  ____ (Dr.), 42
Caruso, Luca, 254
Caruthers, Cheney, 212
Carver
  Thomas, 215
  ____ (Mrs.), 214
Cary, see Carey
Casanbor, Alex., 254
Case
  Charles, 434
  Ed, 434
  George, 254
  M. H., 344
Casey
  Ben, 245
  Hugh W., 253
  John W., 254
  Mary, 253
  Mike, 251
  Thomas A., 400
Cash
  John, 239
  Lit., 244
  William, 244
Cashell
  Emma J., 253
  Eugene, 253
  Joseph, 253
Cashin, Michael, 399
Casio, Geronimo, 253
Caskall, Ellen, 214
Caskey, A. B., 244
Cass
  Abe, 214
  Lewis, 244
Cassady, Emanuel, 254
Cassell, Willie, 246
Cassenella, ____ (Miss), 213
Casserly, James, 404
Cassimere, Jennie, 373
Cassman
  Charles, 263
  Charles (Mrs.), 263
Casson, ____ (Widow), 254
Castaing, Cath., 254
Castello
  Willie, 245
  ____, 214
Caster, Camille, 254
Casteretto, J. B., 253
Casterilli, Joseph, 213
Castillo
  Belinda, 213
  Mike C., 213
Castleman, B. D., 412
Castmill, Henry, 214
Caston
  Bettie, 246
  Charles, 246
  Edith, 246
  Wiggins, 246
  William T., 246

Castopper, Antonie, 254
Castro, Nevvillle, 265
Catalana [Catalona]
  A., 253
  Antonia, 254
  Rileta, 253
Catania, George, 253
Catherine (Empress), 324
Cathey, Bettie, 213
Cathrall, ____ (Dr.), 70
Catleman, B. D., 214
Catlett
  H. C., 251
  ____, 246
Catola, Jean, 254
Catral, Jacob, 254
Catron
  R. R., 154, 214, 407, 416
  Robert R., 166
  ____, 128, 160
Caufield, Martin, 254
Caulfield, Roman, 213
Causey, Laura, 213
Cauvin, Alc., 263
Cavanaugh [Cavangh]
  Martin, 214, 254
  Michael, 400
  W. C., 368, 370, 397
Caw, Herbert, 254
Cawein, ____, 248
Cazale, Adelaide, 253
Cazaloote, Bertrand, 254
Cazant, Alexander, 253
Cazaretta
  Christine, 214
  Peter, 214
Cazeaux
  Emile, 253
  Omile, 254
Cazeres, William, 253
Cazoux, Bernard, 253
Cazzella, Santina, 253
Cearney, Alice (Mrs.), 374
Cecelia (Sister), 158
Cefalu, Concheta, 254
Celite, Johoe, 213
Celsus, 14
Cenles, Dennis, 213
Ceres
  Gabriel, 254
  Marie, 254
Cerf
  Isaac, 249
  Manuel, 249
Cernes, H., 213
Cessaner, J. F., 347
Cessna, Love, 248
Cezerin, Beajio, 264
Chabretto, John, 254
Chabrust, George, 214
Chacoreau, Louis, 253, 254
Chadwick
  Edwin, 316
  Joseph, 254
  Winfred, 254
Chaery, Bertha, 254

Chaillé, Stanford E., 27
Chalan, Julius C., 253
Chalin, Fred, 253
Chalmers
  Charity, 213
  Vernon, 390
  Verona, 213
  _____ (Dr.), 70
Chalmette, George, 214
Chamberlain
  Cora, 239
  Delia (Mrs.), 239
  M. C. (Mrs.), 239
Chamberry, Dupuy de, 16
Chambers
  J. W., 416
  R., 351
  Royal, 242
  Sallie, 213
  Vernon, 214
  William, 246
  _____, 246
Chambora, John, 254
Chamin, Bertha, 265
Champagne
  Abel, 265
  Francis, 265
  Louis, 254
Champlain, George, 214
Champlin, Lou, 264
Chandler
  D. R., 253
  J. F., 213
  James, 214
  Mary T., 264
  W. R., 431
  William, 213, 248
  Willie, 214
  _____ (Dr.), 174
  _____ (Mrs.), 241
Chantelou, Edward, 254
Chanvin
  P., 264
  _____, 264
Chapman
  B. N. (Mrs.), 213
  Henry, 253
  J. F., 253
  John T., 254
  _____, 243
Chappell [Chapel, Chapple]
  Robert W., 245
  R. W., 249
  Simon, 214
Chapsky [Chapski]
  Albert, 254
  Hugo, 253
  L. 408
Chardon, William, 254
Charity Hospital, 32, 33
Charles
  Henry, 253, 254
  S., 254
Charles (Father), 249
Charles IV, 69

Charlton
  Eva L., 254
  Ida L., 254
  T. J., 192
  William, 253
Charto, Jacinno, 254
Charton, J. N., 254
Chartonez, John, 254
Chase
  C., 357
  C. D., 350
  Isaiah, 67
  Ruth W., 215
  W. J., 390, 431
Chastant, Sidney, 264
Chatam, John, 243
Chatard, _____ (Rt. Rev. Bishop), 404
Chavivari, Guiseppe, 246
Chavurgny, Louise, 254
Cheatham, Oliver, 263
Checkapelia, Philip, 253
Cheehan, Laurence, 254
Cheek
  G. A., 213
  Philip M., 212
Cheevers, Ed, 264
Chenowith
  Charles, 245
  John, 245
Chensey, John W., 214
Cherrowillett, Cezar, 254
Cherry, Frank, 246
Chester, Price, 240, 266
Cheves [Chevis]
  C. L., 214
  L. A., 117, 368, 369
  Langdon, 192
  Langdon A., 192
Chevreau, Marie, 254
Chevrin, _____ (Dr.), 25
Chew, J. D., 253, 254
Chiaca, Theo, 254
Chiappetta, Antonio, 254
Chibnall, William, 254
"Chicago John," 221
Chiesa, J. A., 246
Chietta, Pietro, 253
Childress, John, 213
Childs
  Emma, 247
  L. B., 368, 370
Chinn, Walter, 214
Chism, James, 245
Chol, E. Jr., 265
Chopen, Anna, 254
Chopin, _____ (Dr.), 18, 44, 58, 72, 73, 105
Christ, George, 254
Christian, C. (Miss), 251
Christiana, An., 253
Christina, Leonarda, 254
Christonson
  N. P., 215
  Peter, 214
Christopher, John, 253
Christy, Henry, 253

Church
  C. B., 355
  C. H., 213
  John, 253
  Nathan, 346
Cicalla
  N. (Mrs.), 213
  Paul Sr., 214
Cicella, Paul, 213
Cicero, Salvador La., 254
Ciental, Paschal, 253
Cinnetta, Cerelia, 213
Cioccio, Giachin, 254
Clain, August, 253
Clairal, Felicie, 253
Clamous, John, 253
Clampett
  Chalmer, 240
  Harris, 240
  Mollie (Mrs.), 240
  Robert, 240
Clancy [Clancey]
  Daniel, 247
  Maggie, 214
  _____ (Mrs.), 247
Clapham
  George E., 214
  Thomas, 214
Clapp, J. W., 356
Clara, _____ (Mrs.), 214
Clarac, Joseph, 254
Clare
  Posey, 238
  Posey (Mrs.), 238
  Samuel, 249
Clark [Clarke]
  A., 401
  Anna, 213
  Annie, 213, 214
  Arthur, 429
  Barney, 213
  Charley, 213
  D. W. (Mrs.), 245
  E. W. (Mrs.), 214
  Elisha, 244
  Eddie, 215
  Eliza, 213
  Elizabeth, 253
  Ellen, 244
  Emma, 242
  Francis, 214
  G. B., 212
  G. W., 214
  George, 241
  George R., 247
  H., 213
  Harry, 212
  Helen C., 254
  J. H., 355
  J. W. (Mrs.), 163, 374
  James, 244, 263, 429
  Jane, 214
  John, 348
  John B., 358
  Kate, 247
  Kate (Mrs.), 374
  Lee, 265

  Lucy, 215
  Maggie, 253, 254
  Margaret, 254
  Margaret (Mrs.), 212
  Matthew, 247
  Mollie (Mrs.), 214
  Myra May, 254
  Oliver, 263, 264
  R. 214
  R. B., 171, 214, 392, 406
  S. C., 239
  S. C. (Mrs.), 240
  S. R., 117, 165, 214
  Sarah J., 253, 254
  Sarah S., 254
  Smith, 215
  Thaddeus, 215
  Thomas H., 341
  W. A., 251, 266
  W. S., 372
  Walter, 214, 253
  William Gwyn, 214
  Willie W., 214
  _____ (Dr.), 203
  _____ (Mrs.), 251
  _____, 185, 212, 215, 243
Clars, Bridget, 254
Clary
  Cecelia, 244
  Joe, 213
  Joseph M., 254
  Mike, 213
Claude, M. (Mrs.), 253
Clavarri, Charles, 246
Clavery, John, 263
Clavich, Mateo, 253
Clay
  Ann (Mrs.), 214
  C. C., 338
  C. L., 366
  H., 430
  J. L., 369
  John, 250
  John L., 372
  _____ (Miss), 183
Clayer, Charles, 244
Clayton
  Belle, 214
  Ed., 238
  H. W., 416, 434
  Joe, 212
  Joseph, 254
Cleary
  Conn, 213
  J. L., 400
  James, 390
  John D., 214
  Lucy, 212
  M., 213
  Mary, 214
  Mary Ann, 249
  Mary E., 253, 254
  Mike, 213
  _____ (Mrs.), 212
  _____, 213

NAME INDEX

Cleaveland
  L. J. (Mrs.), 373
  W. C., 373
Cleaver, Henry, 253
Cleaverton, W. T., 213
Cleaves
  Charles, 214
  E. L., 213
Cleburne, Adeline, 215
Clece, ____, 214
Cleere [Clere]
  Emma V., 240
  W. P., 214
  W. P. (Mrs.), 215, 240
Cleland
  Bobie, 245
  W. B., 245
Clemens
  Hale, 262
  Henry, 213
  Mary, 262
Clement
  Charles, 254
Clevnille, 265
  Joseph (Mrs.), 265
  Louis, 253
  Theophile, 265
  U. (Mrs.), 265
Clements [Clemments]
  F. T. O., 427
  F. T. O. (Mrs.), 427
  Henry, 421
  J. M., 18
  John, 253, 254
  S. E., 356
  T. F. O., 213
  W. H., 244
  ____ (Mrs.), 432
  ____, 432
Clemmons, H. S., 212
Clere, *see* Cleere
Clesta, Antonio, 254
Cleveland, P. W., 213
Clifford, Mary, 253
Clifton, H., 374
Cline
  W. W., 349
  ____ (Miss), 214
Clinton, James, 395
Clockton
  Josephine, 215
  ____, 215
Clogston, A., 213
Cloney, Miles, 253
Clorezette, Rosette, 254
Close, David, 254
Clouzet, Rosette, 253
Clowers, ____ (Mrs.), 246
Clowery, Primas, 243
Cloyd
  Rose, 240
  T. S., 266, 407
  Thomas S., 212
Cluassen, Octave, 265
Club, Estelle, 401
Clupton, A. L., 346
Coakley, Mary, 244

Coan
  D. W., 336, 380
  S. W., 354
Coate, W. C., 413
Coates
  Almon, 213
  Maud A., 254
  S. A. (Mrs.), 253
Cobb
  Charles S., 251
  E. D. (Mrs.), 215
  Edward, 429
  Eli, 213
  George, 213
  H., 429
  Henry, 213
  Rhoda, 214
  ____ (Sgt.), 113, 429
  ____, 263
Coburn, J., 247
Cochran [Cochrane. Cockran]
  Eugene Jr., 246
  J. W., 355
  James, 253
  Jerome, 27
  Mary A., 253
  Timothy, 399
Cocke, S. (Mrs.), 215
Cockrell
  B. F., 215
  J. (Mrs.), 215
  Richard, 215
Cocorillo, Francis, 264
Codman, ____ (Capt.), 357
Cody
  Alex, 213
  Honora, 244
Coe
  Alice E. (Mrs.), 214
  J. L., 214
  L. H., 213
  Lafayette, 266
  M. J. (Mrs.), 214
  Walter, 214
  William, 395
Coffee [Coffey]
  George B., 254
  Patrick, 251
  William, 251
Coffin
  Francis, 254
  Sam (Mrs.), 246
Coffman
  Charles, 247
  Charles (Mrs.), 247
  Kate, 247
  R., 247
  R. (Mrs.), 247
  ____, 379
Coffrey, F. D., 253
Cogan
  John, 265
  P. (Father), 246
Coggshall, S. W., 254
Coghlen, Cornelius, 404
Coghill, Jackson, 249

Cogswell, C. H., 422
Cohen
  D. L., 374
  E., 419
  F. (Mrs.), 420
  Henry S., 254
  Joseph H., 254
  Lena, 254
  Nidam, 253
  Rebecca, 253
  Solomon J., 254
  ____, 329
Cohman, Mary, 253
Cohn
  H. (Mrs.), 215
  Harris, 214
  Jacob, 212
  Johnny, 250
  ____, 215
Cohupe, Leon, 215
Coker
  Bettie, 246
  Jennie, 246
  Mary, 246
Colbert
  John, 262
  ____ (Mrs.), 262
Cold, Waller, 214
Colden, Henry, 265
Cole
  Alice, 213
  Emily, 214
  Emma, 374
  Frederick, 141, 213, 330, 331, 332, 335
  George, 213
  Gertrude, 212
  Harriet, 213
  Hayden, 214
  Lotta, 251
  R., 213
  Rachel (Mrs.), 212
  Stella, 213
  W. T., 247
  W. T. (Mrs.), 247
Colegoro, Dimetry, 254
Coleman
  A. A., 239
  Adam, 214
  Benjamin, 213
  Cally, 213
  Cullen, 213
  D., 242
  David, 338
  E., 213
  Edward, 215
  Ella, 254
  Emeline, 243
  Frank, 242
  G. S., 360
  Gustave A., 212
  J. M., 214
  Jessie, 214
  Laura, 243
  Lizzie, 239
  Maggie, 238
  S., 213, 266

Sam, 242, 251
  W., 430
  W. L., 368
  Willie, 238
  Wood, 254
  ____ (Dr.), 42
  ____, 214
Coleridge, ____, 311
Colhouer, ____, 302
Colica, Gisvan, 254
Colinsky, Earnest, 254
Collar, ____ (Miss), 213
Collery, Michael, 253
Collier
  Alice, 244
  Bettie, 244
  Genevive C., 254
  James, 244
  John A., 403
Collings, Joseph W., 254
Collins
  C. R., 361
  C. T., 246
  Francis, 253
  George, 214, 248
  J., 254
  J. T., 135
  Jack, 263
  James, 214
  Martin, 409
  Mary, 253
  Matthew, 403
  Patrick, 243
  Peter, 401
  R. A., 248
  Rosalie, 244
  S. H., 368, 370
  Scott, 263
  Thomas, 214
  Tom, 373
  William, 249
  ____ (Miss), 213
Colmam
  D., 408
  B. (Mrs.), 408
  ____, 408
Colome, Henry, 254
Colovan, Charles, 244
Colozero, Annieall, 254
Colter, Mary, 214
Colton, Pat, 214
Coltraro, Callora, 253
Columbus, Christopher, 13, 14
Comanda, Goetano, 254
Comba
  F., 213
  John, 213
  Richard, 214
Combel, Wilfred, 249
Combs
  H. L., 173
  ____ (Mrs. Dr.), 173
Comeaux, James, 263
Comes, Blaise, 254
Comfort, William, 253
Compter, S. A., 254

Compton
  William, 246
  ——— (Mrs.), 245
Comstock
  C. B., 254
  C. M., 213
Conaty, T. J., 404
Concannon, James, 265
Conchela, T. J., 213
Condon
  Mary, 215
  Richard, 254
Cone
  R., 340
  R. J., 357
Conger, C. S., 342
Conget, L. A., 254
Congrela, Bowman, 213
Conklin, C. (Mrs.), 242
Conley [Conly]
  H. E., 427, 432
  Harry, 239
  M., 247
  Mary, 254
  Nancy (Mrs.), 239
Conlin [Conlan]
  Charles, 242
  John, 212
  Maggie, 213
Conn, C. F., 129, 390, 391
Connell [Connel]
  Annie, 214
  Daniel R., 253
  Eliza, 214
  Emma, 214
  F. G., 136
  J. B. M., 251
  James, 247
  Pat, 214
  Patrick, 112
  R., 254
  Thomas, 214
Connelly
  Andrew, 254
  Dennis, 213
  J. B. W., 266
  J. I., 126, 432
  James, 253
  Jane, 213
  John, 253
  John I., 266, 427
  John J., 213
  Kate, 213
  Mary, 213
  Michael, 248
  Michael (Mrs.), 249
  Pete, 215
  Timothy, 213
  ——— (Mrs.), 239, 250
Conner
  C. (Mrs.), 213
  J. W., 214
  James, 213
  Julia, 263
  Lonny, 214
  Maggie, 214

Conners
  Ben, 212
  Frank, 214
  James, 253
  M., 244
  Mike, 213
  Pat, 213
  ———, 253
Connett, A. M., 361
Connigan, Mary, 253
Connington, Burton, 245
Connolly [Conolly]
  Joseph, 254
  Maggie, 253
  T., 400
Connor
  Michael, 253
  ——— (Mrs.), 373
Connors
  D. J., 403
  E. F., 242
  Thomas, 254
Connoway, I. D., 407
Conntee, Ike, 213
Conovan, John, 254
Conover, L. E., 341
Conrad
  Emma, 254
  J. F. (Mrs.), 214
  J. W., 238
  James, 254
  Lena, 253, 254
  Monroe, 214
  ———, 213, 240
Conroy
  Fred, 253
  Thomas, 373
Conry, Fannie, 254
Consadine [Considine]
  John, 112, 213, 391
  ———, 396
Consienne, Adrian, 264
Constance (Sister), 122, 123, 124, 213
Constantine, ———, 253
Conte, Pierre, 254
Converse
  Daisy, 253, 254
  W. H., 254
Conway
  Bridget (Mrs.), 242
  C. (Mrs.), 246
  Clara, 348, 438
  Edwin, 246
  J., 242
  James, 242
  Joseph, 242
  Michael, 254
  Moses, 243
  ——— (Mrs.), 263
  ———, 263
Coockmeyer, Louisa, 254
Cook [Cooke]
  A., 214
  A. F. C., 141, 213, 330, 331, 332, 335
  Adams, 213

  Annie, 150, 155, 159, 190, 213
  B. F., 401
  C. H. (Mrs.), 212
  David, 213
  Eddie, 212
  Ellen, 213
  George, 214
  George (Mrs.), 214
  Henry W., 243
  J. B., 406
  J. L., 251
  J. Reese, 245
  James B., 319
  John, 214
  John Lewis, 254
  Katie, 214
  Levie, 243
  Lucy W., 244
  M. A., 214
  Major F., 373
  Michael, 213
  Peyton, 213
  Richard, 214
  S. D., 213
  Spottswell, 263
  Thomas F., 254
  Thomas N., 254
  W. (Mrs.), 213
  Wallis, 254
  ——— (Mrs.), 246
Cooler, Harriet, 213
Cooley
  ——— (Mrs.), 243
  ———, 214, 243
Coomes, Camille, 264
Coon, G. T., 248
Cooper
  Amelia, 213
  Belle, 242
  D. G., 350
  George, 214, 431
  Ida C., 263
  J. A., 242
  J. C., 350
  J. W., 136, 141, 330, 331, 335
  James, 254
  Katie B., 214
  Milton, 244
  Robert, 247
  Thomas, 213, 263
  W. L., 215
  W. T., 354
Copland, ———, 303
Coplin, James A., 246
Coppersmith, Henry, 253
Copps, J. P., 253
Corbally, T. P., 103
Corbett
  W. D., 251
  W. D. (Mrs.), 251
Corbin, John H., 254
Corcoran, Michael, 399
Cordano, Antonio, 214
Cordes, ——— (Mrs.), 253

Corey
  Joseph, 239
  S. H. (Mrs.), 239
  W. H., 213
Corinthia (Sister), 246
Corisse, Pierre, 254
Corkern
  J. B., 243, 263
  J. B. (Mrs.), 243
  J. F. (Mrs.), 263
Cornatzar, George M. Jr., 239
Corndy, Amelius, 264
Cornelia (Sister), 375
Cornelius
  George, 214
  Philip, 253
Cornellia, Eliza, 214
Corney, James, 246
Corona (Sister), 246
Correrrs
  Concetta, 254
  Concetta G., 254
Corrigan, Mike, 213, 434
Corry, Arthur, 253
Corson
  E. J., 135
  Ed, 407
  Edward E., 214
Cortney, ——— (Mrs.), 249
Corull, James, 254
Corwine, L. P. (Mrs.), 344
Cosenana, Maria, 253
Costello
  Austin, 250
  Miles, 254
Costen, ——— (Mrs.), 215
Costillo, Michael, 215
Costley, T. W., 254
Cottam, R. A., 253
Cotter
  J. B., 404
  William, 403
Cotton, Austin, 214
Cottrell, John, 247
Couch
  H. H. (Mrs.), 214
  James M., 250
  John, 250
Cough, Jack (Mrs.), 251
Coughler, Gus, 247
Coughlin
  James, 254
  Richard, 253
Coulan, James, 254
Couneis, ——— (Mrs.), 253
Countee, D., 214
Countess, Beckie, 213
Court, Atrica, 254
Courteney, T., 264
Courts
  Angie, 214
  Lucy, 214
Cousins, Mary E., 254
Covington
  J. F., 347
  N., 253

NAME INDEX 461

Cowan
  Henry, 245
  J. S. R., 240
  John, 240
  ____, 240
Cowart, W. W., 375
Cowenhovan, H. P., 338
Cowperthwaite, Henry, 254
Cowtwill, Henry, 214
Cox
  A., 214
  E. A. (Mrs.), 214
  George C., 243
  J. J., 263
  James, 250
  James B., 243
  James K., 254
  Joseph, 250
  L. W., 337
  Lelia, 264
  Mitchell, 243
  Sarah, 214
  Susan, 243
  Teresa A., 254
  Thomas, 403
  Thornton, 214
  W. O., 359
  William, 213, 214
  ____ (Mrs.), 214, 246
Coyle
  Mary (Mrs.), 213
  P. J., 213
Coyne
  M. P., 400
  Thomas, 254
  Thomas P., 404
Crabb
  Joe, 434
  John, 433
  John G., 214
  Joseph, 416, 417
  ____, 417, 434
Crabe, Perrie, 254
Craffey, ____ (Mrs.), 375
Craft
  Charles, 253
  John Young, 251
  M. S., 27
Craig
  James A., 263
  R. G., 438
  Sam, 212
Cramer
  E. M., 263
  Martin, 263
  ____, 250
Crammond [Cramond]
  Henry A., 254
  J. E., 253
  J. Emily, 254
Crance, J. W., 344
Crandall [Crandell]
  Delia (Mrs.), 239
  H. E., 190, 416, 433

Crane
  Charles, 213
  Sue V., 347
Craren, Margareth, 254
Crawford
  Cynthia, 214
  E. G., 353
  J. A., 253
  James, 430
  Margaret, 242
  N., 266
  R., 373
  Sallie, 213
  Stephen, 213
  W. M., 240
Crawfore, W. M., 240
Crawley, John B., 399
Crayton, Emma, 242
Creager, C. W., 249
Crecey, Julia, 243
Credon, ____ (Mrs.), 243
Creelambon, L., 254
Crefiril, J., 213
Creighton, Samuel Cook, 215
Creophor, E. T., 263
Crews, George, 254
Cribbins, Joseph, 254
Cricks, Kitty, 213
Crimmens, D., 403
Cringer, Frank, 263
Crisbon, Eliza, 213
Crisman, Randolph, 214
Crittenden, J. A. (Mrs.), 213
Crocker
  Fritz, 213
  ____ (Mrs.), 213
Crockett
  Sam., 245, 247, 249
  ____, 247
Crogan, D., 213
Croghan, David, 251
Crohn, Hattie, 212
Croix, Dela, 253
Croll, Anna M., 254
Cromwell
  George, 247
  John, 247
  N. (Mrs.), 375
  Oliver, 161
  W. A. (Mrs.), 381
  ____ (Mrs.), 214
Cronin [Cronan]
  John, 213, 263
  Maurice, 403
  Patrick, 112
  ____, 263
Crook, George W. L., 213, 411
Cropper, Ernest T., 264
Crops, James M., 246
Crosby
  John H., 250
  Mahala, 213
  Willie J., 250

Cross
  Jacob, 215
  Maliso, 242
Crossette, C. C., 213
Croto, A., 213
Crouch, Mary, 214
Croupra, Norman, 214
Crow, Josie, 250
Crowder
  George, 215
  Nancy, 214
  R. D., 248
  ____ (Miss), 213
  ____ (Mrs.), 213
  ____, 213, 379
Crowell
  H. M., 416, 417, 433
  H. M. (Mrs.), 433
  Henry H., 214
  William, 344
  ____ (Mrs.), 417
  ____, 214, 379, 417, 433
Crowin, Tom, 213
Crowley
  John, 248
  M. H., 402
  Michael, 399
Crowson
  Amanda (Mrs.), 250
  W. E., 250
Croze, Camille de Bres, 254
Cruchen, Stephen, 214
Cruchent
  A. (Mrs.), 253
  Jose, 253
Cruchfield, J. H., 240
Cruikshank, James, 213, 416, 433
Crump
  B. S., 245
  David, 244
  E. H., 245
  William, 245
Crumpeci E., 215
Cruse
  John, 214
  S. P., 213
Crutchen, Rubina, 213
Crutcher
  Charles, 429
  ____ (Pvt.), 113, 429
Cuff, M. J., 374
Cuffey, D. E., 214
Cuilte, Emile, 254
Cullen
  Alice A., 253
  John, 242
  John M., 253
  Mary Ann, 253
  Thomas, 215
  ____, 171
Culligan, Julia, 240
Cullivan
  John, 249
  Walter, 249

Cully [Culley]
  D. A., 243
  M. A. (Mrs.), 243
  R., 214
  R. R., 266
Cummings
  J. J., 213
  Maggie, 213
  Mary (Mrs.), 213
Cummins
  Alex, 213
  James F., 432
  John, 213
  William H., 416
  Yansey, 213
Cundiff
  James B., 253
  Virg. T., 254
Cunepo, Mary (Mrs.), 212
Cunesse, John, 213
Cuney, James, 213
Cunfe, Fran., 254
Cunningham
  Anna (Mrs.), 241
  B. J., 356
  H. (Mrs.), 238
  Hugh, 403
  James, 238, 243
  Lavina, 213
  M. J., 212, 431
  Richard, 214
  Susan, 180
  William, 253
  ____, 214
Curat, Celia, 213
Curia, Dominico, 253
Curien, Armauld, 254
Curlin, Amos, 240
Curran [Curren]
  J., 375
  J. (Mrs.), 375
  James, 404
  Julia, 243
  M. J., 403
  Patrick J., 401
  ____, 251
Curry [Currie]
  A. A., 248
  C. W., 239
  Daniel, 213
  Harry, 373
  Sarah, 263
  Terrence, 253
  Trevanion, 263
Curtis
  C., 244, 266
  C. T., 438
  James, 253
  Jolive, 265
  Lucy, 214
  O. L. (Mrs.), 375
  Truman, 254
Cushing, G. B., 348
Cushman
  C. B. (Mrs.), 245
  M. (Mrs.), 245

W. A., 245
W. R., 245
W. R. (Mrs.), 245
———, 245
Cusmani
C., 247
——— (Mrs.), 247
Custer, George Armstrong, 438
Cuthbert, E. B., 241
Cuthrell, William, 374
Cutrer
Rachael, 264
———, 249
Cutter
Ella J., 254
John, 213
Cutting
B. N., 213, 432, 433
B. N. (Mrs.), 417, 433
Baxter N., 416
Cyrmis, R. A. St., 254
Czapsky, Louis, 214
Czarwick, Anton, 254

D

Daborg, Raymond, 254
Dacy, C. James, 402
Daggen, William, 254
Dagire, ———, 216
Dahl, Charles, 255
Daigre
Delmar, 263
J. D., 263
Dake, J. P., 29
Dale
J. R., 368, 370
William, 251
———, 251
Daley [Daily, Dailey. Daly]
Ely, 372
Harriet, 264
John, 254, 264
John (Mrs.), 264
Lizzie, 264
Mary, 215, 255
Mary A., 254
Mary (Mrs.), 372
Michael, 254
P., 215
Patrick, 254
Patsey, 266
Thomas, 254, 255
———, 245
Dalley, Mary Gonzaga (Sister), 243
Dallman, John, 215
Dalston
Charles, 215
Frank, 215
Dalton
Ambrose G., 216
Elizabeth, 215
H., 415
H. G., 215
J. M., 243, 332, 437

M., 215
Maggie (Mrs.), 215
York, 215
Daltroof, Louis, 143, 172, 185, 295, 376, 416, 418
Dalzell
W. T., 369
——— (Rev. Dr.), 122, 164, 180, 181
Dambelli, John, 255
Damerean, P., 265
D'Amico, Victor, 255
Damilo, L. S., 254
Damstadter
J., 216
J. (Mrs.), 216
Dana, Caleb R., 255
Dance
Belle, 216
———, 216
Dandous, Mary, 254
Dangerfield, Garnett J., 263
Danhauer, E., 255
Daniel
George, 216
Richard, 245
Richard (Mrs.), 245
Daniels
Elvira, 215
H. C., 407
Joseph, 254
Mary, 254
T. O., 265
——— (Mrs.), 407
——— (Rev. Dr.), 121
——— (Rev. Mr.), 164
———, 407
Dannion, William, 395
Danorelle, John, 255
Dansoni, Maria, 254
Dantin, Eugene, 254
Dantoni, Maria, 254
Daoley, Jane (Mrs.), 255
Dapnes, Abraham, 264
Daray, Jeanne, 254
Darby
Jenny (Mrs.), 215
Willie, 107
Dardinnac, J. B. P., 242
Dare, Charles N., 408
Dargin, William, 255
Dargis
Joe, 216
———, 216
Dargle, Julia, 254
Darlin, Thomas A., 254
Darling, ———, 263
Dart
Ben (Mrs.), 245
Julius, 245
Darzie, Kate, 255
Dash, J. H., 358
Dashields, F. S., 374

Dashiell
Frank P., 216
Tate E. (Mrs.), 216
Dasiagne, A., 254
Dau, Charles, 215
Daubauer, George, 255
Daubitz, Paul, 254
Dauccy
Thomas, 216
Thomas C., 216
Daugherty [Daughtry]
Mary, 248
May, 248
P. C. (Mrs.), 247
William, 248
Dauphin, ———, 264
Dauterive, B. B., 254
Dautignan, M., 254
Dautrive, Marie J., 254
Davenport
C. F., 244
Darby, 215
Isham, 243
Pattie, 216
Sam, 254
Thomas F., 255
Daverede, Pierre, 254
Davergne, Octave, 263
Davey
Frank, 215
T. J., 215
Davidson
A., 255
Eva, 265
G. W., 354
J. P., 19
James, 247
John A., 243
——— (Mrs.), 247, 375, 379
Davies
E. M., 343
Mary, 255
R. G., 264
Davine, Mary Ann, 255
Davis
Annie, 242
B., 215
Ben, 245
Ben (Mrs.), 245
Byron, 215
C. C., 215, 354
C. E. (Mrs.), 373
C. (Mrs.), 374
Cally, 248
Carrie, 215
Charity, 215
Charles J., 216
Clarissa, 245
Clayton, 247
D., 242
Dolly, 215
E. A., 216
E. O., 215
Eliza, 249
Ella B., 215
Emma B., 216

F. B., 390, 429
F. S., 359, 438
Felicia, 254
Florence, 215
Frank, 242
G. H., 239
George, 215, 216
Griffin, 215
Gus, 251
H., 215
H. R., 251
H. W., 254
Henry, 429
Hugh R., 248
J. G., 368
James, 215
Jefferson Jr., 190, 216
Jerry, 255
John, 215, 254
John E., 403
Joseph, 255
Josephine, 215, 216
Judge, 245
Kate, 244
Kate (Mrs.), 372
L., 255
Lina A., 255
Lou, 215
Louis, 254
Lulu, 251
Margaret, 243
Maria, 216
Mary, 215
Mary F., 216
Mary F. (Mrs.), 216
Mary J., 255
Mary L., 215
Mary (Mrs.), 215
Minnie, 215
Mira (Mrs.), 249
Oliver, 254
Robert, 215
S. A., 255
S. B., 216
S. W., 216
Sam, 215
Sarah E. (Mrs.), 124
Thad, 216
Theresa, 255
W. C., 424
W. H., 351
W. J., 216
William, 215
——— (Mrs.), 265
———, 215, 249
Davison
E. B., 243
Robert, 250
———, 375
Davizan, Pierre, 255
Davy, Mary L., 215
Dawkens, George, 249
Dawson
Amelia (Mrs.), 215
Annie, 215, 216
Charles, 215
G. R., 368, 369

NAME INDEX 463

H. E., 254
J., 359
J. G., 215
James, 254
John, 170, 215
John (Mrs.), 170
Mary, 216, 372
P., 216
S. R., 117
___ (Dr.), 216
___, 170, 216
Day
  Charlie, 248
  J. S., 390
  John L., 372
  Joseph, 248
  Lillie, 343
  Owen, 216
  Thomas O., 255
  Willie, 248
Dayeson, Pierre, 254
Daymond, Emma, 244
De Chambrey, Dupuy, 294, 295
De Donoto, Ruf., 216
De Graffenreid [De Graffenried]
  E. F., 368
  ___ (Dr.), 168
De Grelman, Charles, 95
De Grey, James, 264
De Hulin, Gordon, 368
De La, Renos M., 254
De Saussure, P. G., 368
Dea, Michael, 215
Deadrick, ___, 379
Deal, John E., 254
Deally, William F., 401
Dean, D. L. (Mrs.), 249
Deano, George, 216
DeAragon, Dennie (Mrs.), 240
Debat, Paul W., 255
DeBlanc, Mary L., 254
DeBodlin, T., 254
Debrula, E. (Mrs.), 216
Decan, George R., 254
Decker
  Eddie, 265
  Henry, 215
  Katie, 255
  Mary, 216
  Theodore, 215
  ___ (Mrs.), 215
Dedelot, Marie, 254
Dedon, Annie, 255
Deering
  H. F. T., 254
  Lavinia, 255
Deety, W. H., 356
Deferes, Marie, 255
Defess, Marie, 254
Defestus, E. C., 255
Defoe, Daniel, 271
Defondellas, Clarina, 263
DeForest, James S., 254
Degan, Laurence, 254

Degat, John, 254
Degelman, Charles, 265
Deike, Albert, 372
Deinheart
  Adam (Mrs.), 248
  Eddie, 249
Deitrick, Ang., 254
Dejan, Gaston E., 254
Dejarnett
  Sallie, 247
  W. A., 381
  ___, 247
Deklyn, B., 427, 432
Delacroix, M. A. (Mrs.), 255
DeLancy, James, 254
Delaney
  John, 255
  Josephine, 242
  Michael, 242, 254
  W. J., 216
  William, 215, 266
  ___ (Mrs.), 215
Delarno, Angelo, 254
Delary, Aug., 254
DeLate, Edward, 254
Delay, J. H., 255
Delespine, ___, 288
Delgad, B. H., 254
Dell, Catherine B., 215
Della, Magdalena (Mrs.), 254
Deltoz, B., 254
Demans, F., 216
Demarchi
  Angelo, 244
  Frank, 246
  Fred, 246
  Louisa, 246
  Thomas, 243
Demerest, George, 255
Demmons, Thomas, 215
Dempsey
  Andy, 248
  Charles, 216
Demuth, Maggie L., 254
Demy [Demmey]
  Farber, 401
  Laura, 245
  ___ (Rev. Father), 402
Dencausse, F., 254
Denerling, G., 254
Deneur, J., 254
Denice, Mabel, 254
Denie, ___, 151
Denn, James, 254
Dennagro, S., 255
Dennett, A. W., 243
Dennis
  D. B., 347
  Harry William, 255
Dennison, W. L., 215
Dennuzio, Natale, 255
Denny, Michael, 254
Denoux
  Henri, 264

Owen, 264
Tanvier, 264
Denson, Thomas, 263
Dent
  Frank Jr., 244
  Giles, 216
DePasquali, Marie, 254
DePelchin, K. (Mrs.), 373
Depke
  Aug., 254
  Frederick H., 254
Depues, H., 264
Derges, May, 215
Dermody, James A., 254
Deroche, Rosa, 255
Derr, Henry W., 254
Derrick
  H. S., 247
  H. S. (Mrs.), 247
Dertel, Louise, 254
Dertilo, ___, 255
Desdunes, M'lde, 254
Desforges, Louis B., 254
Desham, H., 255
Deshane, H., 254
Despommiers, Auguste, 255
Despow, Marie, 254
Dessauer, Fannie, 215
D'Este, Helen, 351
Desuda, Marco, 254
Detham, Augustine, 255
Deveness, L. H. H., 255
Devere, Kate F., 254
Devereux, J. G., 419
Devine
  P. A., 401
  Thomas, 403
Devlin
  B. F., 216
  Charles, 242, 244
  Jack, 255
Devoe, T. W., 349
Devoto
  A., 215
  D., 215
  Davy, 215
Dewar, Norman, 215
Dewey, Ellen, 215
Dewing, W. T., 375
DeWolf [DeWulf]
  D. C., 404
  ___ (Miss), 249
Dexter, George, 244
Deyarman, C. S., 352
Deyleman, John, 254
D'Heremberg, A. (Mrs.), 254
Dias, Ed, 265
Dibble, C. P., 347
Dibetta, Philomena, 254
Dick, Albert, 215
Dickens, ___, 215
Dickerson
  Dennis, 215
  H. N., 216
  Isaac, 215

J. W., 215
P. M., 117, 215
W. P., 216
Dicket, Philip, 255
Dickey
  Dabney, 249
  George, 216, 249
  Mattie, 249
Dickinson [Dickenson]
  B., 429
  J. W., 373
  Phil., 429
Dicks, Eva, 254
Dickson
  E. D., 324
  George, 246
  L. V., 266
  Sallie, 244
  W. H., 374
  William, 425
  ___ (Mrs.), 216
  ___, 303
Dieck, Albert, 369
Diedrich, Aleves, 254
Dielman, M., 255
Diermann
  Barb., 254
  John, 254
  Val., 255
Dies, Lizzie (Mrs.), 216
Dietrich, Barbara, 254
Dietrick
  E. B. G., 254
  W. A. L., 254
Dietz
  Joseph, 255
  Oswald (Mrs.), 239
  Rosanna, 255
Diggins, George, 216
Diggs
  Bennie, 247
  Fanny, 247
  Robert, 242
Dilaruza, Rosa, 254
Dilkenkopier, W., 254
Dillard
  Jim, 215
  Mike, 215
Dille, James, 264
Diller, ___, 245
Dillman, Della (Mrs.), 254
Dillon, Melanie, 255
Dineen [Dinneen]
  B. 400
  James, 403
Dink
  George, 216
  Reverdy, 216
Dionias, Marie, 255
Dionne
  Louis, 265
  Theresa, 265
Dipnes, Abraham, 264
Dirosy, William, 395
Disbia, Oscar M., 254

464   A HISTORY OF THE YELLOW FEVER

Disheroon
  Alice, 248
  William, 248
Dismukes, E. (Mrs.), 374
Dissac, Eugene, 255
Dittmer, H., 375
Ditton, James A., 254
Ditz, Constance, 255
Divestin, M. M., 255
Divincenzo, Antonio, 254
Divine, Bettie, 247
Dix,   (Miss), 325
Dixel, George, 254
Dixie, Mollie, 242
Dixon
  Irwin, 243
  James, 238, 408
  John, 262, 338
  L. V., 92, 238
  Lizzie, 242
  Lu, 374
  Lucas (Mrs.), 264
  Mary, 254
D'Mega, Hen. Estelle, 255
Doak
  B. M., 248
  Johnnie, 247
  Lulu, 247
  ____ (Mrs.), 247
Doane
  A. C., 254
  Albert C., 254
  ____ (Bishop), 191
Doaul, Owen E., 254, 255
Dobbins, A. M. C., 240
Dobbs, Mary, 254
Dobler, C. E., 242
Dodd, A. F., 216
Dodds, Robert, 251
Dodge, Elliot, 246
Dodson
  James, 215
  Lou., 216
  ____, 216
Doereicht, A., 215
Doerr, Lewis, 255
Doherty [Dohertey]
  C. C., 254
  Mark, 401
  Mary C., 215
  Thomas L., 216
Dohery, C., 216
Dohler, Richard M., 244
Dohoney, Michael, 254
Doiron
  A. F., 263
  Elise, 263
Doison
  Annatone, 263
  Elise (Mrs.), 263
Dolan
  Andy, 215
  Ellen, 215
  Frank, 254
  James, 216
  John N., 400
  Maggie, 216

Mike, 215
  Thomas Francis, 215
Dolara (Sister), 215
Dolhonde
  Annette (Mrs.), 374
  C. (Mrs.), 374
Doll, Joseph E., 244
Dolphin, Thomas J., 403
Domerque, J., 254
Domingo, F., 264
Dominic, ____, 216
Dominica (Sister), 150, 158
Dominique, J. (Mrs.), 254
Donagan, Mary, 254
Donahoe, Julia, 254
Donahoo, ____, 172
Donahue [Donaue,
  Donehue, Donohue]
  D., 246
  Ellen, 215
  J. B., 372
  John, 216
  Maggie, 215
  Michael, 254
Donaldson
  A., 348
  Caroline, 215
  Jim, 242
  Mioma K., 255
  Sam, 242
  Sarah, 215
  ____, 215
Doncys, Bernan (Mrs.), 254
Donehiff, F. A., 215
Donevant, George, 251
Donlan, Peter, 216
Donnell, George S., 373
Donnelly [Donneally,
  Donolly, Donnolly]
  Dennis, 215
  George L., 215
  Hattie (Mrs.), 373
  James, 254, 255
  Joanna, 255
  M., 430
  Mary E., 216
  Mary J., 254
  Mina, 215
  Pat, 255
  T. H. (Mrs.), 216
  Thomas, 216, 407
  Thomas H., 215
  ____, 407
Donois, William, 249
Donovan [Donnovan]
  John Jr., 215
  John (Mrs.), 149, 215
  ____ (Mrs.), 150
  ____, 150, 188
Doohan, John J., 400
Dooley
  M., 255
  Mike, 215
  Thomas, 341
Doran
  J., 264
  John, 254, 399

Mary (Mrs.), 372
Michael, 254
  ____, 241
Doravoid, Charley, 216
Dore
  ____ (Mrs.), 249
  ____, 249
Dorenberger, L., 254
Dorgs, Fred, 215
Dorman, George, 246
Dorms, Sim., 216
Dorsey
  Delia, 243
  Fannie, 215
  ____ (Mrs.), 375
Dorson, Robert, 254
Dorva, Jeremiah, 401
Dorwart, Florence Anna,
  243
Dotson, Mary, 216
Dotto, Antonio, 254
Doucet
  Alphonsine, 265
  Mathilda, 265
Doudle, Charles, 254
Doufforg, Alexandre, 254
Dougherty
  J. R. (Mrs.), 245
  Mary E., 244
  N. J., 401
Doughty
  C. F., 254
  Charles, 255
Douglas [Douglass]
  B., 354
  John, 215
  Mattie, 216
  Mollie, 215
  N. E., 375
  Netta, 246
  Rosa, 215
  Sarah (Mrs.), 246
  W. A., 355
  W. E., 431
Doulan, John, 216
Douley, John, 255
Doune, Susan, 254
Dourin, Marie, 255
Doussau, Marie, 255
Dousse, Henry, 254
Dovel, D. E., 255
Dow
  Joseph, 348
  Lorenzo, 429
  Robert, 215
Dowdall, Sidney (Mrs.),
  264
Dowdy, F. H., 216
Dowell
  Frank T., 215
  Greenville, 368
  M. C. (Mrs.), 215
  ____, 13, 14, 15, 16,
    23, 24, 35, 77, 322
  ____ (Dr.), 32, 62, 63,
    72, 301
Dowie, Robert, 254

Dowler, Bennett, 14, 15,
  16, 23, 24, 32, 33,
  34, 35, 36, 42, 43,
  69, 88, 89, 201,
  269, 274, 288, 293,
  294, 295, 296, 297,
  298, 299, 318, 321
Dowling, William, 254
Downey
  E., 399
  Joseph, 216
Downeys, Jean, 254
Downing, A., 344
Downs
  Bettie, 251
  E. L., 245
  James, 215
  Rose, 242
  S. L., 248
  Wiley, 375
  ____ (Mrs.), 215
Doyle
  Agnes, 255
  Bridget, 244
  Emma L., 263
  F., 401
  George, 255
  James, 216
  James W., 254
  Margaret, 254
  Mary, 254, 255
  Nellie, 243
  Patrick, 400
  Thomas, 254
  W. J. P., 170
  William, 254
  ____ (Mrs.), 249
  ____, 249
Dozier, Thomas C., 251
Drach, Ed, 264
Drake
  Archie, 250
  Ethel, 239
  J. P., 325
  L. H., 375
  ____ (Dr.), 34, 311
Drayton, C. T., 430
Dreenerding, Phil., 254
Drehr
  Richard, 264
  ____ (Miss), 264
Drennan
  E. C., 241
  E. C. (Mrs.), 241
Dresler, Thomas, 246
Drew, T., 401
Drewry, James, 255
Dreyfus [Dryfus]
  Benjamin, 216
  Lee, 216
  Lehman, 249
  M., 215
  Samuel, 215, 216, 251
Drier, M., 254
Dries, Elizabeth, 216
Driser, Reinhardt, 215
Driver, V. (Mrs.), 216

NAME INDEX

Drop, N., 254
Drouett, C. M., 254
Druck, Henry, 254
Druillott, Joseph, 254
Drum, Mary I., 255
Drury
   Ellen M., 254
   M. (Mrs.), 374
   Mattie, 215
   W. C., 238
Drushell
   Minnie, 243
   Philip, 243, 244
Dryfus, *see Dreyfus*
Duba, J. S., 254
Dubofer, Charles, 254
Dubois, Michael, 254
Duboretti, John, 254
Dubret, Martha, 254
Dubroca
   Caroline, 263
   Corinne, 263
   Jules V., 263
Duc, John, 254
Duchin, Victor, 254
Duco, Armand, 255
Ducros, ____, 263
Duer
   Jacob, 254, 255
   Michael, 254
Duff, Maggie, 255
Duffel, Clarence F., 264
Duffey [Duffy]
   Alice, 216
   Andrew, 243
   Charles, 332, 437
   Dan, 215
   James, 183, 246, 254
   James V., 215
   John J., 391, 395
   M. E., 264
   Michael, 247
   Owen, 254, 255
   P. J., 216
   Simon B., 216
   Thomas, 399
   Willie, 254
Duffner
   Bernard, 243
   Ella, 242
   Hattie, 243
   Lena, 242, 243
Dufour
   J. B., 254
   Jean B., 255
Dufreshon, Lewis, 255
Dugan [Duggan]
   Albert, 244
   C. F., 242
   Daniel, 215
   G. M., 426
   Louisa, 215
   O. J., 215
   ____ (Lt.), 357
Dugas
   Alece, 264

J., 264
Jerome, 264
Joseph, 265
Luce, 264
Dugerre, Pierre, 254
Duhamel, Calixte, 265
Duke
   Eddie, 216
   Evelina, 264
   Nora, 354
   Thomas E., 403
Dukes
   Robert, 215
   W. C., 216
Dulsheimer, Stella B., 254
Dume, Paul, 216
Dumerges, John, 255
Dummermath
   [Dummermuth],
   John, 254, 255
Dunaki, Lewis, 215
Dunbar, Fay, 242
Duncan
   A. L. (Mrs.), 216
   Annie B., 215
   Blanton, 345
   C. E., 215
   John, 255
   R. T., 421
   Robert, 215
   Thomas F., 255
   William, 368
   ____ (Dr.), 395
   ____, 239
Dunkelberger, J. R., 338
Dunlap
   Amelia, 215
   Eugene, 241
   H., 215
   Howard, 215
   M. A., 263
   M. L., 339
   Sam, 215
   Sue, 241
   ____, 241
Dunn
   Anderson, 216
   Ed, 215
   James A., 401
   Louisa, 254
   Marian, 216
   Mary (Mrs.), 216
   W. S., 216
   ____ (Miss), 250
   ____, 245
Dunneway, Harriet, 215
Dunscomb, S. H., 344
Dupeyron, ____, 275
Dupont
   Gabriel, 254
   J. M., 254
Duprat, Aleck, 254
Dupre, Nenville, 265
Dupree
   Annie, 216
   Bristow, 372
Dupreux, Julia (Mrs.), 254

Duprey, Francois, 254
Duprez, ____ (Dr.), 251
Dupuls
   Louis, 254
   Marie, 254
Dupuy
   Blanche, 255
   Charles, 254
   P., 216
Dupwis, Melanie, 263
Duralde
   J. V. Jr., 263
   Joseph V., 263
   Joseph V. (Mrs.), 263
Durand, A., 255
Durby, Joseph, 254
Durfey, R. W., 246
Durgan, Thomas, 265
Durgin, Daniel, 254
Durke, Oscar, 216
Durring, Lavinia, 254
D'Urville, ____, 201
Durward, G. H., 254
Dusuan, Gustave, 254
Duthilth, A. (Mrs.), 254
Dutilh, August, 254
Dutrey, Marie, 254
Duty, Mary, 215
Duvall [Duval]
   Emma, 244, 246
   Joseph, 215
   Mahala, 248
   ____ (Mrs.), 248
Duzere, Jean N., 254
Dwenger, ____ (Rt. Rev.
   Bishop), 400
Dwight, C. W., 244
Dwyer
   J. W., 249
   James, 374
   Lizzie, 216
   Martin, 215
   Theresa [Teresa], 254, 255
   William, 254
Dyches, Bettie (Mrs.), 216
Dye, James, 245
Dyer
   Margaret B., 215
   Oliver, 243
Dyke
   John, 242
   Virginia, 242
   ____ (Mrs.), 216
Dzmiski, Charles, 216

E

Eagan [Eagen]
   Ann (Mrs.), 255
   Anthony J., 255
   James, 255
   Kate, 255
Early [Earley]
   Angeline, 216
   J. T., 216

John, 216
W. F., 216
Earse, John A., 255
Eartharn, E. J., 240
Easley [Easly]
   E. S., 216
   E. T., 117, 368, 389
   E. V., 248
   ____ (Dr.), 174
Eason, John P., 247, 266
Easterbrook, Frank, 395
Eastman
   John U., 240
   ____, 249
Easton, Thomas, 368
Eaton
   C. H., 422
   E. M., 342
   Joseph, 255
Eaves, Alfred, 255
Eberhard, Bertha, 420
Eberhardt [Ebberhardt]
   C. H., 372
   Ellen, 216
   M. M. (Mrs.), 255
Eberle
   George, 373
   V., 216
Eberts, R., 358
Ebler
   E., 216
   Virginia, 216
Ebner, ____ (Mrs.), 255
Eceffey, D., 216
Echard, Eliza, 251
Echert, Lou, 251
Eciner, Frank, 255
Eckels, W. Y., 348
Ecklott, Sylvanus
   (Brother), 255
Éclair, ____, 25
Eddy
   F., 353
   ____, 216
Edgar
   Irwin, 264
   Irwin (Mrs.), 264
   ____ (Miss), 264
   ____ (Mrs.), 263
   ____, 263
Edington
   Charley, 216
   Gus., 216
Edler
   Alfred, 255
   Louis, 255
Edmonds, Joe, 216
Edmondson [Edmonson]
   E. (Mrs.), 246
   Ellen, 240
   Henry B., 216
   Henry B. (Mrs.), 216
   J. C., 404
   J. H., 136, 142, 216, 329, 330, 331, 333, 335, 376, 377, 380
   Joanna H., 217

Rebecca, 255
———, 216
Edrington, W. H., 243
Edstrom
———(Mrs.), 246
———, 246
Edwards
  Albert, 242
  B. F., 241
  B. T., 245
  C. W., 216
  E. (Mrs.), 216
  F., 344
  Frank, 251
  Freeman, 243
  G. W., 243
  Ida, 251
  James W., 255
  John, 216, 407
  John (Mrs.), 407
  Matilda, 245
  Robert, 216
  T. B., 255
  Thomas, 243
  William, 216
  Willis, 245
  ———(Miss), 263
  ———(Mrs.), 216, 374
  ———, 194, 250, 407
Eels, Daniel P., 352
Eeveran, Benedict, 255
Effert, Jake, 265
Effinger
  Lucie, 255
  Marie, 255
Egan
  Joe, 373
  M. J., 216
  Nancy, 216
  Peter, 97
  Thomas, 216
  ———(Mrs.), 216
Egberts, David, 216
Eggers, William, 255
Eggleston
  John F., 244
  Robert E., 242
Ehler [Ehlers]
  William, 247
  ———(Mrs.), 247
  ———, 247
Ehrenberger, Amelia, 255
Eichberg [Eichburg]
  J., 357
  John L., 407
  John L. (Mrs.), 407
  ———, 407
Eiger, George, 255
Eilert, Lizzie, 216
Eisler, B. A., 216
Eisman
  D., 354
  L. D. Jr., 390
Elder
  A. M., 255
  Alfred, 255
  ———(Mrs.), 375

Eldridge
  Amos, 216
  ———(Lt.), 356
Eler, Elizabeth, 216
Elerman, Joseph, 255
Elernburg, George, 255
Elgere, Ed., 255
Elgire, Edward, 255
Eli, see Ely
Eliert
  Fannie, 216
  Louis, 216
Ell, E. D., 349
Ellert, Lizzie, 216
Ellington, J., 430
Elliott
  A., 32
  A. L., 355
  Annie E., 216
  G. W., 247
  G. W. (Mrs.), 247
  George, 244, 255
  George B., 216, 421
  John D., 216
  Joseph H., 216
  Thomas, 374
  William, 216
  ———(Mrs.), 216
Ellis
  A. K., 244
  J., 216
  Jennie, 216
  Richard, 216
  W. J., 242
Ellison
  Eli, 430
  Laura, 255
  Samuel, 433
Elms, James, 255
Elsenoolin, Nicholas, 255
Elsenson, N., 255
Elsinger, C., 255
Ely [Eli]
  E. G., 248
  Eliza (Mrs.), 248
  Michael, 399
  Nannie, 248
  Smith, 349, 350
Emanuel
  J. M., 375
  Mary, 255
Emerick
  Aleck, 248
  Dan., 248
  Lilly, 248
Emerlein, H. John, 255
Encus, Mary, 255
Endsley, Eddie, 216
Engels, Peter, 216
Engering, Frank, 251
England, W. B., 362
Engle
  Mary (Mrs.), 217
  Nat, 243
  ———, 246
Engleberta (Sister), 375
English, James, 243

Enley, John, 216
Enlow, Clarence, 242
Ennessy, William E., 402
Ennis
  Gus, 431
  John, 216
Enright, John M., 403
Enslen, Henry, 248
Entel, Mary, 242
Entress, Eella, 251
Entriken, Samuel, 255
Enwright, Patrick, 216
Epplett, Thomas, 216
Epps [Epp]
  Fred, 240
  E. A. (Mrs.), 240
  Henry, 245
  Scott, 245
  Tealey, 240
  William (Mrs.), 240
  Wyatt, 216
Erasmus (Brother), 216
Erb
  John, 216
  Philip, 216
Erby, W. E., 216
Erck, Chris, 216
Erdsmandorff, Maria, 255
Erick, Albert, 216
Erlich, A., 216
Erlicher, John, 255
Erlinger, Caroline, 255
Erne, Caroline, 255
Ernest
  G. W., 266
  G. W. (Mrs.), 266
  George M., 251
  George M. (Mrs.), 251
  George W., 424
  George W. (Mrs.), 424
  John Sr., 246
  ———(Mrs.), 240
Erskine
  Alice, 216
  George, 216, 239
  J. H., 216
  John, 96, 105, 163, 265
  John (Mrs.), 265
  John H., 117, 145, 146, 147, 159, 388
  Polexanie, 265
Erwin, William, 239
Escaaz, Jean E., 255
Escat, Alice, 255
Esch, Emma (Mrs.), 216
Eschelman
  Daniel, 247
  Henry, 247
Escobedo, John A., 255
Escoude, Josie, 255
Escudi
  Theophili, 255
  Vincent, 255
Esculapius, see
  Aesculapius
Escuref, John M., 255

Eskridge
  Fox, 248
  W. C., 248
  Walter, 248
  ———, 248, 379
Ess, H., 368
Estapa
  Alphonsine, 249
  Francis, 249
  Josephine, 249
Estebenet, F., 255
Esteberal, Francois, 255
Estes
  B. F., 372
  T. L., 239
Estivan, Marcelin, 265
Estrado
  John, 255
  Paulino, 255
  Raymond, 255
Etchevarne, G., 216
Ethridge
  John, 248
  Mark, 248
Etiena (Sister), 249
Etler, W. W., 356
Etta, ———, 240
Eubanks, Jennie, 255
Euchkins, Eliza, 216
Eudeffries, E., 255
Eugel, John, 255
Eugene, John, 263
Eupel, Barbara, 255
Eurich, Alice, 255
Eustace
  Joseph, 255
  M., 255
Evans
  Allen, 216
  B. F., 255
  C. P., 352
  Charles, 373
  Cora, 216
  Frederick J., 255
  J. T., 341
  L. R. (Mrs.), 248
  Lindsey R., 248
  M. A. R. (Mrs.), 244
  Melon, 216
  ———(Mrs.), 163, 250
  ———, 163, 250
Evarts, William, 425
Evenittz, J. E., 249
Everett
  George, 255
  J. E., 247
  W. E., 216, 250
  William, 135
  ———(Priv.), 130, 429
Everheart, Henry, 216
Evers
  Carrie, 250
  H. M., 255
  Mamie, 250
  W. H. (Mrs.), 250
  William H., 250
Every, Luciana, 255

NAME INDEX

Ewell, _____ (Dr.), 217
Ewing
  Emma, 255
  Frank, 216
  W. J., 239
  William, 247
Ewins, Lizzie, 216
Exememan, M., 263
Exom, Jeff, 216
Exterstein, Aug. W., 255
Eyke
  M. (Mrs.), 216
  Martin, 216, 407
  Martin (Mrs.), 407
Eyrich, Adolphe, 255

F

Faber, Philip, 255
Fabin, John W., 217, 373
Fable, Charles, 255
Fackler, John, 217
Fagans, Ike, 242
Faget, _____ (Dr.), 16
Fahey [Fahy]
  Edward, 217
  J. L., 255
  M. J., 402
Fahrner, Annie, 255
Failionzea, Joseph, 264
Faillomisca, Joe, 264
Fair, Ida Isabelle, 263
Fairbanks
  E., 347
  Ella, 263
Fairchild
  Ella, 249
  Harry B., 249
  William, 264
  William A., 243
  _____, 217
Faires
  J. B., 354
  W. A., 354
Fairie, Robert J. Jr., 263
Fairly, J. D., 248
Falche, Dominico, 255
Falcon
  Antoine, 264
  Hilaire, 264
  Louisa, 264
Falconer
  Howard, 245
  Kinloch, 245
  Thomas A., 245
Fall, William H., 58
Fallar [Faller]
  Hogan, 255
  John, 255
Falligant
  L. A., 29
  Louis A., 27, 316
Fallon
  John, 255
  M. (Mrs.), 373
Falls
  J. N., 355

Lizzie, 217
Rachel, 217
Faltz, F., 218
Falz, Theodore, 218
Fanestine (Sister), 265
Fannin, Francis, 217
Fanning, John A., 400
Fant
  Glenn, 245
  Selden, 245
Fareman, William, 374
Fargo, J. C., 339
Farina, Muncio, 255
Fariss, see Farris
Farmer
  Kate, 239
  Sallie, 239
Farquahar, A. B., 350
Farrar
  Howard, 263
  Willie, 217
Farrell
  Ellen, 218
  Mary, 217
  Michael, 112
  Mike, 218
  Nellie, 217
  Pat, 217
  _____ (Miss), 249
  _____, 107
Farrels, Hugh, 217
Farris [Fariss]
  E., 217
  Ed, 217
  J. B., 217
  J. W., 251
  Tom, 251
  W. H., 421
Farrow, Mollie, 217
Fate, Houston, 243
Faure
  Jean Paul, 255
  Joanna, 255
Fause, V., 217
Faust
  H. Ludwig, 255
  _____ (Mrs.), 248
  _____, 248
Favelora, Angelo, 255
Favrot
  Claude J., 263
  Sidney Joseph, 263
Faw, Nora, 339
Fay
  John, 217
  _____ (Mrs.), 217
Fazelli, Philippi, 255
Fazello, Rose, 255
Fazzi, L., 218
Fazzin, Elizabeth F., 255
Feahney, Kate, 255
Fealey, Sarah (Mrs.), 217
Fearson, Lula A., 255
Featherston
Featherstone [Featherston, Featherstun]
  Abbie, 245

George, 245
Laura, 245, 250
Laura W., 249
M. E. (Mrs.), 245
W. S., 217
W. S. (Mrs.), 245
W. S. Jr., 245
W. T., 266
W. W., 250
Wesley, 245
Willie, 245
_____ (Mrs.), 250
_____, 250
Fedelio, Vicenzo, 255
Feehan
  P. A., 402
  _____ (Bishop), 400, 402, 403
  _____ (Rev. Father), 404
Feelan, William J., 244
Feeney, M. A., 375
Feesser, Charles, 218
Fegilno, Joseph, 242
Feguata, Joseph, 255
Feibleman, Joseph, 243, 263
Feild
  Harry, 247
  Mattie, 247
  Thomas, 247
  _____ (Mrs.), 247
Feithen, _____ (Mrs.), 249
Feldman, Dedrick, 246
Feldstadt, John, 238, 249
Felin, Lizette, 255
Felkins, Eliza, 217
Fell, Harry F., 263
Fellows, _____, 303
Felsenthal, H., 419
Felt, Burney, 262
Felterman, _____ (Mrs.), 264
Felton
  Fort, 217
  J., 430
Femoreau, Vallery, 263
Fends, Ann (Mrs.), 242
Fenero, Andrew, 255
Fennell
  F. M., 245
  J. W., 245
  John, 245
  Sallie, 250
  William, 399
Fenner
  Fred, 247
  _____ (Dr.), 28, 35
Fenney, Denny, 255
Fenny, Michael, 112
Feno, _____ (Dr.), 244
Fensburgh, Charles, 341
Fensley, Susie, 217
Fenwick
  Alice A., 217
  Effie L., 217
  J., 406

J. (Mrs.), 406
L. D. (Mrs.), 217
S. F. (Mrs.), 217
Z. M., 217
_____, 406
Ferana, D., 255
Ferguson
  A., 255
  C. W. (Mrs.), 107
  D., 358
  E. G., 255
  Eliza, 255
  Ellen G., 255
  Harry, 429
  Harry W., 217
  J. F., 242
  Laura, 245
  Mary L., 255
  _____ (Cpl.), 130
Ferina
  Joseph, 255
  Peter, 255
Fernandez
  A., 255
  Anna M., 255
  Margaret, 255
Fernon, John, 255
Ferran, Salvino, 255
Ferrand
  Cozamar, 255
  J. J., 255
Ferrar, Macali, 255
Ferrell, William, 242
Ferrer, Catellina, 255
Ferrett, M. E., 217
Ferrette, Roza, 255
Ferrier, Gabrille, 255
Ferrin, A., 217
Ferring, James, 255
Ferris [Ferriss]
  A. M. (Mrs.), 255
  Eliza N., 361
  _____ (Dr.), 245
  _____ (Mrs. D.), 245
  _____, 245
Ferry
  Douglas, 245
  Joseph, 255
  R. H., 250
  _____ (Mrs. Dr.), 245
  _____, 250
Feta, Valmon, 265
Feuster, Simon, 217
Ficklin, Laura Young, 218
Fiedmann, William, 255
Field
  Clara, 255
  Cora, 217
  Mary (Mrs.), 217
Fieldman, Mary, 217
Fields
  C. H., 374
  Charles, 263
  Dick, 217
  Dora, 217
  Harry, 217
  Henry, 217

Ida, 217
Lizzie, 374
Robert, 217, 374
Sam, 242
____ (Mrs.), 379
____, 217
Fife
　Butler, 248
　Eliza, 248
　William, 248
　____, 248
Fifer
　John S., 433
　William S., 217
Figgerd, Joseph, 217
Filche, ____ (Miss), 347
Filkins, Leonora M., 338
Finacy, M., 218
Finch
　J. W., 266
　J. W. (Mrs.), 245
　John W., 250
Finder, William F., 239
Fine, Henry E., 255
Fink
　Eliza, 359
　Gustave, 217
　____ (Rt. Rev. Bishop), 401
Finley [Finlay]
　Ennis, 217
　Helen, 247
　Robert, 430
　S. L., 355, 422
Finn, Lucy, 218
Finnan, Kate, 217
Finnegan
　C. A., 255
　Michael, 400
　Pat, 246
Finney [Finnie]
　Mike, 217
　W., 218
　W. A., 141
　William, 330, 331, 333, 335, 408
Finnick, Kate, 343
Finster, Jacob, 217
Firth
　Ella, 217
　R. M., 408
　R. N., 217
　Robert F., 217
　W. S., 217
　____, 408
Fishback
　Calvin, 242
　Josephine, 243
Fishel, Lewis (Mrs.), 255
Fisher [Fischer]
　Antonio, 255
　Baville, 217
　C. (Mrs.), 217
　C. G., 185, 390
　Charles, 251
　Charles G., 129, 168, 217, 390, 391

Daniel, 255
Dave, 218
Elizabeth, 255
Frank C., 242
J. F., 217
Jonathan, 251
Joseph W., 426
L., 244, 255
Lena, 249
Louis, 255
Louisa P. G., 255
Martha, 264
Patrick, 217
R., 218
Wesley, 217
____ (Dr.), 168
Fison, Nick, 218
Fitch
　A. B. (Mrs.), 361
　____, 22, 217
Fitchette
　J. V., 246
　____, 246
Fithian, H. E., 217
Fitte, Louisa, 255
Fitz, William, 255
Fitze, Joseph R., 255
Fitzenreiter, ____, 264
Fitzgerald
　A. J., 255
　Clifton, 243
　Eugene, 255
　G., 255
　Jennie (Mrs.), 249
　Jennie N. (Mrs.), 243
　Katie, 255
　P. F., 248
　William J., 399
Fitzgibbon [Fitzgibbons]
　Andrew, 255
　E. (Mrs.), 255
　John, 218
Fitzmaurice, Walter, 402
Fitznuarance, Michael, 255
Fitzpatrick
　Annie E., 244
　Camelia, 255
　J. C., 242
　Joseph, 251
　Jule, 255
　Kate, 255
　Mary, 255
　Mary A., 242
　Mary Eliza, 218
　Thomas, 242
　Willim, 255
Fitzsimmons, Henry B., 399
Fix
　Mina, 255
　Minor, 255
Flack
　Annie M., 255
　B. (Mrs.), 217
　Barbara (Mrs.), 161
　Clara, 161, 217
　George F., 255

Jennie, 161, 217
L. B., 217
Laura, 161, 217
Louisa, 161
T. J., 217
Tom, 161
W. J., 217
Willie, 161
____, 187
Flaget, ____, 15
Flaherty
　E., 340
　G., 217
　James, 238, 249
　P., 403
　____ (Miss), 238, 249
Flake, Catherine, 255
Flannagan [Flanagan, Flannaghan, Flannegan, Flannigan]
　E. M., 375
　Ed, 217
　James, 403
　John, 255
　Joseph, 255
　Katie, 217
　M., 217
　T. (Bro. C.), 255
Flannery
　Dennis, 240
　Dennis (Mrs.), 240
　Mary, 240
　Mike, 217
Flavin
　Garrett, 401
　H., 400
Fleischer
　A., 247
　Adolphe, 247
　____ (Mrs.), 246
Fleming [Flemming]
　Daniel, 430
　J., 218, 401
　Pat. (Mrs.), 239
　W. S., 242
　Will., 217
　William, 255
Fletcher
　Henry, 255
　Mary, 217
Flewellen
　J. H. (Mrs.), 246
　Jane, 246
　Sarah, 246
　Zella, 246
Fliggin, Harvey, 217
Flinch, Joseph, 255
Flint
　Austin Jr., 50
　____, 303
Flippin
　J. R., 356
　John R., 147, 390
　Sam, 248
　Samuel, 248

____ (Mrs.), 248
____, 248
Florentine, D., 255
Flori, Stephano, 255
Florimon, Frank, 255
Florrinon, Francois, 255
Flourade, Florence, 255
Floureade, Catherine, 255
Flowerree, Conway, 243
Flowers
　A. E., 248
　Albert A., 244
　E., 250
　Frederick L., 243
　Jeff, 217
Floyd
　Annie, 243, 263
　R. W., 351
　W. S., 409
Fly, J. H., 246
Flynn
　Annie E., 255
　Ben, 217
　D. P., 217
　Eliza, 217
　Frederick W., 217
　James, 255
　Jessie Louisa, 264
　John R., 372
　Joseph M., 402
　Kate E., 255
　M. E. (Mrs.), 264
　Margaret, 255
　Mary Elizabeth, 264
　Meta, 251
　Robert Emmet, 217
　____, 194, 217
Foerster, Fred, 255
Foester, Paul, 255
Fogarty
　N. J., 368
　Simon, 399
　____ (Dr.), 395
Foisher, Louisa, 255
Fold, Henry, 255
Foley
　Annie, 217
　B. F., 249
　Bate., 217
　D. J., 399
　Edmund J., 255
　Edward, 217
　John, 255
　Margaret J., 242
　Martin, 402
　Mary, 217
　Pat, 240
　Thomas, 217
　William, 255
Folger, Joe, 217
Folk, Amanda, 217
Folks, Julia, 217, 218
Follett, N. C., 343
Folse, Joe, 264
Foltz
　M. A., 354
　S., 406

NAME INDEX

Folz, Sam, 244
Fonlien, G. G., 263
Fontaine, Bennie, 262
Fonvergue [Fonvirgue]
   R., 255
   Raoul, 255
Foote, M. H., 359
Forbes
   Charles, 238
   J. G., 117, 368, 369
   James A., 217
   John, 141
   John C., 148, 217
   ____ (Col.), 288
Forbish, E. E., 373
Force
   F. H., 117, 218
   H. F., 368, 369
Ford
   Alice, 255
   Annie E. (Mrs.), 255
   B., 419
   E. C., 240
   Elizabeth, 217
   Emily (Mrs.), 372
   Hannah, 255
   Harriet, 217
   J., 372
   J. B., 238
   James, 401
   John, 255
   John B., 249
   Laura, 244
   Mary (Mrs.), 373
   Michael, 255
   Pat., 381
   Willie Lee, 217
   ____ (Dr.), 21, 249
   ____, 246, 249
Foreman
   John (Mrs.), 245
   William, 217
Forest [Forrest]
   Annie, 255
   C. G. (Mrs.), 217
   Celestine, 265
   Cyprien, 265
   Felicien, 265
   John J., 255
Forgey, John W., 239
Foriassil, Marie, 255
Formaris, Eugene, 255
Forney, ____, 217
Forrester
   Gus, 247
   Tom, 217
Forrestine
   Sarah A. (Mrs.), 372
   Sarah (Mrs.), 372
Forsythe, J. P., 341
Fort
   James, 245
   L., 243
   Lucy, 245
   Mary C., 255
   Mary E., 218

R. B., 117, 251
R. W., 245
Forter, Arthur B., 255
Fortes, C. H., 265
Fortoricia, A., 255
Fortune, B. W., 251
Foster
   A. J., 348
   Alice, 248
   Annie, 217
   C. W., 374
   Charles, 217, 255
   Clara, 217
   E. B., 136, 217, 330, 331
   E. D., 377
   Edgar, 255
   Edward B., 332
   Edwin B., 141, 334, 335
   Ida, 217
   Mary, 249
   R. B., 344
   Robert J., 400
   Susie, 249
   T., 255
   T. J., 217
   Tipp, 255
   W. H., 352
   William, 217
   Zella E., 255
   ____ (Miss), 347
Foucou, Oval, 255
Fourcade, Catherine, 255
Fourney, Louis, 255
Fourot, A. Frances, 255
Fousse, Carrie, 242
Fowler
   D. F. (Mrs.), 217
   E. (Mrs.), 427
   Fred, 429
   G., 242
   J. J., 427, 402
   J. J. (Mrs.), 217, 432
   Jerry, 217
Fox
   A., 339
   Alf., 217
   H., 419
   James J., 244
   John, 372
   Joseph J. (Mrs.), 249
   Josephine, 246
   L. Cameron, 245
   L. (Mrs.), 250
   Philip, 244
   Thomas, 255
   Tom, 218
   ____, 218
Foy, E. A., 218
Foys
   ____ (Mrs.), 372
   ____, 372
Fraime, P. P., 135, 136
Frainor, Thomas, 242
France, Henry L., 217

Frances (Sister), 122, 124, 170, 188, 217
Franchman, A., 240
Francis
   Amelia, 242
   E. S., 217
   Eddie, 255
   G. (Mrs.), 255
   J., 255
   John W., 299
   Marie, 255
   ____ (Dr.), 288
   ____, 217
Francisco, John H., 255
Franco, Nicols, 255
Frank [Franck]
   A., 255
   C. B., 347
   David, 263
   Eddie, 242
   Frank, 112, 217
   George, 255
   H. L., 419
   James, 217
   Matthew, 242
   Max, 419
   Rosa, 244
   Sol., 217
   Sophia, 263
   ____ (Miss), 217
Frankland, A. E., 136, 438
Franklin
   Ben, 217
   Frank, 217
   Hattie, 217
   Mary, 217
   Miles, 217
   Stephen, 249
   William, 399
Fransciola
   Felix, 438
   Sam, 431
Fransiola, Frank, 217
Franz, Anna, 255
Franze, Ida, 255
Frary, Peter, 217
Fraser, Henry, 240
Fraviga, Lizzie, 217
Frazee, Kate, 217
Frazier [Frayser]
   R. D., 238
   Rudolph, 217
   Ruth, 217
   William, 263
   ____, 238
Freank, J. C., 248
Frederick [Frederic]
   Barbara, 249
   Bernedina, 249
   Charles, 255
   E., 217, 421
   Frank, 255
Frederico, Guiseppe, 255
Freek, John, 255
Freeland, William, 395
Freeman
   H. W., 246

Henry, 217
J. J., 438
John, 240
Lizzie B., 244
   ____, 250
Freenor, Charles, 255
Frege, Emile, 255
Frei
   ____ (Mrs.), 419
   ____, 419
Freitag, Fred, 255
Frelling, Henry, 255
Fremont, Vallery, 263
French
   Bennie, 264
   Fannie V. (Mrs.), 244
   George C., 246
   Hiram, 243
   L. (Mrs.), 247
   Martha, 217
   Robert, 242
   S. Bassett, 425
   W. J., 247
   ____, 247
Frendenthal, Albert, 255
Frenderberg, George, 255
Freney, Lillian, 255
Frennara, Ignazio, 255
Frentil, John, 249
Frenz, W. J., 251
Freret, Armand, 255
Fretby, Michael, 218
Freted, Nicolena, 255
Freundt, Henry, 247
Frey
   A. C., 427
   E. S., 342
Frice, Sophia, 255
Frichette, Jane, 255
Fricke
   George, 217
   Philip G., 217
Friedlob, J., 420
Friedman
   Henry, 217
   Josephine, 217
   Louis, 217
   Lulu, 217
   M., 248
   ____ (Mrs.), 217
   ____, 217
Friend
   E., 420
   Victor, 255
Frierson
   Frank, 376
   L. S., 335
   Lewis [Louis] S., 141, 331, 335
   Louis, 174, 330
Frinster, Caroline, 217
Fritsche, Robert, 255
Fritz
   Emile, 255
   Henry, 217
   John, 217, 406
   John (Mrs.), 406

John D., 255
Lucy E., 217
———, 406
Frizzell, John, 409
Froescher, John G., 263
Froese
  Mary (Mrs.), 217
  R., 217
Frogg, Peter, 264
Froman, William, 218
Fry, Violet, 255
Fuchs
  John, 255
  S. (Mrs.), 217
  Victor D., 217
Fucich, Joseph A., 264
Fuero, Laciano, 255
Fulford, Anna, 265
Fulger, Joseph, 264
Fuller
  B. F., 217, 432
  Benjamin F., 416
Fullerton
  Catherine (Mrs.), 217
  Ed, 217
  Eddie, 217
  H. R., 353
  Mollie, 217
  P. R., 353
Fulner, Auton, 255
Fulsom, Charles, 217
Fulton
  A. M., 255
  D. M., 246
  D. M. (Mrs.), 246
  David, 246
  ———, 246
Fultz, Thomas, 244
Funk [Funck, Funke]
  Doretta, 263
  F., 255
  Fred, 251
  George, 255
  R., 217
Furbish, E. E., 171, 217
Furguson, Louise, 255
Furlong, James, 399
Furstenheim
  H., 390
  Henry, 390
Fust
  Kate (Mrs.), 255
  Mary, 255
Fuzer, A. J., 348

G

Gabbert, C. W., 342
Gabers, B., 218
Gabert, George, 263
Gable
  Bo., 218
  Sophy, 219
Gabler, Elizabeth, 219
Gadd, James, 256
Gaddis
  Thomas, 249
  ——— (Dr.), 247
Gadol, Jean Emile, 256
Gage
  Ben, 248
  H. M., 410, 411, 412, 421
  Marie, 256
  ——— William, 168
  ——— (Dr.), 248
  ———, 248
Gailey, Jane, 263
Gaillard
  J., 374
  ——— (Dr.), 19, 302
Gaillardanno, Alice, 256
Gaillardia, Angelina, 256
Gaillardo, Gaetano, 256
Gain, Eugene, 219
Gaines
  Charles, 373
  ——— (Mrs.), 218
Gaire, Alexandre, 264
Gaitley
  ——— (Mrs.), 245
  ———, 245
Galbreath
  J. J., 355
  W. B., 390
Gale, ———, 263
Galen, 14, 28, 185
Galigman, Mary, 256
Gallagher
  C., 256
  Daniel, 402
  Ed., 255
  Frank, 247
  J. F., 399, 404
  J. P., 135, 256
  John, 263
  Katie, 242
  Morris, 255
  N. A., 399
  P., 256
  Patrick, 402
  Thomas J., 256
Gallaher, James, 219
Gallata, Vincent, 264
Galle, Josephine, 256
Gallenher, N. G., 251
Galley
  Auguste, 218
  Robert, 218
Galling, John (Mrs.), 219
Galloway [Gallaway]
  M. E., 219
  Mary A., 219
  William, 256
Gally, Mary, 256
Galvin, John (Mrs.), 239
Gamble, Frank, 266
Gamgee, ———, 98
Gammel, John, 262
Gammon, Thomas, 256
Gamotis, A., 256
Ganbert, Lem, 265
Gane, Frank, 218
Gannall, B. R., 255
Gannaway, Sue B., 355
Gannon
  Frank, 256
  George, 243
  Stephen [Steven], 256
  William, 243
Gant
  E., 244
  Joseph, 218
Ganter, Frank, 245
Gantreaux, Orvile, 265
Garagnon, Henry, 218
Garaufio, Paulini L., 256
Garbini, G., 256
Garces, Joseph, 256
Garcia
  Anna, 256
  Julia, 256
Garcissi
  Anna, 256
  Joe, 256
  Joseph, 256
Garden, Robert, 218
Gardere, Jennie, 256
Gardner
  C. (Mrs.), 251
  H. C., 218
  H. E., 218
  J. P., 256
  John, 359
  K., 256
  Meta, 251
  R. B., 349
  S., 339
  W. H., 251
  William F., 255
Gardon, Matilda, 256
Gardy, Eliza., 256
Gareissi, Anna, 256
Garesche, Eugene, 219
Garey, see Gary
Garig, William, 263
Garland
  Charles, 218
  Joseph, 218
Garner
  Abb, 247
  Fred, 218
Garney, Henry, 218
Garnon, Fred, 219
Garrera, Antonio, 256
Garrett
  C., 219
  John, 218
  Kenneth Jr., 266
  S. D. (Mrs.), 246
Garris, ——— (Mrs.), 374
Garrison
  Bruce (Mrs.), 395
  Frank, 218
  William, 219
Garrity [Garritty]
  Daniel P., 256
  John, 400
  Mary E., 256
Garrott, M. A., 348
Gartine
  N. U., 246
  ——— (Mrs.), 246
Garvey
  Bridget, 218
  Mary E., 218
Garvin
  J. P., 339
  Joe G., 240
  Mary (Mrs.), 373
  Mike, 219
  R. W., 240
  Sarah, 219
Gary [Garey]
  Bridget, 256
  John, 218, 246
  John W., 218
  ———, 246
Gas, Jennie D., 256
Gascisi, Maria, 256
Gascoigne, William, 342
Gass, Gertrude, 263
Gast, John, 256
Gaston
  C. A., 427, 432
  Charles A., 427
  Jim, 429
  John, 355
  Paul, 256
Gateman, A., 256
Gates
  Aaron, 218
  Frank, 218
  J. E., 425
  Moses, 218
  Ripley, 218
  S. M., 390
  S. M. (Mrs.), 218
  Sam (Mrs.), 218
  Victoria, 218
Gath, James B., 219
Gatlin
  G. W., 218
  Johnson, 218
  ——— (Mrs.), 218
Gatte, Carman, 255
Gatts, John, 256
Gatzen, Eliza, 219
Gauche, Viola, 255
Gaudrey, Vincent E., 374
Gauman, John M., 256
Gauthreaux
  G. (Mrs.), 264
  George, 264
  Leonce, 264
Gauze, Frank, 218
Gaviane, G., 256
Gavlina, Antonie, 255
Gawray, H. M., 218
Gay
  Charles, 256
  Edward J., 256
  Iola, 219
  J. W., 430
  Lucius, 218
Gaylord, G. G., 372

NAME INDEX

Gazara, Pasq., 256
Gealar
  Peter, 245
  ____, 245
Geale, John, 256
Gear, Docia [Dosea], 219, 240
Gearday, Bazil (Mrs.), 256
Geary
  James W., 244
  Mary, 243
  Morris, 243
  Willie, 244
  ____, 243
Gebauer, G., 256
Gebhard, John, 256
Gebhaur, Maggie, 242
Gee
  Joseph C., 218
  ____ (Rev. Mr.), 164
Geehan, Laurence, 256
Geheeb, Charge, 255
Gell, Edward, 256
Gelzer, T. L., 173
Gelzier, ____ (Dr.), 427
Genazzine, Austide, 264
Genella, Oscar F., 244
Geneva, Adesio O., 256
Genevieve, P. (Mrs.), 264
Genoke, Caroline, 219
Gentil, George, 264
Gentry, J. P., 354
Geoghegan
  C. T., 135
  E. T., 135
George, Mary A. (Mrs.), 349
Gerachi, Natalie, 256
Geraghty, Patrick, 399
Geraley, Louise, 256
Gerard
  A., 248, 255
  A. J., 381
  Caroline, 255
  Ellis, 242
  George W., 256
  Lummie, 242
Gerday, Pauline, 256
Gerdine, A. S., 247, 249
Geretz, F., 256
Gerlack
  Franz Jr., 219
  Franz Sr., 219
  Mary, 219
Gerlinger, Lewis, 255
Gerlock, Frederic, 263
German
  Henry, 241
  John, 245
  Lize, 256
Gernelle, Adeline, 247
Gerney, R. G., 430
Gernon, Robert K., 256
Gernou, Julia, 255
Gerson, Reuben, 250
Gerstman, R. A., 347
Gertrude (Sister), 120, 218

Gest, W. H., 342
Getchell
  ____ (Miss), 218
  ____ (Mrs.), 218
  ____, 218
Getta, Asa, 218
Getty, J. H., 374
Getz, Joseph, 352
Geuder, Andre, 256
Ghee Chow Ah, 255
Gheelan, Peter (Mrs.), 246
Ghoen, Fannie, 251
Gholston, ____, 245
Giargi, Joseph, 256
Gibb, Frank, 251
Gibbons
  Edward, 256
  James, 399
  Maggie, 256
  Pat, 255
  William, 373
  ____ (Mrs.), 256
Gibbs [Gibbes]
  A., 246
  C. H., 242
  George, 218
Gibilant, Philip, 375
Gibson
  Charles, 155
  E. W., 126, 218, 266, 427, 432
  E. W. (Mrs.), 432
  Emma, 244
  Frank T., 264
  John Jr., 264
  Julia E. (Mrs.), 427
  Katie, 244
  Mattie, 353
  Nathan, 218
  Thomas, 360
  ____, 244, 262
Giddion, D. P., 249
Giese, A. D., 218
Gift, Sarah J., 219
Gilbert
  C. W., 343
  G., 218
  G. T. A., 374
  J., 395
  James H., 340
  Otto, 256
  Tom, 373
  ____ (Mrs.), 251
Gilchrist, Malcomb, 248
Gill
  Annie, 218
  D. (Mrs.), 250
  George, 356
  Gilbert, 429
  Henry, 219
Gillan, Hugh, 244
Gilland
  L. W., 263
  Lewis, 243
Gillare, Edward, 256
Gillartin, America, 256

Gillem
  Lena, 219
  ____, 219
Gillen
  A. K., 218
  Friday, 218
  J. J., 256
Giller, Eli C., 256
Gillespie
  Michael, 256
  T. D., 354
  ____ (Dr.), 247
  ____ (Mrs.), 247
  ____, 380
Gilliam
  W. A., 240
  ____, 240
Gillis
  Elizabeth, 256
  K. H., 256
  R. H., 256
Gillison, Silva, 374
Gills
  Gilbert, 218
  ____, 218
Gilman
  M., 218
  W. S., 256
  ____ (Capt.), 356
Gilmore
  C., 265
  John, 218
  Louis J. B., 255
  Robert, 256
  William, 219
Gilson, ____, 250
Gilzer, T. L., 368
Gimo, Lorenz, 374
Giovanini
  Dominico, 242
  ____ (Mrs.), 242
Girand, R. A., 400
Girard, Ulger, 255
Girardano, Antonio, 256
Gist, R. C., 218
Gites, William F., 256
Givens, Mary V., 256
Givers, Lewis, 219
Givin, R. G., 218
Glacer, Louis, 256
Gladden, Alfred, 219
Gladinger, W. S., 256
Glancey, Maggie, 218
Glarkman, W. J., 219
Glaser
  Joseph, 251
  R., 251
Glass
  E. (Mrs.), 339
  Edward, 256
  Henry, 256
  J. S., 429
  James, 390
  Matthew A., 219
  Nancy, 242
  R. (Mrs.), 219

____ (Capt.), 275
____ (Mrs.), 256
Glassy
  Charles, 245
  Margaret, 245
Glautzer
  Mary (Mrs.), 218
  William, 218
Glavearo, Mattie, 256
Glaviano, L., 256
Gleason [Gleeson]
  Archie, 218
  Burt, 251
  Hallie, 251
  John, 244, 256
  John A., 256
  M. J. (Mrs.), 218
  Oscar, 239
  P. J., 399
  T. E., 251
Gledhill, G. H., 239
Gleen, J. M., 345
Gleeny, Andrew, 256
Glenn
  L., 400
  Philip, 256
  Samuel, 430
  W. L., 256
Glennon, Benjamin F., 247
Glesse, Mary A., 218
Gliss, Lizetta, 256
Gloetten, Barbara, 256
Glorieux
  A. G., 403
  John, 401
Goal, ____ (Mrs.), 256
Gocke, Anna, 256
Godman, H. R., 249
Goebel
  Fred, 219
  Theodore, 219
Goelsenleuchter, L., 256
Goenner, Clara (Mrs.), 218
Goetz
  J. A. E., 256
  Leno, 218
Goewey, H. M., 126, 266, 426, 432
Gohen
  Fannie, 251
  Margaret, 251
Going
  S. B., 218
  Samuel B., 373
Goldberg, C. (Mrs.), 243
Golden [Goldon]
  Bernard A., 256
  James, 242, 244
  John, 244
  Mike, 243
  Willie, 243
Goldsburg, Caroline (Mrs.), 263
Goldsmith
  Cora, 218
  Henry, 256
  M. (Mrs.), 218

William, 256
——, 183
Goldstein
  Fannie, 219
  S., 239
Goley, Fred, 240
Golmisno, S., 256
Gomez [Gomaz, Gomes]
  Antoine, 242
  Frenzel, 264
  Louis, 374
  Sebastian (Mrs.), 264
Gona, Victor, 264
Gonaux, J. L., 264
Gonzalles [Gonzales]
  Joseph, 249, 264
  Perique (Mrs.), 264
Gooding, John, 218
Goodlet, James R. Jr., 263
Goodloe, G., 264
Goodman
  A., 219
  A. H., 218
  D. (Mrs.), 219
  George, 219
  L., 218
  Robert, 218
  ——, 240
Goodrich
  A. W., 245
  Carrie, 218
  David, 218
  F. W., 243
  William, 218
Goodwin [Goodwyn]
  E. B., 219, 266
  J. R., 390
  Thomas J., 357
  W. G., 239
  William, 246
  —— (Dr.), 191
  —— (Priv.), 130, 429
  ——, 219
Goodyear, D. F., 129, 390, 391, 392, 414, 422
Goosehorn
  Sallie, 248
  Tom, 248
Gordere, Louis, 256
Gordon
  Albert, 219
  Annie, 219
  Charlotte, 219
  G., 244
  G. W., 136, 377
  H. S., 349
  Henry, 256
  Isaac, 219
  James, 241
  John, 219, 368, 411
  Millie, 219
  Missouri, 218
  R. F., 248
  W. R., 248
Gore, Robert, 248
Gorgis, E., 255
Gorgon, E., 430

Gorin, Eugene, 219
Gorman
  J., 256
  James, 240, 256
  John, 255
  Joseph, 218, 256
  Nellie, 240
  Patrick, 218
  Simon, 218
Gormley [Gormly], Ala., 256
Gorrell
  J. G. O., 219, 368, 369
  J. O. G., 117
Goser, Henrietta, 256
Goslin
  Mary Ann, 218
  —— (Mrs.), 218
Goss
  Frank, 218
  Horace, 241
Gossett
  Eliza, 219
  J., 247
Gossweiler, Emilio, 256
Gotchlich
  Amelia, 218
  M. (Mrs.), 218
Gotthelf
  B. H., 245
  B. N., 250
  Morris H., 245
Gouffier, Francois, 256
Gouh, B. C., 246
Gould, L. (Mrs. Dr.), 248
Gouldon, Allen, 245
Gourgoi, J., 256
Goushoff, C. R., 256
Govan, Daniel C., 171
Govern, E. M., 346
Gover, George W., 255
Govin, Eugenie, 372
Goza
  George, 248
  George (Mrs.), 248
Grace, Thomas, 403
Grady
  Thomas, 218, 266
  William, 263
Grafenheim, Jacob, 256
Graff [Graffe]
  Dillon, 256
  J. H., 243
  J. W., 243
  John Jr., 256
  Mary E., 243
Graham
  Blanche, 238
  C. C., 360
  Charles, 241
  D. B., 136
  Hannah, 242
  Hugh, 248
  John, 255
  John F., 255
  L. R., 255
  Lora B., 238

Martindale (Mrs.), 219
  Mattie, 218
  Virgil, 218
  William, 429
  William H., 372
  —— (Miss), 239
Grammer, Ella (Mrs.), 243
Granberry
  George, 247
  George C., 247
  Ida, 247
  Junius, 247
Grand, George L., 263
Graney, James, 255
Granger, W. H., 350
Granna, Anna, 256
Granning, William (Mrs.), 218
Grant
  Claiborne, 218
  G. H. Jr., 218
  George M., 218
  Inez, 218
  Jennie, 218
  John A., 333
  L. H., 416
  L. S., 218
  L. S. (Mrs.), 218
  Lewis, 218
  Margaret, 218
  Martha, 219
  Mary L., 256
  Mary Regis (Sister), 242
  Robert, 218
Graude, Antonio, 256
Grauel, Karl, 256
Graumann, A., 256
Grauna, Antonio, 256
Graurin, Paul, 256
Grauzin, Carrie, 256
Gravely, P. B., 357
Graves
  A. P., 240
  Alonzo Jr., 240
  Eugene, 263
  H. F., 256
  J. (Mrs.), 239
  L. (Mrs.), 374
  Louisa, 243
  N. S., 427, 432
  P. (Mrs.), 240
  Polena, 249
Gray
  A. P., 357
  Anna, 218
  Daniel, 263
  E. L. (Mrs.), 243
  Ed, 247
  Eli, 218
  Ellen, 263
  G. H., 368
  H., 244
  J. C., 247
  J. C. (Mrs.), 247
  J. N., 247
  J. W. (Mrs.), 249

Minerva, 255
  Nervy, 218
  Robert, 218
  Sarah, 244
  Susie, 219
  W. W., 218
  Walker, 218
  Walter, 266
  Willie, 263
  —— (Judge), 379
  —— (Mrs.), 218
  —— (Mrs. Judge), 381
Grayburn, Minnie (Mrs.), 256
Grayson
  Jane, 249
  Lisa, 249
  Steve, 219
Greatna, G. H., 256
Grebe, Louis, 256
Grecco, Angelo, 395
Green [Greene]
  Barnes, 256
  Ben, 243
  C., 218
  Charles, 246
  Charlotte L., 243
  Duncan, 247
  Elizabeth (Mrs.), 219
  Ella, 219
  Ellen, 218
  G. G., 349
  Gayoza, 248
  Grant, 345
  H. J., 368, 370
  Henry, 372
  James, 218
  Jennie, 218
  Jim, 243
  Joe, 219
  John A., 238
  Joseph, 248
  Lizzie, 218, 248
  Mamie, 219
  Margaret, 256
  Margaret (Mrs.), 218
  Martin, 219
  Minnie, 244
  Nat., 219
  Pink, 218
  Pompey, 242
  S. P., 368, 370
  Samuel A., 27
  Simon W., 438
  Stephen, 247
  Thomas, 402
  W. A., 248
  W. H., 218
  William, 264
  —— (Dr.), 180, 181
  —— (Mrs.), 218
  ——, 248
Greenfield
  E. C. (Mrs.), 247
  —— (Miss), 347
Greenpur, Fred, 218
Greenup, John, 251

NAME INDEX

Greenway, W. W., 240
Greer
　Estelle, 248
　Eugenia, 248
　H. C., 338
　Lavinia, 248
　Mary (Mrs.), 248
　Nannie, 239
Grefer, Henry, 256
Gregeris, Demetry, 256
Gregg
　J. C., 218, 266
　Jennie (Mrs.), 219
　Sallie, 219
　Willie, 219
　___ (Mrs.), 166
　___, 166
Greggs, William, 264
Gregor
　C., 353
　Thomas, 219
Gregory
　George, 303
　Isam, 219
　John Henry, 250
　Joseph, 256
　Mag. H. C., 256
　Maggie, 256
　Michael, 256
　Thomas, 256
Grehan [Grehen]
　John R., 434
　John R. (Mrs.), 434
　Larry, 434
　Larry (Mrs.), 434
　William, 218
　___, 434
Grempe, Charles, 219
Gresham, A. H., 135
Groxby, T. A., 429
Grey
　Charles (Sir), 79
　Lizzie, 243
Gribe
　Ann, 218
　Anna, 218
　Fred, 218
Grice, Charles E., 263
Griffin
　Antonio, 218
　Arthur, 239
　Austin, 218
　Calvin, 246
　Charles, 219
　D. T., 266
　Elizabeth, 256
　G. W., 256
　H. (Mrs.), 219
　John, 218, 219, 243, 255
　Martin I. J., 397, 399, 400, 401, 402, 403, 404
　Mary E., 219
　R. S., 219
　T. M., 250
　T. P., 263

Thomas, 404
Thomas P., 263
Tillie, 218
Tom (Mrs.), 250
Tony, 112
William, 218
　___ (Dr.), 247, 249
　___, 218, 219, 249, 355
Griffing, Emma, 248
Griffith, Grace, 255
Grigg, E. S., 339
Griggs, ___ (Mrs.), 219
Grigsby
　J. P., 239
　Mary, 218
　Samuel, 219
　Thomas A., 390
Grimes
　Larry, 218, 266
　M., 374
Grinstead, William, 243
Grisbam, Nora, 256
Griswold
　C. A., 218
　C. A. (Mrs.), 218
Grob, ___, 250
Groch, Fred, 255
Grogan, Edward, 218
Groney, William, 218
Groom, L. A., 256
Grosjean
　Henry, 374
Gross [Gros, Grose]
　H., 265
　I., 265
　J. A., 218
　James, 218
　K. F. (Mrs.), 255
　L., 265
　M. A., 246
　N., 256
　Zephir, 265
　___ (Mrs.), 264
　___, 250
Grossweiler, E. G., 256
Grouse, Frank, 218
Grove
　Ada, 218
　Cog., 241
Groves
　Robert, 238
　___, 218
Grub, J. B., 344
Gruber
　Frederick, 218
　Jacob, 256
Gruelich, J. F., 347
Grunewald, Henry A., 256
Grupe, Charles, 420
Gudenan, Peter, 256
Guderain, Maggie, 256
Gueble, Rene, 256
Guedry
　Leontia, 264
　Paul (Mrs.), 264
Gueitas, Colombau, 256

Guenault, Oscar, 256
Guerchaux, E. D., 255
Guerin
　C., 256
　Isabella, 256
Guerius, Stefano, 256
Guess
　William, 248
　___, 248
Gugel, Henry, 256
Guidrey [Guidray, Guidry]
　Ad., 265
　Aurelien, 263
　Julia, 265
　___, 265
Guigel, John H., 219
Guillot
　A. (Mrs.), 265
　Albertine, 256
　Louis (Mrs.), 265
Guillotte, Edward J., 250
Guinault, Oscar, 256
Guinea, J. L., 218
Guinshorn, F. J., 256
Guirrin, ___ (Mrs.), 255
Guise, Thomas, 242
Guiseppe, Giacommo, 256
Guitlian, ___, 263
Gull, E. A., 255
Gumbel, Francis, 219
Gummer
　Frederick, 218
　John, 218
　Mattie, 218
　___, 218
Gunderson, Andrew (Mrs.), 218
Gunn, Alexander, 376
Gunnell
　Florida, 256
　Sarah, 256
Gunot, Victor H., 263
Gunseead, Oscar, 256
Gunther, Joseph, 256
Guntlach
　___ (Dr.), 241
　___ (Mrs.), 241
Guntz, Peter, 244
Gurdici, A., 218
Gurley, Henry, 218
Gurney, Henry, 218
Gurniot, Heloise, 256
Gurt, Marin, 255
Guscio
　Louisa M., 242
　Peter W., 242
Gusin, Bernard, 403
Gusmanny, Jennie, 218
Gustave, Fondam, 219
Gutenberg, R., 256
Gutheries, ___ (Mrs.), 246
Gutherz
　Fred, 135
　Frederick, 136
Guthrie
　Jerry, 250

Joseph, 256
Michael, 250
Guy, George, 242
Gwynn [Gwinn]
　Indiana, 218
　M. Eliza, 219
　W. H., 240
　William, 218

H

Haack. Julius, 238, 249
Haar, Peter, 257
Haas
　A. B., 344
　Adolphus, 256
　W. B., 419
Habaron, ___, 220
Habbinett, A., 372
Haber
　Emily, 219
　Lena, 257
Habercorn
　Edward, 248
　L. F., 248
Haberg, Louis, 256
Habersham, Matilda, 374
Habicht
　Theodore, 246
　___ (Mrs.), 247
Hack
　M., 221
　___, 250
Hacker, Edward, 256
Hackett
　Harris, 265
　Mary, 219
Hackey, James, 256
Hadaway, James, 240
Haddick
　A. S., 380
　H. T., 247
Hadish, S., 220
Hadsell, A. J., 346
Haeley, Jacob, 248
Haenisch, ___, 303
Haffmeister, Johanna, 251
Hafron, John, 220
Hagaman, M., 256
Hagan
　M. A. (Mrs.), 256
　Mary, 256
　Mary C., 257
　Pat, 257
　Patrick, 257
Hagen, Henry, 257
Haggard [Hagard]
　N. P., 240
　William, 240
Hagge
　John C., 220
　Lewis, 220
Haggerty
　Annie, 220, 221
　J. F., 220
　James, 219
　N., 220

Haggie, John, 220
Hahl, Jacob, 257
Hahn
    Henry, 256, 257
    Moses, 219
    William, 256
Haibthorne, Ida, 257
Haieslaur, Ch., 257
Haight, C. H., 336
Hailinger, A. J., 257
Hainer
    Nancy C., 238
    _____ (Mrs.), 221
Haines
    L. A., 332
    Lewis H., 243
    Smart, 374
    T., 242
    Willie, 242
Haining
    Katie, 243
    Louisa, 244
    Minnie, 243
    S. M., 242
    _____ (Mrs.), 243
Haissig
    Daniel S., 219
    Henry, 219
Haldron, John, 220
Haldrum, Annie, 374
Haley [Haly]
    Charles, 257
    Daniel, 219
    P., 112
    Timothy, 257
    _____ (Mrs.), 221, 245
Hall
    Albert J., 256, 257
    Charles M., 436
    Charles S., 332, 437, 439
    Charlie, 247
    Edwin B., 243
    Esther, 219
    F. K., 248
    George, 248
    George F., 256
    Georgiana, 220
    Henderson, 245
    Henry Sr., 264
    J. D., 349
    J. G., 247, 380
    J. G. (Mrs.), 247
    J. R., 256
    James, 219, 246
    James D., 349
    John, 219, 408
    Joseph, 430
    Lulu, 219
    M. A. (Mrs.), 245
    R. P., 368
    Rosa, 220
    Sarah (Mrs.), 239
    Thomas, 245, 257
    W. W., 247, 380
    W. W. (Mrs.), 247
    William, 220, 265

William H., 243
    _____ (Dr.), 380
    _____ (Mrs.), 265
    _____, 219
Hallahan, Daniel, 403
Hallam
    Mollie, 220
    Sallie, 220
Hallenhead, S. B., 220
Halliday, A., 219
Hallor, Henry C., 257
Halloway, Esther, 240
Hallows
    Eveline, 220
    Joseph, 238, 266
    _____ (Miss), 266
Hallyburton
    Cora (Mrs.), 251
    _____, 251
Halmet, J. M., 347
Halsey
    M. P., 372
    _____ (Judge), 160
Halstead
    R. T., 136
    W. H., 219
Haly, see Haley
Halzucker, P. J., 400
Hamblet, Henry, 256
Hamburger
    Abe, 247
    _____, 174
Hamel, Eliz., 256
Hameron, James V., 220
Hamill, W. E., 373
Hamilton
    A. H., 425
    C., 256
    Charles, 219
    E. M., 373
    Elizabeth, 256
    J., 220
    J. W., 220
    James (Mrs.), 246
    John, 247
    Robert, 256
    Sam, 256
    W. S., 135
    _____ (Mrs.), 374
Hamm, A. B., 355
Hammel, Albert, 239
Hammerson, Pauline, 220
Hammerstein
    Emily, 220
    J., 220
    Julia, 220
    Laura, 220
    _____ (Mrs.), 220
Hammett
    Bessie S., 243
    E. H., 243
Hammock, R. L., 220
Hammond
    Sam, 247
    Sarah, 256
    William, 243
Hammonlough, S., 419

Hammons, Lewis, 241
Hammozed, Ed., 256
Hampton
    C., 220
    Eli, 219
    Wade, 176
Hancock
    G. W., 374
    H. D., 353
    W. W., 251
Handy
    C. G., 240
    Thomas H., 257
Hanenburg, James, 220
Hanes
    Bettie S., 242
    Florence A., 243
Haney, Albert O. C., 256
Hankins
    _____ (Dr.), 248
    _____ (Mrs.), 248
Hanks, G. P., 339
Hanley
    E. P. (Mrs.), 221
    Edward, 221
    Isaac, 242
    Margaret, 220
    Peter, 221
Hanlon, Edward, 399
Hanna
    Noah, 221
    Tisha, 220
Hannart, P., 403
Hannegan [Hannigan]
    Daniel, 403
    John, 220
Hannelia, Antoine, 242
Hanneman, Julius, 257
Hannon, James, 112, 266
Hans, John, 256
Hansburg, Thomas, 256
Hansen, John F., 256
Hanson
    Julia, 219
    M. J., 220
    W. M., 430
    W. N., 113
    William, 219
    _____ (Dr.), 28
Hany, Victor, 256
Hapholdt [Happholdt, Happoldt]
    _____ (Dr.), 20, 46, 243
Haran, Mary (Mrs.), 239
Harbert, John, 429
Harcourt, M. A. (Mrs.), 373
Hardee, Thomas S., 27
Hardeman, Eva, 221
Harder
    Annie, 238, 249
    Ella, 249
    Ellen, 238
    Emile, 256
    Henry, 219
    Mary (Mrs.), 239
Hardin [Harden]
    Ben, 220

Fanny, 256
    Henry, 220
    Lucy, 220
    Monroe, 219
    William, 256
Hardman, Louis, 415
Hardousette, E. L., 256
Hardway, Goodman, 219
Hardwick, Fred, 242
Hardy
    George W., 256
    J., 244
    John, 220
    N. L., 263
Hare
    Filo S., 372
    Henry, 220
    James M., 256, 257
    Maude C., 263
    T. S., 372
    Walter F., 263
Hargan
    Mary L., 256
    Mildred, 219
Hargis, Marie, 265
Hargrove
    H. H., 376
    _____, 185
Haring, Ellen, 248
Harkness, C. D., 239
Harlan
    Gustave, 242
    L. B., 117, 368, 369
Harlt, William, 263
Harman [Harmon]
    Dave, 242
    M. (Mrs.), 372
    William, 220
    William N., 219
Harness, N. P., 251
Harp, Anna (Mrs.), 264
Harper
    Emily, 248
    J. J., 248
    James, 219
    Mattie, 248
    O. B. (Mrs.), 248
    Robert L., 257
    Thomas J., 29
    William, 257
Harpman, F., 419
Harran, William, 256
Harrigan, Patrick, 256
Harriman, F. D. (Mrs.), 124
Harrington
    A., 221
    Andy, 433
    Andy (Mrs.), 433
    H. S., 219
    Mary, 220
    Patrick, 257
    _____ (Mrs.), 245
Harris
    Adolph, 220
    Angeline R., 220
    Annie, 256

NAME INDEX

Bruce, 338
Charles, 245
Davey, 221
E. W., 240
Ed, 220
Elisha, 300
F. J. (Mrs.), 243
Francis, 250
G. C., 353
George, 122, 164
George C., 181, 407
Hal C., 246
Iona A., 257
Isham G., 356
J., 220
J. T., 239
James, 221, 430
Jesse, 220
John, 243
Jordan, 266
Joseph, 257
Kate, 243
L., 256
Leon, 264
Lewis, 220
Louis, 256
M. (Mrs.), 221
Mamie, 220
Margaret D., 244
Matt, 220
Milton, 244
Richard O., 257
Rosa, 220
Ruth, 221
S. C. (Mrs.), 246
Simon, 248
Tip, 429
W. H., 221
Willie, 220
_____, 220, 245
_____ (Pvt.), 113, 429
_____ (Rev. Dr.), 124, 180, 181
_____ (Sen.), 284
Harrison
A., 246
Alabama (Mrs.), 374
C. B. (Mrs.), 243
Caroline, 256
Carter H., 425
Claudia, 256
E. W. B., 256, 257
Edward, 243
G. S., 374
George H., 256
H. C., 374, 376
James, 221
Jordan, 219
Loretta, 256
M. A. V., 257
M. J., 219
R. H., 41
Stella, 256
W. S., 242
_____ (Capt.), 174
_____, 246

Harry
M. G., 352
_____ (Capt.), 238
Harsey, Henry, 256
Harsh, George, 352
Hart
A. M., 257
Charles, 429
Charlotte C., 256
Harry, 248
Hyman (Mrs.), 249
John, 256
Junius, 264
Lena, 264
Stephen, 374
_____, 264
Hartell, Samuel, 256
Harter
George, 246
Jake, 246
Mike, 246
_____, 246
Hartlege, Mollie, 221
Hartley, G. W., 342
Hartman
J. H., 239
J. (Mrs.), 239
John, 239
L., 239
M., 249
Marcella (Mrs.), 247
Margaret, 239
Thomas, 239
Hartner, Margaret, 256
Hartnett, M., 256
Hartnutt, E. J., 256
Hartshorne, _____, 303
Harvey
Clark, 264
J. M., 399
W. W., 221, 429
Willie, 256
_____ (Lt.), 130
_____, 220
Harwell, J. R., 414
Haser, Magdalena, 256
Hashern, L. A., 256
Hasic
Charles, 243
Major, 248
_____, 248
Haskell [Haskill]
Ben, 251
Benjamin, 219
J. C., 192
Rachel, 219
_____ (Judge), 192
_____, 238
Haskin, C. M., 256
Haskins
Charles M., 257
Gus., 241
Gus. Jr., 241
Gus. (Mrs.), 241
_____, 241
Hassan, A., 256
Hassberg, B. (Mrs.), 247

Hasse, Robert, 256
Hassell
S., 244
Samuel J., 243
Hassett, James C., 402
Hasta, Antonio, 256
Hasten, V., 220
Hasting, R. (Mrs.), 245
Hastings, John, 245
Haswell, A. M., 347
Hatch
Emile H., 256
Love, 239
Hatcher, J. S., 221
Hatfield, John L., 342
Hauck, Nicholas, 256
Hauharit, Oscar, 256
Hauk, Louis, 256
Haul, Alfred (Mrs.), 256
Hausche, Robert, 256
Hausell, Maggie M., 256
Hauslauer, Christian, 256
Hausler, Kate, 256
Hausman, Frederick R., 220
Hauton
George A. J., 256
Sophia M., 256
Haven, Sophia, 243
Havenae, E. D., 257
Hawenhauer, H. C., 341
Hawes, L. P., 349
Hawk, Robert, 265
Hawkins
A., 432
A. S., 126, 221, 266, 426
C. S., 352
Emcline, 241
Florence, 219
Frank, 240
Henry, 257
J. M., 338
L., 408
Pres., 221
T. S., 248
Tommy, 248
W. J., 350
_____ (Mrs.), 250
_____, 221, 248, 380, 408
Hawlett, _____ (Capt.), 346
Hawley [Hawly]
Ellen, 256
Isaac H., 221
Pat, 220
Hawthorne, J. S., 422
Hay
Levi, 219
_____, 219
Haycraft, W. A., 246
Hayden
George, 161
James, 220
Maria, 183
Hayes
Bettie, 240

Charlie, 256, 257
G. (Mrs.), 239
Henry, 256, 257
J. P., 403
James, 220, 242
M. W., 351
Mary E., 244
Mary (Mrs.), 372
Patrick, 257
Rutherford B., 170, 390, 391
William, 401
Willie, 264
_____, 239
Haymi, George, 256
Haynes
Loyd A., 437
Nannie, 219
O. B., 429
Richard V., 220
W. B., 221
W. D., 130, 429
Hays
A. J., 238
Belle, 375
Cynda, 220
Emily M., 263
Gabriel, 220
J. B., 375
John R., 343
Mary, 219
R. T. D., 263
Thomas, 220
Timothy, 220
Tobin, 220
_____ (Mrs.), 220
_____, 220
Haywood
C., 353
C. M., 422
Carrie, 256
Hazlett, H., 353, 354
Hazlewood, T. B., 240
Head
John, 256
S. K., 415
Heady [Headey]
F., 368, 369
Francis (Mrs.), 220
Sherman, 117
T. J., 220
Healey [Healy, Heely]
John, 256
M. H., 256
Mary Ann, 256
Michael, 404
Pat, 220, 256
T. C. (Mrs.), 248
Thomas, 256
_____, 248
Heap, Joseph, 256
Heard, T. J., 36, 37
Hearn
Joseph O., 256
Michael A., 374
Hearse, Wilson, 136, 263
Heart, John, 135, 136

Heath
  J. M., 257, 331
  J. W., 186, 220, 330, 332, 335, 406
  J. W. (Mrs.), 406
  James W., 141
  John, 112
  Thomas, 112, 220
  ___, 406
Heathcock, ___ (Mrs.), 241
Heatherly, Mac, 251
Heaton
  J. K., 375
  Nat. E., 257
Heavitson, ___, 250
Hebdon, Thomas, 245
Heber, Thomas, 265
Hebert
  Arthur, 265
  Cecelia C., 263
  Theresa, 265
Hebret, Alfred, 265
Hechmer, John L., 400
Heck, John (Mrs.), 256
Heckle, E. K. (Mrs.), 373
Hedrick
  A. W., 243
  John, 262
Heels, Willie, 256
Heely, see Healey
Heffener, Jerry, 219
Hefferna, Ellen, 402
Heffey, C., 221
Heffner, Frances M., 257
Hefling, L., 353
Heflinger, George, 243
Heggia, Jesse, 375
Heidaw
  John, 219
  ___, 219
Heidel, Robert B., 479
Heidelberg [Heidelburg], Louis, 220, 251, 372
Heidengsfelder, H., 257
Heidenreich, John, 257
Heider
  Fred, 374
  John, 257
Heidson, ___ (Mrs.), 220
Heiman, Moritz, 256
Heimke, F. W., 256
Heiner, ___ (Mrs.), 240
Heines, William, 265
Heino
  Victor, 257
  Victor Sr., 257
Heins, Augustine, 219
Heisch, Catherine, 256
Heissel
  Joanna, 256
  Michael, 257
Heitman, J., 351
Heitt, J. W., 256

Held
  Frank A., 256
  Gerhard, 256
Helflingler, Bertha, 344
Hellburn, M. H., 339
Hellman, Fred, 221
Hellrig, Rudolph, 251
Hellvig, Rudolph, 220
Helmke, Wilhel, 257
Hemard
  Mary, 257
  W. J., 256
Hemmerly, John, 220
Hemmingway, A. T., 342
Hemple
  Eliza, 220
  Willie, 221
Hempstead, Edward, 249
Hempton, ___, 245
Henchel, Louis, 257
Henderson
  A. C., 245
  Jim, 219
  John, 248, 249
  Julia, 241
  Malcomb, 249
  Minnie, 220
  Robert, 219
  Susan, 248
  T., 245
  Thomas J., 425
  Viola, 256
  Virginia, 221
  Virgey, 220
  W., 221
  ___ (Lt. Gov.), 37
  ___ (Mrs.), 221
  ___, 221, 245
Hendricks
  Anna, 251
  Dennis, 219, 265
  F. C. (Mrs.), 219
  J. O., 246, 265
  John, 251
  Louisa, 251
  Sophia (Mrs.), 256
  ___ (Mrs.), 250, 251
  ___, 251
Heneberry, Philip, 402
Henegan, Patrick, 243
Henery, Henry, 219
Henis, A., 256
Henkle, A., 358
Henly, Lena (Mrs.), 239
Hennegan, C. P., 244
Hennessy [Hennessey, Hennesy]
  Charles, 242
  James, 249
  John J., 403
  Kate, 244
  M., 256
  Maggie, 244
  Mary, 243
Henniger
  A., 221
  Fred, 221

Otto, 221
Rosa, 221
Henning
  E. K., 238
  T., 238
Henrich, Emile, 257
Henrick, J. R., 126
Henricle [Henrickle], J. R., 221, 266, 426, 432
Henry
  A. G., 338
  Daniel M., 425
  Elizabeth, 246
  Fannie M., 256
  J., 250
  J. H., 263
  James V., 245
  John C., 219
  John M., 246
  Joseph, 263, 265
  Lizzie, 246
  Lulu, 220
  Mary A., 256
  O. H. P., 256
  Rachael (Mrs.), 246
  S. F. (Mrs.), 372
  William, 256, 410, 411
Heomig, I. M., 221
Heppler, G. A., 373
Herbeline, Blanche, 256
Herbert
  Charles, 256
  J. L., 374
Hereford
  Harriet, 221
  L. S. (Mrs.), 263
  R., 263
Herman
  F., 256
  H., 419
  Lena, 247
  Lizzie, 219
  Max, 220, 421
  ___, 220
Hern, A. S. J., 256
Hernandes, Paschal G., 256
Herndon
  C. L., 256
  John, 240
Hernon, ___ (Mrs.), 264
Herr
  C. J. (Mrs.), 245
  Joseph, 245
  ___, 245
Herriman, A., 256
Herring
  C. Marie, 256
  Mary, 220
Herris, A., 256
Herron
  Cecil, 264
  ___ (Mrs.), 256
Herst, Louis, 263
Hertado, ___, 13, 77

Hertweck
  Max, 251
  Max (Mrs.), 251
Hertz
  L., 219
  ___, 219
Hertzer, John, 257
Hervey, L., 353
Hervinean, Marie (Mrs.), 257
Heryeg, S., 256
Heshburg, Herman, 247
Hespin, John, 251
Hess
  A. J., 245
  Edward, 256
  John L., 256
Hesse, Hester, 219
Hesson, Henry, 219
Hester, Charles A., 348
Hestler
  Maria, 256
  Marie, 257
Hether
  Fred, 264
  Joseph, 264
Hett, Juliana, 256
Heustis, ___ (Dr.), 35
Hewitt
  Henry, 220
  J., 359
  J. H., 359
  Jesse (Mrs.), 221
  Mike, 220
  Peter, 219
  Thomas, 221
  ___ (Miss), 240
  ___ (Dr.), 221
  ___, 221
Heyman
  Howard, 219
  Morris, 219
Heyn, Margaret, 256
Heyser, Jacob, 354
Hick, Emilie, 264
Hickerson, Simon, 220
Hickey
  J. W., 399
  James, 238
Hicklin, William, 220
Hickling
  R., 248
  R. (Mrs.), 248
Hickman, E., 221
Hicks
  Erasmus, 220
  George, 219, 220
  J. B., 220, 368, 369
  John B., 117
  N. M., 373
  N. M. (Mrs.), 373
  R., 429
  Willie, 220
  ___ (Dr.), 240
Hien, Otto, 256
Hiern, Finley B. (Mrs.), 264

NAME INDEX

Higbee, H. H. (Mrs.), 409
Higgerson, Fannie, 220
Higginbotham, Helen A., 256
Higgins
   Albert, 221
   H. C., 220
   James (Mrs.), 245
   William, 220
   ____, 221, 245
Higginson, J. J., 350
High, Mansfield, 220
Highgate, ____, 379
Highland, John N., 221
Highlander, W. D., 356
Highly, Harriet (Mrs.), 256
Hightower
   Daniel, 219
   Francis, 220
   James, 221
   Lewis, 220
   Willie, 219
Higley, A. N., 343
Hilari, Pierre, 257
Hilbert, Henry, 256
Hilborn, Manetta, 256
Hildebrand, ____ (Mrs.), 248
Hilden, Nancy, 263
Hildermandt, B., 374
Hill
   Albert, 219
   Alfred C., 220
   Austin, 219
   E., 350
   E. J., 219
   E. J. (Mrs.), 219
   George, 219
   Harry, 256, 257
   J. E. (Mrs.), 241
   J. S., 240
   J. W., 249
   Lewis, 221
   M. M. C., 244
   Mary, 246
   Mary S., 387
   Mary S. (Mrs.), 374
   Nancy, 239
   R. J., 243
   Sam, 219
   Tom, 219
   W. A. Jr., 431
   W. H., 372
   W. P., 220, 238
   William A., 220
Hilliard [Hillyard]
   Jane, 257
   Mead, 243
   Samuel, 429
Hilton
   Margaret, 220
   Maud, 264
   Peter, 362
Hilyer, Ed, 241
Himes, William E., 256

Hinds
   Ellen (Mrs.), 220
   Jackson, 220
Hineman, A. J., 350
Hines
   John, 256
   W. E., 257
Hinish, Marie, 257
Hinkle
   L., 221
   M. W., 220
Hinson, S., 407
Hinton, Fred, 256
Hippocrates, 14, 28, 185
Hirme, Edward, 256
Hirsch
   Eugene, 257
   Leonard, 244
   ____, 303
Hirsh, Henry, 244
Hiss
   Louisa, 264
   Rosa, 264
   Willie, 264
Hissic, Catherine, 219
Hitchcock
   Ed, 372
   Thomas, 220
Hite, Henry, 219
Hitzfield, William, 220
Hoar, William, 359
Hobbs, J. H., 358
Hobson
   H. R., 238
   Jesse, 220
   ____ (Dr.), 240
Hock, William, 372
Hockstadter, M., 420
Hodge, E. K. (Mrs.), 256
Hodges
   B. M., 220
   E. (Mrs.), 220
   Eugene, 265
   George, 257
   J. W. Jr., 239
   Jennie, 265
   Lovie, 239
   Noel, 265
   T. M., 425
   W. R., 117, 219, 368, 369, 407
Hodgins, John M., 257
Hoehn, Sophie M., 257
Hofer
   Anna, 256
   George, 362
Hoffer
   Josephine (Mrs.), 256
   William, 248
Hoffman
   C., 423
   C. W., 421
   Frooich, 256
   J. P., 410, 415
   Jacob, 219
   John P., 411
   Sam, 265

Hoffmaster, Joanna, 220
Hoffmeister, Lydia, 257
Hofft, L. L., 256
Hogan
   Arthur S., 257
   Callom, 256
   Hattie, 256
   John, 251
   M., 256
   Margaret, 250
   Mary, 266
   Thomas, 262
   Vincent, 256, 257
   William, 245
   ____ (Right Rev. Bishop), 403
Hoge, W. E., 357
Hogey, Jesse, 375
Hogg [Hogge]
   John, 220
   ____ (Mrs.), 220
   ____, 220
Hoggatt
   Philip, 243
   Stacey, 263
   Stacey A., 243
Hoggin, ____ (Mrs.), 220
Hohensee, Andrew J., 264
Hohenwart, Alexander, 245
Hohlin, Amelia, 219
Hoit
   Gustav, 373
   Joseph, 263
Holabeiser, John, 256
Holahan, Mary, 256
Holbrook, M. V., 241
Holcomb [Holcombe]
   Mollie, 220
   William H., 29
Holger, Fritz, 256
Holgern, L. H., 257
Holich, W. P., 256
Hollahan, Mary, 251, 257
Holland
   A. J., 239
   Edward R., 416, 434
   Emily, 256, 257
   Idelle, 434
   James, 264
   John H., 256
   R. C., 219
   T. P., 181, 221, 416, 434
   T. P. (Mrs.), 417, 434
   Vernon, 434
   W. J. L., 246
   ____, 417
Hollenbach, Emma, 257
Hollenberg
   Beno (Mrs.), 149
   C. B., 221
   Carrie (Mrs.), 219
Hollensbud, C. B., 220
Hollenshead, A. S., 433
Holler, Adam, 257
Hollerbach, Ella, 256

Holley [Holly]
   Frank, 248
   Joseph, 221
   Luke, 219
   N., 264
   ____, 264
Hollingsworth, Monroe, 219
Hollman, Charles, 245
Hollywood
   J. (Mrs.), 221
   L., 221
Holman
   George T., 352
   Harry, 220
   Tom, 355
   ____ (Mrs.), 251
Holmes
   Gus, 246
   Henry, 219
   Joe, 244
   Maria, 221
   S., 256
   Willie, 243
   ____ (Rev.), 164
Holsen, Elias, 257
Holst
   George A., 219
   George H., 407
   Theodore, 406
Holston, Martha, 221
Holt
   Herman, 220
   John A., 178, 179, 221, 406, 421
   John A. (Mrs.), 179
   Joseph, 303, 314, 316, 317, 318, 319
   Lewis, 244
   Neal [Neil] B., 179, 219
   R. D., 251
   W. A., 136, 141, 330, 331
   W. H., 335, 380
   ____ (Dr.), 204
   ____ (Mayor), 346
   ____ (Mrs.), 220, 245, 250
   ____, 179, 245
Holtz, T. W., 220
Holzer, Kate, 256
Homan
   George, 242
   William, 112
Homer, 14
Honeycutt, ____ (Rev.), 348
Honlay, Rody, 257
Honlehan, T., 242
Honold, C. A. G., 257
Hoo, Lang, 219
Hood
   E., 373
   Thomas, 126, 158, 266, 426, 432
   Thomas B., 220
   W. B., 431

____ (Miss), 220
____ (Mrs.), 172, 220
____, 172
Hooges, William H., 219
Hooker, E., 430
Hooks
　David, 248
　H. C. (Mrs.), 238
　____ (Mrs.), 248
Hookson, J. V., 343
Hooper, C. M., 346
Hope
　George, 220
　John, 219
　Rachael (Mrs.), 220
　Tim, 112, 220
　Tim (Mrs.), 220
Hopkins
　E. A. (Mrs.), 349
　John, 346
　____, 219
Hopper, James, 219
Hopson, H. R., 117, 240
Horan, Mary, 220
Horasley
　J., 220
　____, 220
Hord, C. C., 251
Hordon, ____, 220
Horigan, L. B., 354
Horn
　Jack, 135
　Maggie, 220
　Maggie (Mrs.), 220
　Mary A., 221
　Mary L., 242
　William, 256
Horshman, G., 353
Horsley
　Benton, 220
　Nellie, 220
　T. T., 220
Horteriche, Master, 256
Horton
　C., 220
　Henrietta, 220
　Nellie, 246
　S. (Mrs.), 373
　W. N., 220
Hosack
　____ (Dr.), 25, 70
　____, 303
Hosbin, Martha, 248
Hose, Thomas, 220
Hoskins
　Ezekiel, 256
　J. J., 360
　John B., 416, 433
　Robert, 250
　W. S. (Mrs.), 250
　____, 165, 250
Hosmar, Chris., 219
Hosrey, Catherine, 257
Hossley, Josephine M., 243
Hotard, James E., 256

Hotchkiss
　R. E., 375
　R. G., 369
　Thomas, 220
　Thomas E., 375, 416
Houder, John, 256
Hought, G., 220
Houghton, M. (Mrs.), 251
Houk
　A. (Mrs.), 250
　R., 250
Houla, Rhoda, 256
Houlihan, Patrick, 257
Houns, Benjamin B., 219
House, Lee, 220
Housman, Charles, 247
Houston
　Alice, 220
　Charles, 219
　Henry H., 353
　Mary, 256
Howard
　C. W. (Mrs.), 221
　Charles, 141, 330, 331, 335
　Frank, 221
　G. P., 404
　George, 263
　George W., 256
　Halsie, 243
　Henry, 220
　Jack, 246
　James, 372
　John, 135, 251, 257, 325
　M. J. (Mrs.), 250
　Willie, 219
Howe
　Isabel, 256
　Mary I. J., 257
　O. M. (Mrs.), 256
　Olympe M. (Mrs.), 257
　R. A., 256
　Thomas, 403
Howell
　Henry, 249
　May Belle, 241
　____ (Rev. Mr.), 240
Howes, Charles J., 256
Howgueltas, F., 256
Howlett, Young, 192
Hubbard
　J. W., 242
　Philip, 242
　T. M., 342
　____ (Maj.), 263
　____ (Mrs.), 263
Hubbert, Cath. (Mrs.), 256
Hubbes, Christian, 256
Huber
　I. J., 112
　J. J., 219
　Rosie, 257
　Theresa, 257
　____ (Mrs.), 248
Hubert
　George, 220

Peter, 256
　____, 220
Hudson
　Anna, 256
　Annie, 256
　James, 219, 373
　John, 219
　Justice, 242
　William, 220
　____, 219
Huener
　Ida S., 242
　William W., 244
Huesman, F. R., 372
Huff
　Frederick C., 257
　Jacob, 256
Huffington
　M., 247
　S., 247
　____ (Mrs.), 381
　____, 379
Hufft, Lenra Lee, 257
Hug, Peter, 221
Huge, Louisa, 256
Hughes
　Barney, 421
　C., 402
　Christopher, 220
　Clara, 374
　Delia, 256
　E. W., 247
　E. W. (Mrs.), 247
　Frank, 241
　Granger, 256, 257
　J. E. (Mrs.), 247
　James, 219, 256
　Jane (Mrs.), 375
　Joe E., 256
　Louis, 356
　Louis (Mrs.), 356
　M. E., 256
　M. H., 257
　Mary, 220, 243, 247
　Michael, 402
　R. G., 256
　W. E., 380
　____ (Dr.), 21
　____ (Miss), 220
　____ (Mrs.), 247
　____, 42, 379
Hughetta (Sister), 181
Hughy
　____ (Dr.), 408
　____ (Mrs. Dr.), 408
　____, 408
Huhn
　John D., 405, 408
　____, 408
Huhner, George, 256
Hulah, William, 220
Huling
　F., 340, 342
　Freeman, 340
Human, Isaac, 249

Humbert
　Jean, 256
　Jeannie, 257
Humblette, ____ (Mrs.), 239
Humboldt, ____, 22, 31
Humes, A. R., 220
Hummel, Ludwig, 248
Humphrey, C. S., 239
Humphreys
　Ben, 248
　D. B. (Mrs.), 248
　Eliza, 240
　Eva, 248
　Warren, 373
Hundermark, Robert A., 242
Hundermonk, Alice V., 242
Hundy, Alice (Mrs.), 257
Huner, Ida W., 243
Hunn
　Alexander, 407
　H. H., 337
Hunnicutt
　Walter, 239
　____ (Mrs.), 239
Hunson, Thomas J., 256
Hunt
　C. P., 390
　Ellen V., 221
　Fannie T., 220
　George, 44
　H. H., 256
　James R. L., 245
　John, 373
　Norman, 243
　T. W., 358
　Tilda, 219
　W. J., 407
　William B., 256
　William W., 220
　____ (Dr.), 35
Hunter
　Carl, 221
　G. W., 374
　George, 220
　Ida, 220
　J. C., 374
　James, 434
　John, 239
　O. B., 256
　R. R., 368, 370
　S. W., 369
　Sallie, 219
　Willie, 220
　____ (Dr.), 175
Huntington
　C. P., 425
　W. H., 362
Huntley, Charles, 246
Hupert, M., 219
Hupp
　Rosa, 256
　William, 256, 257
Hupper, ____ (Mrs.), 220
Hurley
　Ed, 403

NAME INDEX

J. O., 360
John, 257
M., 403
Hurnder, Millie, 220
Hurschman, M., 256
Hurse
____ (Mrs.), 37
____, 37
Hurst, Henry, 219
Hurt
B. F., 240
B. F. (Mrs.), 240
Henry, 220
Julian, 240
Otto, 219
Robert Lee, 240
Thomas, 240
W. S., 240
Huse, Marvin, 57
Huss
Alphonse, 256
Charles, 256
Hussey
A. W., 256
C. S., 350
G. A. C., 256
George H. C., 257
William, 403
Hustead, Louisa, 257
Hustin, A., 219
Hustmell, W., 374
Hutcheson, George W. Jr., 244
Hutchins
R., 220
Thomas A., 219
Hutchinson
Emma, 219
George S., 350
H., 256
Ida F. (Mrs.), 238
Jennie (Mrs.), 220
R., 220
Robert, 160
____ (Mrs.), 245
Hutton, Thomas, 264
Hyde
A. A., 135
H. S., 437
Horace L., 332
John, 220
Serena, 265
Willie, 265
Hyland, Michael, 256
Hyman
M. (Mrs.), 219
William, 221
Hyne, C. C., 349

I

Ibeck, Julius, 372
Ick, B., 429
Icolina
Arcola, 257
Nicola, 257
Idley, Jack, 221

Iglauer
L., 238, 418
____, 265
Ike, Ben., 221
Ilsley, Charles, 264
Imbau, Hortaise, 257
Ingalls
John, 401
____ (Dr.), 117, 221
Ingersol, Merona B. G., 257
Ingleheart, N. G., 355
Ingraham
J., 257
____, 381
Ingram
Eugene, 247
Florence, 248
John (Mrs.), 248
____ (Mrs.), 247
____, 248, 379, 429
Inman, Gabriel J., 257
Innerarity, Catherine, 264
Inwood, Harold, 257
Ipolite, P., 243
Ipsom, Charles, 350
Irby
Amanda D., 221
Sanders, 257
Tom, 248
V. R., 257
Irion, F. M., 429
Ironside, R. B., 351
Irvine, Hugh, 257
Irving, John (Mrs.), 221
Irwin
Charles T., 257
D. C., 257
Emma N., 221
Lottie, 221
P., 337
Peter, 221
R A., 247
R. A. (Mrs.), 247
Isaacs
E., 221
Isaac, 221
John, 262
M., 419
Mattie L., 221
Samuel, 257
W. B., 409
Isbell, Daniel, 221
Isdell, Carrie, 221
Isler, F., 257
Israel
C. B., 264
Estelle, 257
Henry L., 264
Iteibs, Anna, 265
Itreevy, P. W. J., 257
Itro, John, 257
Ittman, Rosa, 257
Ivery, Turner, 221
Ives, J. B., 344
Ivey, J. M., 354

J

Jac, Placide, 257
Jackman, James, 345
Jackson
A., 222, 430
A. S., 263
Al., 222
Anderson, 221
Andrew, 221
C., 265
Clara, 222
Colden, 221
Cora, 222
E., 240
Ella, 222
Florence, 241
George, 222
H., 221
Henry, 243
James, 221
James R., 243
John, 222, 257
Joseph, 257
Julia, 222
L. B., 343
Lou., 222
Louis, 257
M., 221
Mary, 221
Minerva, 221
Mollie, 264
Phil., 221
R. J., 221, 266
Robert L., 221
Samuel H., 257
Sarah, 222, 374
Sol., 222
Thomas J. "Stonewall," 435
Susan, 263
T. D., 429
Townsend, 390
Violet, 243
W. J., 372
William, 244
____ (Mrs.), 221, 222
____, 222
Jacob, Henry, 257
Jacoba, J. C., 408
Jacobi, J. C., 222
Jacobs
Ben, 246
Ben (Mrs.), 246
Dennis, 221
E., 222
Edwin A., 257
Esther, 257
F., 354
George, 420
J. C. (Mrs.), 222
J. (Mrs.), 246
Joe, 221
Joseph, 246
Joseph Jr., 246
Lewis, 257
P., 359

Roberta, 221
____, 246
Jacobson
A., 257
Louis, 257
M., 242
Jacolin, Nicola, 257
Jacornett, Lucie (Mrs.), 257
Jacques, C. N., 401
Jahn, John, 257
James
A. K., 257
Alice J., 221
Amelia (Mrs.), 373
Bushrod W., 29, 313
E. C. (Mrs.), 356
Elvira, 257
F., 348
F. B., 243
Frederick, 257
Harry, 247
Henry, 244
Levi C., 257
Mattie (Mrs.), 247
R. R., 408
Robert, 221
Tucker, 222
William, 257
James I, 270
Jamieson, William, 222
Jamison
E. S., 375
J. D., 243
Janes, Eddie, 221
Janowitz, H., 420
Jaomed, Gaetano, 257
Jardel, H. L., 264
Jarvis
J. T., 339
W. J., 374
____, 222
Jay, Arthur, 257
Jeakle, Samuel, 257
Jeannorut, John, 257
Jeffer, M. J., 257
Jefferson
B., 222
John, 429
Louis, 257
M. S. (Mrs.), 238
Thomas, 222
____, 263
Jeffrey, Amanda, 221
Jeffries
Anna, 257
B. L., 264
J. S. B., 264
John, 299
M. R. (Mrs.), 264
St. Clair, 246
____ (Miss), 264
Jemerson, J. C. (Mrs.), 245
Jeness, Helen, 257
Jenkins
E. (Mrs.), 221
Henry, 221

Julia, 244
Lucinda, 243
Susan (Mrs.), 240
William, 221
—— (Prof.), 203
Jennings
 J., 265
 J. B., 239
 Lafe, 431
 Matthew, 222
 Jenny [Jenney]
 F. W., 221
 ——, 243
Jenore, Augustus, 373
Jensen
 Fred, 257
 Lizzie, 257
Jepson, Sarah, 221
Jerome, E. L. (Mrs.), 221
Jessen, Jerrold, 221
Jett, Carrie L., 257
Jewell [Jewel]
 W., 35
 Wilson, 276, 300
 —— (Gov.), 338
 —— (Mrs.), 249
Jewett, J. R., 342
Jincenor, Lejohn, 257
Jingles
 A., 243
 Mary, 243
 Robert, 244
Jobe
 Jacob, 221
 M. S., 178
 S. M., 222, 330, 331,
  335, 391, 406
 Samuel M., 142, 332,
  335
Jodd
 Bernard P., 263
 Michael, 263
Jodon, F. D., 372
Joete, Joseph, 221
Johanna (Sister), 246
Johausenbach, A., 257
Johl
 Edward, 222
 Henrich, 221
 Mamie, 222
 Mary (Mrs.), 222
 Maxey, 221
 Z. (Mrs.), 221
 ——, 221
Johlisant, Edna, 257
John, Leon T., 257
Johnes, J. J., 257
Johns
 Conrad, 266
 —— (Miss), 415
Johnson
 A. J., 395
 Amanda (Mrs.), 246
 Andro, 257
 Annie, 221, 222, 242
 Annie N., 222
 Antonia, 242

Beatrice, 187
Ben., 221
Benjamin, 372
Bertha (Mrs.), 248
C. Eva, 247
C. H., 409
Caroline, 222
Carrie (Mrs.), 257
Cecil, 257
Charles, 222
Charles E., 257
Christopher, 257
Cora L., 222
Courtney, 222
Cyrus, 221
D. M., 257
Daisy [Daisey], 354,
 355
Ed., 221
Edmund, 222
Edward, 221, 222
Eliza, 222
Elizabeth H., 257
F. (Mrs.), 222
Fannie, 248, 263
Fayette, 222
Frank, 244
Fred, 222, 247
George, 257
Gus, 221
Hal, 245
Handy, 222
Henrietta, 372
Henry, 221, 222, 262
Isaac, 257
J. B., 257
J. B. (Mrs.), 250
J. E. (Mrs.), 242
J. H., 373
J. Jr., 222
J. M., 421
J. P., 355
J. S., 222
Jennie, 222, 240
John, 136, 141, 142,
 185, 221, 243, 257,
 329,
 330, 331, 334, 335,
 348, 363, 376, 384,
 392
Joseph (Mrs.), 250
Julia, 264
Katie, 257
Lizzie, 222
Lucy, 242
M. A., 257
M. C., 344
M. (Mrs.), 222, 250
M. W., 247
Maggie, 246
Margaret (Mrs.), 245,
 372
Maria, 221
Mary, 221, 244, 257
Mary Jane, 221
Mary (Mrs.), 246

Mattie, 221
Nadim, 257
Nannie, 221
Oscar, 257
Peter, 239
Pierce, 222
Robert, 222, 429
S. D., 404
Sallie, 222
Sarah, 222
Sidney, 222
Stephen, 243
T. N., 222
Thomas, 242, 247, 250
Tom, 222
Virginia, 222
W., 243
W. B., 347
W. H. (Mrs.), 247
William, 221, 250
—— (Dr.), 292
—— (Miss), 222
—— (Mrs.), 222
——, 222, 263
Johnston
 Annie, 245
 Isaac, 351
 J. E., 356
 James, 249
 Joe, 245
 Joe (Mrs.), 245
 Sallie, 249
 T. N., 411, 412, 413
 Wesley, 257
 —— (Gen.), 435
 ——, 245
Joiner
 Calvin, 222
 Mary, 222
 Parker, 222
 Joint, Sarah Ann, 257
Jolly [Jolley]
 Andrew H., 263
 Charles E., 263
 Eva Louise, 263
 J. W., 244
 Lawrence, 263
 R. Emmett, 263
Jonan, Alex, 257
Jonas, Leo, 420
Jones
 A. T., 420
 Albert, 221
 Alfred, 222
 Anderson, 221
 Annie (Mrs.), 257
 B., 240
 B. (Miss), 251
 B. P., 374
 Ben, 263
 Bettie, 222
 C., 221, 244
 C. E., 244
 Calvin, 222
 Caroline, 263
 Caroline C., 221
 Catherine, 221

Charles, 221, 257, 263
Clara, 222
D. W., 257
Daisy, 222
Daniel, 221, 222
E. L., 239
Ed. J., 239
Eliza, 222, 248
Emanuel, 372
Emma L. (Mrs.), 373
F., 240
Fall, 239
Fanny, 242
Frank, 222, 413, 425
George, 222, 257, 263
H., 222
H. M., 248
H. (Mrs.), 222
H. T., 245
H. V., 374
Hailey, 221
Hannah, 222
Hattie, 265
Heber, 146, 368
Henrietta, 243
Henry, 245, 249
Henry A., 221
I. H., 221
Irene, 222
J., 244
J. C., 222
J. C. (Mrs.), 245
J. E., 339
J. L., 348
J. W., 395
Jacob, 241
James, 372, 429
Jim, 244
Joe, 242
John, 221, 222
Joseph, 45, 257, 319
Josiah, 248
Lavina, 221
Lena, 221
Lewis [Louis], 222, 257
Littleton, 221
Louisa, 249
M., 406
M. G., 430
M., 222
Mack, 263
Maggie B., 357
Manda, 221
Marcus, 411, 412, 413,
 415
Mary, 257, 415
Mary E., 222
Matilda, 221
Melessa, 222
Milton, 246
Mollie, 221
Monroe, 221
N. M., 390
Nellie, 221, 263
Oscar, 242
P. S., 368
Preston, 222

NAME INDEX

Rachael, 221
Regina G., 263
Richard, 222
Robert, 221, 240, 244
Robert N., 222
Roger, 221
Rossi (Mrs.), 373
S. M., 373
Sarah, 374
Sebastian, 251
Serena B. (Mrs.), 265
Simon N., 360
Susan, 222
T. E., 248
Thomas E., 240
Thomas H. W., 243
Thomas M., 251
V., 240
W. H., 246
W. J., 431
W. R., 243
Walter, 222, 412
William, 246, 372
William John, 257
Willie, 249
_____ (Dr.), 35, 68
_____ (Mrs.), 221, 251
_____, 222, 240, 406
Jordan
B. N., 243
Charles, 257
E., 244
Henry, 222
James, 401
John, 400
John B., 257
M. L. (Mrs.), 244
Joseph
Leon, 264
Mark (Mrs.), 246
Josepha (Sister), 120, 221
Josephine (Sister), 265
Joslin, _____ (Mrs.), 221
Joubert, Emma, 257
Joy, E. L., 349
Joyce
Jennie, 221
John, 257
Patrick, 221
Joyner
William, 222
_____, 44
Juary, Guiseppe, 257
Judah
Charles, 221
G. H., 420
Judd, L. P., 407
Judge, Theodore, 222
Juergen, H. Jr., 257
Jukes, W. C., 222
Jules, Charles, 265
Julius, M. C., 111
Junkerman, _____, 221
Just, M. B., 222
Justus, Dorothia, 257

K

Kadish
S., 222
_____ (Mrs.), 222
_____, 223
Kahn
Charles Jr., 351
Samuel, 243
Kain, see Kane
Kaiser
Eldie, 263
John, 257
Kallaher
C., 222
John, 222
M., 266
Mike, 222
Sarah, 222
Kalmbach
E., 242
R., 243
Kamera
E., 223
Louis, 223
Kampman
E. T., 257
F., 257
Kamsler, Adolph, 249
Kanard, Martin, 243
Kane [Kain, Kayhn]
James, 223
John, 223, 266, 401
Joseph, 263
Patrick, 399
Kanfieldt
E., 223
Ephraim, 223
Kaninski, Joseph, 257
Kanovan, M., 266
Kappes, William, 257
Karcher
Eva, 251
Josie, 251
Mary, 251
Karil, Emile, 257
Karney, John, 242
Karr, _____ (Mrs.), 381
Karrigan, Thomas, 395
Kassava, Adolph, 222
Kates, John S., 223
Kathasena, Emma, 223
Kattman, Clara, 257
Katzenmier, Jacob L., 243
Kaufman [Kauffman]
A., 242
Charles, 257
D. C., 257
Henry, 222
L. (Mrs.), 223
Louis, 222
Samuel, 223
William, 257
_____ (Mrs.), 239
_____, 222
Kaughman, R. C., 257
Kauth, Michael, 244

Kautzer, F., 372
Kavanaugh [Kavenaugh]
Catherine, 257
T. P., 416, 434
Thomas (Mrs.), 248
Kavaney, John, 257
Kay, C. H. D., 257
Kayhn, see Kane
Keaghey, Mary D., 257
Kealhoffer, George, 222
Keane [Kean]
James M., 245
John J., 403
Kearn
Arthur, 222
James, 263
Kearney [Kearny]
Evaline, 257
J. Watts, 257
John W., 401
Lawrence, 257
Martin, 222
Kearns
Frank, 222
Henry, 222
John W., 222
_____ (Mrs.), 222
Kearny, Lawrence, 257
Keary
James C., 222
Martin, 244
Keating
Henry, 249
J. M., 129, 154, 155, 158, 165, 390, 391, 415, 416, 433
Jesse, 264
Katie, 223
M. T., 117, 368, 369
T. M., 181
_____ (Dr.), 370
Keatly, _____ (Mrs.), 241
Keefaber, A. W., 257
Keefe [Keef]
Annie, 222
Dan, 401
J. N., 407
P. H., 401
_____, 222
Keegan
Mary, 257
Mary (Sister), 257
Keeley [Keely]
Annie, 222
Cornelius, 223
James, 241
John, 250
Patrick, 403
Tom, 401
Keenan
Edward, 257
R. J., 403
Sarah (Mrs.), 374
Keene [Keen]
Mary B., 257
Theodore, 257
Keep, Augustus, 350

Keever, M., 257
Keeves, Margaret, 257
Keff, R., 222
Keily, A. M., 403
Keir, A. J., 257
Keistner, M., 251
Keiston, Thomas, 222
Keith
J. H., 257
Robert, 257
Kelher, John, 223
Kelhofer, George, 408
Keller [Kellar]
E., 244
Frank, 404
Louis, 242
Richardson, 264
Sally, 245
William, 257
Kellogg
C. W., 243
O. M., 249
Kelly
A. A., 400
A. M., 403
Ann (Mrs.), 257
Bettie, 240
E., 429
F., 223
Fanny, 247
George, 223
Hannah (Mrs.), 223
Henry, 257
Hugh, 222
Ida, 257
J., 407
J. (Mrs.), 407
James, 222, 223, 246, 433
James P., 373
Jane, 223
Jennie, 222
John, 222, 244
John Jr., 433
John Sr., 433
Luckaby, 222
Lucy, 222
M., 266
Mary, 246, 257
Michael, 222
Thomas, 248
Tillie, 225
William, 257
_____, 395, 407
_____ (Father), 404
_____ (Mrs.), 374, 381, 404
Kelly (Rev. Father), 119, 164
Kelting
John H., 257
Louis, 257
Kelz, Louisa, 257
Kemper, K., 358
Kendall
Alf., 240
Alfred, 266

Anthony, 241
Charles T., 242
G. A., 375
M. E. (Mrs.), 245
Peter, 223, 266
Robert, 223
Samuel, 247
Thomas, 242, 248
W. A., 348
_____, 245
Kenden, _____, 238
Kendrick, Lulu, 247
Keneyld, _____, 422
Kenhue, Aug., 368, 370
Kenneday, G. W., 353
Kennedy
　A. E., 410
　Bridget, 246
　David P., 242
　Edward, 257
　Ellen, 263
　Florence, 223
　George, 348
　Jack, 264
　John, 257
　M., 246, 249
　Mary A., 257
　Peter, 257
　S. D., 250
　S. D. (Mrs.), 250
　Thomas, 257
　W. A., 223
　_____ (Miss), 223
　_____ (Mrs.), 222
　_____, 37, 246
Kenner
　John, 264
　Peter, 257
Kennerly, Martin, 222
Kennott, P. G., 421
Kenney [Kenny]
　Edward S., 257
　James, 257
　Jessie, 239
　John B., 257
　Julia (Mrs.), 239
　Marion, 257
　Pat, 257
　_____, 222
Kennoa, C. E., 265
Kennon
　C. R., 265
　Hubert, 265
Kent, S. J., 257
Kenton, L. M., 352
Kenzler, Louis, 222
Kerberg, John, 401
Kerchner, Alice, 223
Kerger, R. (Mrs.), 223
Kern
　J. E., 257
　William, 257
　William A., 257
Kernan, F. H., 403
Kernell
　Lizzie, 222
　Mamie E., 222

Kerny, Jacob S., 257
Kerr
　A. W., 222
　Charles, 223
　J. H. (Mrs.), 223
　J. M., 222
　James M., 416, 433
　John, 223, 402
　Mollie, 223
　W. E., 257
　William, 223
　_____ (Miss), 338
Kerrigan, J. P., 400
Kersalich, Sam, 257
Kershaw, Thomas, 222
Kerwin, M., 257
Kerzey, A., 257
Kesillen, A., 222
Kessel, Kath., 257
Kessler
　H. S., 437
　W. S., 332
Kester, Susie, 223
Kesterson, C. H., 251
Ketler, B. F., 222
Ketterman, C. F., 222
Kettle
　_____ (Mrs.), 247
　_____, 247
Ketzenmier, J. L., 245
Keutsgel, Joseph, 257
Keyer
　M. J., 126, 222, 426, 432
　Martin J., 222
Keys [Keyes]
　H. M., 332, 436, 437
　M. J., 266
　William, 257
Keyser, A., 223
Kezer, A. R., 243
Khiup, John, 257
Kidd, Virginia, 243
Kidder, G. W., 351
Kiefer, Emile Mary, 257
Kieler, Sophia W. (Mrs.), 257
Kieneman [Kienemann]
　Charles, 257
　George, 257
Kiernan
　Edward, 257
　Francis E., 257
　Kate, 257
Kiesele, Charles, 374
Kiesle
　Charles, 239
　Ed., 239
Kifferel, Joseph, 222
Kilbourne, Henry, 223
Kilbride, Nora, 257
Kilcrease, Dorsey, 248
Kilelia, Annie, 257
Killenea, Thomas J., 257
Killian, R. J., 257
Killum, George, 257

Kilpatrick
　L., 222, 223
　_____, 223
Kim
　Louis, 223
　N., 117
Kimball
　George, 245
　George (Mrs.), 245
　Ida, 223
　S. H., 356
　Sam, 245
Kimbrough [Kimbro]
　A. L., 368, 406
　John, 246
Kincaid
　Emma, 223
　Spencer, 262
Kinchen, Philip, 263
Kind, Bridget, 223
Kindal, Katie, 223
Kindsman, Henry, 345
Kines, Joseph, 223
King
　Albert, 244
　Alexander E., 244
　Amanda, 240
　D., 354
　Ellen, 257
　George E., 425
　H. S., 223, 407
　Henry E., 244
　J. H., 348
　J. W., 410
　James, 239
　John, 243, 245, 401
　L., 245
　Lafayette, 243
　Lewis, 223
　Lizzie, 257
　Margaret, 223
　Maria A., 257
　Mary (Mrs.), 374
　Nicholas, 401
　Robert, 245
　Willie M., 244
　_____, 251
Kingman
　A. D. Jr., 251
　Katie, 251
　Muff, 251
Kingspight, _____, 244
Kinman, Thomas, 223
Kinney
　D. M., 241
　James, 223
　John M., 223
　M. W., 222
　Patrick, 244
　Thomas, 257
　_____, 187
Kinstler
　Amelia, 247
　J., 247
Kinston, Auguste, 222
Kipper, Morris S., 222

Kirby
　Pete, 247
　Pete (Mrs.), 247
　William, 266
　William (Mrs.), 266
　_____ (Dr.), 247, 249
Kirchener, J., 182
Kircheval, E., 223
Kirger, _____ (Mrs.), 251
Kirk
　Fannie, 395
　Sam, 223
Kirkbride, S. M. (Mrs.), 248
Kirkham, Dora E., 257
Kirkland, Harry, 222
Kirwin, Davies, 223
Kisser, John, 257
Kister, Emile, 257
Kitchens, H., 223
Kitchison, _____, 251
Kite
　Lucy (Mrs.), 240
　_____ (Mrs.), 222
Kittrell, John C., 250
Kiutz, Teresa, 257
Klaffki, Andrew, 222
Klarutz, John, 223
Klaw, J. C., 352
Klearheart, John, 223
Kleiber
　Jacob Jr., 249
　Jacob Sr., 249
　Minnie, 247
　_____, 247
Klein [Kline]
　Annie M., 244
　Frank, 264
　Frank H., 242
　John, 222
　Joseph, 257
　Mary C., 243
　Ninion E. Jr., 244
　Patience (Mrs.), 244
　Rosa, 257
　_____, 249
Kleinburry, Louis F., 263
Kleiner
　John, 222
　John R., 222
　Joseph, 222
Kleinhaus, Catherine, 263
Klice, A. J., 241
Kliempeter, W. B., 257
Klinger, David, 257
Klostermeyer, Bertha, 222
Klotz, Lewis, 427, 432
Kluch, John, 244
Knable
　Martin, 245
　Martin (Mrs.), 245
Knapp [Knap]
　A. J., 424
　A. O. (Mrs.), 401
　R. M., 425
　Stephen, 245
　Stephen (Mrs.), 245

NAME INDEX   483

Knatz
  Ferdinand, 257
  Joseph, 257
Kneass, Napoleon B., 106
Knebs, John, 343
Knechel, Aug., 257
Knefter, C., 419
Kney, Charlotte, 223
Knight
  Andy, 222
  Anna, 222
  C. C. (Mrs.), 244
  Joseph (Mrs. Rev.), 264
  Priscilla, 374
  ____ (Mrs.), 222, 263
Knightly, J. W., 344
Knoblock
  Bertha, 265
  Charles, 257
Knoedler, William, 265
Knoff, L., 265
Knooys, Marie L., 257
Knowlton
  C. S., 431
  L. S., 223
  ____ (Col.), 128, 160, 161, 431
Knox
  Charlotte, 223
  Florence, 222
  J. H., 340
  J. M., 247
  Lily, 263
  Louis, 263
  ____ (Capt.), 173
  ____ (Miss), 354
  ____, 263
Kobhause, H. E., 257
Koch
  William, 223
  William Jr., 223
Kochler, Maggie, 257
Koehler
  Ferdinand, 257
  William, 95
Koenig, J. M., 223
Kofford
  Mollie, 223
  Thomas, 223
Kohl, Theodore H., 257
Kohlberg
  J., 330, 331
  Jacob, 142, 335, 419
Kohler, Amelia, 222
Kohlhaas
  Joseph, 265
  ____ (Mrs.), 265
Kohlieldt, Irwin, 223
Koike, Benjamin, 257
Kolb, P., 247
Konenberg, W. F., 399
Koonce, R. M., 240
Korke, Ken, 257
Kormtz, Britton, 402
Kortrecht, Charles, 238
Koser, James, 222
Koswig, Albert, 257

Kottelli, Nicholas, 257
Kounds, B. B., 222
Kozenser, Johanna, 257
Kraft
  Anna, 257
  P., 222
Krail
  Mary J., 257
  Viola, 257
Kratz, John, 257
Kraus [Krause]
  B. (Mrs.), 223
  Cariotta, 223
  Frank, 264
  George, 223
  Jacob, 223
  Lulu, 264
  N., 263
  Wilhelmina, 264
  William, 223
Kreeger, Rosa A., 257
Kreiger
  ____ (Miss), 251
  ____, 251
Kremer, Paul M., 257
Krentle, F., 257
Kress, Eliza, 247
Kretschmar, W. P., 247
Kretz, John, 257
Kringer, Cari, 257
Krinn
  J. (Mrs.), 223
  John, 223
Krobs, Henry, 355
Kroeper, J. G., 257
Kroggman, H. C., 257
Kronopsky, Francis, 257
Krost, E. (Mrs.), 249
Krouse, Jacob, 245
Krowan, Martin F., 404
Krucker, John, 257
Krumpelmann
  [Krumplemann]
  E., 257
  Theodore, 257
Kruner, Martin, 373
Kruse
  H. C., 264
  William, 257
Krutcher, Charles, 222
Kuehne, Augustus, 167
Kuetenmacher, F. A., 257
Kuhn
  Arthur, 222
  J., 399
  Laura, 257
  Paul, 223
Kuhner, Joseph, 257
Kumpf
  Matilda, 223
  William, 223
Kunter, J. K. C., 375
Kuntz
  A. G., 257
  Louis, 242
Kupfer, Edward, 257

Kutsch
  George, 223
  John, 223
  Katie, 223
  Theodore, 223
  Kutz, Frank J., 257
Kyle
  David, 244
  W. D., 246
  ____ (Miss), 246
  ____, 247

L

La Katzenmier, Mamie, 243
La Roche
  R., 299
  ____ (Dr.), 16, 109
  ____, 201, 202, 203, 205
Labadi [Labadie]
  Peter, 257
  ____ (Dr.), 23, 37
  ____ (Mrs.), 224
Labarbe, Gustave, 258
Labesque, J. M. (Mrs.), 224
Labour, J. B., 258
Labre, John B., 257
Labrella, ____ (Maj.), 224
Labrousseau, Julio, 258
Lacassagne, L., 258
Lacaze
  Edward, 258
  Emily T., 258
  Julius, 258
  Michael, 258
Lacey [Lacy]
  A. T., 153, 160, 224, 391
  C. (Mrs.), 223
  Patrick, 258
  ____ (Miss), 251
Lachmund, C. H., 348
Lackey, Joseph, 245
Lacock
  Alice, 247
  Helen, 247
  M., 247
  Mary, 248
Lacosta, Jean, 258
Lacoume, Eulabe, 258
Lacour, Mary De, 258
Lacourage, Benoit, 258
Lacrampe, Antoine, 263
Lacroix, Carrie, 243
Ladd, Charles C., 258
Laduke, Joseph, 258
Laertz, Herman, 373
Lafaett, Mary, 258
Lafargne, Henry, 263
Lafargue
  Emma, 264
  Raoul, 264
Lafayette, ____, 244
Lafon, Joseph L., 257

Lafond, Josephine (Mrs.), 265
Laforte, Jean, 258
Lafosse, J. B., 257
Lafourch, E. B., 258
Lafoze, Rosalie, 258
Lagarde
  Dalilab, 265
  Frank J., 265
  John, 265
Lagenbecker, Leonora, 258
LaGlaise, D., 257
Lagoria, A., 224
Lahen, John, 243
Lahey, Charles, 258
Laine, Eva C., 257
Lair, J. N., 224
Lake
  Annie, 247
  Daniel, 224
  Delia, 247
  Flora, 224
  George (Mrs.), 381
  George W., 247
  George W. (Mrs.), 247
  Peter, 224
  Robert, 224
  Samuel (Mrs.), 239
  William H., 224
  ____, 245, 379
Lala
  Francisco, 258
  John, 258
  Margaret, 258
Lalemana, ____ (Mrs.), 258
Lallemant, ____ (Dr.), 203
Lamar, ____ (Sen.), 296
Lamb
  Annie, 224
  Edward, 224
  L., 223
  Patrick, 244
Lambardi, Emile, 258
Lambert
  A. J., 258
  Alice H., 258
  Cyrille (Mrs.), 243
  James, 258
  Urban, 258
  ____ (Mrs.), 250
Lambig, A. A., 402
Lambricki, Dimitry, 250
Lamkin
  Annie, 247
  Mary, 244
  Nancy (Mrs.), 249
Lamm, ____, 258
Lamon
  John H. Jr., 263
  William R., 263
Lamourant, Philman, 249
Lamy, John, 258
Lanasa, Guiseppe, 258
Land, Richard, 429
Landigan, Richard, 223
Landrake, William, 258

Landreaux, M., 257
Landrum
　George, 224, 433
　Herbert, 128, 160, 433
　Herbert S., 224
　May E., 258
　S., 141, 330, 335, 336, 408, 439, 442, 443
　S. (Mrs.), 408
　_____ (Rev. Dr.), 121, 164, 390
　_____, 408
Landry
　Augustine, 264
　Eupheamia (Mrs.), 264
　I., 264
　Julia, 264
　Mederic, 264
　Stella, 264
　Uloze, 264
　_____, 264
Landsberg, M., 420
Landwehr
　F. W., 257
　M., 258
Lane
　A. C., 373
　Adolphus, 224
　Crawford, 224
　Dennis, 245
　E. T., 339
　Ed., 224
　F. D., 404
　George, 223
　H. B., 223, 266
　Ira, 224
　J. W., 241
　Jesse, 224
　N. V. Jr., 243
　Richard, 224
　T. J., 251
　_____ (Mrs.), 245
　_____ (Pvt.), 113, 429
Lanero, G., 257
Lang
　Augusta, 223
　Martin, 258
Langaballe, R. P., 257
Langboles, E., 258
Lange, _____ (Mrs.), 258
Langell, George, 332
Langford
　C. R., 126, 224, 266, 426, 432
　R., 242
Langham
　Charles (Mrs.), 263
　_____, 263
Langley
　L. M., 247
　S. J. (Mrs.), 265
　W. A., 246
Langstaff
　A. D., 135, 136, 140, 141, 142, 148, 160, 185, 186, 188, 329, 330, 331, 333, 335, 365, 371, 377, 379, 381, 382, 383, 384, 391, 416, 425
Langster, Lucuis, 223
Lanham
　E. H., 408
　E. H. (Mrs.), 408
　E. W., 224
Lanier, Lawrence, 245
Lanigham, Bridget, 223
Lank, Rosa, 258
Lannagan [Lanigan, Lannegan]
　Joseph, 395
　Maggie, 223
　Morris, 223
Lannahan, John, 240
Lannanna, Antonio, 258
Lanphier, J. E., 136
Lantine, Sarah, 258
Lany, Louisa, 224
Lapelsroux, Francis, 258
Lapon, Jean, 258
Lardner, Thomas R., 258
Large
　G., 258
　Jack, 223
Larkin
　D. W., 257
　Dan, 224
　E. J., 262
　J. W., 401
　Michael, 263
Larouche, John, 245
Laroude, John, 257
Larque, Jules, 258
Larry, J. N., 224
Larson [Larsen]
　C. A., 245
　Julius, 258
　P. W., 258
Lasalle, _____ (Mrs.), 223
Lascar, Jennie, 258
Lascascio, Antonio, 257
Lashley, L. C., 374
Laski, _____ (Dr.), 56
Lasmar, Robert, 257
Lassabe
　Bertrand, 249
　Delphine, 249
　Victoria (Sister), 249
Lasse, _____ (Mrs.), 224
Lassell, Minnie (Mrs.), 242
Lastin, A., 223
Lat, C. C., 346
Latch
　Amelia, 223
　Louisa, 223
Latcher
　Barbara E., 243
　John, 244
Latchford, Alvin C., 263
Latemier, Julie, 258
Latena [Lateno, Latina, Latine, Latino]
　John, 258
　Nicola, 257
　R., 257
　Razada, 258
　Rosario, 257
Latham
　G. H., 438
　Tillie, 224
　William, 248
Latherty, Kate, 223
Lathrop
　M., 375
　William, 425
Lathroy, Lyman, 258
Latimer, Mark, 246
Latove, C. (Mrs.), 257
Latrobe, F. C., 345
Latsch, John, 183, 223
Latson, B., 224
Lattien, Julia, 258
Lattin
　John T., 240
　_____ (Miss), 240
Latting, R. G., 360
Latugo, Mag., 258
Laua, D. F., 404
Laughlin
　Mike, 243
　Terrence, 243
Laughton
　J. G., 248
　John C., 258
Lauiza, Nicholas, 257
Launa, A., 348
Laurence
　A. A., 368
　_____ (Mrs.), 395
　_____, 395
Laurens, Henry, 247
Laurent, Emile C., 240
Laurie, Mary A., 251
Lavallee
　Barbara, 258
　Caroline, 258
Lavallen, Catherine, 223
Lavaza, Emma, 224
Lavedon, Pierre, 257
Lavegna, Frank, 223
Lavelle [Laville], M., 257, 401
Laverson, C. (Mrs.), 223
Lavinder
　Frank, 240
　Henry, 240
　Jasper, 240
Lavins, William R., 242
Lawe
　James, 264
　_____, 264
Lawhorn, Jack, 224
Lawler [Lawlor]
　Dan, 249
　Ellen, 249
　Emma, 249
　Henry T. Jr., 258
　Loyola (Sister), 258
　_____ (Miss), 249
Lawraver, A. Rose, 258
Lawrence
　Albert, 248
　Albert (Mrs.), 248
　C., 224
　Ella (Mrs.), 263
　Henry, 242
　Jennie, 224
　Mary E. (Mrs.), 243
　Mary (Sister), 246
　_____ (Dr.), 96
Lawry, Frank B., 258
Laws
　G. L. (Mrs.), 355
　L., 223
Lawson
　Addison, 258
　D. L., 344
　Fred, 224
Lawton
　Eugene, 266
　John, 258
　R. H., 224, 251
　_____, 240
Lay, John, 224
Layden, Margaret, 224
Layne, Enos T., 258
Layton
　M. C. (Mrs.), 240
　W. J., 240
　Willie, 240
　_____, 240
Le Fere, P. A., 239
Le France, Henry, 223
Le Guerre
　Julia E., 223
　Julia H., 223
Lea, Berry, 224
Leach
　H., 250
　John, 224
League, W. H., 240
Leahy, H. L., 401
Leake [Leak]
　W. L., 251
　_____ (Mrs.), 245
Lear, John N., 258
Leary
　Bridget, 258
　Joanna (Mrs.), 223
Leath, Hamilton, 224
Lebaneri, Charles, 258
Lebar, William, 258
Lebatice, Louisa, 258
Lebetgern, Eugene, 258
LeBlanc
　Alba, 264
　C. O., 264
　Ed, 264
　Emilie, 264
　John, 258
　Lawrence, 264
　Paul H., 263
　Rene, 264
　Robert, 263
　Villeneuve, 263
　_____, 264

NAME INDEX

Leblave
  A., 265
  Robert, 265
Leche, Milson A., 258
Leclair, ___, 28
Leclerc, Augusta, 258
Ledbetter
  J. H., 247
  John, 351
Lederz, Constant, 257
Ledet
  Amedee (Mrs.), 265
  Silver, 265
  Sylver, 263
Ledig, Walter A., 258
Leduc, John B., 357
Ledues, Alice, 258
Lee
  A. S. (Mrs.), 246
  Bennett, 223
  Bennie, 223
  Bettie, 224
  Charles, 224
  Charles E., 373
  Cora, 263
  Edward, 112
  Eldora, 241
  George W., 257
  Henry, 258
  J. L., 356
  James, 223
  John M., 355
  Johnnie, 248
  Martha, 263
  Mary Ellie, 258
  Mollie (Mrs.), 257
  Peter B., 415
  Robert E., 129, 435
  Sow, 246
  Susan, 224
  Tish, 224
  William, 258, 263
  ___ (Mrs.), 250, 395
Leech, John, 112
Leedy, Sallie, 247
Lees, Kenny, 246
Lefeim, Robert, 265
Leffal, Wallace, 263
Leffingwell, C. A., 136
Lefort
  W. (Mrs.), 265
  Wallace (Mrs.), 263
Lefranc, Lorena, 258
Legan, Pat, 249
Legare, J. Cecil, 368
Legendre
  Adolphine, 265
  Emile, 265
  Gustave, 265
  Louis, 265
  Louise, 263
Leger, S. E., 340
Legier, Marie C., 258
Leglaize
  Catherine, 258
  Elizabeth, 258
Lego, Charles, 264

Legorini, Lewis, 223
Legras, Edward, 239
Lehbeher, John, 258
Lehleitner, Willie, 258
Lehman [Lehmann]
  Isadore, 258
  Leo, 223
  M. W., 258
  Willie, 224
  Y., 224
  ___, 224, 247
Lehsoy, Maria, 257
Leibing, John, 224
Leidy, Eugene Jr., 238, 245
Leippert, George W., 258
Leisher
  E. E., 248
  Frank, 248
  George, 248
  John, 248
  ___, 248
Leitch
  D., 246
  ___ (Mrs.), 246
Leman
  Henry, 224
  William, 224
Lemants, C., 258
Lembo, Luigi, 258
Lemburg, ___, 240
Lemler, Henry, 247, 249
Lemon
  George W., 223
  H., 407
  Nellie J., 223
  Tom, 223
  W. J., 136
  ___ (Mrs.), 410
  ___, 407
Lemoy, Alexander, 223
Lempasion, Anton, 258
Lenac, Louisa, 250
Lenagh, Patrick, 403
Lenagrau, Lawrence, 258
Lenfant, Eugene, 257
Lenton, James, 258
Leob
  Alex, 264
  S. (Mrs.), 419
Leofold, Maggie M., 242
Leon
  Theodore, 258
  ___ (Mrs.), 239
Leonard
  Freddie, 246
  James, 246
  James (Mrs.), 246
  Janie, 248
  Martin, 374
  Mattie, 246
  Robert (Mrs.), 246
  Rose, 243
  ___ (Mrs.), 250
Leone
  Gossip, 258
  Mary, 258
Leopold, Isaac, 223

Leoron, James, 263
Lepere, Emma, 265
Lerath, Mary, 257
Lerm, John, 258
Leron, Joseph, 265
Lerouge, Anthony F., 258
Leroy, A. H., 411, 413
Lertura, Louise, 224
Lesassier, B. B., 258
Lesko, ___, 258
Leslie
  Charles, 258
  Thomas, 258
Lespominet, J., 257
L'Esponde, Pierre, 258
Lesser, J., 419
Lesseur, Lulu, 245
Lester
  Lulu, 184
  Mollie, 223
  Sallie, 184
  ___, 184
Lestere, Donald, 258
L'Estrange, John J., 399
Letannier, E., 257
Letcher, Fannie, 223
Lethiegae, Henry, 258
Leunis, Moses, 258
Leuschner, R., 257
Levarts, Fannie, 223
Levellier
  Emma, 258
  Joseph, 258
Leveniah, Emilie, 258
Levenson, Frederick, 258
Lever, Catherine, 258
Levere [Leverre]
  R. S. (Mrs.), 224
  Rosetta (Mrs.), 373
Levi, see Levy
Levie, J. R., 242
LeVin, L. J., 372, 376
Levingston, Roy B., 258
Levins, John, 242
Levy [Levi]
  A., 258
  Arthur, 258
  Caroline, 257
  Charles, 257, 263
  E. M., 135
  Ephraim, 224
  J. A. D., 402
  Jacob, 258
  M. C., 258
  Mark, 257
  Mary, 258
  Mina, 263
  Moses, 258
  S., 344, 360
  Samuel J., 257
  Solomon, 258
Lewellyn
  J. C., 257
  Mary, 224
Lewis
  Adeline, 224
  Ann (Mrs.), 257

C., 244
Clara, 224
Frank, 243
Frank C., 243
George, 224
George E., 266
H., 258
H. E. Jr., 243
Henry, 224
J. D., 403
James, 243
John, 224, 257, 258
John E., 238
John J., 258
M. P., 257
Mary, 224
Mary A., 258
Mary (Mrs.), 265
Mason, 224
Nancy, 224
Noel, 224
R. B., 340
S., 265
Thomas, 224
Tom, 113, 430
W. J., 240
___ (Dr.), 245
___ (Rev.), 265
Lewison, ___, 265
Lewlin, Henry, 241
Leydon, Margaret, 224
L'Homme, Leon P., 224
Lichtenfield, E. B., 257
Lichtentein, C., 257
Liddle, J. M. Jr., 250
Lidwell, F. M., 224
Liebel
  Martin, 257
  Theresa, 258
Lieben
  Amelia, 224
  Edward, 223
Liebherr
  F. J., 402
  Frank J., 404
Liebman, Paul, 257
Liet, John, 257
Lightmore, Pope, 224
Lihnbenner, Gus., 223
Lilienthal
  D., 352
  ___ (Dr.), 420
Lilley
  Rosa (Mrs.), 262
  T. W., 262
  Wright, 262
Lilly [Lillie]
  Joe, 224
  Tyre, 248
  W., 223
Limburger, Albert, 395
Lina, B. F., 258
Lincoln
  A., 338
  George, 263
Lindenberger, J. H., 336

Lindenburg
  Annie (Mrs.), 224
  Charles, 224
Lindenstein, Charles, 262
Lindenwood, F., 266
Linderman, ____ (Mrs.), 246
Lindey, Miles, 223
Lindhilen, Gus., 223
Lindley, N. A., 266
Lindner, Aug., 257
Lindo, W. H., 373
Lindon, Charles, 224
Lindsay, Belle, 223
  C., 349
  Charles, 223
  W. T., 223
Linehan, John C., 400
Linen, James A., 353
Ling, Lucy, 223
Lingner, Lizzie, 224
Lingreen, ____, 238
Lining, ____, 303
Link
  Alois, 258
  Louisa, 257
Linkhauer, John, 410, 411, 413, 415
Linkhause, Jacob, 224
Linn, Rosa, 224
Linsey
  Jack, 224
  Joseph, 224
Lippo, M., 258
Lippold, Wiley, 224
Lippseheatz, Theodore, 258
Lipscomb, M. J. (Mrs.), 248
Lirch, Rosini (Mrs.), 223
Lirette, ____, 265
Lirgot, Jacob, 244
List, W. B., 249
Litteray, S. A., 340
Littig, Willie, 223
Little
  C. J., 358
  E. V., 401
  Samuel, 248
  William S., 264
  Willie E., 244
Littlejohn
  Lewis, 224
  W. B., 246
Livingston
  Fannie, 223
  Henry, 223
  J., 59
Llalia, Nicolina, 257
Locassie, Rosalie, 258
Lochert
  M., 257
  Michael, 258
  Regina, 257, 258
  Sebastian, 258
  ____ (Mrs.), 258
Lochmeyer
  A., 223
  William, 223

Lochni, Minnie, 258
Locke [Lock]
  Jasper, 265
  Phoebe, 224
  Robert, 223
  Susie, 224
Lockman, Julius, 247
Lockwood
  D. M., 425
  G. M., 358
Locquet, Ida, 257
Loeb
  Adelbert, 258
  Alex, 264
  Emanuel, 264
  Henry, 264
  Henry L., 258
  Jacob, 223
  Louie, 250
  S. (Mrs.), 419
  ____ (Mrs.), 249
Loechner, Anna, 258
Loeffle
  Charley, 223
  E., 224
Loewenthall, L., 238
Loewer, M. E. (Mrs.), 257
Logan
  Catherine, 223
  J. C., 368
  J. W., 375
  John, 241, 375
  M. E., 258
  ____, 239
Logne, B., 246
Logue, Edward, 246
Lohman
  George, 223
  Henry, 258
  Ida, 223
  Katie, 223
  ____ (Mrs.), 223
Lohmann, Gertrude, 258
Lohr, Rose H., 258
Loiseau, Hyacinthe, 258
Loiseaux, Joseph, 265
Lolinski, L., 224
Lonargan, H., 135
Londen, Edgar G., 257
Lonfield, W. W. (Mrs.), 224
Long
  A., 224, 250
  Edwin, 257, 258
  J. S., 349
  J. W., 342
  Jane, 258
  Jesse, 250
  John, 258
  Luther, 258
  Oscar, 250
  R. A., 246
  Sarah J., 257
  W. E. (Mrs.), 248
Long Hou, 247
Longaret, James, 258

Longerpie
  Y., 263
  ____, 263
Longreen, Peter, 258
Longrois, Louis, 258
Longwell, George, 437
Lonsdale
  J. G., 136, 330, 331, 354
  John G., 224
  John G. Sr., 135, 142, 182, 224, 331, 332, 335
  John G. Sr. (Mrs.), 142, 224
  John G. Jr., 163, 171, 224, 377, 390, 391, 392, 407
  W. J. B., 135, 136, 142, 182, 224, 384
  ____, 142, 185
Lonsford
  John T., 224
  W. W., 224
  ____, 224
Look, Err, 223
Loomis, F. M., 344
Looney
  R. H. A., 223
  William Z., 240
Loop [Loope]
  Annie, 223
  E. Rush, 224
Loos, Julius, 258
Lopez
  Emily, 258
  Margaret, 258
  Philip, 258
  Victor, 258
  ____ (Mrs.), 258
Loranz
  James, 223
  L. M., 223
Loranz (Sister), 224
Lorch
  Adolph, 245, 250
  Henry, 257
  R. P., 258
Lord
  Charles H., 258
  George, 346
Lordeman, Francis, 401
Lorentia (Sister), 245
Lorentz, L. M., 416, 432
Lorie, F. (Mrs.), 258
Loseley, C. H., 347
Losey, Charlie, 265
Lots, Henry J., 258
Lott
  James, 390
  Robert, 223
Lotz, Susan A., 258
Loubert, Clarence, 258
Louden, W. A. Jr., 351
Louder, Andrew J., 248
Loughlin, John, 399

Louis
  Camille, 263
  E., 258
  F. W., 223
  George F., 258
  Louisa, 223
Loutan, Ernest, 258
Love
  Alice, 223
  Annie, 224
  Buddy, 224
  Charley, 224
  Frank E., 243
  Richard, 224
  Robert, 224
  Rosa, 224
Lovell, Nellie (Mrs.), 374
Lovely, Eveline, 223
Lovia, Ida, 265
Lovin, J. J., 406
Lowden, Lawrence D., 258
Lowe
  Esther, 223
  John, 258
  O., 375
Lowell
  Carrie, 223
  Sam., 238
Lowenberg, Abe, 242
Lowenhardt
  Katie (Mrs.), 223
  William, 223
Lowenhaupt
  B., 419
  J., 354
Lowenstein, ____, 349
Lowenthal, M., 420
Lowinsohn, Louis, 258
Lowry [Lowery]
  George F., 250
  H. T., 368, 370
  James, 224
  Lezina, 258
  Lulu, 250
  W. R., 117, 368, 369
  William, 258
  ____ (Mrs.), 250
Loyce, George, 240
Loyd
  Albert Jr., 244
  Annie, 244
  Freddie, 244
  Sophie, 244
  William, 244
Luala, West, 224
Lucarani, J. F., 224
Lucas
  Lou., 224
  M. A., 224
  Robert, 223
  William, 224
Luccarnia, J. R., 112
Lucett, Catherine, 243
Luckett, O. A. Jr., 246
Luddy, John, 374
Ludlow
  Blanche, 258

NAME INDEX

F. W., 224
T. W., 374
Ludson, J. S., 346
Ludy
  Lewis, 224
  _____ (Mrs.), 224
Luetke, Lewis, 224
Luff, M. W., 434
Luiselli (Father), 119
Luizza, Antonio, 258
Luke
  Elizabeth, 258
  J. W., 410
  Peter, 258
Lukenheimer, F., 351
Lulkenie, Joseph, 223
Luluhardt, C. L., 258
Lum, Edward O., 248
Lumpkins
  J. M., 245
  Thomas, 239
Lunch, B., 112
Lundy
  Charles S., 258
  Tom, 224
Lungo, Francisco, 258
Lunn
  Mary E., 258
  Phil. H., 224
  Reno, 224
  Thomas, 224
  William Jr., 224
Lunster, Fred, 224
Lupkin, _____, 224
Luppo
  J., 368, 370
  _____ (Dr.), 178
Lusca, Mateo, 258
Lusher, Charlie, 223
Lusse, _____, 258
Luster, Bettie, 223
Lutcher, Henry G., 258
Lutersbacher, B. A., 257
Luttrell
  Cappie, 251
  John, 251
  _____ (Mrs.), 251
Lutz
  Jacob, 223
  Jacob Sr., 223
  Martha, 395
  S. E. (Mrs.), 224
  _____, 251
Lyle, John, 258
Lyman, H. J., 224
Lynch
  Amelia, 224
  Bernard, 224
  Daniel, 404
  E., 401
  Florence, 400
  James, 223
  Katie, 258
  Mary, 223, 242, 258, 374
  Mary (Mrs.), 223
  Mary M. (Mrs.), 248

Mike, 223
Minerva, 245
Patrick, 399, 400
Virginia, 245
_____ (Mrs.), 223
_____, 274
Lynd, Mike, 223
Lynn, T. J., 389
Lyon, J. E., 249
Lyons
  James, 258
  Larry, 224
  Lizzie, 224
  Robert, 429
  Robert A., 257, 258
  _____ (Dr.), 110
Lyre, Thomas, 258
Lyskle, William, 258
Lyttle [Lytle]
  N. B., 375
  William, 174
Lytus, Dick, 223

M

Maaendina, Antonio, 258
Maag
  George, 226
  George (Mrs.), 226
Maari, B. A. A., 258
Maas, H. (Mrs.), 240
Maberry, Sarah, 243
Mac, Pat, 224
Macazo, Francisco, 259
Macbeth, Mabel, 224
Maccabee [Maccabe],
  J. C., 132, 390, 392
Macdon, Mary Estelle, 263
MacDonald, _____, 226
MacDougal, Charles H., 225
Macelfresh, James, 225
Macether, A., 225
MacEver, William, 245
Mack
  Ann, 227
  Charles, 225
  Charlotte, 244
  James, 258
  Mike, 227
Mackae, George I. J., 259
Mackenzie
  E. S., 225
  Edward, 225
  H., 226
  S. A. (Mrs.), 225
  _____, 225
Mackey, Samuel (Mrs.), 248
Mackin, William, 245
Macklin
  A., 225
  Eliza, 225
  H., 430
Macnamara, John, 225
Macon, Frederick M., 259
Madary, William, 259

Madden
  J. J., 225
  M. C., 399
  William, 225
Maddow, Robert O., 225
Maddox [Madox]
  Charles, 227
  Emma, 406
Madhardt, Elizabeth, 226
Madigan, M. W., 400
Madison
  Charles, 239
  H., 226
  H. M., 373
  J. H., 258
  John, 224
  M., 258
  _____, 227
Madley, Frank, 225
Madsley, John, 225
Magdeline, Julius, 258
Magee
  D. A., 409
  Susan, 225
Magendre, Oscar, 259
Magenta, Santa, 258
Mager, Mary, 259
Maggiore, Antoine, 249
Magher, M., 403
Maginus, Anetta, 225
Magiveny, B., 402
Magoranna, Sarah, 259
Magrath, _____ (Gov.), 192
Magruder, J. T., 246
Maguire
  J. E., 375
  M. M., 337
  Winfred, 258
Mahaffey
  H. J., 226
  L. W., 227
Maher
  James, 225
  Joe, 264
  Mike, 225
  William, 227
Mahin, Joseph, 242
Mahler
  Edward, 258
  Louisa, 265
Mahon, H., 227
Mahoney
  Daniel D., 400
  David, 404
  F. M., 399
  Hannah, 225
  Mary Jane, 258
  Thomas, 259
  _____ (Mrs.), 227
  _____, 227, 264
Mailes, Pauline C., 259
Mailhes, Marie, 258
Mailho, Charles, 259
Mains, Fred, 259
Maiting, Nina, 258
Major, T. W. J., 226
Majorana, Rosa, 258

Majorin, Angelo, 258
Makin
  C. (Mrs.), 373
  Julia, 258
  Patrick, 258
Malasguiva, Luigi, 258
Malci
  Jack, 245
  Lizzie, 245
Malen, F., 265
Maley
  Charles, 258
  Mary A., 227
Mallon, Green, 227
Mallory
  A. H., 227
  L. H., 227
  _____ (Dr.), 47
Malloy
  Charles, 399
  Mary E., 258
Malmont, August, 374
Malone
  A. J., 401
  Albert, 225
  C. C., 226
  C. W., 169
  G. B., 337
  Josie, 225
  Louis, 225
  Maria, 225
  Mike, 225
  Ned., 225
  Robert, 224
  Patrick, 259
  S., 399
  Wesley (Mrs.), 226
Maloney [Malony]
  Edward, 227
  Eliza, 227
  G. B., 353
  Gracie, 227
  James, 259
  Laurent, 258
  Maggie, 227
  Michael, 259
  Patrick, 239
  Peter, 225
  Thomas, 259
  _____ (Miss), 264
Maloy, Belle Lee, 242
Malsi
  Caroline, 227
  Conrad, 225
Maltese, _____ (Mrs.), 225
Malverhill, P. R., 259
Manaby, Joseph, 258
Manala
  Para., 258
  _____ (Mrs.), 258
Manale, Anna, 258
Manassas, Simon, 259
Manatzer
  _____ (Mrs.), 247
  _____, 247
Manches, Gus., 226
Mancoosa, Rosalie, 258

Mandell, Anna, 259
Mandeville, W. R., 378
Mandon, George, 264
Maneisso, D. J., 258
Manely, A. Jr., 400
Manery, James E., 404
Maney, James, 251
Manfree, Tony, 259
Mangle
  Ed, 251
  Ed (Mrs.), 251
Mangum
  A. W., 355
  S. D., 239
  S. D. (Mrs.), 239
Manheim, A., 402
Manierre, Thomas W., 226
Manifold, John, 247
Maniornioux, F., 259
Maniouloux, Eugene, 258
Mankin, H., 259
Manley [Manly]
  Maggie Ellen, 225
  Theresa, 225
  W. J., 247
  Y. R., 225
Manlove, A. R., 242
Mann [Manne]
  Andrew, 430
  Benjamin F., 246
  Charles G., 372
  Eddie, 227
  Eliza, 241
  Henry C., 258
  J. B. (Mrs.), 372
  James, 430
  Joel (Mrs.), 241
  Joseph, 258
  Lelia, 243
  Minnie, 246
  Sallie, 227
Manneaux, Francis, 259
Mannell, John, 243
Manning
  C. P., 402
  Dennis, 259
  George, 226
  Pat, 227
  Regina, 258
  T. D., 368, 369
  T. M., 373
  _____ (Dr.), 245, 356
Mannings, Richard, 373
Mannion, Lawrence, 259
Manroner, Louisa A., 259
Mansfield, S., 438
Mansford
  E. B., 330
  E. J., 135, 136, 225
  Ed, 152
  Edward, 331
  Edward J., 141, 332, 335
  _____, 386
Manton, John, 395

Manuel
  L. (Mrs.), 258
  R. C., 227
Many, James, 225
Manyon, Andrew, 258
Marable, J. T., 368
Maraingues, J., 258
Mararour, Henry, 259
Marble
  E. V., 243
  Robert, 243
Marcault, Maria A., 259
Marcello, Vincent, 259
Marchand, Victoria, 259
Marchant
  C., 372
  Daniel J., 242
Marcus
  Hannah, 244
  John, 244
  Violet, 243
Marcusy, E., 372
Mares, J., 225
Maretilloi, _____ (Lt.), 357
Marett, W. J., 245
Margarette (Sister), 245
Margee, Mary C., 259
Margueritz, E., 242
Marigny
  B., 259
  Blavebe, 259
Marinino, P., 259
Marino
  Salvatore, 259
  Salvatrie, 259
Marion
  George, 226
  Thomas (Mrs.), 247
Marither, M., 250
Marker, Louis, 263
Markey, Josephine, 258
Marks
  A. S. (Mrs.), 355
  Adelaide, 258
  Calhoun, 258
  F., 226
  George, 226
  Gus E., 243
  H., 227
  Isaac, 263
  Jacob, 227, 263
  M., 226, 244
  Moses, 227
  R., 244
  _____ (Mrs.), 226
Marland, _____ (Miss), 361
Marley, Thomas, 430
Marley (Father, Rev. Father), 119, 251
Marlin, E. L., 348
Marlose, S., 249
Marmaduke, J. M., 347
Maron, Reuben, 225
Marona, Joseph, 242
Maronge, Onezippe, 265
Marooney, David, 225

Marrian [Marrion]
  J., 242
  S., 259
Marritia, Frank, 436
Marsden, John, 227
Marsh
  Ed, 240
  Ernestine, 259
  Howard, 239
  Robbie, 226
  S. T., 344
Marshall
  C. K., 71, 125, 438
  E., 390
  E. C., 226
  Henry, 225
  J. A., 259
  Nancy, 248
  Raphael, 247
  Sam, 226
  Sammie, 247
  Samuel, 248
  Thomas F., 381
  Tom F., 247
  William, 246
  _____, 226
Marston
  David, 264
  George, 264
  _____ (Miss), 264
Marteen, Julius, 262
Martella, Rosalie, 258
Martello, Gaetano, 258
Martha, Mary A., 259
Martin
  Anna, 265
  Bertha, 263
  Cornelius, 226
  Eulale, 265
  George M., 259
  Henry, 430
  J. R., 225
  James, 243
  John, 227, 259
  Joseph, 227, 259
  M. P. (Mrs.), 240
  Maria (Mrs.), 226
  Mary, 226
  Michael, 227, 259
  Philip, 259
  Polly, 245
  R. R., 264
  Rose, 259
  Sam, 227
  T., 227
  Theodore, 263
  Thomas, 241
  Tillie, 241
  V. B., 227
  W. H., 248
  William, 249
  _____ (Madame), 258
  _____ (Mrs.), 241
  _____, 249
Martinay [Martiney]
  M. (Mrs.), 263
  Mary G., 258

Martinez, William, 263
Martingley, M. A., 227
Martley, William P., 227
Martz
  _____ (Mr.), 245
  _____ (Mrs.), 245
Marvin, _____, 245
Mary, Moriggo, 259
Mary (Sister), 258
Mary Alphonsa (Sister), 375
Mary Bernadine (Sister), 120
Mary Brigetta (Sister), 253
Mary Dolora (Sister), 120
Mary Eploriam (Sister), 255
Mary Theresa (Sister), 262
Mary Veronica (Sister), 120
Masderville, _____ (Dr.), 69
Maskey, Louisa, 246
Mason
  Charles, 251
  Frederick M., 259
  I. B., 227
  Jack, 227
  Jane, 226
  Jennie, 248
  Luke, 242
  Mary, 242
  Philip, 224
  _____, 225, 227
Massa
  Mary A., 226
  _____ (Mrs.), 227
Massar, J. N., 226
Massengale
  A. S., 227
  Ed, 243
Masser, Teresa, 259
Massey, Joseph, 226
Masseys, Adeline, 258
Masson
  D. B., 258
  Matilda (Mrs.), 258
Mastaiseh, Matt, 259
Matas, Joseph, 259
Matchman, Robert J., 332, 437
Maternus (Father), 119, 165
Mathen, William, 259
Mather, John, 258
Mathers
  Henry, 259
  _____ (Mrs.), 247
Mathes
  J. H., 434
  J. H. (Mrs.), 434
  J. Harvey, 157, 406
  J. Harvey (Mrs.), 406
  _____ (Capt.), 130, 163, 164
Mathews [Matthews]
  A. J., 266
  F. (Mrs.), 225, 226

NAME INDEX 489

F. A., 225
Ferdie, 226
G. W., 347
J. A., 337
J. C., 372
James A., 422
John, 226
Louis, 259
Nancy (Mrs.), 249
Robert, 259
W. D. A., 340
W. S., 406
William, 227
____, 263
Mathewsen, C. C., 259
Mathias, Maggie, 242
Matill, John, 239
Matlock, Carrie V. (Mrs.), 240
Matox, Thomas, 243
Mattel, Charles, 258
Mattson, John, 246
Maucher, A., 225
Maudeville, G. A., 374
Maughan, ____, 245
Maugriocia
 Jena, 259
 Mary, 259
Maumus, A. M., 259
Maunch
 ____ (Mrs.), 251
 ____, 251
Maunord
 B., 226
 ____, 226
Maupin, ____, 171
Maur, Tillie, 227
Maurelian (Brother), 397
Maurer, Phil., 227
Maurin
 Joseph C., 259
 Walter, 264
Maury [Maurey, Maurie]
 Annie, 226
 Edward, 240
 J., 238
 Mary, 238
 ____ (Dr.), 105
Mausen, Charles, 259
Mavorans, J. M., 259
Maxley, Thomas, 430
Maxwell
 D., 404
 John L., 340
May
 Annie, 337, 356
 B. W., 380
 G. S., 249
 Job, 263
 Kate E., 348
 Mintie (Mrs.), 227
 W. B., 226, 248, 408
 W. B. (Mrs.), 248, 408
 William Harrison, 263
 ____, 408
Maya, Fred, 259

Mayer
 Albert, 249
 Bernard, 259
 Caroline, 263
 Fred, 249
 Isadore, 244, 263
 John, 258, 404
 Karl, 259
 Marcus, 263
Mayes, Sam, 226
Mayfield, Helen G., 249
Mayhew
 Bob, 247
 William, 227
 ____, 227
Mayloz, T. W., 264
Maynard, Joseph, 249
Mayne, Mary, 258
Mayner, Joseph E., 259
Mayo
 George, 249
 Martha, 227
 Samuel, 226
Mayre, Ambrose, 429
Mays
 C., 226
 Robert, 244
 Sarah B. F. (Mrs.), 425
Mayse, Henry, 264
Mayson, ____ (Dr.), 250
Mazedye, Jeanetta, 225
Mazelin, George, 262
Mazeron, ____ (Mrs.), 258
Mazetta, Annie, 225
Mazounave, Pierre, 258
McAfee, J. A., 239
McAllister [McAlister]
 A. W., 250
 A. W. (Mrs.), 249
 C. H., 358
 C. K., 247, 249, 250
 C (Mrs.), 247
 Gus, 247
McAnelly, W. T., 227
McArdle, Joseph P., 259
McArey, Michael, 259
McArn, Mary (Mrs.), 372
McArnish, ____, 225
McArthur
 Daniel, 258
 Hugh, 259
 William, 258
McBey
 Alex, 249
 D. (Mrs.), 249
 E. (Mrs.), 249
McBindley, Ed, 225
McBride
 Charles, 241
 Emma, 225
 John, 403
 Margaret, 225
 Mary, 227
 Mary C., 258
 Patrick, 258
 S. F. (Mrs.), 241
 ____ (Mrs.), 241

McCabb, Elizabeth, 259
McCabe
 Annie, 243
 Ella, 243
 James, 227
 Michael, 244
 Patrick, 401
McCadden, Mary Ann, 226
McCain
 George, 226
 John, 258
 William, 251
McCalf, Zac., 226
F. F., 226
McCall
 Ellen (Mrs.), 258
 Henry, 224, 226
 Robert, 227
 Thomas F., 187
 ____ (Dr.), 247
McCallen, P., 404
McCallister, J., 226
McCallum
 Charley, 250
 George C., 250
 James, 242
 James A., 375
 Kate, 250
 M. (Mrs.), 250
 Mary, 250
 W. D., 141, 226, 330, 331, 332, 335
 William, 247
 ____ (Mrs.), 247
 ____, 250
McCammon, Moses, 258
McCampbell
 J., 248
 John, 380
McCann
 Billy, 248
 James, 247
 John, 242
 Thomas J., 399
McCardell, Thomas, 259
McCarthy [McCarthey]
 Dan, 259
 Eugene, 259
 John, 402
McCartney, M. (Mrs.), 227
McCarty
 Alex, 245
 Tim (Mrs.), 251
 ____ (Miss), 250
 ____ (Mrs.), 245, 250
 ____, 245
McCaughey, Edward, 403
McCauley
 J. L., 349
 J. W., 225
 John, 225
 Mary, 258
McCause, W. A., 347
McCavesy, F., 259
McClaffry, Peter, 259
McClain [McClane]
 Jennie, 176

John, 258
R. M. (Mrs.), 355
William, 258
McClann, John, 226
McClannahan [McClanahan]
 H. (Mrs.), 226
 J., 238
 Thomas, 266
McCleary, M. J. (Mrs.), 373
McClellan
 Millie, 225
 W. H., 372
 Wiley, 226
 ____, 225
McClendon
 Matt, 243
 Mattie, 242
McClenon, Mattie, 244
McClintock, Aleck, 259
McClinton, R. H., 248
McCloskey [McClosky]
 George, 259
 Kate Ann, 259
 M. D. (Mrs.), 373
 Mary Ann, 263
McCloy
 G. W., 225
 W. S., 336
McClure
 George, 227
 John, 246
 M. L., 373
 M. (Mrs.), 227
 Mary (Mrs.), 259
 Milton, 342
 Simpson, 248
McCluster, R. H., 248
McCombs, R. H., 224
McConley, James B., 225
McConnell [McConnel]
 A., 225
 Alex, 226
 C. W. (Mrs.), 240
 James, 112, 224, 251, 259
 Tom, 225
 ____ (Mrs.), 258
 ____, 146
McConville, Peter, 258
McCormick [McCormack]
 Andrew, 259
 Anna T., 258
 Charles, 258
 Isaac, 266
 J. D., 352
 John, 225
 M., 266
 Mary, 259
 S. H., 368, 370
 Thomas S., 404
 W., 226
McCorneal
 Tony, 259
 William, 259
McCorshin, Frank, 266
McCoskey, Barney, 246

McCove, George P., 258
McCoy
  A., 430
  Charles, 259
  Hugh, 242
  Levi, 431
  Minnie, 226
  Mollie, 242
  R. J., 227
  Sallie, 226
McCracken
  M., 225
  W. C., 353, 380
McCrady, W. L., 242
McCraven, ____ (Dr.), 42
McCrea, ____, 226
McCreary, George W., 147, 148, 391
McCroskey, H. A., 245
McCrowell, ____ (Mrs.), 227
McCulloch, ____ (Dr.), 305
McCullock
  S. J., 226
  William, 226
McCullom, W. D., 226
McCullough
  Ben., 225
  Ben. (Mrs.), 225
  Bill, 226
  Ellen, 259
  James, 399
  P. P., 404
  Richard, 246
  ____, 225
McCully, W. A., 26, 368
McCune
  James, 258
  Pat, 247
McCurley, Thomas, 226
McCutchem, W. H., 361
McDaniel, John, 265
McDermon, Pat, 246
McDermott
  Frank, 258
  J. J., 259
  James J., 259
  ____ (Mrs.), 245
  ____, 264
McDew, ____, 225
McDonald [McDona'd]
  Alec, 259
  Andrew, 259
  Andy, 249
  Carrie, 241
  Celia, 374
  Charles, 226
  Cornelius, 227
  J. W., 126, 163, 226, 227, 266, 408, 426, 432
  J. W. (Mrs.), 226, 408
  James L., 258
  John, 258
  John A., 263
  Kate, 227
  M. (Mrs.), 373

Mary, 395
Michael, 258
Peter, 226
R. A., 259
R. G., 259
Rosa, 225
Susie, 226
T. C., 135
T. E., 135
Tony, 247
W., 244, 347
William, 259
William R., 226
____ (Dr.), 317
____ (Mrs.), 225, 247, 259, 373
____, 408
McDowell
  Carrie, 226
  Henry, 227
  J. W., 226
  ____ (Mrs.), 225
McElroy
  E., 226
  Martha, 242
  Patrick, 227
  V. H., 407
  V. H. (Mrs.), 407
  W. N., 225
  William, 406, 423, 426
  ____ (Sgt.), 152
  ____, 407
McElwee
  Charles, 239
  S. J., 239
McEnery, Margareth, 258
McEnnis
  J. N., 250
  L. (Mrs.), 250
McEven, Samuel, 258
McEver, J. N., 244
McEwan, John, 259
McFall, Mollie E., 225
McFarland
  Bessie (Mrs.), 250
  Charlie, 250
  Hugh G., 250
  J. T., 336, 368
  Kate, 241
  Mary, 250
  ____ (Dr.), 168, 192
  ____ (Mrs.), 241
  ____, 250
McFeely, John, 427
McField, J., 242
McFreeley, John, 226
McGain, Sam, 259
McGaroc, E. J., 337
McGarvey [McGarvy]
  J. R., 119, 164
  John R., 225
  Mary, 258
McGary, Jane, 245
McGaughey, ____, 240
McGee
  Alexander, 402
  Charles, 226

Martha, 227
P. P. (Mrs.), 338
____ (Miss), 338
McGehee
  F. D., 265
  Harriet, 265
  Margaret, 249
McGeure, ____, 250
McGhee, Tony, 225
McGherry, ____ (Mrs.), 245
McGibbons, M. J., 259
McGill, Daniel, 259
McGilvrey
  David, 226
  J. G. (Mrs.), 225
McGinnis
  Annie, 243
  James, 244
McGinty
  Edward, 400
  G. W., 242
  W. J., 244
McGirk, A., 225
McGiveney, Thomas, 224
McGloin, Charles, 259
McGoey, Mary, 259
McGolrick, James, 401
McGonnegal, E. (Mrs.), 373
McGorks, Alabama, 225
McGoupf, Beverley, 372
McGovern, John, 258
McGowen [McGowan]
  Alfred, 239
  Charlie, 227
  James, 227, 401
  Jane, 227
  Jeff (Mrs.), 245
  Michael, 225
McGrann
  H. J., 416, 417, 433
  H. J. (Mrs.), 417, 433
  ____, 165, 417, 433
McGrath
  Charles P., 259
  Eugene, 400
  John, 259
  Mary Columbia (Sister), 242
  Wallace (Mrs.), 352, 353
McGraty, Barney, 250
McGraw
  Martin, 259
  Nellie, 225
  Sallie, 362
McGregor
  James, 227
  Joseph, 227
  Robert, 226
  S. M., 351
  T. H., 117, 226, 368, 369
  ____ (Dr.), 182
  ____, 224
McGrew, J. E., 368
McGuckin, Henry, 403

McGuin [McGuinn]
  Patrick, 258
  T. S., 402
McGuire
  B. (Mrs.), 259
  Crown (Mrs.), 245
  E. E., 243
  James, 259
  Kate, 258
  M., 259
  Mollie, 244
  Pat, 245
  Willis, 258
McGuirk, Kate G., 259
McGurk, E. A., 399
McHam
  G. B., 244
  H. G., 244
  S. H. (Mrs.), 244
  S. W., 244
McHenry
  George, 259
  W., 242
  W. A., 343
McHugh, James, 245
McIlvaine
  Mary (Mrs.), 224
  ____ (Mrs.), 226
McInnis
  Fannie, 247
  J. A., 245
  John, 249
  Laura (Mrs.), 245
  Mary Belle, 245
McIntosh
  James, 259
  R., 239
  William H., 262
  ____ (Mrs.), 241
McIntyre
  Frank, 372
  William, 259
  Willie, 372
McKahm, T. C., 352
McKain
  John (Mrs.), 225
  ____, 225
McKay
  Catherine, 225
  D. L., 227
  Daniel, 259
  Ida, 249
  Mack, 227
  Mary, 259
  R. H., 240
McKee
  Sallie, 226
  T. M., 408
  T. M. (Mrs.), 408
  ____, 408
McKenly, J., 259
McKenna
  Annie, 242
  Annie (Mrs.), 227, 251
  Delia (Mrs.), 244
  Hugh, 242
  J. R. (Mrs.), 404

NAME INDEX 491

James, 242
John, 402
Louisa, 242
_____, 224
McKenzie, Mary C., 258
McKeogh, M., 425
McKeon
  James, 224
  John E., 238
  M., 227
  Pat, 249, 250
McKernan, James, 403
McKeugh, H. J., 245
McKie
  M. J., 246
  Nath. W., 246
  Zoe, 246
McKim
  J. W., 117, 368, 369
  _____, 342
McKinley
  E. (Mrs.), 225
  _____ (Mrs.), 226
  _____, 180, 225, 226
McKinn
  Mary (Mrs.), 224
  Raleigh, 224
McKinney [McKinnay, McKinnie]
  John, 226
  Lewis, 360
  Maggie, 258
  W. O., 245
  _____ (Mrs. Dr.), 246
McKinstry, G. W., 347
McKissack, Haywood, 245
McKitchen, J. N., 226
McLain [McLane]
  C. (Mrs.), 373
  John W., 225
  Morgan, 226
  Robert, 245
McLashtin, Mary, 259
McLaughlin
  Ann (Mrs.), 258
  Florence, 225
  J. M., 401
  Nicholas, 402
  William, 402
McLean
  Charles T., 248
  Felix (Mrs.), 247
  George H., 248
  James, 247
  John, 225
  Lulu, 247
  Phil, 249
  Thomas, 246
  William T., 248
  _____ (Mrs.), 247
McLemore
  Belle, 226
  John, 227
  Jordan, 225
  Laman, 248
McLennan, Frank, 258

McMahon
  Ann (Mrs.), 224
  C. (Mrs.), 259
  John, 239
  Joseph, 224
  William, 399, 400
McMain, Edith, 263
McMann, A. H., 226
McManus [McMannus]
  A., 259
  A. S., 226
  David, 259
  Emma, 258
  J. H., 244
  John, 258, 259
  M., 242
  Philip, 402
  Samuel, 266
  Samuel W., 226
  Thomas, 259
McMellan, Maggie, 243
McMenema, Francis J., 226
McMert, Lizzie, 258
McMichaels, Thomas, 225
McMicken, M. B., 246
McMillan [McMilen, McMillen, McMillin]
  Clay, 246
  Daniel, 239
  E. J., 227
  E. W., 368
  F. G., 358
  J. W., 408
  M. (Mrs.), 225
  _____ (Mrs.), 379
  William, 227, 379
McMillian
  _____ (Mrs.), 247
  _____, 247
McMorrow, John, 243
McMullen, Chris, 259
McMunson, A. H., 226
McMurray, Mary E., 259
McNair
  Bettie, 246
  David, 246
  David (Mrs.), 246
  Eddie, 246
  L. D. Jr., 246
  L. D. Sr., 246
  Robert, 246
McNally, William, 403
McNamara
  Elizabeth, 259
  John, 226, 266
  John (Mrs.), 266
  L., 226
  L. W., 258
  M., 164, 242
  M. J., 259
  Mary, 258
  Michael, 263
  Thomas, 244
  _____ (Mrs.), 226
  _____, 226

McNamee
  Joseph, 401
  _____ (Mrs.), 169
  _____, 169
McNeese [McNees]
  S. P. (Mrs.), 248
  Sarah (Mrs.), 238
McNeil [McNeal]
  Annie, 226
  Charles, 227
  J. L., 430
  James, 227
  Mattie, 258
  Willie, 226
  _____ (Mrs.), 226, 406
  _____, 258, 406
McNulty, Robert, 226
McPartland, _____, 225
McQuaid, Lizzie, 259
McQuillan [McQuillon]
  Mary, 259
  William, 395
McQuillion, John, 259
McQuinlan, Joseph T., 259
McQuirk, John D., 258
McRendle, Edmonds, 226
McReynolds
  C., 432
  C. W., 427
McShean, John, 226
McSheve, John, 225
McStay, Francis, 258
McStea, Terrence, 258
McSweeney [McSweeny]
  Deborah, 258
  Pat, 259
McTie, John, 346
McTique
  August, 259
  Augusta (Sister), 259
McWhirter, William, 259
McWhorter
  W. J., 263
  _____ (Mrs.), 373
McWilliams
  C., 225
  Cora (Mrs.), 245
  R. A. (Mrs.), 245
  _____, 245
Mead [Meade]
  Francis, 227
  James, 225
  John W., 373
  Lorena, 190
  Lorena (Mrs.), 374
  Richard, 272
  Sarah A., 227
  W. C., 118, 225, 268, 269
  _____, 308
Meadeloon, Em., 258
Meador, James, 248
Meadows, Jane, 225
Meagher
  Charley W., 262
  M., 119

Patrick, 226
  _____ (Rev.), 164
Meaher, Annie, 226
Mears
  D., 404
  Fred., 259
Meath
  John, 226
  Thomas, 226
Medelfreche, P., 259
Meeke [Meek]
  Sallie, 225
  T., 259
Meeks, A. M. (Mrs.), 346
Meh, John, 259
Mehan, James, 402
Mehrents, Gertrude, 258
Meil, Michael, 225
Meinke, Joseph (Mrs.), 258
Meisner, C. F., 247
Melancon, Ada, 264
Melania (Sister), 375
Melbourne, Lou, 259
Mellies, Theresa, 259
Melrusse, M., 264
Melton, Thomas, 225
Melvaney, E., 242
Melville, John, 259
Melvin
  Rebecca (Mrs.), 249
  Robert, 224
Mendel [Mendle]
  Herman, 243
  Israel, 244
  Minnie, 243
  Sigmund, 419
Mendelsohn [Mendelson, Mendelssohn, Mendolsohn]
  C., 259
  J., 259
  J. (Mrs.), 259
  Leon, 263
  Phoebe, 372
Menees, T. W., 368, 369
Menes, T. W., 118
Menken [Menkin]
  N. D., 153, 330, 331, 335
  Nathan D., 141, 170, 225, 332, 335, 418
  Nathan D. (Mrs.), 141
Mentel
  Bosanna L., 259
  Mary (Mrs.), 258
Meny, Henry, 244
Menzies, Caspar, 259
Meredith
  Bettie, 227
  Philip, 401
Merendina, G., 259
Merichen, Henry, 259
Merriam, William, 258
Merricke, Albert, 239
Merrill [Merril]
  De., 264
  J., 337

M. A. (Mrs.), 395
S., 343
William, 225
_____ (Dr.), 42
Merriman, Georgia, 226
Merritt
  G. W., 266
  George R., 225
  Jane, 226
  Jane (Mrs.), 262
Merriwether, Lide, 355
Merton, C., 374
Mesritz, Alex, 258
Messick
  William, 356
  _____, 227
Mester, W. W., 345
Metcalf
  Emmons, 224
  Samuel, 224
Metheny, Robbie, 251
Methua
  A., 244
  J. S., 242
Metlige, Mulita, 259
Metz, James L., 342
Metzler
  Frank, 258
  Thomas Jr., 242
Meumeir, Jule, 259
Meunier, E. J., 259
Meush, Fred, 259
Meyer
  Anton, 259
  Barbara, 259
  Caroline, 227
  Charles, 258
  Charles A., 258
  George, 259
  Henry, 258, 259
  Isadore, 244, 245, 250
  J. G., 339, 340
  J. J., 259
  John, 258
  John F., 259
  Mary E., 243
  Maurice, 242
  Otto, 259
  Rest., 227
  Robert A., 259
  Samuel, 259
  Theresa, 258
  William, 227, 247
Meyers
  A. S., 170
  Adolph, 224, 225
  Charles, 421
  Ed., 227
  Frances, 225
  Fred, 374
  John, 226
  Linda, 227
  Pete., 227
  Thomas, 259
  William, 226, 421
  _____, 395
Meza, J. J. D., 259

Mhoon
  J. G., 227
  M. S., 227
  R. B., 226
  W. J., 227
Michaelis
  Clara, 259
  Ern., 259
Michaels [Michalls, Michels]
  Anette, 259
  Catherine, 259
  Gus., 224
  N., 227
Michand, Paul, 259
Michel
  Annie, 226
  Charles, 171
  Eliziphord, 264
Michot
  E. L., 227
  Eliza, 227
  Eugene, 227
  Lady, 227
  Minnie, 227
Michramers, John, 259
Mickler, Conrad, 258
Middleton
  A. H., 242
  Margaret, 242
Miedner, Mich., 259
Mignon, Philomena, 259
Milam
  E. E., 240
  R. P., 240
Milburne, Ed., 227
Mild, Jacques, 259
Milden, Jennie, 225
Milenus (Father), 225
Miles
  Benjamin F., 263
  Freddie B., 243
  H., 226
  Mike, 395
  Virginia E., 259
  William, 242
  _____ (Mrs.), 373
Milet, Marcellin, 259
Milhot, Louis, 258
Miller
  Alice G., 259
  Andrew, 226
  Anthony, 258
  Auguste, 225
  C. W., 431
  Caroline, 227
  Charles, 258
  D., 225
  E. D. (Mrs.), 245
  E. H., 244
  Ella, 258
  F. W., 259
  Ferdinand, 241
  Ferdinand A., 225
  Frank, 251
  Frank (Mrs.), 251
  Fred, 242

Frederick W., 259
George, 259
George S., 226
Granville, 226
H. G., 409
Henry, 263
Henry A., 244
Ida G., 224
Irwin, 224
J. B., 250
J. R., 336
J. W., 225
James (Mrs.), 245
Jane, 246, 374
Jeff, 246
Jessie, 239
Joe, 224
John, 244, 374
John E., 227, 373
John G. (Mrs.), 225
John H., 224
John J., 347
Joseph, 251
Joseph C., 258
Joseph E., 227
Julius, 263
Laura, 226
Laura W., 240
Leonora, 258
Lige, 246
Louis, 258, 259
Louis S., 258
Lucy, 227
M. E. (Mrs.), 248
Maggie, 259
Margaret, 249
O. H., 343
Phoebe, 227
R. B., 224, 390
Rosalie, 258
Ruby, 258
S. B., 224
S. B. (Mrs.), 225
Sallie, 248
V. R., 240
W. E. (Mrs.), 240
W. W. C., 226
William, 226
William C., 259
William H., 259
_____, 227, 245
Millet [Millett]
  J. M., 258
  John, 251
Millheiser, M., 420
Milliken [Millican]
  C. R., 227
  J. H., 359
Mills, Mollie, 259
Milner, W. R., 298
Milton
  Frank, 226
  J. L., 248, 380
  J. R., 379
Minges, B., 259
Minor [Miner]
  B. B. (Mrs.), 170

Betsy, 243
T. F., 225
Minten, J. R., 354
Minzies, James, 247
Mirable, Nicholas J., 259
Miranda, Beatrice, 263
Miret, N., 259
Miroy, K. Eugene, 259
Mirty, Tennie, 226
Mister, Thomas, 266
Mitche, Mollie (Mrs.), 225
Mitchell
  Avery, 227
  Carrie, 259
  Charles, 248
  Charley, 224
  Frank, 243, 247
  George, 224
  George H., 374, 436
  Harry, 259
  J. H., 225
  J. W., 189
  Jack, 259
  James, 242, 248
  Joe, 225
  John, 247
  John H., 226
  John H. (Mrs.), 226
  John T., 437
  Josephine, 225
  Mary, 248
  Mollie, 225
  Moses, 225, 266
  Neil (Mrs.), 353
  Peter, 258
  R. D., 258
  R. W., 27, 140, 224, 331, 336, 356, 359, 365, 371, 407
  R. W. (Mrs.), 225, 407
  Robert, 244
  S., 224
  Sarah, 259
  Slater, 225
  W., 243
  _____ (Dr.), 21, 53, 69, 70, 72, 116, 128, 156, 163, 181, 190, 191
  _____ (Mrs.), 247
Mittenberger, Odile, 249
Mobray, _____ (Miss), 246
Moch, Millie, 225
Moeller, Louis, 226
Moffat [Moffett]
  Carrie A. (Mrs.), 348
  Charles J., 258
  Edward, 227
  John, 224, 266
  William, 226
Mofford, William, 226
Mogrige, Lottie, 226
Mohl, F., 259
Mohr
  Caroline H., 258
  Edward, 259

NAME INDEX 493

Jacob, 258
Paul, 360
Molaison
　Maria, 259
　Onezippe, 265
　Pauline, 263
Mole, Maria, 247
Molford, W. E., 432
Mollere, Louis, 264
Molloy, E. S., 354
Moltedo, Tarnatore, 242
Molton, Uriah, 225
Moltzgay, V., 259
Momgae, Ettiene, 259
Momus, Mary L., 259
Monaghan, T., 400
Monalxen, William, 258
Moncref, E. A. (Mrs.), 258
Moncusa, Mary T., 258
Mond, Labeire, 259
Monell, ____ (Mrs.), 246
Moneth, Peale, 258
Monette
　Annie K., 244
　G. N. (Mrs.), 258
　Gibson, 245
　J. W., 303
　Sallie (Mrs.), 244
　William E., 245
Monier
　C. V. S., 226
　Frank, 259
　Henry D., 259
Monk, Henry, 247, 249
Monnegan
　Ellen (Mrs.), 227
　M. E., 224
Monnohan, Mary, 246
Monoghan, B. J., 400
Monosterio, J. B. R., 258
Monroe
　Ella, 258
　Lewis, 251
　Mary C., 259
Monsuratt, Oscar, 227
Mont, Ent'mt, 357
Montedonico, John, 258
Monteverdi
　K., 226
　Mary, 226
Montgomery
　B. R., 368, 369
　E., 372
　H., 250
　H. A., 333
　J., 342
　J. D., 226
　James, 333
　Jenny (Mrs.), 262
　John, 246
　John (Mrs.), 246
　Lena, 250
　R. B., 118
　Spencer, 262
　William, 224, 247, 249, 250

William (Mrs.), 247, 249
William (Mrs. Dr.), 250
____, 226
Monticino
　Emanuel, 264
　Emanuel (Mrs.), 264
Montizin, Jean M., 258
Monton, J. (Father), 246
Moode, Henry, 155, 416, 433
Moody
　Eva B., 243
　Fred, 258
　Mary, 226
　William A., 259
　____ (Rev. Dr.), 121
Mook
　Gertie, 419
　Jennie, 419
Moon
　Alice, 226
　Mollie B., 238
　Nelson, 238
　W. J. Jr., 226
　____, 226, 242
Mooney [Moony]
　Bridget, 259
　____ (Rev. Father), 164, 226
　____, 245
Moore
　A. F., 245
　Aula, 345
　B. T., 350
　C. G., 225
　Caroline, 263
　Charles, 225
　Daniel, 244
　Dave, 248
　Duncan, 248
　E., 259
　Ed., 239
　Edward, 225, 259
　Ella, 248
　Emma T., 227
　Ernest, 225
　Eugene, 158
　Eugene W., 171, 258, 433
　G. W., 226, 266
　George, 244
　George W., 67, 68
　H. J., 238, 240
　Hattie, 244
　Henry, 259, 433
　J., 242
　J. H., 356
　J. R., 349
　James, 242
　Jessie, 226
　John, 259, 352, 430
　John F., 259
　John L., 361
　John T., 248
　Knox, 240
　Lloyd, 238

M. B., 240
Maggie, 244
Mary, 259
Mary (Mrs.), 373
Miles, 225
Miller, 225
Richard, 251
Robert, 227
Susan, 259
Thomas E., 258
Virgil V., 225
W. G. Jr., 244
W. H., 227
W. S., 343
W. W., 225
William, 248
William R., 438
____ (Mrs.), 226, 239
Moorehead, Sandy, 243
Mooreman, Randall, 240
Moozinski
　M. J., 249
　____, 249
Moran
　Edward, 112
　Emile G., 259
　Eugene M., 258
　John, 227
　Joseph, 259
　M., 266
　Mary, 258
　Mike, 225
　W. F., 227
Morante, Mattie, 259
Morcali, ____, 225
Mordecai, P. M., 374
Mordinn, John H., 226
Morean, E., 227
Morehouse, Anna, 374
Moreland, R. E., 341
Moreldehouse, Josie, 258
Morell, Robert, 259
Moreney, M. (Mrs.), 226
Morere, William, 250
Morey, D. R. (Mrs.), 259
Morgan
　Annie L., 244
　C. E., 246
　Charles, 246
　Delia, 225
　Eliza, 239
　G. E., 344
　G. H., 347
　George, 246
　Henry, 224
　J. L., 352
　J. P., 349, 350
　John, 225
　L. E., 247
　Ophelia, 263
　Pat, 265
　W. F., 430
　W. T., 239
　Walter, 225
　____ (Mrs.), 226, 246
　____, 167
Morganstein, A., 259

Moriarty, James, 258
Morley, Thomas, 259
Moroney
　John C., 259
　Michael, 401
Morrell [Morrill]
　Ira, 401
　R. R., 225
　Robert, 259
Morris [Morriss]
　Alice (Mrs.), 224
　Betsy, 259
　Bridget, 258
　Charles, 265
　D. (Mrs.), 246
　Dave, 247
　Edward, 240
　Edward T., 258
　Frank, 226, 243
　H. N., 259
　Henry, 258
　James, 224, 225, 259
　James P., 225, 251
　John, 227
　John (Mrs.), 238, 240
　M., 247
　M. (Mrs.), 246, 259
　Margaret A., 259
　Mary, 227
　Robert, 246, 259
　Sally, 345
　____ (Mrs.), 227
　____, 227, 247
Morrison
　Alton, 263
　Channing M., 225
　Eliza J., 243
　Florence, 226
　J. A. (Mrs.), 247
　J. Y., 351
　Joseph A., 248
Morrissey
　Patrick, 258
　Peter, 225
Morrow
　David, 242
　Delia, 244
　J. S., 226
　J. V., 345
　Jennie, 227
　John, 248
　John B., 259
　Julia (Mrs.), 227
　Lutha, 251
Morse
　David, 225
　Lucius D., 29
Mortept, Jean W., 259
Mortequi, Marguerite, 259
Morti, Gus. A., 226
Morton [Morten]
　A. W., 259
　Albert, 227
　Bettie, 226
　Harry, 258
　John, 259
　Lewis, 225

Lizzie, 226
Richard, 242
William, 226
Morzinski
M. J., 247
——, 247
Mosby [Moseby]
C. W., 406
Charles, 227
E. C., 390
Emily, 226
Henry, 373
Mary, 226
S., 390
—— (Mrs.), 227, 406
——, 406
Moser
Charles, 258
May, 258
Moses, 69, 269, 270
Moses
Albert, 226
Alice, 259
Isaac, 259
J. M., 246
Jacob, 258
Jane, 259
John, 241
Max (Mrs.), 258
Nancy, 241
—— (Mrs.), 246
——, 69, 241, 358
Mosfeld, F. L., 259
Mosher, Jacob S., 27
Mosley
Benjamin Frank, 248
Robert J., 248
Moss
A. (Mrs.), 226
David, 266
J. T., 330
John T., 141, 158, 331, 335, 365
Major, 226
Philip, 262
Mossett [Mosset]
Ernam C., 259
Mathilda, 259
Mossinger, —— (Miss), 243
Mosyel, E., 242
Motley, Ike, 225
Mouledons, George, 258
Moulton
Thomas, 251
—— (Mayor), 382
Mount
John, 258
Stephen R., 244
Mousohur, J. D., 259
Movant, Ulysses, 265
Mowbry
R. A., 227
Thomas (Mrs.), 246
Moxon, Frederick B., 259
Moyle, —— (Mrs.) 239
Moynihan, J. W., 403

Mozlet, Frank, 258
Mudd [Mud]
John G., 225
Nathaniel, 251
Mudge, Ephraim C., 249
Mueller, G. W., 227
Muir
Douglas, 431
T. B., 259
Mukes, Mark, 373
Mulcahey, Sophie, 263
Mulder, Daniel, 258
Mulford
H., 332, 437
W. E., 427
Mulhenru, Hugh, 259
Mulholland, David, 259
Mullaney, Peter, 225
Mullaven, ——, 225
Muller
Albert, 224
Chris, 265
Christian, 338
Francis, 259
John, 375
Joseph, 247
Kath., 259
William, 247
——, 249
Mullett, Massy, 226
Mulligan
F., 226
James, 399
Richard, 225
Tom, 226
Mullin[Mullen]
Edward, 341
George, 225, 226
H., 400
Mattie, 243
Michael M., 400
Nicholas, 242
Robert, 378, 381
Willie (Mrs.), 226
Mullins
J. M., 432
John M., 427
Mulready, ——, 250
Mulvahill [Mulvilhill]
Bridget, 243
P. J., 225
Mulvey, Jane A., 259
Mulvin, —— (Mrs.), 374
Muncaster, I., 264
Mundinger, C., 407
Mundz, Mary, 258
Munne [Munn]
Sarah (Mrs.), 250
—— (Mrs.), 373
Munroe [Munro]
Daisy, 243
John W., 243
L., 243
Martha, 259
Munson
A. M., 408
A. M. (Mrs.), 408

Louis, 258
Louisa, 258
Munster
Fred F., 259
Joseph E., 259
Munter, Carl, 227
Murchant, Amy (Mrs.), 249
Murdock
D., 188
Daisy, 372, 387
Lottie, 226
Mure, T. K., 265
Muritzen, Otto, 259
Murphy [Murphey]
A. B., 246
E. K., 395
Eliza, 225
Frank, 224
George, 242
George A., 258
H. C., 276
J. J., 136
J. (Mrs.), 249
J. P., 395
James, 248, 258
Jane, 225
Jeremiah, 227
Jerry, 242, 244
John, 225, 258, 259, 263
Lawrence, 258
Letitia, 242
Louisa, 227
M. G., 259
Margaret, 226
Mary E., 259
Mary (Mrs.), 258
Mollie, 225
Olissa, 225
Owen, 395
Patrick, 259
Philip, 258
R. (Mrs.), 374
R. P., 259
Samuel, 225
Sarah Ann, 259
Smith, 250
T., 259
T. H., 404
Thomas, 242
William, 251
William J., 259
—— (Capt.), 98
—— (Mrs.), 250
Murray
Daniel, 259
Ed, 266
George, 258
Henry, 227
John, 259, 375, 376
Lillie, 258
Mary, 249
Mary Bernadine (Sister), 242
Mollie, 265
Thomas, 259
Willie, 265

Murrell, W. J., 29
Musachiar, Rosella, 259
Muschrous, Ignatius, 263
Muse, Annie, 251
Mustachia, Joseph, 259
Mutter, Thomas H., 171
Myatt
Lewis, 372
M. J. (Mrs.), 372
Myer, see Meyer
Barbara, 259
F. (Mrs.), 373
M., 419
Myers
A. S., 407
A. S. (Mrs.), 407
B. A. (Mrs.), 245
F., 373
H., 244
John, 434
Sallie, 244
——, 152, 407
Myhan, Marie, 259
Mynatt
Henry, 126, 226, 432
Lizzie, 225
Thomas B., 225
W. H., 266, 427
Myrick
E. K., 249
M. A., 265
R. A. (Mrs.), 249

N

Nabers, B. D., 245
Nadeau, Francosis, 259
Nagle
Henry, 259
T. (Mrs.), 228
Naguin
Arthur, 265
Joseph, 265
Louise, 265
—— (Mrs.), 265
Nail
John W., 228
Mary (Mrs.), 228
Nailor, D. B. (Mrs.), 244
Naïve, Jean, 264
Nall
R. B., 54, 395
—— (Dr.), 175
Nance
J. W., 240
James Jr., 248
Spencer, 228
Napier, A., 227
Narbon, Michael, 259
Narf, Emma E., 259
Nash
J. M., 342
M., 350
William J., 399
——, 228
Nason, Henry, 244
Natali, Charles, 259

NAME INDEX

Natchtbrand, J., 227
Nathan, C. H., 244
Naumburg, Benjamin, 259
Nauty, Extreme F., 259
Navailes, Joseph, 259
Navaret, Louis, 259
Naylor, Samuel, 228
Neailly, Joseph, 259
Neal
   C. M., 337
   J. A., 244
   John, 259
   Michael, 251
   ____, 240
Neathery, Mattie, 262
Neeley [Neely]
   Ed., 227
   Frederick, 227
   H. M., 438
   Rosa, 244
Negle, John, 374
Negrotto, D. (Mrs.), 259
Neiding, N., 227
Neighbors, Katie, 227
Neil, M. C. (Mrs.), 228
Neillson, August, 262
Nellums, Tede, 245
Nelm
   Mollie, 228
   William, 228
Nelms, Thomas, 227
Nelson
   A. W. (Mrs. Dr.), 228
   Albert, 227
   Andrew, 227
   C., 265
   C. H., 265
   Cicero, 429
   David, 227
   F. M., 410
   John H., 247
   Julia, 228
   Martha, 227
   Mary, 259
   Mollie, 227
   Murray, 340, 341
   N. J., 247
   N. L., 251
   N. L. (Mrs.), 251
   Otto, 227
   Romeo, 228
   Samuel, 227, 228
   Susan H., 227
   Victor, 228
   W. O., 265
   W. W., 227
   ____ (Dr.), 118, 174, 187
   ____ (Mrs.), 227, 228
Nesmith, William J., 245
Neson
   Libby, 264
   Libby, (Miss), 264
   Libby, (Mrs.), 264
Nessaus, Jules, 259
Netherland
   James Jr., 240

M. E., 244
Parvin, 240
Netzer, Ernest, 259
Neumann, Theo., 259
Neumiller, J., 259
Neville
   G. M., 352
   Mollie, 244
Nevin, Michael, 401
Newbauer, Henrietta, 259
Newbert, G. H., 409
Newburg [Newberg]
   ____ (Mrs.), 348
   ____, 240
Newell [Newall]
   C. R., 432
   Charles, 247
   William, 259
Newhouse
   A. M., 227
   Josephine, 259
   Lee, 259
   Leopold, 259
Newman
   Albert, 259
   Augustus, 245
   Bernard, 248
   Corinne, 248
   Gus, 250
   J. C. (Mrs. Dr.), 245
   James, 227
   L. T. (Mrs.), 248
   M., 375
   Mary (Mrs.), 227
   Sallie (Mrs.), 245
   Sidney, 248
   ____ (Mrs.), 151
Newsom
   A., 250
   Ida, 227
   R. W., 357
Newson, James, 264
Newton, John, 26
Ney
   Henry F., 259
   L., 259
Nicaise
   Abel, 249
   Rebecca, 249
Nichols [Nicholls]
   F. S., 154, 434
   H. S., 259
   Isaac A., 300
   John B., 228
   Madge, 265
   W. B., 239
   W. L., 227
   William, 250, 266
   William L., 228
Nicholson
   J. G., 266
   Mary C., 259
   R. C., 390, 407
   R. G., 240
   Robert, 227, 407
   S. B., 228
   ____ (Mrs.), 302

Nicholvick, Peter, 259
Nicolati, F., 227
Nicolaud, B., 259
Niedel, Michael, 259
Nies, Charles, 259
Niewmann, W., 228
Nightingale, Florence, 325
Niglett, Richard, 36
Nilan, James, 403
Niles, ____ (Mrs.), 249
Nilton, Margaret, 227
Ninut, Joseph, 259
Nivoche, M. E., 375
Nixon, J. O., 297
Noah, Ellen, 228
Nobin, Pat, 259
Noble
   Anna L., 259
   Edward, 259
   Fannie (Mrs.), 246
   Kath., 259
   Mary, 227
   Robert, 228, 266
   Samuel W. H., 259
Nobles, Charles E., 259
Nodler, Emile, 263
Noe
   Arbogast, 259
   George, 246
Noel
   Emma, 227
   T., 227
   ____ (Mrs.), 227
Noeler, Louis, 228
Noisseaux, Joseph, 259
Nolan
   James, 401
   John, 259
   Mary, 227
   Patrick, 248
Noland, Thomas, 244
Nolting, Elizabeth, 259
Nolton, Eugenia, 227
Noonan
   Mary, 228
   ____ (Mrs.), 228
Noonar, John, 227
Norcross, Albert, 259
Norden, Anthony, 259
Norfolk, John Henry, 228
Norman
   A. A. (Mrs.), 228
   James, 430
   Lewis, 228
   Willie F., 228
Norment
   Joseph, 227
   Tom, 227
Norris
   J. B., 244
   John, 227
   Mary E., 227
   ____ (Mrs.), 227
North
   C. B., 354
   George M., 243

Nelson, 228, 266
W. V., 242
Northrup, Rachael E., 228
Norton, Ann, 259
Norvell
   Clement R., 259
   Mattie (Mrs.), 259
   Reed, 259
   Thomas E., 406
   Thomas E. (Mrs.), 406
Norwood, Eliza, 259
Nosley, Mary, 259
Notari, Rosalin, 259
Nott, J. C., 26, 35
Noun, Ernest, 227
Novaille, Charles, 259
Novitzky, Annie, 227
Nowell
   Joseph, 248
   ____ (Mrs.), 248
Noyer, Sophia, 259
Nuberg, Leon, 259
Nugent
   James, 259
   P. C., 118, 228, 368, 369
Nusbaum [Nussbaum]
   Isaac, 420
   J., 259
Nuss, Anna W., 259
Nutall [Nuttal, Nuttall]
   J. H., 368
   James, 245
   James (Mrs.), 245
   M. K., 228
   ____ (Dr.), 169
   ____, 84
Nutting, G. A., 228

O

Oakley
   C. P., 408
   C. P. (Mrs.), 408
   Walter D., 228
   ____, 408
Oates
   Laura, 228
   W. J., 228
Oatis
   Addison, 245
   Amanda, 245
   Fannie, 245
   Jaurdie, 245
   Laura, 245
   Leslie, 245
   Warren, 245
   Willis, 245
Oben
   Emma (Mrs.), 263
   Lulu Maude, 263
Obenchain, J. T. (Mrs.), 241
Oberg, A., 244
Obermeimer, Joe, 228
Obers, Kate, 259

O'Berst [Oberst]
  Catherine, 228
  Julia, 228
  William, 228
Oberti, ____ (Father), 245
Oberts, Sarah, 260
Obhoff, Joseph, 259
Obrey, Sidney, 259
O'Brien [Obrien, O'Bryan]
  Ann (Mrs.), 228
  Benny, 244
  Delia, 260
  Edward, 260
  Emmet, 246
  J., 431
  James, 228, 403, 404
  Jerry, 228, 244, 354
  John, 228
  M., 228, 401
  M. J., 404
  Marian, 260
  Martin, 403
  Mary, 259
  Mary Ann (Mrs.), 260
  Mary M., 259
  Matthew, 399
  O. (Mrs.), 372
  P., 399
  Patrick, 228, 404
  Terrence, 228
  Thomas, 249
  Tim, 244
  Willie, 228
  Willie A., 228
  ____ (Mrs.), 246
  ____, 245
Ochesie, John, 259
Ochner, Martin, 228
Ochs, A., 420
O'Connell
  Anna, 259
  C. (Mrs.), 228
  Dan (Mrs.), 248
  Ellen, 228
  Henry, 259, 260
  John, 228, 337
  Katie, 248
  Mary, 259
  Thomas, 259
O'Connor [O'Conner]
  Bridget, 228
  Charles, 264
  David, 263
  Denis, 404
  J. W., 403
  John, 228
  John Jr., 228
  John Sr., 228
  Mary, 228, 243
  Pat, 403
  Patrick, 400
  Thomas, 259
  ____, 228
O'Connors, John, 259
O'Day, Mike, 248
Odell
  A. D., 426

C. (Mrs.), 228
Ellen, 228
Oden, ____ (Dr.), 249
Odom, Charles, 249
O'Donaghue, D., 400
O'Donnell [)'Donnel]
  A., 259
  B. (Mrs.), 372
  Bridget, 228
  H. R., 399, 400, 401, 404
  John, 404
  Martin, 244
  R. H., 399
  Terrence, 400
  William, 228
  ____ (Mrs.), 228, 239
O'Farrell
  Annie, 228
  Hugh, 228
Offner, Blanche, 265
Offutt, Alfred N., 228
O'Flaherty, Dennis, 375
O'Gara, Mary, 228
Ogden, Lizzie H., 259
O'Gray, Kate (Mrs.), 245
O'Hara
  Clara J., 243
  James T., 228
  John D., 228
  Mary, 343
  Michael, 259
O'Harel, Michael, 240
Oharro, ____, 240
O'Hearn
  H., 228
  Mary, 228
Ohlenschlager, G., 259
O'Keefe
  Anna, 259
  B., 403
  Mamie, 228
  Michael, 401
Olbrecht, ____ (Mrs.), 240
Oldham, Charles, 241
Olds, Joe, 347
O'Leary
  Ignatius, 244
  J. (Mrs.), 228
  John, 228
  Patrick, 247
  William, 401
Oletio, Francisco, 259
Olin
  Amanda, 260
  Heder, 259
  Milo, 168
  W. Milo, 369
  ____ (Judge), 427
Oliva, Helena, 260
Oliver
  Addison, 425
  B. P., 245
  Dan, 245
  I. P., 431
  J. W., 350
  Lou., 228

Louis, 259
Z. P., 228
Oliviera, Bridget, 260
Olloted, Fred, 228
Olmstead, Thomas F., 350
Olson, Dan, 249
O'Malley [O'Maley, O'Mally]
  F. (Sister), 259
  James, 402
  Mary Ann, 228
  ____ (Mrs.), 228
O'Mara, P. H., 400
O'Meara, P. G., 344
O'Neal [O'Neil, O'Neill, Oneill]
  Alice, 228
  Edward, 243
  James, 228, 266, 403
  John, 239
  M., 228, 243
  Maggie (Mrs.), 228
  Mary, 239, 240
  Maurice, 266
  Mike, 251
  N., 244
  Owen, 259
  Patrick, 243
  Thomas, 259
  W. J., 259
  William, 240
  ____, 243
O'Nealey, Patrick, 228
Onetta, G., 228
Onley
  Emma, 228
  John, 228
Onsley, Melissa, 244
Opferkuek, Mary, 259
Oppenheimer
  Henrietta, 260
  J., 259
  S. W., 259
Ording, Gertrude, 228
O'Reilly [O'Reiley]
  J., 404
  James, 399
  M., 431
  P., 404
Oriega, Lewis, 228
Orkus, John, 260
Orloff, Gregory, 324
Orme, F. H., 29
Ormsby, E. S., 343
O'Rourke [O'Rorke]
  J. J., 402
  Michael, 259
  W. H., 242
Orpheus, William, 259
Orr
  A. E., 349, 350
  J. G., 368, 370, 372
Orrington, W. H., 342
Orris, Mary F., 242
Orselle, E., 228
Ortepp, August, 260
Orton, P. A., 359

Osbenchain, J. T., 241
Osborn [Osborne]
  J. T., 259
  Sandy, 251
Oskman, Henry, 228
Oslay, Helen, 228
Osley, ____, 241
Oster, Charles, 259
Osterman, Giovani, 260
O'Sullivan
  D., 243
  F. J., 402
Oswald, Mary J., 260
Otey
  George, 228
  Green, 429
  James H., 170
  James Hervey, 170, 171
  Paul, 170
  Paul H., 117, 147, 228
Ott, J. A., 249
Otto
  A., 228
  A. G., 266
  D. H. (Mrs.), 246
  George, 228
  Wylie, 246
Ourso, ____, 264
Oury
  George, 250
  Lyle, 250
Overall, G. W., 368, 370
Overman, L., 350
Overtel, H., 228
Overton
  John Jr., 355
  Maggie, 251
  Mary J., 251
  W., 430
  ____, 228
Owen
  A. J., 228
  H., 241, 244, 266
  Henry, 228
  Julia, 228
  Minnie, 228
  Thomas, 373
Owens
  Bessie, 228
  Charles, 243
  Dock, 228
  Emma, 228
  Frankie, 243
  James, 228
  Jane, 228
  John, 228
  Julia M., 228
  Lela Lovetta, 248
  Mary, 228
  Mary (Mrs.), 248
  N. J., 240
  N. J. (Mrs.), 240
  Owen, 259
  Pierce, 228
  Thomas, 239, 244
  Thomas J., 228

NAME INDEX

William, 259
William Henry, 248
___ (Mrs.), 240
Oxe, Charles, 375
Ozanne, Isadore, 424

P

Pablo, John, 260
Packer
  C. A., 228
  James, 229
Packert, Dedrick, 260
Pad, John, 228
Paderner, Jean, 260
Page
  A., 244
  E., 372
  G., 229
  G. E., 229
  J. W., 330, 331, 335, 356
  Jesse, 158, 416
  Jesse W. Jr., 141
  John, 347
  M. B., 229
  N., 229
  T., 247
  William, 228
Pagels
  Amelia, 228
  Charles, 228
  Otto, 228
Paillet, Francois, 260
Paine, see Payne
Palezzini, Andrew, 260
Pallo, Mary (Mrs.), 373
Palmasino, D., 260
Palmer
  Dennis, 228
  Elizabeth, 229
  Ella, 229
  George N., 260
  H. L., 229
  J. D., 368
  John, 251, 260
  Lucinda (Mrs.), 229
  Potter, 340
Palthon, M., 260
Pandert, Annie, 228
Panellees, Manuel, 260
Pardien, Charles, 229
Paretti, Jean, 260
Parham
  A. K., 239
  ___ (Miss), 251
Parish
  Brooks, 228
  Charity, 229
  Ella, 240
  L. P., 245
  ___ (Mrs.), 240, 245
Park
  James G., 229
  John, 135
  T. C., 409

Parker
  A. O., 353
  Albert, 244
  Annie, 242
  Charles, 244
  Charlotte, 228
  Cora (Mrs.), 249
  D. A. J., 248
  D. A. J. (Mrs.), 248
  Eli, 228
  G. A., 228
  G. G., 372
  I. S. (Mrs.), 248
  Isaac, 229
  James, 374
  James C., 260
  James G., 229
  John, 239
  Richard, 229
  S., 229
  W., 426
  William L., 247
  ___, 385
Parks [Parkes]
  George, 245
  H. A., 346
  Ida, 229
  J. L., 360
  ___ (Dr.), 26, 110
  ___, 229
Parlen, M. G., 244
Parmer, John, 244
Parsons
  C. C., 122, 156, 164, 228
  C. M., 265
  Charles Carroll, 123
  ___ (Rev. Dr.), 377
  ___ (Rev. Mr.), 121
Partee, C. L., 229
Partlow, F. (Mrs.), 229
Parvangher, C., 242
Pascal, Macrez, 260
Paschal
  Andrew, 229
  Henry, 229
Paschke, Otto, 260
Pascoe, Agnes, 260
Pastor, Mary, 260
Pastorius, John, 260
Patchell
  James, 229
  ___ (Mrs.), 229
Pate, Mark E., 246
Patillo [Patello]
  J. E., 350
  Lucy J., 228
  R. F., 229
  R. H., 229
  W. F., 339
Patrick, J. C., 338
Patten, Amos, 260
Patter, Charles, 229
Patterson
  Harrison, 265
  J. A., 373

Jones, 260
Joseph, 229
Laura B., 228
  N. S., 240
P. M., 361
R. A., 229
R. F., 390
R. J., 399
Smith, 240
Virginia (Mrs.), 240
Willie, 229
  ___ (Mrs.), 229, 260
Patton
  Alexander, 401
  E. S., 228
  Maggie, 229
  R. S. Jr., 248
  R. S. (Mrs.), 248
Paul
  Andrew, 260
  Frank, 246
  Major, 266
  N. P., 229
Paulian, C. F., 260
Pavane, Antonio, 260
Pavice, Picena, 260
Payenne, Jean M., 260
Payler, Samuel A., 424
Payne [Paine]
  Charles, 229
  George, 250
  Henry, 260
  J. W., 173
  J. W. (Mrs.), 173
  James A., 337
  Jennie, 229
  Mary, 228, 229, 373
  Michael, 229
  Narcissa, 229
  William, 250
  ___, 173
Paynes, Mary, 228
Paysse
  Andre, 260
  Jean M., 260
Payton, James, 265
Payzade, Jean B., 260
Peabody
  George N., 229
  J. M., 406
  John M., 171, 172, 229
Peacock
  Mamie, 247
  T. E., 247
  ___, 244, 379
Peale, Mary Belle, 243
Pearcall
  A., 408
  C., 408
  ___, 408
Pearce
  H. M., 368, 369
  Hiram, 163
  Hiram B., 167
Pearl, Emma, 229
Pearsall
  A., 228, 266

Aline, 229
Clara, 229
Pearson
  Albert, 229
  Eliza, 228
  John, 245
  L., 260
  Reed, 241
Pease
  Fannie, 228
  Lucy, 228
  Nancy (Mrs.), 228
Pecante, John (Madame), 264
Peck
  F. B., 229
  ___ (Mrs.), 340
  ___ (Sgt.), 113, 429
Pednour, N. E. J., 260
Pedro
  Joe, 266
  Josie, 260
Peebles
  Clifton, 249
  Ida (Mrs.), 249
  P., 229
  R. A., 376
Peeples
  Berlin, 389
  Fannie, 248
  Isaac, 229
  ___ (Mrs.), 265
  ___, 265
  see also Peoples
Peetz, John, 260
Pefer, Cora, 260
Peilert, Charles, 260
Peix, Frederick, 260
Pelequin, Rosamond, 228
Pellegran, Emile, 229
Pellegrims, Simone, 260
Pelletier, Paul R., 260
Pellip, Peaton W., 260
Pellissier, Martin, 260
Pellrin, C., 242
Pelton, ___ (Mrs.), 242
Pelty
  Johnnie, 250
  ___ (Mrs.), 250
  ___, 250
Pena, Lelia M. S. Dela, 260
Penacchi, Louis, 229
Pendelton, Ed, 373
Pendergrast
  Bridget, 229
  James, 260
  Mary, 260
Penders, Barbara, 229
Pendleton
  Ed., 373
  R. Y., 345
Peniston, John J., 260
Penn
  J. E., 229
  Maggie, 228
  William, 78
  ___, 228

497

Pennell, P. W., 246
Pennington, L. M., 246
Penser, Joseph, 260
Peoples
  Jennie, 228
  Jesse, 229
  John (Mrs.), 248
  W. H., 244
  see also Peebles
Pepper
  G. C., 249
  John P., 260
  Joseph P., 260
  Mattie S. (Mrs.), 249
Pequi, Francois, 260
Perault, F., 260
Percell, Vance P., 429
Peres, Pierre, 260
Perez
  John B., 260
  Letitia, 264
  Santo, 260
Perfect, Ernest, 229
Pericapa, John, 260
Perk, Elvira, 229
Perkins
  Archie, 229
  Henry, 229
  Jefferson, 228
  Mary J., 260
  N. T., 228
  P. A., 239
  P. A. (Mrs.), 239
  Randall, 229
  ____ (Mrs.), 239
Pernal, Joseph Y., 260
Pernett, James E., 260
Perodeau, B. D., 229
Perone, Francisco, 260
Perotti, Vincent, 228
Perregat, Paul, 260
Perriland, Remy, 260
Perrin, Adolph, 265
Perry
  Fred, 246
  Georgiana, 229
  James, 246
  James (Mrs.), 246
  John H., 374
  Leonora, 229
  Lizzie, 244
  Martha E., 242
  Somers, 229
  T. M., 250
  T. P., 247
  T. P. (Mrs.), 246
  Thomas, 260
  ____, 246, 247
Perryman, Reuben, 239
Persey, ____, 400
Person
  Jimmy, 239
  Louisa, 251
  ____, 251
Peter, Thomas, 229
Peters
  E. W. W., 260

  J. C., 248
  John M., 390
  Margaret, 260
  Samuel J., 260
  William, 229
Peterson
  Antoine, 260
  Charles, 260
  John, 229, 395
  John C., 260
  Martha, 229
  O., 260
Petralia, Antonio, 260
Petriman, William, 260
Petro, Felice, 242
Petrus, L. O., 238
Pettetory, Louisa E. E., 260
Pettis, Louisa, 260
Pettit [Pettet]
  Clancy J., 260
  J. T., 390, 438
  Louis, 260
  Sophia (Mrs.), 245
  William D., 263
Pettus, L. O., 241
Petty
  Joe, 266
  Joseph, 229
  ____, 246
Petway, S., 229
Petzetsky, Joseph, 260
Peyton
  P. (Mrs.), 246
  Pat, 246
  Tom, 246
  ____, 246
Pezold, Emil L., 260
Pfaunkucker, H., 260
Pfeifer [Pfeiffer]
  E., 419
  Robert, 345
Pfister, Jacob, 229
Pfortzmeiner, L., 264
Pharow, Phil., 229
Pheffer, E. W., 260
Phelan
  Charles R., 260
  P. H., 229
  ____, 229
Philbert, Philip, 260
Philip
  Archy, 260
  John, 264
Philipin, Theo., 260
Phillips
  A., 340
  A. D., 443
  E. L., 340
  Elizabeth, 260
  F. A., 260
  J. H., 263
  Jennie, 229
  John, 260
  Jules A., 260
  Leonard, 247
  M., 229

  Mary, 229
  Tom, 247
  William, 228
  ____, 181
Philmot, Annie (Mrs.), 229
Philson, Eliza, 229
Phoebus
  J. W., 372
  R. W. K., 229
Piaggio, Victoria, 229
Pichon, Alice, 265
Pickens
  Charles, 260
  James, 229
  Oliver, 229
Pickett [Pickitt]
  J. T., 356
  W. S., 175, 366
Pickle, V., 266
Picot
  J. T., 374
  Victor, 229
Pierce
  F., 430
  Fanny, 243
  Granville M., 263
  H. L., 346
  Harvey, 247
  Hiram M., 118, 229
  J. G., 263
  James O., 359
  K., 375
  K. (Mrs.), 375
  Katie M., 242
  Nellie, 229
  Thomas, 229
Pieroni, ____, 244
Pierre, Antonio, 249
Piez, Joseph, 260
Piggins, Felix, 229
Pike
  Albert, 409
  Z. M., 260
Pilch, ____, 229
Pillman, W. A., 372
Pillow, Gideon J., 238
Pillsbury, ____ (Gov.), 346
Pinch, Xavier, 264
Pinckney, ____, 263
Pinda, Philip, 260
Pinder, Sarah, 395
Pingrey, D., 343
Pinkerton, Allan, 340
Pino, Leonie, 263
Pintz, William, 243
Pipe, O. H., 239
Piper, J. H., 229
Pippen
  Henry, 240
  ____, 240
Pischer, P. H., 358
Pitard, Henry, 260
Pitro, Antonio, 260
Pittman
  John, 368
  Scott, 265

Pitts, E. J., 67
Place
  Gervais, 260
  Mary C., 260
  Paul, 260
Plaggio, Felix, 112
Plain
  Carrie, 229
  Katie, 229
Plaline, Charles, 343
Planchard, John J., 260
Planket, Mary, 260
Platt
  Anna, 247
  W. H., 340
  ____ (Mrs.), 247
Plattsmier, Anna, 260
Pleasant, Dilly, 228
Pledge, ____, 192
Pleitz
  William, 238
  Willie, 241
Pletz, F., 229
Plietz
  ____ (Mrs.), 241
  ____, 241
Plischke, Charles H., 228
Pliske, ____ (Mrs.), 229
Plummer
  Al., 229, 433
  B. F., 229
  B. (Mrs.), 229
  B. T., 408
  B. T. (Mrs.), 408
  Frank, 228, 433
  Margaret, 229
  P. B., 240, 354
  P. B. (Mrs.), 240
  Thad, 431
  William, 250
  ____ (Miss), 229
  ____ (Mrs.), 433
  ____, 408, 433
Plump, Mary, 243
Plunkett, Charles, 251
Plymede, Hugh, 265
Pocai, Henry, 228
Pochon, Jean, 265
Podesta, Angelo, 244
Pogle, Julia (Mrs.), 246
Pohl
  Annie, 228
  Theodore, 229
  Theodore (Mrs.), 229
Pohlman, John, 260
Pohm, ____ (Mrs.), 251
Pohnfich, F., 260
Pointer
  John, 229
  Roxana, 229
Poitevent [Poitevant]
  J. (Mrs.), 247
  Jacob, 247
  M. (Miss), 247
Poleicho, M., 249
Polk
  Amanda, 229

NAME INDEX

Bud, 229
G. (Mrs.), 250
John, 260
Lizzie, 229
Maud, 229
Pollard
   C. R., 407
   Edward M., 251
   J. E., 229
   Nancy L., 229
   ____, 407
Polle, L. (Mrs.), 247
Polleino, V. M., 260
Pollock, Samuel, 228
Polonio, L. (Mrs.), 374
Poltharst, Christian, 260
Pomato, Henry, 229
Pond
   Gertrude, 260
   J. B., 356
Ponder
   John, 260
   Mary, 260
Ponge, Albert, 260
Ponito, Vito, 244
Ponjade, Henry, 260
Pons, Lawrence, 260
Pontico, Marie S., 260
Pool [Poole]
   Annie, 260
   William, 260
Pope
   Edmund, 260
   Edward, 263
   Emmet, 266
   Henry, 260
   James, 263
   Joe, 264
   Rachel, 229
   Willie, 229
Poporny, A., 260
Poppe, George A. A., 375
Poque, Victor, 260
Porello, L., 260
Poretto, S., 260
Porteous, John P., 260
Porter
   Calvin, 243
   D. T., 129, 391, 407
   E. W., 348
   J. F., 136
   James D., 366
   Joseph, 265
   L. A., 239
   W. L., 247
   William, 228, 242
   ____ (Dr.), 25
   ____, 229
Porterfield
   Floyd, 243, 263
   Jeff, 242
Porticq, Antonio, 260
Portonic, Eroga, 374
Poschell, Louis J. C., 260
Posey, H. J., 229
Possati, Peter, 265
Postell, Mattie, 247

Poston, ____, 176
Potfork, Samuel, 260
Potter
   J. C., 245
   John, 228
   John (Mrs.), 245
   N., 305, 307, 310, 311
   Willie, 263
   ____ (Mrs.), 229
Potts
   H., 244
   Martha M., 263
   R. M., 260
   S. C. (Mrs.), 242
   ____ (Dr.), 243
Pouisen, James, 260
Pounder, Frank, 373
Pounds, John, 260
Pourcian, Felix G., 260
Pousylrain, Francois, 263
Powder, S., 244
Powders, R. W., 229
Powell
   Aleck B., 245
   Alexander, 250
   Allie (Mrs.), 249
   Andrew, 229
   Bessie K., 243
   Charley, 228
   Clarence, 245, 250
   Henry, 243
   J. N., 249
   J. W., 248, 249
   James, 399
   John, 378, 381
   M. T., 229
   Robert, 263
   Thomas, 247
   ____ (Mrs.), 263
   ____, 249, 263
Power
   Charles, 402
   Green, 228
   James Silas, 263
   John, 245
   W. A., 399
Powers
   Edward, 228
   J. C., 229
   John H., 228
   Mary, 260
   William, 395
Poyner, ____, 229
Pradelia, Cath., 260
Prather
   G. B., 251
   Hugh, 251
   Hugh L., 251
   R. C., 251
Pratt
   Charles B., 260
   G. W., 359
   Patsey, 228
Precomp, G. L., 228
Prescott
   J. P., 421

O. F., 229, 412, 413
Walter, 229
Presh, Fred, 229
Pressly, ____, 241
Prestel
   Caroline, 249
   Nicholas, 249
Prestice, Dominica, 260
Prestidge [Prestridge]
   J. M. (Mrs.), 248
   James S., 129, 390, 391, 392
Preston
   John, 229
   T. C., 402
   William A., 248
Prewitt
   C. V., 240
   Earnest, 240
   J. H., 240
   J. H. (Mrs.), 240
   Mary (Mrs.), 240
   May, 240
   N. W., 240
   Nannie, 240
   S. E. Jr., 240
Price
   Annie, 228
   B. F., 407
   E. H., 29
   Edward, 228
   Eliza (Mrs.), 248
   H. J., 346
   J. A., 248
   J. C., 434
   J. H., 250
   Joseph, 248
   Maggie, 239
   Mattie, 239
   R. B., 260
   Robert J., 248
   Sarah A., 229
   Susan (Mrs.), 229
   W. R., 356
   William, 260
   ____ (Miss), 338
   ____, 248, 407
Pride, ____ (Mrs.), 229
Priest
   ____ Jr., 249
   ____ Sr., 249
Prilleaux, Adolph, 260
Prince
   Alfred, 260
   Annie, 265
Pringle, ____, 308
Prinz, G. H., 338
Prior, ____ (Maj.), 306
Pritchara, E. J., 260
Pritchard
   J. K., 135
   Maurice, 368, 370
   ____ (Dr.), 155
   ____ (Mrs.), 155
   ____, 155

Pritchett
   F. (Mrs.), 229
   Thomas T., 229
Privett [Privette]
   D. H., 240
   Miles, 228
Probert, George C., 229, 374, 408
Profield, Anne, 264
Profitt, Annie, 264
Propar, Salvador, 264
Prophit, Robert (Mrs.), 246
Protine, Jean W., 260
Proudfit, W. P., 390
Proudfoot, J. R., 372
Prout, Edward, 251
Provenzale, Mike, 229
Pruden
   H. P., 350
   W. D., 351
Pryor
   Bobt., 263
   F. (Mrs.), 247
   Fred, 246
   Green, 228
   James, 228
   Matilda, 228
   Melinda, 228
   Mick, 229
   Nathan, 229
   S. H. (Mrs.), 245
   ____ (Miss), 246
   ____ (Mrs.), 263
   ____, 247
Pucher, P. D., 229
Puches, Charles, 260
Puckett [Pucket]
   George W., 251
   ____, 229
Pugg, W. T., 229
Pugh, Mary Ann, 229
Pugo, ____, 229
Pujo, Marie, 260
Pujol, Anna Louise, 263
Pulham, Doshia, 248
Pullen [Pullin]
   B. K., 406
   B. K. (Mrs.), 406
   Ben K., 194
   Ben K. (Mrs.), 194
   Ben. K. (Mrs.), 240
   Ella, 249
   Minerva, 228
   Ruth W., 248
Pulliam
   George, 240
   Julius, 240
Puneky, Mary M. (Mrs.), 244
Pupor, Josephine, 260
Purcell
   B. J., 344
   Richard, 399
Purdon, James S., 260
Purdy, Chrissa, 229
Purnell
   Bertron, 248

500   A HISTORY OF THE YELLOW FEVER

H. D., 401
H. W., 368
Purse, W. H., 361
Putnam
   George A., 427, 432
   H., 246
   H. B., 247
   S. G., 373
   ____, 431
Putnana, S. G., 229
Pyckard, Lucine, 260
Pyliski, James H., 264
Pym
   ____ (Dr.), 25
   ____, 303
Pyott, James, 260
Pys, Joseph, 260

Q

Quane, John, 260
Quarles, W. R., 357
Querner, Emil, 18
Quick, Walter, 247
Quiggins
   O. J., 245
   ____, 245
Quigley
   Esquire, 192
   H. W., 260
   J. J., 400
   Mary, 229
Quimby, ____ (Dr.), 380, 424
Quin
   Garrett, 399
   Thomas, 403
Quinlan
   D. O. C., 260
   Ed, 403
   Eugene, 229
   John C., 229
   Thomas, 250
   W. J., 349
Quinn
   John, 260
   Mary, 229
   Mike, 229
   Pat, 249
   Thomas, 260
   Thomas R., 244
Quintard
   C. T., 123
   ____ (Right Rev. Dr.), 124

R

Raback, F., 260
Rabb, D. M. (Mrs.), 355
Rabeneck, Richard, 260
Rabenstein, Pike, 230
Rachore, Pierre (Mrs.), 260
Radcliffe, Steven, 230
Rademacher, J., 260
Radjesky
   J., 247

Louis, 246
Rachael, 247
Radt, ____, 230
Rafalsky
   Alexander, 247
   Henry, 248
Raffaci, A., 261
Rafter
   T., 399
   Thomas, 401
Ragan
   Ella, 265
   M., 407
   Rosanna, 243
Raggio
   Amelia, 230
   John, 230
   Lizzie, 231
   Mary R., 230
Ragouso, Joseph, 260
Ragsdale
   B. F., 239
   B. F. (Mrs.), 239
   Claudia, 251
   John, 251
Raid, Susan, 231
Raine, C. H., 429
Raines [Rains], ____ (Dr.), 263, 302
Rainey [Raney]
   Ella, 248
   James P., 243
   Lee B., 240
   P., 230
   William V., 248
Ralph, John, 247
Ralston
   James, 240
   P. A., 330
   Sarah A., 238
   Thomas, 374
   W. Walter, 238
   Walter, 240
Rambaut, G. V., 438
Rampurty, John, 260
Ramsay [Ramsey]
   Cleburne, 230
   ____, 303
Ranburg, John, 230
Rancoske, A., 230
Randall [Randle]
   Fred, 230
   George, 260
   Henry, 231
   Joseph, 260
   Rachael, 230
   W. H., 27
   ____, 231
Rando, Joseph, 261
Randolph
   Evelyn, 338
   Hudson, 230
   Taylor, 231
Randon, Carl, 260
Ranesua, C., 260
Raney, see Rainey
Ranier, Martin, 230

Rank
   P. (Mrs.), 260
   Willie, 260
Rankin
   C. C., 374
   L. (Mrs.), 374
Rankins, Orelia, 243
Ransom
   Mary, 230
   S., 244
   W. Z., 231
   ____, 243
Raoul, Griffin, 249
Rapp
   A. R., 231
   Fred, 260
Raquet, John, 431
Rashell, ____, 243
Rasp, Conrad, 163
Ratchlitz, Julius, 246
Ratcliff, S., 266
Rather, George, 251
Ratigan, Frances, 242
Ratine, Josephine, 260
Rative, Henry, 261
Ratzwell, Louis, 260
Rauer, Marie, 260
Raum, Augusta, 243
Raunch, Henry, 260
Raurind, E., 260
Ravenall, Alfred, 230
Ravenos, A., 230
Raverson, A., 230
Rawes [Raws]
   George (Mrs.), 251
   Millie (Mrs.), 230
Rawlings
   Hennie, 230
   Lou., 231
Rawls, Willie, 231
Ray
   Ben A., 260
   C. W., 230
   Frederick, 263
   J. R., 336
   Lizzie, 260
   Mary M., 260
   R. A., 250
Rayford, Thomas, 231
Raymer, Henry, 260
Raymond
   A. G., 136
   Charles, 239
   E. G., 346
   Fred, 260
   John, 261
   Maggie, 260
   Mary C., 260
Rayner, June, 241
Read
   Clem, 245
   E. P., 230
   Francis, 244
   George, 230
   S. P., 345, 355
   Samuel P., 359
   ____ (Miss), 245

   ____ (Mrs.), 230
   see also Reed, Reid
Reagan [Reagin]
   T., 229
   W. R., 251
Reahardt [Reahart]
   D. G., 141, 330, 331, 335
Reamer, Bella, 260
Rean, J. B., 230
Reardon
   Cohn, 230
   ____ (Mrs.), 240
   ____ (Rev. Father), 230
Reasoner, William, 251
Reasons, Thomas, 246
Rebay
   E. (Mrs.), 243
   George, 243
Reborst, Joe, 249
Rebstock, L., 375
Rechner, Anna, 260
Record
   Corilla, 245
   W. H., 230
Rector, R. S., 239
Redd [Red]
   Aug., 261
   Austin, 230
Redcourt, ____, 230
Redders
   Auguste, 230
   Fred, 260
Reddick, W. L., 231
Redding
   James F., 399
   Wyatt C., 381
   Wyatt M., 247, 380
Reder, Gus., 230, 390, 406
Redford
   A. R., 408
   George R., 231
   M. W., 230
   ____, 408
Reding, W. M., 266
Redman
   M. J., 374
   Margarette, 260
Redmond, Charles, 249
Redon
   Leon S., 260
   Leon S. Jr., 260
Redwood
   Gustave, 260
   R. G., 375
Reed [, Réed, Reede]
   A. F., 373
   Ben., 238
   Benjamin, 240
   C. V., 430
   Charles, 244
   George, 407
   Jane, 240
   John B., 263
   Louisa, 231
   Ross, 231

NAME INDEX

William, 230
___ (Mrs.), 246
___, 263
see also Read, Reid
Reeder
 Joseph, 260
 U. S., 260
Reel, Henry, 260
Reems
 Elizabeth, 260
 Walter, 246
Reese
 H., 246
 M., 419
 Mary, 231
 ___ (Dr.), 296
 ___ (Mrs.), 250
 ___, 246
Reeves
 James J., 260
 R., 373
 S. A., 348
 ___, 241
Reffiy, Hubert, 260
Regan, John C., 400
Regend, Leonie O., 260
Regende, R. R., 260
Reginald (Sister), 158
Regleter, P. B., 358
Regnold, Lewis, 230
Rehkopf
 C., 229
 Fred, 229
Rehorst
 Henry, 249
 Joe, 249
Reiber, A. L., 422
Reichert, Bettie (Mrs.), 260
Reid
 Albert, 260
 Burrell, 244
 D. B., 300
 D. William (Mrs.), 246
 John, 246, 260
 John S., 251
 R. J. Jr., 251
 S. I. (Mrs.), 248
 Susan, 230
 Walter, 230
 see also Read, Reed
Reidehufer, George, 260
Reidel, Robert, 231
Reidling, Rosa, 261
Reif, Sophia, 260
Reilley [Reilly, Reiley, Reily]
 F. T., 437
 Frank W., 332
 George, 264
 James, 230, 401
 Joe, 230
 John A., 264
 Katie, 230
 Martha Hughes, 229
 Mary, 264
 Mike, 230
 Nancy, 231

P., 404
Sarah, 230
Timothy, 260
William, 266
Willie, 264
Reinert, William, 230
Reinerth, ___, 260
Reiney, Caroline J., 231
Reinhardt
 Fred, 260
 H., 260
 Jacques, 260
 John, 373
 John N., 260
 Oscar, 260
 ___ (Dr.), 231
Reinhemier, Lewis, 247
Reinig
 C. (Mrs.), 230, 238
 Caesar, 238
 Moses, 230
Reist, Gustave, 261
Relf, D. O., 261
Relleux, George, 260
Rem, George, 260
Remech, S. K., 260
Remeres, Lavinia, 263
Remington, George W., 260
Remmian, W. T., 340
Rempp, Joseph, 260
Renandin, John, 260
Rench, M. J., 260
Reneau
 Jane, 434
 Lulu, 434
 Maggie, 434
 Russell, 434
 S. L., 416, 434
 Sallie E., 240
 ___ (Miss), 417
 ___, 417
Rengg, Auguste, 229
Renkert, Andrew, 356
Renner
 J. E., 230
 J. G., 118, 368, 369
Rennyson, L. A., 260
Renouard, A., 400
Rentz, John, 230
Resegnet, Louis, 260
Resney, Owen, 238
Rester, Jacob, 230
Restine, Joseph, 260
Restinger, J., 231
Restmeyer
 Frank, 231
 Fred, 112, 230
 Fred (Mrs.), 231
Reston, William, 231
Rettel, Louise, 261
Retwick, ___, 230
Reubenstein, L. B., 421
Reudel, Fred, 374
Reuder, Michael, 260
Reuss, J. M., 39
Reveiley, J., 230
Revel, Henry, 260

Revilla, Angelo, 260
Revoli
 Lizzie, 231
 Lou. (Mrs.), 231
Revoy, Laura, 231
Reyder, Patrick, 229
Reyff, Joseph, 260
Reynard, Barth., 260
Reynaud, Albert G., 263
Reyner, Mary A., 260
Reynick, A. C., 241
Reynolds
 Charles M., 244
 Emma P., 260
 Fannie, 230
 Fannie (Mrs.), 230
 Frank, 230, 431
 H. S., 230, 408
 H. S. (Mrs.), 230, 408
 J. H., 239
 J. S., 260
 James, 242
 James H., 260
 Maggie, 230
 Matt, 244
 Patrick, 399
 R. E., 260
 W. L., 261
Rezzinocco, C. (Mrs.), 230
Rhazes, 14
Rhea, Tom (Mrs.), 250
Rheiffer, Charles, 260
Rhett, Herbert, 428, 429
Rhinehart
 Alex, 251
 Sidney, 251
Rhode, S. W., 136
Rhodes
 A. T., 373
 Cornelia (Mrs.), 240
 E., 260
 L. A., 240
 Louis, 230
Rhoton, Albert C., 263
Riard, Nettie, 260
Ribet, J. M., 265
Rice
 Annie, 230
 Billy, 230
 David, 230
 Henry, 420
 John, 231, 260
 John A., 260
 Lee, 244
 Nora, 251
 W. H., 242
 Will H., 251
 ___ (Rev. Dr.), 240
 ___, 349
Rich, Henry, 230
Richard
 Charles, 265
 Marie, 265
 Percy C., 260
Richards
 Andrew, 243
 Chester, 260

F. S., 136
Grace H., 260
Joe C., 246
Mollie, 231
William, 260
Richardson
 B. A., 230
 E., 344
 G., 260
 G. L., 373
 J. D., 355, 409
 James D., 355
 Jane, 231, 263
 John, 230, 231, 373
 Lucy, 230
 M., 260
 M. S., 260
 Mattie, 231
 S. A., 229
 Sarah (Mrs.), 260
 Stella, 395
 Turner, 230
 William R., 263
 ___ (Capt.), 239
 ___, 230
Richlemann, George, 260
Richmond, George, 230
Rickerty, Lizzie, 260
Rickett, Joseph, 260
Ricks
 Bill, 249
 J. D., 265
 Tena, 260
Ricord, Annie, 230
Riddell, Holma P., 260
Riddle
 Charles V. D., 245
 Lottie Tuley, 245
 Thomas, 245
Ridley
 James (Mrs.), 260
 Jennie, 354
 M. J. (Mrs.), 372
Riedell, ___ (Mrs.), 243
Riel, W. A., 342
Rieule, Simon, 261
Rigby, Thomas H. W., 243
Riggonica, L. N., 230
Rigley, Bill, 243
Rigon, Mary E., 260
Riley
 Dan, 230
 Genevieve, 260
 James, 373
 John, 241
 Louise, 260
 M. H., 390
 Mary, 248, 260
 Mike, 266
 Simon, 260
 Thomas, 261
 ___ (Mrs.), 229
Rilford, Hannah, 230
Rinders, John, 230
Ring
 Dan, 230

Maggie, 229
Moses, 230
Ringer
  Lafayette, 231
  William, 395
  ____ (Mrs.), 260
Ringgold
  ____ (Dr.), 247
  ____ (Mrs. Dr.), 247
  ____, 380
Ringwald
  Edward, 230
  Jesse, 240
  Minnie, 230
  S., 230
  Stella, 238, 239
  ____ (Miss), 230
Rinker, Ann, 229
Rinkers, John, 404
Rinn, Vincent, 230
Rino, Paul, 260
Rioeler, Ida J., 260
Riordan [Riorden]
  C. E., 112
  Daniel, 400
  J. D., 400
  M., 119, 163
  Martin, 164
Ripley, Fred, 230
Risk
  E. F., 230
  E. F. Jr., 411
Ritchie, James M., 260
Ritter
  A. E. (Mrs.), 238
  Alice E., 230
  Alice R., 251
  John, 230
  L., 250
  L. F., 266
  L. R., 251
Ritzens, Willie, 260
Ritzmann, George, 260
Riutte, Julia, 260
Rive, Julius, 260
Rivere, Frank E., 260
Rivers
  Gussie, 231
  Mary, 242
  O. C., 247
  ____, 248
Riviere, J., 154
Rivinac
  Cornelia, 243
  Pierre, 243
Riza, Adam, 253
Roach
  Bill, 230
  J. S., 244
  John, 260
  John D., 242
  P. J., 247
Roark, Katie, 230
Roback, H., 265
Robathoenk, H., 260
Roberson, Bettie, 242
Robert, Henri, 265

Roberts
  Ann Eliza, 230
  C. S., 230, 368, 373
  Emma, 246
  Hannah, 229
  J. S., 240
  John, 230, 266
  Julia (Mrs.), 245
  Sarah, 230
  Susan, 231
  William, 230
  William Y., 260
  ____ (Mrs.), 245
  ____, 230
Robertson
  Adam, 265
  J., 430
  J. D., 230
  J. P., 135, 136
  John, 260
  Leatman F., 260
  Mildred, 260
  Perry, 230
  Rozelle, 260
  T. J., 340
  ____ (Gov.), 273
Robeson, Mary, 230
Robins [Robbins]
  A. M., 230
  Louisa, 260
  S. M., 263
  W. H., 117, 368, 369
  ____ (Dr.), 230
Robinson
  America, 240
  Anderson, 230
  Bart, 372
  Bennie, 229
  C. A., 421
  Cheney, 230
  Clarke, 231
  Ed. H., 239
  Eliza, 230
  Eliza J., 260
  Elizabeth, 260
  Ella, 261
  Emma, 248
  G. F., 353
  G. T., 351, 352
  George, 230, 260
  George P., 261
  Grandison, 230
  H. W., 422
  Isaac, 242
  J. A., 244
  J. H., 351
  James S., 356
  Jane, 230
  John, 373
  Josephine, 260
  Lance, 430
  Lawrence, 230
  M., 230
  Mary, 230
  Nora, 230
  P. C., 260
  P. M., 173

Percy, 230
S. B., 424
S. O., 346
Sophie, 230
Thomas, 260
William, 230
Willis, 231
____, 173
Roblet, Edward Paul, 260
Roche
  Aubert, 271
  David P., 402
  George W., 260
  James, 374
  John H., 260
  Laura, 260
Rochester
  John, 349
  John H., 349, 350
  R. H., 403
Rochet, Joseph, 260
Rockafeller, ____ (Mrs.), 404
Rocker
  August, 260
  Peter, 253
Rockwood, William M., 244
Roddy, Jane, 230
Rodeillior, Alice, 264
Rodgers, see Rogers
Rodites, Salvador, 260
Rodrigney, Emile, 263
Rodriguez [Rodrigue]
  Arthur, 260
  Anna, 264
  Celestine, 264
  H., 264
  Klebert, 264
  Paul, 260
  Victorine, 264
Roe
  Philip, 244
  ____ (Mrs.), 231
Roebecker, John, 260
Roehlet, Otto H., 260
Roehrs, Louise S. M., 260
Roella, Joseph, 260
Roemheld, John, 230
Roeshe
  Charles, 244
  Lizzie, 242
Roesler, Theresa (Mrs.), 373
Roesseler, Louis, 260
Roffignac, J., 321
Rogers
  A., 230
  Alexander, 250
  Anna, 260
  Dennis, 230; Elizabeth, 250
  Emile, 265
  Emily, 230
  Emma, 230
  Flora, 239
  Gid., 241
  Harry, 239

J., 346
J. H., 240
J. M., 117
J. P., 431
James, 260
John, 260
John C., 117, 229
Joseph, 230, 407
Peter, 230
Rebecca, 260
Thomas, 248, 251
Robert, 230
W. B., 429
W. E., 368, 387
W. S., 136, 142, 330, 331, 335
W. T., 341
William H., 403
____ (Capt.), 180
____ (Miss), 351
____, 230
Rognett, Mary (Mrs.), 230
Rogson, J. A., 230
Rohr, N., 260
Roibenack, E., 260
Roice, Josephine, 230
Rokbein, William, 260
Roland, Frank, 260
Rollin, Joseph, 260
Rollins
  Dan, 373
  Marshall, 248
  O. B., 248
Rollman, Otto G., 369, 375
Romango, John, 230
Romer
  Adolph, 260
  Valentine, 260
Romhelt, George, 374
Rommel, Fred, 260
Roney, Patrick H., 260
Rooch
  Delia, 231
  Frank, 230
  George, 230
  Lena, 231
Rooks
  Ellen, 229
  Mamie, 244
Roosart, William, 354
Roosevelt, M. E. (Mrs.), 374
Roost
  Caroline, 242, 244
  Jacob, 242
  Rosaline, 244
Root
  Erwin, 230
  Irvine, 412
Roots [Rootes]
  Harriet A. (Mrs.), 230
  M., 438
Roper
  Ann, 230
  James, 231
  Lizzie, 230
  M. (Mrs.), 231

NAME INDEX

R., 350
Ripley, 349
Rosa
  Franco, 260
  Mary, 260
Rosche, J. H., 260
Rose
  Barry, 248
  Blanche G., 260
  Charles M., 242
  Charles Osman, 349
  Porter, 239, 251
  Walter C., 242
Rose (Sister), 120
Rosebrough [Roseborough]
  D. R. S., 230
  David R. S., 121
  N., 408
  _____ (Rev.), 164
Roselle, Louis, 434
Rosen, F. J., 266
Rosenbaum
  C., 260
  G., 260
  J., 350
  _____ (Mrs.), 260
Rosenstiel, Auguste, 229
Rosenthal, Ralph, 244
Rosone, Antonio, 260
Ross
  Albert, 244
  Anthony, 421
  Benjamin, 230
  C., 230
  Charles H., 263
  Edward, 260
  Elbert, 239
  Elizabeth, 249
  Fannie, 230
  J., 359
  James, 204
  Jesse S., 249
  Jessie, 250
  John, 230
  M. B., 260
  Melissa, 249
  S., 244
  Serena, 240
  U. H., 245
  W. B., 355
  W. N., 249
  _____ (Mrs.), 251
Rossarth, John, 260
Rosseau, S., 260
Rosser
  Hattie, 248
  Ida, 248
  John, 406
Rossi
  John, 231
  Julie (Mrs.), 260
Rossie, Jobe, 260
Rosskam, Leon, 420
Rost, Louisa (Mrs.), 375
Roth
  Angelina, 265
  Gustave, 260, 261

Jacob, 260
John G., 260
Rothass
  George J., 260
  William, 260
Rothschild
  Albert, 243
  Eddie, 243
Rottenberry, H. W. A., 260
Roubillac
  Alph, 260
  Ellen P., 260
Rouen, Pete, 244
Roulhac, George G., 251
Rounds
  Belle, 230
  James Jr., 231
Rourk, Jane, 260
Rous
  Mary A., 260
  Spencer, 260
Roush
  John, 149
  John A., 229, 406
Rousseau
  Edith M., 260
  Monroe, 266
Roussel, Frank, 260
Rousset, Blanche, 261
Roust, Alice C., 260
Roux, J. B., 260
Rowanes, B., 260
Rowell
  H. (Mrs.), 260
  W. Irvine, 260
Rowerty, Frank, 260
Rowland
  _____ (Gen. Supt.), 424
  _____ (Mrs.), 249
Rowley, William, 263
Roxy, Cowan, 245
Royal, Florence L., 359
Royle, M. F., 347, 348
Royster
  F. W. Jr., 230
  L. E., 434
Rozelle
  Louis, 416
  Louisa, 230
Rubenstein, Lena N., 230
Ruby
  Jackson, 230
  Owen (Mrs.), 231
Rucker, B. R., 36
Rucks, James, 249
Rudd
  George, 230
  William A., 230
  _____, 230
Rudenbery, Ada, 260
Rudolph, T., 260
Ruf, Frank, 260
Ruffier, James, 260
Ruffin
  Charley, 230
  Freddie, 231
  J. B., 231

Joe, 231
Marley, 231
  William, 230
William H., 230
Ruffy, Frank, 260
Rugge, Victor, 260
Ruhl [Ruhle]
  E. J., 374
  George (Mrs.), 395
Ruleef, H. H., 260
Rummagio, John, 266
Rummel
  A., 230
  Sophy, 230
  William, 260
Rumples, George, 260
Rundell, A. A., 245
Runge, William, 230
Runolds, M., 265
Runs, Oscar, 230
Runy, Mary E., 260
Ruppel, John, 260
Rush
  Mollie (Mrs.), 248
  R. L., 230
  _____ (Dr.), 70
  _____, 201
Rushing, R. W., 239
Rusk
  Charley, 230
  John, 402
Russell
  Birdie, 229
  Calvin, 244
  Carrie T. (Mrs.), 244
  Essie, 246
  Fred, 265
  G. A., 242
  J. E., 407, 411
  J. (Mrs.), 242
  John, 243
  John H., 358
  Johnnie, 265
  Joseph, 411
  Joseph E., 230, 410
  Maggie, 229
  T. L., 374
  Thomas C., 244
  W., 243
  W. R., 242
  William, 230
  William C., 241
  Zila, 338
  _____ (Mrs.), 250
  _____, 407
Russo, Giovani, 260
Rustin
  _____ (Miss), 231
  _____ (Mrs.), 231
Ruth, Jester, 230
Ruth (Sister), 122, 124, 230
Ruther, Herman, 410
Rutherford, _____ (Dr.), 264
Rutley, Harry, 244
Rutter
  Annie, 231

C., 231
D. P., 191
John, 230
Ruzza, G., 260
Ryan
  Annie L., 244
  Cornelius, 404
  Dennis, 266, 401
  Edward, 243, 261
  Edward (Mrs.), 242
  Elizabeth, 229, 260
  Ellen, 230
  George, 260
  Jack, 231
  James, 229, 230, 231, 260
  James F., 404
  Jennie, 230
  John, 230, 404
  Joseph, 249
  Mary, 242, 266
  Mary E., 261
  Mary (Mrs.), 251, 372
  P., 399
  P. (Father), 239
  P. J., 403
  Phil. (Mrs.), 247
  Sallie L., 244
  Steven, 230
  William, 230, 395
  _____ (Mrs.), 230, 244
  _____, 244
Rylie, M., 244

S

Saachez, Dora, 263
Saaguinetti, Charles, 243
Sabadi, George, 261
Sabala, Mary Ann, 261
Sabat, Peter, 261
Sabathe, Mary, 261
Sabourin, C., 265
Sabrolle
  Mary, 233
  _____, 233
Sackett
  Eddie, 240
  Walter, 240
Sadevia, Salvador, 261
Sadler [Saddler]
  Amos, 247
  Joseph E., 247
  L., 244
  M. B., 362
  Robert, 247
  Rosa, 247
  Sarah, 232
  Walter, 247
  William L., 248
  _____ (Mrs.), 247
Safferans
  A., 232
  James, 232
Sage, J. E., 261
Sagona
  Frank, 242

John, 244
Peter, 242
Saharfea, J., 232
Saidburn, Ellen C., 232
Sailes, Mary (Mrs.), 261
Sakeford, Charles, 231
Saladino, J., 261
Salari
  P. M., 233
  Toney, 233
  ____, 233
Sales, Ellen, 231
Saleu
  G., 406
  ____, 406
Salisa (Sister), 261
Salisbury, J. H., 18
Salles, Gabriel, 261
Salley [Sally]
  C., 242
  Lelia, 243
Salm, J., 373
Salman, Estelle, 261
Saloi
  P., 374
  P. (Mrs.), 374
Salorz, Lydia, 261
Saltalamachi, Frank, 232, 251
Saltanichia, F., 261
Salters, John, 239
Saltglamaohia, Frank, 112
Salvant, Josephine, 261
Salvato, Francisco, 261
Salzeger [Salzeiger]
  H. G., 231, 407
  ____, 407
Sambusetta, Victoria, 233
Sammelson, Aug, 248
Samons, Harriet, 231
Samoo, ____, 232
Sample
  G. F., 368, 369
  Susan, 233
  ____ (Dr.), 56, 175, 233
Sampoon, C., 261
Sampree, Ida, 251
Sampson, Hannah, 261
Samse
  Charles, 251
  F., 251
  F. (Mrs.), 251
  Henry, 251
  Ida (Mrs.), 251
  S., 251
Samson, Joe, 249
Samuels
  H. B., 266
  Henry B., 251
  Ruth M., 261
Sanberg [Sanbarg]
  John, 232
  ____, 231
Sancas, Henri, 261
Sanchey, Isabella, 264

Sancier
  John J., 249
  Leela, 261
Sandberg
  Mary, 183
  ____, 183
Sanden, Matthew, 261
Sanders
  A. P., 248
  A. V. (Mrs.), 249
  Charley, 233
  James M., 261
  Lirey, 264
  M., 233
  Mollie, 248
  Monie J., 261
  O. P., 248
  O. P. (Mrs.), 248
  Richard, 97
Sanderson
  John, 239
  William, 261
  William (Mrs.), 261
Sanford
  George (Mrs.), 246
  William, 261
Sangerson, B. (Mrs.), 261
Sanona, Emma, 232
Sansoucy
  Alfred, 261
  Aug. P., 261
  ____ (Madame), 261
Sappington, ____ (Dr.), 242
Saradet, H., 261
Sarago, John, 232
Sarner, F., 231
Sarrazin, ____, 264
Sarries, J. B., 232
Sartorius, M., 418
Sarvatori, Major, 261
Sassamon, Frank, 233
Satherley, James, 232
Satterfield, Jennie, 248
Sauer
  Ada, 233
  Amelia, 233
  Louis, 233
  Margaret (Mrs.), 233
  Philip Henry, 233
Saul, Jacob, 233
Saunden, Charles, 261
Saunders
  Austin, 245
  B., 356
  Clara, 231
  Fannie, 250
  Fred M., 261
  Hannah, 232
  Jim, 231
  Katie, 243
  M. P. (Mrs.), 250
  P., 250
  R. G., 239
  Ralph, 265
  Sallie, 232
  Thomas B., 231

Willie, 233
  ____ (Dr.), 103, 146
Saupe, Frank, 233
Sausey
  H. A., 265
  Ida A., 265
Sauter, Charles, 231
Sauvé, H. C., 368, 389
Savadras, Vic (Mrs.), 264
Savage
  Henry, 239
  John H., 355
  Rosa, 231
Savard, Charles, 242
Sawyer, A. B., 341
Saxe [Sax]
  Max, 420
  Philip, 261
Saxson, George, 233
Saxton, Robert John, 261
Sayle
  Ed, 429
  Joseph, 247
Sayles, Lucretia, 232
Saylor [Sayler]
  A. D., 347
  Joseph, 232
  Mary, 232
  Thomas E., 261
Sayres, Ann (Mrs.), 372
Scaife [Scafe]
  Alex, 233
  C. T., 354
Scales
  Allie, 233
  Ellen, 233
  George, 231
  James, 233
  Jennie Belle, 246
  Pinkey, 246
Scalley [Scally]
  John, 261
  M. E., 231, 251
Scanlan [Scanlin]
  Francis, 261
  Patrick, 261
  Thomas, 261
  ____ (Mrs.), 247, 248
  ____, 248
Scanlin (Father), 165
Scannell
  J. P., 119, 164
  John M., 244
Scannell (Father), 232
Scarafiatta, Joseph, 233
Scarbonie, Luc, 261
Scarborough
  A. M., 354, 438
  Effie, 264
Scarey, Nella, 261
Scatter, John, 232
Schafer [Schaffer, Schaeffer, Schaefer]
  Alice O., 231
  Aug., 261
  Frank, 261

H. (Mrs.), 251
Henry, 233
Herman, 231
Mary, 261
John, 261
Louis, 243
  ____, 249
Schahill, Mike, 261
Schallary, Thomas, 233
Schalscha
  Hannah, 231
  Ida, 231
Schalscher, Fannie, 231
Schalumbrecht, J. L., 261
Scharf [Scharfe, Scharff]
  Emil, 251
  George, 248
  George (Mrs.), 248
  John P., 261
  ____ (Mrs.), 232
  ____, 232
Schauer, H., 408
Schaul, L. H., 261
Schearer, Thomas, 232
Schefiel, E. (Mrs.), 261
Scheidmantle, H. W., 348
Scheifler
  J. B., 246
  ____ (Mrs.), 246
  ____, 246
Scheimoner, Peter, 261
Scheler, Joseph, 261
Schelin, Carl S., 261
Schelles, John, 261
Schelmann, Eugene, 261
Schenauder, Mary H., 261
Schenck
  P. V., 25, 27
  ____ (Dr.), 109
Schendal
  Bertha, 244
  Marcus, 243
  Maurice, 243
  Minnie, 244
  ____ (Mrs.), 244
Schenrer
  Jacob, 261
  Mary, 261
Scheondorff, F., 261
Schepp, L., 345
Scherbe, Emil, 251
Schere, John, 261
Scherer
  H., 232
  ____, 233
Scherf, Albert, 261
Scherrie, ____ (Mrs.), 233
Scheurmann, Charles, 261
Schevantz, Hermann, 261
Scheveir
  Henry, 239
  Matt, 239
Schibe, Alice, 261
Schiff, Joseph (Mrs.), 261
Schiffersteine, Marie, 265
Schildnedt, C., 261
Schillaght, J., 261

NAME INDEX

Schillect, J., 261
Schiller
  Daniel, 244
  Edward, 416, 417, 433
  Josephine, 232
  M. M., 242
  ___ (Miss), 417
  ___, 165, 417, 433
Schilling
  Ferdinand S., 233
  L., 233
  W. H., 233
Schiro, Antonio, 261
Schlatter, Samuel, 232
Schleimance, Henry, 231
Schleissinger, E., 239
Schlemmer, C. H., 231
Schlenke, H., 399
Schley
  F., 233
  Francis W., 169
  ___ (Mrs.), 169
Schlichte, Edmin, 261
Schlitz, John, 346
Schloeser, Joseph, 261
Schlottman, Charles B., 244
Schlunberg, M., 261
Schluter, A. F., 261
Schmaltz, Julia C., 261
Schmelig, H., 373
Schmeyer, Edward, 233
Schmidt [Schmitt]
  Adam, 244
  C., 261
  C. (Mrs.), 261
  C. J., 375
  John, 373
  Julius, 261
  L. E., 261
  Louis, 261, 373
  Louisa, 242
  Martin, 422
  Sophie, 261
  Susan (Mrs.), 233
Schmoele, William, 17
Schmuck, Peter, 231
Schnable, P. S., 340
Schnackle, Rembrandt, 262
Schnechen, Berge, 261
Schneckler, John, 261
Schnee, George, 239
Schneider [Schnider]
  Andrew, 233
  Aug., 261
  Caroline, 249
  Charles, 245
  Cora, 232
  E., 231
  Henry, 261
  Jacob, 231
  Kate, 232
  Tom, 249
  William, 261
  ___ (Mrs.), 232, 233
  ___, 232

Schneidman
  Jacob, 239
  Louisa, 239
  Sue, 239
Schoen
  Jacob, 261
  Theodore, 261
Schoff, Joseph, 261
Schomillar, M., 261
Schooler
  J. K. (Mrs.), 345
  ___, 345
Schott, John, 261
Schreiner, Fred, 261
Schrider, ___ (Mrs.), 231
Schriever, J. G., 261
Schroeder
  Caroline, 233
  H. L., 233
  Henry, 261
  John, 261
  Mary, 261
Schrumpf, Arthur, 261
Schuldt, William, 261
Schuler
  Martin, 266
  Mollie, 232
  Robert R., 261
  Rosa E., 242
  W. J., 243
Schuling, Henry, 261
Schultz
  Charles, 231
  Emile, 261
  Fred, 232
  John, 231
  William, 374
Schultzele, Margaret, 261
Schulze, A. F., 232
Schumacher
  Benjamin, 244
  E., 261
Schumaker
  Henry, 261
  M. G. (Mrs.), 233
  P., 232
  Peter, 232
  ___, 232
Schummer
  Frank, 261
  Henrich, 261
Schunaman, Aug., 261
Schutz, A. O., 232
Schuyler
  L. S., 232
  Louis S., 121, 122, 164, 180, 181, 191
  M. Roosevelt, 191
  Montgomery, 191
Schwab, Anthony, 231
Schwaner, J., 261
Schwar
  M., 240
  ___, 240
Schwartz
  C. T., 373
  L., 244

M., 249
R. M., 338
Schwarz [Schwarze]
  Edna, 261
  Karl, 261
Schwatzenburg, ___ (Mrs.), 239
Schweitzer, George, 261
Schwennelien, J., 261
Schwink
  Jacob L., 242
  L. T., 242
Scobery, ___ (Mrs.), 239
Scott
  A. E., 355, 361
  C., 346
  Clarinda, 244
  David, 233
  Emma, 232
  Fannie, 232
  G. W., 239
  Garrett, 247
  George, 231
  George R., 261
  Harriett, 243
  John, 261
  Joseph, 45
  Kittie (Mrs.), 250
  Lee C., 250
  Louis, 264
  Louisa, 264
  R. B., 246
  R. H., 241
  Sam, 243
  Thomas, 233
  William, 232, 244, 261
  Willie, 246
  ___, 232, 246, 263, 264
Sconce
  J. C., 407
  J. C. (Mrs.), 407
  ___, 407
Scruggs
  Amanda, 232
  Amy, 240
  Bradford, 232
  Caroline S., 233
  P. T., 121, 233, 238
Scudder, C. D., 238
Sculderhoff, C., 395
Scullin
  Jim, 233
  Patrick, 233
Scully
  Agnes, 231
  Charles, 231
  J. D., 359, 402
  James H., 233
  John, 264
  Pat, 374
  Patrick, 373
  R., 238
Seager, William, 372
Seagrist
  Frank, 251
  Frank (Mrs.), 251

Otto, 251
___, 251
Searing, Robert B., 261
Searles, E. H., 244
Sears
  J. J., 232, 407
  ___, 407
Seavy, H. P., 409
Sebastian, Louise, 261
Sebring
  W. H. (Mrs.), 339
  ___, 339
Seeber, John, 261
Seebolt, Frank, 261
Seeler, Simon, 261
Seepers, Joe, 232
Seerville, Henry, 261
Seibeck, L., 136
Seibel, Daniel, 261
Seibels, E. W., 354
Seibert, Ferdinand, 232
Seifer, M. M., 261
Seigel, Emilie, 261
Seixas, T. J., 362
Selden
  David, 232
  Jim, 231
Selerin, Jean P., 261
Selest, John, 231
Selig, Simon, 241
Selke, Charles, 232
Sellar
  John, 251
  Therese, 251
Sellers
  E. E., 357
  John, 231
  Theresa, 231
Selsey, Ann, 232
Selvin, John, 232
Sely, Charles (Mrs.), 374
Semmes
  Fitz, 246
  P. M., 331
  P. W., 136, 141, 330, 333, 335
Semple, James, 244
Seng, Charles, 231
Senoeuski, A., 261
Senter, D. W. C., 136
Serre, Kate, 261
Serwinski, Aaron, 261
Settle
  Annie, 233
  Louis, 233
Severson, P. C., 232
Sevier
  Peter, 241
  R., 232
Sevin
  Joseph (Mrs.), 265
  Josephine, 265
  Onezipp, 265
Seymour
  Joseph, 231
  Monroe, 231
  Rebecca, 232

Seynanoski, E. Van, 261
Seyple [Seypel]
  Alexander, 245
  Minnie, 233
Shackleford [Shackelford]
  J. N., 250
  Susie, 246
Shaddy, Margaret, 233
Shafer
  A. K. Jr., 248
  Frederick C., 232
Shaftsbury (Lord), 316
Shakeiort, William, 261
Shallack, Anna, 261
Shanahan [Shannahan]
  D. (Mrs.), 246
  Dan, 247, 249
  Dan (Mrs.), 250
  Maggie, 251
Shanders, ____ (Mrs.), 231
Shankle
  E. (Mrs.), 247
  Robert, 247, 248
  W. F., 248
  William, 247
  ____ (Mrs.), 379
Shanks
  H. B., 355
  L., 297
Shanley, J., 403
Shannon
  Annie, 261
  Louis N., 245
  Melinda, 261
  Michael, 261
  S. W., 249
Shardy, Octave, 261
Sharkey, W. L., 375
Sharp [Sharpe]
  Charles P., 243
  Doc, 233
Shaw
  A., 232
  David H., 246
  Edward, 376
  F. G., 243
  Fannie, 232
  Helena, 247
  Henry, 240
  James A., 232
  Katie (Mrs.), 233
  T. B. (Mrs.), 247
  William, 251
  ____, 248
Shawhan, J. N., 261
Shay, Ed., 232
Shea
  John, 399
  Thomas, 231
  William F., 404
Shearer
  Mary, 231
  Oliver W., 261
Sheeley, Gallius, 232

Sheetz
  H. C., 240, 266
  William, 266
Sheffield, T. J., 373
Shefley, John, 231
Sheftall, Benjamin, 368
Shehan
  Alice, 231
  C. (Mrs.), 233
  J. C., 423
  John, 233
  Kate, 233
  M. (Mrs.), 233
Shelby
  Georgia, 232
  Howard, 242
  John, 250
  Matthew, 231
Shelden [Sheldon]
  N. E., 372
  W. J., 375
Shelley, Henry, 232
Shelliday, Sanford, 243
Shelton
  Caroline, 231
  M. A. (Mrs.), 232
  M. L. (Mrs.), 355
  R. W., 233, 408
  R. W. (Mrs.), 233, 408
  ____, 231
Shepherd [Shepard, Sheppard, Shepperd]
  Alexander R., 179, 332, 436, 437
  Annie, 231
  B. E., 232
  Daisy, 233
  Eliza, 243
  Eliza A., 232
  F., 231
  J. H., 423
  Katie, 247
  Laura, 231
  Minnie (Mrs.), 233
  S. H., 422
  S. K., 261
  Sallie B., 240
  Thomas, 231
  W. B., 232, 376
  William, 233, 332, 437
  ____ (Mrs.), 374
Shepley, Martha, 261
Sheppy, W. F., 423
Sheridan [Sheriden]
  E. J., 404
  Hugh, 399
  James A., 261
  Maggie, 261
  Mary, 231
  W. H., 372
Sherk, E. W., 343
Sherlock
  Annie, 261
  James, 261
Sherman [Shermann]
  Dock, 241

  H. B., 248, 349
  Simon, 261
  ____, 248
Sherrod, Fred, 233
Sherron
  John, 251
  Joseph, 251
  Thomas, 251
Sherry
  M. L., 261
  Patrick, 231
Sherwood, Lena, 233
Shewmaker, H. C., 264
Shide, Phil. J., 431
Shiel, John J., 403
Shields
  Charity, 233
  D. A., 242
  Peter, 233, 249
  Viney, 233
Shifferstein, V., 261
Shine, Charlotte, 233
Shines, Bettie, 232
Shinkle, Robert, 266
Shipley, Mathias, 231
Shipling, Martha, 231
Shive, W. H., 233
Shneiper, Ida, 261
Shoemaker
  A., 251
  John, 251
  L. M., 233
  Morris, 233
  ____, 233
Sholner, W. E., 249
Shorey, ____ (Mrs.), 246
Short, William P., 262
Shorter, D., 242
Shortey, Clara Matilda, 232
Shotwell, A. L., 347
Shovenall
  Lena, 240
  ____ (Mrs.), 240
Shreve
  Charles Jr., 248
  Charles (Mrs.), 248
  Charles Sr., 248
Shright, Minnie, 232
Shroyer
  Margaret, 233
  W. P., 233
Shultz
  Henry, 231
  William, 233
Shumaker, Millie, 261
Shurts, ____ (Mrs.), 233
Shute, Frank, 231
Shuter, Emma, 231
Shuto, Edward P., 261
Shuttleworth
  Alfred, 232
  Annie R., 232
  James, 232
Sicollier, Alphonso, 261
Sidley, W. F., 403
Siefker, Mena, 238

Siegel, Frederick H., 261
Sievers, M. (Mrs.), 247
Sigler
  H., 427, 432
  Howell, 432
  Howell (Mrs.), 432
Signaigo, Alice (Mrs.), 248
Sikes, Needham, 347
Silberstein, David, 261
Sill, Henry, 261
Sillivan, Mary, 231
Sillman, Bertha, 261
Silobre, Charles E., 351
Silver, Manuel, 261
Silvermail, L. C., 425
Silverstein
  Lena, 261
  M., 261
Silvery, Sarah (Mrs.), 372
Silvey, Louisa (Mrs.), 375
Sim, F. L., 368
Simmone, Felix D., 261
Simmons
  A. V., 246
  Annie, 240
  H. I., 184, 376, 418
  H. (Mrs.), 261
  Isaac, 429
  J. M., 261
  Jennie, 265
  Jesse, 429
  Julius A., 232
  L., 232
  Mary, 232
  Mattie Lou, 240
  Nannie, 240
  R. S., 240
  R. S. (Mrs.), 240
  Rebecca, 232
  T. Grange, 168
  William, 265
  ____ (Dr.), 427
  ____ (Mrs.), 232
  ____, 172, 185
Simon
  Adolphus, 261
  John, 314
Simonds
  D. (Mrs.), 261
  ____ (Dr.), 33
Simons
  A., 242
  John, 251
  T. G., 368
Simonson, H. J. (Mrs.), 248
Simphondorfer, John, 247
Simpson
  Alfred, 244
  E. A. (Mrs.), 374
  G. W., 239
  J. G., 136
  James R. (Mrs.), 240
  John, 232, 242, 246
  Mary A., 401
  R. A., 135
  ____ (Miss), 354

NAME INDEX 507

Sims [Simms]
  Andrew, 232
  John H., 261
  Lewis, 233
  Lizzie, 232
  M. L. (Mrs.), 233
  Robert, 242
  _____ (Dr.), 380
  _____, 232
Sinclair [Sinklair]
  Lutie, 248
  Robert, 248
Singer
  B., 419
  Christina, 261
  Rosa, 261
  William, 261
Singleton
  Harry, 239
  Mary (Mrs.), 239
  Thomas, 239
  Thomas (Mrs.), 239
Sinnier, Jean B., 261
Sipido, Albert, 261
Sipp, Mary, 231
Sipple, Margaret, 249
Siss, Julia, 232
Sivan, Mollie, 232
Sizer, Henry E., 247
Skelly, Joseph A., 401
Skipwith, E. H., 175
Skire, Antonio, 261
Skoesburg, _____, 245
Skolfield
  Kilhan S., 264
  Pearl, 263
Slack
  Eliza, 232
  J. J., 173
  Jerry, 233
Slagle, Josephine, 231
Slater
  D. C., 408
  D. C. (Mrs.), 408
  E. C., 121, 141, 159, 164, 330, 335, 336, 411, 412
  E. C. (Mrs.), 233, 412
  Mollie, 233
  Oliver H., 261
  Sallie, 233
  _____ (Rev. Dr.), 121, 391
  _____, 408, 412
Sledge
  Caroline, 231
  Henry, 232
  _____ (Mrs.), 233
Sleidger, Fritz, 239
Sleiman, _____ (Miss), 351
Slick, Carl, 232
Slink, _____ (Mrs.), 233
Sloan, Mary, 147
Slocum, Ed., 231
Slugher, A. T., 232
Small
  Effie, 348

F. T., 240
George, 261
George S., 261
M. Louisa, 261
Mary, 232
_____ (Mrs.), 247
Smarr, J. W., 242
Smeck, Jackson, 373
Smith
  A., 264
  Abe, 246
  Ada A., 243
  Adeline, 231
  Aggie, 233
  Albert, 233
  Alfred, 233
  Amelia (Mrs.), 373
  Angus, 233
  Ann, 231
  Annie M., 261
  B., 232
  B. P., 373, 424
  Barbara (Mrs.), 231
  Beauregard, 240
  Bella, 261
  Ben, 430
  Bob, 231, 233
  Burrell, 233
  C., 261
  C. A., 261
  C. A. (Mrs.), 373
  C. J., 375
  C. (Mrs.), 261
  Celia, 261
  Charles, 233, 261, 374
  Charles M., 232, 416, 432
  Charley, 232
  Clara, 233
  Cornelius, 233
  D. B., 342
  Daniel, 400
  Dave, 232
  Dealey, 240
  Dick, 429
  Dorcas, 233
  E. F. (Mrs.), 246
  E. H., 261
  Ed, 266
  Eddie, 246
  Edward, 231, 261
  Eliza, 233
  Emma, 232, 233
  Erla May, 248
  Eva, 261
  F. J., 266
  F. P. (Mrs.), 246
  Frank, 231
  Frank P., 247
  Fred, 261
  G. G., 375
  G. T., 422
  Georgiana, 261
  Gran. W., 401
  Gus, 245
  H., 232, 233
  H. D. (Mrs.), 233

H. G., 233
Henry, 239, 261
Hettie, 232
I. Southwood, 316
Ida, 243
Irving W., 343
Isaac, 352
J. C., 241
J. H., 136, 142, 146, 173, 329, 330, 331, 335, 336, 363, 377, 379
J. J., 233, 404
J. Taylor, 342
J. W., 410
James, 243
James A. (Mrs.), 246
James G., 401
John, 231, 232, 240, 261
John A., 261
John E., 261
John H., 261
Joseph, 261
Josie, 232
Julia, 239
L., 232
Lawrence, 261
M. F., 232
M. (Mrs.), 240
Maggie M., 261
Margaret, 261
Marshall, 243
Martha, 231
Martin, 231
Mary, 231, 261
Mary A., 244
Mary E., 249
Mary R., 261
Matilda, 243
Mattie, 243
Mittie, 246
Mollie, 246
Monti, 246
Nellie, 233, 263
Nelson, 265
O. P., 251
Patrick, 233
Percy, 243
Philip, 233
R. R., 430
R. S., 416, 434
Richard, 155
Robert, 233, 261
Sally, 232
Samuel, 232
Sarah, 261
Southwood, 304
T. M., 368
Tennie, 232
Teresa, 261
Thomas, 264, 430
Tom, 243
Victor, 245
W. C., 233
W. E., 356
W. H., 244, 349, 350

W. J., 106, 136, 137, 138, 140, 141, 146, 151, 161, 329, 330, 331, 333, 334, 335, 336, 365, 377, 378, 381, 386
W. J. Jr., 231
William, 261
William J., 379
William M., 261
Willis, 232
_____ (Dr.), 118
_____ (Mrs.), 190, 231, 239, 246, 248
_____, 151, 231, 232, 233, 264
Smithner, Jacob, 249
Smithson, C. T., 427
Smitta, John, 242
Smoker, John, 242
Smooks, Louis, 232
Smoot
  _____ (Miss), 251
  _____ (Mrs.), 251
Smythe
  Augusta, 264
  W. H., 409
Snead [Sneed]
  Arthur, 238
  Horace H., 243
  J. P. (Mrs.), 250
  John, 261
  Laura, 231
  R., 430
  Thomas F., 336
Sneelan, W. F., 244
Snell
  Albert, 233
  C. V., 421
Snelling, C. Jr., 233
Snigg
  Edward, 233
  Edward J., 416, 433
Snodgrass
  H. C., 248
  _____, 422
Snow
  John, 243
  Robert, 243
Snowberger, Blanche, 247, 249
Snyder [Snider]
  Charles S., 332
  H., 245
  Katie, 232
  Lillie (Mrs.), 245
  S. C., 368
  Sallie, 245
  _____, 245, 250
Soelfker, Mena, 249
Sohm
  Eureka, 251
  John, 251
  Margaret, 231
  Willie, 251
  _____, 251
Soires, Raphael, 264

Sokolosky, Wolf, 244
Solares
  Anthony, 264
  Romain, 261
Sollis
  Henry, 251
  Mary, 251
Solomon
  E., 231
  Fannie, 261
  Morris, 244
  Nicholas, 372
Solomons, Pauline, 251
Somers, T. O., 368
Sommer, Julius, 261
Sommerville [Somerville]
  Allen, 264
  Mary, 264
  R. B., 239, 240
Soners, Charlie, 261
Soniat
  E. E., 261
  Louise E., 261
Sontag, George, 261
Sopp, W. F., 425
Sorry, Mitchell, 232
Souberville, Louis, 261
Soubil, Jean, 261
Soubrier, A., 261
Souhr, Josephine, 232
Soumeillans, H., 261
Southern, W., 232
Southey, William, 232
Southmate, Sarah (Mrs.), 374
Southmayd
  F. B., 329
  G. F., 261
Spahm, S., 261
Spain
  Lucy, 232
  Mary Ann, 233
Spana, Joseph, 261
Spane, Thomas, 240
Sparks, Florence H., 261
Spaulding [Spalding]
  J. B. R., 427
  John B. R., 432
  L. A., 361
  M. F., 347
  ____ (Right Rev.), 341
Speaks, T. B., 247
Spears [Speers]
  Elizabeth (Mrs.), 232
  Joseph, 376
  N W Jr, 407
  Willie, 245
  ____ (Mrs.), 233
  ____, 249
Specht, Joseph, 406
Speckernagle
  [Spickernagle],
  William, 231, 416
Speed
  John K., 438
  Martin, 232

Spellman
  P., 232
  William, 232
Spence, W. F., 261
Spencer
  A. K., 368
  Caroline, 232
  E. W., 344
  Nora, 231
  ____ (Dr.), 395
  ____ (Mrs.), 239, 248
Spengler
  Albert, 244
  Charles C., 243
  Joseph, 243
  Willie, 242
Sperry, Henry, 244
Spess, Robert G., 261
Speyer, Wolfgang, 420
Spicer, Jennie, 233
Spickernagle, William, 416
Spiegel [Spiegle]
  Paul, 429
  ____ (Priv.), 130
  ____, 233
Spillaine, John, 244
Spillman, J., 339
Spiuito, Caesar, 261
Spivey, Jack, 240
Spliedt, C. F., 261
Sprague, Daniel R., 261
Sprausberger, Charles, 231
Spreen, Fred, 261
Sprigg, John, 232
Springer, Andrew J., 402
Springman, Louis, 261
Sprott, W. D., 248
Squan, Victor, 261
Squire, Joseph (Mrs.), 261
Sronce, Jake, 231
St. Clair
  A., 358
  Henry S., 261
  Mary, 261
  T. C., 368, 369
  ____ (Dr.), 240
St. James, Clem, 345
Stacey, G. C., 233
Stack
  Jerry, 250
  Margaret (Mrs.), 232
  Patrick, 261
  ____ (Mrs.), 250
Staffer, C. L., 141, 330, 331, 335
Stafford
  Elizabeth J., 261
  Perry, 372
  R. B., 261
  ____ (Dr.), 246
  ____ (Mrs.), 247
Stahl, Jacob, 261
Stahlen, J. N., 231
Staley, Charlie, 232
Stalin, Helen (Mrs.), 231
Stall, August, 233

Stamps
  ____ (Mrs.), 251
  ____, 251
Stanberg
  Arthur, 232
  Charles, 231
  Ed. A., 231
Standard
  Jessie (Mrs.), 245
  Mary (Mrs.), 244
  Millie (Mrs.), 244
Stanfield
  Fannie, 239
  M. M., 239
  M. M. (Mrs.), 239
  ____ (Mrs.), 239
  ____, 239
Stanford, Tom, 231
Stangel, James, 242
Stanislaus (Sister), 120, 232, 245
Stanley
  J. H., 352
  John R., 233
  May, 261
  Mike, 231, 232
  P. M., 407
  P. M. (Mrs.), 233, 407
  ____, 407
Stann, Rosa, 261
Stanter, N., 261
Stanton
  E. W., 425
  Eliza, 232
  F. B., 425
  Julia (Mrs.), 261
  Lucy A., 232
Starke [Stark]
  Charles E., 261
  W. N., 261
Starks
  H., 242
  Henry, 241
Starrett
  Eddie, 231
  F. E. (Mrs.), 231
Staub, Oswald, 261
Staun, Harry, 240
Stearn [Stearne, Stern]
  M., 261
  Sophia, 261
  T. D., 361
  W. H., 347
Stearns, John E., 374
Steed, W. H., 240
Steefiel, George, 261
Steele [Steel]
  Annie, 246
  C. L., 232
  C. L. (Mrs.), 233
  Francis F., 261
  J. M., 231
  Leda J., 261
  Sam, 243
  W. H., 266
  ____, 231, 233

Steger
  E. A. (Mrs.), 240
  Jack S., 240
Stegman, Joseph, 261
Stehaing, Rebettie, 261
Stehle, Frank, 231
Stein [Stine]
  Martin, 261
  Mary, 233
  Mary M., 261
Steinau, Joseph, 231
Steinberg, E., 247
Steinell, John, 231
Steinhardt, Sarah, 261
Steinkuhl
  C. D., 233
  Henry, 232
  Margaret, 232
Stella (Sister), 245
Stenson, Reese, 232
Stephani, G., 265
Stephens
  C. A., 263
  E. (Mrs.), 251
  Joseph D., 261
  T. B., 349
Stephenson
  Aaron, 390
  Nelson, 233
  Sallie D., 417
  T. F., 261
  W. G., 161, 417, 432, 433
  W. G. (Mrs.), 433
  W. W., 416, 433
  W. W. (Mrs.), 417, 433
  William, 430
  ____, 161, 417, 433
Stepprich, M. D., 261
Steprick, M. D., 261
Sterenberg, L., 261
Sterla, Frederick, 231
Sterlie, Helen, 232
Sterling
  A., 135
  Sandy, 243
Stern, see Stearn
Sterrett, James, 232
Steth, William B., 261
Stetson, Eddie, 231
Stettin, W. A., 348
Stevens
  A. H., 299, 300
  Florence, 261
  Julia Ann, 233
  Samuel, 244
  W. H., 276
  ____, 303
Stevenson
  J. A. Jr., 249
  Jennie, 233
  M., 231
  M. B. (Mrs.), 261
  Mary T., 232
  Robert, 248
  Rufus, 232
  William G., 232, 416

NAME INDEX

____ (Miss), 233
____, 249
Stever, Joseph, 231
Stevers, M. (Mrs.), 247
Steverson, James, 249
Stewart
  Albert, 232
  Annie, 245
  Arthur, 246
  Augustus, 242
  Butler P., 238
  C. Y, 232
  C. Young, 238
  Calvin, 232
  Charles, 233, 431
  D. L., 431
  E. (Mrs.), 239
  Eliza J., 231
  Ellen J., 231
  F., 261
  Frank, 431
  George, 233, 264
  George (Mrs.), 264
  Hugh, 246
  J. R., 240
  J. T., 340
  James, 246
  James H., 246
  James (Mrs.), 250
  Maggie, 231
  Mary, 245
  Maud, 233
  N. M. (Mrs.), 231
  Nettie, 246
  P. B., 232, 266
  S. A., 375
  S. M. (Mrs.), 238
  Sarah W., 232
  T. N., 248
  Thomas, 233
  Thomas H., 261
  W. F., 231
  ____, 239, 250
Sticker
  T., 233
  ____, 233
Stickers, Elvira, 233
Stickley, John, 374
Stickney, James, 232
Stiles, Julian, 372
Stille, P., 22
Stillman, Henry, 154, 231, 434
Stine, see Stein
Stineman, Peter, 245
Stinette, John, 231
Stinkler, R. M., 358
Stinson
  A. F., 240
  A. (Mrs.), 240
  Charles, 240
  Eugene, 240
  Reese, 232
  Samuel, 240
Stith, Oscar N., 244

Stoddard
  A. M., 141, 330, 331, 335, 377, 380
  ____, 395
Stojowski, Julia, 245
Stokes
  J. C. (Mrs.), 247
  James, 247
  John, 232, 247
Stokie, Annie (Mrs.), 233
Stoltz, Paul, 242
Stome, Ida, 233
Stone
  Agnes (Mrs.), 373
  D. L., 247, 249
  E. K., 341
  J. H., 245
  James, 233
  John, 251
  John J., 400
  Melinda, 373
  Mollie J., 355
  Perry S., 246
  Warren, 24, 35, 65
  ____ (Dr.), 26, 42, 297
  ____ (Mrs.), 245
  ____, 15, 118
Stonehouse, Emanuel, 261
Stoner
  Fred, 251
  Kate, 251
Storer, D. H., 299
Storm
  Ad., 438
  Fritz, 240
Stortz, Henry, 261
Storz, John M., 261
Stouder, John, 261
Stovall
  Dinah, 233
  Mollie, 232
Stover
  Dennie, 240
  Mattie, 240
  R. B. (Mrs.), 240
Stowe
  Mellie, 401
  ____ (Mrs.), 233
Stowell, Lyman, 246
Stowits, C. S., 350
Strach, Joe, 375
Strain, ____, 232
Strang, ____, 248
Strange
  Netia, 233
  Tom, 233
Stranger, A., 264
Strattman
  A., 233
  Bernard, 233
Strauberg
  Charles, 231
  Ernest, 231

Strauss [Straus]
  Charles, 263
  Morris, 261
  ____, 245
Straws, Archie (Mrs.), 245
Strayer, C. C., 357, 358
Strealy
  Jerry, 245
  ____, 245
Stream, George, 246
Street
  Fannie, 232
  Nannie, 232
Strehl
  J. A. (Mrs.), 233
  John A., 390
  Mollie, 231
  Sarah R., 232
Stringer
  Abe, 243
  Alfred D., 261
  John, 244
  Mary (Mrs.), 373
Strobel, ____, 303
Strohecker, Lucy (Mrs.), 246
Strong
  G. W., 246
  Henry, 233
  Nancy, 232
  Wash, 244
  ____ (Mrs.), 233
  ____, 231
Strother, Ira B., 261
Strout, Col., 249
Strowbridge
  J. G., 248
  J. (Mrs. Dr.), 248
Strozzi, W. A., 135
Stuart
  Bill, 250
  J. E. B., 435
Stubble, A. M., 242
Stubbs
  Jack, 246
  Phoebe (Mrs.), 246
Stucker, William, 264
Stumpf, C. A., 261
Sturdevant
  A. J., 240
  N., 240
  Peter (Mrs.), 240
  ____ (Miss), 240
  ____ (Mrs.), 231, 241
Sturges [Sturgess]
  E. A., 356
  W. A., 261
Sturm, James, 240
Stutz, Frank, 242
Suarez
  Helen (Mrs.), 249
  Maximo, 261
  Regina M., 249
Suasey
  H. A., 265
  Ida A., 265

Sueck, Louis, 261
Suggs, ____ (Mrs.), 233
Sugure, Timothy, 402
Sullivan
  Cornelius, 401
  Dennis, 112, 232
  Denny, 434
  Ellen, 251
  Helen, 261
  James, 261
  James J., 232
  Jaspar, 233
  Jerry, 232
  John, 261
  John H., 402
  John J., 239
  Joseph, 261
  L. S., 231
  M., 231
  Mary, 232
  Nelson, 233
  P. J., 261
  Pat, 374
  Patrick, 261
  Samuel, 261
  T. O., 399
  Thomas, 261
  Tom, 232
  W. D., 401
  ____ (Miss), 239
  ____ (Mrs.), 231, 233
Summers
  C. E., 246
  C. H., 232
  Margaret (Mrs.), 233
  T. O., 56, 427
  William, 233
Sunberry, ____ (Mrs.), 232
Sundies, William, 232
Supple, James N., 399
Susden, John, 350
Susette [Susete], George, 231, 232
Susman, Julius, 244
Sutbrocker, Antoine, 244
Sutera, Christiana, 261
Sutherland, Charles, 243
Sutton
  Fannie, 232
  George W., 233
  Mollie, 232
  Steve, 246
  Thomas, 232
  ____, 263
Svance, Peter, 340
Swafford, Le Grand, 243
Swan [Swann]
  Auguste, 232
  Booker, 240
  J. T., 342
Swartz, ____ (Mrs.), 248
Swearingen [Swearengen]
  R. M., 27
  ____ (Dr.), 356
Swearinger, E. F., 231
Sweeney [Sweeny]
  Ada, 231

J. H., 232
John, 399
Mary, 239
W. H., 112
W. J., 372
———, 232
Sweetman [Sweetmon]
 C., 261
 Nicholas, 261
 Millie, 261
Swep, Taylor, 233
Swett, William H., 247
Swift
 James, 261
 ———, 232
Swinburne, John, 277
Swint, Lizzie, 232
Swisshelm, Jane G. (Mrs.), 68
Switzer, Mary, 231
Swofford, Ed., 239
Swope, Rebecca, 344
Sword, ———, 191
Swyier, James, 261
Sylvester
 Philip, 248
 Tom, 247
 Walter, 249

T

Taaffee, E. R., 261
Tabany, James T., 402
Tabler, John, 239
Taconi
 Alfred, 249
 Jules, 249
Taffe, Charles F., 243
Taffer, Sophy, 233
Taft, Mattie, 248
Tafuin, Ida, 244
Taggert [Taggart]
 John (Mrs.), 248
 R. L., 234
Tah, Jung Yung, 233
Tainter, H. W., 261
Talbert, W. W., 429
Talbot
 Charles, 262
 F., 430
 Willis, 241
Taleisouer, C. (Mrs.), 261
Tallichet, E. II, 248
Tally
 Annie, 234
 Hugh, 239
Tamme, Emily, 262
Tammie, William, 261
Tamporella, Mich., 262
Tandler, Isaac, 245
Tannehill, C. O., 352
Tanner
 Annie R., 243
 John P., 337
 Sadie L., 243
Tansen, Louis, 261
Tant, James C., 374

Tape, Gerhard, 262
Tarcliff
 Oliver, 265
 Victor (Mrs.), 265
Tarle, Samuel II, 261
Tarrant
 Salvador, 249
 Walter, 261
Tarry, Thomas H., 239
Tarver
 S. J. (Mrs.), 248
 William S., 248
Tashey, E. E., 261
Tate
 Ann, 250
 Bena, 250
 Bob, 250
 David, 234
 Frank, 250
 George E., 424
 J. J., 250
 Jesse M., 234
 Lucy A., 234
 Mark, 266
 Mary, 239
 R. H., 118, 368, 369
 Simpson, 250
 William, 234
 ——— (Dr.), 167
Taut, James, 376
Taylor
 A. W., 234
 Ada, 261
 Ann E. (Mrs.), 234
 Annie (Mrs.), 234
 Ashton, 261
 B., 233
 Bettie, 244
 C. L., 373
 C. M., 355
 Caroline, 234
 Charles, 234, 265
 D. S., 234
 Daniel, 265
 Dave, 234
 Dick, 245
 E. D., 373
 Eddie, 245
 Eliza, 234
 Ensley, 234
 Eugenia, 262
 Henry, 243, 249
 Henry (Mrs.), 249
 Howell L., 262
 I. L., 249
 J. B., 246
 J. Theus, 261
 J. W., 262
 James, 234
 Jennie, 234
 Jesse, 234
 Joe, 234, 241
 John, 262
 John B., 234, 408
 John L., 233
 Lester, 351
 Lou., 234

Louise, 247
Lucy, 234
M., 234
Marshall, 234
Mary Ann, 234
Mary E., 239, 261
Mollie, 240
Nora, 234
Park, 234
Preston, 234
S. A., 423
S. Lester, 336
Samuel, 344
Swift, 234
W. G., 416, 433
W. H., 233
Wash, 240
Will, 165
William, 247
William G., 416
Zack, 244
——— (Dr.), 395
———, 241
Teague, W. H., 266
Teatons, ———, 265
Tebalt, John, 261
Tedro
 Annie (Mrs.), 251
 J. H., 240
 ——— (Mrs.), 240
 ———, 240
Teiglehueter, Cath., 262
Telfer, William, 246
Telford, M. A., 421
Tellair, Sallie (Mrs.), 248
Temple, Horace, 265
Templeman, ——— (Miss), 345
Templet, Josephine, 262
Temps, Willie, 234
Tenfull
 Bettie, 234
 Breton (Mrs.), 234
 Joseph, 234
 Julius, 234
Terpinitz, Edward J., 264
Terrell [Terrill]
 Henrietta, 243
 James, 248
 L. B., 344
Terrio, Octava, 264
Terry
 Andy, 234
 Augustus, 246
 G. C., 339
 Jesse, 234
 John S., 434
 Mary, 262
 Stephen (Mrs.), 124
 T. J., 248
 ———, 246
Tershus, Patrick, 234
Tertron, Jules, 262
Terzia, Steffano, 249
Teutsch, J., 261
Thaler
 Adolph, 248

Adolph (Mrs.), 248
John, 248
Rudolph, 248
Tobias, 248
Thanes, Orillo, 261
Thatcher, W. W., 129, 391
Thayers, Adolph., 234
Thearam, Aleck, 261
Theckler (Sister), 234
Thecla (Sister), 122, 124
Theilgaard, S. C., 248
Theobus, T. V., 234
Theveat
 A., 233
 Bernard, 234
 Noble, 234
Theventh, Robert, 234
Thibant, Christian, 261
Thibodaux [Thibodeaux]
 Angele, 265
 C. (Mrs.), 265
 Edgar, 264
 Elder, 265
 Georgina, 265
 H. (Mrs.), 265
 L., 265
Thilberger, Fred, 262
Thilman, David, 418
Thirreat, William, 261
Thixton
 W. K., 234
 ——— (Mrs.), 234
Thoman, Johannes, 262
Thomas
 A., 153, 234, 421
 Alma, 234
 Ann, 261
 Belle, 243
 Bertha, 264
 Bettie, 234
 C., 354
 C. H., 430
 Caroline (Mrs.), 234
 Casey, 248
 Charles M., 261
 Charlotte, 234
 Coleman, 390
 D., 234
 E. A. (Mrs.), 245
 Ed., 241
 Fred, 429
 Free, 234
 G., 245
 G. M., 243
 George, 240
 H., 234
 Hatch, 234
 Hattie, 234
 Henry, 233, 264
 Ida, 234
 Ignatius, 262
 J. C., 251
 James, 239
 Joe, 234
 John, 187, 234, 244, 248
 John H., 352

NAME INDEX

Laura, 264
Mack, 243
Margaret, 251
Martin, 245
Maud, 262
Pauline, 234
Renie, 234
Richard, 234
S., 244
Sallie, 234, 251
Stella, 244
T. W., 251
Thaddeus N., 251
Viola, 234
___ (Rev. Dr.), 121
___ (Rev. Mr.), 121, 164
___, 234
Thomasson, C. R., 372
Thompkins, La Rue C, 243
Thompson
A. D., 249
A. J., 250
A. R., 234
Aggie, 234
Albert, 240
Alice, 249
Ann Eliza, 234
Annie, 355
Bertha E., 262
Bettie, 250
Celia, 374
Charles, 261, 373
D., 261
D. H., 234
Donnie, 234
E. F., 248
E. L. (Mrs.), 246
Ella, 240
Evan, 240
Georgiana, 264
Ida, 262
J., 240
J. A., 390, 391
Jeff, 243
Jerry, 234, 266
Joanna (Mrs.), 234
John, 250
John (Mrs.), 250
John W., 344
L. A., 248
Lewis, 245
Louis (Mrs.), 245
Mattie (Mrs.), 234
Minerva, 233
N. B., 240
R. A., 128, 154, 160, 161, 234, 390, 431, 433
Samuel, 234
Sarah H. (Mrs.), 376
T. J., 242
Tansey, 234
W. B., 234, 375
W. W., 346
West, 234
William, 266

Willie, 234
___ (Mrs.), 29, 234
Thorn [Thorne]
Ed, 234
Lillie, 233
Thorns, A. C., 246
Thornton
Cal., 264
E., 242
Ellen E. W., 234
G. B., 53, 388
J. J., 348
Luke, 242
___ (Dr.), 138, 140, 389
Thorpe [Thorp]
Adelaide, 262
F. J., 348
Richard, 234
Thrall, J. C., 234, 407, 423
Thrasher, John B., 248
Thrift, Elizabeth (Mrs.), 242
Throols, T., 375
Thrower, Sarah, 372
Throwig, T. Z., 358
Thucydides, 14
Thuer, John K., 262
Thumel, Adolph, 234
Thurber
H., 361
K., 361
Tibbs, Johnson, 234
Tickault, H. L., 348
Tiernan
John, 246
Mike, 245
Tierney [Tiernay]
Charles, 234
M. M., 262
Thomas J., 262
Tierson, Alex, 234
Ties, H. C., 349
Tiggatt, C. M., 358
Tighe
James, 234
James C., 234
Peter A. Jr., 233, 234
Samuel, 234
Tilford, M. A., 234
Tilitz, Helen, 243
Tilley, W. Jr., 247
Tillman, Rosa, 233
Tillson [Tilson]
Elizabeth, 234
F., 234
Samuel, 234
Tilton, R., 234
Timmons, Edward, 262
Tinbeck, ___, 251
Tindall
C. M., 233
R., 242
Tines, Esther, 234
Tinker, J. M., 350
Tinman, Alice, 234
Tinney, J. T., 242

Tithian, Hester E., 234
Titus, Nelson, 251
Tlieller, Cecelia, 244
Tobias, Arthur W., 372
Tobin [Tobyn]
Dennis, 234
Ellen (Mrs.), 234
Mike, 234
Toby, James J., 261
Tocca, Emma, 262
Todd
James, 262
W. R., 245
Toelhe, Mary A., 261
Toka, Frank, 261
Tolivar, Pauline, 262
Toll, John, 261
Tolland, D. W., 262
Tomeney [Tomeny]
Hale, 234
Helen, 234
J. M., 178, 234
J. M. (Mrs.), 178, 234
___, 178
Tomkins, J. H,m 374
Tomlin
G. M., 241
___, 241
Tompkins, R. T., 355
Tong, L. G., 403
Tonmilla, Jean, 262
Tony, Charles, 261
Toof
J. S., 415
John S., 390
S. C., 390
Toohey
Mary, 244
P. J., 244
Topse, Gernard, 261
Torrence, Hugh, 234
Tortorice, Peter, 261
Tutto, Vincenzo, 261
Touce, Mary, 262
Toujet, Margaret, 262
Toulson, Charles, 234
Touman, Hubert, 262
Toups
Clebert, 265
Marie, 265
Overstile (Mrs.), 265
Tournier, J. J., 262
Tourtable, Lucien, 261
Toussaint, M., 261
Touzan, Emile, 262
Towers, Joe, 234
Townley, Dallas, 434
Towns, Earnest, 234
Townsend
Aleck, 234
Candes, 234
D. A., 355
Franklin, 242
J. B., 379
Joseph, 234
Mollie, 234
Robert, 246

Samuel, 112
Willie, 234
___ (Dr.), 272, 274
___ (Miss), 234
___, 303
Townshend, Richard W., 425
Townsley
Florence, 158
Sam., 234, 241
___ (Mrs.), 158, 186
___, 158, 186
Trabert, G. H., 353
Tracy [Tracey]
H. P., 341
John P., 262
L. S., 17
Maggie, 233
Train
George Francis, 165, 166
Thomas, 234
Trainer, Tom (Mrs.), 246
Trammel
George, 247
___ (Mrs.), 246
Trampatore, Cologers, 262
Trark, Anna, 261
Trask, W. L., 154
Trau, V. Alex, 262
Traub, August, 262
Trauth, Caroline (Mrs.), 262
Travers, Katie, 244
Travis, Ann (Mrs.), 244
Trawick, M. T., 261
Traylor, Alber., 261
Traynor, Thomas, 373
Trazey, Peter, 438
Treadwell [Tedwell]
A. B., 409
Gertrude, 234
Tredger, John, 261
Troiforde, R. N., 262
Treil, L. Nado, 262
Trenchard, V., 261
Trevellian, T. C. (Mrs.), 248
Trezevant
J. P., 406
J. T., 354
Pollard, 168
S. P., 234
Tribble
George A., 245
George A. (Mrs.), 245
Trichanard
A. C., 261
G., 261
Trigg
A. B., 247
Allen N., 233
J. M., 373
Marshall, 234
Trimble, Frank, 340
Trindle
Eola Maud, 244

Margaret Belle, 244
William George, 244
Troessard, George A., 262
Trois, John, 262
Tromanovich, S., 262
Trombly
  Aug., 262
  George, 233
Trosclair
  Ida, 265
  Joseph, 265
Troully, Hubert, 262
Trout
  Ira, 182, 336
  Lee, 431
Trueheart, Susan, 234
Truman, H. G., 359
Tryon, W. A., 368
Tscleppert, Robert, 262
Tuck, George H., 341
Tucker
  B. O., 243
  Charles, 234
  Edward, 248
  Francis, 234
  G. W., 368
  Henry, 244
  Lillie, 244
  Mary, 240
  Mary L., 262
  Sallie A. (Mrs.), 234
  Susie, 240
  ____ (Mrs.), 248
Tuerke [Tuerk]
  P., 118, 368, 369
  ____ (Dr.), 167, 168, 234
Tufts, Peter T. E., 234
Tugler, James, 234
Tuhell, C. (Mrs.), 234
Tujague, Bernard, 262
Tullman, K. M., 234
Tumblety, Dennis F., 374
Turgeon, T. D., 265
Turley
  Mike, 234
  Thomas, 422
  Thomas B., 391
Turnan, Kate, 234
Turner
  A., 234
  Aleck (Mrs.), 248
  Charles, 265
  Edna, 234
  Elder, 241
  G. P. M., 107
  Gus H., 261
  Harriet, 241
  Harriet (Mrs.), 241
  Henrietta, 234
  James, 262
  Louis, 244
  Philis., 234
  Robert, 234
  Sallie, 234
  Selby, 234
  Thomas, 233, 234

Vina, 234
____, 234
Turney
  C. R., 261
  H. M., 261
  ____ (Mrs.), 233
Turnipseed, ____ (Dr.), 250
Turpin, John, 262
Tuska, S. (Mrs.), 420
Tuther, Alf, 390
Tvargosky, Delia, 244
Tweedy, Thomas, 234
Twitchell, Grace, 262
Twomey, Ello, 262
Tyler
  Charles, 261
  F. A. Jr., 136
  Scott, 242
Tyson, Nick, 234

U

Ubee, Richard, 262
Uhrman, Martin, 265
Ulard, Gustave, 262
Ulman, M., 419
Ulrich, J., 341
Underhill, W. D., 239
Ungerer, Fritz, 248
Untram, Charles, 235
Unversagt [Unverzagt],
  William, 112, 234
Up, Fanny, 262
Upchurch
  C. H., 234
  C. H. (Mrs.), 234
Updike, P. B., 340
Uphoof, John, 372
Upshaw, E. W., 245
Urban, T., 374
Urdgis, Catherine, 262
Urger, Lena, 262
Uritti, G., 235
Uzell
  J. D., 375
  T. D., 416, 433

V

Vaccari, Vin., 262
Vaccaro
  Alonzo, 235
  Antonio, 262
  Maria, 262
  Nicoletta (Mrs.), 235
Vagelsaenge, J. G., 262
Vaggart, W., 265
Vail, B. M., 248
Vain, Edward, 358
Valconar, Francois, 249
Valencia, Viel, 262
Valentine, ____ (Supt.), 338
Valiente, Pablo, 35
Valier, Thomas, 235
Valkner, Frederick, 235

Vallentine, C. O., 239
Valnote, Poblo, 262
Valuner, Nicholas, 235
Vamote, Joseph, 262
Van Buren, George, 246
Van Dyke, J., 347
Van Epps, Harry, 262
Van Hame, W. C., 235, 372
Van Hook, John, 235
Van Hoove, ____, 262
Van Hooven, A., 262
Van Horn [Van Horne]
  Frank, 416
  Frank (Mrs.), 417
  John, 426
  ____ (Rev.), 357
  ____, 417
Van Ostera, Eva M., 262
Van Troostenberg, ____
  (Rev.), 119, 164
Van Walsh, Daniel, 235
Van Winkle, J., 349
Van Zandt, ____ (Mrs.), 350
Vanburg, John, 235
Vance
  C. F., 355
  Mary, 246
Vandeier, A. J., 338
Vandenburg [Vandenberg]
  Mary A., 243
  Minnie L., 244
Vanderheiden, F. A., 262
Vanderhooder, F., 262
Vandive, Henry, 245
Vanhoostenberg (Father), 235
Vanier
  A., 262
  ____ (Mrs.), 262
Vankunze, C. A., 235
Varillo, John, 239
Varinnani
  Celestine, 264
  Marie, 264
Varley, Thomas, 235
Varnardo, Sammie, 265
Varner, John, 235
Vas, Joseph, 262
Vassali
  P., 249
  ____, 249
Vassalo, J. A., 403
Vassar, M. Jr., 349
Vaudry, J., 375
Vaughn
  A. J., 188
  Harry, 247
  Manuel, 235
Veasey, Ellen, 262
Veaux, Pierre, 262
Veavant, Frederick S., 262
Veazie, H. A., 378
Venable
  Joseph, 235
  W. G., 357
Vendig, S., 420

Venn, Mary L., 235
Venta, J., 262
Venus, Charles F., 262
Verdi, T. S., 29
Verdichizzi, Jo, 262
Verdue, Emile, 264
Verges
  Charles, 262
  Jean P., 262
  John, 262
Vergez, J. Ed., 262
Verhoff, Charles, 262
Verlander, Georgiana, 262
Vermis, P. D., 262
Vernado
  ____ (Mrs.), 249
  ____, 249
Vernier, Charles, 264
Veronica (Sister), 150, 235
Verschoyle, Charles H., 372
Vertner
  J. D., 248
  ____, 248
Vessein, Julia (Mrs.), 262
Viala, A., 402
Vicelli, ____, 249
Vicha, Catherine, 262
Vickers, Sarah, 263
Vicknar, Marie, 262
Vickstron, Larson, 244
Victori (Sister), 245
Vidoo, Amedee, 262
Viendahaar, Lewis, 262
Vienna
  A. J., 355
  Anne E., 264
Vierling, Georgia, 249
Vigard, George, 262
Villere, ____ (Gov.), 295
Vilter
  Bertha, 262
  Max, 262
Vincends, Arthur, 242
Vincent
  Edward, 262
  G., 262
  J. B. P., 262
  Sol., 235
  ____ (Mrs.), 37
Vincent (Sister), 120, 160
Vincentia (Sister), 235
Vincents, Gramilla, 243
Vincil, John D., 409
Vinette, Emanuel, 264
Vining, Rosa, 264
Vinn, Clara C., 235
Vinne, M. N. (Sister), 262
Vinson, ____, 249
Vinston, Wesley, 235
Violet, Thomas, 235
Virgeson
  Kinch, 433
  Kinch (Mrs.), 433
  M., 433
  M. W., 235
Virginia, Mollie, 245

NAME INDEX

Virson, E. E., 247
Vishber, John, 235
Vite, Deserve, 264
Vitola, John, 243
Vitrano, Maria, 262
Vivar, Mary S., 262
Vocheran, Claude, 262
Voconowich, C., 262
Voegele
  H. J., 239
  H. J. (Mrs.), 239
Voeinkle, Louisa, 242
Vogel [Vogl]
  Abe, 373
  G., 262
  Martha (Mrs.), 262
  Moses, 373
Vogeley, Charles, 262
Vogeli
  H. J., 235
  H. J. (Mrs.), 235
Voight
  Clara (Mrs.), 262
  Frantz, 262
Voiscult, Louis, 262
Volger, Violet, 235
Volois, Henry, 262
Volte, Francisco, 262
Volvodich, John, 264
Vondran
  E. J., 248
  E. J. (Mrs.), 249
  Peter, 239, 249
  Peter (Mrs.), 239, 249
Vonwesterhayen, T. B., 262
Voorhees, C. V., 235
Vosbergh, John R., 262
Voslon, Michael, 262
Voss
  Ann, 251
  Ernest, 251
  Mattie A., 262
Vredenburgh, R. V., 438
Vulcon, Henry, 262

W

Wachenfield, Mary, 262
Waddell
  J. D., 339
  J. N., 356
Wade
  A. C., 251
  Sidney Y., 240
  Thomas, 245
  Thruston, 265
Wadley, Frank, 237
Wadsworth, Clara, 243
Waechter, Charles E., 237
Waffon, William, 237
Waggoner [Waggener, Wagoner]
  J. H., 237
  Jesse, 343
  Jesse B., 432

W. S., 237
_____, 236
Wagner
  Elenora, 262
  Frank, 246
  I., 243
  John, 262
  John C., 400
  Mike, 236
Wahl
  Dorothea, 262
  Fred, 262
  S. W., 245
Wain, William, 262
Waite
  Julia, 245
  Willie B., 247
Walch, James, 265
Walden, Jack, 236
Waldron [Waldran]
  E. D., 342
  Elmira, 237
  J. D., 400
  James, 236
  Polly, 236
  W. B., 408
  W. B. (Mrs.), 408
Walds, Ad. J. A., 262
Wales
  Ben, 249
  Hannah, 236
Walheng, John, 262
Walin, Jacques A., 262
Walker
  Alfred, 236
  Alice, 265
  Annie, 237
  Beckie, 236
  C. H., 245
  Cady, 236
  Calvin, 237
  Charles, 262
  Delia, 237
  Ed, 262
  Eddie, 237
  Eli, 245
  Fred, 243
  G. K., 350
  George, 236, 237
  Isaac, 237
  J., 246
  J. B., 249
  Jake H., 240
  James, 241, 245
  Jim, 236
  John, 244
  Joshua, 237
  Laura, 237
  Loring, 265
  M. B. (Mrs.), 237
  Manson, 241
  Martha, 236, 245
  Mary, 262
  Melinda, 238
  N. S., 248
  Robert, 249
  S. F., 237, 239, 406

  Sallie W., 240
  Scott, 236
  Thomas B., 243
  Thomas J., 240
  Tom, 246
  W. I., 360
  W. J., 239, 265, 361
  W. S., 337
  William, 236, 265
  Willie, 235
  _____ (Mrs.), 236
  _____, 248, 249, 263
Wall
  Abe, 247, 265
  Alice, 262
  Dempsey K., 265
  Henry, 262
  John M., 243
  S. B., 245
  Thomas, 246
  William E., 262
Wallace
  B., 237
  Elizabeth, 236
  J. S., 347
  J. W., 372
  James E. W. (Mrs.), 361
  Margueretta, 262
  Mary, 242
  Minnie, 236
  Mollie, 248
  William, 263
  _____ (Miss), 375
Waller
  A. (Mrs.), 248
  Alcina, 265
  Green (Mrs.), 265
  Jessie, 265
  Penn, 265
  _____, 265
Walls, Henry, 236
Walmsley
  Francis P., 242
  George S. Jr., 243
  Julia A., 243
Walsh [Walshe]
  Aggie, 237
  Amelia, 262
  Andrew, 237
  Bridget, 237
  Daniel, 266, 427
  Dennis, 237
  James, 262
  James J., 244
  John, 153, 187, 236, 237, 392
  John Jr., 237
  John L., 262
  Kate, 372
  Katie, 236, 237
  Lillie, 236
  Martin, 119, 164, 236, 237
  Mary E., 262
  P. M., 403
  Patrick, 238

  R., 242
  Richard V., 403
  Thomas, 236
  William, 262, 398
  _____ (Rev. Father), 164
  _____, 153
Walston
  John, 239
  John C., 240
Walter
  Augusta, 262
  Avant, 245
  C., 236
  Frank, 245
  H. W., 245
  Herman, 262
  Jimmy, 245
  Nicholas, 262
Walters
  C., 244
  Margaret (Mrs.), 244
  Stella, 249
Walthall
  W. P., 138
  W. T., 179, 330, 331, 373, 376, 381, 388, 427
  W. T. Jr., 373, 376
  _____ (Mrs.), 179
  _____, 179
Walther
  Charles T., 262
  Henry L., 262
Walton
  Annie, 249
  C., 236
  George, 249
  John, 430
  Joseph, 430
  Tom, 248
Waltz, Charles, 262
Wambaugh, R., 262
Wande, Albert, 236
Wandling, John, 344
Wangenheim, Albert, 262
Wansch, Helena, 262
Warburg, William, 345
Warchiell, Daniel W., 249
Ward
  A. (Mrs.), 247
  Albert, 236
  C. M. (Mrs.), 373
  Clinton Halst., 237
  H. J., 239
  H. S., 374
  H. S. (Mrs.), 374
  Horatio J., 237
  James C., 237
  John, 248, 262
  John J., 262
  Lillie, 236, 237
  Martha, 242
  Mary, 237
  S. J., 238, 413
  Theodore F., 237

Virginia, 237
——, 246
Warden, Nellie, 247
Wardlaw, David A., 237
Wardwell, D. W., 262
Ware
　J. H., 237
　J. N., 238
　John J., 241
　Maria, 241
　P. A., 242
Warfield, John, 262
Warheit, N., 262
Waring
　H. L., 161
　R. P., 330, 331, 335, 376
　R. P. Jr., 335, 372
　Robert P., 142
　T. R., 136, 142, 330, 331, 335, 355
Warle, C. H., 262
Warnaph, C. A., 244
Warne, William, 96
Warnecke
　Caroline, 236
　Fritz, 237
　—— (Mrs.), 236
Warner
　Andrew, 239
　Carrie, 237
　David E., 237
　F., 237
　George, 262
　Leo, 262
　Tom, 236
　—— (Mayor), 361
　——, 171
Warr
　Americus V. Jr., 240
　—— (G.M.), 409
Warren
　D. B., 348
　E. F., 240
　James, 355
　Jennie, 236
　Kate, 239
　Maria (Mrs.), 373
　Mervin, 251
　William, 145
　——, 237
Warrener, Philip, 237
Warring
　B., 237
　H. L., 237
Warrington
　Isaac H., 266
　James, 242
　W. H., 241
Wasche
　Caroline (Mrs.), 237
　Henry, 237
　Louise, 238
Wash, ——, 237
Washburne, Samuel B., 67
Washer, Hattie, 235

Washington
　Boswell, 236
　Charles, 236
　D. W., 431
　E. D. (Mrs.), 237
　Fannie, 243
　G. C., 244
　G. W., 236
　Lucy, 236
　Mary, 249
　Millie, 237
　Pinkie, 236
Wasserman, A., 262
Wassern, Henry, 262
Wasson, J. B., 135
Watenlifer, K., 262
Waterman, M. G., 262
Waters, Sam, 262
Wathan, E. H., 360
Watkins
　Belle, 236
　Ed., 236
　Eliza, 236
　F. G., 376
　Ida, 236
　James, 239
　John, 236
　S., 236
　Thomas, 381
Watson
　C., 262
　E. L., 337
　Edwin C., 343
　G. S., 373
　H. C., 236
　Joshua, 245
　K. P., 152, 236
　P. K., 117
　R. L., 245
　R. L. (Mrs.), 245
　Thomas, 378, 380, 381
　——, 236, 243
Watt, Helen, 244
Watterson, P. M., 247
Watton, Thomas, 379
Watts
　Harriet, 262
　James C. Sr., 245
Waugh, Henry, 262
Wax, Francis N., 264
Way
　S. P., 361
　Samuel (Mrs.), 361
Waycott, Monica, 249
Waynesburgh
　J. W., 408
　J. W. (Mrs.), 408
　John W., 405
　—— (Mrs.), 408
　——, 408
Weager, Annie, 237
Wealey, R., 237
Weatherby [Wetherbee]
　Eva, 246
　James, 240
　L. P., 247
　L. P. (Mrs.), 246

Mabel, 247
Wes, 247
　William, 238, 240
Weatherly, Willie, 244
Weathers
　George, 265
　Joseph, 262
　Richard, 236
Weaver
　Agnes (Sister), 244
　J. B., 239
　J. B. (Mrs.), 239
　John, 262
　John R., 250
　Lafayette, 250
　Sam, 238
　Tommie, 250
　William, 251
　Willie, 250
　—— (Mrs.), 245
Webb
　A., 368
　D. A. (Mrs.), 239
　George, 374
　George S., 237
　Macon, 237
　Mattie, 237
　Nannie, 237
　Thomas, 236
　W. N., 397, 399, 402
　W. Neh., 399, 401
　William, 237
　Willie, 239
　—— (Dr.), 34
　—— (Mrs.), 239, 240
Webber
　Edward, 238
　J. W., 245
　Peter, 245
　—— (Mrs.), 395
　——, 245
Webel, Emma C., 262
Webmeyer, F., 262
Webster, Noah, 14
Weed, H. M. (Mrs.), 373
Weeden, Frederick, 263
Weeks
　Charlie, 248
　Jimmy, 248
Weheren, Annie, 237
Wehle, Stephen, 266
Wehrman
　G., 244
　M. (Mrs.), 244
Weidlau, John, 236
Weigel, Charles, 262
Weigert, Charles, 248
Weihs, Augustus, 249
Weil [Weill]
　Charles, 249
　Gus, 265
　Sam, 264
Weiler, Lillie, 236
Weiling, Jonas, 262
Weimers, C. J., 262
Weinaike, Andrew, 239
Weinang, Fritz, 262

Weiner, Emilie, 262
Weingart, John, 250
Weinnecate, Charles, 239
Weinzentied, Charles, 262
Weir, L. C., 351
Weirich
　—— (Mrs.), 236
　——, 236
Weisch, Jennie, 262
Weisenberg, Joseph, 262
Weiss, John K., 262
Weiter, Fred, 372
Wekman, Margaret, 262
Welch, see Welsh
Welchman, E. C., 404
Wellborn, J. T., 338
Weller, Henry Clay, 237
Wellfonn, Scott, 238
Wellman
　Carey, 238
　M. C., 238
Wellpool, John, 262
Wells
　Alfred, 237
　Francis, 236
　Henry, 249
　J. A., 424
　Jim, 245
　Jim (Mrs.), 245
　John, 237
　John D., 250
　Louis, 399
　M. H., 357
　N. (Mrs.), 237
　Sarah (Mrs.), 250
　——, 237, 249
Welman, C. (Mrs.), 262
Welsh [Welch]
　Bridget (Mrs.), 262
　Charles, 237
　E. A. (Mrs.), 242
　F., 374
　Jennie, 262
　Johanna, 262
　John, 262
　Mary, 236
　Mike, 236
　Minnie W., 262
　Patrick, 262
　S. W., 39, 40
　Sidney, 248
　T. J., 251
　Thomas W., 262
　William, 237, 246, 262
　—— (Mrs.), 263
　—— (Prof.), 248
　——, 263
Weltense, Louis, 262
Wendall, A. G., 368
Wenderlin (Brother), 238
Wendling, George, 262
Werdt, Charlotte, 236
Werlander, J. V., 400
Wermeal, L. (Mrs.), 262
Wernech, Samuel, 340

NAME INDEX   515

Werner
  George, 262
  Mary E., 262
Wernett, Joseph, 262
Wernick, O. O., 262
Wersch, G. C., 135
Wertz
  William H., 262
  ____ (Mrs.), 243
  ____, 245
Wesche, Herman, 244
Wessenberger, Martin, 262
Wesson, Walter, 239
West
  Angeline, 236
  Anthony, 236
  Charles, 374
  Charles N. (Mrs.), 192
  Clotilda, 243
  Henry, 262
  J. H., 242
  J. M., 237
  Jacob S., 39
  Jeanette, 236
  John M., 373
  M. C., 242
  R. R. (Mrs.), 248
  Sarah (Mrs.), 374
  ____ (Mrs.), 242
  ____, 236
Westbrook
  J. L., 368, 370
  W. Ivie, 241
Westenberg, A., 402
Westfield, A. G. H., 236
Westmiller, ____ (Mrs.), 237
Westmoreland, ____ (Dr.), 292
Weston, Richard, 237
Wetherbee, *see Weatherby*
Wetherington, ____, 236
Wetter, Joe, 438
Wettstein, Josephine, 236
Wetzell, Thomas, 332, 437
Weyer
  John, 242
  Joseph, 243
Whall, Aug., 262
Wheat
  Albert, 244
  Peter, 265
  Susie, 242
Wheatley
  Hugh, 238
  P. B., 238
  W. A., 390
  ____ (Cpl.), 130
  ____ (Priv.), 429
Wheeler
  A. J., 157, 236, 406
  A. J. (Mrs.), 406
  Albert, 247
  Andrew J., 126
  J. M., 240
  Joseph K., 409

Mary A., 262
William J., 262
Wheeless
  H. S., 248
  Mary, 248
Whelan, Andrew, 237
Wheles
  J. P., 416, 434
  J. P. (Mrs.), 417, 434
  ____, 417, 434
Wherman
  Lizzie, 243
  Otto, 243
Whipple, E. A. (Mrs.), 237
Whit, Julia, 237
Whitaker, John F., 262
White
  A. J., 355
  A. L., 373
  Bertie, 236
  Burt, 431
  Carey, 429
  D. F., 236
  D. L., 236
  Donny, 237
  E. A., 237, 368, 407
  E. A. (Mrs.), 237, 407
  E. P., 368, 370
  Ellen, 236
  Fannie, 237
  Frank, 236
  George, 122, 164, 248, 262, 355, 408
  Georgianna, 236
  Gottlieb, 237
  Henderson, 237
  Henry, 154, 407, 416, 429, 433
  J. M., 368, 369
  J. M. S., 237
  J. W., 337
  James, 262
  James M., 239
  Jennie L. (Mrs.), 235
  John, 373, 430
  Joseph, 244
  Julia (Mrs.), 237
  K. (Mrs.), 240
  Lon., 236
  Louisa, 237
  M., 237, 239
  Maggie, 244
  Martha, 238
  Mary, 237
  Mary S., 236
  Matilda, 236
  Mollie A., 236
  Nicholas, 262
  R. B. (Mrs.), 240
  R. L. C., 355, 356
  Raymond, 238
  Robert, 236
  S. M., 235
  T. H., 355
  T. M., 355
  W. A., 360
  Weston, 236

William, 246
William W., 406
Z. T., 373, 408
Z. T. (Mrs.), 408
____ (Mrs.), 242, 249
____, 165, 237, 250, 407, 408
Whitehead
  C., 244
  John, 242
  P. F., 242
Whitelaw
  James, 237
  Richard, 241
Whitemore
  Charley, 238
  James, 237
  William, 236
  ____, 237
Whiteside, C., 237
Whitesides, H., 237
Whitfield
  Thomas, 236
  William, 238
Whitford
  A. S. (Mrs.), 238
  C. L. (Mrs.), 237
Whiting, ____, 358
Whitlock, M. G., 339
Whitmore
  E., 434
  Ed, 163
Whitsett, George, 366
Whitten, Joel, 250
Whitter, Mary, 236
Whittleton, Ben., 236
Wichmann, Jacques, 262
Wick
  Sarah W. (Mrs.), 262
Wickham, James, 246
Wicks, G. H. (Mrs.), 337
Widney
  Charles, 264
  Mary A., 264
Widrig, George J., 236
Wiesenfeldt
  L., 247
  L. (Mrs.), 247
Wiggering, John, 262
Wiggin, James, 237
Wiggins
  Elizabeth R., 262
  Jackson, 264
Wiggs, Jesse P., 239
Wight
  Charles, 262
  Frank, 262
  John, 262
Wighthert, Garcana, 262
Wilbur [Wilber]
  H. W., 262
  R. H., 349
Wilburne
  Jane, 237
  Ned, 237
Wilcox
  Nancy, 235

S. H., 237
____ (Mrs.), 246
Wild
  Am., 262
  Ed., 236
  Jacob, 374
Wildberger
  John, 236
  Stella, 236
  ____, 429
Wilder
  Hattie, 236
  J. M., 342
  ____, 236
Wildy, J. M., 343
Wile
  Emanuel, 248
  M., 248
Wiley
  A., 353
  John, 237
  Minerva, 249
  O. C., 338
  W., 236
  W. H., 266
  William, 237
  ____, 237
Wilhelmina (Sister), 120, 236
Wilhelmine, Elizabeth, 262
Wilhere, M. F., 401
Wilkenson, *see Wilkinson*
Wilker, John, 237
Wilkerson
  J. (Mrs.), 263
  W. N., 366
Wilkes
  ____ (Dr.), 34, 395
  ____ (Mrs.), 34
  ____, 34
Wilkings, J. R., 247
Wilkins
  F. G., 375
  Gilbert A. (Mrs.), 192
  J. R., 080
  James S., 438
  John, 249
  Jones, 245
  Leroy B., 250
  Louis, 262
  Mary E., 262
  Sharp, 235
Wilkinson [Wilkenson]
  Benjamin, 264
  P. A. (Mrs.), 239
  Thomas C., 262
Wilks, A. B., 368
Willard, M. E., 237
Willbrath, Aug., 262
Willet, Henry, 262
Willett [Willette]
  E. D., 362
  E. Miles, 368
  Eliza, 236
  J. H., 239
  ____ (Dr.), 146, 158
Willhart, ____ (Miss), 236

Willheit
  Adolph, 237
  E., 237
Willhoft, ____, 249
Williams
  A., 236
  Addie, 238
  Alfred, 262
  Alice, 262
  Andy, 372
  Annie, 236, 262
  Annie M., 262
  Annie (Mrs.), 262
  Arthur, 346
  Ben., 237
  Ben (Mrs.), 248
  Bettie, 242
  Biddy, 236
  Billy, 236
  Bussey, 237
  C. S., 339
  Caroline, 236, 237
  Carrie, 244
  Carter, 243
  Charles, 236, 237, 247, 251
  Chas., 238
  D. H., 346
  Dan, 236, 246
  Dan (Mrs.), 246
  Davie, 237
  E., 266
  E. (Mrs.), 237
  Ed., 236
  Ed (Mrs.), 263
  Eddie, 236
  Edward, 236
  Emma, 238, 240
  Eugene, 262
  Fannie, 239
  Fanny (Mrs.), 262
  Frank, 236, 375
  Fred, 237
  George, 237, 249
  H., 237
  Hatch, 237
  Henry, 236, 242, 246, 262
  Henry G., 372
  Isaac, 248
  Isabel, 237
  J. A., 247
  J. Calvin, 246
  J. (Mrs.), 250
  J. P., 239
  J. R., 375
  J. T., 355
  James, 237
  Jane, 238
  Joe, 147
  John, 237, 262, 332, 374
  Joseph, 262
  Josephine G., 264
  Julius Wilson, 264
  Katie, 236
  Lewis, 243
  Lillie, 262
  Lizzie, 236
  Lou, 244
  Louis, 236
  M. W., 238
  Maggie, 236, 262
  Margaret, 236
  Marry, 235
  Martin, 437
  Mary Ella, 264
  Mattie, 244
  Michael, 262
  Mollie, 236
  Nancy, 237
  Nannie, 236
  Nannie H., 237
  Peter, 237, 246
  Pinckney, 262
  R., 244
  R. B., 118, 236, 368, 369
  R. E., 262
  R. H., 374
  R. Sr., 248
  R. T., 248
  Robert E., 237
  S., 262
  S. E. (Mrs.), 236
  S. W., 395
  Sam, 237, 243
  Samuel E., 262
  Sarah, 237, 242
  Sarah G., 237
  T., 264
  T. E., 368
  Thomas, 355
  Vina, 241
  W. H., 262
  W. T., 237
  Walker, 237
  Wallace, 238, 266
  Walter, 236, 246
  Wash, 237
  ____ (Mrs.), 238, 241
  ____, 236, 237, 264
Williamson
  Alice, 240
  C. M., 251
  F. E., 262
  Frank E., 262
  Frederick, 236
  M. T., 424
  Spencer, 240
  T. J., 338
  W. B., 263
  Warren, 262
  ____, 236
Willingham
  Ellen, 243
  Matt, 244
Willis
  Clara A., 264
  Douglas, 264
  E. B., 243
  E. Bryant, 245
  H. Richards, 357
  P. C. (Mrs.), 264
  W. A., 127, 163
  Wesley, 241
  William, 237, 390, 391
  ____ (Supt.), 391
Wills
  Alfred, 241
  W. T., 241
  Walter C., 236
Wilshire
  A. T., 245
  ____, 381
Wilson
  Andrew, 236, 240, 247
  Cora, 245
  Cora A., 262
  D. Leet, 353
  David, 236
  E., 374
  George H., 262
  Helen B., 237
  Henrietta, 238
  Henry, 236, 429
  Irene, 264
  J., 407
  J. (Mrs.), 407
  J. C., 242
  Jack, 408
  James, 237
  Joe, 240
  John, 237, 238
  John O., 236
  John Sr., 240
  L., 422
  Laura C., 237
  Lucy, 242
  M. A., 244
  M. A. (Mrs.), 246
  M. M. (Mrs.), 236
  Mary, 264
  Mary Ella, 237
  Mollie, 236, 245
  N. H., 236
  Nancy, 237
  Nathan, 237
  Norvell W., 262
  R., 242
  Robert, 243
  Thomas, 262
  Thomas J., 403
  Timothy, 342
  Trevel., 264
  W. H., 351
  W. P., 136
  W. W., 237
  William, 262
  Willie, 245
  Wood, 237
  ____ (Mrs.), 236, 237, 245, 247
  ____, 245
Wiltenmuth, John, 262
Wiltze, Ralph, 239
Wimberly [Wimberley]
  A. H., 237
  ____, 408
Winans, J. T., 400
Winant, M., 236
Winburn, Hugh, 245
Winbush, Lucelia, 243
Winchester
  Floy, 237
  Louisa, 238
Wind, Charles, 237
Winder, Francisa, 237
Windex, Andrew, 236
Windler
  Frank, 236
  John, 236
Windling, Frank, 236
Winfield, Morris, 242
Winford, Thomas, 236
Winfred, Henry, 236
Wing, George, 245
Wingfield
  Walter, 249
  Willie, 249
Winkelman (Sister), 120
Winkleman, J. H., 360
Winland, C. W., 429
Winn
  Charles, 266
  Fred, 236, 251
  James, 429
  W. B., 368, 370
Winson
  S., 237
  ____ (Mrs.), 237
Winstead, T. H., 262
Winstein, A., 262
Winston
  Brown, 244
  Charles, 236
  Ed, 241
  John, 244
  Laura, 236
  Lucy, 235
Winter
  C. A. (Mrs.), 247
  Charles, 237
  J. H., 351
  Jack, 247
  Sam, 250
  Shirley, 247
  T. E., 247
  ____, 236
Winterberger, Mary, 262
Winters
  C. A., 249
  Charley, 237
  Eddie, 249
  Emmet, 235, 239
  Esquire, 107
  J., 373
  Jack, 249, 250
  Jimmie, 150
  Thomas, 236
  Thomas Jr., 236
  ____, 249
Winva, ____ (Mrs.), 240
Wischer, Bernard, 262
Wise
  Bob, 249
  Julius, 368, 418

NAME INDEX

Minor, 236
William, 262
Wisely, Julia, 237
Wiseman
  Catherine, 262
  Robert, 264
  W. J., 239
Wishe
  A., 237
  A. (Mrs.), 237
Wiskerman, W. C., 372
Wissner, S. L., 341
Wistar, ____, 303
Withe, W. (Mrs.), 236
Withers, Gertrude, 250
Withrow, James, 352
Witt, Albert C., 262
Witte, Wilhelm, 237
Wizohski, Henry, 262
Wockerborth, Adolph, 262
Woeller, L., 236
Woern, Louisa, 237
Wogan, Louis G., 262
Wolcott, Rosa, 262
Wolf [Wolfe, Wolff]
  Albert, 399
  Angelina (Mrs.), 381
  Anna (Mrs.), 236
  Annie S. D., 249
  Eva, 262
  Gustave A., 236
  Henry, 249
  John W., 262
  Leon, 264
  Lizzie, 264
  Mary J. F., 243
  Meyer, 249
  Rosalie, 265
  Willie, 262
  Willis K., 262
  ____ (Mrs.), 247
  ____, 237
Wolfert, Fred, 262
Wolfolk, Avery, 347
Wolfork, ____ (Dr.), 247
Womble
  Jordan, 351
  Jordan Jr., 351
Wong, Chin Foo, 375
Wood
  Annie M., 243
  Benjamin, 347
  Charlotte M., 262
  Emma, 241
  G. V., 243
  George B., 299
  Hunter, 345
  I. K., 248
  J., 408
  J. K., 266
  J. K. (Mrs.), 266
  Jesse, 390
  John, 237
  John W., 235
  Jonathan, 237
  L. H., 373
  Lizzie, 236

Louis, 236
Mattie C., 238
Spencer R., 241
W. C., 262
W. H., 354, 438
W. L., 422
Wright, 236
  ____ (Miss), 352
  ____ (Most Rev. Archbishop), 402
  ____ (Mrs.), 237, 249
  ____, 249
Woodfall, Henry, 236
Woodfold
  B., 237
  James, 237
Woodington, E. J., 372
Woodlock
  H. P., 433
  ____, 165, 433
Woodran, Armistead, 236
Woodruff
  Andrew, 238
  G. W., 339
  J. W., 244
  W. C., 236
  William, 361, 362
Woods
  Ann Emily, 264
  Annie, 240
  Carrie N. (Mrs.), 239
  Emma, 238
  George W., 237, 432, 433
  George W. (Mrs.), 433
  J. K., 239
  James, 240
  John, 248, 374
  John H., 264
  Joseph, 262
  Josephine, 236
  Katie, 240
  Martha, 237
  Mary, 237
  Massie, 237
  Mollie, 240
  Pat, 241
  Rosina, 262
  Sophia W. (Mrs.), 243
  W. E., 395
  W. J., 240
  W. S. (Mrs.), 237
  Willie, 240
  Zinnie, 236
  ____ (Mrs.), 236
Woodsen, Philip, 262
Woodsworth
  ____ (Mrs.), 236
  ____, 236
Woodward
  A., 239, 265
  A. B., 236
  J. D., 237
  J. W., 117
  ____ (Dr.), 162
  ____, 236
Woodwen, D., 375

Woodworth
  John M., 27
  Mabel, 262
  ____ (Dr.), 105
Wooldridge, Amanda, 251
Woolfolk
  R. F., 368, 370
  ____, 380
Wooten, Willie, 245
Work, Charles A., 262
Worsham
  Clifford, 237, 251
  E. R. T., 237, 407
  Ed, 186
Worsmick, ____ (Mrs.), 237
Worsneck, Joseph, 237
Worth
  H., 237
  Pauline, 262
Worthberg, Nuevia (Mrs.), 262
Worthey, B., 243
Wosterberg, ____, 244
Wray
  John H., 236
  ____ (Mrs.), 236
Wright
  A., 238
  A. D., 372
  A. L., 239
  Anderson, 242
  Belle (Mrs.), 355
  Casper, 237
  Charles, 427
  E. K., 338, 352
  E. S., 425
  H. L., 401
  Hardin, 238
  Henry, 237
  James, 248
  Jessie (Mrs.), 237
  John, 248
  King, 237
  Lucy, 240
  Luke E., 129, 131, 132, 390, 391, 397
  M. M. (Mrs.), 248
  Mack, 248
  Mary, 349, 395
  Mary A., 262
  Mary (Mrs.), 373
  Nelson, 429
  Robert, 262
  Robert A., 236
  Ruth J., 262
  Tom, 236
  W. H., 373
  William, 401
  Willie, 236
  ____ (Dr.), 339
  ____ (Gen.), 127
  ____ (Mrs.), 237
  ____, 236, 248, 262
Wuaranara, S., 262
Wuernasa, Mic. A., 262
Wuerpel, Ada O., 262

Wunder, M. L., 262
Wunsch, Josephine, 264
Wupperman, A., 238
Wuvman, ____ (Dr.), 249
Wyley [Wylie]
  Patrick, 262
  William T., 262
Wyman
  L. W., 373
  ____ (Lt.), 356
  ____ (U. S. Asst. Surg.), 437
Wyrth, Henry J., 262

Y

Yaegan, John, 262
Yancey
  Lou., 238
  William, 245
  ____ (Mrs.), 245
  ____, 245
Yarbo, J. J., 239
Yarborough [Yarbrough]
  Harriet, 372
  J. S., 250
  J. S. (Mrs.), 250
Yates
  Charles, 248
  Esther, 238
  Frank, 238
  J., 368
  ____ (Gov.), 437
  ____ (Mayor), 349
Yeager, Tillie, 238
Yearger
  Pompey, 429
  Walter, 238
Yegge, Louis, 238
Yerby, A. N., 238
Yerdel, J., 356
Yerger
  Arthur R., 247
  George S., 243
  Julia, 243
Yob, Henry, 262
Yonge, Easton, 427
Yonkers, ____ (Mrs.), 238
Yonkha, Margaret, 251
Yore
  V. M., 332
  Vincent M., 437
York
  F. P., 238
  John, 262
  Will O., 238
Youcum, Sophia, 247
Young [Youngee]
  Alex, 241
  Alex Jr., 241
  Anna, 262
  Annie, 238
  Annie R., 262
  Casey, 284, 391, 425
  Charles, 262
  Daisy, 246
  E. T., 368

Ed., 238
Fannie, 238
H. M., 348
Henry, 264
James B., 357
John, 238, 239, 243
Louise, 262
M., 238
Martha, 241
Mathew, 250
Peter, 262
R. L., 400
Robert A., 247
Robert A. (Mrs.), 247
S. O., 368
Thomas, 238, 248
Thomas (Mrs. Dr.), 248
William, 262
_____ (Mrs.), 246
_____, 251, 264
Youngblut, E. J., 262
Younger, Addie, 238
Youngz, Agnes, 262
Yowell, Squire, 245
Yuille, Kittie (Mrs.), 262
Yung, Magdalena, 262

Z

Zable, Ernest, 262
Zack, _____ (Mrs.), 107
Zaconi, Gaeltane, 262
Zadeck
  Ben, 250
  Ben (Mrs.), 250

J. H., 436
_____, 250
Zahn, George A., 264
Zamanta, M., 262
Zanna, Mary E., 238
Zanona, Mary N., 238
Zappa, Henry, 262
Zehring
  J. C., 406
  J. C. (Mrs.), 406
  John, 238
  _____, 238, 406
Zeigler, _____, 351
Zella, Coniconda, 262
Zellman, Isawra, 262
Zemmer, Theodore, 262
Zenobia (Sister), 246
Zent, John, 406
Zenzer, W., 262
Zerega
  Alber, 262
  Charles, 262
  Maud A., 262
Zetlmann, Andrew, 262
Zichici, G., 262
Zignsticker, F. A., 403
Zill, Annie V., 262
Zimmerman
  E., 346
  Jake, 242
  L. E., 349
  Sophy, 238
  _____, 238
Zlidel, Franz, 262
Zoanne, Baptiste, 238

Zoeller, Mina (Mrs.), 262
Zolenka, Maggie, 251
Zollinger
  Alois, 243
  Valentine, 244
Zoyer, Tillie, 238
Zucker, Gussie (Mrs.), 242
Zundt, Joseph, 249

Aleck, 246
Angela, 252
Annie, 212
Annie May, 337
Belle, 212
Birdie, 212
Blanche, 212
Camelia, 173
Camille, 254
Charles, 213
Clark, 438
Crissie, 213
Cronius, 214
Daisey, 215
Dennis, 184
Ellen, 216
Fannie, 217
Frank, 217
Gary, 251
Ida, 221
Isaac, 221
Jake, 222
Jennie, 222

Jessie, 222
Joanna, 222
John, 222
John, see Chicago John
Josephine, 222, 257
Leon, 224
Lissa, 249
Lott, 224
Maggie, 251
Manuel, 251
Margaret, 226
Maria, 246
Martha, 225
Mary, 225, 226
Mary Ann, 225
Mike, 226
Mingo, 250
Nick, 433
Peter, 229
Ray, 251
Riffi, 230
Samuel, 249
Telfy, 230
Will, 237
Zach., 239

GENERAL INDEX

A

Academy of Science, 283
Africa, 13, 15, 20, 29, 44, 56, 77
  Mauritius, 27, 28
Alabama, 36, 77, 337, 363, 414
  Andalusia, 338
  Athens, 92, 250, 337, 338
    Presbyterian Church, 337
  Auburn, 338
  Baldwin Co., 371, 372
  Birmingham
    Birmingham Sunday School, 338
    L. & N. Rail Road, 337
    Presbyterian Church, 360
  Blount Springs, 337
  Bolling, 338
  Brownsboro, 371, 372
  Cahawba, 88
  Childersburg, 338
    Wood & Powell, 338
  Citronelle, 88
  Columbiana, 338
  Coosa Station, 338
  Courtland, 93, 173, 250, 338, 361
  Crawford, 338
  Cullman, 338
  Cussetta, 338
  Decatur, 93, 250, 337, 342, 426, 427
  Demopolis, 88
    Marengo Lodge #283, I.O.B.B., 419
  Dog River Cotton Factory, 88
  Evergreen, 338
  Florence, 93, 250, 251, 337
  Fort Claiborne, 83
  Fort Morgan Island, 91
  Fort St. Stephen, 83
  Gadsden, 338
  Greensboro, 338
    Colored Baptist Church, 338
    Colored M. C. Church, 338
  Greenville, 338, 419
  Guntersville, 338
  Hamburg, 338
  Hebena Sabbath School, 338
  Holywood, 88
  Huntingdon, 338
  Huntsville, 94, 251, 337, 338
    J. M. Hamette & Co., 338
    J. Neil & Bro., 337
    Knights of Honor Relief Committee, 421
    Madison I.O.O.F., 337
  Leighton, 94, 239
  Madison, 338
    Madison Lodge #329 (Masonic), 409
  Marion, Church of Marion, 338
  Mobile, 22, 29, 78, 83, 84, 85, 86, 87, 88, 89, 90, 92, 94, 138, 173, 179, 251, 303, 318, 329, 330, 368, 371, 373, 379, 380, 382, 384, 427, 438
    Can't-Get-Away Club, 179, 337, 338, 376, 378, 381, 382, 385, 386, 387
    Hebrew Benevolent Society, 419
    Ladies' Benevolent Society, 419
  Monterallo, 338
  Montgomery, 88, 89, 90, 91, 92, 303, 338, 401, 419, 426
    Fire Department, 338
    Relief Committee, 338
  Montvale, 409, 419
  Mooresville, 338
  New Harmony, 338
  Oak Bowery, 338
  Opelika, 337, 338
    Baptist Church, 338
    Methodist Church, 338
    Presbyterian Church, 338
  Oxford, 338
    Hartwell Lodge #101, 409
  Oxmoor, 338
  Pierceville Sabbath School, 362
  Planton, 338
  Prattsville, 338
    Daniel Pratt Gin Co., 338
  Richmond, 338
  Scottsboro, 422
  Selma, 88, 337
    Brass Band, 338
    Literary Society, 338
  Spring Creek Church, 338
  Spring Hill, 98
  Spring Valley M. E. Church, 338
  Stevenson, 96, 117, 251, 337, 367, 369
  Troy, 338
    Hebrew Relief Association, 338
  Tuscaloosa, 97, 251, 338
  Tuscumbia [Tuscambia], 97, 179, 238, 251, 337, 350, 414
    Baptist Association, 338
    Crescent Lodge #413, Knights of Honor, 422
    Insane Asylum, 338
    J. H. Pitts [Fitts] & Co., 337, 338
  Tuskegee, 371, 375
    Union Springs Baptist Sunday School, 338
  Uniontown, 338
    Colored Baptist Church and Sunday School, 338
    Concordia Lodge #152, 419
  Verbena, 338
  Vienna, 338
  Warrior, Success Lodge #773, Knights of Honor, 422
  Weaver Station, 338
  Wheeler, 337
  Whistler, 97, 251
Alabama River, 83
Alaska, 363
Allopathic Commission, see Woodworth Commission
American Express, 348
American Philosophical Society, 70
American Public Health Association, 325
Anchor Line Packet Co., vi
Ancient Order of Workingmen, vi
Andrew Jackson Lodge (Masonic), 409
Arabia, 269
Argentina, Buenos Ayres, 77
Arizona, 337, 363
  Prescott Barracks, 337
Arkansas, 36, 77, 187, 269, 293, 337, 363, 408, 414
  Alma, 337
  Arkadelphia, 337, 368, 371, 372
  Atkins, 337

Augusta, 92, 250, 337
Austin, 409
Batesville Chapter R.A.M., 337
Bell Grove Children's Public School, 337
Bell Point Lodge F. & A. M., 337
Bentonville, 337
Boonesboro
   Cave Hill Masonic Lodge, 337
Camden
   Riverside Lodge #959, Knights of Honor, 422
Bradley Co., 337
Camden Presbyterian Church, 337
Carlilse, 337
Cincinnati, 337
Clarendon, 337
Clarksville, 337
Columbia, 88
Conway, 337
Dardanelle, 337
   Bright Star Lodge #212 (Masonic), 410
   Dardanelle Chapter #64 (Masonic), 409
   Presbyterian Sunday School, 337
Des Arc, 337
Dover Relief Committee, 337
Duvall's Bluff, 426
Fayetteville Musical Club, 337
Forrest City, 337, 419
   St. Francis Lodge #492, Knights of Honor, 422
Fort Smith, 32, 84, 337
Fulton, 337
Golden Lake, 250
Grand Chapter (Masonic), 409
Grand Lake, 88
Grand Lodge (Masonic), 409, 410
Haynes' Bluff, 250
Helena, 250, 371, 373, 426
Hope, Cotton Blossom Minstrels, 337
Hopefield, 185, 250, 368, 369
Hot Springs, 117, 368, 369, 371, 373, 389, 419
   Crystal Lodge, Knights of Honor, 337
   D. B. Elliott & Co., 337
   G. C. Hotel, 337
   Order Royal Arcanum, 337
Indian Bay, H. H. Silverman & Co., 337
Jacksonport, 337
   Jacksonport Lodge (Masonic), 409
Little Rock, 92, 117, 368, 369, 370, 371, 373, 389
   Adelphi Lodge #1159, Knights of Honor, 422
   Colored Masons Lodge #2, 337
   Democrat, 174
   Germania Lodge #910, Knights of Honor, 422
   Howard Association, 337
   J. F. Hill Lodge #270 (Masonic), 410
   Little Rock Lodge #452, Knights of Honor, 422
   Little Rock Lodge #454, Knights of Honor, 422
   Rose City Lodge #1090, Knights of Honor, 422
   M. E. Church, 337
   Spring Street M. E. Church, 337
   Typographical Union, 415
Locksburg, 337
Malvern Union Sabbath School, 337
Marianna [Mariana], 337, 426
   Lee Lodge #713, Knights of Honor, 422
Mineral Springs, 337
Monticello, 337
Napoleon, 88
Newport, 371, 373

Osceola, 337
   Osceola Lodge #27 (Masonic), 409
Ozark, 337
   Ozark Lodge #79 (Masonic), 410
   Ozark Methodist Sunday School, 337
   Union Sabbath School, 337
Pecan Point, 337
Phillips [Philips] Co., 171, 235, 238
Pine Bluff, 337, 371, 373, 426, 409
   Colored Sabbath School, 337
   Phoenix Lodge #279, I.O.B.B., 419
   Presbyterian Sabbath School, 337
   United Brothers Friendship, 337
Prescott, 337
   Kyle & Cassidy, 337
   St. James Church, 337
Quitman, 337
Russellville, 337
Searcy, 337
South Dardanelle M. E. Church, 337
Terrene, 96, 250
Van Buren, 337
   Colored Temperance Union, 337
   Episcopal Sabbath School, 337
   Trinity Sabbath School, 337
   Warren Relief Committee, 337
Washington, 337
Arkansas River, 84
Ascension Island, 28
Asia, 13, 56, 77
Associated Press, 166, 367, 412
Association for Relief of French Residents, 423
Australia, 13, 77, 116
Austria, Vienna, 277

B

Balize, 67
Baltic, 272
Bann, 25, 28
Belgium, 119
Bellevue Hospital, 65, 297
Benner Relief Fund, 438
Bermuda, 56, 84, 97
Black Sea, 279
Bolivia, 77
Brazil, 14, 16, 23, 24, 77, 97, 117, 204, 315
   Fortaleza, 117
   Lagoa-funda Cemetery, 117
   Para, 67, 97
   Rio de Janeiro, 15, 35, 97, 98, 203, 301, 302, 318
   San Juan Baptista Cemetery, 117
Brazos River, 36
British Guiana, 77, 290

C

C., C., C., & I. Rail Road, 352
C., S. & C. Rail Road, 352
California, 115, 338, 363, 414
   Anglo California Bank, 338
   Fresno, Clark, Dixon & Redlock, 338
   Los Angeles, 338, 368, 370
   Modesta, 338
   Puebla, 338
   Riversdale, 338

GENERAL INDEX

San Francisco, 329, 371, 375, 419
   Citizens' Committee, 338
   St. Joseph's Total Abstinence Benevolent & L. Society, 403
Santa Barbara, 338
Santa Cruz, C. B. A. Society, 403
Stockton
   Irish American Benevolent Society, 403
   St. Mary's Temperance Society, 403
Tulare Co., 338
Watsonville, 338
Camp Burke, 302
Camp Duffy, 391, 395
Camp Griffin, 175, 391
Camp Morris Henderson, 391
Camp Smith, 175, 391
Camp Wade, 175, 391
Camp Wright, 391, 442
Canada, 77, 200, 363, 376
   Bootha, 204
   British Columbia, 414
   New Brunswick, 414
      Carleton Temperance Society, 400
      St. John's, 348, 403, 415
      St. Malachy's Total Abstinence R. Society, 403
   Nova Scotia, 414
      Halifax, 89, 94
   Ontario, 348
      London, 361, 362
      Shulenberg, 348
      St. Catherine's, 348
         Spring Bank Hotel, 349
      St. Thomas, 348
         Presbyterian Church, 348
   Prince Albert Land, 204
   Quebec, 14, 82, 303
   Toronto, Typographical Union, 415
Catholic Total Abstinence Union of America, 396
Central Rail Road, 40
China, 204
Clermont, 348
Code of Marine Hygiene, 300
Colorado, 338, 363, 414
   Black Hawk, 338
   Boulder, First National Bank, 338
   Cañon City, 338
   Central City, 338
      St. James M. E. Sunday School, 338
      Warren Camp #2, K. of N. W.
   Colton, 338
   Denver, 338
      C. T. Benevolent Society, 400
      Relief Committee, 338
      St. Joseph's Catholic Total Abstinence Benevolent Society, 400
      Typographical Union, 415
   Georgetown Presbyterian Sunday School, 338
   Golden, 338
      Relief Fund, 338
   Greely, 362
   Leadville, Winnennick Mine, 338
   Nederland, 338
   Pueblo, 338
   Rock Ridge, 338
   Russell Gulch Sunday School, 338

Stockton, 338
Susan City, 338
Columbia, 77
Congressional Yellow Fever Commission, 314
Connecticut, 77, 338, 363, 414
   Ansonia F.M.T. A. Society, 399
   Bridgeport
      Abraham Lodge #80, I.O.B.B., 419
      F. M. Y. M. Total Abstinence and Benevolent Society, 399
   Bristol Presbyterian Church, 338
   Chatham (Middlesex Co.), 79
   Danbury, St. Vincent de Paul Total Abstinence Benevolent Society, 400
   Fair Haven, St. Francis Total Abstinence Benevolent Society, 400
   Greenville, 338
   Hartford, 79, 80, 123, 329, 338, 371, 373, 409
      Bureau of Relief, 123
      Collins & Co., 425
      St. Peter's Total Abstinence and Benevolent Society, 400
      Y.M.C.A., 338
   Meriden, 338
      St. Patrick's M. R. Society, 401
      St. Rose's Total Abstinence Benevolent Society, 401
   Middlesex Co., 79
   Middletown, 84, 401
   Mystic Bridge, St. Patrick's Total Abstinence Benevolent Society, 401
   New Britain, 338
   New Haven, 78, 79, 81, 82, 84, 203, 338
      Relief Committee, 338
      Typographical Union, 415
   New London, 79, 203, 362, 404
      St. John's Benevolent Society, 402
      Star of the Sea Total Abstinence Benevolent Society, 402
   Norwalk, 80, 338
   Norwich, 81
      Typographical Union, 415
   Rockville F. M. Total Abstinence Benevolent Society, 403
   Southington, St. Thomas' Total Abstinence Benevolent Society, 403
   Stamford, 78, 338
      St. Patrick's Total Abstinence Society, 403
   Stonington, 80
   Thames River, 80
   West Winstead, 404
   Willimantic, St. Joseph's Temperance Society, 404
Constantinople, 27, 275, 277, 324
Corona Lodge #537 Knights of Honor, 422
Cuba, 22, 92, 97
   Cienfuego, 35
   Havana, 25, 26, 30, 31, 35, 40, 69, 71, 79, 81, 82, 83, 84, 86, 92, 105, 202, 303, 329
      Belot Hospital, 86
Cyrene Commandery, 408

D

Dakota Territory, 338, 363, 414
   Bismark, 338
      Whitney Opera House, 338

Black Hill, 339
  Deadwood, 339
  Fort Buford, 339
  Fort Rice, 339
  Lead City, 339
  Spearfish, 339
Damascus, 14
Delaware, 77, 339, 363, 414
  Brandywine, St. Joseph's Benevolent Society, 399
  Lewes, 94
  New Castle, 80, 339
    Catholic Total Abstinence Society, 402
  Wilmington, 80, 81, 360, 361, 404
    St. Mary's Benevolent Society, 404
    St. Michael's Benevolent Society, 404
    St. Peter's Benevolent Society, 404
    St. Peter's Female Benevolent Society, 404
Delaware Bay, 80
Delaware River, 80, 82, 273
Delawater Breakwater, 266
District of Columbia, see Washington, D.C.
Doolittle, Webster & Co., 361
Du West Church, 348

E

East India, 19
Egypt, 277
  Cairo, 307
Episcopal Brotherhood of St. John the Evangelist, 191
Ethiopia, 307, 309

F

Florida, 22, 36, 77, 164, 200, 339, 363, 369
  Apalachicola, 85
  Apalachicola Bay, 85
  Bronson, 339
  Cedar Keys, 92
  Crescent City, 339
  Crystal Lake, 339
  Fernanda, 368
  Fernandina [Fernandino], 92, 93, 266, 366, 371, 372
  Fort Barrancas, 92
  Fort Pickens, 92
  Fort Reed, 339
  Fort Taylor, 26
  Gainesville, 92
  Jacksonville, 90, 371, 373
    Sun and Press, 339
  Key West, 26, 85, 86, 88, 89, 91, 92, 94
  Lake City, 339
  Live Oak, 339
  Mariana, 339
  Matanzas Sound, 82, 86
  Milton, 88, 90, 92
  Palatka, 339
  Pensacola, 26, 35, 78, 83, 84, 85, 86, 87, 88, 89, 90, 91, 92, 95, 274
    Germania Fire Co., 339
    Knowles & Brent, 339
  Quincy, 339
    Nickly Club, 339
  St. Augustine, 82, 84, 86, 288, 339
  St. Barnabas P. E. Mission, 339
  St. Joseph, 86
  Suwanee, 86

Suwanee River, 86
Tallahassee Citizens' Aid Committee, 339
Tampa, 86, 88, 92
Tampa Bay, 86
Tortugas, 91
Toulon, 272
Fourth Annual Quarantine Commission, 276
France, 14, 77, 116, 271, 279, 329
  Bayonne, 85
  Marseilles, 272
  Paris, 16, 23, 275, 320, 329
    Academy of Medicine, 275
    College of Physicians, 35
    College of Surgery, 14
    European Congress, 300
Fredonia Lodge #225 (Masonic), 409
Free Sons of Israel, 348

G

Georgia, 77, 339, 340, 363, 414
  Albany, 339
    Benevolent Association, 339
    Micha Lodge #147, I.O.B.B., 419
  Americus, 168, 368
  Athens, 339, 419
    Burns' Silver Cornet Band, 339
  Atlanta, 29, 292, 369, 404, 419
    Atlanta Benevolent Society, 419
    Concordia Association, 339
    Gate City Lodge #346, Knights of Honor, 421
    Georgia Lodge #127, Knights of Honor, 422
    Relief Committee, 339
    Rossini Musical Club, 339
    Scientific Association, 361
  Augusta, 86, 89, 168, 339, 340, 369, 371, 372, 422, 427
    Board of Trustees, Masons, 339
    Central Rail Road, 339
    Citizens' Relief Committee, 339, 340
    Colored Church, 339
    Harmony Church, 339
    Mord Society #1, 339
  Bainbridge, 92
    Rossini Musical Club, 339
  Brunswick, 340, 360, 371, 372
    Catholic Benevolent Society, 399
    Ladies' Relief Association, 360
  Buena Vista, 339
  Cairo, 339
  Canton Baptist Church, 339
  Cartersville, 339, 362
  Cave Springs, 339
    Ladies' Association, 339
  Cedartown, 339
    Cedartown Lodge #273, Knights of Honor, 422
  Centre Village, 339
  Clark's Station, 340
  Cobb Co., 371, 372
    Baptist Church, 339
  Columbus, 329, 339, 368, 410
    Columbus Lodge #77, I.O.B.B., 419
    Columbus Manufacturing Co., 340
    St. Luke's Episcopal Church, 339
    Young Men's Christian Union, 399

GENERAL INDEX   523

Congress
  Methodist Sabbath School, 339
  Presbyterian Church, 339
Covington, Golden Fleece Lodge #6, F. & A. M., 340
Cuthbert, 339
Dalton, 93, 266
  National Hotel, 339
Decatur, 339
Dublin, 339
East Point M. E. Sunday School, 339
Eulalee Presbyterian Sabbath School, 339
Gainesville, 339
  Piedmont Aid Association, 339
Greensboro, 339
  Brass Band, 339
Greenville, 339
Griffin, 339, 410
  Presbyterian Sunday School, 339
Guysboro, 339
Guyton, 339
Hamilton
  Masonic Lodge, 339
  M. E. Sunday School, 339
Hawkinsville, 339
Hickory Head Baptist Church, 339
Hopkinsville, 339
Jefferson, 339
Louisville, 339
Lumber City, 339
Macon, 339, 371, 373
  Congregation Beth Israel, 419
  Malachi Lodge #146, I.O.B.B., 419
  Relief Committee, 339
  St. Vincent de Paul Benevolent Society, 401
  Typographical Union, 415
Madison, 339
Marietta, 339
  Colored Baptist Church, 339
  Corgill & Co., 339
  Cornet Band, 339
  Kenesaw Lodge #33, 409
Maxwell, 339
McIntosh Union Sunday School, 339
Newman, 339
Perry, 339
Pike Co., 339
Pine Bluff Baptist Church, 339
Quitman, 339
Rockdale, Smyrna Sabbath School, 339
Rome, 339
  Oostanaula Lodge, 409
  Y.M.C.A., 339
Saraham, 410
Savannah, 29, 81, 83, 84, 85, 88, 89, 90, 92, 117,
    168, 188, 192, 200, 203, 322, 329, 336, 368,
    369, 371, 373, 376, 419, 427, 438, 440
  Georgia Lodge #151, K.S.B., 419
  Hebrew Benevolent Society, 419
  Joseph Lodge #76, I.O.B.B., 419
  News, 192
  Relief Committee, 339
  Savannah Lodge #317, I.O.B.B., 419
  St. Patrick's Total Abstinence Benevolent
    Society, 403
St. Mary's, 83

Thomasson
  Colored Church, 340
  Irving & Neal, 339
Thomasville, 339, 367, 419
  Georgia Lodge #207, I.O.B.B., 419
Tunnell Hill, 339
Valdosta, 339
Warrenton, 339
  Relief Committee, 339
Washington, 339
West Point, 339
German Bass Club (Effingham), 348
German National Bank, 365
Germany, 38, 116, 119
  Berlin, 320
  Heidelberg, 168
Golconda Lodge #131 (Masonic), 409
Grapeland, 348
Great Britain, 291
  England, 25, 77, 82, 116, 170, 191, 203, 270, 273,
    289, 293, 316, 320, 323
  Gazette (Pall Mall), 203
  Health Board, 25
  Liverpool, 67, 105, 173, 329, 348
  London, 89, 117, 204, 205, 271, 309, 314, 320,
    329
    Brown, Shipley & Co., 348
    Fever Hospital, 304
    Standard, 177, 435
  Over Darwen, 320
  Oxford, Cowley, 191
  Southampton, 88
Guernsey, 273
Jersey, 273
Royal Astronomical Society, 205
Royal Historical Society, 204
Scilly Islands, 273
Scotland, 273, 408
  Edinburgh, 167
Statistical Society, 204
Greece
  Athens, 14
  Syracuse, 14
Greenbush, 348
Gulf of Guinea, Fernando Po, 315
Gulf of Mexico, 22, 36

H

Hebrew Hospital Association, 126, 141, 417
Hebrew Relief Association, 420
Holland, 271
Homeopathic Yellow Fever Commission of 1878, 29, 70,
    71, 312, 325, 326
Honduras, 77
Howard Association, v, 50, 51, 56, 59, 106, 109, 112,
    116, 122, 129, 130, 132, 133, 135, 136, 137,
    138, 139, 140, 141, 143, 146, 148, 149, 151,
    152, 153, 154, 155, 158, 160, 161, 162, 168,
    172, 173, 174, 175, 178, 179, 180, 182, 184,
    185, 186, 187, 189, 190, 191, 193, 295, 328,
    329, 330, 332, 333, 366, 367, 370, 371, 375,
    376, 435, 439
  Commissary Department, 392
  Druggists, 369
  Infirmaries, 389

Medical Corps, v, 331, 365, 367, 369
Medical Directory, 175
Medical Society, 181
Nurse Department, 371, 376
Visiting Corps, 125

I

Idaho, 363
Illinois, 77, 200, 340, 341, 363, 414, 415
   Aledo, 334
   Alton, 340, 341
      Congregational Church, 340
      Hope Hose Co., 340
   Altoona, 422
   Anna, 341
   Arcola, 340, 341
   Arlington Heights, 341, 342
   Astoria Lodge #100 (Masonic), 410
   Atlanta Temperance Union, 342
   Aurora, 340, 419
      F.M.T.A. and B. Society, 399
      German M. E. Church, 341
      Trinity Episcopal Church, 341
      Union Baptist Church, 340
   Barry (Pike Co.), 340
      Baptist Church, 342
   Belknap Relief Committee, 341
   Belle Flower, 341
   Belleville, 341
   Bennett, 342
   Bethallo, 342
      Relief Association, 341
   Bethel United Presbyterian Congregation, 341
   Biggsville, 341
   Blandensville, 341
   Bloomington
      Free Congregational Society, 341
      Presbyterian Church, 340
      St. Patrick's Total Abstinence and Benevolent Society, 399
   Blue Island Citizens' Relief Committee, 341
   Bradford, 341
   Bunker Hill, 340
   Burnside, 342
   Bushnell, 340, 342
      Reformed Church, 341
   Butler, 341
   Cairo, 92, 93, 96, 371, 372
      Knights F. M. C. Total Abstinence Society, 399
      St. Patrick's Benevolent Society, 399
   Cambridge, 342
   Carbondale, 340, 341
      Reynolds Chapter #75, 410
      Union Sabbath School, 341
   Carlinville, 340, 341, 342
      Silver Lodge, Knights of Honor, 341
   Carlyle Lodge #38, I.O.O.F., 340
   Carni, 340, 341, 342
   Carrollton, 340, 341
      Presbyterian Church & Sunday School, 341
   Carthage A. O. U. W., 341
   Cayuga, 340, 341
   Cedarville, 341
   Centralia, 341, 362
      Centralia Lodge #201 (Masonic), 409
   Champaign, 340, 341
      United Sons of Erin, 399, 400
   Channahow, 341
   Charleston
      Baptist Congregation Sunday School, 340
      Presbyterian Congregation Sunday School, 340
   Chenoa, 340
   Chester, Cole, Brothers & Co., 340
   Chicago, 38, 44, 104, 173, 292, 326, 329, 340, 341, 342, 360, 361, 371, 372, 376, 409, 415, 419, 425
      All Saints Society, Catholic Total Abstinence Union, 400
      Baptist Church, 341
      Blake, Walker & Co., 360
      Catholic Young Men's Society, Catholic Total Abstinence Union, 400
      Chicago Bakery Co., 360
      Crane Brothers Manufacturing Co., 341
      Deborah Verein, 419
      Elgin Club, 342
      Holy Family Society, Catholic Total Abstinence Union, 400
      Home National Bank, 341
      Illinois Lodge #264, I.O.B.B., 419
      I.O.B.B., 419
      Irving Literary Society, 341
      Journal, 415
      K. I. P., 400
      Merchants National Bank, 340
      National Society, Catholic Total Abstinence Union, 400
      Owl Club, 341
      Relief Committee, 332, 341
      Sacred Heart Society, Catholic Total Abstinence Union, 400
      Sinai Congregation, 419
      Sisters of Peace, 419
      St. James' Society, Catholic Total Abstinence Union, 400
      Total Abstinence Societies, 400
      Tribune, 185, 188, 189
      Typographical Union, 415
      Washington Ice Co., 360
      Y.M.C.A., 341
      Young Men's Society, Catholic Total Abstinence Union, 400
      Zion Society, 419
   Chillicothe, 341
   Clay City, 341
   Clinton, 340
   Cobden, 340
   Collensville, 341
   Danville, 341, 342
   Decatur, 341
      Bethlehem C. P. Church, 342
      Good Templars, 340
      Stapp's Chapel M. E. Church, 340
   DeKalb, 340
   Douglas, 340
   DuPage, Red School House Sabbath School, 342
   Duquoin
      Duquoin Lodge #234 (Masonic), 409
      Presbyterian Church, 341
      Relief Committee, 341
   Durant, 340
   Edwardsville, 340, 342

Effingham
  Baptist Church, 341
  Hero Lodge #991, Knights of Honor, 422
El Paso, 340
  F. M. Total Abstinence Society, 400
Elgin, 340, 341, 361
  Board of Trade, 340
  Insane Hospital, 341
Elmwood, 341
Englewood, 341
  Citizens' Relief Committee, 341
Eugenie, 342
Eureka, 340, 341
Fairbury, 400
Fairfield, 340, 341, 342
Farmington, 341
Forreston, 341
Franklin, 341
Freeport, 340
  Centennial Lodge, I.O.G.T., 340
  Germania Association, 341
  Second Presbyterian Sabbath School, 340
  Union Band, 340
Fremont, 341
Fulton, 342
Galesboro, 340, 341
  Altha Lodge, 341
  Chapter #46, R.A.M., 340
  Commandery 8, K. T., 340
  Masons, 341
Geneseo, 340
Gibson City, 340
Gilman, 340
Glendale, 341
Golconda, 340, 341, 360
  J. W. McCoy & Son, 340
Grand Island, 340
Grand Ridge Presbyterian Church, 341
Grant Tower, 340, 342
Graysville, 341
Griggsville, 340
  Congregational Church, 341
Hamburg, National Christian Temperance Union, 341
Hardin, 341
Havana, 341
Hazleton German Church, 362
Henderson Presbyterian Sunday School, 341
Hennepin, 340, 341
Henry, 340
Huntsville Shiloh Church, 342
Iverdale, 341
  Catholic Church, 341
Jacksonville, 342, 409
  Relief Fund, 341
Jerseyville, 425
  Jerseyville Chapter #140, 409
Joliet, 340
  F. M. Total Abstinence and Benevolent Society, 401
  Prison, 341
  St. Mary's Catholic Church, 341
  St. Patrick's Benevolent Society, 401
Kankakee, 340, 342
  Ladies' Literary Association, 340
Kansas, 419
Keithsburg, 340

Kirkwood, 340, 341
La Harpe, 341
La Salle
  St. Patrick's Benevolent Society, 401
  St. Patrick's Total Abstinence Benevolent Society, 401
  Zine City Fire Co., 342
Lemont
  Citizen's Relief Association, 341
  F. M. Total Abstinence Society, 401
Leroy, 340
Lexington, 340
Lima Choral Society, 340
Lincoln, 341
  F. M. Total Abstinence Society, 401
Litchfield, 340, 341
Lockport, 341
  Congregational Church, 341
Lostant, F. M. Temperance Society, 401
Macomb, 341
  Camp Creek Presbyterian Church, 342
Marion, 342
  Fellowship Lodge #89 (Masonic), 409
Mason City Benevolent Association, 341
Mattoon, 340, 410
Maywood, 340
McLean Co. Coal Co., 341
McLeansboro, 341
  Knights of Honor, 341
Mendota, 340, 341
  Irish Catholic Benevolent Society, 401
  Literary Society, 340
Metropolis, 340
  E. G. Whires & Co., 360
Minooka, 341
Monmouth, 340, 342
  Gennesee League, 340
Mound City, 340
Mount Carmel, 340, 341, 342
  Y.M.C.A., 340
Mount Morris, 342
Mount Sterling, 341
Mount Vernon, 341
Murpheysboro, 340
Nashville, 340
Neponset, 340
Newton, 341
Nokomis, 341
North Chicago Rolling Mill, 341
Oakland, 341
Oden, 340
Olmsted Lodge, I.O.G.T, 340
Olney, 341
Onarga, 341
Orion, 342
Ottawa F. M. Total Abstinence Society, 402
Ottumwa, 340, 342
Owance, 341
Paris, 340, 341
  Citizens' Relief Committee, 341
  Edgar Co. Agricultural Board, 340
Paxton
  A. B. L. Society, 341
  Choral Society, 341
Payson, 341
Peking, 341
  Benevolent Association, 341

Pelmont M. E. Sabbath School, 341
Peoria, 340, 341, 361, 408
   Board of Trade, 340, 341
   Congregational Church, 341
   German Banking Association, 341
   St. Patrick's Church, 403
   Typographical Union, 415
Perry, 340, 342
Peru, 341
Petersburg, 340
Pike Co., 340
Plainfield, 340, 342
Plano, 340
Plumb Creek Presbyterian Church, 341
Pluto, 341
Plymouth, 341
Polo, 341
Princeton, 341, 425
Providence Congregational Church, 341
Quincy, 340, 341, 361, 362, 419
   Humboldt Lodge #61, 340
   Old John Robinson's Circus, 340
   Typographical Union, 415
Rattan, 342
Red Bird, 340
Rochelle C. & I. Rail Road, 341
Rock Island, 340, 341, 342
   Relief Committee, 340
   St. Patrick's Benevolent Society, 403
Rockford, 425
   Rockford Rifles, 425
Rood House, 341
Roseville A.O.U.W., 341
Salem, 341, 342
Sandoval, 340
Seward Congregational Church, 341
Shannon, 341
Shawneetown, 96, 340, 425
Sheffield, Lyford & Sprague, 342
South Evanston
   M. E. Church, 340
   M. E. Sunday School, 341
Sparta, 341
   Randle School, 341
   United Presbyterian Congregation, 341
Springfield, 340, 341, 342, 419
   Asylum for Feeble-Minded Children, 340
   Ellwood Commandery #6, 409
   F. M. Total Abstinence Benevolent Society, 403
   Peerless Lodge #493, Knights of Honor, 422
   State Prison, 340
   Typographical Union, 415
   Tyrian Lodge & Chapter, 409
St. Claire Co., 340
St. Joseph, 340
St. Louis, Illinois Lodge #268, Knights of Honor, 422
Sterling, 340
   Citizens' Relief Committee, 341
Streeter, Ladies Relief Association, 340
Tazewell Co., 341
Tishkilwa, 340
Troy, 341
Urbana, 340
Vandalia, 341
Vermillion Co., 341
Vermont, 341

Verona, 342
Vienna, 341
Virden, Union Lodge, Knights of Honor, 341
Virginia, 341
Walnut Grove, 342
Warrensburg, 341
Warsaw, 340
Washington Citizens' Relief Committee, 341
Waterloo, 362
Waukegon, 340
   Methodist Society, 340
Waverly, 340, 341
Wenona F. M. Total Abstinence Society, 404
Whitehall, 341
Williams, 340
Williamstown, 341
Willow Hill, 341
Windsor Station, 340
Wine Hill, 342
Wyanet Congregational Church, 342
Xenia, 341
Independent Order of Mutual Aiders [Aid], vi, 423
India, 23, 27, 116, 316
   Calcutta, 270
Indian Territory, 77, 344, 363
Indiana, 77, 341, 342, 363, 414
   Anadusko, 343
   Anderson, 342, 343
      Irish Benevolent Society, 399
   Attica, 342
      Attica Lodge #18 (Masonic), 410
   Aurora
      Relief Association, 343
      Universalist Church, 342
   Bean Blossom, F. & A. M. Lodge #687, 342
   Bedford, 342
      Christian Church, 342
   Bloomington, 342, 343, 360
   Bourbon, 343
   Clayton, 342
   Cloverdale, 342
   Columbus, St. John's Lodge #20 (Masonic), 409
   Connersville, St. Patrick's Benevolent Society, 400
   Cresco Congregational Sunday School, 342
   Crown Point Gesang Verien, 342
   Decatur, 343
   Edinburgh, 342
   Edwardsport, 342
   Evansville, 147, 342
      Brownell, Graville & Co., 342
      Catholic Hibernian Benevolent Society, 400
      E. & T. H. Rail Road Co., 342
      Evansville Public Schools, 342
      K.S.B., 419
   Fort Wayne, 400, 419
      Ft. Wayne Lodge #14, I.O.O.F., 342
      Hamilton Bank, 342
      Hebrew Congregation, 342
      Typographical Union, 415
   Ft. Wayne, 368, 369
   Goodland, 342
   Greencastle, 342
      Ladies of the Presbyterian Church, 342
   Greensburg Y.M.C.A., 342
   Greenville, 342
   Hagerstown Dramatic Club, 343
   Hanover College, 342

GENERAL INDEX 527

Huntingdon, 342
Indianapolis, 329, 342, 343, 361, 368, 373, 404, 409, 419, 422
  Fletcher & Sharpe, 342
  Indianapolis Lodge #14, Knights of Honor, 422
  Marion Lodge #601, Knights of Honor, 422
  Rapier Commandery, 342
  Soda Bottling Co., 362
  St. John's Church, 400
  St. Patrick's Total Abstinence Benevolent Society, 400
  Tree of Life Society, 419
  Wabash Relief Comm., 342
  Woodburn Wheel Co., 342
Jeffersonville
  Mitchell & Reed, 342
  St. Augustine's Benevolent Society, 401
Kentland, 362
Kingston M. E. Church, 342
Knightstown, 342
Kokomo, 342
  F. M. Total Abstinence and Benevolent Society, 401
La Fayette Commandery #3, 409
La Gro, Tuscan Lodge #143 (Masonic), 410
Lafayette, 342, 343, 415
  Barzillai Lodge #111, I.O.B.B., 419
  St. Michael's Total Abstinence Benevolent Society, 401
Laporte
  John Hilt & Co., 360
  Y. M. Association, 342
  Y.M.C.A., 342
Lawrenceburg [Laurenceburg], 342
Lavergne, 425
Ligonier, 419
Logansport, 342, 343
  Relief Committee, 342
Louisville, 342
Madison, 342
  First Presbyterian Church, 342
  German M. E. Church, 342
  United Presbyterian Church, 342
  W. Trow & Co., 342
Manckport, 342
Marion, 342
  Sweetser Bank, 342
Michigan City, 343
  Y.M.C.A., 342
Mishawaka Christian Church, 343
Mitchell, 342
Mt. Vernon, 419
  Concord Leiderkranz, 342
  Order of the Eastern Star, 361
  Rebecca Verein, 419
New Albany, 95, 96, 342
  Doric Lodge, A.O.U.W., 342
  St. Patrick's Benevolent Society, 402
North Vernon, 342
Orleans, 342
  Red Ribbon Club, 342
Oxford, 342
Paoli Brass Band, 342
Peru, 343
Plymouth
  Hebrew Ladies' Benevolent Society, 342
  Relief Committee, 343

Queensville, 342
Richmond
  Coffin Manufacturing Co., 361
  First National Bank, 342
  Gaar, Scott & Co., 342
  Grace M. E. Church, 342
  J. M. Hutton & Co., 342
  Relief Association, 362
Rochester, 342, 343
Rockport, 342, 368
  C. R. & S. Rail Road, 343
Rockville, 342
Roswood, 371, 373
Rushville
  Immaculate Conception Total Abstinence Society, 403
  Presbyterian Sunday School, 342
Saline City, 370
Seymour, 342
  St. Ambrose Benevolent Society, 403
  Woolen Mills, 342
Shelbyville, 342, 343
South Bend, 343, 362
  St. Joseph's Total Abstinence Benevolent Society, 403
Spiceland, Friends' Sabbath School, 343
Springland, 342
State Centre, 342
Stony Point, 343
Tell City
  Chair-makers' Union, 342
  Combs, Hartman & Co., 343
  Relief Association, 343
  South Western Furniture Association, 343
Terre Haute, 342, 343, 368, 371, 375
  Graves Sabbath School, 342
  Hibernian Catholic Benevolent Society, 404
  Knights F. M., 404
  St. Joseph's Society, 404
Tipton, 343
Union City, 343
Vevay, 342
Vincennes, 343, 404
  Mission Sabbath School, 342
Wabash, S.P., D.R., St. P. Total Abstinence and Benevolent Society, 404
Washington, 343
  Charity Lodge, F. & A. M., 342
Whitestown, 342
Worthington, 342
  Masonic Fraternity, 343
Zionsville, 342
International Sanitary Convention (Vienna), 277
I.O.O.F., vi, 126, 138, 146, 172, 381, vi
  Special Relief Fund, 415
  Yellow Fever Fund, 414
Iowa, 343, 363, 414
  Adel Presbyterian Church, 343
  Alkader, 343
  Allentown, 343
  Ames
    Chones Club, 343
    Iowa Agricultural Society, 425
  Anamosa, 343
  Atlantic, 343
  Bedford, 343
  Belle Plain, 343

Blue Glass, 343
Bonapart [Bonaparte], 343, 426
Boone, 344
    Presbyterian Church, 343
Boonsboro Lodge # 79, I. O. O. F., 343
Burlington, 343
    Burlington *Hawkeye*, 343
    Land Depot, C. B. & Q. Rail Road, 343
Cascade Baptist Church, 343
Cedar Falls, 344
Cedar Rapids, 343, 422
    Crescent Lodge #25 (Masonic), 409
    Mount Hermon Lodge #263 (Masonic), 409
Centerville, 344
    Lodge #76, 343
Charles City, 343
    Congregational Church, 343
Charlotte, T. C. Total Abstinence Benevolent Society of St. Mary's, 400
Cherokee, 343
Clarinda, 343
    Children's Band of Hope, 343
    Old School Presbyterian Church, 343
Clinton, 343
    First Baptist Church, 343
    Roman Catholic Total Abstinence Society, 399
College Springs Congregational Church, 343
Columbus Junction Sunday School, 343
Council Bluffs, 343, 400
    Howard Association, 344
    Officer & Percy, 343, 425
Crawfordsville United Presbyterian Congregation, 344
Creston, 343, 361
    Executive Committee, 361
Davenport, 343, 344
    Hibernian Benevolent Society, 400
    St. Margaret's Total Abstinence Society, 400
    St. Mary's Church Total Abstinence Benevolent Society, 400
    St. Patrick's Benevolent Society, 400
De Witt, 343
Dennison [Denison], 343
Des Moines, 343
    Asleway Sabbath School, 343
    Cater, Hussy & Culry, 343
    Congregational Sunday School, 343
    Ft. D. & D. Rail Road, 344
    First Baptist Sabbath School, 343
    Hebrew Congregation, 343
    Plymouth Church, 343
Dexter, 343
Dubuque, C. B. Society, 400
Durant, 343
Earlham, 400
Earlville, 344
Eldorado Sunday School, 343
Elkador Catholic Total Abstinence Society, 400
Emmetsburg, 343
Exira First Congregational Church, 343
Fort Madison, 343
    Presbyterian Church & Sunday School, 343
Garden Grove Presbyterian Church, 343
Garner, Concord Sabbath School, 343
Glenwood, 343
Grinnell, 343
Hopkinton, Lennox College Inst., 343

Indianola Ladies' Relief Association, 343
Jasper Co., Buena Vista Sunday School, 344
Jefferson, 344
Joust City First Congregational Church, 343
Kellogg, 344
    Congregational Church, 343
    M. E. Sabbath School, 343
Keokuk, 343
    Keokuk Lodge #544, Knights of Honor, 422
Keosauqua Congregational Church, 343
Knoxville M. E. Sunday School, 343
Lansing, 343
Leeds Grove
    Congregational Church, 343
    Methodist Church, 343
Leetsville Relief Committee, 362
Lisbon, 343
    Evangelical Lutheran Church, 343
Lyons, 343
Marshall, 343
Marshalltown, 344
Mason City, 343
McGregor, 343
    Congregational Church, 343
Mechanicsville, 343
Morning Sun, 343
Mt. Vernon
    M. E. Church, 343
    Presbyterian Church & Sunday School, 343
Muscatine, 343
    Board of Trade, 343
    Catholic Mutual Aid Society, 401
    First Baptist Sabbath School, 343
    German Church & Sunday School, 343
    High Prairie M. E. Church, 344
    Ladies' Reading Club, 344
    M. E. Sabbath School, 343
    Ninth St. Mission Sunday School, 343
    Solders' Reunion, 344
National State Bank, 343
Navarre Relief Association, 343
Nevada, 343
    M. E. Church, 343
    Presbyterian Sabbath School, 343
Newton, 343
Onawa, Vesper Lodge #223 (Masonic), 409
Onona, 425
Oskaloosa, 343
    Baldwin Bros., 343
    Cong. Presbyterian Church, 343
Page Co. Presbyterian Church Relief Committee, 344
Pella, 343
Pine Creek, 343
Red Oak, 343
Riverton Baptist Sabbath School, 343
Rowley, 343
Russell, 343
Sabula [Sebula], 343
    Congregational Sunday School, 343
    Methodist Church, 343
Sibley, 343
Sigourney, 343
Sioux City, 343, 409
    Tootle, Livingston & Co., 343
Tama City, 343
Vail, 343

GENERAL INDEX 529

Walcott Lodge #13, A. O. U. W., 343
Washington United Presbyterian Congregation, 344
Waterford Presbyterian Church and Sunday School, 343
Waterloo Young People's Christian Association, 343
Waverly, 344
Indian Territory, Ft. Reno, 344
Ireland, 119
  Co. Tipperary, 119
Irish Catholic Benevolent Union, 396, 398
Italy, 77
  Florence, 270
  Leghorn, 81, 82, 202, 290
  Pisa, 290
  Rome, 14
  Sardinia, 270
  Venice, 270
Iraq, Baghdad, 324

K

Kansas, 344, 363, 414
  Atchison, 344
    Atchison Liederkranz, 344
    Catholic Benevolent Irish Society, 399
    Hebrew Ladies' Society, 344
  Augusta, 344
  Burlingham, 344
  Burlington National Bank, 344
  Cherokee Union Sabbath School, 343
  Clyde Station, 344
  Coffeeville, 344
  Council Grove, 343
    M. E. Society, 343
  Dodge City, 344
  Douglass, 344
  Edgarton, 344
  Effingham, 344
  Fort Scott, 409
  Ft. Hayes, 344
  Ft. McPherson, 344
  Ft. Scott, 344
  Ft. Wallace, 344
  Garnett, 344
  Girard, 344
  Grand Lodge (Masonic), 409
  Holton, 344
    Banner Sunday School, 344
    Co. Sabbath School, 344
    German Church, 344
  Howard Association, 344
  Humboldt City Schools, 344
  Hutchinson, 344
  Independence, 368
  Junction City, Harmony Fire Co., 344
  Kansas City, 175, 344
  La Crosse, 344
  Lawrence, 344
    Plymouth Congregational Church, 344
  Leavenworth, 344, 401, 409, 419
    Emmet Benevolent Society, 344
    Israelites, 344
    Military Prison, 344
    Quartermaster Dept., 344
  LesCygne, 344
    M. E. Church and Sunday School, 344
  Manhattan, Webster Literary Society, 344
  McPherson, 344
    Centennial Lodge #138, I.O.O.F, 344
  Newton, 344
  Nortonville United Presbyterian Church and Sunday School, 344
  Olathe, 344
  Osage City, 344
  Osborne, 344
  Oskaloosa, 344
  Oswego, 409
  Otawah [Ottawa], 344
    Otawah Lodge #7 (Masonic), 409
  Paoli, 344
  Parsons, 344
  Raymond, 344
  Salina Liederkranz, 344
  St. Marys, 344
  Topeka, 344
    Catholic Benevolent Society, 404
    Presbyterian Church, 344
    S. Barnum & Co., 419
    Turn-Verein, 344
  Wanego, 344
  Wichita, 344
    Eagle, 344
  Winchester United Presbyterian Sunday School, 344
  Wyandotte, 344, 409, 410
    L. U. B., 344
    Wyandotte Chapter #6, 409
Kentucky, 36, 56, 77, 119, 138, 164, 200, 344, 345, 363, 371, 373, 409, 414
  Allensville, 361
  Allenville [Allanville], 344, 360
  Ashland
    Norton Iron Works, 425
    Poagee Lodge #325 (Masonic), 409
  Big Clifty, 345
  Bowling Green, 93, 251, 345, 371, 372
    Green and Barren River Navigation Co., 344
    Relief Association, 345
    St. Joseph's Benevolent Society, 399
    Warren Lodge #248, Knights of Honor, 422
  Burgen, 345
  Cadiz, 344
  Caldwell Co. Southern Relief Fund, 345
  Carlisle, 344, 345
  Carrollton, Jno. W. Howe & Son, 344
  Caseyville, 344, 360, 409
  Chicago
    St. Francis Catholic Total Abstinence Society, 399
    St. Francis Church, 399
  Clinton, 93
  Columbus, Iron Banks Lodge #802, Knights of Honor, 422
  Covington, 344, 371, 372
    Covington Chapter #35, 409
    Golden Rule Lodge #345 (Masonic), 409
    Valley Lodge #58, A. O. U. W., 345
  Cynthiana, 345, 409
    Methodist Sunday School, 345
  Danville, 93, 251
    Boyle Lodge #385, Knights of Honor, 422
  Dayton, 345
  Dixon, 345

Elizabethtown, Hardin Lodge #249, Knights of Honor, 422
Elkton, 344
    Baptist Sunday School, 345
    Relief Committee, 345, 361
Fillmore, 93
Fisherville, 368
Flemingsburg, 345
Frankfort, 345
    St. Joseph's Catholic Benevolent Society, 400
Franklin, 345
    Antioch Church, 345
    Franklin Lodge #320, Knights of Honor, 422
    Relief Committee, 344
Fulton, 93, 251
Georgetown, 344
    Vernon Lodge #14 (Masonic), 409
Ghent, 345
Glasgow, 344, 345
    Christian Church, 345
    Glasgow Lodge #263, Knights of Honor, 422
Georgetown Christian Church, 422
Greelyboro, 345
Greenville, Muhlenberg Lodge #908, Knights of Honor, 422
Guthrie, 427
Hadensville Relief Committee, 344
Harrodsburg, 119, 164
    Relief Committee, 345
Henderson, 344, 345, 409
    Dixon Lodge #569, Knights of Honor, 422
Hickman, 31, 56, 94, 251, 437
Hopkinsville, 118, 345, 371, 373, 400
    A. O. U. W., 344
    Christian Lodge #820, Knights of Honor, 422
    Colored Baptist Church, 345
    Colored Benevolent Association, 344
    Evergreen Lodge #28, Knights of Pythias, 344
    Methodist Colored Church, 344
Huber Station Presbyterian Congregation, 344
Jassamine
    Relief Association, 345
    Southern Relief Committee, 345
Jewish Relief Fund, 344
Jordan Station, 251
Knottsville, St. Lawrence Catholic Total Abstinence Society, 401
Lagrange, Amo Lodge #274, Knights of Honor, 422
Lairs Station, 345
    Broadwell Union Sunday School, 345
Lebanon, 361, 362
Lexington, 344, 345
    Broadway St. Christian Church, 344
    Centennial Lodge #40, A. O. U. W., 344
    Main Street Sunday School, 345
    Mutual Lodge #1, A. O. U. W., 344
    Northern Bank of Lexington, 345
    Old Jassamin Church, 345
    Phantom Lodge #15, Knights of Pythias, 344
    Una Lodge #518, Knights of Honor, 422
Logan Co., Adairsville Lodge, 410
Louisiana
    Saw Mill Co., 360
    Talmage Lake Ice Co., 360
Louisville, 15, 17, 19, 29, 43, 48, 92, 94, 95, 119, 164, 238, 251, 290, 302, 329, 330, 344, 345,
355, 360, 366, 370, 371, 373, 376, 384, 398, 409, 415, 419, 426
Arminius Lodge #7, Knights of Honor, 422
Centennial Lodge #200, Knights of Honor, 422
Central Lodge #164, Knights of Honor, 422
Clearing-House Committee, 362
Confederate Relief Committee, 345
Courier-Journal, 162, 180, 185, 187, 189, 190, 415, 438
Erskine & Erskine, 344
Excelsior Lodge #4, Knights of Honor, 422
Golden Lodge #1, Knights of Honor, 422
Hall & Eddy, 360
Jefferson Lodge #5, Knights of Honor, 422
John H. Barnd & Co., 360
Kentucky Distillery Co., 360
L. C. & L. Rail Road Co., 344
Lewis Gage & Co., 360
Louisville Clearing House Committee, 344, 345
Louisville Coffin Co., 360
Louisville Medical College, 174
Louisville Yellow Fever Hospital, 57
Mystic Lodge #212, Knights of Honor, 422
Northern Bank of Kentucky, 345
R. E. Lee Lodge #6, Knights of Honor, 422
Relief Association, 345
Royal Insurance Agency, 344
St. Alphonsus Total Abstinence Society, 401
St. Cecelia's Benevolent Society, 401
St. Francis Total Abstinence Society, 401
St. Patrick's Total Abstinence Society, 401
W. B. Hoke Lodge #177, Knights of Honor, 422
W. C. A., 345
Werne & Barnum, 172
Western Fin. Corp., 345
William S. Kene & Co., 360
Yellow Fever Committee, 419
Yellow Fever Hospital, 57
Marion, 345
Marion Co. Relief Committee, 361
Marysville, 401
Mayfield, 345
Maysville, 344, 345
    Mess. Wheats & Co., 345
McHenry, 345
    Good Templars, 345
Nelson Co., St. Vincent's Church, 402
New Haven, 371, 373
    St. Catherine's Total Abstinence Benevolent Society & C., 402
Newport
    Board of Education, 344
    Christian Church Sunday School, 345
    Masons, 345
Nicholasville
    Relief Association, 345
    Southern Relief Committee, 345
North Middleton, 345
Otawah Chapter, 409
    Franklin Lodge #18 (Masonic), 409
Owensboro, 345
    St. Stephen's Total Abstinence Society, 402
Paducah, 344, 371, 373, 404
    Bernheim & Co., 419
    Congregational Church, 345
    Harmony Lodge #149, I.O.B.B., 419

GENERAL INDEX

P. & D. Rail Road, 344
Washington Lodge #455, Knights of Honor, 422
Paris, 345
   Honor Lodge #559, Knights of Honor, 344
   Rescue Fire Co., 345
   Southern Relief Association, 345
   St. Patrick's Benevolent Society, 403
Pembroke, 344, 345
Penhope, 345
Petersburgh, 345
Pewee Valley, 345
Pleasanton, 345
Princeton, 422
Russellville, 344
   Masonic Relief Committee, 410
Sardis M. E. Church, 345
Shelbyville, 345
   Catholic M. A. Society, 403
   Post Office, 345
South Carrollton, 343
Springfield, Mizpah Lodge #822, Knights of Honor, 422
Sulphur Springs, 368
Trenton, 251, 345
Versailles, 410
Warsaw, 345
Whiteville, St. Mary's Total Abstinence Society, 404
Winchester, 345
Wingo, 345
   Relief Association, 345
Woodburn, 345, 368, 369
   Cedar Bluff College, 345
Knights of Honor, vi, 126, 138, 172
   Central Relief Committee, 421
Knights of Pythias, vi, 126, 138, 146, 174

L

L & D Rail Road, 348
Ladies' Relief Association, 348
Levant, 270, 345
L. N. & Great Southern Rail Road, *see Memphis & Louisville Rail Road*
Locust Grove Church, 348
Louisiana, 36, 42, 77, 86, 91, 92, 179, 180, 188, 190, 295, 299, 345, 363, 376
   Alexandria, 38, 84, 85, 86, 87, 88, 89, 90
   Algiers, 87, 88, 90, 93
   Ascension Parish, 84, 93
   Baton Rouge, 83, 84, 85, 86, 87, 89, 90, 92, 263, 264, 269
   Bay of St. Louis, 84, 85
   Bayou Goula, 92, 264
   Bayou Sara, 87, 88, 92
   Berwick City, 92
   Brashear City, 67
   Broussard, 93
   Brule Sacramento, 264
   Buras, 93
   Burat Settlement, 87, 89
   Canaan Landing, 93
   Carrollton, 90
   Centreville, 88, 90
   Clinton, 43, 88, 93, 264
   Cloutierville, 89
   Cook's Landing, 93
   Covington, 87, 168
   Delhi, 93, 262
   Delta, 262
   Donaldsonville, 85, 93, 264
   Dunboyne Plantation, 93, 263
   English Turn, 273
   Franklin, 86, 89, 90, 96, 145
   Goodrich Landing, 263
   Gretna, 93, 263
   Hammond, 345
   Harrisonburg, 94, 263
   Henderson's Landing, 94, 263
   Jeanneretts, 89
   Jesuits' Bend, 89
   La Fourche [Lafourche] Crossing, 94, 263
   Labadieville, 94
   Lafayette, 87
   Lagonda, 263
   Lake Providence, 89
   Mandeville, 87, 94
   McDonoughville, 90
   Monroe, 345
   Natchitoches, 86, 89
   New Iberia, 86, 91, 92
   New Orleans, 16, 18, 19, 24, 25, 26, 28, 29, 30, 32, 33, 35, 36, 37, 38, 39, 40, 42, 43, 44, 59, 66, 67, 69, 71, 72, 78, 79, 80, 81, 82, 83, 84, 85, 86, 138, 145, 152, 166, 173, 179, 180, 190, 200, 201, 252, 253, 254, 255, 256, 257, 258, 259, 260, 261, 262, 269, 272, 273, 274, 276, 287, 289, 290, 291, 292, 293, 294, 296, 297, 298, 302, 303, 304, 314, 316, 318, 319, 321, 322, 325, 326, 329, 334, 351, 354, 357, 361, 367, 368, 371, 373, 377, 378, 379, 380, 381, 386, 389, 413, 435, 438, 440
      American Cotton Tie Association, 345
      Board of Health, 15, 33, 58, 105, 290, 316, 317
      Canal Carondelet, 42, 321
      Charity Hospital, 32, 33, 274
      Commission of 1853, 15, 16, 34
      Daily Delta, 292
      Democrat, 329
      Howard Association, 340, 343, 345, 357, 358, 378, 381
      J. B. Laffitte & Co., 348
      State National Bank, 356
      Times, 44, 72
      Walthall Infirmary, 48
   Omega Landing, 263
   Opelousas, 85, 86, 87, 89, 91
   Paincourtville, 95
   Pass Christian, 87, 89, 90, 95, 264
   Pattersonville, 89, 90, 95, 264
   Pecan Grove, 263
   Plaquemine, 86, 87, 89, 90, 95, 264
   Point-a-la-Hache [Heche], 89, 96, 264
   Point Pleasant, 96
   Port Barre, 92
   Port Barrow, 264
   Port Eds, 96
   Port Hudson, 86, 87, 96
   Raleigh Landing, 263
   Richoc, 96
   Saint Francisville, 83
   Shreveport, 26, 42, 67, 89, 92, 118, 164, 181, 189, 276, 296, 345, 369, 371, 375, 376, 419
      E. & B. Jacobs, 345
      Jordan Lodge #102, O.K.S.B., 419

Louisiana Lodge #107, I.O.B.B., 419
Shreveport Ward Committee, 345
St. Paul's Colored Church, 345
Southwest Pass, 96, 264
St. Gabriel, 96
St. James' Parish, 96, 264, 345
St. John Baptiste, 89
St. Martinsville, 86
St. Mary's Parish, 89
Tallulah, 96, 263
Tangipahoa [Tangipaha], 96, 264, 265
Teche River, 86
Terre Aux Boeuf, 265
Thibodeaux Parish, 87, 89, 96, 265
Tipton Co., 168
Trenton, 89
Vidalia, 89
Ville Platte, 92
Washington, 86, 88, 89, 91
West Feliciana Parish, 83, 84, 85, 86, 87, 89
West Pascagoula, F. Guatier & Sons, 345
West Plaquemine, 93
White Haven, 263
Wingaw Bay, 83
Louisville & Memphis Rail Road, 333
Louisville & Nashville Rail Road, 266, 423
Louisville Rail Road, 179, 180
Lynch's Station, 348

M

M. & C. Rail Road *see Memphis & Charleston Rail Road*
Maine, 77, 345, 363, 414
 Bangor, St. John's Church Total Abstinence and Benevolent Society, 399
 Bath, 345
 Portland, 345
  Typographical Union, 415
 South Portland, Norwich Comm., 345
 Waterville, 345
Mansfield Valley, 401
Maryland, 77, 345, 363, 414
 Baltimore, 79, 80, 81, 82, 84, 104, 119, 192, 276, 305, 318, 322, 329, 330, 345, 367, 371, 372, 409, 427
  Adams Express Co., 345
  Baltimore Hebrew Benevolent Society, 419
  Deaf & Dumb Institute, 345
  Ira Pleasants & Son, 345
  J. J. Nicholson & Sons, 345
  Lord Baltimore Lodge #275, Knights of Honor, 421
  Maryland Lodge #1133, Knights of Honor, 422
  St. Ignatius Benevolent Society, 399
  St. John Evangelist Temperance Society, 399
  Typographical Union, 415
  Wilson Burns & Co., 345
 Baltimore Co., 311
 Carlisle, 425
 Chestertown, 345
 Elizabeth City, 425
 Frostburg, St. Joseph's Benevolent Society, 400
 Hancock, St. Peter's Temperance and Benevolent Society, 400
 Havre de Grace, St. John the Baptist Society, 400
 Mount Savage, St. Patrick's Benevolent Society, 401
 Oakland, 345
 Port Deposit, St. Joseph's Benevolent Society, 403
 Westernport
  F. M. Young Men's Society, 404
  St. Peter's Total Abstinence Benevolent Society, 404
Masonic Jewel, 157
Mason's Depot, 360
Massachusetts, 77, 272, 346, 363, 414
 Ayer, Irish Benevolent Society, 399
 Barnardstown, 346
 Blackstone, St. Paul's Total Abstinence Society, 399
 Bolton, 93
 Boston, 37, 77, 78, 79, 80, 81, 82, 84, 97, 98, 103, 109, 293, 300, 318, 320, 329, 346, 422
  Cambridge Station, 415
  Cathedral T.A.B. Society, 399
  F.M. No. 2 of St. James, 399
  F.M. No. 2, Sts. Peter & Paul, 399
  Mendelssohn Lodge #25, I.O.B.B., 419
  St. Augustine's Total Abstinence & M. B. Society, 399
  St. James Society, 399
  St. Stephen's T.A. Society, 399
  Sts. Peter & Paul Total Abstinence Benevolent Society, 399
 Bridgewater F.M.T. Society, 399
 Brookfield, Brewster, Henry & Co., 346
 Buzzard's Bay, 80
 Byram, 93
 Cambridge
  F. M. Society of St. John's, 399
  Idlewild House, 346
  St. Paul's Total Abstinence Benevolent Society, 399
  St. Peter's Temperance Society, 399
 Clinton, St. John's Church, 399
 Coleraine, Congregational Church, 346
 East Cambridge, St. John's Society, 400
 Framingham [Farmingham], St. John's Episcopal Church, 400
 Grand Lodge (Masonic), 409
 Greenfield
  Citizen's Committee, 346
  First Congregational Society, 346
 Holliston, 78
 Lawrence, St. Mary's Association of Prayer, 401
 Lowell, 346
  Executive Comm., 346
  St. Patrick's Church, 401
 Lynn, Citizens' Relief Comm., 346
 Middlesex Co., 78
 Milbury, F. M. Total Abstinence and Benevolent Society, 401
 Nantucket, 78
 New Bedford, 80, 81
 Newburyport, 79, 346
 North Adams, F. M. Total Abstinence Society, 402
 North Attleboro, 346
 North Brockfield, American Society of Hibernians, 402
 Northampton, F. M. Total Abstinence and Benevolent Society, 402
 Norwood, 402

GENERAL INDEX

Pittsfield
  F. M. Total Abstinence Society, 403
  St. Joseph's C. Union, 403
Quincy, 346
  St. John's Temperance Society, 403
Salem, 80
  Relief Committee, 346
Shelburne Falls, 346
South Hadley Falls, St. Patrick's Temperance Association, 346
Springfield, 329
  Sacred Heart Temperance Society, 403
Taunton, 404
  Catholic Benevolent Society, 404
Waltham, 404
West Brookfield, Total Abstinence Benevolent Society, 404
West Quincy, St. Mary's C. Total Abstinence & M. R. Society, 404
Worcester
  Citizens' Relief Committee, 404
  F. M. Temperance Society, 404
  I. C. Benevolent Society, 404
  St. John's Church, 404
Medical Gazette, 296
Medical News, 43
Medical Repository, 70
Medina, 81
Memoir on Contagion, 305
Memphis & Charleston Rail Road, 94, 105, 142, 147, 179, 180, 266, 333, 336, vi
Memphis & Louisville Rail Road, 142, 147, 336, vi
Memphis & Ohio River Packet Co., vi
Memphis & Tennessee Rail Road, 173, 334, 390, vi
Minneapolis & St. Paul Rail Road, 340
Menken Bros., 350
Merchants' Magazine, 276
Mexico, 13, 14, 15, 16, 77
  Tampico, 15, 36, 289, 290
  Vera Cruz, 36, 39, 40, 80, 81, 92, 289, 290, 302, 303
    Hospital of St. Sebastian, 81
  Yucatan, 22
Michigan, 346, 347, 363, 414
  Adrian, St. Patrick's Benevolent Society, 399
  Alamo, Congregational Church, 347
  Allegan, 347
  Amanda, Reformed Church, 347
  Ann Arbor, 347
    Congregational Church, 346
    Red Ribbon Reform Club, 346, 347
  Battle Creek, 361
  Bay City, 346
    Bay City Lodge #129 (Masonic), 409
    St. James' Roman Catholic Total Abstinence and Benevolent Society, 399
  Big Rapids, 347
  Blissfield, 346
  Bridgeport, 422
  Chelsea, 346
  Coldwater, 346, 347
    Anderson & Sandridge, 348
  Decatur, 346
  Detroit, 346, 347, 368, 370, 371, 372
    Abraham Lincoln Lodge #710, Knights of Honor, 422
    Charity Lodge #14, I. O. F. S. I., 419
    Clark Bros., 360
    Congregation Beth El, 419
    Free Press, 346, 347
    Hibernian Benevolent Society, 400
    Second National Bank, 346
    Terchheimer Bros., 360
    Toof & Co., 360
    Typographical Union, 415
  Dexter, 346
    Women's Christian Temperance Union, 346
  East Saginaw, 415
    Courier, 415
    First Presbyterian Church, 346
    St. Joseph's Catholic Total Abstinence Society, 400
  Flint, Citizens' Relief Comm., 347
  Masonic Fraternity, 346
  Grand Blanc, Red Ribbon Club, 347
  Grand Haven, 346
    Cutler House, 346
  Grand Rapids, 346, 347
    Gymnasium Club, 346
    Nathan Church, 346
  Greenville, 346
  Hanover, M. E. Church, 347
  Hartford, 346
  Hastings, 346
  Henderson, 346
  Hersey, 346
  Holland, 346
  Houghton Co., 400
  Ishpening
    Old Soldiers' and Sailors' Club, 346
    St. Patrick's Catholic Benevolent Society, 400
  Jackson, 346, 371, 373
    Michigan State Prison, 346
    South Jackson Sunday School, 347
  Kalamazoo, 346
    Reformed Dutch Church, 346
  L. Ause, 346
  Lansing, 346, 347
  Mackinac, 346
  Manistee, German Aid Society, 347
  Marquette, 347
  Marshall, 346, 347
  Mason, Dudley House, 346
  Michigamme, Hibernian Aid Society, 401
  Monroe, 346, 347, 362
  Muskegon, 346, 347
  Negaunee, St. Patrick's Benevolent Society, 402
  Niesland, Reformed Church and Sunday School, 347
  Novi, 346
  Otsego, 347
  Paw Paw, 347
  Port Hudson, St. Patrick's Society, 403
  Port Huron, 346
    Custom House, 346
  Portland, 346
  Quincy, 346
    Michigan State Fire Association, 346
  Reed City, Relief Committee, 347
  Rochester, Congregational Church, 346
  Rockford, 347
  Romeo, 346, 347
  Sault Ste Marie, First Presbyterian Church, 347
  St. Clair, 346
    Palmer Lodge #20, Knights of Pythias, 346

St. Joseph [St. Joe]
   Fire Co., 346
   Ladies' Relief Society, 346
Wilmington, 346
Zilwaukee, 346, 347
Military
   Bluff City Cornet Band, 428, 430
   Bluff City Grays, 130, 147, 175, 184, 390, 394, 428, 429
   Brown's Zouaves, 391
   Chickasaw Guards, 130, 156, 355
   McClellan[d] Guards, 113, 147, 391, 394, 428, 429
   U. S. Army, 20, 283, 286, 437
      3rd Infantry, 346
      8th Cavalry, Co. F, 356
      10th Infantry, 357
         Co. D, 356
      13th Infantry, 332
      24th Infantry, 357
         Co. D, 356
         Co. E, 356
         Co. H, 356
   U. S. Marine Hospital Service, 283, 286
   U. S. Navy, 67, 283, 286, 304
   U. S. Signal Corps, 426
   Zouave Guards, 113, 428, 429
Minnesota, 346, 363, 414
   Alexandria, Congregational Church & Society, 346
   Austin, F.M.T.A. Society, 399
   Belle Creek, F. M. Total Abstinence Society, 399
   Benson, St. Malachy's Total Abstinence and Benevolent Society, 399
   Belle Plaine, 346
   Fairbault, 346
   Farmington, 346
   Kasson, 422
      North Star Lodge #803, Knights of Honor, 422
   Mankato, 346
   Minneapolis, 346, 368
      C. & G. W. Scott, 346
      Father Mathew Society, 401
      First Presbyterian Church, 346
      Police Department, 346
      R. Reis & Gumbach, 419
      Total Abstinence Society, 401
   Northfield, 346
      Spaulding Congregational Sunday School, 346
      Town Line Sunday School, 346
   Pilot Grove, Union Sunday School, 346
   Red Wing, 346
      Cataract Engine Co., 346
   Rochester, 346
   St. Cloud, Prebyterian Sunday School, 346
   St. Paul, 44, 346, 360, 403
      Cathedral Benevolent Society, 403
      F. M. Total Abstinence Society, 403
      Locomotive Brotherhood, St. Paul Div., 346
      State Fair, 346
   Stillwater
      City Council, 346
      Crusaders' Society, 403
      F. M. Total Abstinence Society, 403
   Winebago City, 346
   Winona, 346
      Congregational Church, 346
      F. M. Total Abstinence Society, 404

Presbyterian Church, 346
St. Thomas' Church, 404
Mississippi, 36, 77, 174, 179, 269, 293, 348, 363, 389, 414
Austin, 56, 175, 368, 369
Bay St. Louis, 84, 85, 88, 92, 249
Beachland, 250
Bennett's Landing, 348
Biloxi, 78, 86, 87, 89, 90, 93, 250
Bolton, 249
Bovina, 93, 249
Brandon, 89
Brookhaven, 419
Brookhaven Lodge #291, 408
Canton, 90, 93, 246, 337, 340, 351, 352, 354
Cardiff Landing, 249
Carrollton, 250
Cayuga, 93, 250
Charlestown, 348
Christian, 87
Clarksdale, 348
Clifton, 89
Clinton, 68
Coldwater, 348
   Anderson & Sandridge, 348
Columbia, 348
Columbus, 348
Como, 348
Cooper's Wells, 90, 296
Corinth, 348, 419
Courtland, Sabbath School, 348
Cox's Landing, 93
Dry Grove, 93, 94, 246
Duck Hill, 93
Durant, 93
Edward's Depot, 93
Fort Adams, 89
Friar's Point, 93, 249, 348
Galman Station, 94
Garner Station, 94
Grand Gulf, 89
Grand Junction, 371, 373
Greenville, 93, 169, 246, 247
Greenwood, 89
Grenada, 31, 93, 106, 137, 138, 140, 146, 151, 154, 161, 173, 175, 239, 247, 248, 330, 331, 334, 335, 337, 338, 339, 340, 341, 342, 344, 346, 347, 348, 349, 350, 351, 353, 354, 355, 356, 357, 361, 377, 378, 379, 380, 386, 413, 414, 426
Handsboro, 94, 249
Harrison Co., Beauvoir Station, 381
Haynes Bluff, 94
Hernando, 94, 157, 238, 239, 248, 249, 379
Hinds Co., 246
   Lebanon District, 246
Holliston, 78
Holly Springs, 93, 94, 134, 238, 245, 246, 340, 342, 345, 349, 350, 356, 357
Horn Lake, 44, 238, 249, 348, 367, 371, 373
Iuka, 164, 238
Jackson, 34, 89, 93, 94, 247, 371, 373
Jacksonville, 89
Jonestown, 191, 367
King's Point, 94
Kosciusko, 419
Lake, 94, 250

GENERAL INDEX 535

Lawrence Station, 94
Lebanon Church, 94
Logtown, 94
Macomb City, 371, 373
Madison College, 174
Masons, 175, 179
McCombs City, 94
McNairy, 94
Meridian, 94, 248
Michigan City, 94
Mississippi City, 94, 179, 249
Morgan City, 94, 249
Mulatto Bayou, 95
Natchez, 37, 42, 83, 84, 85, 86, 87, 89, 90, 145, 269, 298, 325, 348, 371, 373, 402
   D. G. Lodge # 7, I.O.B.B., 419
   Ezra Lodge #134, I.O.B.B., 419
   Marine Hospital, 86
   Natchez Democrat, 37
   Phoenix Insurance Co., 348
New Iberia, 25
Ocean Springs, 95, 249
Olive Branch, 348
Osyka, 249
Oxford, 348
Ozyka, 95
Pascagoula, 26, 89, 92, 95
Pearlington, 95, 249
Petit Gulf Hills, 89
Phoenix, 348
Port Gibson, 89, 96, 145, 248, 353
Refuge Landing, 96
Ricohoc [Richoc], 249
Rocky Springs, 96, 248
Rodney, 85, 87, 89
Senatobia, 96, 249, 348, 354, 426
Shieldsboro, 84, 85, 86
Smith's Station, 249
St. Louis, 118, 200, 326, 329, 332, 361, 409
   Christ Church, 191
   Globe-Democrat, 415
   Knights P. M., 403
Stevenson's Plantation, 249
Stoneville, 96, 249
Sulphur Springs, 249
Summit, 96, 249
Sunflower, 96, 249
Terrene, 436
Terry, 96, 249
Vaiden, 368, 369
Valley Home, 97, 250
Valley Horn, 97
Vicksburg, 29, 71, 86, 87, 90, 92, 93, 95, 97, 179, 242, 243, 244, 298, 325, 332, 333, 337, 351, 352, 354, 357, 371, 375, 435, 436, 437, 438
Howard Association, 436
Marine Hospital, 332
Warren Co., 244, 245
Washington, 36, 37, 85
Water Valley, 97, 246, 350
West Pascagoula, F. Gautier & Sons, 345
Whitsell's Landing, 83
Winona, 97, 250
Winterville, 250
Woodville, 87, 88, 89, 90
Yazoo City, 89, 97, 246

Mississippi & Tennessee Rail Road, 54, 105, 106, 142, 179, 180, 266, 302, 333, 336, 377, 428
Mississippi Central Rail Road, 378
Mississippi River, 34, 83, 84, 85, 86, 179, 292, 318, 321, 326, 332, 436, 438
Mississippi Valley, 269, 298, 314
Missouri, 36, 77, 347, 348, 363, 414
   Appleton City, 347
   Aullville, 347
   Booneville, 347
   Breckinridge, Good Templars, 347
   Brunswick, 347
   Butler, 347
   Cambridge, 347
   Cape Girardeau, 347, 399
   Carrollton, 347
      Presbyterian Church, 347
   Chamois, 347
   Charleston, 347
   Chillicothe, M. E. Church, 347
   Clarksville, 347
   Columbia, 347
   Commerce, 347
   Craig, 347
   Edina
      Christian Sunday School, 347
      Dramatic Association, 347
      Presbyterian Church, 347
   Fayette, 347
   Frederickstown, Marcus Lodge #110 (Masonic), 409
   Fulton, 347
   Glasgow Bridge, 347
   Gunn City, 348
   Hannibal
      Appleton Lodge, Knights of Pythias, 347
      West Ely Lodge, S. of T., 347
   Higginsville, 347
   Holden, M. E. Church, 347
   Huntsville, 347
   Hyattville, 347
   Independence, 26, 347, 348
      Baptist Church, 348
   Jefferson, 347
   Jefferson City, 347
   Joplin, 347
   Kansas City, 347, 368, 370
      Board of Trade, 347
      German Association, 347
      I. C. Benevolent Society, 401
   Kirksville, 347
   Kirkwood, 348
   Lamar, 347
   Lancaster, 347
   Lee's Summit Union Christian Aid Association, 348
   Lexington, 347, 348
      Relief Committee, 347
      Southern Relief Committee, 348
   Liberty, 347
   Ligonier Lodge #185, F. & A. M., 347
   Marshall, 347, 348
      Salt Pond Baptist Church, 347
   Marysville, 347
   Maysville, 347
   Mecklin, M. E. Church, 347
   Memphis, 347
   Mexico, 347
      Fire Co., 347

Mineral Point, 419
Moberly, 347
    Avery Wolfolk & Co., 347
    Irish Catholic Benevolent Society, 401
Modoc, 347
Monroe City, 347
Monsterratt, 347
Monticello, 347
Montrose, 347
Mt. Vernon, 347
Neoshonie, 347
New Design (St. Louis Co.,), 34, 79
New Madrid, 347
Otterville, 347
Page City, 347
Palmyra, 347, 348
    Fabius Fair Association, 348
Platte City Sabbath School, 347
Plattsburg, 347
    St. Mary's Catholic Total Abstinence Society, 403
Potosi, 347
Princeton, 347
Rockport, 347
Sedalia, 347, 348
    Catholic Benevolent Society, 403
Shelbina, 347
Sikeston, 347
Somer Hill Congregational Church and Sunday School, 347
Springfield, 347
    First Baptist Church and Sunday School, 359
St. Joseph [St. Joe], 347, 348, 403
    Relief Association, 347
    Relief Committee, 347, 348
    Southern Relief Association, 348
    Typographical Union, 415
St. Louis, 21, 25, 27, 34, 38, 79, 89, 90, 96, 104, 117, 171, 179, 191, 200, 239, 265, 303, 326, 329, 332, 347, 348, 366, 368, 369, 371, 375, 409, 410, 415, 419, 436
    Appleton, Noyes & Maude, 347
    Benton Lodge I.O.O.F., 347
    Burton, 348
    Chatopa Lodge #73 (Masonic), 409
    Christ Church, 191
    Church Birmingham, 347
    D. G. Lodge #2, I.O.F.S.I., 419
    Dozier, Weyl & Co., 360
    Evening Post, 437
    Globe Democrat, 347
    Great Western Glass Co., 348
    Gymnastic Association, 348
    Hebrew Y. M. Lit. Society, 347
    Hibernian Benevolent Society, 403
    Immaculate Conception Total Abstinence Benevolent Society of Iron Mountain, 403
    Kirtland, Humphreys & Mitchell, 359
    Lincoln Lodge #430, Knights of Honor, 422
    Merchants' Exchange, 347, 360
    Relief Committee, 347
    Missouri Lodge #25, I.O.F.S.I., 419
    Nations Bank, 346
    Peabody Association, 360
    Pleasant Hill, 347
    Relief Committee [Fund], 347
    Republican, 170
    Schiller Lodge #400, Knights of Honor, 422
    Sedalia, 347
    U. C. St. Vincent de Paul Society, 403
    Watson & Gilliland, 347
St. Louis Co., 79
Sturgeon, 347
Trenton M. E. Church and Sunday School, 347
Unionville, 347
Virginia City, 368, 370
Warrensburg, 347
Warrenton, 347
Warsaw, 347
Washington, 426
Weston
    Presbyterian Church, 347
    Relief Fund, 347
Windsor, 347
Mobile & Montgomery Rail Road, 337
Mobile & Ohio Rail Road, 88
Montana, 178, 346, 363
    Fort Benton, 346
    Fort Ellis
        St. Mary's Society, 400
    Helena, 410
        Masons, 346
        St. Patrick's Catholic Benevolent Total Abstinence Society, 400
    Pioneer City, 410
    Virginia City, 346
Montana Territory, 414
Montgomery Co.
    Lovely Mount Post Office, 360
Montpelier, 14
Mossy Creek College, 443
Mound City, 96
Mount Pleasant Lodge #57 (Masonic), 409

N

National Board of Health, 51, 283, 284, 285, 286, 287
Nebraska, 348, 349, 363, 414
    Ashland, 349
    Beatrice, 349
        Executive Comm., 349
    Blair, 349
    Brownsville, 349
    Clarksville, 349
    Columbus
        Monitor Lodge #879, Knights of Honor, 422
    Crete, 349
        Crete Dramatic Club, 349
        M. E. Church, 349
    Elk Horn Valley, 349
    Eureka R. A. M. Chapter 5, 348
    Fairfield, 349
        Union Sabbath School, 349
    Fairmont, 349
    Fremont, 349
        Davidson & Sheridan, 349
        Fremont Lodge #859, Knights of Honor, 422
    Hastings, 349
    Humboldt, 349
    Lincoln, 349, 368
    Nebraska City, 349
        Nebraska City #925, Knights of Honor, 422
    North Platte, 349
        Brass Band, 349

GENERAL INDEX

Relief Committee, 349
String Band, 349
Omaha, 163, 348, 349, 371, 373
  Conductors' Brotherhood, 348
  Omaha Lodge #829, Knights of Honor, 422
  Omaha Mission, 349
Pawnee City, 349
  Methodist Church, 349
Plattsmouth, 349
  Plattsmouth Lodge #1043, Knights of Honor, 422
  St. Luke's Episcopal Church, 349, 361
Sidney, Bank of Nebraska, 349
Teckmah, 349
  Presbyterian Church, 349
  Union Sabbath School, 349
Wahoo, Saunders Lodge #974, Knights of Honor, 422
Nevada, 115, 363
  Carson, 348
  Central City, 348
  Eureka, 348
    Chapter #5, R. A. M., 348
  Ft. McPherson, 348
  Gold Hill, 348
    Parker Lodge, I.O.O.F., 348
  Renova, Reno Lodge #13 (Masonic), 409
  Tuscarora, 410
  Virginia City, 348, 410
    Good Templars, 348
    Virginia & Truckee Rail Road, 348
New Grenada, 14, 79
New Hampshire, 77, 363, 414
  Dover, 425
    St. Mary's Catholic Total Abstinence Society, 400
  Fisherville, St. John's Catholic Total Abstinence Society, 400
  Hampton, 348
  Keene, St. Bernard's Total Abstinence Society, 401
  Manchester, 348
    Citizen's Relief Committee, 348
    St. John Catholic Total Abstinence and Benevolent Society, 401
    St. Paul's Catholic Total Abstinence Society, 401
  Milton Mills, 348
  Nashua, St. Mary's Society, 402
  Portsmouth, 80, 81, 97, 98, 348
  Salmon Falls
    St. Mary's C. Total Abstinence Benevolent Society, 403
New Jersey, 77, 156, 239, 349, 363, 414
  Bayonne, 349
    First Reformed Sunday School Bible Class, 349
  Bernardsville, 399
  Bordentown, Hibernian Total Abstinence Benevolent Society, 399
  Burlington, 80
  Camden, 404
    St. Joseph's Benevolent Society, 400
  Courtland Wagon Manufacturing Co., 349
  Elizabeth, 349
    Trinity Church, 349
    First Baptist Church, 349
  Freehold, 349
  Gloucester City, 82

  St. Mary's Society, 400
  Young Men's Catholic Benevolent Society, 400
  Haledon, 362
  Hightstown, 349
  Hoboken, 164, 180, 181, 191, 349
    Church of the Holy Innocents, 191
    Noah Lodge #185, I.O.B.B., 420
  Jersey City
    St. Bridget's Total Abstinence Benevolent Society, 401
    St. Michael's Total Abstinence Benevolent Society, 401
  Monmouth, Committee of Monmouth, 349
  Montclair, 349
  New Brunswick, 371, 373
  New Market Baptist Church, 349
  Newark, 191, 349, 422
    House of Prayer, 191
    St. John's Church, 402
    St. Patrick's Cathedral, 402
    Typographical Union, 415
    Young Men's Hebrew Association, 420
  Orange, 349
    St. John's Total Abstinence Society, 402
  Patterson, 349, 362
    F. M. Total Abstinence Benevolent Society, 403
    St. Patrick's Total Abstinence Benevolent Society, 403
  Perth Amboy, 83
  Plainfield, 349
    Ancient Order of Hibernians, Div. No. 4, 403
    St. Mary's Catholic Total Abstinence and Benevolent Society, 403
    Y.M.C.A., 349
  Port Elizabeth, 80
  Red Bank, 349
  Salem, St. Mary's Church, 403
  Somerville, 349
    St. John's Church, 349
  Summit C. Total Abstinence Society, 403
  Trenton, 349
    Prospect St. Presbyterian Church, 349
    Red Stocking Assembly, 404
    Relief Fund, 349
    St. John's Church, 404
    Typographical Union, 415
    Young Men's League, Catholic Total Abstinence, 404
  Woodbury, 80, 349
New Mexico, 363
  Santa Fe, 348
New York, 77, 181, 200, 201, 203, 266, 272, 273, 274, 276, 277, 278, 299, 302, 353, 363, 414
  Afton, 350
  Albany, 78, 80, 191, 329, 350, 361
    St. Peter's Church, 191
  Amsterdam, 349, 350
    Relief Fund, 350
  Avon, 349
  Bath, 350
    First Presbyterian Church, 350
  Binghamton, 350
    Democratic Co. Convention, 350
    First Presbyterian Church & Society, 350
    German Evangelical Society, 350
    St. Patrick's Total Abstinence and Benevolent Society, 399

Birmingham, 350
Brooklyn, 83, 85, 90, 93, 277, 349, 350
   Board of Health, 104
   Citizens' Relief Committee, 350
   St. James' Total Abstinence Society, 399
   Sts. Peter and Paul Church, 399
   Union Lodge #31, I.O.F.S.I., 420
Brooklyn Heights, 290
Buffalo, 203, 329, 425
   F.M. Total Abstinence and Benevolent Society, 399
   St. John Baptist Benevolent Society, 399
   St. Joseph's Total Abstinence Benevolent Society, 399
   Typographical Union, 415
Cairo, 78, 79, 81
Catskill, 78, 79, 81, 349
Cayuga Falls, 408
Cazenovia, 349
Cohoes, St. Bernard's Total Abstinence Benevolent Society, 400
Elmira, 349
Essex Ferry, 400
Fairport, 350
Fort Hamilton, 275
Fredonia, 350
Freemansburg, 349, 350
   Baptist Church, 350
   Presbyterian Church, 349
Frewsburg, 350
Gaines, 350
   Universalist Church, 350
Gainesville, 350
   Presbyterian Sunday School, 350
General Relief Committee, 426
Geneseo, 350
   Livingston Co., 350
Geneva, 191, 400
Governor's Island, 17, 25, 26, 90, 92
Gowanus, 90
Greenfield (Saratoga Co.), 80
Half Moon, 350
Harlem, 349, 350
Hobart College, 191
Hoffman Island, 277
Homer, 349
Hoosac Falls F. M. Total Abstinence and Benevolent Society, 400
Hudson, 350
Hudson River, 78, 123
Huntington (Suffolk Co.), 79, 80
Huntington Bay, 79
Irvington, 400
Jamestown, 349, 350
Kianstone, 350
   Congregational Society, 350
Kingston, St. Joseph's Total Abstinence and Benevolent Society, 401
Ladies of Albion, 350
Leroy [Le Roy], 349
   St. Patrick's Society, 401
Lima, 350
Little Falls, 350
Lockport, 94, 350
   Episcopal Church, 350
   Relief Committee, 350

Long Island, 275, 350
   Bay Ridge, 90, 275
Long Island Sound, 80
Martinsburgh, 350
Medina, 350
Mount Vernon, 360
Mt. Morris, 350
   St. John's Episcopal Church, 350
New Haven, 350
   Congregational Church, 350
New York City, 17, 29, 50, 60, 70, 77, 78, 79, 80, 81, 82, 83, 84, 85, 86, 117, 281, 288, 292, 293, 296, 315, 318, 320, 322, 326, 329, 349, 350, 354, 368, 369, 370, 371, 373, 415, 420, 426, 427, 437
   Akiba Eger Lodge #26, K.S.B., 420
   Allen & B., 349
   Booth's Theater, 165
   Bulletin, 415
   Chamber of Commerce, 349, 350, 360
   Charles T. White & Co., 350
   Christian at Work, 350
   Christian Church, 350
   Church of the Holy Innocents Temperance Society, 401
   Condensed Milk Co., 350
   Cotton Exchange, 349
   D. J. Garth, Son & Co., 349
   Drexel, Morgan & Co., 349, 350
   Exchange Relief Committee, 349
   Fourth National Bank, 350
   Goldsmith & Plant, 350
   H. & K. Thurbur, 361
   H. B. Claflin & Co., 350
   Herald, 349, 350, 415
   Insurance Monitor, 349
   Irish Brigade Officer's Association, 401
   J. S. Warren & Co., 349
   Jackson & O'Hara, 349
   Ludlow & Co., 350
   Marine Hospital, 80, 81, 82, 83, 84, 85, 86, 87, 88, 89, 90
   Miller & Eastmead, 425
   Moore, Tingue & Co., 350
   Mt. Sinai Lodge, I.O.B.B., 420
   New York Stock Exchange, 349, 350
   O. Lanfer & Co., 349
   Salance & Grosyear, 349
   St. Michael's Roman Catholic Total Abstinence Benevolent Society, 401
   St. Vincent de Paul Society, 402
   Stationers' Board of Trade, 350
   Strauss & Arenstein, 350
   Temple Emanuel, 420
   Thomas French & Sons, 359
   Times, 177, 291, 350, 435
   Transfiguration Roman Catholic Total Abstinence Benevolent Society, 401
   Typographical Union, 415
   Wall Street, 101
   William Zinsser & Co., 360
   Yellow Fever Relief Committee, 420
   Young Ladies' Charitable Union, 420
Newark, 350
   Presbyterian Church, 350
Olean, 350
Orange Co., 81

Oswego, 350, 422
  Ames Iron Works, 425
  Co. F., 48th Regiment, 350
Peekskill, 361
Poughkeepsie, 349, 350, 362
  St. Peter's Total Abstinence Benevolent Society, 403
Queensborough (Orange Co.), 81
Red Hook, 90
Rochester, 349, 350, 403, 420
  Advertiser, 415
  Blumenthal & S., 350
  Congregational Church, 350
  J. Cunningham, Son & Co., 349
  Security Lodge #164, 349
  St. Patrick's Benevolent Society, 403
  Typographical Union, 415
Saratoga Co., 80
Saugerties, 420
Seguin's Point, 278
Seneca Falls F. M. Total Abstinence Society, 403
Spencerport, 350
  Congregational Church, 350
  M. E. Church, 350
  Presbyterian Church, 350
Staten Island, 273, 290
  Stapleton, 87
  Tompkinsville, 87
Suffolk Co., 79
Syracuse, 349, 350
  Israelites of Syracuse, 349
Troy, 349, 350
  Ladies' Hebrew Benevolent Society, 420
Utica, 349
  Daniel Krouse & Sons, 349
  Morning Herald & Gazette, 350
  Typographical Union, 415
Weedsport, 350
West Bank, 276, 277
West Neck (Suffolk Co.), 79
West Point, 82
  U. S. Military Academy, 156
West Troy, 350
  St. P. F. M. Total Abstinence Benevolent Society, 404
Westfield, 350, 362
  Presbyterian Church, 350
White Plains, 350
  Relief Committee, 350
Williamsburg, 349
  Friendly Sons of St. Patrick, 349
Windsor, 350
  Union Temperance, 350
World, 191, 415
Yellow Hook, 90
Yonkers, Immaculate Conception Total Abstinence Society, 404
North Carolina, 77, 200, 363, 414
  Ashboro, 351
  Asheville, 350
  Battery Wagner, Morris Island, 192
  Beaufort, 90, 91, 92
  Black Run Congregation Chapel, 351
  Bristol, 351
  Charlotte, 350, 351, 371, 372, 376
    Hill Chapel Lodge, 351
    J. R. Holland and Co., 351
    Ladies' Aid Association, 350
    Lidell & Co., 351
    Presbyterian Church, 351
    R. Chambers, 351
  Charlotteville Military Institute, 351
  Clinton, 351
    Southern Relief Fund, 351
  Concord
    Cannon, Fitser & Wadsworth, 351
    Hoover & Love, 351
  Dallas, 351
  Deanville, 351
  Durham, 351
  Edenton, 350, 351
  Ely City Church, 351
  Faulkland, 351
  Forrestville, 351
    Baptist Church, 351
  Franklin, 351
    Junaluskee Lodge, A. F. & A. M., 351
  Goldsboro, 362, 419
  Graham, 351
  Greensboro, 351
    Buffalo Church, 351
  Halesville, 350
  Halifax, 350, 351
  Hamfield Presbyterian Church, 350
  Henderson, 350
    Colored M. E. Church, 351
  Hendersonville, 351
  Hillsboro, 351
    Presbyterian Church, 351
  Jonesborough, 351
  Kingston, 350, 419
  Lawrenceburg, 351
    Presbyterian Church, 351
  Lisleville, 351
    Baptist Church, 351
  Lumberton, 362
  Manly, 350
  Marion, 351
  Mebanville, 350
    Presbyterian Church, 350
  Mecklenburg Presbyterian Church, 351
  Meuse River, 80
  Moncure, 351
  Monroe, 351
    M. E. Church, 351
    Methodist Church, 351
    Presbyterian Church, 351
  Morrisville, 351
  Mount Monroe
    Centre Church, 351
  New Berne, 80, 91
  Newbern, 351
  Oxford, 350, 351
    T. D. Crawford & Co., 351
  Pineville, 350
  Raleigh, 350, 351
    Academy of Medicine, 351
    Arylee Church, 351
    Colored Congregational Church, 350
    Hebrew Union, 350
    Ladies' Relief Association, 350
    Southern Express Co., 350
    St. John's Benevolent Society, 403
    Typographical Union, 415

Ridgeway, 350
Rockingham, 351
  Great Falls Manufacturing Co., 351
Roxboro, 351
Salusbury [sic], 351
Scotland Neck, 351
  Scotland Neck Lodge #68, 351
Smithville, 91
Snow Hill, 351
St. Louisberg, 351
Statesville, 351
  Piedmont Lodge #558, Knights of Honor, 422
Tar River, 80
Tarboro Congregation Bnai Israel, 419
Thomasville, 351
Troy, 350
  T. O. Troy Co. Shops, 350
Wake Forrest, 350
Warrenton, 351
Washington, 80
Weldon, 351
Wentworth, 351
Weston, 410
Whitakers, 351
  Speights Chapel Sunday School, 351
Whitesville, 351
Wilmington, 79, 80, 84, 91, 276, 350, 351, 371, 375
  Manhattan Lodge #158, K.S.B., 419
  North State Lodge #222, I.O.B.B., 419
  Southern Relief Association, 351
Windsor, 350
Winston, Brown & Brother, 359

O

Oceanica, 201
Ohio, 36, 77, 167, 200, 363, 371, 373, 414
  Akron, 410, 427
    F.M. Society, 399
    Harmonic Association, 352
    St. Vincent de Paul Brotherhood, 399
  Alliance First Presbyterian Church, 352
  Arcadia M. E. Sunday School, 352
  Ashland
    Relief Committee, 353
    Sunday Schools, 352
  Ashtabula
    Baptist Congregation, 352
    Congregational Congregation, 352
  Athens, 352
  Beach City, 352
  Bellaire, 352
    Bellmont United Presbyterian Church, 352
  Belleville, 352
  Belpre, Congregational Church, 352
  Bench City, 352
  Beverly Temperance Union, 351
  Bluffton, 352
    Sunday Schools, 352
  Bucyrus, 352
  Burton Congregational Society, 353
  Cadiz, 352
  Caledonia, 93
  Canal Dover, Southern Relief Fund, 352
  Canal Fulton, 352
  Canton, 352
    German Relief Society, 352
  Cardington, Tymochtee Tribe 1, 352
  Carrollton, 352, 353
  Chillicothe, 351, 352, 353, 371, 372, 426
  Cincinnati, 58, 92, 93, 104, 108, 118, 150, 163, 167, 238, 265, 329, 351, 352, 353, 360, 362, 368, 369, 370, 371, 372, 415, 420, 426
    Albert Fisher & Co., 362
    Alpha Lodge #37, Knights of Honor, 422
    Board of Health, 95
    Davis, Gould & Co., 351
    Enquirer, 415
    Episcopal Church of the Advent, 351
    Evans, Lippincott & Cunningham, 351
    General Relief Committee (I.O.O.F.), 414
    Germania Lodge #38, Knights of Honor, 422
    Grand Lodge #2, I.O.B.B., 420
    Israelite and Deborah, 420
    Knights of Honor Relief Committee, 422
    Leath Orphan Asylum, 362
    Panoli Oil Works, 351
    Relief Committee, 351, 352
    Royer Wheel Co., 352
    Seasongood & Sons, 420
    Southern Relief Association, 351
    Southern Relief Committee, 336, 353, 420
    Stix, Krouse & Co., 420
    Third Presbyterian Church, 351
    Typographical Union, 415
    Welsh Congregational Church, 351
  Cleveland, 18, 351, 352, 361, 371, 372, 404
    Daughters of Israel, 420
    Free Sons of Israel, 351
    Hebrew Relief Committee, 420
    Holy Family Church, 399
    King Solomon Lodge #23, I.O.F.S.I., 420
    Knights of Erin, 399
    Knights St. Joseph, 399
    Relief Committee, 351
    Southern Relief Committee, 420
    St. Malachy's Total Abstinence and M.R. Society, 399
    St. Patrick's Society, 399
  Clyde, 352
  Coalville, 352
  Columbia, 167
  Columbus, 117, 167, 351, 368, 369
    Relief Committee, 351
    St. Patrick's Church, 399
    Typographical Union, 415
  Congress City, 352
  Wayne Presbyterian Church, 352
  Conneaut, 353
  Coshocton, 351, 352
    Disciple Church, 351
  Crawford Co., 353
  Crestline, 352
  Cumberland
    Buffalo Presbyterian Church, 352
    Presbyterian Sunday School, 352
  Cuyahoga Falls, 352
  Dayton, 93, 351, 368, 370, 371, 372, 420
    Beckel House, 351
    Dayton Lodge #23, Knights of Honor, 422
    Disabled Volunteer Soldiers, 351
    Equitable Loan and Savings Association, 351
    Firemans Insurance Co., 351
    Hibernian Benevolent Society, 402

GENERAL INDEX 541

Mendelssohn Quartette Club, 351
Merchants National Bank, 351
National Military Homes, 402
Philips House, 351
Reed Commandery #6, 410
Relief Committee, 352
Defiance, 352
Del Roy Presbyterian Church, 353
Dennison, St. Patrick's Society, 400
Dresden, 352
Dunkirk, 352
Eaton, 352
Elyria, St. Joseph's Benevolent Society, 400
Erie Co., 353
Findlay, 351, 353
Fostoria, 352, 425
   Hayes House, 352
   Jay & Silvermail, 352
Four Corners, 352
Freedonia, 352
Gainsville, Lodge #375 (Masonic), 409
Galion, 352
Gallatin, King Solomon Lodge #64 (Masonic), 409
Gallipolis, 32, 79, 93, 95, 265, 306
Garrettsville, 361
Genesee, 352
Geneva, 352
Gnadenhutten Singing Choir, 352
Greenville, St. Patrick's Benevolent Society, 400
Hamilton, 351, 371, 373
Hanoverton, 351
   Presbyterian Church, 351
Harlem Springs, M. E. Church, 353
Hudson, 400
Huntsburg Congregational Church, 353
Irondale, 352
Ironton, 352
   Congregational Church, 352
Jamestown United Presbyterian Church, 352
Kansas, 352
Kellogsville, 352
Kelly's Island
   Congregational Church, 352
   Ladies' Sewing Society, 351
Kent, St. Vincent de Paul Society, 401
Kenton, 352
Lancaster, 352
Lawrence, 352
Leesburg
   M. E. Sunday School, 352
   Murphy Temperance Congregation, 352
Leetonia, St. Patrick's Society, 401
Lima, 352
Logan, 351, 352
London, 352, 353
   Episcopal Society, 351
Londonville, 352
Loveland, Murdoch Club, 352
Madisonville, 352
Mantua, 352
Marietta
   Congregational Church, 352
   Fourth Street Presbyterian Church, 352
   Soldiers' Relief Union Fund, 352
   Soldiers' Reunion, 352
Marion Relief Committee, 352
Martin's Ferry, 351

Marysville
   Dramatic Club, 351
   Sabbath School, 352
Massillon, 352
   German Benevolent Association, 352
   St. Patrick's Irish Catholic Benevolent Society, 401
Middletown, 352
   St. Patrick's Benevolent Society, 401
Milan (Erie Co.), 353
   Case, Mills, Gricks, and Fay, 353
Millersburg, 352
   U. P. Church, 352
Mooresville, 352
Mount Gilead, 351
Mount Pleasant, 353
   Quaker Meeting, 352
Mount Vernon, 351
Mt. Vernon
   Citizens' Committee, 352
   St. Vincent de Paul Benevolent Society, 401
New Bremen, 352
New Castle, 352
New Comerstown Lutheran Church, 352
New Lexington, 352
New Lisbon, 352
New Philadelphia, 351
Newark, 351, 371, 373
   Citizens' Relief Fund, 398, 402
Newport, 352
North Fairfield, 352
Norwalk, 352
   Commandery, 408
   Union Church, 352
Ottawa, 352
Painesville, 352
   First National Bank, 352
   St. James Episcopal Church, 351
Paulding, 352
Perryville [Perrysville], 352
   Greentown Academy, 352
Powhattan, 352
Puqua, St. Patrick's Benevolent Society, 403
Quaker City, Sand Hill Sunday School, 352
Ravenna, 351, 352, 353
   Catholic Total Abstinence and Benevolent Society, 403
Rome Presbyterian Church and Sunday School, 352
Rushcreek United Presbyterian Church, 352
Rushsylvania Relief, P. S. S., 352
Salem Reformed Church, 352
Sandusky, 351, 352
Sardina, H. C. Dramatic Club, 352
Sardrina Presbyterian Church, 352
Savannah
   Methodist Church, 352
   Post Office, 352
   Presbyterian Church and Sunday School, 352
   United Presbyterian Congregational, 352
Shannon, 352
Smithville, 352
Somerset, 352
Springfield, 352, 404
   Champion Machine Co., 351
   Friendly Sons Society, 403
   James Leffel & Co., 351

Knights of St. Patrick, 403
Young Men's Hibernian Society, 403
St. Mary's, 352
Steubenville
    Golden Rule Lodge, I.O.O.F., 351
    Relief Committee, 351
Sugar Creek German Baptist Society, 353
Summerfield, 353
Tarlton M. E. Sunday School, 352
Thornton United Presbyterian Church, 352
Tiffin, St. Patrick's Total Abstinence and Benevolent Society, 404
Toledo, 351, 404
    Citizens' Relief Committee, 352, 420
    St. Vincent de Paul Society, 404
    Toledo Lodge #73, Knights of Honor, 422
    Typographical Union, 415
Troy, 351
    Franklin Lodge #14, 409
Uniontown Reformed Presbyterian Church, 352
Upper Sandusky, 352
Urbana, 362
    Letter 87, 352
    Relief Association, 353
    United Sons of Hibernia Society, 404
Urichsville, 352
Versailles Dramatic Society, 352
Waktonica Cross Roads, 352
Waranochs Reformed Presbyterian Church, 352
Warren Co., Miss.
    1st Presbyterian Church, 352
    Christ Church, 352
Warsaw, Jefferson Presbyterian Church, 352
Wauseon, 362
West Alexandria, 353
West Jefferson, 352
West Middlebury Relief Association, 352
West Salem Presbyterian Church, 353
Weston, 352
White Cottage, 352
Wilmington
    Relief Association, 351, 352
Wooster, 351
    First Presbyterian Church, 352
    United Presbyterian Congregation, 352
Worcester Citizens' Relief, 398
Worthington Presbyterian Church, 352
Xenia, 351, 352, 404
Youngstown, 352
    St. Anne's Total Abstinence Society, 404
    St. Columba's Church, 404
Zanesville, 351, 352
    F. M. Total Abstinence Society, 404
    Helen D'Este Troupe, 351
    St. Patrick's Benevolent Society, 404
    St. Thomas' Benevolent A. Society, 404
Ohio River, 32, 79
Orange, 37
Orangeburg, 348
Oregon, 115, 178, 363
    Astoria, 353
    Portland, 329, 353
        F. M. Total Abstinence and Benevolent Society, 403
Orient, 316

P

Palestine, 269
Pattisonville, 348
Pennsylvania, 70, 77, 273, 311, 363, 414
    Allegheny, Sholem Lodge #154, I.O.B.B., 420
    Allegheny City Temperance Society, 399
    Allegheny Co., Baldwyne Lodge #374, 408
    Allentown, St. Patrick's Society, 399
    Altoona, 353, 354
        Citizens' Committee, 353
        Southern Relief Fund, 353
    Anot F.M. Society, 399
    Bald Eagle Valley, 80
    Baldwin, 353
    Barclay, St. Patrick's Total Abstinence and Benevolent Society, 399
    Beaver Falls, 353
        Relief Committee, 353
    Bellefonte, 353
    Blairsville, Sts. Simon and Jude Benevolent Society, 399
    Blossburgh, Catholic Total Abstinence Society, 399
    Butler, 399, 422
        Butler Lodge #272, 409
    Cannonsburg
        Chartier's Presbyterian Church, 353
        Presbyterian Church, 353
    Centralia, St. Ignatius Total Abstinence and Benevolent Society, 399
    Centre Co., 80
    Chambersburg, 354
    Chester, 80
        Immaculate Heart Society, 399
        St. Michael's Benevolent Society, 399
    Chester Co., 82
    Connellsville Total Abstinence and Benevolent Society, 399
    Corry
        Ely Lodge #45, Knights of Honor, 422
        St. Thomas' Benevolent Society, 399
    Dallsburg, 353
    Drifton
        St. Anne's Total Abstinence and Benevolent Society, 400
        St. Patrick's Benevolent Society, 400
    Easton, 353, 361
        St. Bernard's Benevolent Society, 400
    Edenberg, Jones Bros., 400
    Edinburg, 353
    Elmira F. M. Total Abstinence Society, 400
    Emlenton, 353
    Erie, 415
        Gorgee & Sell, 425
        I. A. B. A. Society, 400
        I.O.K.S.B., 420
        Park Opera House, 425
    Falls of Schuylkill
        Rev. Thomas Fox Benevolent Society, 402
    Fisher's Island, 273
    Fort Mifflin, 273
    Foxburg, 353
    Frankfort Presbyterian Church, 353
    Franklin, 353
        Fire Insurance Co., 353
        Relief Committee, 353

GENERAL INDEX   543

Germantown, St. Vincent de Paul Total Abstinence Benevolent Society, 400
Gettysburg, 435
Girard, 353
Greensburg, 353
Greenville United Presbyterian Church Sunday School, 353
Harrisburg, 81
Hillsville, Zone Baptist Church, 353
Holmesburg
   St. Dominic's Benevolent Society, 400
   St. Dominic's Total Abstinence Benevolent Society, 400
Honesdale F. M. Total Abstinence Society, 400
Jefferson School, 171
Johnstown, 353
Kellyville
   St. Charles Total Abstinence Benevolent Society, 401
   St. Mary's Benevolent Society, 401
Kensington (Philadelphia Co.), 79
Kittanning, 353
Lancaster St. Bernard's Benevolent Society, 401
Lansford, 353
Lebanon, 353
   Presbyterian Church, 353
Line Run Disciples Church, 353
Lisburn, 81
Macungie, 353
Mahanoy City, St. Joseph's Total Abstinence Society, 401
Mahanoy Plane, St. Patrick's Total Abstinence Benevolent Society, 401
Manayunk
   St. John Baptist Total Abstinence Benevolent Society, 401
   St. Patrick's Benevolent Society, 401
   St. Patrick's Society, 401
Marcus Hook, 80
McKeesport, 353
   Emp. Nat. Tube Works, 353
   St. Joseph's Benevolent Society, 401
Meadville
   A. & G. W. Rail Road, 353
   Citizens' Relief Committee, 353
   Delameter & Co., 353, 354
Media, 401
Mercer, 353
Miles Grove, Grace Episcopal Church, 353
Millerstown, 353
   I.O.O.F., 353
   Knights of Honor, 353
Moosic, St. Mary's Total Abstinence Society, 401
Morris Run, St. Joseph's Total Abstinence Benevolent Society, 401
Morristown Presbyterian Sunday School, 353
Mt. Carmel, St. Mary's Roman Catholic Benevolent Society, 401
Mt. Pleasant, Chartier's Presbyterian Church, 353
Mud Island, 273
New Bethlehem Total Abstinence Benevolent Society, 402
New Castle, 353
Nittany (Centre Co.), 80
North East, 425
   Lake Shore Seminary, 354, 362

Oil City, 353
Oil Exchange, 353
St. Joseph's Temperance Society, 402
Typographical Union, 415
Parker City, 353
Petrolia, 353
Philadelphia, 17, 18, 29, 35, 77, 78, 79, 80, 81, 82, 83, 84, 89, 90, 92, 95, 104, 109, 158, 171, 201, 203, 266, 272, 273, 276, 290, 293, 295, 296, 299, 302, 303, 313, 315, 318, 320, 322, 326, 329, 353, 362, 402, 404, 420
Ancient Order of Hibernians, Div. No. 1, 402
Ancient Order of Hibernians, Div. No. 7, 402
Annunciation C. Total Abstinence Society, 402
Archbishop Carroll Benevolent Society, 402
Archbishop MacHale Benevolent Society, 402
Aushai Emeth Sabbath-School, 420
Bishop Wood Benevolent Society, 402
Citizens' Relief Committee, 402
College of Physicians, 35
Congregation House Israel, 420
Congregation Mickve Israel, 420
Congregation Rodef Sholem, 420
Covenant Lodge #66, K.S.B., 420
Cremeiux Lodge #83, I.O.B.B., 420
D. G. Lodge # 4, K.S.B., 420
D. G. Lodge # 6, I.O.B.B., 420
Daniel Carroll Benevolent Society, 402
Dr. Moriarty Benevolent Society, 402
Era Lodge #7, I.O.F.S.I., 420
Etz Chaim Lodge #205, I.O.B.B., 420
Father Barbelin Benevolent Society, 402
Father Burke Benevolent Society, 402
Father Mark Crane Benevolent Society, 402
Franklin Club, 420
Franklin Lodge #32, I.O.F.S.I., 420
Franklin Lodge #43, K.S.B., 420
Garrick Literary Association, 420
Grand Lodge, K.S.B., 420
Hance Bros. & White, 360
Har Moriah Lodge #10, I.O.B.B., 420
Har Nevoh Lodge #12, I.O.B.B., 420
Hebrew Sunday School, 420
Hiram Lodge #46, K.C.B., 420
I. C. B. U. Convention Delegates, 402
Immaculate Conception T. H. Benevolent Society, 402
James D. Howley Benevolent Society, 402
Jeshurun Lodge #59, I.O.B.B., 420
Jewish Temple, 420
John Lee Carroll Benevolent Society, 402
Kensington Catholic Society, 402
Keystone M. and F. Benevolent Society, 402
Leah Lodge #3, F. D. of I., 420
Meyers & Co., 404
Mordecai Lodge #36, K.S.B., 420
National Catholic Benevolent Society, 402
Our Lady of Lourdes Benevolent Society, 402
Philadelphia National Catholic Benevolent Society, 402
Posdamer & Co., 420
Puis IX Benevolent Society, 402
Rebecca Lodge, K.S.B., 420
Rev. Thomas Fox Benevolent Society, 402
S. Vendig & G. H. Judah, 420
Sacred Heart Total Abstinence Benevolent Society, 402

St. Agnes Female Benevolent Society, 402
St. Cecelia's Benevolent Society, 402
St. Cecilia's Total Abstinence Benevolent Society, 402
St. Charles Total Abstinence Society, 402
St. Edward's Benevolent Society, 402
St. Elizabeth Benevolent Society, 402
St. Michael's Total Abstinence Benevolent Society, 402
St. Monica Female Benevolent Society, 402
St. Paul's Pioneer Corps, 402
St. Paul's Total Abstinence Benevolent Society, 402
St. Philip Neri Total Abstinence Benevolent Society, 402
Typographical Union, 415
Waterman's Benevolent Society, 402
Philadelphia Co., 79
Phoenixville, St. Mary and St. Joseph Society, 403
Pittsburgh, 95, 104, 329, 359, 371, 373, 426
   Brotherhood of St. Mary of Con., 402
   Cincinnati & St. Louis Rail Road, 353
   Citizens' Relief, 398
   Dispatch, 353
   Emerald Benevolent Society, 402
   German National Bank, 420
   Jericho Lodge #44, I.O.B.B., 420
   Johnson Lodge, I.O.O.F., 354
   Pittsburg Relief Committee, 402
   Relief Committee, 353
   Rook & O'Neil, 353
   St. Agnes Total Abstinence and Benevolent Society, 402
   St. Bridget's Total Abstinence and Benevolent Society, 402
   Total Abstinence and Benevolent Society, 402
   Typographical Union, 415
Pittston F. M. Society, 403
Plymouth, St. Vincent Total Abstinence Benevolent Society, 403
Pottsville, 353
   Union Lodge #124, I.O.B.B., 420
Providence, St. Thaddeus F. M. Total Abstinence Benevolent Society, 402
Queenstown, 353
Reading Southern Relief Fund, 353
Renova, St. Joseph's Benevolent Society, 403
Roaring Springs, Morrison, Bare & Caps, 353
Scranton, 353
   F. M. Total Abstinence Benevolent Society, 403
Selin's Grove, 353, 354
Sharon, 353
   F. M. Total Abstinence and Benevolent Society, 403
South Bethlehem Catholic Benevolent Society, 403
Southwark (Philadelphia Co.), 79
St. Petersburg, 353
Stempton, Workingmen's Benevolent Society, 403
Swarthmore, F. M. Benevolent Society, 403
Titusville, African M. E. Church, 353
Tryburgh, 353
Tyrone, 353
   1st Presbyterian Sunday School, 353
Washington, 353
   1st Presbyterian Church, 353
   2nd Presbyterian Church, 353
   East Buffalo Presbyterian Church, 353

   Hopewell Lodge, I.O.O.F., 353
   Relief Committee, 354
   West Alexandria, Chartier's Presbyterian Church, 353
   West Chester, St. Agnes' Total Abstinence Benevolent Society, 404
Wilkesbarre
   F. M. C. Total Abstinence Society, 404
   F. M. Total Abstinence Benevolent Society, 404
   Rodef Sholem Lodge #129, I.O.B.B., 420
   Wyoming Lodge #16, I.O.F.S.I., 420
Williamsburg, 353
Williamsport, 354
   Lodge #4, I.O.F.S.I., 420
   Lodge #16, I.O.F.S.I., 420
   Lodge #17, I.O.F.S.I., 420
   Lodge #19, I.O.F.S.I., 420
   Montefoire Lodge #108, K.S.B., 420
   St. Patrick's Benevolent Society, 404
York, 353, 404
Persia, 204, 277
Peru, 77, 84
Pinkerton Agency, 173
Pomeroy, 95
Port du Passage, 85
Portugal, 77, 271
   Lisbon, 26, 110
President's Island, 105, 430
Prince Albert Land, 204
Public Health Association, 387

R

Red River, 84, 85, 86
Reidenville, 348
Rhine River, 14
Rhode Island, 77, 363, 414
   Ashton, St. Joseph's Total Abstinence Society, 399
   Black Island, 81
   Bristol, 79, 354
   St. Mary's Total Abstinence Society, 399
   Central Falls, Sacred Heart Total Abstinence Society, 399
   Dover, 354
   Long Island Sound, 81
   Narragansett Bay, 79
   Newport, 82, 354
   Pawtucket
      St. Joseph's Total Abstinence and Benevolent Society, 403
      St. Mary's Total Abstinence and Benevolent Society, 403
   Pawtucket River, 80, 82
   Providence, 79, 80, 82, 109, 329, 354
      Board of Trade, 354
      St. Patrick's Church, 354
      Sts. Peter & Paul Conference, 402
   Westerly, 80, 82
   Woonsocket, F. M. Total Abstinence Society, 404
Richmond College, 171
Rio del Norte, 36
Rocky Mount, 348
Rogersville, 362
Royal Academy of Medicine, 25
Russellville Relief Committee, 348
Russia, 23, 204
   Moscow, 324

GENERAL INDEX

S

San Lucas, 80
Sanitarian, 313
Sanitary Congress, 275
Santa Cruz, 97, 98
Schuylkill River, 273
Searsville Baptist Church, 348
Ships
 Bann, 25, 28
 Borrusa, 105
 Chambers (National Relief Boat), 332
 Cherokee, 292
 De Russy (U. S. Snag Boat), 340
 Delaware, 80, 301
 Dolphin, 35
 Edward Henry, 67
 George O. Baker, 189
 Golden Crown, 93, 96, 107, 145
 Gomez, 87
 Herculean, 67
 HMS Bullfinch, 94
 John A. Scudder, 96
 John D. Porter, 95, 96, 145
 John M. Chambers (National Relief Boat), 179 332, 436, 437
 Mandarin, 35
 Mary Houston, 95, 96
 Millie (Barque), 315
 Nyanza, 67
 Plymouth, 97, 98, 304
 Ruthven, 39
 Sudder, 105
 Viscount Canning, 98
South Carolina, 70, 77, 87, 88, 90, 363, 414
 Anderson, 354
  G. A. Reformed Presbyterian Church, 354
  Good Hope Presbyterian Church, 354
 Bancroft, 354
 Beaufort, 92
 Bennettsville
  Baptist Church, 354
  M. E. Church, 354
  Town Council, 354
 Charleston, 15, 20, 28, 35, 78, 79, 80, 81, 82, 83, 84, 85, 86, 87, 88, 89, 90, 91, 92, 109, 168, 203, 313, 318, 322, 329, 354, 368, 371, 372, 427, 438
  Academy of Music, 354
  City Council, 354
  Congregation Beth Elohim, 419
  Dan Lodge #93, I.O.B.B., 419
  Irish Volunteers, 399
  News & Courier, 354
  Riordan & Dawson, 354
  St. Joseph's Total Abstinence Benevolent Society, 399
 Chester
  Ebenezer M. E. Church, 354
  Pleasant Grove Church, 354
 Cokesburg, 354
 Columbia, 90, 354
  Richland Lodge #39 (Masonic), 409
  Southern Express Co., 354
  Typographical Union, 415
 Edgefield, 354
  Belle Lodge No. 22, I.O.G.T., 354
 Ellenton, Riple Lodge (Masonic), 409
 Florence, 354
 Fort Moultrie, 88, 90
 Gastoria, 354
 Greenville, 354
  Baptist Church, 354
  Christ Church, 354
  Colored Ladies' Relief Association, 354
  Ladies' Colored Relief Association, 354
 Greenwood, 354
 Hilton Head, 91
 Horea Path, 354
 Langley, 354
 Laurens, 354
  M. E. Church, 354
  Musical Club, 354
  Laurens Court House, 354
  Lewisville United Cong. Reformed Presbyterian Church, 354
 Liberty Hill, 354
 Marion Town Council, 354
 Mount Bethel Methodist Church, 354
 Mt. Pleasant, 83, 87, 88, 90
 Newberg, 354
 Newberry, 362
  Amity Lodge #87, 409
  Y. M. C. A., 359
 Pawnee City United Presbyterian Church, 354
 Pleasant Grove, 354
 Port Royal, 188, 354, 371, 373
 Rock Hill, 354
  Moise Guards, 354
 Rockville, 354
 Sedalia, 354
 Seneca City Baptist Church, 354
 South Cheraw M. E. Church, 354
 Spartanburg, 354
 Townsville, 354
 Unionville, 354
 Waccaniwa All Saints' Parish, 354
 Wainsboro', 354
 Winnsboro', 354
  Lebanon Presbyterian Church, 354
South Carolina Supreme Court, 192
South Pole, 201
Southern Express Co., 127, 162, 336, 391, 418, vi
Southern Relief Fund, 361
Spain, 14, 35, 36, 69, 77, 82, 271, 288, 296
 Andalusia, 202
 Barcelona, 81, 84, 202
  Seminary Hospital, 84
 Cadiz, 26, 35, 78, 80, 82, 83
  Cadiz Hospital, 80
 Carlotta, 84
 Carthagena, 82, 83
 Ecija, 80, 82
 Gibraltar, 36, 82, 83, 85, 202, 290
 Malaga, 82, 84
 Palma, 84
 Puerto Santa Maria, 80
 Sedonia, 81
 Seville, 35, 80, 81, 83
  General Hospital, 81
  Santa Caridad, 81
 Siguenza, 84

Tortosa, 84
Xeres [Zeres], 80, 83, 84
St. Elmo Commandery, 408
St. Nicholas, 79
St. Simon's Mills, 348
Standish Creek, 273
Stewart Co., Moriah Grove Lodge #301 (Masonic), 409
Stillman Valley, 348
Stones River National Bank, 348
Sweden, 340

T

Table Talk, 311
Telegraphers' Aid Association, 426
Tennessee, 36, 77, 170, 200, 269, 280, 282, 284, 293, 363, 376, 414
    Adams' Station, 409
    Alamo Methodist Church, 355
    Athens, 354, 355
    Atoka, Salem Church, 361
    Bailey's Station, 238
    Bartlett, 92, 238, 239, 355
    Beech Grove, 92
    Beersheba, 355
    Bell Buckle, 355
    Bell's, 361
    Bell's Depot, 92, 239
        Belleville Minstrels, 360
        Bell's Depot Minstrels, 356
    Benton, 355, 422
    Bethel Springs, 93, 239
    Bolivar, 239, 354
        Colored Relief Association, 355
        Colored Relief Society, 355
    Braden, 362
    Bristol, 356
    Brownsville, 117, 238, 241, 333, 341, 348, 349, 354, 356, 367, 369, 376, 414
        Colored Benevolent Society, 355
        Lea & Cowan, 360
    Buntyn, 93, 238
    Buntyn Station, 190
    Callawha Institute, 355
    Camden, Benton Co. Aid Association, 355
    Camp Benjes, 177
    Camp Father Mathew, 177, 391, 395, 396, 398
    Camp Joe Williams [Camp Joe, Camp William], 54, 55, 56, 130, 147, 148, 158, 175, 176, 177, 184, 302, 390, 393, 395, 396, 428, 430, 442
        Camp Retreat, 394
        Camp Willis, 394
    Capersville, 238
    Capleville, 415
    Carbon, 355
    Carbondale, 356
    Careyville, Oriental Lodge #532, Knights of Honor, 422
    Cedar Grove, 238, 239
    Cedar Springs
        Sunday School, 355
    Center Point, 356
    Chapel Hill, 355
    Chattanooga, 29, 92, 118, 239, 355, 368, 369, 399, 414, 420
        Relief Committee, 354, 355
        Relief Fund, 356
    Chelsea, 153, 160
    Cherry Station, 238
    Chickamauga, 131
    Christiana, 355
    Clarksville [Clarkesville], 354, 355, 356, 399
        Lagrange Warehouse Association, 355
        Tobacco Board of Trade, 355
    Cleveland, 355, 371, 372
        Relief Association, 355
        Y. M. C. A., 355
    Collierville [Colliersville], 93, 179, 239, 354, 355, 368, 371, 372, 376
    Columbia, 355, 409, 420
        Central Lodge #253, Knights of Honor, 422
        First National Bank, 355
        Holding & Anderson, 360
        Maury Co. Lodge No. 423, I. O. G. T., 355
        Relief Committee, 355
    Concord
        Freedmans' Sunday School, 356
        Sabbath School, 361
    Cornersville, 238
    County, 238
    Covington, 36, 93, 182, 238, 239, 354, 355, 360
    Cowan, 355
        Goshen Church, 356
    Dandridge, 355
    Danville F. & A. M. Lodge, No. 208, 355
    Dyer Station
        Rehobath Church, 356
        Roll Ellen Aid Society, 355
    Dyersburg, 356, 420
        Hess Lodge #93 (Masonic), 409
    Eagle Machine Co., 355
    Elizabethtown, 362
    Erin, 93, 239, 333
    Falcon, 355
    Farmington, 355
    Fayette Co., 238
        Mount Moriah Lodge #309 (Masonic), 410
    Fayetteville Lodge #181, Knights of Honor, 422
    Fishersville, Morning Sun Council, No. 258, 355
    Franklin, 355, 356, 360, 361, 371, 372
    Frayser's [Frayser] Station, 93, 238, 239
    Fulton, 356
    Gadsden, 93, 239, 354
    Gainesville, 355
    Gallatin, 355
        Citizens' Committee, 355
    Galloway, 179, 239
    Galway, 93
    Gardner's Station, 239
    Garner, 179
    Germantown, 94, 105, 238, 239, 240
    Giles Co., 355
        Mt. Moriah Presbyterian Church, 355
    Gill's Station, 93, 240
    Gills Station, 93
    Grand Encampment (I.O.O.F.), 413
    Grand Junction, 94, 130, 192, 240, 355, 357
    Grand Lodge (I.O.O.F.), 410
    Hebrew Hospital Association, 355
    Henderson, 355
    Hickman, 31, 179
    Hollow Rock, 361

GENERAL INDEX

Houston, Lone Star Lodge #210, I.O.B.B., 420
Humboldt, 238, 355
Huntingdon, 240
Huntington, 355
Jackson, 240, 354, 355, 371, 373, 401, 409, 420, 426
   Catholic M. Benevolent Society, 401
   Tribune & Sun, 192
Jasper, 355
Johnsonville, Caldwell Lodge #273 (Masonic), 410
Kenton Methodist Sunday School, 355
Kingston Springs, 355
Knox Co., Concordia Sunday School, 355
Knoxville, 94, 292, 371, 373
   Car Wheel Co., 354
   E. T. Va. & G. Rail Road, 354
   Hebrew Congregation, 354
   I.O.O.F., 414
   Knoxville Iron Co., 355
   Teutonia Lodge #141, Knights of Honor, 421, 422
Ladies' Tabernacle, 355
Lagrange, 238, 239, 350, 355
Lebanon, 356, 368
   Citizens' Board of Relief, 355
Lewisburg, 355
   Relief Committee, 355
Limestone, 356
   Limestone Lodge # 1132, Knights of Honor, 421
London, 356
Lookout Mountain, 238
Lynchburg, Talley & Eaton, 360
Macon Depot, 354
Martin, 94
Mason, 94, 239, 240, 333
McKenzie, 94, 238, 240, 360, 426
McMinnville, 355
   Warren House, 354
Memphis, 17, 20, 21, 24, 26, 28, 29, 30, 31, 32, 34, 36, 39, 42, 43, 44, 46, 51, 53, 54, 56, 67, 72, 89, 90, 91, 92, 93, 94, 95, 96, 97, 98, 101, 102, 104, 105, 106, 108, 121, 122, 128, 133, 134, 135, 136, 138, 141, 142, 145, 147, 149, 153, 154, 155, 158, 159, 160, 161, 162, 163, 164, 165, 166, 167, 170, 171, 173, 178, 179, 180, 181, 182, 183, 185, 187, 188, 189, 190, 191, 192, 202, 238, 281, 288, 293, 295, 296, 297, 298, 302, 319, 320, 321, 322, 324, 328, 329, 330, 331, 332, 333, 334, 335, 336, 349, 352, 354, 355, 356, 359, 360, 366, 367, 368, 369, 370, 376, 377, 378, 379, 381, 382, 383, 387, 388, 393, 395, 398, 401, 409, 410, 420, 425, 426, 427, 435, 436, 440
   A. A. Patten & Co., 355
   A. Vacarro & Co., 438
   Angerona Lodge #168, 406
   Appeal, 127, 149, 150, 153, 154, 155, 156, 157, 158, 159, 160, 161, 165, 166, 168, 170, 174, 175, 176, 177, 179, 181, 183, 193, 384, 391, 428, 430, 431, 432, 435, 436, 438
   Ashbrook & White, 438
   Avalanche, 127, 128, 149, 150, 151, 153, 154, 155, 156, 160, 161, 166, 169, 170, 172, 177, 178, 179, 182, 379, 432, 433, 435
   B. Lowenstein & Bros. [B. Lowenstein & Co.], 360, 438
   Bank of Commerce, 178
   Bejac & Co., 360
   Board of Health, 103, 105, 136, 143, 145, 146, 147, 148, 149, 150, 151, 159, 174, 330, 331, 334, 377, 382, 383, 411, 412
   Board of Special Relief (I.O.O.F.), 410, 412
   Bohlen, Huse & Co., 438
   Bowles & Son, 438
   Brooks, Neely & Co., 438
   Brown & Jones, 438
   Bulletin, 154
   Burwinkle & Struwing, 355
   C. B. Carter & Co., 438
   C. P. Hunt & Co., 438
   C. W. Goyer & Co., 355
   Cage & Fisher, 438
   Calvary Cemetery, 396
   Calvary Church, 164
   Central Baptist Church, 160, 439
   Chamberlain House, 378, 381
   Chapel Hill Cemetery, 176
   Charity Hospital, 298
   Chelsea Lodge #280, Knights of Honor, 421, 422
   Chickasaw Bluffs, 319
   Chickasaw Lodge #8 (I.O.O.F.), 410, 413
   Church (Episcopal) Home, 188
   Church of the Good Shepherd, 164
   Church Orphan's Home, 162
   Citizens' Relief Association, v, 55, 111, 112, 121, 125, 127, 129, 130, 131, 132, 133, 149, 163, 164, 165, 168, 171
   Citizens' Relief Committee, v, 55, 111, 112, 121, 125, 127, 129, 130, 131, 132, 133, 149, 163, 164, 165, 168, 171, 177, 180, 184, 185, 188, 193, 324, 360, 390, 391, 392, 393, 395, 397, 398, 405, 414, 418, 420, 425
   City Hospital, 53, 106, 331
   City Oil Works, 355
   Clark, Johnson & Co., 360
   Colored Orphan Asylum, 392
   Cooper & Co., 438
   Court Street Infirmary, 167, 180
   Day & Proudfit, 438
   De Soto Lodge #299, 407
   Diamond Lodge #583, Knights of Honor, 421, 422
   E. M. Apperson & Co., 438
   Elmwood Cemetery, 116, 158, 167, 170, 173, 176, 181, 182, 185, 187, 190, 194, 332, 405
   Estes, Doan Co., 438
   Evening Ledger [Ledger], 127, 130, 137, 138, 154, 157, 163, 164, 165, 166, 181, 432, 434, 435
   Fader, Jacobs & Co., 390, 438
   Father Mathew Association [Society], 355, 396
   Ferguson & Hampson, 438
   First Colored Baptist Church, 355
   First National Bank, 349, 391
   First Presbyterian Church, 164
   Flaherty & Sullivan, 174, 188, 356
   Fort Pickering, 133, 153, 155, 178, 183, 187, 321
   Fountain Lodge #296, Knights of Honor, 421, 422
   Furstenheim & Wellford, 438
   G. Falls & Co., 390, 438
   G. W. Jones & Co., 354
   Gayoso Encampment #3 (I.O.O.F.), 413
   Gazette, 175
   General Council, 102, 103

German Free Protestant Church, 153
Germania Lodge #369, Knights of Honor, 421, 422
Goodbar & Co., 438
Goodlett & Co., 355
Goyer & Co., 438
Grace Church, 156
Grace Church Parish, 164
Greenlaw Opera House, 390
Grubbs, Austin & Berry, 438
Guy, Dillard & Co., 438
Hadden and Avery, 438
Happy Hollow, 382, 384
Harris, Mallory & Co., 438
Hebrew Orphan Asylum, 392
Hen-and-Chicken Island, 189
Hill & Mitchell, 438
Hill, Fontaine & Co., 396, 438
Howard Association, 51, 56, 333, 334, 336, 364, 365, 377, 378, 379, 380, 381, 382, 383, 384, 386, 387, 391, 392, 395, 397, 398, 405, 414, 416, 418, 420
Howard Medical Society, 175
Infirmary, 384, 385
Irish Literary Society, 425
J. F. Frank & Co., 438
J. Fargason & Co., 438
J. Gavin & Co., 438
J. H. Coffee & Co., 438
J. J. Busby & Co., 438
J. M. James and Sons, 438
J. S. Richardson & Co., 438
J. W. Jefferson & Co., 438
Jewish Synagogue, 169
Johnson & Vance, 438
Joyner, Lemon [Lemmon] & Gale, 354, 355, 438
Kahn & Freiburg, 354
Kilwinning Lodge #341, 407
Knights of Honor, 411
L. & N. Rail Road Shops, 354
LaSalette Academy, 150, 158
Leath Orphan Asylum, 167, 171, 392
Leila Scott Lodge # 289, 407
Linden Street Christian Church, 355
Lodge #6 (I.O.O.F.), 410
Lodge #187 (I.O.O.F.), 410
Louisville Depot, 184
M. L. Meacham & Co., 360, 438
Mammoth Cotton Press, 438
Marine Hospital, 138
Market Street Infirmary, 387
Martin & Co., 438
Masonic Relief Board, 107, 405, 406, 409
Masonic Relief Committee, 411
Memphis Cotton Exchange, 438
Memphis Fire Department, 390
Memphis Lodge #196, Knights of Honor, 421, 422
Menkin & Brother, 172
Mitchell, Hoffman & Co., 438
Mosby & Hunt, 161
National Cemetery, 193
Oliver Finnie & Co., 438
Orgill Bros. & Co., 390, 438
Park Avenue Lodge #362, 405, 408
Peabody Hotel, 143, 163, 167, 171, 181, 185, 386
Pearce, Suggs & Co., 438

Physicians' Infirmary, 181
Porter, Taylor & Co., 356, 390, 438
Post Office, 430
President's Island, 105, 430
R. G. Craig & Co., 360
R. G. Latting & Co., 360
Randle, Heath & Co., 354
Relief Committee, 381
Rice, Stix & Co., 355, 438
S. C. Tool & Co., 356
Schoolfield, Hanauer & Co., 360, 438
Schwab & Co., 438
Second Presbyterian Church, 167
Sisterhood of St. Mary, 123
Sisters of Charity, 148
Sisters of St. Joseph, 397
St. Agnes, 157
St. Andrew's Society, 148
St. Bridgets Church, 164, 398
St. Lazarus Church, 156, 164
St. Mary's Cathedral, 162, 164, 181
St. Mary's Church, 119
St. Mary's Episcopal Church, 122, 123
St. Mary's (German) Franciscan Church, 164, 165
St. Mary's Orphan Asylum, 392
St. Patrick's Church, 161, 163, 164, 395
St. Peter's, 164, 165
St. Peter's Orphan Asylum, 392
Telegraph Aid Association, 415
Telegraph Office, 431
Thomas H. Allen & Co., 355, 438
Townsend, Woolly & Co., 438
Typographical Union #11, 415, 416
  Relief Committee, 415, 416
U. & P. Bank, 348
Union Cotton Compress Association, 438
Unity Lodge #217, Knights of Honor, 421, 422
W. & S. Jack & Co., 356
W. B. Galbreath & Co., 438
W. J. Chase & Co., 360
W. S. Bruce & Co., 438
W. S. Jack & Co., 438
Walker Brothers & Co., 438
Wills & Wildberger, 360, 438
Woodruff & Co., 355
Middleton, Adams Lodge #246 (Masonic), 409
Midway Sunday School, 355
Milan, 94, 192, 193, 239
Morristown, 360
Moscow, 94, 164, 179, 240, 357, 420
Murfreesboro, 117, 238, 240, 355, 368, 369, 370
Nashville, 29, 34, 56, 95, 117, 118, 165, 240, 311, 325, 354, 355, 366, 367, 368, 369, 371, 373, 402, 409, 413, 414, 420, 426, 427
  Banner, 314, 355
  Citizens' Relief Committee, 355
  Davidson Co. Medical Society, 34
  G. A. Dickell & Co., 354
  Hibernian Society, 402
  St. Joseph's Total Abstinence Benevolent Society, 402
  Typographical Union, 415
  Valentino & Co., 355
New Memphis, 397
Newborn, 368, 370
Newport, 355, 361

GENERAL INDEX   549

Nubbin Ridge, 95, 240
Oakland Sunday School, 355
Ottawah City Relief Committee, 355
Paris, 95, 179, 240, 333, 425, 426
Plunkett, Isom & Co., 356
Prospect Lodge #456 (Masonic), 409
Pulaski, 355, 403
  Bethel Lodge, No. 194, F.& A. M, 355
  Cumberland Presbyterian Church, 355
  Olio Club & Musical Society, 355, 356
Raleigh, 96, 238, 239, 240, 335, 395
Ralston, 355, 361
Rammer, 355
River, 238
Rodgersville, 355
Roll Ellen Aid Society, 356
Rossville, 238, 240
Ruthersford Station I.O.O.F., 414
Saulsbury, Berlin Lodge #170, 409
Serieville Relief Committee, 356
Sevierville Mountain Lodge #197, 409
Shelby Co., 187, 360, 368, 370, 392
Shelby Depot, 240
Somerville, 96, 238, 239, 240, 354
South Memphis Lodge #118, 406
Special Relief Committee (I.O.O.F.), 415
Spring Hill, 355
Stevenson, 193
Stewart Creek, 355
Tipton Co., 368, 369
Trenton Presbyterian Church, 355
Trezevant, 239, 361
Tullahoma, 354, 355
Union Sunday School, 355
Union City, 240
Unionville, 355
Walton Hills, 355
Washington, 179
Waverly, 361
Waverly Station, 163
White Haven, 97, 302
White Pine, 361
  Colly & Graves, 356
Whitehaven Station, 105
Whiteville, 355
Williston, 97, 240, 357
Winchester, 97, 355
  M. E. Church South, 355
Withe, 333
Withe Depot, 240
Wolf Creek, 362
Wood Lawn Mills, 360
Wythe, 356
Wythe Depot, 97, 238, 355
Tennessee State Medical Society, 317
Texas, 36, 39, 40, 77, 167, 180, 200, 269, 363, 376, 414
  Alleyton, 91
  Anderson, 91
  Austin, 91, 356, 369, 371, 372
    Austin Lodge #418, Knights of Honor, 422
    Fire Department, 357
    Masonic Fraternity, 356
    Typographical Union, 415
  Bastrop, 91, 356
    M. E. Sunday School, 356
  Beaumont, 91
    Young Men's Aid Association, 356
  Bell Co.
    Little Elm Grange (Harrisville), 357
  Oenaville, 357
  Bellville, 90
    Citizens' Committee, 357
  Belton, 356
  Benham Dramatic Club, 356
  Brazos River, 86
  Brazoria, 90
  Breckenridge, 356
  Brenham, 91, 371, 372
  Brennan, 356
    Colored M. E. Church, 356
  Brownsville, 89, 90, 91, 93, 147, 150, 179
  Brownwood, 356
  Buffalo Bayou, 37
  Caldwell Baptist Church, 356
  Calvert, 42, 91, 357
  Cameron M. E. Church & Sunday School, 357
  Carthage, 356
  Casqueville Baptist Church, 356
  Chapel Hill, 91
  Cieres Co., 357
  Clarksville, 356, 357
  Clebourne, Heard, Allen & Rainer, 356
  Cold Springs Citizens' Committee, 357
  Colorado Commandery, No. 4, 356
  Columbia, 41, 86, 92
    Cornet Band, 357
  Columbus, 41, 92, 371, 372
  Corpus Christi, 39, 91, 92, 371, 372
  Corsicana, 92, 357
  Cotton Gin, 357
  Courtney, 356
  Crockett, 356
  Cypress City, 89, 90
  Dallas, 174, 356, 360, 361, 362, 371, 372
    Exchange Bank, 356
  Dallas Co., Leyene Lodge, A. F. M., 357
  Danville, 91
  Dennison, 356, 368, 371, 372
    R. A. Chapter, 356
    Vorwarts Society, 356
  Denton, 357
  DeWitt Co., 357
  Douglasville Methodist Sunday School, 356
  Edinburgh, 90
  Elmo, 361
  Ennis, Mark, Lallimer & Co., 356
  Flatinia Citizens' Relief Association, 356
  Fort McIntosh, 357
  Fort Point, 37
  Fort Worth, 356, 357, 371, 372, 420
    Christian Church, 356
    Fort Worth Chapter, 409
    Fort Worth Lodge #148 (Masonic), 409
  Gainesville, 356
  Galveston, 23, 25, 32, 36, 37, 39, 86, 87, 89, 90, 91, 301, 329, 356, 368, 371, 372, 400, 438
    Galveston Historical Society, 301
    Hebrew Benevolent Society, 420
    Ladies' Hebrew Benevolent Society, 420
    Typographical Union, 415
  Georgetown, San Gabriel Lodge, 89, A. F. & A. M., 357
  Goliad, 91
  Granbury, 356

Greenville M. E. Church, 356
Hackley, 89
Hampstead, 91
Harrisburg, 91
Hearne Relief Committee, 357
Hebrew Benevolent Society, 420
Hempstead, 356
Henderson, 356
    Colored M. E. Church, 356
Hickory Grove Church, 357
Honey Grove, 357
Houston, 36, 37, 40, 42, 86, 87, 89, 90, 91, 92, 356, 368, 371, 373, 427
    H. & T. C. Rail Road, 356
    M. E. Church & Sunday School, 356
    St. Joseph's Total Abstinence Benevolent Society, 400
    Street Rail Road, 356
Howard, 356
Huntingdon, 356
Huntsville, 91, 356
Independence, 91
Indianola, 25, 39, 88, 89, 90, 91
    Temperance Friends, 400
Jefferson, 357
Kaufman, 357
Lagrange, 91, 94
Lancaster, 362
Laredo, 356
Ledbetter, W. B. McClellan & Son, 357
Leon & Blum, 420
Liberty, 39, 91
Liverpool, 89
Longpoint, 368
Longview, 357
    Baptist Church, 356
    Baptist Sunday School, 356
    Christian Church, 356
    T. J. Harrison & Co., 356
Luling, 357
    Dixie Minstrels, 357
    Relief Committee, 357
Marshall, 303, 371, 373
Matagorda, 91, 357
McKinney, 356
Meansville, 39
Mexia
    Baptist Church, 356
    Forest Glade Church, 356
    Prairie Grove Sunday School, 356
Millican, 91, 356
Minneola Lodge, No. 511, Knights of Honor, 356
Mongolia, 357
Mosquito Island, 37
Navasota [Navisota], 37, 68, 91
New Bronfelds, 356
Old Town, 91
Orange, 37
    Social Club, 356
Palestine, 356
    Int. & Gt. N. Rail Road, 356
    Methodist E. Church, 356
Paoli Lodge, No. 28, I.O.W.M., 356
Paris, 356, 371, 373
    Paris Commandery, No. 9, 356
    Relief Association, 356
Pilot Point Christ's Church, 356

Pittsburg, 357
Platinia
    Moulton Chapter, 356
    Moulton Lodge, 356
Port Lavaca, 91
Post Oak Grove Baptist Church, 357
Richmond, 89, 90
Rio Grande City, 91
Rockdale, 356
Rockville, 356
Round Rock, 117, 356, 368, 369, 371, 373
Rusk, 356
Sabine City, 91
Saluria, 89
San Antonio, 356, 368, 371, 375
San Augustine, 357
San Saba, 356
Seguin, 356
Sherman, 356, 368, 369, 371, 375
    Sam Houston Fire Co., No. 1, 356
Stephensville, 356
Tehaucana, Trinity University, 362
Terrell, 356, 357
Texarkana, 356
Troy, 357
Tyler, 357
Valley View, 356
Victoria, 91, 356, 371, 375
Waco, 356, 357
Washa, 356
Washington, 36, 37
Waxahatchie, 357
    Christian Church, 356
    Cumberland Church, 356
Weathersford [Weatherford], 356, 357, 359
Weimar, 356
    Osage Church, 357
Wellburn, 356
Will's Point Relief Committee, 361
Windham Presbyterian Church, 357
Tombigbee River, 83
Treatise on Fever, 304
Turkey, 279
Typographical Union of Canada, 415
Typographical Union of the United States, 415

U

Union & Bay State Manufacturing Co., 350
United States Bank, 192
Uruguay, Montivideo, 14
Utah
    Frisco, 357
    Henry Clay Society, 357
    Ogden, 357
    Park City Mining Camp, 357
    Salt Lake City, 357, 415
        Ladies' Relief Association, 357
    Stockton, 357
    Tribune, 425
    Wild Dutchman Camp, 357
Utah Territory, 363, 414

V

Valley Mills Baptist Church, 348

GENERAL INDEX   551

Venezuela, 14
 Caraccas, 202
Vermont, 77, 178, 363
 Bakersfield, 358
 Bellows Falls St. Patrick's Society, 399
 Burlington, 200, 358
 North Bennington, 358
 Woodstock, 358
Virginia, 77, 363, 369, 414
 Abingdon, 92, 238, 266
 Abington, 357
 Alexandria, 81, 357, 358, 360
  Hebrew Society, 357
  Washington Lodge, 408
 Appomattox River, 80
 Bangs, 361
 Big Creek, 359
 Big Lick, 362
 Bland Court House, 357
 Bluestone, 358
 Bonsack, Bonsack & Kiser, 361
 Bristol Second Presbyterian Church, 357
 Broadway, 361
 Bufordsville, 357
 Cappahosic Sunday School, 358
 Cedar Creek, 361
 Charleston, 361
 Charlottesville, 357
  Charlottesville Lodge #55 (Masonic), 409
  Relief Committee, 362
 Christiansburg, 357
 City Point, 80
 Clark Co., 358
  Old Chapel, 358
 Covington, 357
 Culpeper, St. Stephen's Episcopal Church, 357
 Danville, 357
  Knights of the Crescent, 357
  Methodist E. Church, 357
  Musical Club, 357
  Presbyterian Church, 357
 De Paince, 361
 Dublin, 358
  Emanuel P. E. Church, 358
 Edinburg, 361
 Fairfax, 357
  Good Templars, 358
 Fairfax Court House, Good Templars, 357
 Fairfield Court House, 357
 Falmouth, 357
 Farmville, W. G. Venable & Bro., 358
 Fauquier Co., Leed's Church, 357
 Fincastle, 357
  Pierce Sabbath School, 358
 Forrest, 361
 Fort Monroe
  Munster Lodge #199 (Masonic), 409
  St. John's Chapter #57, 409
 Fredericksburg
  Conway, Gordon & Garnett, 358
  Disbursing Committee, 357
 Glade Springs, 357, 362
 Gordonsville, 358
 Gosport, 90
 Halltown, 361
 Hampton Roads, 92
 Harrisonburg, 357, 358, 361
 Howard Association, 357
 James River, 80
 Kenton, 361
 Leesburg, 358
 Lexington, 192, 357, 358
 Liberty
  Baptist Sunday School, 357
  Ladies' Aid Society, 357
 Linville, 361
 Luray, Lafayette Lodge, 137, F. & A. M., 357
 Lynchburg, 357
  Catholic Church, 357
  Hill City Lodge #173 (Masonic), 410
  Mansfield & Loyd, 357
  St. J. Benevolent Society, 401
  St. Patrick's Benevolent Society, 401
 Mathews Court House, 357
 Middleton, 361
 Millbrook, 361
 Montgomery Co., Virginia May Lodge #233, 409
 Mount Crawford, 361
 Mount Sidway, 361
 Mouth of Wilson, 358
 New Market, 358
 Newtown, 361
  Methodist Relief Association, 361
 Norfolk, 35, 78, 79, 80, 81, 82, 84, 85, 88, 90, 95, 98, 275, 276, 303, 371, 373, 376, 382, 402, 440
  Howard Association, 357
  Norfolk Lodge #1 (Masonic), 409
  Rollins, Whitcher & Co., 360
  Y. M. C. A., 357
 Nottoway Co., 357, 358
 Orange Co., 368, 370
 Orange Court House, 358
 Orkney Springs, 425
 Pampalia City, South Side Masonic Lodge, 191, 357
 Pedlar Mills, St. Luke's Church, 358
 Petersburg, 80, 361, 409, 435
  Congregation Rodef Sholem, 420
  St. Joseph's Catholic Benevolent Society, 403
 Portsmouth, 88, 90, 371, 373, 425
  St. Patrick's Benevolent Society, 403
 Rappahannock Station, 357
 Richmond, 96, 171, 329, 330, 357, 371, 373, 387, 403, 409, 420, 425, 435, 438
  Catholic Benevolent Society, 403
  Congregation Beth Ahaba, 420
  Ladies' Hebrew Benevolent Association, 420
  St. Peter's C. Total Abstinence Benevolent Society, 403
  Typographical Union, 415
  Valentine Meat Juice Works, 360
 Richmond & P. Rail Road, 357
 Rockbridge Co., 358
 Rockingham Co., 357
 Rural Retreat, 362
 Salem, 357, 358
  Y.M.C.A., 358
 Scott's Creek, 90
 Sidney Lodge No. 119, 358
 Statesville, 361
 Staunton, 357, 358, 361
  Catholic Hibernian Benevolent Society, 403
  I.O.O.F., 414
  Lodge No. 13, 357
  Stonewall Brigade Band, 357

Stephen's Cove, 361
Stephenson, 361
Strasburg, 361
Sulphur Springs, 357
Summit Point, 361
Tazewell Court House, 357, 358
Timberville, 361
Virginia Military Institute, 192
Warrenton Junction, 357
White Sulphur Springs, 357
Winchester, 81, 82, 358, 361
    Little Girls Bazaar, 358

W

Wabash Rail Road Machine Shops, 348
Washington, D. C., 29, 97, 200, 283, 329, 358, 363, 371, 375, 409, 415, 425, 436
    Capital Lodge #131, K.S.B., 419
    East Washington Citizen's Relief Committee, 358
    East Washington Relief Association, 358
    Evening Star, 358
    Government Printing Office, 415
    Grace Agular Lodge #117, I.O.B.B., 419
    Hibernian Benevolent Society, 404
    Marine Hospital, 105
    National Relief Committee, 436, 437
    Relief Committee, 332, 425
    U. S. Dept. of the Interior, 358
    U. S. Government Printing Office, 358
    U. S. Treasury, 358
Washoe Typographical Union, 415
Well's Fargo & Co., 338, 403
West Indies [West India Islands], 13, 14, 15, 16, 20, 22, 24, 26, 28, 29, 56, 77, 81, 82, 83, 97, 103, 142, 183, 202, 203, 272, 288, 313, 315, 316, 414
    Antilles, 28
    Barbadoes, 15, 82, 83, 84, 86, 87
    Basseterie, 86, 87
    Boa Vista, 87
    Cayenne, 87
    Demarara, 110
        Georgetown, 86
        Seaman's Hospital, 86
    Dominica, 86, 87, 203
    Guadaloupe, 79, 80, 81, 85, 86, 87, 97
    Haiti [Hayti], 106
    Jamaica, 15, 27, 81, 83, 84, 85, 203, 289, 290
        Kingston, 290, 302
    Leeward Islands, 79
    Martinique, 81, 83, 84, 85, 86, 202
    Port Royal, 88
    Porto Sal Rey, 87
    San Domingo [Santo Domingo], 13, 78, 79, 80, 81, 97, 106
    St. Christopher, 83
    St. Lucia, 77
    St. Thomas, 88, 290
    Trinidad, 83
    Windward Islands, 79
West Virginia, 77, 363
    Bob Town, 358
    Charleston, 358
    Fairmont Ladies' Relief Association, 358
    Fairview, 358
    Grafton, Hibernian Benevolent Society, 400
    Guyandotte, 358
    Hinton, 358
    Huntington [Huntingdon], 358
        Catholic Aid Society, 400
        Wyandotte Chapter #70, 409
    Martinsburg [Martinsburgh], 358
        St. Joseph's Society, 401
        St. Patrick's Society, 401
    Moundsville, 358
    Parkersburg, 358
        St. Patrick's M. R. Society, 403
    Phillippi, 358
    Piedmont, 358
        Eureka Lodge #643, Knights of Honor, 422
    Plattenburg, 358
    Point Pleasant, 358
    Raymond Coal Co., 358
    St. Albans, 358
    Triadelphia, St. Mary's Y. A. Benevolent Society, 404
    Wellsburg, 358
    Wheeling, 358
        Alpha Lodge #424, Knights of Honor, 422
        Hail City Boat Club, 358
        J. H. Hobbs, Brockermier & Co., 358
        La Belle Iron Works, 358
        Lutheran Sunday School, 358
        Relief Committee, 358
Western Associated Press, 160
Western Methodist, 161
Western Star Lodge #2 (Masonic), 410
Western Union Telegraph Co., 128, 336, 363, 418, vi
White River, 145, 436
Wilkerson & Co., 366
Winchester Music Club, 348
Wisconsin, 363, 414
    Appleton, 358, 359
        St. Patrick's T.A.B. Society, 399
    Ashland, 358
    Atkinson A. O. U. W., 358
    Beloit, 358
    Bennington, 359
    Boscobel, 358
    Burlington, 358, 359
    Chippewa Falls, 359
    Columbus, 359
    Darlington, 359
        Relief Committee, 358
    De Pere Temple of Honor, No. 82, 359, 400
    Delafield, 358
    Duwanda, 409
    Elkhorn, 358, 359
    Evansville, 358
    Fond du Lac, 358, 361
        St. Patrick's Benevolent Society, 400
    Geneva Lake
        Dramatic Club, 358
        Laurel Band Class, 362
    Green Bay, 359
        First Presbyterian Church, 358
    Horicon, 359
    Janesville, 358, 359
        Temple of Honor, 358
    Jefferson, 358
        German M. E. Church, 359
    Kenosha, 358
    La Crosse, 359

Lake Mills, 359
Madison, 358
　State Journal, 358
Manitoowoc Citizens' Association, 358
Mazomanie, 358
Menasha, 358
Mexico, 358
Milwaukee, 188, 329, 358, 371, 373, 401, 420
　Hibernian Benevolent Society, 401
　Jewett & Sherman, 358
　Joseph Schlitz Brewing Co., 358
　Ladies' Committee, 358
　Ladies' Emanuel Society, 420
　Sentinel, 358
　Southside Relief Association, 358
　T. H. Chapman & Co., 358
Mineral Point, 359
Monroe, 359
　Relief Committee, 358
Oconomowac [Oconomowoc]
　Draper Hall, 358
　St. Jerome Total Abstinence and Benevolent
　　Society, 402
Oconto, St. John's C. Total Abstinence and
　Benevolent Society, 402
Oshkosh, 359
　St. Peter's Church, 402
　St. Peter's Total Abstinence Society, 402
Pactogue, 358
Pewaukee, 359
Plattsville, 358, 359
Plymouth, 359
Prairie Du Chien, 358
　M. E. Church, 358
Prescott, 358
Pt. Washington, Merchants & Manufacturing
　Association, 358
Racine, 358
　Citizens' Relief Committee, 358

Ripon
　Fairwater Baptist Church, 359
　St. Patrick's C. Total Abstinence Benevolent
　　Society, 403
River Falls, 359
Schofield Mills, 359
Sheboygan, 358
Sheboygan Falls, 359
　Harmony Chapter, 409
St. Pierre, 88
Stephens Point
　Ladies' Benevolent Association, 358
　Ogema Temple of Honor, 359
　Presbyterian Sunday School, 358
　Shaurette Lodge, No. 92, I. O. O. F., 358
Stevens' Point, 403
Stockton, St. John's Total Abstinence Society, 403
Tomah, 358
Two Rivers, 358
Washington, 359
Watertown, 358, 359
Waukegan, 359
　Baptist Church, 358
Waukesha
　Citizens' Relief Committee, 359
　Volunteer Fire Department, 358
Wauwatosa Relief Association, 358
Whitewater, 359
　Congregational Church, 358
　St. Patrick's C. Total Abstinence Society, 404
Woodworth Commission [Allopathic Commission], 27,
　29, 316
World (New York), 191, 415
Wyoming, 363
Wyoming Territory, 414
　Cheyenne, 359
　Easton, 359
　Fort A. D. Russell, 359
　Laramie City, 359

www.ingramcontent.com/pod-product-compliance
Lightning Source LLC
Chambersburg PA
CBHW060907300426
44112CB00011B/1380